DATE DUE

COURT RULES

AND

PROCEDURE

VOLUME II – FEDERAL

2015

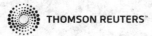
THOMSON REUTERS

Mat#41608324

ISBN: 978–0–314–67339–8

PREFACE

Illinois Court Rules and Procedure, Volume II – Federal, 2015, includes rules and associated material governing practice before the Illinois federal courts. It replaces the 2014 edition and any accompanying supplements. It is current with amendments received through April 1, 2015.

For additional information or research assistance, call the West reference attorneys at 1-800-REF-ATTY (1-800-733-2889). Contact West's editorial department directly with your questions and suggestions by e-mail at west.editor@thomson.com.

THE PUBLISHER

May 2015

TABLE OF CONTENTS

FEDERAL
RULES OF CIVIL PROCEDURE
FOR THE
UNITED STATES DISTRICT COURTS

Effective September 16, 1938
Including Amendments Effective December 1, 2014

1

TITLE I. SCOPE OF RULES; FORM OF ACTION

RULE 1. SCOPE AND PURPOSE

These rules govern the procedure in all civil actions and proceedings in the United States district courts, except as stated in Rule 81. They should be construed and administered to secure the just, speedy, and inexpensive determination of every action and proceeding.

(Amended December 29, 1948, effective October 20, 1949; February 28, 1966, effective July 1, 1966; April 22, 1993, effective December 1, 1993; April 30, 2007, effective December 1, 2007.)

RULE 2. ONE FORM OF ACTION

There is one form of action—the civil action.

(Amended April 30, 2007, effective December 1, 2007.)

TITLE II. COMMENCING AN ACTION; SERVICE OF PROCESS, PLEADINGS, MOTIONS, AND ORDERS

RULE 3. COMMENCING AN ACTION

A civil action is commenced by filing a complaint with the court.

(Amended April 30, 2007, effective December 1, 2007.)

RULE 4. SUMMONS

(a) Contents; Amendments.

(1) *Contents.* A summons must:

(A) name the court and the parties;

(B) be directed to the defendant;

(C) state the name and address of the plaintiff's attorney or—if unrepresented—of the plaintiff;

(D) state the time within which the defendant must appear and defend;

(E) notify the defendant that a failure to appear and defend will result in a default judgment against the defendant for the relief demanded in the complaint;

(F) be signed by the clerk; and

(G) bear the court's seal.

(2) *Amendments.* The court may permit a summons to be amended.

(b) Issuance. On or after filing the complaint, the plaintiff may present a summons to the clerk for signature and seal. If the summons is properly completed, the clerk must sign, seal, and issue it to the plaintiff for service on the defendant. A summons—or a copy of a summons that is addressed to multiple defendants—must be issued for each defendant to be served.

(c) Service.

(1) *In General.* A summons must be served with a copy of the complaint. The plaintiff is responsible for having the summons and complaint served within the time allowed by Rule 4(m) and must furnish the necessary copies to the person who makes service.

(2) *By Whom.* Any person who is at least 18 years old and not a party may serve a summons and complaint.

(3) *By a Marshal or Someone Specially Appointed.* At the plaintiff's request, the court may order that service be made by a United States marshal or deputy marshal or by a person specially appointed by the court. The court must so order if the plaintiff is authorized to proceed in forma pauperis under 28 U.S.C. § 1915 or as a seaman under 28 U.S.C. § 1916.

(d) Waiving Service.

(1) *Requesting a Waiver.* An individual, corporation, or association that is subject to service under Rule 4(e), (f), or (h) has a duty to avoid unnecessary expenses of serving the summons. The plaintiff may notify such a defendant that an action has been commenced and request that the defendant waive service of a summons. The notice and request must:

(A) be in writing and be addressed:

(i) to the individual defendant; or

(ii) for a defendant subject to service under Rule 4(h), to an officer, a managing or general agent, or any other agent authorized by appointment or by law to receive service of process;

(B) name the court where the complaint was filed;

(C) be accompanied by a copy of the complaint, two copies of a waiver form, and a prepaid means for returning the form;

3

(D) inform the defendant, using text prescribed in Form 5, of the consequences of waiving and not waiving service;

(E) state the date when the request is sent;

(F) give the defendant a reasonable time of at least 30 days after the request was sent—or at least 60 days if sent to the defendant outside any judicial district of the United States—to return the waiver; and

(G) be sent by first-class mail or other reliable means.

(2) *Failure to Waive.* If a defendant located within the United States fails, without good cause, to sign and return a waiver requested by a plaintiff located within the United States, the court must impose on the defendant:

(A) the expenses later incurred in making service; and

(B) the reasonable expenses, including attorney's fees, of any motion required to collect those service expenses.

(3) *Time to Answer After a Waiver.* A defendant who, before being served with process, timely returns a waiver need not serve an answer to the complaint until 60 days after the request was sent—or until 90 days after it was sent to the defendant outside any judicial district of the United States.

(4) *Results of Filing a Waiver.* When the plaintiff files a waiver, proof of service is not required and these rules apply as if a summons and complaint had been served at the time of filing the waiver.

(5) *Jurisdiction and Venue Not Waived.* Waiving service of a summons does not waive any objection to personal jurisdiction or to venue.

(e) Serving an Individual Within a Judicial District of the United States. Unless federal law provides otherwise, an individual—other than a minor, an incompetent person, or a person whose waiver has been filed—may be served in a judicial district of the United States by:

(1) following state law for serving a summons in an action brought in courts of general jurisdiction in the state where the district court is located or where service is made; or

(2) doing any of the following:

(A) delivering a copy of the summons and of the complaint to the individual personally;

(B) leaving a copy of each at the individual's dwelling or usual place of abode with someone of suitable age and discretion who resides there; or

(C) delivering a copy of each to an agent authorized by appointment or by law to receive service of process.

(f) Serving an Individual in a Foreign Country. Unless federal law provides otherwise, an individual—other than a minor, an incompetent person, or a person whose waiver has been filed—may be served at a place not within any judicial district of the United States:

(1) by any internationally agreed means of service that is reasonably calculated to give notice, such as those authorized by the Hague Convention on the Service Abroad of Judicial and Extrajudicial Documents;

(2) if there is no internationally agreed means, or if an international agreement allows but does not specify other means, by a method that is reasonably calculated to give notice:

(A) as prescribed by the foreign country's law for service in that country in an action in its courts of general jurisdiction;

(B) as the foreign authority directs in response to a letter rogatory or letter of request; or

(C) unless prohibited by the foreign country's law, by:

(i) delivering a copy of the summons and of the complaint to the individual personally; or

(ii) using any form of mail that the clerk addresses and sends to the individual and that requires a signed receipt; or

(3) by other means not prohibited by international agreement, as the court orders.

(g) Serving a Minor or an Incompetent Person. A minor or an incompetent person in a judicial district of the United States must be served by following state law for serving a summons or like process on such a defendant in an action brought in the courts of general jurisdiction of the state where service is made. A minor or an incompetent person who is not within any judicial district of the United States must be served in the manner prescribed by Rule 4(f)(2)(A), (f)(2)(B), or (f)(3).

(h) Serving a Corporation, Partnership, or Association. Unless federal law provides otherwise or the defendant's waiver has been filed, a domestic or foreign corporation, or a partnership or other unincorporated association that is subject to suit under a common name, must be served:

(1) in a judicial district of the United States:

(A) in the manner prescribed by Rule 4(e)(1) for serving an individual; or

(B) by delivering a copy of the summons and of the complaint to an officer, a managing or general agent, or any other agent authorized by appointment or by law to receive service of process and—if the agent is one authorized by statute and the statute so requires—

by also mailing a copy of each to the defendant; or

(2) at a place not within any judicial district of the United States, in any manner prescribed by Rule 4(f) for serving an individual, except personal delivery under (f)(2)(C)(i).

(i) Serving the United States and Its Agencies, Corporations, Officers, or Employees.

(1) *United States.* To serve the United States, a party must:

(A)(i) deliver a copy of the summons and of the complaint to the United States attorney for the district where the action is brought—or to an assistant United States attorney or clerical employee whom the United States attorney designates in a writing filed with the court clerk—or

(ii) send a copy of each by registered or certified mail to the civil-process clerk at the United States attorney's office;

(B) send a copy of each by registered or certified mail to the Attorney General of the United States at Washington, D.C.; and

(C) if the action challenges an order of a nonparty agency or officer of the United States, send a copy of each by registered or certified mail to the agency or officer.

(2) *Agency; Corporation; Officer or Employee Sued in an Official Capacity.* To serve a United States agency or corporation, or a United States officer or employee sued only in an official capacity, a party must serve the United States and also send a copy of the summons and of the complaint by registered or certified mail to the agency, corporation, officer, or employee.

(3) *Officer or Employee Sued Individually.* To serve a United States officer or employee sued in an individual capacity for an act or omission occurring in connection with duties performed on the United States' behalf (whether or not the officer or employee is also sued in an official capacity), a party must serve the United States and also serve the officer or employee under Rule 4(e), (f), or (g).

(4) *Extending Time.* The court must allow a party a reasonable time to cure its failure to:

(A) serve a person required to be served under Rule 4(i)(2), if the party has served either the United States attorney or the Attorney General of the United States; or

(B) serve the United States under Rule 4(i)(3), if the party has served the United States officer or employee.

(j) Serving a Foreign, State, or Local Government.

(1) *Foreign State.* A foreign state or its political subdivision, agency, or instrumentality must be served in accordance with 28 U.S.C. § 1608.

(2) *State or Local Government.* A state, a municipal corporation, or any other state-created governmental organization that is subject to suit must be served by:

(A) delivering a copy of the summons and of the complaint to its chief executive officer; or

(B) serving a copy of each in the manner prescribed by that state's law for serving a summons or like process on such a defendant.

(k) Territorial Limits of Effective Service.

(1) *In General.* Serving a summons or filing a waiver of service establishes personal jurisdiction over a defendant:

(A) who is subject to the jurisdiction of a court of general jurisdiction in the state where the district court is located;

(B) who is a party joined under Rule 14 or 19 and is served within a judicial district of the United States and not more than 100 miles from where the summons was issued; or

(C) when authorized by a federal statute.

(2) *Federal Claim Outside State–Court Jurisdiction.* For a claim that arises under federal law, serving a summons or filing a waiver of service establishes personal jurisdiction over a defendant if:

(A) the defendant is not subject to jurisdiction in any state's courts of general jurisdiction; and

(B) exercising jurisdiction is consistent with the United States Constitution and laws.

(l) Proving Service.

(1) *Affidavit Required.* Unless service is waived, proof of service must be made to the court. Except for service by a United States marshal or deputy marshal, proof must be by the server's affidavit.

(2) *Service Outside the United States.* Service not within any judicial district of the United States must be proved as follows:

(A) if made under Rule 4(f)(1), as provided in the applicable treaty or convention; or

(B) if made under Rule 4(f)(2) or (f)(3), by a receipt signed by the addressee, or by other evidence satisfying the court that the summons and complaint were delivered to the addressee.

(3) *Validity of Service; Amending Proof.* Failure to prove service does not affect the validity of service. The court may permit proof of service to be amended.

(m) Time Limit for Service. If a defendant is not served within 120 days after the complaint is filed, the court—on motion or on its own after notice to the plaintiff—must dismiss the action without prejudice against that defendant or order that service be made within a specified time. But if the plaintiff shows good cause for the failure, the court must extend the time for service for an appropriate period. This subdivision (m) does not apply to service in a foreign country under Rule 4(f) or 4(j)(1).

(n) Asserting Jurisdiction over Property or Assets.

(1) *Federal Law.* The court may assert jurisdiction over property if authorized by a federal statute. Notice to claimants of the property must be given as provided in the statute or by serving a summons under this rule.

(2) *State Law.* On a showing that personal jurisdiction over a defendant cannot be obtained in the district where the action is brought by reasonable efforts to serve a summons under this rule, the court may assert jurisdiction over the defendant's assets found in the district. Jurisdiction is acquired by seizing the assets under the circumstances and in the manner provided by state law in that district.

(Amended January 21, 1963, effective July 1, 1963; February 28, 1966, effective July 1, 1966; April 29, 1980, effective August 1, 1980; amended by Pub.L. 97-462, § 2, January 12, 1983, 96 Stat. 2527, effective 45 days after January 12, 1983; amended March 2, 1987, effective August 1, 1987; April 22, 1993, effective December 1, 1993; April 17, 2000, effective December 1, 2000; April 30, 2007, effective December 1, 2007.)

RULE 4.1.　SERVING OTHER PROCESS

(a) In General. Process—other than a summons under Rule 4 or a subpoena under Rule 45—must be served by a United States marshal or deputy marshal or by a person specially appointed for that purpose. It may be served anywhere within the territorial limits of the state where the district court is located and, if authorized by a federal statute, beyond those limits. Proof of service must be made under Rule 4(*l*).

(b) Enforcing Orders: Committing for Civil Contempt. An order committing a person for civil contempt of a decree or injunction issued to enforce federal law may be served and enforced in any district. Any other order in a civil-contempt proceeding may be served only in the state where the issuing court is located or elsewhere in the United States within 100 miles from where the order was issued.

(Adopted April 22, 1993, effective December 1, 1993; amended April 30, 2007, effective December 1, 2007.)

RULE 5.　SERVING AND FILING PLEADINGS AND OTHER PAPERS

(a) Service: When Required.

(1) *In General.* Unless these rules provide otherwise, each of the following papers must be served on every party:

(A) an order stating that service is required;

(B) a pleading filed after the original complaint, unless the court orders otherwise under Rule 5(c) because there are numerous defendants;

(C) a discovery paper required to be served on a party, unless the court orders otherwise;

(D) a written motion, except one that may be heard ex parte; and

(E) a written notice, appearance, demand, or offer of judgment, or any similar paper.

(2) *If a Party Fails to Appear.* No service is required on a party who is in default for failing to appear. But a pleading that asserts a new claim for relief against such a party must be served on that party under Rule 4.

(3) *Seizing Property.* If an action is begun by seizing property and no person is or need be named as a defendant, any service required before the filing of an appearance, answer, or claim must be made on the person who had custody or possession of the property when it was seized.

(b) Service: How Made.

(1) *Serving an Attorney.* If a party is represented by an attorney, service under this rule must be made on the attorney unless the court orders service on the party.

(2) *Service in General.* A paper is served under this rule by:

(A) handing it to the person;

(B) leaving it:

(i) at the person's office with a clerk or other person in charge or, if no one is in charge, in a conspicuous place in the office; or

(ii) if the person has no office or the office is closed, at the person's dwelling or usual place of abode with someone of suitable age and discretion who resides there;

(C) mailing it to the person's last known address—in which event service is complete upon mailing;

(D) leaving it with the court clerk if the person has no known address;

(E) sending it by electronic means if the person consented in writing—in which event service is complete upon transmission, but is not effective if the serving party learns that it did not reach the person to be served; or

(F) delivering it by any other means that the person consented to in writing—in which event service is complete when the person making service delivers it to the agency designated to make delivery.

(3) *Using Court Facilities.* If a local rule so authorizes, a party may use the court's transmission facilities to make service under Rule 5(b)(2)(E).

(c) Serving Numerous Defendants.

(1) *In General.* If an action involves an unusually large number of defendants, the court may, on motion or on its own, order that:

(A) defendants' pleadings and replies to them need not be served on other defendants;

(B) any crossclaim, counterclaim, avoidance, or affirmative defense in those pleadings and replies to them will be treated as denied or avoided by all other parties; and

(C) filing any such pleading and serving it on the plaintiff constitutes notice of the pleading to all parties.

(2) *Notifying Parties.* A copy of every such order must be served on the parties as the court directs.

(d) Filing.

(1) *Required Filings; Certificate of Service.* Any paper after the complaint that is required to be served—together with a certificate of service—must be filed within a reasonable time after service. But disclosures under Rule 26(a)(1) or (2) and the following discovery requests and responses must not be filed until they are used in the proceeding or the court orders filing: depositions, interrogatories, requests for documents or tangible things or to permit entry onto land, and requests for admission.

(2) *How Filing Is Made—In General.* A paper is filed by delivering it:

(A) to the clerk; or

(B) to a judge who agrees to accept it for filing, and who must then note the filing date on the paper and promptly send it to the clerk.

(3) *Electronic Filing, Signing, or Verification.* A court may, by local rule, allow papers to be filed, signed, or verified by electronic means that are consistent with any technical standards established by the Judicial Conference of the United States. A local rule may require electronic filing only if reasonable exceptions are allowed. A paper filed electronically in compliance with a local rule is a written paper for purposes of these rules.

(4) *Acceptance by the Clerk.* The clerk must not refuse to file a paper solely because it is not in the form prescribed by these rules or by a local rule or practice.

(Amended January 21, 1963, effective July 1, 1963; March 30, 1970, effective July 1, 1970; April 29, 1980, effective August 1, 1980; March 2, 1987, effective August 1, 1987; April 30, 1991, effective December 1, 1991; April 22, 1993, effective December 1, 1993; April 23, 1996, effective December 1, 1996; April 17, 2000, effective December 1, 2000; April 23, 2001, effective December 1, 2001; April 12, 2006, effective December 1, 2006; April 30, 2007, effective December 1, 2007.)

RULE 5.1. CONSTITUTIONAL CHALLENGE TO A STATUTE—NOTICE, CERTIFICATION, AND INTERVENTION

(a) Notice by a Party. A party that files a pleading, written motion, or other paper drawing into question the constitutionality of a federal or state statute must promptly:

(1) file a notice of constitutional question stating the question and identifying the paper that raises it, if:

(A) a federal statute is questioned and the parties do not include the United States, one of its agencies, or one of its officers or employees in an official capacity; or

(B) a state statute is questioned and the parties do not include the state, one of its agencies, or one of its officers or employees in an official capacity; and

(2) serve the notice and paper on the Attorney General of the United States if a federal statute is questioned—or on the state attorney general if a state statute is questioned—either by certified or registered mail or by sending it to an electronic address designated by the attorney general for this purpose.

(b) Certification by the Court. The court must, under 28 U.S.C. § 2403, certify to the appropriate attorney general that a statute has been questioned.

(c) Intervention; Final Decision on the Merits. Unless the court sets a later time, the attorney general may intervene within 60 days after the notice is filed or after the court certifies the challenge, whichever is earlier. Before the time to intervene expires, the court may reject the constitutional challenge, but may not enter a final judgment holding the statute unconstitutional.

(d) No Forfeiture. A party's failure to file and serve the notice, or the court's failure to certify, does not forfeit a constitutional claim or defense that is otherwise timely asserted.

(Adopted April 12, 2006, effective December 1, 2006; amended April 30, 2007, effective December 1, 2007.)

RULE 5.2. PRIVACY PROTECTION FOR FILINGS MADE WITH THE COURT

(a) Redacted Filings. Unless the court orders otherwise, in an electronic or paper filing with the court that contains an individual's social-security number, taxpayer-identification number, or birth date, the name of an individual known to be a minor, or a financial-account number, a party or nonparty making the filing may include only:

(1) the last four digits of the social-security number and taxpayer-identification number;

(2) the year of the individual's birth;

(3) the minor's initials; and

(4) the last four digits of the financial-account number.

(b) Exemptions from the Redaction Requirement. The redaction requirement does not apply to the following:

(1) a financial-account number that identifies the property allegedly subject to forfeiture in a forfeiture proceeding;

(2) the record of an administrative or agency proceeding;

(3) the official record of a state-court proceeding;

(4) the record of a court or tribunal, if that record was not subject to the redaction requirement when originally filed;

(5) a filing covered by Rule 5.2(c) or (d); and

(6) a pro se filing in an action brought under 28 U.S.C. §§ 2241, 2254, or 2255.

(c) Limitations on Remote Access to Electronic Files; Social–Security Appeals and Immigration Cases. Unless the court orders otherwise, in an action for benefits under the Social Security Act, and in an action or proceeding relating to an order of removal, to relief from removal, or to immigration benefits or detention, access to an electronic file is authorized as follows:

(1) the parties and their attorneys may have remote electronic access to any part of the case file, including the administrative record;

(2) any other person may have electronic access to the full record at the courthouse, but may have remote electronic access only to:

(A) the docket maintained by the court; and

(B) an opinion, order, judgment, or other disposition of the court, but not any other part of the case file or the administrative record.

(d) Filings Made Under Seal. The court may order that a filing be made under seal without redaction. The court may later unseal the filing or order the person who made the filing to file a redacted version for the public record.

(e) Protective Orders. For good cause, the court may by order in a case:

(1) require redaction of additional information; or

(2) limit or prohibit a nonparty's remote electronic access to a document filed with the court.

(f) Option for Additional Unredacted Filing Under Seal. A person making a redacted filing may also file an unredacted copy under seal. The court must retain the unredacted copy as part of the record.

(g) Option for Filing a Reference List. A filing that contains redacted information may be filed together with a reference list that identifies each item of redacted information and specifies an appropriate identifier that uniquely corresponds to each item listed. The list must be filed under seal and may be amended as of right. Any reference in the case to a listed identifier will be construed to refer to the corresponding item of information.

(h) Waiver of Protection of Identifiers. A person waives the protection of Rule 5.2(a) as to the person's own information by filing it without redaction and not under seal.

(Adopted April 30, 2007, effective December 1, 2007.)

RULE 6. COMPUTING AND EXTENDING TIME; TIME FOR MOTION PAPERS

(a) Computing Time. The following rules apply in computing any time period specified in these rules, in any local rule or court order, or in any statute that does not specify a method of computing time.

(1) *Period Stated in Days or a Longer Unit.* When the period is stated in days or a longer unit of time:

(A) exclude the day of the event that triggers the period;

(B) count every day, including intermediate Saturdays, Sundays, and legal holidays; and

(C) include the last day of the period, but if the last day is a Saturday, Sunday, or legal holiday, the period continues to run until the end of the next day that is not a Saturday, Sunday, or legal holiday.

(2) *Period Stated in Hours.* When the period is stated in hours:

(A) begin counting immediately on the occurrence of the event that triggers the period;

(B) count every hour, including hours during intermediate Saturdays, Sundays, and legal holidays; and

(C) if the period would end on a Saturday, Sunday, or legal holiday, the period continues to run until the same time on the next day that is not a Saturday, Sunday, or legal holiday.

(3) *Inaccessibility of the Clerk's Office.* Unless the court orders otherwise, if the clerk's office is inaccessible:

(A) on the last day for filing under Rule 6(a)(1), then the time for filing is extended to the first accessible day that is not a Saturday, Sunday, or legal holiday; or

(B) during the last hour for filing under Rule 6(a)(2), then the time for filing is extended to the same time on the first accessible day that is not a Saturday, Sunday, or legal holiday.

(4) *"Last Day" Defined.* Unless a different time is set by a statute, local rule, or court order, the last day ends:

(A) for electronic filing, at midnight in the court's time zone; and

(B) for filing by other means, when the clerk's office is scheduled to close.

(5) *"Next Day" Defined.* The "next day" is determined by continuing to count forward when the period is measured after an event and backward when measured before an event.

(6) *"Legal Holiday" Defined.* "Legal holiday" means:

(A) the day set aside by statute for observing New Year's Day, Martin Luther King Jr.'s Birthday, Washington's Birthday, Memorial Day, Independence Day, Labor Day, Columbus Day, Veterans' Day, Thanksgiving Day, or Christmas Day;

(B) any day declared a holiday by the President or Congress; and

(C) for periods that are measured after an event, any other day declared a holiday by the state where the district court is located.

(b) **Extending Time.**

(1) *In General.* When an act may or must be done within a specified time, the court may, for good cause, extend the time:

(A) with or without motion or notice if the court acts, or if a request is made, before the original time or its extension expires; or

(B) on motion made after the time has expired if the party failed to act because of excusable neglect.

(2) *Exceptions.* A court must not extend the time to act under Rules 50(b) and (d), 52(b), 59(b), (d), and (e), and 60(b).

(c) **Motions, Notices of Hearing, and Affidavits.**

(1) *In General.* A written motion and notice of the hearing must be served at least 14 days before the time specified for the hearing, with the following exceptions:

(A) when the motion may be heard ex parte;

(B) when these rules set a different time; or

(C) when a court order—which a party may, for good cause, apply for ex parte—sets a different time.

(2) *Supporting Affidavit.* Any affidavit supporting a motion must be served with the motion. Except as Rule 59(c) provides otherwise, any opposing affidavit must be served at least 7 days before the hearing, unless the court permits service at another time.

(d) **Additional Time After Certain Kinds of Service.** When a party may or must act within a specified time after service and service is made under Rule 5(b)(2)(C), (D), (E), or (F), 3 days are added after the period would otherwise expire under Rule 6(a).

(Amended December 27, 1946, effective March 19, 1948; January 21, 1963, effective July 1, 1963; February 28, 1966, effective July 1, 1966; December 4, 1967, effective July 1, 1968; March 1, 1971, effective July 1, 1971; April 28, 1983, effective August 1, 1983; April 29, 1985, effective August 1, 1985; March 2, 1987, effective August 1, 1987; April 29, 1999, effective December 1, 1999; April 23, 2001, effective December 1, 2001; April 25, 2005, effective December 1, 2005; April 30, 2007, effective December 1, 2007; March 26, 2009, effective December 1, 2009.)

TITLE III. PLEADINGS AND MOTIONS

RULE 7. PLEADINGS ALLOWED; FORM OF MOTIONS AND OTHER PAPERS

(a) **Pleadings.** Only these pleadings are allowed:

(1) a complaint;

(2) an answer to a complaint;

(3) an answer to a counterclaim designated as a counterclaim;

(4) an answer to a crossclaim;

(5) a third-party complaint;

(6) an answer to a third-party complaint; and

(7) if the court orders one, a reply to an answer.

(b) **Motions and Other Papers.**

(1) *In General.* A request for a court order must be made by motion. The motion must:

(A) be in writing unless made during a hearing or trial;

(B) state with particularity the grounds for seeking the order; and

(C) state the relief sought.

(2) *Form.* The rules governing captions and other matters of form in pleadings apply to motions and other papers.

(Amended December 27, 1946, effective March 19, 1948; January 21, 1963, effective July 1, 1963; April 28, 1983, effective August 1, 1983; April 30, 2007, effective December 1, 2007.)

RULE 7.1.   DISCLOSURE STATEMENT

(a) **Who Must File; Contents.** A nongovernmental corporate party must file two copies of a disclosure statement that:

(1) identifies any parent corporation and any publicly held corporation owning 10% or more of its stock; or

(2) states that there is no such corporation.

(b) **Time to File; Supplemental Filing.** A party must:

(1) file the disclosure statement with its first appearance, pleading, petition, motion, response, or other request addressed to the court; and

(2) promptly file a supplemental statement if any required information changes.

(Adopted April 29, 2002, effective December 1, 2002; April 30, 2007, effective December 1, 2007.)

RULE 8.   GENERAL RULES OF PLEADING

(a) **Claim for Relief.** A pleading that states a claim for relief must contain:

(1) a short and plain statement of the grounds for the court's jurisdiction, unless the court already has jurisdiction and the claim needs no new jurisdictional support;

(2) a short and plain statement of the claim showing that the pleader is entitled to relief; and

(3) a demand for the relief sought, which may include relief in the alternative or different types of relief.

(b) **Defenses; Admissions and Denials.**

(1) *In General.* In responding to a pleading, a party must:

(A) state in short and plain terms its defenses to each claim asserted against it; and

(B) admit or deny the allegations asserted against it by an opposing party.

(2) *Denials—Responding to the Substance.* A denial must fairly respond to the substance of the allegation.

(3) *General and Specific Denials.* A party that intends in good faith to deny all the allegations of a pleading—including the jurisdictional grounds—may do so by a general denial. A party that does not intend to deny all the allegations must either specifically deny designated allegations or generally deny all except those specifically admitted.

(4) *Denying Part of an Allegation.* A party that intends in good faith to deny only part of an allegation must admit the part that is true and deny the rest.

(5) *Lacking Knowledge or Information.* A party that lacks knowledge or information sufficient to form a belief about the truth of an allegation must so state, and the statement has the effect of a denial.

(6) *Effect of Failing to Deny.* An allegation—other than one relating to the amount of damages—is admitted if a responsive pleading is required and the allegation is not denied. If a responsive pleading is not required, an allegation is considered denied or avoided.

(c) **Affirmative Defenses.**

(1) *In General.* In responding to a pleading, a party must affirmatively state any avoidance or affirmative defense, including:

- accord and satisfaction;
- arbitration and award;
- assumption of risk;
- contributory negligence;
- duress;
- estoppel;
- failure of consideration;
- fraud;
- illegality;
- injury by fellow servant;
- laches;
- license;
- payment;
- release;
- res judicata;
- statute of frauds;
- statute of limitations; and
- waiver.

(2) *Mistaken Designation.* If a party mistakenly designates a defense as a counterclaim, or a counterclaim as a defense, the court must, if justice requires, treat the pleading as though it were correctly designated, and may impose terms for doing so.

(d) Pleading to Be Concise and Direct; Alternative Statements; Inconsistency.

(1) *In General.* Each allegation must be simple, concise, and direct. No technical form is required.

(2) *Alternative Statements of a Claim or Defense.* A party may set out 2 or more statements of a claim or defense alternatively or hypothetically, either in a single count or defense or in separate ones. If a party makes alternative statements, the pleading is sufficient if any one of them is sufficient.

(3) *Inconsistent Claims or Defenses.* A party may state as many separate claims or defenses as it has, regardless of consistency.

(e) Construing Pleadings. Pleadings must be construed so as to do justice.

(Amended February 28, 1966, effective July 1, 1966; March 2, 1987, effective August 1, 1987; April 30, 2007, effective December 1, 2007; April 28, 2010, effective December 1, 2010.)

RULE 9. PLEADING SPECIAL MATTERS

(a) Capacity or Authority to Sue; Legal Existence.

(1) *In General.* Except when required to show that the court has jurisdiction, a pleading need not allege:

(A) a party's capacity to sue or be sued;

(B) a party's authority to sue or be sued in a representative capacity; or

(C) the legal existence of an organized association of persons that is made a party.

(2) *Raising Those Issues.* To raise any of those issues, a party must do so by a specific denial, which must state any supporting facts that are peculiarly within the party's knowledge.

(b) Fraud or Mistake; Conditions of Mind. In alleging fraud or mistake, a party must state with particularity the circumstances constituting fraud or mistake. Malice, intent, knowledge, and other conditions of a person's mind may be alleged generally.

(c) Conditions Precedent. In pleading conditions precedent, it suffices to allege generally that all conditions precedent have occurred or been performed. But when denying that a condition precedent has occurred or been performed, a party must do so with particularity.

(d) Official Document or Act. In pleading an official document or official act, it suffices to allege that the document was legally issued or the act legally done.

(e) Judgment. In pleading a judgment or decision of a domestic or foreign court, a judicial or quasi-judicial tribunal, or a board or officer, it suffices to plead the judgment or decision without showing jurisdiction to render it.

(f) Time and Place. An allegation of time or place is material when testing the sufficiency of a pleading.

(g) Special Damages. If an item of special damage is claimed, it must be specifically stated.

(h) Admiralty or Maritime Claim.

(1) *How Designated.* If a claim for relief is within the admiralty or maritime jurisdiction and also within the court's subject-matter jurisdiction on some other ground, the pleading may designate the claim as an admiralty or maritime claim for purposes of Rules 14(c), 38(e), and 82 and the Supplemental Rules for Admiralty or Maritime Claims and Asset Forfeiture Actions. A claim cognizable only in the admiralty or maritime jurisdiction is an admiralty or maritime claim for those purposes, whether or not so designated.

(2) *Designation for Appeal.* A case that includes an admiralty or maritime claim within this subdivision (h) is an admiralty case within 28 U.S.C. § 1292(a)(3).

(Amended February 28, 1966, effective July 1, 1966; December 4, 1967, effective July 1, 1968; March 30, 1970, effective July 1, 1970; March 2, 1987, effective August 1, 1987; April 11, 1997, effective December 1, 1997; April 12, 2006, effective December 1, 2006; April 30, 2007, effective December 1, 2007.)

RULE 10. FORM OF PLEADINGS

(a) Caption; Names of Parties. Every pleading must have a caption with the court's name, a title, a file number, and a Rule 7(a) designation. The title of the complaint must name all the parties; the title of other pleadings, after naming the first party on each side, may refer generally to other parties.

(b) Paragraphs; Separate Statements. A party must state its claims or defenses in numbered paragraphs, each limited as far as practicable to a single set of circumstances. A later pleading may refer by number to a paragraph in an earlier pleading. If doing so would promote clarity, each claim founded on a separate transaction or occurrence—and each defense other than a denial—must be stated in a separate count or defense.

(c) Adoption by Reference; Exhibits. A statement in a pleading may be adopted by reference elsewhere in the same pleading or in any other pleading or motion. A copy of a written instrument that is an exhibit to a pleading is a part of the pleading for all purposes.

(Amended April 30, 2007, effective December 1, 2007.)

RULE 11. SIGNING PLEADINGS, MOTIONS, AND OTHER PAPERS; REPRESENTATIONS TO THE COURT; SANCTIONS

(a) Signature. Every pleading, written motion, and other paper must be signed by at least one attorney of record in the attorney's name—or by a party personally if the party is unrepresented. The paper must state the signer's address, e-mail address, and telephone number. Unless a rule or statute specifically states otherwise, a pleading need not be verified or accompanied by an affidavit. The court must strike an unsigned paper unless the omission is promptly corrected after being called to the attorney's or party's attention.

(b) Representations to the Court. By presenting to the court a pleading, written motion, or other paper—whether by signing, filing, submitting, or later advocating it—an attorney or unrepresented party certifies that to the best of the person's knowledge, information, and belief, formed after an inquiry reasonable under the circumstances:

　(1) it is not being presented for any improper purpose, such as to harass, cause unnecessary delay, or needlessly increase the cost of litigation;

　(2) the claims, defenses, and other legal contentions are warranted by existing law or by a nonfrivolous argument for extending, modifying, or reversing existing law or for establishing new law;

　(3) the factual contentions have evidentiary support or, if specifically so identified, will likely have evidentiary support after a reasonable opportunity for further investigation or discovery; and

　(4) the denials of factual contentions are warranted on the evidence or, if specifically so identified, are reasonably based on belief or a lack of information.

(c) Sanctions.

　(1) *In General.* If, after notice and a reasonable opportunity to respond, the court determines that Rule 11(b) has been violated, the court may impose an appropriate sanction on any attorney, law firm, or party that violated the rule or is responsible for the violation. Absent exceptional circumstances, a law firm must be held jointly responsible for a violation committed by its partner, associate, or employee.

　(2) *Motion for Sanctions.* A motion for sanctions must be made separately from any other motion and must describe the specific conduct that allegedly violates Rule 11(b). The motion must be served under Rule 5, but it must not be filed or be presented to the court if the challenged paper, claim, defense, contention, or denial is withdrawn or appropriately corrected within 21

days after service or within another time the court sets. If warranted, the court may award to the prevailing party the reasonable expenses, including attorney's fees, incurred for the motion.

　(3) *On the Court's Initiative.* On its own, the court may order an attorney, law firm, or party to show cause why conduct specifically described in the order has not violated Rule 11(b).

　(4) *Nature of a Sanction.* A sanction imposed under this rule must be limited to what suffices to deter repetition of the conduct or comparable conduct by others similarly situated. The sanction may include nonmonetary directives; an order to pay a penalty into court; or, if imposed on motion and warranted for effective deterrence, an order directing payment to the movant of part or all of the reasonable attorney's fees and other expenses directly resulting from the violation.

　(5) *Limitations on Monetary Sanctions.* The court must not impose a monetary sanction:

　　(A) against a represented party for violating Rule 11(b)(2); or

　　(B) on its own, unless it issued the show-cause order under Rule 11(c)(3) before voluntary dismissal or settlement of the claims made by or against the party that is, or whose attorneys are, to be sanctioned.

　(6) *Requirements for an Order.* An order imposing a sanction must describe the sanctioned conduct and explain the basis for the sanction.

(d) Inapplicability to Discovery. This rule does not apply to disclosures and discovery requests, responses, objections, and motions under Rules 26 through 37.

(Amended April 28, 1983, effective August 1, 1983; March 2, 1987, effective August 1, 1987; April 22, 1993, effective December 1, 1993; April 30, 2007, effective December 1, 2007.)

RULE 12. DEFENSES AND OBJECTIONS: WHEN AND HOW PRESENTED; MOTION FOR JUDGMENT ON THE PLEADINGS; CONSOLIDATING MOTIONS; WAIVING DEFENSES; PRETRIAL HEARING

(a) Time to Serve a Responsive Pleading.

　(1) *In General.* Unless another time is specified by this rule or a federal statute, the time for serving a responsive pleading is as follows:

　　(A) A defendant must serve an answer:

　　　(i) within 21 days after being served with the summons and complaint; or

(ii) if it has timely waived service under Rule 4(d), within 60 days after the request for a waiver was sent, or within 90 days after it was sent to the defendant outside any judicial district of the United States.

(B) A party must serve an answer to a counterclaim or crossclaim within 21 days after being served with the pleading that states the counterclaim or crossclaim.

(C) A party must serve a reply to an answer within 21 days after being served with an order to reply, unless the order specifies a different time.

(2) *United States and Its Agencies, Officers, or Employees Sued in an Official Capacity.* The United States, a United States agency, or a United States officer or employee sued only in an official capacity must serve an answer to a complaint, counterclaim, or crossclaim within 60 days after service on the United States attorney.

(3) *United States Officers or Employees Sued in an Individual Capacity.* A United States officer or employee sued in an individual capacity for an act or omission occurring in connection with duties performed on the United States' behalf must serve an answer to a complaint, counterclaim, or crossclaim within 60 days after service on the officer or employee or service on the United States attorney, whichever is later.

(4) *Effect of a Motion.* Unless the court sets a different time, serving a motion under this rule alters these periods as follows:

(A) if the court denies the motion or postpones its disposition until trial, the responsive pleading must be served within 14 days after notice of the court's action; or

(B) if the court grants a motion for a more definite statement, the responsive pleading must be served within 14 days after the more definite statement is served.

(b) **How to Present Defenses.** Every defense to a claim for relief in any pleading must be asserted in the responsive pleading if one is required. But a party may assert the following defenses by motion:

(1) lack of subject-matter jurisdiction;

(2) lack of personal jurisdiction;

(3) improper venue;

(4) insufficient process;

(5) insufficient service of process;

(6) failure to state a claim upon which relief can be granted; and

(7) failure to join a party under Rule 19.

A motion asserting any of these defenses must be made before pleading if a responsive pleading is allowed. If a pleading sets out a claim for relief that does not require a responsive pleading, an opposing party may assert at trial any defense to that claim. No defense or objection is waived by joining it with one or more other defenses or objections in a responsive pleading or in a motion.

(c) **Motion for Judgment on the Pleadings.** After the pleadings are closed—but early enough not to delay trial—a party may move for judgment on the pleadings.

(d) **Result of Presenting Matters Outside the Pleadings.** If, on a motion under Rule 12(b)(6) or 12(c), matters outside the pleadings are presented to and not excluded by the court, the motion must be treated as one for summary judgment under Rule 56. All parties must be given a reasonable opportunity to present all the material that is pertinent to the motion.

(e) **Motion for a More Definite Statement.** A party may move for a more definite statement of a pleading to which a responsive pleading is allowed but which is so vague or ambiguous that the party cannot reasonably prepare a response. The motion must be made before filing a responsive pleading and must point out the defects complained of and the details desired. If the court orders a more definite statement and the order is not obeyed within 14 days after notice of the order or within the time the court sets, the court may strike the pleading or issue any other appropriate order.

(f) **Motion to Strike.** The court may strike from a pleading an insufficient defense or any redundant, immaterial, impertinent, or scandalous matter. The court may act:

(1) on its own; or

(2) on motion made by a party either before responding to the pleading or, if a response is not allowed, within 21 days after being served with the pleading.

(g) **Joining Motions.**

(1) *Right to Join.* A motion under this rule may be joined with any other motion allowed by this rule.

(2) *Limitation on Further Motions.* Except as provided in Rule 12(h)(2) or (3), a party that makes a motion under this rule must not make another motion under this rule raising a defense or objection that was available to the party but omitted from its earlier motion.

(h) **Waiving and Preserving Certain Defenses.**

(1) *When Some Are Waived.* A party waives any defense listed in Rule 12(b)(2)-(5) by:

(A) omitting it from a motion in the circumstances described in Rule 12(g)(2); or

(B) failing to either:

  (i) make it by motion under this rule; or

  (ii) include it in a responsive pleading or in an amendment allowed by Rule 15(a)(1) as a matter of course.

(2) *When to Raise Others.* Failure to state a claim upon which relief can be granted, to join a person required by Rule 19(b), or to state a legal defense to a claim may be raised:

  (A) in any pleading allowed or ordered under Rule 7(a);

  (B) by a motion under Rule 12(c); or

  (C) at trial.

(3) *Lack of Subject–Matter Jurisdiction.* If the court determines at any time that it lacks subject-matter jurisdiction, the court must dismiss the action.

(i) Hearing Before Trial. If a party so moves, any defense listed in Rule 12(b)(1)-(7)—whether made in a pleading or by motion—and a motion under Rule 12(c) must be heard and decided before trial unless the court orders a deferral until trial.

(Amended December 27, 1946, effective March 19, 1948; January 21, 1963, effective July 1, 1963; February 28, 1966, effective July 1, 1966; March 2, 1987, effective August 1, 1987; April 22, 1993, effective December 1, 1993; April 17, 2000, effective December 1, 2000; April 30, 2007, effective December 1, 2007; March 26, 2009, effective December 1, 2009.)

RULE 13. COUNTERCLAIM AND CROSSCLAIM

(a) Compulsory Counterclaim.

(1) *In General.* A pleading must state as a counterclaim any claim that—at the time of its service—the pleader has against an opposing party if the claim:

  (A) arises out of the transaction or occurrence that is the subject matter of the opposing party's claim; and

  (B) does not require adding another party over whom the court cannot acquire jurisdiction.

(2) *Exceptions.* The pleader need not state the claim if:

  (A) when the action was commenced, the claim was the subject of another pending action; or

  (B) the opposing party sued on its claim by attachment or other process that did not establish personal jurisdiction over the pleader on that claim, and the pleader does not assert any counterclaim under this rule.

(b) Permissive Counterclaim. A pleading may state as a counterclaim against an opposing party any claim that is not compulsory.

(c) Relief Sought in a Counterclaim. A counterclaim need not diminish or defeat the recovery sought by the opposing party. It may request relief that exceeds in amount or differs in kind from the relief sought by the opposing party.

(d) Counterclaim Against the United States. These rules do not expand the right to assert a counterclaim—or to claim a credit—against the United States or a United States officer or agency.

(e) Counterclaim Maturing or Acquired After Pleading. The court may permit a party to file a supplemental pleading asserting a counterclaim that matured or was acquired by the party after serving an earlier pleading.

(f) [Abrogated]

(g) Crossclaim Against a Coparty. A pleading may state as a crossclaim any claim by one party against a coparty if the claim arises out of the transaction or occurrence that is the subject matter of the original action or of a counterclaim, or if the claim relates to any property that is the subject matter of the original action. The crossclaim may include a claim that the coparty is or may be liable to the cross-claimant for all or part of a claim asserted in the action against the cross-claimant.

(h) Joining Additional Parties. Rules 19 and 20 govern the addition of a person as a party to a counterclaim or crossclaim.

(i) Separate Trials; Separate Judgments. If the court orders separate trials under Rule 42(b), it may enter judgment on a counterclaim or crossclaim under Rule 54(b) when it has jurisdiction to do so, even if the opposing party's claims have been dismissed or otherwise resolved.

(Amended December 27, 1946, effective March 19, 1948; January 21, 1963, effective July 1, 1963; February 28, 1966, effective July 1, 1966; March 2, 1987, effective August 1, 1987; April 30, 2007, effective December 1, 2007; March 26, 2009, effective December 1, 2009.)

RULE 14. THIRD–PARTY PRACTICE

(a) When a Defending Party May Bring in a Third Party.

(1) *Timing of the Summons and Complaint.* A defending party may, as third-party plaintiff, serve a summons and complaint on a nonparty who is or may be liable to it for all or part of the claim against it. But the third-party plaintiff must, by motion, obtain the court's leave if it files the third-party complaint more than 14 days after serving its original answer.

(2) *Third–Party Defendant's Claims and Defenses.* The person served with the summons and third-party complaint—the "third-party defendant":

  (A) must assert any defense against the third-party plaintiff's claim under Rule 12;

  (B) must assert any counterclaim against the third-party plaintiff under Rule 13(a), and may assert any counterclaim against the third-party plaintiff under Rule 13(b) or any crossclaim against another third-party defendant under Rule 13(g);

  (C) may assert against the plaintiff any defense that the third-party plaintiff has to the plaintiff's claim; and

  (D) may also assert against the plaintiff any claim arising out of the transaction or occurrence that is the subject matter of the plaintiff's claim against the third-party plaintiff.

(3) *Plaintiff's Claims Against a Third–Party Defendant.* The plaintiff may assert against the third-party defendant any claim arising out of the transaction or occurrence that is the subject matter of the plaintiff's claim against the third-party plaintiff. The third-party defendant must then assert any defense under Rule 12 and any counterclaim under Rule 13(a), and may assert any counterclaim under Rule 13(b) or any crossclaim under Rule 13(g).

(4) *Motion to Strike, Sever, or Try Separately.* Any party may move to strike the third-party claim, to sever it, or to try it separately.

(5) *Third–Party Defendant's Claim Against a Nonparty.* A third-party defendant may proceed under this rule against a nonparty who is or may be liable to the third-party defendant for all or part of any claim against it.

(6) *Third–Party Complaint In Rem.* If it is within the admiralty or maritime jurisdiction, a third-party complaint may be in rem. In that event, a reference in this rule to the "summons" includes the warrant of arrest, and a reference to the defendant or third-party plaintiff includes, when appropriate, a person who asserts a right under Supplemental Rule C(6)(a)(i) in the property arrested.

(b) **When a Plaintiff May Bring in a Third Party.** When a claim is asserted against a plaintiff, the plaintiff may bring in a third party if this rule would allow a defendant to do so.

(c) **Admiralty or Maritime Claim.**

  (1) *Scope of Impleader.* If a plaintiff asserts an admiralty or maritime claim under Rule 9(h), the defendant or a person who asserts a right under Supplemental Rule C(6)(a)(i) may, as a third-party plaintiff, bring in a third-party defendant who may be wholly or partly liable—either to the plaintiff or to the third-party plaintiff—for remedy over, contribution, or otherwise on account of the same transaction, occurrence, or series of transactions or occurrences.

  (2) *Defending Against a Demand for Judgment for the Plaintiff.* The third-party plaintiff may demand judgment in the plaintiff's favor against the third-party defendant. In that event, the third-party defendant must defend under Rule 12 against the plaintiff's claim as well as the third-party plaintiff's claim; and the action proceeds as if the plaintiff had sued both the third-party defendant and the third-party plaintiff.

(Amended December 27, 1946, effective March 19, 1948; January 21, 1963, effective July 1, 1963; February 28, 1966, effective July 1, 1966; March 2, 1987, effective August 1, 1987; April 17, 2000, effective December 1, 2000; April 12, 2006, effective December 1, 2006; April 30, 2007, effective December 1, 2007; March 26, 2009, effective December 1, 2009.)

RULE 15. AMENDED AND SUPPLEMENTAL PLEADINGS

(a) **Amendments Before Trial.**

  (1) *Amending as a Matter of Course.* A party may amend its pleading once as a matter of course within:

    (A) 21 days after serving it, or

    (B) if the pleading is one to which a responsive pleading is required, 21 days after service of a responsive pleading or 21 days after service of a motion under Rule 12(b), (e), or (f), whichever is earlier.

  (2) *Other Amendments.* In all other cases, a party may amend its pleading only with the opposing party's written consent or the court's leave. The court should freely give leave when justice so requires.

  (3) *Time to Respond.* Unless the court orders otherwise, any required response to an amended pleading must be made within the time remaining to respond to the original pleading or within 14 days after service of the amended pleading, whichever is later.

(b) **Amendments During and After Trial.**

  (1) *Based on an Objection at Trial.* If, at trial, a party objects that evidence is not within the issues raised in the pleadings, the court may permit the pleadings to be amended. The court should freely permit an amendment when doing so will aid in presenting the merits and the objecting party fails to satisfy the court that the evidence would prejudice that party's action or defense on the merits. The court may grant a

continuance to enable the objecting party to meet the evidence.

(2) *For Issues Tried by Consent.* When an issue not raised by the pleadings is tried by the parties' express or implied consent, it must be treated in all respects as if raised in the pleadings. A party may move—at any time, even after judgment—to amend the pleadings to conform them to the evidence and to raise an unpleaded issue. But failure to amend does not affect the result of the trial of that issue.

(c) Relation Back of Amendments.

(1) *When an Amendment Relates Back.* An amendment to a pleading relates back to the date of the original pleading when:

(A) the law that provides the applicable statute of limitations allows relation back;

(B) the amendment asserts a claim or defense that arose out of the conduct, transaction, or occurrence set out—or attempted to be set out—in the original pleading; or

(C) the amendment changes the party or the naming of the party against whom a claim is asserted, if Rule 15(c)(1)(B) is satisfied and if, within the period provided by Rule 4(m) for serving the summons and complaint, the party to be brought in by amendment:

(i) received such notice of the action that it will not be prejudiced in defending on the merits; and

(ii) knew or should have known that the action would have been brought against it, but for a mistake concerning the proper party's identity.

(2) *Notice to the United States.* When the United States or a United States officer or agency is added as a defendant by amendment, the notice requirements of Rule 15(c)(1)(C)(i) and (ii) are satisfied if, during the stated period, process was delivered or mailed to the United States attorney or the United States attorney's designee, to the Attorney General of the United States, or to the officer or agency.

(d) Supplemental Pleadings. On motion and reasonable notice, the court may, on just terms, permit a party to serve a supplemental pleading setting out any transaction, occurrence, or event that happened after the date of the pleading to be supplemented. The court may permit supplementation even though the original pleading is defective in stating a claim or defense. The court may order

that the opposing party plead to the supplemental pleading within a specified time.

(Amended January 21, 1963, effective July 1, 1963; February 28, 1966, effective July 1, 1966; March 2, 1987, effective August 1, 1987; April 30, 1991, effective December 1, 1991; amended by Pub.L. 102–198, § 11, December 9, 1991, 105 Stat. 1626; amended April 22, 1993, effective December 1, 1993; April 30, 2007, effective December 1, 2007; March 26, 2009, effective December 1, 2009.)

RULE 16.   PRETRIAL CONFERENCES; SCHEDULING; MANAGEMENT

(a) Purposes of a Pretrial Conference. In any action, the court may order the attorneys and any unrepresented parties to appear for one or more pretrial conferences for such purposes as:

(1) expediting disposition of the action;

(2) establishing early and continuing control so that the case will not be protracted because of lack of management;

(3) discouraging wasteful pretrial activities;

(4) improving the quality of the trial through more thorough preparation; and

(5) facilitating settlement.

(b) Scheduling.

(1) *Scheduling Order.* Except in categories of actions exempted by local rule, the district judge—or a magistrate judge when authorized by local rule—must issue a scheduling order:

(A) after receiving the parties' report under Rule 26(f); or

(B) after consulting with the parties' attorneys and any unrepresented parties at a scheduling conference or by telephone, mail, or other means.

(2) *Time to Issue.* The judge must issue the scheduling order as soon as practicable, but in any event within the earlier of 120 days after any defendant has been served with the complaint or 90 days after any defendant has appeared.

(3) *Contents of the Order.*

(A) *Required Contents.* The scheduling order must limit the time to join other parties, amend the pleadings, complete discovery, and file motions.

(B) *Permitted Contents.* The scheduling order may:

(i) modify the timing of disclosures under Rules 26(a) and 26(e)(1);

(ii) modify the extent of discovery;

(iii) provide for disclosure or discovery of electronically stored information;

(iv) include any agreements the parties reach for asserting claims of privilege or of protection as trial-preparation material after information is produced;

(v) set dates for pretrial conferences and for trial; and

(vi) include other appropriate matters.

(4) *Modifying a Schedule.* A schedule may be modified only for good cause and with the judge's consent.

(c) **Attendance and Matters for Consideration at a Pretrial Conference.**

(1) *Attendance.* A represented party must authorize at least one of its attorneys to make stipulations and admissions about all matters that can reasonably be anticipated for discussion at a pretrial conference. If appropriate, the court may require that a party or its representative be present or reasonably available by other means to consider possible settlement.

(2) *Matters for Consideration.* At any pretrial conference, the court may consider and take appropriate action on the following matters:

(A) formulating and simplifying the issues, and eliminating frivolous claims or defenses;

(B) amending the pleadings if necessary or desirable;

(C) obtaining admissions and stipulations about facts and documents to avoid unnecessary proof, and ruling in advance on the admissibility of evidence;

(D) avoiding unnecessary proof and cumulative evidence, and limiting the use of testimony under Federal Rule of Evidence 702;

(E) determining the appropriateness and timing of summary adjudication under Rule 56;

(F) controlling and scheduling discovery, including orders affecting disclosures and discovery under Rule 26 and Rules 29 through 37;

(G) identifying witnesses and documents, scheduling the filing and exchange of any pretrial briefs, and setting dates for further conferences and for trial;

(H) referring matters to a magistrate judge or a master;

(I) settling the case and using special procedures to assist in resolving the dispute when authorized by statute or local rule;

(J) determining the form and content of the pretrial order;

(K) disposing of pending motions;

(L) adopting special procedures for managing potentially difficult or protracted actions that may involve complex issues, multiple parties, difficult legal questions, or unusual proof problems;

(M) ordering a separate trial under Rule 42(b) of a claim, counterclaim, crossclaim, third-party claim, or particular issue;

(N) ordering the presentation of evidence early in the trial on a manageable issue that might, on the evidence, be the basis for a judgment as a matter of law under Rule 50(a) or a judgment on partial findings under Rule 52(c);

(O) establishing a reasonable limit on the time allowed to present evidence; and

(P) facilitating in other ways the just, speedy, and inexpensive disposition of the action.

(d) **Pretrial Orders.** After any conference under this rule, the court should issue an order reciting the action taken. This order controls the course of the action unless the court modifies it.

(e) **Final Pretrial Conference and Orders.** The court may hold a final pretrial conference to formulate a trial plan, including a plan to facilitate the admission of evidence. The conference must be held as close to the start of trial as is reasonable, and must be attended by at least one attorney who will conduct the trial for each party and by any unrepresented party. The court may modify the order issued after a final pretrial conference only to prevent manifest injustice.

(f) **Sanctions.**

(1) *In General.* On motion or on its own, the court may issue any just orders, including those authorized by Rule 37(b)(2)(A)(ii)-(vii), if a party or its attorney:

(A) fails to appear at a scheduling or other pretrial conference;

(B) is substantially unprepared to participate—or does not participate in good faith—in the conference; or

(C) fails to obey a scheduling or other pretrial order.

(2) *Imposing Fees and Costs.* Instead of or in addition to any other sanction, the court must order the party, its attorney, or both to pay the reasonable expenses—including attorney's fees—incurred because of any noncompliance with this rule, unless the noncompliance was substantially justified or other circumstances make an award of expenses unjust.

(Amended April 28, 1983, effective August 1, 1983; March 2, 1987, effective August 1, 1987; April 22, 1993, effective December 1, 1993; April 12, 2006, effective December 1, 2006; April 30, 2007, effective December 1, 2007.)

TITLE IV. PARTIES

RULE 17. PLAINTIFF AND DEFENDANT; CAPACITY; PUBLIC OFFICERS

(a) Real Party in Interest.

(1) *Designation in General.* An action must be prosecuted in the name of the real party in interest. The following may sue in their own names without joining the person for whose benefit the action is brought:

(A) an executor;

(B) an administrator;

(C) a guardian;

(D) a bailee;

(E) a trustee of an express trust;

(F) a party with whom or in whose name a contract has been made for another's benefit; and

(G) a party authorized by statute.

(2) *Action in the Name of the United States for Another's Use or Benefit.* When a federal statute so provides, an action for another's use or benefit must be brought in the name of the United States.

(3) *Joinder of the Real Party in Interest.* The court may not dismiss an action for failure to prosecute in the name of the real party in interest until, after an objection, a reasonable time has been allowed for the real party in interest to ratify, join, or be substituted into the action. After ratification, joinder, or substitution, the action proceeds as if it had been originally commenced by the real party in interest.

(b) Capacity to Sue or Be Sued. Capacity to sue or be sued is determined as follows:

(1) for an individual who is not acting in a representative capacity, by the law of the individual's domicile;

(2) for a corporation, by the law under which it was organized; and

(3) for all other parties, by the law of the state where the court is located, except that:

(A) a partnership or other unincorporated association with no such capacity under that state's law may sue or be sued in its common name to enforce a substantive right existing under the United States Constitution or laws; and

(B) 28 U.S.C. §§ 754 and 959(a) govern the capacity of a receiver appointed by a United States court to sue or be sued in a United States court.

(c) Minor or Incompetent Person.

(1) *With a Representative.* The following representatives may sue or defend on behalf of a minor or an incompetent person:

(A) a general guardian;

(B) a committee;

(C) a conservator; or

(D) a like fiduciary.

(2) *Without a Representative.* A minor or an incompetent person who does not have a duly appointed representative may sue by a next friend or by a guardian ad litem. The court must appoint a guardian ad litem—or issue another appropriate order—to protect a minor or incompetent person who is unrepresented in an action.

(d) Public Officer's Title and Name. A public officer who sues or is sued in an official capacity may be designated by official title rather than by name, but the court may order that the officer's name be added.

(Amended December 27, 1946, effective March 19, 1948; December 29, 1948, effective October 20, 1949; February 28, 1966, effective July 1, 1966; March 2, 1987, effective August 1, 1987; April 25, 1988, effective August 1, 1988; amended by Pub.L. 100–690, Title VII, § 7049, November 18, 1988, 102 Stat. 4401 (although amendment by Pub.L. 100–690 could not be executed due to prior amendment by Court order which made the same change effective August 1, 1988); April 30, 2007, effective December 1, 2007.)

RULE 18. JOINDER OF CLAIMS

(a) In General. A party asserting a claim, counterclaim, crossclaim, or third-party claim may join, as independent or alternative claims, as many claims as it has against an opposing party.

(b) Joinder of Contingent Claims. A party may join two claims even though one of them is contingent on the disposition of the other; but the court may grant relief only in accordance with the parties' relative substantive rights. In particular, a plaintiff may state a claim for money and a claim to set aside a conveyance that is fraudulent as to that plaintiff, without first obtaining a judgment for the money.

(Amended February 28, 1966, effective July 1, 1966; March 2, 1987, effective August 1, 1987; April 30, 2007, effective December 1, 2007.)

RULE 19. REQUIRED JOINDER OF PARTIES

(a) Persons Required to Be Joined if Feasible.

(1) *Required Party.* A person who is subject to service of process and whose joinder will not

deprive the court of subject-matter jurisdiction must be joined as a party if:

(A) in that person's absence, the court cannot accord complete relief among existing parties; or

(B) that person claims an interest relating to the subject of the action and is so situated that disposing of the action in the person's absence may:

(i) as a practical matter impair or impede the person's ability to protect the interest; or

(ii) leave an existing party subject to a substantial risk of incurring double, multiple, or otherwise inconsistent obligations because of the interest.

(2) *Joinder by Court Order.* If a person has not been joined as required, the court must order that the person be made a party. A person who refuses to join as a plaintiff may be made either a defendant or, in a proper case, an involuntary plaintiff.

(3) *Venue.* If a joined party objects to venue and the joinder would make venue improper, the court must dismiss that party.

(b) **When Joinder Is Not Feasible.** If a person who is required to be joined if feasible cannot be joined, the court must determine whether, in equity and good conscience, the action should proceed among the existing parties or should be dismissed. The factors for the court to consider include:

(1) the extent to which a judgment rendered in the person's absence might prejudice that person or the existing parties;

(2) the extent to which any prejudice could be lessened or avoided by:

(A) protective provisions in the judgment;

(B) shaping the relief; or

(C) other measures;

(3) whether a judgment rendered in the person's absence would be adequate; and

(4) whether the plaintiff would have an adequate remedy if the action were dismissed for nonjoinder.

(c) **Pleading the Reasons for Nonjoinder.** When asserting a claim for relief, a party must state:

(1) the name, if known, of any person who is required to be joined if feasible but is not joined; and

(2) the reasons for not joining that person.

(d) **Exception for Class Actions.** This rule is subject to Rule 23.

(Amended February 28, 1966, effective July 1, 1966; March 2, 1987, effective August 1, 1987; April 30, 2007, effective December 1, 2007.)

RULE 20. PERMISSIVE JOINDER OF PARTIES

(a) **Persons Who May Join or Be Joined.**

(1) *Plaintiffs.* Persons may join in one action as plaintiffs if:

(A) they assert any right to relief jointly, severally, or in the alternative with respect to or arising out of the same transaction, occurrence, or series of transactions or occurrences; and

(B) any question of law or fact common to all plaintiffs will arise in the action.

(2) *Defendants.* Persons—as well as a vessel, cargo, or other property subject to admiralty process in rem—may be joined in one action as defendants if:

(A) any right to relief is asserted against them jointly, severally, or in the alternative with respect to or arising out of the same transaction, occurrence, or series of transactions or occurrences; and

(B) any question of law or fact common to all defendants will arise in the action.

(3) *Extent of Relief.* Neither a plaintiff nor a defendant need be interested in obtaining or defending against all the relief demanded. The court may grant judgment to one or more plaintiffs according to their rights, and against one or more defendants according to their liabilities.

(b) **Protective Measures.** The court may issue orders—including an order for separate trials—to protect a party against embarrassment, delay, expense, or other prejudice that arises from including a person against whom the party asserts no claim and who asserts no claim against the party.

(Amended February 28, 1966, effective July 1, 1966; March 2, 1987, effective August 1, 1987; April 30, 2007, effective December 1, 2007.)

RULE 21. MISJOINDER AND NONJOINDER OF PARTIES

Misjoinder of parties is not a ground for dismissing an action. On motion or on its own, the court may at any time, on just terms, add or drop a party. The court may also sever any claim against a party.

(Amended April 30, 2007, effective December 1, 2007.)

RULE 22. INTERPLEADER

(a) **Grounds.**

(1) *By a Plaintiff.* Persons with claims that may expose a plaintiff to double or multiple liability

may be joined as defendants and required to interplead. Joinder for interpleader is proper even though:

(A) the claims of the several claimants, or the titles on which their claims depend, lack a common origin or are adverse and independent rather than identical; or

(B) the plaintiff denies liability in whole or in part to any or all of the claimants.

(2) *By a Defendant.* A defendant exposed to similar liability may seek interpleader through a crossclaim or counterclaim.

(b) **Relation to Other Rules and Statutes.** This rule supplements—and does not limit—the joinder of parties allowed by Rule 20. The remedy this rule provides is in addition to—and does not supersede or limit—the remedy provided by 28 U.S.C. §§ 1335, 1397, and 2361. An action under those statutes must be conducted under these rules.

(Amended December 29, 1948, effective October 20, 1949; March 2, 1987, effective August 1, 1987; April 30, 2007, effective December 1, 2007.)

RULE 23. CLASS ACTIONS

(a) **Prerequisites.** One or more members of a class may sue or be sued as representative parties on behalf of all members only if:

(1) the class is so numerous that joinder of all members is impracticable;

(2) there are questions of law or fact common to the class;

(3) the claims or defenses of the representative parties are typical of the claims or defenses of the class; and

(4) the representative parties will fairly and adequately protect the interests of the class.

(b) **Types of Class Actions.** A class action may be maintained if Rule 23(a) is satisfied and if:

(1) prosecuting separate actions by or against individual class members would create a risk of:

(A) inconsistent or varying adjudications with respect to individual class members that would establish incompatible standards of conduct for the party opposing the class; or

(B) adjudications with respect to individual class members that, as a practical matter, would be dispositive of the interests of the other members not parties to the individual adjudications or would substantially impair or impede their ability to protect their interests;

(2) the party opposing the class has acted or refused to act on grounds that apply generally to the class, so that final injunctive relief or corresponding declaratory relief is appropriate respecting the class as a whole; or

(3) the court finds that the questions of law or fact common to class members predominate over any questions affecting only individual members, and that a class action is superior to other available methods for fairly and efficiently adjudicating the controversy. The matters pertinent to these findings include:

(A) the class members' interests in individually controlling the prosecution or defense of separate actions;

(B) the extent and nature of any litigation concerning the controversy already begun by or against class members;

(C) the desirability or undesirability of concentrating the litigation of the claims in the particular forum; and

(D) the likely difficulties in managing a class action.

(c) **Certification Order; Notice to Class Members; Judgment; Issues Classes; Subclasses.**

(1) *Certification Order.*

(A) *Time to Issue.* At an early practicable time after a person sues or is sued as a class representative, the court must determine by order whether to certify the action as a class action.

(B) *Defining the Class; Appointing Class Counsel.* An order that certifies a class action must define the class and the class claims, issues, or defenses, and must appoint class counsel under Rule 23(g).

(C) *Altering or Amending the Order.* An order that grants or denies class certification may be altered or amended before final judgment.

(2) *Notice.*

(A) *For (b)(1) or (b)(2) Classes.* For any class certified under Rule 23(b)(1) or (b)(2), the court may direct appropriate notice to the class.

(B) *For (b)(3) Classes.* For any class certified under Rule 23(b)(3), the court must direct to class members the best notice that is practicable under the circumstances, including individual notice to all members who can be identified through reasonable effort. The notice must clearly and concisely state in plain, easily understood language:

(i) the nature of the action;

(ii) the definition of the class certified;

(iii) the class claims, issues, or defenses;

(iv) that a class member may enter an appearance through an attorney if the member so desires;

(v) that the court will exclude from the class any member who requests exclusion;

(vi) the time and manner for requesting exclusion; and

(vii) the binding effect of a class judgment on members under Rule 23(c)(3).

(3) *Judgment.* Whether or not favorable to the class, the judgment in a class action must:

(A) for any class certified under Rule 23(b)(1) or (b)(2), include and describe those whom the court finds to be class members; and

(B) for any class certified under Rule 23(b)(3), include and specify or describe those to whom the Rule 23(c)(2) notice was directed, who have not requested exclusion, and whom the court finds to be class members.

(4) *Particular Issues.* When appropriate, an action may be brought or maintained as a class action with respect to particular issues.

(5) *Subclasses.* When appropriate, a class may be divided into subclasses that are each treated as a class under this rule.

(d) **Conducting the Action.**

(1) *In General.* In conducting an action under this rule, the court may issue orders that:

(A) determine the course of proceedings or prescribe measures to prevent undue repetition or complication in presenting evidence or argument;

(B) require—to protect class members and fairly conduct the action—giving appropriate notice to some or all class members of:

(i) any step in the action;

(ii) the proposed extent of the judgment; or

(iii) the members' opportunity to signify whether they consider the representation fair and adequate, to intervene and present claims or defenses, or to otherwise come into the action;

(C) impose conditions on the representative parties or on intervenors;

(D) require that the pleadings be amended to eliminate allegations about representation of absent persons and that the action proceed accordingly; or

(E) deal with similar procedural matters.

(2) *Combining and Amending Orders.* An order under Rule 23(d)(1) may be altered or amended from time to time and may be combined with an order under Rule 16.

(e) **Settlement, Voluntary Dismissal, or Compromise.** The claims, issues, or defenses of a certified class may be settled, voluntarily dismissed, or compromised only with the court's approval. The following procedures apply to a proposed settlement, voluntary dismissal, or compromise:

(1) The court must direct notice in a reasonable manner to all class members who would be bound by the proposal.

(2) If the proposal would bind class members, the court may approve it only after a hearing and on finding that it is fair, reasonable, and adequate.

(3) The parties seeking approval must file a statement identifying any agreement made in connection with the proposal.

(4) If the class action was previously certified under Rule 23(b)(3), the court may refuse to approve a settlement unless it affords a new opportunity to request exclusion to individual class members who had an earlier opportunity to request exclusion but did not do so.

(5) Any class member may object to the proposal if it requires court approval under this subdivision (e); the objection may be withdrawn only with the court's approval.

(f) **Appeals.** A court of appeals may permit an appeal from an order granting or denying class-action certification under this rule if a petition for permission to appeal is filed with the circuit clerk within 14 days after the order is entered. An appeal does not stay proceedings in the district court unless the district judge or the court of appeals so orders.

(g) **Class Counsel.**

(1) *Appointing Class Counsel.* Unless a statute provides otherwise, a court that certifies a class must appoint class counsel. In appointing class counsel, the court:

(A) must consider:

(i) the work counsel has done in identifying or investigating potential claims in the action;

(ii) counsel's experience in handling class actions, other complex litigation, and the types of claims asserted in the action;

(iii) counsel's knowledge of the applicable law; and

(iv) the resources that counsel will commit to representing the class;

(B) may consider any other matter pertinent to counsel's ability to fairly and adequately represent the interests of the class;

(C) may order potential class counsel to provide information on any subject pertinent to the appointment and to propose terms for attorney's fees and nontaxable costs;

(D) may include in the appointing order provisions about the award of attorney's fees or nontaxable costs under Rule 23(h); and

(E) may make further orders in connection with the appointment.

(2) *Standard for Appointing Class Counsel.* When one applicant seeks appointment as class counsel, the court may appoint that applicant only if the applicant is adequate under Rule 23(g)(1) and (4). If more than one adequate applicant seeks appointment, the court must appoint the applicant best able to represent the interests of the class.

(3) *Interim Counsel.* The court may designate interim counsel to act on behalf of a putative class before determining whether to certify the action as a class action.

(4) *Duty of Class Counsel.* Class counsel must fairly and adequately represent the interests of the class.

(h) Attorney's Fees and Nontaxable Costs. In a certified class action, the court may award reasonable attorney's fees and nontaxable costs that are authorized by law or by the parties' agreement. The following procedures apply:

(1) A claim for an award must be made by motion under Rule 54(d)(2), subject to the provisions of this subdivision (h), at a time the court sets. Notice of the motion must be served on all parties and, for motions by class counsel, directed to class members in a reasonable manner.

(2) A class member, or a party from whom payment is sought, may object to the motion.

(3) The court may hold a hearing and must find the facts and state its legal conclusions under Rule 52(a).

(4) The court may refer issues related to the amount of the award to a special master or a magistrate judge, as provided in Rule 54(d)(2)(D).

(Amended February 28, 1966, effective July 1, 1966; March 2, 1987, effective August 1, 1987; April 24, 1998, effective December 1, 1998; March 27, 2003, effective December 1, 2003; April 30, 2007, effective December 1, 2007; March 26, 2009, effective December 1, 2009.)

RULE 23.1.   DERIVATIVE ACTIONS

(a) Prerequisites. This rule applies when one or more shareholders or members of a corporation or an unincorporated association bring a derivative action to enforce a right that the corporation or association may properly assert but has failed to enforce. The derivative action may not be maintained if it appears that the plaintiff does not fairly and adequately represent the interests of shareholders or members who are similarly situat-

ed in enforcing the right of the corporation or association.

(b) Pleading Requirements. The complaint must be verified and must:

(1) allege that the plaintiff was a shareholder or member at the time of the transaction complained of, or that the plaintiff's share or membership later devolved on it by operation of law;

(2) allege that the action is not a collusive one to confer jurisdiction that the court would otherwise lack; and

(3) state with particularity:

(A) any effort by the plaintiff to obtain the desired action from the directors or comparable authority and, if necessary, from the shareholders or members; and

(B) the reasons for not obtaining the action or not making the effort.

(c) Settlement, Dismissal, and Compromise. A derivative action may be settled, voluntarily dismissed, or compromised only with the court's approval. Notice of a proposed settlement, voluntary dismissal, or compromise must be given to shareholders or members in the manner that the court orders.

(Adopted February 28, 1966, effective July 1, 1966; amended March 2, 1987, effective August 1, 1987; April 30, 2007, effective December 1, 2007.)

RULE 23.2.   ACTIONS RELATING TO UNINCORPORATED ASSOCIATIONS

This rule applies to an action brought by or against the members of an unincorporated association as a class by naming certain members as representative parties. The action may be maintained only if it appears that those parties will fairly and adequately protect the interests of the association and its members. In conducting the action, the court may issue any appropriate orders corresponding with those in Rule 23(d), and the procedure for settlement, voluntary dismissal, or compromise must correspond with the procedure in Rule 23(e).

(Adopted February 28, 1966, effective July 1, 1966; amended April 30, 2007, effective December 1, 2007.)

RULE 24.   INTERVENTION

(a) Intervention of Right. On timely motion, the court must permit anyone to intervene who:

(1) is given an unconditional right to intervene by a federal statute; or

(2) claims an interest relating to the property or transaction that is the subject of the action, and is so situated that disposing of the action may as a practical matter impair or impede the movant's ability to protect its interest, unless existing parties adequately represent that interest.

(b) Permissive Intervention.

  (1) *In General.* On timely motion, the court may permit anyone to intervene who:

    (A) is given a conditional right to intervene by a federal statute; or

    (B) has a claim or defense that shares with the main action a common question of law or fact.

  (2) *By a Government Officer or Agency.* On timely motion, the court may permit a federal or state governmental officer or agency to intervene if a party's claim or defense is based on:

    (A) a statute or executive order administered by the officer or agency; or

    (B) any regulation, order, requirement, or agreement issued or made under the statute or executive order.

  (3) *Delay or Prejudice.* In exercising its discretion, the court must consider whether the intervention will unduly delay or prejudice the adjudication of the original parties' rights.

(c) Notice and Pleading Required. A motion to intervene must be served on the parties as provided in Rule 5. The motion must state the grounds for intervention and be accompanied by a pleading that sets out the claim or defense for which intervention is sought.

(Amended December 27, 1946, effective March 19, 1948; December 29, 1948, effective October 20, 1949; January 21, 1963, effective July 1, 1963; February 28, 1966, effective July 1, 1966; March 2, 1987, effective August 1, 1987; April 30, 1991, effective December 1, 1991; April 12, 2006, effective December 1, 2006; April 30, 2007, effective December 1, 2007.)

RULE 25. SUBSTITUTION OF PARTIES

(a) Death.

  (1) *Substitution if the Claim Is Not Extinguished.* If a party dies and the claim is not extinguished, the court may order substitution of the proper party. A motion for substitution may be made by any party or by the decedent's successor or representative. If the motion is not made within 90 days after service of a statement noting the death, the action by or against the decedent must be dismissed.

  (2) *Continuation Among the Remaining Parties.* After a party's death, if the right sought to be enforced survives only to or against the remaining parties, the action does not abate, but proceeds in favor of or against the remaining parties. The death should be noted on the record.

  (3) *Service.* A motion to substitute, together with a notice of hearing, must be served on the parties as provided in Rule 5 and on nonparties as provided in Rule 4. A statement noting death must be served in the same manner. Service may be made in any judicial district.

(b) Incompetency. If a party becomes incompetent, the court may, on motion, permit the action to be continued by or against the party's representative. The motion must be served as provided in Rule 25(a)(3).

(c) Transfer of Interest. If an interest is transferred, the action may be continued by or against the original party unless the court, on motion, orders the transferee to be substituted in the action or joined with the original party. The motion must be served as provided in Rule 25(a)(3).

(d) Public Officers; Death or Separation from Office. An action does not abate when a public officer who is a party in an official capacity dies, resigns, or otherwise ceases to hold office while the action is pending. The officer's successor is automatically substituted as a party. Later proceedings should be in the substituted party's name, but any misnomer not affecting the parties' substantial rights must be disregarded. The court may order substitution at any time, but the absence of such an order does not affect the substitution.

(Amended December 29, 1948, effective October 20, 1949; April 17, 1961, effective July 19, 1961; January 21, 1963, effective July 1, 1963; March 2, 1987, effective August 1, 1987; April 30, 2007, effective December 1, 2007.)

TITLE V. DISCLOSURES AND DISCOVERY

RULE 26. DUTY TO DISCLOSE; GENERAL PROVISIONS GOVERNING DISCOVERY

(a) Required Disclosures.

  (1) *Initial Disclosure.*

    (A) *In General.* Except as exempted by Rule 26(a)(1)(B) or as otherwise stipulated or ordered by the court, a party must, without awaiting a discovery request, provide to the other parties:

      (i) the name and, if known, the address and telephone number of each individual likely to have discoverable information—along with the subjects of that information—that the disclosing party may use to support its claims or defenses, unless the use would be solely for impeachment;

(ii) a copy—or a description by category and location—of all documents, electronically stored information, and tangible things that the disclosing party has in its possession, custody, or control and may use to support its claims or defenses, unless the use would be solely for impeachment;

(iii) a computation of each category of damages claimed by the disclosing party—who must also make available for inspection and copying as under Rule 34 the documents or other evidentiary material, unless privileged or protected from disclosure, on which each computation is based, including materials bearing on the nature and extent of injuries suffered; and

(iv) for inspection and copying as under Rule 34, any insurance agreement under which an insurance business may be liable to satisfy all or part of a possible judgment in the action or to indemnify or reimburse for payments made to satisfy the judgment.

(B) *Proceedings Exempt from Initial Disclosure.* The following proceedings are exempt from initial disclosure:

(i) an action for review on an administrative record;

(ii) a forfeiture action in rem arising from a federal statute;

(iii) a petition for habeas corpus or any other proceeding to challenge a criminal conviction or sentence;

(iv) an action brought without an attorney by a person in the custody of the United States, a state, or a state subdivision;

(v) an action to enforce or quash an administrative summons or subpoena;

(vi) an action by the United States to recover benefit payments;

(vii) an action by the United States to collect on a student loan guaranteed by the United States;

(viii) a proceeding ancillary to a proceeding in another court; and

(ix) an action to enforce an arbitration award.

(C) *Time for Initial Disclosures—In General.* A party must make the initial disclosures at or within 14 days after the parties' Rule 26(f) conference unless a different time is set by stipulation or court order, or unless a party

objects during the conference that initial disclosures are not appropriate in this action and states the objection in the proposed discovery plan. In ruling on the objection, the court must determine what disclosures, if any, are to be made and must set the time for disclosure.

(D) *Time for Initial Disclosures—For Parties Served or Joined Later.* A party that is first served or otherwise joined after the Rule 26(f) conference must make the initial disclosures within 30 days after being served or joined, unless a different time is set by stipulation or court order.

(E) *Basis for Initial Disclosure; Unacceptable Excuses.* A party must make its initial disclosures based on the information then reasonably available to it. A party is not excused from making its disclosures because it has not fully investigated the case or because it challenges the sufficiency of another party's disclosures or because another party has not made its disclosures.

(2) *Disclosure of Expert Testimony.*

(A) *In General.* In addition to the disclosures required by Rule 26(a)(1), a party must disclose to the other parties the identity of any witness it may use at trial to present evidence under Federal Rule of Evidence 702, 703, or 705.

(B) *Witnesses Who Must Provide a Written Report.* Unless otherwise stipulated or ordered by the court, this disclosure must be accompanied by a written report—prepared and signed by the witness—if the witness is one retained or specially employed to provide expert testimony in the case or one whose duties as the party's employee regularly involve giving expert testimony. The report must contain:

(i) a complete statement of all opinions the witness will express and the basis and reasons for them;

(ii) the facts or data considered by the witness in forming them;

(iii) any exhibits that will be used to summarize or support them;

(iv) the witness's qualifications, including a list of all publications authored in the previous 10 years;

(v) a list of all other cases in which, during the previous 4 years, the witness testified as an expert at trial or by deposition; and

(vi) a statement of the compensation to be paid for the study and testimony in the case.

(C) *Witnesses Who Do Not Provide a Written Report.* Unless otherwise stipulated or ordered by the court, if the witness is not required to provide a written report, this disclosure must state:

(i) the subject matter on which the witness is expected to present evidence under Federal Rule of Evidence 702, 703, or 705; and

(ii) a summary of the facts and opinions to which the witness is expected to testify.

(D) *Time to Disclose Expert Testimony.* A party must make these disclosures at the times and in the sequence that the court orders. Absent a stipulation or a court order, the disclosures must be made:

(i) at least 90 days before the date set for trial or for the case to be ready for trial; or

(ii) if the evidence is intended solely to contradict or rebut evidence on the same subject matter identified by another party under Rule 26(a)(2)(B) or (C), within 30 days after the other party's disclosure.

(E) *Supplementing the Disclosure.* The parties must supplement these disclosures when required under Rule 26(e).

(3) *Pretrial Disclosures.*

(A) *In General.* In addition to the disclosures required by Rule 26(a)(1) and (2), a party must provide to the other parties and promptly file the following information about the evidence that it may present at trial other than solely for impeachment:

(i) the name and, if not previously provided, the address and telephone number of each witness—separately identifying those the party expects to present and those it may call if the need arises;

(ii) the designation of those witnesses whose testimony the party expects to present by deposition and, if not taken stenographically, a transcript of the pertinent parts of the deposition; and

(iii) an identification of each document or other exhibit, including summaries of other evidence—separately identifying those items the party expects to offer and those it may offer if the need arises.

(B) *Time for Pretrial Disclosures; Objections.* Unless the court orders otherwise, these disclosures must be made at least 30 days before trial. Within 14 days after they are made, unless the court sets a different time, a party may serve and promptly file a list of the following objections: any objections to the use under Rule 32(a) of a deposition designated by another party under Rule 26(a)(3)(A)(ii); and any objection, together with the grounds for it, that may be made to the admissibility of materials identified under Rule 26(a)(3)(A)(iii). An objection not so made—except for one under Federal Rule of Evidence 402 or 403—is waived unless excused by the court for good cause.

(4) *Form of Disclosures.* Unless the court orders otherwise, all disclosures under Rule 26(a) must be in writing, signed, and served.

(b) Discovery Scope and Limits.

(1) *Scope in General.* Unless otherwise limited by court order, the scope of discovery is as follows: Parties may obtain discovery regarding any nonprivileged matter that is relevant to any party's claim or defense—including the existence, description, nature, custody, condition, and location of any documents or other tangible things and the identity and location of persons who know of any discoverable matter. For good cause, the court may order discovery of any matter relevant to the subject matter involved in the action. Relevant information need not be admissible at the trial if the discovery appears reasonably calculated to lead to the discovery of admissible evidence. All discovery is subject to the limitations imposed by Rule 26(b)(2)(C).

(2) *Limitations on Frequency and Extent.*

(A) *When Permitted.* By order, the court may alter the limits in these rules on the number of depositions and interrogatories or on the length of depositions under Rule 30. By order or local rule, the court may also limit the number of requests under Rule 36.

(B) *Specific Limitations on Electronically Stored Information.* A party need not provide discovery of electronically stored information from sources that the party identifies as not reasonably accessible because of undue burden or cost. On motion to compel discovery or for a protective order, the party from whom discovery is sought must show that the information is not reasonably accessible because of undue burden or cost. If that showing is made, the court may nonetheless order discovery from such sources if the requesting party shows good cause, considering the limitations of Rule 26(b)(2)(C). The court may specify conditions for the discovery.

(C) *When Required.* On motion or on its own, the court must limit the frequency or extent of discovery otherwise allowed by these rules or by local rule if it determines that:

(i) the discovery sought is unreasonably cumulative or duplicative, or can be obtained from some other source that is more convenient, less burdensome, or less expensive;

(ii) the party seeking discovery has had ample opportunity to obtain the information by discovery in the action; or

(iii) the burden or expense of the proposed discovery outweighs its likely benefit, considering the needs of the case, the amount in controversy, the parties' resources, the importance of the issues at stake in the action, and the importance of the discovery in resolving the issues.

(3) *Trial Preparation: Materials.*

(A) *Documents and Tangible Things.* Ordinarily, a party may not discover documents and tangible things that are prepared in anticipation of litigation or for trial by or for another party or its representative (including the other party's attorney, consultant, surety, indemnitor, insurer, or agent). But, subject to Rule 26(b)(4), those materials may be discovered if:

(i) they are otherwise discoverable under Rule 26(b)(1); and

(ii) the party shows that it has substantial need for the materials to prepare its case and cannot, without undue hardship, obtain their substantial equivalent by other means.

(B) *Protection Against Disclosure.* If the court orders discovery of those materials, it must protect against disclosure of the mental impressions, conclusions, opinions, or legal theories of a party's attorney or other representative concerning the litigation.

(C) *Previous Statement.* Any party or other person may, on request and without the required showing, obtain the person's own previous statement about the action or its subject matter. If the request is refused, the person may move for a court order, and Rule 37(a)(5) applies to the award of expenses. A previous statement is either:

(i) a written statement that the person has signed or otherwise adopted or approved; or

(ii) a contemporaneous stenographic, mechanical, electrical, or other recording—or a transcription of it—that recites substantially verbatim the person's oral statement.

(4) *Trial Preparation: Experts.*

(A) *Deposition of an Expert Who May Testify.* A party may depose any person who has been identified as an expert whose opinions may be presented at trial. If Rule

26(a)(2)(B) requires a report from the expert, the deposition may be conducted only after the report is provided.

(B) *Trial–Preparation Protection for Draft Reports or Disclosures.* Rules 26(b)(3)(A) and (B) protect drafts of any report or disclosure required under Rule 26(a)(2), regardless of the form in which the draft is recorded.

(C) *Trial–Preparation Protection for Communications Between a Party's Attorney and Expert Witnesses.* Rules 26(b)(3)(A) and (B) protect communications between the party's attorney and any witness required to provide a report under Rule 26(a)(2)(B), regardless of the form of the communications, except to the extent that the communications:

(i) relate to compensation for the expert's study or testimony;

(ii) identify facts or data that the party's attorney provided and that the expert considered in forming the opinions to be expressed; or

(iii) identify assumptions that the party's attorney provided and that the expert relied on in forming the opinions to be expressed.

(D) *Expert Employed Only for Trial Preparation.* Ordinarily, a party may not, by interrogatories or deposition, discover facts known or opinions held by an expert who has been retained or specially employed by another party in anticipation of litigation or to prepare for trial and who is not expected to be called as a witness at trial. But a party may do so only:

(i) as provided in Rule 35(b); or

(ii) on showing exceptional circumstances under which it is impracticable for the party to obtain facts or opinions on the same subject by other means.

(E) *Payment.* Unless manifest injustice would result, the court must require that the party seeking discovery:

(i) pay the expert a reasonable fee for time spent in responding to discovery under Rule 26(b)(4)(A) or (D); and

(ii) for discovery under (D), also pay the other party a fair portion of the fees and expenses it reasonably incurred in obtaining the expert's facts and opinions.

(5) *Claiming Privilege or Protecting Trial-Preparation Materials.*

(A) *Information Withheld.* When a party withholds information otherwise discoverable by claiming that the information is privileged or subject to protection as trial-preparation material, the party must:

 (i) expressly make the claim; and

 (ii) describe the nature of the documents, communications, or tangible things not produced or disclosed—and do so in a manner that, without revealing information itself privileged or protected, will enable other parties to assess the claim.

(B) *Information Produced.* If information produced in discovery is subject to a claim of privilege or of protection as trial-preparation material, the party making the claim may notify any party that received the information of the claim and the basis for it. After being notified, a party must promptly return, sequester, or destroy the specified information and any copies it has; must not use or disclose the information until the claim is resolved; must take reasonable steps to retrieve the information if the party disclosed it before being notified; and may promptly present the information to the court under seal for a determination of the claim. The producing party must preserve the information until the claim is resolved.

(c) Protective Orders.

(1) *In General.* A party or any person from whom discovery is sought may move for a protective order in the court where the action is pending—or as an alternative on matters relating to a deposition, in the court for the district where the deposition will be taken. The motion must include a certification that the movant has in good faith conferred or attempted to confer with other affected parties in an effort to resolve the dispute without court action. The court may, for good cause, issue an order to protect a party or person from annoyance, embarrassment, oppression, or undue burden or expense, including one or more of the following:

(A) forbidding the disclosure or discovery;

(B) specifying terms, including time and place, for the disclosure or discovery;

(C) prescribing a discovery method other than the one selected by the party seeking discovery;

(D) forbidding inquiry into certain matters, or limiting the scope of disclosure or discovery to certain matters;

(E) designating the persons who may be present while the discovery is conducted;

(F) requiring that a deposition be sealed and opened only on court order;

(G) requiring that a trade secret or other confidential research, development, or commercial information not be revealed or be revealed only in a specified way; and

(H) requiring that the parties simultaneously file specified documents or information in sealed envelopes, to be opened as the court directs.

(2) *Ordering Discovery.* If a motion for a protective order is wholly or partly denied, the court may, on just terms, order that any party or person provide or permit discovery.

(3) *Awarding Expenses.* Rule 37(a)(5) applies to the award of expenses.

(d) Timing and Sequence of Discovery.

(1) *Timing.* A party may not seek discovery from any source before the parties have conferred as required by Rule 26(f), except in a proceeding exempted from initial disclosure under Rule 26(a)(1)(B), or when authorized by these rules, by stipulation, or by court order.

(2) *Sequence.* Unless, on motion, the court orders otherwise for the parties' and witnesses' convenience and in the interests of justice:

(A) methods of discovery may be used in any sequence; and

(B) discovery by one party does not require any other party to delay its discovery.

(e) Supplementing Disclosures and Responses.

(1) *In General.* A party who has made a disclosure under Rule 26(a)—or who has responded to an interrogatory, request for production, or request for admission—must supplement or correct its disclosure or response:

(A) in a timely manner if the party learns that in some material respect the disclosure or response is incomplete or incorrect, and if the additional or corrective information has not otherwise been made known to the other parties during the discovery process or in writing; or

(B) as ordered by the court.

(2) *Expert Witness.* For an expert whose report must be disclosed under Rule 26(a)(2)(B), the party's duty to supplement extends both to information included in the report and to information given during the expert's deposition. Any additions or changes to this information must be disclosed by the time the party's pretrial disclosures under Rule 26(a)(3) are due.

(f) Conference of the Parties; Planning for Discovery.

(1) *Conference Timing.* Except in a proceeding exempted from initial disclosure under Rule 26(a)(1)(B) or when the court orders otherwise, the parties must confer as soon as practicable—

and in any event at least 21 days before a scheduling conference is to be held or a scheduling order is due under Rule 16(b).

(2) Conference Content; Parties' Responsibilities. In conferring, the parties must consider the nature and basis of their claims and defenses and the possibilities for promptly settling or resolving the case; make or arrange for the disclosures required by Rule 26(a)(1); discuss any issues about preserving discoverable information; and develop a proposed discovery plan. The attorneys of record and all unrepresented parties that have appeared in the case are jointly responsible for arranging the conference, for attempting in good faith to agree on the proposed discovery plan, and for submitting to the court within 14 days after the conference a written report outlining the plan. The court may order the parties or attorneys to attend the conference in person.

(3) Discovery Plan. A discovery plan must state the parties' views and proposals on:

(A) what changes should be made in the timing, form, or requirement for disclosures under Rule 26(a), including a statement of when initial disclosures were made or will be made;

(B) the subjects on which discovery may be needed, when discovery should be completed, and whether discovery should be conducted in phases or be limited to or focused on particular issues;

(C) any issues about disclosure or discovery of electronically stored information, including the form or forms in which it should be produced;

(D) any issues about claims of privilege or of protection as trial-preparation materials, including—if the parties agree on a procedure to assert these claims after production— whether to ask the court to include their agreement in an order;

(E) what changes should be made in the limitations on discovery imposed under these rules or by local rule, and what other limitations should be imposed; and

(F) any other orders that the court should issue under Rule 26(c) or under Rule 16(b) and (c).

(4) Expedited Schedule. If necessary to comply with its expedited schedule for Rule 16(b) conferences, a court may by local rule:

(A) require the parties' conference to occur less than 21 days before the scheduling conference is held or a scheduling order is due under Rule 16(b); and

(B) require the written report outlining the discovery plan to be filed less than 14 days after the parties' conference, or excuse the parties

from submitting a written report and permit them to report orally on their discovery plan at the Rule 16(b) conference.

(g) Signing Disclosures and Discovery Requests, Responses, and Objections.

(1) Signature Required; Effect of Signature. Every disclosure under Rule 26(a)(1) or (a)(3) and every discovery request, response, or objection must be signed by at least one attorney of record in the attorney's own name—or by the party personally, if unrepresented—and must state the signer's address, e-mail address, and telephone number. By signing, an attorney or party certifies that to the best of the person's knowledge, information, and belief formed after a reasonable inquiry:

(A) with respect to a disclosure, it is complete and correct as of the time it is made; and

(B) with respect to a discovery request, response, or objection, it is:

(i) consistent with these rules and warranted by existing law or by a nonfrivolous argument for extending, modifying, or reversing existing law, or for establishing new law;

(ii) not interposed for any improper purpose, such as to harass, cause unnecessary delay, or needlessly increase the cost of litigation; and

(iii) neither unreasonable nor unduly burdensome or expensive, considering the needs of the case, prior discovery in the case, the amount in controversy, and the importance of the issues at stake in the action.

(2) Failure to Sign. Other parties have no duty to act on an unsigned disclosure, request, response, or objection until it is signed, and the court must strike it unless a signature is promptly supplied after the omission is called to the attorney's or party's attention.

(3) Sanction for Improper Certification. If a certification violates this rule without substantial justification, the court, on motion or on its own, must impose an appropriate sanction on the signer, the party on whose behalf the signer was acting, or both. The sanction may include an order to pay the reasonable expenses, including attorney's fees, caused by the violation.

(Amended December 27, 1946, effective March 19, 1948; January 21, 1963, effective July 1, 1963; February 28, 1966, effective July 1, 1966; March 30, 1970, effective July 1, 1970; April 29, 1980, effective August 1, 1980; April 28, 1983, effective August 1, 1983; March 2, 1987, effective August 1, 1987; April 22, 1993, effective December 1, 1993; April 17, 2000, effective December 1, 2000; April 12, 2006, effective December 1, 2006; April 30, 2007, effective December 1, 2007; April 28, 2010, effective December 1, 2010.)

RULE 27. DEPOSITIONS TO PERPETUATE TESTIMONY

(a) Before an Action Is Filed.

(1) *Petition.* A person who wants to perpetuate testimony about any matter cognizable in a United States court may file a verified petition in the district court for the district where any expected adverse party resides. The petition must ask for an order authorizing the petitioner to depose the named persons in order to perpetuate their testimony. The petition must be titled in the petitioner's name and must show:

(A) that the petitioner expects to be a party to an action cognizable in a United States court but cannot presently bring it or cause it to be brought;

(B) the subject matter of the expected action and the petitioner's interest;

(C) the facts that the petitioner wants to establish by the proposed testimony and the reasons to perpetuate it;

(D) the names or a description of the persons whom the petitioner expects to be adverse parties and their addresses, so far as known; and

(E) the name, address, and expected substance of the testimony of each deponent.

(2) *Notice and Service.* At least 21 days before the hearing date, the petitioner must serve each expected adverse party with a copy of the petition and a notice stating the time and place of the hearing. The notice may be served either inside or outside the district or state in the manner provided in Rule 4. If that service cannot be made with reasonable diligence on an expected adverse party, the court may order service by publication or otherwise. The court must appoint an attorney to represent persons not served in the manner provided in Rule 4 and to cross-examine the deponent if an unserved person is not otherwise represented. If any expected adverse party is a minor or is incompetent, Rule 17(c) applies.

(3) *Order and Examination.* If satisfied that perpetuating the testimony may prevent a failure or delay of justice, the court must issue an order that designates or describes the persons whose depositions may be taken, specifies the subject matter of the examinations, and states whether the depositions will be taken orally or by written interrogatories. The depositions may then be taken under these rules, and the court may issue orders like those authorized by Rules 34 and 35. A reference in these rules to the court where an action is pending means, for purposes of this rule, the court where the petition for the deposition was filed.

(4) *Using the Deposition.* A deposition to perpetuate testimony may be used under Rule 32(a) in any later-filed district-court action involving the same subject matter if the deposition either was taken under these rules or, although not so taken, would be admissible in evidence in the courts of the state where it was taken.

(b) Pending Appeal.

(1) *In General.* The court where a judgment has been rendered may, if an appeal has been taken or may still be taken, permit a party to depose witnesses to perpetuate their testimony for use in the event of further proceedings in that court.

(2) *Motion.* The party who wants to perpetuate testimony may move for leave to take the depositions, on the same notice and service as if the action were pending in the district court. The motion must show:

(A) the name, address, and expected substance of the testimony of each deponent; and

(B) the reasons for perpetuating the testimony.

(3) *Court Order.* If the court finds that perpetuating the testimony may prevent a failure or delay of justice, the court may permit the depositions to be taken and may issue orders like those authorized by Rules 34 and 35. The depositions may be taken and used as any other deposition taken in a pending district-court action.

(c) Perpetuation by an Action. This rule does not limit a court's power to entertain an action to perpetuate testimony.

(Amended December 27, 1946, effective March 19, 1948; December 29, 1948, effective October 20, 1949; March 1, 1971, effective July 1, 1971; March 2, 1987, effective August 1, 1987; April 25, 2005, effective December 1, 2005; April 30, 2007, effective December 1, 2007; March 26, 2009, effective December 1, 2009.)

RULE 28. PERSONS BEFORE WHOM DEPOSITIONS MAY BE TAKEN

(a) Within the United States.

(1) *In General.* Within the United States or a territory or insular possession subject to United States jurisdiction, a deposition must be taken before:

(A) an officer authorized to administer oaths either by federal law or by the law in the place of examination; or

(B) a person appointed by the court where the action is pending to administer oaths and take testimony.

(2) *Definition of "Officer"*. The term "officer" in Rules 30, 31, and 32 includes a person appointed by the court under this rule or designated by the parties under Rule 29(a).

(b) In a Foreign Country.

(1) *In General.* A deposition may be taken in a foreign country:

    (A) under an applicable treaty or convention;

    (B) under a letter of request, whether or not captioned a "letter rogatory";

    (C) on notice, before a person authorized to administer oaths either by federal law or by the law in the place of examination; or

    (D) before a person commissioned by the court to administer any necessary oath and take testimony.

(2) *Issuing a Letter of Request or a Commission.* A letter of request, a commission, or both may be issued:

    (A) on appropriate terms after an application and notice of it; and

    (B) without a showing that taking the deposition in another manner is impracticable or inconvenient.

(3) *Form of a Request, Notice, or Commission.* When a letter of request or any other device is used according to a treaty or convention, it must be captioned in the form prescribed by that treaty or convention. A letter of request may be addressed "To the Appropriate Authority in [name of country]." A deposition notice or a commission must designate by name or descriptive title the person before whom the deposition is to be taken.

(4) *Letter of Request—Admitting Evidence.* Evidence obtained in response to a letter of request need not be excluded merely because it is not a verbatim transcript, because the testimony was not taken under oath, or because of any similar departure from the requirements for depositions taken within the United States.

(c) Disqualification. A deposition must not be taken before a person who is any party's relative, employee, or attorney; who is related to or employed by any party's attorney; or who is financially interested in the action.

(Amended December 27, 1946, effective March 19, 1948; January 21, 1963, effective July 1, 1963; April 29, 1980, effective August 1, 1980; March 2, 1987, effective August 1, 1987; April 22, 1993, effective December 1, 1993; April 30, 2007, effective December 1, 2007.)

RULE 29. STIPULATIONS ABOUT DISCOVERY PROCEDURE

Unless the court orders otherwise, the parties may stipulate that:

(a) a deposition may be taken before any person, at any time or place, on any notice, and in the manner specified—in which event it may be used in the same way as any other deposition; and

(b) other procedures governing or limiting discovery be modified—but a stipulation extending the time for any form of discovery must have court approval if it would interfere with the time set for completing discovery, for hearing a motion, or for trial.

(Amended March 30, 1970, effective July 1, 1970; April 22, 1993, effective December 1, 1993; April 30, 2007, effective December 1, 2007.)

RULE 30. DEPOSITIONS BY ORAL EXAMINATION

(a) When a Deposition May Be Taken.

(1) *Without Leave.* A party may, by oral questions, depose any person, including a party, without leave of court except as provided in Rule 30(a)(2). The deponent's attendance may be compelled by subpoena under Rule 45.

(2) *With Leave.* A party must obtain leave of court, and the court must grant leave to the extent consistent with Rule 26(b)(2):

    (A) if the parties have not stipulated to the deposition and:

      (i) the deposition would result in more than 10 depositions being taken under this rule or Rule 31 by the plaintiffs, or by the defendants, or by the third-party defendants;

      (ii) the deponent has already been deposed in the case; or

      (iii) the party seeks to take the deposition before the time specified in Rule 26(d), unless the party certifies in the notice, with supporting facts, that the deponent is expected to leave the United States and be unavailable for examination in this country after that time; or

    (B) if the deponent is confined in prison.

(b) Notice of the Deposition; Other Formal Requirements.

(1) *Notice in General.* A party who wants to depose a person by oral questions must give reasonable written notice to every other party. The notice must state the time and place of the deposition and, if known, the deponent's name and address. If the name is unknown, the notice

must provide a general description sufficient to identify the person or the particular class or group to which the person belongs.

(2) **Producing Documents.** If a subpoena duces tecum is to be served on the deponent, the materials designated for production, as set out in the subpoena, must be listed in the notice or in an attachment. The notice to a party deponent may be accompanied by a request under Rule 34 to produce documents and tangible things at the deposition.

(3) **Method of Recording.**

(A) *Method Stated in the Notice.* The party who notices the deposition must state in the notice the method for recording the testimony. Unless the court orders otherwise, testimony may be recorded by audio, audiovisual, or stenographic means. The noticing party bears the recording costs. Any party may arrange to transcribe a deposition.

(B) *Additional Method.* With prior notice to the deponent and other parties, any party may designate another method for recording the testimony in addition to that specified in the original notice. That party bears the expense of the additional record or transcript unless the court orders otherwise.

(4) **By Remote Means.** The parties may stipulate—or the court may on motion order—that a deposition be taken by telephone or other remote means. For the purpose of this rule and Rules 28(a), 37(a)(2), and 37(b)(1), the deposition takes place where the deponent answers the questions.

(5) **Officer's Duties.**

(A) *Before the Deposition.* Unless the parties stipulate otherwise, a deposition must be conducted before an officer appointed or designated under Rule 28. The officer must begin the deposition with an on-the-record statement that includes:

(i) the officer's name and business address;

(ii) the date, time, and place of the deposition;

(iii) the deponent's name;

(iv) the officer's administration of the oath or affirmation to the deponent; and

(v) the identity of all persons present.

(B) *Conducting the Deposition; Avoiding Distortion.* If the deposition is recorded non-stenographically, the officer must repeat the items in Rule 30(b)(5)(A)(i)-(iii) at the beginning of each unit of the recording medium. The deponent's and attorneys' appearance or demeanor must not be distorted through recording techniques.

(C) *After the Deposition.* At the end of a deposition, the officer must state on the record that the deposition is complete and must set out any stipulations made by the attorneys about custody of the transcript or recording and of the exhibits, or about any other pertinent matters.

(6) **Notice or Subpoena Directed to an Organization.** In its notice or subpoena, a party may name as the deponent a public or private corporation, a partnership, an association, a governmental agency, or other entity and must describe with reasonable particularity the matters for examination. The named organization must then designate one or more officers, directors, or managing agents, or designate other persons who consent to testify on its behalf; and it may set out the matters on which each person designated will testify. A subpoena must advise a nonparty organization of its duty to make this designation. The persons designated must testify about information known or reasonably available to the organization. This paragraph (6) does not preclude a deposition by any other procedure allowed by these rules.

(c) **Examination and Cross–Examination; Record of the Examination; Objections; Written Questions.**

(1) **Examination and Cross–Examination.** The examination and cross-examination of a deponent proceed as they would at trial under the Federal Rules of Evidence, except Rules 103 and 615. After putting the deponent under oath or affirmation, the officer must record the testimony by the method designated under Rule 30(b)(3)(A). The testimony must be recorded by the officer personally or by a person acting in the presence and under the direction of the officer.

(2) **Objections.** An objection at the time of the examination—whether to evidence, to a party's conduct, to the officer's qualifications, to the manner of taking the deposition, or to any other aspect of the deposition—must be noted on the record, but the examination still proceeds; the testimony is taken subject to any objection. An objection must be stated concisely in a nonargumentative and nonsuggestive manner. A person may instruct a deponent not to answer only when necessary to preserve a privilege, to enforce a limitation ordered by the court, or to present a motion under Rule 30(d)(3).

(3) **Participating Through Written Questions.** Instead of participating in the oral examination, a party may serve written questions in a sealed envelope on the party noticing the deposition, who must deliver them to the officer. The offi-

cer must ask the deponent those questions and record the answers verbatim.

(d) Duration; Sanction; Motion to Terminate or Limit.

  (1) *Duration.* Unless otherwise stipulated or ordered by the court, a deposition is limited to 1 day of 7 hours. The court must allow additional time consistent with Rule 26(b)(2) if needed to fairly examine the deponent or if the deponent, another person, or any other circumstance impedes or delays the examination.

  (2) *Sanction.* The court may impose an appropriate sanction—including the reasonable expenses and attorney's fees incurred by any party—on a person who impedes, delays, or frustrates the fair examination of the deponent.

  (3) *Motion to Terminate or Limit.*

    (A) *Grounds.* At any time during a deposition, the deponent or a party may move to terminate or limit it on the ground that it is being conducted in bad faith or in a manner that unreasonably annoys, embarrasses, or oppresses the deponent or party. The motion may be filed in the court where the action is pending or the deposition is being taken. If the objecting deponent or party so demands, the deposition must be suspended for the time necessary to obtain an order.

    (B) *Order.* The court may order that the deposition be terminated or may limit its scope and manner as provided in Rule 26(c). If terminated, the deposition may be resumed only by order of the court where the action is pending.

    (C) *Award of Expenses.* Rule 37(a)(5) applies to the award of expenses.

(e) Review by the Witness; Changes.

  (1) *Review; Statement of Changes.* On request by the deponent or a party before the deposition is completed, the deponent must be allowed 30 days after being notified by the officer that the transcript or recording is available in which:

    (A) to review the transcript or recording; and

    (B) if there are changes in form or substance, to sign a statement listing the changes and the reasons for making them.

  (2) *Changes Indicated in the Officer's Certificate.* The officer must note in the certificate prescribed by Rule 30(f)(1) whether a review was requested and, if so, must attach any changes the deponent makes during the 30–day period.

(f) Certification and Delivery; Exhibits; Copies of the Transcript or Recording; Filing.

  (1) *Certification and Delivery.* The officer must certify in writing that the witness was duly sworn and that the deposition accurately records the witness's testimony. The certificate must accompany the record of the deposition. Unless the court orders otherwise, the officer must seal the deposition in an envelope or package bearing the title of the action and marked "Deposition of [witness's name]" and must promptly send it to the attorney who arranged for the transcript or recording. The attorney must store it under conditions that will protect it against loss, destruction, tampering, or deterioration.

  (2) *Documents and Tangible Things.*

    (A) *Originals and Copies.* Documents and tangible things produced for inspection during a deposition must, on a party's request, be marked for identification and attached to the deposition. Any party may inspect and copy them. But if the person who produced them wants to keep the originals, the person may:

      (i) offer copies to be marked, attached to the deposition, and then used as originals—after giving all parties a fair opportunity to verify the copies by comparing them with the originals; or

      (ii) give all parties a fair opportunity to inspect and copy the originals after they are marked—in which event the originals may be used as if attached to the deposition.

    (B) *Order Regarding the Originals.* Any party may move for an order that the originals be attached to the deposition pending final disposition of the case.

  (3) *Copies of the Transcript or Recording.* Unless otherwise stipulated or ordered by the court, the officer must retain the stenographic notes of a deposition taken stenographically or a copy of the recording of a deposition taken by another method. When paid reasonable charges, the officer must furnish a copy of the transcript or recording to any party or the deponent.

  (4) *Notice of Filing.* A party who files the deposition must promptly notify all other parties of the filing.

(g) Failure to Attend a Deposition or Serve a Subpoena; Expenses. A party who, expecting a deposition to be taken, attends in person or by an attorney may recover reasonable expenses for attending, including attorney's fees, if the noticing party failed to:

  (1) attend and proceed with the deposition; or

(2) serve a subpoena on a nonparty deponent, who consequently did not attend.

(Amended January 21, 1963, effective July 1, 1963; March 30, 1970, effective July 1, 1970; March 1, 1971, effective July 1, 1971; November 20, 1972, effective July 1, 1975; April 29, 1980, effective August 1, 1980; March 2, 1987, effective August 1, 1987; April 22, 1993, effective December 1, 1993; April 17, 2000, effective December 1, 2000; April 30, 2007, effective December 1, 2007.)

RULE 31. DEPOSITIONS BY WRITTEN QUESTIONS

(a) When a Deposition May Be Taken.

(1) *Without Leave.* A party may, by written questions, depose any person, including a party, without leave of court except as provided in Rule 31(a)(2). The deponent's attendance may be compelled by subpoena under Rule 45.

(2) *With Leave.* A party must obtain leave of court, and the court must grant leave to the extent consistent with Rule 26(b)(2):

(A) if the parties have not stipulated to the deposition and:

(i) the deposition would result in more than 10 depositions being taken under this rule or Rule 30 by the plaintiffs, or by the defendants, or by the third-party defendants;

(ii) the deponent has already been deposed in the case; or

(iii) the party seeks to take a deposition before the time specified in Rule 26(d); or

(B) if the deponent is confined in prison.

(3) *Service; Required Notice.* A party who wants to depose a person by written questions must serve them on every other party, with a notice stating, if known, the deponent's name and address. If the name is unknown, the notice must provide a general description sufficient to identify the person or the particular class or group to which the person belongs. The notice must also state the name or descriptive title and the address of the officer before whom the deposition will be taken.

(4) *Questions Directed to an Organization.* A public or private corporation, a partnership, an association, or a governmental agency may be deposed by written questions in accordance with Rule 30(b)(6).

(5) *Questions from Other Parties.* Any questions to the deponent from other parties must be served on all parties as follows: cross-questions, within 14 days after being served with the notice and direct questions; redirect questions, within 7 days after being served with cross-questions; and recross-questions, within 7 days after being served with redirect questions. The court may, for good cause, extend or shorten these times.

(b) Delivery to the Officer; Officer's Duties. The party who noticed the deposition must deliver to the officer a copy of all the questions served and of the notice. The officer must promptly proceed in the manner provided in Rule 30(c), (e), and (f) to:

(1) take the deponent's testimony in response to the questions;

(2) prepare and certify the deposition; and

(3) send it to the party, attaching a copy of the questions and of the notice.

(c) Notice of Completion or Filing.

(1) *Completion.* The party who noticed the deposition must notify all other parties when it is completed.

(2) *Filing.* A party who files the deposition must promptly notify all other parties of the filing.

(Amended March 30, 1970, effective July 1, 1970; March 2, 1987, effective August 1, 1987; April 22, 1993, effective December 1, 1993; April 30, 2007, effective December 1, 2007.)

RULE 32. USING DEPOSITIONS IN COURT PROCEEDINGS

(a) Using Depositions.

(1) *In General.* At a hearing or trial, all or part of a deposition may be used against a party on these conditions:

(A) the party was present or represented at the taking of the deposition or had reasonable notice of it;

(B) it is used to the extent it would be admissible under the Federal Rules of Evidence if the deponent were present and testifying; and

(C) the use is allowed by Rule 32(a)(2) through (8).

(2) *Impeachment and Other Uses.* Any party may use a deposition to contradict or impeach the testimony given by the deponent as a witness, or for any other purpose allowed by the Federal Rules of Evidence.

(3) *Deposition of Party, Agent, or Designee.* An adverse party may use for any purpose the deposition of a party or anyone who, when deposed, was the party's officer, director, managing agent, or designee under Rule 30(b)(6) or 31(a)(4).

(4) *Unavailable Witness.* A party may use for any purpose the deposition of a witness, whether or not a party, if the court finds:

(A) that the witness is dead;

(B) that the witness is more than 100 miles from the place of hearing or trial or is outside the United States, unless it appears that the witness's absence was procured by the party offering the deposition;

(C) that the witness cannot attend or testify because of age, illness, infirmity, or imprisonment;

(D) that the party offering the deposition could not procure the witness's attendance by subpoena; or

(E) on motion and notice, that exceptional circumstances make it desirable—in the interest of justice and with due regard to the importance of live testimony in open court—to permit the deposition to be used.

(5) *Limitations on Use.*

(A) *Deposition Taken on Short Notice.* A deposition must not be used against a party who, having received less than 14 days' notice of the deposition, promptly moved for a protective order under Rule 26(c)(1)(B) requesting that it not be taken or be taken at a different time or place—and this motion was still pending when the deposition was taken.

(B) *Unavailable Deponent; Party Could Not Obtain an Attorney.* A deposition taken without leave of court under the unavailability provision of Rule 30(a)(2)(A)(iii) must not be used against a party who shows that, when served with the notice, it could not, despite diligent efforts, obtain an attorney to represent it at the deposition.

(6) *Using Part of a Deposition.* If a party offers in evidence only part of a deposition, an adverse party may require the offeror to introduce other parts that in fairness should be considered with the part introduced, and any party may itself introduce any other parts.

(7) *Substituting a Party.* Substituting a party under Rule 25 does not affect the right to use a deposition previously taken.

(8) *Deposition Taken in an Earlier Action.* A deposition lawfully taken and, if required, filed in any federal- or state-court action may be used in a later action involving the same subject matter between the same parties, or their representatives or successors in interest, to the same extent as if taken in the later action. A deposition previously taken may also be used as allowed by the Federal Rules of Evidence.

(b) Objections to Admissibility. Subject to Rules 28(b) and 32(d)(3), an objection may be made at a hearing or trial to the admission of any deposition testimony that would be inadmissible if the witness were present and testifying.

(c) Form of Presentation. Unless the court orders otherwise, a party must provide a transcript of any deposition testimony the party offers, but may provide the court with the testimony in nontranscript form as well. On any party's request, deposition testimony offered in a jury trial for any purpose other than impeachment must be presented in nontranscript form, if available, unless the court for good cause orders otherwise.

(d) Waiver of Objections.

(1) *To the Notice.* An objection to an error or irregularity in a deposition notice is waived unless promptly served in writing on the party giving the notice.

(2) *To the Officer's Qualification.* An objection based on disqualification of the officer before whom a deposition is to be taken is waived if not made:

(A) before the deposition begins; or

(B) promptly after the basis for disqualification becomes known or, with reasonable diligence, could have been known.

(3) *To the Taking of the Deposition.*

(A) *Objection to Competence, Relevance, or Materiality.* An objection to a deponent's competence—or to the competence, relevance, or materiality of testimony—is not waived by a failure to make the objection before or during the deposition, unless the ground for it might have been corrected at that time.

(B) *Objection to an Error or Irregularity.* An objection to an error or irregularity at an oral examination is waived if:

(i) it relates to the manner of taking the deposition, the form of a question or answer, the oath or affirmation, a party's conduct, or other matters that might have been corrected at that time; and

(ii) it is not timely made during the deposition.

(C) *Objection to a Written Question.* An objection to the form of a written question under Rule 31 is waived if not served in writing on the party submitting the question within the time for serving responsive questions or, if the question is a recross-question, within 7 days after being served with it.

(4) *To Completing and Returning the Deposition.* An objection to how the officer transcribed the testimony—or prepared, signed, certified, sealed, endorsed, sent, or otherwise dealt with the deposition—is waived unless a motion to suppress is made promptly after the error or irregularity becomes known or, with reasonable diligence, could have been known.

(Amended March 30, 1970, effective July 1, 1970; November 20, 1972, effective July 1, 1975; April 29, 1980, effective August 1, 1980; March 2, 1987, effective August 1, 1987; April 22, 1993, effective December 1, 1993; April 30, 2007, effective December 1, 2007; March 26, 2009, effective December 1, 2009.)

RULE 33. INTERROGATORIES TO PARTIES

(a) In General.

(1) *Number.* Unless otherwise stipulated or ordered by the court, a party may serve on any other party no more than 25 written interrogatories, including all discrete subparts. Leave to serve additional interrogatories may be granted to the extent consistent with Rule 26(b)(2).

(2) *Scope.* An interrogatory may relate to any matter that may be inquired into under Rule 26(b). An interrogatory is not objectionable merely because it asks for an opinion or contention that relates to fact or the application of law to fact, but the court may order that the interrogatory need not be answered until designated discovery is complete, or until a pretrial conference or some other time.

(b) Answers and Objections.

(1) *Responding Party.* The interrogatories must be answered:

(A) by the party to whom they are directed; or

(B) if that party is a public or private corporation, a partnership, an association, or a governmental agency, by any officer or agent, who must furnish the information available to the party.

(2) *Time to Respond.* The responding party must serve its answers and any objections within 30 days after being served with the interrogatories. A shorter or longer time may be stipulated to under Rule 29 or be ordered by the court.

(3) *Answering Each Interrogatory.* Each interrogatory must, to the extent it is not objected to, be answered separately and fully in writing under oath.

(4) *Objections.* The grounds for objecting to an interrogatory must be stated with specificity. Any ground not stated in a timely objection is waived unless the court, for good cause, excuses the failure.

(5) *Signature.* The person who makes the answers must sign them, and the attorney who objects must sign any objections.

(c) Use. An answer to an interrogatory may be used to the extent allowed by the Federal Rules of Evidence.

(d) Option to Produce Business Records. If the answer to an interrogatory may be determined by examining, auditing, compiling, abstracting, or summarizing a party's business records (including electronically stored information), and if the burden of deriving or ascertaining the answer will be substantially the same for either party, the responding party may answer by:

(1) specifying the records that must be reviewed, in sufficient detail to enable the interrogating party to locate and identify them as readily as the responding party could; and

(2) giving the interrogating party a reasonable opportunity to examine and audit the records and to make copies, compilations, abstracts, or summaries.

(Amended December 27, 1946, effective March 19, 1948; March 30, 1970, effective July 1, 1970; April 29, 1980, effective August 1, 1980; April 22, 1993, effective December 1, 1993; April 12, 2006, effective December 1, 2006; April 30, 2007, effective December 1, 2007.)

RULE 34. PRODUCING DOCUMENTS, ELECTRONICALLY STORED INFORMATION, AND TANGIBLE THINGS, OR ENTERING ONTO LAND, FOR INSPECTION AND OTHER PURPOSES

(a) In General. A party may serve on any other party a request within the scope of Rule 26(b):

(1) to produce and permit the requesting party or its representative to inspect, copy, test, or sample the following items in the responding party's possession, custody, or control:

(A) any designated documents or electronically stored information—including writings, drawings, graphs, charts, photographs, sound recordings, images, and other data or data compilations—stored in any medium from which information can be obtained either directly or, if necessary, after translation by the responding party into a reasonably usable form; or

(B) any designated tangible things; or

(2) to permit entry onto designated land or other property possessed or controlled by the responding party, so that the requesting party may inspect, measure, survey, photograph, test, or sample the property or any designated object or operation on it.

(b) Procedure.

(1) *Contents of the Request.* The request:

(A) must describe with reasonable particularity each item or category of items to be inspected;

(B) must specify a reasonable time, place, and manner for the inspection and for performing the related acts; and

(C) may specify the form or forms in which electronically stored information is to be produced.

(2) *Responses and Objections.*

(A) *Time to Respond.* The party to whom the request is directed must respond in writing within 30 days after being served. A shorter or longer time may be stipulated to under Rule 29 or be ordered by the court.

(B) *Responding to Each Item.* For each item or category, the response must either state that inspection and related activities will be permitted as requested or state an objection to the request, including the reasons.

(C) *Objections.* An objection to part of a request must specify the part and permit inspection of the rest.

(D) *Responding to a Request for Production of Electronically Stored Information.* The response may state an objection to a requested form for producing electronically stored information. If the responding party objects to a requested form—or if no form was specified in the request—the party must state the form or forms it intends to use.

(E) *Producing the Documents or Electronically Stored Information.* Unless otherwise stipulated or ordered by the court, these procedures apply to producing documents or electronically stored information:

(i) A party must produce documents as they are kept in the usual course of business or must organize and label them to correspond to the categories in the request;

(ii) If a request does not specify a form for producing electronically stored information, a party must produce it in a form or forms in which it is ordinarily maintained or in a reasonably usable form or forms; and

(iii) A party need not produce the same electronically stored information in more than one form.

(c) Nonparties. As provided in Rule 45, a nonparty may be compelled to produce documents and tangible things or to permit an inspection.

(Amended December 27, 1946, effective March 19, 1948; March 30, 1970, effective July 1, 1970; April 29, 1980, effective August 1, 1980; March 2, 1987, effective August 1, 1987; April 30, 1991, effective December 1, 1991; April 22, 1993, effective December 1, 1993; April 12, 2006, effective December 1, 2006; April 30, 2007, effective December 1, 2007.)

RULE 35. PHYSICAL AND MENTAL EXAMINATIONS

(a) Order for an Examination.

(1) *In General.* The court where the action is pending may order a party whose mental or physical condition—including blood group—is in controversy to submit to a physical or mental examination by a suitably licensed or certified examiner. The court has the same authority to order a party to produce for examination a person who is in its custody or under its legal control.

(2) *Motion and Notice; Contents of the Order.* The order:

(A) may be made only on motion for good cause and on notice to all parties and the person to be examined; and

(B) must specify the time, place, manner, conditions, and scope of the examination, as well as the person or persons who will perform it.

(b) Examiner's Report.

(1) *Request by the Party or Person Examined.* The party who moved for the examination must, on request, deliver to the requester a copy of the examiner's report, together with like reports of all earlier examinations of the same condition. The request may be made by the party against whom the examination order was issued or by the person examined.

(2) *Contents.* The examiner's report must be in writing and must set out in detail the examiner's findings, including diagnoses, conclusions, and the results of any tests.

(3) *Request by the Moving Party.* After delivering the reports, the party who moved for the examination may request—and is entitled to receive—from the party against whom the examination order was issued like reports of all earlier or later examinations of the same condition. But those reports need not be delivered by the party with custody or control of the person examined if the party shows that it could not obtain them.

(4) *Waiver of Privilege.* By requesting and obtaining the examiner's report, or by deposing the examiner, the party examined waives any privilege it may have—in that action or any other action involving the same controversy—concerning testimony about all examinations of the same condition.

(5) *Failure to Deliver a Report.* The court on motion may order—on just terms—that a party deliver the report of an examination. If the report is not provided, the court may exclude the examiner's testimony at trial.

(6) *Scope.* This subdivision (b) applies also to an examination made by the parties' agreement, unless the agreement states otherwise. This subdivision does not preclude obtaining an examiner's report or deposing an examiner under other rules.

(Amended March 30, 1970, effective July 1, 1970; March 2, 1987, effective August 1, 1987; amended by Pub.L. 100–690, Title VII, § 7047(b), November 18, 1988, 102 Stat. 4401; amended April 30, 1991, effective December 1, 1991; April 30, 2007, effective December 1, 2007.)

RULE 36. REQUESTS FOR ADMISSION

(a) Scope and Procedure.

(1) *Scope.* A party may serve on any other party a written request to admit, for purposes of the pending action only, the truth of any matters within the scope of Rule 26(b)(1) relating to:

(A) facts, the application of law to fact, or opinions about either; and

(B) the genuineness of any described documents.

(2) *Form; Copy of a Document.* Each matter must be separately stated. A request to admit the genuineness of a document must be accompanied by a copy of the document unless it is, or has been, otherwise furnished or made available for inspection and copying.

(3) *Time to Respond; Effect of Not Responding.* A matter is admitted unless, within 30 days after being served, the party to whom the request is directed serves on the requesting party a written answer or objection addressed to the matter and signed by the party or its attorney. A shorter or longer time for responding may be stipulated to under Rule 29 or be ordered by the court.

(4) *Answer.* If a matter is not admitted, the answer must specifically deny it or state in detail why the answering party cannot truthfully admit or deny it. A denial must fairly respond to the substance of the matter; and when good faith requires that a party qualify an answer or deny only a part of a matter, the answer must specify the part admitted and qualify or deny the rest. The answering party may assert lack of knowledge or information as a reason for failing to admit or deny only if the party states that it has made reasonable inquiry and that the information it knows or can readily obtain is insufficient to enable it to admit or deny.

(5) *Objections.* The grounds for objecting to a request must be stated. A party must not object solely on the ground that the request presents a genuine issue for trial.

(6) *Motion Regarding the Sufficiency of an Answer or Objection.* The requesting party may move to determine the sufficiency of an answer or objection. Unless the court finds an objection justified, it must order that an answer be served. On finding that an answer does not comply with this rule, the court may order either that the matter is admitted or that an amended answer be served. The court may defer its final decision until a pretrial conference or a specified time before trial. Rule 37(a)(5) applies to an award of expenses.

(b) **Effect of an Admission; Withdrawing or Amending It.** A matter admitted under this rule is conclusively established unless the court, on motion, permits the admission to be withdrawn or amended. Subject to Rule 16(e), the court may permit withdrawal or amendment if it would promote the presentation of the merits of the action and if the court is not persuaded that it would prejudice the requesting party in maintaining or defending the action on the merits. An admission under this rule is not an admission for any other purpose and cannot be used against the party in any other proceeding.

(Amended December 27, 1946, effective March 19, 1948; March 30, 1970, effective July 1, 1970; March 2, 1987, effective August 1, 1987; April 22, 1993, effective December 1, 1993; April 30, 2007, effective December 1, 2007.)

RULE 37. FAILURE TO MAKE DISCLO-SURES OR TO COOPERATE IN DIS-COVERY; SANCTIONS

(a) Motion for an Order Compelling Disclosure or Discovery.

(1) *In General.* On notice to other parties and all affected persons, a party may move for an order compelling disclosure or discovery. The motion must include a certification that the movant has in good faith conferred or attempted to confer with the person or party failing to make disclosure or discovery in an effort to obtain it without court action.

(2) *Appropriate Court.* A motion for an order to a party must be made in the court where the action is pending. A motion for an order to a nonparty must be made in the court where the discovery is or will be taken.

(3) *Specific Motions.*

(A) *To Compel Disclosure.* If a party fails to make a disclosure required by Rule 26(a), any other party may move to compel disclosure and for appropriate sanctions.

(B) *To Compel a Discovery Response.* A party seeking discovery may move for an order compelling an answer, designation, production, or inspection. This motion may be made if:

(i) a deponent fails to answer a question asked under Rule 30 or 31;

(ii) a corporation or other entity fails to make a designation under Rule 30(b)(6) or 31(a)(4);

(iii) a party fails to answer an interrogatory submitted under Rule 33; or

(iv) a party fails to respond that inspection will be permitted—or fails to permit inspection—as requested under Rule 34.

(C) *Related to a Deposition.* When taking an oral deposition, the party asking a question may complete or adjourn the examination before moving for an order.

(4) *Evasive or Incomplete Disclosure, Answer, or Response.* For purposes of this subdivision (a), an evasive or incomplete disclosure, answer, or response must be treated as a failure to disclose, answer, or respond.

(5) *Payment of Expenses; Protective Orders.*

(A) *If the Motion Is Granted (or Disclosure or Discovery Is Provided After Filing).* If the motion is granted—or if the disclosure or requested discovery is provided after the motion was filed—the court must, after giving an opportunity to be heard, require the party or deponent whose conduct necessitated the motion, the party or attorney advising that conduct, or both to pay the movant's reasonable expenses incurred in making the motion, including attorney's fees. But the court must not order this payment if:

(i) the movant filed the motion before attempting in good faith to obtain the disclosure or discovery without court action;

(ii) the opposing party's nondisclosure, response, or objection was substantially justified; or

(iii) other circumstances make an award of expenses unjust.

(B) *If the Motion Is Denied.* If the motion is denied, the court may issue any protective order authorized under Rule 26(c) and must, after giving an opportunity to be heard, require the movant, the attorney filing the motion, or both to pay the party or deponent who opposed the motion its reasonable expenses incurred in opposing the motion, including attorney's fees. But the court must not order this payment if the motion was substantially justified or other circumstances make an award of expenses unjust.

(C) *If the Motion Is Granted in Part and Denied in Part.* If the motion is granted in part and denied in part, the court may issue any pro-

tective order authorized under Rule 26(c) and may, after giving an opportunity to be heard, apportion the reasonable expenses for the motion.

(b) **Failure to Comply with a Court Order.**

(1) *Sanctions Sought in the District Where the Deposition Is Taken.* If the court where the discovery is taken orders a deponent to be sworn or to answer a question and the deponent fails to obey, the failure may be treated as contempt of court. If a deposition-related motion is transferred to the court where the action is pending, and that court orders a deponent to be sworn or to answer a question and the deponent fails to obey, the failure may be treated as contempt of either the court where the discovery is taken or the court where the action is pending.

(2) *Sanctions Sought in the District Where the Action Is Pending.*

(A) *For Not Obeying a Discovery Order.* If a party or a party's officer, director, or managing agent—or a witness designated under Rule 30(b)(6) or 31(a)(4)—fails to obey an order to provide or permit discovery, including an order under Rule 26(f), 35, or 37(a), the court where the action is pending may issue further just orders. They may include the following:

(i) directing that the matters embraced in the order or other designated facts be taken as established for purposes of the action, as the prevailing party claims;

(ii) prohibiting the disobedient party from supporting or opposing designated claims or defenses, or from introducing designated matters in evidence;

(iii) striking pleadings in whole or in part;

(iv) staying further proceedings until the order is obeyed;

(v) dismissing the action or proceeding in whole or in part;

(vi) rendering a default judgment against the disobedient party; or

(vii) treating as contempt of court the failure to obey any order except an order to submit to a physical or mental examination.

(B) *For Not Producing a Person for Examination.* If a party fails to comply with an order under Rule 35(a) requiring it to produce another person for examination, the court may issue any of the orders listed in Rule 37(b)(2)(A)(i)-(vi), unless the disobedient party shows that it cannot produce the other person.

(C) *Payment of Expenses.* Instead of or in addition to the orders above, the court must order the disobedient party, the attorney advising that party, or both to pay the reasonable expenses, including attorney's fees, caused by the failure, unless the failure was substantially justified or other circumstances make an award of expenses unjust.

(c) **Failure to Disclose, to Supplement an Earlier Response, or to Admit.**

(1) *Failure to Disclose or Supplement.* If a party fails to provide information or identify a witness as required by Rule 26(a) or (e), the party is not allowed to use that information or witness to supply evidence on a motion, at a hearing, or at a trial, unless the failure was substantially justified or is harmless. In addition to or instead of this sanction, the court, on motion and after giving an opportunity to be heard:

(A) may order payment of the reasonable expenses, including attorney's fees, caused by the failure;

(B) may inform the jury of the party's failure; and

(C) may impose other appropriate sanctions, including any of the orders listed in Rule 37(b)(2)(A)(i)-(vi).

(2) *Failure to Admit.* If a party fails to admit what is requested under Rule 36 and if the requesting party later proves a document to be genuine or the matter true, the requesting party may move that the party who failed to admit pay the reasonable expenses, including attorney's fees, incurred in making that proof. The court must so order unless:

(A) the request was held objectionable under Rule 36(a);

(B) the admission sought was of no substantial importance;

(C) the party failing to admit had a reasonable ground to believe that it might prevail on the matter; or

(D) there was other good reason for the failure to admit.

(d) **Party's Failure to Attend Its Own Deposition, Serve Answers to Interrogatories, or Respond to a Request for Inspection.**

(1) *In General.*

(A) *Motion; Grounds for Sanctions.* The court where the action is pending may, on motion, order sanctions if:

(i) a party or a party's officer, director, or managing agent—or a person designated under Rule 30(b)(6) or 31(a)(4)—fails, after being served with proper notice, to appear for that person's deposition; or

(ii) a party, after being properly served with interrogatories under Rule 33 or a request for inspection under Rule 34, fails to serve its answers, objections, or written response.

(B) *Certification.* A motion for sanctions for failing to answer or respond must include a certification that the movant has in good faith conferred or attempted to confer with the party failing to act in an effort to obtain the answer or response without court action.

(2) *Unacceptable Excuse for Failing to Act.* A failure described in Rule 37(d)(1)(A) is not excused on the ground that the discovery sought was objectionable, unless the party failing to act has a pending motion for a protective order under Rule 26(c).

(3) *Types of Sanctions.* Sanctions may include any of the orders listed in Rule 37(b)(2)(A)(i)-(vi). Instead of or in addition to these sanctions, the court must require the party failing to act, the attorney advising that party, or both to pay the reasonable expenses, including attorney's fees, caused by the failure, unless the failure was substantially justified or other circumstances make an award of expenses unjust.

(e) **Failure to Provide Electronically Stored Information.** Absent exceptional circumstances, a court may not impose sanctions under these rules on a party for failing to provide electronically stored information lost as a result of the routine, good-faith operation of an electronic information system.

(f) **Failure to Participate in Framing a Discovery Plan.** If a party or its attorney fails to participate in good faith in developing and submitting a proposed discovery plan as required by Rule 26(f), the court may, after giving an opportunity to be heard, require that party or attorney to pay to any other party the reasonable expenses, including attorney's fees, caused by the failure.

(Amended December 29, 1948, effective October 20, 1949; March 30, 1970, effective July 1, 1970; April 29, 1980, effective August 1, 1980; amended by Pub.L. 96–481, Title II, § 205(a), October 21, 1980, 94 Stat. 2330, effective October 1, 1981; amended March 2, 1987, effective August 1, 1987; April 22, 1993, effective December 1, 1993; April 17, 2000, effective December 1, 2000; April 12, 2006, effective December 1, 2006; April 30, 2007, effective December 1, 2007; April 16, 2013, effective December 1, 2013.)

TITLE VI. TRIALS

RULE 38. RIGHT TO A JURY TRIAL; DEMAND

(a) Right Preserved. The right of trial by jury as declared by the Seventh Amendment to the Constitution—or as provided by a federal statute—is preserved to the parties inviolate.

(b) Demand. On any issue triable of right by a jury, a party may demand a jury trial by:

(1) serving the other parties with a written demand—which may be included in a pleading—no later than 14 days after the last pleading directed to the issue is served; and

(2) filing the demand in accordance with Rule 5(d).

(c) Specifying Issues. In its demand, a party may specify the issues that it wishes to have tried by a jury; otherwise, it is considered to have demanded a jury trial on all the issues so triable. If the party has demanded a jury trial on only some issues, any other party may—within 14 days after being served with the demand or within a shorter time ordered by the court—serve a demand for a jury trial on any other or all factual issues triable by jury.

(d) Waiver; Withdrawal. A party waives a jury trial unless its demand is properly served and filed. A proper demand may be withdrawn only if the parties consent.

(e) Admiralty and Maritime Claims. These rules do not create a right to a jury trial on issues in a claim that is an admiralty or maritime claim under Rule 9(h).

(Amended February 28, 1966, effective July 1, 1966; March 2, 1987, effective August 1, 1987; April 22, 1993, effective December 1, 1993; April 30, 2007, effective December 1, 2007; March 26, 2009, effective December 1, 2009.)

RULE 39. TRIAL BY JURY OR BY THE COURT

(a) When a Demand Is Made. When a jury trial has been demanded under Rule 38, the action must be designated on the docket as a jury action. The trial on all issues so demanded must be by jury unless:

(1) the parties or their attorneys file a stipulation to a nonjury trial or so stipulate on the record; or

(2) the court, on motion or on its own, finds that on some or all of those issues there is no federal right to a jury trial.

(b) When No Demand Is Made. Issues on which a jury trial is not properly demanded are to be tried by the court. But the court may, on motion, order a jury trial on any issue for which a jury might have been demanded.

(c) Advisory Jury; Jury Trial by Consent. In an action not triable of right by a jury, the court, on motion or on its own:

(1) may try any issue with an advisory jury; or

(2) may, with the parties' consent, try any issue by a jury whose verdict has the same effect as if a jury trial had been a matter of right, unless the action is against the United States and a federal statute provides for a nonjury trial.

(Amended April 30, 2007, effective December 1, 2007.)

RULE 40. SCHEDULING CASES FOR TRIAL

Each court must provide by rule for scheduling trials. The court must give priority to actions entitled to priority by a federal statute.

(Amended April 30, 2007, effective December 1, 2007.)

RULE 41. DISMISSAL OF ACTIONS

(a) Voluntary Dismissal.

(1) *By the Plaintiff.*

(A) *Without a Court Order.* Subject to Rules 23(e), 23.1(c), 23.2, and 66 and any applicable federal statute, the plaintiff may dismiss an action without a court order by filing:

(i) a notice of dismissal before the opposing party serves either an answer or a motion for summary judgment; or

(ii) a stipulation of dismissal signed by all parties who have appeared.

(B) *Effect.* Unless the notice or stipulation states otherwise, the dismissal is without prejudice. But if the plaintiff previously dismissed any federal- or state-court action based on or including the same claim, a notice of dismissal operates as an adjudication on the merits.

(2) *By Court Order; Effect.* Except as provided in Rule 41(a)(1), an action may be dismissed at the plaintiff's request only by court order, on terms that the court considers proper. If a defendant has pleaded a counterclaim before being served with the plaintiff's motion to dismiss, the action may be dismissed over the defendant's objection only if the counterclaim can remain pending for independent adjudication. Unless the order states otherwise, a dismissal under this paragraph (2) is without prejudice.

(b) Involuntary Dismissal; Effect. If the plaintiff fails to prosecute or to comply with these rules or a court order, a defendant may move to dismiss the action or any claim against it. Unless the dismissal order states otherwise, a dismissal under this subdivision (b) and any dismissal not under this rule—except one for lack of jurisdiction, improper venue, or failure to join a party under Rule 19—operates as an adjudication on the merits.

(c) Dismissing a Counterclaim, Crossclaim, or Third–Party Claim. This rule applies to a dismissal of any counterclaim, crossclaim, or third-party claim. A claimant's voluntary dismissal under Rule 41(a)(1)(A)(i) must be made:

    (1) before a responsive pleading is served; or

    (2) if there is no responsive pleading, before evidence is introduced at a hearing or trial.

(d) Costs of a Previously Dismissed Action. If a plaintiff who previously dismissed an action in any court files an action based on or including the same claim against the same defendant, the court:

    (1) may order the plaintiff to pay all or part of the costs of that previous action; and

    (2) may stay the proceedings until the plaintiff has complied.

(Amended December 27, 1946, effective March 19, 1948; January 21, 1963, effective July 1, 1963; February 28, 1966, effective July 1, 1966; December 4, 1967, effective July 1, 1968; March 2, 1987, effective August 1, 1987; April 30, 1991, effective December 1, 1991; April 30, 2007, effective December 1, 2007.)

RULE 42. CONSOLIDATION; SEPARATE TRIALS

(a) Consolidation. If actions before the court involve a common question of law or fact, the court may:

    (1) join for hearing or trial any or all matters at issue in the actions;

    (2) consolidate the actions; or

    (3) issue any other orders to avoid unnecessary cost or delay.

(b) Separate Trials. For convenience, to avoid prejudice, or to expedite and economize, the court may order a separate trial of one or more separate issues, claims, crossclaims, counterclaims, or third-party claims. When ordering a separate trial, the court must preserve any federal right to a jury trial.

(Amended February 28, 1966, effective July 1, 1966; April 30, 2007, effective December 1, 2007.)

RULE 43. TAKING TESTIMONY

(a) In Open Court. At trial, the witnesses' testimony must be taken in open court unless a federal statute, the Federal Rules of Evidence, these rules, or other rules adopted by the Supreme Court provide otherwise. For good cause in compelling circumstances and with appropriate safeguards, the court may permit testimony in open court by contemporaneous transmission from a different location.

(b) Affirmation Instead of an Oath. When these rules require an oath, a solemn affirmation suffices.

(c) Evidence on a Motion. When a motion relies on facts outside the record, the court may hear the matter on affidavits or may hear it wholly or partly on oral testimony or on depositions.

(d) Interpreter. The court may appoint an interpreter of its choosing; fix reasonable compensation to be paid from funds provided by law or by one or more parties; and tax the compensation as costs.

(Amended February 28, 1966, effective July 1, 1966; November 20, 1972, and December 18, 1972, effective July 1, 1975; March 2, 1987, effective August 1, 1987; April 23, 1996, effective December 1, 1996; April 30, 2007, effective December 1, 2007.)

RULE 44. PROVING AN OFFICIAL RECORD

(a) Means of Proving.

    (1) *Domestic Record.* Each of the following evidences an official record—or an entry in it—that is otherwise admissible and is kept within the United States, any state, district, or commonwealth, or any territory subject to the administrative or judicial jurisdiction of the United States:

      (A) an official publication of the record; or

      (B) a copy attested by the officer with legal custody of the record—or by the officer's deputy—and accompanied by a certificate that the officer has custody. The certificate must be made under seal:

        (i) by a judge of a court of record in the district or political subdivision where the record is kept; or

        (ii) by any public officer with a seal of office and with official duties in the district or political subdivision where the record is kept.

    (2) *Foreign Record.*

      (A) *In General.* Each of the following evidences a foreign official record—or an entry in it—that is otherwise admissible:

(i) an official publication of the record; or

(ii) the record—or a copy—that is attested by an authorized person and is accompanied either by a final certification of genuineness or by a certification under a treaty or convention to which the United States and the country where the record is located are parties.

(B) *Final Certification of Genuineness.* A final certification must certify the genuineness of the signature and official position of the attester or of any foreign official whose certificate of genuineness relates to the attestation or is in a chain of certificates of genuineness relating to the attestation. A final certification may be made by a secretary of a United States embassy or legation; by a consul general, vice consul, or consular agent of the United States; or by a diplomatic or consular official of the foreign country assigned or accredited to the United States.

(C) *Other Means of Proof.* If all parties have had a reasonable opportunity to investigate a foreign record's authenticity and accuracy, the court may, for good cause, either:

(i) admit an attested copy without final certification; or

(ii) permit the record to be evidenced by an attested summary with or without a final certification.

(b) Lack of a Record. A written statement that a diligent search of designated records revealed no record or entry of a specified tenor is admissible as evidence that the records contain no such record or entry. For domestic records, the statement must be authenticated under Rule 44(a)(1). For foreign records, the statement must comply with (a)(2)(C)(ii).

(c) Other Proof. A party may prove an official record—or an entry or lack of an entry in it—by any other method authorized by law.

(Amended February 28, 1966, effective July 1, 1966; March 2, 1987, effective August 1, 1987; April 30, 1991, effective December 1, 1991; April 30, 2007, effective December 1, 2007.)

RULE 44.1. DETERMINING FOREIGN LAW

A party who intends to raise an issue about a foreign country's law must give notice by a pleading or other writing. In determining foreign law, the court may consider any relevant material or source, including testimony, whether or not submitted by a party or admissible under the Federal Rules of Evidence. The court's determination must be treated as a ruling on a question of law.

(Adopted February 28, 1966, effective July 1, 1966; amended November 20, 1972, effective July 1, 1975; March 2, 1987, effective August 1, 1987; April 30, 2007, effective December 1, 2007.)

RULE 45. SUBPOENA

(a) In General.

(1) *Form and Contents.*

(A) *Requirements—In General.* Every subpoena must:

(i) state the court from which it issued;

(ii) state the title of the action and its civil-action number;

(iii) command each person to whom it is directed to do the following at a specified time and place: attend and testify; produce designated documents, electronically stored information, or tangible things in that person's possession, custody, or control; or permit the inspection of premises; and

(iv) set out the text of Rule 45(d) and (e).

(B) *Command to Attend a Deposition—Notice of the Recording Method.* A subpoena commanding attendance at a deposition must state the method for recording the testimony.

(C) *Combining or Separating a Command to Produce or to Permit Inspection; Specifying the Form for Electronically Stored Information.* A command to produce documents, electronically stored information, or tangible things or to permit the inspection of premises may be included in a subpoena commanding attendance at a deposition, hearing, or trial, or may be set out in a separate subpoena. A subpoena may specify the form or forms in which electronically stored information is to be produced.

(D) *Command to Produce; Included Obligations.* A command in a subpoena to produce documents, electronically stored information, or tangible things requires the responding person to permit inspection, copying, testing, or sampling of the materials.

(2) *Issuing Court.* A subpoena must issue from the court where the action is pending.

(3) *Issued by Whom.* The clerk must issue a subpoena, signed but otherwise in blank, to a party who requests it. That party must complete it before service. An attorney also may issue and sign a subpoena if the attorney is authorized to practice in the issuing court.

(4) *Notice to Other Parties Before Service.* If the subpoena commands the production of documents, electronically stored information, or tangible things or the inspection of premises before trial, then before it is served on the person to whom it is directed, a notice and a copy of the subpoena must be served on each party.

(b) Service.

(1) *By Whom and How; Tendering Fees.* Any person who is at least 18 years old and not a party may serve a subpoena. Serving a subpoena requires delivering a copy to the named person and, if the subpoena requires that person's attendance, tendering the fees for 1 day's attendance and the mileage allowed by law. Fees and mileage need not be tendered when the subpoena issues on behalf of the United States or any of its officers or agencies.

(2) *Service in the United States.* A subpoena may be served at any place within the United States.

(3) *Service in a Foreign Country.* 28 U.S.C. § 1783 governs issuing and serving a subpoena directed to a United States national or resident who is in a foreign country.

(4) *Proof of Service.* Proving service, when necessary, requires filing with the issuing court a statement showing the date and manner of service and the names of the persons served. The statement must be certified by the server.

(c) Place of Compliance.

(1) *For a Trial, Hearing, or Deposition.* A subpoena may command a person to attend a trial, hearing, or deposition only as follows:

(A) within 100 miles of where the person resides, is employed, or regularly transacts business in person; or

(B) within the state where the person resides, is employed, or regularly transacts business in person, if the person

(i) is a party or a party's officer; or

(ii) is commanded to attend a trial and would not incur substantial expense.

(2) *For Other Discovery.* A subpoena may command:

(A) production of documents, electronically stored information, or tangible things at a place within 100 miles of where the person resides, is employed, or regularly transacts business in person; and

(B) inspection of premises at the premises to be inspected.

(d) Protecting a Person Subject to a Subpoena; Enforcement.

(1) *Avoiding Undue Burden or Expense; Sanctions.* A party or attorney responsible for issuing and serving a subpoena must take reasonable steps to avoid imposing undue burden or expense on a person subject to the subpoena. The court for the district where compliance is required must enforce this duty and impose an appropriate sanction—which may include lost earnings and reasonable attorney's fees—on a party or attorney who fails to comply.

(2) *Command to Produce Materials or Permit Inspection.*

(A) *Appearance Not Required.* A person commanded to produce documents, electronically stored information, or tangible things, or to permit the inspection of premises, need not appear in person at the place of production or inspection unless also commanded to appear for a deposition, hearing, or trial.

(B) *Objections.* A person commanded to produce documents or tangible things or to permit inspection may serve on the party or attorney designated in the subpoena a written objection to inspecting, copying, testing, or sampling any or all of the materials or to inspecting the premises—or to producing electronically stored information in the form or forms requested. The objection must be served before the earlier of the time specified for compliance or 14 days after the subpoena is served. If an objection is made, the following rules apply:

(i) At any time, on notice to the commanded person, the serving party may move the court for the district where compliance is required for an order compelling production or inspection.

(ii) These acts may be required only as directed in the order, and the order must protect a person who is neither a party nor a party's officer from significant expense resulting from compliance.

(3) *Quashing or Modifying a Subpoena.*

(A) *When Required.* On timely motion, the court for the district where compliance is required must quash or modify a subpoena that:

(i) fails to allow a reasonable time to comply;

(ii) requires a person to comply beyond the geographical limits specified in Rule 45(c);

(iii) requires disclosure of privileged or other protected matter, if no exception or waiver applies; or

(iv) subjects a person to undue burden.

(B) *When Permitted.* To protect a person subject to or affected by a subpoena, the court for the district where compliance is required may, on motion, quash or modify the subpoena if it requires:

   (i) disclosing a trade secret or other confidential research, development, or commercial information; or

   (ii) disclosing an unretained expert's opinion or information that does not describe specific occurrences in dispute and results from the expert's study that was not requested by a party.

  (C) *Specifying Conditions as an Alternative.* In the circumstances described in Rule 45(d)(3)(B), the court may, instead of quashing or modifying a subpoena, order appearance or production under specified conditions if the serving party:

   (i) shows a substantial need for the testimony or material that cannot be otherwise met without undue hardship; and

   (ii) ensures that the subpoenaed person will be reasonably compensated.

(e) **Duties in Responding to a Subpoena.**

  (1) *Producing Documents or Electronically Stored Information.* These procedures apply to producing documents or electronically stored information:

   (A) *Documents.* A person responding to a subpoena to produce documents must produce them as they are kept in the ordinary course of business or must organize and label them to correspond to the categories in the demand.

   (B) *Form for Producing Electronically Stored Information Not Specified.* If a subpoena does not specify a form for producing electronically stored information, the person responding must produce it in a form or forms in which it is ordinarily maintained or in a reasonably usable form or forms.

   (C) *Electronically Stored Information Produced in Only One Form.* The person responding need not produce the same electronically stored information in more than one form.

   (D) *Inaccessible Electronically Stored Information.* The person responding need not provide discovery of electronically stored information from sources that the person identifies as not reasonably accessible because of undue burden or cost. On motion to compel discovery or for a protective order, the person responding must show that the information is not reasonably accessible because of undue burden or cost. If that showing is made, the court may nonetheless order discovery from such sources if the requesting party shows good cause, considering the limitations of Rule 26(b)(2)(C). The court may specify conditions for the discovery.

  (2) *Claiming Privilege or Protection.*

   (A) *Information Withheld.* A person withholding subpoenaed information under a claim that it is privileged or subject to protection as trial-preparation material must:

   (i) expressly make the claim; and

   (ii) describe the nature of the withheld documents, communications, or tangible things in a manner that, without revealing information itself privileged or protected, will enable the parties to assess the claim.

   (B) *Information Produced.* If information produced in response to a subpoena is subject to a claim of privilege or of protection as trial-preparation material, the person making the claim may notify any party that received the information of the claim and the basis for it. After being notified, a party must promptly return, sequester, or destroy the specified information and any copies it has; must not use or disclose the information until the claim is resolved; must take reasonable steps to retrieve the information if the party disclosed it before being notified; and may promptly present the information under seal to the court for the district where compliance is required for a determination of the claim. The person who produced the information must preserve the information until the claim is resolved.

(f) **Transferring a Subpoena–Related Motion.** When the court where compliance is required did not issue the subpoena, it may transfer a motion under this rule to the issuing court if the person subject to the subpoena consents or if the court finds exceptional circumstances. Then, if the attorney for a person subject to a subpoena is authorized to practice in the court where the motion was made, the attorney may file papers and appear on the motion as an officer of the issuing court. To enforce its order, the issuing court may transfer the order to the court where the motion was made.

(g) **Contempt.** The court for the district where compliance is required—and also, after a motion is transferred, the issuing court—may hold in contempt a person who, having been served, fails without adequate excuse to obey the subpoena or an order related to it.

(Amended December 27, 1946, effective March 19, 1948; December 29, 1948, effective October 20, 1949; March 30, 1970, effective July 1, 1970; April 29, 1980, effective August 1, 1980; April 29, 1985, effective August 1, 1985; March 2, 1987, effective August 1, 1987; April 30, 1991, effective December 1, 1991; April 25, 2005, effective December 1, 2005; April 12, 2006, effective December 1, 2006; April 30, 2007, effective December 1, 2007; April 16, 2013, effective December 1, 2013.)

RULE 46. OBJECTING TO A RULING OR ORDER

A formal exception to a ruling or order is unnecessary. When the ruling or order is requested or made, a party need only state the action that it wants the court to take or objects to, along with the grounds for the request or objection. Failing to object does not prejudice a party who had no opportunity to do so when the ruling or order was made.

(Amended March 2, 1987, effective August 1, 1987; April 30, 2007, effective December 1, 2007.)

RULE 47. SELECTING JURORS

(a) **Examining Jurors.** The court may permit the parties or their attorneys to examine prospective jurors or may itself do so. If the court examines the jurors, it must permit the parties or their attorneys to make any further inquiry it considers proper, or must itself ask any of their additional questions it considers proper.

(b) **Peremptory Challenges.** The court must allow the number of peremptory challenges provided by 28 U.S.C. § 1870.

(c) **Excusing a Juror.** During trial or deliberation, the court may excuse a juror for good cause.

(Amended February 28, 1966, effective July 1, 1966; April 30, 1991, effective December 1, 1991; April 30, 2007, effective December 1, 2007.)

RULE 48. NUMBER OF JURORS; VERDICT; POLLING

(a) **Number of Jurors.** A jury must begin with at least 6 and no more than 12 members, and each juror must participate in the verdict unless excused under Rule 47(c).

(b) **Verdict.** Unless the parties stipulate otherwise, the verdict must be unanimous and must be returned by a jury of at least 6 members.

(c) **Polling.** After a verdict is returned but before the jury is discharged, the court must on a party's request, or may on its own, poll the jurors individually. If the poll reveals a lack of unanimity or lack of assent by the number of jurors that the parties stipulated to, the court may direct the jury to deliberate further or may order a new trial.

(Amended April 30, 1991, effective December 1, 1991; April 30, 2007, effective December 1, 2007; March 26, 2009, effective December 1, 2009.)

RULE 49. SPECIAL VERDICT; GENERAL VERDICT AND QUESTIONS

(a) **Special Verdict.**

(1) *In General.* The court may require a jury to return only a special verdict in the form of a special written finding on each issue of fact. The court may do so by:

(A) submitting written questions susceptible of a categorical or other brief answer;

(B) submitting written forms of the special findings that might properly be made under the pleadings and evidence; or

(C) using any other method that the court considers appropriate.

(2) *Instructions.* The court must give the instructions and explanations necessary to enable the jury to make its findings on each submitted issue.

(3) *Issues Not Submitted.* A party waives the right to a jury trial on any issue of fact raised by the pleadings or evidence but not submitted to the jury unless, before the jury retires, the party demands its submission to the jury. If the party does not demand submission, the court may make a finding on the issue. If the court makes no finding, it is considered to have made a finding consistent with its judgment on the special verdict.

(b) **General Verdict with Answers to Written Questions.**

(1) *In General.* The court may submit to the jury forms for a general verdict, together with written questions on one or more issues of fact that the jury must decide. The court must give the instructions and explanations necessary to enable the jury to render a general verdict and answer the questions in writing, and must direct the jury to do both.

(2) *Verdict and Answers Consistent.* When the general verdict and the answers are consistent, the court must approve, for entry under Rule 58, an appropriate judgment on the verdict and answers.

(3) *Answers Inconsistent with the Verdict.* When the answers are consistent with each other but one or more is inconsistent with the general verdict, the court may:

(A) approve, for entry under Rule 58, an appropriate judgment according to the answers, notwithstanding the general verdict;

(B) direct the jury to further consider its answers and verdict; or

(C) order a new trial.

(4) *Answers Inconsistent with Each Other and the Verdict.* When the answers are inconsistent with each other and one or more is also inconsistent with the general verdict, judgment must not be entered; instead, the court must direct

the jury to further consider its answers and verdict, or must order a new trial.

(Amended January 21, 1963, effective July 1, 1963; March 2, 1987, effective August 1, 1987; April 30, 2007, effective December 1, 2007.)

RULE 50. JUDGMENT AS A MATTER OF LAW IN A JURY TRIAL; RELATED MOTION FOR A NEW TRIAL; CONDITIONAL RULING

(a) Judgment as a Matter of Law.

(1) *In General.* If a party has been fully heard on an issue during a jury trial and the court finds that a reasonable jury would not have a legally sufficient evidentiary basis to find for the party on that issue, the court may:

 (A) resolve the issue against the party; and

 (B) grant a motion for judgment as a matter of law against the party on a claim or defense that, under the controlling law, can be maintained or defeated only with a favorable finding on that issue.

(2) *Motion.* A motion for judgment as a matter of law may be made at any time before the case is submitted to the jury. The motion must specify the judgment sought and the law and facts that entitle the movant to the judgment.

(b) Renewing the Motion After Trial; Alternative Motion for a New Trial. If the court does not grant a motion for judgment as a matter of law made under Rule 50(a), the court is considered to have submitted the action to the jury subject to the court's later deciding the legal questions raised by the motion. No later than 28 days after the entry of judgment—or if the motion addresses a jury issue not decided by a verdict, no later than 28 days after the jury was discharged—the movant may file a renewed motion for judgment as a matter of law and may include an alternative or joint request for a new trial under Rule 59. In ruling on the renewed motion, the court may:

(1) allow judgment on the verdict, if the jury returned a verdict;

(2) order a new trial; or

(3) direct the entry of judgment as a matter of law.

(c) Granting the Renewed Motion; Conditional Ruling on a Motion for a New Trial.

(1) *In General.* If the court grants a renewed motion for judgment as a matter of law, it must also conditionally rule on any motion for a new trial by determining whether a new trial should be granted if the judgment is later vacated or reversed. The court must state the grounds for conditionally granting or denying the motion for a new trial.

(2) *Effect of a Conditional Ruling.* Conditionally granting the motion for a new trial does not affect the judgment's finality; if the judgment is reversed, the new trial must proceed unless the appellate court orders otherwise. If the motion for a new trial is conditionally denied, the appellee may assert error in that denial; if the judgment is reversed, the case must proceed as the appellate court orders.

(d) Time for a Losing Party's New–Trial Motion. Any motion for a new trial under Rule 59 by a party against whom judgment as a matter of law is rendered must be filed no later than 28 days after the entry of the judgment.

(e) Denying the Motion for Judgment as a Matter of Law; Reversal on Appeal. If the court denies the motion for judgment as a matter of law, the prevailing party may, as appellee, assert grounds entitling it to a new trial should the appellate court conclude that the trial court erred in denying the motion. If the appellate court reverses the judgment, it may order a new trial, direct the trial court to determine whether a new trial should be granted, or direct the entry of judgment.

(Amended January 21, 1963, effective July 1, 1963; March 2, 1987, effective August 1, 1987; April 30, 1991, effective December 1, 1991; April 22, 1993, effective December 1, 1993; April 27, 1995, effective December 1, 1995; April 12, 2006, effective December 1, 2006; April 30, 2007, effective December 1, 2007; March 26, 2009, effective December 1, 2009.)

RULE 51. INSTRUCTIONS TO THE JURY; OBJECTIONS; PRESERVING A CLAIM OF ERROR

(a) Requests.

(1) *Before or at the Close of the Evidence.* At the close of the evidence or at any earlier reasonable time that the court orders, a party may file and furnish to every other party written requests for the jury instructions it wants the court to give.

(2) *After the Close of the Evidence.* After the close of the evidence, a party may:

 (A) file requests for instructions on issues that could not reasonably have been anticipated by an earlier time that the court set for requests; and

 (B) with the court's permission, file untimely requests for instructions on any issue.

(b) Instructions. The court:

(1) must inform the parties of its proposed instructions and proposed action on the requests be-

fore instructing the jury and before final jury arguments;

(2) must give the parties an opportunity to object on the record and out of the jury's hearing before the instructions and arguments are delivered; and

(3) may instruct the jury at any time before the jury is discharged.

(c) Objections.

(1) *How to Make.* A party who objects to an instruction or the failure to give an instruction must do so on the record, stating distinctly the matter objected to and the grounds for the objection.

(2) *When to Make.* An objection is timely if:

(A) a party objects at the opportunity provided under Rule 51(b)(2); or

(B) a party was not informed of an instruction or action on a request before that opportunity to object, and the party objects promptly after learning that the instruction or request will be, or has been, given or refused.

(d) Assigning Error; Plain Error.

(1) *Assigning Error.* A party may assign as error:

(A) an error in an instruction actually given, if that party properly objected; or

(B) a failure to give an instruction, if that party properly requested it and—unless the court rejected the request in a definitive ruling on the record—also properly objected.

(2) *Plain Error.* A court may consider a plain error in the instructions that has not been preserved as required by Rule 51(d)(1) if the error affects substantial rights.

(Amended March 2, 1987, effective August 1, 1987; March 27, 2003, effective December 1, 2003; April 30, 2007, effective December 1, 2007.)

RULE 52. FINDINGS AND CONCLUSIONS BY THE COURT; JUDGMENT ON PARTIAL FINDINGS

(a) Findings and Conclusions.

(1) *In General.* In an action tried on the facts without a jury or with an advisory jury, the court must find the facts specially and state its conclusions of law separately. The findings and conclusions may be stated on the record after the close of the evidence or may appear in an opinion or a memorandum of decision filed by the court. Judgment must be entered under Rule 58.

(2) *For an Interlocutory Injunction.* In granting or refusing an interlocutory injunction, the court must similarly state the findings and conclusions that support its action.

(3) *For a Motion.* The court is not required to state findings or conclusions when ruling on a motion under Rule 12 or 56 or, unless these rules provide otherwise, on any other motion.

(4) *Effect of a Master's Findings.* A master's findings, to the extent adopted by the court, must be considered the court's findings.

(5) *Questioning the Evidentiary Support.* A party may later question the sufficiency of the evidence supporting the findings, whether or not the party requested findings, objected to them, moved to amend them, or moved for partial findings.

(6) *Setting Aside the Findings.* Findings of fact, whether based on oral or other evidence, must not be set aside unless clearly erroneous, and the reviewing court must give due regard to the trial court's opportunity to judge the witnesses' credibility.

(b) Amended or Additional Findings. On a party's motion filed no later than 28 days after the entry of judgment, the court may amend its findings—or make additional findings—and may amend the judgment accordingly. The motion may accompany a motion for a new trial under Rule 59.

(c) Judgment on Partial Findings. If a party has been fully heard on an issue during a nonjury trial and the court finds against the party on that issue, the court may enter judgment against the party on a claim or defense that, under the controlling law, can be maintained or defeated only with a favorable finding on that issue. The court may, however, decline to render any judgment until the close of the evidence. A judgment on partial findings must be supported by findings of fact and conclusions of law as required by Rule 52(a).

(Amended December 27, 1946, effective March 19, 1948; January 21, 1963, effective July 1, 1963; April 28, 1983, effective August 1, 1983; April 29, 1985, effective August 1, 1985; April 30, 1991, effective December 1, 1991; April 22, 1993, effective December 1, 1993; April 27, 1995, effective December 1, 1995; April 30, 2007, effective December 1, 2007; March 26, 2009, effective December 1, 2009.)

RULE 53. MASTERS

(a) Appointment.

(1) *Scope.* Unless a statute provides otherwise, a court may appoint a master only to:

(A) perform duties consented to by the parties;

(B) hold trial proceedings and make or recommend findings of fact on issues to be decided without a jury if appointment is warranted by:

(i) some exceptional condition; or

(ii) the need to perform an accounting or resolve a difficult computation of damages; or

(C) address pretrial and posttrial matters that cannot be effectively and timely addressed by an available district judge or magistrate judge of the district.

(2) *Disqualification.* A master must not have a relationship to the parties, attorneys, action, or court that would require disqualification of a judge under 28 U.S.C. § 455, unless the parties, with the court's approval, consent to the appointment after the master discloses any potential grounds for disqualification.

(3) *Possible Expense or Delay.* In appointing a master, the court must consider the fairness of imposing the likely expenses on the parties and must protect against unreasonable expense or delay.

(b) Order Appointing a Master.

(1) *Notice.* Before appointing a master, the court must give the parties notice and an opportunity to be heard. Any party may suggest candidates for appointment.

(2) *Contents.* The appointing order must direct the master to proceed with all reasonable diligence and must state:

(A) the master's duties, including any investigation or enforcement duties, and any limits on the master's authority under Rule 53(c);

(B) the circumstances, if any, in which the master may communicate ex parte with the court or a party;

(C) the nature of the materials to be preserved and filed as the record of the master's activities;

(D) the time limits, method of filing the record, other procedures, and standards for reviewing the master's orders, findings, and recommendations; and

(E) the basis, terms, and procedure for fixing the master's compensation under Rule 53(g).

(3) *Issuing.* The court may issue the order only after:

(A) the master files an affidavit disclosing whether there is any ground for disqualification under 28 U.S.C. § 455; and

(B) if a ground is disclosed, the parties, with the court's approval, waive the disqualification.

(4) *Amending.* The order may be amended at any time after notice to the parties and an opportunity to be heard.

(c) Master's Authority.

(1) *In General.* Unless the appointing order directs otherwise, a master may:

(A) regulate all proceedings;

(B) take all appropriate measures to perform the assigned duties fairly and efficiently; and

(C) if conducting an evidentiary hearing, exercise the appointing court's power to compel, take, and record evidence.

(2) *Sanctions.* The master may by order impose on a party any noncontempt sanction provided by Rule 37 or 45, and may recommend a contempt sanction against a party and sanctions against a nonparty.

(d) Master's Orders. A master who issues an order must file it and promptly serve a copy on each party. The clerk must enter the order on the docket.

(e) Master's Reports. A master must report to the court as required by the appointing order. The master must file the report and promptly serve a copy on each party, unless the court orders otherwise.

(f) Action on the Master's Order, Report, or Recommendations.

(1) *Opportunity for a Hearing; Action in General.* In acting on a master's order, report, or recommendations, the court must give the parties notice and an opportunity to be heard; may receive evidence; and may adopt or affirm, modify, wholly or partly reject or reverse, or resubmit to the master with instructions.

(2) *Time to Object or Move to Adopt or Modify.* A party may file objections to—or a motion to adopt or modify—the master's order, report, or recommendations no later than 21 days after a copy is served, unless the court sets a different time.

(3) *Reviewing Factual Findings.* The court must decide de novo all objections to findings of fact made or recommended by a master, unless the parties, with the court's approval, stipulate that:

(A) the findings will be reviewed for clear error; or

(B) the findings of a master appointed under Rule 53(a)(1)(A) or (C) will be final.

(4) *Reviewing Legal Conclusions.* The court must decide de novo all objections to conclusions of law made or recommended by a master.

(5) *Reviewing Procedural Matters.* Unless the appointing order establishes a different standard of review, the court may set aside a master's ruling on a procedural matter only for an abuse of discretion.

(g) Compensation.

(1) *Fixing Compensation.* Before or after judgment, the court must fix the master's compensation on the basis and terms stated in the ap-

pointing order, but the court may set a new basis and terms after giving notice and an opportunity to be heard.

(2) *Payment.* The compensation must be paid either:

(A) by a party or parties; or

(B) from a fund or subject matter of the action within the court's control.

(3) *Allocating Payment.* The court must allocate payment among the parties after considering the nature and amount of the controversy, the parties' means, and the extent to which any party is more responsible than other parties for

the reference to a master. An interim allocation may be amended to reflect a decision on the merits.

(h) **Appointing a Magistrate Judge.** A magistrate judge is subject to this rule only when the order referring a matter to the magistrate judge states that the reference is made under this rule.

(Amended February 28, 1966, effective July 1, 1966; April 28, 1983, effective August 1, 1983; March 2, 1987, effective August 1, 1987; April 30, 1991, effective December 1, 1991; April 22, 1993, effective December 1, 1993; March 27, 2003, effective December 1, 2003; April 30, 2007, effective December 1, 2007; March 26, 2009, effective December 1, 2009.)

TITLE VII. JUDGMENT

RULE 54. JUDGMENT; COSTS

(a) **Definition; Form.** "Judgment" as used in these rules includes a decree and any order from which an appeal lies. A judgment should not include recitals of pleadings, a master's report, or a record of prior proceedings.

(b) **Judgment on Multiple Claims or Involving Multiple Parties.** When an action presents more than one claim for relief—whether as a claim, counterclaim, crossclaim, or third-party claim—or when multiple parties are involved, the court may direct entry of a final judgment as to one or more, but fewer than all, claims or parties only if the court expressly determines that there is no just reason for delay. Otherwise, any order or other decision, however designated, that adjudicates fewer than all the claims or the rights and liabilities of fewer than all the parties does not end the action as to any of the claims or parties and may be revised at any time before the entry of a judgment adjudicating all the claims and all the parties' rights and liabilities.

(c) **Demand for Judgment; Relief to Be Granted.** A default judgment must not differ in kind from, or exceed in amount, what is demanded in the pleadings. Every other final judgment should grant the relief to which each party is entitled, even if the party has not demanded that relief in its pleadings.

(d) **Costs; Attorney's Fees.**

(1) *Costs Other Than Attorney's Fees.* Unless a federal statute, these rules, or a court order provides otherwise, costs—other than attorney's fees—should be allowed to the prevailing party. But costs against the United States, its officers, and its agencies may be imposed only to the extent allowed by law. The clerk may tax costs on 14 days' notice. On motion served within the

next 7 days, the court may review the clerk's action.

(2) *Attorney's Fees.*

(A) *Claim to Be by Motion.* A claim for attorney's fees and related nontaxable expenses must be made by motion unless the substantive law requires those fees to be proved at trial as an element of damages.

(B) *Timing and Contents of the Motion.* Unless a statute or a court order provides otherwise, the motion must:

(i) be filed no later than 14 days after the entry of judgment;

(ii) specify the judgment and the statute, rule, or other grounds entitling the movant to the award;

(iii) state the amount sought or provide a fair estimate of it; and

(iv) disclose, if the court so orders, the terms of any agreement about fees for the services for which the claim is made.

(C) *Proceedings.* Subject to Rule 23(h), the court must, on a party's request, give an opportunity for adversary submissions on the motion in accordance with Rule 43(c) or 78. The court may decide issues of liability for fees before receiving submissions on the value of services. The court must find the facts and state its conclusions of law as provided in Rule 52(a).

(D) *Special Procedures by Local Rule; Reference to a Master or a Magistrate Judge.* By local rule, the court may establish special procedures to resolve fee-related issues without extensive evidentiary hearings. Also, the court may refer issues concerning the value of services to a special master under Rule 53 without regard to the limitations of Rule

53(a)(1), and may refer a motion for attorney's fees to a magistrate judge under Rule 72(b) as if it were a dispositive pretrial matter.

(E) *Exceptions.* Subparagraphs (A)-(D) do not apply to claims for fees and expenses as sanctions for violating these rules or as sanctions under 28 U.S.C. § 1927.

(Amended December 27, 1946, effective March 19, 1948; April 17, 1961, effective July 19, 1961; March 2, 1987, effective August 1, 1987; April 22, 1993, effective December 1, 1993; April 29, 2002, effective December 1, 2002; March 27, 2003, effective December 1, 2003; April 30, 2007, effective December 1, 2007; March 26, 2009, effective December 1, 2009.)

RULE 55. DEFAULT; DEFAULT JUDGMENT

(a) **Entering a Default.** When a party against whom a judgment for affirmative relief is sought has failed to plead or otherwise defend, and that failure is shown by affidavit or otherwise, the clerk must enter the party's default.

(b) **Entering a Default Judgment.**

(1) *By the Clerk.* If the plaintiff's claim is for a sum certain or a sum that can be made certain by computation, the clerk—on the plaintiff's request, with an affidavit showing the amount due—must enter judgment for that amount and costs against a defendant who has been defaulted for not appearing and who is neither a minor nor an incompetent person.

(2) *By the Court.* In all other cases, the party must apply to the court for a default judgment. A default judgment may be entered against a minor or incompetent person only if represented by a general guardian, conservator, or other like fiduciary who has appeared. If the party against whom a default judgment is sought has appeared personally or by a representative, that party or its representative must be served with written notice of the application at least 7 days before the hearing. The court may conduct hearings or make referrals—preserving any federal statutory right to a jury trial—when, to enter or effectuate judgment, it needs to:

(A) conduct an accounting;

(B) determine the amount of damages;

(C) establish the truth of any allegation by evidence; or

(D) investigate any other matter.

(c) **Setting Aside a Default or a Default Judgment.** The court may set aside an entry of default for good cause, and it may set aside a default judgment under Rule 60(b).

(d) **Judgment Against the United States.** A default judgment may be entered against the United States, its officers, or its agencies only if the claimant establishes a claim or right to relief by evidence that satisfies the court.

(Amended March 2, 1987, effective August 1, 1987; April 30, 2007, effective December 1, 2007; March 26, 2009, effective December 1, 2009.)

RULE 56. SUMMARY JUDGMENT

(a) **Motion for Summary Judgment or Partial Summary Judgment.** A party may move for summary judgment, identifying each claim or defense—or the part of each claim or defense—on which summary judgment is sought. The court shall grant summary judgment if the movant shows that there is no genuine dispute as to any material fact and the movant is entitled to judgment as a matter of law. The court should state on the record the reasons for granting or denying the motion.

(b) **Time to File a Motion.** Unless a different time is set by local rule or the court orders otherwise, a party may file a motion for summary judgment at any time until 30 days after the close of all discovery.

(c) **Procedures.**

(1) *Supporting Factual Positions.* A party asserting that a fact cannot be or is genuinely disputed must support the assertion by:

(A) citing to particular parts of materials in the record, including depositions, documents, electronically stored information, affidavits or declarations, stipulations (including those made for purposes of the motion only), admissions, interrogatory answers, or other materials; or

(B) showing that the materials cited do not establish the absence or presence of a genuine dispute, or that an adverse party cannot produce admissible evidence to support the fact.

(2) *Objection That a Fact Is Not Supported by Admissible Evidence.* A party may object that the material cited to support or dispute a fact cannot be presented in a form that would be admissible in evidence.

(3) *Materials Not Cited.* The court need consider only the cited materials, but it may consider other materials in the record.

(4) *Affidavits or Declarations.* An affidavit or declaration used to support or oppose a motion must be made on personal knowledge, set out facts that would be admissible in evidence, and show that the affiant or declarant is competent to testify on the matters stated.

(d) When Facts Are Unavailable to the Nonmovant. If a nonmovant shows by affidavit or declaration that, for specified reasons, it cannot present facts essential to justify its opposition, the court may:

(1) defer considering the motion or deny it;

(2) allow time to obtain affidavits or declarations or to take discovery; or

(3) issue any other appropriate order.

(e) Failing to Properly Support or Address a Fact. If a party fails to properly support an assertion of fact or fails to properly address another party's assertion of fact as required by Rule 56(c), the court may:

(1) give an opportunity to properly support or address the fact;

(2) consider the fact undisputed for purposes of the motion;

(3) grant summary judgment if the motion and supporting materials—including the facts considered undisputed—show that the movant is entitled to it; or

(4) issue any other appropriate order.

(f) Judgment Independent of the Motion. After giving notice and a reasonable time to respond, the court may:

(1) grant summary judgment for a nonmovant;

(2) grant the motion on grounds not raised by a party; or

(3) consider summary judgment on its own after identifying for the parties material facts that may not be genuinely in dispute.

(g) Failing to Grant All the Requested Relief. If the court does not grant all the relief requested by the motion, it may enter an order stating any material fact—including an item of damages or other relief—that is not genuinely in dispute and treating the fact as established in the case.

(h) Affidavit or Declaration Submitted in Bad Faith. If satisfied that an affidavit or declaration under this rule is submitted in bad faith or solely for delay, the court—after notice and a reasonable time to respond—may order the submitting party to pay the other party the reasonable expenses, including attorney's fees, it incurred as a result. An offending party or attorney may also be held in contempt or subjected to other appropriate sanctions.

(Amended December 27, 1946, effective March 19, 1948; January 21, 1963, effective July 1, 1963; March 2, 1987, effective August 1, 1987; April 30, 2007, effective December 1, 2007; March 26, 2009, effective December 1, 2009; April 28, 2010, effective December 1, 2010.)

RULE 57. DECLARATORY JUDGMENT

These rules govern the procedure for obtaining a declaratory judgment under 28 U.S.C. § 2201. Rules 38 and 39 govern a demand for a jury trial. The existence of another adequate remedy does not preclude a declaratory judgment that is otherwise appropriate. The court may order a speedy hearing of a declaratory-judgment action.

(Amended December 29, 1948, effective October 20, 1949; April 30, 2007, effective December 1, 2007.)

RULE 58. ENTERING JUDGMENT

(a) Separate Document. Every judgment and amended judgment must be set out in a separate document, but a separate document is not required for an order disposing of a motion:

(1) for judgment under Rule 50(b);

(2) to amend or make additional findings under Rule 52(b);

(3) for attorney's fees under Rule 54;

(4) for a new trial, or to alter or amend the judgment, under Rule 59; or

(5) for relief under Rule 60.

(b) Entering Judgment.

(1) *Without the Court's Direction.* Subject to Rule 54(b) and unless the court orders otherwise, the clerk must, without awaiting the court's direction, promptly prepare, sign, and enter the judgment when:

(A) the jury returns a general verdict;

(B) the court awards only costs or a sum certain; or

(C) the court denies all relief.

(2) *Court's Approval Required.* Subject to Rule 54(b), the court must promptly approve the form of the judgment, which the clerk must promptly enter, when:

(A) the jury returns a special verdict or a general verdict with answers to written questions; or

(B) the court grants other relief not described in this subdivision (b).

(c) Time of Entry. For purposes of these rules, judgment is entered at the following times:

(1) if a separate document is not required, when the judgment is entered in the civil docket under Rule 79(a); or

(2) if a separate document is required, when the judgment is entered in the civil docket under Rule 79(a) and the earlier of these events occurs:

(A) it is set out in a separate document; or

(B) 150 days have run from the entry in the civil docket.

(d) Request for Entry. A party may request that judgment be set out in a separate document as required by Rule 58(a).

(e) Cost or Fee Awards. Ordinarily, the entry of judgment may not be delayed, nor the time for appeal extended, in order to tax costs or award fees. But if a timely motion for attorney's fees is made under Rule 54(d)(2), the court may act before a notice of appeal has been filed and become effective to order that the motion have the same effect under Federal Rule of Appellate Procedure 4(a)(4) as a timely motion under Rule 59.

(Amended December 27, 1946, effective March 19, 1948; January 21, 1963, effective July 1, 1963; April 22, 1993, effective December 1, 1993; April 29, 2002, effective December 1, 2002; April 30, 2007, effective December 1, 2007.)

RULE 59. NEW TRIAL; ALTERING OR AMENDING A JUDGMENT

(a) In General.

(1) *Grounds for New Trial.* The court may, on motion, grant a new trial on all or some of the issues—and to any party—as follows:

  (A) after a jury trial, for any reason for which a new trial has heretofore been granted in an action at law in federal court; or

  (B) after a nonjury trial, for any reason for which a rehearing has heretofore been granted in a suit in equity in federal court.

(2) *Further Action After a Nonjury Trial.* After a nonjury trial, the court may, on motion for a new trial, open the judgment if one has been entered, take additional testimony, amend findings of fact and conclusions of law or make new ones, and direct the entry of a new judgment.

(b) Time to File a Motion for a New Trial. A motion for a new trial must be filed no later than 28 days after the entry of judgment.

(c) Time to Serve Affidavits. When a motion for a new trial is based on affidavits, they must be filed with the motion. The opposing party has 14 days after being served to file opposing affidavits. The court may permit reply affidavits.

(d) New Trial on the Court's Initiative or for Reasons Not in the Motion. No later than 28 days after the entry of judgment, the court, on its own, may order a new trial for any reason that would justify granting one on a party's motion. After giving the parties notice and an opportunity to be heard, the court may grant a timely motion for a new trial for a reason not stated in the motion. In either event, the court must specify the reasons in its order.

(e) Motion to Alter or Amend a Judgment. A motion to alter or amend a judgment must be filed no later than 28 days after the entry of the judgment.

(Amended December 27, 1946, effective March 19, 1948; February 28, 1966, effective July 1, 1966; April 27, 1995, effective December 1, 1995; April 30, 2007, effective December 1, 2007; March 26, 2009, effective December 1, 2009.)

RULE 60. RELIEF FROM A JUDGMENT OR ORDER

(a) Corrections Based on Clerical Mistakes; Oversights and Omissions. The court may correct a clerical mistake or a mistake arising from oversight or omission whenever one is found in a judgment, order, or other part of the record. The court may do so on motion or on its own, with or without notice. But after an appeal has been docketed in the appellate court and while it is pending, such a mistake may be corrected only with the appellate court's leave.

(b) Grounds for Relief from a Final Judgment, Order, or Proceeding. On motion and just terms, the court may relieve a party or its legal representative from a final judgment, order, or proceeding for the following reasons:

(1) mistake, inadvertence, surprise, or excusable neglect;

(2) newly discovered evidence that, with reasonable diligence, could not have been discovered in time to move for a new trial under Rule 59(b);

(3) fraud (whether previously called intrinsic or extrinsic), misrepresentation, or misconduct by an opposing party;

(4) the judgment is void;

(5) the judgment has been satisfied, released or discharged; it is based on an earlier judgment that has been reversed or vacated; or applying it prospectively is no longer equitable; or

(6) any other reason that justifies relief.

(c) Timing and Effect of the Motion.

(1) *Timing.* A motion under Rule 60(b) must be made within a reasonable time—and for reasons (1), (2), and (3) no more than a year after the entry of the judgment or order or the date of the proceeding.

(2) *Effect on Finality.* The motion does not affect the judgment's finality or suspend its operation.

(d) Other Powers to Grant Relief. This rule does not limit a court's power to:

(1) entertain an independent action to relieve a party from a judgment, order, or proceeding;

(2) grant relief under 28 U.S.C. § 1655 to a defendant who was not personally notified of the action; or

(3) set aside a judgment for fraud on the court.

(e) Bills and Writs Abolished. The following are abolished: bills of review, bills in the nature of bills of review, and writs of coram nobis, coram vobis, and audita querela.

(Amended December 27, 1946, effective March 19, 1948; December 29, 1948, effective October 20, 1949; March 2, 1987, effective August 1, 1987; April 30, 2007, effective December 1, 2007.)

RULE 61. HARMLESS ERROR

Unless justice requires otherwise, no error in admitting or excluding evidence—or any other error by the court or a party—is ground for granting a new trial, for setting aside a verdict, or for vacating, modifying, or otherwise disturbing a judgment or order. At every stage of the proceeding, the court must disregard all errors and defects that do not affect any party's substantial rights.

(Amended April 30, 2007, effective December 1, 2007.)

RULE 62. STAY OF PROCEEDINGS TO ENFORCE A JUDGMENT

(a) Automatic Stay; Exceptions for Injunctions, Receiverships, and Patent Accountings. Except as stated in this rule, no execution may issue on a judgment, nor may proceedings be taken to enforce it, until 14 days have passed after its entry. But unless the court orders otherwise, the following are not stayed after being entered, even if an appeal is taken:

(1) an interlocutory or final judgment in an action for an injunction or a receivership; or

(2) a judgment or order that directs an accounting in an action for patent infringement.

(b) Stay Pending the Disposition of a Motion. On appropriate terms for the opposing party's security, the court may stay the execution of a judgment—or any proceedings to enforce it—pending disposition of any of the following motions:

(1) under Rule 50, for judgment as a matter of law;

(2) under Rule 52(b), to amend the findings or for additional findings;

(3) under Rule 59, for a new trial or to alter or amend a judgment; or

(4) under Rule 60, for relief from a judgment or order.

(c) Injunction Pending an Appeal. While an appeal is pending from an interlocutory order or final judgment that grants, dissolves, or denies an injunction, the court may suspend, modify, restore, or grant an injunction on terms for bond or other terms that secure the opposing party's rights. If the judgment appealed from is rendered by a statutory three-judge district court, the order must be made either:

(1) by that court sitting in open session; or

(2) by the assent of all its judges, as evidenced by their signatures.

(d) Stay with Bond on Appeal. If an appeal is taken, the appellant may obtain a stay by supersedeas bond, except in an action described in Rule 62(a)(1) or (2). The bond may be given upon or after filing the notice of appeal or after obtaining the order allowing the appeal. The stay takes effect when the court approves the bond.

(e) Stay Without Bond on an Appeal by the United States, Its Officers, or Its Agencies. The court must not require a bond, obligation, or other security from the appellant when granting a stay on an appeal by the United States, its officers, or its agencies or on an appeal directed by a department of the federal government.

(f) Stay in Favor of a Judgment Debtor Under State Law. If a judgment is a lien on the judgment debtor's property under the law of the state where the court is located, the judgment debtor is entitled to the same stay of execution the state court would give.

(g) Appellate Court's Power Not Limited. This rule does not limit the power of the appellate court or one of its judges or justices:

(1) to stay proceedings—or suspend, modify, restore, or grant an injunction—while an appeal is pending; or

(2) to issue an order to preserve the status quo or the effectiveness of the judgment to be entered.

(h) Stay with Multiple Claims or Parties. A court may stay the enforcement of a final judgment entered under Rule 54(b) until it enters a later judgment or judgments, and may prescribe terms necessary to secure the benefit of the stayed judgment for the party in whose favor it was entered.

(Amended December 27, 1946, effective March 19, 1948; December 29, 1948, effective October 20, 1949; April 17, 1961, effective July 19, 1961; March 2, 1987, effective August 1, 1987; April 30, 2007, effective December 1, 2007; March 26, 2009, effective December 1, 2009.)

RULE 62.1. INDICATIVE RULING ON A MOTION FOR RELIEF THAT IS BARRED BY A PENDING APPEAL

(a) Relief Pending Appeal. If a timely motion is made for relief that the court lacks authority to grant because of an appeal that has been docketed and is pending, the court may:

  (1) defer considering the motion;

  (2) deny the motion; or

  (3) state either that it would grant the motion if the court of appeals remands for that purpose or that the motion raises a substantial issue.

(b) Notice to the Court of Appeals. The movant must promptly notify the circuit clerk under Federal Rule of Appellate Procedure 12.1 if the district court states that it would grant the motion or that the motion raises a substantial issue.

(c) Remand. The district court may decide the motion if the court of appeals remands for that purpose.

(Added March 26, 2009, effective December 1, 2009.)

RULE 63. JUDGE'S INABILITY TO PROCEED

If a judge conducting a hearing or trial is unable to proceed, any other judge may proceed upon certifying familiarity with the record and determining that the case may be completed without prejudice to the parties. In a hearing or a nonjury trial, the successor judge must, at a party's request, recall any witness whose testimony is material and disputed and who is available to testify again without undue burden. The successor judge may also recall any other witness.

(Amended March 2, 1987, effective August 1, 1987; April 30, 1991, effective December 1, 1991; April 30, 2007, effective December 1, 2007.)

TITLE VIII. PROVISIONAL AND FINAL REMEDIES

RULE 64. SEIZING A PERSON OR PROPERTY

(a) Remedies Under State Law—In General. At the commencement of and throughout an action, every remedy is available that, under the law of the state where the court is located, provides for seizing a person or property to secure satisfaction of the potential judgment. But a federal statute governs to the extent it applies.

(b) Specific Kinds of Remedies. The remedies available under this rule include the following—however designated and regardless of whether state procedure requires an independent action:

- arrest;
- attachment;
- garnishment;
- replevin;
- sequestration; and
- other corresponding or equivalent remedies.

(Amended April 30, 2007, effective December 1, 2007.)

RULE 65. INJUNCTIONS AND RESTRAINING ORDERS

(a) Preliminary Injunction.

  (1) *Notice.* The court may issue a preliminary injunction only on notice to the adverse party.

  (2) *Consolidating the Hearing with the Trial on the Merits.* Before or after beginning the hearing on a motion for a preliminary injunction, the court may advance the trial on the merits and consolidate it with the hearing. Even when consolidation is not ordered, evidence that is received on the motion and that would be admissible at trial becomes part of the trial record and

need not be repeated at trial. But the court must preserve any party's right to a jury trial.

(b) Temporary Restraining Order.

  (1) *Issuing Without Notice.* The court may issue a temporary restraining order without written or oral notice to the adverse party or its attorney only if:

    (A) specific facts in an affidavit or a verified complaint clearly show that immediate and irreparable injury, loss, or damage will result to the movant before the adverse party can be heard in opposition; and

    (B) the movant's attorney certifies in writing any efforts made to give notice and the reasons why it should not be required.

  (2) *Contents; Expiration.* Every temporary restraining order issued without notice must state the date and hour it was issued; describe the injury and state why it is irreparable; state why the order was issued without notice; and be promptly filed in the clerk's office and entered in the record. The order expires at the time after entry—not to exceed 14 days—that the court sets, unless before that time the court, for good cause, extends it for a like period or the adverse party consents to a longer extension. The reasons for an extension must be entered in the record.

  (3) *Expediting the Preliminary–Injunction Hearing.* If the order is issued without notice, the motion for a preliminary injunction must be set for hearing at the earliest possible time, taking precedence over all other matters except hearings on older matters of the same character. At the hearing, the party who obtained the order must proceed with the motion; if the party does not, the court must dissolve the order.

(4) *Motion to Dissolve.* On 2 days' notice to the party who obtained the order without notice— or on shorter notice set by the court—the adverse party may appear and move to dissolve or modify the order. The court must then hear and decide the motion as promptly as justice requires.

(c) **Security.** The court may issue a preliminary injunction or a temporary restraining order only if the movant gives security in an amount that the court considers proper to pay the costs and damages sustained by any party found to have been wrongfully enjoined or restrained. The United States, its officers, and its agencies are not required to give security.

(d) **Contents and Scope of Every Injunction and Restraining Order.**

(1) *Contents.* Every order granting an injunction and every restraining order must:

(A) state the reasons why it issued;

(B) state its terms specifically; and

(C) describe in reasonable detail—and not by referring to the complaint or other document—the act or acts restrained or required.

(2) *Persons Bound.* The order binds only the following who receive actual notice of it by personal service or otherwise:

(A) the parties;

(B) the parties' officers, agents, servants, employees, and attorneys; and

(C) other persons who are in active concert or participation with anyone described in Rule 65(d)(2)(A) or (B).

(e) **Other Laws Not Modified.** These rules do not modify the following:

(1) any federal statute relating to temporary restraining orders or preliminary injunctions in actions affecting employer and employee;

(2) 28 U.S.C. § 2361, which relates to preliminary injunctions in actions of interpleader or in the nature of interpleader; or

(3) 28 U.S.C. § 2284, which relates to actions that must be heard and decided by a three-judge district court.

(f) **Copyright Impoundment.** This rule applies to copyright-impoundment proceedings.

(Amended December 27, 1946, effective March 19, 1948; December 29, 1948, effective October 20, 1949; February 28, 1966, effective July 1, 1966; March 2, 1987, effective August 1, 1987; April 23, 2001, effective December 1, 2001; April 30, 2007, effective December 1, 2007; March 26, 2009, effective December 1, 2009.)

RULE 65.1. PROCEEDINGS AGAINST A SURETY

Whenever these rules (including the Supplemental Rules for Admiralty or Maritime Claims and Asset Forfeiture Actions) require or allow a party to give security, and security is given through a bond or other undertaking with one or more sureties, each surety submits to the court's jurisdiction and irrevocably appoints the court clerk as its agent for receiving service of any papers that affect its liability on the bond or undertaking. The surety's liability may be enforced on motion without an independent action. The motion and any notice that the court orders may be served on the court clerk, who must promptly mail a copy of each to every surety whose address is known.

(Adopted February 28, 1966, effective July 1, 1966; amended March 2, 1987, effective August 1, 1987; April 12, 2006, effective December 1, 2006; April 30, 2007, effective December 1, 2007.)

RULE 66. RECEIVERS

These rules govern an action in which the appointment of a receiver is sought or a receiver sues or is sued. But the practice in administering an estate by a receiver or a similar court-appointed officer must accord with the historical practice in federal courts or with a local rule. An action in which a receiver has been appointed may be dismissed only by court order.

(Amended December 27, 1946, effective March 19, 1948; December 29, 1948, effective October 20, 1949; April 30, 2007, effective December 1, 2007.)

RULE 67. DEPOSIT INTO COURT

(a) **Depositing Property.** If any part of the relief sought is a money judgment or the disposition of a sum of money or some other deliverable thing, a party—on notice to every other party and by leave of court—may deposit with the court all or part of the money or thing, whether or not that party claims any of it. The depositing party must deliver to the clerk a copy of the order permitting deposit.

(b) **Investing and Withdrawing Funds.** Money paid into court under this rule must be deposited and withdrawn in accordance with 28 U.S.C. §§ 2041 and 2042 and any like statute. The money must be deposited in an interest-bearing account or invested in a court-approved, interest-bearing instrument.

(Amended December 29, 1948, effective October 20, 1949; April 28, 1983, effective August 1, 1983; April 30, 2007, effective December 1, 2007.)

RULE 68. OFFER OF JUDGMENT

(a) Making an Offer; Judgment on an Accepted Offer. At least 14 days before the date set for trial, a party defending against a claim may serve on an opposing party an offer to allow judgment on specified terms, with the costs then accrued. If, within 14 days after being served, the opposing party serves written notice accepting the offer, either party may then file the offer and notice of acceptance, plus proof of service. The clerk must then enter judgment.

(b) Unaccepted Offer. An unaccepted offer is considered withdrawn, but it does not preclude a later offer. Evidence of an unaccepted offer is not admissible except in a proceeding to determine costs.

(c) Offer After Liability is Determined. When one party's liability to another has been determined but the extent of liability remains to be determined by further proceedings, the party held liable may make an offer of judgment. It must be served within a reasonable time—but at least 14 days—before the date set for a hearing to determine the extent of liability.

(d) Paying Costs After an Unaccepted Offer. If the judgment that the offeree finally obtains is not more favorable than the unaccepted offer, the offeree must pay the costs incurred after the offer was made.

(Amended December 27, 1946, effective March 19, 1948; February 28, 1966, effective July 1, 1966; March 2, 1987, effective August 1, 1987; April 30, 2007, effective December 1, 2007; March 26, 2009, effective December 1, 2009.)

RULE 69. EXECUTION

(a) In General.

(1) _Money Judgment; Applicable Procedure._ A money judgment is enforced by a writ of execution, unless the court directs otherwise. The procedure on execution—and in proceedings supplementary to and in aid of judgment or execution—must accord with the procedure of the state where the court is located, but a federal statute governs to the extent it applies.

(2) _Obtaining Discovery._ In aid of the judgment or execution, the judgment creditor or a successor in interest whose interest appears of record may obtain discovery from any person—including the judgment debtor—as provided in these rules or by the procedure of the state where the court is located.

(b) Against Certain Public Officers. When a judgment has been entered against a revenue officer in the circumstances stated in 28 U.S.C. § 2006, or against an officer of Congress in the circumstances stated in 2 U.S.C. § 118,[1] the judgment must be satisfied as those statutes provide.

(Amended December 29, 1948, effective October 20, 1949; March 30, 1970, effective July 1, 1970; March 2, 1987 effective August 1, 1987; April 30, 2007, effective December 1, 2007.)

1 Now editorially reclassified 2 U.S.C. § 5503.

RULE 70. ENFORCING A JUDGMENT FOR A SPECIFIC ACT

(a) Party's Failure to Act; Ordering Another to Act. If a judgment requires a party to convey land, to deliver a deed or other document, or to perform any other specific act and the party fails to comply within the time specified, the court may order the act to be done—at the disobedient party's expense—by another person appointed by the court. When done, the act has the same effect as if done by the party.

(b) Vesting Title. If the real or personal property is within the district, the court—instead of ordering a conveyance—may enter a judgment divesting any party's title and vesting it in others. That judgment has the effect of a legally executed conveyance.

(c) Obtaining a Writ of Attachment or Sequestration. On application by a party entitled to performance of an act, the clerk must issue a writ of attachment or sequestration against the disobedient party's property to compel obedience.

(d) Obtaining a Writ of Execution or Assistance. On application by a party who obtains a judgment or order for possession, the clerk must issue a writ of execution or assistance.

(e) Holding in Contempt. The court may also hold the disobedient party in contempt.

(Amended April 30, 2007, effective December 1, 2007.)

RULE 71. ENFORCING RELIEF FOR OR AGAINST A NONPARTY

When an order grants relief for a nonparty or may be enforced against a nonparty, the procedure for enforcing the order is the same as for a party.

(Amended March 2, 1987, effective August 1, 1987; April 30, 2007, effective December 1, 2007.)

TITLE IX. SPECIAL PROCEEDINGS

RULE 71.1. CONDEMNING REAL OR PERSONAL PROPERTY

(a) Applicability of Other Rules. These rules govern proceedings to condemn real and personal property by eminent domain, except as this rule provides otherwise.

(b) Joinder of Properties. The plaintiff may join separate pieces of property in a single action, no matter whether they are owned by the same persons or sought for the same use.

(c) Complaint.

(1) *Caption.* The complaint must contain a caption as provided in Rule 10(a). The plaintiff must, however, name as defendants both the property—designated generally by kind, quantity, and location—and at least one owner of some part of or interest in the property.

(2) *Contents.* The complaint must contain a short and plain statement of the following:

  (A) the authority for the taking;

  (B) the uses for which the property is to be taken;

  (C) a description sufficient to identify the property;

  (D) the interests to be acquired; and

  (E) for each piece of property, a designation of each defendant who has been joined as an owner or owner of an interest in it.

(3) *Parties.* When the action commences, the plaintiff need join as defendants only those persons who have or claim an interest in the property and whose names are then known. But before any hearing on compensation, the plaintiff must add as defendants all those persons who have or claim an interest and whose names have become known or can be found by a reasonably diligent search of the records, considering both the property's character and value and the interests to be acquired. All others may be made defendants under the designation "Unknown Owners."

(4) *Procedure.* Notice must be served on all defendants as provided in Rule 71.1(d), whether they were named as defendants when the action commenced or were added later. A defendant may answer as provided in Rule 71.1(e). The court, meanwhile, may order any distribution of a deposit that the facts warrant.

(5) *Filing; Additional Copies.* In addition to filing the complaint, the plaintiff must give the clerk at least one copy for the defendants' use and additional copies at the request of the clerk or a defendant.

(d) Process.

(1) *Delivering Notice to the Clerk.* On filing a complaint, the plaintiff must promptly deliver to the clerk joint or several notices directed to the named defendants. When adding defendants, the plaintiff must deliver to the clerk additional notices directed to the new defendants.

(2) *Contents of the Notice.*

  (A) *Main Contents.* Each notice must name the court, the title of the action, and the defendant to whom it is directed. It must describe the property sufficiently to identify it, but need not describe any property other than that to be taken from the named defendant. The notice must also state:

    (i) that the action is to condemn property;

    (ii) the interest to be taken;

    (iii) the authority for the taking;

    (iv) the uses for which the property is to be taken;

    (v) that the defendant may serve an answer on the plaintiff's attorney within 21 days after being served with the notice;

    (vi) that the failure to so serve an answer constitutes consent to the taking and to the court's authority to proceed with the action and fix the compensation; and

    (vii) that a defendant who does not serve an answer may file a notice of appearance.

  (B) *Conclusion.* The notice must conclude with the name, telephone number, and e-mail address of the plaintiff's attorney and an address within the district in which the action is brought where the attorney may be served.

(3) *Serving the Notice.*

  (A) *Personal Service.* When a defendant whose address is known resides within the United States or a territory subject to the administrative or judicial jurisdiction of the United States, personal service of the notice (without a copy of the complaint) must be made in accordance with Rule 4.

  (B) *Service by Publication.*

    (i) A defendant may be served by publication only when the plaintiff's attorney files a certificate stating that the attorney believes the defendant cannot be personally served, because after diligent inquiry within the state where the complaint is filed, the defendant's place of residence is still unknown or, if known, that it is beyond the territorial limits of personal service. Service is then made by publishing the notice—once a week for at least 3 successive weeks—in a newspaper published in the county where the property is located or, if there is no such newspaper, in a newspaper with general circulation where the property is located. Before the last publication, a copy of the notice must also be mailed to every defendant who cannot be personally served but whose place of residence is then known. Unknown owners may be served by publication in the same manner by a notice addressed to "Unknown Owners."

(ii) Service by publication is complete on the date of the last publication. The plaintiff's attorney must prove publication and mailing by a certificate, attach a printed copy of the published notice, and mark on the copy the newspaper's name and the dates of publication.

(4) *Effect of Delivery and Service.* Delivering the notice to the clerk and serving it have the same effect as serving a summons under Rule 4.

(5) *Amending the Notice; Proof of Service and Amending the Proof.* Rule 4(a)(2) governs amending the notice. Rule 4(*l*) governs proof of service and amending it.

(e) **Appearance or Answer.**

(1) *Notice of Appearance.* A defendant that has no objection or defense to the taking of its property may serve a notice of appearance designating the property in which it claims an interest. The defendant must then be given notice of all later proceedings affecting the defendant.

(2) *Answer.* A defendant that has an objection or defense to the taking must serve an answer within 21 days after being served with the notice. The answer must:

(A) identify the property in which the defendant claims an interest;

(B) state the nature and extent of the interest; and

(C) state all the defendant's objections and defenses to the taking.

(3) *Waiver of Other Objections and Defenses; Evidence on Compensation.* A defendant waives all objections and defenses not stated in its answer. No other pleading or motion asserting an additional objection or defense is allowed. But at the trial on compensation, a defendant—whether or not it has previously appeared or answered—may present evidence on the amount of compensation to be paid and may share in the award.

(f) **Amending Pleadings.** Without leave of court, the plaintiff may—as often as it wants—amend the complaint at any time before the trial on compensation. But no amendment may be made if it would result in a dismissal inconsistent with Rule 71.1(i)(1) or (2). The plaintiff need not serve a copy of an amendment, but must serve notice of the filing, as provided in Rule 5(b), on every affected party who has appeared and, as provided in Rule 71.1(d), on every affected party who has not appeared. In addition, the plaintiff must give the clerk at least one copy of each amendment for the defendants' use, and additional copies at the request of the clerk or a defendant. A defendant may appear or answer in the time and manner and with the same effect as provided in Rule 71.1(e).

(g) **Substituting Parties.** If a defendant dies, becomes incompetent, or transfers an interest after being joined, the court may, on motion and notice of hearing, order that the proper party be substituted. Service of the motion and notice on a nonparty must be made as provided in Rule 71.1(d)(3).

(h) **Trial of the Issues.**

(1) *Issues Other Than Compensation; Compensation.* In an action involving eminent domain under federal law, the court tries all issues, including compensation, except when compensation must be determined:

(A) by any tribunal specially constituted by a federal statute to determine compensation; or

(B) if there is no such tribunal, by a jury when a party demands one within the time to answer or within any additional time the court sets, unless the court appoints a commission.

(2) *Appointing a Commission; Commission's Powers and Report.*

(A) *Reasons for Appointing.* If a party has demanded a jury, the court may instead appoint a three-person commission to determine compensation because of the character, location, or quantity of the property to be condemned or for other just reasons.

(B) *Alternate Commissioners.* The court may appoint up to two additional persons to serve as alternate commissioners to hear the case and replace commissioners who, before a decision is filed, the court finds unable or disqualified to perform their duties. Once the commission renders its final decision, the court must discharge any alternate who has not replaced a commissioner.

(C) *Examining the Prospective Commissioners.* Before making its appointments, the court must advise the parties of the identity and qualifications of each prospective commissioner and alternate, and may permit the parties to examine them. The parties may not suggest appointees, but for good cause may object to a prospective commissioner or alternate.

(D) *Commission's Powers and Report.* A commission has the powers of a master under Rule 53(c). Its action and report are determined by a majority. Rule 53(d), (e), and (f) apply to its action and report.

(i) Dismissal of the Action or a Defendant.

(1) *Dismissing the Action.*

(A) *By the Plaintiff.* If no compensation hearing on a piece of property has begun, and if the plaintiff has not acquired title or a lesser interest or taken possession, the plaintiff may, without a court order, dismiss the action as to that property by filing a notice of dismissal briefly describing the property.

(B) *By Stipulation.* Before a judgment is entered vesting the plaintiff with title or a lesser interest in or possession of property, the plaintiff and affected defendants may, without a court order, dismiss the action in whole or in part by filing a stipulation of dismissal. And if the parties so stipulate, the court may vacate a judgment already entered.

(C) *By Court Order.* At any time before compensation has been determined and paid, the court may, after a motion and hearing, dismiss the action as to a piece of property. But if the plaintiff has already taken title, a lesser interest, or possession as to any part of it, the court must award compensation for the title, lesser interest, or possession taken.

(2) *Dismissing a Defendant.* The court may at any time dismiss a defendant who was unnecessarily or improperly joined.

(3) *Effect.* A dismissal is without prejudice unless otherwise stated in the notice, stipulation, or court order.

(j) Deposit and Its Distribution.

(1) *Deposit.* The plaintiff must deposit with the court any money required by law as a condition to the exercise of eminent domain and may make a deposit when allowed by statute.

(2) *Distribution; Adjusting Distribution.* After a deposit, the court and attorneys must expedite the proceedings so as to distribute the deposit and to determine and pay compensation. If the

compensation finally awarded to a defendant exceeds the amount distributed to that defendant, the court must enter judgment against the plaintiff for the deficiency. If the compensation awarded to a defendant is less than the amount distributed to that defendant, the court must enter judgment against that defendant for the overpayment.

(k) Condemnation Under a State's Power of Eminent Domain. This rule governs an action involving eminent domain under state law. But if state law provides for trying an issue by jury—or for trying the issue of compensation by jury or commission or both—that law governs.

(*l* **) Costs.** Costs are not subject to Rule 54(d).

(Adopted April 30, 1951, effective August 1, 1951; amended January 21, 1963, effective July 1, 1963; April 29, 1985, effective August 1, 1985; March 2, 1987, effective August 1, 1987; April 25, 1988, effective August 1, 1988; amended by Pub.L. 100–690, Title VII, § 7050, November 18, 1988, 102 Stat. 4401 (although amendment by Pub.L. 100–690 could not be executed due to prior amendment by Court order which made the same change effective August 1, 1988); amended April 22, 1993, effective December 1, 1993; March 27, 2003, effective December 1, 2003; April 30, 2007, effective December 1, 2007; March 26, 2009, effective December 1, 2009.)

RULE 72. MAGISTRATE JUDGES: PRETRIAL ORDER

(a) Nondispositive Matters. When a pretrial matter not dispositive of a party's claim or defense is referred to a magistrate judge to hear and decide, the magistrate judge must promptly conduct the required proceedings and, when appropriate, issue a written order stating the decision. A party may serve and file objections to the order within 14 days after being served with a copy. A party may not assign as error a defect in the order not timely objected to. The district judge in the case must consider timely objections and modify or set aside any part of the order that is clearly erroneous or is contrary to law.

(b) Dispositive Motions and Prisoner Petitions.

(1) *Findings and Recommendations.* A magistrate judge must promptly conduct the required proceedings when assigned, without the parties' consent, to hear a pretrial matter dispositive of a claim or defense or a prisoner petition challenging the conditions of confinement. A record must be made of all evidentiary proceedings and may, at the magistrate judge's discretion, be made of any other proceedings. The magistrate judge must enter a recommended disposition, including, if appropriate, proposed findings of fact. The clerk must promptly mail a copy to each party.

(2) *Objections.* Within 14 days after being served with a copy of the recommended disposition, a party may serve and file specific written objections to the proposed findings and recommendations. A party may respond to another party's objections within 14 days after being served with a copy. Unless the district judge orders otherwise, the objecting party must promptly arrange for transcribing the record, or whatever portions of it the parties agree to or the magistrate judge considers sufficient.

(3) *Resolving Objections.* The district judge must determine de novo any part of the magistrate judge's disposition that has been properly objected to. The district judge may accept, reject, or modify the recommended disposition; receive further evidence; or return the matter to the magistrate judge with instructions.

(Former Rule 72 abrogated December 4, 1967, effective July 1, 1968; new Rule 72 adopted April 28, 1983, effective August 1, 1983; amended April 30, 1991, effective December 1, 1991; April 22, 1993, effective December 1, 1993; April 30, 2007, effective December 1, 2007; March 26, 2009, effective December 1, 2009.)

RULE 73. MAGISTRATE JUDGES: TRIAL BY CONSENT; APPEAL

(a) Trial by Consent. When authorized under 28 U.S.C. § 636(c), a magistrate judge may, if all parties consent, conduct a civil action or proceeding, including a jury or nonjury trial. A record must be made in accordance with 28 U.S.C. § 636(c)(5).

(b) Consent Procedure.

(1) *In General.* When a magistrate judge has been designated to conduct civil actions or proceedings, the clerk must give the parties written notice of their opportunity to consent under 28 U.S.C. § 636(c). To signify their consent, the parties must jointly or separately file a statement consenting to the referral. A district judge or magistrate judge may be informed of a party's response to the clerk's notice only if all parties have consented to the referral.

(2) *Reminding the Parties About Consenting.* A district judge, magistrate judge, or other court official may remind the parties of the magistrate judge's availability, but must also advise them that they are free to withhold consent without adverse substantive consequences.

(3) *Vacating a Referral.* On its own for good cause—or when a party shows extraordinary circumstances—the district judge may vacate a referral to a magistrate judge under this rule.

(c) Appealing a Judgment. In accordance with 28 U.S.C. § 636(c)(3), an appeal from a judgment entered at a magistrate judge's direction may be taken to the court of appeals as would any other appeal from a district-court judgment.

(Former Rule 73 abrogated December 4, 1967, effective July 1, 1968; new Rule 73 adopted April 28, 1983, effective August 1, 1983; amended March 2, 1987, effective August 1, 1987; April 22, 1993, effective December 1, 1993; April 11, 1997, effective December 1, 1997; April 30, 2007, effective December 1, 2007.)

RULE 74. METHOD OF APPEAL FROM MAGISTRATE JUDGE TO DISTRICT JUDGE UNDER TITLE 28, U.S.C. § 636(c)(4) AND RULE 73(d) [ABROGATED]

(Former Rule 74 abrogated December 4, 1967, effective July 1, 1968; new Rule 74 adopted April 28, 1983, effective August 1, 1983; amended April 22, 1993, effective December 1, 1993; abrogated April 11, 1997, effective December 1, 1997; April 30, 2007, effective December 1, 2007.)

RULE 75. PROCEEDINGS ON APPEAL FROM MAGISTRATE JUDGE TO DISTRICT JUDGE UNDER RULE 73(d) [ABROGATED]

(Former Rule 75 abrogated December 4, 1967, effective July 1, 1968; new Rule 75 adopted April 28, 1983, effective August 1, 1983; amended March 2, 1987, effective August 1, 1987; April 22, 1993, effective December 1, 1993; abrogated April 11, 1997, effective December 1, 1997; April 30, 2007, effective December 1, 2007.)

RULE 76. JUDGMENT OF THE DISTRICT JUDGE ON THE APPEAL UNDER RULE 73(d) AND COSTS [ABROGATED]

(Former Rule 76 abrogated December 4, 1967, effective July 1, 1968; new Rule 76 adopted April 28, 1983, effective August 1, 1983; amended April 22, 1993, effective December 1, 1993; abrogated April 11, 1997, effective December 1, 1997; April 30, 2007, effective December 1, 2007.)

TITLE X. DISTRICT COURTS AND CLERKS: CONDUCTING BUSINESS; ISSUING ORDERS

RULE 77. CONDUCTING BUSINESS; CLERK'S AUTHORITY; NOTICE OF AN ORDER OR JUDGMENT

(a) **When Court Is Open.** Every district court is considered always open for filing any paper, issuing and returning process, making a motion, or entering an order.

(b) **Place for Trial and Other Proceedings.** Every trial on the merits must be conducted in open court and, so far as convenient, in a regular courtroom. Any other act or proceeding may be done or conducted by a judge in chambers, without the attendance of the clerk or other court official, and anywhere inside or outside the district. But no hearing—other than one ex parte—may be conducted outside the district unless all the affected parties consent.

(c) **Clerk's Office Hours; Clerk's Orders.**

(1) *Hours.* The clerk's office—with a clerk or deputy on duty—must be open during business hours every day except Saturdays, Sundays, and legal holidays. But a court may, by local rule or order, require that the office be open for specified hours on Saturday or a particular legal holiday other than one listed in Rule 6(a)(6)(A).

(2) *Orders.* Subject to the court's power to suspend, alter, or rescind the clerk's action for good cause, the clerk may:

(A) issue process;

(B) enter a default;

(C) enter a default judgment under Rule 55(b)(1); and

(D) act on any other matter that does not require the court's action.

(d) **Serving Notice of an Order or Judgment.**

(1) *Service.* Immediately after entering an order or judgment, the clerk must serve notice of the entry, as provided in Rule 5(b), on each party who is not in default for failing to appear. The clerk must record the service on the docket. A party also may serve notice of the entry as provided in Rule 5(b).

(2) *Time to Appeal Not Affected by Lack of Notice.* Lack of notice of the entry does not affect the time for appeal or relieve—or authorize the court to relieve—a party for failing to appeal within the time allowed, except as allowed by Federal Rule of Appellate Procedure (4)(a).

(Amended December 27, 1946, effective March 19, 1948; January 21, 1963, effective July 1, 1963; December 4, 1967, effective July 1, 1968; March 1, 1971, effective July 1, 1971; March 2, 1987, effective August 1, 1987; April 30, 1991, effective December 1, 1991; April 23, 2001, effective December 1, 2001; April 30, 2007, effective December 1, 2007; April 25, 2014, effective December 1, 2014.)

RULE 78. HEARING MOTIONS; SUBMISSION ON BRIEFS

(a) **Providing a Regular Schedule for Oral Hearings.** A court may establish regular times and places for oral hearings on motions.

(b) **Providing for Submission on Briefs.** By rule or order, the court may provide for submitting and determining motions on briefs, without oral hearings.

(Amended March 2, 1987, effective August 1, 1987; April 30, 2007, effective December 1, 2007.)

RULE 79. RECORDS KEPT BY THE CLERK

(a) **Civil Docket.**

(1) *In General.* The clerk must keep a record known as the "civil docket" in the form and manner prescribed by the Director of the Administrative Office of the United States Courts with the approval of the Judicial Conference of the United States. The clerk must enter each civil action in the docket. Actions must be assigned consecutive file numbers, which must be noted in the docket where the first entry of the action is made.

(2) *Items to be Entered.* The following items must be marked with the file number and entered chronologically in the docket:

(A) papers filed with the clerk;

(B) process issued, and proofs of service or other returns showing execution; and

(C) appearances, orders, verdicts, and judgments.

(3) *Contents of Entries; Jury Trial Demanded.* Each entry must briefly show the nature of the paper filed or writ issued, the substance of each proof of service or other return, and the substance and date of entry of each order and judgment. When a jury trial has been properly

demanded or ordered, the clerk must enter the word "jury" in the docket.

(b) Civil Judgments and Orders. The clerk must keep a copy of every final judgment and appealable order; of every order affecting title to or a lien on real or personal property; and of any other order that the court directs to be kept. The clerk must keep these in the form and manner prescribed by the Director of the Administrative Office of the United States Courts with the approval of the Judicial Conference of the United States.

(c) Indexes; Calendars. Under the court's direction, the clerk must:

(1) keep indexes of the docket and of the judgments and orders described in Rule 79(b); and

(2) prepare calendars of all actions ready for trial, distinguishing jury trials from nonjury trials.

(d) Other Records. The clerk must keep any other records required by the Director of the Administrative Office of the United States Courts with the approval of the Judicial Conference of the United States.

(Amended December 27, 1946, effective March 19, 1948; December 29, 1948, effective October 20, 1949; January 21, 1963, effective July 1, 1963; April 30, 2007, effective December 1, 2007.)

RULE 80. STENOGRAPHIC TRANSCRIPT AS EVIDENCE

If stenographically reported testimony at a hearing or trial is admissible in evidence at a later trial, the testimony may be proved by a transcript certified by the person who reported it.

(Amended December 27, 1946, effective March 19, 1948; April 30, 2007, effective December 1, 2007.)

TITLE XI. GENERAL PROVISIONS

RULE 81. APPLICABILITY OF THE RULES IN GENERAL; REMOVED ACTIONS

(a) Applicability to Particular Proceedings.

(1) *Prize Proceedings.* These rules do not apply to prize proceedings in admiralty governed by 10 U.S.C. §§ 7651–7681.

(2) *Bankruptcy.* These rules apply to bankruptcy proceedings to the extent provided by the Federal Rules of Bankruptcy Procedure.

(3) *Citizenship.* These rules apply to proceedings for admission to citizenship to the extent that the practice in those proceedings is not specified in federal statutes and has previously conformed to the practice in civil actions. The provisions of 8 U.S.C. § 1451 for service by publication and for answer apply in proceedings to cancel citizenship certificates.

(4) *Special Writs.* These rules apply to proceedings for habeas corpus and for quo warranto to the extent that the practice in those proceedings:

(A) is not specified in a federal statute, the Rules Governing Section 2254 Cases, or the Rules Governing Section 2255 Cases; and

(B) has previously conformed to the practice in civil actions.

(5) *Proceedings Involving a Subpoena.* These rules apply to proceedings to compel testimony or the production of documents through a subpoena issued by a United States officer or agency under a federal statute, except as otherwise provided by statute, by local rule, or by court order in the proceedings.

(6) *Other Proceedings.* These rules, to the extent applicable, govern proceedings under the following laws, except as these laws provide other procedures:

(A) 7 U.S.C. §§ 292, 499g(c), for reviewing an order of the Secretary of Agriculture;

(B) 9 U.S.C., relating to arbitration;

(C) 15 U.S.C. § 522, for reviewing an order of the Secretary of the Interior;

(D) 15 U.S.C. § 715d(c), for reviewing an order denying a certificate of clearance;

(E) 29 U.S.C. §§ 159, 160, for enforcing an order of the National Labor Relations Board;

(F) 33 U.S.C. §§ 918, 921, for enforcing or reviewing a compensation order under the Longshore and Harbor Workers' Compensation Act; and

(G) 45 U.S.C. § 159, for reviewing an arbitration award in a railway-labor dispute.

(b) Scire Facias and Mandamus. The writs of scire facias and mandamus are abolished. Relief previously available through them may be obtained by appropriate action or motion under these rules.

(c) Removed Actions.

(1) *Applicability.* These rules apply to a civil action after it is removed from a state court.

(2) *Further Pleading.* After removal, repleading is unnecessary unless the court orders it. A defendant who did not answer before removal must answer or present other defenses or objections under these rules within the longest of these periods:

(A) 21 days after receiving—through service or otherwise—a copy of the initial pleading stating the claim for relief;

(B) 21 days after being served with the summons for an initial pleading on file at the time of service; or

(C) 7 days after the notice of removal is filed.

(3) ***Demand for a Jury Trial.***

(A) *As Affected by State Law.* A party who, before removal, expressly demanded a jury trial in accordance with state law need not renew the demand after removal. If the state law did not require an express demand for a jury trial, a party need not make one after removal unless the court orders the parties to do so within a specified time. The court must so order at a party's request and may so order on its own. A party who fails to make a demand when so ordered waives a jury trial.

(B) *Under Rule 38.* If all necessary pleadings have been served at the time of removal, a party entitled to a jury trial under Rule 38 must be given one if the party serves a demand within 14 days after:

(i) it files a notice of removal; or

(ii) it is served with a notice of removal filed by another party.

(d) **Law Applicable.**

(1) *"State Law" Defined.* When these rules refer to state law, the term "law" includes the state's statutes and the state's judicial decisions.

(2) *"State" Defined.* The term "state" includes, where appropriate, the District of Columbia and any United States commonwealth or territory.

(3) *"Federal Statute" Defined in the District of Columbia.* In the United States District Court for the District of Columbia, the term "federal statute" includes any Act of Congress that applies locally to the District.

(Amended December 28, 1939, effective April 3, 1941; December 27, 1946, effective March 19, 1948; December 29, 1948, effective October 20, 1949; April 30, 1951, effective August 1, 1951; January 21, 1963, effective July 1, 1963; February 28, 1966, effective July 1, 1966; December 4, 1967, effective July 1, 1968; March 1, 1971, effective July 1, 1971; March 2, 1987, effective August 1, 1987; April 23, 2001, effective December 1, 2001; April 29, 2002, effective December 1, 2002; April 30, 2007, effective December 1, 2007; March 26, 2009, effective December 1, 2009.)

RULE 82. JURISDICTION AND VENUE UNAFFECTED

These rules do not extend or limit the jurisdiction of the district courts or the venue of actions in those courts. An admiralty or maritime claim under Rule

9(h) is not a civil action for purposes of 28 U.S.C. §§ 1391–1392.

(Amended December 29, 1948, effective October 20, 1949; February 28, 1966, effective July 1, 1966; April 23, 2001, effective December 1, 2001; April 30, 2007, effective December 1, 2007.)

RULE 83. RULES BY DISTRICT COURTS; JUDGE'S DIRECTIVES

(a) **Local Rules.**

(1) *In General.* After giving public notice and an opportunity for comment, a district court, acting by a majority of its district judges, may adopt and amend rules governing its practice. A local rule must be consistent with—but not duplicate—federal statutes and rules adopted under 28 U.S.C. §§ 2072 and 2075, and must conform to any uniform numbering system prescribed by the Judicial Conference of the United States. A local rule takes effect on the date specified by the district court and remains in effect unless amended by the court or abrogated by the judicial council of the circuit. Copies of rules and amendments must, on their adoption, be furnished to the judicial council and the Administrative Office of the United States Courts and be made available to the public.

(2) *Requirement of Form.* A local rule imposing a requirement of form must not be enforced in a way that causes a party to lose any right because of a nonwillful failure to comply.

(b) **Procedure When There Is No Controlling Law.** A judge may regulate practice in any manner consistent with federal law, rules adopted under 28 U.S.C. §§ 2072 and 2075, and the district's local rules. No sanction or other disadvantage may be imposed for noncompliance with any requirement not in federal law, federal rules, or the local rules unless the alleged violator has been furnished in the particular case with actual notice of the requirement.

(Amended April 29, 1985, effective August 1, 1985; April 27, 1995, effective December 1, 1995; April 30, 2007, effective December 1, 2007.)

RULE 84. FORMS

The forms in the Appendix suffice under these rules and illustrate the simplicity and brevity that these rules contemplate.

(Amended December 27, 1946, effective March 19, 1948; April 30, 2007, effective December 1, 2007.)

RULE 85. TITLE

These rules may be cited as the Federal Rules of Civil Procedure.

(Amended April 30, 2007, effective December 1, 2007.)

RULE 86. EFFECTIVE DATES

(a) In General. These rules and any amendments take effect at the time specified by the Supreme Court, subject to 28 U.S.C. § 2074. They govern:

    (1) proceedings in an action commenced after their effective date; and

    (2) proceedings after that date in an action then pending unless:

    (A) the Supreme Court specifies otherwise; or

    (B) the court determines that applying them in a particular action would be infeasible or work an injustice.

(b) December 1, 2007 Amendments. If any provision in Rules 1–5.1, 6–73, or 77–86 conflicts with another law, priority in time for the purpose of 28 U.S.C. § 2072(b) is not affected by the amendments taking effect on December 1, 2007.

(Amended December 27, 1946, effective March 19, 1948; December 29, 1948, effective October 20, 1949; April 17, 1961, effective July 19, 1961; January 21, 1963, and March 18, 1963, effective July 1, 1963; April 30, 2007, effective December 1, 2007.)

APPENDIX OF FORMS

(See Rule 84)

FORM 1. CAPTION

(Use on every summons, complaint, answer, motion, or other document.)

United States District Court
for the
_____ District of _____

A B, Plaintiff	)
	)
v.	)
	) Civil Action No. _____
C D, Defendant	)
	)
v.	)
	)
E F, Third–Party Defendant	)
(Use if needed.)	)

(Name of Document)

(Added Apr. 30, 2007, eff. Dec. 1, 2007.)

FORM 2. DATE, SIGNATURE, ADDRESS, E–MAIL ADDRESS, AND TELEPHONE NUMBER

(Use at the conclusion of pleadings and other papers that require a signature.)

Date _____

_____
(Signature of the attorney or unrepresented party)

_____
(Printed name)

_____
(Address)

_____
(E-mail address)

_____
(Telephone number)

(Added Apr. 30, 2007, eff. Dec. 1, 2007.)

FORM 3. SUMMONS

(Caption—See Form 1.)

To *name the defendant*:

A lawsuit has been filed against you.

Within 21 days after service of this summons on you (not counting the day you received it), you must serve on the plaintiff an answer to the attached complaint or a motion under Rule 12 of the Federal Rules of Civil Procedure. The answer or motion must be served on the plaintiff's attorney, _____, whose address is _____. If you fail to do so, judgment by default will be entered against you for the relief demanded in the complaint. You also must file your answer or motion with the court.

Date _____

_____
Clerk of Court

(Court Seal)

(*Use 60 days if the defendant is the United States or a United States agency, or is an officer or employee of the United States allowed 60 days by Rule 12(a)(3).*)

(Added Apr. 30, 2007, eff. Dec. 1, 2007, and amended Mar. 26, 2009, eff. Dec. 1, 2009.)

FORM 4. SUMMONS ON A THIRD-PARTY COMPLAINT

(Caption—See Form 1.)

To *name the third-party defendant*:

A lawsuit has been filed against defendant _____, who as third-party plaintiff is making this claim against you to pay part or all of what [he] may owe to the plaintiff _____.

Within 21 days after service of this summons on you (not counting the day you received it), you must serve on the plaintiff and on the defendant an answer to the attached third-party complaint or a motion under Rule 12 of the Federal Rules of Civil Procedure. The answer or motion must be served on the defendant's attorney, _____, whose address is, _____, and also on the plaintiff's attorney, _____, whose address is, _____. If you fail to do so, judgment by default will be entered against you for the relief demanded in the third-party complaint. You also must file the answer or motion with the court and serve it on any other parties.

A copy of the plaintiff's complaint is also attached. You may—but are not required to—respond to it.

Date _____

_____
Clerk of Court

(Court Seal)

(Added Apr. 30, 2007, eff. Dec. 1, 2007, and amended Mar. 26, 2009, eff. Dec. 1, 2009.)

FORM 5. NOTICE OF A LAWSUIT AND REQUEST
TO WAIVE SERVICE OF A SUMMONS

(Caption—See Form 1.)

To *(name the defendant—or if the defendant is a corporation, partnership, or association name an officer or agent authorized to receive service)*:

Why are you getting this?

A lawsuit has been filed against you, or the entity you represent, in this court under the number shown above. A copy of the complaint is attached.

This is not a summons, or an official notice from the court. It is a request that, to avoid expenses, you waive formal service of a summons by signing and returning the enclosed waiver. To avoid these expenses, you must return the signed waiver within *(give at least 30 days or at least 60 days if the defendant is outside any judicial district of the United States)* from the date shown below, which is the date this notice was sent. Two copies of the waiver form are enclosed, along with a stamped, self-addressed envelope or other prepaid means for returning one copy. You may keep the other copy.

What happens next?

If you return the signed waiver, I will file it with the court. The action will then proceed as if you had been served on the date the waiver is filed, but no summons will be served on you and you will have 60 days from the date this notice is sent (see the date below) to answer the complaint (or 90 days if this notice is sent to you outside any judicial district of the United States).

If you do not return the signed waiver within the time indicated, I will arrange to have the summons and complaint served on you. And I will ask the court to require you, or the entity you represent, to pay the expenses of making service.

Please read the enclosed statement about the duty to avoid unnecessary expenses.

I certify that this request is being sent to you on the date below.

(Date and sign—See Form 2.)

(Added Apr. 30, 2007, eff. Dec. 1, 2007.)

FORM 6. WAIVER OF THE SERVICE OF SUMMONS

(Caption—See Form 1.)

To *name the plaintiff's attorney or the unrepresented plaintiff*:

I have received your request to waive service of a summons in this action along with a copy of the complaint, two copies of this waiver form, and a prepaid means of returning one signed copy of the form to you.

I, or the entity I represent, agree to save the expense of serving a summons and complaint in this case.

I understand that I, or the entity I represent, will keep all defenses or objections to the lawsuit, the court's jurisdiction, and the venue of the action, but that I waive any objections to the absence of a summons or of service.

I also understand that I, or the entity I represent, must file and serve an answer or a motion under Rule 12 within 60 days from _____, the date when this request was sent (or 90 days if it was sent outside the United States). If I fail to do so, a default judgment will be entered against me or the entity I represent.

(Date and sign—See Form 2.)

(Attach the following to Form 6.)

Duty to Avoid Unnecessary Expenses of Serving a Summons

Rule 4 of the Federal Rules of Civil Procedure requires certain defendants to cooperate in saving unnecessary expenses of serving a summons and complaint. A defendant who is located in the United States and who fails to return a signed waiver of service requested by a plaintiff located in the United States will be required to pay the expenses of service, unless the defendant shows good cause for the failure.

"Good cause" does *not* include a belief that the lawsuit is groundless, or that it has been brought in an improper venue, or that the court has no jurisdiction over this matter or over the defendant or the defendant's property.

If the waiver is signed and returned, you can still make these and all other defenses and objections, but you cannot object to the absence of a summons or of service.

If you waive service, then you must, within the time specified on the waiver form, serve an answer or a motion under Rule 12 on the plaintiff and file a copy with the court. By signing and returning the waiver form, you are allowed more time to respond than if a summons had been served.

(Added Apr. 30, 2007, eff. Dec. 1, 2007.)

FORM 7. STATEMENT OF JURISDICTION

a. (*For diversity-of-citizenship jurisdiction.*) The plaintiff is [a citizen of *Michigan*] [a corporation incorporated under the laws of *Michigan* with its principal place of business in *Michigan*]. The defendant is [a citizen of *New York*] [a corporation incorporated under the laws of *New York* with its principal place of business in *New York*]. The amount in controversy, without interest and costs, exceeds the sum or value specified by 28 U.S.C. § 1332.

b. (*For federal-question jurisdiction.*) This action arises under [the United States Constitution, *specify the article or amendment and the section*] [a United States treaty *specify*] [a federal statute, ___ U.S.C. § ___].

c. (*For a claim in the admiralty or maritime jurisdiction.*) This is a case of admiralty or maritime jurisdiction. (*To invoke admiralty status under Rule 9(h) use the following:* This is an admiralty or maritime claim within the meaning of Rule 9(h).)

(Added Apr. 30, 2007, eff. Dec. 1, 2007.)

FORM 8. STATEMENT OF REASONS FOR OMITTING A PARTY

(*If a person who ought to be made a party under Rule 19(a) is not named, include this statement in accordance with Rule 19(c).*)

This complaint does not join as a party *name* who [is not subject to this court's personal jurisdiction] [cannot be made a party without depriving this court of subject-matter jurisdiction] because *state the reason.*

(Added Apr. 30, 2007, eff. Dec. 1, 2007.)

FORM 9. STATEMENT NOTING A PARTY'S DEATH

(Caption—See Form 1.)

In accordance with Rule 25(a) *name the person,* who is [a party to this action] [a representative of or successor to the deceased party] notes the death during the pendency of this action of *name*, [*describe as party* in this action].

(Date and sign—See Form 2.)

(Added Apr. 30, 2007, eff. Dec. 1, 2007.)

FORM 10.   COMPLAINT TO RECOVER A SUM CERTAIN

(Caption—See Form 1.)

1.   (Statement of Jurisdiction—See Form 7.)

(Use one or more of the following as appropriate and include a demand for judgment.)

(a) On a Promissory Note

2.   On *date,* the defendant executed and delivered a note promising to pay the plaintiff on *date* the sum of $_____ with interest at the rate of ___ percent. A copy of the note [is attached as Exhibit A] [is summarized as follows: _____.]

3.   The defendant has not paid the amount owed.

(b) On an Account

2.   The defendant owes the plaintiff $_____ according to the account set out in Exhibit A.

(c) For Goods Sold and Delivered

2.   The defendant owes the plaintiff $_____ for goods sold and delivered by the plaintiff to the defendant from *date* to *date.*

(d) For Money Lent

2.   The defendant owes the plaintiff $_____ for money lent by the plaintiff to the defendant on *date.*

(e) For Money Paid by Mistake

2.   The defendant owes the plaintiff $_____ for money paid by mistake to the defendant on *date* under these circumstances: *describe with particularity in accordance with Rule 9(b).*

(f) For Money Had and Received

2.   The defendant owes the plaintiff $_____ for money that was received from *name* on *date* to be paid by the defendant to the plaintiff.

Demand for Judgment

Therefore, the plaintiff demands judgment against the defendant for $_____, plus interest and costs.

(Date and sign—See Form 2.)

(Added Apr. 30, 2007, eff. Dec. 1, 2007.)

FORM 11. COMPLAINT FOR NEGLIGENCE

(Caption—See Form 1.)

1. (Statement of Jurisdiction—See Form 7.)

2. On *date*, at *place*, the defendant negligently drove a motor vehicle against the plaintiff.

3. As a result, the plaintiff was physically injured, lost wages or income, suffered physical and mental pain, and incurred medical expenses of $_____.

Therefore, the plaintiff demands judgment against the defendant for $_____, plus costs.

(Date and sign—See Form 2).

(Added Apr. 30, 2007, eff. Dec. 1, 2007.)

FORM 12. COMPLAINT FOR NEGLIGENCE WHEN THE PLAINTIFF DOES NOT KNOW WHO IS RESPONSIBLE

(Caption—See Form 1.)

1. (Statement of Jurisdiction—See Form 7.)

2. On *date*, at *place*, defendant *name* or defendant *name* or both of them willfully or recklessly or negligently drove, or caused to be driven, a motor vehicle against the plaintiff.

3. As a result, the plaintiff was physically injured, lost wages or income, suffered mental and physical pain, and incurred medical expenses of $_____.

Therefore, the plaintiff demands judgment against one or both defendants for $_____, plus costs.

(Date and sign—See Form 2.)

(Added Apr. 30, 2007, eff. Dec. 1, 2007.)

FORM 13. COMPLAINT FOR NEGLIGENCE UNDER THE FEDERAL EMPLOYERS' LIABILITY ACT

(Caption—See Form 1.)

1. (Statement of Jurisdiction—See Form 7.)

2. At the times below, the defendant owned and operated in interstate commerce a railroad line that passed through a tunnel located at _____.

3. On *date*, the plaintiff was working to repair and enlarge the tunnel to make it convenient and safe for use in interstate commerce.

4. During this work, the defendant, as the employer, negligently put the plaintiff to work in a section of the tunnel that the defendant had left unprotected and unsupported.

5. The defendant's negligence caused the plaintiff to be injured by a rock that fell from an unsupported portion of the tunnel.

6. As a result, the plaintiff was physically injured, lost wages or income, suffered mental and physical pain, and incurred medical expenses of $_____.

Therefore, the plaintiff demands judgment against the defendant for $_____, and costs.

(Date and sign—See Form 2.)

(Added Apr. 30, 2007, eff. Dec. 1, 2007.)

FORM 14. COMPLAINT FOR DAMAGES UNDER THE MERCHANT MARINE ACT

(Caption—See Form 1.)

1. (Statement of Jurisdiction—See Form 7.)

2. At the times below, the defendant owned and operated the vessel *name* and used it to transport cargo for hire by water in interstate and foreign commerce.

3. On *date*, at *place*, the defendant hired the plaintiff under seamen's articles of customary form for a voyage from _____ to _____ and return at a wage of $_____ a month and found, which is equal to a shore worker's wage of $_____ a month.

4. On *date*, the vessel was at sea on the return voyage. (*Describe the weather and the condition of the vessel.*)

5. (*Describe as in Form 11 the defendant's negligent conduct.*)

6. As a result of the defendant's negligent conduct and the unseaworthiness of the vessel, the plaintiff was physically injured, has been incapable of any gainful activity, suffered mental and physical pain, and has incurred medical expenses of $_____.

Therefore, the plaintiff demands judgment against the defendant for $_____, plus costs.

(Date and sign—See Form 2.)

(Added Apr. 30, 2007, eff. Dec. 1, 2007.)

FORM 15.   COMPLAINT FOR THE CONVERSION OF PROPERTY

(Caption—See Form 1.)

1.   (Statement of Jurisdiction—See Form 7.)

2.   On *date*, at *place*, the defendant converted to the defendant's own use property owned by the plaintiff. The property converted consists of *describe*.

3.   The property is worth $_____.

Therefore, the plaintiff demands judgment against the defendant for $_____, plus costs.

(Date and sign—See Form 2.)

(Added Apr. 30, 2007, eff. Dec. 1, 2007.)

FORM 16.   THIRD–PARTY COMPLAINT

(Caption—See Form 1.)

1.   Plaintiff *name* has filed against defendant *name* a complaint, a copy of which is attached.

2.   *(State grounds entitling defendant's name to recover from third-party defendant's name for (all or an identified share) of any judgment for plaintiff's name against defendant's name.)*

Therefore, the defendant demands judgment against *third-party defendant's name* for *all or an identified share* of sums that may be adjudged against the defendant in the plaintiff's favor.

(Date and sign—See Form 2.)

(Added Apr. 30, 2007, eff. Dec. 1, 2007.)

FORM 17. COMPLAINT FOR SPECIFIC PERFORMANCE OF A CONTRACT TO CONVEY LAND

(Caption—See Form 1.)

1. (Statement of Jurisdiction—See Form 7.)

2. On *date*, the parties agreed to the contract [attached as Exhibit A][summarize the contract].

3. As agreed, the plaintiff tendered the purchase price and requested a conveyance of the land, but the defendant refused to accept the money or make a conveyance.

4. The plaintiff now offers to pay the purchase price.

Therefore, the plaintiff demands that:

(a) the defendant be required to specifically perform the agreement and pay damages of $_____, plus interest and costs, or

(b) if specific performance is not ordered, the defendant be required to pay damages of $_____, plus interest and costs.

(Date and sign—See Form 2.)

(Added Apr. 30, 2007, eff. Dec. 1, 2007.)

FORM 18. COMPLAINT FOR PATENT INFRINGEMENT

(Caption—See Form 1.)

1. (Statement of Jurisdiction—See Form 7.)

2. On *date*, United States Letters Patent No. _____ were issued to the plaintiff for an invention in an *electric motor*. The plaintiff owned the patent throughout the period of the defendant's infringing acts and still owns the patent.

3. The defendant has infringed and is still infringing the Letters Patent by making, selling, and using *electric motors* that embody the patented invention, and the defendant will continue to do so unless enjoined by this court.

4. The plaintiff has complied with the statutory requirement of placing a notice of the Letters Patent on all *electric motors* it manufactures and sells and has given the defendant written notice of the infringement.

Therefore, the plaintiff demands:

(a) a preliminary and final injunction against the continuing infringement;

(b) an accounting for damages; and

(c) interest and costs.

(Date and sign—See Form 2.)

(Added Apr. 30, 2007, eff. Dec. 1, 2007.)

FORM 19. COMPLAINT FOR COPYRIGHT INFRINGEMENT AND UNFAIR COMPETITION

(Caption—See Form 1.)

1. (Statement of Jurisdiction—See Form 7.)

2. Before *date*, the plaintiff, a United States citizen, wrote a book entitled _____.

3. The book is an original work that may be copyrighted under United States law. A copy of the book is attached as Exhibit A.

4. Between *date* and *date*, the plaintiff applied to the copyright office and received a certificate of registration dated _____ and identified as *date, class, number*.

5. Since *date*, the plaintiff has either published or licensed for publication all copies of the book in compliance with the copyright laws and has remained the sole owner of the copyright.

6. After the copyright was issued, the defendant infringed the copyright by publishing and selling a book entitled _____, which was copied largely from the plaintiff's book. A copy of the defendant's book is attached as Exhibit B.

7. The plaintiff has notified the defendant in writing of the infringement.

8. The defendant continues to infringe the copyright by continuing to publish and sell the infringing book in violation of the copyright, and further has engaged in unfair trade practices and unfair competition in connection with its publication and sale of the infringing book, thus causing irreparable damage.

Therefore, the plaintiff demands that:

(a) until this case is decided the defendant and the defendant's agents be enjoined from disposing of any copies of the defendant's book by sale or otherwise;

(b) the defendant account for and pay as damages to the plaintiff all profits and advantages gained from unfair trade practices and unfair competition in selling the defendant's book, and all profits and advantages gained from infringing the plaintiff's copyright (but no less than the statutory minimum);

(c) the defendant deliver for impoundment all copies of the book in the defendant's possession or control and deliver for destruction all infringing copies and all plates, molds, and other materials for making infringing copies;

(d) the defendant pay the plaintiff interest, costs, and reasonable attorney's fees; and

(e) the plaintiff be awarded any other just relief.

(Date and sign—See Form 2.)

(Added Apr. 30, 2007, eff. Dec. 1, 2007.)

FORM 20.　COMPLAINT FOR INTERPLEADER AND DECLARATORY RELIEF

(Caption—See Form 1.)

1. (Statement of Jurisdiction—See Form 7.)

2. On *date*, the plaintiff issued a life insurance policy on the life of *name* with *name* as the named beneficiary.

3. As a condition for keeping the policy in force, the policy required payment of a premium during the first year and then annually.

4. The premium due on *date* was never paid, and the policy lapsed after that date.

5. On *date*, after the policy had lapsed, both the insured and the named beneficiary died in an automobile collision.

6. Defendant *name* claims to be the beneficiary in place of *name* and has filed a claim to be paid the policy's full amount.

7. The other two defendants are representatives of the deceased persons' estates. Each defendant has filed a claim on behalf of each estate to receive payment of the policy's full amount.

8. If the policy was in force at the time of death, the plaintiff is in doubt about who should be paid.

Therefore, the plaintiff demands that:

  (a) each defendant be restrained from commencing any action against the plaintiff on the policy;

  (b) a judgment be entered that no defendant is entitled to the proceeds of the policy or any part of it, but if the court determines that the policy was in effect at the time of the insured's death, that the defendants be required to interplead and settle among themselves their rights to the proceeds, and that the plaintiff be discharged from all liability except to the defendant determined to be entitled to the proceeds; and

  (c) the plaintiff recover its costs.

(Date and sign—See Form 2.)

(Added Apr. 30, 2007, eff. Dec. 1, 2007.)

FORM 21. COMPLAINT ON A CLAIM FOR A DEBT AND TO SET ASIDE A FRAUDULENT CONVEYANCE UNDER RULE 18(b)

(Caption—See Form 1.)

1. (Statement of Jurisdiction—See Form 7.)

2. On *date*, defendant *name* signed a note promising to pay to the plaintiff on *date* the sum of $_____ with interest at the rate of ___ percent. [The pleader may, but need not, attach a copy or plead the note verbatim.]

3. Defendant *name* owes the plaintiff the amount of the note and interest.

4. On *date*, defendant *name* conveyed all defendant's real and personal property *if less than all, describe it fully* to defendant *name* for the purpose of defrauding the plaintiff and hindering or delaying the collection of the debt.

Therefore, the plaintiff demands that:

  (a) judgment for $_____, plus costs, be entered against defendant(s) *name(s)*; and

  (b) the conveyance to defendant *name* be declared void and any judgment granted be made a lien on the property.

(Date and sign—See Form 2.)

(Added Apr. 30, 2007, eff. Dec. 1, 2007.)

FORM 30.   ANSWER PRESENTING DEFENSES UNDER RULE 12(b)

(Caption—See Form 1.)

Responding to Allegations in the Complaint

1.   Defendant admits the allegations in paragraphs _____.
2.   Defendant lacks knowledge or information sufficient to form a belief about the truth of the allegations in paragraphs _____.
3.   Defendant admits *identify part of the allegation* in paragraph _____ and denies or lacks knowledge or information sufficient to form a belief about the truth of the rest of the paragraph.

Failure to State a Claim

4.   The complaint fails to state a claim upon which relief can be granted.

Failure to Join a Required Party

5.   If there is a debt, it is owed jointly by the defendant and *name* who is a citizen of _____. This person can be made a party without depriving this court of jurisdiction over the existing parties.

Affirmative Defense—Statute of Limitations

6.   The plaintiff's claim is barred by the statute of limitations because it arose more than _____ years before this action was commenced.

Counterclaim

7.   *(Set forth any counterclaim in the same way a claim is pleaded in a complaint. Include a further statement of jurisdiction if needed.)*

Crossclaim

8.   *(Set forth a crossclaim against a coparty in the same way a claim is pleaded in a complaint. Include a further statement of jurisdiction if needed.)*

(Date and sign—See Form 2.)

(Added Apr. 30, 2007, eff. Dec. 1, 2007.)

FORM 31. ANSWER TO A COMPLAINT FOR MONEY HAD AND RECEIVED WITH A COUNTERCLAIM FOR INTERPLEADER

(Caption—See Form 1.)

Response to the Allegations in the Complaint
(See Form 30.)

Counterclaim for Interpleader

1. The defendant received from *name* a deposit of $_____.

2. The plaintiff demands payment of the deposit because of a purported assignment from *name*, who has notified the defendant that the assignment is not valid and who continues to hold the defendant responsible for the deposit.

Therefore, the defendant demands that:

   (a) *name* be made a party to this action;

   (b) the plaintiff and *name* be required to interplead their respective claims;

   (c) the court decide whether the plaintiff or *name* or either of them is entitled to the deposit and discharge the defendant of any liability except to the person entitled to the deposit; and

   (d) the defendant recover costs and attorney's fees.

(Date and sign—See Form 2.)

(Added Apr. 30, 2007, eff. Dec. 1, 2007.)

FORM 40. MOTION TO DISMISS UNDER RULE 12(B) FOR LACK OF JURISDICTION, IMPROPER VENUE, INSUFFICIENT SERVICE OF PROCESS, OR FAILURE TO STATE A CLAIM

(Caption—See Form 1.)

The defendant moves to dismiss the action because:

1. the amount in controversy is less than the sum or value specified by 28 U.S.C. § 1332;

2. the defendant is not subject to the personal jurisdiction of this court;

3. venue is improper (this defendant does not reside in this district and no part of the events or omissions giving rise to the claim occurred in the district);

4. the defendant has not been properly served, as shown by the attached affidavits of _____; or

5. the complaint fails to state a claim upon which relief can be granted.

(Date and sign—See Form 2.)

(Added Apr. 30, 2007, eff. Dec. 1, 2007.)

FORM 41. MOTION TO BRING IN A THIRD–PARTY DEFENDANT

(Caption—See Form 1.)

The defendant, as third-party plaintiff, moves for leave to serve on *name* a summons and third-party complaint, copies of which are attached.

(Date and sign—See Form 2.)

(Added Apr. 30, 2007, eff. Dec. 1, 2007.)

FORM 42. MOTION TO INTERVENE AS A DEFENDANT UNDER RULE 24

(Caption—See Form 1.)

1. *name* moves for leave to intervene as a defendant in this action and to file the attached answer.

(State grounds under Rule 24(a) or (b).)

2. The plaintiff alleges patent infringement. We manufacture and sell to the defendant the articles involved, and we have a defense to the plaintiff's claim.

3. Our defense presents questions of law and fact that are common to this action.

(Date and sign—See Form 2.)

[An Intervener's Answer must be attached. See Form 30.]

(Added Apr. 30, 2007, eff. Dec. 1, 2007.)

FORM 50. REQUEST TO PRODUCE DOCUMENTS AND TANGIBLE THINGS, OR TO ENTER ONTO LAND UNDER RULE 34

(Caption—See Form 1.)

The plaintiff *name* requests that the defendant *name* respond within ____ days to the following requests:

1. To produce and permit the plaintiff to inspect and copy and to test or sample the following documents, including electronically stored information:

   (Describe each document and the electronically stored information, either individually or by category.)

   (State the time, place, and manner of the inspection and any related acts.)

2. To produce and permit the plaintiff to inspect and copy—and to test or sample—the following tangible things:

   (Describe each thing, either individually or by category.)

   (State the time, place, and manner of the inspection and any related acts.)

3. To permit the plaintiff to enter onto the following land to inspect, photograph, test, or sample the property or an object or operation on the property.

   (Describe the property and each object or operation.)

   (State the time and manner of the inspection and any related acts.)

(Date and sign—See Form 2.)

(Added Apr. 30, 2007, eff. Dec. 1, 2007.)

FORM 51. REQUEST FOR ADMISSIONS UNDER RULE 36

(Caption—See Form 1.)

The plaintiff *name* asks the defendant *name* to respond within 30 days to these requests by admitting, for purposes of this action only and subject to objections to admissibility at trial:

1. The genuineness of the following documents, copies of which [are attached] [are or have been furnished or made available for inspection and copying].

   (List each document.)

2. The truth of each of the following statements:

   (List each statement.)

(Date and sign—See Form 2.)

(Added Apr. 30, 2007, eff. Dec. 1, 2007.)

FORM 52.   REPORT OF THE PARTIES' PLANNING MEETING

(Caption—See Form 1.)

1. The following persons participated in a Rule 26(f) conference on   *date*   by *state the method of conferring*   :

2. Initial Disclosures. The parties [have completed] [will complete by   *date*] the initial disclosures required by Rule 26(a)(1).

3. Discovery Plan. The parties propose this discovery plan:

(Use separate paragraphs or subparagraphs if the parties disagree.)

   (a) Discovery will be needed on these subjects: *(describe)*

   (b) Disclosure or discovery of electronically stored information should be handled as follows: *(briefly describe the parties' proposals, including the form or forms for production.)*

   (c) The parties have agreed to an order regarding claims of privilege or of protection as trial-preparation material asserted after production, as follows: *(briefly describe the provisions of the proposed order.)*

   (d) (Dates for commencing and completing discovery, including discovery to be commenced or completed before other discovery.)

   (e) (Maximum number of interrogatories by each party to another party, along with dates the answers are due.)

   (f) (Maximum number of requests for admission, along with the dates responses are due.)

   (g) (Maximum number of depositions for each party.)

   (h) (Limits on the length of depositions, in hours.)

   (i) (Dates for exchanging reports of expert witnesses.)

   (j) (Dates for supplementations under Rule 26(e).)

4. Other Items:

   (a) (A date if the parties ask to meet with the court before a scheduling order.)

   (b) (Requested dates for pretrial conferences.)

   (c) (Final dates for the plaintiff to amend pleadings or to join parties.)

   (d) (Final dates for the defendant to amend pleadings or to join parties.)

   (e) (Final dates to file dispositive motions.)

   (f) (State the prospects for settlement.)

   (g) (Identify any alternative dispute resolution procedure that may enhance settlement prospects.)

   (h) (Final dates for submitting Rule 26(a)(3) witness lists, designations of witnesses whose testimony will be presented by deposition, and exhibit lists.)

   (i) (Final dates to file objections under Rule 26(a)(3).)

   (j) (Suggested trial date and estimate of trial length.)

   (k) (Other matters.)

(Date and sign—see Form 2.)

(Added Apr. 30, 2007, eff. Dec. 1, 2007. As amended Apr. 28, 2010, eff. Dec. 1, 2010.)

FORM 60.   NOTICE OF CONDEMNATION

(Caption—See Form 1.)

To *name the defendant*.

1. A complaint in condemnation has been filed in the United States District Court for the _____District of _____, to take property to use for *purpose*. The interest to be taken is *describe*. The court is located in the United States courthouse at this address: _____.

2. The property to be taken is described below. You have or claim an interest in it.

(Describe the property.)

3. The authority for taking this property is *cite*.

4. If you want to object or present any defense to the taking you must serve an answer on the plaintiff's attorney within 21 days [after being served with this notice][from *(insert the date of the last publication of notice)*]. Send your answer to this address: _____.

5. Your answer must identify the property in which you claim an interest, state the nature and extent of that interest, and state all your objections and defenses to the taking. Objections and defenses not presented are waived.

6. If you fail to answer you consent to the taking and the court will enter a judgment that takes your described property interest.

7. Instead of answering, you may serve on the plaintiff's attorney a notice of appearance that designates the property in which you claim an interest. After you do that, you will receive a notice of any proceedings that affect you. Whether or not you have previously appeared or answered, you may present evidence at a trial to determine compensation for the property and share in the overall award.

(Date and sign—See Form 2.)

(Added Apr. 30, 2007, eff. Dec. 1, 2007, and amended Mar. 26, 2009, eff. Dec. 1, 2009.)

FORM 61. COMPLAINT FOR CONDEMNATION

(Caption—See Form 1; name as defendants the property and at least one owner.)

1. (Statement of Jurisdiction—See Form 7.)
2. This is an action to take property under the power of eminent domain and to determine just compensation to be paid to the owners and parties in interest.
3. The authority for the taking is _____.
4. The property is to be used for _____.
5. The property to be taken is (*describe in enough detail for identification—or attach the description and state "is described in Exhibit A, attached."*)
6. The interest to be acquired is _____.
7. The persons known to the plaintiff to have or claim an interest in the property are: _____. (*For each person include the interest claimed.*)
8. There may be other persons who have or claim an interest in the property and whose names could not be found after a reasonably diligent search. They are made parties under the designation "Unknown Owners."

Therefore, the plaintiff demands judgment:

  (a) condemning the property;

  (b) determining and awarding just compensation; and

  (c) granting any other lawful and proper relief.

(Date and sign—See Form 2.)

(Added Apr. 30, 2007, eff. Dec. 1, 2007.)

FORM 70. JUDGMENT ON A JURY VERDICT

(Caption—See Form 1.)

This action was tried by a jury with Judge _____ presiding, and the jury has rendered a verdict.

It is ordered that:

[the plaintiff *name* recover from the defendant *name* the amount of $_____ with interest at the rate of ___%, along with costs.]

[the plaintiff recover nothing, the action be dismissed on the merits, and the defendant *name* recover costs from the plaintiff *name*.]

Date _____

_____

Clerk of Court

(Added Apr. 30, 2007, eff. Dec. 1, 2007.)

FORM 71. JUDGMENT BY THE COURT WITHOUT A JURY

(Caption—See Form 1.)

This action was tried by Judge _____ without a jury and the following decision was reached:

It is ordered that [the plaintiff *name* recover from the defendant *name* the amount of $_____, with prejudgment interest at the rate of ___%, postjudgment interest at the rate of ___%, along with costs.] [the plaintiff recover nothing, the action be dismissed on the merits, and the defendant *name* recover costs from the plaintiff *name*.]

Date_____

_____
Clerk of Court

(Added Apr. 30, 2007, eff. Dec. 1, 2007.)

FORM 80. NOTICE OF A MAGISTRATE JUDGE'S AVAILABILITY

1. A magistrate judge is available under title 28 U.S.C. § 636(c) to conduct the proceedings in this case, including a jury or nonjury trial and the entry of final judgment. But a magistrate judge can be assigned only if all parties voluntarily consent.

2. You may withhold your consent without adverse substantive consequences. The identity of any party consenting or withholding consent will not be disclosed to the judge to whom the case is assigned or to any magistrate judge.

3. If a magistrate judge does hear your case, you may appeal directly to a United States court of appeals as you would if a district judge heard it.

A form called *Consent to an Assignment to a United States Magistrate Judge* is available from the court clerk's office.

(Added Apr. 30, 2007, eff. Dec. 1, 2007.)

FORM 81. CONSENT TO AN ASSIGNMENT
TO A MAGISTRATE JUDGE

(Caption—See Form 1.)

I voluntarily consent to have a United States magistrate judge conduct all further proceedings in this case, including a trial, and order the entry of final judgment. (Return this form to the court clerk—not to a judge or magistrate judge.)

Date_____

_____
Signature of the Party

(Added Apr. 30, 2007, eff. Dec. 1, 2007.)

FORM 82. ORDER OF ASSIGNMENT TO A MAGISTRATE JUDGE

(Caption—See Form 1.)

With the parties' consent it is ordered that this case be assigned to United States Magistrate Judge _____ of this district to conduct all proceedings and enter final judgment in accordance with 28 U.S.C. § 636(c).

Date _____

_____
United States District Judge

(Added Apr. 30, 2007, eff. Dec. 1, 2007.)

SUPPLEMENTAL RULES FOR ADMIRALTY OR MARITIME CLAIMS AND ASSET FORFEITURE ACTIONS

RULE A. SCOPE OF RULES

(1) These Supplemental Rules apply to:

(A) the procedure in admiralty and maritime claims within the meaning of Rule 9(h) with respect to the following remedies:

(i) maritime attachment and garnishment,

(ii) actions in rem,

(iii) possessory, petitory, and partition actions, and

(iv) actions for exoneration from or limitation of liability;

(B) forfeiture actions in rem arising from a federal statute; and

(C) the procedure in statutory condemnation proceedings analogous to maritime actions in rem, whether within the admiralty and maritime jurisdiction or not. Except as otherwise provided, references in these Supplemental Rules to actions in rem include such analogous statutory condemnation proceedings.

(2) The Federal Rules of Civil Procedure also apply to the foregoing proceedings except to the extent that they are inconsistent with these Supplemental Rules.

(Added Feb. 28, 1966, eff. July 1, 1966, and amended Apr. 12, 2006, eff. Dec. 1, 2006.)

RULE B. IN PERSONAM ACTIONS: ATTACHMENT AND GARNISHMENT

(1) **When Available; Complaint, Affidavit, Judicial Authorization, and Process.** In an in personam action:

(a) If a defendant is not found within the district when a verified complaint praying for attachment and the affidavit required by Rule B(1)(b) are filed, a verified complaint may contain a prayer for process to attach the defendant's tangible or intangible personal property—up to the amount sued for—in the hands of garnishees named in the process.

(b) The plaintiff or the plaintiff's attorney must sign and file with the complaint an affidavit stating that, to the affiant's knowledge, or on information and belief, the defendant cannot be found within the district. The court must review the complaint and affidavit and, if the conditions of this Rule B appear to exist, enter an order so stating and authorizing process of attachment and garnishment. The clerk

may issue supplemental process enforcing the court's order upon application without further court order.

(c) If the plaintiff or the plaintiff's attorney certifies that exigent circumstances make court review impracticable, the clerk must issue the summons and process of attachment and garnishment. The plaintiff has the burden in any post-attachment hearing under Rule E(4)(f) to show that exigent circumstances existed.

(d)(i) If the property is a vessel or tangible property on board a vessel, the summons, process, and any supplemental process must be delivered to the marshal for service.

(ii) If the property is other tangible or intangible property, the summons, process, and any supplemental process must be delivered to a person or organization authorized to serve it, who may be (A) a marshal; (B) someone under contract with the United States; (C) someone specially appointed by the court for that purpose; or, (D) in an action brought by the United States, any officer or employee of the United States.

(e) The plaintiff may invoke state-law remedies under Rule 64 for seizure of person or property for the purpose of securing satisfaction of the judgment.

(2) **Notice to Defendant.** No default judgment may be entered except upon proof—which may be by affidavit—that:

(a) the complaint, summons, and process of attachment or garnishment have been served on the defendant in a manner authorized by Rule 4;

(b) the plaintiff or the garnishee has mailed to the defendant the complaint, summons, and process of attachment or garnishment, using any form of mail requiring a return receipt; or

(c) the plaintiff or the garnishee has tried diligently to give notice of the action to the defendant but could not do so.

(3) **Answer.**

(a) **By Garnishee.** The garnishee shall serve an answer, together with answers to any interrogatories served with the complaint, within 21 days after service of process upon the garnishee. Interrogatories to the garnishee may be served with the complaint without leave of court. If the garnishee refuses or neglects to answer on oath as to the debts, credits, or effects of the defendant in the garnishee's hands, or any interrogatories concerning such debts, credits, and effects that may be propounded by the plaintiff, the court may award compulsory process against the garnishee. If the garnishee admits any debts, credits, or effects, they shall be held in the garnishee's hands or paid into the registry of the court, and shall be held in either case subject to the further order of the court.

(b) By Defendant. The defendant shall serve an answer within 30 days after process has been executed, whether by attachment of property or service on the garnishee.

(Added Feb. 28, 1966, eff. July 1, 1966, and amended Apr. 29, 1985, eff. Aug. 1, 1985; Mar. 2, 1987, eff. Aug. 1, 1987; Apr. 17, 2000, eff. Dec. 1, 2000; Apr. 25, 2005, eff. Dec. 1, 2005; Mar. 26, 2009, eff. Dec. 1, 2009.)

RULE C. IN REM ACTIONS: SPECIAL PROVISIONS

(1) When Available. An action in rem may be brought:

(a) To enforce any maritime lien;

(b) Whenever a statute of the United States provides for a maritime action in rem or a proceeding analogous thereto.

Except as otherwise provided by law a party who may proceed in rem may also, or in the alternative, proceed in personam against any person who may be liable.

Statutory provisions exempting vessels or other property owned or possessed by or operated by or for the United States from arrest or seizure are not affected by this rule. When a statute so provides, an action against the United States or an instrumentality thereof may proceed on in rem principles.

(2) Complaint. In an action in rem the complaint must:

(a) be verified;

(b) describe with reasonable particularity the property that is the subject of the action; and

(c) state that the property is within the district or will be within the district while the action is pending.

(3) Judicial Authorization and Process.

(a) Arrest Warrant.

(i) The court must review the complaint and any supporting papers. If the conditions for an in rem action appear to exist, the court must issue an order directing the clerk to issue a warrant for the arrest of the vessel or other property that is the subject of the action.

(ii) If the plaintiff or the plaintiff's attorney certifies that exigent circumstances make court review impracticable, the clerk must promptly issue a summons and a warrant for the arrest of the vessel or other property that is the subject of the action. The plaintiff has the burden in any post-arrest hearing under Rule E(4)(f) to show that exigent circumstances existed.

(b) Service.

(i) If the property that is the subject of the action is a vessel or tangible property on board a vessel, the warrant and any supplemental process must be delivered to the marshal for service.

(ii) If the property that is the subject of the action is other property, tangible or intangible, the warrant and any supplemental process must be delivered to a person or organization authorized to enforce it, who may be: (A) a marshal; (B) someone under contract with the United States; (C) someone specially appointed by the court for that purpose; or, (D) in an action brought by the United States, any officer or employee of the United States.

(c) Deposit in Court. If the property that is the subject of the action consists in whole or in part of freight, the proceeds of property sold, or other intangible property, the clerk must issue—in addition to the warrant—a summons directing any person controlling the property to show cause why it should not be deposited in court to abide the judgment.

(d) Supplemental Process. The clerk may upon application issue supplemental process to enforce the court's order without further court order.

(4) Notice. No notice other than execution of process is required when the property that is the subject of the action has been released under Rule E(5). If the property is not released within 14 days after execution, the plaintiff must promptly—or within the time that the court allows—give public notice of the action and arrest in a newspaper designated by court order and having general circulation in the district, but publication may be terminated if the property is released before publication is completed. The notice must specify the time under Rule C(6) to file a statement of interest in or right against the seized property and to answer. This rule does not affect the notice requirements in an action to foreclose a preferred ship mortgage under 46 U.S.C. §§ 31301 et seq., as amended.

(5) Ancillary Process. In any action in rem in which process has been served as provided by this rule, if any part of the property that is the subject of the action has not been brought within the control of the court because it has been removed or sold, or because it is intangible property in the hands of a person who has not been served with process, the court may, on motion, order any person having possession or control of such property or its proceeds to show cause why it should not be delivered into the custody of the marshal or other person or organization having a warrant for the arrest of the property, or paid into court to abide the judgment; and, after hearing, the court may enter such judgment as law and justice may require.

(6) Responsive Pleading; Interrogatories.

(a) Statement of Interest; Answer. In an action in rem:

(i) a person who asserts a right of possession or any ownership interest in the property that is the subject of the action must file a verified statement of right or interest:

(A) within 14 days after the execution of process, or

(B) within the time that the court allows;

(ii) the statement of right or interest must describe the interest in the property that supports the person's demand for its restitution or right to defend the action;

(iii) an agent, bailee, or attorney must state the authority to file a statement of right or interest on behalf of another; and

(iv) a person who asserts a right of possession or any ownership interest must serve an answer within 21 days after filing the statement of interest or right.

(b) Interrogatories. Interrogatories may be served with the complaint in an in rem action without leave of court. Answers to the interrogatories must be served with the answer to the complaint.

(Added Feb. 28, 1966, eff. July 1, 1966, and amended Apr. 29, 1985, eff. Aug. 1, 1985; Mar. 2, 1987, eff. Aug. 1, 1987; Apr. 30, 1991, eff. Dec. 1, 1991; Apr. 17, 2000, eff. Dec. 1, 2000; Apr. 29, 2002, eff. Dec. 1, 2002; Apr. 25, 2005, eff. Dec. 1, 2005; Apr. 12, 2006, eff. Dec. 1, 2006; Apr. 23, 2008, eff. Dec. 1, 2008; Mar. 26, 2009, eff. Dec. 1, 2009.)

RULE D. POSSESSORY, PETITORY, AND PARTITION ACTIONS

In all actions for possession, partition, and to try title maintainable according to the course of the admiralty practice with respect to a vessel, in all actions so maintainable with respect to the possession of cargo or other maritime property, and in all actions by one or more part owners against the others to obtain security for the return of the vessel from any voyage undertaken without their consent, or by one or more part owners against the others to obtain possession of the vessel for any voyage on giving security for its safe return, the process shall be by a warrant of arrest of the vessel, cargo, or other property, and by

notice in the manner provided by Rule B(2) to the adverse party or parties.

(Added Feb. 28, 1966, eff. July 1, 1966.)

RULE E. ACTIONS IN REM AND QUASI IN REM: GENERAL PROVISIONS

(1) Applicability. Except as otherwise provided, this rule applies to actions in personam with process of maritime attachment and garnishment, actions in rem, and petitory, possessory, and partition actions, supplementing Rules B, C, and D.

(2) Complaint; Security.

(a) Complaint. In actions to which this rule is applicable the complaint shall state the circumstances from which the claim arises with such particularity that the defendant or claimant will be able, without moving for a more definite statement, to commence an investigation of the facts and to frame a responsive pleading.

(b) Security for Costs. Subject to the provisions of Rule 54(d) and of relevant statutes, the court may, on the filing of the complaint or on the appearance of any defendant, claimant, or any other party, or at any later time, require the plaintiff, defendant, claimant, or other party to give security, or additional security, in such sum as the court shall direct to pay all costs and expenses that shall be awarded against the party by any interlocutory order or by the final judgment, or on appeal by any appellate court.

(3) Process.

(a) In admiralty and maritime proceedings process in rem or of maritime attachment and garnishment may be served only within the district.

(b) Issuance and Delivery. Issuance and delivery of process in rem, or of maritime attachment and garnishment, shall be held in abeyance if the plaintiff so requests.

(4) Execution of Process; Marshal's Return; Custody of Property; Procedures for Release.

(a) In General. Upon issuance and delivery of the process, or, in the case of summons with process of attachment and garnishment, when it appears that the defendant cannot be found within the district, the marshal or other person or organization having a warrant shall forthwith execute the process in accordance with this subdivision (4), making due and prompt return.

(b) Tangible Property. If tangible property is to be attached or arrested, the marshal or other person or organization having the warrant shall take it into the marshal's possession for safe custody. If the character or situation of the property is such that the taking of actual possession is impracticable, the marshal or other person executing the process shall affix a copy thereof to the property in a conspicuous place and leave a copy of the complaint and process with the person having possession or the person's agent. In furtherance of the marshal's custody of any vessel the marshal is authorized to make a written request to the collector of customs not to grant clearance to such vessel until notified by the marshal or deputy marshal or by the clerk that the vessel has been released in accordance with these rules.

(c) Intangible Property. If intangible property is to be attached or arrested the marshal or other person or organization having the warrant shall execute the process by leaving with the garnishee or other obligor a copy of the complaint and process requiring the garnishee or other obligor to answer as provided in Rules B(3)(a) and C(6); or the marshal may accept for payment into the registry of the court the amount owed to the extent of the amount claimed by the plaintiff with interest and costs, in which event the garnishee or other obligor shall not be required to answer unless alias process shall be served.

(d) Directions With Respect to Property in Custody. The marshal or other person or organization having the warrant may at any time apply to the court for directions with respect to property that has been attached or arrested, and shall give notice of such application to any or all of the parties as the court may direct.

(e) Expenses of Seizing and Keeping Property; Deposit. These rules do not alter the provisions of Title 28, U.S.C., § 1921, as amended, relative to the expenses of seizing and keeping property attached or arrested and to the requirement of deposits to cover such expenses.

(f) Procedure for Release From Arrest or Attachment. Whenever property is arrested or attached, any person claiming an interest in it shall be entitled to a prompt hearing at which the plaintiff shall be required to show why the arrest or attachment should not be vacated or other relief granted consistent with these rules. This subdivision shall have no application to suits for seamen's wages when process is issued upon a certification of sufficient cause filed pursuant to Title 46, U.S.C. §§ 603 and 604[2] or to actions by the United States for forfeitures for violation of any statute of the United States.

(5) Release of Property.

(a) Special Bond. Whenever process of maritime attachment and garnishment or process in rem is issued the execution of such process shall be stayed, or the property released, on the giving of security, to be approved by the court or clerk, or by stipulation of the parties, conditioned to answer the judgment of the court or of any appellate court.

The parties may stipulate the amount and nature of such security. In the event of the inability or refusal of the parties so to stipulate the court shall fix the principal sum of the bond or stipulation at an amount sufficient to cover the amount of the plaintiff's claim fairly stated with accrued interest and costs; but the principal sum shall in no event exceed (i) twice the amount of the plaintiff's claim or (ii) the value of the property on due appraisement, whichever is smaller. The bond or stipulation shall be conditioned for the payment of the principal sum and interest thereon at 6 per cent per annum.

(b) General Bond. The owner of any vessel may file a general bond or stipulation, with sufficient surety, to be approved by the court, conditioned to answer the judgment of such court in all or any actions that may be brought thereafter in such court in which the vessel is attached or arrested. Thereupon the execution of all such process against such vessel shall be stayed so long as the amount secured by such bond or stipulation is at least double the aggregate amount claimed by plaintiffs in all actions begun and pending in which such vessel has been attached or arrested. Judgments and remedies may be had on such bond or stipulation as if a special bond or stipulation had been filed in each of such actions. The district court may make necessary orders to carry this rule into effect, particularly as to the giving of proper notice of any action against or attachment of a vessel for which a general bond has been filed. Such bond or stipulation shall be indorsed by the clerk with a minute of the actions wherein process is so stayed. Further security may be required by the court at any time.

If a special bond or stipulation is given in a particular case, the liability on the general bond or stipulation shall cease as to that case.

(c) Release by Consent or Stipulation; Order of Court or Clerk; Costs. Any vessel, cargo, or other property in the custody of the marshal or other person or organization having the warrant may be released forthwith upon the marshal's acceptance and approval of a stipulation, bond, or other security, signed by the party on whose behalf the property is detained or the party's attorney and expressly authorizing such release, if all costs and charges of the court and its officers shall have first been paid. Otherwise no property in the custody of the marshal, other person or organization having the warrant, or other officer of the court shall be released without an order of the court; but such order may be entered as of course by the clerk, upon the giving of approved security as provided by law and these rules, or upon the dismissal or discontinuance of the action; but the marshal or other person or organization having the warrant shall not deliver any property so released until the costs and charges of the officers of the court shall first have been paid.

(d) Possessory, Petitory, and Partition Actions. The foregoing provisions of this subdivision (5) do not apply to petitory, possessory, and partition actions. In such cases the property arrested shall be released only by order of the court, on such terms and conditions and on the giving of such security as the court may require.

(6) Reduction or Impairment of Security. Whenever security is taken the court may, on motion and hearing, for good cause shown, reduce the amount of security given; and if the surety shall be or become insufficient, new or additional sureties may be required on motion and hearing.

(7) Security on Counterclaim.

(a) When a person who has given security for damages in the original action asserts a counterclaim that arises from the transaction or occurrence that is the subject of the original action, a plaintiff for whose benefit the security has been given must give security for damages demanded in the counterclaim unless the court for cause shown, directs otherwise. Proceedings on the original claim must be stayed until this security is given unless the court directs otherwise.

(b) The plaintiff is required to give security under Rule E(7)(a) when the United States or its corporate instrumentality counterclaims and would have been required to give security to respond in damages if a private party but is relieved by law from giving security.

(8) Restricted Appearance. An appearance to defend against an admiralty and maritime claim with respect to which there has issued process in rem, or process of attachment and garnishment, may be expressly restricted to the defense of such claim, and in that event is not an appearance for the purposes of any other claim with respect to which such process is not available or has not been served.

(9) Disposition of Property; Sales.

(a) Interlocutory Sales; Delivery.

(i) On application of a party, the marshal, or other person having custody of the property, the court may order all or part of the property sold— with the sales proceeds, or as much of them as will satisfy the judgment, paid into court to await further orders of the court—if:

(A) the attached or arrested property is perishable, or liable to deterioration, decay, or injury by being detained in custody pending the action;

(B) the expense of keeping the property is excessive or disproportionate; or

(C) there is an unreasonable delay in securing release of the property.

(ii) In the circumstances described in Rule E(9)(a)(i), the court, on motion by a defendant or a person filing a statement of interest or right under Rule C(6), may order that the property, rather than being sold, be delivered to the movant upon giving security under these rules.

(b) Sales; Proceeds. All sales of property shall be made by the marshal or a deputy marshal, or by other person or organization having the warrant, or by any other person assigned by the court where the marshal or other person or organization having the warrant is a party in interest; and the proceeds of sale shall be forthwith paid into the registry of the court to be disposed of according to law.

(10) Preservation of Property. When the owner or another person remains in possession of property attached or arrested under the provisions of Rule E(4)(b) that permit execution of process without taking actual possession, the court, on a party's motion or on its own, may enter any order necessary to preserve the property and to prevent its removal.

(Added Feb. 28, 1966, eff. July 1, 1966, and amended Apr. 29, 1985, eff. Aug. 1, 1985; Mar. 2, 1987, eff. Aug. 1, 1987; Apr. 30, 1991, eff. Dec. 1, 1991; Apr. 17, 2000, eff. Dec. 1, 2000; Apr. 12, 2006, eff. Dec. 1, 2006.)

2 Repealed by Pub. L. 98–89, § 4(b), Aug. 26, 1983, 97 Stat. 600, section 1 of which enacted Title 46, Shipping.

RULE F. LIMITATION OF LIABILITY

(1) Time for Filing Complaint; Security. Not later than six months after receipt of a claim in writing, any vessel owner may file a complaint in the appropriate district court, as provided in subdivision (9) of this rule, for limitation of liability pursuant to statute. The owner (a) shall deposit with the court, for the benefit of claimants, a sum equal to the amount or value of the owner's interest in the vessel and pending freight, or approved security therefor, and in addition such sums, or approved security therefor, as the court may from time to time fix as necessary to carry out the provisions of the statutes as amended; or (b) at the owner's option shall transfer to a trustee to be appointed by the court, for the benefit of claimants, the owner's interest in the vessel and pending freight, together with such sums, or approved security therefor, as the court may from time to time fix as necessary to carry out the provisions of the statutes as amended. The plaintiff shall also give security for costs and, if the plaintiff elects to give security, for interest at the rate of 6 percent per annum from the date of the security.

(2) Complaint. The complaint shall set forth the facts on the basis of which the right to limit liability is asserted and all facts necessary to enable the court to determine the amount to which the owner's liability shall be limited. The complaint may demand exoneration from as well as limitation of liability. It shall state the voyage if any, on which the demands sought to be limited arose, with the date and place of its termination; the amount of all demands including all unsatisfied liens or claims of lien, in contract or in tort or otherwise, arising on that voyage, so far as known to the plaintiff, and what actions and proceedings, if any, are pending thereon; whether the vessel was damaged, lost, or abandoned, and, if so, when and where; the value of the vessel at the close of the voyage or, in case of wreck, the value of her wreckage, strippings, or proceeds, if any, and where and in whose possession they are; and the amount of any pending freight recovered or recoverable. If the plaintiff elects to transfer the plaintiff's interest in the vessel to a trustee, the complaint must further show any prior paramount liens thereon, and what voyages or trips, if any, she has made since the voyage or trip on which the claims sought to be limited arose, and any existing liens arising upon any such subsequent voyage or trip, with the amounts and causes thereof, and the names and addresses of the lienors, so far as known; and whether the vessel sustained any injury upon or by reason of such subsequent voyage or trip.

(3) Claims Against Owner; Injunction. Upon compliance by the owner with the requirements of subdivision (1) of this rule all claims and proceedings against the owner or the owner's property with respect to the matter in question shall cease. On application of the plaintiff the court shall enjoin the further prosecution of any action or proceeding against the plaintiff or the plaintiff's property with respect to any claim subject to limitation in the action.

(4) Notice to Claimants. Upon the owner's compliance with subdivision (1) of this rule the court shall issue a notice to all persons asserting claims with respect to which the complaint seeks limitation, admonishing them to file their respective claims with the clerk of the court and to serve on the attorneys for the plaintiff a copy thereof on or before a date to be named in the notice. The date so fixed shall not be less than 30 days after issuance of the notice. For cause shown, the court may enlarge the time within which claims may be filed. The notice shall be published in such newspaper or newspapers as the court may direct once a week for four successive weeks prior to the date fixed for the filing of claims. The plaintiff not later than the day of second publication shall also mail a copy of the notice to every person known to have made any claim against the vessel or the plaintiff arising out of the voyage or trip on which the claims sought to be limited arose. In cases involving death a copy of such notice shall be mailed to the decedent at the decedent's last known address, and also to any person who shall be known to have made any claim on account of such death.

(5) Claims and Answer. Claims shall be filed and served on or before the date specified in the notice provided for in subdivision (4) of this rule. Each claim shall specify the facts upon which the claimant relies in support of the claim, the items thereof, and the dates on which the same accrued. If a claimant desires to contest either the right to exoneration from or the right to limitation of liability the claimant shall file and serve an answer to the complaint unless the claim has included an answer.

(6) Information to be Given Claimants. Within 30 days after the date specified in the notice for filing claims, or within such time as the court thereafter may allow, the plaintiff shall mail to the attorney for each claimant (or if the claimant has no attorney to the claimant) a list setting forth (a) the name of each claimant, (b) the name and address of the claimant's attorney (if the claimant is known to have one), (c) the nature of the claim, i.e., whether property loss, property damage, death, personal injury etc., and (d) the amount thereof.

(7) Insufficiency of Fund or Security. Any claimant may by motion demand that the funds deposited in court or the security given by the plaintiff be increased on the ground that they are less than the value of the plaintiff's interest in the vessel and pending freight. Thereupon the court shall cause due appraisement to be made of the value of the plaintiff's interest in the vessel and pending freight; and if the court finds that the deposit or security is either insufficient or excessive it shall order its increase or reduction. In like manner any claimant may demand that the deposit or security be increased on the ground that it is insufficient to carry out the provisions of the statutes relating to claims in respect of loss of life or bodily injury; and, after notice and hearing, the court may similarly order that the deposit or security be increased or reduced.

(8) Objections to Claims: Distribution of Fund. Any interested party may question or controvert any claim without filing an objection thereto. Upon determination of liability the fund deposited or secured, or the proceeds of the vessel and pending freight, shall be divided pro rata, subject to all relevant provisions of law, among the several claimants in proportion to the amounts of their respective claims, duly proved, saving, however, to all parties any priority to which they may be legally entitled.

(9) Venue; Transfer. The complaint shall be filed in any district in which the vessel has been attached or arrested to answer for any claim with respect to which the plaintiff seeks to limit liability; or, if the vessel has not been attached or arrested, then in any district in which the owner has been sued with respect to any such claim. When the vessel has not been attached or arrested to answer the matters aforesaid, and suit has not been commenced against the owner, the proceedings may be had in the district in which the vessel may be, but if the vessel is not within any district and no suit has been commenced in any district, then the complaint may be filed in any district.

For the convenience of parties and witnesses, in the interest of justice, the court may transfer the action to any district; if venue is wrongly laid the court shall dismiss or, if it be in the interest of justice, transfer the action to any district in which it could have been brought. If the vessel shall have been sold, the proceeds shall represent the vessel for the purposes of these rules.

(Added Feb. 28, 1966, eff. July 1, 1966, and amended Mar. 2, 1987, eff. Aug. 1, 1987.)

RULE G. FORFEITURE ACTIONS IN REM

(1) **Scope.** This rule governs a forfeiture action in rem arising from a federal statute. To the extent that this rule does not address an issue, Supplemental Rules C and E and the Federal Rules of Civil Procedure also apply.

(2) **Complaint.** The complaint must:

(a) be verified;

(b) state the grounds for subject-matter jurisdiction, in rem jurisdiction over the defendant property, and venue;

(c) describe the property with reasonable particularity;

(d) if the property is tangible, state its location when any seizure occurred and—if different—its location when the action is filed;

(e) identify the statute under which the forfeiture action is brought; and

(f) state sufficiently detailed facts to support a reasonable belief that the government will be able to meet its burden of proof at trial.

(3) **Judicial Authorization and Process.**

(a) **Real Property.** If the defendant is real property, the government must proceed under 18 U.S.C. § 985.

(b) **Other Property; Arrest Warrant.** If the defendant is not real property:

(i) the clerk must issue a warrant to arrest the property if it is in the government's possession, custody, or control;

(ii) the court—on finding probable cause—must issue a warrant to arrest the property if it is not in the government's possession, custody, or control and is not subject to a judicial restraining order; and

(iii) a warrant is not necessary if the property is subject to a judicial restraining order.

(c) **Execution of Process.**

(i) The warrant and any supplemental process must be delivered to a person or organization authorized to execute it, who may be: (A) a marshal or any other United States officer or employee; (B) someone under contract with the United States; or (C) someone specially appointed by the court for that purpose.

(ii) The authorized person or organization must execute the warrant and any supplemental process on property in the United States as soon as practicable unless:

(A) the property is in the government's possession, custody, or control; or

(B) the court orders a different time when the complaint is under seal, the action is stayed before the warrant and supplemental process are executed, or the court finds other good cause.

(iii) The warrant and any supplemental process may be executed within the district or, when authorized by statute, outside the district.

(iv) If executing a warrant on property outside the United States is required, the warrant may be transmitted to an appropriate authority for serving process where the property is located.

(4) **Notice.**

(a) **Notice by Publication.**

(i) **When Publication Is Required.** A judgment of forfeiture may be entered only if the government has published notice of the action within a reasonable time after filing the complaint or at a time the court orders. But notice need not be published if:

(A) the defendant property is worth less than $1,000 and direct notice is sent under Rule G(4)(b) to every person the government can reasonably identify as a potential claimant; or

(B) the court finds that the cost of publication exceeds the property's value and that other means of notice would satisfy due process.

(ii) **Content of the Notice.** Unless the court orders otherwise, the notice must:

(A) describe the property with reasonable particularity;

(B) state the times under Rule G(5) to file a claim and to answer; and

(C) name the government attorney to be served with the claim and answer.

(iii) **Frequency of Publication.** Published notice must appear:

(A) once a week for three consecutive weeks; or

(B) only once if, before the action was filed, notice of nonjudicial forfeiture of the same property was published on an official internet government forfeiture site for at least 30 consecutive days, or in a newspaper of general circulation for three consecutive weeks in a district where publication is authorized under Rule G(4)(a)(iv).

(iv) Means of Publication. The government should select from the following options a means of publication reasonably calculated to notify potential claimants of the action:

(A) if the property is in the United States, publication in a newspaper generally circulated in the district where the action is filed, where the property was seized, or where property that was not seized is located;

(B) if the property is outside the United States, publication in a newspaper generally circulated in a district where the action is filed, in a newspaper generally circulated in the country where the property is located, or in legal notices published and generally circulated in the country where the property is located; or

(C) instead of (A) or (B), posting a notice on an official internet government forfeiture site for at least 30 consecutive days.

(b) Notice to Known Potential Claimants.

(i) Direct Notice Required. The government must send notice of the action and a copy of the complaint to any person who reasonably appears to be a potential claimant on the facts known to the government before the end of the time for filing a claim under Rule G(5)(a)(ii)(B).

(ii) Content of the Notice. The notice must state:

(A) the date when the notice is sent;

(B) a deadline for filing a claim, at least 35 days after the notice is sent;

(C) that an answer or a motion under Rule 12 must be filed no later than 21 days after filing the claim; and

(D) the name of the government attorney to be served with the claim and answer.

(iii) Sending Notice.

(A) The notice must be sent by means reasonably calculated to reach the potential claimant.

(B) Notice may be sent to the potential claimant or to the attorney representing the potential claimant with respect to the seizure of the property or in a related investigation, administrative forfeiture proceeding, or criminal case.

(C) Notice sent to a potential claimant who is incarcerated must be sent to the place of incarceration.

(D) Notice to a person arrested in connection with an offense giving rise to the forfeiture who is not incarcerated when notice is sent may be sent to the address that person last gave to the agency that arrested or released the person.

(E) Notice to a person from whom the property was seized who is not incarcerated when notice is sent may be sent to the last address that person gave to the agency that seized the property.

(iv) When Notice Is Sent. Notice by the following means is sent on the date when it is placed in the mail, delivered to a commercial carrier, or sent by electronic mail.

(v) Actual Notice. A potential claimant who had actual notice of a forfeiture action may not oppose or seek relief from forfeiture because of the government's failure to send the required notice.

(5) Responsive Pleadings.

(a) Filing a Claim.

(i) A person who asserts an interest in the defendant property may contest the forfeiture by filing a claim in the court where the action is pending. The claim must:

(A) identify the specific property claimed;

(B) identify the claimant and state the claimant's interest in the property;

(C) be signed by the claimant under penalty of perjury; and

(D) be served on the government attorney designated under Rule G(4)(a)(ii)(C) or (b)(ii)(D).

(ii) Unless the court for good cause sets a different time, the claim must be filed:

(A) by the time stated in a direct notice sent under Rule G(4)(b);

(B) if notice was published but direct notice was not sent to the claimant or the claimant's attorney, no later than 30 days after final publication of newspaper notice or legal notice under Rule G(4)(a) or no later than 60 days after the first day of publication on an official internet government forfeiture site; or

(C) if notice was not published and direct notice was not sent to the claimant or the claimant's attorney:

(1) if the property was in the government's possession, custody, or control when the complaint was filed, no later than 60 days after the filing, not counting any time when the complaint was under seal or when the action was stayed before execution of a warrant issued under Rule G(3)(b); or

(2) if the property was not in the government's possession, custody, or control when the complaint was filed, no later than 60 days after the government complied with 18 U.S.C. § 985(c) as to real property, or 60 days after process was executed on the property under Rule G(3).

(iii) A claim filed by a person asserting an interest as a bailee must identify the bailor, and if filed on the bailor's behalf must state the authority to do so.

(b) **Answer.** A claimant must serve and file an answer to the complaint or a motion under Rule 12 within 21 days after filing the claim. A claimant waives an objection to in rem jurisdiction or to venue if the objection is not made by motion or stated in the answer.

(6) **Special Interrogatories.**

(a) **Time and Scope.** The government may serve special interrogatories limited to the claimant's identity and relationship to the defendant property without the court's leave at any time after the claim is filed and before discovery is closed. But if the claimant serves a motion to dismiss the action, the government must serve the interrogatories within 21 days after the motion is served.

(b) **Answers or Objections.** Answers or objections to these interrogatories must be served within 21 days after the interrogatories are served.

(c) **Government's Response Deferred.** The government need not respond to a claimant's motion to dismiss the action under Rule G(8)(b) until 21 days after the claimant has answered these interrogatories.

(7) **Preserving, Preventing Criminal Use, and Disposing of Property; Sales.**

(a) **Preserving and Preventing Criminal Use of Property.** When the government does not have actual possession of the defendant property the court, on motion or on its own, may enter any order necessary to preserve the property, to prevent its removal or encumbrance, or to prevent its use in a criminal offense.

(b) **Interlocutory Sale or Delivery.**

(i) **Order to Sell.** On motion by a party or a person having custody of the property, the court may order all or part of the property sold if:

(A) the property is perishable or at risk of deterioration, decay, or injury by being detained in custody pending the action;

(B) the expense of keeping the property is excessive or is disproportionate to its fair market value;

(C) the property is subject to a mortgage or to taxes on which the owner is in default; or

(D) the court finds other good cause.

(ii) **Who Makes the Sale.** A sale must be made by a United States agency that has authority to sell the property, by the agency's contractor, or by any person the court designates.

(iii) **Sale Procedures.** The sale is governed by 28 U.S.C. §§ 2001, 2002, and 2004, unless all parties, with the court's approval, agree to the sale, aspects of the sale, or different procedures.

(iv) **Sale Proceeds.** Sale proceeds are a substitute res subject to forfeiture in place of the property that was sold. The proceeds must be held in an interest-bearing account maintained by the United States pending the conclusion of the forfeiture action.

(v) **Delivery on a Claimant's Motion.** The court may order that the property be delivered to the claimant pending the conclusion of the action if the claimant shows circumstances that would permit sale under Rule G(7)(b)(i) and gives security under these rules.

(c) **Disposing of Forfeited Property.** Upon entry of a forfeiture judgment, the property or proceeds from selling the property must be disposed of as provided by law.

(8) **Motions.**

(a) **Motion To Suppress Use of the Property as Evidence.** If the defendant property was seized, a party with standing to contest the lawfulness of the seizure may move to suppress use of the property as evidence. Suppression does not affect forfeiture of the property based on independently derived evidence.

(b) **Motion To Dismiss the Action.**

(i) A claimant who establishes standing to contest forfeiture may move to dismiss the action under Rule 12(b).

(ii) In an action governed by 18 U.S.C. § 983(a)(3)(D) the complaint may not be dismissed on the ground that the government did not have adequate evidence at the time the complaint was filed to establish the forfeitability of the property. The sufficiency of the complaint is governed by Rule G(2).

(c) **Motion To Strike a Claim or Answer.**

(i) At any time before trial, the government may move to strike a claim or answer:

(A) for failing to comply with Rule G(5) or (6), or

(B) because the claimant lacks standing.

(ii) The motion:

(A) must be decided before any motion by the claimant to dismiss the action; and

95

(B) may be presented as a motion for judgment on the pleadings or as a motion to determine after a hearing or by summary judgment whether the claimant can carry the burden of establishing standing by a preponderance of the evidence.

(d) Petition To Release Property.

(i) If a United States agency or an agency's contractor holds property for judicial or nonjudicial forfeiture under a statute governed by 18 U.S.C. § 983(f), a person who has filed a claim to the property may petition for its release under § 983(f).

(ii) If a petition for release is filed before a judicial forfeiture action is filed against the property, the petition may be filed either in the district where the property was seized or in the district where a warrant to seize the property issued. If a judicial forfeiture action against the property is later filed in another district—or if the government shows that the action will be filed in another district—the petition may be transferred to that district under 28 U.S.C. § 1404.

(e) Excessive Fines. A claimant may seek to mitigate a forfeiture under the Excessive Fines Clause of the Eighth Amendment by motion for summary judgment or by motion made after entry of a forfeiture judgment if:

(i) the claimant has pleaded the defense under Rule 8; and

(ii) the parties have had the opportunity to conduct civil discovery on the defense.

(9) Trial. Trial is to the court unless any party demands trial by jury under Rule 38.

(Added Apr. 12, 2006, eff. Dec. 1, 2006, and amended Mar. 26, 2009, eff. Dec. 1, 2009.)

INDEX TO
FEDERAL RULES OF CIVIL PROCEDURE

FEDERAL RULES OF EVIDENCE

Including Amendments Effective December 1, 2014

ARTICLE I. GENERAL PROVISIONS

RULE 101. SCOPE; DEFINITIONS

(a) Scope. These rules apply to proceedings in United States courts. The specific courts and proceedings to which the rules apply, along with exceptions, are set out in Rule 1101.

(b) Definitions. In these rules:

(1) "civil case" means a civil action or proceeding;

(2) "criminal case" includes a criminal proceeding;

(3) "public office" includes a public agency;

(4) "record" includes a memorandum, report, or data compilation;

(5) a "rule prescribed by the Supreme Court" means a rule adopted by the Supreme Court under statutory authority; and

(6) a reference to any kind of written material or any other medium includes electronically stored information.

(Pub.L. 93–595, § 1, Jan. 2, 1975, 88 Stat. 1929; Mar. 2, 1987, eff. Oct. 1, 1987; Apr. 25, 1988, eff. Nov. 1, 1988; Apr. 22, 1993, eff. Dec. 1, 1993; Apr. 26, 2011, eff. Dec. 1, 2011.)

RULE 102. PURPOSE

These rules should be construed so as to administer every proceeding fairly, eliminate unjustifiable expense and delay, and promote the development of evidence law, to the end of ascertaining the truth and securing a just determination.

(Pub.L. 93–595, § 1, Jan. 2, 1975, 88 Stat.1929; Apr. 26, 2011, eff. Dec. 1, 2011.)

RULE 103. RULINGS ON EVIDENCE

(a) Preserving a Claim of Error. A party may claim error in a ruling to admit or exclude evidence only if the error affects a substantial right of the party and:

(1) if the ruling admits evidence, a party, on the record:

(A) timely objects or moves to strike; and

(B) states the specific ground, unless it was apparent from the context; or

(2) if the ruling excludes evidence, a party informs the court of its substance by an offer of proof, unless the substance was apparent from the context.

(b) Not Needing to Renew an Objection or Offer of Proof. Once the court rules definitively on the record—either before or at trial—a party need not renew an objection or offer of proof to preserve a claim of error for appeal.

(c) Court's Statement About the Ruling; Directing an Offer of Proof. The court may make any statement about the character or form of the evidence, the objection made, and the ruling. The court may direct that an offer of proof be made in question-and-answer form.

(d) Preventing the Jury from Hearing Inadmissible Evidence. To the extent practicable, the court must conduct a jury trial so that inadmissible evidence is not suggested to the jury by any means.

(e) Taking Notice of Plain Error. A court may take notice of a plain error affecting a substantial right, even if the claim of error was not properly preserved.

(Pub.L. 93–595, § 1, Jan. 2, 1975, 88 Stat. 1929; Apr. 17, 2000, eff. Dec. 1, 2000; Apr. 26, 2011, eff. Dec. 1, 2011.)

RULE 104. PRELIMINARY QUESTIONS

(a) In General. The court must decide any preliminary question about whether a witness is qualified, a privilege exists, or evidence is admissible. In so deciding, the court is not bound by evidence rules, except those on privilege.

(b) Relevance That Depends on a Fact. When the relevance of evidence depends on whether a fact exists, proof must be introduced sufficient to support a finding that the fact does exist. The court may admit the proposed evidence on the condition that the proof be introduced later.

(c) Conducting a Hearing So That the Jury Cannot Hear It. The court must conduct any hearing on a preliminary question so that the jury cannot hear it if:

(1) the hearing involves the admissibility of a confession;

(2) a defendant in a criminal case is a witness and so requests; or

(3) justice so requires.

(d) Cross–Examining a Defendant in a Criminal Case. By testifying on a preliminary question, a defendant in a criminal case does not become subject to cross-examination on other issues in the case.

(e) Evidence Relevant to Weight and Credibility. This rule does not limit a party's right to introduce before the jury evidence that is relevant to the weight or credibility of other evidence.

(Pub.L. 93–595, § 1, Jan. 2, 1975, 88 Stat.1930; Mar. 2, 1987, eff. Oct. 1, 1987; Apr. 26, 2011, eff. Dec. 1, 2011.)

RULE 105. LIMITING EVIDENCE THAT IS NOT ADMISSIBLE AGAINST OTHER PARTIES OR FOR OTHER PURPOSES

If the court admits evidence that is admissible against a party or for a purpose—but not against another party or for another purpose—the court, on timely request, must restrict the evidence to its proper scope and instruct the jury accordingly.

(Pub.L. 93–595, § 1, Jan. 2, 1975, 88 Stat. 1930; Apr. 26, 2011, eff. Dec. 1, 2011.)

RULE 106. REMAINDER OF OR RELATED WRITINGS OR RECORDED STATEMENTS

If a party introduces all or part of a writing or recorded statement, an adverse party may require the introduction, at that time, of any other part—or any other writing or recorded statement—that in fairness ought to be considered at the same time.

(Pub.L. 93–595, § 1, Jan. 2, 1975, 88 Stat. 1930; Mar. 2, 1987, eff. Oct. 1, 1987; Apr. 26, 2011, eff. Dec. 1, 2011.)

ARTICLE II. JUDICIAL NOTICE

RULE 201. JUDICIAL NOTICE OF ADJUDICATIVE FACTS

(a) Scope. This rule governs judicial notice of an adjudicative fact only, not a legislative fact.

(b) Kinds of Facts That May Be Judicially Noticed. The court may judicially notice a fact that is not subject to reasonable dispute because it:

(1) is generally known within the trial court's territorial jurisdiction; or

(2) can be accurately and readily determined from sources whose accuracy cannot reasonably be questioned.

(c) Taking Notice. The court:

(1) may take judicial notice on its own; or

(2) must take judicial notice if a party requests it and the court is supplied with the necessary information.

(d) Timing. The court may take judicial notice at any stage of the proceeding.

(e) Opportunity to Be Heard. On timely request, a party is entitled to be heard on the propriety of taking judicial notice and the nature of the fact to be noticed. If the court takes judicial notice before notifying a party, the party, on request, is still entitled to be heard.

(f) Instructing the Jury. In a civil case, the court must instruct the jury to accept the noticed fact as conclusive. In a criminal case, the court must instruct the jury that it may or may not accept the noticed fact as conclusive.

(Pub.L. 93–595, § 1, Jan. 2, 1975, 88 Stat. 1930; Apr. 26, 2011, eff. Dec. 1, 2011.)

ARTICLE III. PRESUMPTIONS IN CIVIL CASES

RULE 301. PRESUMPTIONS IN CIVIL CASES GENERALLY

In a civil case, unless a federal statute or these rules provide otherwise, the party against whom a presumption is directed has the burden of producing evidence to rebut the presumption. But this rule does not shift the burden of persuasion, which remains on the party who had it originally.

(Pub.L. 93–595, § 1, Jan. 2, 1975, 88 Stat. 1931; Apr. 26, 2011, eff. Dec. 1, 2011.)

RULE 302. APPLYING STATE LAW TO PRESUMPTIONS IN CIVIL CASES

In a civil case, state law governs the effect of a presumption regarding a claim or defense for which state law supplies the rule of decision.

(Pub.L. 93–595, § 1, Jan. 2, 1975, 88 Stat. 1931; Apr. 26, 2011, eff. Dec. 1, 2011.)

ARTICLE IV. RELEVANCE AND ITS LIMITS

RULE 401. TEST FOR RELEVANT EVIDENCE

Evidence is relevant if:

(a) it has any tendency to make a fact more or less probable than it would be without the evidence; and

(b) the fact is of consequence in determining the action.

(Pub.L. 93–595, § 1, Jan. 2, 1975, 88 Stat.1931; Apr. 26, 2011, eff. Dec. 1, 2011.)

RULE 402. GENERAL ADMISSIBILITY OF RELEVANT EVIDENCE

Relevant evidence is admissible unless any of the following provides otherwise:

- the United States Constitution;
- a federal statute;
- these rules; or
- other rules prescribed by the Supreme Court.

Irrelevant evidence is not admissible.

(Pub.L. 93–595, § 1, Jan. 2, 1975, 88 Stat. 1931; Apr. 26, 2011, eff. Dec. 1, 2011.)

RULE 403. EXCLUDING RELEVANT EVIDENCE FOR PREJUDICE, CONFUSION, WASTE OF TIME, OR OTHER REASONS

The court may exclude relevant evidence if its probative value is substantially outweighed by a danger of one or more of the following: unfair prejudice, confusing the issues, misleading the jury, undue delay, wasting time, or needlessly presenting cumulative evidence.

(Pub.L. 93–595, § 1, Jan. 2, 1975, 88 Stat. 1932; Apr. 26, 2011, eff. Dec. 1, 2011.)

RULE 404. CHARACTER EVIDENCE; CRIMES OR OTHER ACTS

(a) Character Evidence.

(1) *Prohibited Uses.* Evidence of a person's character or character trait is not admissible to prove that on a particular occasion the person acted in accordance with the character or trait.

(2) *Exceptions for a Defendant or Victim in a Criminal Case.* The following exceptions apply in a criminal case:

(A) a defendant may offer evidence of the defendant's pertinent trait, and if the evidence is admitted, the prosecutor may offer evidence to rebut it;

(B) subject to the limitations in Rule 412, a defendant may offer evidence of an alleged victim's pertinent trait, and if the evidence is admitted, the prosecutor may:

(i) offer evidence to rebut it; and

(ii) offer evidence of the defendant's same trait; and

(C) in a homicide case, the prosecutor may offer evidence of the alleged victim's trait of peacefulness to rebut evidence that the victim was the first aggressor.

(3) *Exceptions for a Witness.* Evidence of a witness's character may be admitted under Rules 607, 608, and 609.

(b) Crimes, Wrongs, or Other Acts.

(1) *Prohibited Uses.* Evidence of a crime, wrong, or other act is not admissible to prove a person's character in order to show that on a particular occasion the person acted in accordance with the character.

(2) ***Permitted Uses; Notice in a Criminal Case.*** This evidence may be admissible for another purpose, such as proving motive, opportunity, intent, preparation, plan, knowledge, identity, absence of mistake, or lack of accident. On request by a defendant in a criminal case, the prosecutor must:

(A) provide reasonable notice of the general nature of any such evidence that the prosecutor intends to offer at trial; and

(B) do so before trial—or during trial if the court, for good cause, excuses lack of pretrial notice.

(Pub.L. 93–595, § 1, Jan. 2, 1975, 88 Stat.1932; Mar. 2, 1987, eff. Oct. 1, 1987; Apr. 30, 1991, eff. Dec. 1, 1991; Apr. 17, 2000, eff. Dec. 1, 2000; Apr. 12, 2006, eff. Dec. 1, 2006; Apr. 26, 2011, eff. Dec. 1, 2011.)

RULE 405. METHODS OF PROVING CHARACTER

(a) **By Reputation or Opinion.** When evidence of a person's character or character trait is admissible, it may be proved by testimony about the person's reputation or by testimony in the form of an opinion. On cross-examination of the character witness, the court may allow an inquiry into relevant specific instances of the person's conduct.

(b) **By Specific Instances of Conduct.** When a person's character or character trait is an essential element of a charge, claim, or defense, the character or trait may also be proved by relevant specific instances of the person's conduct.

(Pub.L. 93–595, § 1, Jan. 2, 1975, 88 Stat. 1932; Mar. 2, 1987, eff. Oct. 1, 1987; Apr. 26, 2011, eff. Dec. 1, 2011.)

RULE 406. HABIT; ROUTINE PRACTICE

Evidence of a person's habit or an organization's routine practice may be admitted to prove that on a particular occasion the person or organization acted in accordance with the habit or routine practice. The court may admit this evidence regardless of whether it is corroborated or whether there was an eyewitness.

(Pub.L. 93–595, § 1, Jan. 2, 1975, 88 Stat. 1932; Apr. 26, 2011, eff. Dec. 1, 2011.)

RULE 407. SUBSEQUENT REMEDIAL MEASURES

When measures are taken that would have made an earlier injury or harm less likely to occur, evidence of the subsequent measures is not admissible to prove:

- negligence;

- culpable conduct;
- a defect in a product or its design; or
- a need for a warning or instruction.

But the court may admit this evidence for another purpose, such as impeachment or—if disputed—proving ownership, control, or the feasibility of precautionary measures.

(Pub.L. 93–595, § 1, Jan. 2, 1975, 88 Stat. 1932; Apr. 11, 1997, eff. Dec. 1, 1997; Apr. 26, 2011, eff. Dec. 1, 2011.)

RULE 408. COMPROMISE OFFERS AND NEGOTIATIONS

(a) **Prohibited Uses.** Evidence of the following is not admissible—on behalf of any party—either to prove or disprove the validity or amount of a disputed claim or to impeach by a prior inconsistent statement or a contradiction:

(1) furnishing, promising, or offering—or accepting, promising to accept, or offering to accept—a valuable consideration in compromising or attempting to compromise the claim; and

(2) conduct or a statement made during compromise negotiations about the claim—except when offered in a criminal case and when the negotiations related to a claim by a public office in the exercise of its regulatory, investigative, or enforcement authority.

(b) **Exceptions.** The court may admit this evidence for another purpose, such as proving a witness's bias or prejudice, negating a contention of undue delay, or proving an effort to obstruct a criminal investigation or prosecution.

(Pub.L. 93–595, § 1, Jan. 2, 1975, 88 Stat. 1933; Apr. 12, 2006, eff. Dec. 1, 2006; Apr. 26, 2011, eff. Dec. 1, 2011.)

RULE 409. OFFERS TO PAY MEDICAL AND SIMILAR EXPENSES

Evidence of furnishing, promising to pay, or offering to pay medical, hospital, or similar expenses resulting from an injury is not admissible to prove liability for the injury.

(Pub.L. 93–595, § 1, Jan. 2, 1975, 88 Stat.1933; Apr. 26, 2011, eff. Dec. 1, 2011.)

RULE 410. PLEAS, PLEA DISCUSSIONS, AND RELATED STATEMENTS

(a) **Prohibited Uses.** In a civil or criminal case, evidence of the following is not admissible against the defendant who made the plea or participated in the plea discussions:

(1) a guilty plea that was later withdrawn;

(2) a nolo contendere plea;

(3) a statement made during a proceeding on either of those pleas under Federal Rule of Criminal Procedure 11 or a comparable state procedure; or

(4) a statement made during plea discussions with an attorney for the prosecuting authority if the discussions did not result in a guilty plea or they resulted in a later-withdrawn guilty plea.

(b) Exceptions. The court may admit a statement described in Rule 410(a)(3) or (4):

(1) in any proceeding in which another statement made during the same plea or plea discussions has been introduced, if in fairness the statements ought to be considered together; or

(2) in a criminal proceeding for perjury or false statement, if the defendant made the statement under oath, on the record, and with counsel present.

(Pub.L. 93–595, § 1, Jan. 2, 1975, 88 Stat. 1933; Pub.L. 94–149, § 1(9), Dec. 12, 1975, 89 Stat. 805; Apr. 30, 1979, eff. Dec. 1, 1980; Apr. 26, 2011, eff. Dec. 1, 2011.)

RULE 411. LIABILITY INSURANCE

Evidence that a person was or was not insured against liability is not admissible to prove whether the person acted negligently or otherwise wrongfully. But the court may admit this evidence for another purpose, such as proving a witness's bias or prejudice or proving agency, ownership, or control.

(Pub.L. 93–595, § 1, Jan. 2, 1975, 88 Stat.1933; Mar. 2, 1987, eff. Oct. 1, 1987; Apr. 26, 2011, eff. Dec. 1, 2011.)

RULE 412. SEX–OFFENSE CASES: THE VICTIM'S SEXUAL BEHAVIOR OR PREDISPOSITION

(a) Prohibited Uses. The following evidence is not admissible in a civil or criminal proceeding involving alleged sexual misconduct:

(1) evidence offered to prove that a victim engaged in other sexual behavior; or

(2) evidence offered to prove a victim's sexual predisposition.

(b) Exceptions.

(1) *Criminal Cases.* The court may admit the following evidence in a criminal case:

(A) evidence of specific instances of a victim's sexual behavior, if offered to prove that someone other than the defendant was the source of semen, injury, or other physical evidence;

(B) evidence of specific instances of a victim's sexual behavior with respect to the person accused of the sexual misconduct, if offered by the defendant to prove consent or if offered by the prosecutor; and

(C) evidence whose exclusion would violate the defendant's constitutional rights.

(2) *Civil Cases.* In a civil case, the court may admit evidence offered to prove a victim's sexual behavior or sexual predisposition if its probative value substantially outweighs the danger of harm to any victim and of unfair prejudice to any party. The court may admit evidence of a victim's reputation only if the victim has placed it in controversy.

(c) Procedure to Determine Admissibility.

(1) *Motion.* If a party intends to offer evidence under Rule 412(b), the party must:

(A) file a motion that specifically describes the evidence and states the purpose for which it is to be offered;

(B) do so at least 14 days before trial unless the court, for good cause, sets a different time;

(C) serve the motion on all parties; and

(D) notify the victim or, when appropriate, the victim's guardian or representative.

(2) *Hearing.* Before admitting evidence under this rule, the court must conduct an in camera hearing and give the victim and parties a right to attend and be heard. Unless the court orders otherwise, the motion, related materials, and the record of the hearing must be and remain sealed.

(d) Definition of "Victim." In this rule, "victim" includes an alleged victim.

(Added Pub.L. 95–540, § 2(a), Oct. 28, 1978, 92 Stat. 2046, and amended Pub.L. 100–690, Title VII, § 7046(a), Nov. 18, 1988, 102 Stat. 4400; Apr. 29, 1994, eff. Dec. 1, 1994; Pub.L. 103–322, Title IV, § 40141(b), Sept. 13, 1994, 108 Stat. 1919; Apr. 26, 2011, eff. Dec. 1, 2011.)

RULE 413. SIMILAR CRIMES IN SEXUAL–ASSAULT CASES

(a) Permitted Uses. In a criminal case in which a defendant is accused of a sexual assault, the court may admit evidence that the defendant committed any other sexual assault. The evidence may be considered on any matter to which it is relevant.

(b) Disclosure to the Defendant. If the prosecutor intends to offer this evidence, the prosecutor must disclose it to the defendant, including witnesses' statements or a summary of the expected testimony. The prosecutor must do so at least 15 days before trial or at a later time that the court allows for good cause.

(c) Effect on Other Rules. This rule does not limit the admission or consideration of evidence under any other rule.

(d) Definition of "Sexual Assault." In this rule and Rule 415, "sexual assault" means a crime under federal law or under state law (as "state" is defined in 18 U.S.C. § 513) involving:

(1) any conduct prohibited by 18 U.S.C. chapter 109A;

(2) contact, without consent, between any part of the defendant's body—or an object—and another person's genitals or anus;

(3) contact, without consent, between the defendant's genitals or anus and any part of another person's body;

(4) deriving sexual pleasure or gratification from inflicting death, bodily injury, or physical pain on another person; or

(5) an attempt or conspiracy to engage in conduct described in subparagraphs (1)–(4).

(Added Pub.L. 103–322, Title XXXII, § 320935(a), Sept. 13, 1994, 108 Stat. 2136; Apr. 26, 2011, eff. Dec. 1, 2011.)

RULE 414.   SIMILAR CRIMES IN CHILD– MOLESTATION CASES

(a) Permitted Uses. In a criminal case in which a defendant is accused of child molestation, the court may admit evidence that the defendant committed any other child molestation. The evidence may be considered on any matter to which it is relevant.

(b) Disclosure to the Defendant. If the prosecutor intends to offer this evidence, the prosecutor must disclose it to the defendant, including witnesses' statements or a summary of the expected testimony. The prosecutor must do so at least 15 days before trial or at a later time that the court allows for good cause.

(c) Effect on Other Rules. This rule does not limit the admission or consideration of evidence under any other rule.

(d) Definition of "Child" and "Child Molestation." In this rule and Rule 415:

(1) "child" means a person below the age of 14; and

(2) "child molestation" means a crime under federal law or under state law (as "state" is defined in 18 U.S.C. § 513) involving:

(A) any conduct prohibited by 18 U.S.C. chapter 109A and committed with a child;

(B) any conduct prohibited by 18 U.S.C. chapter 110;

(C) contact between any part of the defendant's body—or an object—and a child's genitals or anus;

(D) contact between the defendant's genitals or anus and any part of a child's body;

(E) deriving sexual pleasure or gratification from inflicting death, bodily injury, or physical pain on a child; or

(F) an attempt or conspiracy to engage in conduct described in subparagraphs (A)–(E).

(Added Pub.L. 103–322, Title XXXII, § 320935(a), Sept. 13, 1994, 108 Stat. 2135; Apr. 26, 2011, eff. Dec. 1, 2011.)

RULE 415.   SIMILAR ACTS IN CIVIL CASES INVOLVING SEXUAL ASSAULT OR CHILD MOLESTATION

(a) Permitted Uses. In a civil case involving a claim for relief based on a party's alleged sexual assault or child molestation, the court may admit evidence that the party committed any other sexual assault or child molestation. The evidence may be considered as provided in Rules 413 and 414.

(b) Disclosure to the Opponent. If a party intends to offer this evidence, the party must disclose it to the party against whom it will be offered, including witnesses' statements or a summary of the expected testimony. The party must do so at least 15 days before trial or at a later time that the court allows for good cause.

(c) Effect on Other Rules. This rule does not limit the admission or consideration of evidence under any other rule.

(Added Pub.L. 103–322, Title XXXII, § 320935(a), Sept. 13, 1994, 108 Stat. 2137; Apr. 26, 2011, eff. Dec. 1, 2011.)

ARTICLE V.   PRIVILEGES

RULE 501.   PRIVILEGE IN GENERAL

The common law—as interpreted by United States courts in the light of reason and experience—governs a claim of privilege unless any of the following provides otherwise:

• the United States Constitution;

• a federal statute; or

• rules prescribed by the Supreme Court.

But in a civil case, state law governs privilege regarding a claim or defense for which state law supplies the rule of decision.

(Pub.L. 93–595, § 1, Jan. 2, 1975, 88 Stat. 1933; Apr. 26, 2011, eff. Dec. 1, 2011.)

RULE 502. ATTORNEY–CLIENT PRIVILEGE AND WORK PRODUCT; LIMITATIONS ON WAIVER

The following provisions apply, in the circumstances set out, to disclosure of a communication or information covered by the attorney-client privilege or work-product protection.

(a) Disclosure Made in a Federal Proceeding or to a Federal Office or Agency; Scope of a Waiver. When the disclosure is made in a federal proceeding or to a federal office or agency and waives the attorney-client privilege or work-product protection, the waiver extends to an undisclosed communication or information in a federal or state proceeding only if:

(1) the waiver is intentional;

(2) the disclosed and undisclosed communications or information concern the same subject matter; and

(3) they ought in fairness to be considered together.

(b) Inadvertent Disclosure. When made in a federal proceeding or to a federal office or agency, the disclosure does not operate as a waiver in a federal or state proceeding if:

(1) the disclosure is inadvertent;

(2) the holder of the privilege or protection took reasonable steps to prevent disclosure; and

(3) the holder promptly took reasonable steps to rectify the error, including (if applicable) following Federal Rule of Civil Procedure 26(b)(5)(B).

(c) Disclosure Made in a State Proceeding. When the disclosure is made in a state proceeding and is not the subject of a state-court order concerning waiver, the disclosure does not operate as a waiver in a federal proceeding if the disclosure:

(1) would not be a waiver under this rule if it had been made in a federal proceeding; or

(2) is not a waiver under the law of the state where the disclosure occurred.

(d) Controlling Effect of a Court Order. A federal court may order that the privilege or protection is not waived by disclosure connected with the litigation pending before the court—in which event the disclosure is also not a waiver in any other federal or state proceeding.

(e) Controlling Effect of a Party Agreement. An agreement on the effect of disclosure in a federal proceeding is binding only on the parties to the agreement, unless it is incorporated into a court order.

(f) Controlling Effect of This Rule. Notwithstanding Rules 101 and 1101, this rule applies to state proceedings and to federal court-annexed and federal court-mandated arbitration proceedings, in the circumstances set out in the rule. And notwithstanding Rule 501, this rule applies even if state law provides the rule of decision.

(g) Definitions. In this rule:

(1) "attorney-client privilege" means the protection that applicable law provides for confidential attorney-client communications; and

(2) "work-product protection" means the protection that applicable law provides for tangible material (or its intangible equivalent) prepared in anticipation of litigation or for trial.

(Pub.L. 110–322, § 1(a), Sept. 19, 2008, 122 Stat. 3537; Apr. 26, 2011, eff. Dec. 1, 2011.)

ARTICLE VI. WITNESSES

RULE 601. COMPETENCY TO TESTIFY IN GENERAL

Every person is competent to be a witness unless these rules provide otherwise. But in a civil case, state law governs the witness's competency regarding a claim or defense for which state law supplies the rule of decision.

(Pub.L. 93–595, § 1, Jan. 2, 1975, 88 Stat.1934; Apr. 26, 2011, eff. Dec. 1, 2011.)

RULE 602. NEED FOR PERSONAL KNOWLEDGE

A witness may testify to a matter only if evidence is introduced sufficient to support a finding that the witness has personal knowledge of the matter. Evidence to prove personal knowledge may consist of the witness's own testimony. This rule does not apply to a witness's expert testimony under Rule 703.

(Pub.L. 93–595, § 1, Jan. 2, 1975, 88 Stat. 1934; Mar. 2, 1987, eff. Oct. 1, 1987; Apr. 25, 1988, eff. Nov. 1, 1988; Apr. 26, 2011, eff. Dec. 1, 2011.)

RULE 603. OATH OR AFFIRMATION TO TESTIFY TRUTHFULLY

Before testifying, a witness must give an oath or affirmation to testify truthfully. It must be in a form designed to impress that duty on the witness's conscience.

(Pub.L. 93–595, § 1, Jan. 2, 1975, 88 Stat. 1934; Mar. 2, 1987, eff. Oct. 1, 1987; Apr. 26, 2011, eff. Dec. 1, 2011.)

RULE 604. INTERPRETER

An interpreter must be qualified and must give an oath or affirmation to make a true translation.

(Pub.L. 93–595, § 1, Jan. 2, 1975, 88 Stat. 1934; Mar. 2, 1987, eff. Oct. 1, 1987; Apr. 26, 2011, eff. Dec. 1, 2011.)

RULE 605. JUDGE'S COMPETENCY AS A WITNESS

The presiding judge may not testify as a witness at the trial. A party need not object to preserve the issue.

(Pub.L. 93–595, § 1, Jan. 2, 1975, 88 Stat. 1934; Apr. 26, 2011, eff. Dec. 1, 2011.)

RULE 606. JUROR'S COMPETENCY AS A WITNESS

(a) **At the Trial.** A juror may not testify as a witness before the other jurors at the trial. If a juror is called to testify, the court must give a party an opportunity to object outside the jury's presence.

(b) **During an Inquiry Into the Validity of a Verdict or Indictment.**

(1) **Prohibited Testimony or Other Evidence.** During an inquiry into the validity of a verdict or indictment, a juror may not testify about any statement made or incident that occurred during the jury's deliberations; the effect of anything on that juror's or another juror's vote; or any juror's mental processes concerning the verdict or indictment. The court may not receive a juror's affidavit or evidence of a juror's statement on these matters.

(2) **Exceptions.** A juror may testify about whether:

(A) extraneous prejudicial information was improperly brought to the jury's attention;

(B) an outside influence was improperly brought to bear on any juror; or

(C) a mistake was made in entering the verdict on the verdict form.

(Pub.L. 93–595, § 1, Jan. 2, 1975, 88 Stat. 1934; Pub.L. 94–149, § 1(10), Dec. 12, 1975, 89 Stat. 805; Mar. 2, 1987, eff. Oct. 1, 1987; Apr. 12, 2006, eff. Dec. 1, 2006; Apr. 26, 2011, eff. Dec. 1, 2011.)

RULE 607. WHO MAY IMPEACH A WITNESS

Any party, including the party that called the witness, may attack the witness's credibility.

(Pub.L. 93–595, § 1, Jan. 2, 1975, 88 Stat.1934; Mar. 2, 1987, eff. Oct. 1, 1987; Apr. 26, 2011, eff. Dec. 1, 2011.)

RULE 608. A WITNESS'S CHARACTER FOR TRUTHFULNESS OR UNTRUTHFULNESS

(a) **Reputation or Opinion Evidence.** A witness's credibility may be attacked or supported by testimony about the witness's reputation for having a character for truthfulness or untruthfulness, or by testimony in the form of an opinion about that character. But evidence of truthful character is admissible only after the witness's character for truthfulness has been attacked.

(b) **Specific Instances of Conduct.** Except for a criminal conviction under Rule 609, extrinsic evidence is not admissible to prove specific instances of a witness's conduct in order to attack or support the witness's character for truthfulness. But the court may, on cross-examination, allow them to be inquired into if they are probative of the character for truthfulness or untruthfulness of:

(1) the witness; or

(2) another witness whose character the witness being cross-examined has testified about.

By testifying on another matter, a witness does not waive any privilege against self-incrimination for testimony that relates only to the witness's character for truthfulness.

(Pub.L. 93–595, § 1, Jan. 2, 1975, 88 Stat.1935; Mar. 2, 1987, eff. Oct. 1, 1987; Apr. 25, 1988, eff. Nov. 1, 1988; Mar. 27, 2003, eff. Dec. 1, 2003; Apr. 26, 2011, eff. Dec. 1, 2011.)

RULE 609. IMPEACHMENT BY EVIDENCE OF A CRIMINAL CONVICTION

(a) **In General.** The following rules apply to attacking a witness's character for truthfulness by evidence of a criminal conviction:

(1) for a crime that, in the convicting jurisdiction, was punishable by death or by imprisonment for more than one year, the evidence:

(A) must be admitted, subject to Rule 403, in a civil case or in a criminal case in which the witness is not a defendant; and

(B) must be admitted in a criminal case in which the witness is a defendant, if the probative value of the evidence outweighs its prejudicial effect to that defendant; and

(2) for any crime regardless of the punishment, the evidence must be admitted if the court can readily determine that establishing the elements of the crime required proving—or the witness's admitting—a dishonest act or false statement.

(b) **Limit on Using the Evidence After 10 Years.** This subdivision (b) applies if more than 10 years have passed since the witness's conviction or release from confinement for it, whichever is later. Evidence of the conviction is admissible only if:

(1) its probative value, supported by specific facts and circumstances, substantially outweighs its prejudicial effect; and

(2) the proponent gives an adverse party reasonable written notice of the intent to use it so that the party has a fair opportunity to contest its use.

(c) **Effect of a Pardon, Annulment, or Certificate of Rehabilitation.** Evidence of a conviction is not admissible if:

(1) the conviction has been the subject of a pardon, annulment, certificate of rehabilitation, or other equivalent procedure based on a finding that the person has been rehabilitated, and the person has not been convicted of a later crime punishable by death or by imprisonment for more than one year; or

(2) the conviction has been the subject of a pardon, annulment, or other equivalent procedure based on a finding of innocence.

(d) **Juvenile Adjudications.** Evidence of a juvenile adjudication is admissible under this rule only if:

(1) it is offered in a criminal case;

(2) the adjudication was of a witness other than the defendant;

(3) an adult's conviction for that offense would be admissible to attack the adult's credibility; and

(4) admitting the evidence is necessary to fairly determine guilt or innocence.

(e) **Pendency of an Appeal.** A conviction that satisfies this rule is admissible even if an appeal is pending. Evidence of the pendency is also admissible.

(Pub.L. 93–595, § 1, Jan. 2, 1975, 88 Stat.1935; Mar. 2, 1987, eff. Oct. 1, 1987; Jan. 26, 1990, eff. Dec. 1, 1990; Apr. 12, 2006, eff. Dec. 1, 2006; Apr. 26, 2011, eff. Dec. 1, 2011.)

RULE 610. RELIGIOUS BELIEFS OR OPINIONS

Evidence of a witness's religious beliefs or opinions is not admissible to attack or support the witness's credibility.

(Pub.L. 93–595, § 1, Jan. 2, 1975, 88 Stat.1936; Mar. 2, 1987, eff. Oct. 1, 1987; Apr. 26, 2011, eff. Dec. 1, 2011.)

RULE 611. MODE AND ORDER OF EXAMINING WITNESSES AND PRESENTING EVIDENCE

(a) **Control by the Court; Purposes.** The court should exercise reasonable control over the mode and order of examining witnesses and presenting evidence so as to:

(1) make those procedures effective for determining the truth;

(2) avoid wasting time; and

(3) protect witnesses from harassment or undue embarrassment.

(b) **Scope of Cross–Examination.** Cross-examination should not go beyond the subject matter of the direct examination and matters affecting the witness's credibility. The court may allow inquiry into additional matters as if on direct examination.

(c) **Leading Questions.** Leading questions should not be used on direct examination except as necessary to develop the witness's testimony. Ordinarily, the court should allow leading questions:

(1) on cross-examination; and

(2) when a party calls a hostile witness, an adverse party, or a witness identified with an adverse party.

(Pub.L. 93–595, § 1, Jan. 2, 1975, 88 Stat. 1936; Mar. 2, 1987, eff. Oct. 1, 1987; Apr. 26, 2011, eff. Dec. 1, 2011.)

RULE 612. WRITING USED TO REFRESH A WITNESS'S MEMORY

(a) **Scope.** This rule gives an adverse party certain options when a witness uses a writing to refresh memory:

(1) while testifying; or

(2) before testifying, if the court decides that justice requires the party to have those options.

(b) **Adverse Party's Options; Deleting Unrelated Matter.** Unless 18 U.S.C. § 3500 provides otherwise in a criminal case, an adverse party is entitled to have the writing produced at the hearing, to inspect it, to cross-examine the witness about it, and to introduce in evidence any portion that relates to the witness's testimony. If the producing party claims that the writing includes unrelated matter, the court must examine the writing in camera, delete any unrelated portion, and order that the rest be delivered to the adverse party. Any portion deleted over objection must be preserved for the record.

(c) **Failure to Produce or Deliver the Writing.** If a writing is not produced or is not delivered as ordered, the court may issue any appropriate order. But if the prosecution does not comply in a criminal case, the court must strike the witness's testimony or—if justice so requires—declare a mistrial.

(Pub.L. 93–595, § 1, Jan. 2, 1975, 88 Stat. 1936; Mar. 2, 1987, eff. Oct. 1, 1987; Apr. 26, 2011, eff. Dec. 1, 2011.)

RULE 613. WITNESS'S PRIOR STATEMENT

(a) Showing or Disclosing the Statement During Examination. When examining a witness about the witness's prior statement, a party need not show it or disclose its contents to the witness. But the party must, on request, show it or disclose its contents to an adverse party's attorney.

(b) Extrinsic Evidence of a Prior Inconsistent Statement. Extrinsic evidence of a witness's prior inconsistent statement is admissible only if the witness is given an opportunity to explain or deny the statement and an adverse party is given an opportunity to examine the witness about it, or if justice so requires. This subdivision (b) does not apply to an opposing party's statement under Rule 801(d)(2).

(Pub.L. 93–595, § 1, Jan. 2, 1975, 88 Stat.1936; Mar. 2, 1987, eff. Oct. 1, 1987; Apr. 25, 1988, eff. Nov. 1, 1988; Apr. 26, 2011, eff. Dec. 1, 2011.)

RULE 614. COURT'S CALLING OR EXAMINING A WITNESS

(a) Calling. The court may call a witness on its own or at a party's request. Each party is entitled to cross-examine the witness.

(b) Examining. The court may examine a witness regardless of who calls the witness.

(c) Objections. A party may object to the court's calling or examining a witness either at that time or at the next opportunity when the jury is not present.

(Pub.L. 93–595, § 1, Jan. 2, 1975, 88 Stat.1937; Apr. 26, 2011, eff. Dec. 1, 2011.)

RULE 615. EXCLUDING WITNESSES

At a party's request, the court must order witnesses excluded so that they cannot hear other witnesses' testimony. Or the court may do so on its own. But this rule does not authorize excluding:

(a) a party who is a natural person;

(b) an officer or employee of a party that is not a natural person, after being designated as the party's representative by its attorney;

(c) a person whose presence a party shows to be essential to presenting the party's claim or defense; or

(d) a person authorized by statute to be present.

(Pub.L. 93–595, § 1, Jan. 2, 1975, 88 Stat.1937; Mar. 2, 1987, eff. Oct. 1, 1987; Apr. 25, 1988, eff. Nov. 1, 1988; Pub.L. 100–690, Nov. 18, 1988, Title VII, § 7075(a), 102 Stat. 4405; Apr. 24, 1998, eff. Dec. 1, 1998; Apr. 26, 2011, eff. Dec. 1, 2011.)

ARTICLE VII. OPINIONS AND EXPERT TESTIMONY

RULE 701. OPINION TESTIMONY BY LAY WITNESSES

If a witness is not testifying as an expert, testimony in the form of an opinion is limited to one that is:

(a) rationally based on the witness's perception;

(b) helpful to clearly understanding the witness's testimony or to determining a fact in issue; and

(c) not based on scientific, technical, or other specialized knowledge within the scope of Rule 702.

(Pub.L. 93–595, § 1, Jan. 2, 1975, 88 Stat.1937; Mar. 2, 1987, eff. Oct. 1, 1987; Apr. 17, 2000, eff. Dec. 1, 2000; Apr. 26, 2011, eff. Dec. 1, 2011.)

RULE 702. TESTIMONY BY EXPERT WITNESSES

A witness who is qualified as an expert by knowledge, skill, experience, training, or education may testify in the form of an opinion or otherwise if:

(a) the expert's scientific, technical, or other specialized knowledge will help the trier of fact to understand the evidence or to determine a fact in issue;

(b) the testimony is based on sufficient facts or data;

(c) the testimony is the product of reliable principles and methods; and

(d) the expert has reliably applied the principles and methods to the facts of the case.

(Pub.L. 93–595, § 1, Jan. 2, 1975, 88 Stat. 1937; Apr. 17, 2000, eff. Dec. 1, 2000; Apr. 26, 2011, eff. Dec. 1, 2011.)

RULE 703. BASES OF AN EXPERT'S OPINION TESTIMONY

An expert may base an opinion on facts or data in the case that the expert has been made aware of or personally observed. If experts in the particular field would reasonably rely on those kinds of facts or data in forming an opinion on the subject, they need not be admissible for the opinion to be admitted. But if the facts or data would otherwise be inadmissible, the proponent of the opinion may disclose them to the jury only if their probative value in helping the jury evaluate the opinion substantially outweighs their prejudicial effect.

(Pub.L. 93–595, § 1, Jan. 2, 1975, 88 Stat.1937; Mar. 2, 1987, eff. Oct. 1, 1987; Apr. 17, 2000, eff. Dec. 1, 2000; Apr. 26, 2011, eff. Dec. 1, 2011.)

RULE 704. OPINION ON AN ULTIMATE ISSUE

(a) In General—Not Automatically Objectionable. An opinion is not objectionable just because it embraces an ultimate issue.

(b) Exception. In a criminal case, an expert witness must not state an opinion about whether the defendant did or did not have a mental state or condition that constitutes an element of the crime charged or of a defense. Those matters are for the trier of fact alone.

(Pub.L. 93–595, § 1, Jan. 2, 1975, 88 Stat. 1937; Pub.L. 98–473, Title IV, § 406, Oct. 12, 1984, 98 Stat. 2067; Apr. 26, 2011, eff. Dec. 1, 2011.)

RULE 705. DISCLOSING THE FACTS OR DATA UNDERLYING AN EXPERT'S OPINION

Unless the court orders otherwise, an expert may state an opinion—and give the reasons for it—without first testifying to the underlying facts or data. But the expert may be required to disclose those facts or data on cross-examination.

(Pub.L. 93–595, § 1, Jan. 2, 1975, 88 Stat. 1938; Mar. 2, 1987, eff. Oct. 1, 1987; Apr. 22, 1993, eff. Dec. 1, 1993; Apr. 26, 2011, eff. Dec. 1, 2011.)

RULE 706. COURT–APPOINTED EXPERT WITNESSES

(a) Appointment Process. On a party's motion or on its own, the court may order the parties to show cause why expert witnesses should not be appointed and may ask the parties to submit nominations. The court may appoint any expert that the parties agree on and any of its own choosing. But the court may only appoint someone who consents to act.

(b) Expert's Role. The court must inform the expert of the expert's duties. The court may do so in writing and have a copy filed with the clerk or may do so orally at a conference in which the parties have an opportunity to participate. The expert:

(1) must advise the parties of any findings the expert makes;

(2) may be deposed by any party;

(3) may be called to testify by the court or any party; and

(4) may be cross-examined by any party, including the party that called the expert.

(c) Compensation. The expert is entitled to a reasonable compensation, as set by the court. The compensation is payable as follows:

(1) in a criminal case or in a civil case involving just compensation under the Fifth Amendment, from any funds that are provided by law; and

(2) in any other civil case, by the parties in the proportion and at the time that the court directs—and the compensation is then charged like other costs.

(d) Disclosing the Appointment to the Jury. The court may authorize disclosure to the jury that the court appointed the expert.

(e) Parties' Choice of Their Own Experts. This rule does not limit a party in calling its own experts.

(Pub.L. 93–595, § 1, Jan. 2, 1975, 88 Stat.1938; Mar. 2, 1987, eff. Oct. 1, 1987; Apr. 26, 2011, eff. Dec. 1, 2011.)

ARTICLE VIII. HEARSAY

RULE 801. DEFINITIONS THAT APPLY TO THIS ARTICLE; EXCLUSIONS FROM HEARSAY

(a) Statement. "Statement" means a person's oral assertion, written assertion, or nonverbal conduct, if the person intended it as an assertion.

(b) Declarant. "Declarant" means the person who made the statement.

(c) Hearsay. "Hearsay" means a statement that:

(1) the declarant does not make while testifying at the current trial or hearing; and

(2) a party offers in evidence to prove the truth of the matter asserted in the statement.

(d) Statements That Are Not Hearsay. A statement that meets the following conditions is not hearsay:

(1) A Declarant–Witness's Prior Statement. The declarant testifies and is subject to cross-examination about a prior statement, and the statement:

(A) is inconsistent with the declarant's testimony and was given under penalty of perjury at a trial, hearing, or other proceeding or in a deposition;

(B) is consistent with the declarant's testimony and is offered:

(i) to rebut an express or implied charge that the declarant recently fabricated it or acted from a recent improper influence or motive in so testifying; or

    (ii) to rehabilitate the declarant's credibility as a witness when attacked on another ground; or

    (C) identifies a person as someone the declarant perceived earlier.

(2) **An Opposing Party's Statement.** The statement is offered against an opposing party and:

    (A) was made by the party in an individual or representative capacity;

    (B) is one the party manifested that it adopted or believed to be true;

    (C) was made by a person whom the party authorized to make a statement on the subject;

    (D) was made by the party's agent or employee on a matter within the scope of that relationship and while it existed; or

    (E) was made by the party's coconspirator during and in furtherance of the conspiracy.

The statement must be considered but does not by itself establish the declarant's authority under (C); the existence or scope of the relationship under (D); or the existence of the conspiracy or participation in it under (E).

(Pub.L. 93–595, § 1, Jan. 2, 1975, 88 Stat.1938; Pub.L. 94–113, § 1, Oct. 16, 1975, 89 Stat. 576; Mar. 2, 1987, eff. Oct. 1, 1987; Apr. 11, 1997, eff. Dec. 1, 1997; Apr. 26, 2011, eff. Dec. 1, 2011; Apr. 25, 2014, eff. Dec. 1, 2014.)

RULE 802. THE RULE AGAINST HEARSAY

Hearsay is not admissible unless any of the following provides otherwise:

- a federal statute;
- these rules; or
- other rules prescribed by the Supreme Court.

(Pub.L. 93–595, § 1, Jan. 2, 1975, 88 Stat. 1939; Apr. 26, 2011, eff. Dec. 1, 2011.)

RULE 803. EXCEPTIONS TO THE RULE AGAINST HEARSAY—REGARDLESS OF WHETHER THE DECLARANT IS AVAILABLE AS A WITNESS

The following are not excluded by the rule against hearsay, regardless of whether the declarant is available as a witness:

(1) **Present Sense Impression.** A statement describing or explaining an event or condition, made while or immediately after the declarant perceived it.

(2) **Excited Utterance.** A statement relating to a startling event or condition, made while the declarant was under the stress of excitement that it caused.

(3) **Then–Existing Mental, Emotional, or Physical Condition.** A statement of the declarant's then-existing state of mind (such as motive, intent, or plan) or emotional, sensory, or physical condition (such as mental feeling, pain, or bodily health), but not including a statement of memory or belief to prove the fact remembered or believed unless it relates to the validity or terms of the declarant's will.

(4) **Statement Made for Medical Diagnosis or Treatment.** A statement that:

    (A) is made for—and is reasonably pertinent to—medical diagnosis or treatment; and

    (B) describes medical history; past or present symptoms or sensations; their inception; or their general cause.

(5) **Recorded Recollection.** A record that:

    (A) is on a matter the witness once knew about but now cannot recall well enough to testify fully and accurately;

    (B) was made or adopted by the witness when the matter was fresh in the witness's memory; and

    (C) accurately reflects the witness's knowledge.

If admitted, the record may be read into evidence but may be received as an exhibit only if offered by an adverse party.

(6) **Records of a Regularly Conducted Activity.** A record of an act, event, condition, opinion, or diagnosis if:

    (A) the record was made at or near the time by—or from information transmitted by—someone with knowledge;

    (B) the record was kept in the course of a regularly conducted activity of a business, organization, occupation, or calling, whether or not for profit;

    (C) making the record was a regular practice of that activity;

    (D) all these conditions are shown by the testimony of the custodian or another qualified witness, or by a certification that complies with Rule 902(11) or (12) or with a statute permitting certification; and

    (E) the opponent does not show that the source of information or the method or circumstances of preparation indicate a lack of trustworthiness.

(7) **Absence of a Record of a Regularly Conducted Activity.** Evidence that a matter is not included in a record described in paragraph (6) if:

(A) the evidence is admitted to prove that the matter did not occur or exist;

(B) a record was regularly kept for a matter of that kind; and

(C) the opponent does not show that the possible source of the information or other circumstances indicate a lack of trustworthiness.

(8) Public Records. A record or statement of a public office if:

(A) it sets out:

(i) the office's activities;

(ii) a matter observed while under a legal duty to report, but not including, in a criminal case, a matter observed by law-enforcement personnel; or

(iii) in a civil case or against the government in a criminal case, factual findings from a legally authorized investigation; and

(B) the opponent does not show that the source of information or other circumstances indicate a lack of trustworthiness.

(9) Public Records of Vital Statistics. A record of a birth, death, or marriage, if reported to a public office in accordance with a legal duty.

(10) Absence of a Public Record. Testimony—or a certification under Rule 902—that a diligent search failed to disclose a public record or statement if:

(A) the testimony or certification is admitted to prove that

(i) the record or statement does not exist; or

(ii) a matter did not occur or exist, if a public office regularly kept a record or statement for a matter of that kind; and

(B) in a criminal case, a prosecutor who intends to offer a certification provides written notice of that intent at least 14 days before trial, and the defendant does not object in writing within 7 days of receiving the notice—unless the court sets a different time for the notice or the objection.

(11) Records of Religious Organizations Concerning Personal or Family History. A statement of birth, legitimacy, ancestry, marriage, divorce, death, relationship by blood or marriage, or similar facts of personal or family history, contained in a regularly kept record of a religious organization.

(12) Certificates of Marriage, Baptism, and Similar Ceremonies. A statement of fact contained in a certificate:

(A) made by a person who is authorized by a religious organization or by law to perform the act certified;

(B) attesting that the person performed a marriage or similar ceremony or administered a sacrament; and

(C) purporting to have been issued at the time of the act or within a reasonable time after it.

(13) Family Records. A statement of fact about personal or family history contained in a family record, such as a Bible, genealogy, chart, engraving on a ring, inscription on a portrait, or engraving on an urn or burial marker.

(14) Records of Documents That Affect an Interest in Property. The record of a document that purports to establish or affect an interest in property if:

(A) the record is admitted to prove the content of the original recorded document, along with its signing and its delivery by each person who purports to have signed it;

(B) the record is kept in a public office; and

(C) a statute authorizes recording documents of that kind in that office.

(15) Statements in Documents That Affect an Interest in Property. A statement contained in a document that purports to establish or affect an interest in property if the matter stated was relevant to the document's purpose—unless later dealings with the property are inconsistent with the truth of the statement or the purport of the document.

(16) Statements in Ancient Documents. A statement in a document that is at least 20 years old and whose authenticity is established.

(17) Market Reports and Similar Commercial Publications. Market quotations, lists, directories, or other compilations that are generally relied on by the public or by persons in particular occupations.

(18) Statements in Learned Treatises, Periodicals, or Pamphlets. A statement contained in a treatise, periodical, or pamphlet if:

(A) the statement is called to the attention of an expert witness on cross-examination or relied on by the expert on direct examination; and

(B) the publication is established as a reliable authority by the expert's admission or testimony, by another expert's testimony, or by judicial notice.

If admitted, the statement may be read into evidence but not received as an exhibit.

(19) Reputation Concerning Personal or Family History. A reputation among a person's family by blood, adoption, or marriage—or among a person's associates or in the community—concerning the person's birth, adoption, legitimacy, ancestry, marriage, divorce, death, relationship by blood, adoption, or marriage, or similar facts of personal or family history.

(20) Reputation Concerning Boundaries or General History. A reputation in a community—arising before the controversy—concerning boundaries of land in the community or customs that affect the land, or concerning general historical events important to that community, state, or nation.

(21) Reputation Concerning Character. A reputation among a person's associates or in the community concerning the person's character.

(22) Judgment of a Previous Conviction. Evidence of a final judgment of conviction if:

(A) the judgment was entered after a trial or guilty plea, but not a nolo contendere plea;

(B) the conviction was for a crime punishable by death or by imprisonment for more than a year;

(C) the evidence is admitted to prove any fact essential to the judgment; and

(D) when offered by the prosecutor in a criminal case for a purpose other than impeachment, the judgment was against the defendant.

The pendency of an appeal may be shown but does not affect admissibility.

(23) Judgments Involving Personal, Family, or General History, or a Boundary. A judgment that is admitted to prove a matter of personal, family, or general history, or boundaries, if the matter:

(A) was essential to the judgment; and

(B) could be proved by evidence of reputation.

(24) [Other Exceptions.] [Transferred to Rule 807.]

(Pub.L. 93–595, § 1, Jan. 2, 1975, 88 Stat. 1939; Pub.L. 94–149, § 1(11), Dec. 12, 1975, 89 Stat. 805; Mar. 2, 1987, eff. Oct. 1, 1987; Apr. 11, 1997, eff. Dec. 1, 1997; Apr. 17, 2000, eff. Dec. 1, 2000; Apr. 26, 2011, eff. Dec. 1, 2011; Apr. 16, 2013, eff. Dec. 1, 2013; Apr. 25, 2014, eff. Dec. 1, 2014.)

RULE 804. EXCEPTIONS TO THE RULE AGAINST HEARSAY—WHEN THE DECLARANT IS UNAVAILABLE AS A WITNESS

(a) Criteria for Being Unavailable. A declarant is considered to be unavailable as a witness if the declarant:

(1) is exempted from testifying about the subject matter of the declarant's statement because the court rules that a privilege applies;

(2) refuses to testify about the subject matter despite a court order to do so;

(3) testifies to not remembering the subject matter;

(4) cannot be present or testify at the trial or hearing because of death or a then-existing infirmity, physical illness, or mental illness; or

(5) is absent from the trial or hearing and the statement's proponent has not been able, by process or other reasonable means, to procure:

(A) the declarant's attendance, in the case of a hearsay exception under Rule 804(b)(1) or (6); or

(B) the declarant's attendance or testimony, in the case of a hearsay exception under Rule 804(b)(2), (3), or (4).

But this subdivision (a) does not apply if the statement's proponent procured or wrongfully caused the declarant's unavailability as a witness in order to prevent the declarant from attending or testifying.

(b) The Exceptions. The following are not excluded by the rule against hearsay if the declarant is unavailable as a witness:

(1) Former Testimony. Testimony that:

(A) was given as a witness at a trial, hearing, or lawful deposition, whether given during the current proceeding or a different one; and

(B) is now offered against a party who had—or, in a civil case, whose predecessor in interest had—an opportunity and similar motive to develop it by direct, cross-, or redirect examination.

(2) Statement Under the Belief of Imminent Death. In a prosecution for homicide or in a civil case, a statement that the declarant, while believing the declarant's death to be imminent, made about its cause or circumstances.

(3) Statement Against Interest. A statement that:

(A) a reasonable person in the declarant's position would have made only if the person believed it to be true because, when made, it was so contrary to the declarant's proprietary or pecuniary interest or had so great a tendency to invalidate the declarant's claim against someone else or to expose the declarant to civil or criminal liability; and

(B) is supported by corroborating circumstances that clearly indicate its trustworthiness, if it is offered in a criminal case as one that tends to expose the declarant to criminal liability.

(4) Statement of Personal or Family History. A statement about:

(A) the declarant's own birth, adoption, legitimacy, ancestry, marriage, divorce, relationship by blood, adoption, or marriage, or similar facts of personal or family history, even though the declarant had no way of acquiring personal knowledge about that fact; or

(B) another person concerning any of these facts, as well as death, if the declarant was related to the person by blood, adoption, or marriage or was so intimately associated with the person's family that the declarant's information is likely to be accurate.

(5) **[Other Exceptions.]** [Transferred to Rule 807.]

(6) **Statement Offered Against a Party That Wrongfully Caused the Declarant's Unavailability.** A statement offered against a party that wrongfully caused—or acquiesced in wrongfully causing—the declarant's unavailability as a witness, and did so intending that result.

(Pub.L. 93–595, § 1, Jan. 2, 1975, 88 Stat. 1942; Pub.L. 94–149, § 1(12), (13), Dec. 12, 1975, 89 Stat. 806; Mar. 2, 1987, eff. Oct. 1, 1987; Pub.L. 100–690, Title VII, § 7075(b), Nov. 18, 1988, 102 Stat. 4405; Apr. 11, 1997, eff. Dec. 1, 1997; Apr. 28, 2010, eff. Dec. 1, 2010; Apr. 26, 2011, eff. Dec. 1, 2011.)

RULE 805. HEARSAY WITHIN HEARSAY

Hearsay within hearsay is not excluded by the rule against hearsay if each part of the combined statements conforms with an exception to the rule.

(Pub.L. 93–595, § 1, Jan. 2, 1975, 88 Stat. 1943; Apr. 26, 2011, eff. Dec. 1, 2011.)

RULE 806. ATTACKING AND SUPPORTING THE DECLARANT'S CREDIBILITY

When a hearsay statement—or a statement described in Rule 801(d)(2)(C), (D), or (E)—has been admitted in evidence, the declarant's credibility may be attacked, and then supported, by any evidence that would be admissible for those purposes if the declarant had testified as a witness. The court may admit evidence of the declarant's inconsistent statement or conduct, regardless of when it occurred or whether the declarant had an opportunity to explain or deny it. If the party against whom the statement was admitted calls the declarant as a witness, the party may examine the declarant on the statement as if on cross-examination.

(Pub.L. 93–595, § 1, Jan. 2, 1975, 88 Stat. 1943; Mar. 2, 1987, eff. Oct. 1, 1987; Apr. 11, 1997, eff. Dec. 1, 1997; Apr. 26, 2011, eff. Dec. 1, 2011.)

RULE 807. RESIDUAL EXCEPTION

(a) **In General.** Under the following circumstances, a hearsay statement is not excluded by the rule against hearsay even if the statement is not specifically covered by a hearsay exception in Rule 803 or 804:

(1) the statement has equivalent circumstantial guarantees of trustworthiness;

(2) it is offered as evidence of a material fact;

(3) it is more probative on the point for which it is offered than any other evidence that the proponent can obtain through reasonable efforts; and

(4) admitting it will best serve the purposes of these rules and the interests of justice.

(b) **Notice.** The statement is admissible only if, before the trial or hearing, the proponent gives an adverse party reasonable notice of the intent to offer the statement and its particulars, including the declarant's name and address, so that the party has a fair opportunity to meet it.

(Added Apr. 11, 1997, eff. Dec. 1, 1997; Apr. 26, 2011, eff. Dec. 1, 2011.)

ARTICLE IX. AUTHENTICATION AND IDENTIFICATION

RULE 901. AUTHENTICATING OR IDENTIFYING EVIDENCE

(a) **In General.** To satisfy the requirement of authenticating or identifying an item of evidence, the proponent must produce evidence sufficient to support a finding that the item is what the proponent claims it is.

(b) **Examples.** The following are examples only—not a complete list—of evidence that satisfies the requirement:

(1) **Testimony of a Witness with Knowledge.** Testimony that an item is what it is claimed to be.

(2) **Nonexpert Opinion About Handwriting.** A nonexpert's opinion that handwriting is genuine, based on a familiarity with it that was not acquired for the current litigation.

(3) **Comparison by an Expert Witness or the Trier of Fact.** A comparison with an authenticated specimen by an expert witness or the trier of fact.

(4) **Distinctive Characteristics and the Like.** The appearance, contents, substance, internal patterns, or other distinctive characteristics of the item, taken together with all the circumstances.

(5) **Opinion About a Voice.** An opinion identifying a person's voice—whether heard firsthand or through mechanical or electronic transmission or recording—based on hearing the voice at any time under circumstances that connect it with the alleged speaker.

(6) Evidence About a Telephone Conversation. For a telephone conversation, evidence that a call was made to the number assigned at the time to:

(A) a particular person, if circumstances, including self-identification, show that the person answering was the one called; or

(B) a particular business, if the call was made to a business and the call related to business reasonably transacted over the telephone.

(7) Evidence About Public Records. Evidence that:

(A) a document was recorded or filed in a public office as authorized by law; or

(B) a purported public record or statement is from the office where items of this kind are kept.

(8) Evidence About Ancient Documents or Data Compilations. For a document or data compilation, evidence that it:

(A) is in a condition that creates no suspicion about its authenticity;

(B) was in a place where, if authentic, it would likely be; and

(C) is at least 20 years old when offered.

(9) Evidence About a Process or System. Evidence describing a process or system and showing that it produces an accurate result.

(10) Methods Provided by a Statute or Rule. Any method of authentication or identification allowed by a federal statute or a rule prescribed by the Supreme Court.

(Pub.L. 93–595, § 1, Jan. 2, 1975, 88 Stat.1943; Apr. 26, 2011, eff. Dec. 1, 2011.)

RULE 902. EVIDENCE THAT IS SELF–AUTHENTICATING

The following items of evidence are self-authenticating; they require no extrinsic evidence of authenticity in order to be admitted:

(1) Domestic Public Documents That Are Sealed and Signed. A document that bears:

(A) a seal purporting to be that of the United States; any state, district, commonwealth, territory, or insular possession of the United States; the former Panama Canal Zone; the Trust Territory of the Pacific Islands; a political subdivision of any of these entities; or a department, agency, or officer of any entity named above; and

(B) a signature purporting to be an execution or attestation.

(2) Domestic Public Documents That Are Not Sealed but Are Signed and Certified. A document that bears no seal if:

(A) it bears the signature of an officer or employee of an entity named in Rule 902(1)(A); and

(B) another public officer who has a seal and official duties within that same entity certifies under seal—or its equivalent—that the signer has the official capacity and that the signature is genuine.

(3) Foreign Public Documents. A document that purports to be signed or attested by a person who is authorized by a foreign country's law to do so. The document must be accompanied by a final certification that certifies the genuineness of the signature and official position of the signer or attester—or of any foreign official whose certificate of genuineness relates to the signature or attestation or is in a chain of certificates of genuineness relating to the signature or attestation. The certification may be made by a secretary of a United States embassy or legation; by a consul general, vice consul, or consular agent of the United States; or by a diplomatic or consular official of the foreign country assigned or accredited to the United States. If all parties have been given a reasonable opportunity to investigate the document's authenticity and accuracy, the court may, for good cause, either:

(A) order that it be treated as presumptively authentic without final certification; or

(B) allow it to be evidenced by an attested summary with or without final certification.

(4) Certified Copies of Public Records. A copy of an official record—or a copy of a document that was recorded or filed in a public office as authorized by law—if the copy is certified as correct by:

(A) the custodian or another person authorized to make the certification; or

(B) a certificate that complies with Rule 902(1), (2), or (3), a federal statute, or a rule prescribed by the Supreme Court.

(5) Official Publications. A book, pamphlet, or other publication purporting to be issued by a public authority.

(6) Newspapers and Periodicals. Printed material purporting to be a newspaper or periodical.

(7) Trade Inscriptions and the Like. An inscription, sign, tag, or label purporting to have been affixed in the course of business and indicating origin, ownership, or control.

(8) Acknowledged Documents. A document accompanied by a certificate of acknowledgment that is lawfully executed by a notary public or another officer who is authorized to take acknowledgments.

(9) Commercial Paper and Related Documents. Commercial paper, a signature on it, and related documents, to the extent allowed by general commercial law.

(10) Presumptions Under a Federal Statute. A signature, document, or anything else that a federal statute declares to be presumptively or prima facie genuine or authentic.

(11) Certified Domestic Records of a Regularly Conducted Activity. The original or a copy of a domestic record that meets the requirements of Rule 803(6)(A)–(C), as shown by a certification of the custodian or another qualified person that complies with a federal statute or a rule prescribed by the Supreme Court. Before the trial or hearing, the proponent must give an adverse party reasonable written notice of the intent to offer the record—and must make the record and certification available for inspection—so that the party has a fair opportunity to challenge them.

(12) Certified Foreign Records of a Regularly Conducted Activity. In a civil case, the original or a copy of a foreign record that meets the requirements of Rule 902(11), modified as follows: the certification, rather than complying with a federal statute or Supreme Court rule, must be signed in a manner that, if falsely made, would subject the maker to a criminal penalty in the country where the certification is signed. The proponent must also meet the notice requirements of Rule 902(11).

(Pub.L. 93–595, § 1, Jan. 2, 1975, 88 Stat. 1944; Mar. 2, 1987, eff. Oct. 1, 1987; Apr. 25, 1988, eff. Nov. 1, 1988; Apr. 17, 2000, eff. Dec. 1, 2000; Apr. 26, 2011, eff. Dec. 1, 2011.)

RULE 903. SUBSCRIBING WITNESS'S TESTIMONY

A subscribing witness's testimony is necessary to authenticate a writing only if required by the law of the jurisdiction that governs its validity.

(Pub.L. 93–595, § 1, Jan. 2, 1975, 88 Stat.1945; Apr. 26, 2011, eff. Dec. 1, 2011.)

ARTICLE X. CONTENTS OF WRITINGS, RECORDINGS, AND PHOTOGRAPHS

RULE 1001. DEFINITIONS THAT APPLY TO THIS ARTICLE

In this article:

(a) A "writing" consists of letters, words, numbers, or their equivalent set down in any form.

(b) A "recording" consists of letters, words, numbers, or their equivalent recorded in any manner.

(c) A "photograph" means a photographic image or its equivalent stored in any form.

(d) An "original" of a writing or recording means the writing or recording itself or any counterpart intended to have the same effect by the person who executed or issued it. For electronically stored information, "original" means any printout—or other output readable by sight—if it accurately reflects the information. An "original" of a photograph includes the negative or a print from it.

(e) A "duplicate" means a counterpart produced by a mechanical, photographic, chemical, electronic, or other equivalent process or technique that accurately reproduces the original.

(Pub.L. 93–595, § 1, Jan. 2, 1975, 88 Stat. 1945; Apr. 26, 2011, eff. Dec. 1, 2011.)

RULE 1002. REQUIREMENT OF THE ORIGINAL

An original writing, recording, or photograph is required in order to prove its content unless these rules or a federal statute provides otherwise.

(Pub.L. 93–595, § 1, Jan. 2, 1975, 88 Stat. 1946; Apr. 26, 2011, eff. Dec. 1, 2011.)

RULE 1003. ADMISSIBILITY OF DUPLICATES

A duplicate is admissible to the same extent as the original unless a genuine question is raised about the original's authenticity or the circumstances make it unfair to admit the duplicate.

(Pub.L. 93–595, § 1, Jan. 2, 1975, 88 Stat. 1946; Apr. 26, 2011, eff. Dec. 1, 2011.)

RULE 1004. ADMISSIBILITY OF OTHER EVIDENCE OF CONTENT

An original is not required and other evidence of the content of a writing, recording, or photograph is admissible if:

(a) all the originals are lost or destroyed, and not by the proponent acting in bad faith;

(b) an original cannot be obtained by any available judicial process;

(c) the party against whom the original would be offered had control of the original; was at that time put on notice, by pleadings or otherwise, that the original would be a subject of proof at the trial or hearing; and fails to produce it at the trial or hearing; or

(d) the writing, recording, or photograph is not closely related to a controlling issue.

(Pub.L. 93–595, § 1, Jan. 2, 1975, 88 Stat. 1946; Mar. 2, 1987, eff. Oct. 1, 1987; Apr. 26, 2011, eff. Dec. 1, 2011.)

RULE 1005. COPIES OF PUBLIC RECORDS TO PROVE CONTENT

The proponent may use a copy to prove the content of an official record—or of a document that was recorded or filed in a public office as authorized by law—if these conditions are met: the record or document is otherwise admissible; and the copy is certified as correct in accordance with Rule 902(4) or is testified to be correct by a witness who has compared it with the original. If no such copy can be obtained by reasonable diligence, then the proponent may use other evidence to prove the content.

(Pub.L. 93–595, § 1, Jan. 2, 1975, 88 Stat. 1946; Apr. 26, 2011, eff. Dec. 1, 2011.)

RULE 1006. SUMMARIES TO PROVE CONTENT

The proponent may use a summary, chart, or calculation to prove the content of voluminous writings, recordings, or photographs that cannot be conveniently examined in court. The proponent must make the originals or duplicates available for examination or copying, or both, by other parties at a reasonable time and place. And the court may order the proponent to produce them in court.

(Pub.L. 93–595, § 1, Jan. 2, 1975, 88 Stat. 1946; Apr. 26, 2011, eff. Dec. 1, 2011.)

RULE 1007. TESTIMONY OR STATEMENT OF A PARTY TO PROVE CONTENT

The proponent may prove the content of a writing, recording, or photograph by the testimony, deposition, or written statement of the party against whom the evidence is offered. The proponent need not account for the original.

(Pub.L. 93–595, § 1, Jan. 2, 1975, 88 Stat. 1947; Mar. 2, 1987, eff. Oct. 1, 1987; Apr. 26, 2011, eff. Dec. 1, 2011.)

RULE 1008. FUNCTIONS OF THE COURT AND JURY

Ordinarily, the court determines whether the proponent has fulfilled the factual conditions for admitting other evidence of the content of a writing, recording, or photograph under Rule 1004 or 1005. But in a jury trial, the jury determines—in accordance with Rule 104(b)—any issue about whether:

(a) an asserted writing, recording, or photograph ever existed;

(b) another one produced at the trial or hearing is the original; or

(c) other evidence of content accurately reflects the content.

(Pub.L. 93–595, § 1, Jan. 2, 1975, 88 Stat. 1947; Apr. 26, 2011, eff. Dec. 1, 2011.)

ARTICLE XI. MISCELLANEOUS RULES

RULE 1101. APPLICABILITY OF THE RULES

(a) To Courts and Judges. These rules apply to proceedings before:

- United States district courts;
- United States bankruptcy and magistrate judges;
- United States courts of appeals;
- the United States Court of Federal Claims; and
- the district courts of Guam, the Virgin Islands, and the Northern Mariana Islands.

(b) To Cases and Proceedings. These rules apply in:

- civil cases and proceedings, including bankruptcy, admiralty, and maritime cases;
- criminal cases and proceedings; and
- contempt proceedings, except those in which the court may act summarily.

(c) Rules on Privilege. The rules on privilege apply to all stages of a case or proceeding.

(d) Exceptions. These rules—except for those on privilege—do not apply to the following:

(1) the court's determination, under Rule 104(a), on a preliminary question of fact governing admissibility;

(2) grand-jury proceedings; and

(3) miscellaneous proceedings such as:

- extradition or rendition;

- issuing an arrest warrant, criminal summons, or search warrant;

- a preliminary examination in a criminal case;

- sentencing;

- granting or revoking probation or supervised release; and

- considering whether to release on bail or otherwise.

(e) Other Statutes and Rules. A federal statute or a rule prescribed by the Supreme Court may provide for admitting or excluding evidence independently from these rules.

(Pub.L. 93–595, § 1, Jan. 2, 1975, 88 Stat. 1947; Pub.L. 94–149, § 1(14), Dec. 12, 1975, 89 Stat. 806; Pub.L. 95–598, Title II, § 251, Nov. 6, 1978, 92 Stat. 2673; Pub.L. 97–164, Title I, § 142, Apr. 2, 1982, 96 Stat. 45; Mar. 2, 1987, eff. Oct. 1, 1987; Apr. 25, 1988, eff. Nov. 1, 1988; Pub.L. 100–690, Title VII, § 7075(c), Nov. 18, 1988, 102 Stat. 4405; Apr. 22, 1993, eff. Dec. 1, 1993; Apr. 26, 2011, eff. Dec. 1, 2011.)

RULE 1102. AMENDMENTS

These rules may be amended as provided in 28 U.S.C. § 2072.

(Pub.L. 93–595, § 1, Jan. 2, 1975, 88 Stat.1948; Apr. 30, 1991, eff. Dec. 1, 1991; Apr. 26, 2011, eff. Dec. 1, 2011.)

RULE 1103. TITLE

These rules may be cited as the Federal Rules of Evidence.

(Pub.L. 93–595, § 1, Jan. 2, 1975, 88 Stat.1948; Apr. 26, 2011, eff. Dec. 1, 2011.)

INDEX TO
FEDERAL RULES OF EVIDENCE

FEDERAL RULES OF APPELLATE PROCEDURE

Effective July 1, 1968
Including Amendments Effective December 1, 2014

TITLE I. APPLICABILITY OF RULES

RULE 1. SCOPE OF RULES; DEFINITION; TITLE

(a) Scope of Rules.

(1) These rules govern procedure in the United States courts of appeals.

(2) When these rules provide for filing a motion or other document in the district court, the procedure must comply with the practice of the district court.

(b) Definition. In these rules, "state" includes the District of Columbia and any United States commonwealth or territory.

(c) Title. These rules are to be known as the Federal Rules of Appellate Procedure.

(As amended Apr. 30, 1979, eff. Aug. 1, 1979; Apr. 25, 1989, eff. Dec. 1, 1989; Apr. 29, 1994, eff. Dec. 1, 1994; Apr. 24, 1998, eff. Dec. 1, 1998; Apr. 29, 2002, eff. Dec. 1, 2002; Apr. 28, 2010, eff. Dec. 1, 2010.)

RULE 2. SUSPENSION OF RULES

On its own or a party's motion, a court of appeals may—to expedite its decision or for other good cause—suspend any provision of these rules in a particular case and order proceedings as it directs, except as otherwise provided in Rule 26(b).

(As amended Apr. 24, 1998, eff. Dec. 1, 1998.)

TITLE II. APPEAL FROM A JUDGMENT OR ORDER OF A DISTRICT COURT

RULE 3. APPEAL AS OF RIGHT— HOW TAKEN

(a) Filing the Notice of Appeal.

(1) An appeal permitted by law as of right from a district court to a court of appeals may be taken only by filing a notice of appeal with the district clerk within the time allowed by Rule 4. At the time of filing, the appellant must furnish the clerk with enough copies of the notice to enable the clerk to comply with Rule 3(d).

(2) An appellant's failure to take any step other than the timely filing of a notice of appeal does not affect the validity of the appeal, but is ground only for the court of appeals to act as it considers appropriate, including dismissing the appeal.

(3) An appeal from a judgment by a magistrate judge in a civil case is taken in the same way as an appeal from any other district court judgment.

(4) An appeal by permission under 28 U.S.C. § 1292(b) or an appeal in a bankruptcy case may be taken only in the manner prescribed by Rules 5 and 6, respectively.

(b) Joint or Consolidated Appeals.

(1) When two or more parties are entitled to appeal from a district-court judgment or order, and their interests make joinder practicable, they may file a joint notice of appeal. They may then proceed on appeal as a single appellant.

(2) When the parties have filed separate timely notices of appeal, the appeals may be joined or consolidated by the court of appeals.

(c) Contents of the Notice of Appeal.

(1) The notice of appeal must:

(A) specify the party or parties taking the appeal by naming each one in the caption or body of the notice, but an attorney representing more than one party may describe those parties with such terms as "all plaintiffs," "the defendants," "the plaintiffs A, B, et al.," or "all defendants except X";

(B) designate the judgment, order, or part thereof being appealed; and

(C) name the court to which the appeal is taken.

(2) A pro se notice of appeal is considered filed on behalf of the signer and the signer's spouse and minor children (if they are parties), unless the notice clearly indicates otherwise.

(3) In a class action, whether or not the class has been certified, the notice of appeal is sufficient if it names one person qualified to bring the appeal as representative of the class.

(4) An appeal must not be dismissed for informality of form or title of the notice of appeal, or for failure to name a party whose intent to appeal is otherwise clear from the notice.

(5) Form 1 in the Appendix of Forms is a suggested form of a notice of appeal.

(d) Serving the Notice of Appeal.

(1) The district clerk must serve notice of the filing of a notice of appeal by mailing a copy to each party's counsel of record—excluding the appellant's—or, if a party is proceeding pro se, to the party's last known address. When a defendant in a criminal case appeals, the clerk must also serve a copy of the notice of appeal on the defendant, either by personal service or by mail addressed to the defendant. The clerk must promptly send a copy of the notice of appeal and of the docket entries—and any later docket entries—to the clerk of the court of appeals named in the notice. The district clerk must note, on each copy, the date when the notice of appeal was filed.

(2) If an inmate confined in an institution files a notice of appeal in the manner provided by Rule 4(c), the district clerk must also note the date when the clerk docketed the notice.

(3) The district clerk's failure to serve notice does not affect the validity of the appeal. The clerk must note on the docket the names of the parties to whom the clerk mails copies, with the date of mailing. Service is sufficient despite the death of a party or the party's counsel.

(e) Payment of Fees. Upon filing a notice of appeal, the appellant must pay the district clerk all required fees. The district clerk receives the appellate docket fee on behalf of the court of appeals.

(As amended Apr. 30, 1979, eff. Aug. 1, 1979; Mar. 10, 1986, eff. July 1, 1986; Apr. 25, 1989, eff. Dec. 1, 1989; Apr. 22, 1993, eff. Dec. 1, 1993; Apr. 29, 1994, eff. Dec. 1, 1994; Apr. 24, 1998, eff. Dec. 1, 1998.)

[RULE 3.1. APPEAL FROM A JUDGMENT OF A MAGISTRATE JUDGE IN A CIVIL CASE (Abrogated Apr. 24, 1998, eff. Dec. 1, 1998)]

RULE 4. APPEAL AS OF RIGHT— WHEN TAKEN

(a) Appeal in a Civil Case.

(1) Time for Filing a Notice of Appeal.

(A) In a civil case, except as provided in Rules 4(a)(1)(B), 4(a)(4), and 4(c), the notice of appeal required by Rule 3 must be filed with the district clerk within 30 days after entry of the judgment or order appealed from.

(B) The notice of appeal may be filed by any party within 60 days after entry of the judgment or order appealed from if one of the parties is:

(i) the United States;

(ii) a United States agency;

(iii) a United States officer or employee sued in an official capacity; or

(iv) a current or former United States officer or employee sued in an individual capacity for an act or omission occurring in connection with duties performed on the United States' behalf— including all instances in which the United States represents that person when the judgment or order is entered or files the appeal for that person.

(C) An appeal from an order granting or denying an application for a writ of error coram nobis is an appeal in a civil case for purposes of Rule 4(a).

(2) Filing Before Entry of Judgment. A notice of appeal filed after the court announces a decision or order—but before the entry of the judgment or order—is treated as filed on the date of and after the entry.

(3) Multiple Appeals. If one party timely files a notice of appeal, any other party may file a notice of appeal within 14 days after the date when the first notice was filed, or within the time otherwise prescribed by this Rule 4(a), whichever period ends later.

(4) Effect of a Motion on a Notice of Appeal.

(A) If a party timely files in the district court any of the following motions under the Federal Rules of Civil Procedure, the time to file an appeal runs for all parties from the entry of the order disposing of the last such remaining motion:

(i) for judgment under Rule 50(b);

(ii) to amend or make additional factual findings under Rule 52(b), whether or not granting the motion would alter the judgment;

(iii) for attorney's fees under Rule 54 if the district court extends the time to appeal under Rule 58;

(iv) to alter or amend the judgment under Rule 59;

(v) for a new trial under Rule 59; or

(vi) for relief under Rule 60 if the motion is filed no later than 28 days after the judgment is entered.

(B)(i) If a party files a notice of appeal after the court announces or enters a judgment—but before it disposes of any motion listed in Rule

4(a)(4)(A)—the notice becomes effective to appeal a judgment or order, in whole or in part, when the order disposing of the last such remaining motion is entered.

(ii) A party intending to challenge an order disposing of any motion listed in Rule 4(a)(4)(A), or a judgment's alteration or amendment upon such a motion, must file a notice of appeal, or an amended notice of appeal—in compliance with Rule 3(c)—within the time prescribed by this Rule measured from the entry of the order disposing of the last such remaining motion.

(iii) No additional fee is required to file an amended notice.

(5) Motion for Extension of Time.

(A) The district court may extend the time to file a notice of appeal if:

(i) a party so moves no later than 30 days after the time prescribed by this Rule 4(a) expires; and

(ii) regardless of whether its motion is filed before or during the 30 days after the time prescribed by this Rule 4(a) expires, that party shows excusable neglect or good cause.

(B) A motion filed before the expiration of the time prescribed in Rule 4(a)(1) or (3) may be ex parte unless the court requires otherwise. If the motion is filed after the expiration of the prescribed time, notice must be given to the other parties in accordance with local rules.

(C) No extension under this Rule 4(a)(5) may exceed 30 days after the prescribed time or 14 days after the date when the order granting the motion is entered, whichever is later.

(6) Reopening the Time to File an Appeal. The district court may reopen the time to file an appeal for a period of 14 days after the date when its order to reopen is entered, but only if all the following conditions are satisfied:

(A) the court finds that the moving party did not receive notice under Federal Rule of Civil Procedure 77(d) of the entry of the judgment or order sought to be appealed within 21 days after entry;

(B) the motion is filed within 180 days after the judgment or order is entered or within 14 days after the moving party receives notice under Federal Rule of Civil Procedure 77(d) of the entry, whichever is earlier; and

(C) the court finds that no party would be prejudiced.

(7) Entry Defined.

(A) A judgment or order is entered for purposes of this Rule 4(a):

(i) if Federal Rule of Civil Procedure 58(a) does not require a separate document, when the judgment or order is entered in the civil docket under Federal Rule of Civil Procedure 79(a); or

(ii) if Federal Rule of Civil Procedure 58(a) requires a separate document, when the judgment or order is entered in the civil docket under Federal Rule of Civil Procedure 79(a) and when the earlier of these events occurs:

● the judgment or order is set forth on a separate document, or

● 150 days have run from entry of the judgment or order in the civil docket under Federal Rule of Civil Procedure 79(a).

(B) A failure to set forth a judgment or order on a separate document when required by Federal Rule of Civil Procedure 58(a) does not affect the validity of an appeal from that judgment or order.

(b) Appeal in a Criminal Case.

(1) Time for Filing a Notice of Appeal.

(A) In a criminal case, a defendant's notice of appeal must be filed in the district court within 14 days after the later of:

(i) the entry of either the judgment or the order being appealed; or

(ii) the filing of the government's notice of appeal.

(B) When the government is entitled to appeal, its notice of appeal must be filed in the district court within 30 days after the later of:

(i) the entry of the judgment or order being appealed; or

(ii) the filing of a notice of appeal by any defendant.

(2) Filing Before Entry of Judgment. A notice of appeal filed after the court announces a decision, sentence, or order—but before the entry of the judgment or order—is treated as filed on the date of and after the entry.

(3) Effect of a Motion on a Notice of Appeal.

(A) If a defendant timely makes any of the following motions under the Federal Rules of Criminal Procedure, the notice of appeal from a judgment of conviction must be filed within 14 days after the entry of the order disposing of the last such remaining motion, or within 14 days after the entry of the judgment of conviction, whichever period ends later. This provision applies to a timely motion:

(i) for judgment of acquittal under Rule 29;

(ii) for a new trial under Rule 33, but if based on newly discovered evidence, only if the motion is made no later than 14 days after the entry of the judgment; or

(iii) for arrest of judgment under Rule 34.

(B) A notice of appeal filed after the court announces a decision, sentence, or order—but before it disposes of any of the motions referred to in Rule 4(b)(3)(A)—becomes effective upon the later of the following:

(i) the entry of the order disposing of the last such remaining motion; or

(ii) the entry of the judgment of conviction.

(C) A valid notice of appeal is effective—without amendment—to appeal from an order disposing of any of the motions referred to in Rule 4(b)(3)(A).

(4) Motion for Extension of Time. Upon a finding of excusable neglect or good cause, the district court may—before or after the time has expired, with or without motion and notice—extend the time to file a notice of appeal for a period not to exceed 30 days from the expiration of the time otherwise prescribed by this Rule 4(b).

(5) Jurisdiction. The filing of a notice of appeal under this Rule 4(b) does not divest a district court of jurisdiction to correct a sentence under Federal Rule of Criminal Procedure 35(a), nor does the filing of a motion under 35(a) affect the validity of a notice of appeal filed before entry of the order disposing of the motion. The filing of a motion under Federal Rule of Criminal Procedure 35(a) does not suspend the time for filing a notice of appeal from a judgment of conviction.

(6) Entry Defined. A judgment or order is entered for purposes of this Rule 4(b) when it is entered on the criminal docket.

(c) Appeal by an Inmate Confined in an Institution.

(1) If an inmate confined in an institution files a notice of appeal in either a civil or a criminal case, the notice is timely if it is deposited in the institution's internal mail system on or before the last day for filing. If an institution has a system designed for legal mail, the inmate must use that system to receive the benefit of this rule. Timely filing may be shown by a declaration in compliance with 28 U.S.C. § 1746 or by a notarized statement, either of which must set forth the date of deposit and state that first-class postage has been prepaid.

(2) If an inmate files the first notice of appeal in a civil case under this Rule 4(c), the 14–day period provided in Rule 4(a)(3) for another party to file a notice of appeal runs from the date when the district court dockets the first notice.

(3) When a defendant in a criminal case files a notice of appeal under this Rule 4(c), the 30–day period for the government to file its notice of appeal runs from the entry of the judgment or order appealed from or from the district court's docketing of the defendant's notice of appeal, whichever is later.

(d) Mistaken Filing in the Court of Appeals. If a notice of appeal in either a civil or a criminal case is mistakenly filed in the court of appeals, the clerk of that court must note on the notice the date when it was received and send it to the district clerk. The notice is then considered filed in the district court on the date so noted.

(As amended Apr. 30, 1979, eff. Aug. 1, 1979; Nov. 18, 1988, Pub.L. 100–690, Title VII, § 7111, 102 Stat. 4419; Apr. 30, 1991, eff. Dec. 1, 1991; Apr. 22, 1993, eff. Dec. 1, 1993; Apr. 27, 1995, eff. Dec. 1, 1995; Apr. 24, 1998, eff. Dec. 1, 1998; Apr. 29, 2002, eff. Dec. 1, 2002; Apr. 25, 2005, eff. Dec. 1, 2005; Mar. 26, 2009, eff. Dec. 1, 2009; Apr. 28, 2010, eff. Dec. 1, 2010; Apr. 26, 2011, eff. Dec. 1, 2011.)

RULE 5.   APPEAL BY PERMISSION

(a) Petition for Permission to Appeal.

(1) To request permission to appeal when an appeal is within the court of appeals' discretion, a party must file a petition for permission to appeal. The petition must be filed with the circuit clerk with proof of service on all other parties to the district-court action.

(2) The petition must be filed within the time specified by the statute or rule authorizing the appeal or, if no such time is specified, within the time provided by Rule 4(a) for filing a notice of appeal.

(3) If a party cannot petition for appeal unless the district court first enters an order granting permission to do so or stating that the necessary conditions are met, the district court may amend its order, either on its own or in response to a party's motion, to include the required permission or statement. In that event, the time to petition runs from entry of the amended order.

(b) Contents of the Petition; Answer or Cross– Petition; Oral Argument.

(1) The petition must include the following:

(A) the facts necessary to understand the question presented;

(B) the question itself;

(C) the relief sought;

(D) the reasons why the appeal should be allowed and is authorized by a statute or rule; and

(E) an attached copy of:

(i) the order, decree, or judgment complained of and any related opinion or memorandum, and

(ii) any order stating the district court's permission to appeal or finding that the necessary conditions are met.

(2) A party may file an answer in opposition or a cross-petition within 10 days after the petition is served.

(3) The petition and answer will be submitted without oral argument unless the court of appeals orders otherwise.

(c) Form of Papers; Number of Copies. All papers must conform to Rule 32(c)(2). Except by the court's permission, a paper must not exceed 20 pages, exclusive of the disclosure statement, the proof of service, and the accompanying documents required by Rule 5(b)(1)(E). An original and 3 copies must be filed unless the court requires a different number by local rule or by order in a particular case.

(d) Grant of Permission; Fees; Cost Bond; Filing the Record.

(1) Within 14 days after the entry of the order granting permission to appeal, the appellant must:

(A) pay the district clerk all required fees; and

(B) file a cost bond if required under Rule 7.

(2) A notice of appeal need not be filed. The date when the order granting permission to appeal is entered serves as the date of the notice of appeal for calculating time under these rules.

(3) The district clerk must notify the circuit clerk once the petitioner has paid the fees. Upon receiving this notice, the circuit clerk must enter the appeal on the docket. The record must be forwarded and filed in accordance with Rules 11 and 12(c).

(As amended Apr. 30, 1979, eff. Aug. 1, 1979; Apr. 29, 1994, eff. Dec. 1, 1994; Apr. 24, 1998, eff. Dec. 1, 1998; Apr. 29, 2002, eff. Dec. 1, 2002; Mar. 26, 2009, eff. Dec. 1, 2009.)

[RULE 5.1. APPEAL BY LEAVE UNDER 28 U.S.C. § 636(c)(5) (Abrogated Apr. 24, 1998, eff. Dec. 1, 1998)]

RULE 6. APPEAL IN A BANKRUPTCY CASE

(a) Appeal From a Judgment, Order, or Decree of a District Court Exercising Original Jurisdiction in a Bankruptcy Case. An appeal to a court of appeals from a final judgment, order, or decree of a district court exercising jurisdiction under 28 U.S.C. § 1334 is taken as any other civil appeal under these rules.

(b) Appeal From a Judgment, Order, or Decree of a District Court or Bankruptcy Appellate Panel

Exercising Appellate Jurisdiction in a Bankruptcy Case.

(1) Applicability of Other Rules. These rules apply to an appeal to a court of appeals under 28 U.S.C. § 158(d)(1) from a final judgment, order, or decree of a district court or bankruptcy appellate panel exercising appellate jurisdiction under 28 U.S.C. § 158(a) or (b), but with these qualifications:

(A) Rules 4(a)(4), 4(b), 9, 10, 11, 12(c), 13–20, 22–23, and 24(b) do not apply;

(B) the reference in Rule 3(c) to "Form 1 in the Appendix of Forms" must be read as a reference to Form 5;

(C) when the appeal is from a bankruptcy appellate panel, "district court," as used in any applicable rule, means "appellate panel"; and

(D) in Rule 12.1, "district court" includes a bankruptcy court or bankruptcy appellate panel.

(2) Additional Rules. In addition to the rules made applicable by Rule 6(b)(1), the following rules apply:

(A) Motion for Rehearing.

(i) If a timely motion for rehearing under Bankruptcy Rule 8022 is filed, the time to appeal for all parties runs from the entry of the order disposing of the motion. A notice of appeal filed after the district court or bankruptcy appellate panel announces or enters a judgment, order, or decree—but before disposition of the motion for rehearing—becomes effective when the order disposing of the motion for rehearing is entered.

(ii) If a party intends to challenge the order disposing of the motion—or the alteration or amendment of a judgment, order, or decree upon the motion—then the party, in compliance with Rules 3(c) and 6(b)(1)(B), must file a notice of appeal or amended notice of appeal. The notice or amended notice must be filed within the time prescribed by Rule 4—excluding Rules 4(a)(4) and 4(b)—measured from the entry of the order disposing of the motion.

(iii) No additional fee is required to file an amended notice.

(B) The Record on Appeal.

(i) Within 14 days after filing the notice of appeal, the appellant must file with the clerk possessing the record assembled in accordance with Bankruptcy Rule 8009—and serve on the appellee—a statement of the issues to be presented on appeal and a designation of the record to be certified and made available to the circuit clerk.

(ii) An appellee who believes that other parts of the record are necessary must, within 14 days after being served with the appellant's designation, file with the clerk and serve on the appellant a designation of additional parts to be included.

(iii) The record on appeal consists of:

● the redesignated record as provided above;

● the proceedings in the district court or bankruptcy appellate panel; and

● a certified copy of the docket entries prepared by the clerk under Rule 3(d).

(C) Making the Record Available.

(i) When the record is complete, the district clerk or bankruptcy-appellate-panel clerk must number the documents constituting the record and promptly make it available to the circuit clerk. If the clerk makes the record available in paper form, the clerk will not send documents of unusual bulk or weight, physical exhibits other than documents, or other parts of the record designated for omission by local rule of the court of appeals, unless directed to do so by a party or the circuit clerk. If unusually bulky or heavy exhibits are to be made available in paper form, a party must arrange with the clerks in advance for their transportation and receipt.

(ii) All parties must do whatever else is necessary to enable the clerk to assemble the record and make it available. When the record is made available in paper form, the court of appeals may provide by rule or order that a certified copy of the docket entries be made available in place of the redesignated record. But any party may request at any time during the pendency of the appeal that the redesignated record be made available.

(D) Filing the Record. When the district clerk or bankruptcy-appellate-panel clerk has made the record available, the circuit clerk must note that fact on the docket. The date noted on the docket serves as the filing date of the record. The circuit clerk must immediately notify all parties of the filing date.

(c) Direct Review by Permission Under 28 U.S.C. § 158(d)(2).

(1) Applicability of Other Rules. These rules apply to a direct appeal by permission under 28 U.S.C. § 158(d)(2), but with these qualifications:

(A) Rules 3–4, 5(a)(3), 6(a), 6(b), 8(a), 8(c), 9–12, 13–20, 22–23, and 24(b) do not apply;

(B) as used in any applicable rule, "district court" or "district clerk" includes—to the extent appropriate—a bankruptcy court or bankruptcy appellate panel or its clerk; and

(C) the reference to "Rules 11 and 12(c)" in Rule 5(d)(3) must be read as a reference to Rules 6(c)(2)(B) and (C).

(2) Additional Rules. In addition, the following rules apply:

(A) The Record on Appeal. Bankruptcy Rule 8009 governs the record on appeal.

(B) Making the Record Available. Bankruptcy Rule 8010 governs completing the record and making it available.

(C) Stays Pending Appeal. Bankruptcy Rule 8007 applies to stays pending appeal.

(D) Duties of the Circuit Clerk. When the bankruptcy clerk has made the record available, the circuit clerk must note that fact on the docket. The date noted on the docket serves as the filing date of the record. The circuit clerk must immediately notify all parties of the filing date.

(E) Filing a Representation Statement. Unless the court of appeals designates another time, within 14 days after entry of the order granting permission to appeal, the attorney who sought permission must file a statement with the circuit clerk naming the parties that the attorney represents on appeal.

(Added Apr. 25, 1989, eff. Dec. 1, 1989, and amended Apr. 30, 1991, eff. Dec. 1, 1991; Apr. 22, 1993, eff. Dec. 1, 1993; Apr. 24, 1998, eff. Dec. 1, 1998; Mar. 26, 2009, eff. Dec. 1, 2009; Apr. 25, 2014, eff. Dec. 1, 2014.)

RULE 7. BOND FOR COSTS ON APPEAL IN A CIVIL CASE

In a civil case, the district court may require an appellant to file a bond or provide other security in any form and amount necessary to ensure payment of costs on appeal. Rule 8(b) applies to a surety on a bond given under this rule.

(As amended Apr. 30, 1979, eff. Aug. 1, 1979; Apr. 24, 1998, eff. Dec. 1, 1998.)

RULE 8. STAY OR INJUNCTION PENDING APPEAL

(a) Motion for Stay.

(1) Initial Motion in the District Court. A party must ordinarily move first in the district court for the following relief:

(A) a stay of the judgment or order of a district court pending appeal;

(B) approval of a supersedeas bond; or

(C) an order suspending, modifying, restoring, or granting an injunction while an appeal is pending.

(2) Motion in the Court of Appeals; Conditions on Relief. A motion for the relief mentioned in Rule 8(a)(1) may be made to the court of appeals or to one of its judges.

(A) The motion must:

(i) show that moving first in the district court would be impracticable; or

(ii) state that, a motion having been made, the district court denied the motion or failed to afford the relief requested and state any reasons given by the district court for its action.

(B) The motion must also include:

(i) the reasons for granting the relief requested and the facts relied on;

(ii) originals or copies of affidavits or other sworn statements supporting facts subject to dispute; and

(iii) relevant parts of the record.

(C) The moving party must give reasonable notice of the motion to all parties.

(D) A motion under this Rule 8(a)(2) must be filed with the circuit clerk and normally will be considered by a panel of the court. But in an exceptional case in which time requirements make that procedure impracticable, the motion may be made to and considered by a single judge.

(E) The court may condition relief on a party's filing a bond or other appropriate security in the district court.

(b) Proceeding Against a Surety. If a party gives security in the form of a bond or stipulation or other undertaking with one or more sureties, each surety submits to the jurisdiction of the district court and irrevocably appoints the district clerk as the surety's agent on whom any papers affecting the surety's liability on the bond or undertaking may be served. On motion, a surety's liability may be enforced in the district court without the necessity of an independent action. The motion and any notice that the district court prescribes may be served on the district clerk, who must promptly mail a copy to each surety whose address is known.

(c) Stay in a Criminal Case. Rule 38 of the Federal Rules of Criminal Procedure governs a stay in a criminal case.

(As amended Mar. 10, 1986, eff. July 1, 1986; Apr. 27, 1995, eff. Dec. 1, 1995; Apr. 24, 1998, eff. Dec. 1, 1998.)

RULE 9. RELEASE IN A CRIMINAL CASE

(a) Release Before Judgment of Conviction.

(1) The district court must state in writing, or orally on the record, the reasons for an order regarding the release or detention of a defendant in a criminal case. A party appealing from the order must file with the court of appeals a copy of the district court's order and the court's statement of reasons as soon as practicable after filing the notice of appeal. An appellant who questions the factual basis for the district court's order must file a transcript of the release proceedings or an explanation of why a transcript was not obtained.

(2) After reasonable notice to the appellee, the court of appeals must promptly determine the appeal on the basis of the papers, affidavits, and parts of the record that the parties present or the court requires. Unless the court so orders, briefs need not be filed.

(3) The court of appeals or one of its judges may order the defendant's release pending the disposition of the appeal.

(b) Release After Judgment of Conviction. A party entitled to do so may obtain review of a district-court order regarding release after a judgment of conviction by filing a notice of appeal from that order in the district court, or by filing a motion in the court of appeals if the party has already filed a notice of appeal from the judgment of conviction. Both the order and the review are subject to Rule 9(a). The papers filed by the party seeking review must include a copy of the judgment of conviction.

(c) Criteria for Release. The court must make its decision regarding release in accordance with the applicable provisions of 18 U.S.C. §§ 3142, 3143, and 3145(c).

(As amended Apr. 24, 1972, eff. Oct. 1, 1972; Oct. 12, 1984, Pub.L. 98–473, Title II, § 210, 98 Stat. 1987; Apr. 29, 1994, eff. Dec. 1, 1994; Apr. 24, 1998, eff. Dec. 1, 1998.)

RULE 10. THE RECORD ON APPEAL

(a) Composition of the Record on Appeal. The following items constitute the record on appeal:

(1) the original papers and exhibits filed in the district court;

(2) the transcript of proceedings, if any; and

(3) a certified copy of the docket entries prepared by the district clerk.

(b) The Transcript of Proceedings.

(1) Appellant's Duty to Order. Within 14 days after filing the notice of appeal or entry of an order disposing of the last timely remaining motion of a type specified in Rule 4(a)(4)(A), whichever is later, the appellant must do either of the following:

(A) order from the reporter a transcript of such parts of the proceedings not already on file as the appellant considers necessary, subject to a local rule of the court of appeals and with the following qualifications:

(i) the order must be in writing;

(ii) if the cost of the transcript is to be paid by the United States under the Criminal Justice Act, the order must so state; and

(iii) the appellant must, within the same period, file a copy of the order with the district clerk; or

(B) file a certificate stating that no transcript will be ordered.

(2) Unsupported Finding or Conclusion. If the appellant intends to urge on appeal that a finding or conclusion is unsupported by the evidence or is contrary to the evidence, the appellant must include in the record a transcript of all evidence relevant to that finding or conclusion.

(3) Partial Transcript. Unless the entire transcript is ordered:

(A) the appellant must—within the 14 days provided in Rule 10(b)(1)—file a statement of the issues that the appellant intends to present on the appeal and must serve on the appellee a copy of both the order or certificate and the statement;

(B) if the appellee considers it necessary to have a transcript of other parts of the proceedings, the appellee must, within 14 days after the service of the order or certificate and the statement of the issues, file and serve on the appellant a designation of additional parts to be ordered; and

(C) unless within 14 days after service of that designation the appellant has ordered all such parts, and has so notified the appellee, the appellee may within the following 14 days either order the parts or move in the district court for an order requiring the appellant to do so.

(4) Payment. At the time of ordering, a party must make satisfactory arrangements with the reporter for paying the cost of the transcript.

(c) Statement of the Evidence When the Proceedings Were Not Recorded or When a Transcript Is Unavailable. If the transcript of a hearing or trial is unavailable, the appellant may prepare a statement of the evidence or proceedings from the best available means, including the appellant's recollection. The statement must be served on the appellee, who may serve objections or proposed amendments within 14 days after being served. The statement and any objections or proposed amendments must then be submitted to the district court for settlement and approval. As settled and approved, the statement must be included by the district clerk in the record on appeal.

(d) Agreed Statement as the Record on Appeal. In place of the record on appeal as defined in Rule 10(a), the parties may prepare, sign, and submit to the district court a statement of the case showing how the issues presented by the appeal arose and were decided in the district court. The statement must set forth only those facts averred and proved or sought to be proved that are essential to the court's resolution of the issues. If the statement is truthful, it—together with any additions that the district court may consider necessary to a full presentation of the issues on appeal—must be approved by the district court and must then be certified to the court of appeals as the record on appeal. The district clerk must then send it to the circuit clerk within the time provided by Rule 11. A copy of the agreed statement may be filed in place of the appendix required by Rule 30.

(e) Correction or Modification of the Record.

(1) If any difference arises about whether the record truly discloses what occurred in the district court, the difference must be submitted to and settled by that court and the record conformed accordingly.

(2) If anything material to either party is omitted from or misstated in the record by error or accident, the omission or misstatement may be corrected and a supplemental record may be certified and forwarded:

(A) on stipulation of the parties;

(B) by the district court before or after the record has been forwarded; or

(C) by the court of appeals.

(3) All other questions as to the form and content of the record must be presented to the court of appeals.

(As amended Apr. 30, 1979, eff. Aug. 1, 1979; Mar. 10, 1986, eff. July 1, 1986; Apr. 30, 1991, eff. Dec. 1, 1991; Apr. 22, 1993, eff. Dec. 1, 1993; Apr. 27, 1995, eff. Dec. 1, 1995; Apr. 24, 1998, eff. Dec. 1, 1998; Mar. 26, 2009, eff. Dec. 1, 2009.)

RULE 11.   FORWARDING THE RECORD

(a) Appellant's Duty. An appellant filing a notice of appeal must comply with Rule 10(b) and must do whatever else is necessary to enable the clerk to assemble and forward the record. If there are multiple appeals from a judgment or order, the clerk must forward a single record.

(b) Duties of Reporter and District Clerk.

(1) Reporter's Duty to Prepare and File a Transcript. The reporter must prepare and file a transcript as follows:

(A) Upon receiving an order for a transcript, the reporter must enter at the foot of the order the date of its receipt and the expected completion date and send a copy, so endorsed, to the circuit clerk.

(B) If the transcript cannot be completed within 30 days of the reporter's receipt of the order, the reporter may request the circuit clerk to grant additional time to complete it. The clerk must note on the docket the action taken and notify the parties.

(C) When a transcript is complete, the reporter must file it with the district clerk and notify the circuit clerk of the filing.

(D) If the reporter fails to file the transcript on time, the circuit clerk must notify the district judge and do whatever else the court of appeals directs.

(2) District Clerk's Duty to Forward. When the record is complete, the district clerk must number the documents constituting the record and send them promptly to the circuit clerk together with a list of the documents correspondingly numbered and reasonably identified. Unless directed to do so by a party or the circuit clerk, the district clerk will not send to the court of appeals documents of unusual bulk or weight, physical exhibits other than documents, or other parts of the record designated for omission by local rule of the court of appeals. If the exhibits are unusually bulky or heavy, a party must arrange with the clerks in advance for their transportation and receipt.

(c) Retaining the Record Temporarily in the District Court for Use in Preparing the Appeal. The parties may stipulate, or the district court on motion may order, that the district clerk retain the record temporarily for the parties to use in preparing the papers on appeal. In that event the district clerk must certify to the circuit clerk that the record on appeal is complete. Upon receipt of the appellee's brief, or earlier if the court orders or the parties agree, the appellant must request the district clerk to forward the record.

(d) [Abrogated.]

(e) Retaining the Record by Court Order.

(1) The court of appeals may, by order or local rule, provide that a certified copy of the docket entries be forwarded instead of the entire record. But a party may at any time during the appeal request that designated parts of the record be forwarded.

(2) The district court may order the record or some part of it retained if the court needs it while the appeal is pending, subject, however, to call by the court of appeals.

(3) If part or all of the record is ordered retained, the district clerk must send to the court of appeals a copy of the order and the docket entries together with the parts of the original record allowed by the district court and copies of any parts of the record designated by the parties.

(f) Retaining Parts of the Record in the District Court by Stipulation of the Parties. The parties may agree by written stipulation filed in the district court that designated parts of the record be retained in the district court subject to call by the court of appeals or request by a party. The parts of the record so designated remain a part of the record on appeal.

(g) Record for a Preliminary Motion in the Court of Appeals. If, before the record is forwarded, a party makes any of the following motions in the court of appeals:

- for dismissal;

- for release;

- for a stay pending appeal;

- for additional security on the bond on appeal or on a supersedeas bond; or

- for any other intermediate order—

the district clerk must send the court of appeals any parts of the record designated by any party.

(As amended Apr. 30, 1979, eff. Aug. 1, 1979; Mar. 10, 1986, eff. July 1, 1986; Apr. 24, 1998, eff. Dec. 1, 1998.)

RULE 12.　DOCKETING THE APPEAL; FILING A REPRESENTATION STATEMENT; FILING THE RECORD

(a) Docketing the Appeal. Upon receiving the copy of the notice of appeal and the docket entries from the district clerk under Rule 3(d), the circuit clerk must docket the appeal under the title of the district-court action and must identify the appellant, adding the appellant's name if necessary.

(b) Filing a Representation Statement. Unless the court of appeals designates another time, the attorney who filed the notice of appeal must, within 14 days after filing the notice, file a statement with the circuit clerk naming the parties that the attorney represents on appeal.

(c) Filing the Record, Partial Record, or Certificate. Upon receiving the record, partial record, or district clerk's certificate as provided in Rule 11, the circuit clerk must file it and immediately notify all parties of the filing date.

(As amended Apr. 30, 1979, eff. Aug. 1, 1979; Mar. 10, 1986, eff. July 1, 1986; Apr. 22, 1993, eff. Dec. 1, 1993; Apr. 24, 1998, eff. Dec. 1, 1998; Mar. 26, 2009, eff. Dec. 1, 2009.)

RULE 12.1. REMAND AFTER AN INDICATIVE RULING BY THE DISTRICT COURT ON A MOTION FOR RELIEF THAT IS BARRED BY A PENDING APPEAL

(a) **Notice to the Court of Appeals.** If a timely motion is made in the district court for relief that it lacks authority to grant because of an appeal that has been docketed and is pending, the movant must promptly notify the circuit clerk if the district court states either that it would grant the motion or that the motion raises a substantial issue.

(b) **Remand After an Indicative Ruling.** If the district court states that it would grant the motion or that the motion raises a substantial issue, the court of appeals may remand for further proceedings but retains jurisdiction unless it expressly dismisses the appeal. If the court of appeals remands but retains jurisdiction, the parties must promptly notify the circuit clerk when the district court has decided the motion on remand.

(Added Mar. 26, 2009, eff. Dec. 1, 2009.)

TITLE III. APPEALS FROM THE UNITED STATES TAX COURT

RULE 13. APPEALS FROM THE TAX COURT

(a) **Appeal as of Right.**

(1) **How Obtained; Time for Filing a Notice of Appeal.**

(A) An appeal as of right from the United States Tax Court is commenced by filing a notice of appeal with the Tax Court clerk within 90 days after the entry of the Tax Court's decision. At the time of filing, the appellant must furnish the clerk with enough copies of the notice to enable the clerk to comply with Rule 3(d). If one party files a timely notice of appeal, any other party may file a notice of appeal within 120 days after the Tax Court's decision is entered.

(B) If, under Tax Court rules, a party makes a timely motion to vacate or revise the Tax Court's decision, the time to file a notice of appeal runs from the entry of the order disposing of the motion or from the entry of a new decision, whichever is later.

(2) **Notice of Appeal; How Filed.** The notice of appeal may be filed either at the Tax Court clerk's office in the District of Columbia or by mail addressed to the clerk. If sent by mail the notice is considered filed on the postmark date, subject to § 7502 of the Internal Revenue Code, as amended, and the applicable regulations.

(3) **Contents of the Notice of Appeal; Service; Effect of Filing and Service.** Rule 3 prescribes the contents of a notice of appeal, the manner of service, and the effect of its filing and service. Form 2 in the Appendix of Forms is a suggested form of a notice of appeal.

(4) **The Record on Appeal; Forwarding; Filing.**

(A) Except as otherwise provided under Tax Court rules for the transcript of proceedings, the appeal is governed by the parts of Rules 10, 11, and 12 regarding the record on appeal from a district court, the time and manner of forwarding and filing, and the docketing in the court of appeals.

(B) If an appeal is taken to more than one court of appeals, the original record must be sent to the court named in the first notice of appeal filed. In an appeal to any other court of appeals, the appellant must apply to that other court to make provision for the record.

(b) **Appeal by Permission.** An appeal by permission is governed by Rule 5.

(As amended Apr. 30, 1979, eff. Aug. 1, 1979; Apr. 29, 1994, eff. Dec. 1, 1994; Apr. 24, 1998, eff. Dec. 1, 1998; Apr. 16, 2013, eff. Dec. 1, 2013.)

RULE 14. APPLICABILITY OF OTHER RULES TO APPEALS FROM THE TAX COURT

All provisions of these rules, except Rules 4, 6–9, 15–20, and 22–23, apply to appeals from the Tax Court. References in any applicable rule (other than Rule 24(a)) to the district court and district clerk are to be read as referring to the Tax Court and its clerk.

(As amended Apr. 24, 1998, eff. Dec. 1, 1998; Apr. 16, 2013, eff. Dec. 1, 2013.)

TITLE IV. REVIEW OR ENFORCEMENT OF AN ORDER OF AN ADMINISTRATIVE AGENCY, BOARD, COMMISSION, OR OFFICER

RULE 15. REVIEW OR ENFORCEMENT OF AN AGENCY ORDER—HOW OBTAINED; INTERVENTION

(a) Petition for Review; Joint Petition.

(1) Review of an agency order is commenced by filing, within the time prescribed by law, a petition for review with the clerk of a court of appeals authorized to review the agency order. If their interests make joinder practicable, two or more persons may join in a petition to the same court to review the same order.

(2) The petition must:

(A) name each party seeking review either in the caption or the body of the petition—using such terms as "et al.," "petitioners," or "respondents" does not effectively name the parties;

(B) name the agency as a respondent (even though not named in the petition, the United States is a respondent if required by statute); and

(C) specify the order or part thereof to be reviewed.

(3) Form 3 in the Appendix of Forms is a suggested form of a petition for review.

(4) In this rule "agency" includes an agency, board, commission, or officer; "petition for review" includes a petition to enjoin, suspend, modify, or otherwise review, or a notice of appeal, whichever form is indicated by the applicable statute.

(b) Application or Cross–Application to Enforce an Order; Answer; Default.

(1) An application to enforce an agency order must be filed with the clerk of a court of appeals authorized to enforce the order. If a petition is filed to review an agency order that the court may enforce, a party opposing the petition may file a cross-application for enforcement.

(2) Within 21 days after the application for enforcement is filed, the respondent must serve on the applicant an answer to the application and file it with the clerk. If the respondent fails to answer in time, the court will enter judgment for the relief requested.

(3) The application must contain a concise statement of the proceedings in which the order was entered, the facts upon which venue is based, and the relief requested.

(c) Service of the Petition or Application. The circuit clerk must serve a copy of the petition for review, or an application or cross-application to enforce an agency order, on each respondent as prescribed by Rule 3(d), unless a different manner of service is prescribed by statute. At the time of filing, the petitioner must:

(1) serve, or have served, a copy on each party admitted to participate in the agency proceedings, except for the respondents;

(2) file with the clerk a list of those so served; and

(3) give the clerk enough copies of the petition or application to serve each respondent.

(d) Intervention. Unless a statute provides another method, a person who wants to intervene in a proceeding under this rule must file a motion for leave to intervene with the circuit clerk and serve a copy on all parties. The motion—or other notice of intervention authorized by statute—must be filed within 30 days after the petition for review is filed and must contain a concise statement of the interest of the moving party and the grounds for intervention.

(e) Payment of Fees. When filing any separate or joint petition for review in a court of appeals, the petitioner must pay the circuit clerk all required fees.

(As amended Apr. 22, 1993, eff. Dec. 1, 1993; Apr. 24, 1998, eff. Dec. 1, 1998; Mar. 26, 2009, eff. Dec. 1, 2009.)

RULE 15.1. BRIEFS AND ORAL ARGUMENT IN A NATIONAL LABOR RELATIONS BOARD PROCEEDING

In either an enforcement or a review proceeding, a party adverse to the National Labor Relations Board proceeds first on briefing and at oral argument, unless the court orders otherwise.

(Added Mar. 10, 1986, eff. July 1, 1986, and amended Apr. 24, 1998, eff. Dec. 1, 1998.)

RULE 16. THE RECORD ON REVIEW OR ENFORCEMENT

(a) Composition of the Record. The record on review or enforcement of an agency order consists of:

(1) the order involved;

(2) any findings or report on which it is based; and

(3) the pleadings, evidence, and other parts of the proceedings before the agency.

(b) Omissions From or Misstatements in the Record. The parties may at any time, by stipulation, supply any omission from the record or correct a misstatement, or the court may so direct. If necessary, the court may direct that a supplemental record be prepared and filed.

(As amended Apr. 24, 1998, eff. Dec. 1, 1998.)

RULE 17. FILING THE RECORD

(a) Agency to File; Time for Filing; Notice of Filing. The agency must file the record with the circuit clerk within 40 days after being served with a petition for review, unless the statute authorizing review provides otherwise, or within 40 days after it files an application for enforcement unless the respondent fails to answer or the court orders otherwise. The court may shorten or extend the time to file the record. The clerk must notify all parties of the date when the record is filed.

(b) Filing—What Constitutes.

(1) The agency must file:

(A) the original or a certified copy of the entire record or parts designated by the parties; or

(B) a certified list adequately describing all documents, transcripts of testimony, exhibits, and other material constituting the record, or describing those parts designated by the parties.

(2) The parties may stipulate in writing that no record or certified list be filed. The date when the stipulation is filed with the circuit clerk is treated as the date when the record is filed.

(3) The agency must retain any portion of the record not filed with the clerk. All parts of the record retained by the agency are a part of the record on review for all purposes and, if the court or a party so requests, must be sent to the court regardless of any prior stipulation.

(As amended Apr. 24, 1998, eff. Dec. 1, 1998.)

RULE 18. STAY PENDING REVIEW

(a) Motion for a Stay.

(1) Initial Motion Before the Agency. A petitioner must ordinarily move first before the agency for a stay pending review of its decision or order.

(2) Motion in the Court of Appeals. A motion for a stay may be made to the court of appeals or one of its judges.

(A) The motion must:

(i) show that moving first before the agency would be impracticable; or

(ii) state that, a motion having been made, the agency denied the motion or failed to afford the relief requested and state any reasons given by the agency for its action.

(B) The motion must also include:

(i) the reasons for granting the relief requested and the facts relied on;

(ii) originals or copies of affidavits or other sworn statements supporting facts subject to dispute; and

(iii) relevant parts of the record.

(C) The moving party must give reasonable notice of the motion to all parties.

(D) The motion must be filed with the circuit clerk and normally will be considered by a panel of the court. But in an exceptional case in which time requirements make that procedure impracticable, the motion may be made to and considered by a single judge.

(b) Bond. The court may condition relief on the filing of a bond or other appropriate security.

(As amended Apr. 24, 1998, eff. Dec. 1, 1998.)

RULE 19. SETTLEMENT OF A JUDGMENT ENFORCING AN AGENCY ORDER IN PART

When the court files an opinion directing entry of judgment enforcing the agency's order in part, the agency must within 14 days file with the clerk and serve on each other party a proposed judgment conforming to the opinion. A party who disagrees with the agency's proposed judgment must within 10 days file with the clerk and serve the agency with a proposed judgment that the party believes conforms to the opinion. The court will settle the judgment and direct entry without further hearing or argument.

(As amended Mar. 10, 1986, eff. July 1, 1986; Apr. 24, 1998, eff. Dec. 1, 1998; Mar. 26, 2009, eff. Dec. 1, 2009.)

RULE 20. APPLICABILITY OF RULES TO THE REVIEW OR ENFORCEMENT OF AN AGENCY ORDER

All provisions of these rules, except Rules 3–14 and 22–23, apply to the review or enforcement of an agency order. In these rules, "appellant" includes a petitioner or applicant, and "appellee" includes a respondent.

(As amended Apr. 24, 1998, eff. Dec. 1, 1998.)

TITLE V. EXTRAORDINARY WRITS

RULE 21. WRITS OF MANDAMUS AND PROHIBITION, AND OTHER EXTRAORDINARY WRITS

(a) Mandamus or Prohibition to a Court: Petition, Filing, Service, and Docketing.

(1) A party petitioning for a writ of mandamus or prohibition directed to a court must file a petition with the circuit clerk with proof of service on all parties to the proceeding in the trial court. The party must also provide a copy to the trial-court judge. All parties to the proceeding in the trial court other than the petitioner are respondents for all purposes.

(2)(A) The petition must be titled "In re [name of petitioner]."

(B) The petition must state:

(i) the relief sought;

(ii) the issues presented;

(iii) the facts necessary to understand the issue presented by the petition; and

(iv) the reasons why the writ should issue.

(C) The petition must include a copy of any order or opinion or parts of the record that may be essential to understand the matters set forth in the petition.

(3) Upon receiving the prescribed docket fee, the clerk must docket the petition and submit it to the court.

(b) Denial; Order Directing Answer; Briefs; Precedence.

(1) The court may deny the petition without an answer. Otherwise, it must order the respondent, if any, to answer within a fixed time.

(2) The clerk must serve the order to respond on all persons directed to respond.

(3) Two or more respondents may answer jointly.

(4) The court of appeals may invite or order the trial-court judge to address the petition or may invite an amicus curiae to do so. The trial-court judge may request permission to address the petition but may not do so unless invited or ordered to do so by the court of appeals.

(5) If briefing or oral argument is required, the clerk must advise the parties, and when appropriate, the trial-court judge or amicus curiae.

(6) The proceeding must be given preference over ordinary civil cases.

(7) The circuit clerk must send a copy of the final disposition to the trial-court judge.

(c) Other Extraordinary Writs. An application for an extraordinary writ other than one provided for in Rule 21(a) must be made by filing a petition with the circuit clerk with proof of service on the respondents. Proceedings on the application must conform, so far as is practicable, to the procedures prescribed in Rule 21(a) and (b).

(d) Form of Papers; Number of Copies. All papers must conform to Rule 32(c)(2). Except by the court's permission, a paper must not exceed 30 pages, exclusive of the disclosure statement, the proof of service, and the accompanying documents required by Rule 21(a)(2)(C). An original and 3 copies must be filed unless the court requires the filing of a different number by local rule or by order in a particular case.

(As amended Apr. 29, 1994, eff. Dec. 1, 1994; Apr. 23, 1996, eff. Dec. 1, 1996; Apr. 24, 1998, eff. Dec. 1, 1998; Apr. 29, 2002, eff. Dec. 1, 2002.)

TITLE VI. HABEAS CORPUS; PROCEEDINGS IN FORMA PAUPERIS

RULE 22. HABEAS CORPUS AND SECTION 2255 PROCEEDINGS

(a) Application for the Original Writ. An application for a writ of habeas corpus must be made to the appropriate district court. If made to a circuit judge, the application must be transferred to the appropriate district court. If a district court denies an application made or transferred to it, renewal of the application before a circuit judge is not permitted. The applicant may, under 28 U.S.C. § 2253, appeal to the court of appeals from the district court's order denying the application.

(b) Certificate of Appealability.

(1) In a habeas corpus proceeding in which the detention complained of arises from process issued by a state court, or in a 28 U.S.C. § 2255 proceeding, the applicant cannot take an appeal unless a circuit justice or a circuit or district judge issues a certificate of appealability under 28 U.S.C. § 2253(c). If an applicant files a notice of appeal, the district clerk must send to the court of appeals the certificate (if any) and the statement described in Rule 11(a) of the Rules Governing Proceedings Under 28 U.S.C. § 2254 or § 2255 (if any), along with the notice of appeal and the file of the district-court proceedings. If the district judge has denied

the certificate, the applicant may request a circuit judge to issue it.

(2) A request addressed to the court of appeals may be considered by a circuit judge or judges, as the court prescribes. If no express request for a certificate is filed, the notice of appeal constitutes a request addressed to the judges of the court of appeals.

(3) A certificate of appealability is not required when a state or its representative or the United States or its representative appeals.

(As amended Pub.L. 104–132, Title I, § 103, Apr. 24, 1996, 110 Stat. 1218; Apr. 24, 1998, eff. Dec. 1, 1998; Mar. 26, 2009, eff. Dec. 1, 2009.)

RULE 23. CUSTODY OR RELEASE OF A PRISONER IN A HABEAS CORPUS PROCEEDING

(a) **Transfer of Custody Pending Review.** Pending review of a decision in a habeas corpus proceeding commenced before a court, justice, or judge of the United States for the release of a prisoner, the person having custody of the prisoner must not transfer custody to another unless a transfer is directed in accordance with this rule. When, upon application, a custodian shows the need for a transfer, the court, justice, or judge rendering the decision under review may authorize the transfer and substitute the successor custodian as a party.

(b) **Detention or Release Pending Review of Decision Not to Release.** While a decision not to release a prisoner is under review, the court or judge rendering the decision, or the court of appeals, or the Supreme Court, or a judge or justice of either court, may order that the prisoner be:

(1) detained in the custody from which release is sought;

(2) detained in other appropriate custody; or

(3) released on personal recognizance, with or without surety.

(c) **Release Pending Review of Decision Ordering Release.** While a decision ordering the release of a prisoner is under review, the prisoner must—unless the court or judge rendering the decision, or the court of appeals, or the Supreme Court, or a judge or justice of either court orders otherwise—be released on personal recognizance, with or without surety.

(d) **Modification of the Initial Order on Custody.** An initial order governing the prisoner's custody or release, including any recognizance or surety, continues in effect pending review unless for special reasons shown to the court of appeals or the Supreme Court, or to a judge or justice of either court, the order is modified or an independent order regarding custody, release, or surety is issued.

(As amended Mar. 10, 1986, eff. July 1, 1986; Apr. 24, 1998, eff. Dec. 1, 1998.)

RULE 24. PROCEEDING IN FORMA PAUPERIS

(a) **Leave to Proceed In Forma Pauperis.**

(1) **Motion in the District Court.** Except as stated in Rule 24(a)(3), a party to a district-court action who desires to appeal in forma pauperis must file a motion in the district court. The party must attach an affidavit that:

(A) shows in the detail prescribed by Form 4 of the Appendix of Forms the party's inability to pay or to give security for fees and costs;

(B) claims an entitlement to redress; and

(C) states the issues that the party intends to present on appeal.

(2) **Action on the Motion.** If the district court grants the motion, the party may proceed on appeal without prepaying or giving security for fees and costs, unless a statute provides otherwise. If the district court denies the motion, it must state its reasons in writing.

(3) **Prior Approval.** A party who was permitted to proceed in forma pauperis in the district-court action, or who was determined to be financially unable to obtain an adequate defense in a criminal case, may proceed on appeal in forma pauperis without further authorization, unless:

(A) the district court—before or after the notice of appeal is filed—certifies that the appeal is not taken in good faith or finds that the party is not otherwise entitled to proceed in forma pauperis and states in writing its reasons for the certification or finding; or

(B) a statute provides otherwise.

(4) **Notice of District Court's Denial.** The district clerk must immediately notify the parties and the court of appeals when the district court does any of the following:

(A) denies a motion to proceed on appeal in forma pauperis;

(B) certifies that the appeal is not taken in good faith; or

(C) finds that the party is not otherwise entitled to proceed in forma pauperis.

(5) **Motion in the Court of Appeals.** A party may file a motion to proceed on appeal in forma pauperis in the court of appeals within 30 days after service of the notice prescribed in Rule 24(a)(4). The

motion must include a copy of the affidavit filed in the district court and the district court's statement of reasons for its action. If no affidavit was filed in the district court, the party must include the affidavit prescribed by Rule 24(a)(1).

(b) Leave to Proceed In Forma Pauperis on Appeal from the United States Tax Court or on Appeal or Review of an Administrative–Agency Proceeding. A party may file in the court of appeals a motion for leave to proceed on appeal in forma pauperis with an affidavit prescribed by Rule 24(a)(1):

(1) in an appeal from the United States Tax Court; and

(2) when an appeal or review of a proceeding before an administrative agency, board, commission, or officer proceeds directly in the court of appeals.

(c) Leave to Use Original Record. A party allowed to proceed on appeal in forma pauperis may request that the appeal be heard on the original record without reproducing any part.

(As amended Apr. 30, 1979, eff. Aug. 1, 1979; Mar. 10, 1986, eff. July 1, 1986; Apr. 24, 1998, eff. Dec. 1, 1998; Apr. 29, 2002, eff. Dec. 1, 2002; Apr. 16, 2013, eff. Dec. 1, 2013.)

TITLE VII. GENERAL PROVISIONS

RULE 25. FILING AND SERVICE

(a) Filing.

(1) Filing with the Clerk. A paper required or permitted to be filed in a court of appeals must be filed with the clerk.

(2) Filing: Method and Timeliness.

(A) In general. Filing may be accomplished by mail addressed to the clerk, but filing is not timely unless the clerk receives the papers within the time fixed for filing.

(B) A brief or appendix. A brief or appendix is timely filed, however, if on or before the last day for filing, it is:

(i) mailed to the clerk by First–Class Mail, or other class of mail that is at least as expeditious, postage prepaid; or

(ii) dispatched to a third-party commercial carrier for delivery to the clerk within 3 days.

(C) Inmate filing. A paper filed by an inmate confined in an institution is timely if deposited in the institution's internal mailing system on or before the last day for filing. If an institution has a system designed for legal mail, the inmate must use that system to receive the benefit of this rule. Timely filing may be shown by a declaration in compliance with 28 U.S.C. § 1746 or by a notarized statement, either of which must set forth the date of deposit and state that first-class postage has been prepaid.

(D) Electronic filing. A court of appeals may by local rule permit or require papers to be filed, signed, or verified by electronic means that are consistent with technical standards, if any, that the Judicial Conference of the United States establishes. A local rule may require filing by electronic means only if reasonable exceptions are allowed. A paper filed by electronic means in compliance with a local rule constitutes a written paper for the purpose of applying these rules.

(3) Filing a Motion with a Judge. If a motion requests relief that may be granted by a single judge, the judge may permit the motion to be filed with the judge; the judge must note the filing date on the motion and give it to the clerk.

(4) Clerk's Refusal of Documents. The clerk must not refuse to accept for filing any paper presented for that purpose solely because it is not presented in proper form as required by these rules or by any local rule or practice.

(5) Privacy Protection. An appeal in a case whose privacy protection was governed by Federal Rule of Bankruptcy Procedure 9037, Federal Rule of Civil Procedure 5.2, or Federal Rule of Criminal Procedure 49.1 is governed by the same rule on appeal. In all other proceedings, privacy protection is governed by Federal Rule of Civil Procedure 5.2, except that Federal Rule of Criminal Procedure 49.1 governs when an extraordinary writ is sought in a criminal case.

(b) Service of All Papers Required. Unless a rule requires service by the clerk, a party must, at or before the time of filing a paper, serve a copy on the other parties to the appeal or review. Service on a party represented by counsel must be made on the party's counsel.

(c) Manner of Service.

(1) Service may be any of the following:

(A) personal, including delivery to a responsible person at the office of counsel;

(B) by mail;

(C) by third-party commercial carrier for delivery within 3 days; or

(D) by electronic means, if the party being served consents in writing.

(2) If authorized by local rule, a party may use the court's transmission equipment to make electronic service under Rule 25(c)(1)(D).

(3) When reasonable considering such factors as the immediacy of the relief sought, distance, and cost, service on a party must be by a manner at least as expeditious as the manner used to file the paper with the court.

(4) Service by mail or by commercial carrier is complete on mailing or delivery to the carrier. Service by electronic means is complete on transmission, unless the party making service is notified that the paper was not received by the party served.

(d) Proof of Service.

(1) A paper presented for filing must contain either of the following:

(A) an acknowledgment of service by the person served; or

(B) proof of service consisting of a statement by the person who made service certifying:

(i) the date and manner of service;

(ii) the names of the persons served; and

(iii) their mail or electronic addresses, facsimile numbers, or the addresses of the places of delivery, as appropriate for the manner of service.

(2) When a brief or appendix is filed by mailing or dispatch in accordance with Rule 25(a)(2)(B), the proof of service must also state the date and manner by which the document was mailed or dispatched to the clerk.

(3) Proof of service may appear on or be affixed to the papers filed.

(e) Number of Copies. When these rules require the filing or furnishing of a number of copies, a court may require a different number by local rule or by order in a particular case.

(As amended Mar. 10, 1986, eff. July 1, 1986; Apr. 30, 1991, eff. Dec. 1, 1991; Apr. 22, 1993, eff. Dec. 1, 1993; Apr. 29, 1994, eff. Dec. 1, 1994; Apr. 23, 1996, eff. Dec. 1, 1996; Apr. 24, 1998, eff. Dec. 1, 1998; Apr. 29, 2002, eff. Dec. 1, 2002; Apr. 12, 2006, eff. Dec. 1, 2006; Apr. 30, 2007, eff. Dec. 1, 2007; Mar. 26, 2009, eff. Dec. 1, 2009.)

RULE 26. COMPUTING AND EXTENDING TIME

(a) Computing Time. The following rules apply in computing any time period specified in these rules, in any local rule or court order, or in any statute that does not specify a method of computing time.

(1) Period Stated in Days or a Longer Unit. When the period is stated in days or a longer unit of time:

(A) exclude the day of the event that triggers the period;

(B) count every day, including intermediate Saturdays, Sundays, and legal holidays; and

(C) include the last day of the period, but if the last day is a Saturday, Sunday, or legal holiday, the period continues to run until the end of the next day that is not a Saturday, Sunday, or legal holiday.

(2) Period Stated in Hours. When the period is stated in hours:

(A) begin counting immediately on the occurrence of the event that triggers the period;

(B) count every hour, including hours during intermediate Saturdays, Sundays, and legal holidays; and

(C) if the period would end on a Saturday, Sunday, or legal holiday, the period continues to run until the same time on the next day that is not a Saturday, Sunday, or legal holiday.

(3) Inaccessibility of the Clerk's Office. Unless the court orders otherwise, if the clerk's office is inaccessible:

(A) on the last day for filing under Rule 26(a)(1), then the time for filing is extended to the first accessible day that is not a Saturday, Sunday, or legal holiday; or

(B) during the last hour for filing under Rule 26(a)(2), then the time for filing is extended to the same time on the first accessible day that is not a Saturday, Sunday, or legal holiday.

(4) "Last Day" Defined. Unless a different time is set by a statute, local rule, or court order, the last day ends:

(A) for electronic filing in the district court, at midnight in the court's time zone;

(B) for electronic filing in the court of appeals, at midnight in the time zone of the circuit clerk's principal office;

(C) for filing under Rules 4(c)(1), 25(a)(2)(B), and 25(a)(2)(C)—and filing by mail under Rule 13(b)—at the latest time for the method chosen for delivery to the post office, third-party commercial carrier, or prison mailing system; and

(D) for filing by other means, when the clerk's office is scheduled to close.

(5) "Next Day" Defined. The "next day" is determined by continuing to count forward when the period is measured after an event and backward when measured before an event.

(6) "Legal Holiday" Defined. "Legal holiday" means:

(A) the day set aside by statute for observing New Year's Day, Martin Luther King Jr.'s Birthday, Washington's Birthday, Memorial Day, Independence Day, Labor Day, Columbus Day, Veterans' Day, Thanksgiving Day, or Christmas Day;

(B) any day declared a holiday by the President or Congress; and

(C) for periods that are measured after an event, any other day declared a holiday by the state where either of the following is located: the district court that rendered the challenged judgment or order, or the circuit clerk's principal office.

(b) Extending Time. For good cause, the court may extend the time prescribed by these rules or by its order to perform any act, or may permit an act to be done after that time expires. But the court may not extend the time to file:

(1) a notice of appeal (except as authorized in Rule 4) or a petition for permission to appeal; or

(2) a notice of appeal from or a petition to enjoin, set aside, suspend, modify, enforce, or otherwise review an order of an administrative agency, board, commission, or officer of the United States, unless specifically authorized by law.

(c) Additional Time after Service. When a party may or must act within a specified time after service, 3 days are added after the period would otherwise expire under Rule 26(a), unless the paper is delivered on the date of service stated in the proof of service. For purposes of this Rule 26(c), a paper that is served electronically is not treated as delivered on the date of service stated in the proof of service.

(As amended Mar. 1, 1971, eff. July 1, 1971; Mar. 10, 1986, eff. July 1, 1986; Apr. 25, 1989, eff. Dec. 1, 1989; Apr. 30, 1991, eff. Dec. 1, 1991; Apr. 23, 1996, eff. Dec. 1, 1996; Apr. 24, 1998, eff. Dec. 1, 1998; Apr. 29, 2002, eff. Dec. 1, 2002; Apr. 25, 2005, eff. Dec. 1, 2005; Mar. 26, 2009, eff. Dec. 1, 2009.)

RULE 26.1.   CORPORATE DISCLOSURE STATEMENT

(a) Who Must File. Any nongovernmental corporate party to a proceeding in a court of appeals must file a statement that identifies any parent corporation and any publicly held corporation that owns 10% or more of its stock or states that there is no such corporation.

(b) Time for Filing; Supplemental Filing. A party must file the Rule 26.1(a) statement with the principal brief or upon filing a motion, response, petition, or answer in the court of appeals, whichever occurs first, unless a local rule requires earlier filing. Even if the statement has already been filed, the party's principal brief must include the statement before the table of contents. A party must supplement its statement whenever the information that must be disclosed under Rule 26.1(a) changes.

(c) Number of Copies. If the Rule 26.1(a) statement is filed before the principal brief, or if a supplemental statement is filed, the party must file an original and 3 copies unless the court requires a different number by local rule or by order in a particular case.

(Added Apr. 25, 1989, eff. Dec. 1, 1989, and amended Apr. 30, 1991, eff. Dec. 1, 1991; Apr. 29, 1994, eff. Dec. 1, 1994; Apr. 24, 1998, eff. Dec. 1, 1998; Apr. 29, 2002, eff. Dec. 1, 2002.)

RULE 27.   MOTIONS

(a) In General.

(1) Application for Relief. An application for an order or other relief is made by motion unless these rules prescribe another form. A motion must be in writing unless the court permits otherwise.

(2) Contents of a Motion.

(A) Grounds and relief sought. A motion must state with particularity the grounds for the motion, the relief sought, and the legal argument necessary to support it.

(B) Accompanying documents.

(i) Any affidavit or other paper necessary to support a motion must be served and filed with the motion.

(ii) An affidavit must contain only factual information, not legal argument.

(iii) A motion seeking substantive relief must include a copy of the trial court's opinion or agency's decision as a separate exhibit.

(C) Documents barred or not required.

(i) A separate brief supporting or responding to a motion must not be filed.

(ii) A notice of motion is not required.

(iii) A proposed order is not required.

(3) Response.

(A) Time to file. Any party may file a response to a motion; Rule 27(a)(2) governs its contents. The response must be filed within 10 days after service of the motion unless the court shortens or extends the time. A motion authorized by Rules 8, 9, 18, or 41 may be granted before the 10–day period runs only if the court gives reasonable notice to the parties that it intends to act sooner.

(B) Request for affirmative relief. A response may include a motion for affirmative relief. The time to respond to the new motion, and to reply to that response, are governed by Rule 27(a)(3)(A) and (a)(4). The title of the response must alert the court to the request for relief.

(4) Reply to Response. Any reply to a response must be filed within 7 days after service of the response. A reply must not present matters that do not relate to the response.

(b) Disposition of a Motion for a Procedural Order. The court may act on a motion for a procedural order—including a motion under Rule 26(b)—at any time without awaiting a response, and may, by rule or by order in a particular case, authorize its clerk to act on specified types of procedural motions. A party adversely affected by the court's, or the clerk's, action may file a motion to reconsider, vacate, or modify that action. Timely opposition filed after the motion is granted in whole or in part does not constitute a request to reconsider, vacate, or modify the disposition; a motion requesting that relief must be filed.

(c) Power of a Single Judge to Entertain a Motion. A circuit judge may act alone on any motion, but may not dismiss or otherwise determine an appeal or other proceeding. A court of appeals may provide by rule or by order in a particular case that only the court may act on any motion or class of motions. The court may review the action of a single judge.

(d) Form of Papers; Page Limits; and Number of Copies.

    (1) Format.

        (A) Reproduction. A motion, response, or reply may be reproduced by any process that yields a clear black image on light paper. The paper must be opaque and unglazed. Only one side of the paper may be used.

        (B) Cover. A cover is not required, but there must be a caption that includes the case number, the name of the court, the title of the case, and a brief descriptive title indicating the purpose of the motion and identifying the party or parties for whom it is filed. If a cover is used, it must be white.

        (C) Binding. The document must be bound in any manner that is secure, does not obscure the text, and permits the document to lie reasonably flat when open.

        (D) Paper size, line spacing, and margins. The document must be on 8½ by 11 inch paper. The text must be double-spaced, but quotations more than two lines long may be indented and single-spaced. Headings and footnotes may be single-spaced. Margins must be at least one inch on all four sides. Page numbers may be placed in the margins, but no text may appear there.

        (E) Typeface and type styles. The document must comply with the typeface requirements of Rule 32(a)(5) and the type-style requirements of Rule 32(a)(6).

    (2) Page Limits. A motion or a response to a motion must not exceed 20 pages, exclusive of the corporate disclosure statement and accompanying documents authorized by Rule 27(a)(2)(B), unless the court permits or directs otherwise. A reply to a response must not exceed 10 pages.

    (3) Number of Copies. An original and 3 copies must be filed unless the court requires a different number by local rule or by order in a particular case.

(e) Oral Argument. A motion will be decided without oral argument unless the court orders otherwise.

(As amended Apr. 30, 1979, eff. Aug. 1, 1979; Apr. 25, 1989, eff. Dec. 1, 1989; Apr. 29, 1994, eff. Dec. 1, 1994; Apr. 24, 1998, eff. Dec. 1, 1998; Apr. 29, 2002, eff. Dec. 1, 2002; Apr. 25, 2005, eff. Dec. 1, 2005; Mar. 26, 2009, eff. Dec. 1, 2009.)

RULE 28. BRIEFS

(a) Appellant's Brief. The appellant's brief must contain, under appropriate headings and in the order indicated:

    (1) a corporate disclosure statement if required by Rule 26.1;

    (2) a table of contents, with page references;

    (3) a table of authorities—cases (alphabetically arranged), statutes, and other authorities—with references to the pages of the brief where they are cited;

    (4) a jurisdictional statement, including:

        (A) the basis for the district court's or agency's subject-matter jurisdiction, with citations to applicable statutory provisions and stating relevant facts establishing jurisdiction;

        (B) the basis for the court of appeals' jurisdiction, with citations to applicable statutory provisions and stating relevant facts establishing jurisdiction;

        (C) the filing dates establishing the timeliness of the appeal or petition for review; and

        (D) an assertion that the appeal is from a final order or judgment that disposes of all parties' claims, or information establishing the court of appeals' jurisdiction on some other basis;

    (5) a statement of the issues presented for review;

    (6) a concise statement of the case setting out the facts relevant to the issues submitted for review, describing the relevant procedural history, and identifying the rulings presented for review, with appropriate references to the record (see Rule 28(e));

    (7) a summary of the argument, which must contain a succinct, clear, and accurate statement of the arguments made in the body of the brief, and which must not merely repeat the argument headings;

    (8) the argument, which must contain:

(A) appellant's contentions and the reasons for them, with citations to the authorities and parts of the record on which the appellant relies; and

(B) for each issue, a concise statement of the applicable standard of review (which may appear in the discussion of the issue or under a separate heading placed before the discussion of the issues);

(9) a short conclusion stating the precise relief sought; and

(10) the certificate of compliance, if required by Rule 32(a)(7).

(b) Appellee's Brief. The appellee's brief must conform to the requirements of Rule 28(a)(1)–(8) and (10), except that none of the following need appear unless the appellee is dissatisfied with the appellant's statement:

(1) the jurisdictional statement;

(2) the statement of the issues;

(3) the statement of the case; and

(4) the statement of the standard of review.

(c) Reply Brief. The appellant may file a brief in reply to the appellee's brief. Unless the court permits, no further briefs may be filed. A reply brief must contain a table of contents, with page references, and a table of authorities—cases (alphabetically arranged), statutes, and other authorities—with references to the pages of the reply brief where they are cited.

(d) References to Parties. In briefs and at oral argument, counsel should minimize use of the terms "appellant" and "appellee." To make briefs clear, counsel should use the parties' actual names or the designations used in the lower court or agency proceeding, or such descriptive terms as "the employee," "the injured person," "the taxpayer," "the ship," "the stevedore."

(e) References to the Record. References to the parts of the record contained in the appendix filed with the appellant's brief must be to the pages of the appendix. If the appendix is prepared after the briefs are filed, a party referring to the record must follow one of the methods detailed in Rule 30(c). If the original record is used under Rule 30(f) and is not consecutively paginated, or if the brief refers to an unreproduced part of the record, any reference must be to the page of the original document. For example:

- Answer p. 7;
- Motion for Judgment p. 2;
- Transcript p. 231.

Only clear abbreviations may be used. A party referring to evidence whose admissibility is in controversy must cite the pages of the appendix or of the transcript at which the evidence was identified, offered, and received or rejected.

(f) Reproduction of Statutes, Rules, Regulations, etc. If the court's determination of the issues presented requires the study of statutes, rules, regulations, etc., the relevant parts must be set out in the brief or in an addendum at the end, or may be supplied to the court in pamphlet form.

(g) [Reserved]

(h) [Deleted]

(i) Briefs in a Case Involving Multiple Appellants or Appellees. In a case involving more than one appellant or appellee, including consolidated cases, any number of appellants or appellees may join in a brief, and any party may adopt by reference a part of another's brief. Parties may also join in reply briefs.

(j) Citation of Supplemental Authorities. If pertinent and significant authorities come to a party's attention after the party's brief has been filed—or after oral argument but before decision—a party may promptly advise the circuit clerk by letter, with a copy to all other parties, setting forth the citations. The letter must state the reasons for the supplemental citations, referring either to the page of the brief or to a point argued orally. The body of the letter must not exceed 350 words. Any response must be made promptly and must be similarly limited.

(As amended Apr. 30, 1979, eff. Aug. 1, 1979; Mar. 10, 1986, eff. July 1, 1986; Apr. 25, 1989, eff. Dec. 1, 1989; Apr. 30, 1991, eff. Dec. 1, 1991; Apr. 22, 1993, eff. Dec. 1, 1993; Apr. 29, 1994, eff. Dec. 1, 1994; Apr. 24, 1998, eff. Dec. 1, 1998; Apr. 29, 2002, eff. Dec. 1, 2002; Apr. 25, 2005, eff. Dec. 1, 2005; Apr. 16, 2013, eff. Dec. 1, 2013.)

RULE 28.1. CROSS–APPEALS

(a) Applicability. This rule applies to a case in which a cross-appeal is filed. Rules 28(a)–(c), 31(a)(1), 32(a)(2), and 32(a)(7)(A)–(B) do not apply to such a case, except as otherwise provided in this rule.

(b) Designation of Appellant. The party who files a notice of appeal first is the appellant for the purposes of this rule and Rules 30 and 34. If notices are filed on the same day, the plaintiff in the proceeding below is the appellant. These designations may be modified by the parties' agreement or by court order.

(c) Briefs. In a case involving a cross-appeal:

(1) Appellant's Principal Brief. The appellant must file a principal brief in the appeal. That brief must comply with Rule 28(a).

(2) Appellee's Principal and Response Brief. The appellee must file a principal brief in the cross-appeal and must, in the same brief, respond to the principal brief in the appeal. That appellee's brief must comply with Rule 28(a), except that the brief need not include a statement of the case unless the appellee is dissatisfied with the appellant's statement.

(3) Appellant's Response and Reply Brief. The appellant must file a brief that responds to the principal brief in the cross-appeal and may, in the same brief, reply to the response in the appeal. That brief must comply with Rule 28(a)(2)–(8) and (10), except that none of the following need appear unless the appellant is dissatisfied with the appellee's statement in the cross-appeal:

    (A) the jurisdictional statement;

    (B) the statement of the issues;

    (C) the statement of the case; and

    (D) the statement of the standard of review.

(4) Appellee's Reply Brief. The appellee may file a brief in reply to the response in the cross-appeal. That brief must comply with Rule 28(a)(2)–(3) and (10) and must be limited to the issues presented by the cross-appeal.

(5) No Further Briefs. Unless the court permits, no further briefs may be filed in a case involving a cross-appeal.

(d) Cover. Except for filings by unrepresented parties, the cover of the appellant's principal brief must be blue; the appellee's principal and response brief, red; the appellant's response and reply brief, yellow; the appellee's reply brief, gray; an intervenor's or amicus curiae's brief, green; and any supplemental brief, tan. The front cover of a brief must contain the information required by Rule 32(a)(2).

(e) Length.

(1) Page Limitation. Unless it complies with Rule 28.1(e)(2) and (3), the appellant's principal brief must not exceed 30 pages; the appellee's principal and response brief, 35 pages; the appellant's response and reply brief, 30 pages; and the appellee's reply brief, 15 pages.

(2) Type–Volume Limitation.

    (A) The appellant's principal brief or the appellant's response and reply brief is acceptable if:

      (i) it contains no more than 14,000 words; or

      (ii) it uses a monospaced face and contains no more than 1,300 lines of text.

    (B) The appellee's principal and response brief is acceptable if:

      (i) it contains no more than 16,500 words; or

      (ii) it uses a monospaced face and contains no more than 1,500 lines of text.

    (C) The appellee's reply brief is acceptable if it contains no more than half of the type volume specified in Rule 28.1(e)(2)(A).

(3) Certificate of Compliance. A brief submitted under Rule 28.1(e)(2) must comply with Rule 32(a)(7)(C).

(f) Time to Serve and File a Brief. Briefs must be served and filed as follows:

    (1) the appellant's principal brief, within 40 days after the record is filed;

    (2) the appellee's principal and response brief, within 30 days after the appellant's principal brief is served;

    (3) the appellant's response and reply brief, within 30 days after the appellee's principal and response brief is served; and

    (4) the appellee's reply brief, within 14 days after the appellant's response and reply brief is served, but at least 7 days before argument unless the court, for good cause, allows a later filing.

(As added April 25, 2005, eff. Dec. 1, 2005, and amended Mar. 26, 2009, eff. Dec. 1, 2009; Apr. 16, 2013, eff. Dec. 1, 2013.)

RULE 29. BRIEF OF AN AMICUS CURIAE

(a) When Permitted. The United States or its officer or agency or a state may file an amicus-curiae brief without the consent of the parties or leave of court. Any other amicus curiae may file a brief only by leave of court or if the brief states that all parties have consented to its filing.

(b) Motion for Leave to File. The motion must be accompanied by the proposed brief and state:

    (1) the movant's interest; and

    (2) the reason why an amicus brief is desirable and why the matters asserted are relevant to the disposition of the case.

(c) Contents and Form. An amicus brief must comply with Rule 32. In addition to the requirements of Rule 32, the cover must identify the party or parties supported and indicate whether the brief supports affirmance or reversal. An amicus brief need not comply with Rule 28, but must include the following:

    (1) if the amicus curiae is a corporation, a disclosure statement like that required of parties by Rule 26.1;

    (2) a table of contents, with page references;

    (3) a table of authorities—cases (alphabetically arranged), statutes, and other authorities—with references to the pages of the brief where they are cited;

    (4) a concise statement of the identity of the amicus curiae, its interest in the case, and the source of its authority to file;

(5) unless the amicus curiae is one listed in the first sentence of Rule 29(a), a statement that indicates whether:

(A) a party's counsel authored the brief in whole or in part;

(B) a party or a party's counsel contributed money that was intended to fund preparing or submitting the brief; and

(C) a person—other than the amicus curiae, its members, or its counsel—contributed money that was intended to fund preparing or submitting the brief and, if so, identifies each such person;

(6) an argument, which may be preceded by a summary and which need not include a statement of the applicable standard of review; and

(7) a certificate of compliance, if required by Rule 32(a)(7).

(d) **Length.** Except by the court's permission, an amicus brief may be no more than one-half the maximum length authorized by these rules for a party's principal brief. If the court grants a party permission to file a longer brief, that extension does not affect the length of an amicus brief.

(e) **Time for Filing.** An amicus curiae must file its brief, accompanied by a motion for filing when necessary, no later than 7 days after the principal brief of the party being supported is filed. An amicus curiae that does not support either party must file its brief no later than 7 days after the appellant's or petitioner's principal brief is filed. A court may grant leave for later filing, specifying the time within which an opposing party may answer.

(f) **Reply Brief.** Except by the court's permission, an amicus curiae may not file a reply brief.

(g) **Oral Argument.** An amicus curiae may participate in oral argument only with the court's permission.

(As amended Apr. 24, 1998, eff. Dec. 1, 1998; Apr. 28, 2010, eff. Dec. 1, 2010.)

RULE 30.　APPENDIX TO THE BRIEFS

(a) **Appellant's Responsibility.**

(1) **Contents of the Appendix.** The appellant must prepare and file an appendix to the briefs containing:

(A) the relevant docket entries in the proceeding below;

(B) the relevant portions of the pleadings, charge, findings, or opinion;

(C) the judgment, order, or decision in question; and

(D) other parts of the record to which the parties wish to direct the court's attention.

(2) **Excluded Material.** Memoranda of law in the district court should not be included in the appendix unless they have independent relevance. Parts of the record may be relied on by the court or the parties even though not included in the appendix.

(3) **Time to File; Number of Copies.** Unless filing is deferred under Rule 30(c), the appellant must file 10 copies of the appendix with the brief and must serve one copy on counsel for each party separately represented. An unrepresented party proceeding in forma pauperis must file 4 legible copies with the clerk, and one copy must be served on counsel for each separately represented party. The court may by local rule or by order in a particular case require the filing or service of a different number.

(b) **All Parties' Responsibilities.**

(1) **Determining the Contents of the Appendix.** The parties are encouraged to agree on the contents of the appendix. In the absence of an agreement, the appellant must, within 14 days after the record is filed, serve on the appellee a designation of the parts of the record the appellant intends to include in the appendix and a statement of the issues the appellant intends to present for review. The appellee may, within 14 days after receiving the designation, serve on the appellant a designation of additional parts to which it wishes to direct the court's attention. The appellant must include the designated parts in the appendix. The parties must not engage in unnecessary designation of parts of the record, because the entire record is available to the court. This paragraph applies also to a cross-appellant and a cross-appellee.

(2) **Costs of Appendix.** Unless the parties agree otherwise, the appellant must pay the cost of the appendix. If the appellant considers parts of the record designated by the appellee to be unnecessary, the appellant may advise the appellee, who must then advance the cost of including those parts. The cost of the appendix is a taxable cost. But if any party causes unnecessary parts of the record to be included in the appendix, the court may impose the cost of those parts on that party. Each circuit must, by local rule, provide for sanctions against attorneys who unreasonably and vexatiously increase litigation costs by including unnecessary material in the appendix.

(c) **Deferred Appendix.**

(1) **Deferral Until After Briefs Are Filed.** The court may provide by rule for classes of cases or by order in a particular case that preparation of the appendix may be deferred until after the briefs have been filed and that the appendix may be filed 21 days after the appellee's brief is served. Even though the filing of the appendix may be deferred,

Rule 30(b) applies; except that a party must designate the parts of the record it wants included in the appendix when it serves its brief, and need not include a statement of the issues presented.

(2) References to the Record.

(A) If the deferred appendix is used, the parties may cite in their briefs the pertinent pages of the record. When the appendix is prepared, the record pages cited in the briefs must be indicated by inserting record page numbers, in brackets, at places in the appendix where those pages of the record appear.

(B) A party who wants to refer directly to pages of the appendix may serve and file copies of the brief within the time required by Rule 31(a), containing appropriate references to pertinent pages of the record. In that event, within 14 days after the appendix is filed, the party must serve and file copies of the brief, containing references to the pages of the appendix in place of or in addition to the references to the pertinent pages of the record. Except for the correction of typographical errors, no other changes may be made to the brief.

(d) Format of the Appendix. The appendix must begin with a table of contents identifying the page at which each part begins. The relevant docket entries must follow the table of contents. Other parts of the record must follow chronologically. When pages from the transcript of proceedings are placed in the appendix, the transcript page numbers must be shown in brackets immediately before the included pages. Omissions in the text of papers or of the transcript must be indicated by asterisks. Immaterial formal matters (captions, subscriptions, acknowledgments, etc.) should be omitted.

(e) Reproduction of Exhibits. Exhibits designated for inclusion in the appendix may be reproduced in a separate volume, or volumes, suitably indexed. Four copies must be filed with the appendix, and one copy must be served on counsel for each separately represented party. If a transcript of a proceeding before an administrative agency, board, commission, or officer was used in a district-court action and has been designated for inclusion in the appendix, the transcript must be placed in the appendix as an exhibit.

(f) Appeal on the Original Record Without an Appendix. The court may, either by rule for all cases or classes of cases or by order in a particular case, dispense with the appendix and permit an appeal to proceed on the original record with any copies of the record, or relevant parts, that the court may order the parties to file.

(As amended Mar. 30, 1970, eff. July 1, 1970; Mar. 10, 1986, eff. July 1, 1986; Apr. 30, 1991, eff. Dec. 1, 1991; Apr. 29, 1994, eff. Dec. 1, 1994; Apr. 24, 1998, eff. Dec. 1, 1998; Mar. 26, 2009, eff. Dec. 1, 2009.)

RULE 31. SERVING AND FILING BRIEFS

(a) Time to Serve and File a Brief.

(1) The appellant must serve and file a brief within 40 days after the record is filed. The appellee must serve and file a brief within 30 days after the appellant's brief is served. The appellant may serve and file a reply brief within 14 days after service of the appellee's brief but a reply brief must be filed at least 7 days before argument, unless the court, for good cause, allows a later filing.

(2) A court of appeals that routinely considers cases on the merits promptly after the briefs are filed may shorten the time to serve and file briefs, either by local rule or by order in a particular case.

(b) Number of Copies. Twenty-five copies of each brief must be filed with the clerk and 2 copies must be served on each unrepresented party and on counsel for each separately represented party. An unrepresented party proceeding in forma pauperis must file 4 legible copies with the clerk, and one copy must be served on each unrepresented party and on counsel for each separately represented party. The court may by local rule or by order in a particular case require the filing or service of a different number.

(c) Consequence of Failure to File. If an appellant fails to file a brief within the time provided by this rule, or within an extended time, an appellee may move to dismiss the appeal. An appellee who fails to file a brief will not be heard at oral argument unless the court grants permission.

(As amended Mar. 30, 1970, eff. July 1, 1970; Mar. 10, 1986, eff. July 1, 1986; Apr. 29, 1994, eff. Dec. 1, 1994; Apr. 24, 1998, eff. Dec. 1, 1998; Apr. 29, 2002, eff. Dec. 1, 2002; Mar. 26, 2009, eff. Dec. 1, 2009.)

RULE 32. FORM OF BRIEFS, APPENDICES, AND OTHER PAPERS

(a) Form of a Brief.

(1) Reproduction.

(A) A brief may be reproduced by any process that yields a clear black image on light paper. The paper must be opaque and unglazed. Only one side of the paper may be used.

(B) Text must be reproduced with a clarity that equals or exceeds the output of a laser printer.

(C) Photographs, illustrations, and tables may be reproduced by any method that results in a good copy of the original; a glossy finish is acceptable if the original is glossy.

(2) Cover. Except for filings by unrepresented parties, the cover of the appellant's brief must be blue; the appellee's, red; an intervenor's or amicus curiae's, green; any reply brief, gray; and any supplemental brief, tan. The front cover of a brief must contain:

(A) the number of the case centered at the top;

(B) the name of the court;

(C) the title of the case (see Rule 12(a));

(D) the nature of the proceeding (e.g., Appeal, Petition for Review) and the name of the court, agency, or board below;

(E) the title of the brief, identifying the party or parties for whom the brief is filed; and

(F) the name, office address, and telephone number of counsel representing the party for whom the brief is filed.

(3) Binding. The brief must be bound in any manner that is secure, does not obscure the text, and permits the brief to lie reasonably flat when open.

(4) Paper Size, Line Spacing, and Margins. The brief must be on 8½ by 11 inch paper. The text must be double-spaced, but quotations more than two lines long may be indented and single-spaced. Headings and footnotes may be single-spaced. Margins must be at least one inch on all four sides. Page numbers may be placed in the margins, but no text may appear there.

(5) Typeface. Either a proportionally spaced or a monospaced face may be used.

(A) A proportionally spaced face must include serifs, but sans-serif type may be used in headings and captions. A proportionally spaced face must be 14–point or larger.

(B) A monospaced face may not contain more than 10½ characters per inch.

(6) Type Styles. A brief must be set in a plain, roman style, although italics or boldface may be used for emphasis. Case names must be italicized or underlined.

(7) Length.

(A) Page limitation. A principal brief may not exceed 30 pages, or a reply brief 15 pages, unless it complies with Rule 32(a)(7)(B) and (C).

(B) Type-volume limitation.

(i) A principal brief is acceptable if:

● it contains no more than 14,000 words; or

● it uses a monospaced face and contains no more than 1,300 lines of text.

(ii) A reply brief is acceptable if it contains no more than half of the type volume specified in Rule 32(a)(7)(B)(i).

(iii) Headings, footnotes, and quotations count toward the word and line limitations. The corporate disclosure statement, table of contents, table of citations, statement with respect to oral argument, any addendum containing statutes, rules or regulations, and any certificates of counsel do not count toward the limitation.

(C) Certificate of compliance.

(i) A brief submitted under Rules 28.1(e)(2) or 32(a)(7)(B) must include a certificate by the attorney, or an unrepresented party, that the brief complies with the type-volume limitation. The person preparing the certificate may rely on the word or line count of the word-processing system used to prepare the brief. The certificate must state either:

● the number of words in the brief; or

● the number of lines of monospaced type in the brief.

(ii) Form 6 in the Appendix of Forms is a suggested form of a certificate of compliance. Use of Form 6 must be regarded as sufficient to meet the requirements of Rules 28.1(e)(3) and 32(a)(7)(C)(i).

(b) Form of an Appendix. An appendix must comply with Rule 32(a)(1), (2), (3), and (4), with the following exceptions:

(1) The cover of a separately bound appendix must be white.

(2) An appendix may include a legible photocopy of any document found in the record or of a printed judicial or agency decision.

(3) When necessary to facilitate inclusion of odd-sized documents such as technical drawings, an appendix may be a size other than 8½ by 11 inches, and need not lie reasonably flat when opened.

(c) Form of Other Papers.

(1) Motion. The form of a motion is governed by Rule 27(d).

(2) Other Papers. Any other paper, including a petition for panel rehearing and a petition for hearing or rehearing en banc, and any response to such a petition, must be reproduced in the manner prescribed by Rule 32(a), with the following exceptions:

(A) A cover is not necessary if the caption and signature page of the paper together contain the information required by Rule 32(a)(2). If a cover is used, it must be white.

(B) Rule 32(a)(7) does not apply.

(d) Signature. Every brief, motion, or other paper filed with the court must be signed by the party filing the paper or, if the party is represented, by one of the party's attorneys.

(e) Local Variation. Every court of appeals must accept documents that comply with the form requirements of this rule. By local rule or order in a particular case a court of appeals may accept documents that do not meet all of the form requirements of this rule.

(As amended Apr. 24, 1998, eff. Dec. 1, 1998; Apr. 29, 2002, eff. Dec. 1, 2002; Apr. 25, 2005, eff. Dec. 1, 2005.)

RULE 32.1. CITING JUDICIAL DISPOSITIONS

(a) Citation Permitted. A court may not prohibit or restrict the citation of federal judicial opinions, orders, judgments, or other written dispositions that have been:

(i) designated as "unpublished," "not for publication," "non-precedential," "not precedent," or the like; and

(ii) issued on or after January 1, 2007.

(b) Copies Required. If a party cites a federal judicial opinion, order, judgment, or other written disposition that is not available in a publicly accessible electronic database, the party must file and serve a copy of that opinion, order, judgment, or disposition with the brief or other paper in which it is cited.

(Added Apr. 12, 2006, eff. Dec. 1, 2006.)

RULE 33. APPEAL CONFERENCES

The court may direct the attorneys—and, when appropriate, the parties—to participate in one or more conferences to address any matter that may aid in disposing of the proceedings, including simplifying the issues and discussing settlement. A judge or other person designated by the court may preside over the conference, which may be conducted in person or by telephone. Before a settlement conference, the attorneys must consult with their clients and obtain as much authority as feasible to settle the case. The court may, as a result of the conference, enter an order controlling the course of the proceedings or implementing any settlement agreement.

(As amended Apr. 29, 1994, eff. Dec. 1, 1994; Apr. 24, 1998, eff. Dec. 1, 1998.)

RULE 34. ORAL ARGUMENT

(a) In General.

(1) **Party's Statement.** Any party may file, or a court may require by local rule, a statement explaining why oral argument should, or need not, be permitted.

(2) **Standards.** Oral argument must be allowed in every case unless a panel of three judges who have examined the briefs and record unanimously agrees that oral argument is unnecessary for any of the following reasons:

(A) the appeal is frivolous;

(B) the dispositive issue or issues have been authoritatively decided; or

(C) the facts and legal arguments are adequately presented in the briefs and record, and the decisional process would not be significantly aided by oral argument.

(b) Notice of Argument; Postponement. The clerk must advise all parties whether oral argument will be scheduled, and, if so, the date, time, and place for it, and the time allowed for each side. A motion to postpone the argument or to allow longer argument must be filed reasonably in advance of the hearing date.

(c) Order and Contents of Argument. The appellant opens and concludes the argument. Counsel must not read at length from briefs, records, or authorities.

(d) Cross-Appeals and Separate Appeals. If there is a cross-appeal, Rule 28.1(b) determines which party is the appellant and which is the appellee for purposes of oral argument. Unless the court directs otherwise, a cross-appeal or separate appeal must be argued when the initial appeal is argued. Separate parties should avoid duplicative argument.

(e) Nonappearance of a Party. If the appellee fails to appear for argument, the court must hear appellant's argument. If the appellant fails to appear for argument, the court may hear the appellee's argument. If neither party appears, the case will be decided on the briefs, unless the court orders otherwise.

(f) Submission on Briefs. The parties may agree to submit a case for decision on the briefs, but the court may direct that the case be argued.

(g) Use of Physical Exhibits at Argument; Removal. Counsel intending to use physical exhibits other than documents at the argument must arrange to place them in the courtroom on the day of the argument before the court convenes. After the argument, counsel must remove the exhibits from the courtroom, unless the court directs otherwise. The clerk may destroy or dispose of the exhibits if counsel does not reclaim them within a reasonable time after the clerk gives notice to remove them.

(As amended Apr. 30, 1979, eff. Aug. 1, 1979; Mar. 10, 1986, eff. July 1, 1986; Apr. 30, 1991, eff. Dec. 1, 1991; Apr. 22, 1993, eff. Dec. 1, 1993; Apr. 24, 1998, eff. Dec. 1, 1998; Apr. 25, 2005, eff. Dec. 1, 2005.)

RULE 35. EN BANC DETERMINATION

(a) When Hearing or Rehearing En Banc May Be Ordered. A majority of the circuit judges who are in regular active service and who are not disqualified may order that an appeal or other proceeding be heard or reheard by the court of appeals en banc. An en banc hearing or rehearing is not favored and ordinarily will not be ordered unless:

    (1) en banc consideration is necessary to secure or maintain uniformity of the court's decisions; or

    (2) the proceeding involves a question of exceptional importance.

(b) Petition for Hearing or Rehearing En Banc. A party may petition for a hearing or rehearing en banc.

    (1) The petition must begin with a statement that either:

        (A) the panel decision conflicts with a decision of the United States Supreme Court or of the court to which the petition is addressed (with citation to the conflicting case or cases) and consideration by the full court is therefore necessary to secure and maintain uniformity of the court's decisions; or

        (B) the proceeding involves one or more questions of exceptional importance, each of which must be concisely stated; for example, a petition may assert that a proceeding presents a question of exceptional importance if it involves an issue on which the panel decision conflicts with the authoritative decisions of other United States Courts of Appeals that have addressed the issue.

    (2) Except by the court's permission, a petition for an en banc hearing or rehearing must not exceed 15 pages, excluding material not counted under Rule 32.

    (3) For purposes of the page limit in Rule 35(b)(2), if a party files both a petition for panel rehearing and a petition for rehearing en banc, they are considered a single document even if they are filed separately, unless separate filing is required by local rule.

(c) Time for Petition for Hearing or Rehearing En Banc. A petition that an appeal be heard initially en banc must be filed by the date when the appellee's brief is due. A petition for a rehearing en banc must be filed within the time prescribed by Rule 40 for filing a petition for rehearing.

(d) Number of Copies. The number of copies to be filed must be prescribed by local rule and may be altered by order in a particular case.

(e) Response. No response may be filed to a petition for an en banc consideration unless the court orders a response.

(f) Call for a Vote. A vote need not be taken to determine whether the case will be heard or reheard en banc unless a judge calls for a vote.

(As amended Apr. 30, 1979, eff. Aug. 1, 1979; Apr. 29, 1994, eff. Dec. 1, 1994; Apr. 24, 1998, eff. Dec. 1, 1998; Apr. 25, 2005, eff. Dec. 1, 2005.)

RULE 36. ENTRY OF JUDGMENT; NOTICE

(a) Entry. A judgment is entered when it is noted on the docket. The clerk must prepare, sign, and enter the judgment:

    (1) after receiving the court's opinion—but if settlement of the judgment's form is required, after final settlement; or

    (2) if a judgment is rendered without an opinion, as the court instructs.

(b) Notice. On the date when judgment is entered, the clerk must serve on all parties a copy of the opinion—or the judgment, if no opinion was written—and a notice of the date when the judgment was entered.

(As amended Apr. 24, 1998, eff. Dec. 1, 1998; Apr. 29, 2002, eff. Dec. 1, 2002.)

RULE 37. INTEREST ON JUDGMENT

(a) When the Court Affirms. Unless the law provides otherwise, if a money judgment in a civil case is affirmed, whatever interest is allowed by law is payable from the date when the district court's judgment was entered.

(b) When the Court Reverses. If the court modifies or reverses a judgment with a direction that a money judgment be entered in the district court, the mandate must contain instructions about the allowance of interest.

(As amended Apr. 24, 1998, eff. Dec. 1, 1998.)

RULE 38. FRIVOLOUS APPEAL— DAMAGES AND COSTS

If a court of appeals determines that an appeal is frivolous, it may, after a separately filed motion or notice from the court and reasonable opportunity to respond, award just damages and single or double costs to the appellee.

(As amended Apr. 29, 1994, eff. Dec. 1, 1994; Apr. 24, 1998, eff. Dec. 1, 1998.)

RULE 39. COSTS

(a) Against Whom Assessed. The following rules apply unless the law provides or the court orders otherwise:

    (1) if an appeal is dismissed, costs are taxed against the appellant, unless the parties agree otherwise;

    (2) if a judgment is affirmed, costs are taxed against the appellant;

    (3) if a judgment is reversed, costs are taxed against the appellee;

(4) if a judgment is affirmed in part, reversed in part, modified, or vacated, costs are taxed only as the court orders.

(b) Costs For and Against the United States. Costs for or against the United States, its agency, or officer will be assessed under Rule 39(a) only if authorized by law.

(c) Costs of Copies. Each court of appeals must, by local rule, fix the maximum rate for taxing the cost of producing necessary copies of a brief or appendix, or copies of records authorized by Rule 30(f). The rate must not exceed that generally charged for such work in the area where the clerk's office is located and should encourage economical methods of copying.

(d) Bill of Costs: Objections; Insertion in Mandate.

(1) A party who wants costs taxed must—within 14 days after entry of judgment—file with the circuit clerk, with proof of service, an itemized and verified bill of costs.

(2) Objections must be filed within 14 days after service of the bill of costs, unless the court extends the time.

(3) The clerk must prepare and certify an itemized statement of costs for insertion in the mandate, but issuance of the mandate must not be delayed for taxing costs. If the mandate issues before costs are finally determined, the district clerk must—upon the circuit clerk's request—add the statement of costs, or any amendment of it, to the mandate.

(e) Costs on Appeal Taxable in the District Court. The following costs on appeal are taxable in the district court for the benefit of the party entitled to costs under this rule:

(1) the preparation and transmission of the record;

(2) the reporter's transcript, if needed to determine the appeal;

(3) premiums paid for a supersedeas bond or other bond to preserve rights pending appeal; and

(4) the fee for filing the notice of appeal.

(As amended Apr. 30, 1979, eff. Aug. 1, 1979; Mar. 10, 1986, eff. July 1, 1986; Apr. 24, 1998, eff. Dec. 1, 1998; Mar. 26, 2009, eff. Dec. 1, 2009.)

RULE 40. PETITION FOR PANEL REHEARING

(a) Time to File; Contents; Answer; Action by the Court if Granted.

(1) **Time.** Unless the time is shortened or extended by order or local rule, a petition for panel rehearing may be filed within 14 days after entry of judgment. But in a civil case, unless an order shortens or extends the time, the petition may be filed by any party within 45 days after entry of judgment if one of the parties is:

(A) the United States;

(B) a United States agency;

(C) a United States officer or employee sued in an official capacity; or

(D) a current or former United States officer or employee sued in an individual capacity for an act or omission occurring in connection with duties performed on the United States' behalf—including all instances in which the United States represents that person when the court of appeals' judgment is entered or files the petition for that person.

(2) **Contents.** The petition must state with particularity each point of law or fact that the petitioner believes the court has overlooked or misapprehended and must argue in support of the petition. Oral argument is not permitted.

(3) **Answer.** Unless the court requests, no answer to a petition for panel rehearing is permitted. But ordinarily rehearing will not be granted in the absence of such a request.

(4) **Action by the Court.** If a petition for panel rehearing is granted, the court may do any of the following:

(A) make a final disposition of the case without reargument;

(B) restore the case to the calendar for reargument or resubmission; or

(C) issue any other appropriate order.

(b) Form of Petition; Length. The petition must comply in form with Rule 32. Copies must be served and filed as Rule 31 prescribes. Unless the court permits or a local rule provides otherwise, a petition for panel rehearing must not exceed 15 pages.

(As amended Apr. 30, 1979, eff. Aug. 1, 1979; Apr. 29, 1994, eff. Dec. 1, 1994; Apr. 24, 1998, eff. Dec. 1, 1998; Apr. 26, 2011, eff. Dec. 1, 2011.)

RULE 41. MANDATE: CONTENTS; ISSUANCE AND EFFECTIVE DATE; STAY

(a) Contents. Unless the court directs that a formal mandate issue, the mandate consists of a certified copy of the judgment, a copy of the court's opinion, if any, and any direction about costs.

(b) When Issued. The court's mandate must issue 7 days after the time to file a petition for rehearing expires, or 7 days after entry of an order denying a timely petition for panel rehearing, petition for rehearing en banc, or motion for stay of mandate, whichever is later. The court may shorten or extend the time.

(c) Effective Date. The mandate is effective when issued.

(d) Staying the Mandate.

(1) On Petition for Rehearing or Motion. The timely filing of a petition for panel rehearing, petition for rehearing en banc, or motion for stay of mandate, stays the mandate until disposition of the petition or motion, unless the court orders otherwise.

(2) Pending Petition for Certiorari.

(A) A party may move to stay the mandate pending the filing of a petition for a writ of certiorari in the Supreme Court. The motion must be served on all parties and must show that the certiorari petition would present a substantial question and that there is good cause for a stay.

(B) The stay must not exceed 90 days, unless the period is extended for good cause or unless the party who obtained the stay files a petition for the writ and so notifies the circuit clerk in writing within the period of the stay. In that case, the stay continues until the Supreme Court's final disposition.

(C) The court may require a bond or other security as a condition to granting or continuing a stay of the mandate.

(D) The court of appeals must issue the mandate immediately when a copy of a Supreme Court order denying the petition for writ of certiorari is filed.

(As amended Apr. 29, 1994, eff. Dec. 1, 1994; Apr. 24, 1998, eff. Dec. 1, 1998; Apr. 29, 2002, eff. Dec. 1, 2002; Mar. 26, 2009, eff. Dec. 1, 2009.)

RULE 42. VOLUNTARY DISMISSAL

(a) Dismissal in the District Court. Before an appeal has been docketed by the circuit clerk, the district court may dismiss the appeal on the filing of a stipulation signed by all parties or on the appellant's motion with notice to all parties.

(b) Dismissal in the Court of Appeals. The circuit clerk may dismiss a docketed appeal if the parties file a signed dismissal agreement specifying how costs are to be paid and pay any fees that are due. But no mandate or other process may issue without a court order. An appeal may be dismissed on the appellant's motion on terms agreed to by the parties or fixed by the court.

(As amended Apr. 24, 1998, eff. Dec. 1, 1998.)

RULE 43. SUBSTITUTION OF PARTIES

(a) Death of a Party.

(1) After Notice of Appeal Is Filed. If a party dies after a notice of appeal has been filed or while a proceeding is pending in the court of appeals, the decedent's personal representative may be substituted as a party on motion filed with the circuit clerk by the representative or by any party. A party's motion must be served on the representative in accordance with Rule 25. If the decedent has no representative, any party may suggest the death on the record, and the court of appeals may then direct appropriate proceedings.

(2) Before Notice of Appeal Is Filed—Potential Appellant. If a party entitled to appeal dies before filing a notice of appeal, the decedent's personal representative—or, if there is no personal representative, the decedent's attorney of record—may file a notice of appeal within the time prescribed by these rules. After the notice of appeal is filed, substitution must be in accordance with Rule 43(a)(1).

(3) Before Notice of Appeal Is Filed—Potential Appellee. If a party against whom an appeal may be taken dies after entry of a judgment or order in the district court, but before a notice of appeal is filed, an appellant may proceed as if the death had not occurred. After the notice of appeal is filed, substitution must be in accordance with Rule 43(a)(1).

(b) Substitution for a Reason Other Than Death. If a party needs to be substituted for any reason other than death, the procedure prescribed in Rule 43(a) applies.

(c) Public Officer: Identification; Substitution.

(1) Identification of Party. A public officer who is a party to an appeal or other proceeding in an official capacity may be described as a party by the public officer's official title rather than by name. But the court may require the public officer's name to be added.

(2) Automatic Substitution of Officeholder. When a public officer who is a party to an appeal or other proceeding in an official capacity dies, resigns, or otherwise ceases to hold office, the action does not abate. The public officer's successor is automatically substituted as a party. Proceedings following the substitution are to be in the name of the substituted party, but any misnomer that does not affect the substantial rights of the parties may be disregarded. An order of substitution may be entered at any time, but failure to enter an order does not affect the substitution.

(As amended Mar. 10, 1986, eff. July 1, 1986; Apr. 24, 1998, eff. Dec. 1, 1998.)

RULE 44. CASE INVOLVING A CONSTITUTIONAL QUESTION WHEN THE UNITED STATES OR THE RELEVANT STATE IS NOT A PARTY

(a) Constitutional Challenge to Federal Statute. If a party questions the constitutionality of an Act of Congress in a proceeding in which the United States or its agency, officer, or employee is not a party in an official capacity, the questioning party must give written notice to the circuit clerk immediately upon the filing of the record or as soon as the question is raised in the court of appeals. The clerk must then certify that fact to the Attorney General.

(b) Constitutional Challenge to State Statute. If a party questions the constitutionality of a statute of a State in a proceeding in which that State or its agency, officer, or employee is not a party in an official capacity, the questioning party must give written notice to the circuit clerk immediately upon the filing of the record or as soon as the question is raised in the court of appeals. The clerk must then certify that fact to the attorney general of the State.

(As amended Apr. 24, 1998, eff. Dec. 1, 1998; Apr. 29, 2002, eff. Dec. 1, 2002.)

RULE 45. CLERK'S DUTIES

(a) General Provisions.

(1) Qualifications. The circuit clerk must take the oath and post any bond required by law. Neither the clerk nor any deputy clerk may practice as an attorney or counselor in any court while in office.

(2) When Court Is Open. The court of appeals is always open for filing any paper, issuing and returning process, making a motion, and entering an order. The clerk's office with the clerk or a deputy in attendance must be open during business hours on all days except Saturdays, Sundays, and legal holidays. A court may provide by local rule or by order that the clerk's office be open for specified hours on Saturdays or on legal holidays other than New Year's Day, Martin Luther King, Jr.'s Birthday, Washington's Birthday, Memorial Day, Independence Day, Labor Day, Columbus Day, Veterans' Day, Thanksgiving Day, and Christmas Day.

(b) Records.

(1) The Docket. The circuit clerk must maintain a docket and an index of all docketed cases in the manner prescribed by the Director of the Administrative Office of the United States Courts. The clerk must record all papers filed with the clerk and all process, orders, and judgments.

(2) Calendar. Under the court's direction, the clerk must prepare a calendar of cases awaiting argument. In placing cases on the calendar for argument, the clerk must give preference to appeals in criminal cases and to other proceedings and appeals entitled to preference by law.

(3) Other Records. The clerk must keep other books and records required by the Director of the Administrative Office of the United States Courts, with the approval of the Judicial Conference of the United States, or by the court.

(c) Notice of an Order or Judgment. Upon the entry of an order or judgment, the circuit clerk must immediately serve a notice of entry on each party, with a copy of any opinion, and must note the date of service on the docket. Service on a party represented by counsel must be made on counsel.

(d) Custody of Records and Papers. The circuit clerk has custody of the court's records and papers. Unless the court orders or instructs otherwise, the clerk must not permit an original record or paper to be taken from the clerk's office. Upon disposition of the case, original papers constituting the record on appeal or review must be returned to the court or agency from which they were received. The clerk must preserve a copy of any brief, appendix, or other paper that has been filed.

(As amended Mar. 1, 1971, eff. July 1, 1971; Mar. 10, 1986, eff. July 1, 1986; Apr. 24, 1998, eff. Dec. 1, 1998; Apr. 29, 2002, eff. Dec. 1, 2002; Apr. 25, 2005, eff. Dec. 1, 2005.)

RULE 46. ATTORNEYS

(a) Admission to the Bar.

(1) Eligibility. An attorney is eligible for admission to the bar of a court of appeals if that attorney is of good moral and professional character and is admitted to practice before the Supreme Court of the United States, the highest court of a state, another United States court of appeals, or a United States district court (including the district courts for Guam, the Northern Mariana Islands, and the Virgin Islands).

(2) Application. An applicant must file an application for admission, on a form approved by the court that contains the applicant's personal statement showing eligibility for membership. The applicant must subscribe to the following oath or affirmation:

"I, _____, do solemnly swear [or affirm] that I will conduct myself as an attorney and counselor of this court, uprightly and according to law; and that I will support the Constitution of the United States."

(3) Admission Procedures. On written or oral motion of a member of the court's bar, the court will act on the application. An applicant may be admitted by oral motion in open court. But, unless the court orders otherwise, an applicant need not appear before the court to be admitted. Upon admission, an applicant must pay the clerk the fee prescribed by local rule or court order.

(b) Suspension or Disbarment.

(1) **Standard.** A member of the court's bar is subject to suspension or disbarment by the court if the member:

(A) has been suspended or disbarred from practice in any other court; or

(B) is guilty of conduct unbecoming a member of the court's bar.

(2) **Procedure.** The member must be given an opportunity to show good cause, within the time prescribed by the court, why the member should not be suspended or disbarred.

(3) **Order.** The court must enter an appropriate order after the member responds and a hearing is held, if requested, or after the time prescribed for a response expires, if no response is made.

(c) Discipline. A court of appeals may discipline an attorney who practices before it for conduct unbecoming a member of the bar or for failure to comply with any court rule. First, however, the court must afford the attorney reasonable notice, an opportunity to show cause to the contrary, and, if requested, a hearing.

(As amended Mar. 10, 1986, eff. July 1, 1986; Apr. 24, 1998, eff. Dec. 1, 1998.)

RULE 47. LOCAL RULES BY COURTS OF APPEALS

(a) Local Rules.

(1) Each court of appeals acting by a majority of its judges in regular active service may, after giving appropriate public notice and opportunity for comment, make and amend rules governing its practice. A generally applicable direction to parties or lawyers regarding practice before a court must be in a local rule rather than an internal operating procedure or standing order. A local rule must be consistent with—but not duplicative of—Acts of Congress and rules adopted under 28 U.S.C. § 2072 and must conform to any uniform numbering sys-

tem prescribed by the Judicial Conference of the United States. Each circuit clerk must send the Administrative Office of the United States Courts a copy of each local rule and internal operating procedure when it is promulgated or amended.

(2) A local rule imposing a requirement of form must not be enforced in a manner that causes a party to lose rights because of a nonwillful failure to comply with the requirement.

(b) Procedure When There Is No Controlling Law. A court of appeals may regulate practice in a particular case in any manner consistent with federal law, these rules, and local rules of the circuit. No sanction or other disadvantage may be imposed for noncompliance with any requirement not in federal law, federal rules, or the local circuit rules unless the alleged violator has been furnished in the particular case with actual notice of the requirement.

(As amended Apr. 27, 1995, eff. Dec. 1, 1995; Apr. 24, 1998, eff. Dec. 1, 1998.)

RULE 48. MASTERS

(a) Appointment; Powers. A court of appeals may appoint a special master to hold hearings, if necessary, and to recommend factual findings and disposition in matters ancillary to proceedings in the court. Unless the order referring a matter to a master specifies or limits the master's powers, those powers include, but are not limited to, the following:

(1) regulating all aspects of a hearing;

(2) taking all appropriate action for the efficient performance of the master's duties under the order;

(3) requiring the production of evidence on all matters embraced in the reference; and

(4) administering oaths and examining witnesses and parties.

(b) Compensation. If the master is not a judge or court employee, the court must determine the master's compensation and whether the cost is to be charged to any party.

(As amended Apr. 29, 1994, eff. Dec. 1, 1994; Apr. 24, 1998, eff. Dec. 1, 1998.)

APPENDIX OF FORMS
FORM 1. NOTICE OF APPEAL TO A COURT OF APPEALS FROM A JUDGMENT OR ORDER OF A DISTRICT COURT

United States District Court for the _____
District of _____
File Number _____

A.B., *Plaintiff*   )
)
       v.   ) *Notice of Appeal*
)
C.D., *Defendant*   )

Notice is hereby given that [____(here name all parties taking the appeal)____, (plaintiffs) (defendants) in the above named case,[1]] hereby appeal to the United States Court of Appeals for the _____ Circuit (from the final judgment) (from an order (describing it)) entered in this action on the _____ day of _____, 20___.

(s) _____
                Attorney for [_____]
                [Address:_____]

(As amended Apr. 22, 1993, eff. Dec. 1, 1993; Mar. 27, 2003, eff. Dec. 1, 2003.)

1 See Rule 3(c) for permissible ways of identifying appellants.

FORM 2. NOTICE OF APPEAL TO A COURT OF APPEALS FROM A DECISION OF THE UNITED STATES TAX COURT

UNITED STATES TAX COURT

Washington, D.C.

A.B., Petitioner	)	
	)	
v.	)	Docket No. _____
	)	
Commissioner of Internal	)	
Revenue, Respondent	)	

Notice of Appeal

Notice is hereby given that [____ here name all parties taking the appeal [1] ____], hereby appeals to the United States Court of Appeals for the _____ Circuit from (that part of) the decision of this court entered in the above captioned proceeding on the _____ day of _____, 20___ (relating to _____).

(s)   _____

           Counsel for [_____]

           [Address:_____]

(As amended Apr. 22, 1993, eff. Dec. 1, 1993; Mar. 27, 2003, eff. Dec. 1, 2003.)

[1] See Rule 3(c) for permissible ways of identifying appellants.

FORM 3. PETITION FOR REVIEW OF ORDER OF AN AGENCY, BOARD, COMMISSION OR OFFICER

United States Court of Appeals for the _____ Circuit

A.B., Petitioner	)	
	)	
v.	)	Petition for Review
XYZ Commission, Respondent	)	

[____(here name all parties bringing the petition[1])____] hereby petitions the court for review of the Order of the XYZ Commission (describe the order) entered on _____, 20___.

[(s)] _____

Attorney for Petitioners

Address:_____

(As amended Apr. 22, 1993, eff. Dec. 1, 1993; Mar. 27, 2003, eff. Dec. 1, 2003.)

[1] See Rule 15.

FORM 4. AFFIDAVIT ACCOMPANYING MOTION FOR PERMISSION TO APPEAL IN FORMA PAUPERIS

United States District Court
for the
_____ District of _____

<Name(s) of plaintiff(s),>	)
	)
Plaintiff(s)	)
	)
v.	)
	) Case No. <Number>
<Name(s) of defendant(s),>	)
	)
Defendant	)
	)

AFFIDAVIT ACCOMPANYING MOTION
FOR PERMISSION TO APPEAL IN FORMA PAUPERIS

Affidavit in Support of Motion

I swear or affirm under penalty of perjury that, because of my poverty, I cannot prepay the docket fees of my appeal or post a bond for them. I believe I am entitled to redress. I swear or affirm under penalty of perjury under United States laws that my answers on this form are true and correct. (28 U.S.C. § 1746; 18 U.S.C. § 1621.)

Signed: _____

Instructions

Complete all questions in this application and then sign it. Do not leave any blanks: if the answer to a question is "0," "none," or "not applicable (N/A)," write in that response. If you need more space to answer a question or to explain your answer, attach a separate sheet of paper identified with your name, your case's docket number, and the question number.

Date: _____

My issues on appeal are:

1.   For both you and your spouse estimate the average amount of money received from each of the following sources during the past 12 months. Adjust any amount that was received weekly, biweekly, quarterly, semiannually, or annually to show the monthly rate. Use gross amounts, that is, amounts before any deductions for taxes or otherwise.

Income source	Average monthly amount during the past 12 months		Amount expected next month	
	You	Spouse	You	Spouse
Employment	$_____	$_____	$_____	$_____
Self-employment	$_____	$_____	$_____	$_____
Income from real property (such as rental income)	$_____	$_____	$_____	$_____
Interest and dividends	$_____	$_____	$_____	$_____
Gifts	$_____	$_____	$_____	$_____
Alimony	$_____	$_____	$_____	$_____
Child support	$_____	$_____	$_____	$_____

Retirement (such as social security, pensions, annuities, insurance)	$_____	$_____	$_____	$_____
Disability (such as social security, insurance payments)	$_____	$_____	$_____	$_____
Unemployment payments	$_____	$_____	$_____	$_____
Public-assistance (such as welfare)	$_____	$_____	$_____	$_____
Other (specify): _____	$_____	$_____	$_____	$_____
Total monthly income:	$_____	$_____	$_____	$_____

2. List your employment history for the past two years, most recent employer first. (Gross monthly pay is before taxes or other deductions.)

Employer	Address	Dates of employment	Gross monthly pay
_____	_____	_____	_____
_____	_____	_____	_____

3. List your spouse's employment history for the past two years, most recent employer first. (Gross monthly pay is before taxes or other deductions.)

Employer	Address	Dates of employment	Gross monthly pay
_____	_____	_____	_____
_____	_____	_____	_____

4. How much cash do you and your spouse have? $_____
Below, state any money you or your spouse have in bank accounts or in any other financial institution.

Financial institution	Type of account	Amount you have	Amount your spouse has
_____	_____	$_____	$_____
_____	_____	$_____	$_____
_____	_____	$_____	$_____

If you are a prisoner seeking to appeal a judgment in a civil action or proceeding, you must attach a statement certified by the appropriate institutional officer showing all receipts, expenditures, and balances during the last six months in your institutional accounts. If you have multiple accounts, perhaps because you have been in multiple institutions, attach one certified statement of each account.

5. List the assets, and their values, which you own or your spouse owns. Do not list clothing and ordinary household furnishings.

Home	(Value)	Other real estate	(Value)	Motor vehicle #1	(Value)
_____		_____		Make & year: _____	
_____		_____		Model: _____	
_____		_____		Registration #: _____	

Motor vehicle #2	(Value)	Other assets	(Value)	Other assets	(Value)
Make & year: _____		_____		_____	
Model: _____		_____		_____	
Registration #: _____		_____		_____	

6. State every person, business, or organization owing you or your spouse money, and the amount owed.

Person owing you or your spouse money	Amount owed to you	Amount owed to your spouse
_____	_____	_____
_____	_____	_____

7. State the persons who rely on you or your spouse for support.

Name [or, if under 18, initials only]	Relationship	Age
_____	_____	_____
_____	_____	_____

8. Estimate the average monthly expenses of you and your family. Show separately the amounts paid by your spouse. Adjust any payments that are made weekly, biweekly, quarterly, semiannually, or annually to show the monthly rate.

	You	Your Spouse
Rent or home-mortgage payment (include lot rented for mobile home)	$_____	$_____
Are real-estate taxes included? ☐ Yes ☐ No		
Is property insurance included? ☐ Yes ☐ No		
Utilities (electricity, heating fuel, water, sewer, and telephone)	$_____	$_____
Home maintenance (repairs and upkeep)	$_____	$_____
Food	$_____	$_____
Clothing	$_____	$_____
Laundry and dry-cleaning	$_____	$_____
Medical and dental expenses	$_____	$_____
Transportation (not including motor vehicle payments)	$_____	$_____
Recreation, entertainment, newspapers, magazines, etc.	$_____	$_____
Insurance (not deducted from wages or included in mortgage payments)		
Homeowner's or renter's:	$_____	$_____
Life:	$_____	$_____
Health:	$_____	$_____
Motor Vehicle:	$_____	$_____
Other: _____	$_____	$_____
Taxes (not deducted from wages or included in mortgage payments) (specify): __	$_____	$_____
Installment payments		
Motor Vehicle	$_____	$_____
Credit card (name): _____	$_____	$_____
Department store (name): _____	$_____	$_____
Other: _____	$_____	$_____
Alimony, maintenance, and support paid to others	$_____	$_____
Regular expenses for operation of business, profession, or farm (attach detailed statement)	$_____	$_____
Other (specify): _____	$_____	$_____
Total monthly expenses:	$_____	$_____

9. Do you expect any major changes to your monthly income or expenses or in your assets or liabilities during the next 12 months?

☐ Yes ☐ No   If yes, describe on an attached sheet.

10. Have you spent—or will you be spending—any money for expenses or attorney fees in connection with this lawsuit?

☐ Yes ☐ No   If yes, how much? $_____

11. Provide any other information that will help explain why you cannot pay the docket fees for your appeal.

12. State the city and state of your legal residence.

_____

_____

Your daytime phone number: (___) _____
Your age: _____ Your years of schooling: _____
Last four digits of your social-security number: _____

(As amended Apr. 24, 1998, eff. Dec. 1, 1998; Apr. 28, 2010, eff. Dec. 1, 2010; Apr. 16, 2013, eff. Dec. 1, 2013.)

FORM 5. NOTICE OF APPEAL TO A COURT OF APPEALS FROM A JUDGMENT OR ORDER OF A DISTRICT COURT OR A BANKRUPTCY APPELLATE PANEL

United States District Court for the ....

District of ....

In re   )
)
....................................,   )
              Debtor   )
)   File No...........
....................................,   )
             Plaintiff   )
)
               v.   )
)
....................................,   )
             Defendant   )

Notice of Appeal to
United States Court of Appeals
        for the .... Circuit
........................., the plaintiff [or defendant or other party] appeals to
the United States Court of Appeals for the .... Circuit from
the final judgment [or order or decree] of the district court for the district of ...
[or bankruptcy appellate panel of the .... circuit], entered in this case
on ...., 20.... [here describe the judgment, order, or decree] ....
     The parties to the judgment [or order or decree] appealed from and the names
and addresses of their respective attorneys are as follows:

                                    Dated ....
                                    Signed ....
                                            Attorney for Appellant

                                    Address: ....
                                    ....

(Added Apr. 25, 1989, eff. Dec. 1, 1989; Mar. 27, 2003, eff. Dec. 1, 2003.)

FORM 6.   CERTIFICATE OF COMPLIANCE WITH RULE 32(a)

Certificate of Compliance With Type-Volume Limitation, Typeface
Requirements, and Type Style Requirements

1.   This brief complies with the type-volume limitation of Fed. R. App. P.
32(a)(7)(B) because:

☐ this brief contains [*state the number of*] words, excluding the parts of the brief
exempted by Fed. R. App. P. 32(a)(7)(B)(iii), *or*

☐ this brief uses a monospaced typeface and contains [*state the number of*] lines
of text, excluding the parts of the brief exempted by Fed. R. App. P.
32(a)(7)(B)(iii).

2.   This brief complies with the typeface requirements of Fed. R. App. P. 32(a)(5)
and the type style requirements of Fed. R. App. P. 32(a)(6) because:

☐ this brief has been prepared in a proportionally spaced typeface using [*state
name and version of word processing program*] in [*state font size and name of
type style*], *or*

☐ this brief has been prepared in a monospaced typeface using [*state name and
version of word processing program*] with [*state number of characters per inch
and name of type style*].

(s)_____

Attorney for _____

Dated: _____

(Added Apr. 29, 2002, eff. Dec. 1, 2002.)

INDEX TO
FEDERAL RULES OF APPELLATE PROCEDURE

UNITED STATES COURT OF APPEALS
FOR THE
SEVENTH CIRCUIT

Including Amendments Received Through
April 1, 2015

APPENDICES

APPENDIX OF FORMS TO FEDERAL RULES OF APPELLATE PROCEDURE

APPENDIX OF FORMS TO THE CIRCUIT RULES

OPERATING PROCEDURES

THE PLAN OF THE UNITED STATES COURT OF APPEALS FOR THE SEVENTH CIRCUIT TO SUPPLEMENT THE PLANS OF THE SEVERAL UNITED STATES DISTRICT COURTS WITHIN THE SEVENTH CIRCUIT

STANDARDS FOR PROFESSIONAL CONDUCT WITHIN THE SEVENTH FEDERAL JUDICIAL CIRCUIT

ELECTRONIC CASE FILING

RULES FOR JUDICIAL–CONDUCT AND JUDICIAL–DISABILITY PROCEEDINGS

ARTICLE I. GENERAL PROVISIONS

ARTICLE II. INITIATION OF A COMPLAINT

ARTICLE III. REVIEW OF A COMPLAINT BY THE CHIEF JUDGE

TITLE I. APPLICABILITY OF RULES

FRAP 1. SCOPE OF RULES; TITLE

[For text of rule, see the Federal Rules of Appellate Procedure]

RULE 1. SCOPE OF RULES

These rules govern procedure in the United States Court of Appeals for the Seventh Circuit. They are to be known as the Circuit Rules of the United States Court of Appeals for the Seventh Circuit.
[Amended effective December 1, 1997.]

FRAP 2. SUSPENSION OF RULES

[For text of rule, see the Federal Rules of Appellate Procedure]

RULE 2. SUSPENSION OF CIRCUIT RULES

In the interest of expediting decision or for other good cause, the court may suspend the requirements of these Circuit Rules.

TITLE II. APPEAL FROM A JUDGMENT OR ORDER OF A DISTRICT COURT

FRAP 3. APPEAL AS OF RIGHT— HOW TAKEN

[For text of rule, see the Federal Rules of Appellate Procedure]

RULE 3. NOTICE OF APPEAL, DOCKETING FEE, DOCKETING STATEMENT, AND DESIGNATION OF COUNSEL OF RECORD

(a) Forwarding Copy of Notice of Appeal. When the clerk of the district court transmits to the clerk of this court a copy of the notice of appeal, the district court clerk shall include any docketing statement. In civil cases the clerk of the district court shall include the judgments or orders under review, any transcribed oral statement of reasons, opinion, memoran-dum of decision, findings of fact, and conclusions of law.

(b) Dismissal of Appeal for Failure to Pay Docketing Fee. If a proceeding is docketed without pre-payment of the docketing fee, the appellant shall pay the fee within 14 days after docketing. If the appellant fails to do so, the clerk is authorized to dismiss the appeal.

(c)(1) *Docketing Statement.* The appellant must serve on all parties a docketing statement and file it with the clerk of the district court at the time of the filing of the notice of appeal or with the clerk of this court within seven days of filing the notice of appeal. The docketing statement must comply with the re-quirements of Circuit Rule 28(a). If there have been prior or related appellate proceedings in the case, or if the party believes that the earlier appellate proceed-ings are sufficiently related to the new appeal, the statement must identify these proceedings by caption and number. The statement also must describe any prior litigation in the district court that, although not appealed, (a) arises out of the same criminal conviction, or (b) has been designated by the district court as satisfying the criteria of 28 U.S.C. § 1915(g). If any of the parties to the litigation appears in an official capacity, the statement must identify the current occupant of the office. The docketing statement in a collateral attack on a criminal conviction must identify the prisoner's current place of confinement and its current warden; if the prisoner has been released, the statement must describe the nature of any ongoing custody (such as supervised release) and identify the custodian. If the docketing statement is not complete and correct, the appellee must provide a complete one to the court of appeals clerk within 14 days after the date of the filing of the appellant's docketing statement.

(2) Failure to file the docketing statement within 14 days of the filing of the notice of appeal will lead to the imposition of a $100 fine on counsel. Failure to file the statement within 28 days of the filing of the notice of appeal will be treated as abandonment of the appeal, and the appeal will be dismissed. When the appeal is docketed, the court will remind the litigants of these provisions.

(d) **Counsel of Record.** The attorney whose name appears on the docketing statement or other document first filed by that party in this court will be deemed counsel of record, and a separate notice of appearance need not be filed. If the name of more than one attorney is shown, the attorney who is counsel of record must be clearly identified. (There can be only one counsel of record.) If no attorney is so identified, the court will treat the first listed as counsel of record. The court will send documents only to the counsel of record for each party, who is responsible for transmitting them to other lawyers for the same party. The docketing statement or other document must provide the post office address, email address and telephone number of counsel of record. The names of other members of the Bar of this Court and, if desired, their post office and email addresses, may be added but counsel of record must be clearly identified. An attorney representing a party who will not be filing a document shall enter a separate notice of appearance as counsel of record indicating the name of the party represented. Counsel of record may not withdraw, without consent of the court, unless another counsel of record is simultaneously substituted.

[Amended effective February 1, 1992; June 1, 1995; January 1, 1997; December 1, 1997; December 1, 1998; December 1, 2014.]

FRAP 3.1 APPEAL FROM A JUDGMENT OF A MAGISTRATE JUDGE IN A CIVIL CASE [ABROGATED]

[For text of rule, see the Federal Rules of Appellate Procedure]

FRAP 4. APPEAL AS OF RIGHT— WHEN TAKEN

[For text of rule, see the Federal Rules of Appellate Procedure]

FRAP 5. APPEAL BY PERMISSION

[For text of rule, see the Federal Rules of Appellate Procedure]

FRAP 6. APPEAL IN A BANKRUPTCY CASE FROM A FINAL JUDGMENT, ORDER, OR DECREE OF A DISTRICT COURT OR BANKRUPTCY APPELLATE PANEL

[For text of rule, see the Federal Rules of Appellate Procedure]

FRAP 7. BOND FOR COSTS ON APPEAL IN A CIVIL CASE

[For text of rule, see the Federal Rules of Appellate Procedure]

FRAP 8. STAY OR INJUNCTION PENDING APPEAL

[For text of rule, see the Federal Rules of Appellate Procedure]

RULE 8. MOTIONS FOR STAYS AND INJUNCTIONS PENDING APPEAL

Counsel's obligation under Fed. R. App. P. 8(a) to provide this court with the reasons the district judge gave for denying relief includes an obligation to supply any statement of reasons by a magistrate judge or bankruptcy judge. Filing with the motion a copy of the order or memorandum of decision in which the reasons were stated, or if they were stated orally in open court, a copy of the transcript of proceedings is preferred; but, in an emergency, if such a copy is not available, counsel's statement of the reasons given by the district or bankruptcy court will suffice.

[Amended effective December 1, 1997.]

FRAP 9. RELEASE IN A CRIMINAL CASE

[For text of rule, see the Federal Rules of Appellate Procedure]

RULE 9. MOTIONS CONCERNING CUSTODY PENDING TRIAL OR APPEAL

(a) All requests for release from custody pending trial shall be by motion. The defendant shall file a notice of appeal followed by a motion.

(b) All requests to reverse orders granting bail or enlargement pending trial or appeal shall be by motion. The government shall file a notice of appeal followed by a motion.

(c) All requests for release from custody after sentencing and pending the disposition of the appeal shall be by motion in the main case. There is no need for a separate notice of appeal.

(d) Any motion filed under this rule shall be accompanied by a memorandum of law.

[Amended effective February 1, 1992.]

FRAP 10. THE RECORD ON APPEAL

[For text of rule, see the Federal Rules of Appellate Procedure]

RULE 10. PREPARATION OF RECORD IN DISTRICT COURT APPEALS

(a) Record Preparation Duties. The clerk of the district court shall prepare within 14 days of filing the notice of appeal the original papers, transcripts filed in the district court, and exhibits received or offered in evidence (with the exceptions listed below). The transcript of a deposition is "filed" within the meaning of this rule, and an exhibit is "received or offered," to the extent that it is tendered to the district court in support of a brief or motion, whether or not the rules of the district court treat deposition transcripts or exhibits as part of the record. These materials may be designated as part of the record on appeal without the need for a motion under Fed. R. App. P. 10(e). Counsel must ensure that exhibits and transcripts to be included in the record which are not in the possession of the district court clerk are furnished to the clerk within fourteen days after the filing of the notice of appeal. The following items will not be included in a record unless specifically requested by a party by item and date of filing within fourteen days after the notice of appeal is filed or unless specifically ordered by this court:

    briefs and memoranda,

    notices of filings,

    subpoenas,

    summonses,

    motions to extend time,

    affidavits and admissions of service and mailing,

    notices of settings,

    depositions and notices, and

    jury lists.

(b) Correction or Modification of Record. A motion to correct or modify the record pursuant to Rule 10(e), Fed. R. App. P., or a motion to strike matter from the record on the ground that it is not properly a part thereof shall be presented first to the district court. That court's order ruling on the motion will be transmitted to this court as part of the record.

(c) Order or Certification with Regard to Transcript. Counsel and court reporters are to utilize the form prescribed by this court when ordering transcripts or certifying that none will be ordered. For specific requirements, see Rules 10(b) and 11(b), Fed. R. App. P.

(d) Ordering Transcripts in Criminal Cases.

(1) *Transcripts in Criminal Justice Act Cases.* At the time of the return of a verdict of guilty or, in the case of a bench trial, an adjudication of guilt in a criminal case in which the defendant is represented by counsel appointed under the Criminal Justice Act (C.J.A.), counsel for the defendant shall request a transcript of testimony and other relevant proceedings by completing a C.J.A. Form No. 24 and giving it to the district judge. If the district judge believes an appeal is probable, the judge shall order transcribed so much of the proceedings as the judge believes necessary for an appeal. The transcript shall be filed with the clerk of the district court within 40 days after the return of a verdict of guilty or, in the case of a bench trial, the adjudication of guilt or within seven days after sentencing, whichever occurs later. If the district judge decides not to order the transcript at that time, the judge shall retain the C.J.A. Form No. 24 without ruling. If a notice of appeal is filed later, appointed counsel or counsel for a defendant allowed after trial to proceed on appeal in forma pauperis shall immediately notify the district judge of the filing of a notice of appeal and file or renew the request made on C.J.A. Form No. 24 for a free transcript.

(2) *Transcripts in Other Criminal Cases.* Within 14 days after filing the notice of appeal in other criminal cases, the appellant or appellant's counsel shall deposit with the court reporter the estimated cost of the transcript ordered pursuant to Rule 10(b), Fed. R. App. P., unless the district court orders that the transcript be paid for by the United States. A non-indigent appellant must pay a pro rata share of the cost of a transcript prepared at the request of an indigent co-defendant under the Criminal Justice Act unless the district court determines that fairness requires a different division of the cost. Failure to comply with this paragraph will be cause for dismissal of the appeal.

(e) Indexing of Transcript. The transcript of proceedings to be transmitted to this court as part of the record on appeal (and any copies prepared for the use of the court or counsel in the case on appeal) shall be produced by the reporter in a volume or volumes, with the pages consecutively numbered throughout all volumes. The transcript of proceedings, or the first volume thereof, shall contain a suitable index, which shall refer to the number of the volume as well as the page, shall be cumulative for all volumes, and shall include the following information:

(1) An alphabetical list of witnesses, giving the pages on which the direct and each other examination of each witness begins.

(2) A list of exhibits by number, with a brief description of each exhibit indicating the nature of its contents, and with a reference to the pages of the transcript where each exhibit has been identified, offered, and received or rejected.

(3) A list of other significant portions of the trial such as opening statements, arguments to the jury, and instructions, with a reference to the page where each begins.

When the record includes transcripts of more than one trial or other distinct proceeding, and it would be cumbersome to apply this paragraph to all the transcripts taken together as one, the rule may be applied separately to each transcript of one trial or other distinct proceeding.

(f) Presentence Reports. The presentence report is part of the record on appeal in every criminal case. The district court should transmit this report under seal, unless it has already been placed in the public record in the district court. If the report is transmitted under seal, the report may not be included in the appendix to the brief or the separate appendix under Fed. R. App. P. 30 and Circuit Rule 30. Counsel of record may review the presentence report at the clerk's office but may not review the probation officer's written comments and any other portion submitted in camera to the trial judge.

(g) Effect of Omissions from the Record on Appeal. When a party's argument is countered by a contention of waiver for failure to raise the point in the trial court or before an agency, the party opposing the waiver contention must give the record cite where the point was asserted and also ensure that the record before the court of appeals contains the relevant document or transcript.

[Amended effective February 1, 1992; June 1, 1995; January 1, 1996; December 1, 2009; December 1, 2014.]

FRAP 11.   FORWARDING THE RECORD

[For text of rule, see the Federal Rules of Appellate Procedure]

RULE 11.   RECORD ON APPEAL

(a) Record Transmission. When the appeal is ready for scheduling for oral argument or submission, the clerk of the court of appeals will notify the district court clerk to transmit the record to the court of appeals. The parties may agree or the court of appeals may order that the record be sent to the clerk of the court of appeals at an earlier time. But in no event shall the clerk of the district court transmit bulky items, currency, securities, liquids, drugs, weapons, or similar items without a specific order of this court.

(b) Transcript and Other Supplemental Transmissions. When trial or hearing transcripts, or other parts of the record, are filed with the clerk of the district court (or exhibits that have been retained in the district court for use in preparation of the transcript are returned to the clerk) after initial transmission of the record, they shall be immediately transmitted to this court and filed as a supplemental record without the requirement of this court's order. This immediate transmission meets the requirements of Rule 11(b), Fed. R. App. P., that the court reporter notify the clerk of the court of appeals that the transcript has been filed with the clerk of the district court.

(c) Extension of Time.

(1) *Requests for Extension to be Addressed to Court of Appeals.* All requests for extension of time for filing the record or parts thereof shall be addressed to the court of appeals.

(2) *Extension of Time for Preparation of Transcript.* Any request by a court reporter for an exten-

sion of time longer than 30 days from the date the transcript was first ordered must be filed with the clerk of this court on a form prescribed by the court. The request must include the date the transcript was ordered, the reasons for both that request, and any previous requests for extensions of time, and a certificate that all parties or their counsel have been sent a copy of the request. If the request is for an extension of time longer than 60 days from the date the transcript was first ordered, it must include a statement from the district judge who tried the case or the chief judge of the district court that the request has been brought to that judge's attention and that steps are being taken to insure that all ordered transcripts will be promptly prepared.

(d) Withdrawal of Record. During the time allowed for the preparation and filing of a brief, an attorney for a party or a party acting pro se may withdraw any record not in electronic format upon giving a receipt to the clerk who has physical custody of the record. Once a panel of judges is assigned, a non-electronic record may not be withdrawn without an order of the court. Original exhibits may not be withdrawn but may be examined only in the clerk's office. The party who has withdrawn a non-electronic record may not file a brief or petition for rehearing until the record has been returned to the clerk's office from which it was withdrawn. Except as provided above, non-electronic records shall not be taken from a clerk's office without leave of this court on written motion. Failure of a party to return non-electronic records to the clerk may be treated as contempt of this court. When the party withdrawing the record is incarcerated, the clerk who has physical custody of the record, on order of this court, will send the record to the warden of the institution with the request that the record be made available to the party under super-

vised conditions and be returned to the respective clerk before a specified date.

[Amended effective February 1, 1992; December 1, 2014.]

FRAP 12. DOCKETING THE APPEAL; FILING A REPRESENTATION STATEMENT; FILING THE RECORD

[For text of rule, see the Federal Rules of Appellate Procedure]

RULE 12. DOCKETING THE APPEAL

(a) Docketing. The clerk will notify counsel and parties acting pro se of the date the appeal is docketed.

(b) Caption. The parties on appeal shall be designated in the title of the cause in court as they appeared in the district court, with the addition of identification of appellant and appellee, for example, John Smith, Plaintiff–Appellee v. William Jones, Defendant–Appellant. Actions seeking habeas corpus shall be designated "Petitioner v. Custodian" and not "United States ex rel. Petitioner v. Custodian".

[Amended effective January 1, 1990; February 1, 1992; December 1, 1997.]

FRAP 12.1. REMAND AFTER AN INDICATIVE RULING BY THE DISTRICT COURT ON A MOTION FOR RELIEF THAT IS BARRED BY A PENDING APPEAL

[For text of rule, see the Federal Rules of Appellate Procedure]

TITLE III. APPEALS FROM THE UNITED STATES TAX COURT

FRAP 13. APPEALS FROM THE TAX COURT

[For text of rule, see the Federal Rules of Appellate Procedure]

FRAP 14. APPLICABILITY OF OTHER RULES TO APPEALS FROM THE TAX COURT

[For text of rule, see the Federal Rules of Appellate Procedure]

TITLE IV. REVIEW OR ENFORCEMENT OF AN ORDER OF AN ADMINISTRATIVE AGENCY, BOARD, COMMISSION, OR OFFICER

FRAP 15. REVIEW OR ENFORCEMENT OF AN AGENCY ORDER—HOW OBTAINED; INTERVENTION

[For text of rule, see the Federal Rules of Appellate Procedure]

FRAP 15.1. BRIEFS AND ORAL ARGUMENT IN A NATIONAL LABOR RELATIONS BOARD PROCEEDING

[For text of rule, see the Federal Rules of Appellate Procedure]

FRAP 16. THE RECORD ON REVIEW OR ENFORCEMENT

[For text of rule, see the Federal Rules of Appellate Procedure]

FRAP 17. FILING THE RECORD

[For text of rule, see the Federal Rules of Appellate Procedure]

FRAP 18. STAY PENDING REVIEW

[For text of rule, see the Federal Rules of Appellate Procedure]

FRAP 19. SETTLEMENT OF A JUDGMENT ENFORCING AN AGENCY ORDER IN PART

[For text of rule, see the Federal Rules of Appellate Procedure]

FRAP 20. APPLICABILITY OF RULES TO THE REVIEW OR ENFORCEMENT OF AN AGENCY ORDER

[For text of rule, see the Federal Rules of Appellate Procedure]

TITLE V. EXTRAORDINARY WRITS

FRAP 21. WRITS OF MANDAMUS AND PROHIBITION, AND OTHER EXTRAORDINARY WRITS

[For text of rule, see the Federal Rules of Appellate Procedure]

TITLE VI. HABEAS CORPUS; PROCEEDINGS IN FORMA PAUPERIS

FRAP 22. HABEAS CORPUS AND SECTION 2255 PROCEEDINGS

[For text of rule, see the Federal Rules of Appellate Procedure]

RULE 22. DEATH PENALTY CASES

(a) Operation and Scope.

(1) This rule applies to all cases involving persons under sentence of capital punishment.

(2) Cases within the scope of this rule will be assigned to a panel as soon as the appeal is docketed. The panel to which a case is assigned will handle all substantial matters pertaining to the case, including certificates of appealability, stays of execution, consideration of the merits, second or successive petitions, remands from the Supreme Court of the United States, and associated procedural matters. If a judge on the panel is unavailable to participate, another judge may be substituted.

(3) Pursuant to 18 U.S.C. § 3006A, and 18 U.S.C. § 3599, 28 U.S.C. § 2254(h), and 28 U.S.C. § 2255(g), appellate counsel shall be appointed for any person under a sentence of death who is financially unable to obtain representation, requests that counsel be appointed, and does not already have counsel appointed by a state under 28 U.S.C. § 2261.

(4) The panel to which a case is assigned may make changes in procedure and scheduling in any case when justice so requires.

(b) Notice of Appeal and Required Documents.

(1) The district court clerk must notify the clerk of this court by telephone immediately upon the filing of a notice of appeal of a case within the scope of this rule. In all cases within the scope of this rule, the district court clerk must immediately transmit the record to the court of appeals. A supplemental record may be sent later if items are not currently available.

(2) Upon receipt of the record from the district court clerk, or any petition, application or motion invoking the jurisdiction of this court, the clerk of this court shall docket the appeal. The panel will be immediately notified.

(3) Upon filing a notice of appeal, the appellant shall immediately transmit to the court a copy of, or a citation to, each state or federal court opinion, memorandum decision, order, transcript of oral statement of reasons, or judgment involving an issue to be presented on appeal to this court. If a document or transcript is needed and is not immediately available, appellant shall submit an affidavit as to the decision and reasons given by the court. Appellant shall file the document or transcript as soon as it is available.

(c) Briefs.

(1) Unless the court sets another schedule, the following time limitations apply.

(A) On direct appeal in a federal criminal prosecution, the appellant shall serve and file a brief within 63 days after the date on which the appeal is docketed. The appellee shall serve and file a brief within 49 days after service of the brief by the appellant. The appellant may serve and file a reply brief within 21 days after service of the brief by the appellee.

(B) In all other cases within the scope of this rule the appellant will have 28 days from the date on which the notice of appeal is filed to file and serve a brief. The appellee then will have 21 days from the service of the brief to file and serve a brief. Within seven days after service of the appellee's brief, appellant may file and serve a reply brief.

(2) If an issue is raised that was not presented at a prior stage of the litigation (for example, in the district court, the appropriate state court, or this court on a prior appeal), the party raising the issue must state why the issue was not raised and why relief should nonetheless be granted.

(d) Submission and Oral Argument.

(1) The court will hear oral argument in every direct appeal in a federal criminal prosecution and in every appeal from the decision concerning an initial petition under 28 U.S.C. § 2254 in a state case. In

any other case, a request for oral argument will be evaluated under the standards of Fed. R. App. P. 34(a).

(2) Oral argument will be held expeditiously after the filing of the reply brief.

(3) The merits of an appeal may be decided summarily if the panel decides that an appeal is frivolous. In such a case, the panel may issue a single opinion deciding both the merits of the appeal and the motion for a stay of execution.

(e) Opinion or Order.

(1) The panel's decision shall be made without undue delay. In cases to which 28 U.S.C. § 2266 applies, the panel's decision will be issued no later than 120 days after the date the reply brief was filed.

(2) In cases in which an execution date has been set and not stayed, the panel will release the decision with dispatch to allow the losing party time to ask for rehearing or consideration by the Supreme Court.

(f) Panel or En Banc Rehearing.

(1) Any active judge of the court may, within 14 days after filing of the opinion, notify the panel and the clerk to hold issuance of the mandate and poll the court for en banc consideration. If the mandate has already issued, it may be recalled by the panel or by the en banc court. All judges are to vote within 14 days after the request for the vote on en banc consideration. A judge unable by reason of illness or absence to act within the time allowed by this rule may extend the time to act for a reasonable period upon written notice to the other judges. Unless within 30 days after the petition for rehearing, or the answer to the petition (if one has been requested), is filed, a majority of the panel, or of the judges in active service, has voted to grant rehearing or rehearing en banc, the court will enter an order denying the petition.

(2) If the court decides to rehear an appeal en banc, the appeal will be scheduled for oral argument expeditiously and decided within the time allowed by 28 U.S.C. § 2266(c).

(g) Second or Successive Petitions or Appeals. A second or successive petition or appeal will be assigned to the panel that handled the first appeal, motion for stay of execution, application for certificate of appealability or other prayer for relief. A motion for leave to commence a second or successive case is governed by Circuit Rule 22.2 and likewise will be assigned to the original panel.

(h) Stay of Execution.

(1) A stay of execution is granted automatically (A) on direct appeal in a federal criminal prosecution by Fed. R. Crim. P. 38(a), and (B) in some state cases by

28 U.S.C. § 2262(a). A stay of execution is forbidden in some state cases by 28 U.S.C. § 2262(b) and (c). All requests with respect to stays of execution over which the court possesses discretion, or in which any party contends that § 2262 or Rule 38(a) has not been followed, must be made by motion under this rule.

(2) An appellant may not file a motion to stay execution or to vacate a stay of execution unless there is an appeal accompanied by a certificate of appealability or a request that this court issue a certificate of appealability together with a copy of the district judge's statement as to why the certificate should not issue. The request for a certificate of appealability and the motion to stay execution shall be decided together.

(3) The movant shall file the motion and shall immediately notify opposing counsel by telephone. If the following documents have not yet been filed with this court as part of the record, a copy of each shall be filed with each copy of the motion:

(i) certificate of appealability;

(ii) the complaint, petition or motion seeking relief in the district court and the response thereto;

(iii) the district court decision on the merits;

(iv) the motion in the district court to stay execution or vacate stay of execution and the response thereto; and

(v) the district court decision on the motion to stay execution or vacate stay of execution.

If any required document cannot be filed, the movant shall state the reason for the omission.

(4) If an issue is raised that was not presented at a prior stage of the litigation (for example, in the district court, the appropriate state court, or this court on a prior appeal), the party raising the issue must state why the issue was not raised and why relief should nonetheless be granted.

(5) If the attorney for the government has no objection to the motion for stay, the court shall enter an order staying the execution.

(6) Parties shall endeavor to file motions with the clerk during normal business hours. Parties having emergency motions during nonbusiness hours shall call the clerk's telephone number for recorded instructions. The clerk shall promptly notify, by telephone, the designated representatives of the appropriate governmental body or counsel for petitioner of any such motions or other communications received by the clerk during nonbusiness hours. Each side must keep the clerk informed of the home and office telephone

number and email address of one attorney who will serve as emergency representative.

(7) An order of the panel granting or denying a motion to issue or vacate a stay of execution shall set forth the reasons for its decision.

(i) Clerk's List of Cases. The clerk shall maintain a list by jurisdiction of cases within the scope of this rule.

(j) Notification of State Supreme Court Clerk. The clerk shall send to the state supreme court a copy of the final decision in any habeas corpus case within the scope of this rule.

[Amended effective January 1, 1990; February 1, 1992; June 1, 1995; May 30, 1996; January 1, 1997; December 1, 2009; December 1, 2014.]

RULE 22.2 SUCCESSIVE PETITIONS FOR COLLATERAL REVIEW

(a) A request under 28 U.S.C. § 2244(b) or the final paragraph of 28 U.S.C. § 2255 for leave to file a second or successive petition must include the following information and attachments, in this order:

(1) A disclosure statement, if required by Circuit Rule 26.1.

(2) A short narrative statement of all claims the person wishes to present for decision. This statement must disclose whether any of these claims has been presented previously to any state or federal court and, if it was, how each court to which it was presented resolved it. If the claim has not previously been presented to a federal court, the applicant must state either:

(A) That the claim depends on a new rule of constitutional law, made retroactive to cases on collateral review by the Supreme Court; or

(B) That the factual predicate for the claim could not have been discovered previously through the exercise of due diligence and that the facts, if proven and viewed in light of the evidence as a whole, would be sufficient to establish by clear and convincing evidence that no reasonable fact-finder would have found the applicant guilty of the crime, had there been no constitutional error.

(3) A short narrative statement explaining how the person proposes to establish the requirements mentioned above. An applicant who relies on a new rule of constitutional law must identify the new rule, the

case that establishes that rule, and the decision of the Supreme Court that holds this new rule applicable to cases on collateral review.

(4) Copies of all opinions rendered by any state or federal court previously rendered in the criminal prosecution, any appeal, and any collateral attack.

(5) Copies of all prior petitions or motions for collateral review.

(b) A copy of the application, together with all attachments, must be served on the attorney for the appropriate government agency at the same time as the application is filed with the court. The application must include a certificate stating who was served, by what means, and when. If the application is made by a prisoner who is not represented by counsel, filing and service may be made under the terms of Fed. R. App. P. 4(c).

(c) Except in capital cases in which execution is imminent, the attorney for the custodian (in state cases) or the United States Attorney (in federal cases) may file a response within 14 days. When an execution is imminent, the court will not wait for a response. A response must include copies of any petitions or opinions that the applicant omitted from the papers.

(d) The applicant may file a reply memorandum within 14 days of the response, after which the request will be submitted to a panel of the court for decision.

(e) An applicant's failure to supply the information and documents required by this rule will lead the court to dismiss the application, but without prejudice to its renewal in proper form.

[Adopted effective May 30, 1996. Amended December 1, 2001; December 1, 2009.]

FRAP 23. CUSTODY OR RELEASE OF A PRISONER IN A HABEAS CORPUS PROCEEDING

[For text of rule, see the Federal Rules of Appellate Procedure]

FRAP 24. PROCEEDING IN FORMA PAUPERIS

[For text of rule, see the Federal Rules of Appellate Procedure]

TITLE VII. GENERAL PROVISIONS

FRAP 25. FILING AND SERVICE

*[For text of rule, see the Federal Rules
of Appellate Procedure]*

RULE 25. ELECTRONIC FILING

(a) All documents must be filed and served electronically.

(b) Subsection (a) does not apply to documents submitted by unrepresented litigants who are not themselves lawyers. Nor may documents be served electronically on unrepresented parties who are not lawyers. Filing by, and service on, these unrepresented litigants must be accomplished by paper copies in compliance with national and circuit rules other than this Rule 25.

(c) Any party may request by motion an exemption from this rule. The motion, which need not be filed or served electronically, must provide a good reason. A motion for exemption must be filed at least seven days before the brief, petition, or other document is due.

(d) Electronic filing is accomplished via the court's website, www.ca7.uscourts.gov. The procedures for filing are specified on the website, and paper copies of the procedures may be obtained from the Clerk. Paper copies of documents are required (and will be accepted) only to the extent provided in these e-filing procedures.

[Amended effective May 1, 2011.]

FRAP 26. COMPUTING AND EXTENDING TIME

*[For text of rule, see the Federal Rules
of Appellate Procedure]*

RULE 26. EXTENSIONS OF TIME TO FILE BRIEFS

Extensions of time to file briefs are not favored. A request for an extension of time shall be in the form of a motion supported by affidavit. The date the brief is due shall be stated in the motion. The affidavit must disclose facts which establish to the satisfaction of the court that with due diligence, and giving priority to the preparation of the brief, it will not be possible to file the brief on time.

In addition, if the time for filing the brief has been previously extended, the affidavit shall set forth the filing date of any prior motions and the court's ruling thereon. All factual statements required by this rule shall be set forth with specificity. Generalities, such as that the purpose of the motion is not for delay, or that counsel is too busy will not be sufficient.

Grounds that may merit consideration are:

(1) Engagement in other litigation, provided such litigation is identified by caption, number, and court, and there is set forth (a) a description of action taken on a request for continuance or deferment of other litigation; (b) an explanation of the reasons why other litigation should receive priority over the case in which the petition is filed; and (c) other relevant circumstances including why other associated counsel cannot either prepare the brief for filing or, in the alternative, relieve the movant's counsel of the other litigation claimed as a ground for extension.

(2) The matter under appeal is so complex that an adequate brief cannot reasonably be prepared by the date the brief is due, provided that the complexity is factually demonstrated in the affidavit.

(3) Extreme hardship to counsel will result unless an extension is granted, in which event the nature of the hardship must be set forth in detail.

The motion shall be filed at least seven days before the brief is due, unless it is made to appear in the motion that the facts which are the basis of the motion did not exist earlier or were not, or with due diligence could not have been, known earlier to the movant's counsel. Notice of the fact that an extension will be sought must be given to the opposing counsel together with a copy of the motion prior to the filing thereof.

In criminal cases, or in other cases in which a party may be in custody (including military service), a statement must be set forth in the affidavit as to the custodial status of the party, including the conditions of the party's bail, if any.

[Amended December 1, 2009.]

FRAP 26.1. CORPORATE DISCLOSURE STATEMENT

*[For text of rule, see the Federal Rules
of Appellate Procedure]*

RULE 26.1 DISCLOSURE STATEMENT

(a) Who Must File. Each attorney for a nongovernmental party or amicus curiae, and each private attorney representing a governmental party, must file a separate statement under this rule. A party or amicus required to file a corporate disclosure statement under Fed. R. App. P. 26.1 may combine the information required by subsection (b) of this rule with the statement required by the national rule. A disclosure statement constitutes an attorney's appearance. An attorney filing a disclosure statement need not file a representation statement under Fed. R. App. P. 12(b).

(b) Contents of Statement. The statement must disclose the names of all law firms whose partners or associates have appeared for the party or amicus in the case (including proceedings in the district court or before an administrative agency) or are expected to appear in this court. If any litigant is using a pseudonym, the statement must disclose the litigant's true name. A disclosure required by the preceding sentence will be kept under seal. Attorneys are encouraged to use the disclosure statement form posted on the Court of Appeals' website.

(c) Time for Filing. The statement under this rule and Fed. R. App. P. 26.1 must be filed no later than 21 days after docketing the appeal, with a party's first motion or response to an adversary's motion, or when directed by the court, whichever time is earliest. A disclosure statement for each attorney for a nongovernmental party or amicus curiae, and each private attorney representing a governmental party, also must accompany any petition for permission to appeal under Fed. R. App. P. 5 and must be included with a second or successive petition for collateral review, an appellant's brief, an appellee's brief, a brief of amicus curiae, and any petition for rehearing en banc. See Cir. R. 22.2(a)(1); Fed. R. App. P. 28(a)(1), (b); Fed. R. App. P. 29(c)(1); Cir. R. 35.

(d) Duty to Update. Counsel must file updated disclosure statements under this rule and Fed. R. App. P. 26.1 within 14 days of any change in the information required to be disclosed.

[Adopted effective March 23, 1999. Amended effective December 1, 2001; December 1, 2014.]

FRAP 27. MOTIONS

[For text of rule, see the Federal Rules of Appellate Procedure]

RULE 27. EMERGENCY FILINGS

Counsel who anticipate the need for emergency action while the Clerk's office is closed should alert the Clerk's office during business hours, and at the earliest possible time. Although documents seeking emergency relief must be filed in compliance with Circuit Rule 25, failure to provide advance notice may delay action by the court. Counsel should not expect that electronic filings will be read and acted on outside business hours, unless arrangements for the emergency filing have been made in advance.

[Amended effective May 1, 2011.]

FRAP 28. BRIEFS

[For text of rule, see the Federal Rules of Appellate Procedure]

RULE 28. BRIEFS

Briefs must conform to Fed. R. App. P. 28 and the additional provisions in Circuit Rules 12(b), 30 and 52.

The following requirements supplement those in the corresponding provisions of Fed. R. App. P. 28:

(a) Appellant's Jurisdictional Statement. The jurisdictional statement in appellant's brief, see Fed. R. App. P. 28(a)(4), must contain the following details:

(1) The statement concerning the district court's jurisdiction shall identify the provision of the constitution or federal statute involved if jurisdiction is based on the existence of a federal question. If jurisdiction depends on diversity of citizenship, the statement shall identify the jurisdictional amount and the citizenship of each party to the litigation. If any party is a corporation, the statement shall identify both the state of incorporation and the state in which the corporation has its principal place of business. If any party is an unincorporated association or partnership the statement shall identify the citizenship of all members. The statement shall supply similar details concerning the invocation of supplemental jurisdiction or other sources of jurisdiction.

(2) The statement concerning appellate jurisdiction shall identify the statutory provision believed to confer jurisdiction on this court and the following particulars:

(i) The date of entry of the judgment or decree sought to be reviewed.

(ii) The filing date of any motion for a new trial or alteration of the judgment or any other motion claimed to toll the time within which to appeal.

(iii) The disposition of such a motion and the date of its entry.

(iv) The filing date of the notice of appeal (together with information about an extension of time if one was granted).

(v) If the case is a direct appeal from the decision of a magistrate judge, the dates on which each party consented in writing to the entry of final judgment by the magistrate judge.

(3) If the appeal is from an order other than a final judgment which adjudicates all of the claims with respect to all parties, counsel shall provide the information necessary to enable the court to determine whether the order is immediately appealable. Elaboration will be necessary in the following cases although the list is illustrative rather than exhaustive:

(i) If any claims or parties remain for disposition in the district court, identify the nature of these claims and the ground on which an appeal may be taken in advance of the final judgment. If there has been a certificate under Fed. R. Civ. P. 54(b) or if this is an appeal by permission under 28 U.S.C. § 1292(b), give the particulars and describe the relation between the claims or parties subject to the appeal and the claims or parties remaining in the district court.

(ii) If the ground of jurisdiction is the "collateral order doctrine," describe how the order meets each of the criteria of that doctrine: finality, separability from the merits of the underlying action, and practical unreviewability on appeal from a final judgment. Cite pertinent cases establishing the appealability of orders of the character involved.

(iii) If the order sought to be reviewed remands a case to a bankruptcy judge or administrative agency, explain what needs to be done on remand and why the order is nonetheless "final."

(iv) Whenever some issues or parties remain before the district court, give enough information to enable the court to determine whether the order is appealable. Appeals from orders granting or staying arbitration or abstaining from decision as well as appeals from the grant or denial of injunctions require careful exposition of jurisdictional factors.

(b) Appellee's Jurisdictional Statement. The appellee's brief shall state explicitly whether or not the jurisdictional summary in the appellant's brief is complete and correct. If it is not, the appellee shall provide a complete jurisdictional summary.

(c) [Deleted]

(d) Briefs in Multiple Appeals.

(1) If a cross-appeal is filed, the clerk will designate which party will file the opening brief, and will set a briefing schedule in accordance with Fed. R. App. P. 28.1.

(2) The court will entertain motions for realignment of the briefing schedule and enlargement of the number of pages when the norm established by this rule proves inappropriate. Because it is improper to take a cross-appeal in order to advance additional arguments in support of a judgment, the court will not grant motions under this subsection by cross-appellants that do not seek to enlarge their rights under the judgment.

(3) Captions of Briefs in Multiple Appeals. When two or more parties file cross-appeals or other separate but related appeals, the briefs shall bear the appellate case numbers and captions of all related appeals.

(e) Citation of Supplemental Authority. Counsel shall file the original letter and ten copies of supplemental authorities drawn to the court's attention under Fed. R. App. P. 28(j).

(f) Citation to the United States Reports. Citation to the opinions of the Supreme Court of the United States must include the Volume and page of the United States Reports, once the citation is available.

[Amended effective February 1, 1992; June 1, 1995; December 1, 1997; December 1, 1998; December 1, 2014.]

FRAP 28.1.   CROSS–APPEALS

[For text of rule, see the Federal Rules of Appellate Procedure]

FRAP 29.   BRIEF OF AN AMICUS CURIAE

[For text of rule, see the Federal Rules of Appellate Procedure]

FRAP 30.   APPENDIX TO THE BRIEFS

[For text of rule, see the Federal Rules of Appellate Procedure]

RULE 30.   APPENDICES

(a) Contents. The appellant shall submit, bound with the main brief, an appendix containing the judgment or order under review and any opinion, memorandum of decision, findings of fact and conclusions of law, or oral statement of reasons delivered by the trial court or administrative agency upon the rendering of that judgment, decree, or order.

(b) Additional Contents. The appellant shall also include in an appendix:

(1) Copies of any other opinions, orders, or oral rulings in the case that address the issues sought to be raised. If the appellant's brief challenges any oral ruling, the portion of the transcript containing the judge's rationale for that ruling must be included in the appendix.

(2) Copies of any opinions or orders in the case rendered by magistrate judges or bankruptcy judges that address the issues sought to be raised.

(3) Copies of all opinions, orders, findings of fact and conclusions of law rendered in the case by administrative agencies (including their administrative law judges and adjudicative officers such as administrative appeals judges, immigration judges, members of boards and commissions, and others who serve functionally similar roles). This requirement applies whether the original review of the administrative decision is in this court or was conducted by the district court.

(4) If this is a collateral attack on a criminal conviction, then the appendix also must include copies of all opinions by any federal court or state appellate court previously rendered in the criminal prosecution, any appeal, and any earlier collateral attack.

(5) An order concerning a motion for new trial, alteration or amendment of the judgment, rehearing, and other relief sought under Rules 52(a) or 59, Fed. R. Civ. P.

(6) Any other short excerpts from the record, such as essential portions of the pleading or charge, disput-

ed provisions of a contract, pertinent pictures, or brief portions of the transcript, that are important to a consideration of the issues raised on appeal.

(7) The documents in (b) may also be placed in the appendix bound with the brief if these documents when added to the required appendix in (a) do not exceed fifty pages.

(c) Appendix to the brief of a Cross–Appellant. The brief of a cross-appellant must comply with this rule, but it need not include materials contained in the appendix of the appellant.

(d) Statement That All Required Materials Are in Appendix. The appendix to each appellant's brief shall contain a statement that all of the materials required by parts (a) and (b) of this rule are included. If there are no materials within the scope of parts (a) and (b) of this rule, counsel shall so certify.

(e) Stipulated Joint Appendix and Supplemental Appendices. The parties may file a stipulated joint appendix. A supplemental appendix, containing material not included in an appendix previously filed, may be filed with the appellee's brief. An appendix should not be lengthy, and costs for a lengthy appendix will not be awarded.

(f) Indexing of Appendix. If a party elects to file an appendix containing portions of the transcript of proceedings, it shall contain an index of the portions of the transcript contained therein in the form and detail described in Circuit Rule 10(e) as well as a complete table of contents.

[Amended effective December 1, 1997; December 1, 1998.]

FRAP 31. SERVING AND FILING BRIEFS

[For text of rule, see the Federal Rules of Appellate Procedure]

RULE 31. FILING OF BRIEFS AND FAILURE TO TIMELY FILE BRIEFS

(a) Time for Filing Briefs. Except in agency cases, the time for filing briefs shall run from the date the appeal is docketed, regardless of the completeness of the record at the time of docketing, unless the court orders otherwise.

(b) Number of Briefs Required. The clerk of this court is authorized to accept 15 copies of briefs as substantial compliance with Rule 31(b), Fed. R. App. P. Appointed counsel shall also file 15 copies.

(c) Failure of Appellant to File Brief. When an appellant's original brief is not filed when it is due, the procedure shall be as follows:

(1) *All Criminal Cases in Which the Defendant Has Counsel and Civil Cases With Court–Appointed Counsel.* The clerk shall enter an order directing counsel to show cause within 14 days why disciplinary action should not be taken. The court will then take appropriate action.

(2) *All Other Cases.* The clerk shall enter an order directing counsel, or a pro se appellant, to show cause why the appeal should not be dismissed. The court will then take appropriate action.

(d) Failure of Appellee to File Brief. When an appellee's brief is not filed on time, the clerk shall enter an order requiring the appellee to show cause within 14 days why the case should not be treated as ready for oral argument or submission and the appellee denied oral argument. The court will then take appropriate action.

(e) [Rescinded]

[Amended effective February 1, 1992; January 1, 1997; December 1, 2001; May 1, 2011.]

FRAP 32. FORM OF BRIEFS, APPENDICES, AND OTHER PAPERS

[For text of rule, see the Federal Rules of Appellate Procedure]

RULE 32. FORM OF A BRIEF

(a) A brief need not comply with the portion of Fed. R. App. P. 32(a)(3) requiring it to "lie reasonably flat when open." A brief's binding is acceptable if it is secure and does not obscure the text.

(b) A brief need not comply with the 14–point–type requirement in Fed. R. App. P. 32(a)(5)(A). A brief is acceptable if proportionally spaced type is 12 points or larger in the body of the brief, and 11 points or larger in footnotes.

[Amended effective January 1, 1990; February 1, 1992; January 1, 1996; January 1, 1997; June, 1997; December 1, 1997; December 1, 1998; December 1, 2001.]

FRAP 32.1. CITING JUDICIAL DISPOSITIONS

[For text of rule, see the Federal Rules of Appellate Procedure]

RULE 32.1 PUBLICATION OF OPINIONS

(a) Policy. It is the policy of the circuit to avoid issuing unnecessary opinions.

(b) Publication. The court may dispose of an appeal by an opinion or an order. Opinions, which may be signed or per curiam, are released in printed form, are published in the Federal Reporter, and constitute the law of the circuit. Orders, which are unsigned, are released in photocopied form, are not published in the Federal Reporter, and are not treated as precedents. Every order bears the legend: "Nonprecedential disposition. To be cited only in accordance with Fed. R. App. P. 32.1."

(c) Motion to Change Status. Any person may request by motion that an order be reissued as an opinion. The motion should state why this change would be appropriate.

(d) Citation of Older Orders. No order of this court issued before January 1, 2007, may be cited except to support a claim of preclusion (res judicata or collateral estoppel) or to establish the law of the case from an earlier appeal in the same proceeding.

[Effective January 1, 2007.]

FRAP 33. APPEAL CONFERENCES

[For text of rule, see the Federal Rules of Appellate Procedure]

RULE 33. PREHEARING CONFERENCE

At the conference the court may, among other things, examine its jurisdiction, simplify and define issues, consolidate cases, establish the briefing schedule, set limitations on the length of briefs, and explore the possibility of settlement.

[Amended effective February 1, 1992.]

FRAP 34. ORAL ARGUMENT

[For text of rule, see the Federal Rules of Appellate Procedure]

RULE 34. ORAL ARGUMENT

(a) Notice to Clerk. The names of counsel intending to argue orally shall be furnished to the clerk not later than five business days before the argument.

(b) Calendar.

(1) The calendar for a particular day will generally consist of six appeals scheduled for oral argument at 9:30 a.m. The amount of time allotted for oral argument will be set based on the nature of the case. The clerk will notify counsel of the allocation approximately 21 days before the argument. The types of cases listed below are to be given priority, though the sequence of listing here is not intended to indicate relative priority among the types of cases.

(i) Appeal from an order of confinement after refusal of an immunized witness to testify before the grand jury. (These appeals must be decided within 30 days.) 28 U.S.C. § 1826.

(ii) Criminal Appeals. Rule 45(b), Fed R. App. P.

(iii) Appeals from orders refusing or imposing conditions of release, which will be heard without the necessity of briefs. Rule 9, Fed. R. App. P.

(iv) Appeals involving issues of public importance.

(v) Habeas corpus and 28 U.S.C. § 2255 appeals.

(vi) Appeals from the granting, denying, or modifying of injunctions.

(vii) Petitions for writs of mandamus and prohibition and other extraordinary writs. Rule 21(b) and (c), Fed. R. App. P.

(viii) "Any other action if good cause therefore is shown. For purposes of this subsection, 'good cause' is shown if a right under the Constitution of the United States or a Federal Statute (including rights under section 552 of Title 5) would be maintained in a factual context that indicates that a request for expedited consideration has merit." 28 U.S.C. § 1657.

(2) Consideration will be given to requests addressed to the clerk by out-of-town counsel to schedule more than one appeal for oral argument the same day in order to minimize travel time and expenses.

(3) Requests by counsel, made in advance of the scheduling of an appeal for oral argument, that the court avoid scheduling the oral argument for a particular day or week will be respected, if possible.

(4) Once an appeal has been scheduled for oral argument, the court will not ordinarily reschedule it. Requests under subparagraphs (2) and (3) of this paragraph should therefore be made as early as possible. Counsel should have in mind that, when practicable, criminal appeals are scheduled for oral argument shortly after the appellant's brief is filed and civil appeals shortly after the appellee's brief is filed.

(c) Divided Argument Not Favored. Divided arguments on behalf of a single party or multiple parties with the same interests are not favored by the court. When such arguments are nevertheless divided or when more than one counsel argues on the same side for parties with differing interests, the time allowed shall be apportioned between such counsel in their own discretion. If counsel are unable to agree, the court will allocate the time.

(d) Preparation. In preparing for oral arguments, counsel should be mindful that this court follows the practice of reading briefs prior to oral argument.

(e) Waiver or Postponement. Any request for waiver or postponement of a scheduled oral argument must be made by formal motion, with proof of service on all other counsel or parties. Postponements will be granted only in extraordinary circumstances.

(f) Statement Concerning Oral Argument. A party may include, as part of a principal brief, a short statement explaining why oral argument is (or is not) appropriate under the criteria of Fed. R. App. P. 34(a).

(g) Citation of Authorities at Oral Argument. Counsel may not cite or discuss a case at oral argument unless the case has been cited in one of the briefs or drawn to the attention of the court and opposing counsel by a filing under Fed R. App. P. 28(j). The filing may be made on the day of oral argument, if absolutely necessary, but should be made sooner.

(h) Argument by Law Student. The court may permit a law student to present oral argument under supervision of a member of this court's bar, with the client's written approval, if the representation is part of a program of an accredited law school. The supervising attorney's motion must be filed at least 14 days before the date on which argument is to be held and must state the reasons why presentation of argument by a law student is appropriate.

[Amended effective January 1, 1996; December 1, 1997; December 1, 2001; December 1, 2009; December 1, 2014.]

FRAP 35. EN BANC DETERMINATION

[For text of rule, see the Federal Rules of Appellate Procedure]

RULE 35. PETITIONS FOR REHEARING EN BANC

Every petition for rehearing en banc, and every brief of an amicus curiae supporting or opposing a petition for rehearing en banc, must include a statement providing the information required by Fed. R. App. P. 26.1 and Circuit Rule 26.1 as of the date the petition is filed.

[Adopted effective June 1, 1995. Amended effective January 1, 1996; December 1, 1998; March 23, 1999.]

FRAP 36. ENTRY OF JUDGMENT; NOTICE

[For text of rule, see the Federal Rules of Appellate Procedure]

RULE 36. REASSIGNMENT OF REMANDED CASES

Whenever a case tried in a district court is remanded by this court for a new trial, it shall be reassigned by the district court for trial before a judge other than the judge who heard the prior trial unless the remand order directs or all parties request that the same judge retry the case. In appeals which are not subject to this rule by its terms, this court may nevertheless direct in its opinion or order that this rule shall apply on remand.

FRAP 37. INTEREST ON JUDGMENTS

[For text of rule, see the Federal Rules of Appellate Procedure]

FRAP 38. FRIVOLOUS APPEALS— DAMAGES AND COSTS

[For text of rule, see the Federal Rules of Appellate Procedure]

FRAP 39. COSTS

[For text of rule, see the Federal Rules of Appellate Procedure]

RULE 39. COSTS OF PRINTING BRIEFS AND APPENDICES

The cost of printing or otherwise producing copies of briefs and appendices shall not exceed the maximum rate per page as established by the clerk of the court of appeals. If a commercial printing process has been used, a copy of the bill must be attached to the itemized and verified bill of costs filed and served by the party.

FRAP 40. PETITION FOR PANEL REHEARING

[For text of rule, see the Federal Rules of Appellate Procedure]

RULE 40. PETITIONS FOR REHEARING

(a) Table of Contents. The petition for rehearing shall include a table of contents with page references and a table of cases (alphabetically arranged), statutes and other authorities cited, with reference to the pages of the brief where they are cited.

(b) Number of Copies. Fifteen copies of a petition for rehearing shall be filed, except that 30 shall be filed if the petitioner suggests rehearing en banc.

(c) Time for Filing After Decision in Agency Case. The date on which this court enters a final order or files a dispositive opinion is the date of the "entry of judgment" for the purpose of commencing the period for filing a petition for rehearing in accordance with Fed. R. App. P. 40, notwithstanding the fact that a formal detailed judgment is entered at a later date.

(d) Time for Filing After Decision From the Bench. The time limit for filing a petition for rehearing shall run from the date of this court's written order following a decision from the bench.

(e) Rehearing Sua Sponte Before Decision. A proposed opinion approved by a panel of this court adopting a position which would overrule a prior decision of this court or create a conflict between or among circuits shall not be published unless it is first circulated among the active members of this court and a majority of them do not vote to rehear en banc the issue of whether the position should be adopted. In the discretion of the panel, a proposed opinion which would establish a new rule or procedure may be similarly circulated before it is issued. When the position is adopted by the panel after compliance with this procedure, the opinion, when published, shall contain a footnote worded, depending on the circumstances, in substance as follows:

This opinion has been circulated among all judges of this court in regular active service. (No judge favored, or, A majority did not favor) a rehearing en banc on the question of (e.g., overruling *Doe v. Roe*).

[Amended effective June 1, 1995; January 1, 1996; January 1, 1997; December 1, 1997.]

FRAP 41. MANDATE: CONTENTS; ISSUANCE AND EFFECTIVE DATE; STAY

[For text of rule, see the Federal Rules of Appellate Procedure]

RULE 41. IMMEDIATE ISSUANCE OF MANDATE AFTER CERTAIN DISPOSITIONS

The mandate will issue immediately when an appeal is dismissed (1) voluntarily, (2) for failure to pay the docket fee, (3) for failure to file the docketing statement under Circuit Rule 3(c), or (4) for failure by the appellant to file a brief.

[Amended effective February 1, 1992; June 1, 1995; December 1, 1998.]

FRAP 42. VOLUNTARY DISMISSAL

[For text of rule, see the Federal Rules of Appellate Procedure]

FRAP 43. SUBSTITUTION OF PARTIES

[For text of rule, see the Federal Rules of Appellate Procedure]

RULE 43. CHANGE IN PUBLIC OFFICES

Whenever any of the parties to the litigation appears in an official capacity and there is a change in the occupant of the office after the filing of the Rule 3(c)(1) docketing statement, the official-capacity litigant (other than a member of the Cabinet) must notify the court of the identity of the new occupant of the office. Similarly, in collateral attacks on confinement,

the parties must notify the court of any change in custodian or custodial status.

[Adopted effective June 1, 1995.]

FRAP 44. CASE INVOLVING A CONSTITUTIONAL QUESTION WHERE UNITED STATES IS NOT A PARTY

[For text of rule, see the Federal Rules of Appellate Procedure]

FRAP 45. CLERK'S DUTIES

[For text of rule, see the Federal Rules of Appellate Procedure]

RULE 45. FEES

(a) **Fees To Be Collected by the Clerk.** All fees collected by the clerk shall be in accordance with the Court of Appeals Miscellaneous Fee Schedule established by the Judicial Conference of the United States under 28 U.S.C. § 1913. No other fees for miscellaneous services than those prescribed by the Judicial Conference of the United States shall be charged or collected by any clerk of court.

(b) **Fees To Be Paid in Advance.** The clerk shall not be required to docket any proceeding or perform any other service until all fees due to the clerk have been paid, except at the direction of a judge of this court or at the instance of a party who is entitled to proceed without prepayment of fees.

[Amended effective November 1, 2003; December 1, 2014.]

FRAP 46. ATTORNEYS

[For text of rule, see the Federal Rules of Appellate Procedure]

RULE 46. ATTORNEYS

(a) **Admission.** The lead attorney for all parties represented by counsel in this court must be admitted to practice in this court. Counsel have thirty days from docketing of the matter in this court to comply. In addition, any attorney who orally argues an appeal must be admitted to practice in this court. An applicant for admission to the bar of this court shall file with the clerk an application on the form furnished by the clerk. The oath or affirmation thereon may be taken before any officer authorized by federal or state law to administer an oath. When an appropriate application and motion have been filed and fee tendered, if a fee be required, the clerk shall present the papers to an active or senior circuit judge for action in chambers unless the applicant requests admission in open court. If admission is in open court, the applicant must appear in person and the sponsor shall make an oral motion in support of the written application. If admission is in chambers, the applicant and sponsor need not appear.

(b) Admission Fees. The prescribed fee for admission is a $15.00 local fee* plus a national fee prescribed by the Court of Appeals Miscellaneous Fee Schedule, except that attorneys who have been appointed by the district court or this court to represent a party on appeal in forma pauperis, law clerks to judges of this court or the district courts, and attorneys employed by the United States or any agency thereof need not pay the fee. The clerk shall receive the $15.00 local fee as trustee of the lawyers fund and shall deposit it in a bank designated by the court. Payments from the fund shall be made for the purchase of law books, for library conveniences, or other court purposes, by checks duly signed by the clerk as trustee and countersigned by two judges of this court.

(c) Government Attorneys. Attorneys for any federal, state or local government office or agency may appear before this court in connection with their official duties without being formally admitted to practice before the court.

(d) Striking a Name From the Roll of Attorneys. Whenever it is shown to this court that any members of its bar have been disbarred or suspended from practice, or their names have been stricken from the roll of attorneys, in any state, or the District of Columbia, they will be forthwith suspended from practice before this court. They will thereupon be afforded the opportunity to show cause, within 30 days, why their names should not be stricken from the roll of attorneys admitted to practice before this court. Upon the attorney's response to the rule to show cause, or upon the expiration of the 30 days if no response is made, this court will enter an appropriate order.

[Amended effective January 1, 1991; December 1, 2014.]

   * [**Publisher's Note:** For the mostcurrent admission fee charged by the Court, contact the Clerk's Office. *See also* the Federal Courts Miscellaneous Fee Schedules, *post.*]

FRAP 47. LOCAL RULES BY COURTS OF APPEALS

[For text of rule, see the Federal Rules of Appellate Procedure]

RULE 47. ADVISORY COMMITTEE

The court shall appoint an Advisory Committee to provide a forum for continuing study of the procedures of the court and to serve as a conduit between members of the bar who have suggestions for change and the court, which retains ultimate responsibility for effectuating change. The committee shall consist of one district judge, one law school professor, and two

attorneys from each state of the circuit, Illinois, Indiana, and Wisconsin, and, as ex officio members, the President and First–Vice-President of the Seventh Circuit Bar Association, the Circuit Executive, the Senior Staff Attorney, and the Clerk of this court. The district judges, attorneys, and law school professors on the committee shall serve three-year terms with the appointments being staggered.

The court shall appoint a chairman from the membership of the committee to serve for a two-year term. The advisory committee shall promulgate its own rules, and call its own meetings. The advisory committee shall arrange for notice of proposed rule changes and shall consider comments received. From time to time, as it deems necessary or advisable, it shall make recommendations to the circuit council or to the court. Suggestions for consideration by the advisory committee may be filed with the clerk of this court.

[Amended effective February 1, 1992.]

FRAP 48. MASTERS

[For text of rule, see the Federal Rules of Appellate Procedure]

RULE 50. JUDGES TO GIVE REASONS WHEN DISMISSING A CLAIM, GRANTING SUMMARY JUDGMENT, OR ENTERING AN APPEALABLE ORDER

Whenever a district court resolves any claim or counterclaim on the merits, terminates the litigation in its court (as by remanding or transferring the case, or denying leave to proceed in forma pauperis with or without prejudice), or enters an interlocutory order that may be appealed to the court of appeals, the judge shall give his or her reasons, either orally on the record or by written statement. The court urges the parties to bring to this court's attention as soon as possible any failure to comply with this rule.

[Amended effective May 1, 1993; June 1, 1995.]

RULE 51. SUMMARY DISPOSITION OF CERTAIN APPEALS BY CONVICTED PERSONS; WAIVER OF APPEAL

(a) Duties of Criminal Trial Counsel. Trial counsel in a criminal case, whether retained or appointed by the district court, is responsible for the continued representation of the client desiring to appeal unless specifically relieved by the court of appeals upon a motion to withdraw. Such relief shall be freely granted. If trial counsel was appointed by the district court and a notice of appeal has been filed, trial counsel will be appointed as appellate counsel without further proof of the client's eligibility for appointed counsel. If the client was not found to be eligible for Criminal Justice Act representation in the district court but appears to qualify on appeal, trial counsel must immediately assist the client in filing in the district court a motion to proceed as one who is financially unable to obtain an adequate defense in a criminal case. This motion must be accompanied by an affidavit containing substantially the same information as contained in Form 4 of the Appendix to the Federal Rules of Appellate Procedure. If the motion is granted, the court of appeals will appoint trial counsel as appellate counsel unless the district court informs the court of appeals that new counsel should be appointed. If the motion is denied by the district court, trial counsel may file a similar motion in the court of appeals. Counsel may have additional duties under Part V of the Circuit's Plan implementing the Criminal Justice Act of 1964.

(b) Withdrawal of Court–Appointed Counsel in a Criminal Case. When representing a convicted person in a proceeding to review the conviction, court-appointed counsel who files a brief characterizing an appeal as frivolous and moves to withdraw (see *Anders v. California*, 386 U.S. 738 (1967); *United States v. Edwards*, 777 F.2d 364 (7th Cir. 1985)) shall file with the brief a proof of service which also indicates the current address of the client. Except as provided in paragraph (g) of this rule, the clerk shall then send to the client by certified mail, return receipt requested, a copy of the brief and motion, with a notice in substantially the form set out in Appendix I to these rules. The same procedures shall be followed by court-appointed counsel and the clerk when a motion to dismiss the appeal has been filed by the appellee and the appellant's counsel believes that any argument that could be made in opposition to the motion would be frivolous.

(c) Time for Filing Motion to Withdraw in a Criminal Case. Any motion to withdraw for good cause (other than the frivolousness of an appeal) must be filed in the court of appeals within 14 days of the notice of appeal. The court of appeals will make all appellate appointments.

(d) Notice of Motion to Dismiss Pro Se Appeal. When a convicted person appears pro se in a proceeding to review the conviction, and the government moves to dismiss the appeal for a reason other than failure to file a brief on time, the clerk shall, unless paragraph (e) of this rule applies, send to the convicted person by certified mail, return receipt requested, a copy of the motion with a notice in substantially the form set out in Appendix II to these rules.

(e) Dismissal if No Response. If no response to a notice under paragraph (a) or (b) of this rule is received within 30 days after the mailing, the appeal may be dismissed.

(f) Voluntary Waiver of Appeal. Notwithstanding the preceding paragraphs, if the convicted person consents to dismissal of the appeal after consultation with appellate counsel, the appeal may be dismissed upon the filing of a motion accompanied by an executed acknowledgment and consent in substantially the form set out in Appendix III to these rules. See Rule 42(b), Fed. R. App. P.

(g) Incompetent Appellant. If, in a case in which paragraph (a) or (b) of this rule would otherwise be applicable, the convicted person has been found incompetent or there is reason to believe that person is incompetent, the motion shall so state and the matter shall be referred directly to the court by the clerk for such action as law and justice may require.

[Former Circuit Rule 4 redesignated Circuit Rule 51(a) and (c) and amended effective December 1, 1997. Amended December 1, 1998; December 1, 2009.]

RULE 52. CERTIFICATION OF QUESTIONS OF STATE LAW

(a) When the rules of the highest court of a state provide for certification to that court by a federal court of questions arising under the laws of that state which will control the outcome of a case pending in the federal court, this court, sua sponte or on motion of a party, may certify such a question to the state court in accordance with the rules of that court, and may stay the case in this court to await the state court's decision of the question certified. The certification will be made after the briefs are filed in this court. A motion for certification shall be included in the moving party's brief.

(b) If the state court decides the certified issue, then within 21 days after the issuance of its opinion the parties must file in this court statements of their positions about what action this court should take to complete the resolution of the appeal.

[Amended December 1, 1998.]

RULE 53. PLAN FOR PUBLICATION OF OPINIONS OF THE SEVENTH CIRCUIT PROMULGATED PURSUANT TO RESOLUTION OF THE JUDICIAL CONFERENCE OF THE UNITED STATES [RESCINDED DEC. 27, 2006, EFF. JAN. 1, 2007. SEE, NOW, LOCAL RULE 32.1]

RULE 54. REMANDS FROM SUPREME COURT

When the Supreme Court remands a case to this court for further proceedings, counsel for the parties shall, within 21 days after the issuance of a certified copy of the Supreme Court's judgment pursuant to its Rule 45.3, file statements of their positions as to the action which ought to be taken by this court on remand.

[Amended effective December 1, 1997.]

RULE 55. PROHIBITION OF PHOTOGRAPHS AND BROADCASTS

The taking of photographs in, or radio or television broadcasting from the courtroom or any other place on the 27th floor or judges' chambers or corridors adjacent thereto on the 26th floor of the Federal Courthouse located at 219 South Dearborn Street, Chicago, Illinois, without permission of the court, is prohibited.

RULE 56. OPPORTUNITY TO OBJECT AND MAKE PROPOSALS ON THE RECORD

(a) **Opportunity to State Objections and Their Rationale.** Whenever a rule of court requires concrete proposals or objections and reasons in order to preserve a claim for appeal (e.g., Fed. R. Civ. P. 51, Fed. R. Crim. P. 30, Fed R. Evid. 103(a)), the judge must ensure that parties have an adequate opportunity to put their proposals, objections, and reasons on the record. When the judge entertains proposals or objections off the record (for example, a sidebar conference or a jury instruction conference in chambers), as soon as practicable the judge must offer an opportunity to summarize on the record the proposal or objection discussed, and the reasons for the proposal or objection. The judge then must state the ruling made.

(b) **Waiver.** Parties offered an opportunity to make a record under part (a) of this rule must use it in order to preserve a position for appeal. No proposal, objection, or reason may be urged as a ground of appeal unless placed on the record. A lawyer who believes that he or she has not been given an adequate opportunity to make a record under this rule must so state on the record. This rule does not alter any obligation imposed by any other rule to make concrete proposals or to state objections and reasons in order to preserve a claim for appeal.

[Adopted effective June 1, 1995.]

RULE 57. REMANDS FOR REVISION OF JUDGMENT

A party who during the pendency of an appeal has filed a motion under Fed. R. Civ. P. 60(a) or 60(b), Fed. R. Crim. P. 35(b), or any other rule that permits the modification of a final judgment, should request the district court to indicate whether it is inclined to grant the motion. If the district court so indicates, this court will remand the case for the purpose of modifying the judgment. Any party dissatisfied with the judgment as modified must file a fresh notice of appeal.

[Adopted effective January 1, 1996.]

RULE 60. SEVENTH CIRCUIT JUDICIAL CONFERENCE

(a) **Purpose of the Conference.** Each year the Chief Judge shall call a circuit judicial conference in accordance with 28 U.S.C. § 333 for the purpose of considering the business of courts and advising means of improving the administration of justice within the circuit. The Chief Judge shall designate the location of the conference and either preside at it or designate officers of the Seventh Circuit Bar Association, or others, to preside.

(b) **Members of the Conference.** Each active Circuit, District, Bankruptcy, and Magistrate Judge of the Circuit shall be a member of the conference. The following shall be members of the conference and are encouraged to attend: (1) Senior Circuit, District and Bankruptcy Judges; (2) Circuit Executive, Deputy Circuit Executive, Senior Staff Attorney for the Seventh Circuit, staff attorneys and law clerks to all Circuit, District, Bankruptcy, and Magistrate Judges; (3) Clerks of the Court of Appeals, District Courts and Bankruptcy Courts in the Circuit; (4) United States Attorneys in the Circuit and their legal staffs; (5) Federal Defenders in the Circuit and their legal staffs; (6) Members of the Seventh Circuit Bar Association; (7) Special guests invited by the Chief Judge or by the President of the Seventh Circuit Bar Association with the approval of the Chief Judge; (8) United States Trustees in the Circuit and their legal staffs.

(c) **Planning of the Conference.** The Judicial Conference shall be planned by a committee composed of eight persons, four judges appointed annually by the Chief Judge from the active judges in the Circuit and four members of the Seventh Circuit Bar Association appointed annually by the President of the Bar Association. The Chief Judge, after consultation with the President of the Bar Association, shall designate one of the members to chair the committee.

(d) **Executive Session.** All or part of one day of the conference shall be designated by the Chief Judge as an executive session to be attended only by active Circuit, District and Bankruptcy Judges, Magistrate Judges and other court personnel.

(e) **Record of the Conference.** The Clerk of the Court of Appeals shall make and preserve a record of the proceedings at the Judicial Conference.

[Amended effective January 1, 1990; December 1, 1997; December 1, 2003.]

APPENDICES

APPENDIX OF FORMS TO FEDERAL RULES
OF APPELLATE PROCEDURE

FORM 1. NOTICE OF APPEAL TO A COURT OF APPEALS FROM A JUDGMENT OR ORDER OF A DISTRICT COURT

[For text of form, see the Federal Rules of Appellate Procedure]

FORM 2. NOTICE OF APPEAL TO A COURT OF APPEALS FROM A DECISION OF THE UNITED STATES TAX COURT

[For text of form, see the Federal Rules of Appellate Procedure]

FORM 3. PETITION FOR REVIEW OF ORDER OF AN AGENCY, BOARD, COMMISSION OR OFFICER

[For text of form, see the Federal Rules of Appellate Procedure]

FORM 4. AFFIDAVIT ACCOMPANYING MOTION FOR PERMISSION TO APPEAL IN FORMA PAUPERIS

[For text of form, see the Federal Rules of Appellate Procedure]

FORM 5. NOTICE OF APPEAL TO A COURT OF APPEALS FROM A JUDGMENT OR ORDER OF A DISTRICT COURT OR A BANKRUPTCY APPELLATE PANEL

[For text of form, see the Federal Rules of Appellate Procedure]

FORM 6. CERTIFICATE OF COMPLIANCE WITH RULE 32(a)

[For text of form, see the Federal Rules of Appellate Procedure]

APPENDIX OF FORMS TO THE CIRCUIT RULES

APPENDIX I. NOTICE RE: DEFENDANT COUNSEL'S MOTION FOR LEAVE TO WITHDRAW UNDER CIRCUIT RULE 51(b)

To: _____
(Name)

_____
(Street Address or Prison Box)

_____
(City, State, Zip Code)

You are the appellant in a case now pending in this court:

Case No. _____

_____

v.

_____

Your attorney filed a brief on _____, 20___, stating a belief that your appeal is frivolous and requesting permission to withdraw from the case. Please be advised as follows:

1) You have 30 days from the date this notice was mailed in which to raise any points that you choose which show why your conviction should be set aside.

2) If you do not respond within the 30 days, the court may affirm or dismiss your appeal. An affirmance or dismissal would mean that your case would be finally decided against you.

3) If you want to make a showing why the court should not affirm or dismiss your appeal and believe that there is a very good reason why you will not be able to file your objections with the court within the 30-day limit, you should *immediately* write to the court and ask for additional time up to 30 days. If additional time is granted, you must file your reasons why the court should not affirm or dismiss your appeal before your additional time expires.

4) You do not have a right to another attorney unless this court finds that your showing requires that your case be further briefed or argued. If the court finds that your case should be further briefed or argued, an attorney will be appointed for you who will argue your appeal.

If you want to write to this court, you should address your letter to:

Clerk of the Court
United States Court of Appeals
219 South Dearborn Street
Chicago, Illinois 60604

Be sure, when writing, to show clearly the name and number of your case.

Notice mailed _____, 20___

_____
Deputy Clerk, U.S. Court of Appeals

Attorney for appellant

_____
(Name)

_____
(Street Address)

_____
(City, State, Zip Code)

_____
(Area Code and Telephone Number)

APPENDIX II. FORM OF NOTICE FOR MOTION FOR DISMISSAL UNDER CIRCUIT RULE 51(d)

To: _____
(Name)

_____
(Street Address or Prison Box)

_____
(City, State, Zip Code)

You are the appellant in a case now pending in this court:

Case No. _____

_____

v.

_____

A motion was filed by the opposing party on _____, 20___, which asks the court to dismiss your appeal. You have 30 days in which to answer the motion. Please be advised as follows:

1) You have a right to answer. You can either agree to the requested dismissal or object to the motion.

2) If you object, you should explain your objections carefully and show why you contend the court should hear your case.

3) If you agree that your case should be dismissed, you should write the court immediately that you agree.

4) If you do not respond within 30 days after this notice was mailed, the court may affirm or dismiss your appeal. An affirmance or dismissal would mean that your case would be finally decided against you.

5) If you want to file objections and feel that there is a very good reason why you will not be able to file your objections with the court within the 30-day limit, you should *immediately* write to the court and ask for additional time up to 30 days. If additional time is granted, you must file your objections before your additional time expires.

6) If you are appealing from a conviction and upon receiving notice of motion for dismissal of your appeal you desire an attorney, you should immediately
   (a) employ an attorney if you can afford one; or
   (b) request this court to appoint an attorney for you if you cannot afford one.

The court will appoint an attorney if it concludes that your appeal is not frivolous.

If you want to write to this court, you should address your letter to:

Clerk of the Court
United States Court of Appeals
219 South Dearborn Street
Chicago, Illinois 60604

Be sure, when writing, to show clearly the name and number of your case.

Notice mailed _____, 20___.

_____
Deputy Clerk, U.S. Court of Appeals

_____
Attorney for appellant

_____
(Name)

_____
(Street Address)

(City, State, Zip Code)

(Area Code and Telephone Number)

APPENDIX III. FORM OF ACKNOWLEDGMENT OF ATTORNEY'S MOTION FOR DISMISSAL AND CONSENT TO THE DISMISSAL OF THE APPEAL

Case No. _____

_____

v.

_____

To: Clerk of the Court
         United States Court of Appeals
         219 South Dearborn Street
         Chicago, Illinois 60604

     I have been informed of my attorney's intention to move to dismiss my appeal.

     I concur in my attorney's decision and hereby waive all rights to object or raise any points on appeal.

                          _____
                                     (Name)

                          _____
               (Street Address or Prison Box)

                          _____
                   (City, State, Zip Code)

OPERATING PROCEDURES

INTRODUCTION

These are procedures for the court's internal operations. The court may dispense with their use in particular cases. Litigants acquire no rights under these procedures.

IOP 1. MOTIONS

(a) Number of Judges Necessary to Determine Motions.

(1) *Ordinary Practice.* At least two judges shall act on requests for bail, denials of certificates of appealability, and denials of leave to proceed on appeal in forma pauperis. Ordinarily three judges shall act to dismiss or otherwise finally determine an appeal or other proceeding, unless the dismissal is by stipulation or is for procedural reasons. Three judges shall also act to deny a motion to expedite an appeal when the denial may result in the mooting of the appeal. All other motions shall be entertained by a single judge in accordance with the practice set forth in paragraph (c). In the interest of expediting a decision or for other good cause, a fewer number of judges than provided in these procedures may decide any motion.

(2) *En Banc Requests.* If en banc consideration of a motion is requested, no more than the normal number of judges required for such a motion need act on it. If en banc reconsideration of the decision on a motion is requested, the motion will be considered by the same judge or judges who acted on the motion originally and, if and to the extent necessary to constitute a panel of three, one or more members of the motions panel. A judge may request that any motion be considered by the court en banc.

(b) Selection of Judges to Determine Motions.

The responsibility to handle motions shall be rotated among the judges. If a single judge to whom a motion is presented orders a response, the motion and response will ordinarily be presented to the same judge for ruling.

(c) Motion Practice.

(1) *Motions That May Require Immediate Action.* A staff attorney will read upon filing the following motions (whether labeled emergency or not): (i) for bond; (ii) for injunction; (iii) for stay of injunction; (iv) for stay of an agency order; (v) to dismiss appeals not by agreement; (vi) for leave to appeal from an interlocutory order pursuant to 28 U.S.C. § 1292(b); (vii) to stay or recall the mandate; (viii) to supplement the record; and (ix) all other emergency motions. If the motion requires immediate action, it will be taken to the motions judge and, if necessary, a panel. If it does not require immediate action, the staff attorney will wait up to fourteen days for a response to be filed before taking the motion to the motions judge or panel.

(2) *Routine Motions.* Routine motions (see subparagraph (7)) will be given to court staff who will read the motion and any affidavit in support thereof as well as any response to the motion. The designated staff member is then authorized, acting pursuant to such general directions and criteria as the court prescribes, to prepare an order in the name of the court either granting or denying the motion or requesting a response to the motion. If the designated staff member has any questions about what action should be taken, the motions judge will be consulted. Once a panel has been assigned for the oral argument or submission of an appeal, or after an appeal has actually been orally argued or submitted for decision without oral argument, the court staff should consult the presiding judge on motions that would otherwise be considered routine.

(3) *Nonroutine Motions.* A staff attorney shall read each nonroutine motion (see subparagraph (7)) and then present it to the motions judge and, if necessary, the motions panel. The judge or panel will then advise the staff attorney as to the decision and direct that an order be prepared accordingly. The staff attorney will then prepare the order. If the order states detailed reasons for the decision, the staff attorney will take the original of the order to the motions judge or one of the judges on the motions panel to read and approve. The same procedure will be followed whenever a judge asks to see the prepared order before it is released.

(4) *Duties of Clerk of Court.* When an order is in final form and ready for release, copies of the order will be reproduced and mailed to the litigants and to any other persons who are affected by the order, such as the district court clerk, the district judge, the United States Marshal, *et al.* The clerk will make certain that the language of the order is technically proper.

(5) *Automatic Reconsideration When Response Filed After Ruling.* If a response to a motion is properly filed after the court has ruled on the motion adversely to the respondent, the motion and response will be reconsidered and a new order stating this fact and ruling on the motion shall be issued.

(6) *Record Keeping.* The clerk shall keep a record of all orders by date of entry and also place a copy of each order in the file folder of the appeal.

(7) *Classification of Motions and Actions by Court.* Motions and actions of the court are classified for purposes of this paragraph as follows:

Type	Classification
To extend time or to file instanter	Routine
To consolidate appeals	Routine
To hold briefing in abeyance	Routine
To expedite or schedule briefing	
(But see 1(a) supra.)	Routine
To intervene as of right	Routine
To withdraw exhibits for preparation of a brief by counsel of record or party appearing pro se prior to case being scheduled for oral argument	Routine
To listen to tapes of oral argument under supervision of the clerk's office	Routine
To withdraw as counsel in criminal cases when other counsel has filed or is simultaneously filing an appearance	Routine
To withdraw as counsel in civil cases	Routine
To correct error in the caption of a case	Routine
To withdraw a previously filed motion before the court has acted upon it	Routine
To file a deferred appendix	Routine
(generally denied)	
To dismiss by agreement (except in cases to which panels have already been assigned)	Routine
To supplement record	
(if no objection)	Routine
(with an item before district court)	Routine
(with item not clearly before district court)	Routine
(to deny with leave to renew after moving to correct record in district court pursuant to Fed. R. App. P.10(e))	Routine
For leave to appeal in forma pauperis (if denied without prejudice to renewal after district court denial)	Routine
(if denied for any other reason)	Nonroutine
(if granted)	Nonroutine
For leave to file brief amicus curiae	Nonroutine
For leave to file oversized brief	Nonroutine
To stay or recall mandate	Nonroutine
For appointment of counsel	Nonroutine
To postpone oral argument	Nonroutine
For certificate of appealability	
(if denied)	Nonroutine
(if granted)	Nonroutine
For leave to commence second or successive collateral attack	Nonroutine
To dismiss, not by agreement	Nonroutine
For bond, injunction, or stay of injunction	Nonroutine
To reconsider any order of court	
(other than pursuant to subparagraph (5))	Nonroutine
For leave to appeal from interlocutory order, pursuant to 28 U.S.C. § 1292(b)	Nonroutine
All other motions	Nonroutine

The following actions by the court shall be handled similarly to the stated procedures for routine or nonroutine motions:

Issuance of orders to show cause pursuant to Circuit Rule 31(c) and (d)	Routine
Discharge of rules to show cause under Fed. R. App.P. 31(c) and Circuit Rule 31(c) and (d)	
(granting discharge)	Routine
(denying discharge)	Nonroutine

Type	Classification
Orders pursuant to Fed. R. App. P. 34 . . . . Nonroutine	

(8) The clerk is authorized to reject repetitious motions to reconsider.

[Amended effective December 1, 2009.]

IOP 2. TITLES AND PRECEDENCE OF JUDGES

(a) Except to the extent required by law, the court does not distinguish between judges in regular active service and senior judges with respect to title, precedence, and eligibility to participate in the court's decisions.

(b) Judges hold precedence in this sequence for the purpose of presiding at a session of the court: (1) Circuit Justice; (2) the Chief Judge of the circuit; (3) the judge of this circuit in regular active service with the greatest seniority according to the terms of 28 U.S.C. § 45(b). Every panel includes at least one circuit judge in regular active service, so no further provision for the selection of a presiding judge is necessary.

(c) Subject to part (b) of this rule, judges have precedence and are listed on opinions in the following order: (1) Circuit Justice; (2) Chief Judge of the circuit; (3) Associate Justice (Retired); (4) Circuit Judges by seniority of commission (without distinction between judges of this and other circuits); (5) District Judges by seniority of commission.

(d) Clerk's office personnel will ensure that all orders and opinions comply with this rule. The Clerk's office also will ensure that the description of the panel is consistent and conforms to the appropriate model: "X, Chief Judge, and Y and Z, Circuit Judges"; "X, Y, and Z, Circuit Judges"; "X and Y, Circuit Judges, and Z, District Judge."

IOP 3. ISSUANCE OF OPINIONS

(a) When an opinion is ready for release, the author will send the opinion (together with any concurring or dissenting opinions) to the printer immediately.

(b) The Clerk's office will provide each writing judge with page proofs of the opinion. Each judge will review the proofs promptly. If within three business days the Clerk's office has not received a response, the Clerk will call to inquire about the status of the opinion.

(c) The Clerk's office will release the opinion immediately after receipt of the printed copies, unless the writing judge has asked the clerk to delay release to permit the judge to check the corrected proofs against the printed opinion.

IOP 4. INCLUSION OF COSTS [ABROGATED]

[Abrogated effective October 22, 1996]

IOP 5. HEARINGS AND REHEARINGS EN BANC

(a) **Request for Answer and Subsequent Request for Vote.** If a petition for rehearing en banc is filed, a request for an answer (which may be made by any Seventh Circuit judge in regular active service or by any member of the panel that rendered the decision sought to be reheard) must be made within 14 days after the electronic filing of the en banc petition. If an answer is requested, the clerk shall notify the prevailing party that an answer be filed within 14 days from the date of the court's request. Within 10 days of the electronic filing of the answer, any judge entitled to request an answer, may request a vote on the petition for rehearing en banc.

(b) **Request for Vote When No Answer Requested.** Ordinarily an answer will be requested prior to a request for a vote. A request for a vote on the petition (which may be made by any judge entitled to request an answer) must be made within 14 days from the electronic filing of the petition. If a vote is so requested, the clerk shall notify the prevailing party that an answer to the petition is due within 14 days.

(c) **Notification to File Answer.** The judge who requests an answer pursuant to paragraph (a) or who requests a vote pursuant to paragraph (b) shall be responsible for having the clerk notify the prevailing party to file an answer to the petition.

(d) **Voting.**

(1) *Majority.* A simple majority of the voting active judges is required to grant a rehearing en banc.

(2) *Time for Voting.* Judges are expected to vote within 14 days of the request for a vote or within 14 days of the filing of the answer pursuant to the request for a vote, whichever is later.

(e) **Preparation of Order.** After the vote is completed, the authoring judge, or the presiding judge of the panel if the author is a visiting judge, will prepare and send to the clerk an appropriate order. Minority positions will be noted in the denial of a petition for rehearing en banc or the denial of a petition for rehearing unless the judges in the minority request otherwise. Minority positions will not be noted in orders granting a rehearing or rehearing en banc unless so requested by the minority judge. An order granting rehearing en banc should specifically state that the original panel's decision is thereby vacated.

(f) Participants in Rehearings En Banc. Only Seventh Circuit active judges and any Seventh Circuit senior judge who was a member of the original panel may participate in rehearings en banc.

(g) Similar Procedures for Hearings En Banc. Similar voting procedures and time limits shall apply for requests for hearings en banc except that a staff attorney may circulate such a request.

(h) Distribution of Petitions. Petitions for rehearing that do not suggest rehearing en banc are distributed only to the panel. Petitions for rehearing en banc are distributed to all judges entitled to vote on the petition.

[Amended effective December 1, 2009.]

IOP 6. PANEL ASSIGNMENTS IN CERTAIN CASES

(a) Remands From the Supreme Court. A case remanded by the Supreme Court to this court for further proceedings will ordinarily be reassigned to the same panel that heard the case previously. If a member of that panel was a visiting judge and it is inconvenient for the visitor to participate further, that judge may be replaced by designation or by lot, as the chief judge directs.

(b) Successive Appeals. Briefs in a subsequent appeal in a case in which the court has heard an earlier appeal will be sent to the panel that heard the prior appeal. That panel will decide the successive appeal on the merits unless there is no overlap in the issues presented. When the subsequent appeal presents different issues but involves the same essential facts as the earlier appeal, the panel will decide the subsequent appeal unless it concludes that considerations of judicial economy do not support retaining the case. If the panel elects not to decide the new appeal, it will return the case for reassignment at random. If the original panel retains the successive appeal, it will notify the circuit executive whether oral argument is necessary. If oral argument is scheduled, any visiting judge will be replaced by a member of this court designated by lot. Cases that have been heard by the court en banc are outside the scope of this procedure, and successive appeals will be assigned at random unless the en banc court directs otherwise.

(c) Successive Collateral Attacks. An application for leave to file a second or successive petition under 28 U.S.C. § 2254 or § 2255 (see also 28 U.S.C. § 2244(b) and Circuit Rule 22.2) will be assigned to the panel that heard the prior appeal. If there was no appeal in the prior case, the application will be assigned to the current motions panel.

(d) Certain Cases Before Motion Panels. When a motion panel decides that a motion or petition should be set for oral argument or the appeal expedited, it may recommend to the chief judge that the matter be assigned for argument and decision to the same panel. In the absence of such a recommendation, the matter will ordinarily be assigned in the same manner as other appeals.

IOP 7. ROUTINE ACTION BY THE CLERK

(a) Dismissal for Failure to Prosecute. Statutes and rules of court call for the parties to take specified steps at particular times, and the court treats failure to take some of these steps as failure to prosecute, leading to dismissal. Failure to pay the docket fee, failure to file the docketing statement required by Circuit Rule 3(c), and failure by the appellant or petitioner to file a brief, amount to abandonment of the appeal.

(1) Seven days after the docket fee, docketing statement, or brief is due, the Clerk will send a notice, by certified mail, reminding the party of the obligation. The notice will inform the party about the consequence of continued delay in satisfying the obligation.

(2) If the party or counsel does not respond within 21 days of the date of the notice, the Clerk will enter an order dismissing the appeal for want of prosecution. In a criminal appeal with appointed counsel, however, the Clerk will not dismiss the appeal but will instead discharge the lawyer and appoint new counsel. When counsel is discharged under this procedure, the Clerk also will enter an order requiring the lawyer to show cause why abandonment of the client should not lead to disbarment.

(3) If the party responds within 21 days but does not comply with the obligation, or if the Clerk has not received a receipt showing delivery of the notice, a staff attorney will present the papers to the motions panel for decision.

(b) Removal From the List of Attorneys Authorized to Practice. States within the jurisdiction of this circuit send the court lists of attorneys who have been suspended from practice, disbarred, or resigned to prevent consideration of a pending ethical complaint. As a rule, these attorneys have had ample opportunity to contest that adverse action and do not oppose parallel action by other jurisdictions, leading to routine handling in this court.

(1) Promptly after learning that a member of this court's bar has been suspended for a year or more, has been disbarred, or has resigned from the bar of a jurisdiction in which the attorney is authorized to practice, the Clerk will send a notice, by certified mail, directing the lawyer to explain within 30 days why this court should not strike him from the roll of attorneys authorized to practice.

(2) If the lawyer does not respond within 30 days, or if the lawyer consents to the proposed disposition, the Clerk will enter an order removing the lawyer

from the roll of attorneys authorized to practice in this court.

(3) If the lawyer responds within 30 days but does not consent to the proposed disposition, or if within that time the Clerk has not received a receipt showing delivery of the notice, a staff attorney will present the papers to the motions panel for decision.

(c) Review of the Clerk's Action. A petition for rehearing contesting the entry of a routine order under this operating procedure will be treated as a motion and referred to the motions panel. An order by the motions panel permitting the appeal to continue has the effect of reinstating the appeal, and the Clerk will reset the briefing schedule accordingly.

IOP 8.   MULTIPLE APPEALS

When multiple parties to the same case have taken appeals, the court's senior staff attorney will review the docketing statements filed under Circuit Rule 3 and issue a scheduling order governing the filing of briefs.

When multiple appellants have the same or a closely related interest in the appeal, the senior staff attorney ordinarily will provide for the filing of a joint opening brief, with provision in appropriate cases for separate individual briefs to present points that do not concern all appellants. When the parties have filed cross appeals, the scheduling order usually will call on the party principally aggrieved by the judgment to file the opening brief. For example, when the judgment holds the defendant liable and the plaintiff's cross appeal concerns the amount of damages or an award of attorney's fees, the defendant normally will file the opening brief.

IOP 9.   PRESUMPTIVE TIMES
FOR ACTION

Expeditious preparation and release of opinions and orders is important not only to litigants ("Justice delayed is justice denied") but also to the operation of the court. Delay in the preparation of or response to opinions means that other judges must reread the briefs and re-study the record in order to act conscientiously on their colleagues' drafts. Dispatch in circulating drafts and responding to a colleague's circulations therefore reduces duplicative work and improves the quality of justice. With these considerations in mind, the court establishes the following presumptive times for action, anticipating that in most cases judges will take less time but understanding that circumstances may make it imprudent to adhere to these norms mechanically. Every judge should, and may, take the time required for adequate study and reflection.

(a) A judge assigned to write a draft after a case has been identified at conference as suitable for dispo-

sition by a brief unpublished order should circulate the draft to the other members of the panel within 21 days of the date the case was argued or submitted.

(b) A judge assigned to write a published opinion should circulate the draft to the other members of the panel within 90 days of the date the case was argued or submitted. When the case is unusually complex, extended research is required, or other special circumstances apply, however, the writing judge may extend this time to 180 days by giving appropriate notice to the other members of the panel.

(c) Responding to drafts circulated by other judges is the first order of business. Every judge should respond by approval, memorandum suggesting changes, or notice that a separate opinion is under active consideration within 14 days of the circulation of a draft.

(d) As a rule, writing separate concurring or dissenting opinions takes precedence over all business other than initial responses to newly circulated drafts. Separate opinions should be circulated to the panel within 28 days after the initial response described in part (c) of this procedure.

(e) Once the opinion has issued, judges should act promptly on any further motions. In particular, members of the panel should vote within 14 days on any petition for rehearing. Under Operating Procedure 5, judges have 14 days to request a response to a petition for rehearing en banc, and 14 days to call for a vote on the petition once the response has been received. Once a judge has called for a vote, all other judges should register their votes within 14 days. Once this time (including extensions described below) has passed, and sufficient votes have been received to grant or deny the petition for rehearing or petition for rehearing en banc, the court will enter an order to that effect without waiting for additional responses.

(f) Each judge should establish a tickler system designed to ensure adherence to these norms. When one chambers does not receive a draft, vote or response within the time presumptively established, secretaries or law clerks should inquire. This step not only catches communications lost in transmission but also serves as a backup reminder system.

(g) A judge who believes that additional time is required to permit full consideration should notify the other members of the panel to that effect. If the judge believes that more than 30 days (in the case of opinions) or 14 days (in the case of other actions), in addition to the time presumptively established by this procedure, is essential, the judge also should notify the chief judge of the delay and the reasons for it.

(h) The presiding judge of a panel should reassign the case if the judge initially assigned to draft the order or opinion has not circulated the draft within the time provided by parts (a) and (b) of this procedure, plus the extra time allowed by part (g), unless in consultation with the assigned author and the chief judge the presiding judge decides that reassignment would delay disposition still further.

(i) If two members of the panel have agreed on an opinion, and the third member does not respond within the time provided by part (c), or does not complete a separate opinion within the time presumptively established by parts (d) and (g), the writing judge should inquire of the third member whether a response is imminent. If further delay is anticipated, the majority should issue the opinion with a notation that the third judge reserves the right to file a separate opinion later.

(j) When the presumptive time for action established by this procedure is 14 days, the time may be extended on notice that a judge is unavailable to act on judicial business. The time specified by this notice

is added to the time presumptively established by this procedure.

[Amended effective December 1, 2009.]

IOP 10. SEALING PORTIONS OF THE RECORD

(a) **Requirement of Judicial Approval.** Except to the extent portions of the record are required to be sealed by statute (e.g., 18 U.S.C. § 3509(d)) or a rule of procedure (e.g., Fed. R. Crim. P. 6(e), Circuit Rule 26.1(b)), every document filed in or by this court (whether or not the document was sealed in the district court) is in the public record unless a judge of this court orders it to be sealed.

(b) **Delay in Disclosure.** Documents sealed in the district court will be maintained under seal in this court for 14 days, to afford time to request the approval required by section (a) of this procedure.

THE PLAN OF THE UNITED STATES COURT OF APPEALS FOR THE SEVENTH CIRCUIT TO SUPPLEMENT THE PLANS OF THE SEVERAL UNITED STATES DISTRICT COURTS WITHIN THE SEVENTH CIRCUIT

INTRODUCTION

Pursuant to the approval of the Judicial Council of the Seventh Circuit, the United States Court of Appeals for the Seventh Circuit adopts the following Plan for furnishing representation for persons financially unable to obtain adequate representation in the cases and situations defined in the Criminal Justice Act of 1964, as amended, 18 U.S.C. § 3006A ("Act"), and 21 U.S.C. § 848(q), and the *Guidelines for the Administration of the Criminal Justice Act*, Volume VII, *Guide to Judiciary Policies and Procedures* ("CJA Guidelines"). This Plan supplements the plans heretofore adopted by the several United States District Courts within the Seventh Circuit and approved in final form by the Judicial Council of the Seventh Circuit.

Representation shall include counsel and investigative, expert, and other services necessary for an adequate defense.

I. STATEMENT OF POLICY

The Judicial Council recognizes that the successful operation of this plan will require the active and continual cooperation of members of the bar, appropriate bar associations and legal aid agencies. In particular, it is expected that the advice and assistance of the Seventh Circuit Bar Association will contribute greatly to the successful working of this Plan.

The judges, circuit executive, clerk, all federal public defender organizations and community defender organizations, and private attorneys appointed under the CJA should comply with the *CJA Guidelines* approved by the Judicial Conference of the United States and/or its Committee on Defender Services and with the Plan.

The payment of compensation to counsel under the Act, in most cases, probably will be something less than compensatory. Service of counsel by appointment under the Act will continue to require a substantial measure of dedication and public service. The responsibility of members of the bar to accept appointments and to serve in these cases is the same as it traditionally has been in the past and is in no way lessened by the passage of the Act. We have complete confidence in the professional integrity of the bar to fulfill this responsibility.

In the administration of this Plan, the Court will be particularly careful to safeguard against the opportunity for any charges of fiscal laxity, favoritism or other abuse which may cast a shadow on the general judicial system. The public funds involved will be expended with characteristic judicial responsibility.

It is deemed advisable at all times to coordinate efficiently the operation of this Plan with the several state courts to the end that there be a proper cooperation between the federal and state judicial systems.

The Court will welcome any proper and approved plan of cooperation whereby the services of advanced law school students may be made available to provide legal research assistance to appointed counsel, thereby to furnish such assistance to appointed counsel who may find it helpful and to broaden the interest and capabilities of law school students in the field of criminal law.

Finally, and most important, the Plan shall be administered so that those accused of crime will not, because they are financially unable to pay for adequate representation, be deprived of any element of representation necessary to enable them to have a fair opportunity to be heard on appeal in this Court.

II. PREPARATION OF PANEL OF ATTORNEYS

1. The Clerk of this Court, under the direction and supervision and with approval of the Court, shall forthwith prepare and maintain a panel of practicing attorneys, or attorneys from a bar association, legal aid agency, or defender organization furnishing representation pursuant to the Plan, in areas of the principal places of holding district court within the Seventh Circuit, who are deemed competent to provide adequate representation on appeal for persons qualifying under the Act. The Clerk of this Court shall reexamine the panel of attorneys annually to assure that it is kept current at all times.

2. Attorneys for the panel shall be selected without regard to race, color, creed, or membership in any organized bar association.

3. The Clerk shall solicit the assistance of the Seventh Circuit Bar Association, law schools, and any other appropriate bar association, in the preparation and maintenance of the panel of attorneys.

4. Additions to and removals from the panel of attorneys may be made at any time by the Court or any active member thereof.

5. The clerk of court shall provide each appointed attorney a copy of this Plan upon the attorney's first appointment under the CJA or designation as a mem-

ber of the panel and shall also make available to them a current copy of the *Guidelines*.

III. DETERMINATION OF NEED FOR APPOINTMENT OF COUNSEL

1. In all cases where the defendant was found by the district court to be financially unable to obtain adequate representation, the Court may accept this finding and appoint an attorney without further proof. *But see* Fed. R. App. P. 24(a).

2. At any time before or after the appointment of counsel, the Court may examine or reexamine the financial status of the defendant. If the Court finds upon such inquiry that the defendant is financially able to employ counsel or make partial payment for his representation, then the Court may make an order appropriate under the circumstances denying or terminating such appointment pursuant to subsection (c) of the Act, or requiring such partial payment to be made pursuant to subsection (f) of the Act, as the interests of justice may dictate.

3. In determining the need for appointment of counsel under the Act, the Courts shall not be governed by a requirement of indigence on the part of the defendant, but rather by his financial inability to employ counsel, in harmony with Congressional intent in formulating this program of assistance to those found to be in need within the spirit and purpose of the Act.

IV. APPOINTMENT OF COUNSEL

1. Counsel furnishing representation under the Plan shall be selected from a panel of attorneys designated or approved by the Court, or from a bar association, legal aid agency, or defender organization furnishing representation pursuant to the Plan. When the Court determines that the appointment of an attorney who is not a member of the panel is in the interest of justice, judicial economy, or continuity of representation, or there is some other exceptional circumstance warranting his or her appointment, the attorney may be admitted to the panel and appointed to represent the individual. Agreeable with the directives of the Judicial Conference of the United States, at least 25% of all such appointments shall be assigned to members of the private bar. Such order of appointment of counsel may be entered by the current motion judge or by any active member of the Court.

2. In all cases on appeal where the defendant was represented in the district court by court appointed counsel, such counsel shall continue to represent the defendant on appeal, unless and until relieved by order of this Court. The Court may, in appropriate cases, designate such counsel to continue on appeal.

3. At the time such appeals are docketed in this Court, the Clerk shall notify defendant's court appointed trial counsel that he shall continue such representation of defendant in this Court unless and until relieved by order of this Court, and shall request such trial counsel to advise the Court whether he desires to continue such representation throughout the appeal.

4. In appeals under the Act involving more than one defendant, if the Court finds the need, because of conflicting interests of certain defendants or where circumstances otherwise warrant, separate counsel may be appointed for any one or more of the defendants as may be required for their adequate representation.

5. The Court may, in its discretion, at any stage of the proceedings on appeal, substitute one appointed attorney for another.

6. If, at any stage of the proceedings on appeal, the Court finds the defendant is financially unable to pay counsel whom he has retained, the Court may appoint counsel as provided in subsection (b) of the Act and authorize payment as provided in subsection (d) of the Act and the *CJA Guidelines*, pursuant to subsection (c) of the Act.

7. More than one attorney may be appointed in any case determined by the Court to be extremely difficult. In a capital case, at least two attorneys should be appointed. Except as provided by section 848(q)(7) of title 21, U.S.C., at least one attorney appointed in a capital case shall meet the experience qualifications required by section 848(q)(6) of title 21, U.S.C. Pursuant to section 848(q)(7), the presiding judicial officer, for good cause, may appoint an attorney who may not qualify under section 848(q)(6), but who has the background, knowledge, and experience necessary to represent the defendant properly in a capital case, giving due consideration to the seriousness of the possible penalty and to the unique and complex nature of the litigation.

8. The selection of counsel to represent any person under the Act shall remain the sole and exclusive responsibility of the Court.

V. DUTIES OF APPOINTED COUNSEL

1. The services to be rendered a defendant by counsel appointed under the Act shall be reasonably commensurate with those rendered if counsel were privately employed, having regard for the circumstances of each case and as the interests of justice may require.

2. If, at any stage of the proceedings on appeal, appointed counsel obtains information that a client is financially able to make payment, in whole or in part, for legal or other services in connection with his or her representation, and the source of the attorney's information is not protected as a privileged communication, counsel shall advise the Court.

3. After an adverse decision on appeal by this Court, appointed counsel shall advise the defendant in writing of his right to seek review of such decision by the Supreme Court of the United States. If, after consultation (by correspondence, or otherwise), the represented person requests it and there are reasonable grounds for counsel properly to do so, the appointed attorney must prepare and file a petition for writ of certiorari and other necessary and appropriate documents and must continue to represent the defendant until relieved by the Supreme Court. Counsel who conclude that reasonable grounds for filing a petition for writ of certiorari do not exist must promptly inform the defendant, who may by motion request this Court to direct counsel to seek certiorari.

4. Attorneys appointed pursuant to any provisions of the Act shall conform to the highest standards of professional conduct, including but not limited to the provisions of the American Bar Association's Model Rules of Professional Conduct.

5. Appointed appellate attorneys have a duty to continue to represent their clients after remand to the district court. An attorney appointed for the appeal who is unable to continue at the trial level should move in the district court for withdrawal and appointment of trial counsel.

6. Attorneys appointed in a federal death penalty case, unless replaced by similarly qualified counsel upon the attorney's own motion or upon motion of the defendant, shall represent the defendant throughout every stage of the available judicial proceedings, including all available post-conviction process, together with applications for stays of execution and other appropriate motions and procedures, and shall also represent the defendant in proceedings for executive or other clemency as may be available to the defendant.

VI. PAYMENT OF CLAIMS FOR COMPENSATION AND EXPENSES

1. An attorney, bar association, legal aid agency, or community defender organization appointed by the Court pursuant to the Plan shall be compensated for their services and reimbursed for their expenses reasonably incurred within the limitations and subject to the conditions of subsection (d) of the Act.

2. The hourly rates of compensation fixed by the Act are designated and intended to be maximum rates only and shall be treated as such.

3. No appointed representative under the Plan shall accept a payment from or on behalf of the person represented in this Court without prior authorization by a United States circuit judge on the form provided for such purpose. All such authorized payments shall be received subject to the directions contained in such order and pursuant to the provisions of subsection (f) of the Act.

4. Each appointed representative under the Plan shall be entitled to reimbursement for expenses reasonably incurred for travel and out-of-pocket expenditures. Travel by privately owned automobile should be claimed at the rate per mile set forth in the *Travel and Transportation* regulations, Volume I, *Guide to Judiciary Policies and Procedures*, plus parking fees and tolls. Transportation other than by privately owned automobile should be claimed on an actual cost basis. Per diem in lieu of subsistence is not allowable. Meals and lodging expenses, which are reasonably incurred based upon the prevailing limitations placed upon travel and subsistence expenses of federal judiciary employees in accordance with existing travel regulations, as well as telephone toll calls, telegrams and copying (except printing), are reimbursable. Non-reimbursable items include general office overhead, personal items for the person represented, filing fees, and printing. (A person represented under the Act is not required to pay filing fees.)

5. An appointed attorney or other authorized legal entity shall not incur any expense subject to claim for reimbursement in excess of $300 except for necessary travel and maintenance to and from this Court for hearing on oral argument, without prior Court approval. In the event it is deemed necessary to provide an appendix of the record on appeal of more than 50 pages, they shall first petition the Court for authority to incur such expense and obtain approval therefor.

6. All claims for compensation and reimbursement for expenses reasonably incurred shall be itemized and prepared on prescribed forms and filed with the Clerk of this Court. All such claims should be filed promptly and in any event not more than 30 days after the conclusion of such services.

7. A panel of judges hearing an appeal, or any active member of the Court if designated by such panel, shall, in each instance, fix the compensation and allow the reimbursement for expenses to be paid to the appointed representative as provided in the Act. After such approval, the Clerk of this Court shall forthwith forward such claims to the Director of the Administrative Office of the United States Courts for payment.

8. Counsel's time and expenses involved in the preparation of a petition for a writ of certiorari shall be considered as applicable to the case before this Court, and should be vouchered as such.

VII. MISCELLANEOUS

1. The United States Court of Appeals shall submit a report of the appointment of counsel to the Administrative Office of the United States Courts in such form and at such times as the Judicial Confer-

ence of the United States may direct, and otherwise comply with such rules, regulations, and guidelines governing the operation of Plans formulated by the Judicial Conference of the United States, pursuant to subsection (h) of the Act.

2. Where standard forms have been prescribed and distributed by the Director of the Administrative Office of the United States Courts, such forms shall be used, where applicable, in all proceedings under this Plan.

3. Amendments to the Plan may be made from time to time by the Judicial Council of this circuit, and such amendments shall be forwarded immediately to the Administrative Office of the United States Courts.

VIII. EFFECTIVE DATE

This Plan shall become effective January 1, 1991. Approved and adopted by the Seventh Circuit Judicial Council on December 3, 1990. As amended January 1, 1996.

STANDARDS FOR PROFESSIONAL CONDUCT WITHIN THE SEVENTH FEDERAL JUDICIAL CIRCUIT

Adopted December 14, 1992

Preamble

A lawyer's conduct should be characterized at all times by personal courtesy and professional integrity in the fullest sense of those terms. In fulfilling our duty to represent a client vigorously as lawyers, we will be mindful of our obligations to the administration of justice, which is a truth-seeking process designed to resolve human and societal problems in a rational, peaceful, and efficient manner.

A judge's conduct should be characterized at all times by courtesy and patience toward all participants. As judges we owe to all participants in a legal proceeding respect, diligence, punctuality, and protection against unjust and improper criticism or attack.

Conduct that may be characterized as uncivil, abrasive, abusive, hostile, or obstructive impedes the fundamental goal of resolving disputes rationally, peacefully, and efficiently. Such conduct tends to delay and often to deny justice.

The following standards are designed to encourage us, judges and lawyers, to meet our obligations to each other, to litigants and to the system of justice, and thereby achieve the twin goals of civility and professionalism, both of which are hallmarks of a learned profession dedicated to public service.

We expect judges and lawyers will make a mutual and firm commitment to these standards. Voluntary adherence is expected as part of a commitment by all participants to improve the administration of justice throughout this Circuit.

These standards shall not be used as a basis for litigation or for sanctions or penalties. Nothing in these standards supersedes or detracts from existing disciplinary codes or alters existing standards of conduct against which lawyer negligence may be determined.

These standards should be reviewed and followed by all judges and lawyers participating in any proceeding, in this Circuit. Copies may be made available to clients to reinforce our obligation to maintain and foster these standards.

LAWYERS' DUTIES TO OTHER COUNSEL

1. We will practice our profession with a continuing awareness that our role is to advance the legitimate interests of our clients. In our dealings with others we will not reflect the ill feelings of our clients. We will treat all other counsel, parties, and witnesses in a civil and courteous manner, not only in court, but also in all other written and oral communications.

2. We will not, even when called upon by a client to do so, abuse or indulge in offensive conduct directed to other counsel, parties, or witnesses. We will abstain from disparaging personal remarks or acrimony toward other counsel, parties, or witnesses. We will treat adverse witnesses and parties with fair consideration.

3. We will not encourage or knowingly authorize any person under our control to engage in conduct that would be improper if we were to engage in such conduct.

4. We will not, absent good cause, attribute bad motives or improper conduct to other counsel or bring the profession into disrepute by unfounded accusations of impropriety.

5. We will not seek court sanctions without first conducting a reasonable investigation and unless fully justified by the circumstances and necessary to protect our client's lawful interests.

6. We will adhere to all express promises and to agreements with other counsel, whether oral or in writing, and will adhere in good faith to all agreements implied by the circumstances or local customs.

7. When we reach an oral understanding on a proposed agreement or a stipulation and decide to commit it to writing, the drafter will endeavor in good faith to state the oral understanding accurately and completely. The drafter will provide the opportunity for review of the writing to other counsel. As drafts are exchanged between or among counsel, changes from prior drafts will be identified in the draft or otherwise explicitly brought to the attention of other counsel. We will not include in a draft matters to which there has been no agreement without explicitly advising other counsel in writing of the addition.

8. We will endeavor to confer early with other counsel to assess settlement possibilities. We will not falsely hold out the possibility of settlement as a means to adjourn discovery or to delay trial.

9. In civil actions, we will stipulate to relevant matters if they are undisputed and if no good faith advocacy basis exists for not stipulating.

10. We will not use any form of discovery or discovery scheduling as a means of harassment.

11. We will make good faith efforts to resolve by agreement our objections to matters contained in pleadings and discovery requests and objections.

12. We will not time the filing or service of motions or pleadings in any way that unfairly limits another party's opportunity to respond.

13. We will not request an extension of time solely for the purpose of unjustified delay or to obtain a tactical advantage.

14. We will consult other counsel regarding scheduling matters in a good faith effort to avoid scheduling conflicts.

15. We will endeavor to accommodate previously scheduled dates for hearings, depositions, meetings, conferences, vacations, seminars, or other functions that produce good faith calendar conflicts on the part of other counsel. If we have been given an accommodation because of a calendar conflict, we will notify those who have accommodated us as soon as the conflict has been removed.

16. We will notify other counsel and, if appropriate, the court or other persons, at the earliest possible time when hearings, depositions, meetings, or conferences are to be canceled or postponed. Early notice avoids unnecessary travel and expense of counsel and may enable the court to use the previously reserved time for other matters.

17. We will agree to reasonable requests for extensions of time and for waiver of procedural formalities, provided our clients' legitimate rights will not be materially or adversely affected.

18. We will not cause any default or dismissal to be entered without first notifying opposing counsel, when we know his or her identity.

19. We will take depositions only when actually needed to ascertain facts or information or to perpetuate testimony. We will not take depositions for the purposes of harassment or to increase litigation expenses.

20. We will not engage in any conduct during a deposition that would not be appropriate in the presence of a judge.

21. We will not obstruct questioning during a deposition or object to deposition questions unless necessary under the applicable rules to preserve an objection or privilege for resolution by the court.

22. During depositions we will ask only those questions we reasonably believe are necessary for the prosecution or defense of an action.

23. We will carefully craft document production requests so they are limited to those documents we reasonably believe are necessary for the prosecution or defense of an action. We will not design production requests to place an undue burden or expense on a party.

24. We will respond to document requests reasonably and not strain to interpret the request in an artificially restrictive manner to avoid disclosure of relevant and non-privileged documents. We will not produce documents in a manner designed to hide or obscure the existence of particular documents.

25. We will carefully craft interrogatories so they are limited to those matters we reasonably believe are necessary for the prosecution or defense of an action, and we will not design them to place an expense or undue burden or expense on a party.

26. We will respond to interrogatories reasonably and will not strain to interpret them in an artificially restrictive manner to avoid disclosure of relevant and non-privileged information.

27. We will base our discovery objections on a good faith belief in their merit and will not object solely for the purpose of withholding or delaying the disclosure of relevant information.

28. When a draft order is to be prepared by counsel to reflect a court ruling, we will draft an order that accurately and completely reflects the court's ruling. We will promptly prepare and submit a proposed order to other counsel and attempt to reconcile any differences before the draft order is presented to the court.

29. We will not ascribe a position to another counsel that counsel has not taken or otherwise seek to create an unjustified inference based on counsel's statements or conduct.

30. Unless specifically permitted or invited by the court, we will not send copies of correspondence between counsel to the court.

LAWYERS' DUTIES TO THE COURT

1. We will speak and write civilly and respectfully in all communications with the court.

2. We will be punctual and prepared for all court appearances so that all hearings, conferences, and trials may commence on time; if delayed, we will notify the court and counsel, if possible.

3. We will be considerate of the time constraints and pressures on the court and court staff inherent in their efforts to administer justice.

4. We will not engage in any conduct that brings disorder or disruption to the courtroom. We will advise our clients and witnesses appearing in court of the proper conduct expected and required there and, to the best of our ability, prevent our clients and witnesses from creating disorder or disruption.

5. We will not knowingly misrepresent, mischaracterize, misquote, or miscite facts or authorities in any oral or written communication to the court.

6. We will not write letters to the court in connection with a pending action, unless invited or permitted by the court.

7. Before dates for hearings or trials are set, or if that is not feasible, immediately after such date has been set, we will attempt to verify the availability of necessary participants and witnesses so we can promptly notify the court of any likely problems.

8. We will act and speak civilly to court marshals, clerks, court reporters, secretaries, and law clerks with an awareness that they, too, are an integral part of the judicial system.

COURTS' DUTIES TO LAWYERS

1. We will be courteous, respectful, and civil to lawyers, parties, and witnesses. We will maintain control of the proceedings, recognizing that judges have both the obligation and the authority to insure that all litigation proceedings are conducted in a civil manner.

2. We will not employ hostile, demeaning, or humiliating words in opinions or in written or oral communications with lawyers, parties, or witnesses.

3. We will be punctual in convening all hearings, meetings, and conferences; if delayed, we will notify counsel, if possible.

4. In scheduling all hearings, meetings and conferences we will be considerate of time schedules of lawyers, parties, and witnesses.

5. We will make all reasonable efforts to decide promptly all matters presented to us for decision.

6. We will give the issues in controversy deliberate, impartial, and studied analysis and consideration.

7. While endeavoring to resolve disputes efficiently, we will be considerate of the time constraints and pressures imposed on lawyers by the exigencies of litigation practice.

8. We recognize that a lawyer has a right and a duty to present a cause fully and properly, and that a litigant has a right to a fair and impartial hearing. Within the practical limits of time, we will allow lawyers to present proper arguments and to make a complete and accurate record.

9. We will not impugn the integrity or professionalism of any lawyer on the basis of the clients whom or the causes which a lawyer represents.

10. We will do our best to insure that court personnel act civilly toward lawyers, parties, and witnesses.

11. We will not adopt procedures that needlessly increase litigation expense.

12. We will bring to lawyers' attention uncivil conduct which we observe.

JUDGES' DUTIES TO EACH OTHER

1. We will be courteous, respectful, and civil in opinions, ever mindful that a position articulated by another judge is the result of that judge's earnest effort to interpret the law and the facts correctly.

2. In all written and oral communications, we will be abstain from disparaging personal remarks or criticisms, or sarcastic or demeaning comments about another judge.

3. We will endeavor to work with other judges in an effort to foster a spirit of cooperation in our mutual goal of enhancing the administration of justice.

ELECTRONIC CASE FILING

(a) Scope of Electronic Filing.

(1) The court has adopted a Case Management/Electronic Case Filing (CM/ECF) system. The system enables the filing of documents submitted, signed or verified by electronic means that comply with procedures established by the court. Participation is mandatory for attorneys practicing in this court.

(2) Except as otherwise prescribed by local rule or order, all cases are assigned to the court's electronic filing system.

(3) Except as otherwise prescribed by local rule or court order, all briefs, appendices, motions, petitions for rehearing, and other documents filed in any case with the court by an Attorney Filing User registered as set forth under Circuit Rules/Electronic Case Filing (ECF) procedures, must be filed electronically using the electronic filing system.

(4) Paper copies are required for briefs, appendices and petitions for rehearing as provided in Paragraph (h)(2) of these procedures, but not for other pleadings unless specifically requested by the Court.

(5) Upon the court's request, an Attorney Filing User must promptly provide the Clerk, in a format designated by the court, an identical electronic version of any paper document previously filed in the same case by that Attorney Filing User.

(b) Eligibility, Registration, Passwords.

(1) Attorneys who intend to practice in this court, including those regularly admitted or admitted pro hac vice to the bar of the court and attorneys authorized to represent the United States without being admitted to the bar of this court, must register as Attorney Filing Users of the court's electronic filing system.

(2) Registration requirements are defined in the Electronic Case Filing (ECF) User Manual.

(3) Registration as an Attorney Filing User constitutes consent to electronic service of all documents as provided in these ECF Procedures and the Federal Rules of Appellate Procedure.

(4) Attorney Filing Users agree to protect the security of their passwords and immediately notify the PACER Service Center and the Clerk if they learn that their password has been compromised. Attorney Filing Users may be sanctioned for failure to comply with this provision.

(5) The court may terminate or sanction an Attorney Filing User's electronic filing privileges for abusing the system by an inordinate number of filings, filings of excessive size, or other failures to comply with the electronic filing procedures and standards.

(c) Implications of Electronic Filing.

(1) Electronic transmission of a document to the electronic filing system consistent with these procedures, together with the transmission of a Notice of Docket Activity from the court, constitutes filing of the document under the Federal Rules of Appellate Procedure and the local rules of this court, and constitutes entry of the document on the docket kept by the Clerk under Fed. R. App. P. 36 and 45(b).

(2) If the court requires a party to file a motion for leave to file, both the motion and document at issue should be submitted electronically. The underlying document should be tendered as an attachment to the motion and will be filed if the court so directs.

(3) Electronic documents must be in Portable Document Format (PDF). All documents must be generated by printing to PDF from the original word processing file, so that the text of the digital document is searchable. PDF images created by scanning paper documents are not searchable and may be used only for appendix or reference materials not available in PDF format.

(4) When a document has been filed electronically, the official record is the electronic document stored by the court, and the filing party is bound by the document as filed. Except in the case of documents first filed in paper form and subsequently submitted electronically under these procedures, a document filed electronically is deemed filed at the date and time stated on the Notice of Docket Activity from the court. Filing must be completed before midnight, Central Time, to be considered timely filed, unless otherwise ordered by the court.

(d) Service of Documents by Electronic Means.

(1) The Notice of Docket Activity that is generated by the court's electronic filing system constitutes service of the filed document on all Attorney Filing Users. Parties who are not Attorney Filing Users must be served with a copy of any document filed electronically in accordance with the Federal Rules of Appellate Procedure and the local rules. If the document is not available electronically, the filer must use an alternative method of service.

(2) The Notice of Docket Activity generated by the court's electronic filing system does not replace the certificate of service required by Fed. R. App. P. 25.

(e) Entry of Court–Issued Documents.

(1) Except as otherwise provided by local rule or court order, all orders, decrees, judgments, and proceedings of the court relating to cases filed and maintained in the CM/ECF system will be filed in accordance with these procedures, which will constitute

entry on the docket kept by the Clerk under Fed. R. App. P. 36 and 45(b).

(2) Any order or other court-issued document filed electronically without the original signature of a judge or authorized court personnel has the same force and effect as if a judge or the Clerk had signed a paper copy of the order.

(3) Orders also may be issued as "text-only" entries on the docket, without an attached document. Such orders are official and binding.

(f) Attachments and Exhibits to Motions and Original Proceedings.

(1) Attorney Filing Users must submit all documents referenced as exhibits or attachments in electronic form within any file size limits the Clerk may prescribe, as well as any paper copies the Clerk specifies. See ECF User Manual for specifics.

(2) An Attorney Filing User must submit as exhibits or attachments only those excerpts of the referenced documents that are directly germane to the matter under consideration by the court. Excerpted material must be clearly and prominently identified as such.

(3) The court may require parties to file additional excerpts or the complete document.

(g) Sealed Documents.

(1) A motion to file documents under seal must be filed electronically unless prohibited by law, local rule, or court order.

(2) Proposed sealed materials must be filed electronically by following the directions provided with the electronic filing system. Failure to follow these directions will result in public disclosure of sensitive material. Attorney Filing Users are responsible for ensuring that sealed materials are filed appropriately.

(3) If the court grants the motion, the order of the court authorizing the filing of documents under seal may be filed electronically unless prohibited by law.

(4) Documents ordered placed under seal may be filed traditionally in paper or electronically, as authorized by the court. If filed traditionally, a paper copy of the authorizing order must be attached to the documents under seal and delivered to the Clerk.

(h) Briefs, Appendices and Petitions for Rehearing.

(1) A brief, appendix and petition for rehearing (and any answer filed thereto) will be considered timely once it is submitted to the court's electronic filing system. It will be considered filed on the court's docket only after a review for compliance with applicable rules, acceptance by the Clerk, and issuance of a Notice of Docket Activity.

(2) Filers are also required to submit the necessary number of duplicate paper copies of briefs, appendices and petitions for rehearing, in accordance with Fed. R. App. P. 30(a)(3) and Circuit Rules 31(b) and 40(b). Duplicate paper copies must be received by the Clerk within seven days of the Notice of Docket Activity generated upon acceptance of the electronic brief or appendices. Duplicate paper copies of petitions for rehearing must be submitted within three days of the Notice of Docket Activity.

(i) Signatures.

(1) The user log-in and password required to submit documents to the electronic filing system serve as the Attorney Filing User's signature on all electronic documents filed with the court. They also serve as a signature for purposes of the Federal Rules of Appellate Procedure, the local rules of this court, and any other purpose for which a signature is required in connection with proceedings before this court.

(2) The name of the Attorney Filing User under whose log-in and password the document is submitted must be preceded by an "s/" and typed in the space where the signature would otherwise appear.

(3) No Attorney Filing User or other person may knowingly permit or cause to permit an Attorney Filing User's log-in and password to be used by anyone other than an authorized agent of the Attorney Filing User.

(4) Documents requiring signatures of more than one party must be electronically filed either by: (A) submitting a scanned document containing all necessary signatures; (B) representing the consent of the other parties on the document; (C) identifying on the document the parties whose signatures are required and submitting a notice of endorsement by the other parties no later than three business days after filing; or (D) in any other manner approved by the court.

(5) Electronically represented signatures of all parties and Attorney Filing Users as described above are presumed to be valid signatures. If any party, counsel of record, or Attorney Filing User objects to the representation of his or her signature on an electronic document as described above, he or she must, within 14 days, file a notice setting forth the basis of the objection.

(j) Notice of Court Orders and Judgments.

(1) Immediately upon the entry of an order or judgment in a case assigned to the electronic filing system, the Clerk will electronically transmit a Notice of Docket Activity to Attorney Filing Users in the case.

(2) Electronic transmission of the Notice of Docket Activity constitutes the notice and service of the opinion or order required by Fed. R. App. P. 36(b) and 45(c).

(3) The Clerk must give notice in paper form to a person who has not consented to electronic service in accordance with the Federal Rules of Appellate Procedure.

(k) Technical Failures. An Attorney Filing User whose filing is made untimely as the result of a technical failure may seek appropriate relief from the court by filing a motion.

(*l*) Public Access.

(1) Parties must refrain from including, or must partially redact where inclusion is necessary, the following personal data identifiers from all documents filed with the court, including exhibits thereto, whether filed electronically or in paper, unless otherwise ordered by the court:

(A) Social Security Numbers. If an individual's Social Security number must be included, only the last four digits of that number should be used.

(B) Names of Minor Children. If the involvement of a minor child must be mentioned, only the initials of that child should be used.

(C) Dates of Birth. If an individual's date of birth must be included, only the year should be used.

(D) Financial Account Numbers. If financial account numbers are relevant, only the last four digits of these numbers should be used.

(E) Home Addresses. In criminal cases, if a home address must be included, only the city and state should be listed.

(2) In compliance with the E–Government Act of 2002, a party wishing to file a document containing the personal data identifiers listed above may:

(A) File an un-redacted version of the document under seal, or

(B) File a reference list under seal.

(i) The reference list must contain the complete personal data identifier(s) and the redacted identifier(s) used in its(their) place in the filing.

(ii) All references in the case to the redacted identifiers included in the reference list will be construed to refer to the corresponding complete personal data identifier.

(iii) The reference list must be filed under seal, and may be amended as of right.

(3) The un-redacted version of the document or the reference list must be retained by the court as part of the record. The court may, however, still require the party to file a redacted copy for the public file.

(4) The responsibility for redacting these personal identifiers rests solely with counsel and the parties. The Clerk will not review each pleading for compliance with this rule.

(m) Hyperlinks.

(1) Electronically filed documents may contain the following types of hyperlinks:

(A) Hyperlinks to other portions of the same document; and

(B) Hyperlinks to a location on the Internet that contains a source document for a citation.

(2) Hyperlinks to cited authority may not replace standard citation format. Complete citations must be included in the text of the filed document. A hyperlink, or any site to which it refers, will not be considered part of the record. Hyperlinks are simply convenient mechanisms for accessing material cited in a filed document.

(3) The court accepts no responsibility for, and does not endorse, any product, organization, or content at any hyperlinked site, or at any site to which that site might be linked. The court accepts no responsibility for the availability or functionality of any hyperlink.

[Amended effective May 24, 2011.]

RULES FOR JUDICIAL–CONDUCT AND JUDICIAL–DISABILITY PROCEEDINGS

PREFACE

These Rules were promulgated by the Judicial Conference of the United States, after public comment, pursuant to 28 U.S.C. §§ 331 and 358, to establish standards and procedures for addressing complaints filed by complainants or identified by chief judges, under the Judicial Conduct and Disability Act, 28 U.S.C. §§ 351–364.

ARTICLE I. GENERAL PROVISIONS

RULE 1. SCOPE

These Rules govern proceedings under the Judicial Conduct and Disability Act, 28 U.S.C. §§ 351–364 (the Act), to determine whether a covered judge has engaged in conduct prejudicial to the effective and expeditious administration of the business of the courts or is unable to discharge the duties of office because of mental or physical disability.

[Adopted March 11, 2008, effective April 10, 2008.]

Commentary on Rule 1

In September 2006, the Judicial Conduct and Disability Act Study Committee, appointed in 2004 by Chief Justice Rehnquist and known as the "Breyer Committee," presented a report, known as the "Breyer Committee Report," 239 F.R.D. 116 (Sept. 2006), to Chief Justice Roberts that evaluated implementation of the Judicial Conduct and Disability Act of 1980, 28 U.S.C. §§ 351–364. The Breyer Committee had been formed in response to criticism from the public and the Congress regarding the effectiveness of the Act's implementation. The Executive Committee of the Judicial Conference directed the Judicial Conference Committee on Judicial Conduct and Disability to consider the recommendations made by the Breyer Committee and to report on their implementation to the Conference.

The Breyer Committee found that it could not evaluate implementation of the Act without establishing interpretive standards, Breyer Committee Report, 239 F.R.D. at 132, and that a major problem faced by chief judges in implementing the Act was the lack of authoritative interpretive standards. Id. at 212–15. The Breyer Committee then established standards to guide its evaluation, some of which were new formulations and some of which were taken from the "Illustrative Rules Governing Complaints of Judicial Misconduct and Disability," discussed below. The principal standards used by the Breyer Committee are in Appendix E of its Report. Id. at 238.

Based on the findings of the Breyer Committee, the Judicial Conference Committee on Judicial Conduct and Disability concluded that there was a need for the Judicial Conference to exercise its power under Section 358 of the Act to fashion standards guiding the various officers and bodies who must exercise responsibility under the Act. To that end, the Judicial Conference Committee proposed rules that were based largely on Appendix E of the Breyer Committee Report and the Illustrative Rules.

The Illustrative Rules were originally prepared in 1986 by the Special Committee of the Conference of Chief Judges of the United States Courts of Appeals, and were subsequently revised and amended, most recently in 2000, by the predecessor to the Committee on Judicial Conduct and Disability. The Illustrative Rules were adopted, with minor variations, by circuit judicial councils, to govern complaints under the Judicial Conduct and Disability Act.

After being submitted for public comment pursuant to 28 U.S.C. § 358(c), the present Rules were promulgated by the Judicial Conference on March 11, 2008.

RULE 2. EFFECT AND CONSTRUCTION

(a) **Generally.** These Rules are mandatory; they supersede any conflicting judicial-council rules. Judicial councils may promulgate additional rules to implement the Act as long as those rules do not conflict with these Rules.

(b) **Exception.** A Rule will not apply if, when performing duties authorized by the Act, a chief judge, a special committee, a judicial council, the Judicial Conference Committee on Judicial Conduct and Disability, or the Judicial Conference of the United States expressly finds that exceptional circumstances render application of that Rule in a particular proceeding manifestly unjust or contrary to the purposes of the Act or these Rules.

[Adopted March 11, 2008, effective April 10, 2008.]

Commentary on Rule 2

Unlike the Illustrative Rules, these Rules provide mandatory and nationally uniform provisions governing the substantive and procedural aspects of misconduct and disability proceedings under the Act. The mandatory nature of these Rules is authorized by 28 U.S.C. § 358(a) and (c). Judicial councils retain the power to promulgate rules consistent with these Rules. For example, a local rule may authorize the electronic distribution of materials pursuant to Rule 8(b).

Rule 2(b) recognizes that unforeseen and exceptional circumstances may call for a different approach in particular cases.

RULE 3. DEFINITIONS

(a) **Chief Judge.** "Chief judge" means the chief judge of a United States Court of Appeals, of the United States Court of International Trade, or of the United States Court of Federal Claims.

(b) Circuit Clerk. "Circuit clerk" means a clerk of a United States court of appeals, the clerk of the United States Court of International Trade, the clerk of the United States Court of Federal Claims, or the circuit executive of the United States Court of Appeals for the Federal Circuit.

(c) Complaint. A complaint is:

(1) a document that, in accordance with Rule 6, is filed by any person in his or her individual capacity or on behalf of a professional organization; or

(2) information from any source, other than a document described in (c) (1), that gives a chief judge probable cause to believe that a covered judge, as defined in Rule 4, has engaged in misconduct or may have a disability, whether or not the information is framed as or is intended to be an allegation of misconduct or disability.

(d) Court of Appeals, District Court, and District Judge. "Courts of appeals," "district court," and "district judge," where appropriate, include the United States Court of Federal Claims, the United States Court of International Trade, and the judges thereof.

(e) Disability. "Disability" is a temporary or permanent condition rendering a judge unable to discharge the duties of the particular judicial office. Examples of disability include substance abuse, the inability to stay awake during court proceedings, or a severe impairment of cognitive abilities.

(f) Judicial Council and Circuit. "Judicial council" and "circuit," where appropriate, include any courts designated in 28 U.S.C. § 363.

(g) Magistrate Judge. "Magistrate judge," where appropriate, includes a special master appointed by the Court of Federal Claims under 42 U.S.C. § 300aa–12(c).

(h) Misconduct. Cognizable misconduct:

(1) is conduct prejudicial to the effective and expeditious administration of the business of the courts. Misconduct includes, but is not limited to:

(A) using the judge's office to obtain special treatment for friends or relatives;

(B) accepting bribes, gifts, or other personal favors related to the judicial office;

(C) having improper discussions with parties or counsel for one side in a case;

(D) treating litigants or attorneys in a demonstrably egregious and hostile manner;

(E) engaging in partisan political activity or making inappropriately partisan statements;

(F) soliciting funds for organizations; or

(G) violating other specific, mandatory standards of judicial conduct, such as those pertaining to

restrictions on outside income and requirements for financial disclosure.

(2) is conduct occurring outside the performance of official duties if the conduct might have a prejudicial effect on the administration of the business of the courts, including a substantial and widespread lowering of public confidence in the courts among reasonable people.

(3) does not include:

(A) an allegation that is directly related to the merits of a decision or procedural ruling. An allegation that calls into question the correctness of a judge's ruling, including a failure to recuse, without more, is merits-related. If the decision or ruling is alleged to be the result of an improper motive, e.g., a bribe, ex parte contact, racial or ethnic bias, or improper conduct in rendering a decision or ruling, such as personally derogatory remarks irrelevant to the issues, the complaint is not cognizable to the extent that it attacks the merits.

(B) an allegation about delay in rendering a decision or ruling, unless the allegation concerns an improper motive in delaying a particular decision or habitual delay in a significant number of unrelated cases.

(i) Subject Judge. "Subject judge" means any judge described in Rule 4 who is the subject of a complaint.

[Adopted March 11, 2008, effective April 10, 2008.]

Commentary on Rule 3

Rule 3 is derived and adapted from the Breyer Committee Report and the Illustrative Rules.

Unless otherwise specified or the context otherwise indicates, the term "complaint" is used in these Rules to refer both to complaints identified by a chief judge under Rule 5 and to complaints filed by complainants under Rule 6.

Under the Act, a "complaint" may be filed by "any person" or "identified" by a chief judge. See 28 U.S.C. § 351(a) and (b). Under Rule 3(c)(1), complaints may be submitted by a person, in his or her individual capacity, or by a professional organization. Generally, the word "complaint" brings to mind the commencement of an adversary proceeding in which the contending parties are left to present the evidence and legal arguments, and judges play the role of an essentially passive arbiter. The Act, however, establishes an administrative, inquisitorial process. For example, even absent a complaint under Rule 6, chief judges are expected in some circumstances to trigger the process—"identify a complaint," see 28 U.S.C. § 351(b) and Rule 5—and conduct an investigation without becoming a party. See 28 U.S.C. § 352(a); Breyer Committee Report, 239 F.R.D. at 214; Illustrative Rule 2(j). Even when a complaint is filed by someone other than the chief judge, the complainant lacks many rights that a litigant would have, and the chief judge, instead of being limited to the "four corners of the complaint," must, under Rule 11, proceed as though misconduct or disability has been alleged where the complainant reveals information of misconduct or disability but does not claim it as such. See Breyer Committee Report, 239 F.R.D. at 183–84.

An allegation of misconduct or disability filed under Rule 6 is a "complaint," and the Rule so provides in subsection (c)(1). However, both the nature of the process and the use of the term "identify" suggest that the word "complaint" covers more than a document formally triggering the process. The process relies on chief judges considering known information and triggering the process when appropriate. "Identifying" a "complaint," therefore, is best understood as the chief judge's concluding that information known to the judge constitutes probable cause to believe that misconduct occurred or a disability exists, whether or not the information is framed as, or intended to be an accusation. This definition is codified in (c)(2).

Rule 3(e) relates to disability and provides only the most general definition, recognizing that a fact-specific approach is the only one available.

The phrase "prejudicial to the effective and expeditious administration of the business of the courts" is not subject to precise definition, and subsection (h)(1) therefore provides some specific examples. Although the Code of Conduct for United States Judges may be informative, its main precepts are highly general; the Code is in many potential applications aspirational rather than a set of disciplinary rules. Ultimately, the responsibility for determining what constitutes misconduct under the statute is the province of the judicial council of the circuit subject to such review and limitations as are ordained by the statute and by these Rules.

Even where specific, mandatory rules exist—for example, governing the receipt of gifts by judges, outside earned income, and financial disclosure obligations—the distinction between the misconduct statute and the specific, mandatory rules must be borne in mind. For example, an inadvertent, minor violation of any one of these Rules, promptly remedied when called to the attention of the judge, might still be a violation but might not rise to the level of misconduct under the statute. By contrast, a pattern of such violations of the Code might well rise to the level of misconduct.

An allegation can meet the statutory standard even though the judge's alleged conduct did not occur in the course of the performance of official duties. The Code of Conduct for United States Judges expressly covers a wide range of extra-official activities, and some of these activities may constitute misconduct. For example, allegations that a judge solicited funds for a charity or participated in a partisan political event are cognizable under the Act.

On the other hand, judges are entitled to some leeway in extra-official activities. For example, misconduct may not include a judge being repeatedly and publicly discourteous to a spouse (not including physical abuse) even though this might cause some reasonable people to have diminished confidence in the courts. Rule 3(h)(2) states that conduct of this sort is covered, for example, when it might lead to a "substantial and widespread" lowering of such confidence.

Rule 3(h)(3)(A) tracks the Act, 28 U.S.C. § 352(b)(1)(A)(ii), in excluding from the definition of misconduct allegations "[d]irectly related to the merits of a decision or procedural ruling." This exclusion preserves the independence of judges in the exercise of judicial power by ensuring that the complaint procedure is not used to collaterally attack the substance of a judge's ruling. Any allegation that calls into question the correctness of an official action of a judge—

without more—is merits-related. The phrase "decision or procedural ruling" is not limited to rulings issued in deciding Article III cases or controversies. Thus, a complaint challenging the correctness of a chief judge's determination to dismiss a prior misconduct complaint would be properly dismissed as merits-related—in other words, as challenging the substance of the judge's administrative determination to dismiss the complaint—even though it does not concern the judge's rulings in Article III litigation. Similarly, an allegation that a judge had incorrectly declined to approve a Criminal Justice Act voucher is merits-related under this standard.

Conversely, an allegation—however unsupported—that a judge conspired with a prosecutor to make a particular ruling is not merits-related, even though it "relates" to a ruling in a colloquial sense. Such an allegation attacks the propriety of conspiring with the prosecutor and goes beyond a challenge to the correctness—"the merits"—of the ruling itself. An allegation that a judge ruled against the complainant because the complainant is a member of a particular racial or ethnic group, or because the judge dislikes the complainant personally, is also not merits-related. Such an allegation attacks the propriety of arriving at rulings with an illicit or improper motive. Similarly, an allegation that a judge used an inappropriate term to refer to a class of people is not merits-related even if the judge used it on the bench or in an opinion; the correctness of the judge's rulings is not at stake. An allegation that a judge treated litigants or attorneys in a demonstrably egregious and hostile manner while on the bench is also not merits-related.

The existence of an appellate remedy is usually irrelevant to whether an allegation is merits-related. The merits-related ground for dismissal exists to protect judges' independence in making rulings, not to protect or promote the appellate process. A complaint alleging an incorrect ruling is merits-related even though the complainant has no recourse from that ruling. By the same token, an allegation that is otherwise cognizable under the Act should not be dismissed merely because an appellate remedy appears to exist (for example, vacating a ruling that resulted from an improper ex parte communication). However, there may be occasions when appellate and misconduct proceedings overlap, and consideration and disposition of a complaint under these Rules may be properly deferred by a chief judge until the appellate proceedings are concluded in order to avoid, inter alia, inconsistent decisions.

Because of the special need to protect judges' independence in deciding what to say in an opinion or ruling, a somewhat different standard applies to determine the merits-relatedness of a non-frivolous allegation that a judge's language in a ruling reflected an improper motive. If the judge's language was relevant to the case at hand—for example a statement that a claim is legally or factually "frivolous"—then the judge's choice of language is presumptively merits-related and excluded, absent evidence apart from the ruling itself suggesting an improper motive. If, on the other hand, the challenged language does not seem relevant on its face, then an additional inquiry under Rule 11 is necessary.

With regard to Rule 3(h)(3)(B), a complaint of delay in a single case is excluded as merits-related. Such an allegation may be said to challenge the correctness of an official action of the judge—in other words, assigning a low priority to deciding the particular case. But, by the same token, an allegation of a habitual pattern of delay in a significant number of unrelated cases, or an allegation of deliberate delay in a single case arising out of an illicit motive, is not merits-related.

The remaining subsections of Rule 3 provide technical definitions clarifying the application of the Rules to the various kinds of courts covered.

RULE 4. COVERED JUDGES

A complaint under these Rules may concern the actions or capacity only of judges of United States courts of appeals, judges of United States district courts, judges of United States bankruptcy courts, United States magistrate judges, and judges of the courts specified in 28 U.S.C. § 363.

[Adopted March 11, 2008, effective April 10, 2008.]

Commentary on Rule 4

This Rule tracks the Act. Rule 8(c) and (d) contain provisions as to the handling of complaints against persons not covered by the Act, such as other court personnel, or against both covered judges and noncovered persons.

ARTICLE II. INITIATION OF A COMPLAINT

RULE 5. IDENTIFICATION OF A COMPLAINT

(a) Identification. When a chief judge has information constituting reasonable grounds for inquiry into whether a covered judge has engaged in misconduct or has a disability, the chief judge may conduct an inquiry, as he or she deems appropriate, into the accuracy of the information even if no related complaint has been filed. A chief judge who finds probable cause to believe that misconduct has occurred or that a disability exists may seek an informal resolution that he or she finds satisfactory. If no informal resolution is achieved or is feasible, the chief judge may identify a complaint and, by written order stating the reasons, begin the review provided in Rule 11. If the evidence of misconduct is clear and convincing and no informal resolution is achieved or is feasible, the chief judge must identify a complaint. A chief judge must not decline to identify a complaint merely because the person making the allegation has not filed a complaint under Rule 6. This Rule is subject to Rule 7.

(b) Noncompliance With Rule 6(d). Rule 6 complaints that do not comply with the requirements of Rule 6(d) must be considered under this Rule.

[Adopted March 11, 2008, effective April 10, 2008.]

Commentary on Rule 5

This Rule is adapted from the Breyer Committee Report, 239 F.R.D. at 245–46.

The Act authorizes the chief judge, by written order stating reasons, to identify a complaint and thereby dispense with the filing of a written complaint. See 28 U.S.C. § 351(b). Under Rule 5, when a chief judge becomes aware of information constituting reasonable grounds to inquire into possible misconduct or disability on the part of a covered judge, and no formal complaint has been filed, the chief judge has the power in his or her discretion to begin an appropriate inquiry. A chief judge's decision whether to informally seek a resolution and/or to identify a complaint is guided by the results of that inquiry. If the chief judge concludes that there is probable cause to believe that misconduct has occurred or a disability exists, the chief judge may seek an informal resolution, if feasible, and if failing in that, may identify a complaint. Discretion is accorded largely for the reasons police officers and prosecutors have discretion in making arrests or bringing charges. The matter may be trivial and isolated, based on marginal evidence, or otherwise highly unlikely to lead to a misconduct or disability finding. On the other hand, if the inquiry leads the chief judge to conclude that there is clear and convincing evidence of misconduct or a disability, and no satisfactory informal resolution has been achieved or is feasible, the chief judge is required to identify a complaint.

An informal resolution is one agreed to by the subject judge and found satisfactory by the chief judge. Because an informal resolution under Rule 5 reached before a complaint is filed under Rule 6 will generally cause a subsequent Rule 6 complaint alleging the identical matter to be concluded, see Rule 11(d), the chief judge must be sure that the resolution is fully appropriate before endorsing it. In doing so, the chief judge must balance the seriousness of the matter against the particular judge's alacrity in addressing the issue. The availability of this procedure should encourage attempts at swift remedial action before a formal complaint is filed.

When a complaint is identified, a written order stating the reasons for the identification must be provided; this begins the process articulated in Rule 11. Rule 11 provides that once the chief judge has identified a complaint, the chief judge, subject to the disqualification provisions of Rule 25, will perform, with respect to that complaint, all functions assigned to the chief judge for the determination of complaints filed by a complainant.

In high-visibility situations, it may be desirable for the chief judge to identify a complaint without first seeking an informal resolution (and then, if the circumstances warrant, dismiss or conclude the identified complaint without appointment of a special committee) in order to assure the public that the allegations have not been ignored.

A chief judge's decision not to identify a complaint under Rule 5 is not appealable and is subject to Rule 3(h)(3)(A), which excludes merits-related complaints from the definition of misconduct.

A chief judge may not decline to identify a complaint solely on the basis that the unfiled allegations could be raised by one or more persons in a filed complaint, but none of these persons has opted to do so.

Subsection (a) concludes by stating that this Rule is "subject to Rule 7." This is intended to establish that only: (i) the chief judge of the home circuit of a potential subject judge, or (ii) the chief judge of a circuit in which misconduct is alleged to have occurred in the course of official business while the potential subject judge was sitting by designation, shall have the power or a duty under this Rule to identify a complaint.

Subsection (b) provides that complaints filed under Rule 6 that do not comply with the requirements of Rule 6(d), must be considered under this Rule. For instance, if a complaint has been filed but the form submitted is unsigned, or the truth of the statements therein are not verified in writing under penalty of perjury, then a chief judge must nevertheless consider the allegations as known information, and proceed to follow the process described in Rule 5(a).

RULE 6. FILING A COMPLAINT

(a) Form. A complainant may use the form reproduced in the appendix to these Rules or a form designated by the rules of the judicial council in the circuit in which the complaint is filed. A complaint form is also available on each court of appeals' website or may be obtained from the circuit clerk or any district court or bankruptcy court within the circuit. A form is not necessary to file a complaint, but the complaint must be written and must include the information described in (b).

(b) Brief Statement of Facts. A complaint must contain a concise statement that details the specific facts on which the claim of misconduct or disability is based. The statement of facts should include a description of:

(1) what happened;

(2) when and where the relevant events happened;

(3) any information that would help an investigator check the facts; and

(4) for an allegation of disability, any additional facts that form the basis of that allegation.

(c) Legibility. A complaint should be typewritten if possible. If not typewritten, it must be legible. An illegible complaint will be returned to the complainant with a request to resubmit it in legible form. If a resubmitted complaint is still illegible, it will not be accepted for filing.

(d) Complainant's Address and Signature; Verification. The complainant must provide a contact address and sign the complaint. The truth of the statements made in the complaint must be verified in writing under penalty of perjury. If any of these requirements are not met, the complaint will be accepted for filing, but it will be reviewed under only Rule 5(b).

(e) Number of Copies; Envelope Marking. The complainant shall provide the number of copies of the complaint required by local rule. Each copy should be in an envelope marked "Complaint of Misconduct" or "Complaint of Disability." The envelope must not show the name of any subject judge.

[Adopted March 11, 2008, effective April 10, 2008.]

Commentary on Rule 6

The Rule is adapted from the Illustrative Rules and is self-explanatory.

RULE 7. WHERE TO INITIATE COMPLAINTS

(a) Where to File. Except as provided in (b),

(1) a complaint against a judge of a United States court of appeals, a United States district court, a United States bankruptcy court, or a United States magistrate judge must be filed with the circuit clerk in the jurisdiction in which the subject judge holds office.

(2) a complaint against a judge of the United States Court of International Trade or the United States Court of Federal Claims must be filed with the respective clerk of that court.

(3) a complaint against a judge of the United States Court of Appeals for the Federal Circuit must be filed with the circuit executive of that court.

(b) Misconduct in Another Circuit; Transfer. If a complaint alleges misconduct in the course of official business while the subject judge was sitting on a court by designation under 28 U.S.C. §§ 291–293 and 294(d), the complaint may be filed or identified with the circuit clerk of that circuit or of the subject judge's home circuit. The proceeding will continue in the circuit of the first-filed or first-identified complaint. The judicial council of the circuit where the complaint was first filed or first identified may transfer the complaint to the subject judge's home circuit or to the circuit where the alleged misconduct occurred, as the case may be.

[Adopted March 11, 2008, effective April 10, 2008.]

Commentary on Rule 7

Title 28 U.S.C. § 351 states that complaints are to be filed with "the clerk of the court of appeals for the circuit." However, in many circuits, this role is filled by circuit executives. Accordingly, the term "circuit clerk," as defined in Rule 3(b) and used throughout these Rules, applies to circuit executives.

Section 351 uses the term "the circuit" in a way that suggests that either the home circuit of the subject judge or the circuit in which misconduct is alleged to have occurred is the proper venue for complaints. With an exception for judges sitting by designation, the Rule requires the identifying or filing of a misconduct or disability complaint in the circuit in which the judge holds office, largely based on the administrative perspective of the Act. Given the Act's emphasis on the future conduct of the business of the courts, the circuit in which the judge holds office is the appropriate forum because that circuit is likely best able to influence a judge's future behavior in constructive ways.

However, when judges sit by designation, the non-home circuit has a strong interest in redressing misconduct in the course of official business, and where allegations also involve a member of the bar—ex parte contact between an attorney and a judge, for example—it may often be desirable to have the judicial and bar misconduct proceedings take place in the same venue. Rule 7(b), therefore, allows transfer to, or filing or identification of a complaint in, the non-home circuit. The proceeding may be transferred by the judicial council of the filing or identified circuit to the other circuit.

RULE 8. ACTION BY CLERK

(a) Receipt of Complaint. Upon receiving a complaint against a judge filed under Rule 5 or 6, the circuit clerk must open a file, assign a docket number according to a uniform numbering scheme promulgated by the Judicial Conference Committee on Judicial Conduct and Disability, and acknowledge the complaint's receipt.

(b) Distribution of Copies. The clerk must promptly send copies of a complaint filed under Rule 6 to the chief judge or the judge authorized to act as chief judge under Rule 25(f), and copies of complaints filed under Rule 5 or 6 to each subject judge. The clerk must retain the original complaint. Any further distribution should be as provided by local rule.

(c) Complaints Against Noncovered Persons. If the clerk receives a complaint about a person not holding an office described in Rule 4, the clerk must not accept the complaint for filing under these Rules.

(d) Receipt of Complaint About a Judge and Another Noncovered Person. If a complaint is received about a judge described in Rule 4 and a person not holding an office described in Rule 4, the clerk must accept the complaint for filing under these Rules only with regard to the judge and must inform the complainant of the limitation.

[Adopted March 11, 2008, effective April 10, 2008.]

Commentary on Rule 8

This Rule is adapted from the Illustrative Rules and is largely self-explanatory.

The uniform docketing scheme described in subsection (a) should take into account potential problems associated with a complaint that names multiple judges. One solution may be to provide separate docket numbers for each subject judge. Separate docket numbers would help avoid difficulties in tracking cases, particularly if a complaint is dismissed with respect to some, but not all, of the named judges.

Complaints against noncovered persons are not to be accepted for processing under these Rules but may, of course, be accepted under other circuit rules or procedures for grievances.

RULE 9. TIME FOR FILING OR IDENTIFYING A COMPLAINT

A complaint may be filed or identified at any time. If the passage of time has made an accurate and fair

investigation of a complaint impractical, the complaint must be dismissed under Rule 11(c)(1)(E).

[Adopted March 11, 2008, effective April 10, 2008.]

Commentary on Rule 9

This Rule is adapted from the Act, 28 U.S.C. §§ 351, 352(b)(1)(A)(iii), and the Illustrative Rules.

RULE 10. ABUSE OF THE COMPLAINT PROCEDURE

(a) Abusive Complaints. A complainant who has filed repetitive, harassing, or frivolous complaints, or has otherwise abused the complaint procedure, may be restricted from filing further complaints. After giving the complainant an opportunity to show cause in writing why his or her right to file further complaints should not be limited, a judicial council may prohibit, restrict, or impose conditions on the complainant's use of the complaint procedure. Upon written request of the complainant, the judicial council may revise or withdraw any prohibition, restriction, or condition previously imposed.

(b) Orchestrated Complaints. When many essentially identical complaints from different complainants are received and appear to be part of an orchestrated campaign, the chief judge may recommend that the judicial council issue a written order instructing the circuit clerk to accept only a certain number of such complaints for filing and to refuse to accept further ones. The clerk must send a copy of any such order to anyone whose complaint was not accepted.

[Adopted March 11, 2008, effective April 10, 2008.]

Commentary on Rule 10

This Rule is adapted from the Illustrative Rules.

Rule 10(a) provides a mechanism for a judicial council to restrict the filing of further complaints by a single complainant who has abused the complaint procedure. In some instances, however, the complaint procedure may be abused in a manner for which the remedy provided in Rule 10(a) may not be appropriate. For example, some circuits have been inundated with submissions of dozens or hundreds of essentially identical complaints against the same judge or judges, all submitted by different complainants. In many of these instances, persons with grievances against a particular judge or judges used the Internet or other technology to orchestrate mass complaint-filing campaigns against them. If each complaint submitted as part of such a campaign were accepted for filing and processed according to these Rules, there would be a serious drain on court resources without any benefit to the adjudication of the underlying merits.

A judicial council may, therefore, respond to such mass filings under Rule 10(b) by declining to accept repetitive complaints for filing, regardless of the fact that the complaints are nominally submitted by different complainants. When the first complaint or complaints have been dismissed on the merits, and when further, essentially identical submissions follow, the judicial council may issue a second order noting that these are identical or repetitive complaints, directing the circuit clerk not to accept these complaints or any further such complaints for filing, and directing the clerk to send each putative complainant copies of both orders.

ARTICLE III. REVIEW OF A COMPLAINT BY THE CHIEF JUDGE

RULE 11. REVIEW BY THE CHIEF JUDGE

(a) Purpose of Chief Judge's Review. When a complaint is identified by the chief judge or is filed, the chief judge must review it unless the chief judge is disqualified under Rule 25. If the complaint contains information constituting evidence of misconduct or disability, but the complainant does not claim it as such, the chief judge must treat the complaint as if it did allege misconduct or disability and give notice to the subject judge. After reviewing the complaint, the chief judge must determine whether it should be:

(1) dismissed;

(2) concluded on the ground that voluntary corrective action has been taken;

(3) concluded because intervening events have made action on the complaint no longer necessary; or

(4) referred to a special committee.

(b) Inquiry by Chief Judge. In determining what action to take under Rule 11(a), the chief judge may conduct a limited inquiry. The chief judge, or a designee, may communicate orally or in writing with the complainant, the subject judge, and any others who may have knowledge of the matter, and may review transcripts or other relevant documents. In conducting the inquiry, the chief judge must not determine any reasonably disputed issue.

(c) Dismissal.

(1) *Allowable Grounds.* A complaint must be dismissed in whole or in part to the extent that the chief judge concludes that the complaint:

(A) alleges conduct that, even if true, is not prejudicial to the effective and expeditious administration of the business of the courts and does not indicate a mental or physical disability resulting in inability to discharge the duties of judicial office;

(B) is directly related to the merits of a decision or procedural ruling;

(C) is frivolous;

(D) is based on allegations lacking sufficient evidence to raise an inference that misconduct has occurred or that a disability exists;

(E) is based on allegations which are incapable of being established through investigation;

(F) has been filed in the wrong circuit under Rule 7; or

(G) is otherwise not appropriate for consideration under the Act.

(2) *Disallowed Grounds.* A complaint must not be dismissed solely because it repeats allegations of a previously dismissed complaint if it also contains material information not previously considered and does not constitute harassment of the subject judge.

(d) Corrective Action. The chief judge may conclude the complaint proceeding in whole or in part if:

(1) an informal resolution under Rule 5 satisfactory to the chief judge was reached before the complaint was filed under Rule 6, or

(2) the chief judge determines that the subject judge has taken appropriate voluntary corrective action that acknowledges and remedies the problems raised by the complaint.

(e) Intervening Events. The chief judge may conclude the complaint proceeding in whole or in part upon determining that intervening events render some or all of the allegations moot or make remedial action impossible.

(f) Appointment of Special Committee. If some or all of the complaint is not dismissed or concluded, the chief judge must promptly appoint a special committee to investigate the complaint or any relevant portion of it and to make recommendations to the judicial council. Before appointing a special committee, the chief judge must invite the subject judge to respond to the complaint either orally or in writing if the judge was not given an opportunity during the limited inquiry. In the chief judge's discretion, separate complaints may be joined and assigned to a single special committee. Similarly, a single complaint about more than one judge may be severed and more than one special committee appointed.

(g) Notice of Chief Judge's Action; Petitions for Review.

(1) *When Special Committee Is Appointed.* If a special committee is appointed, the chief judge must notify the complainant and the subject judge that the matter has been referred to a special committee and identify the members of the committee. A copy of the order appointing the special committee must be sent to the Judicial Conference Committee on Judicial Conduct and Disability.

(2) *When Chief Judge Disposes of Complaint Without Appointing Special Committee.* If the chief judge disposes of the complaint under Rule 11(c), (d), or (e), the chief judge must prepare a supporting memorandum that sets forth the reasons for the disposition. Except as authorized by 28 U.S.C. § 360, the memorandum must not include the name of the complainant or of the subject judge. The order and the supporting memorandum, which may be one document, must be provided to the complainant, the subject judge, and the Judicial Conference Committee on Judicial Conduct and Disability.

(3) *Right of Petition for Review.* If the chief judge disposes of a complaint under Rule 11(c), (d), or (e), the complainant and subject judge must be notified of the right to petition the judicial council for review of the disposition, as provided in Rule 18. If a petition for review is filed, the chief judge must promptly transmit all materials obtained in connection with the inquiry under Rule 11(b) to the circuit clerk for transmittal to the judicial council.

(h) Public Availability of Chief Judge's Decision. The chief judge's decision must be made public to the extent, at the time, and in the manner provided in Rule 24.

[Adopted March 11, 2008, effective April 10, 2008.]

Commentary on Rule 11

Subsection (a) lists the actions available to a chief judge in reviewing a complaint. This subsection provides that where a complaint has been filed under Rule 6, the ordinary doctrines of waiver do not apply. A chief judge must identify as a complaint any misconduct or disability issues raised by the factual allegations of the complaint even if the complainant makes no such claim with regard to those issues. For example, an allegation limited to misconduct in fact-finding that mentions periods during a trial when the judge was asleep must be treated as a complaint regarding disability. Some formal order giving notice of the expanded scope of the proceeding must be given to the subject judge.

Subsection (b) describes the nature of the chief judge's inquiry. It is based largely on the Breyer Committee Report, 239 F.R.D. at 243–45. The Act states that dismissal is appropriate "when a limited inquiry . . . demonstrates that the allegations in the complaint lack any factual foundation or are conclusively refuted by objective evidence." 28 U.S.C. § 352(b)(1)(B). At the same time, however, Section 352(a) states that "[t]he chief judge shall not undertake to make findings of fact about any matter that is reasonably in dispute." These two statutory standards should be read together, so that a matter is not "reasonably" in dispute if a limited inquiry shows that the allegations do not constitute misconduct or disability, that they lack any reliable factual foundation, or that they are conclusively refuted by objective evidence.

In conducting a limited inquiry under subsection (b), the chief judge must avoid determinations of reasonably disputed issues, including reasonably disputed issues as to whether the facts alleged constitute misconduct or disability, which are ordinarily left to a special committee and the judicial council. An allegation of fact is ordinarily not "refuted" simply because the subject judge denies it. The limited inquiry must reveal something more in the way of refutation before it is appropriate to dismiss a complaint that is otherwise cognizable. If it is the complainant's word against the subject judge's—in other words, there is simply no other significant evidence of what happened or of the complainant's unreliability—then there must be a special-committee investigation. Such a credibility issue is a matter "reasonably in dispute" within the meaning of the Act.

However, dismissal following a limited inquiry may occur when the complaint refers to transcripts or to witnesses and the chief judge determines that the transcripts and witnesses all support the subject judge. Breyer Committee Report, 239 F.R.D. at 243. For example, consider a complaint alleging that the subject judge said X, and the complaint mentions, or it is independently clear, that five people may have heard what the judge said. Id. The chief judge is told by the subject judge and one witness that the judge did not say X, and the chief judge dismisses the complaint without questioning the other four possible witnesses. Id. In this example, the matter remains reasonably in dispute. If all five witnesses say the judge did not say X, dismissal is appropriate, but if potential witnesses who are reasonably accessible have not been questioned, then the matter remains reasonably in dispute. Id.

Similarly, under (c)(1)(A), if it is clear that the conduct or disability alleged, even if true, is not cognizable under these Rules, the complaint should be dismissed. If that issue is reasonably in dispute, however, dismissal under (c)(1)(A) is inappropriate.

Essentially, the standard articulated in subsection (b) is that used to decide motions for summary judgment pursuant to Fed. R. Civ. P. 56. Genuine issues of material fact are not resolved at the summary judgment stage. A material fact is one that "might affect the outcome of the suit under the governing law," and a dispute is "genuine" if "the evidence is such that a reasonable jury could return a verdict for the nonmoving party." *Anderson v. Liberty Lobby*, 477 U.S. 242, 248 (1986). Similarly, the chief judge may not resolve a genuine issue concerning a material fact or the existence of misconduct or a disability when conducting a limited inquiry pursuant to subsection (b).

Subsection (c) describes the grounds on which a complaint may be dismissed. These are adapted from the Act, 28 U.S.C. § 352(b), and the Breyer Committee Report, 239 F.R.D. at 239–45. Subsection (c)(1)(A) permits dismissal of an allegation that, even if true, does not constitute misconduct or disability under the statutory standard. The proper standards are set out in Rule 3 and discussed in the Commentary on that Rule. Subsection (c)(1)(B) permits dismissal of complaints related to the merits of a decision by a subject judge; this standard is also governed by Rule 3 and its accompanying Commentary.

Subsections (c)(1)(C)–(E) implement the statute by allowing dismissal of complaints that are "frivolous, lacking sufficient evidence to raise an inference that misconduct has occurred, or containing allegations which are incapable of being established through investigation." 28 U.S.C. § 352(b)(1)(A)(iii).

Dismissal of a complaint as "frivolous," under Rule 11(c)(1)(C), will generally occur without any inquiry beyond the face of the complaint. For instance, when the allegations are facially incredible or so lacking in indicia of reliability that no further inquiry is warranted, dismissal under this subsection is appropriate.

A complaint warranting dismissal under Rule 11(c)(1)(D) is illustrated by the following example. Consider a complainant who alleges an impropriety and asserts that he knows of it because it was observed and reported to him by a person who is identified. The judge denies that the event occurred. When contacted, the source also denies it. In such a case, the chief judge's proper course of action may turn on whether the source had any role in the allegedly improper conduct. If the complaint was based on a lawyer's statement that he or she had an improper ex parte contact with a judge, the lawyer's denial of the impropriety might not be taken as wholly persuasive, and it would be appropriate to conclude that a real factual issue is raised. On the other hand, if the complaint quoted a disinterested third party and that disinterested party denied that the statement had been made, there would be no value in opening a formal investigation. In such a case, it would be appropriate to dismiss the complaint under Rule 11(c)(1)(D).

Rule 11(c)(1)(E) is intended, among other things, to cover situations when no evidence is offered or identified, or when the only identified source is unavailable. Breyer Committee Report, 239 F.R.D. at 243. For example, a complaint alleges that an unnamed attorney told the complainant that the judge did X. Id. The subject judge denies it. The chief judge requests that the complainant (who does not purport to have observed the judge do X) identify the unnamed witness, or that the unnamed witness come forward so that the chief judge can learn the unnamed witness's account. Id. The complainant responds that he has spoken with the unnamed witness, that the unnamed witness is an attorney who practices in federal court, and that the unnamed witness is unwilling to be identified or to come forward. Id. at 243–44. The allegation is then properly dismissed as containing allegations that are incapable of being established through investigation. Id.

If, however, the situation involves a reasonable dispute over credibility, the matter should proceed. For example, the complainant alleges an impropriety and alleges that he or she observed it and that there were no other witnesses; the subject judge denies that the event occurred. Unless the complainant's allegations are facially incredible or so lacking indicia of reliability warranting dismissal under Rule 11(c)(1)(C), a special committee must be appointed because there is a material factual question that is reasonably in dispute.

Dismissal is also appropriate when a complaint is filed so long after an alleged event that memory loss, death, or changes to unknown residences prevent a proper investigation.

Subsection (c)(2) indicates that the investigative nature of the process prevents the application of claim preclusion principles where new and material evidence becomes available. However, it also recognizes that at some point a renewed investigation may constitute harassment of the subject judge and should be foregone, depending of course on the seriousness of the issues and the weight of the new evidence.

Rule 11(d) implements the Act's provision for dismissal if voluntary appropriate corrective action has been taken. It is largely adapted from the Breyer Committee Report, 239

F.R.D. 244–45. The Act authorizes the chief judge to conclude the proceedings if "appropriate corrective action has been taken." 28 U.S.C. § 352(b)(2). Under the Rule, action taken after the complaint is filed is "appropriate" when it acknowledges and remedies the problem raised by the complaint. Breyer Committee Report, 239 F.R.D. at 244. Because the Act deals with the conduct of judges, the emphasis is on correction of the judicial conduct that was the subject of the complaint. Id. Terminating a complaint based on corrective action is premised on the implicit understanding that voluntary self-correction or redress of misconduct or a disability is preferable to sanctions. Id. The chief judge may facilitate this process by giving the subject judge an objective view of the appearance of the judicial conduct in question and by suggesting appropriate corrective measures. Id. Moreover, when corrective action is taken under Rule 5 satisfactory to the chief judge before a complaint is filed, that informal resolution will be sufficient to conclude a subsequent complaint based on the identical conduct.

"Corrective action" must be voluntary action taken by the subject judge. Breyer Committee Report, 239 F.R.D. at 244. A remedial action directed by the chief judge or by an appellate court without the participation of the subject judge in formulating the directive or without the subject judge's subsequent agreement to such action does not constitute the requisite voluntary corrective action. Id. Neither the chief judge nor an appellate court has authority under the Act to impose a formal remedy or sanction; only the judicial council can impose a formal remedy or sanction under 28 U.S.C. § 354(a)(2). Id. Compliance with a previous council order may serve as corrective action allowing conclusion of a later complaint about the same behavior. Id.

Where a judge's conduct has resulted in identifiable, particularized harm to the complainant or another individual, appropriate corrective action should include steps taken by that judge to acknowledge and redress the harm, if possible, such as by an apology, recusal from a case, or a pledge to refrain from similar conduct in the future. Id. While the Act is generally forward-looking, any corrective action should, to the extent possible, serve to correct a specific harm to an individual, if such harm can reasonably be remedied. Id. In some cases, corrective action may not be "appropriate" to justify conclusion of a complaint unless the complainant or other individual harmed is meaningfully apprised of the nature of the corrective action in the chief judge's order, in a direct communication from the subject judge, or otherwise. Id.

Voluntary corrective action should be proportionate to any plausible allegations of misconduct in the complaint. The form of corrective action should also be proportionate to any sanctions that a judicial council might impose under Rule 20(b), such as a private or public reprimand or a change in case assignments. Breyer Committee Report, 239 F.R.D at 244–45. In other words, minor corrective action will not suffice to dispose of a serious matter. Id.

Rule 11(e) implements Section 352(b)(2) of the Act, which permits the chief judge to "conclude the proceeding," if "action on the complaint is no longer necessary because of intervening events," such as a resignation from judicial office. Ordinarily, however, stepping down from an administrative post such as chief judge, judicial-council member, or court-committee chair does not constitute an event rendering unnecessary any further action on a complaint alleging judicial misconduct. Breyer Committee Report, 239 F.R.D. at 245.

As long as the subject of the complaint performs judicial duties, a complaint alleging judicial misconduct must be addressed. Id.

If a complaint is not disposed of pursuant to Rule 11(c), (d), or (e), a special committee must be appointed. Rule 11(f) states that a subject judge must be invited to respond to the complaint before a special committee is appointed, if no earlier response was invited.

Subject judges, of course, receive copies of complaints at the same time that they are referred to the chief judge, and they are free to volunteer responses to them. Under Rule 11(b), the chief judge may request a response if it is thought necessary. However, many complaints are clear candidates for dismissal even if their allegations are accepted as true, and there is no need for the subject judge to devote time to a defense.

The Act requires that the order dismissing a complaint or concluding the proceeding contain a statement of reasons and that a copy of the order be sent to the complainant. 28 U.S.C. § 352(b). Rule 24, dealing with availability of information to the public, contemplates that the order will be made public, usually without disclosing the names of the complainant or the subject judge. If desired for administrative purposes, more identifying information can be included in a non-public version of the order.

When complaints are disposed of by chief judges, the statutory purposes are best served by providing the complainant with a full, particularized, but concise explanation, giving reasons for the conclusions reached. See also Commentary on Rule 24, dealing with public availability.

Rule 11(g) provides that the complainant and subject judge must be notified, in the case of a disposition by the chief judge, of the right to petition the judicial council for review. A copy of a chief judge's order and memorandum, which may be one document, disposing of a complaint must be sent by the circuit clerk to the Judicial Conference Committee on Judicial Conduct and Disability.

ARTICLE IV. INVESTIGATION AND REPORT BY SPECIAL COMMITTEE

RULE 12. COMPOSITION OF SPECIAL COMMITTEE

(a) Membership. Except as provided in (e), a special committee appointed under Rule 11(f) must consist of the chief judge and equal numbers of circuit and district judges. If the complaint is about a district judge, bankruptcy judge, or magistrate judge, then, when possible, the district-judge members of the committee must be from districts other than the district of the subject judge. For the courts named in 28 U.S.C. § 363, the committee must be selected from the judges serving on the subject judge's court.

(b) Presiding Officer. When appointing the committee, the chief judge may serve as the presiding officer or else must designate a committee member as the presiding officer.

(c) Bankruptcy Judge or Magistrate Judge as Adviser. If the subject judge is a bankruptcy judge or magistrate judge, he or she may, within 14 days after being notified of the committee's appointment, ask the chief judge to designate as a committee adviser another bankruptcy judge or magistrate judge, as the case may be. The chief judge must grant such a request but may otherwise use discretion in naming the adviser. Unless the adviser is a Court of Federal Claims special master appointed under 42 U.S.C. § 300aa–12(c), the adviser must be from a district other than the district of the subject bankruptcy judge or subject magistrate judge. The adviser cannot vote but has the other privileges of a committee member.

(d) Provision of Documents. The chief judge must certify to each other member of the committee and to any adviser copies of the complaint and statement of facts in whole or relevant part, and any other relevant documents on file.

(e) Continuing Qualification of Committee Members. A member of a special committee who was qualified to serve when appointed may continue to serve on the committee even though the member relinquishes the position of chief judge, active circuit judge, or active district judge, as the case may be, but only if the member continues to hold office under Article III, Section 1, of the Constitution of the United States, or under 28 U.S.C. § 171.

(f) Inability of Committee Member to Complete Service. If a member of a special committee can no longer serve because of death, disability, disqualification, resignation, retirement from office, or other reason, the chief judge must decide whether to appoint a replacement member, either a circuit or district judge as needed under (a). No special committee appointed under these Rules may function with only a single member, and the votes of a two-member committee must be unanimous.

(g) Voting. All actions by a committee must be by vote of a majority of all members of the committee.

[Adopted March 11, 2008, effective April 10, 2008.]

Commentary on Rule 12

This Rule is adapted from the Act and the Illustrative Rules.

Rule 12 leaves the size of a special committee flexible, to be determined on a case-by-case basis. The question of committee size is one that should be weighed with care in view of the potential for consuming the members' time; a large committee should be appointed only if there is a special reason to do so.

Although the Act requires that the chief judge be a member of each special committee, 28 U.S.C. § 353(a)(1), it does not require that the chief judge preside. Accordingly, Rule 12(b) provides that if the chief judge does not preside, he or she must designate another committee member as the presiding officer.

Rule 12(c) provides that the chief judge must appoint a bankruptcy judge or magistrate judge as an adviser to a special committee at the request of a bankruptcy or magistrate subject judge.

Subsection (c) also provides that the adviser will have all the privileges of a committee member except a vote. The adviser, therefore, may participate in all deliberations of the committee, question witnesses at hearings, and write a separate statement to accompany the special committee's report to the judicial council.

Rule 12(e) provides that a member of a special committee who remains an Article III judge may continue to serve on the committee even though the member's status otherwise changes. Thus, a committee that originally consisted of the chief judge and an equal number of circuit and district judges, as required by the law, may continue to function even though changes of status alter that composition. This provision reflects the belief that stability of membership will contribute to the quality of the work of such committees.

Stability of membership is also the principal concern animating Rule 12(f), which deals with the case in which a special committee loses a member before its work is complete. The Rule permits the chief judge to determine whether a replacement member should be appointed. Generally, appointment of a replacement member is desirable in these situations unless the committee has conducted evidentiary hearings before the vacancy occurs. However, cases may arise in which a committee is in the late stages of its work, and in which it would be difficult for a new member to play a meaningful role. The Rule also preserves the collegial character of the committee process by prohibiting a single surviving member from serving as a committee and by providing that a committee of two surviving members will, in essence, operate under a unanimity rule.

Rule 12(g) provides that actions of a special committee must be by vote of a majority of all the members. All the members of a committee should participate in committee decisions. In that circumstance, it seems reasonable to require that committee decisions be made by a majority of the membership, rather than a majority of some smaller quorum.

RULE 13. CONDUCT OF AN INVESTIGATION

(a) Extent and Methods of Special–Committee Investigation. Each special committee must determine the appropriate extent and methods of the investigation in light of the allegations of the complaint. If, in the course of the investigation, the committee has cause to believe that the subject judge may have engaged in misconduct or has a disability that is beyond the scope of the complaint, the committee must refer the new matter to the chief judge for action under Rule 5 or Rule 11.

(b) Criminal Conduct. If the committee's investigation concerns conduct that may be a crime, the committee must consult with the appropriate prosecutorial authorities to the extent permitted by the Act to avoid compromising any criminal investigation. The committee has final authority over the timing and extent of its investigation and the formulation of its recommendations.

(c) Staff. The committee may arrange for staff assistance to conduct the investigation. It may use existing staff of the judicial branch or may hire special staff through the Director of the Administrative Office of the United States Courts.

(d) Delegation of Subpoena Power; Contempt. The chief judge may delegate the authority to exercise the committee's subpoena powers. The judicial council or special committee may institute a contempt proceeding under 28 U.S.C. § 332(d) against anyone who fails to comply with a subpoena.

[Adopted March 11, 2008, effective April 10, 2008.]

Commentary on Rule 13

This Rule is adapted from the Illustrative Rules.

Rule 13, as well as Rules 14, 15, and 16, are concerned with the way in which a special committee carries out its mission. They reflect the view that a special committee has two roles that are separated in ordinary litigation. First, the committee has an investigative role of the kind that is characteristically left to executive branch agencies or discovery by civil litigants. 28 U.S.C. § 353(c). Second, it has a formalized fact-finding and recommendation-of-disposition role that is characteristically left to juries, judges, or arbitrators. Id. Rule 13 generally governs the investigative stage. Even though the same body has responsibility for both roles under the Act, it is important to distinguish between them in order to ensure that appropriate rights are afforded at appropriate times to the subject judge.

One of the difficult questions that can arise is the relationship between proceedings under the Act and criminal investigations. Rule 13(b) assigns responsibility for coordination to the special committee in cases in which criminal conduct is suspected, but gives the committee the authority to determine the appropriate pace of its activity in light of any criminal investigation.

Title 28 U.S.C. § 356(a) provides that a special committee will have full subpoena powers as provided in 28 U.S.C. § 332(d). Section 332(d)(1) provides that subpoenas will be issued on behalf of judicial councils by the circuit clerk "at the direction of the chief judge of the circuit or his designee." Rule 13(d) contemplates that, where the chief judge designates someone else as presiding officer of a special committee, the presiding officer also be delegated the authority to direct the circuit clerk to issue subpoenas related to committee proceedings. That is not intended to imply, however, that the decision to use the subpoena power is exercisable by the presiding officer alone. See Rule 12(g).

RULE 14. CONDUCT OF HEARINGS BY SPECIAL COMMITTEE

(a) Purpose of Hearings. The committee may hold hearings to take testimony and receive other evidence, to hear argument, or both. If the committee is investigating allegations against more than one judge, it may hold joint or separate hearings.

(b) Committee Evidence. Subject to Rule 15, the committee must obtain material, nonredundant evidence in the form it considers appropriate. In the committee's discretion, evidence may be obtained by committee members, staff, or both. Witnesses offering testimonial evidence may include the complainant and the subject judge.

(c) Counsel for Witnesses. The subject judge has the right to counsel. The special committee has discretion to decide whether other witnesses may have counsel present when they testify.

(d) Witness Fees. Witness fees must be paid as provided in 28 U.S.C. § 1821.

(e) Oath. All testimony taken at a hearing must be given under oath or affirmation.

(f) Rules of Evidence. The Federal Rules of Evidence do not apply to special-committee hearings.

(g) Record and Transcript. A record and transcript must be made of all hearings.

[Adopted March 11, 2008, effective April 10, 2008.]

Commentary on Rule 14

This Rule is adapted from Section 353 of the Act and the Illustrative Rules.

Rule 14 is concerned with the conduct of fact-finding hearings. Special-committee hearings will normally be held only after the investigative work has been completed and the committee has concluded that there is sufficient evidence to warrant a formal fact-finding proceeding. Special-committee proceedings are primarily inquisitorial rather than adversarial. Accordingly, the Federal Rules of Evidence do not apply to such hearings. Inevitably, a hearing will have something of an adversary character. Nevertheless, that tendency should be moderated to the extent possible. Even though a proceeding will commonly have investigative and hearing stages, committee members should not regard themselves as prosecutors one day and judges the next. Their duty—and that of their staff—is at all times to be impartial seekers of the truth.

Rule 14(b) contemplates that material evidence will be obtained by the committee and presented in the form of affidavits, live testimony, etc. Staff or others who are organizing the hearings should regard it as their role to present evidence representing the entire picture. With respect to testimonial evidence, the subject judge should normally be called as a committee witness. Cases may arise in which the judge will not testify voluntarily. In such cases, subpoena powers are available, subject to the normal testimonial privileges. Although Rule 15(c) recognizes the subject judge's statutory right to call witnesses on his or her own behalf, exercise of this right should not usually be necessary.

RULE 15. RIGHTS OF SUBJECT JUDGE

(a) Notice.

(1) *Generally.* The subject judge must receive written notice of:

(A) the appointment of a special committee under Rule 11(f);

(B) the expansion of the scope of an investigation under Rule 13(a);

(C) any hearing under Rule 14, including its purposes, the names of any witnesses the committee intends to call, and the text of any statements that have been taken from those witnesses.

(2) *Suggestion of Additional Witnesses.* The subject judge may suggest additional witnesses to the committee.

(b) Report of the Special Committee. The subject judge must be sent a copy of the special committee's report when it is filed with the judicial council.

(c) Presentation of Evidence. At any hearing held under Rule 14, the subject judge has the right to present evidence, to compel the attendance of witnesses, and to compel the production of documents. At the request of the subject judge, the chief judge or the judge's designee must direct the circuit clerk to issue a subpoena to a witness under 28 U.S.C. § 332(d)(1). The subject judge must be given the opportunity to cross-examine committee witnesses, in person or by counsel.

(d) Presentation of Argument. The subject judge may submit written argument to the special committee and must be given a reasonable opportunity to present oral argument at an appropriate stage of the investigation.

(e) Attendance at Hearings. The subject judge has the right to attend any hearing held under Rule 14 and to receive copies of the transcript, of any documents introduced, and of any written arguments submitted by the complainant to the committee.

(f) Representation by Counsel. The subject judge may choose to be represented by counsel in the exercise of any right enumerated in this Rule. As provided in Rule 20(e), the United States may bear the costs of the representation.

[Adopted March 11, 2008, effective April 10, 2008.]

Commentary on Rule 15

This Rule is adapted from the Act and the Illustrative Rules.

The Act states that these Rules must contain provisions requiring that "the judge whose conduct is the subject of a complaint ... be afforded an opportunity to appear (in person or by counsel) at proceedings conducted by the investigating panel, to present oral and documentary evidence, to compel the attendance of witnesses or the production of documents, to cross-examine witnesses, and to present argument orally or in writing." 28 U.S.C. § 358(b)(2). To implement this provision, Rule 15(e) gives the judge the right to attend any hearing held for the purpose of receiving evidence of record or hearing argument under Rule 14.

The Act does not require that the subject judge be permitted to attend all proceedings of the special committee. Accordingly, the Rules do not give a right to attend other proceedings—for example, meetings at which the committee is engaged in investigative activity, such as interviewing persons to learn whether they ought to be called as witnesses or examining for relevance purposes documents delivered pursuant to a subpoena duces tecum, or meetings in which the committee is deliberating on the evidence or its recommendations.

RULE 16. RIGHTS OF COMPLAINANT IN INVESTIGATION

(a) Notice. The complainant must receive written notice of the investigation as provided in Rule 11(g)(1). When the special committee's report to the judicial council is filed, the complainant must be notified of the filing. The judicial council may, in its discretion, provide a copy of the report of a special committee to the complainant.

(b) Opportunity to Provide Evidence. If the committee determines that the complainant may have evidence that does not already exist in writing, a representative of the committee must interview the complainant.

(c) Presentation of Argument. The complainant may submit written argument to the special committee. In its discretion, the special committee may permit the complainant to offer oral argument.

(d) Representation by Counsel. A complainant may submit written argument through counsel and, if permitted to offer oral argument, may do so through counsel.

(e) Cooperation. In exercising its discretion under this Rule, a special committee may take into account the degree of the complainant's cooperation in preserving the confidentiality of the proceedings, including the identity of the subject judge.

[Adopted March 11, 2008, effective April 10, 2008.]

Commentary on Rule 16

This Rule is adapted from the Act and the Illustrative Rules.

In accordance with the view of the process as fundamentally administrative and inquisitorial, these Rules do not give the complainant the rights of a party to litigation, and leave the complainant's role largely to the discretion of the special committee. However, Rule 16(b) provides that, where a special committee has been appointed and it determines that the complainant may have additional evidence, the complainant must be interviewed by a representative of the committee. Such an interview may be in person or by telephone, and the representative of the committee may be either a member or staff.

Rule 16 does not contemplate that the complainant will ordinarily be permitted to attend proceedings of the special committee except when testifying or presenting oral argument. A special committee may exercise its discretion to permit the complainant to be present at its proceedings, or to permit the complainant, individually or through counsel, to participate in the examination or cross-examination of witnesses.

The Act authorizes an exception to the normal confidentiality provisions where the judicial council in its discretion provides a copy of the report of the special committee to the complainant and to the subject judge. 28 U.S.C. § 360(a)(1). However, the Rules do not entitle the complainant to a copy of the special committee's report.

In exercising their discretion regarding the role of the complainant, the special committee and the judicial council should protect the confidentiality of the complaint process. As a consequence, subsection (e) provides that a special committee may consider the degree to which a complainant has cooperated in preserving the confidentiality of the proceedings in determining what role beyond the minimum required by these Rules should be given to that complainant.

RULE 17. SPECIAL–COMMITTEE REPORT

The committee must file with the judicial council a comprehensive report of its investigation, including findings and recommendations for council action. The report must be accompanied by a statement of the vote by which it was adopted, any separate or dissenting statements of committee members, and the record of any hearings held under Rule 14. A copy of the report and accompanying statement must be sent to the Judicial Conference Committee on Judicial Conduct and Disability.

[Adopted March 11, 2008, effective April 10, 2008.]

Commentary on Rule 17

This Rule is adapted from the Illustrative Rules and is self-explanatory. The provision for sending a copy of the special-committee report and accompanying statement to the Judicial Conference Committee is new.

ARTICLE V. JUDICIAL–COUNCIL REVIEW

RULE 18. PETITIONS FOR REVIEW OF CHIEF JUDGE DISPOSITIONS UNDER RULE 11(C), (D), OR (E)

(a) Petitions for Review. After the chief judge issues an order under Rule 11(c), (d), or (e), a complainant or subject judge may petition the judicial council of the circuit to review the order. By rules promulgated under 28 U.S.C. § 358, the judicial council may refer a petition for review filed under this Rule to a panel of no fewer than five members of the council, at least two of whom must be district judges.

(b) When to File; Form; Where to File. A petition for review must be filed in the office of the circuit clerk within 35 days of the date on the clerk's letter informing the parties of the chief judge's order. The petition should be in letter form, addressed to the circuit clerk, and in an envelope marked "Misconduct Petition" or "Disability Petition." The name of the subject judge must not be shown on the envelope. The letter should be typewritten or otherwise legible. It should begin with "I hereby petition the judicial council for review of ..." and state the reasons why the petition should be granted. It must be signed.

(c) Receipt and Distribution of Petition. A circuit clerk who receives a petition for review filed within the time allowed and in proper form must:

(1) acknowledge its receipt and send a copy to the complainant or subject judge, as the case may be;

(2) promptly distribute to each member of the judicial council, or its relevant panel, except for any member disqualified under Rule 25, or make available in the manner provided by local rule, the following materials:

    (A) copies of the complaint;

    (B) all materials obtained by the chief judge in connection with the inquiry;

    (C) the chief judge's order disposing of the complaint;

    (D) any memorandum in support of the chief judge's order;

    (E) the petition for review; and

    (F) an appropriate ballot;

(3) send the petition for review to the Judicial Conference Committee on Judicial Conduct and Disability. Unless the Judicial Conference Committee requests them, the clerk will not send copies of the materials obtained by the chief judge.

(d) Untimely Petition. The clerk must refuse to accept a petition that is received after the deadline in (b).

(e) Timely Petition Not in Proper Form. When the clerk receives a petition filed within the time allowed but in a form that is improper to a degree that would substantially impair its consideration by the judicial council—such as a document that is ambiguous about whether it is intended to be a petition for review—the clerk must acknowledge its receipt, call the filer's attention to the deficiencies, and give the filer the opportunity to correct the deficiencies within 21 days of the date of the clerk's letter about the deficiencies or within the original deadline for filing the petition, whichever is later. If the deficiencies are corrected within the time allowed, the clerk will proceed according to paragraphs (a) and (c) of this Rule. If the deficiencies are not corrected, the clerk must reject the petition.

[Adopted March 11, 2008, effective April 10, 2008.]

Commentary on Rule 18

Rule 18 is adapted largely from the Illustrative Rules.

Subsection (a) permits a subject judge, as well as the complainant, to petition for review of a chief judge's order dismissing a complaint under Rule 11(c), or concluding that appropriate corrective action or intervening events have remedied or mooted the problems raised by the complaint pursuant to Rule 11(d) or (e). Although the subject judge may ostensibly be vindicated by the dismissal or conclusion of a complaint, a chief judge's order may include language disagreeable to the subject judge. For example, an order may dismiss a complaint, but state that the subject judge did in fact engage in misconduct. Accordingly, a subject judge may wish to object to the content of the order and is given the opportunity to petition the judicial council of the circuit for review.

Subsection (b) contains a time limit of thirty-five days to file a petition for review. It is important to establish a time limit on petitions for review of chief judges' dispositions in order to provide finality to the process. If the complaint requires an investigation, the investigation should proceed; if it does not, the subject judge should know that the matter is closed.

The standards for timely filing under the Federal Rules of Appellate Procedure should be applied to petitions for review. See Fed. R. App. P. 25(a)(2)(A) and (C).

Rule 18(e) provides for an automatic extension of the time limit imposed under subsection (b) if a person files a petition that is rejected for failure to comply with formal requirements.

RULE 19. JUDICIAL–COUNCIL DISPOSITION OF PETITIONS FOR REVIEW

(a) Rights of Subject Judge. At any time after a complainant files a petition for review, the subject judge may file a written response with the circuit clerk. The clerk must promptly distribute copies of the response to each member of the judicial council or of the relevant panel, unless that member is disqualified under Rule 25. Copies must also be distributed to the chief judge, to the complainant, and to the Judicial Conference Committee on Judicial Conduct and Disability. The subject judge must not otherwise communicate with individual council members about the matter. The subject judge must be given copies of any communications to the judicial council from the complainant.

(b) Judicial–Council Action. After considering a petition for review and the materials before it, a judicial council may:

(1) affirm the chief judge's disposition by denying the petition;

(2) return the matter to the chief judge with directions to conduct a further inquiry under Rule 11(b) or to identify a complaint under Rule 5;

(3) return the matter to the chief judge with directions to appoint a special committee under Rule 11(f); or

(4) in exceptional circumstances, take other appropriate action.

(c) Notice of Council Decision. Copies of the judicial council's order, together with any accompanying memorandum in support of the order or separate concurring or dissenting statements, must be given to the complainant, the subject judge, and the Judicial Conference Committee on Judicial Conduct and Disability.

(d) Memorandum of Council Decision. If the council's order affirms the chief judge's disposition, a supporting memorandum must be prepared only if the judicial council concludes that there is a need to supplement the chief judge's explanation. A memorandum supporting a council order must not include the name of the complainant or the subject judge.

(e) Review of Judicial–Council Decision. If the judicial council's decision is adverse to the petitioner, and if no member of the council dissented on the ground that a special committee should be appointed under Rule 11(f), the complainant must be notified that he or she has no right to seek review of the decision. If there was a dissent, the petitioner must be informed that he or she can file a petition for review under Rule 21(b) solely on the issue of whether a special committee should be appointed.

(f) Public Availability of Judicial–Council Decision. Materials related to the council's decision must be made public to the extent, at the time, and in the manner set forth in Rule 24.

[Adopted March 11, 2008, effective April 10, 2008.]

Commentary on Rule 19

This Rule is largely adapted from the Act and is self-explanatory.

The council should ordinarily review the decision of the chief judge on the merits, treating the petition for review for all practical purposes as an appeal. The judicial council may respond to a petition by affirming the chief judge's order, remanding the matter, or, in exceptional cases, taking other appropriate action.

RULE 20. JUDICIAL–COUNCIL CONSIDERATION OF REPORTS AND RECOMMENDATIONS OF SPECIAL COMMITTEES

(a) Rights of Subject Judge. Within 21 days after the filing of the report of a special committee, the subject judge may send a written response to the members of the judicial council. The judge must also be given an opportunity to present argument through counsel, written or oral, as determined by the council. The judge must not otherwise communicate with council members about the matter.

(b) Judicial–Council Action.

(1) *Discretionary Actions.* Subject to the judge's rights set forth in subsection (a), the judicial council may:

(A) dismiss the complaint because:

(i) even if the claim is true, the claimed conduct is not conduct prejudicial to the effective and expeditious administration of the business of the courts and does not indicate a mental or physical disability resulting in inability to discharge the duties of office;

(ii) the complaint is directly related to the merits of a decision or procedural ruling;

(iii) the facts on which the complaint is based have not been established; or

(iv) the complaint is otherwise not appropriate for consideration under 28 U.S.C. §§ 351–364.

(B) conclude the proceeding because appropriate corrective action has been taken or intervening events have made the proceeding unnecessary.

(C) refer the complaint to the Judicial Conference of the United States with the council's recommendations for action.

(D) take remedial action to ensure the effective and expeditious administration of the business of the courts, including:

(i) censuring or reprimanding the subject judge, either by private communication or by public announcement;

(ii) ordering that no new cases be assigned to the subject judge for a limited, fixed period;

(iii) in the case of a magistrate judge, ordering the chief judge of the district court to take action specified by the council, including the initiation of removal proceedings under 28 U.S.C. § 631(i) or 42 U.S.C. § 300aa–12(c)(2);

(iv) in the case of a bankruptcy judge, removing the judge from office under 28 U.S.C. § 152(e);

(v) in the case of a circuit or district judge, requesting the judge to retire voluntarily with the provision (if necessary) that ordinary length-of-service requirements will be waived; and

(vi) in the case of a circuit or district judge who is eligible to retire but does not do so, certifying the disability of the judge under 28 U.S.C. § 372(b) so that an additional judge may be appointed.

(E) take any combination of actions described in (b)(1)(A)–(D) of this Rule that is within its power.

(2) *Mandatory Actions.* A judicial council must refer a complaint to the Judicial Conference if the council determines that a circuit judge or district judge may have engaged in conduct that:

(A) might constitute ground for impeachment; or

(B) in the interest of justice, is not amenable to resolution by the judicial council.

(c) **Inadequate Basis for Decision.** If the judicial council finds that a special committee's report, recommendations, and record provide an inadequate basis for decision, it may return the matter to the committee for further investigation and a new report, or it may conduct further investigation. If the judicial council decides to conduct further investigation, the subject judge must be given adequate prior notice in writing of that decision and of the general scope and purpose of the additional investigation. The judicial council's conduct of the additional investigation must generally accord with the procedures and powers set forth in Rules 13 through 16 for the conduct of an investigation by a special committee.

(d) **Council Vote.** Council action must be taken by a majority of those members of the council who are not disqualified. A decision to remove a bankruptcy judge from office requires a majority vote of all the members of the council.

(e) **Recommendation for Fee Reimbursement.** If the complaint has been finally dismissed or concluded under (b)(1)(A) or (B) of this Rule, and if the subject judge so requests, the judicial council may recommend that the Director of the Administrative Office of the United States Courts use funds appropriated to the Judiciary to reimburse the judge for reasonable expenses incurred during the investigation, when those expenses would not have been incurred but for the requirements of the Act and these Rules. Reasonable expenses include attorneys' fees and expenses related to a successful defense or prosecution of a proceeding under Rule 21(a) or (b).

(f) **Council Action.** Council action must be by written order. Unless the council finds that extraordinary reasons would make it contrary to the interests of justice, the order must be accompanied by a memorandum setting forth the factual determinations on which it is based and the reasons for the council action. The order and the supporting memorandum must be provided to the complainant, the subject judge, and the Judicial Conference Committee on Judicial Conduct and Disability. The complainant and the subject judge must be notified of any right to review of the judicial council's decision as provided in Rule 21(b).

[Adopted March 11, 2008, effective April 10, 2008.]

Commentary on Rule 20

This Rule is largely adapted from the Illustrative Rules.

Rule 20(a) provides that within twenty-one days after the filing of the report of a special committee, the subject judge may address a written response to all of the members of the judicial council. The subject judge must also be given an opportunity to present oral argument to the council, personally or through counsel. The subject judge may not otherwise communicate with council members about the matter.

Rule 20(c) provides that if the judicial council decides to conduct an additional investigation, the subject judge must be given adequate prior notice in writing of that decision and of the general scope and purpose of the additional investigation. The conduct of the investigation will be generally in accordance with the procedures set forth in Rules 13 through 16 for the conduct of an investigation by a special committee. However, if hearings are held, the council may limit testimony or the presentation of evidence to avoid unnecessary repetition of testimony and evidence before the special committee.

Rule 20(d) provides that council action must be taken by a majority of those members of the council who are not disqualified, except that a decision to remove a bankruptcy judge from office requires a majority of all the members of the council as required by 28 U.S.C. § 152(e). However, it is inappropriate to apply a similar rule to the less severe actions that a judicial council may take under the Act. If some members of the council are disqualified in the matter, their disqualification should not be given the effect of a vote against council action.

With regard to Rule 20(e), the judicial council, on the request of the subject judge, may recommend to the Director of the Administrative Office of the United States Courts that the subject judge be reimbursed for reasonable expenses, including attorneys' fees, incurred. The judicial council has the authority to recommend such reimbursement where, after investigation by a special committee, the complaint has been finally dismissed or concluded under subsection (b)(1)(A) or (B) of this Rule. It is contemplated that such reimbursement may be provided for the successful prosecution or defense of a proceeding under Rule 21(a) or (b), in other words, one that results in a Rule 20(b)(1)(A) or (B) dismissal or conclusion.

Rule 20(f) requires that council action normally be supported with a memorandum of factual determinations and reasons and that notice of the action be given to the complainant and the subject judge. Rule 20(f) also requires that the notification to the complainant and the subject judge include notice of any right to petition for review of the council's decision under Rule 21(b).

ARTICLE VI.   REVIEW BY JUDICIAL CONFERENCE COMMITTEE ON CONDUCT AND DISABILITY

RULE 21.   COMMITTEE ON JUDICIAL CONDUCT AND DISABILITY

(a) **Review by Committee.** The Committee on Judicial Conduct and Disability, consisting of seven members, considers and disposes of all petitions for review under (b) of this Rule, in conformity with the Committee's jurisdictional statement. Its disposition of petitions for review is ordinarily final. The Judicial Conference of the United States may, in its sole discretion, review any such Committee decision, but a complainant or subject judge does not have a right to this review.

(b) **Reviewable Matters.**

(1) *Upon Petition.* A complainant or subject judge may petition the Committee for review of a judicial-council order entered in accordance with:

(A) Rule 20(b)(1)(A), (B), (D), or (E); or

(B) Rule 19(b)(1) or (4) if one or more members of the judicial council dissented from the order on the ground that a special committee should be appointed under Rule 11(f); in that event, the Committee's review will be limited to the issue of whether a special committee should be appointed.

(2) *Upon Committee's Initiative.* At its initiative and in its sole discretion, the Committee may review any judicial-council order entered under Rule 19(b)(1) or (4), but only to determine whether a special committee should be appointed. Before undertaking the review, the Committee must invite that judicial council to explain why it believes the appointment of a special committee is unnecessary, unless the reasons are clearly stated in the judicial council's order denying the petition for review. If the Committee believes that it would benefit from a submission by the subject judge, it may issue an appropriate request. If the Committee determines that a special committee should be appointed, the Committee must issue a written decision giving its reasons.

(c) **Committee Vote.** Any member of the Committee from the same circuit as the subject judge is disqualified from considering or voting on a petition for review. Committee decisions under (b) of this Rule must be by majority vote of the qualified Committee members. If only six members are qualified to vote on a petition for review, the decision must be made by a majority of a panel of five members drawn from a randomly selected list that rotates after each decision by a panel drawn from the list. The mem-

bers who will determine the petition must be selected based on committee membership as of the date on which the petition is received. Those members selected to hear the petition should serve in that capacity until final disposition of the petition, whether or not their term of committee membership has ended. If only four members are qualified to vote, the Chief Justice must appoint, if available, an ex-member of the Committee or, if not, another United States judge to consider the petition.

(d) **Additional Investigation.** Except in extraordinary circumstances, the Committee will not conduct an additional investigation. The Committee may return the matter to the judicial council with directions to undertake an additional investigation. If the Committee conducts an additional investigation, it will exercise the powers of the Judicial Conference under 28 U.S.C. § 331.

(e) **Oral Argument; Personal Appearance.** There is ordinarily no oral argument or personal appearance before the Committee. In its discretion, the Committee may permit written submissions from the complainant or subject judge.

(f) **Committee Decisions.** Committee decisions under this Rule must be transmitted promptly to the Judicial Conference of the United States. Other distribution will be by the Administrative Office at the direction of the Committee chair.

(g) **Finality.** All orders of the Judicial Conference or of the Committee (when the Conference does not exercise its power of review) are final.

[Adopted March 11, 2008, effective April 10, 2008.]

Commentary on Rule 21

This Rule is largely self-explanatory.

Rule 21(a) is intended to clarify that the delegation of power to the Judicial Conference Committee on Judicial Conduct and Disability to dispose of petitions does not preclude review of such dispositions by the Conference. However, there is no right to such review in any party.

Rules 21(b)(1)(B) and (b)(2) are intended to fill a jurisdictional gap as to review of dismissals or conclusions of complaints under Rule 19(b)(1) or (4). Where one or more members of a judicial council reviewing a petition have dissented on the ground that a special committee should have been appointed, the complainant or subject judge has the right to petition for review by the Committee but only as to that issue. Under Rule 21(b)(2), the Judicial Conference Committee on Judicial Conduct and Disability may review such a dismissal or conclusion in its sole discretion, whether or not such a dissent occurred, and only as to the appointment of a special committee. No party has a right to such review, and such review will be rare.

Rule 21(c) provides for review only by Committee members from circuits other than that of the subject judge. To avoid tie votes, the Committee will decide petitions for review by rotating panels of five when only six members are qualified. If only four members are qualified, the Chief Justice must appoint an additional judge to consider that petition for review.

Under this Rule, all Committee decisions are final in that they are unreviewable unless the Judicial Conference, in its discretion, decides to review a decision. Committee decisions, however, do not necessarily constitute final action on a complaint for purposes of Rule 24.

RULE 22. PROCEDURES FOR REVIEW

(a) Filing a Petition for Review. A petition for review of a judicial-council decision may be filed by sending a brief written statement to the Judicial Conference Committee on Judicial Conduct and Disability, addressed to:

> Judicial Conference Committee on Judicial Conduct and Disability
>
> Attn: Office of General Counsel
>
> Administrative Office of the United States Courts
>
> One Columbus Circle, NE
>
> Washington, D.C. 20544

The Administrative Office will send a copy of the petition to the complainant or subject judge, as the case may be.

(b) Form and Contents of Petition for Review. No particular form is required. The petition must contain a short statement of the basic facts underlying the complaint, the history of its consideration before the appropriate judicial council, a copy of the judicial council's decision, and the grounds on which the petitioner seeks review. The petition for review must specify the date and docket number of the judicial-council order for which review is sought. The petitioner may attach any documents or correspondence arising in the course of the proceeding before the judicial council or its special committee. A petition should not normally exceed 20 pages plus necessary attachments.

(c) Time. A petition must be submitted within 63 days of the date of the order for which review is sought.

(d) Copies. Seven copies of the petition for review must be submitted, at least one of which must be signed by the petitioner or his or her attorney. If the petitioner submits a signed declaration of inability to pay the expense of duplicating the petition, the Administrative Office must accept the original petition and must reproduce copies at its expense.

(e) Action on Receipt of Petition for Review. The Administrative Office must acknowledge receipt of a petition for review submitted under this Rule, notify the chair of the Judicial Conference Committee on Judicial Conduct and Disability, and distribute the petition to the members of the Committee for their deliberation.

[Adopted March 11, 2008, effective April 10, 2008.]

Commentary on Rule 22

Rule 22 is self-explanatory.

ARTICLE VII. MISCELLANEOUS RULES

RULE 23. CONFIDENTIALITY

(a) General Rule. The consideration of a complaint by the chief judge, a special committee, the judicial council, or the Judicial Conference Committee on Judicial Conduct and Disability is confidential. Information about this consideration must not be disclosed by any judge or employee of the judicial branch or by any person who records or transcribes testimony except as allowed by these Rules. In extraordinary circumstances, a chief judge may disclose the existence of a proceeding under these Rules when necessary to maintain public confidence in the federal judiciary's ability to redress misconduct or disability.

(b) Files. All files related to complaints must be separately maintained with appropriate security precautions to ensure confidentiality.

(c) Disclosure in Decisions. Except as otherwise provided in Rule 24, written decisions of the chief judge, the judicial council, or the Judicial Conference Committee on Judicial Conduct and Disability, and dissenting opinions or separate statements of members of the council or Committee may contain information and exhibits that the authors consider appropriate for inclusion, and the information and exhibits may be made public.

(d) Availability to Judicial Conference. On request of the Judicial Conference or its Committee on Judicial Conduct and Disability, the circuit clerk must furnish any requested records related to a complaint. For auditing purposes, the circuit clerk must provide access to the Committee to records of proceedings under the Act at the site where the records are kept.

(e) Availability to District Court. If the judicial council directs the initiation of proceedings for removal of a magistrate judge under Rule 20(b)(1)(D)(iii), the circuit clerk must provide to the chief judge of the district court copies of the report of the special committee and any other documents and records that were before the judicial council at the time of its decision. On request of the chief judge of the district court, the judicial council may authorize release to that chief judge of any other records relating to the investigation.

(f) Impeachment Proceedings. If the Judicial Conference determines that consideration of impeachment may be warranted, it must transmit the record of all relevant proceedings to the Speaker of the House of Representatives.

(g) Subject Judge's Consent. If both the subject judge and the chief judge consent in writing, any materials from the files may be disclosed to any person. In any such disclosure, the chief judge may require that the identity of the complainant, or of witnesses in an investigation conducted by a chief judge, a special committee, or the judicial council, not be revealed.

(h) Disclosure in Special Circumstances. The Judicial Conference, its Committee on Judicial Conduct and Disability, or a judicial council may authorize disclosure of information about the consideration of a complaint, including the papers, documents, and transcripts relating to the investigation, to the extent that disclosure is justified by special circumstances and is not prohibited by the Act. Disclosure may be made to judicial researchers engaged in the study or evaluation of experience under the Act and related modes of judicial discipline, but only where the study or evaluation has been specifically approved by the Judicial Conference or by the Judicial Conference Committee on Judicial Conduct and Disability. Appropriate steps must be taken to protect the identities of the subject judge, the complainant, and witnesses from public disclosure. Other appropriate safeguards to protect against the dissemination of confidential information may be imposed.

(i) Disclosure of Identity by Subject Judge. Nothing in this Rule precludes the subject judge from acknowledging that he or she is the judge referred to in documents made public under Rule 24.

(j) Assistance and Consultation. Nothing in this Rule precludes the chief judge or judicial council acting on a complaint filed under the Act from seeking the help of qualified staff or from consulting other judges who may be helpful in the disposition of the complaint.

[Adopted March 11, 2008, effective April 10, 2008.]

Commentary on Rule 23

Rule 23 was adapted from the Illustrative Rules.

The Act applies a rule of confidentiality to "papers, documents, and records of proceedings related to investigations conducted under this chapter" and states that they may not be disclosed "by any person in any proceeding," with enumerated exceptions. 28 U.S.C. § 360(a). Three questions arise: Who is bound by the confidentiality rule, what proceedings are subject to the rule, and who is within the circle of people who may have access to information without breaching the rule?

With regard to the first question, Rule 23(a) provides that judges, employees of the judicial branch, and those persons involved in recording proceedings and preparing transcripts are obliged to respect the confidentiality requirement. This of course includes subject judges who do not consent to identification under Rule 23(i).

With regard to the second question, Rule 23(a) applies the rule of confidentiality broadly to consideration of a complaint at any stage.

With regard to the third question, there is no barrier of confidentiality among a chief judge, judicial council, the Judicial Conference, and the Judicial Conference Committee on Judicial Conduct and Disability. Each may have access to any of the confidential records for use in their consideration of a referred matter, a petition for review, or monitoring the administration of the Act. A district court may have similar access if the judicial council orders the district court to initiate proceedings to remove a magistrate judge from office, and Rule 23(e) so provides.

In extraordinary circumstances, a chief judge may disclose the existence of a proceeding under these Rules. The disclosure of such information in high-visibility or controversial cases is to reassure the public that the federal judiciary is capable of redressing judicial misconduct or disability. Moreover, the confidentiality requirement does not prevent the chief judge from "communicat[ing] orally or in writing with . . . [persons] who may have knowledge of the matter," as part of a limited inquiry conducted by the chief judge under Rule 11(b).

Rule 23 recognizes that there must be some exceptions to the Act's confidentiality requirement. For example, the Act requires that certain orders and the reasons for them must be made public. 28 U.S.C. § 360(b). Rule 23(c) makes it explicit that memoranda supporting chief judge and council orders, as well as dissenting opinions and separate statements, may contain references to information that would otherwise be confidential and that such information may be made public. However, subsection (c) is subject to Rule 24(a) which provides the general rule regarding the public availability of decisions. For example, the name of a subject judge cannot be made public in a decision if disclosure of the name is prohibited by that Rule.

The Act makes clear that there is a barrier of confidentiality between the judicial branch and the legislative. It provides that material may be disclosed to Congress only if it is believed necessary to an impeachment investigation or trial of a judge. 28 U.S.C. § 360(a)(2). Accordingly, Section 355(b) of the Act requires the Judicial Conference to transmit the record of the proceeding to the House of Representatives if the Conference believes that impeachment of a subject judge may be appropriate. Rule 23(f) implements this requirement.

The Act provides that confidential materials may be disclosed if authorized in writing by the subject judge and by the chief judge. 28 U.S.C. § 360(a)(3). Rule 23(g) implements this requirement. Once the subject judge has consented to the disclosure of confidential materials related to a complaint, the chief judge ordinarily will refuse consent only to the extent necessary to protect the confidentiality interests of the complainant or of witnesses who have testified in investigatory proceedings or who have provided information in response to a limited inquiry undertaken pursuant to Rule 11. It will generally be necessary, therefore, for the chief judge to require that the identities of the complainant or of such witnesses, as well as any identifying information, be shielded in any materials disclosed, except insofar as the chief judge has secured the consent of the complainant or of a particular witness to disclosure, or there is a demonstrated need for disclosure of the information that, in the judgment of the chief judge, outweighs the confidentiality interest of the complainant or of a particular witness (as may be the case where the complainant is delusional or where the complainant or a particular witness has already demonstrated a lack of concern about maintaining the confidentiality of the proceedings).

Rule 23(h) permits disclosure of additional information in circumstances not enumerated. For example, disclosure may be appropriate to permit a prosecution for perjury based on testimony given before a special committee. Another example might involve evidence of criminal conduct by a judge discovered by a special committee.

Subsection (h) also permits the authorization of disclosure of information about the consideration of a complaint, including the papers, documents, and transcripts relating to the investigation, to judicial researchers engaged in the study or evaluation of experience under the Act and related modes of judicial discipline. The Rule envisions disclosure of information from the official record of complaint proceedings to a limited category of persons for appropriately authorized research purposes only, and with appropriate safeguards to protect individual identities in any published research results that ensue. In authorizing disclosure, the judicial council may refuse to release particular materials when such release would be contrary to the interests of justice, or that constitute purely internal communications. The Rule does not envision disclosure of purely internal communications between judges and their colleagues and staff.

Under Rule 23(j), chief judges and judicial councils may seek staff assistance or consult with other judges who may be helpful in the process of complaint disposition; the confidentiality requirement does not preclude this. The chief judge, for example, may properly seek the advice and assistance of another judge who the chief judge deems to be in the best position to communicate with the subject judge in an attempt to bring about corrective action. As another example, a new chief judge may wish to confer with a predecessor to learn how similar complaints have been handled. In consulting with other judges, of course, the chief judge should disclose information regarding the complaint only to the extent the chief judge deems necessary under the circumstances.

RULE 24. PUBLIC AVAILABILITY OF DECISIONS

(a) General Rule; Specific Cases. When final action has been taken on a complaint and it is no longer subject to review, all orders entered by the chief judge and judicial council, including any supporting memoranda and any dissenting opinions or separate statements by members of the judicial council, must be made public, with the following exceptions:

(1) if the complaint is finally dismissed under Rule 11(c) without the appointment of a special committee, or if it is concluded under Rule 11(d) because of voluntary corrective action, the publicly available materials must not disclose the name of the subject judge without his or her consent.

(2) if the complaint is concluded because of intervening events, or dismissed at any time after a special committee is appointed, the judicial council must determine whether the name of the subject judge should be disclosed.

(3) if the complaint is finally disposed of by a privately communicated censure or reprimand, the publicly available materials must not disclose either the name of the subject judge or the text of the reprimand.

(4) if the complaint is finally disposed of under Rule 20(b)(1)(D) by any action other than private censure or reprimand, the text of the dispositive order must be included in the materials made public, and the name of the subject judge must be disclosed.

(5) the name of the complainant must not be disclosed in materials made public under this Rule unless the chief judge orders disclosure.

(b) Manner of Making Public. The orders described in (a) must be made public by placing them in a publicly accessible file in the office of the circuit clerk or by placing the orders on the court's public website. If the orders appear to have precedential value, the chief judge may cause them to be published. In addition, the Judicial Conference Committee on Judicial Conduct and Disability will make available on the Federal Judiciary's website, www.uscourts.gov, selected illustrative orders described in paragraph (a), appropriately redacted, to provide additional information to the public on how complaints are addressed under the Act.

(c) Orders of Judicial Conference Committee. Orders of this Committee constituting final action in a complaint proceeding arising from a particular circuit will be made available to the public in the office of the clerk of the relevant court of appeals. The Committee will also make such orders available on the Federal Judiciary's website, www.uscourts.gov. When authorized by the Committee, other orders related to complaint proceedings will similarly be made available.

(d) Complaints Referred to the Judicial Conference of the United States. If a complaint is referred to the Judicial Conference under Rule 20(b)(1)(C) or 20(b)(2), materials relating to the complaint will be made public only if ordered by the Judicial Conference.

[Adopted March 11, 2008, effective April 10, 2008.]

Commentary on Rule 24

Rule 24 is adapted from the Illustrative Rules and the recommendations of the Breyer Committee.

The Act requires the circuits to make available only written orders of a judicial council or the Judicial Conference imposing some form of sanction. 28 U.S.C. § 360(b). The Judicial Conference, however, has long recognized the desirability of public availability of a broader range of orders and other materials. In 1994, the Judicial Conference "urge[d] all circuits and courts covered by the Act to submit to the West Publishing Company, for publication in Federal Reporter 3d, and to Lexis all orders issued pursuant to [the Act] that are deemed by the issuing circuit or court to have significant precedential value to other circuits and courts covered by the Act." Report of the Proceedings of the Judicial Conference of the United States, Mar. 1994, at 28. Following this recommendation, the 2000 revision of the Illustrative Rules contained a public availability provision very similar to Rule 24. In 2002, the Judicial Conference again voted to encourage the circuits "to submit non-routine public orders disposing of complaints of judicial misconduct or disability for publication by on-line and print services." Report of the Proceedings of the Judicial Conference of the United States, Sept. 2002, at 58. The Breyer Committee Report further emphasized that "[p]osting such orders on the judicial branch's public website would not only benefit judges directly, it would also encourage scholarly commentary and analysis of the orders." Breyer Committee Report, 239 F.R.D. at 216. With these considerations in mind, Rule 24 provides for public availability of a wide range of materials.

Rule 24 provides for public availability of orders of the chief judge, the judicial council, and the Judicial Conference Committee on Judicial Conduct and Disability and the texts of any memoranda supporting their orders, together with any dissenting opinions or separate statements by members of the judicial council. However, these orders and memoranda are to be made public only when final action on the complaint has been taken and any right of review has been exhausted. The provision that decisions will be made public only after final action has been taken is designed in part to avoid public disclosure of the existence of pending proceedings. Whether the name of the subject judge is disclosed will then depend on the nature of the final action. If the final action is an order predicated on a finding of misconduct or disability (other than a privately communicated censure or reprimand) the name of the judge must be made public. If the final action is dismissal of the complaint, the name of the subject judge must not be disclosed. Rule 24(a)(1) provides that where a proceeding is concluded under Rule 11(d) by the chief judge on the basis of voluntary corrective action, the name of the subject judge must not be disclosed. Shielding the name of the subject judge in this circumstance should encourage informal disposition.

If a complaint is dismissed as moot, or because intervening events have made action on the complaint unnecessary, after appointment of a special committee, Rule 24(a)(2) allows the judicial council to determine whether the subject judge will be identified. In such a case, no final decision has been rendered on the merits, but it may be in the public interest—particularly if a judicial officer resigns in the course of an investigation—to make the identity of the judge known.

Once a special committee has been appointed, and a proceeding is concluded by the full council on the basis of a remedial order of the council, Rule 24(a)(4) provides for disclosure of the name of the subject judge.

Finally, Rule 24(a)(5) provides that the identity of the complainant will be disclosed only if the chief judge so orders. Identifying the complainant when the subject judge is not identified would increase the likelihood that the identity of the subject judge would become publicly known, thus circumventing the policy of nondisclosure. It may not always be practicable to shield the complainant's identity while making public disclosure of the judicial council's order and supporting memoranda; in some circumstances, moreover, the complainant may consent to public identification.

RULE 25. DISQUALIFICATION

(a) General Rule. Any judge is disqualified from participating in any proceeding under these Rules if the judge, in his or her discretion, concludes that circumstances warrant disqualification. If the complaint is filed by a judge, that judge is disqualified from participating in any consideration of the complaint except to the extent that these Rules provide for a complainant's participation. A chief judge who has identified a complaint under Rule 5 is not automatically disqualified from considering the complaint.

(b) Subject Judge. A subject judge is disqualified from considering the complaint except to the extent that these Rules provide for participation by a subject judge.

(c) Chief Judge Not Disqualified From Considering a Petition for Review of a Chief Judge's Order. If a petition for review of a chief judge's order entered under Rule 11(c), (d), or (e) is filed with the judicial council in accordance with Rule 18, the chief judge is not disqualified from participating in the council's consideration of the petition.

(d) Member of Special Committee Not Disqualified. A member of the judicial council who serves on a special committee, including the chief judge, is not disqualified from participating in council consideration of the committee's report.

(e) Subject Judge's Disqualification After Appointment of a Special Committee. Upon appointment of a special committee, the subject judge is automatically disqualified from participating in any proceeding arising under the Act or these Rules as a member of any special committee, the judicial council of the circuit, the Judicial Conference of the United States, and the Judicial Conference Committee on Judicial Conduct and Disability. The disqualification continues until all proceedings on the complaint against the subject judge are finally terminated with no further right of review.

(f) Substitute for Disqualified Chief Judge. If the chief judge is disqualified from participating in consideration of the complaint, the duties and responsibilities of the chief judge under these Rules must be assigned to the most-senior active circuit judge not disqualified. If all circuit judges in regular active service are disqualified, the judicial council may determine whether to request a transfer under Rule 26, or, in the interest of sound judicial administration, to permit the chief judge to dispose of the complaint on the merits. Members of the judicial council who are named in the complaint may participate in this determination if necessary to obtain a quorum of the judicial council.

(g) Judicial–Council Action When Multiple Judges Are Disqualified. Notwithstanding any other provision in these Rules to the contrary,

(1) a member of the judicial council who is a subject judge may participate in its disposition if:

(A) participation by one or more subject judges is necessary to obtain a quorum of the judicial council;

(B) the judicial council finds that the lack of a quorum is due to the naming of one or more judges in the complaint for the purpose of disqualifying that judge or judges, or to the naming of one or more judges based on their participation in a decision excluded from the definition of misconduct under Rule 3(h)(3); and

(C) the judicial council votes that it is necessary, appropriate, and in the interest of sound judicial administration that one or more subject judges be eligible to act.

(2) otherwise disqualified members may participate in votes taken under (g)(1)(B) and (g)(1)(C).

(h) Disqualification of Members of the Judicial Conference Committee. No member of the Judicial Conference Committee on Judicial Conduct and Disability is disqualified from participating in any proceeding under the Act or these Rules because of consultations with a chief judge, a member of a special committee, or a member of a judicial council about the interpretation or application of the Act or these Rules, unless the member believes that the consultation would prevent fair-minded participation.

[Adopted March 11, 2008, effective April 10, 2008.]

Commentary on Rule 25

Rule 25 is adapted from the Illustrative Rules.

Subsection (a) provides the general rule for disqualification. Of course, a judge is not disqualified simply because the subject judge is on the same court. However, this subsection recognizes that there may be cases in which an appearance of bias or prejudice is created by circumstances other than an association with the subject judge as a colleague. For example, a judge may have a familial relationship with a complainant or subject judge. When such circumstances exist, a judge may, in his or her discretion, conclude that disqualification is warranted.

Subsection (e) makes it clear that the disqualification of the subject judge relates only to the subject judge's participation in any proceeding arising under the Act or these Rules as a member of a special committee, judicial council,

Judicial Conference, or the Judicial Conference Committee. The Illustrative Rule, based on Section 359(a) of the Act, is ambiguous and could be read to disqualify a subject judge from service of any kind on each of the bodies mentioned. This is undoubtedly not the intent of the Act; such a disqualification would be anomalous in light of the Act's allowing a subject judge to continue to decide cases and to continue to exercise the powers of chief circuit or district judge. It would also create a substantial deterrence to the appointment of special committees, particularly where a special committee is needed solely because the chief judge may not decide matters of credibility in his or her review under Rule 11.

While a subject judge is barred by Rule 25(b) from participating in the disposition of the complaint in which he or she is named, Rule 25(e) recognizes that participation in proceedings arising under the Act or these Rules by a judge who is the subject of a special committee investigation may lead to an appearance of self-interest in creating substantive and procedural precedents governing such proceedings; Rule 25(e) bars such participation.

Under the Act, a complaint against the chief judge is to be handled by "that circuit judge in regular active service next senior in date of commission." 28 U.S.C. § 351(c). Rule 25(f) provides that seniority among judges other than the chief judge is to be determined by date of commission, with the result that complaints against the chief judge may be routed to a former chief judge or other judge who was appointed earlier than the chief judge. The Rules do not purport to prescribe who is to preside over meetings of the judicial council. Consequently, where the presiding member of the judicial council is disqualified from participating under these Rules, the order of precedence prescribed by Rule 25(f) for performing "the duties and responsibilities of the chief circuit judge under these Rules" does not apply to determine the acting presiding member of the judicial council. That is a matter left to the internal rules or operating practices of each judicial council. In most cases the most senior active circuit judge who is a member of the judicial council and who is not disqualified will preside.

Sometimes a single complaint is filed against a large group of judges. If the normal disqualification rules are observed in such a case, no court of appeals judge can serve as acting chief judge of the circuit, and the judicial council will be without appellate members. Where the complaint is against all circuit and district judges, under normal rules no member of the judicial council can perform the duties assigned to the council under the statute.

A similar problem is created by successive complaints arising out of the same underlying grievance. For example, a complainant files a complaint against a district judge based on alleged misconduct, and the complaint is dismissed by the chief judge under the statute. The complainant may then file a complaint against the chief judge for dismissing the first complaint, and when that complaint is dismissed by the next senior judge, still a third complaint may be filed. The threat is that the complainant will bump down the seniority ladder until, once again, there is no member of the court of appeals who can serve as acting chief judge for the purpose of the next complaint. Similarly, complaints involving the merits of litigation may involve a series of decisions in which many judges participated or in which a rehearing en banc was denied by the court of appeals, and the complaint may name a majority of the judicial council as subject judges.

In recognition that these multiple-judge complaints are virtually always meritless, the judicial council is given discretion to determine: (1) whether it is necessary, appropriate, and in the interest of sound judicial administration to permit the chief judge to dispose of a complaint where it would otherwise be impossible for any active circuit judge in the circuit to act, and (2) whether it is necessary, appropriate, and in the interest of sound judicial administration, after appropriate findings as to need and justification are made, to permit subject judges of the judicial council to participate in the disposition of a petition for review where it would otherwise be impossible to obtain a quorum.

Applying a rule of necessity in these situations is consistent with the appearance of justice. See, e.g., In re Complaint of Doe, 2 F.3d 308 (8th Cir. Jud. Council 1993) (invoking the rule of necessity); In re Complaint of Judicial Misconduct, No. 91–80464 (9th Cir. Jud. Council 1992) (same). There is no unfairness in permitting the chief judge to dispose of a patently insubstantial complaint that names all active circuit judges in the circuit.

Similarly, there is no unfairness in permitting subject judges, in these circumstances, to participate in the review of a chief judge's dismissal of an insubstantial complaint. The remaining option is to assign the matter to another body. Among other alternatives, the council may request a transfer of the petition under Rule 26. Given the administrative inconvenience and delay involved in these alternatives, it is desirable to request a transfer only if the judicial council determines that the petition is substantial enough to warrant such action.

In the unlikely event that a quorum of the judicial council cannot be obtained to consider the report of a special committee, it would normally be necessary to request a transfer under Rule 26.

Rule 25(h) recognizes that the jurisdictional statement of the Judicial Conference Committee contemplates consultation between members of the Committee and judicial participants in proceedings under the Act and these Rules. Such consultation should not automatically preclude participation by a member in that proceeding.

RULE 26. TRANSFER TO ANOTHER JUDICIAL COUNCIL

In exceptional circumstances, a chief judge or a judicial council may ask the Chief Justice to transfer a proceeding based on a complaint identified under Rule 5 or filed under Rule 6 to the judicial council of another circuit. The request for a transfer may be made at any stage of the proceeding before a reference to the Judicial Conference under Rule 20(b)(1)(C) or 20(b)(2) or a petition for review is filed under Rule 22. Upon receiving such a request, the Chief Justice may refuse the request or select the transferee judicial council, which may then exercise the powers of a judicial council under these Rules.

[Adopted March 11, 2008, effective April 10, 2008.]

Commentary on Rule 26

Rule 26 is new; it implements the Breyer Committee's recommended use of transfers. Breyer Committee Report, 239 F.R.D. at 214–15.

Rule 26 authorizes the transfer of a complaint proceeding to another judicial council selected by the Chief Justice. Such transfers may be appropriate, for example, in the case of a serious complaint where there are multiple disqualifications among the original council, where the issues are highly visible and a local disposition may weaken public confidence in the process, where internal tensions arising in the council as a result of the complaint render disposition by a less involved council appropriate, or where a complaint calls into question policies or governance of the home court of appeals. The power to effect a transfer is lodged in the Chief Justice to avoid disputes in a council over where to transfer a sensitive matter and to ensure that the transferee council accepts the matter.

Upon receipt of a transferred proceeding, the transferee council shall determine the proper stage at which to begin consideration of the complaint—for example, reference to the transferee chief judge, appointment of a special committee, etc.

RULE 27. WITHDRAWAL OF COMPLAINTS AND PETITIONS FOR REVIEW

(a) Complaint Pending Before Chief Judge. With the chief judge's consent, a complainant may withdraw a complaint that is before the chief judge for a decision under Rule 11. The withdrawal of a complaint will not prevent a chief judge from identifying or having to identify a complaint under Rule 5 based on the withdrawn complaint.

(b) Complaint Pending Before Special Committee or Judicial Council. After a complaint has been referred to a special committee for investigation and before the committee files its report, the complainant may withdraw the complaint only with the consent of both the subject judge and either the special committee or the judicial council.

(c) Petition for Review. A petition for review addressed to a judicial council under Rule 18, or the Judicial Conference Committee on Judicial Conduct and Disability under Rule 22 may be withdrawn if no action on the petition has been taken.

[Adopted March 11, 2008, effective April 10, 2008.]

Commentary on Rule 27

Rule 27 is adapted from the Illustrative Rules and treats the complaint proceeding, once begun, as a matter of public business rather than as the property of the complainant. Accordingly, the chief judge or the judicial council remains responsible for addressing any complaint under the Act, even a complaint that has been formally withdrawn by the complainant.

Under subsection 27(a), a complaint pending before the chief judge may be withdrawn if the chief judge consents. Where the complaint clearly lacked merit, the chief judge may accordingly be saved the burden of preparing a formal order and supporting memorandum. However, the chief judge may, or be obligated under Rule 5, to identify a complaint based on allegations in a withdrawn complaint.

If the chief judge appoints a special committee, Rule 27(b) provides that the complaint may be withdrawn only with the consent of both the body before which it is pending (the special committee or the judicial council) and the subject judge. Once a complaint has reached the stage of appointment of a special committee, a resolution of the issues may be necessary to preserve public confidence. Moreover, the subject judge is given the right to insist that the matter be resolved on the merits, thereby eliminating any ambiguity that might remain if the proceeding were terminated by withdrawal of the complaint.

With regard to all petitions for review, Rule 27(c) grants the petitioner unrestricted authority to withdraw the petition. It is thought that the public's interest in the proceeding is adequately protected, because there will necessarily have been a decision by the chief judge and often by the judicial council as well in such a case.

RULE 28.   AVAILABILITY OF RULES AND FORMS

These Rules and copies of the complaint form as provided in Rule 6(a) must be available without charge in the office of the clerk of each court of appeals, district court, bankruptcy court, or other federal court whose judges are subject to the Act. Each court must also make these Rules and the complaint form available on the court's website, or provide an Internet link to the Rules and complaint form that are available on the appropriate court of appeals' website.

[Adopted March 11, 2008, effective April 10, 2008.]

RULE 29.   EFFECTIVE DATE

These Rules will become effective 30 days after promulgation by the Judicial Conference of the United States.

[Adopted March 11, 2008, effective April 10, 2008.]

APPENDIX

COMPLAINT FORM

Judicial Council of the _____ Circuit

COMPLAINT OF JUDICIAL MISCONDUCT OR DISABILITY

To begin the complaint process, complete this form and prepare the brief statement of facts described in item 5 (below). The RULES FOR JUDICIAL–CONDUCT AND JUDICIAL–DISABILITY PROCEEDINGS, adopted by the Judicial Conference of the United States, contain information on what to include in a complaint (Rule 6), where to file a complaint (Rule 7), and other important matters. The rules are available in federal court clerks' offices, on individual federal courts' Web sites, and on www.uscourts. gov.

Your complaint (this form and the statement of facts) should be typewritten and must be legible. For the number of copies to file, consult the local rules or clerk's office of the court in which your complaint is required to be filed. Enclose each copy of the complaint in an envelope marked "COMPLAINT OF MISCONDUCT" or "COMPLAINT OF DISABILITY" and submit it to the appropriate clerk of court. **Do not put the name of any judge on the envelope.**

1. Name of Complainant: _____
   Contact Address: _____

   Daytime telephone: (_____) _____

2. Name(s) of Judge(s): _____
   Court: _____

3. Does this complaint concern the behavior of the judge(s) in a particular lawsuit or lawsuits?
          [ ] Yes   [ ] No
   If "yes," give the following information about each lawsuit:
   Court: _____
   Case Number: _____
   Docket number of any appeal to the _____ Circuit: _____
   Are (were) you a party or lawyer in the lawsuit?
   [ ] Party   [ ] Lawyer   [ ] Neither

   If you are (were) a party and have (had) a lawyer, give the lawyer's name, address, and telephone number:
   _____
   _____
   _____

4. Have you filed any lawsuits against the judge?
          [ ] Yes   [ ] No
   If "yes," give the following information about each such lawsuit:
   Court: _____
   Case Number: _____
   Present status of lawsuit: _____
   Name, address, and telephone number of your lawyer for the lawsuit against the judge:
   _____
   _____
   _____

   Court to which any appeal has been taken in the lawsuit against the judge:
   _____

   Docket number of the appeal: _____
   Present status of the appeal: _____

5.   **Brief Statement of Facts.**   Attach a brief statement of the specific facts on which the claim of judicial misconduct or disability is based.   Include what happened, when and where it happened, and any information that would help an investigator check the facts.   If the complaint alleges judicial disability, also include any additional facts that form the basis of that allegation.

6.   **Declaration and signature:**

    I declare under penalty of perjury that the statements made in this complaint are true and correct to the best of my knowledge.

    (Signature)_____   (Date)_____

[Adopted March 11, 2008, effective April 10, 2008.]

INDEX TO
UNITED STATES COURT OF APPEALS
FOR THE SEVENTH CIRCUIT

UNITED STATES DISTRICT COURT FOR THE NORTHERN DISTRICT OF ILLINOIS

Including Amendments Received Through
April 1, 2015

LOCAL GENERAL RULES

LR 1 TO LR 2. [RESERVED]

LR 3.1. DESIGNATION SHEET

(a) Plaintiff's Counsel to File Designation Sheet. At the time of filing a case, plaintiff's counsel, or if the case is filed pro se, the plaintiff shall file with the original papers a completed designation sheet (civil cover sheet). If the case is filed by a person in custody, the staff law clerk or prisoner correspondence clerk shall complete the designation sheet.

(b) List of Associated Bankruptcy Matters. Pursuant to LR40.3.1, the person filing the petition for withdrawal of reference, report and recommendation, appeal, motion for leave to appeal, or application for a writ shall complete the designation sheet required by LR3.1 and shall include on the sheet a list of any associated bankruptcy cases, adversary proceedings, non-core proceedings, appeals or motions for leave to appeal, or application for a writ from such proceedings previously assigned to one or more district judges.

(c) Identification of Multidistrict Litigation Proceedings. Where a case is filed as a tag-along to a multidistrict litigation (MDL) proceeding that is before a judge of this Court, the person filing the designation sheet shall, at the same time, file an affidavit identifying the number assigned to the MDL proceeding by the Judicial Panel on Multidistrict Litigation and the name of the presiding judge.

[Effective September 1, 1999. Amended effective February 25, 2005; April 2, 2012.]

LR 3.2. NOTIFICATION OF AFFILIATES—DISCLOSURE STATEMENT

Definition. For purposes of this rule, "affiliate" is defined to include:

A. In the case of a corporation, any entity owning more than 5% of the corporation.

B. In the case of a general partnership, joint venture, LLC, LLLP, or LLP, any member.

C. In the case of any other unincorporated association, any corporate member.

If any such affiliate is itself a partnership, joint venture, LLC, LLLP, LLP or any other unincorporated association, its "affiliates" (as defined above) shall also be included within the definition of "affiliate."

(a) Who Must File. Any nongovernmental party, other than an individual or sole proprietorship, shall file a statement identifying all its publicly held affiliates. If a non-governmental party has no publicly held affiliates, a statement shall be filed to that effect.

(b) Time for Filing. A party must file the statement with the complaint or answer, or upon filing a motion, response, or petition, whichever occurs first. The statement is to be attached to the document being filed. A supplement to the statement shall be filed within a reasonable period of time of any change in the information reported.

[NOTE: Rule 3.2 was amended by General Order of November 3, 2000, on December 1, 2006 by press release of November 20, 2006, by General Order of April 20, 2007.]

[Effective September 1, 1999. Amended effective November 3, 2000; December 1, 2006; April 20, 2007.]

LR 3.3. PAYMENT OF FEES IN ADVANCE; IN FORMA PAUPERIS MATTERS; SANCTIONS

(a) Definitions The following definitions shall apply to this rule:

(1) "IFP petition" means a petition for leave to proceed in forma pauperis, i.e., without prepayment of prescribed fees.

(2) "Financial affidavit" means the form of affidavit of financial status prescribed by the Court.

(b) Prepayment Required. Any document submitted for filing for which a filing fee is required must be accompanied either by the appropriate fee or an IFP petition. Notwithstanding this provision, the clerk will file any document including a complaint in a civil action, a notice of appeal, or other document for which a filing fee is prescribed, without prepayment, but such filings shall be subject to the sanctions set forth in section (e) of this Rule.

(c) Filing In Forma Pauperis. The IFP petition and the financial affidavit shall be filed and assigned to a judge. The complaint shall be stamped received as of the date presented. The clerk shall promptly forward the IFP petition and all other papers to the judge to whom it is assigned.

(d) Date of Filing. If the judge grants the IFP petition, the complaint shall be filed as of the date of the judge's order except that where the complaint must be filed within a time limit and the order granting leave to file is entered after the expiration of that time limit, the complaint shall be deemed to have been filed:

(1) in the case of any plaintiff in custody, as of the time of the plaintiff's delivery of the complaint to the custodial authorities for transmittal to the court; or

(2) in the case of any other plaintiff, as of the time the complaint was received by the clerk.

(e) Notice of Fees Due; Sanctions. Upon denial of an IFP petition, the clerk shall notify the person filing the documents of the amount of fees due. If the required fees are not paid within 15 days of the date of such notification, or within such other time as may be fixed by the court, the clerk shall notify the judge before whom the matter is pending of the nonpayment. The court may then apply such sanctions as it determines necessary including dismissal of the action.

(f) Order Granting IFP Petition. Where an order is entered granting the IFP petition, that order shall, unless otherwise ordered by the court, stand as authority for the United States Marshal to serve summonses without prepayment of the required fees.

[Effective September 1, 1999.]

LR 3.4. NOTICE OF CLAIMS INVOLVING PATENTS OR TRADEMARKS

In order to assist the clerk in complying with the requirement to notify the commissioner, any party filing a pleading, complaint, or counterclaim which raises for the first time a claim arising under the patent and trademark laws of the United States (U.S. Code, Titles 15 and 35) shall file with the pleading, complaint, or counterclaim a separate notice of claims involving patents or trademarks. That notice shall include for each patent the information required by 35 U.S.C. § 290; and for each trademark the information required by 15 U.S.C. § 1116(c).

[Effective September 1, 1999.]

LR 4. SERVICE IN IN FORMA PAUPERIS CASES

In civil matters in which the plaintiff is authorized to proceed in forma pauperis pursuant to 28 U.S.C. § 1915, service shall be accomplished in the manner set forth in the subsections below.

(a) Service upon the United States, an agency of the United States, or officials of the United States or its agencies in their official capacity, shall be accomplished by plaintiff by registered or certified mail pursuant to Fed.R.Civ.P.4(i), except in certain cases under the Social Security Act that are described in subsection (b).

(b) Where a complaint for administrative review is filed pursuant to 42 U.S.C. § 405(g) concerning benefits under the Social Security Act, unless otherwise ordered, by agreement with the United States Attorney, no service of initial process (*i.e.*, summons and complaint) shall be required in any case (not limited to in forma pauperis cases). The Social Security Administration will treat notification through the court's Case Management and Electronic Filing System (CM/ECF) as service under Rule 4 of the Federal Rules of Civil Procedure.

(c) In all cases where a petitioner has filed a habeas corpus petition under 28 U.S.C. § 2254, regardless of whether or not the $5 filing fee has been paid, service will be pursuant to the agreement, set forth in Appendix 1 to these Local Rules, between the Attorney General of Illinois and the Court.

(d) In any action in which the U.S. Marshal has been designated to effectuate service, the U.S. Marshal is requested to send the complaint and appropriate papers for waiver of service to the named defendant (including defendant federal officials sued in their individual capacities) pursuant to Rule 4(d). If a defendant neither returns the waiver nor files a responsive pleading within the required time, the Court will notify the U.S. Marshal of the need for personal service on that defendant. If the U.S. Marshal then effects personal service on the defendant, the Court will impose the costs of service on the defendant consistent with Fed.R.Civ.P. 4(d)(2).

(e) In actions in which the U.S. Marshal has been designated to effectuate service pursuant to this rule, the following time limits shall apply to waiver of service notice and requests:

(1) The notice and request for waiver of service shall allow the defendant a reasonable time to return the waiver, which shall be 30 days after the date on which the request is sent or 60 days after that date if the defendant is addressed outside any judicial district of the United States.

(2) A defendant that, before being served with process, timely returns a waiver so requested, is not

required to serve an answer to the complaint until 60 days after the date on which the request for waiver of service was sent, or 90 days after that date if the defendant was addressed outside any judicial district of the United States.

[Effective September 1, 1999. Amended effective October 2, 2012.]

LR 5.1. PLACE OF FILING; DIVISION

Except as otherwise ordered, all filings shall be made in the divisional office of the division to which the case is assigned provided that a document initiating a case that should be filed in one of the divisions of this Court may be presented for filing to the assignment clerk of the other division. In such instances, the person filing the document should clearly indicate that it is to be filed in the other division. The case will be numbered and assigned as if it were filed in the proper division. Following the assignment, the clerk will promptly forward the papers to the proper divisional office.

[Effective September 1, 1999.]

LR 5.2. FORM OF DOCUMENTS FILED

(a) Electronic Filing Permitted. The court will accept for filing documents submitted, signed, or verified by electronic means that comply with procedures established by the court as set forth in the General Order on Electronic Case Filing or other similar order.

Where a document is submitted in an electronic format pursuant to procedures established by the court, submitted in both electronic and paper formats, or submitted in paper and subsequently produced in an electronic format by court staff, the electronic version shall be the court's official record. Where a document is submitted in paper format without an electronic version being produced, the paper version shall be the court's official record. Where the electronic version of a document is a redacted version of an unredacted paper document, the unredacted paper version shall be the court's official record.

(b) Redaction of Transcripts Filed Electronically. If a party or an attorney for a party files a written request to redact specific portions of a transcript pursuant to either Federal Rule of Civil Procedure 5.2 or Federal Rule of Criminal Procedure 49.1, the court reporter is ordered by the Court to make that redaction. Any other redaction request must be made by motion to the court.

(c) Paper and Font Size. Each paper original filed and each paper judge's copy shall be flat and unfolded on opaque, unglazed, white paper 8½ × 11 inches in size. It shall be plainly written, typed, printed, or prepared by means of a duplicating process, without erasures or interlineations which materially deface it.

Where the document is typed, line spacing will be at least 2.0 lines. Where it is typed or printed,

(1) the size of the type in the body of the text shall be 12 points and that in footnotes, no less than 11 points, and

(2) the margins, left-hand, right-hand, top, and bottom, shall each be a minimum of 1 inch.

(d) Binding and Tabs. Each paper original shall be bound or secured at the top edge of the document by a staple or a removable metal paper fastener inserted through two holes. A paper original shall not have a front or back cover. A paper original shall not have protruding tabs. Exhibits or tabs that are part of the paper original shall be indicated in bold type on a single sheet of paper placed immediately before the corresponding exhibit or attachment. Unless not reasonably feasible, exhibits to paper originals shall be 8½ × 11 inches in size. A judge's paper copy shall be bound on the left side and shall include protruding tabs for exhibits. A list of exhibits must be provided for each document that contains more than one exhibit.

(e) Documents Not Complying May be Stricken. Any document that does not comply with this rule shall be filed subject to being stricken by the court.

(f) Judge's Copy. Each person or party filing a paper version of a pleading, motion, or document, other than an appearance form, motion to appear pro hac vice, or return of service, shall file, in addition to the original, a copy for use by the court, with the exception of documents filed by Persons in Custody. A Person in Custody need not file a judge's copy. Where a filing is made electronically of a pleading, motion, or document other than an appearance form or return of service, a paper copy shall be provided for the judge within one business day, if the electronically filed document, including all exhibits, exceeds ten pages in length; provided, however, that any judge may, by standing order or by order in any case, dispense with this requirement for documents of greater length or, in the alternative, may direct that counsel submit a paper copy of any filing, regardless of length. Delivery of paper copies by overnight mail satisfies this requirement. Every judge's paper copy must be bound and tabbed as required by subsection (d).

[Effective September 1, 1999. Amended effective December 20, 2004; April 20, 2006; September 23, 2008; June 24, 2009; February 4, 2010; January 31, 2012; May 18, 2012; June 24, 2013; October 21, 2013; November 22, 2013.]

LR 5.3. NOTICE OF MOTIONS AND OBJECTIONS

(a) Service. Except in the case of an emergency or unless otherwise ordered, written notice of the intent to present a motion, or an objection to a magistrate judge's order or report under F.R.Civ.P. 72, specifying the date on which the motion or objection is to be presented, a copy of the motion or objection and any accompanying documents must be served as follows:

(1) *Personal Service.* Personal service must be accomplished no later than 4:00 p.m. of the second business day preceding the date of presentment. Personal service shall include actual delivery within the time specified by this section by a service organization providing for delivery within a specified time (e.g., overnight service) or by electronic transmission pursuant to F.R.Civ.P. 5(b)(2)(D) and 5(b)(3).

(2) *Mail Service.* Where the service is by mail, the notice and documents shall be mailed at least seven days before the date of presentment. Ex parte motions and agreed motions or objections may be presented without notice.

(b) Presentment. Every motion or objection shall be accompanied by a notice of presentment specifying the date and time on which, and judge before whom, the motion or objection is to be presented. The date of presentment shall be not more than 14 days following the date on which the motion or objection is delivered to the court pursuant to LR78.1.

[NOTE: Rule 5.3 was amended by General Order of October 2, 2002, by General Order of March 27, 2003, and by General Order of November 19, 2009.]

[Effective September 1, 1999. Amended effective October 2, 2002; March 27, 2003; November 19, 2009.]

LR 5.4. MOTIONS: FILING NOTICE & MOTION

Filing of papers shall be with the clerk unless a particular judge has provided for filing in the judge's chambers. The clerk shall maintain a list of the delivery requirements of each judge and post a copy in a public area of the clerk's office.

Where a motion is delivered to the clerk that does not comply with the scheduling requirements established by the judge pursuant to LR78.1 or is scheduled before a judge who, pursuant to this rule, has directed that the motions are to be delivered to the minute clerk assigned to the judge or to the judge's chambers, the clerk shall inform the person offering the motion of the correct procedure. If the person insists on delivering it to the clerk, the clerk shall accept it and attach to it a note indicating that the person delivering it was advised of the scheduling or delivery requirements.

[Effective September 1, 1999.]

LR 5.5. PROOF OF SERVICE

(a) General. Proof of service of all papers required or permitted to be served shall, unless some other method is expressly required by these rules or the Federal Rules of Civil Procedure, be made in the following manner:

(1) if the person serving the papers is an attorney of record in the case, by certificate;

(2) if the person serving the papers is not an attorney of record in the case, by affidavit, or by written acknowledgment of service, or by any other proof satisfactory to the court.

(3) if the case is one for which the General Order on Electronic Case Filing applies, in the manner set forth in that General Order under the heading entitled "Service of Documents by Electronic Means".

(b) Certificate of Service. Each document other than one filed ex parte shall be accompanied by a certificate of service indicating the date and manner of services and a statement that copies of documents required to be served by Fed.R.Civ.P. 5(a) have been served. Where the service was by FAX, the certificate shall be accompanied by a copy of the transaction statement produced by the FAX machine. Such transaction statement shall include the date and time of service, the telephone number to which the documents were transmitted, and an acknowledgment from the receiving FAX machine that the transmission was received or, in the event that the receiving FAX machine did not produce the acknowledgment to the transmitting FAX machine, an affidavit or, if by an attorney, a certificate setting forth the date and time of service and telephone number to which documents were transmitted.

(c) Filing by FAX Not Permitted. Documents to be filed with the court may not be transmitted to the court by FAX. The only means of filing documents with the court by electronic means is in accordance with LR5.2(a) and the General Order on Electronic Case Filing or other similar order.

(d) Ex Parte Motion. A motion for an ex parte order shall be accompanied by an affidavit showing cause therefor and stating whether or not a previous application for similar relief has been made.

[NOTE: Rule 5.5 was amended by General Order of December 20, 2004.]

[Effective September 1, 1999. Amended effective December 20, 2004.]

LR 5.6. FILING DOCUMENTS BY NON-PARTIES

No pleading, motion [except for motion to intervene], or other document shall be filed in any case by any person who is not a party thereto, unless approved by the court. Absent such an order, the clerk shall not accept any document tendered by a person who is not a party. Should any such document be accepted inadvertently or by mistake in the absence of such an order, it may be stricken by the court on its own motion and without notice.

[Effective September 1, 1999.]

LR 5.7. FILING CASES UNDER SEAL

(a) General. The clerk is authorized to accept a complaint for filing and treat that complaint and the accompanying papers as if they were restricted pursuant to LR26.2 where the complaint is accompanied by a written request containing the following:

(1) the name, address, and signature of the party or counsel making the request;

(2) a statement indicating that the party believes that due to special circumstance which the party will promptly bring to the attention of the judge to whom the case is to be assigned, it is necessary to restrict access to the case at filing;

(3) a statement that the party is aware that absent an order extending or setting aside the sealing, the file and its contents will become public on the seventh day following the date of filing; and

(4) the attorney's or party's e-mail address if the attorney or party is registered as a Filing User of electronic case filing, the caption of the case, and the title of the document.

Absent any order to the contrary, the contents of the case file shall be treated as restricted documents as defined by LR26.2 for seven days following the day on which the complaint was filed. Except as otherwise ordered, on the seventh day the file will no longer be treated as restricted.

(b) Filings Under 31 U.S.C. § 3730. The procedures set forth in section (a) shall also be followed in filing complaints *in camera* pursuant to 31 U.S.C. § 3730 with the following modifications:

(1) the person presenting the complaint for filing *in camera* shall state in the instructions to the assignment clerk that the complaint is being filed pursuant to 31 U.S.C. § 3730; and

(2) unless otherwise ordered by the court, the matter shall remain restricted for the period specified in 31 U.S.C. § 3730.

[NOTE: Rule 5.7 was amended by General Order of April 20, 2004, and by General Order of November 19, 2009.]

[Effective September 1, 1999. Amended effective April 20, 2004; November 19, 2009.]

Committee Comments

LR5.7 is amended to ensure it is in compliance with LR26.2—Restricted Documents

LR 5.8. FILING MATERIALS UNDER SEAL

Any document to be filed under seal shall be filed in compliance with procedures established by the Clerk of Court and approved by the Executive Committee. Where pursuant to court order as* a restricted or sealed document as defined by LR26.2 is not filed electronically, it must be accompanied by a cover sheet which shall include the following:

(A) the caption of the case, including the case number;

(B) the title "Sealed Document Pursuant to LR26.2";

(C) a statement indicating that the document is filed under seal in accordance with an order of court and the date of that order; and

(D) the signature of the attorney of record or unrepresented party filing the document, the attorney's or party's name and address, including e-mail address if the attorney or party is registered as a Filing User of electronic case filing, and the title of the document.

Any document purporting to be a sealed document as defined in LR26.2 that is not filed in compliance with such procedures shall be processed like any other document. In such instances, where the document has not been filed electronically, the clerk is authorized to open the sealed envelope and remove the materials for processing.

[NOTE: Rule 5.8 was amended by General Order of April 20, 2004, November 5, 2009, May 18, 2012]

[Effective September 1, 1999. Amended effective April 20, 2004; November 5, 2009; May 18, 2012.]

* So in original.

LR 5.9 SERVICE BY ELECTRONIC MEANS

In accordance with the General Order on Electronic Case Filing and subject to the provisions of Fed. R.Civ.P. 5(b)(3), the Notice of Electronic Filing that is issued through the court's Electronic Case Filing System will constitute service under Fed.R.Civ.P. 5(b)(2)(D) and Fed.R.Crim.P. 49(b) as to all Filing Users in a case assigned to the court's Electronic Case Filing System.

[NOTE: Rule 5.9 was established by General Order of December 20, 2004.]

[Effective December 20, 2004.]

LR 6. [RESERVED]

LR 7.1. BRIEFS: PAGE LIMIT

Neither a brief in support of or in opposition to any motion nor objections to a report and recommendation or order of a magistrate judge or special master shall exceed 15 pages without prior approval of the court. Briefs that exceed the 15 page limit must have a table of contents with the pages noted and a table of cases. Any brief or objection that does not comply with this rule shall be filed subject to being stricken by the court.

[Effective September 1, 1999.]

LR 8.1. SOCIAL SECURITY CASES: NOTICE OF SOCIAL SECURITY NUMBER

Where a complaint for judicial review is filed pursuant to 42 U.S.C. § 405(g) and/or 42 U.S.C. § 1383(c)(3);

(a) The complaint shall include the full Social Security number of the plaintiff, including that of a minor plaintiff not otherwise identified by his or her full name. If the plaintiff's application for Social Security benefits was filed on another person's wage-record, that person's Social Security number shall also be included in the complaint.

(b) The Social Security Administration's filing of the certified administrative record, in and of itself, shall suffice as the agency's answer to the complaint.

[Effective September 1, 1999. Amended effective November 20, 2006; October 2, 2012; January 31, 2014; May 22, 2014.]

LR 9.1. THREE–JUDGE CASES

The party instituting an action requiring a three-judge court shall advise the clerk that such a court is requested and shall specify the statute involved. In such cases counsel shall furnish the clerk with three additional copies of all pleadings filed and all briefs submitted.

[Effective September 1, 1999.]

LR 10.1. RESPONSIVE PLEADINGS

Responsive pleadings shall be made in numbered paragraphs each corresponding to and stating a concise summary of the paragraph to which it is directed.

[Effective September 1, 1999.]

LR 11 TO LR 15. [RESERVED]

LR 16.1. PRETRIAL PROCEDURES

(a) Standing Order & Form. Pursuant to Fed. R.Civ.P. 16, the Court has adopted a standing order on pretrial procedures together with model pretrial order forms. Copies of the standing order and forms shall be available from the clerk [*see* Appendix]. The procedures set forth in the standing order, except for the need to prepare the pretrial order itself, shall apply to all civil cases except for those in categories enumerated in section (b) of this rule. As to all other cases, a pretrial order shall be prepared whenever the judge to whom a case is assigned so orders.

(b) Exempted Classes of Cases. The pretrial procedures adopted pursuant to section (a) of this rule shall not apply to the following classes of civil cases (The statistical nature of suit ("NS") codes are shown in parentheses following the class of cases.):

(1) Recovery of overpayments and student loan cases (NS: 150, 152, 153);

(2) Mortgage foreclosure cases (NS: 220);

(3) Prisoner petitions (NS: 510, 520, 530, 540, 550);

(4) U.S. forfeiture/penalty cases (NS: 610, 620, 630, 640, 650, 660, 690);

(5) Bankruptcy appeals and transfers (NS: 420, 421);

(6) Deportation reviews (NS: 460);

(7) ERISA: Collections of Delinquent Contributions;

(8) Social Security reviews (NS: 861, 862, 863, 864, 865);

(9) Tax suits & IRS third party (NS: 870, 871);

(10) Customer challenges 12 U.S.C. § 3410 (NS: 875); or

(11) Cases brought under the Agricultural Acts, Economic Stabilization Act, Energy Allocation Act, Freedom of Information Act, Appeal of Fee Determination Under Equal Access to Justice Act, NARA Title II (NS: 891, 892, 894, 895, 900, 970).

Notwithstanding the provisions of this rule, a pretrial order shall be prepared whenever the judge to whom a case is assigned so orders.

Effective September 1, 1999; Amended effective October 4, 2006.

[Adopted June 26, 1985. Amended November 27, 1991; March 9, 1995.]

LR 16.2. PRETRIAL CONFERENCES AND STATUS HEARINGS

At the discretion of the court pretrial conferences or status hearings held pursuant to Fed.R.Civ.P. 16(a) may be conducted by telephone or other appropriate means. The court may require parties to provide written status reports in advance of any such hearing.

[Effective September 1, 1999.]

LR 16.3. VOLUNTARY MEDIATION PROGRAM

(a) Program Established. A program for voluntary mediation is established for cases arising under the Federal Trademark Act of 1946, 15 U.S.C. §§ 1051–1127 ("the Lanham Act").

(b) Procedures. The voluntary mediation program shall follow the procedures approved by the Executive Committee. The procedures outline the responsibilities of counsel and the parties in cases that are eligible for the mediation program. Copies of the procedures may be obtained from the clerk. [*see* Appendix]

(c) Confidentiality. All mediation proceedings, including any statement made by any party, attorney or other participant, shall, in all respects, be privileged and not reported, recorded, placed in evidence, made known to the trial court or jury, or construed for any purpose as an admission. No party shall be bound by anything done or said at the conference unless a settlement is reached, in which event the settlement shall be reduced to writing and shall be binding upon all parties.

[Effective September 1, 1999.]

LR 16.4. SCHEDULING IN SOCIAL SECURITY CASES

In cases brought pursuant to 42 U.S.C. § 405(g) for benefits under the Social Security Act, the following schedule is established unless otherwise ordered:

(a) Plaintiff's brief in support of reversing or remanding the decision subject to review is due within 60 days of the filing of the administrative record (no motion required).

(b) The Social Security Administration's motion to affirm the decision subject to review and its brief in support are due 45 days after plaintiff's brief is filed.

(c) Plaintiff's reply brief, if any, is due 14 days after defendant's brief is filed.

[Effective October 2, 2012. Amended effective January 31, 2014.]

LR 17.1. ACTIONS BY OR ON BEHALF OF INFANTS OR INCOMPETENTS

Any proposed settlement of an action brought by or on behalf of an infant or incompetent shall not become final without written approval by the court in the form of an order, judgment or decree. The court may authorize payment of reasonable attorney's fees and expenses from the amount realized in such an action.

[Effective September 1, 1999.]

LR 18 TO LR 23. [RESERVED]

LR 24.1. NOTICE OF CLAIMS OF UNCONSTITUTIONALITY

In order to assist the court in its statutory duty under 28 U.S.C. § 2403, counsel raising a question of the constitutionality of an Act of Congress affecting the public interest shall promptly advise the court in writing of such fact.

[Effective September 1, 1999.]

LR 25. [RESERVED]

LR 26.1. SCHEDULING CONFERENCE

Rule 26(f) meetings may be conducted by telephone. Unless otherwise ordered by the court (1) parties need not present a written report outlining the discovery plan at the preliminary pretrial conference, and (2) the initial status hearing shall be the scheduling conference referred to in Fed.R.Civ.P. 26(f).

[NOTE: Rule 26.1 was amended by General Order of November 30, 2000]

[Effective September 1, 1999. Amended effective December 1, 2000.]

LR 26.2. SEALED DOCUMENTS

(a) Definitions. As used in this rule the term:

"Sealed document" means a document that the court has directed be maintained under seal electronically or, where the court allows a sealed document to be filed non-electronically, within a sealed enclosure such that access to the document requires breaking the seal of the enclosure; and

"Sealing order" means any order restricting access to one or more documents filed or to be filed with the court.

(b) Sealing Order. The court may for good cause shown enter an order directing that one or more documents be filed under seal. No attorney or party may file a document under seal without order of court specifying the particular document or portion of a document that may be filed under seal.

(c) Sealing Motion for Documents filed Electronically. Any party wishing to file a document or portion of a document electronically under seal in connection with a motion, brief or other submission must: (1) provisionally file the document electronically under seal; (2) file electronically at the same time a public-record version of the brief, motion or other submission with only the sealed document excluded; and (3) move the court for leave to file the document under seal. The sealing motion must be filed before or simultaneously with the provisional filing of the document under seal, and must be noticed for presentment promptly thereafter. Any document filed under seal without such a sealing motion may be stricken by the court without notice.

(d) Sealing Motion for Documents not filed Electronically. Where the court has permitted documents to be filed non-electronically, the party seeking to file a document under seal must, before filing the document, move the court for a sealing order specifying the particular document or portion of a document to be filed under seal. The final paragraph of the order shall state the following information: (1) the identity of the persons, if any, who are to have access to the documents without further order of court; and (2) instructions for the disposition of the restricted documents following the conclusion of the case. A copy of the sealing order must be included with any document presented for filing under seal. The attorney or party submitting a restricted document must file it in a sealed enclosure that conspicuously states on the face of the enclosure the attorney's or party's name and address, including e-mail address if the attorney is registered as a Filing User of electronic case filing, the caption of the case, and the title of the document.

(e) Copies Served on Counsel and Judge's Paper Courtesy Copy. Any sealed document served on any other party and any judge's paper courtesy copy must be a complete version, without any redactions made to create the public-record version unless otherwise ordered for good cause shown.

(f) Docket Entries. The court may on written motion and for good cause shown enter an order directing that the docket entry for a sealed document show only that a sealed document was filed without any notation indicating its nature. Unless the Court directs otherwise, a sealed document shall be filed pursuant to procedures referenced by Local Rule 5.8.

(g) Inspection of Sealed Documents. The clerk shall maintain a record in a manner provided for by internal operating procedures approved by the Court of persons permitted access to sealed documents that have not been filed electronically. Such procedures may require anyone seeking access to show identification and to sign a statement to the effect that they have been authorized to examine the sealed document.

(h) Disposition of Sealed Non-electronic Documents. When a case is closed in which an order was entered pursuant to section (b) of this rule, the clerk shall maintain the documents filed under seal non-electronically as sealed documents for a period of 63 days following the final disposition including appeals. Except where the court in response to a request of a party made pursuant to this section or on its own motion orders otherwise, at the end of the 63 day period the clerk shall notify the attorney or party who filed the documents that the documents must be retrieved from the clerk's office within 30 days of notification. If the parties do not retrieve the sealed documents within 30 days, the clerk shall destroy the documents.

[Effective September 1, 1999. Amended effective April 20, 2006; May 26, 2006; November 5, 2009; October 2, 2012.]

LR 26.3. DISCOVERY MATERIALS OFFERED IN EVIDENCE AS EXHIBIT

Except as provided by this rule, discovery materials, including disclosure of expert testimony, shall not be filed with the court. The party serving the discovery materials or taking the deposition shall retain the original and be custodian of it. The court, on its own motion, on motion of any party, or on application by a non-party, may require the filing of any discovery materials or may make provisions for a person to obtain a copy at that person's own expense.

Where discovery materials are offered into evidence as an exhibit, the attorney producing them will retain them unless the court orders them deposited with the clerk. Where the court orders them deposited, they will be treated as exhibits subject to the provisions of LR79.1.

[Effective September 1, 1999.]

LR 26.4. TESTIMONY FOR USE IN FOREIGN TRIBUNALS

Where an interested person requests to take the testimony or statement of any person pursuant to 28 U.S.C. § 1782 for use in a proceeding in a foreign or international tribunal, notice to the parties before the foreign or international tribunal must be provided except where the requesting party shows cause why notice could not be given. Where the request is sought by a letter rogatory or request made by a foreign or international tribunal, the request may be made ex parte.

[Effective September 1, 1999. Amended effective June 2, 2011.]

LR 27.1. DEPOSITIONS: FEES FOR ATTORNEYS APPOINTED TO REPRESENT ABSENT PARTY

An order appointing an attorney to represent the absent expected adversary party and to cross-examine the proposed witness pursuant to Fed.R.Civ.P. 27(a)(2) shall set the attorney's compensation including expenses. The compensation so set shall be paid by the petitioner prior to the appearance of the appointed attorney at the examination.

[Effective September 1, 1999.]

LR 28 TO LR 32. [RESERVED]

LR 33.1. INTERROGATORIES; FORM OF ANSWER; OBJECTIONS

A party answering interrogatories shall set forth immediately preceding each answer a full statement of the interrogatory to which the party is responding.

When objecting to an interrogatory or to the answer to an interrogatory, a party shall set forth the interrogatory or the interrogatories and answer thereto immediately preceding the objection.

[Effective September 1, 1999.]

LR 34 TO LR 36.   [RESERVED]

LR 37.1.   CONTEMPTS

(a) Commencing Proceedings. A proceeding to adjudicate a person in civil contempt of court, including a case provided for in Fed.R.Civ.P. 37(b)(2)(D), shall be commenced by the service of a notice of motion or order to show cause. The affidavit upon which such notice of motion or order to show cause is based shall set out with particularity the misconduct complained of, the claim, if any, for damages occasioned thereby, and such evidence as to the amount of damages as may be available to the moving party. A reasonable counsel fee, necessitated by the contempt proceeding, may be included as an item of damage. Where the alleged contemnor has appeared in the action by an attorney, the notice of motion or order to show cause and the papers upon which it is based may be served upon that attorney; otherwise service shall be made personally, in the manner provided for by Fed.R.Civ.P. 4 for the service of a summons. If an order to show cause is sought, such order may, upon necessity shown therefor, direct the United States marshal to arrest the alleged contemnor. The order shall fix the amount of bail and shall require that any bond signed by the alleged contemnor include as a condition of release that the alleged contemnor will comply with any order of the court directing the contemnor to surrender.

(b) Trial. If the alleged contemnor puts in issue the alleged misconduct giving rise to the contempt proceedings or the damages thereby occasioned, the alleged contemnor shall upon demand therefor be entitled to have oral evidence taken thereon, either before the court or before a master appointed by the court. When by law the alleged contemnor is entitled to a trial by jury, unless a written jury demand is filed by the alleged contemnor on or before the return day or adjourned day of the application, the alleged contemnor will be deemed to have waived a trial by jury.

(c) Order Where Found in Contempt. In the event the alleged contemnor is found to be in contempt of court, an order shall be entered—

(1) reciting or referring to the verdict or findings of fact upon which the adjudication is based;

(2) setting forth the amount of damages to which the complainant is entitled;

(3) fixing the fine, if any, imposed by the court, which fine shall include the damages found, and naming the person to whom such fine shall be payable;

(4) stating any other conditions, the performance whereof will operate to purge the contempt; and

(5) directing the arrest of the contemnor by the United States marshal and the confinement of the contemnor until the performance of the condition fixed in the order and the payment of the fine, or until the contemnor be otherwise discharged pursuant to law.

Unless the order otherwise specifies, the place of confinement shall be either the Chicago Metropolitan Correctional Center in Chicago, Illinois, or the Winnebago County jail in Rockford, Illinois. No party shall be required to pay or to advance to the marshal any expenses for the upkeep of the prisoner. Upon such an order, no person shall be detained in prison by reason of non-payment of the fine for a period exceeding 6 months. A certified copy of the order committing the contemnor shall be sufficient warrant to the marshal for the arrest and confinement. The aggrieved party shall also have the same remedies against the property of the contemnor as if the order awarding the fine were a final judgment.

(d) Discharge Where No Contempt. Where a finding of no contempt is entered, the alleged contemnor shall be discharged from the proceeding. The court may in its discretion for good cause shown enter judgment against the complainant and for the alleged contemnor for the latter's costs and disbursements and a reasonable counsel fee.

[Effective September 1, 1999.]

LR 37.2.   MOTION FOR DISCOVERY AND PRODUCTION; STATEMENT OF EFFORTS TO REACH AN ACCORD

To curtail undue delay and expense in the administration of justice, this court shall hereafter refuse to hear any and all motions for discovery and production of documents under Rules 26 through 37 of the Federal Rules of Civil Procedure, unless the motion includes a statement (1) that after consultation in person or by telephone and good faith attempts to resolve differences they are unable to reach an accord, or (2) counsel's attempts to engage in such consultation were unsuccessful due to no fault of counsel's. Where the consultation occurred, this statement shall recite, in addition, the date, time and place of such conference, and the names of all parties participating therein. Where counsel was unsuccessful in engaging in such consultation, the statement shall recite the efforts made by counsel to engage in consultation.

[Effective September 1, 1999.]

LR 38 TO LR 39.   [RESERVED]

LR 40.1.   ASSIGNMENT OF CASES: GENERAL

(a) General. The rules of this Court and any procedures adopted by the Court that deal with the assignment and reassignment of cases shall be construed to secure an equitable distribution of cases, both in quantity and kind, among the judges. Except as specifically provided by the rules of this Court or by procedures adopted by the Court, the assignment of cases shall be by lot.

(b) Supervision of Assignment System. The assignment of cases to calendars and judges and the preparation of calendars and supplements thereto shall be done solely under the direction of the Executive Committee by the clerk or a deputy clerk who is designated by the clerk as an assignment clerk.

(c) Contempt. Any person who violates the case assignment procedures shall be punished for contempt of court.

(d) Condition of Reassignment. No case shall be transferred or reassigned from the calendar of a judge of this Court to the calendar of any other judge except as provided by the rules of this Court or as ordered by the Executive Committee.

(e) Calendars. In each Division of the Court there shall be criminal, civil and Executive Committee calendars. The cases on the criminal and civil calendars of the court shall be assigned among the judges in the manner prescribed by the rules of this Court. The cases so assigned shall constitute the calendars of the judges. The calendar of the Executive Committee shall consist of the following classes and categories of cases:

(1) civil cases to be transferred to another judge or district for multidistrict litigation pursuant to procedures adopted by the Court;

(2) criminal cases to be held on the Committee's Fugitive Calendar pursuant to procedures adopted by the Court;

(3) such cases as are assigned to the Executive Committee for purposes of reassignment; and

(4) such other cases as the Executive Committee directs be assigned to its calendar.

(f) Calendar of Departing Judge. Cases on the calendar of a judge who dies, resigns, or retires ("departing judge") shall be reassigned as soon as possible under the direction of the Executive Committee, pro rata by lot among the remaining judges, provided that the Committee may direct that such calendar be transferred in its entirety or in part to form the calendar of a newly-appointed district judge where the departing judge was a district judge, or to form the calendar of a newly-appointed magistrate judge where the departing judge was a magistrate judge. Referrals pending before a departing magistrate judge shall be considered returned to the calendar of the district judge before whom the underlying case is pending, provided that the Executive Committee may direct that they be maintained as a calendar

for a newly-appointed magistrate judge. Where a judge wishes to re-refer a case returned to that judge's calendar pursuant to this section, the procedure set forth in LR72.1 shall be followed except that where the Executive Committee approves the referral, it shall direct the clerk to assign it by lot.

(g) Calendar for New Judge. A calendar shall be prepared for a newly-appointed judge ("new judge") to which cases shall be transferred by lot, under the direction of the Executive Committee in such number as it may determine. Where the new judge is a magistrate judge, the calendar shall include referrals made pursuant to LR72.1 and LCrR50.3(d) and cases assigned pursuant to LR73.1 which shall be transferred by lot, under the direction of the Executive Committee in such number as it may determine. The new magistrate judge will be the designated magistrate judge in all matters on that judge's calendar. Where a magistrate judge is appointed to succeed a leaving magistrate judge, the Executive Committee may direct that the new judge be the designated magistrate judge in all cases in which the former was the designated magistrate judge at the time of the former's death, retirement, or resignation. Once a referral has been transferred to a newly appointed judge, as part of the new calendar, it remains with the new judge "as the designated judge".

[Effective September 1, 1999.]

Committee Comment

28 U.S.C. § 137 provides in part as follows:

The business of the court having more than one judge shall be divided among the judges as provided by the rules and orders of the court. The chief judge of the district shall be responsible for the observance of such rules and orders, and shall divide the business and assign the cases so far as such rules and orders do not otherwise prescribe.

This Court has used a random assignment system for more than 50 years. As stated in section (a), an important goal of the system is to achieve "an equitable distribution of cases, both in quantity and kind, among the judges." Over the years the system grew in complexity. In part, this was a result of increases in the size of the Court, the complexity of its organization and the size of its caseload. It was also a result of a more sophisticated understanding of how the "equitable distribution" should be achieved.

An equally important goal is implicit in the sanctions found in section (c). This is that no one should be able to manipulate the assignment system in order to determine in advance which judge will get a case where the assignment is by lot.

As part of the process of renumbering the rules to comply with the uniform system adopted by the Judicial Conference of the United States in March 1996, the Court significantly revised its assignment rules. Much of the detail formerly included in local General Rules 2.00 and 2.44, the former assignment rules, has been moved from the rules to procedures adopted by general order. Because of the importance of the assignment system, the Court included this summary to provide parties and counsel with a basic overview of the way in which cases are assigned in this Court. The Court is divided into two division: the Eastern at Chicago and the Western at Rockford. Eastern and Western Division cases can be distinguished by their case numbers. Case numbers in the Eastern Division start with the number 1 each year. In the Western Division they start with 50,001.

There are 22 district judgeships and 10 magistrate judgeships authorized for the Court. One district judgeship and one magistrate judgeship are authorized for the Western Division, the remainder are all authorized for the Eastern Division. Cases filed in the Western Division are generally assigned to the Western Division judge. The magistrate judge of that division usually supervises pretrial matters in civil cases.

Most of the provisions of the random assignment system apply only to the Eastern Division. For assignment purposes civil cases are grouped into categories, usually by the type of case. The case types chosen for each category are expected over the long run to generate about the same amount of judicial work. Criminal cases are grouped in a similar fashion.

The current assignment system is computer based. A separate assignment deck is kept for each category. (Prior to the introduction of the computerized assignment system, physical decks of assignment cards were used. The terms "assignment deck" and even "assignment card" continue in use as metaphors to describe the manner in which the computer operates.) In the deck the name of each regular active judge on full assignment appears an equal number of times. The name of the chief judge appears half as often as a regular active judge. The ratios for senior judges depend on the caseloads they are carrying, varying from being no different from that of a regular active judge, to a one-half share less than all of the categories.

As part of filing a new case, the assignment clerk enters the case category information into the assignment system. The system keeps track of cases processed and automatically shows the next available case number.

Once the case number and category are verified, the computer uses a shuffle procedure to pick a name from one of the unused names remaining in the assignment deck for the category selected. For obvious security reasons, the deputies assigning the cases do not have access to the software that sets up the assignment decks. The deputies responsible for setting up the decks do not assign cases. This system together with the changes in the make up of the deck due to equalization and the shuffling of the names prior to the actual assignment assures that staff cannot determine in advance the name of the judge to whom a case will be assigned.

The assignment system also handles the reassignment of cases. Cases are reassigned for a variety of reasons. The most frequent is the need to reassign a case because it is related to one pending on another judge's calendar. Recusals result in reassignments or equalization. When a new judge takes office, cases are reassigned from the calendars of sitting judges.

When a judge leaves, the cases on the judge's calendar are reassigned among sitting judges. There are even provisions in the procedures for reassignments due to errors made at assignment. When a judge is appointed to the Court an initial calendar is prepared. It consists of civil cases equal in number to the average number of civil and criminal cases pending on the calendars of sitting judges. The new judge gets only civil cases in the initial calendar. A civil case that was twice previously reassigned to form a new calendar cannot be reassigned a third time for that reason. Any civil case in which the trial is in process or has been held and the case is awaiting final ruling also cannot be reassigned. The remaining cases are arranged in case number order and a random selection is made. In this way the age distribution of the cases on the new judge's initial calendar reflects the average age distribution of all civil cases pending. Such a distribution serves to provide the new judge with a calendar that is reasonably close to the average in terms of workload.

LR 40.2. ASSIGNMENT PROCEDURES

(a) Assigning New Cases. The assignment clerk shall file each new case in accordance with procedures approved by the Court.

(b) Cases Filed After Hours. A judge accepting a case for filing as an emergency matter outside of the normal business hours of the clerk's office shall cause the initiating documents to be delivered to the clerk's office as early as practicable on the next business day. On receipt of the initiating documents, the assignment clerk shall process the case in accordance with section (a).

(c) Mail-In Cases. All cases received through the mail for filing shall be filed and assigned in accordance with section (a). The process of filing and assignment shall be completed on the day of receipt, provided that all necessary initiating documents and filing fees are submitted.

[Effective September 1, 1999.]

LR 40.3. DIRECT ASSIGNMENT OF CASES

(a) To Executive Committee. The following cases or categories of cases shall be assigned to the calendar of the Executive Committee on filing:

(1) Disciplinary cases brought pursuant to LR83.25 through LR83.31; and

(2) Such other cases as the chief judge may direct.

(b) To Specific Judge. In each of the following instances, the assignment clerk shall assign the case to a judge in the manner specified:

(1) *Cases Filed by Persons in Custody.* Any petition for writ of habeas corpus ("habeas corpus petition") or any complaint brought under the Civil Rights Act or 28 U.S.C. § 1331 challenging the terms or the conditions of confinement ("civil rights complaint") filed by or on behalf of a person in custody shall be assigned in the same manner as other civil cases except that—

(A) a subsequent habeas corpus petition shall be assigned to the judge to whom the most recently filed petition was assigned;

(B) a subsequent civil rights complaint shall be assigned to the judge to whom the most recently filed complaint was assigned;

(C) a habeas corpus petition to be assigned by lot shall be assigned to a judge other than the judge or judges to whom civil rights complaints filed by or on behalf of the petitioner have been assigned; and

(D) a civil rights complaint to be assigned by lot shall be assigned to a judge other than the judge or judges to whom habeas corpus petitions filed by or on behalf of the plaintiff have been assigned.

(2) *Re-filing of Cases Previously Dismissed.* When a case is dismissed with prejudice or without, and a second case is filed involving the same parties and relating to the same subject matter, the second case shall be assigned to the judge to whom the first case was assigned. The designation sheet presented at the time the second case is filed shall indicate the number of the earlier case and the name of the judge to whom it was assigned.

(3) *Removal of Cases Previously Remanded.* When a case previously remanded is again removed, it shall be assigned to the judge who previously ordered it to be remanded.

(4) *Petitions to Enforce Summonses Issued by the Internal Revenue Service.* Where two or more petitions to enforce summonses issued by the Internal Revenue Service ("I.R.S.") are presented for filing and the summonses involve the same taxpayer, the first petition shall be assigned by lot in accordance with the rules of this Court and any other petition shall be assigned directly to the judge to whom the first was assigned. The person presenting such petitions for filing shall notify the assignment clerk that they involve the same taxpayer. This section of shall not be construed as authorizing the direct assignment of petitions to enforce administrative process other than summonses issued by the I.R.S.

(5) *Cases Filed to Enforce, Modify, or Vacate Judgment.* Proceedings to enforce, modify, or vacate a judgment should be brought within the case in which the judgment was entered. If a separate case is filed for the purpose of enforcing, modifying, or vacating a judgment entered in a case previously filed in this District, the case shall be assigned directly to the judge to whom the earlier case was assigned.

(6) *Tag-Along Cases in Multidistrict Proceedings.* Where a civil case is filed as a potential tag-along action to a multidistrict litigation ("MDL") proceeding pending in the district, it shall be assigned directly to the judge handling the MDL proceeding. The judge handling the MDL proceeding may, at that judge's discretion, transfer to the Executive Committee for reassignment by lot any case assigned pursuant to this Rule that either—

(A) the MDL Panel determines should not be included in the MDL proceeding, or

(B) the judge assigned to the MDL proceeding determines pursuant to Rule 13 of the Rules of Procedure of the Judicial Panel on Multidistrict Litigation is not a tag-along case, or

(C) requires trial following the completion of the consolidated discovery.

(c) Direct Assignment in Social Security Cases. In a proceeding for judicial review of a final decision by the Commissioner of Social Security pursuant to 42 U.S.C. § 405(g), when a district judge or magistrate judge remands the case for further administrative proceedings, any subsequent proceedings in the district court involving that matter shall be assigned to the district and magistrate judge to which the preceding action for judicial review was originally assigned.

[Effective September 1, 1999. Amended effective October 4, 2006.]

Comment

The inclusion of section (c) will ensure that the judicial officer who originally decided to remand the case be assigned to review any subsequent appeals after remand to the Social Security Administration.

LR 40.3.1   ASSIGNMENTS INVOLVING BANKRUPTCY

(a) Referral to Bankruptcy Judges. Pursuant to 28 U.S.C. § 157(a), all cases under Title 11 U.S.C. and all proceedings arising under Title 11 U.S.C. or arising in or related to any cases under Title 11 U.S.C. are referred to the bankruptcy judges of this District.

(b) Assignment by Lot. Except as provided by sections (c) and (d), each of the following items shall be assigned by lot to a district judge:

(1) motions pursuant to 28 U.S.C. § 157(d) (including a recommendation by a bankruptcy judge) for the withdrawal of the reference of a bankruptcy ("B") case, or of a contested matter or adversary ("A") proceeding within a bankruptcy case;

(2) objections to proposed findings of fact and conclusions of law of a bankruptcy judge filed pursuant to 28 U.S.C. § 157(a)(1);

(3) appeals pursuant to 28 U.S.C. § 158(a)(1);

(4) motions for leave to appeal pursuant to 28 U.S.C. § 158(a)(3); and

(5) applications for a writ of mandamus or a similar writ in connection with a bankruptcy case, contested matter, or adversary proceeding.

All such assignments shall be made using the Civil II assignment category, except that objections to proposed findings and conclusions shall be assigned using the Civil III assignment category. The clerk is directed to assign a case so designated to the judge on whose calendar the previously filed case was assigned.

(c) Direct assignment for rehearing. Whenever there is activity in bankruptcy court following a district judge's consideration of any of the items described in section (b), any subsequent proceedings in the district court involving that item shall be assigned to the district judge who considered the item initially.

(d) Relatedness. The provisions of LR 40.4 are applicable to the items described in section (b).

(e) Designation Sheet. The person filing any of the items described in paragraph (b) shall complete the designation sheet required by LR3.1 and include on the sheet a designation of any such item, previously heard by the district court, that the filer believes would require direct assignment of the filing pursuant to this rule.

[Effective April 25, 2005. Amended effective December 23, 2014.]

LR 40.4. RELATED CASES; REASSIGNMENT OF CASES AS RELATED

(a) Definitions. Two or more civil cases may be related if one or more of the following conditions are met:

(1) the cases involve the same property;

(2) the cases involve some of the same issues of fact or law;

(3) the cases grow out of the same transaction or occurrence; or

(4) in class action suits, one or more of the classes involved in the cases is or are the same.

(b) Conditions for Reassignment. A case may be reassigned to the calendar of another judge if it is found to be related to an earlier-numbered case assigned to that judge and each of the following criteria is met:

(1) both cases are pending in this Court;

(2) the handling of both cases by the same judge is likely to result in a substantial saving of judicial time and effort;

(3) the earlier case has not progressed to the point where designating a later filed case as related would be likely to delay the proceedings in the earlier case substantially; and

(4) the cases are susceptible of disposition in a single proceeding.

(c) Motion To Reassign. A motion for reassignment based on relatedness may be filed by any party to a case. The motion shall—

(1) set forth the points of commonality of the cases in sufficient detail to indicate that the cases are related within the meaning of section (a), and

(2) indicate the extent to which the conditions required by section (b) will be met if the cases are found to be related.

A copy of the complaint or other relevant pleading in each of the higher-numbered cases that are the subject of the motion shall be attached to the motion.

The motion shall be filed in the lowest-numbered case of the claimed related set and noticed before the judge assigned to that case. Where all of the cases claimed to be related are assigned to magistrate judges on consent, then the motion shall be filed with the magistrate judge before whom the lowest-numbered case is pending. Where one or more of the cases claimed to be related is assigned to a magistrate judge on consent and one or more of the remaining cases is assigned to a district judge, the motion shall be filed with the district judge having the lowest-numbered case.

In order that all parties to a proceeding be permitted to respond on the questions of relatedness and possible reassignment, such motions should not generally be filed until after the answer or motions in lieu of answer have been filed in each of the proceedings involved.

(d) Ruling on Motion. The judge to whom the motion is presented may consult with the judge or judges before whom the other case or cases are pending. The judge shall enter an order finding whether or not the cases are related within the meaning of the rules of this Court and, if they are, whether the higher-numbered case or cases should be reassigned.

Where the judge finds that the cases are related and that reassignment should take place, a copy of that finding will be forwarded to the Executive Committee together with a request that the Committee reassign the higher-numbered case or cases.

A copy of any finding that cases either are or are not related and, if they are, that reassignment should or should not take place shall also be sent to each of the judges on whose calendar one or more of the higher-numbered cases is or are pending. Any judge to whom one or more of the cases involved is or are assigned may seek a review of the finding by the Executive Committee. The order entered by the Committee following review shall be final.

[Effective September 1, 1999. Amended effective November 2, 2010.]

LR 40.5. REMANDS; PROCEDURES FOR FOLLOWING APPEALS

(a) General. This rule shall not apply to remands resulting from appeals of summary judgments or in-

terlocutory orders unless the mandate or order remanding the case indicates that it is to be reassigned
to a judge other than the judge to whom the case was
previously assigned ("prior judge"). Whenever a
mandate from the Court of Appeals for the Federal
Circuit or the Seventh Circuit is filed with the clerk
indicating that the case appealed is remanded for a
new trial, the case shall be assigned to the Executive
Committee, except

(1) if the mandate or accompanying opinion indicates that the case is to be retried by the prior
judge, then the case shall remain on that judge's
calendar, or

(2) where the prior judge is no longer sitting and
the case is an Eastern Division case, it will be
reassigned by lot, or

(3) where the prior judge is no longer sitting and
the case is a Western Division case, it will be
assigned to the Western Division judge.

(b) Notice by Clerk. When a case is reassigned to
the Executive Committee pursuant to section (a), the
clerk shall forthwith notify all parties of record by
mail that the mandate has been filed and that unless a
stipulation is filed by all parties within 14 days after
the date of the notice indicating that all parties wish
the case returned to the prior judge, the case will be
reassigned to another judge.

(c) Reassignment. When a stipulation is filed indicating that the parties wish the case assigned to the
prior judge, the Executive Committee shall reassign
the case to that judge. When no such stipulation is
filed, the Executive Committee shall direct that the
case be reassigned to a judge other than the prior
judge. A case reassigned pursuant to this rule shall
be treated for assignment purposes as a new case.
The judge receiving the case is not authorized to
transfer a similar case to the Executive Committee for
reassignment to the prior judge.

[Effective September 1, 1999. Amended effective November
19, 2009.]

LR 41.1. DISMISSAL FOR WANT OF PROSECUTION OR BY DEFAULT

Cases which have been inactive for more than six
months may be dismissed for want of prosecution.

An order of dismissal for want of prosecution or an
order of default may be entered if counsel fails to
respond to a call of the case set by order of court.
Notice of the court call shall be by publication or as
otherwise provided by the court. In the Eastern Division publication shall be in the Chicago Daily Law
Bulletin unless the court provides otherwise.

[Effective September 1, 1999. Amended effective February
4, 2010.]

LR 42 TO LR 44. [RESERVED]

LR 45.1 ATTACHING A NOTE TO THE SUBPOENA PERMITTED

The validity of the subpoena shall not be affected by
attaching or delivering of a note or other memorandum containing instructions to a witness regarding the
exact date, time, and place the witness is required to
appear.

[Effective September 1, 1999.]

LR 46. [RESERVED]

LR 47.1. JURIES

(a) General. The chief judge shall from time to
time enter such orders as may be required to summon
petit jurors for the court. Except as provided for in
section (b), petit jurors shall be assigned to a single
jury pool and reassigned for service upon the request
of each judge. The jury pool shall be under the
supervision of the clerk. Unless otherwise ordered a
copy of the jury list showing the name, town and ZIP
code of each juror summoned shall be available for
viewing on the first day of the service period.

(b) Separate Panels. Where the extraordinary nature of a trial indicates that administrative efficiency
will be improved and substantial judicial time will be
saved through the use of a separate panel of petit
jurors, the chief judge may, at the request of the trial
judge, direct that such a separate jury panel be summoned.

(c) Qualification Forms are Confidential. Juror
qualification forms completed by the jurors shall be
confidential. Such forms shall not be made available
for inspection except upon order of the chief judge or
upon order of the assigned judge in connection with
the preparation or presentation of a motion challenging compliance with selection procedures pursuant to
28 U.S.C. § 1867. Orders directing that the juror
qualification forms be made available for inspection
shall specify the terms of the inspection, including the
forms to be inspected, the names of the persons
authorized to make the inspection, and any conditions
required regarding the release of information contained on the forms.

[Effective September 1, 1999.]

LR 48 TO LR 52. [RESERVED]

LR 53.1. MASTERS

(a) Appointment. The court may grant a motion
for the appointment of a master in a civil action where
the parties stipulate in writing to such an appointment. The stipulation shall indicate whether the master is to report upon particular issues or upon all the

issues. The procedure covering such a reference shall be the same as that governing any other reference to a master.

A judge may appoint the designated magistrate judge or, with the approval of the Executive Committee, a magistrate judge other than the designated magistrate judge to perform the duties of a special master.

Whenever an order of reference to a master is entered, the attorney procuring the order shall, at the time of filing thereof, deposit with the clerk a copy to be furnished to the master. On docketing the order, the clerk shall promptly send the copy to the master.

(b) Master May Sit Outside District. A master may sit within or outside of the District. If the master is requested to sit outside the District for the convenience of a party and there is opposition thereto by another party, the master may make an order for the holding of the hearing, or a part thereof, outside the District, upon such terms and conditions as shall be just.

(c) Motions Regarding Report. A motion to confirm or to reject, in whole or in part, a report of a master shall be heard by the judge appointing such master.

[Effective September 1, 1999.]

LR 54.1. TAXATION OF COSTS

(a) Time to File. Within 30 days of the entry of a judgment allowing costs, the prevailing party shall file a bill of costs with the clerk and serve a copy of the bill on each adverse party. If the bill of costs is not filed within 30 days, costs other than those of the clerk, taxable pursuant to 28 U.S.C. § 1920, shall be deemed waived. The court may, on motion filed within the time provided for the filing of the bill of costs, extend the time for filing the bill.

(b) Transcript Costs. Subject to the provisions of Fed.R.Civ.P. 54(d), the expense of any prevailing party in necessarily obtaining all or any part of a transcript for use in a case, for purposes of a new trial, or amended findings, or for appeal shall be taxable as costs against the adverse party. If in taxing costs the clerk finds that a transcript or deposition was necessarily obtained, the costs of the transcript or deposition shall not exceed the regular copy rate as established by the Judicial Conference of the United States and in effect at the time the transcript or deposition was filed unless some other rate was previously provided for by order of court. Court reporter appearance fees may be awarded in addition to the per page limit, but the fees shall not exceed the published rates on the Court website unless another rate was previously provided by order of court. Except as otherwise ordered by the court, only the cost of the original of such transcript or deposition together with the cost

of one copy each where needed by counsel and, for depositions, the copy provided to the court shall be allowed.

(c) Bond Premiums. If costs shall be awarded by the court to either or any party then the reasonable premiums or expenses paid on all bonds or stipulations or other security given by the party in that suit shall be taxed as part of the costs of that party.

(d) Fee of Special Master. After a master's compensation and disbursements have been allowed by the court, the prevailing party may pay such compensation and disbursements, and on payment the amount thereof shall be a taxable cost against the unsuccessful party or parties. Where, however, the court directs by order the parties against whom, or the proportion in which such compensation and disbursements shall be charged, or the fund or subject matter out of which they shall be paid, the party making the payment to the master shall be entitled to tax such compensation and disbursements only against such parties and in such proportions as the court has directed, and to payment of such taxable cost only out of such fund or subject matter as the court has directed.

[Effective September 1, 1999. Amended effective May 24, 2013.]

Committee Comment

This Rule has been amended in response to the Seventh Circuit Court of Appeals decision in *Harney v. City of Chicago*, ___ F.3d ___, 2012 WL 6097336 *10 (7th Cir. Dec. 10. 2012), in which the Court of Appeals recommended adoption of "an amendment of that rule [LR54.1] clarifying the availability of court reporter appearance fees over and above the allowable per page amount."

LR 54.2. JURY COSTS FOR UNUSED PANELS

If for any reason attributable to counsel or parties, including a settlement or change of plea, the court is unable to commence a jury trial as scheduled where a panel of prospective jurors has reported to the courthouse for the voir dire, the court may assess against counsel or parties responsible all or part of the cost of the panel. Any monies collected as a result of said assessment shall be paid to the clerk who shall promptly remit them to the Treasurer of the United States.

[Effective September 1, 1999.]

LR 54.3. ATTORNEY'S FEES AND RELATED NON-TAXABLE EXPENSES

(a) Definitions; General. For the purposes of this rule—

(1) "Fee motion" means a motion, complaint or any other pleading seeking only an award of attorney's fees and related nontaxable expenses,

(2) "Movant" means the party filing the fee motion,

(3) "Respondent" means a party from whom the movant seeks payment, and

(4) "Related nontaxable expenses" means any expense for which a prevailing party may seek reimbursement other than costs that are taxed by the clerk pursuant to Fed.R.Civ.P. 54(d)(1).

Unless otherwise ordered by the court, this rule does not apply to motions for sanctions under Fed. R.Civ.P. 11 or other sanctions provisions.

Sections (d) through (g) govern a fee motion that would be paid by a party to the litigation rather than out of a fund already created by judgment or by settlement.

(b) Time to File. Either before or after the entry of judgment the court may enter an order with respect to the filing of a fee motion pursuant to Fed. R.Civ.P. 54. Unless the court's order includes a different schedule for such filing, the motion shall be filed in accordance with the provisions of this rule and shall be filed and served no later than 91 days after the entry of the judgment or settlement agreement on which the motion is founded. If the court has not entered such an order before a motion has been filed pursuant to Fed.R.Civ.P. 54(d)(2)(B), then after such filing the court may order the parties to comply with the procedure set out in this rule as a post-filing rather than as a pre-filing procedure.

(c) Effect on Appeals. The filing of a fee motion shall not stop the running of the time for appeal of any judgment on which the motion is founded.

Where the parties reach an agreement as to the award and the award is to be based on a judgment, unless the agreement provides otherwise, it shall affect neither a party's right to appeal the fee order resulting from the agreement nor a party's right to seek a subsequent increase, decrease or vacation of the agreed award in the event the underlying judgment is reversed or modified by subsequent judicial proceedings or settlement.

The time requirements of Fed.R.Civ.P. 59 are not changed by this rule.

(d) Pre–Motion Agreement. The parties involved shall confer and attempt in good faith to agree on the amount of fees or related nontaxable expenses that should be awarded prior to filing a fee motion.

During the attempt to agree, the parties shall, upon request, provide the following information to each other:

(1) The movant shall provide the respondent with the time and work records on which the motion will be

based, and shall specify the hours for which compensation will and will not be sought. These records may be redacted to prevent disclosure of material protected by the attorney-client privilege or work product doctrine.

(2) The movant shall inform the respondent of the hourly rates that will be claimed for each lawyer, paralegal, or other person. If the movant's counsel or other billers have performed any legal work on an hourly basis during the period covered by the motion, the movant shall provide representative business records sufficient to show the types of litigation in which such hourly rates were paid and the rates that were paid in each type. If the movant's counsel has been paid on an hourly basis in the case in question or in litigation of the same type as the case in question, records showing the rates paid for those services must be provided. If the movant will rely on other evidence to establish appropriate hourly rates, such as evidence of rates charged by attorneys of comparable experience and qualifications or evidence of rates used in previous awards by courts or administrative agencies, the movant shall provide such other evidence.

(3) The movant shall furnish the evidence that will be used to support the related nontaxable expenses to be sought by the motion.

(4) The movant shall provide the respondent with the above information within 21 days of the judgment or settlement agreement upon which the motion is based, unless the court sets a different schedule.

(5) If no agreement is reached after the above information has been furnished, the respondent shall, within 21 days of receipt of that information, disclose the total amount of attorney's fees paid by respondent (and all fees billed but unpaid at the time of the disclosure and all time as yet unbilled and expected to be billed thereafter) for the litigation and shall furnish the following additional information as to any matters (rates, hours, or related nontaxable expenses) that remain in dispute:

(A) the time and work records (if such records have been kept) of respondent's counsel pertaining to the litigation, which records may be redacted to prevent disclosure of material protected by the attorney-client privilege or work product doctrine;

(B) evidence of the hourly rates for all billers paid by respondent during the litigation;

(C) evidence of the specific expenses incurred or billed in connection with the litigation, and the total amount of such expenses; and

(D) any evidence the respondent will use to oppose the requested hours, rates, or related nontaxable expenses.

By providing the opposing party with information under this rule about the party's hours, billing rates and related nontaxable expenses, no party shall be deemed to make any admission or waive any argument about the relevance or effect of such information in determining an appropriate award.

Within 14 days after the above exchange of information is completed and before the motion is filed, the parties shall specifically identify all hours, billing rates, or related nontaxable expenses (if any) that will and will not be objected to, the basis of any objections, and the specific hours, billing rates, and related nontaxable expenses that in the parties' respective views are reasonable and should be compensated. The parties will thereafter attempt to resolve any remaining disputes.

All information furnished by any party under this section shall be treated as strictly confidential by the party receiving the information. The information shall be used solely for purposes of the fee litigation, and shall be disclosed to other persons, if at all, only in court filings or hearings related to the fee litigation. A party receiving such information who proposes to disclose it in a court filing or hearing shall provide the party furnishing it with prior written notice and a reasonable opportunity to request an appropriate protective order.

(e) Joint Statement. If any matters remain in dispute after the above steps are taken, the parties, prior to the filing of the fee motion, shall prepare a joint statement listing the following:

(1) the total amount of fees and related nontaxable expenses claimed by the moving party (If the fee request is based on the "lodestar" method, the statement shall include a summary table giving the name, claimed hours, claimed rates, and claimed totals for each biller.);

(2) the total amount of fees and/or related nontaxable expenses that the respondent deems should be awarded (If the fees are contested, the respondent shall include a similar table giving respondent's position as to the name, compensable hours, appropriate rates, and totals for each biller listed by movant.);

(3) a brief description of each specific dispute remaining between the parties as to the fees or expenses; and

(4) a statement disclosing—

(A) whether the motion for fees and expenses will be based on a judgment or on a settlement of the underlying merits dispute, and

(B) if the motion will be based on a judgment, whether respondent has appealed or intends to appeal that judgment.

The parties shall cooperate to complete preparation of the joint statement no later than 70 days after the entry of the judgment or settlement agreement on which the motion for fees will be based, unless the court orders otherwise.

(f) Fee Motion. The movant shall attach the joint statement to the fee motion. Unless otherwise allowed by the court, the motion and any supporting or opposing memoranda shall limit their argument and supporting evidentiary matter to disputed issues.

(g) Motion for Instructions. A motion may be filed seeking instructions from the court where it appears that the procedures set forth in this rule cannot be followed within the time limits established by the rule or by order of court because of—

(1) the inability of the parties to resolve a dispute over what materials are to be turned over or the meaning of a provision of the rule,

(2) the failure of one or more of the parties to provide information required by the rule, or

(3) other disputes between the parties that cannot be resolved after good faith attempts.

The motion shall state with specificity the nature of the dispute or items not turned over and the attempts made to resolve the dispute or to obtain the items. The motion must be filed not later than 14 days following the expiration of the time within which the matter in dispute or the materials not turned over should have been delivered in accordance with the time table set out in this rule or in the court's order.

The court may on motion filed pursuant to this section, or on its own initiative, modify any time schedule provided for by this rule.

[Effective September 1, 1999. Amended effective July 6, 2000; February 4, 2010.]

LR 54.4. JUDGMENT OF FORECLOSURE

Except as otherwise directed by the court, any form of judgment of foreclosure presented for approval by the court shall contain the following statement with respect to attorneys' fees:

The court has approved the portion of the lien attributable to attorneys' fees only for purposes of the foreclosure sale, and not for purposes of determining the amount required to be paid personally by defendant in the event of redemption by defendant, or a deficiency judgment, or otherwise. In the event of redemption by defendant or for purposes of any personal deficiency judgment, this court reserves the right to review the amount of attorneys' fees to be included for either purpose. Plaintiff's counsel is required to notify defendant of the provisions of this paragraph.

[Effective September 1, 1999.]

LR 54.5. STIPULATION REGARDING PAYMENT OF FEES AND COSTS NOT PREPAID

(a) Stipulation. Where, pursuant to 28 U.S.C. § 1915, 28 U.S.C. § 1916 or 45 U.S.C. § 153(b), a plaintiff seeks to commence a civil action without paying fees and costs or giving security for them, the plaintiff and, if represented, counsel for the plaintiff, shall file with the complaint a stipulation that the recovery, if any, in the action shall be paid to the clerk, who shall pay from it the filing fees and other costs not previously paid and remit the balance to the plaintiff or counsel for plaintiff in accordance with section (b).

(b) Notification of Payment. Whenever money shall be paid to the clerk of this Court in compliance with section (a), the clerk shall notify the judge to whom the case is assigned of the amount paid and of any fees prescribed by statute, including those established by the Judicial Conference of the United States, which were not collected because plaintiff was permitted to maintain an action without prepayment of such fees. The judge shall thereupon enter an order directing the clerk to pay from the amount such fees and costs as were not prepaid and to remit the balance to plaintiff or counsel for plaintiff.

[Effective September 1, 1999.]

LR 55.   [RESERVED]

LR 56.1.   MOTIONS FOR SUMMARY JUDGMENT

(a) Moving Party. With each motion for summary judgment filed pursuant to Fed.R.Civ.P. 56 the moving party shall serve and file—

(1) any affidavits and other materials referred to in Fed.R.Civ.P. 56(e);

(2) a supporting memorandum of law; and

(3) a statement of material facts as to which the moving party contends there is no genuine issue and that entitle the moving party to a judgment as a matter of law, and that also includes:

(A) a description of the parties, and

(B) all facts supporting venue and jurisdiction in this Court.

The statement referred to in (3) shall consist of short numbered paragraphs, including within each paragraph specific references to the affidavits, parts of the record, and other supporting materials relied upon to support the facts set forth in that paragraph. Failure to submit such a statement constitutes grounds for denial of the motion. Absent prior leave of Court, a movant shall not file more than 80 separately-numbered statements of undisputed material fact.

If additional material facts are submitted by the opposing party pursuant to section (b), the moving .party may submit a concise reply in the form prescribed in that section for a response. All material facts set forth in the statement filed pursuant to

section (b)(3)(C) will be deemed admitted unless controverted by the statement of the moving party.

(b) Opposing Party. Each party opposing a motion filed pursuant to Fed.R.Civ.P. 56 shall serve and file—

(1) any opposing affidavits and other materials referred to in Fed.R.Civ.P. 56(e);

(2) a supporting memorandum of law; and

(3) a concise response to the movant's statement that shall contain:

(A) numbered paragraphs, each corresponding to and stating a concise summary of the paragraph to which it is directed, and

(B) a response to each numbered paragraph in the moving party's statement, including, in the case of any disagreement, specific references to the affidavits, parts of the record, and other supporting materials relied upon, and

(C) a statement, consisting of short numbered paragraphs, of any additional facts that require the denial of summary judgment, including references to the affidavits, parts of the record, and other supporting materials relied upon. Absent prior leave of Court, a respondent to a summary judgment motion shall not file more than 40 separately-numbered statements of additional facts. All material facts set forth in the statement required of the moving party will be deemed to be admitted unless controverted by the statement of the opposing party.

[NOTE: Rule 56.1 was adopted by General Order of April 20, 2006]

[Effective September 1, 1999;   amended effective April 20, 2006.]

Committee Comment

Local Rule 56.1 is revised to set forth limits on the number of statements of fact that may be offered in connection with a summary judgment motion. The judges of this Court have observed that parties frequently include in their LR56.1 statements facts that are unnecessary to the motion and/or are disputed. The judges' observation is that in the vast majority of cases, a limit of 80 asserted statements of fact and 40 assertions of additional statements of fact will be more than sufficient to determine whether the case is appropriate for summary judgment. The number of statements of fact has been set in light of the requirement of section (a)(3), which requires that only "material facts" be set down. A party may seek leave to file more asserted statements of fact or additional fact, upon a showing that the complexity of the case requires a relaxation of the 80 or 40 statement limit.

LR 56.2.   NOTICE TO PRO SE LITIGANTS OPPOSING SUMMARY JUDGMENT

Any party moving for summary judgment against a party proceeding pro se shall serve and file as a separate document, together with the papers in support of the motion, a "Notice to Pro Se Litigant Opposing Motion for Summary Judgment" in the form indicated below. Where the pro se party is not the plaintiff, the movant should amend the form notice as necessary to reflect that fact.

NOTICE TO PRO SE LITIGANT OPPOSING MOTION FOR SUMMARY JUDGMENT

The defendant has moved for summary judgment against you. This means that the defendant is telling the judge that there is no disagreement about the important facts of the case. The defendant is also claiming that there is no need for a trial of your case and is asking the judge to decide that the defendant should win the case based on its written argument about what the law is.

In order to defeat the defendant's request, you need to do one of two things: you need to show that there is a dispute about important facts and a trial is needed to decide what the actual facts are *or* you need to explain why the defendant is wrong about what the law is.

Your response must comply with Rule 56(e) of the Federal Rules of Civil Procedure and Local Rule 56.1 of this court. These rules are available at any law library. Your Rule 56.1 statement needs to have numbered paragraphs responding to each paragraph in the defendant's statement of facts. If you disagree with any fact offered by the defendant, you need to explain how and why you disagree with the defendant. You also need to explain how the documents or declarations that you are submitting support your version of the facts. If you think that some of the facts offered by the defendant are immaterial or irrelevant, you need to explain why you believe that those facts should not be considered.

In your response, you must also describe and *include* copies of documents which show why you disagree with the defendant about the facts of the case. You may rely upon your own declaration or the declarations of other witnesses. A declaration is a signed statement by a witness. The declaration *must* end with the following phrase: "I declare under penalty of perjury under the laws of the United States that the foregoing is true and correct," and *must* be dated. If you do not provide the Court with evidence that shows that there is a dispute about the facts, the judge will be required to assume that the defendant's factual contentions are true, and, if the defendant is also correct about the law, your case will be dismissed.

If you choose to do so, you may offer the Court a list of facts that you believe are in dispute and require a trial to decide. Your list of disputed facts should be supported by your documents or declarations. It is important that you comply fully with these rules and respond to each fact offered by the defendant, and explain how your documents or declarations support

your position. If you do not do so, the judge will be forced to assume that you do not dispute the facts which you have not responded to.

Finally, you should explain why you think the defendant is wrong about what the law is.

[NOTE: Rule 56.2 was adopted by General Order of November 3, 2000]

[Effective November 3, 2000.]

LR 57.   [RESERVED]

LR 58.1.   SATISFACTION OF JUDGMENT

The clerk shall enter the satisfaction of a judgment in any of the following circumstances:

(1) upon the filing of a statement of satisfaction of the judgment executed and acknowledged by:

(A) the judgment-creditor, or

(B) by a legal representative or assignee of the judgment-creditor who files evidence of their authority, or

(C) if the filing is within two years of the entry of the judgment, by the attorney or proctor of record for the judgment-creditor.

(2) upon payment to the court of the amount of the judgment plus interest and costs;

(3) if the judgment-creditor is the United States, upon the filing of a statement of satisfaction executed by the United States attorney;

(4) in an admiralty proceeding, upon issuance of an order of satisfaction, such order to be made on the consent of the proctors if such consent be given within two years from the entry of the decree; or

(5) upon receipt of a certified copy of a statement of satisfaction entered in another district.

[Effective September 1, 1999.]

LR 59 TO LR 61.   [RESERVED]

LR 62.1.   SUPERSEDEAS BOND

The bond shall be conditioned for the satisfaction of the judgment in full together with costs, interest, and damages for delay, if for any reason the appeal is dismissed or if the judgment is affirmed, and to satisfy in full such modification of the judgment and such costs, interest, and damages as the appellate court may adjudge and award.

A supersedeas bond, where the judgment is for a sum of money only, shall be in the amount of the judgment plus one year's interest at the rate provided in 28 U.S.C. § 1961, plus $500 to cover costs. If in conformance with LR65.1, the bond may be approved by the clerk. The bond amount fixed hereunder is without prejudice to any party's right to seek timely judicial determination of a higher or lower amount.

[Effective September 1, 1999.]

LR 63 TO LR 64. [RESERVED]

LR 65.1. SURETIES ON BONDS

(a) **General.** Bonds and similar undertakings may be executed by the surety or sureties alone, except in bankruptcy and criminal cases or where a different procedure is prescribed by law. No member of the bar nor any officer or employee of this Court shall act as surety in any action or proceeding in this court.

(b) **Security.** Except as otherwise provided by law, every bond or similar undertaking must be secured by one of the following:

(1) the deposit of cash or obligations of the United States in the amount of the bond, or

(2) the undertaking or guaranty of a corporate surety holding a certificate of authority from the Secretary of the Treasury, or

(3) the undertaking or guaranty of two individual residents of the Northern District of Illinois, provided that each individual surety shall file an affidavit of justification, which shall list the following information:

(a) the surety's full name, occupation, residence and business addresses, and

(b) a statement showing that the surety owns real or personal property within this District which, after excluding property exempt from execution and deducting the surety's debts, liabilities and other obligations (including those which may arise by virtue of acting as surety on other bonds or undertakings), is properly valued at no less than twice the amount of the bond, or

(4) an unconditional letter of credit is an approved form of security and shall be submitted on LR65.1 Form of Letter of Credit, or on a form agreed to by the parties.

[Effective September 1, 1999. Amended effective July 1, 2008.]

LR 65.2. APPROVAL OF BONDS BY THE CLERK

Except in criminal cases, or where another procedure is prescribed by law, the clerk may approve bonds without an order of court if—

(1) the amount of the bond has been fixed by a judge, by court rule, or by statute, and

(2) the bond is secured in accordance with LR65.1(b).

[Effective September 1, 1999.]

LR 65.3. SECURITY FOR COSTS

Upon good cause shown, the court may order the filing of a bond as security for costs. Except as ordered by the court, the bond will be secured in compliance with LR65.1. The bond shall be conditioned to secure the payment of all fees which the party filing it must pay by law to the clerk, marshal or other officer of the court and all costs of the action which the party filing it may be directed to pay to any other party.

[Effective September 1, 1999.]

LR 65.1.1. NOTICE OF MOTION TO ENFORCE LIABILITY OF SUPERSEDEAS BOND

Whenever a notice of motion to enforce the liability of a surety upon an appeal or a supersedeas bond is served upon the clerk pursuant to Fed.R.Civ.P. 65.1, the party making such motion shall deposit with the clerk one additional copy for each surety to be served.

[Effective September 1, 1999.]

LR 66.1. RECEIVERS; ADMINISTRATION OF ESTATES

(a) **General.** The administration of estates by receivers or other officers shall be similar to that in bankruptcy cases except that the court in its discretion shall—

(1) fix the allowance of compensation of receivers or similar officers, their counsel, and any others appointed to aid in the administration of the estate, and

(2) direct the manner in which the estate shall be administered, including the conduct of its business, the discovery and acquirement of its assets, and the formation of reorganization plans.

(b) **Reports by Receiver.** Unless otherwise ordered, a receiver, or other similar officer appointed by this Court, shall as soon as practicable after appointment, but in any event not later than 21 days thereafter, file an inventory of all property, real, personal or mixed, of which the receiver has taken possession or control, together with a list of the then known liabilities of the estate and a report explaining such inventory.

Thereafter and until discharged, the receiver shall file a current report every four months, unless the court fixes some other filing interval. The current report and account shall list the receipts and disbursements and summarize the activities of the receiver.

[Effective September 1, 1999. Amended effective November 19, 2009.]

LR 67.1. INVESTMENT OF FUNDS DEPOSITED WITH CLERK

All funds ordered deposited with the clerk pursuant to 28 U.S.C. § 2041 for deposit in the registry fund of the Court shall be deposited in the registry account, provided that the Court in exceptional circumstances may for good cause shown direct the clerk to hold the funds deposited in some other form of interest bearing investment. Where the Court so orders, the order shall specify—

(1) the reason or reasons for such alternative form of investment,

(2) the amount to be invested,

(3) the type of account or instrument in which the funds are to be invested, and

(4) the term of the investment.

[Effective September 1, 1999.]

LR 68. [RESERVED]

LR 69.1. NOTICE OF SALE

The notice of a proposed sale of property directed to be made by an order or judgment of the court in a civil action need not, unless otherwise ordered by the court, set out the terms of sale specified in the order or judgment. The notice will be sufficient if in substantially the following form:

United States District Court
Northern District of Illinois
_____Division

NOTICE OF SALE

Pursuant to *(order or judgment)* of the United States District Court for the Northern District of Illinois, _____ Division, filed in the office of the clerk of that Court on *(date)* in the cause entitled *(name and docket number)* the undersigned will sell at public sale at *(place of sale)* on *(date and hour of sale)* the property in said *(order or judgment)* described and therein directed to be sold, to which *(order or judgment)* reference is made for the terms of sale and for a description of the property which may be briefly described as follows:

_____

_____

_____

Dated: (date)

The notice need not describe the property by metes and bounds or otherwise in detail and will be sufficient if in general terms it identifies the property by specifying its nature and location. However, it shall state the approximate acreage of any real estate outside the limits of any town or city, the street, lot and block number of any real estate within any town or city, the termini of any railroad and a general statement of the character of any improvements upon the property.

[Effective September 1, 1999.]

LR 70 TO LR 71. [RESERVED]

LR 72.1. DESIGNATED MAGISTRATE JUDGES: REFERRALS

At the time any case is filed and assigned to a district judge in the Eastern Division, the name of a magistrate judge shall also be assigned in accordance with the procedures adopted pursuant to LR40.2(a) when applicable. The magistrate judge so assigned shall be the designated magistrate judge for that case. Whenever a new case is assigned to a district judge directly and not by lot pursuant to LR40.3(b), the designated magistrate judge for the case originally assigned by lot will be the designated magistrate judge for the later filed case.

Any judge wishing to refer a matter in a civil case pending on that judge's calendar to a magistrate judge may do so following procedures approved by the Executive Committee.

Where two or more cases are related, the designated magistrate judge in the lowest-numbered case of the set of related cases will be the designated magistrate judge for all cases in the set. The designated magistrate judge in the lowest-numbered case will remain the designated magistrate judge for the set as long as any cases in the set are pending.

Except as ordered by the Executive Committee, the reassignment of a case from one district judge to another shall not change the designated magistrate judge for that case.

[Effective September 1, 1999. Amended effective May 31, 2011.]

LR 73.1. MAGISTRATE JUDGES: REASSIGNMENT ON CONSENT

(a) **Procedure for Parties to Consent to Appear Before a Magistrate Judge.** Consent forms filed by parties will be maintained by the plaintiff or plaintiff's counsel until such time as all parties or their counsel have signed the form. At such time as the consent form has been signed by all of the parties, a single joint statement indicating that all parties have consented must be filed electronically with the Court, unless the assigned judge or magistrate judge allows the parties to file a single paper consent form in court. If a case in which a consent has been filed is reassigned to a magistrate judge other than the magistrate judge designated pursuant to Local Rule 72.1, the parties may object within 21 days of such reassignment. If a timely objection is filed by any party, the case will be reassigned to the district judge before whom it was last pending. If no objection has been filed within 21 days, the parties will be deemed to have consented to the reassignment.

(b) Reassignment of Case. Any judge wishing to reassign a case pending on that judge's calendar to a magistrate judge following the consent by all parties to have the magistrate judge conduct any and all proceedings in that case will transfer the case to the calendar of the designated magistrate judge.

(c) Consent to Enter Judgment. A magistrate judge is authorized to enter a final judgment for a sum certain to which all the parties have consented in writing or a judgment of dismissal to which all of the parties have stipulated in writing, provided that the parties indicate their consent to the entry of the judgment by the magistrate judge either in writing or in open court at the time of the entry of the judgment.

(d) Limited Consents. Parties may consent to the transfer of part of a proceeding to a magistrate judge to act pursuant to 28 U.S.C. § 636(c). Such consents shall be filed in the same manner as the consents for a transfer of the entire proceeding. Upon notification of the filing of such consents by the parties, the district judge may transfer that portion of the case covered by the consents for reassignment to the Executive Committee in accordance with the procedures adopted pursuant to LR40.2(a). If the Committee approves the reassignment, the motion may be reassigned to the calendar of the designated magistrate judge. Where such a reassignment is made, the case shall remain on the calendar of the district judge.

[Effective September 1, 1999. Amended effective October 4, 2006; May 24, 2013.]

Comment

The consent form referred to in section (a) may be found on the District Court website (www.ilnd.uscourts.gov) with instructions for completion.

LR 74 TO LR 76.   [RESERVED]

LR 77.1.   PLACES OF HOLDING COURT

The regular places of holding court in this District shall be the Everett McKinley Dirksen Federal Courthouse at Chicago for the Eastern Division and the United States Courthouse at Rockford for the Western Division.

No judge of this Court shall hold a special session or sessions of the court at a location or locations other than the regular places of holding court, without first having obtained permission from the Executive Committee, provided, that if an emergency matter arises at night, on Saturdays or Sundays or holidays, a judge may entertain motions or petitions at a place other than a regular place of holding court.

[Effective September 1, 1999.]

LR 77.2.   EMERGENCIES; EMERGENCY JUDGES

(a) Definitions. For the purpose of these rules—

(1) "Emergency judge" means the judge assigned to perform the duties of emergency judge specified by any local rule or procedure adopted by the Court,

(2) "Emergency magistrate judge" means the magistrate judge assigned to perform the duties of emergency magistrate judge specified by any local rule or procedure adopted by the Court, and

(3) "Emergency matter" means a matter of such a nature that the delay in hearing it that would result from its being treated as any other matter would cause serious and irreparable harm to one or more of the parties to the proceeding provided that requests for continuances or leave to file briefs or interrogatories in excess of the limits prescribed by these rules will normally be entertained as emergency matters only during the summer sessions, and

(4) "Summer session" means the fourteen-week period beginning on the first Monday in June.

(b) Duties of Emergency Judge. The emergency judge is responsible for hearing all emergency matters not previously assigned to a judge of this Court that arise outside of the regular business hours of the Court, except for discovery motions as set forth in subsection (c) below.

During regular office hours other than in the summer session, the emergency judge will not hear emergency matters arising out of the cases assigned to the calendar of another judge where that judge is sitting, except on approval of the chief judge at the request of the judge to whom the case is assigned. The emergency judge will also hear the following matters or preside at the following ceremonies:

(1) petitions for admission brought by attorneys wishing to be admitted to practice before the Court;

(2) requests for review or de novo determinations of matters directly assigned to the duty magistrate brought pursuant to LCrR50.4;

(3) petitions presented by the United States Immigration and Naturalization Service;

(4) ceremonies for the mass admission of attorneys to the bar of this Court; and

(5) ceremonies for the administration of the oath of allegiance to newly naturalized citizens.

(c) Any emergency matter involving discovery or requests for protective orders that would otherwise be brought before the emergency judge are referred and shall be brought before the magistrate judge assigned to the case (or the emergency magistrate judge when the assigned magistrate judge is not sitting).

(d) Duties of Emergency Magistrate Judge. The emergency magistrate judge is responsible for hearing any emergency matter arising in a case referred or assigned to a magistrate judge when that magistrate judge is not sitting.

(e) Western Division. A party in a case filed in or to be filed in the Western Division with an emergency matter should first contact the Western Division judge, or in that judge's absence, the Western Division magistrate judge. If neither can be reached, then the emergency judge is authorized to handle the matter.

[Effective September 1, 1999. Amended effective April 1, 2002; May 11, 2009.]

Committee Comment

In general, matters are to be presented to the judge to whom the case is assigned. Under procedures adopted by the Court, if a judge anticipates being absent temporarily, that judge will designate another judge to hear the absent judge's call. The name of the designated judge is posted on the door of the courtroom regularly used by the absent judge. It is also likely to be listed in the Chicago Daily Law Bulletin.

If the absent judge did not designate another judge or where both the absent judge and the designated judge are unavailable, an emergency matter can then be taken before the emergency judge. If the emergency judge should also be unavailable, the matter can be brought to the attention of the chief judge. The chief judge is the chairperson of the Executive Committee, the Court's calendar committee. In that role the chief judge can instruct the parties as to which judge should hear the matter.

While emergency matters arising outside of regular business hours are rare, it is not unusual that a party can anticipate that happening. An example is ongoing negotiations which, if they do not reach agreement, will lead one of the parties to seek injunctive relief and the negotiations must be concluded by a point in time that lies outside of regular business hours, e.g., midnight on a Saturday. In such instances the party should make every effort to contact the chambers of the emergency judge and inform staff of the potential emergency. In this way arrangements can be made that will give greater assurance that the emergency judge will be available in the event that the emergency matter does in fact occur. If an emergency matter occurs outside of regular business hours and the party has not made prior arrangements with the emergency judge, a telephone number is published in the Chicago Daily Law Bulletin for contacting a member of the staff of the emergency judge.

LR 77.3. CLERK TO SIGN CERTAIN ORDERS

The clerk shall sign orders of the following classes without submission to the court:

(1) consent orders extending for not more than 21 days in any instance the time to file the record on appeal and to docket the appeal in the appellate court, except in criminal cases;

(2) orders of discontinuance, or dismissal on consent, except in bankruptcy proceedings and in causes to which Rules 23(c) and 66 of the Federal Rules of Civil Procedure apply; and

(3) consent orders satisfying decrees or canceling bonds.

[Effective September 1, 1999. Amended effective November 19, 2009.]

LR 78.1. MOTIONS: FILING IN ADVANCE OF HEARING

Except where a judge fixes a different time in accordance with this rule, the original of any motion shall be filed by 4:30 p.m. of the *second* business day preceding the date of presentment.

A judge may fix a time for delivery longer than that provided by this rule, or elect to hear motions less frequently than daily, or both. In those instances where a judge elects to fix a longer delivery time, or hear motions less frequently than daily, or both, the judge shall notify the clerk in writing of the practice to be adopted. The clerk shall maintain a list of the current motion practices of each of the judges at the assignment desk.

[Effective September 1, 1999; Amended effective October 13, 2004.]

LR 78.2. MOTIONS: DENIAL FOR FAILURE TO PROSECUTE

Where the moving party, or if the party is represented by counsel, counsel for the moving party, delivers a motion or objection to a magistrate judge's order or report without the notice required by LR5.3(b) and fails to serve notice of a date of presentment within 14 days of delivering the copy of the motion or objection to the court as provided by LR5.4, the court may on its own initiative deny the motion or objection.

[Effective September 1, 1999. Amended effective February 28, 2007; November 19, 2009.]

LR 78.3. MOTIONS: BRIEFING SCHEDULES; ORAL ARGUMENTS; FAILURE TO FILE BRIEF

The court may set a briefing schedule. Oral argument may be allowed in the court's discretion.

Failure to file a supporting or answering memorandum shall not be deemed to be a waiver of the motion or a withdrawal of opposition thereto, but the court on its own motion or that of a party may strike the motion or grant the same without further hearing.

Failure to file a reply memorandum within the requisite time shall be deemed a waiver of the right to file.

[Effective September 1, 1999.]

LR 78.4. MOTIONS: COPIES OF EVIDENTIARY MATTER TO BE SERVED

Where evidentiary matter, in addition to affidavits permitted or required under Rules 5 or 6 of the Federal Rules of Civil Procedure, will be submitted in support of a motion, copies thereof shall be served with the notice of motion.

[Effective September 1, 1999.]

LR 78.5. MOTIONS: REQUEST FOR DECISION; REQUEST FOR STATUS REPORT

Any party may on notice provided for by LR5.3 call a motion to the attention of the court for decision.

Any party may also request the clerk to report on the status of any motion on file for at least seven months without a ruling or on file and fully briefed for at least sixty days. Such requests will be in writing. On receipt of a request the clerk will promptly verify that the motion is pending and meets the criteria fixed by this section. If it is not pending or does not meet the criteria, the clerk will so notify the person making the request. If it is pending and does meet the criteria, the clerk will thereupon notify the judge before whom the motion is pending that a request has been received for a status report on the motion. The clerk will not disclose the name of the requesting party to the judge. If the judge provides information on the status of the motion, the clerk will notify all parties. If the judge does not provide any information within ten days of the clerk's notice to the judge, the clerk will notify all parties that the motion is pending and that it has been called to the judge's attention.

[Effective September 1, 1999.]

LR 79.1. RECORDS OF THE COURT

(a) **Retention of Exhibits.** Exhibits shall be retained by the attorney producing them unless the court orders them deposited with the clerk. In proceedings before a master or other like officer, the officer may elect to include exhibits with the report.

(b) **Availability of Exhibits.** Exhibits retained by counsel are subject to orders of the court. Upon request, counsel shall make the exhibits or copies thereof available to any other party to enable that party to designate or prepare the record on appeal.

(c) **Removal of Exhibits.** Exhibits deposited with the clerk shall be removed by the party responsible for them—

(1) 90 days after a final decision is rendered if no appeal is taken from that decision, or

(2) where an appeal is taken, within 30 days after the mandate of the reviewing court is filed.

A party failing to comply with this rule shall be notified by the clerk to remove the exhibits. If a party fails to remove the exhibits within 30 days following such notice, the material shall be sold by the marshal at public or private sale or disposed of as the court directs. The net proceeds of the sale shall be paid into the registry of the Court.

(d) **Withdrawal of Records.** Pleadings and records filed and exhibits deposited with the clerk shall not be withdrawn from the custody of the Court except as provided by these rules or upon order of court. Parties withdrawing their exhibits from the court's custody and persons withdrawing items pursuant to an order of court shall give the clerk a signed receipt identifying the material taken, which receipt shall be filed.

[Effective September 1, 1999.]

LR 79.2. REDEMPTION FROM JUDICIAL SALES

The clerk shall maintain a listing in which shall be recorded any certificate of purchase issued by the United States marshal, master in chancery or other officer of this court, together with any certificate of redemption from such sale, the costs thereof to be taxed in the cause in which the sale is made.

[Effective September 1, 1999.]

LR 80. [RESERVED]

LR 81.1. COMPLAINTS UNDER THE CIVIL RIGHTS ACT, 42 U.S.C. § 1983, BY PERSONS IN CUSTODY

Pro se complaints brought under the Civil Rights Act, 42 U.S.C. § 1983, by persons in custody shall be in writing, signed and certified. Such complaints shall be on forms supplied by the Court.

[Effective September 1, 1999.]

LR 81.2 REMOVALS; REMANDS OF REMOVALS

After the entry of an order remanding a case to a state court pursuant to 28 U.S.C. § 1447(c) the clerk shall not transmit the certified copy of the remand order for 14 days following the date of docketing that order unless the court ordering the remand directs the clerk to transmit the certified copy of the order at an earlier date.

The filing of a petition for reconsideration of such order shall not stop the remand of the case unless the court orders otherwise.

[Effective March 13, 2008.]

LR 81.3. HABEAS CORPUS PROCEEDINGS BY PERSONS IN CUSTODY

(a) Approved Form. Petitions for writs of habeas corpus filed pursuant to 28 U.S.C. § 2241 and § 2254 and motions filed pursuant to 28 U.S.C. § 2255 shall, when filed by persons in custody, be submitted on forms approved by the Executive Committee. The clerk will supply copies of the approved forms to any person requesting them.

(b) Capital Punishment Cases. Post conviction petitions filed pursuant to 28 U.S.C. § 2254 and § 2255 by or on behalf of a petitioner under sentence of capital punishment shall proceed in accordance with the *District Court Rules for the Disposition of Post Conviction Petitions Brought Pursuant to 28 U.S.C. § 2254 and § 2255 in Cases Involving Petitioners Under a Sentence of Capital Punishment* adopted by the Judicial Council of the Seventh Circuit.

(c) Filing Outside of Business Hours. Counsel for the petitioner and counsel for any other person or group seeking leave to file amicus briefs or motions should communicate with either the chief deputy clerk or the senior staff attorney promptly after counsel's appointment to establish procedures to be used in the event of an emergency. Should an emergency arise before such procedures have been established and at a time that the clerk's office is not open, counsel should use the phone number listed in the *Chicago Daily Law Bulletin* for after hours emergencies. [That number is (312) 514–9622.]

(d) § 2255 Motions. The clerk shall cause a civil case number to be assigned to any motion filed pursuant to 28 U.S.C. § 2255. Except where otherwise ordered, a separate file and docket of the pleadings filed in connection with such motions shall be maintained under the civil case number. The clerk shall cause a docket entry to be made on the criminal docket indicating the filing of any § 2255 motion and the civil case number assigned to the motion. The docket entry will also indicate that a file and docket with that civil case number is maintained for filing and docketing the motion and pleadings associated with the § 2255 motion.

[Effective September 1, 1999.]

LR 81.4. HABEAS CORPUS PROCEEDINGS IN REMOVAL CASES

(a) Appeal From Immigration Judge. Where an appeal from an order of an Immigration Judge is permitted by law, the petition must show that the alien has taken such an appeal to the Board of Immigration Appeals and that the appeal has been denied.

(b) Petition. In complying with the requirements of 28 U.S.C. § 2242, the petitioner shall specify the acts which have deprived the petitioner of a fair hearing or other reasons entitling petitioner to the relief sought. To the extent practicable, the petition shall state the following:

(1) that the facts recited have been obtained from the records of the Immigration and Naturalization Service; or

(2) that access to such records has been refused, in which event the petition shall state when and by whom application was made and refused; or

(3) that the interval between the notice of removal and the date of removal is too short to allow an examination of the records.

The petition shall further set forth the dates of the notice and the affirmance of the orders, the date set for departure, and the basis for inability to make the necessary examination.

(c) Service of Writ and Stay of Order. The writ shall be addressed to, and must be personally served upon, the officer who has actual physical custody of the alien. Service may not be made upon a master after a ship has cast off her moorings. Service may not be made upon a captain of an aircraft after an alien has boarded the aircraft and the aircraft door is closed. Service of the writ does not stay the removal of an alien pending the Court's decision on the writ, unless the Court orders otherwise.

[NOTE: Rule 81.4 was amended by General Order of January 31, 2000]

[Effective September 1, 1999. Amended effective January 31, 2000.]

LR 82. [RESERVED]

LR 83.1. COURT FACILITIES: LIMITATIONS ON USE

(a) Court Environs Defined. For the purpose of this rule the term "court environs" shall refer to the following areas:

(1) in Chicago in the Courthouse:

(A) the 6th through the 8th floors, and the 10th through the 25th floors, inclusive;

(B) the offices of the Pretrial Services Department of this Court on the 15th floor, and the public corridors immediately adjacent to those offices;

(C) the central jury assembly lounge, south elevator banks, and corridors leading from one to the other on the 2nd floor; and

(D) the immediate areas surrounding the elevators on the 1st floor;

(2) in Chicago but not in the Courthouse, the offices of the Probation Department of this Court located at 55 East Monroe Street;

(3) in the Eastern Division but not in Chicago, the immediate area surrounding the courtroom on the 2nd floor of the Federal Building and Courthouse at Joliet; and

(4) in Rockford in the Courthouse:

(A) the entire 5th and 6th floors:

(B) the 1st floor areas to include the Bankruptcy Court clerk's office, the offices of Probation and Pretrial Services, and the public corridors immediately adjacent to those offices;

(C) the 2nd floor jury assembly room, grand jury room. District Court clerk's office, and the public corridors immediately adjacent to those offices;

(D) the 3rd floor Bankruptcy Court courtrooms, the mediation rooms, the 4th floor Bankruptcy Court chambers, and the corridors immediately adjacent to those spaces.

(b) **Soliciting & Loitering Prohibited.** Soliciting and loitering within the court environs is prohibited. The unapproved congregating of groups or the causing of a disturbance or nuisance within the courthouses of this Court is prohibited. Picketing or parading outside of the courthouses of this Court is prohibited only when such picketing or parading obstructs or impedes the orderly administration of justice.

(c) **No Cameras or Recorders.** Except as provided for in section (e) below, the taking of photographs, radio and television broadcasting or taping in the court environs during the progress of or in connection with judicial proceedings including proceedings before a United States magistrate judge, whether or not court is actually in session, is prohibited.

(d) **Marshal to Enforce.** The United States marshal and the Custodian of the courthouses shall enforce sections (b) and (c) of this rule, either by ejecting violators from the courthouse or by causing them to appear before one of the judges of this Court for a hearing and the imposition of such punishment as the court may deem proper.

(e) **Limited Exception for Video Recording Pilot Program.** Proceedings being recorded as part of the video recording pilot program approved by the Judicial Conference of the United States Courts in September of 2010 are exempted from the provisions of section (c) of this Rule. Such recordings must comply with guidelines for the pilot program approved by the Judicial Conference. These guidelines allow recordings by Court cameras only. No other recordings are allowed.

[Effective September 1, 1999. Amended effective November 2, 2010; June 8, 2011; January 31, 2012; June 29, 2012.]

LR 83.2. OATH OF MASTER, COMMISSIONER, ETC. [DELETED]

Deleted June 2, 2011 per General Order 11–0012.

[Effective September 1, 1999. Amended effective May 19, 2011. Deleted effective June 2, 2011.]

LR 83.3. PUBLICATION OF ADVERTISEMENTS

Except in sales of realty or interests therein, publication of any notice or advertisement required by law or rule of court shall be made in a newspaper of general circulation, in the city of Chicago when the case is pending in the Eastern Division, and in a newspaper of general circulation in the cities of Freeport or Rockford when the case is pending in the Western Division. Additional notices or advertisements may be published via the Internet or e-mail, or such other means as ordered by the court.

[Effective September 1, 1999. Amended effective June 2, 2011.]

LR 83.4. TRANSFERS OF CASES UNDER 28 U.S.C. §§ 1404, 1406, 1412

When an order is entered directing the clerk to transfer a case to another district pursuant to the provisions of 28 U.S.C. §§ 1404, 1406, or 1412, the clerk shall delay the transfer of the case for 14 days following the date of docketing the order of transfer, provided that where the court directs that the case be transferred forthwith, no such delay shall be made. In effecting the transfer, the clerk shall transmit the original of all documents, including the order of transfer, and a certified copy of the docket. The clerk shall note on the docket the date of the transfer.

The filing of a petition for reconsideration of an order of transfer shall not serve to stop the transfer of the case. The court on its own motion or on motion of the party filing a petition for reconsideration may direct the clerk not to complete the transfer process until a date certain or further order of court.

[Effective September 1, 1999.]

LR 83.5. CONFIDENTIALITY OF ALTERNATIVE DISPUTE RESOLUTION PROCEEDINGS

Pursuant to 28 U.S.C. § 652(d), all non-binding alternative dispute resolution ("ADR") proceedings referred or approved by any judicial officer of this court in a case pending before such judicial officer, including any act or statement made by any party, attorney or other participant, shall, in all respects, be privileged and not reported, recorded, placed in evidence, made known to the trial court or jury (without consent of all parties), or construed for any purpose as an admission in the case referred or in any case or proceeding. No participant in the ADR proceedings shall be bound by anything done or said at the ADR conference unless a settlement is reached, in which event the settlement shall be reduced to writing or otherwise memorialized and shall be binding upon all parties to the settlement.

[NOTE: Rule 83.5 was adopted by General Order of November 30, 2000]

[Effective November 30, 2000.]

LR 83.6 TO LR 83.9   [RESERVED]

LR 83.10.   GENERAL BAR

(a) **Qualifications.** An applicant for admission to the bar of this Court must be a member in good standing of the bar of the highest court of any state of the United States or of the District of Columbia.

(b) **Petition Form.** The Executive Committee will approve a form of petition to be used by anyone applying for admission to practice. Copies of the approved form will be provided on request by the clerk.

(c) **Filing Petition.** Each person applying for admission to practice shall electronically file with the clerk a completed petition for admission on the approved form.

The petitioner must electronically file with the petition the following in pdf format:

(1) a certificate from the highest court of a state of the United States or of the District of Columbia that the petitioner is a member in good standing of the bar of that court; and

(2) the affidavits of two attorneys who are currently and for at least two years have been members in good standing of the bar of the highest court of any state of the United States or of the District of Columbia and who have known the applicant for at least one year.

(d) **Screening the Petition.** The clerk, under the supervision of the Executive Committee, will screen each petition to assure that it is filed on the correct form, has been completed and contains sufficient information to establish that the petitioner meets the qualifications required for the general bar, and is accompanied by the required affidavits of sponsors and a current indication of good standing. Where these requirements are met, an indication to that effect will be placed on the petition and the petitioner

will be notified that the petition is approved. Where the requirements are not met, the petition will be returned to the applicant with appropriate instructions.

(e) **Taking the Oath.** Petitioners may choose whether or not to appear in person to be admitted. If a petitioner does not wish to appear in person to be sworn in, the petitioner's signature by the "Oath of Office" must be notarized. If a petitioner does not have his/her "Oath of Office" signature notarized and wishes to appear in person to be admitted, then within 30 days of the petition being approved pursuant to section (d), the petitioner will appear before a judge of this Court or a magistrate judge to take the oath or affirmation required for admission. Petitioner may make arrangements to appear before a judge of this Court or a magistrate judge in order to take the oath or affirmation. In such circumstances petitioner must be accompanied by an attorney who is a member in good standing of the bar of this Court. That attorney will move the admission of the petitioner.

(f) **Admission Fee.** Each petitioner shall pay an admission fee upon the filing of the petition, provided that in the event the petitioner is not admitted, the petitioner may request that the fee be refunded. The amount of the fee shall be established by the court in conjunction with the fee prescribed by the Judicial Conference of the United States pursuant to 28 U.S.C. § 1914.

(g) **Certificate of Admission.** On receipt of completed petition form indicating that the petitioner has taken the oath of office, or on receipt of the attorney's own motion accompanied by a copy of the attorney's Certificate of Admission to Practice in another District of Illinois and by the attorney's certification that the attorney is admitted in that district and that his or her right to practice law is not suspended by order of court in any jurisdiction, the clerk shall promptly issue a certificate indicating that petitioner has been admitted to the general bar of this Court and add petitioner's name in the list of attorneys admitted to that bar.

[Effective September 1, 1999. Amended effective December 20, 2004; January 24, 2008; April 3, 2009; November 2, 2010.]

LR 83.11.   TRIAL BAR

(a) **Definitions.** The following definitions shall apply to this rule:

(1) The term "testimonial proceedings" refers to proceedings that meet all of the following criteria:

(A) they are evidentiary proceedings in which all testimony is given under oath and a record is made of the testimony;

(B) the witness or witnesses are subject to cross-examination;

(C) a presiding officer is present;

(D) the parties to such proceedings are generally represented by attorneys; and

(E) where a proceeding was held before an administrative agency, the findings and determinations of the agency are based upon the proceeding and are reviewable for sufficiency of evidence by a court of record.

Procedures limited to taking the deposition of a witness do not constitute testimonial proceedings for the purposes of this rule,

(2) The term "qualifying trial" refers to an evidentiary proceeding that meets the following criteria:

(A) it lasts at least one day;

(B) it must be a trial or hearing involving substantial testimonial proceedings going to the merits; and

(C) it must be held in open court before one of the following: a judge or magistrate judge of a United States district court; a judge of a United States bankruptcy court; a judge of the United States Tax Court; a judge of a trial court of record of a state, the District of Columbia, or a territory of the United States; or any administrative law judge.

(3) The term "participation units" shall mean a qualifying trial in which the petitioner participated as the lead counsel or the assistant to the lead counsel.

(4) The term "observation unit" shall mean a qualifying trial the petitioner observed while being supervised by a supervising attorney who consulted with the observer about the trial. At the time of the observation the supervising attorney must either have been a member of the trial bar of this Court or have had previous trial experience equivalent to at least 4 participation units.

(5) The term "simulation unit" shall mean a trial advocacy program in which the focus is experiential, as contrasted to lecture in which the petitioner satisfactorily participated either as a law school or a continuing legal education course.

(6) The term "training unit of the District Court" shall mean participation in a training seminar officially sanctioned by the Court.

(7) The term "qualifying unit of trial experience" shall include any of the following: participation units, observation units, simulation units, and training units. A petitioner shall be credited the following qualifying units of trial experience for the experience indicated:

(A) for each participation unit, 2 units where the trial lasted 9 days or less, 3 units where the trial lasted from 10 to 12 full days, and 4 units where the trial lasted 13 or more full days;

(B) for each observation unit, 1 unit;

(C) for each simulation unit, 2 units; and

(D) for each training unit of the District Court, 1 unit.

(8) The term "required trial experience" shall mean not less than 4 qualifying units of trial experience.

(9) The term "pro bono panel" shall refer to a panel of members of the trial bar selected pursuant to LR83.35(b) for the purpose of representing or assisting in the representation of parties unable to afford to hire a member of the trial bar.

(NOTE: See Regulations promulgated by the District Admissions Committee for additional material relating to admissions. The Regulations are located in the Appendix to the local Rules.)

(b) Qualifications. An applicant for admission to the trial bar of this Court must be a member in good standing of the general bar of this Court and provide evidence of having the required trial experience. Anyone wishing to apply for admission to the trial bar who is not a member of the bar of this Court may apply for admission to both bars simultaneously.

(c) Petition Form. The Executive Committee will approve a form of petition to be used by anyone applying for admission to the trial bar. Copies of the approved form will be provided on request by the clerk.

(d) Screening the Petition. The clerk, under the supervision of the Executive Committee, will screen each petition to assure that it is filed on the correct form, has been completed, and contains sufficient information to establish that the petitioner meets the qualifications required for the trial bar. Where these requirements are met, an indication to that effect will be placed on the petition and the petitioner will be notified that the petition is approved. Where the requirements are not met, the petition will be returned to the applicant with appropriate instructions.

(e) Admission Fee. Each petitioner shall pay an admission fee upon the filing of the petition, provided that in the event the petitioner is not admitted, the petitioner may request that the fee be refunded. The amount of the fee shall be established by the court. The clerk shall deposit the fee in the District Court Fund.

(f) Duty to Supervise. Every member of the trial bar shall be available to be assigned by the court to supervise attorneys who are in the process of obtaining observation units needed to qualify for membership in the trial bar. Such assignments shall be made in a manner so as to allocate the responsibility imposed by this rule equally among all members of the trial bar.

(g) Duty to Accept Assignments. Each member of the trial bar shall be available for assignment by the court to represent or assist in the representation of those who cannot afford to hire a member of the trial bar. Assignments under this rule shall be made in a manner such that no member of the trial bar shall be required to accept more than one assignment during any 12 month period.

(h) Withdrawal from Trial Bar. A member of the trial bar may, on motion for good cause shown, voluntarily withdraw from said bar. Such motion shall be filed with the clerk for presentation to the Executive Committee. Where the motion to withdraw is made by a member of the current pro bono panel the name of the attorney will be removed from the pro bono panel if the motion is granted.

(i) Reinstatement. Any attorney permitted to withdraw as a member of the trial bar pursuant to section (h) who wishes to be reinstated must file a petition for reinstatement with the clerk for presentation to the Executive Committee. Where the attorney was a member of a pro bono panel at the time the petition to withdraw was filed, the petition for reinstatement shall include a statement indicating the attorney's present willingness and ability to accept an assignment under LR83.35 through LR83.49. If the committee grants the motion in such an instance, it shall direct that the attorney be included in the pro bono panel and remain there for one year or until the attorney is assigned, whichever comes first.

[Effective September 1, 1999. Amended effective June 24, 2009; November 2, 2010; May 24, 2013.]

LR 83.12. APPEARANCE OF ATTORNEYS GENERALLY

(a) Who May Appear. Except as provided in LR83.14 and LR83.15 and as otherwise provided in this rule, only members in good standing of the general bar of this Court may enter appearance of parties, file pleadings, motions or other documents, sign stipulations or receive payments upon judgments, decrees or orders. Attorneys admitted to the trial bar may appear alone in all matters. Attorneys admitted to the general bar, but not to the trial bar, may appear in association with a member of the trial bar in all matters and may appear alone except as otherwise provided by this rule. The following officers appearing in their official capacity shall be entitled to appear in all matters before the court without admission to the trial bar of this Court: the Attorney General of the United States, the United States Attorney for the Northern District of Illinois, the attorney general or other highest legal officer of any state, and the state's attorney of any county in the State of Illinois. This exception to membership in the trial bar shall apply to such persons as hold the above-described offices during their terms of office, and to their assistants.

(b) Testimonial Proceedings. An attorney who is a member of the trial bar may appear alone during testimonial proceedings. An attorney who is a member of the bar, but not of the trial bar, may appear during testimonial proceedings only if accompanied by a member of the trial bar who is serving as advisor. For the purposes of this rule the definition of the term "testimonial proceedings" is the same as in LR83.11(a)(1).

(c) Criminal Proceedings. An attorney who is a member of the trial bar may appear alone on behalf of a defendant in a criminal proceeding. An attorney who is a member of the general bar, but not a member of the trial bar, may (1) appear as lead counsel for a defendant in a criminal proceeding only if accompanied by a member of the trial bar who is serving as advisor and (2) sign pleadings, motions or other documents filed on behalf of the defendant only if they are co-signed by a member of the trial bar.

(d) Waiver. A judge may grant permission in a civil or criminal proceeding pending before that judge to an attorney admitted to the general bar, but not to the trial bar, to appear alone in any aspect of the matter only upon written request by the client and a showing that the interests of justice are best served by waiving the experience requirements otherwise required by these rules. Such permission shall apply only to the proceeding in which it was granted. Granting of such permission shall be limited to exceptional circumstances.

[Effective September 1, 1999. Amended effective June 24, 2009.]

LR 83.13. REPRESENTATION BY SUPERVISED SENIOR LAW STUDENTS

A student in a law school who has been certified by the Administrative Director of Illinois Courts to render services in accordance with Rule 711 of the Rules of the Illinois Supreme Court may perform such services in this Court under like conditions and under the supervision of a member of the trial bar of this Court. In addition to the agencies specified in paragraph (b) of said Rule 711, the law school student may render such services with the United States Attorney for this District, the legal staff of any agency of the United States government or the Federal Defender Program for this District including any of its staff or panel attorneys or, with the prior approval of the assigned judge on a case-by-case basis, any member of the trial bar of this Court.

[Effective September 1, 1999.]

LR 83.14. APPEARANCE BY ATTORNEYS NOT MEMBERS OF THE BAR

A member in good standing of the bar of the highest court of any state or of any United States district court may, upon motion, be permitted to argue or try a particular case in whole or in part subject to the requirements of LR83.12. A petition for admission under this rule shall be on a form approved by the Executive Committee. The clerk shall provide copies of such forms on request.

The fee for admission under this Rule shall be established by the Court. The fee shall be paid to the clerk who shall deposit it in the District Court Fund.

A petition for admission under this rule may be presented by the petitioner. No admission under this rule shall become effective until such time as the fee has been paid.

[Effective September 1, 1999. Amended effective May 31, 2011.]

LR 83.15. LOCAL COUNSEL: DESIGNATION FOR SERVICE

(a) **Designation.** An attorney not having an office within this District ("nonresident attorney") shall appear before this Court only upon having designated as local counsel a member of the bar of this Court having an office within this District upon whom service of papers may be made. Such designation shall be made at the time the initial notice or pleading is filed by the nonresident attorney. Local counsel shall file an appearance but is not required to participate in the case beyond the extent required of an attorney designated pursuant to this rule.

(b) **Penalties.** Where the nonresident attorney tenders documents without the required designation of local counsel, the clerk shall process them as if the designation were filed and shall promptly notify the attorney in writing that the designation must be made within 30 days. If the attorney fails to file the designation within that time, the documents filed by the attorney may be stricken by the court.

(c) **Duties of Local Counsel.** Local counsel shall be responsible for receiving service of notices, pleadings, and other documents and promptly notifying the nonresident attorney of their receipt and contents. In emergencies, local counsel may appear on behalf of the nonresident attorney. This rule does not require local counsel to handle any substantive aspects of the litigation. Such matters may be handled by the nonresident attorney under LR83.12 or LR83.14. Nor does the rule require local counsel to sign any pleading, motion or other paper (*See* Fed.R.Civ.P. 11).

[Effective September 1, 1999. Amended effective April 30, 2008.]

LR 83.16. APPEARANCE FORMS

(a) **General.** The Executive Committee will approve the format of the appearance form to be used. The clerk shall provide copies of the forms on request.

(b) **Who Must File.** Except as otherwise provided in these rules, an appearance form shall be filed by every attorney, including senior students admitted pursuant to LR83.13 and attorneys admitted pursuant to LR83.14, who represents a party in any proceeding brought in this Court, whether before a judge or magistrate judge. No appearance form need be filed by the United States Attorney or any Assistant United States Attorney where the appearance is on behalf of the United States, any agency thereof or one of its officials. The United States Attorney's Office is required to provide the name of a designated Assistant United States Attorney who is to receive electronic notices of Court proceedings in addition to the notices received by the United States Attorney's central e-mail account.

(c) **Appearance by Firms Prohibited.** Appearance forms are to list only the name of an individual attorney. The clerk is directed to bring to the attention of the assigned judge any appearance form listing a firm of attorneys rather than an individual attorney. For the purposes of this rule, an individual attorney who practices as a professional corporation may file the appearance as the professional corporation.

(d) **When To Be Filed.** An attorney required by these rules to file an appearance form shall file it prior to or simultaneously with the filing of any motion, brief or other document in a proceeding before a judge or magistrate judge of this Court, or at the attorney's initial appearance before a judge or magistrate judge of this Court, whichever occurs first.

Where the appearance is filed by an attorney representing a criminal defendant in a proceeding before a judge or magistrate judge, the attorney shall serve a copy of the appearance on the United States attorney.

(e) **Penalties.** If it is brought to the attention of the clerk that an attorney who has filed documents or appeared in court has not filed the appearance form required by this rule, the clerk will notify the judge or magistrate judge before whom the proceedings are pending. An attorney who fails to file an appearance form where required to do so by this rule may be sanctioned.

(f) **Emergency Appearances.** An attorney may appear before a judge or magistrate judge without filing an appearance form as required by this rule where the purpose of the appearance is to stand in for an attorney who has filed or is required to file such a form and the latter attorney is unable to appear because of an emergency.

(g) **Attorney ID Numbers.** The number issued to members of the Illinois bar by the Illinois Attorney Registration and Disciplinary Commission, or such other number as may be approved by the Executive Committee, shall serve as the identification number. The clerk shall be responsible for issuing identification numbers to attorneys who are not members of the Illinois bar.

[Effective September 1, 1999. Amended effective April 20, 2007; June 24, 2009.]

LR 83.17. WITHDRAWAL, ADDITION, AND SUBSTITUTION OF COUNSEL

Once an attorney has filed an appearance form pursuant to LR83.16, that attorney is the attorney of record for the party represented for all purposes incident to the proceeding in which the appearance was filed. The attorney of record may not withdraw, nor may any other attorney file an appearance on behalf of the same party or as a substitute for the attorney of record, without first obtaining leave of court, except that substitutions or additions may be made without motion where both counsel are of the same firm. Where the appearance indicates that pursuant to these rules a member of the trial bar is acting as a supervisor or is accompanying a member of the bar, the member of the trial bar included in the appearance may not withdraw, nor may another member be added or substituted, without first obtaining leave of court.

[Effective September 1, 1999.]

LR 83.18. TRANSFER TO INACTIVE STATUS

(a) Automatic Transfer. When a member of the general bar of this Court is transferred to inactive status by the highest court of any state of the United States or the District of Columbia, the order transferring the attorney to inactive status shall stand as the order transferring the attorney to inactive status in this Court.

Upon being made aware of any order that would automatically transfer a member of the general bar to inactive status, the clerk shall promptly notify the attorney of the provisions of this rule. The notice will also indicate the order upon which automatic transfer to inactive status is being based.

Within 21 days of the mailing of the notice by the clerk, the attorney subject to automatic transfer to inactive status may file a motion with the Executive Committee requesting that the automatic transfer not take place. The motion shall indicate the reasons for the request.

(b) Motion for Transfer. An attorney may, in the absence of disciplinary proceedings, file a motion with the Executive Committee requesting transfer to inactive status. The Committee may appoint the United States attorney or any other attorney to conduct an investigation and make recommendations to the Committee as to whether the motion should be granted.

(c) Practice of Law Prohibited. An attorney who has been transferred to inactive status may not engage in the practice of law before this Court until restored to active status.

(d) Automatic Reinstatement. When an attorney has been transferred to inactive status by the highest court of any state of the United States or the District of Columbia solely for nonpayment of registration fees and has been reinstated upon payment of registration fees, that attorney will automatically be reinstated to the roll of attorneys of this Court upon receipt of notification by the clerk of that court.

(e) Reinstatement. An attorney who has been transferred to inactive status may file a petition for reinstatement with the Executive Committee. Unless the motion to reinstate is granted by the Committee, the attorney shall be granted a hearing.

(f) Disciplinary Proceedings. Disciplinary proceedings may be commenced against an attorney in inactive status. If a disciplinary proceeding is pending against an attorney at the time the attorney is transferred to inactive status, the Executive Committee shall determine whether the disciplinary proceeding is to proceed or is to be held in abeyance until further order of the Committee.

[Effective September 1, 1999.]

LR 83.19 TO LR 83.24 [RESERVED]

LR 83.25. DISCIPLINARY PROCEEDINGS GENERALLY

(a) Definitions. The following definitions shall apply to the disciplinary rules:

(1) The term "another court" shall mean any other court of the United States or of the District of Columbia, or of any state, territory, commonwealth, or possession of the United States.

(2) The term "complaint of misconduct" shall mean any document in which it is alleged that an attorney practicing before this Court is guilty of misconduct.

(3) The term "discipline" shall include disbarment, suspension from practice before this Court, reprimand or censure, and such other disciplinary action as the circumstances may warrant, including, but not limited to, restitution of funds, satisfactory completion of educational programs, compliance with treatment programs, and community service. The term discipline is not intended to include sanctions or contempt.

(4) The term "misconduct" shall mean any act or omission by an attorney admitted to practice before this Court that violates the applicable Code of Conduct.

(b) Executive Committee. The Executive Committee shall serve as the disciplinary committee of the Court.

(c) Jurisdiction. Nothing contained in these rules shall be construed to deny such powers as are necessary for a judge, magistrate judge or bankruptcy judge of this Court to maintain control over proceedings conducted before that judge, magistrate judge or bankruptcy judge, such as proceedings for contempt under LR37.1, Fed.R.Crim.P. 42 or, 18 U.S.C. §§ 401 and 402.

(d) Attorneys Admitted Under LR83.14. An attorney who is not a member of the bar of this Court who, pursuant to LR83.14, petitions to appear or is permitted to appear in this Court for purposes of a particular proceeding (pro hac vice), shall be deemed thereby to have conferred disciplinary jurisdiction upon this Court for any alleged misconduct of that attorney arising in the course of or in the preparation for such proceeding.

(e) Confidentiality. Proceedings before the Executive Committee shall be confidential, except that the Committee may in the interests of justice and on such terms it deems appropriate authorize the clerk to produce, disclose, release, inform, report, or testify to any information, reports, investigations, documents, evidence or transcripts in the clerk's possession. Where a disciplinary proceeding is assigned to a judge of this Court pursuant to these rules, the record and hearings in the proceeding before that judge shall be public, unless for good cause that judge shall in writing order otherwise.

Final orders in disciplinary matters shall be a matter of public record and may be published at the direction of the Executive Committee or the assigned judge.

(f) Filing. An answer to a rule to show cause, a statement of charges, and any other document filed in connection with a disciplinary proceeding before the Executive Committee shall be filed with the attorney admissions coordinator or such other deputy clerk as the clerk may in writing designate.

[Effective September 1, 1999. Amended effective May 31, 2011.]

Committee Comment

A proceeding to discipline a member of the bar of this Court can arise in one of three ways: another court disciplines the attorney; the attorney is convicted of a serious crime; or a complaint is filed alleging misconduct on the part of the attorney. Traditionally, most disciplinary proceedings have been reciprocal proceedings, i.e., proceedings initiated following the discipline of the attorney by another court. The next largest group of disciplinary proceedings consist of those initiated by the conviction of an attorney in this Court for a serious crime.

The Executive Committee is the disciplinary committee of the Court. In those circumstances where an evidentiary hearing may be required as part of the disciplinary proceeding, the Committee may direct that the proceeding be assigned by lot to an individual judge (LR83.28(e)).

As section (c) indicates, the disciplinary rules are not intended to diminish or usurp the authority of a judge in maintaining order in that judge's courtroom or in enforcing compliance with that judge's orders. Disciplinary proceedings are not alternatives to contempt proceedings.

LR83.14 establishes the procedures for admitting an attorney who wishes to appear *pro hac vice.* Section (d) of LR83.25 provides that such attorneys are subject to the same discipline as attorneys who are members of the general bar of the Court.

Section (e) of this rule provides that in general disciplinary proceedings are confidential. Any final orders imposing discipline are public. In those instances where a proceeding is assigned to an individual judge, it becomes at that point like any other civil proceeding, a matter of public record. As with any other civil case, there may be exceptional circumstances where some or all of the record or hearings should not be made public. Section (e) permits this.

Section (f) makes explicit what has been a practice of long standing: materials relating to disciplinary proceedings before the Executive Committee are to be filed with the Attorney Admissions Coordinator. This procedure enables more effective control over the documents in disciplinary proceedings, a control necessary to assure that the confidentiality of such proceedings is maintained. In addition, the coordinator serves as a source of information on procedure for attorneys involved in disciplinary proceedings.

LR 83.26. DISCIPLINE OF ATTORNEYS DISCIPLINED BY OTHER COURTS

(a) Duty to Notify. Any attorney admitted to practice before this Court shall, upon being subjected to public discipline by another court, promptly inform the Clerk of this Court of such action.

(b) Disciplinary Order as Evidence. Except as provided in section (e), the final adjudication in another court that an attorney has been guilty of misconduct shall establish conclusively the misconduct for purposes of a disciplinary proceeding in this Court.

(c) Rule to Show Cause. Upon the filing of a certified or exemplified copy of a judgment or order demonstrating that an attorney admitted to practice before this court has been disciplined by another court, the Executive Committee shall forthwith enter an order directing that the attorney inform the Committee of any claim by that attorney predicated upon the grounds set forth in section (e) that the imposition of the identical discipline by this Court would be unwarranted and the reasons for such a claim. The order will also provide that the response, if any, is to be filed with the clerk within 14 days of service. A certified copy of the order and a copy of the judgment or order from the other court will be served on the attorney by certified mail.

(d) Effect of Stay of Imposition of Discipline in Other Court. In the event the discipline imposed in the other jurisdiction has been stayed, any reciprocal discipline imposed in this Court shall be deferred until such stay expires.

(e) Imposition of Discipline; Exceptions. Upon the expiration of 14 days from service of the notice issued pursuant to the provisions of section (b), the Executive Committee shall immediately impose the identical discipline unless the attorney demonstrates, or the Executive Committee finds—

(1) that the procedure before the other court was so lacking in notice or opportunity to be heard as to constitute a deprivation of due process; or

(2) that there was such a infirmity of proof establishing the misconduct as to give rise to the clear conviction that this Court could not, consistent with its duty, accept as final the conclusion on that subject; or

(3) that the imposition of the same discipline by this Court would result in injustice; or

(4) that the misconduct established is deemed by this Court to warrant different discipline.

If the Executive Committee determines that any of those elements exist, it shall enter such other order as it deems appropriate.

[Effective September 1, 1999. Amended effective January 30, 2009.]

LR 83.27. DISCIPLINE OF CONVICTED ATTORNEYS

(a) Automatic Suspension. Upon the filing with this Court of a certified copy of a judgment of conviction demonstrating that any attorney admitted to practice before the Court has been convicted of a serious crime in this or another court, the Executive Committee shall enter an order immediately suspending that attorney, until final disposition of a disciplinary proceeding to be commenced upon such conviction. Such order shall be entered regardless of whether the conviction resulted from a plea of guilty or nolo contendere or from a verdict after trial or otherwise, and regardless of the pendency of any appeal. A copy of such order shall immediately be served upon the attorney. Upon good cause shown, the Executive Committee may set aside such order when it appears in the interest of justice to do so.

(b) Judgment of Conviction as Evidence. A certified copy of a judgment of conviction of any attorney for any crime shall be conclusive evidence of the commission of that crime in any disciplinary proceeding instituted against that attorney based upon the conviction.

(c) Executive Committee to Institute Disciplinary Proceedings. Upon the filing of a certified copy of a judgment of conviction of an attorney for a serious crime, the Executive Committee shall, in addition to suspending that attorney in accordance with the provi-

sions of this rule, institute a disciplinary proceeding in which the sole issue to be determined shall be the extent of the final discipline to be imposed as a result of the conduct resulting in the conviction. Each disciplinary proceeding so instituted will not be concluded until all appeals from the conviction are concluded.

(d) Proceedings Where Attorney Convicted of Other Than Serious Crime. Upon the filing of a certified copy of a judgment of conviction of an attorney for a crime not constituting a serious crime, the Executive Committee may, but is not required to, initiate a disciplinary proceeding.

(e) Reinstatement Where Conviction Reversed. An attorney suspended pursuant to section (a) will be reinstated immediately upon the filing of a certificate demonstrating that the underlying conviction of a serious crime has been reversed, but the reinstatement will not terminate any disciplinary proceeding then pending against the attorney. The disposition of such proceeding shall be determined by the Executive Committee on the basis of all available evidence pertaining to both guilt and the extent of discipline to be imposed.

[Effective September 1, 1999.]

LR 83.28. DISCIPLINE OF ATTORNEYS FOR MISCONDUCT

(a) Complaint of Misconduct. Any complaint of misconduct shall be filed with the chief judge. The complaint may be in the form of a letter. The chief judge shall refer it to the Executive Committee for consideration and appropriate action.

(b) Action by Executive Committee. On receipt of a complaint of misconduct the Committee may forward a copy to the attorney and ask for a response within a time set by the Committee. On the basis of the complaint of misconduct and any response, the Committee may:

(1) determine that the complaint merits no further action, or

(2) direct that formal disciplinary proceedings be commenced, or

(3) take such other action as the Committee deems appropriate, including the assignment of an attorney pursuant to LR83.29.

(c) Statement of Charges; Service. To initiate formal disciplinary proceedings based on allegations of misconduct, the Executive Committee shall issue a statement of charges. In addition to setting forth the charges, the statement of charges shall include an order requiring the attorney to show cause, within 14 days after service why the attorney should not be disciplined.

Upon the issuance the statement of charges, the clerk shall forthwith mail two copies to the last known address of the attorney. One copy shall be mailed by certified mail restricted to addressee only, return receipt requested. The other copy shall be mailed by first class mail, If the statement is returned as undeliverable, the clerk shall so notify the Executive Committee, The Executive Committee may direct that further attempts at service be made, either personal service by a private process server or by the United States marshal, or by publication. Personal service shall be accomplished in the manner provided by Fed.R.Civ.P. 5(b) for service other than by mail. Service by publication shall be accomplished by publishing a copy of the rule to show cause portion of the statement in accordance with the provisions of LR83.3, Except as otherwise directed by the Executive Committee, the division of the Court in which the notice is to be published will be as follows:

(1) where the last known address of the attorney is located in the District, the division in which the address is located; or,

(2) where no address is known or the last known address is outside of the District, the Eastern Division.

(d) **Answer; Declaration.** The attorney shall file with the answer to the statement of charges a declaration identifying all courts before which the attorney is admitted to practice. The form of the declaration shall be established by the Executive Committee.

(e) **Assignment to Individual Judge.** Following the filing of the answer to the statement of charges, if the Executive Committee determines that an evidentiary hearing is required, the proceeding shall be assigned by lot for a prompt hearing before a judge of this Court. The assigned judge shall not be one who was a member of the Executive Committee that determined that an evidentiary hearing was required. The decision of the assigned judge shall be final.

(f) **Disbarment on Consent.** Any attorney admitted to practice before this Court who is the subject of an investigation into, or a pending proceeding involving, allegations of misconduct may consent to disbarment, but only by delivering a declaration stating that the attorney desires to consent to disbarment and that:

(1) the attorney's consent is freely and voluntarily rendered;

(2) the attorney is not being subjected to coercion or duress;

(3) the attorney is fully aware of the implications of so consenting;

(4) the attorney is aware that there is presently pending an investigation or proceeding involving allegations that there exist grounds for the attorney's

discipline, the nature of which the attorney shall specifically set forth; and

(5) the attorney acknowledges that the material facts so alleged are true.

Upon receipt of the required declaration, the Executive Committee shall enter an order disbarring the attorney. The order of disbarring the attorney on consent shall be a matter of public record. However, the declaration shall not be publicly disclosed or made available for use in any other proceeding except where the Executive Committee orders such release after finding it to be required in the interests of justice.

[Effective September 1, 1999. Amended effective January 30, 2009; May 24, 2013.]

LR 83.29. ASSIGNMENT OF COUNSEL

(a) **Assignment.** The Executive Committee or the judge to whom the case is assigned may assign one or more attorneys to investigate allegations of misconduct, to prosecute disciplinary proceedings, or in conjunction with a reinstatement petition filed by a disciplined attorney. The United States attorney or an assistant United States attorney, the administrator of the Attorney Registration and Disciplinary Commission of the Supreme Court of Illinois or a designee of the administrator, or a member of the bar of this Court may be assigned. Once assigned, an attorney may not resign unless permission to do so is given by the Executive Committee or the judge to whom the case is assigned.

(b) **Subpoenas.** An attorney assigned under section (a) may, with the approval of the Executive Committee or the presiding judge, cause subpoenas to be issued during the proceedings. Any subpoenas issued pursuant to this rule shall be returnable before the Executive Committee or the presiding judge.

[Effective September 1, 1999. Amended effective May 24, 2013.]

LR 83.30. REINSTATEMENT

(a) **Automatic & by Petition.** An attorney suspended for 3 months or less shall be automatically reinstated at the end of the period of suspension. An attorney suspended for more than 3 months or disbarred may not resume practice until reinstated by order of the Executive Committee.

(b) **Petition for Reinstatement.** A petition for reinstatement may be filed under the following conditions:

(1) *By a Suspended Attorney:* An attorney who has been suspended for a period of more than 3 months may petition for reinstatement at any time following the conclusion of the period of suspension.

(2) *By a Disbarred Attorney:* A petition to reinstate a disbarred attorney may not be filed until at least 5

years has elapsed from the effective date of the disbarment.

Following an adverse decision upon a petition for reinstatement a period of at least 1 year must elapse from the date of the order denying reinstatement before a subsequent petition for reinstatement may be filed.

Petitions for reinstatement shall be filed with the attorney admissions coordinator or such other deputy as the clerk may in writing designate. The Executive Committee may grant the petition without hearing, decide the petition based on a hearing before the Committee, or assign the matter for prompt hearing before, and decision by, a judge of this Court. Where the Committee directs that the petition be assigned to a judge, the assignment will be in the same manner as provided by LR83.28(e) for the assignment of a statement of charges alleging misconduct.

(c) Hearing. A petition for reinstatement will be included on the agenda of the first meeting of the Executive Committee scheduled for not less than 7 days from the time the petition is filed. At that meeting the Committee will consider whether to grant the petition, schedule a hearing, or direct that it be assigned to a judge. Where a hearing is to be held and the Executive Committee has directed that the matter be assigned to a judge, it shall be scheduled for a date not less than 30 days from the date of assignment.

(d) Burden of Proof. At the hearing the petitioner shall have the burden of demonstrating by clear and convincing evidence that the petitioner has the requisite character and fitness for admission to practice law before this Court and that the petitioner's resumption of the practice of law will not be detrimental to the integrity and standing of the bar or to the administration of justice, or subversive of the public interest.

(e) Duties of Counsel. Where an attorney is appointed pursuant to LR83.29, cross-examination of the witnesses of the petitioner and the submission of evidence in opposition to the petition, if any, shall be by that attorney.

(f) Conditions of Reinstatement. The petition for reinstatement shall be denied if the petitioner fails to demonstrate fitness to resume the practice of law. If the petitioner is found fit to resume the practice of law, the judgment shall reinstate the petitioner, but may make reinstatement conditional upon the making of partial or complete restitution to parties harmed by the conduct of petitioner which led to the suspension or disbarment. If the petitioner has been suspended or disbarred for 5 years or more, reinstatement may be conditioned, in the discretion of the Executive Committee or the judge before whom the matter is heard, upon the furnishing or proof of competency and learning in the law. Such proof may include certification by the bar examiners of a state or other jurisdiction of the attorney's successful completion of an examination

for admission to practice subsequent to the date of suspension or disbarment.

[Effective September 1, 1999.]

LR 83.31.   DUTIES OF THE CLERK [*SEE* INTERNAL OPERATING PROCEDURE 8]

LR 83.32 TO LR 83.34   [RESERVED]

LR 83.35.   PRO BONO PROGRAM

(a) Definitions. The following definitions shall apply to the pro bono rules:

(1) The term "assignment of counsel" shall mean the assignment of a member of the trial bar to represent a party who lacks the resources to retain counsel by any other means. Such assignment shall only be in a civil action or appeal and shall not include any assignment made pursuant to the Criminal Justice Act of 1964, 18 U.S.C. § 3006A.

(2) The term "judge" shall mean the judge to whom the action is assigned. It shall include a magistrate judge where the assignment is made in a civil case assigned to a magistrate judge for all purposes pursuant to 28 U.S.C. § 636(c) or referred for evidentiary hearings pursuant to 28 U.S.C. § 636(b)(1)(B).

(3) The term "panel" shall mean those members of the trial bar who have volunteered for assignment and those whose names were selected pursuant to section (b).

(4) The terms "pro bono rules" and "pro bono program" shall refer to LR83.35 through 83.49.

(b) Creating the Panel. From time to time, the clerk shall select names at random from the trial bar to create a panel. Except as otherwise provided by the pro bono rules, the clerk shall select members from the trial bar who have not been included on an earlier panel.

(c) Notification to Panel. Following the selection of a panel the clerk shall notify each member and obtain from each the following information:

(1) counsel's prior civil trial experience, including a general indication of the number of trials and areas of trial experience;

(2) counsel's ability to consult and advise in languages other than English;

Such information as is supplied by counsel may be amended at any time by letter.

(d) Exemptions. A member of the trial bar

(1) whose principal place of business is outside of this District, or

(2) who is employed full-time as an attorney for an agency of the United States, a state, a county, or any sub-division thereof, or

(3) who is employed full-time as an attorney by a not-for-profit legal aid organization shall, when selected for a panel, be removed from it and returned to the pool. However, such action shall not preclude counsel from being selected for a subsequent panel.

(e) Volunteers. A member of the trial bar may volunteer to be included in a panel. Whenever a volunteer is assigned, the clerk as part of the notification process will ask the volunteer to elect one of the following options:

(1) the volunteer's name will be moved to the end of the list of names on the panel, or

(2) the volunteer's name will be removed from the panel and either replaced after a specified time period or at the request of the volunteer. The clerk will make a similar request of any volunteer whose name has been on a panel for 12 months and who has not been assigned during that time.

[Effective September 1, 1999. Amended effective January 26, 2012; May 24, 2013.]

Committee Comment:

Pursuant to LR83.11(g) each member of the trial bar has the responsibility to serve as an assigned attorney in pro se matters. The pro se rules provide for the reimbursement of expenses of counsel assigned under those rules. The admission fees collected when counsel join the trial bar form a major source of the funds used to pay the expenses.

The procedures for assignment involve selecting from a current panel. The panel is formed annually. The names are selected in such a manner that no member of the trial bar is selected for a subsequent panel until all other members have been selected. The only exemption from being included on a panel is the limited one granted to members of the groups specified in section (d).

Committee Comment

Pursuant to LR83.11(g) each member of the trial bar has the responsibility to serve as an appointed attorney in pro se matters. The pro se rules provide for the reimbursement of expenses of counsel appointed under those rules. The admission fees collected when counsel join the trial bar form a major source of the funds used to pay the expenses.

The procedures for appointment involve selecting from a current panel. The panel is formed annually. The names are selected in such a manner that no member of the trial bar is selected for a subsequent panel until all other members have been selected. The only exemption from being included on a panel is the limited one granted to members of the groups specified in section (d).

LR 83.36. ASSIGNMENT PROCEDURES

(a) Application. Any application for the assignment of counsel by a party appearing pro se shall be on a form approved by the Executive Committee. The application shall include a form of affidavit stating the party's efforts, if any, to obtain counsel by means other than assignment and indicating any prior pro bono assignments of counsel to represent the party in cases brought in this Court including both pending and previously terminated actions. A completed copy of the affidavit of financial status in the form required by LR3.3(a)(2) shall be attached to the application. A pro se party who was ineligible for assigned counsel at the outset of the litigation who later becomes eligible by reason of changed circumstances may apply for assignment of counsel within a reasonable time after the change in circumstances has occurred.

(b) Notice of Assignment. After counsel has been selected, the clerk shall forthwith send to counsel written notice of the assignment. In addition to notifying counsel, the clerk shall also notify all of the parties to the action of the assignment and include with such notification the name, address, and telephone number of the assignee.

(c) Making Private Counsel Court–Assigned. Where a party is represented by counsel and because of the party's financial condition both the party and counsel wish to change the nature of the representation to court- assigned representation in order that counsel may be eligible for reimbursement of expenses from the District Court Fund pursuant to LR83.40, counsel may petition the court to be court-assigned counsel. Any such petition shall indicate that if the court grants the petition, any existing fee agreements between the party and counsel shall no longer be enforceable and any subsequent fee agreements between the party and counsel may only be made in accordance with the provisions of LR83.41. In ruling on the petition, the judge shall grant it only if the judge would have granted an application filed under this rule had the party not been represented by counsel. Where the party is represented by more than one counsel, any order of assignment under this section shall preclude prospective operation of fee agreements with all such counsel but shall appoint only those counsel wishing to be assigned.

[Effective September 1, 1999. Amended effective May 31, 2011; January 31, 2012; May 24, 2013.]

LR 83.37. DUTIES & RESPONSIBILITIES OF ASSIGNED COUNSEL

Upon receiving notice of the assignment, counsel shall forthwith file an appearance in accordance with LR83.12 in the action to which counsel is assigned. Promptly following the filing of an appearance, counsel shall communicate with the newly-represented party concerning the action or appeal. In addition to a full discussion of the merits of the dispute, counsel shall explore with the party any possibilities of resolving the dispute in other forums, including but not limited to administrative forums. If after consultation with counsel the party decides to prosecute or defend the action or appeal, counsel shall proceed to represent the party in the action or appeal unless or until the attorney-client relationship is terminated as provided by these rules.

Except where the assignment is terminated pursuant to LR83.38 or LR83.39, each assigned counsel shall represent the party in the action from the date counsel enters an appearance until a final judgment is entered in the action. If the matter is remanded to an administrative forum, the assigned counsel shall, unless given leave to withdraw by the judge, continue to represent the party in any proceeding, judicial or administrative, that may ensue upon an order of remand. The assigned counsel is not required by these rules to continue to represent a party on appeal should the party represented wish to appeal from a final judgment.

Upon assignment for purposes of settlement assistance, the attorney will assist in preparing for the settlement conference, participate in the settlement conference on behalf of the pro se litigant, and draft a settlement agreement and corresponding motion to dismiss, if appropriate. Assistance under the Settlement Assistance Program will be limited only to the effort to settle the case and will not extend to any other part of the litigation process.

[Effective September 1, 1999. Amended effective May 31, 2011; May 24, 2013.]

LR 83.38. RELIEF FROM ASSIGNMENT

(a) Grounds; Application. After assignment counsel may apply to be relieved of an order of assignment only on the following grounds or on such other grounds as the assigning judge finds adequate for good cause shown:

(1) Some conflict of interest precludes counsel from accepting the responsibilities of representing the party in the action.

(2) In counsel's opinion, counsel is not competent to represent the party in the particular type of action assigned.

(3) Some personal incompatibility or a substantial disagreement on litigation strategy exists between counsel and the party.

(4) Because of the temporary burden of other professional commitments involved in the practice of law, counsel lacks the time necessary to represent the party.

(5) In counsel's opinion the party is proceeding for purpose of harassment or malicious injury, or the party's claims or defenses are not warranted under existing law and cannot be supported by good faith argument for extension, modification, or reversal of existing law.

Any application by assigned counsel for relief from an order of assignment on any of the grounds set forth in this section shall be made to the judge promptly after the attorney becomes aware of the existence of such grounds, or within such additional period as may be permitted by the judge for good cause shown,

(b) Order Granting Relief. If an application for relief from an order of assignment is granted, the judge may issue an order directing the assignment of another counsel to represent the party. Such assignment shall be made in accordance with the procedures set forth in LR83.36. Alternatively, the judge shall have the discretion not to issue a further order of assignment, in which case the party shall be permitted to prosecute or defend the action pro se.

Where the judge enters an order granting relief from an order of assignment on the grounds that counsel lacks the time to represent the party due to a temporary burden of other professional commitments, the name of counsel so relieved shall, except as otherwise provided in the order, automatically be included among the names selected for the next panel.

[Effective September 1, 1999. Amended effective May 24, 2013.]

LR 83.39. DISCHARGE OF ASSIGNED COUNSEL ON REQUEST OF PARTY

Any party for whom counsel has been assigned shall be permitted to request the judge to discharge that counsel from the representation and to assign another. Such request shall be made promptly after the party becomes aware of the reasons giving rise to the request, or within such additional period as may be permitted by the judge for good cause shown.

When such a request is supported by good cause, such as personal incompatibility or a substantial disagreement on litigation strategy between the party and assigned counsel, the judge shall forthwith issue an order discharging and relieving assigned counsel from further representation of the party in the action or appeal. Following the entry of such an order of discharge, the judge may in the judge's discretion either enter or not enter a further order directing the assignment of another counsel to represent the party. In any action where the judge discharges assigned counsel but does not issue a further order of assignment, the party shall be permitted to proceed pro se.

In any action where a second counsel is assigned and subsequently discharged upon request of a party, no additional assignment shall be made except on a strong showing of good cause. Any assignments made following the entry of an order of discharge shall be made in accordance with the procedures set forth in LR83.36.

[Effective September 1, 1999. Amended effective May 24, 2013.]

LR 83.40.   EXPENSES

The party shall bear the cost of any expenses of the litigation or appeal to the extent reasonably feasible in light of the party's financial condition. Such expenses shall include, but not be limited to discovery expenses, subpoena and witness fees, and transcript expenses. It shall be permissible for appointed counsel or the firm with which counsel is affiliated to advance part or all of the payment of any such expenses without requiring that the party remain ultimately liable for such expenses, except out of the proceeds of any recovery. However, the attorney or firm shall not be required to advance the payment of such expenses.

Expenses incurred by counsel appointed pursuant to LR83.36 or the firm with which counsel is affiliated may be reimbursed from the District Court Fund in accordance with the provisions of the *Regulations Governing the Reimbursement of Expenses in Pro Bono Cases*. The clerk will provide copies of the *Regulations* and the *Plan for the Administration of the District Court Fund* on request.

[Effective September 1, 1999.]

LR 83.41.   ATTORNEY'S FEES

(a) **Party's Ability to Pay.** Where as part of the process of appointing counsel the judge finds that the party is able to pay for legal services in whole or in part but that appointment is justified, the judge shall include in the order of appointment provisions for any fee arrangement between the party and the appointed counsel.

If appointed counsel discovers after appointment that the party is able to pay for legal services in whole or in part, counsel shall bring that information to the attention of the judge. Thereupon the judge may either (1) authorize the party and counsel to enter into a fee agreement subject to the judge's approval, or (2) relieve counsel from the responsibilities of the order of appointment and either permit the party to retain an attorney or to proceed pro se.

(b) **Fee Agreements.** If appointed counsel wishes to negotiate a fee arrangement with the client, counsel must do so at the outset of the representation. Any such fee arrangement is subject to all applicable rules and canons of professional conduct. Any fee agreement that appointed counsel and the client may reach must be submitted to the court for review and approval before the agreement becomes effective, and is subject to revision by the court.

(c) **Allowance of Fees.** Upon appropriate application by appointed counsel, the judge may award attorney's fees to appointed counsel for services rendered in the action as authorized by applicable statute, regulation, rule, or other provision of law, including case law.

[Effective September 1, 1999. Amended effective January 31, 2012.]

LR 83.42 TO LR 83.49   [RESERVED]

LR 83.50.   RULES OF PROFESSIONAL CONDUCT

Applicable disciplinary rules are the Model Rules adopted by the American Bar Association. On any matter not addressed by the ABA Model Rules or for which the ABA Model Rules are inconsistent with the Rules of Professional Conduct, a lawyer admitted to practice in Illinois is governed by the Illinois Rules of Professional Conduct, as adopted by the Illinois Supreme Court, and a lawyer not admitted to practice in Illinois is bound by the Rules of Professional Conduct for the state in which the lawyer's principal office is located. Notwithstanding the foregoing, limited scope appearances of attorneys, as set forth in Illinois Supreme Court Rules 11(e), 13(c)(6), 13(c)(7), 137(e) and any comparable rules of other states, are not permitted in matters before this Court. Any attorney seeking to enter a limited appearance on behalf of a party may do so only with leave of Court.

[Effective June 2, 2011. Amended effective May 22, 2014.]

LR 83.50.1 TO LR 83.58.4   [RESERVED]

LR 83.58.5.   JURISDICTION

Any lawyer practicing before this Court is subject to the disciplinary authority of this Court although also engaged in practice elsewhere.

[Effective September 1, 1999.]

Committee Comment

In addition to the fact that Illinois lawyers practice in Illinois state courts as well as in this Court, in modern practice lawyers frequently act outside the territorial limits of the jurisdiction in which they are licensed to practice, either in another state or outside the United States. In doing so, they remain subject to the governing authority of this Court as well as the state jurisdiction in which they are licensed to practice.

Where the lawyer is licensed to practice law before two courts which impose conflicting obligations, applicable rules of choice of law may govern the situation. This Court's adoption of rules differing to some extent from the Illinois Rules has been intended, to the maximum extent possible, to minimize, or avoid entirely, such conflicting obligations.

LOCAL ADMIRALTY RULES

LRSup A.1. LOCAL ADMIRALTY RULES; APPLICATION OF LOCAL CIVIL RULES

Local rules numbered as LRSupA.1, LRSupB.1, etc., are associated with the Supplemental Rules For Certain Admiralty and Maritime Claims of the Federal Rules of Civil Procedure. They may be referred to as the "local admiralty rules." The terms "Supplemental Rule" and "Supplemental Rules" as used within the local admiralty rules shall refer to one or all of the Supplemental Rules for Certain Admiralty Claims of the Federal Rules of Civil Procedure.

The local civil rules of this Court shall apply to admiralty and maritime claims to the extent they are not inconsistent with the local admiralty rules.

[Effective September 1, 1999.]

LRSup B.1. ATTACHMENTS & GARNISHMENTS: SPECIAL PROVISIONS

(a) Suits Filed In Forma Pauperis. In suits in forma pauperis no process in rem shall issue except upon proof of 24 hours' notice to the owner of the property or his agent, of the filing of the complaint unless allowed by the court.

(b) Service. In actions in personam where the debts, credits or effects named in any process of maritime attachment and garnishment are not delivered up to the marshal by the garnishee or are denied by him to be the property of the defendant it shall be a sufficient service of such process to leave a copy thereof with such garnishee, or at his usual residence or place of business, with notice of the property attached. On return by the marshal, the plaintiff may proceed to a hearing and final judgment in the cause on providing proof to the satisfaction of the court that the property belongs to defendant.

In actions in rem, process against freight or proceeds of property in possession of any person may be served in the same manner.

(c) Judgment of Default. On the expiration of the time to answer, if no pleading under Fed.R.Civ.P. 12 has been filed, the plaintiff may have an ex parte hearing of the cause and a judgment without notice, except that:

(1) if an appearance has been filed, 7 days' notice of the hearing shall be given by the plaintiff to all persons who have appeared; and

(2) final judgment shall not enter against arrested or attached property until it is shown by affidavit that notice of the motion has been given to the owner of the property, if known to the plaintiff, or otherwise to the owner's agent, if known and to any holder of any security interest in the vessel arrested or attached, recorded in the records of the United States Coast Guard.

The notice shall be by first class mail to the mailing address of record or to the last known address. Failure to give notice as provided by this rule may be grounds for setting aside the default under applicable rules, but shall not affect title to property sold under a judgment.

[Effective September 1, 1999. Amended effective November 19, 2009.]

LRSup C.1. ACTIONS IN REM: SPECIAL PROVISIONS

(a) Publication; Notice of Sale. The notice required by section (4) of Supplemental Rule C shall be published at least once and shall contain the fact and date of the arrest, the name of the Court, the title of the cause, the nature of the action, the amount demanded, the name of the marshal, the name and address of the attorney for the plaintiff, and a statement that claimants must file their claims pursuant to Supplemental Rule C(6) with the clerk within 14 days after the date of first publication or within such additional time as may be allowed by the court and must file and serve their answers within 21 days after the filing of their claims. The notice shall also state that all interested persons should file claims and answers within the times so fixed; otherwise default will be noted and condemnation ordered.

When property remains in custody of the marshal the cause will not be heard until after publication of notice of arrest shall have been made in that cause or in some other pending cause in which the property is held in custody. No final judgment shall be entered ordering the condemnation and sale of non-perishable property, arrested under process in rem, unless publication of notice of arrest in that cause shall have been duly made.

Unless otherwise ordered as provided by law, notice of sale of the property in suits in rem shall be published daily for at least 7 days before sale.

All publication shall be made in a newspaper of general circulation in the City of Chicago.

(b) Time Within Which to Show Cause. A summons issued pursuant to Supplemental Rule C(3) dealing with freight or the proceeds of property sold or other intangible property, shall set the date by which the person having control of the funds is to show cause. The date shall be at least 10 days after service of the summons. The court, for good cause shown, may shorten the period.

(c) Property in Possession of Collector of Customs. In suits in rem when property is in the possession or custody of the collector of customs the person or organization to whom the clerk delivered the warrant of arrest shall deliver a copy of the process to the collector together with notice of the arrest of the property therein described and require the collector to detain such property in custody until the further order of the court. This requirement shall be in addition to any publication of process made pursuant to section (a).

(d) Limitations on Claims Made After Sale. In proceedings in rem, claims upon the proceeds of sale of property under a final judgment order or decree, except for seamen's wages, will not be admitted in behalf of lienors who file complaints or petitions after the sale, to the prejudice of lienors who filed complaints or petitions before the sale, but shall be limited to the remnants and surplus, unless for cause shown it shall be otherwise ordered.

[Effective September 1, 1999. Amended effective November 19, 2009.]

LRSup D.   [RESERVED]

LRSup E.1.   ACTIONS IN REM AND QUASI IN REM: GENERAL PROVISIONS

(a) Security for Costs. Each plaintiff other than the United States shall file a security for cost bond or stipulation in the amount of $250 conditioned that the principal shall pay all costs awarded by this or any appellate court, except as ordered by court.

Municipal corporations within this District shall not be required to file such bond unless ordered by court pursuant to Supplemental Rule E(2)(b).

(b) Stipulations. Whenever the owner or owners of any vessel shall execute and deliver to the clerk a general bond or stipulation as provided by Supplemental Rule E(5)(b) conditioned to answer the judgment of the court in all or any actions that may be brought thereafter in such court in which the vessel is attached or arrested, notice of the process shall be given to the principal and surety or sureties in said bond by service of a copy thereof by the marshal upon each of the persons named in said bond. Failure to receive such notice shall in no wise affect the liability under such bond; all other notices shall be given and the cause proceed as if such vessel had been taken into actual custody.

All stipulations shall contain the consent of the stipulators, that if the party, for whose benefit the stipulation is filed recover, the judgment may be entered against them for an amount not exceeding the amount named in such stipulation.

(c) Notice & Approval. Stipulators may justify on short notice before a magistrate judge, the clerk, or a notary public, who, if required by an adverse party, shall examine the sureties under oath as to their sufficiency, and annex their depositions to the bond or stipulation.

In all cases where the surety on bonds or stipulations is not a corporate surety holding a certificate of authority of the Secretary of the Treasury and the bond or stipulation is not approved by the parties, reasonable notice of the application for approval by the court or clerk shall be given.

[Effective September 1, 1999.]

LRSup E.2.   APPRAISAL

In case of seizure of property in behalf of the United States, an appraisal for the purpose of bonding may be had by any party in interest, on giving seven days' notice of motion for the appointment of appraisers. If the parties or their attorneys and the United States attorney are present in court, such motion may be made instanter, after seizure and without notice.

Orders for the appraisal of property under arrest or attachment at the suite of a private party may be entered as of course, at the instance of any party interested, or upon the consent of the attorneys for the respective parties.

Unless otherwise ordered, only one appraiser shall be appointed. Where the respective parties do not agree in writing, the judge shall name the appraiser.

The appraiser shall give one day's notice of the time and place of making the appraisal to the attorneys in the action. The appraisal shall be filed with the clerk.

[Effective September 1, 1999. Amended effective November 19, 2009.]

LRSup E.3.   SAFEKEEPING OF VESSELS; MOVEMENT WITHIN PORT

Upon seizure of any vessel, the marshal shall make appropriate arrangements for the safekeeping of the vessel. The marshal may require the party at whose instance the vessel is to be seized to pay any costs as incurred.

Upon the request of the claimant of the vessel or of the owner, charterer, master or other person in control of the vessel at the time it was seized, and with the consent of the party at whose instance the vessel was seized, the marshal may appoint the master of the vessel as custodian and may permit the vessel to be worked and shifted within the District without further order of court.

[Effective September 1, 1999.]

LRSup E.4. JUDICIAL SALE

(a) Marshal's Account of Sale. When any money shall come to the hands of the marshal under or by virtue of any order or process of the court, he shall forthwith present to the clerk a bill of his charges showing the time he received the money. After the filing of the bill of charges and upon the taxation thereof he shall forthwith pay to the clerk the amount of said money less his charges as taxed. An account of all property sold under the order or judgment of this Court shall be returned by the marshal and filed in the clerk's office, with the execution or other process under which the sale was made.

(b) Conditions of Sale. When a vessel is sold under an order or judgment of this Court pursuant to Supplemental Rules E(9)(b) or E(9)(c), the marshal shall make his account of the property sold as provided in section (a) and shall prepare a certificate of sale showing the name and address of the highest bidder. Such sale shall be subject to approval and confirmation by the court or rejection by the court, upon motion and showing of good cause therefor, which motion may be made by the plaintiff, or by any party of record, or by the highest bidder. It shall be the responsibility of the plaintiff, or such other party of record who desires that the sale be approved and confirmed, to prepare and present to the court from the pleadings in the case, or from other sources, a description of the vessel for purpose of identification as an aid to the United States Coast Guard properly to record and index the vessel on its records, or to enable the vessel to be registered or numbered under the Illinois Boat Registration and Safety Act or such other state or federal statute as may be applicable. The description may include the name of the vessel, its official number, if any, its state identification number, if any, its dimensions, the name of the former owner, the ownership interest to be transferred, and the name and address of the purchaser who shall have been the successful bidder at the sale.

(c) Marshal's Bill of Sale. If and when the court approves and confirms the sale, the order approving and confirming such sale shall direct the marshal to issue a marshal's bill of sale containing appropriate identification and description of the vessel so that the same may be recorded pursuant to any applicable regulations of the United States Coast Guard or other government agency.

[Effective September 1, 1999.]

LOCAL CRIMINAL RULES

LCrR 1.1. ADOPTION OF RULES

These rules apply to the conduct of criminal proceedings in this Court. They may be referred to as "local criminal rules" or, where reference is to a specific rule, "LCrR.[number]."

Unless otherwise indicated, reference in these rules to the United States attorney shall also include an assistant United States attorney and an assistant United States attorney general.

Reference in these rules to defendant's attorney is in no way intended to preclude a defendant from proceeding pro se, in which case a reference to defendant's attorney applies to defendant.

[Effective September 1, 1999.]

LCrR 1.2. APPLICABILITY OF LOCAL CIVIL RULES

In all criminal proceedings, the Civil Rules of this Court shall be followed insofar as they are applicable.

[Effective September 1, 1999.]

LCrR 2 to 4. [RESERVED]

LCrR 5.1. DUTY MAGISTRATE JUDGE: EASTERN DIVISION

The magistrate judge designated as emergency magistrate judge pursuant to LR77.2 shall serve as duty magistrate judge.

Magistrate judges in this district shall have the power to perform all duties set forth in the United States Code and the Federal Rules of Criminal Procedure.

[Effective September 1, 1999.]

LCrR 6.1. CHIEF JUDGE TO SUPERVISE GRAND JURY

The chief judge shall supervise the operations of the grand jury, including empaneling and charging each grand jury at the commencement of its term, providing whatever services it may require, including a convenient place for its deliberations, entering all appropriate orders it requests, and discharging it upon completion of its deliberations or at the end of its term. All matters pertaining to grand juries shall be heard by the chief judge or his or her designee.

[Effective September 1, 1999.]

LCrR 6.2. RECORDS OF THE GRAND JURIES IN THE POSSESSION OF THE CLERK

The following documents relating to grand juries shall be public records:

(1) orders empaneling grand juries;

(2) orders returning indictments;

(3) orders extending the period of service of grand juries; and

(4) orders discharging grand juries.

The clerk is authorized to provide to an attorney who has filed an appearance in a criminal case pending in this Court a copy of any motions, orders, or documents relating to any grand jury subpoena issued in the grand jury proceeding from which the case arose against the person on whose behalf the attorney is appearing.

All other records maintained by the clerk relating to grand juries are restricted documents and shall be available only on order of the chief judge. This includes grand jury subpoenas, transcripts of testimony, the clerk's docket of grand jury proceedings, motions and orders relating to grand jury subpoenas, true bills, and no bills.

[Effective September 1, 1999. Amended effective February 28, 2007.]

LCrR 7 to LCrR 9.   [RESERVED]

LCrR 10.1.   ARRAIGNMENTS

Following the filing of an indictment or information the clerk shall promptly enter a minute order setting the date of arraignment. Where the defendant is not in custody, the arraignment shall be conducted on or before 7 days after the date of filing, unless the judge to whom the case is assigned orders that the arraignment shall be held within a shorter period of time. Where the defendant is in custody, the arraignment shall be set for no later than the second business day following such filing. Copies of the minute order setting the arraignment shall be mailed to each defendant and attorney for the defendant if their addresses are known. If their addresses are not known, the copies shall be attached to the copy of the indictment or information to be served on the defendant.

[Effective September 1, 1999.]

LCrR 11.1.   PLEAS BY CORPORATE DEFENDANTS

When the defendant in a criminal proceeding is other than a natural person, any plea other than a plea of not guilty shall be entered by an authorized officer, director or managing agent of the defendant, or by counsel, provided counsel is authorized to do so by virtue of a specific corporate resolution to that effect from the defendant's board of directors.

[Effective September 1, 1999.]

LCrR 12.1.   PRETRIAL MOTIONS

(a) **Time.** All pretrial motions and supporting briefs shall be filed within the time set by the court. If the court does not set a time, pretrial motions shall be filed within 21 days from the date of arraignment.

(b) **Additional Discovery.** In the event that a party moves for additional discovery or inspection following the discovery conference required by LCrR 16.1(a), the motion shall be filed within 7 days of the conference or, if the court has set a later date for the filing of pretrial motions, the later date. The motion shall contain:

(1) a statement that the required conference was held;

(2) the date the conference was held;

(3) the name of opposing counsel with whom the conference was held; and

(4) the statement that agreement could not be reached concerning the discovery or inspection that is the subject of the motion.

The court will not hear a motion for additional discovery or inspection if it does not conform to the procedural requisites of this section.

[Effective September 1, 1999.]

LCrR 13 to LCrR 15.   [RESERVED]

LCrR 16.1.   PRETRIAL DISCOVERY AND INSPECTION

(a) **Discovery Conference.** Within 7 days after the arraignment the United States attorney and the defendant's attorney shall confer and attempt to agree on a timetable and procedures for the following:

(1) inspecting, copying, or photographing any of the information subject to disclosure pursuant to Fed. R.Crim.P. 16;

(2) preserving the written notes of government agents;

(3) identification and notification of evidence the United States attorney intends to introduce pursuant to Federal Rule of Evidence 404(b);

(4) the filing of a proffer made within the scope of U.S. v. Santiago, 582 F.2d 1128 (7th Cir., 1978);

(5) the filing of materials subject to 18 U.S.C. § 3500; and

(6) any other preliminary matters where such agreement would serve to expedite the orderly trial of the case.

(b) **Declination of Disclosure.** If in the judgment of the United States attorney or of the defendant's attorney, it would not be in the interests of justice to make any one or more of the disclosures set forth in Fed.R.Crim.P. 16 and requested by counsel, disclosure may be declined. A declination shall be in writing, directed to opposing counsel. The declination shall specify the types of disclosures that are declined. It shall be signed personally by the United States attorney or the first assistant United States attorney or the defendant's counsel, as appropriate. It shall be served on opposing counsel and a copy filed with the court within 5 days of the discovery conference held pursuant to section (a).

[Effective September 1, 1999.]

LCrR 17 to LCrR 30. [RESERVED]

LCrR 31.1. CONTACT WITH JURORS

After the conclusion of a trial, no party, agent or attorney shall communicate with any members of the petit jury before which the case was tried without first receiving permission of the court.

[Effective September 1, 1999.]

LCrR 32.1. PRESENTENCE INVESTIGATIONS

(a) Application of Rule. This rule shall be effective in all cases in which a determination of guilt is made on or after the date of its adoption.

(b) Definitions. The following definitions shall apply to this rule:

(1) "business day" shall include any day other than a Saturday, a Sunday, or a legal holiday as defined by Fed.R.Crim.P. 45(a);

(2) "day" (except where used in the term "business day") shall refer to all days, including Saturdays, Sundays, and legal holidays as defined by Fed. R.Crim.P. 45(a);

(3) "determination of guilt" shall mean the entry of a judgment of conviction whether by plea or after trial;

(4) "Guidelines" shall mean the United States Sentencing Guidelines and Policy Statements promulgated pursuant to 28 U.S.C. § 944;

(5) "probation officer" shall mean the probation officer assigned to prepare the presentence investigation report; and

(6) "report" shall mean the presentence investigation report.

(c) Scheduling of Hearing. Upon the determination of guilt, the court shall set a date for the sentencing hearing. The hearing shall be set not less than 84 days after the determination of guilt. Any motion to modify the time limits in this Rule must be made at the time the sentencing hearing date is set.

(d) Notifying Probation Department. Following determination of guilt, the attorney for the defendant and the defendant, unless in custody, shall report immediately to the probation department to begin the presentence investigation.

If the defendant is incarcerated, the attorney for the defendant shall report to the probation department and provide the information needed to begin the presentence investigation.

Within one business day following determination of guilt, the court's courtroom deputy shall forward a presentence referral form to the probation department. Defendant shall participate in an interview, if any, with the probation department, within 14 days after the determination of guilt. Failure to schedule the interview within this period does not affect any of the other dates set forth herein.

(e) Submission of Versions. Not more than 14 days after the determination of guilt, the attorney for the government shall submit to the probation officer its version of the offense conduct. Not more than 7 days after submission of the government's version of the offense conduct, the attorney for each defendant shall submit a version of the offense conduct to the probation officer. The attorneys shall serve copies of their versions upon opposing counsel and upon the attorney for any co-defendant as to whom a determination of guilt has been made. Within 7 days after the receipt of the co-defendants' versions, each co-defendant's attorney shall submit to the probation officer and serve upon all counsel that defendant's version of the offense conduct as it relates to the defendants' respective roles in the offense. Failure to submit a version of the offense conduct within 7 days after the government's submission of its version of the offense conduct may constitute waiver of the right to have such material considered within the PSR, and the probation officer will have the right to make determinations without regard to a defendant's version of the offense conduct submitted after that date.

(f) Presentence Investigation Report. Not later than 35 days prior to sentencing, the probation officer shall complete and issue the presentence investigation report to the court, the defendant and defense counsel, and counsel for the government. The recommendation of the presentence report shall be submitted initially only to the Court, but the Court may, in its discretion, and with notice to the Probation Office, direct disclosure of the recommendation to the defendant and defense counsel, and counsel for the government, as well. The recommendation section shall not include any factual information not already contained in the other sections of the report.

(g) Position Paper. Not later than 14 days prior to sentencing, counsel for the defendant shall file with the Court and the probation officer objections, if any, to the Presentence Investigation Report, and a sentencing memorandum. The Government will have leave to respond 7 days thereafter. The parties' submissions shall specify—

(1) any factor important to the sentencing determination that is reasonably in dispute,

(2) any additional material information affecting the sentencing ranges established by the Guidelines, and

(3) any other objections or corrections to the report.

Any objection or correction not filed at that time shall be deemed waived, unless for good cause shown the court permits it to be raised at the sentencing hearing. The attorneys shall serve copies of the position papers upon opposing counsel and upon the attorney for any co-defendant as to whom a determination of guilt has been made.

(h) Responsibility of Attorneys to Review Presentence Investigation Report. Counsel for the defendant shall meet with the defendant to read and discuss the report at a reasonable time prior to the date set for submission of objections and sentencing memorandum. Counsel for the government shall examine the final report at a reasonable time prior to the date set for the government's submission.

(i) Report and Letters. Letters to the court regarding the case or defendant shall be disclosed promptly to the probation department and all counsel.

(j) Availability of Report. The report shall not be disclosed to any person or agency without the written permission of the sentencing judge. Upon notice of appeal, the probation department shall, with notification to the sentencing judge, forward under seal and apart from the appellate public file, a copy of the report to the clerk of the appellate court where it shall be available upon request for review by attorneys for the defendant and the government. Upon completion of all appellate matters, the report and the recommendation shall be returned to the probation department. Unauthorized copying, dissemination, or disclosure of the contents of the report in violation of these rules may be treated as contempt of court and punished accordingly.

[Effective September 1, 1999. Amended effective October 1, 2002; December 23, 2002; December 20, 2004; October 26, 2005; November 19, 2009; October 25, 2012; October 21, 2013.]

Committee Comment to 2013 Amendment

The Rule is amended in response to language in *United States v. Peterson*, 711 F.3d 770 (7th Cir. 2013) suggesting that parties should be permitted to "evaluate any analysis that might form the basis of a judicial determination."

Committee Comment to 2012 Amendment

The Rule is amended to render it consistent with Federal Rule of Criminal Procedure 32(f) and to set reasonable deadlines for the parties' submissions to the court.

Committee Comment to 2002 Amendment

Prior to its most recent amendment, the rule had required the probation officer to "mail a preliminary report, without

the recommendation to the defendant, the defendant's attorney and the attorney for the government." The above-quoted language did not expressly require that the recommendation be kept confidential. It merely prevented its early disclosure. We believe that the phrase "without the recommendation" was included in the prior rule because it reflected the long-standing practice of confidentiality. This commonly accepted practice had existed for decades. All district courts in this Circuit treat the recommendations as confidential. Nevertheless, elimination of the phrase has led to uncertainty over the continuing confidentiality of the recommendations.

[NOTE: Criminal Rule 32.1 was amended by General Orders of October 1, 2002, December 23, 2002, September 30, 2003, October 26, 2005, November 19, 2009, and October 25, 2012]

LCrR 32.1.1. PETITIONS & REPORTS RELATING TO MODIFICATION OF TERMS OF PROBATION OR SUPERVISED RELEASE

The probation department will file with the court any petitions or reports dealing with alleged violations or modification of conditions of probation or supervised release. The probation department will also file with such petition or report a proof of service indicating that a copy of such petition or report has been served upon the United States attorney, to the defendant, and, if the defendant is represented, to the defendant's attorney.

[Effective September 1, 1999.]

LCrR 32.3. CONFIDENTIALITY OF RECORDS RELATING TO PRESENTENCE INVESTIGATION REPORTS AND PROBATION SUPERVISION

Records maintained by the probation department of this Court relating to the preparation of presentence investigation reports and the supervision of persons on probation or supervised release are confidential. Information contained in the records that is relied on by the probation department to prepare presentence investigation or supervision reports may be released only by order of the court. Requests for such information shall be by written petition establishing with particularity the need for specific information contained in such records. A court order is not necessary to obtain criminal history information, which the probation department shall make available to counsel of record upon request.

When a demand by way of a subpoena or other judicial process is made of a probation officer either for testimony concerning information contained in such records or for the records or copies of the records, the probation officer may petition the court for instructions. The probation officer shall neither disclose the information nor provide the records or copies of the records except on order of this Court or as provided in LCrR32.1.

[Effective September 1, 1999. Amended effective January 30, 2009.]

LCrR 33 to LCrR 45. [RESERVED]

LCrR 44.1. INTERIM CJA PAYMENTS

In a case in which representation of a criminal defendant is projected to be unusually complex and lengthy, an attorney appointed pursuant to the Criminal Justice Act ("CJA Attorney") may seek approval for interim payments. A motion for such approval must cite this local criminal rule and justify the request on the basis of the hardship to counsel in undertaking the representation for a period of the projected length without compensation, pursuant to the Guidelines for the Administration of the Criminal Justice Act. ¶2.30. The motion must certify the CJA Attorney's acceptance of the following requirements:

1. Counsel shall submit quarterly, or on a schedule approved by the Court, to the Clerk of Court an interim. CJA form 20 "Appointment of and Authority to Pay Court Appointed Counsel." The first interim voucher shall reflect all compensation claimed and reimbursable expenses incurred, from the effective date of the- appointment through the date in which the first interim voucher is submitted.

2. Each voucher shall include the time period covered and shall be consecutively numbered.

3. Interim vouchers shall be submitted quarterly, or on a schedule approved by the Court, even in those periods for which little or no compensation or expenses are claimed.

4. All interim vouchers shall be supported by detailed and itemized statements of attorney time and expenses. Each voucher shall include the total amount of money requested to date.

5. The Court will review the interim vouchers when submitted, particularly with regard to the amount of time claimed, and will authorize compensation to be paid for 80 percent of the approved number of hours. This compensation will be determined by multiplying 80 percent of the approved number of hours by the applicable rate. Counsel should note that the interim payments are partial tentative payments and the final payment may be adjusted if necessary by the Court.

6. Within 45 days of the conclusion of the representation, counsel shall submit a final voucher seeking payment of the 20% balance withheld from the earlier interim vouchers, as well as payment for the representation provided during the final interim period. After reviewing the final voucher, the Court will submit it to the Chief Judge of the Circuit or his or her delegate for review and approval.

7. Counsel may be reimbursed for out-of-pocket expenses reasonably incurred incident to the representation.

8. Although the statute and applicable regulations do not place a monetary limit on the amount of expenses that can be incurred, counsel should incur no single expense item in excess of $500.00 without prior approval of the Court. Such approval may by sought be filing an ex parte application with the Clerk, stating the nature of the expense, the estimated cost, and the reason the expense is necessary to the representation. An application seeking such approval may be filed in camera, if necessary.

9. Recurring expenses, such as telephone toll calls, photocopying and photographs, which may aggregate more than $500 on one or more interim vouchers, are not considered a single item expense requiring prior court approval.

10. Telephone toll calls, photocopying, and photographs may be reimbursable expenses if reasonably incurred.

11. General office overhead, such as rent, secretarial help, and normal telephone service is not a reimbursable expense, nor are items of a personal nature.

12. Expenses for service of subpoenas on fact witnesses are not reimbursable, but rather are governed by Rule 17 of the FED.R.CRIM.P. and 28 U.S.C. § 1825.

13. In some instances, travel may be required for purposes of consulting with the client or with predecessor counsel, interviewing witnesses or experts, etc. In such circumstances, where travel is required outside the County of Cook for cases assigned to the Eastern Division, or outside the County of Winnebago for cases assigned to the Western Division, travel expenses, such as airfare, mileage, parking fee, meals and lodging, can be claimed as itemized expenses. If expenses relating to a single trip will exceed a total of $500.00, counsel must seek prior Court approval. Actual expenses incurred for meals and lodging in the course of such travel must conform to the prevailing government travel regulations imposed on federal judiciary employees for official travel.

14. CJA Attorneys are bound by the regulations of the Criminal Justice Act set forth in (1) 18 U.S.C. § 3006A; (2) the Plan of the United States District Court for the Northern District of Illinois, available through the Clerk of Court; and (3) Guidelines for the Administration of the Criminal Justice Act, published by the Administrative Office of the U.S. Courts, also available through the Clerk of Court. Should these references fail to provide the desired clarification or direction, counsel should address their inquiry directly to this Court and its staff.

[Effective September 23, 2014.]

LCrR 46.1. BAIL BONDS

(a) **Who May Approve Bonds.** When the amount of bail has been set by the judge or magistrate judge, a bond, whether secured by the defendant's own recognizance or by a surety may be approved by a magistrate judge, the clerk, or one of the officers specified in 18 U.S.C. § 3041, *provided* that only a judge may admit to bail or otherwise release a person charged with an offense punishable by death.

(b) **Refund of Cash Deposit.** Where a defendant's bond is secured by depositing cash with the clerk, the cash shall be refunded when the conditions of the bond have been performed and the defendant has been discharged from all obligations thereon. However, if the sentence includes a fine or costs, the sentence shall constitute a lien in favor of the United States on the amount deposited to secure the bond. In such instances the amount deposited can be refunded only by order of court. No such lien shall attach when someone other than the defendant has deposited the cash and refund is directed to someone other than the defendant.

At the time the cash deposit is made, the person furnishing the cash ("the depositor") shall be given a receipt by the clerk. The depositor shall at the time of the deposit indicate in writing the name and address of the person to whom the cash is to be refunded. This shall be done on Form LCrR46.1. The depositor may change the designation of the person to receive the refund by completing a new form and filing it with a fiscal deputy in the clerk's office at any time before the refund is made.

A refund to a person other than the depositor shall be made only pursuant to an order of court.

[Effective September 1, 1999.]

LCrR 46.2. PRETRIAL SERVICES AGENCY

The Pretrial Services Agency of this Court ("Agency") shall perform the following functions:

(1) collect, verify and report promptly to the district or magistrate judge information pertaining to the pretrial release of each person charged with an offense, including any drug testing information, and recommend appropriate release conditions;

(2) review and modify the reports and recommendations made in (1) above for persons seeking release pursuant to 18 U.S.C. § 3145;

(3) supervise persons released into its custody;

(4) with the cooperation of the Administrative Office of the United States Courts, and with the approval of the Attorney General, operate or contract for the operation of appropriate facilities for the custody or care of persons released under Chapter 207 of Title 18

of the United States Code, including, but not limited to, residential halfway houses, drug addiction and alcoholism treatment centers and counseling services;

(5) inform the court of all apparent violations of pretrial release conditions or arrests of persons released to its custody or under its supervision and recommend appropriate modifications of release conditions;

(6) serve as coordinator for other local agencies which serve or are eligible to serve as custodians under Chapter 207 of Title 18 of the United States Code and advise the court as to the eligibility, availability and capacity of such agencies;

(7) assist persons released on bond in securing any necessary employment, medical, legal, or social services;

(8) prepare, in cooperation with the United States marshal and the United States attorney, such pretrial detention reports as are required by the provisions of the Federal Rules of Criminal Procedure relating to the supervision of detention pending trial; and

(9) perform such other functions as the court may assign from time to time.

[Effective September 1, 1999.]

LCrR 46.3. NOTIFYING PRETRIAL SERVICES AGENCY OF ARREST AND FILING OF CASE

(a) **Arrest or Confinement.** The Pretrial Services Agency ("Agency") shall be notified (1) by the arresting officer, or (2) by the officer receiving the defendant if the defendant was arrested by local officers and subsequently turned over to federal officers, as soon as practicable following the arrest or transfer, of the facts of such arrest or transfer, the name of the defendant, the charge upon which the defendant has been arrested or transferred, and the place wherein the defendant is being detained.

(b) **Filing of Case.** Immediately following the filing of a complaint the magistrate judge shall cause a copy of it to be forwarded to the Agency. The clerk shall cause a copy of each indictment or information filed to be forwarded to the Agency immediately following the filing, provided that if the indictment is suppressed, the clerk shall cause the copy to be forwarded immediately following the release of the suppression.

[Effective September 1, 1999.]

LCrR 46.4. CONFIDENTIALITY OF PRETRIAL SERVICES INFORMATION AND REPORTS

(a) **General.** The information obtained in the course of performing pretrial services functions in relation to a particular accused shall be used only for the purposes of release determination and shall otherwise be confidential. Each pretrial services report shall be made available to the attorney for the accused and the attorney for the Government in connection with a pretrial release or detention hearing, a pretrial release revocation proceeding, or any judicial proceeding to modify the conditions of release. The pretrial services report should not be disclosed to other parties by the attorney for the defendant or the attorney for the Government. Any copies of the pretrial services report so disclosed shall be returned to the pretrial services officer at the conclusion of the hearing.

(b) Prohibition of Disclosure. Unless authorized by the regulations as established by the Director of the Administrative Office, or ordered by the judicial officer for good cause shown, a pretrial services officer shall not disclose pretrial services information. This prohibition on unauthorized disclosure applies whether such disclosure is sought through the direct testimony of the pretrial services officer or by means of a subpoena, subpoena duces tecum, or other form of judicial process.

The term "pretrial services information" shall include any information whether recorded or not, that is obtained or developed by a pretrial services officer in the course of performing a pretrial services investigation, preparing the pretrial services report, performing any post-release of post-detention investigation, or supervising a defendant released pursuant to chapter 207 of Title 18, United States Code. The term does not include any information appearing in the public records of the court.

Any disclosure of pretrial services information permitted under the provisions of these regulations or ordered by the judicial officer shall be limited to the minimum information necessary to carry out the purpose of the disclosure.

[Effective September 1, 1999.]

LCrR 47.1.   MOTIONS

(a) Notice and Presentation. Except as provided in section (c) of this rule, LR5.3 and LR78.1 shall apply to motions filed in criminal cases and proceedings.

(b) Briefing Motions. A contested motion shall be accompanied by a short, concise brief in support of the motion, together with citations of authority. An original and a copy of the motion and brief shall be filed. The clerk shall forward the copy to the judge unless otherwise ordered by the court. The opposing party shall file an answering brief within 14 days of receiving the supporting brief. The moving party may file a reply brief within 7 days of receipt of the answering brief.

Failure to file a supporting or answering brief shall not be deemed a waiver of the motion or a withdrawal of opposition thereto, but the court on its own motion or that of a party may strike or grant the motion without further hearing. Failure to file reply brief within the requisite time shall be deemed a waiver of the right to file.

The court may by order excuse the filing of supporting, answering, or reply briefs, and may shorten or extend the time fixed by this rule filing briefs.

Any party may on notice call the motion or matter to the attention of the court for a decision. When requested, oral argument may be allowed in the Court's discretion.

(c) Exceptions. The following motions are not subject to the provisions of section (a) of this rule:

(1) *Pretrial Motions.* Motions filed pursuant to LCrR12.1 are not subject to the requirements of this rule.

(2) *Ex Parte Motions.* The original, signed motion shall be presented to the court at the hearing. Copies of the stipulated motions shall be served on all parties as soon thereafter as practicable.

[Effective September 1, 1999. Amended effective October 13, 2004; November 19, 2009.]

LCrR 48 to LCrR 49.   [RESERVED]

LCrR 50.1.   RELATED CASES: REASSIGNMENT OF CASES AS RELATED

Two or more criminal cases may be related if all of the defendants named in each of the cases are the same and none of the cases includes defendants not named in any of the other cases. A case may be reassigned to the calendar of another judge as related if it is found to be related to another case and it meets the criteria established by LR40.4(b) for reassigning civil cases. The procedures set out in LR40.4(c) and (d) shall be followed where the reassignment of a criminal case based on relatedness is sought.

[Effective September 1, 1999.]

LCrR 50.2.   DIRECT ASSIGNMENTS: CRIMINAL

In each of the following instances, the assignment clerk shall assign the case to a judge in the manner specified:

(1) Criminal Contempt Cases Arising Out of Grand Jury Proceedings. Any criminal contempt case arising out of grand jury proceedings shall be assigned to the chief judge at the time of filing. If the chief judge determines that such case should be heard by some other judge, it will be transferred to the

Executive Committee with a recommendation that it be assigned by lot to some other judge.

(2) Interception of Wire and Oral Communications. All requests for authorization for interceptions of wire and oral communications or other investigatory matters arising under Chapter 119 of Title 18 of the U.S. Code shall be brought before the chief judge. Any civil suppressed cases arising out of such requests shall be assigned directly to the calendar of the chief judge.

(3) Cases Arising Out of Failure to Appear. Where an information or indictment is filed in which the principal charge is that the defendant failed to appear in a criminal proceeding in this Court, the information or indictment shall be assigned directly to the same calendar as that to which the earlier criminal proceeding is assigned.

(4) Superseding Indictments or Informations. The United States attorney will indicate on the designation sheet filed with each indictment or information whether or not it supersedes a pending indictment or information. A superseding indictment or information will be filed in the same case as the superseded indictment or information. Where it supersedes more than one indictment or information, it will be filed in the case which was first assigned to a district judge.

For the purpose of this subsection, an indictment or information supersedes an earlier filed indictment or information if at least one of the defendants in the later filed indictment or information is charged with at least one of the charges brought against the same defendant in an earlier filed indictment or information.

(5) Criminal Cases Where Pre-indictment Assignment Made. Where a proceeding arising out of a criminal complaint is required to be heard by a district judge and is assigned by lot to a district judge prior to the filing of the indictment or information associated with the complaint, the indictment or information shall be assigned directly to the calendar of the judge to whom the proceeding was assigned. Where the indictment would have been assigned using a category different from the one used to assign the criminal complaint, appropriate equalization will be made.

[Effective September 1, 1999.]

LCrR 50.3. MAGISTRATE JUDGES: ASSIGNMENTS AND REFERRALS

(a) Misdemeanors. Where a magistrate judge has not previously been designated pursuant to LR72.1, informations filed or indictments returned in the Eastern Division alleging the commission of a misdemeanor shall be assigned by lot among the magistrate judges sitting in that division. Similar informations filed or indictments returned in the Western Division shall be assigned to the magistrate judge sitting in division.

(b) Federal Enclave Magistrate Judge. From time to time the presiding magistrate judge shall approve a schedule designating the periods during which each of the magistrate judges sitting in the Eastern Division will serve as the federal enclave magistrate judge. The federal enclave magistrate judge will conduct trials of all misdemeanors which arise in federal enclaves.

(c) Designation at Filing. Whenever a criminal case is filed in the Eastern Division and assigned to the calendar of a district judge, the clerk shall designate a magistrate judge in the manner provided in LR72.1. Where an indictment or information arises out of one or more criminal complaints, the designated magistrate judge shall be the magistrate to whom the earliest of those complaints was assigned. Where multiple defendants in a single complaint assigned to a magistrate judge are subsequently charged in more than one indictment or information arising out of that complaint, the designated magistrate judge for each such case shall be the magistrate judge to whom the complaint was assigned.

(d) Referrals. The procedures used to refer a matter in a criminal case to a magistrate judge shall be the same as those used to refer a civil case pursuant to LR72.1, provided that where a judge notifies the clerk in writing that the judge wishes to have criminal cases routinely referred to a magistrate judge for conducting arraignments and other pretrial matters, such notification shall act as a referral in lieu of the procedures specified in LR72.1. The clerk shall promptly notify the designated magistrate judge of the filing of any indictment or information assigned to the calendar of a judge who has filed a notice of routine reference.

(e) Forfeiture of Collateral Hearings. Hearings and other matters relating to violation notices and forfeiture of collateral proceedings pursuant to LCrR58.1 shall be handled in the Eastern Division by the magistrate judge designated as federal enclave magistrate judge on the day the hearings are scheduled and in the Western Division by the magistrate judge sitting in that division.

(f) Right to Proceed Before District Judge. If a proceeding assigned directly to a magistrate judge is such that a party to the proceeding has the right to proceed before a district judge and that party fails to waive that right, then the proceeding shall be reassigned to a district judge pursuant to LCrR50.4(b) as if it were an appeal from a judgment of a magistrate judge. The magistrate judge shall notify the clerk in writing of the failure to waive. The clerk will reassign the proceeding promptly following the receipt of that notice.

[Effective September 1, 1999. Amended effective January 31, 2001; June 23, 2006.]

LCrR 50.4. MAGISTRATE JUDGES: REVIEWS AND APPEALS

(a) **Duty Magistrate Judge.** Where a review is requested of an order entered by the duty magistrate judge in proceedings directly assigned pursuant to LCrR5.1, the review shall be heard by the emergency judge. The request for review shall be brought to the attention of the emergency judge by the party seeking review as soon as practicable following the entry of the order by the magistrate judge. The party seeking review shall be responsible for notifying the other parties involved in the proceeding that a review will be requested and for notifying them of the time the review is noticed before the emergency judge.

(b) **CVB and Misdemeanor.** Appeals from final judgments entered by a magistrate judge in violation notice and forfeiture of collateral proceedings and misdemeanor cases shall be assigned by lot to a judge of this Court. For assignment purposes, such appeals shall be considered as cases in the magistrate judge class established by the procedures adopted pursuant to LR40.2. The assignments of a judge shall be made when the appeal is filed with the clerk pursuant to Fed.R.Crim.P. 58(g)(2).

[Effective September 1, 1999.]

LCrR 51 to LCrR 56. [RESERVED]

LCrR 57.1. ATTORNEYS: FILING APPEARANCES

Each attorney representing a defendant in a criminal proceeding shall file an appearance. The appearance must be filed prior to or simultaneously with the filing of any motion, brief or other document or at the initial court appearance, whichever occurs first. A copy of the appearance shall be served on the United States attorney.

The filing of an appearance in a pre-indictment proceeding does not relieve an attorney from filing an appearance in a subsequent proceeding should an indictment be returned or an information filed against the defendant. A copy of the appearance in the subsequent proceedings shall also be served on the United States attorney.

The appearance shall be on the form prescribed by LR83.16.

[Effective September 1, 1999.]

LCrR 57.2. RELEASE OF INFORMATION BY COURTHOUSE PERSONNEL

All courtroom and courthouse personnel, including, but not limited to, deputy marshals, court security officers, minute clerks, court reporters, pretrial services officers, probation officers, and clerical personnel of the offices of the United States marshal, the clerk of court, the probation department, and pretrial services, shall not disclose to any person, without authorization by the court, information relating to a pending criminal case that is not part of the public record. In particular, all such personnel shall not divulge any information concerning arguments and hearings held in chambers or otherwise outside the presence of the public.

[Effective September 1, 1999.]

LCrR 58.1. PETTY OFFENSES; CENTRAL VIOLATIONS BUREAU

(a) **Executive Committee.** Orders establishing the amount of collateral to be posted by defendants alleged to have committed petty offenses and those cases in which the collateral may be accepted in lieu of appearances may be entered by the Executive Committee acting for the Court.

(b) **Collateral In Lieu of Appearance.** Collateral may be posted by a defendant in lieu of appearance where the charge is one of the petty offenses listed in an order entered pursuant to (a) of this rule. The collateral shall be in the amount specified in that order. Collateral may not be posted by a defendant in lieu of appearance either—

(1) where the petty offense involved or contributed to an accident which resulted in personal injury or damage to property in excess of $100, or

(2) for a subsequent offense not arising out of the same facts or sequence of events which resulted in the original offense.

(c) **Forfeiture of Collateral.** Posting collateral pursuant to section (b) of this rule signifies that the defendant neither contests the charge nor requests a hearing before the designated magistrate judge. The failure of the defendant to appear shall result in the forfeiture of the amount posted. Such forfeiture shall be tantamount to a finding of guilty. The clerk shall certify the record of any conviction of a traffic violation to the proper state authority as required by the applicable state statute.

(d) **Central Violations Bureau (CVB).** The clerk shall maintain a central violations bureau (CVB). All agencies issuing violation notices shall prepare the notices in the form prescribed by the Director of the Administrative Office of the United States Courts. Agencies shall promptly submit to the CVB the original and one copy of any violation notice issued or any which the agency wishes to be voided or dismissed.

(e) Dismissals and Voids. No violation notice may be dismissed or voided except by order of court. Requests to dismiss or void made by agencies shall be submitted to the CVB. The CVB shall notify the United States attorney of the request. The United States attorney shall present the request to the designated magistrate judge at a regular call of violation notices.

[Effective September 1, 1999.]

LOCAL PATENT RULES

PREAMBLE

These Local Patent Rules provide a standard structure for patent cases that will permit greater predictability and planning for the Court and the litigants. These Rules also anticipate and address many of the procedural issues that commonly arise in patent cases. The Court's intention is to eliminate the need for litigants and judges to address separately in each case procedural issues that tend to recur in the vast majority of patent cases.

The Rules require, along with a party's disclosures under Federal Rule of Civil Procedure 26(a)(1), meaningful disclosure of each party's contentions and support for allegations in the pleadings. Complaints and counterclaims in most patent cases are worded in a bare-bones fashion, necessitating discovery to flesh out the basis for each party's contentions. The Rules require the parties to provide the particulars behind allegations of infringement, non-infringement, and invalidity at an early date. Because Federal Rule of Civil Procedure 11 requires a party to have factual and legal support for allegations in its pleadings, early disclosure of the basis for each side's allegations will impose no unfair hardship and will benefit all parties by enabling a focus on the contested issues at an early stage of the case. The Rules' supplementation of the requirements of Rule 26(a)(1) and other Federal Rules is also appropriate due to the various ways in which patent litigation differs from most other civil litigation, including its factual complexity; the routine assertion of counterclaims; the need for the Court to construe, and thus for the parties to identify, disputed language in patent claims; and the variety of ways in which a patent may be infringed or invalid.

The initial disclosures required by the Rules are not intended to confine a party to the contentions it makes at the outset of the case. It is not unusual for a party in a patent case to learn additional grounds for claims of infringement, non-infringement, and invalidity as the case progresses. After a reasonable period for fact discovery, however, each party must provide a final statement of its contentions on relevant issues, which the party may thereafter amend only "upon a showing of good cause and absence of unfair prejudice, made in timely fashion following discovery of the basis for the amendment." LPR 3.4.

The Rules also provide a standardized structure for claim construction proceedings, requiring the parties to identify and exchange position statements regarding disputed claim language before presenting disputes to the Court. The Rules contemplate that claim construction will be done, in most cases, toward the end of fact discovery. The committee of lawyers and judges that drafted and proposed the Rules considered placing claim construction at both earlier and later spots in the standard schedule. The decision to place claim construction near the end of fact discovery is premised on the determination that claim construction is more likely to be a meaningful process that deals with the truly significant disputed claim terms if the parties have had sufficient time, via the discovery process, to ascertain what claim terms really matter and why and can identify (as the Rules require) which are outcome determinative. The Rules' placement of claim construction near the end of fact discovery does not preclude the parties from proposing or the Court from requiring an earlier claim construction in a particular case. This may be appropriate in, for example, a case in which it is apparent at an early stage that the outcome will turn on one claim term or a small number of terms that can be identified without a significant amount of fact discovery.

Finally, the Rules provide for a standardized protective order that is deemed to be in effect upon the initiation of the lawsuit. This is done for two reasons. First, confidentiality issues abound in patent litigation. Second, early entry of a protective order is critical to enable the early initial disclosures of patent-related contentions that the Rules require. Absent a "default" protective order, the making of initial disclosures, and thus the entire schedule, would be delayed while the parties negotiated a protective order. The parties may, either at the outset of the case or later, seek a revised protective order that is more tailored to their case. Because, however, the Rules provide for automatic entry of the default protective order, the desire to negotiate a more tailored version is not a basis to delay the disclosure and discovery schedule that the Rules contemplate.

[Effective October 1, 2009.]

1. SCOPE OF RULES

LPR 1.1   APPLICATION AND CONSTRUCTION

These Rules ("LPR") apply to all cases filed in or transferred to this District after their effective date in which a party makes a claim of infringement, non-infringement, invalidity, or unenforceability of a utility patent. The Court may apply all or part of the LPR to any such case already pending on the effective date of the LPR. The Court may modify the obligations and deadlines of the LPR based on the circumstances of any particular case. If a party files, prior to the Claim Construction Proceedings provided for in LPR Section 5, a motion that raises claim construction issues, the Court may defer the motion until after the Claim Construction Proceedings.

[Effective October 1, 2009.]

LPR 1.2.   INITIAL SCHEDULING CONFERENCE

In their conference pursuant to Fed. R. Civ. P. 26(f), the parties must discuss and address those matters found in the form scheduling order contained in LPR Appendix "A." A completed proposed version of the scheduling order is to be presented to the Court within seven (7) days after the Rule 26(f) conference or at such other time as the Court directs. Paragraphs 4(e), 7(c) and 7(d) of the form scheduling order shall be included, without alteration, in this proposed scheduling order.

[Effective October 1, 2009. Amended effective March 1, 2013.]

LPR 1.3.   FACT DISCOVERY

Fact discovery shall commence upon the date for the Initial Disclosures under LPR 2.1 and shall be completed twenty-eight (28) days after the date for exchange of claim terms and phrases under LPR 4.1. Fact discovery may resume upon entry of a claim construction ruling and shall end forty-two (42) days after entry of the claim construction ruling.

[Effective October 1, 2009. Amended effective March 1, 2013.]

Comment

The Rule states that resumption of fact discovery upon entry of a claim construction ruling "may" occur. The Rule does not provide that discovery shall automatically resume as a matter of right. It is intended that parties seeking further discovery following the claim construction ruling shall submit a motion explaining why further discovery is necessitated by the claim construction ruling.

LPR 1.4   CONFIDENTIALITY

The protective order found in LPR Appendix B shall be deemed to be in effect as of the date for each party's Initial Disclosures. Any party may move the Court to modify the Appendix B protective order for good cause. The filing of such a motion does not affect the requirement for or timing of any of the disclosures required by the LPR.

[Effective October 1, 2009.]

LPR 1.5   CERTIFICATION OF DISCLOSURES

All disclosures made pursuant to LPR 2.2, 2.3, 2.4, 2.5, 3.1, and 3.2 must be dated and signed by counsel of record (or by the party if unrepresented by counsel) and are subject to the requirements of Federal Rules of Civil Procedure 11 and 26(g).

[Effective October 1, 2009.]

LPR 1.6   ADMISSIBILITY OF DISCLOSURES

The disclosures provided for in LPR 2.2, 2.3, 2.4, and 2.5 are inadmissible as evidence on the merits.

[Effective October 1, 2009.]

Comment

The purpose of the initial disclosures pursuant to LPR 2.2–2.5 is to identify the likely issues in the case, to enable the parties to focus and narrow their discovery requests. Permitting use of the initial disclosures as evidence on the merits would defeat this purpose. A party may make reference to the initial disclosures for any other appropriate purpose.

LPR 1.7   RELATIONSHIP TO FEDERAL RULES OF CIVIL PROCEDURE

A party may not object to mandatory disclosures under Federal Rule of Civil Procedure 26(a) or to a discovery request on the ground that it conflicts with or is premature under the LPR, except to the following categories of requests and disclosures:

(a) requests for a party's claim construction position;

(b) requests to the patent claimant for a comparison of the asserted claims and the accused apparatus, device, process, method, act, or other instrumentality;

(c) requests to an accused infringer for a comparison of the asserted claims and the prior art;

(d) requests to an accused infringer for its non-infringement contentions; and

(e) requests to the patent claimant for its contentions regarding the presence of claim elements in the prior art.

Federal Rule of Civil Procedure 26's requirements concerning supplementation of disclosure and discovery responses apply to all disclosures required under the LPR.

[Effective October 1, 2009.]

2. PATENT INITIAL DISCLOSURES

LPR 2.1 INITIAL DISCLOSURES

The plaintiff and any defendant that files an answer or other response to the complaint shall exchange their initial disclosures under Federal Rule of Civil Procedure 26(a)(1) ("Initial Disclosures") within fourteen (14) days after the defendant files its answer or other response, provided, however, if defendant asserts a counterclaim for infringement of another patent, the Initial Disclosures shall be within fourteen (14) days after the plaintiff files its answer or other response to that counterclaim. As used in this Rule, the term "document" has the same meaning as in Federal Rule of Civil Procedure 34(a):

(a) A party asserting a claim of patent infringement shall produce or make the following available for inspection and copying along with its Initial Disclosures, to the extent they are in the party's possession, custody or control.

(1) all documents concerning any disclosure, sale or transfer, or offer to sell or transfer, of any item embodying, practicing or resulting from the practice of the claimed invention prior to the date of application for the patent in suit. Production of a document pursuant to this Rule is not an admission that the document evidences or is prior art under 35 U.S.C. § 102;

(2) all documents concerning the conception, reduction to practice, design, and development of each claimed invention, which were created on or before the date of application for the patent in suit or a priority date otherwise identified for the patent in suit, whichever is earlier;

(3) all documents concerning communications to and from the U.S. Patent Office for each patent in suit and for each patent on which a claim for priority is based; and

(4) all documents concerning ownership of the patent rights by the party asserting patent infringement.

The producing party shall separately identify by production number which documents correspond to each category.

(b) A party opposing a claim of patent infringement shall produce or make the following available for inspection and copying, along with its Initial Disclosures:

(1) documents sufficient to show the operation and construction of all aspects or elements of each accused apparatus, product, device, component, process, method or other instrumentality identified with specificity in the pleading of the party asserting patent infringement; and

(2) a copy of each item of prior art of which the party is aware that allegedly anticipates each asserted patent and its related claims or renders them obvious or, if a copy is unavailable, a description sufficient to identify the prior art and its relevant details.

[Effective October 1, 2009.]

LPR 2.2 INITIAL INFRINGEMENT CONTENTIONS

A party claiming patent infringement must serve on all parties "Initial Infringement Contentions" containing the following information within fourteen (14) days after the Initial Disclosure under LPR 2.1:

(a) identification each claim of each patent in suit that is allegedly infringed by the opposing party, including for each claim the applicable statutory subsection of 35 U.S.C. § 271;

(b) separately for each asserted claim, identification of each accused apparatus, product, device, process, method, act, or other instrumentality ("Accused Instrumentality") of the opposing party of which the party claiming infringement is aware. Each Accused Instrumentality must be identified by name, if known, or by any product, device, or apparatus which, when used, allegedly results in the practice of the claimed method or process;

(c) a chart identifying specifically where each element of each asserted claim is found within each Accused Instrumentality, including for each element that such party contends is governed by 35 U.S.C. § 112(6), a description of the claimed function of that element and the identity of the structure(s), act(s), or material(s) in the Accused Instrumentality that performs the claimed function;

(d) identification of whether each element of each asserted claim is claimed to be present in the Accused Instrumentality literally or under the doctrine of equivalents. For any claim under the doctrine of equivalents, the Initial Infringement Contentions must include an explanation of each function, way, and result that is equivalent and why any differences are not substantial;

(e) For each claim that is alleged to have been indirectly infringed, an identification of any direct infringement and a description of the acts of the alleged indirect infringer that contribute to or are inducing that direct infringement. If alleged direct infringement is based on joint acts of multiple parties, the role of each such party in the direct infringement must be described;

(f) for any patent that claims priority to an earlier application, the priority date to which each asserted claim allegedly is entitled;

(g) identification of the basis for any allegation of willful infringement; and

(h) if a party claiming patent infringement wishes to preserve the right to rely, for any purpose, on the assertion that its own or its licensee's apparatus, product, device, process, method, act, or other instrumentality practices the claimed invention, the party must identify, separately for each asserted patent, each such apparatus, product, device, process, method, act, or other instrumentality that incorporates or reflects that particular claim, including whether it is marked with the patent number.

[Effective October 1, 2009.]

Comment

LPR 2.2–2.5 supplements the initial disclosures required by Federal Rule of Civil Procedure 26(a)(1). As stated in the comment to LPR 1.6, the purpose of these provisions is to require the parties to identify the likely issues in the case, to enable them to focus and narrow their discovery requests. To accomplish this purpose, the parties' disclosures must be meaningful—as opposed to boilerplate—and non-evasive. These provisions should be construed accordingly when applied to particular cases.

LPR 2.3   INITIAL NON–INFRINGEMENT, UNENFORCEABILITY AND INVALIDITY CONTENTIONS

Each party opposing a claim of patent infringement or asserting invalidity or unenforceability shall serve upon all parties its "Initial Non–Infringement, Unenforceability and Invalidity Contentions" within fourteen (14) days after service of the Initial Infringement Contentions. Such Initial Contentions shall be as follows:

(a) Non–Infringement Contentions shall contain a chart, responsive to the chart required by LPR 2.2(c), that identifies as to each identified element in each asserted claim, to the extent then known by the party opposing infringement, whether such element is present literally or under the doctrine of equivalents in each Accused Instrumentality and, if not, the reason for such denial and the relevant distinctions.

(b) Invalidity Contentions must contain the following information to the extent then known to the party asserting invalidity:

(1) identification, with particularity, of each item of prior art that allegedly anticipates each asserted claim or renders it obvious. Each prior art patent shall be identified by its number, country of origin, and date of issue. Each prior art publication must be identified by its title, date of publication, and where feasible, author and publisher. Prior art under 35 U.S.C. § 102(b) shall be identified by specifying the item offered for sale or publicly used or known, the date the offer or use took place or the information became known, and the identity of the person or entity which made the use or which made and received the offer, or the person or entity which made the information known or to whom it was made known. Prior art under 35 U.S.C. § 102(f) shall be identified by providing the name of the person(s) from whom and the circumstances under which the invention or any part of it was derived. Prior art under 35 U.S.C. § 102(g) shall be identified by providing the identities of the person(s) or entities involved in and the circumstances surrounding the making of the invention before the patent applicant(s);

(2) a statement of whether each item of prior art allegedly anticipates each asserted claim or renders it obvious. If a combination of items of prior art allegedly makes a claim obvious, each such combination, and the reasons to combine such items must be identified;

(3) a chart identifying where specifically in each alleged item of prior art each element of each asserted claim is found, including for each element that such party contends is governed by 35 U.S.C. § 112(6), a description of the claimed function of that element and the identity of the structure(s), act(s), or material(s) in each item of prior art that performs the claimed function; and

(4) a detailed statement of any grounds of invalidity based on indefiniteness under 35 U.S.C. § 112(2) or enablement or written description under 35 U.S.C. § 112(1).

(c) Unenforceability contentions shall identify the acts allegedly supporting and all bases for the assertion of unenforceability.

[Effective October 1, 2009.]

Comment

LPR 2.2–2.5 supplements the initial disclosures required by Federal Rule of Civil Procedure 26(a)(1). As stated in the comment to LPR 1.6, the purpose of these provisions is to require the parties to identify the likely issues in the case, to enable them to focus and narrow their discovery requests. To accomplish this purpose, the parties' disclosures must be meaningful—as opposed to boilerplate—and non-evasive.

These provisions should be construed accordingly when applied to particular cases.

LPR 2.4 DOCUMENT PRODUCTION ACCOMPANYING INITIAL INVALIDITY CONTENTIONS

With the Initial Non–Infringement and Invalidity Contentions under LPR 2.3, the party opposing a claim of patent infringement shall supplement its Initial Disclosures and, in particular, must produce or make available for inspection and copying:

(a) any additional documentation showing the operation of any aspects or elements of an Accused Instrumentality identified by the patent claimant in its LPR 2.2 chart; and

(b) a copy of any additional items of prior art identified pursuant to LPR 2.3 that does not appear in the file history of the patent(s) at issue.

[Effective October 1, 2009.]

Comment

LPR 2.2–2.5 supplements the initial disclosures required by Federal Rule of Civil Procedure 26(a)(1). As stated in the comment to LPR 1.6, the purpose of these provisions is to require the parties to identify the likely issues in the case, to enable them to focus and narrow their discovery requests. To accomplish this purpose, the parties' disclosures must be meaningful—as opposed to boilerplate—and non-evasive. These provisions should be construed accordingly when applied to particular cases.

LPR 2.5 INITIAL RESPONSE TO INVALIDITY CONTENTIONS

Within fourteen (14) days after service of the Initial Non–Infringement and Invalidity Contentions under LPR 2.3, each party claiming patent infringement shall serve upon all parties its "Initial Response to Invalidity Contentions." The Initial Response to Invalidity Contentions shall contain a chart, responsive to the chart required by LPR 2.3(b)(3), that states as to each identified element in each asserted claim, to the extent then known, whether the party admits to the identity of elements in the prior art and, if not, the reason for such denial.

[Effective October 1, 2009.]

Comment

LPR 2.2–2.5 supplements the initial disclosures required by Federal Rule of Civil Procedure 26(a)(1). As stated in the comment to LPR 1.6, the purpose of these provisions is to require the parties to identify the likely issues in the case, to enable them to focus and narrow their discovery requests. To accomplish this purpose, the parties' disclosures must be meaningful—as opposed to boilerplate—and non-evasive. These provisions should be construed accordingly when applied to particular cases.

LPR 2.6 DISCLOSURE REQUIREMENT IN PATENT CASES INITIATED BY COMPLAINT FOR DECLARATORY JUDGMENT

In a case initiated by a complaint for declaratory judgment in which a party files a pleading seeking a judgment that a patent is not infringed, is invalid, or is unenforceable, LPR 2.2 and 2.3 shall not apply unless a party makes a claim for patent infringement. If no claim of infringement is made, the party seeking a declaratory judgment must comply with LPR 2.3 and 2.4 within twenty-eight (28) days after the Initial Disclosures.

[Effective October 1, 2009.]

3. FINAL CONTENTIONS

LPR 3.1. FINAL INFRINGEMENT, UNENFORCEABILITY AND INVALIDITY CONTENTIONS

A party claiming patent infringement must serve on all parties "Final Infringement Contentions" containing the information required by LPR 2.2 (a)–(h) within twenty-one (21) weeks after the due date for service of Initial Infringement Contentions. Each party asserting invalidity or unenforceability of a patent claim shall serve on all other parties, no later than the same time that the Final Infringement Contentions are due, "Final Unenforceability and Invalidity Contentions" containing the information required by LPR 2.3(b) and (c). Final Invalidity Contentions may rely on more than twenty-five (25) prior art references only by order of the Court upon a showing of good cause and absence of unfair prejudice to opposing parties.

[Effective October 1, 2009. Amended effective March 1, 2013.]

LPR 3.2. FINAL NON-INFRINGEMENT, ENFORCEABILITY AND VALIDITY CONTENTIONS

Each party asserting non-infringement of a patent claim shall serve on all other parties "Final Non-infringement Contentions" within twenty-eight (28) days after service of the Final Infringement Contentions, containing the information called for in LPR 2.3(a). Each party asserting patent infringement shall serve, at the same time the "Final Non–Infringement Contentions" are due, Final Contentions in Response to any "Final Unenforceability and Invalidity Contentions."

[Effective October 1, 2009. Amended effective March 1, 2013.]

LPR 3.3 DOCUMENT PRODUCTION ACCOMPANYING FINAL INVALIDITY CONTENTIONS

With the Final Invalidity Contentions, the party asserting invalidity of any patent claim shall produce or make available for inspection and copying: a copy or sample of all prior art identified pursuant to LPR 3.2, to the extent not previously produced, that does not appear in the file history of the patent(s) at issue. If any such item is not in English, an English translation of the portion(s) relied upon shall be produced. The translated portion of the non-English prior art shall be sufficient to place in context the particular matter upon which the party relies.

The producing party shall separately identify by production number which documents correspond to each category.

[Effective October 1, 2009.]

LPR 3.4. AMENDMENT OF FINAL CONTENTIONS

A party may amend its Final Infringement Contentions; Final Non-infringement, Unenforceability and Invalidity Contentions; or Final Contentions in Response to any Unenforceability and Invalidity Contentions only by order of the Court upon a showing of good cause and absence of unfair prejudice to opposing parties, made promptly upon discovery of the basis for the amendment. An example of a circumstance that may support a finding of good cause, absent undue prejudice to the non-moving party, includes a claim construction by the Court different from that proposed by the party seeking amendment. A motion to amend final contentions due to a claim construction ruling shall be filed, with proposed amendment(s), within fourteen (14) days of the entry of such ruling.

The duty to supplement discovery responses does not excuse the need to obtain leave of court to amend contentions.

[Effective October 1, 2009. Amended effective March 1, 2013.]

LPR 3.5 FINAL DATE TO SEEK STAY PENDING REEXAMINATION

Absent exceptional circumstances, no party may file a motion to stay the lawsuit pending reexamination in the U.S. Patent Office after the due date for service of the Final Contentions pursuant to LPR 3.2.

[Effective October 1, 2009.]

LPR 3.6 DISCOVERY CONCERNING OPINIONS OF COUNSEL

(a) The substance of a claim of reliance on advice of counsel offered in defense to a charge of willful infringement, and other information within the scope of a waiver of the attorney-client privilege based upon disclosure of such advice, is not subject to discovery until thirty-five (35) days prior to the close of the period of fact discovery that, under LPR 1.3, follows the court's claim construction ruling.

(b) On the day advice of counsel information becomes discoverable under LPR 3.6(a), a party claiming reliance on advice of counsel shall disclose to all other parties the following:

(1) All written opinions of counsel upon which the party will rely;

(2) All information provided to the attorney in connection with the advice;

(3) All written attorney work product developed in preparing the opinion that the attorney disclosed to the client; and

(4) Identification of the date, sender and recipient of all written and oral communications with the attorney or law firm concerning the subject matter of the advice by counsel.

(c) After advice of counsel information becomes discoverable under LPR 3.6(a), a party claiming willful infringement may take the deposition of any attorneys preparing or rendering the advice relied upon and any persons who received or claims to have relied upon such advice.

(d) This Rule does not address whether materials other than those listed in LPR 3.6(b)(1–4) are subject to discovery or within the scope of any waiver of the attorney client privilege.

[Effective October 1, 2009.]

4. CLAIM CONSTRUCTION PROCEEDINGS

LPR 4.1 EXCHANGE OF PROPOSED CLAIM TERMS TO BE CONSTRUED ALONG WITH PROPOSED CONSTRUCTIONS

(a) Within fourteen (14) days after service of the Final Contentions pursuant to LPR 3.2, each party shall serve a list of (i) the claim terms and phrases the party contends the Court should construe; (ii) the party's proposed constructions; (iii) identification of any claim element that the party contends is governed by 35 U.S.C. § 112(6); and (iv) the party's description of the function of that element, and the structure(s), act(s), or material(s) corresponding to that element, identified by column and line number with respect to the asserted patent(s).

(b) Within seven (7) days after the exchange of claim terms and phrases, the parties must meet and confer and agree upon no more than ten (10) terms or phrases to submit for construction by the court. No more than ten (10) terms or phrases may be presented to the Court for construction absent prior leave of court upon a showing of good cause. The assertion of multiple non-related patents shall, in an appropriate case, constitute good cause. If the parties are unable to agree upon ten terms, then five shall be allocated to all plaintiffs and five to all defendants. For each term to be presented to the Court, the parties must certify whether it is outcome-determinative.

[Effective October 1, 2009.]

Comment

In some cases, the parties may dispute the construction of more than ten terms. But because construction of outcome-determinative or otherwise significant claim terms may lead to settlement or entry of summary judgment, in the majority of cases the need to construe other claim terms of lesser importance may be obviated. The limitation to ten claim terms to be presented for construction is intended to require the parties to focus upon outcome-determinative or otherwise significant disputes.

LPR 4.2 CLAIM CONSTRUCTION BRIEFS

(a) Within thirty-five (35) days after the exchange of terms set forth in LPR 4.1, the parties opposing infringement shall file their Opening Claim Construction Brief, which may not exceed twenty-five (25) pages absent prior leave of court. The brief shall identify any intrinsic evidence with citation to the Joint Appendix under LPR 4.2(b) and shall separately identify any extrinsic evidence the party contends supports its proposed claim construction. If a party offers the testimony of a witness to support its claim construction, it must include with its brief a sworn declaration by the witness setting forth the substance of the witness' proposed testimony, and promptly make the witness available for deposition concerning the proposed testimony.

(b) On the date for filing the Opening Claim Construction Brief, the parties shall file a Joint Appendix containing the patent(s) in dispute and the prosecution history for each patent. The prosecution history must be paginated, and all parties must cite to the Joint Appendix when referencing the materials it contains. Any party may file a separate appendix to its claim construction brief containing other supporting materials.

(c) Within twenty-eight (28) days after filing of the Opening Claim Construction brief, the parties claiming infringement shall file their Responsive Claim Construction Brief, which may not exceed twenty-five (25) pages absent prior leave of Court. The brief shall identify any intrinsic evidence with citation to the Joint Appendix under LPR 4.2(b) and shall separately identify any extrinsic evidence the party contends supports its proposed claim construction. If a party offers the testimony of a witness to support its claim construction, it must include with its brief a sworn declaration by the witness setting forth the substance of the witness's proposed testimony and promptly make the witness available for deposition concerning the proposed testimony, in which case the date for the filing of a Reply Claim Construction brief shall be extended by seven (7) calendar days. The brief shall also describe all objections to any extrinsic evidence identified in the Opening Claim Construction Brief.

(d) Within fourteen (14) days after filing of the Responsive Claim Construction Brief, the parties opposing infringement shall file their Reply Claim Construction Brief, which may not exceed fifteen (15) pages absent prior leave of Court. The brief shall describe all objections to any extrinsic evidence identified in the Opening Claim Construction Brief.

(e) The presence of multiple alleged infringers with different products or processes shall, in an appropriate case, constitute good cause for allowing additional pages in the Opening, Responsive, or Reply Claim Construction Briefs or for allowing separate briefing as to different alleged infringers.

(f) Within seven (7) days after filing of the Reply Claim Construction Brief, the parties shall file (1) a joint claim construction chart that sets forth each claim term and phrase addressed in the claim construction briefs; each party's proposed construction, and (2) a joint status report containing the parties' proposals for the nature and form of the claim construction hearing pursuant to LPR 4.3.

[Effective October 1, 2009.]

Comment

The committee opted for consecutive claim construction briefs rather than simultaneous briefs, concluding that consecutive briefing is more likely to promote a meaningful exchange regarding the contested points. For the same reason, the committee opted to have the alleged infringer file the opening claim construction brief. Patent holders are more likely to argue for a "plain meaning" construction or for non-construction of disputed terms; alleged infringers tend to be less likely to do so.

The Rules provide for three briefs (opening, response, and reply), not four, due to the likelihood of a claim construction hearing or argument. The Court's determination not to hold a hearing or argument may constitute a basis to permit a surreply brief by the patent holder. A judge may choose not to require a reply brief.

LPR 4.3   CLAIM CONSTRUCTION HEARING

Unless the Court orders otherwise, a claim construction oral argument or hearing may be held within twenty-eight (28) days after filing of the Reply Claim Construction Brief. Either before or after the filing of claim construction briefs, the Court shall issue an order describing the schedule and procedures for a claim construction hearing. Any exhibits, including demonstrative exhibits, to be used at a claim construction hearing must be exchanged no later than three (3) days before the hearing.

[Effective October 1, 2009.]

5.   EXPERT WITNESSES

LPR 5.1.   DISCLOSURE OF EXPERTS AND EXPERT REPORTS

Unless the Court orders otherwise,

(a) for issues other than claim construction to which expert testimony shall be directed, expert witness disclosures and depositions shall be governed by this Rule;

(b) within twenty-one (21) days after the claim construction ruling or the close of discovery after the claim construction ruling, whichever is later, each party shall make its initial expert witness disclosures required by Federal Rule of Civil Procedure 26 on issues for which it bears the burden of proof;

(c) within thirty-five (35) days after the date for initial expert reports, each party shall make its rebuttal expert witness disclosures required by Federal Rule of Civil Procedure 26 on the issues for which the opposing party bears the burden of proof.

[Effective October 1, 2009. Amended effective March 1, 2013.]

LPR 5.2   DEPOSITIONS OF EXPERTS

Depositions of expert witnesses shall be completed within thirty-five (35) days after exchange of expert rebuttal disclosures.

[Effective October 1, 2009.]

LPR 5.3   PRESUMPTION AGAINST SUPPLEMENTATION OF REPORTS

Amendments or supplementation to expert reports after the deadlines provided herein are presumptively prejudicial and shall not be allowed absent prior leave of court upon a showing of good cause that the amendment or supplementation could not reasonably have been made earlier and that the opposing party is not unfairly prejudiced.

[Effective October 1, 2009.]

6.   DISPOSITIVE MOTIONS

LPR 6.1   FINAL DAY FOR FILING DISPOSITIVE MOTIONS

All dispositive motions shall be filed within twenty-eight (28) days after the scheduled date for the end of expert discovery.

[Effective October 1, 2009.]

Comment

This Rule does not preclude a party from moving for summary judgment at an earlier stage of the case if circumstances warrant. It is up to the trial judge to determine whether to consider an "early" summary judgment motion. See also LPR 1.1 (judge may defer a motion raising claim construction issues until after claim construction hearing is held).

APPENDIX A. REPORT OF THE PARTIES' PLANNING MEETING

UNITED STATES DISTRICT COURT
for the
NORTHERN DISTRICT OF ILLINOIS

<table>
<tr><td><Name(s) of plaintiff(s)>,</td><td>)</td><td></td></tr>
<tr><td></td><td>)</td><td></td></tr>
<tr><td>Plaintiff(s)</td><td>)</td><td></td></tr>
<tr><td></td><td>)</td><td></td></tr>
<tr><td>v.</td><td>)</td><td></td></tr>
<tr><td></td><td>)</td><td>Civil Action No. <Number></td></tr>
<tr><td><Name(s) of defendant(s)>,</td><td>)</td><td></td></tr>
<tr><td></td><td>)</td><td></td></tr>
<tr><td>Defendant(s)</td><td>)</td><td></td></tr>
<tr><td></td><td>)</td><td></td></tr>
</table>

REPORT OF THE PARTIES' PLANNING MEETING

1. The following persons participated in a Rule 26(f) conference on <Date> by <State the method of conferring>:

   <Name>, representing the <plaintiff>

   <Name>, representing the <defendant>

2. Initial Disclosures. The parties [have completed] [will complete by <Date>] the initial disclosures required by Rule 26(a)(1).

3. Disclosures and Discovery Pursuant to Local Patent Rules. The parties acknowledge that the requirements of the Local Patent Rules apply to this case.

4. Additional Discovery Plan. The parties propose the following in addition to the discovery plan and schedules addressed in the Local Patent Rules:

   (a) <Maximum number of interrogatories by each party to another party, along with the dates the answers are due.>

   (b) <Maximum number of requests for admission, along with the dates responses are due.>

   (c) <Maximum number of factual depositions by each party.>

   (d) <Limits on the length of depositions, in hours.>

   (e) Discovery is permitted with respect to claims of willful infringement and defenses of patent invalidity or unenforceability not pleaded by a party, where the evidence needed to support these claims or defenses is in whole or in part in the hands of another party.

5. Alternative Discovery Plan. The parties propose a discovery plan that differs from that provided in the Local Patent Rules, for the reasons described with particularity in Exhibit 1 to this Report:

   <Use separate paragraphs or subparagraphs if the parties disagree.>

6. Other Dates:

   (a) <Dates for supplementations under Rule 26(e).>

   (b) <A date if the parties ask to meet with the court before a scheduling order.>

   (c) <Requested dates for pretrial conferences.>

   (d) <Final dates for the plaintiff to amend pleadings or to join parties.>

   (e) <Final dates for the defendant to amend pleadings or to join parties.>

   (f) <Final dates for submitting Rule 26(a)(3) witness lists, designations of witnesses whose testimony will be presented by deposition, and exhibit lists.>

(g) <Final dates to file objections under Rule 26(a)(3).>

7.   Other Items:

(a) <State the prospects for settlement.>

(b) <Identify any alternative dispute resolution procedure that may enhance settlement prospects.>

(c) Communications between a party's attorney and a testifying expert relating to the issues on which he/she opines, or to the basis or grounds in support of or countering the opinion, are subject to discovery by the opposing party only to the extent provided in Rule 26(b)(4)(B) and (C).

(d) In responding to discovery requests, each party shall construe broadly terms of art used in the patent field (e.g., "prior art", "best mode", "on sale"), and read them as requesting discovery relating to the issue as opposed to a particular definition of the term used. Compliance with this provision is not satisfied by the respondent including a specific definition of the term in its response, and limiting the response to that definition.

(e) The parties [agree/do not agree] the video "An Introduction to the Patent System" distributed by the Federal Judicial Center, should be shown to the jurors in connection with its preliminary jury instructions.

(f) The parties [agree/do not agree] that the provisions of Sections 3A, B and C of the America Invents Act concerning the revisions to 35 U.S.C. §§ 102, 103 apply to all patents-in-suit in this case. In the event of disagreement, note the potential contention here:

(g) <Other matters.>

Date: <Date>   <Signature of the attorney or unrepresented party>

_____

<Printed name>
<Address><E-mail address>
<Telephone number>

Date: <Date>   <Signature of the attorney or unrepresented party>

_____

<Printed name>
<Address>
<E-mail address>
<Telephone number>

[Effective October 1, 2009. Amended effective March 1, 2011.]

APPENDIX B.   PROTECTIVE ORDER

IN THE UNITED STATES DISTRICT COURT
FOR THE NORTHERN DISTRICT OF ILLINOIS

EASTERN DIVISION

_____,	)	
	)	
Plaintiff[s],	)	
	)	
vs.	)	Case No. _____
	)	
_____,	)	
	)	
Defendant[s].	)	

PROTECTIVE ORDER

The Court enters the following protective order pursuant to Federal Rule of Civil Procedure 26(c)(1).

1. Findings. The Court finds that the parties to this case may request or produce information involving trade secrets or confidential research and development or commercial information, the disclosure of which is likely to cause harm to the party producing such information.

2. Definitions.

a. "Party" means a named party in this case. "Person" means an individual or an entity. "Producer" means a person who produces information via the discovery process in this case. "Recipient" means a person who receives information via the discovery process in this case.

b. "Confidential" information is information concerning a person's business operations, processes, and technical and development information within the scope of Rule 26(c)(1)(G), the disclosure of which is likely to harm that person's competitive position, or the disclosure of which would contravene an obligation of confidentiality to a third person or to a Court.

c. "Highly Confidential" information is information within the scope of Rule 26(c)(1)(G) that is current or future business or technical trade secrets and plans more sensitive or strategic than Confidential information, the disclosure of which is likely to significantly harm that person's competitive position, or the disclosure of which would contravene an obligation of confidentiality to a third person or to a Court.

d. Information is not Confidential or Highly Confidential if it is disclosed in a printed publication, is known to the public, was known to the recipient without obligation of confidentiality before the producer disclosed it, or is or becomes known to the recipient by means not constituting a breach of this Order. Information is likewise not Confidential or Highly Confidential if a person lawfully obtained it independently of this litigation.

3. Designation of information as Confidential or Highly Confidential.

a. A person's designation of information as Confidential or Highly Confidential means that the person believes in good faith, upon reasonable inquiry, that the information qualifies as such.

b. A person designates information in a document or thing as Confidential or Highly Confidential by clearly and prominently marking it on its face as "CONFIDENTIAL" or "HIGHLY CONFIDENTIAL." A producer may make documents or things containing Confidential or Highly Confidential information available for inspection and copying without marking them as confidential without forfeiting a claim of confidentiality, so long as the producer causes copies of the documents or things to be marked as Confidential or Highly Confidential before providing them to the recipient.

c. A person designates information in deposition testimony as Confidential or Highly Confidential by stating on the record at the deposition that the information is Confidential or Highly Confidential or by advising the opposing party and the stenographer and videographer in writing, within fourteen days after receipt of the deposition transcript, that the information is Confidential or Highly Confidential.

d. A person's failure to designate a document, thing, or testimony as Confidential or Highly Confidential does not constitute forfeiture of a claim of confidentiality as to any other document, thing, or testimony.

e. A person who has designated information as Confidential or Highly Confidential may withdraw the designation by written notification to all parties in the case.

f. If a party disputes a producer's designation of information as Confidential or Highly Confidential, the party shall notify the producer in writing of the basis for the dispute, identifying the specific document[s] or thing[s] as to which the designation is disputed and proposing a new designation for such materials. The party and the producer shall then meet and confer to attempt to resolve the dispute without involvement of the Court. If they cannot resolve the dispute, the proposed new designation shall be applied fourteen (14) days after notice of the dispute unless within that fourteen day period the producer files a motion with the Court to maintain the producer's designation. The producer bears the burden of proving that the information is properly designated as Confidential or Highly Confidential. The information shall remain subject to the producer's Confidential or Highly Confidential designation until the Court rules on the dispute. A party's failure to contest a designation of information as Confidential or Highly Confidential is not an admission that the information was properly designated as such.

4. Use and disclosure of Confidential [or Highly Confidential] information.

a. Confidential and Highly Confidential information may be used exclusively for purposes of this litigation, subject to the restrictions of this order.

b. Absent written permission from the producer or further order by the Court, the recipient may not disclose Confidential information to any person other than the following: (i) a party's outside counsel of record, including necessary paralegal, secretarial and clerical personnel assisting such counsel; (ii) a party's in-house counsel; (iii) a party's officers and employees directly involved in this case whose access to the information is reasonably required to supervise, manage, or participate in this case; (iv) a stenographer and videographer recording testimony concerning the information; (v) subject to the provisions of paragraph 4(d) of this order, experts and consultants and their staff whom a party employs for purposes of this litigation only; and (vi) the Court and personnel assisting the Court.

c. Absent written permission from the producer or further order by the Court, the recipient may not disclose Highly Confidential information to any person other than those identified in paragraph 4(b)(i), (iv), (v), and (vi).

d. A party may not disclose Confidential or Highly Confidential information to an expert or consultant pursuant to paragraph 4(b) or 4(c) of this order until after the expert or consultant has signed an undertaking in the form of Appendix 1 to this Order. The party obtaining the undertaking must serve it on all other parties within ten days after its execution. At least ten days before the first disclosure of Confidential or Highly Confidential information to an expert or consultant (or member of their staff), the party proposing to make the disclosure must serve the producer with a written identification of the expert or consultant and a copy of his or her curriculum vitae. If the producer has good cause to object to the disclosure (which does not include challenging the qualifications of the expert or consultant), it must serve the party proposing to make the disclosure with a written objection within ten days after service of the identification. Unless the parties resolve the dispute within ten days after service of the objection, the producer must move the Court promptly for a ruling, and the Confidential or Highly Confidential information may not be disclosed to the expert or consultant without the Court's approval.

e. Notwithstanding paragraph 4(a) and (b), a party may disclose Confidential or Highly Confidential information to: (i) any employee or author of the producer; (ii) any person, no longer affiliated with the producer, who authored the information in whole or in part; and (iii) any person who received the information before this case was filed.

f. A party who wishes to disclose Confidential or Highly Confidential information to a person not authorized under paragraph 4(b) or 4(c) must first make a reasonable attempt to obtain the producer's permission. If the party is unable to obtain permission, it may move the Court to obtain permission.

5. **Copies.** A party producing documents as part of discovery must, upon request, furnish the requesting party with one copy of the documents it requests, at the requesting party's expense. Before copying, the parties must agree upon the rate at which the requesting party will be charged for copying.

6. **Inadvertent Disclosure.** Inadvertent disclosures of material protected by the attorney-client privilege or the work product doctrine shall be handled in accordance with Federal Rule of Evidence 502.

7. **Filing with the Court.**

a. This protective order does not, by itself, authorize the filing of any document under seal. No document may be filed under seal without prior leave of court. A party wishing to file under seal a document containing Confidential or Highly Confidential information must move the Court, consistent with Local Rule 26.2(b) and prior to the due date for the document, for permission to file the document under seal. If a party obtains permission to file a document under seal, it must also (unless excused by the Court) file a public-record version that excludes any Confidential or Highly Confidential information.

b. If a party wishes to file in the public record a document that another producer has designated as Confidential or Highly Confidential, the party must advise the producer of the document no later than five business days before the document is due to be filed, so that the producer may move the Court to require the document to be filed under seal.

c. Pursuant to Local Rule 5.8, any document filed under seal must be accompanied by a cover sheet disclosing (i) the caption of the case, including the case number; (ii) the title "Restricted Document Pursuant to Local Rule 26.2;" (iii) a statement that the document is filed as restricted in accordance with a court order and the date of the order; and (iv) the signature of the attorney of record filing the document.

8. **Document Disposal.** Upon the conclusion of this case, each party must return to the producer all documents and copies of documents containing the producer's Confidential [or Highly Confidential] information, and must destroy all notes, memoranda, or other materials derived from or in any way revealing confidential or highly confidential information. Alternatively, if the producer agrees, the party may destroy all documents and copies of documents containing the producer's Confidential or Highly Confidential information. The party returning and/or destroying the producer's Confidential and Highly Confidential information must promptly certify in writing its compliance with the requirements of this paragraph. Notwithstanding the requirements of this paragraph, a party and its counsel may retain one complete set of all documents filed with the Court, remaining subject to all requirements of this order.

9. **Originals.** A legible photocopy of a document may be used as the "original" for all purposes in this action. The actual "original," in whatever form the producing

party has it, must be made available to any other party within ten days after a written request.

10. Survival of obligations. This order's obligations regarding Confidential and Highly Confidential information survive the conclusion of this case.

IN THE UNITED STATES DISTRICT COURT

FOR THE NORTHERN DISTRICT OF ILLINOIS

EASTERN DIVISION

_____,	)	
	)	
Plaintiff[s],	)	
	)	
vs.	)	Case No. _____
	)	
_____,	)	
	)	
Defendant[s].	)	

UNDERTAKING OF *[insert name]*

I, *[insert person's name]* , state the following under penalties of perjury as provided by law:

I have been retained by *[insert party's name]* , as an expert or consultant in connection with this case. I will be receiving Confidential [and Highly Confidential] information that is covered by the Court's protective order dated *[fill in date]*. I have read the Court's protective order and understand that the Confidential [and Highly Confidential] information is provided pursuant to the terms and conditions in that order.

I agree to be bound by the Court's protective order. I agree to use the Confidential [and Highly Confidential] information solely for purposes of this case. I understand that neither the Confidential [and Highly Confidential] information nor any notes concerning that information may be disclosed to anyone that is not bound by the Court's protective order. I agree to return the Confidential [and Highly Confidential] information and any notes concerning that information to the attorney for *[insert name of retaining party]* or to destroy the information and any notes at that attorney's request.

I submit to the jurisdiction of the Court that issued the protective order for purposes of enforcing that order. I give up any objections I might have to that Court's jurisdiction over me or to the propriety of venue in that Court.

_____

Signature

Subscribed and sworn to
before me this _____ day
of _____, 20___

_____

Notary Public

[Effective October 1, 2009.]

LOCAL PATENT RULES FOR ELECTRONICALLY STORED INFORMATION

LPR ESI 1.1. (PURPOSE)

These Local Patent Rules for Electronically Stored Information ("Rules") supplement all other discovery rules and orders. The purpose of these Rules is to assist courts in the administration of Federal Rule of Civil Procedure 1, to secure the just, speedy, and inexpensive determination of every civil case, and to promote, whenever possible, the early resolution of disputes regarding the discovery of electronically stored information ("ESI") without Court intervention.

[Effective March 13, 2013.]

LPR ESI 1.2. (COOPERATION)

(a) Counsel shall cooperate in all aspects of seeking and responding to discovery requests.

(b) The failure of counsel or the parties to litigation to cooperate in facilitating and reasonably limiting discovery requests and responses will be considered in cost-shifting determinations.

[Effective March 13, 2013.]

LPR ESI 1.3. (DISCOVERY PLAN)

The standard set forth in Fed. R. Civ. P. 26(b)(2)(C) should be applied in each case when formulating a discovery plan. To further the application of the standard set forth in Fed. R. Civ. P. 26(b)(2)(C) in discovery, requests for production of ESI and related responses should be reasonably targeted, clear, and as specific as practicable.

[Effective March 13, 2013.]

LPR ESI 1.4. (PRIVILEGE AND WAIVER)

(a) Pursuant to Federal Rule of Evidence 502(d), the production of a privileged or work product protected ESI is not a waiver in the pending case or in any other federal or state proceeding.

(b) The mere production of ESI in a litigation as part of a mass production shall not itself constitute a waiver for any purpose.

(c) A producing party that requests the return of ESI on the ground that it is privileged or work product protected must provide the receiving party with the information required by Federal Rule of Civil Procedure 26(b)(5)(A) within 7 days of the request for return.

(d) The receiving party must return, sequester, or destroy ESI that the producing party claims is privi-

leged or work product protected as provided in Rule 26(b)(5)(B) and may use such ESI only to challenge the claim of privilege or protection.

[Effective March 13, 2013.]

LPR ESI 2.1. (DUTY TO MEET AND CONFER ON DISCOVERY AND TO IDENTIFY DISPUTES FOR EARLY RESOLUTION)

(a) Prior to the initial status conference with the Court, counsel shall meet and discuss the application of the discovery process set forth in the Federal Rules of Civil Procedure and these Rules to their specific case.

(b) If the parties have disputes regarding ESI that counsel for the parties are unable to resolve, the parties shall present those disputes to the Court at the initial status conference pursuant to Fed. R. Civ. P. Rule 16(b), or as soon as possible thereafter.

(c) Prior to the presentation of disputes to the court, each party shall designate an individual as e-discovery liaison. The e-discovery liaison shall participate in the meet and confer held to resolve the dispute. Regardless of whether the e-discovery liaison(s) is an attorney (in-house or outside counsel), a third party consultant, or an employee of the party, the e-discovery liaison(s) must:

1. be prepared to participate in e-discovery dispute resolution;

2. be knowledgeable about the party's e-discovery efforts;

3. be, or have reasonable access to those who are, familiar with the party's electronic systems and capabilities in order to explain those systems and answer relevant questions; and be, or have reasonable access to those who are, knowledgeable about the technical aspects of e-discovery, including electronic document storage, organization, and format issues, and relevant information retrieval technology, including search methodology.

(d) The Court may modify the obligations and deadlines of these Rules based on the circumstances of any particular case. The parties shall jointly submit any proposed modifications within 30 days after the Federal Rule of Civil Procedure 16 conference. If the parties cannot resolve their disagreements regarding these modifications, the parties shall submit their competing proposals and a summary of their dispute.

(e) If the Court determines that any counsel or party in a case has failed to cooperate and participate in good faith in the meet and confer process or is impeding the purpose of these Rules, the Court may require additional discussions prior to the commencement of discovery, and may impose sanctions, if appropriate.

[Effective March 13, 2013.]

LPR ESI 2.2. (PRESERVATION REQUESTS AND ORDERS)

(a) Appropriate preservation requests and preservation orders further the goals of these Rules. Vague and overly broad preservation requests do not further the goals of these Rules and are therefore disfavored. Vague and overly broad preservation orders should not be sought or entered. The information sought to be preserved through the use of a preservation letter request or order should be reasonable in scope and mindful of the factors set forth in Rule 26(b)(2)(C).

(b) To the extent counsel or a party requests preservation of ESI through the use of a preservation letter, such requests should attempt to ensure the preservation of relevant and discoverable information and to facilitate cooperation between requesting and receiving counsel and parties by transmitting specific and useful information. Examples of such specific and useful information include, but are not limited to:

(1) names of the parties;

(2) factual background of the potential legal claim(s) and identification of potential cause(s) of action;

(3) names of potential witnesses and other people reasonably anticipated to have relevant evidence;

(4) relevant time period; and

(5) other information that may assist the responding party in assessing what information to preserve.

(c) If the recipient of a preservation request chooses to respond, that response should provide the requesting counsel or party with useful information regarding the preservation efforts undertaken by the responding party. Examples of such useful and specific information include, but are not limited to, information that:

(1) identifies what information the responding party is willing to preserve and the steps being taken in response to the preservation letter;

(2) identifies any disagreement(s) with the request to preserve; and;

(3) identifies any further preservation issues that were not raised.

(d) Nothing in these Rules shall be construed as requiring the sending of a preservation request or requiring the sending of a response to such a request.

[Effective March 13, 2013.]

LPR ESI 2.3. (SCOPE OF PRESERVATION)

(a) Every party to litigation and its counsel are responsible for taking reasonable and proportionate steps to preserve relevant and discoverable ESI within its possession, custody or control. Determining which steps are reasonable and proportionate in particular litigation is a fact specific inquiry that will vary from case to case. The parties and counsel should address preservation issues at the outset of a case, and should continue to address them as the case progresses and their understanding of the issues and the facts improves.

(b) Discovery concerning the preservation and collection efforts of another party may be appropriate but, if used unadvisedly, can also contribute to the unnecessary expense and delay and may inappropriately implicate work product and attorney-client privileged matter. Accordingly, prior to initiating such discovery a party shall confer with the party from whom the information is sought concerning: (i) the specific need for such discovery, including its relevance to issues likely to arise in the litigation; and (ii) the suitability of alternative means for obtaining the information. Nothing herein exempts deponents on merits issues from answering questions concerning the preservation and collection of their documents, ESI, and tangible things.

(c) The parties and counsel should come to the meet and confer conference prepared to discuss the claims and defenses in the case including specific issues, time frame, potential damages, and targeted discovery that each anticipates requesting. In addition, the parties and counsel should be prepared to discuss reasonably foreseeable preservation issues that relate directly to the information that the other party is seeking. The parties and counsel need not raise every conceivable issue that may arise concerning their preservation efforts; however, the identification of any such preservation issues should be specific.

(d) The following categories of ESI generally are not discoverable in most cases, and if any party intends to request the preservation or production of these categories, then that intention should be discussed at the meet and confer or as soon thereafter as practicable:

(1) "deleted," "slack," "fragmented," or "unallocated" data on hard drives;

(2) random access memory (RAM) or other ephemeral data;

(3) on-line access data such as temporary internet files, history, cache, cookies, etc.;

(4) data in metadata fields that are frequently updated automatically, such as last-opened dates;

(5) backup data that is substantially duplicative of data that is more accessible elsewhere; and

(6) other forms of ESI whose preservation requires extraordinary affirmative measures that are not utilized in the ordinary course of business.

(e) If there is a dispute concerning the scope of a party's preservation efforts, the parties or their counsel must meet and confer and fully explain their reasons for believing that additional efforts are, or are not, reasonable and proportionate, pursuant to Rule 26(b)(2)(C). If the parties are unable to resolve a preservation issue, then the issue should be raised promptly with the Court.

[Effective March 13, 2013.]

LPR ESI 2.4. (IDENTIFICATION OF ESI)

(a) At the Rule 26(f) conference or as soon thereafter as possible, counsel or the parties shall discuss potential methodologies for identifying ESI for production.

(b) Topics for discussion may include, but are not limited to, any plans to:

(1) eliminate duplicative ESI and whether such elimination will occur only within each particular custodian's data set or whether it will occur across all custodians;

(2) filter data based on file type, date ranges custodian, search terms, or other similar parameters; and

(3) use keyword searching, mathematical or thesaurus-based topic or concept clustering, or other advanced culling technologies.

[Effective March 13, 2013.]

LPR ESI 2.5. (PRODUCTION FORMAT)

(a) At the Rule 26(f) conference, counsel and the parties should make a good faith effort to agree on the format(s) for production of ESI (whether native or some other reasonably usable form). If counsel or the parties are unable to resolve a production format issue, then the issue should be raised promptly with the Court.

(b) The parties should confer on whether ESI stored in a database or a database management system can be produced by querying the database for discoverable information, resulting in a report or a reasonably usable and exportable electronic file for review by the requesting counsel or party.

(c) The general presumption is that meta-data is not requested and need not be produced, unless a special request is made.

(d) ESI and other tangible or hard copy documents that are not text-searchable need not be made text-searchable.

(e) If a party requests production in a format other than the one most convenient for the producing party, the requesting party is responsible for the incremental cost of creating its copy of requested information. Counsel or the parties are encouraged to discuss cost sharing for optical character recognition (OCR) or other upgrades of paper documents or non-text-searchable electronic images that may be contemplated by each party.

[Effective March 13, 2013.]

LPR ESI 2.6. (EMAIL PRODUCTION REQUESTS)

(a) General ESI production requests under Federal Rules of Civil Procedure 34 and 45 shall not include email or other forms of electronic correspondence (collectively "email"). To obtain emails parties must propound specific email production requests.

(b) Email production requests shall be phased to occur after the parties have exchanged initial disclosures and basic documentation about the patents, the prior art, the accused instrumentalities, and the relevant finances. While this provision does not require the production of such information, the Court encourages prompt and early production of this information to promote efficient and economical streamlining of the case.

(c) Email production requests shall identify the custodian, search terms, and time frame. The parties shall cooperate to identify the proper custodians, proper search terms and proper timeframe.

(d) Each requesting party shall limit its email production requests to a total of five custodians per producing party for all such requests. The parties may jointly agree to modify this limit without the Court's leave. The Court shall consider contested requests for up to five additional custodians per producing party, upon showing a distinct need based on the size, complexity, and issues of this specific case. Should a party serve email production requests for additional custodians beyond the limits agreed to by the parties or granted by the Court pursuant to this paragraph, the requesting party shall bear all reasonable costs caused by such additional discovery.

(e) Each requesting party shall limit its email production requests to a total of five search terms per custodian per party. The parties may jointly agree to modify this limit without the Court's leave. The Court shall consider contested requests for up to five additional search terms per custodian, upon showing a distinct need based on the size, complexity, and issues of this specific case. The search terms shall be narrowly tailored to particular issues. Indiscriminate terms, such as the producing company's name or its product name, are inappropriate unless combined with narrowing search criteria that sufficiently reduce the risk of overproduction. A conjunctive combination of multiple words or phrases (e.g., "computer" and "system") narrows the search and shall count as a single search term. A disjunctive combination of multiple words or phrases (e.g., "computer" or "system") broadens the search, and thus each word or phrase shall count as a separate search term unless they are variants of the same word. Use of narrowing search criteria (e.g., "and," "but not," "w/x") is encouraged to limit the production and shall be considered when determining whether to shift costs for disproportionate discovery. Should a party serve email production requests with search terms beyond the limits agreed to by the parties or granted by the Court pursuant to this paragraph, the requesting party shall bear all reasonable costs caused by such additional discovery.

[Effective March 13, 2013.]

INTERNAL OPERATING PROCEDURES
OF THE
UNITED STATES DISTRICT COURT
NORTHERN DISTRICT OF ILLINOIS

INTRODUCTION

These are procedures for the court's internal operations. They are intended to supplement the *Guide to Judiciary Policies and Procedures* and the local rules. They set out the procedures generally to be used by chambers and the clerk's office in performing certain administrative tasks. While the procedures are public and available on request, litigants acquire no rights under them. The Court's web page, www.ilnd.uscourts. gov, provides procedures used in the chambers of each of the judges. A current copy of these procedures and any proposed changes is also available at that site.

IOP 1. MEETINGS OF DISTRICT JUDGES

(a) **Meetings of the District Judges.** The judges of this Court shall establish the policies of the Court, determine its programs and adopt and promulgate its rules at their official meetings. The regular active and senior judges shall assemble not less than once a month for such official meetings except as they determine otherwise. Each judge attending the meeting, whether active or senior, shall be entitled to vote on matters brought before the meeting, except as otherwise required by statute.

(b) **Secretary of the Court**. At the September meeting the least senior regular active judge who has not previously served as secretary shall be designated as secretary of the Court. The secretary shall make and maintain the official minutes of the judges' meetings. The secretary, if unable to attend the meeting, shall make arrangements for another judge to act as secretary and inform the chief judge of such arrangements.

IOP 2. EXECUTIVE COMMITTEE

(a) **Duties & Responsibilities**. This Court shall administer and conduct its business by action of its Executive Committee. The Executive Committee shall prescribe its own rules of procedure. Each of the members other than the non-voting members shall have one vote. The presiding chief judge or acting chief judge may vote in the case of a tie.

The members of the Executive Committee shall meet not less than once a month, except as they otherwise determine. Such meetings shall be prior to the regular monthly meetings of the Court. The chief judge may call the members of the Committee to attend a special meeting where a ruling of the Com-

mittee is required and such ruling cannot be delayed until the next scheduled regular meeting.

The Executive Committee shall report a summary of its actions and activities to the Court at regularly scheduled meetings of the judges. Decisions and actions of the Executive Committee taken on behalf of the Court may be approved or disapproved by a majority of the judges of the Court.

(b) **Composition of the Executive Committee**. The Executive Committee shall be composed of the chief judge, the acting chief judge, four regular active judges of the Court, the presiding magistrate judge, and the clerk of the Court. The chief judge, the acting chief judge, the presiding magistrate judge, and the clerk will be non-voting members of the Executive Committee. The chief judge or, in the absence of the chief judge, the acting chief judge, shall preside over the meetings of the Executive Committee. The clerk shall serve as secretary to the Executive Committee.

Membership in the Executive Committee shall be rotated among the regular active judge of the Court in order of seniority. Except as otherwise provided by this section, the term of each regular active judge other than one holding non-voting membership shall start on 15 September and end on 14 September four years later. As the term of such a member of the Executive Committee expires or terminates for any reason, the regular active judge with the most seniority who has not served on the Executive Committee shall become a member. When all the regular active judges of the Court have served one term, membership shall be rotated on the basis of seniority of the active judges then members of this Court, provided that the chief judge may not serve as both a four year term member and *ex officio*. When a judge assumes an unexpired term vacated by another judge, that judge shall serve for four years starting on the day following the last day of service of the judge who failed to complete a four year term.

IOP 3. LIAISON JUDGES AND COMMITTEES

The administrative business of the Court will be accomplished through liaison judges and such committees as the Court or the chief judge shall create. The chief judge shall make the assignments of liaison judges and members of committees created by the chief judge. The judges so assigned shall serve until such time as the chief judge designates a successor. Members of committees created by the Court shall be appointed and served in the manner provided for in the general order creating such committee.

Each liaison judge and committee shall be responsible for maintaining effective liaison with the departments or agencies or areas of special concern that constitute the administrative area to which the judge or committee was assigned. From time to time each liaison judge or committee shall report to the Court on the activities of the administrative area concerned and make any recommendations for actions on the part of the Court that the liaison judge or committee deems necessary.

From time to time the chief judge after consulting the full Court will cause to be published an order listing the administrative areas to which liaison judges or committees are to be assigned together with any committees of the Court other than the Executive Committee. Such order will also indicate the names of the judges designated as liaison judges or as members of a committee.

IOP 4. PRESIDING MAGISTRATE JUDGE

The chief judge shall appoint from among the full-time magistrate judges a presiding magistrate judge. The presiding magistrate judge shall preside at any meeting of the magistrate judges, shall serve as an *ex-officio* member of the executive committee, shall be responsible for maintaining liaison on matters pertaining to magistrate judges with the district judge designated as liaison judge to magistrate judges, and shall be responsible for performing such other duties as the chief judge directs. The order of appointment will fix the length of the appointment which shall not exceed two years.

IOP 5. MEETINGS OF MAGISTRATE JUDGES

The presiding magistrate judge shall call meetings of the magistrate judges not less often than quarterly for the purpose of discussing matters of common interest to the magistrate judges in the performance of their duties.

IOP 6. DESIGNATED ACTING CHIEF JUDGE

The judges of this Court hereby prescribe that if the chief judge is temporarily unable to perform the chief judge's duties, these duties shall be performed by the judge identified in 28 U.S.C. § 136(e), unless the chief judge has designated another judge in active service, who consents to the designation, is present in the district, and is able and qualified to serve, as the designated acting chief judge. The designated acting chief judge shall assume all duties and responsibilities of the chief judge during the designated time period.

IOP 7. MAGISTRATE JUDGE EXTENDED SERVICE RECALL

(a) An eligible magistrate judge who wishes to be recalled to office as provided for by 28 U.S.C. Section 636(h) shall make such a request in writing to the Chief Judge of the Court. The request shall specify the judicial workload the magistrate judge wishes to carry while in recall status.

(b) Where the Chief Judge receives such a request, it shall be forwarded to the full Court for consideration. In such instances, the Court shall consider the needs of the Court and the current judicial capacity of the applicant; and the clerk of court shall provide a report addressing space and facilities considerations affected by the recall, in addition to information concerning magistrate judge utilization.

(c) Where the Court approves a request for the recall of a magistrate judge, the request shall be forwarded to the Circuit Council of the Seventh Circuit in accordance with the Judicial Conference Guidelines.

[Effective February 25, 2010.]

IOP 8. ASSIGNMENT OF PRO BONO ATTORNEYS IN CIVIL CASES INTERNAL OPERATING PROCEDURES

(a) **Order of Assignment.** Whenever the judge concludes that the assignment of counsel is warranted, the judge shall enter an order pursuant to 28 U.S.C. § 1915(e) directing the assignment of counsel to represent the pro se party. The judge may specify in the order of assignment an area of expertise or preference so that the clerk may select a prospective assignee who indicated such area, if one is available. The order shall be transmitted forthwith to the clerk. If service of the summons and complaint has not yet been made, an order directing service by the United States marshal or by other appropriate method of service shall accompany the assignment order.

The selection of a member of the panel for assignment pursuant to the assignment order will normally be made in accordance with section (e). However, the judge may determine that an assignment be made in any of the following manners:

(1) Where the pro se party has one or more other cases pending before this Court in which counsel has been assigned, the judge may determine it to be appropriate that counsel assigned in such other case or cases be assigned to represent the pro se party in the case before the judge.

(2) Where the judge finds that the nature of the case requires specific expertise and among the panel members available for assignment there are some with the required expertise, the judge may direct the clerk to select counsel from among those included in

the group or may designate a specific member of the group.

(3) Where the judge finds that the nature of the case requires specific expertise and none of the panel members available for assignment has indicated that expertise, the judge may assign counsel with the required expertise who is not on the panel.

In order to assist the judge in determining whether or not to make a direct assignment under (1) of this section, the clerk shall provide on request the case number, case title, presiding judge, and name of counsel assigned of each case currently pending before the Court in which the pro se party has had counsel assigned.

(b) Selection of Attorney to be Assigned. Except where another method of assignment is ordered pursuant to section (d), the clerk, on receipt of the order of assignment, shall select a name from the panel in the following manner:

(1) Where the order specifies a particular area of expertise or a preference, the clerk shall select the first available panel member indicating such expertise or preference. If no such person is found, the next available person listed on the panel shall be selected.

(2) Where the order does not specify any area of expertise or preference, the clerk shall select the first available person listed on the panel. (Adopted 06/02/11)

[Effective May 19, 2011. Amended effective May 24, 2013; November 24, 2014.]

IOP 9. DUTIES OF THE CLERK IN ATTORNEY DISCIPLINARY PROCEEDINGS

(a) Certification of Conviction in Another Court. Upon being informed that an attorney admitted to practice before this Court has been convicted of any crime, the clerk shall determine whether the clerk of the court in which such conviction occurred has forwarded a certificate of such conviction to this Court. If a certificate has not been forwarded, the clerk of this Court shall promptly obtain a certificate and file it with this Court.

(b) Discipline Imposed in Another Court. Upon being informed that an attorney admitted to practice before this Court has been subjected to discipline by another court, the clerk shall determine whether a certified or exemplified copy of the disciplinary judgment or order has been filed with this Court, and if not, the clerk shall promptly obtain a certified or exemplified copy of the disciplinary judgment or order and file it with this Court.

(c) Conviction or Discipline in this Court. Whenever it appears that any person who is admitted to practice law in any other jurisdiction or before any

other court has been convicted of a crime, or disbarred, or suspended, or censured, or disbarred on consent by this Court, the clerk shall, within 14 days of that conviction, disbarment, suspension, censure, or disbarment on consent, transmit to the disciplinary authority in such other jurisdiction, or for such other court—

(1) a certificate of the conviction or a certified or exemplified copy of the judgment or order of disbarment, suspension, censure, or disbarment on consent, and

(2) the last known office and residence addresses of the defendant or respondent.

(d) ABA National Discipline Data Bank. The clerk shall promptly notify the National Discipline Data Bank operated by the American Bar Association of any order imposing public discipline upon any attorney admitted to practice before this Court.

(e) Record of Disciplinary Actions. The clerk shall note the entry of an order imposing disciplinary sanctions or reinstating a disciplined attorney on the record of that attorney included in the index of attorneys admitted to the bar of this Court.

[Effective June 2, 2011.]

IOP 10. CASE NUMBERS AND CASE CATEGORIES

(a) Classes Of Cases. All cases filed in this Court shall be assigned to one of the following six classes of cases:

(1) *adversary proceedings* which include any cases initiated by the filing of an adversary complaint in a bankruptcy proceeding pursuant to the provisions of the Bankruptcy Act or of the Bankruptcy Code;

(2) *bankruptcy cases* which include any cases initiated by the filing of a petition pursuant to the provisions of the Bankruptcy Code;

(3) *criminal cases* which include any cases initiated (A) by the filing of a complaint, an information or an indictment for the punishment of a crime against the United States, including cases instituted under the Federal Juvenile Delinquency Act, removal cases and complaints for the apprehension of a material witness or (B) by the issuing of a rule to show cause why a person should not be held in contempt where criminal contempt is involved, including such contempts arising from grand jury proceedings;

(4) *disciplinary proceedings* which include any cases involving the discipline of members of the bar of this Court pursuant to LR83.25, *et seq.*;

(5) *magistrate judge cases* which include (A) any cases initiated before a magistrate judge by documents other than a criminal complaint, including but not limited to search warrants, orders appointing

counsel where no complaint has been filed and inspection of warrants, but not generally including petty offenses based on violation notices, and (B) any petty offense proceeding based on the issuance of a violation notice in which the defendant does not waive the right to trial before a district judge and the case is referred to the district court for trial; and

(6) civil cases which include (A) any other case or matters initiated by the filing of an application, complaint or petition, (B) any appeal from an order entered by a bankruptcy judge, and (C) any certificates for contempt filed by a magistrate judge or by a bankruptcy judge.

(b) Case Numbers. Each case, upon the filing of the initial paper, shall be given a case number which shall indicate the year in which it was filed, the class to which it belongs, and a sequence number, as follows:

(1) the year of filing will be indicated by the use of the last two digits of the calendar year in which the initial paper is filed;

(2) the class to which the case belongs will be indicated by use of the letter A, B, CR, D, M or C, to indicate, respectively, the classes of adversary proceedings, bankruptcy cases, criminal cases, disciplinary proceedings, magistrate judge cases, or civil cases;

(3) the sequence number will be the next available number taken from the appropriate case number series. In each of the two Divisions of the Court there shall be eleven consecutive number series, one for each class of cases other than disciplinary proceedings and one for disciplinary proceedings. The number series in the Eastern Division and the number series for disciplinary proceedings will start each year with the number 1. The number series in the Western Division will start with the number 50,001.

(c) Exceptions to Numbering System in Criminal Cases. An indictment or information that arises out of offenses charged in one or more previously filed criminal complaints shall be designated by the same case number as the earliest filed complaint. Any indictment or information that supersedes an earlier filed indictment or information as defined by subsection (4) of LCrR50.2 shall be designated by the same case number as that of the superseded indictment or information.

In order to identify clearly and uniquely each defendant named in a criminal complaint, indictment, or information, each defendant listed in the caption of the original complaint, indictment, or information shall be assigned a number such that the first listed defendant shall be defendant 1, the second, defendant 2, etc. Where pursuant to this section an indictment or information is designated by the same case number as either an earlier filed criminal complaint or a superseded indictment or information, each defendant in-

cluded in the later filed indictment or information who was included in the earlier filed complaint, indictment, or information shall be assigned the same defendant number as was assigned at the earlier filing. Where a defendant included in the earlier filed complaint, indictment, or information is not included in the later filed indictment or information, the number assigned to that defendant will be skipped. Where one or more defendants are included in the later filed indictment or information who were not included in the earlier filed complaint, indictment, or information, defendant numbers shall be assigned starting with the lowest number not assigned at the time of the filing of the initial complaint, indictment, or information.

IOP 11. FILING & ASSIGNMENT OF NEW CASES

(a) Filing Procedures. The assignment clerk shall file each new case in the following manner:

(1) Except where the case was accepted for filing by the emergency judge outside of regular business hours and the date and time of filing are already noted, the date and time of filing shall be stamped or written on the cover of the documents initiating the case.

(2) The appropriate case number shall be stamped on the initiating document.

(3) The case number and assignment category shall be entered into the computerized assignment system and the case shall be assigned.

(4) A magistrate judge shall be designated for the case in the manner provided for by section (c).

(5) Except as provided for in section (f) below, the name of the district judge to whom the case is assigned and, where applicable, the name of the designated magistrate judge shall be stamped on the initiating documents.

Where two or more indictments or informations are presented to the assignment clerk for assignment, the order in which they are to be filed and assigned shall be according to their grand jury numbers, the earliest such number being assigned first. Where indictments returned by two or more grand juries are presented for filing at the same time, the indictments of the older grand jury shall be taken first. If two grand juries were impaneled in the same month, the indictments of the special grand jury shall be taken first.

(b) Assignment of Cases: Eastern Division. The clerk shall maintain an automated assignment system for the assignment and reassignment of cases in the Eastern Division. All cases filed in the Eastern Division shall be by assigned using the automated assignment system.

For the purposes of assigning cases to the calendars of the judges serving in the Eastern Division, the civil and criminal cases shall be divided into the categories indicated:

(1) *Criminal Cases:* (A) Criminal I, (B) Criminal II, (C) Criminal III, (D) Criminal IV, and (F) Criminal V; and

(2) *Civil Cases:* (A) Civil I, (B) Civil II, (C) Civil III, (D) Civil IV, (E) Civil V, (F) Civil VI, (G) Civil VII, (H) certificates for contempt filed by bankruptcy judges pursuant to Rule 920 of the National Bankruptcy Rules and certificates for contempt filed by magistrate judges.

In addition, those magistrate judge cases involving petty offenses based on the issuance of violation notices wherein defendants did not waive their right to trial before a judge of the district court which are referred to a judge of the district court shall constitute a separate assignment category.

The Executive Committee shall establish the types of cases to be included in Criminal categories I, II, III, IV, and V and in Civil categories I, II, III, IV, V, VI, and VII. A master list of the types of cases included in those categories shall be used by the assignment clerk in the assignment of civil and criminal cases.

The automated assignment system shall provide a separate process for assigning cases in each of the enumerated categories. In each process the name of each judge of this Court, other than the chief judge or any senior judge, shall appear an equal number of times. The sequence of judges' names within each block shall be kept secret. The process shall record for each case assigned the case number, the assignment category, and date and time of the assignment.

A motion for the return of property filed pursuant to FRCrP41(e) after an indictment or information has been filed in a criminal case shall be directly assigned to the district judge before whom the criminal case was last pending. If that judge is no longer sitting, the motion shall be assigned by lot to a district judge.

Whenever it appears that a case has been assigned by lot that should have been assigned directly under the provisions of this section, the judge receiving the case shall transfer it to the Executive Committee for reassignment to the calendar of the judge to whom it should have been assigned directly.

The automated assignment system will at the time of the reassignment of any case introduce any equalization required. The equalization will take the form of an adjustment to the appropriate assignment process that will treat the reassignment as a new assignment to the judge receiving the case and negate the assignment of the case to the judge reassigning it. Unless otherwise ordered by the Executive Committee in the order of reassignment, such equalization will apply in each of the following instances:

(1) where a case is reassigned as related pursuant to LR40.4;

(2) to correct an assignment error where a case that should have been assigned directly pursuant to LR40.3 was assigned by lot;

(3) where a case is reassigned following a result of a recusal with equalization pursuant to IOP13(f); or

(4) where the order of reassignment directs that the reassignment be with equalization.

The clerk shall periodically report to the Executive Committee on the performance of the automated assignment system. Such report shall include a summary of any assignments or reassignments for which equalization is required in addition to any automatic equalization authorized by these procedures. Where it determines additional equalization is required, the Executive Committee will enter an appropriate order.

Records of the system shall be preserved for five years except as otherwise ordered by the Executive Committee.

(c) Designation Cycles for Magistrate Judges. There shall be a separate designation cycle for magistrate judges for civil and criminal cases each of the assignment categories specified in IOP11(b), provided that the Executive Committee may direct that two or more of the categories other than Civil I, II, and III, and Criminal I, II, and III be combined into a single designation cycle. Each designation cycle shall consist of the name of each of the magistrate judges assigned to the Eastern Division. Whenever a new case is assigned to a district judge using one of the assignment decks enumerated above, the clerk shall randomly designate a magistrate judge from the designation cycle for that type of case as the magistrate judge in the case. Whenever pursuant to LR40.3(b) or LCrR50.2 a new case is assigned to a district judge directly and not by lot, the magistrate judge designated for the case originally assigned by lot will be designated for the later filed case. The provisions of this section notwithstanding, where an indictment or information arises out of one or more criminal complaints, the designated magistrate judge shall be the magistrate judge to whom the earliest of those complaints was assigned. Where multiple defendants in a single complaint assigned to a magistrate judge are subsequently charged in more than one indictment or information arising out of that complaint, the designated magistrate judge for each such case shall be the magistrate judge to whom the complaint was assigned.

(d) Assignment of Cases: Western Division. Cases in the Western Division shall at filing be assigned to the district judge and referred generally to the magistrate judge whose duty stations are in that division, provided that the district judge may in any case set aside the initial general reference to the magistrate judge.

(e) Duties under the Federal Debt Collection Procedures Act. Pursuant to 28 U.S.C. § 3008, the Court assigns its duties in proceedings under Chapter 176 of Title 28 of the United States Code, the Federal Debt Collection Procedures Act, ("FDCPA") in all civil cases to the United States Magistrate Judges of this Court.

When relief under the FDCPA is sought by the United States, all necessary documents shall be submitted to the designated magistrate. If no magistrate judge has been previously designated, or where the designated magistrate judge is no longer sitting, a magistrate judge shall be designated as provided for by section (c). The designated magistrate shall supervise proceedings, decide all nondispositive matters, and prepare a report and recommendation in all dispositive matters. If the designated magistrate judge enters a report and recommendation on a dispositive motion, the clerk shall assign the case by lot to a district judge if one has not been previously assigned.

If the parties consent to the reassignment of the proceedings to a magistrate judge, the clerk shall reassign the case to the designated magistrate judge without the entry of a separate Executive Committee reassignment order.

(f) Assignment of Student Loan and Veteran Education Loan Cases. When a complaint is filed on behalf of the Department of Education or the Veterans' Department alleging a failure to repay a student loan or a failure to repay an educational overpayment, the person filing the complaint shall indicate its nature to the assignment clerk. When a complaint of this type is filed, the assignment clerk shall designate a magistrate judge as provided for by section (c) above and shall assign the case generally to the United States magistrate judges. When necessary, the designated magistrate judge shall supervise pretrial proceedings, which may include the preparation of a report and recommendation for the disposition of any motion for injunctive relief, for judgment on the pleadings, for summary judgment, or to dismiss for any reason.

If the parties consent to the reassignment of the case to a magistrate judge, the clerk shall reassign the case to the designated magistrate judge without the entry of a separate Executive Committee reassignment order. If the magistrate judge enters the pretrial order or issues a report and recommendation on a dispositive motion, the clerk shall assign the case by lot to a district judge.

Where a case requires the involvement of a magistrate judge and no magistrate judge has been previously designated, or where the designated magistrate judge is no longer sitting, a magistrate judge shall be designated as provided for by section (c).

[Amended February 7, 2002; April 3, 2002; June 4, 2009.]

IOP 12. WESTERN DIVISION BACKUP JUDGE

(a) Selection. A regular active judge, whose duty station is the Eastern Division and who is not currently serving as chief judge, shall serve as the Western Division backup judge. The judge shall serve as backup judge for a period of 1 year commencing on the first day of January. Unless an Eastern Division judge volunteers and is so designated by the Chief Judge, the backup judge shall be selected from among the eligible regular active judges on the basis of seniority, the most senior being selected first. No judge eligible to serve as the backup judge shall serve a second term until all other eligible judges have served at least once. No judge who has been in office for less than 6 months is eligible to serve as the backup judge.

(b) Reassignment of Cases. Any case in which the judge assigned to the Western Division enters a recusal will be transferred to the Executive Committee for reassignment to the judge serving as Western Division backup judge. The Executive Committee will reassign the case to the calendar of the judge acting as backup judge as of the date of the Committee's order. The order of reassignment will also provide that the backup judge receive equalization for each case so reassigned in the form of a skip in the assignment of new cases in the same category.

IOP 13. REASSIGNMENTS AND TRANSFERS

(a) Multi-District Litigation. When it is brought to the attention of the Executive Committee that proceedings similar to those in a case pending in this District are pending in one or more other districts and that coordinated or consolidated pretrial discovery proceedings should be conducted, the Committee will notify each judge upon whose calendars such cases appear of the proceedings in the other district or districts. Each such judge will transfer the case or cases to the calendar of the Executive Committee. The Committee will reassign the cases to a judge designated by the Committee for the purpose of hearing and determining any and all motions in connection with such multi-district litigation. The judge to whom the cases are so assigned shall have the power to transfer them for the purpose of discovery to another district, either in this or in another circuit, when it is deemed necessary to promote multi-district discovery, provided that in those instances where the transfer of cases to other districts is being considered by the Panel for Multi–District Litigation, the cases shall not be transferred until such time as the Panel has made its determination.

Cases reassigned under this procedure that require trial following the completion of the consolidated discovery shall be transferred to the Executive Committee for reassignment to the judge from whose calendar they were initially transferred. If that judge is no longer sitting, the cases shall be reassigned by lot.

(b) Fugitive Calendar. The Executive Committee shall maintain a calendar called the Fugitive Calendar. Defendants in criminal cases shall be assigned to that calendar in accordance with the procedures set out in this section. Where appropriate, the term "judge" used in this section shall mean both district judge and magistrate judge.

(1) *Reassignment of Cases to the Fugitive Calendar.* Whenever a defendant in a criminal case is fugitive for more than 30 consecutive days or whenever short of said 30 days the judge determines that a defendant is fugitive, the judge to whom the case is assigned shall transfer the defendant to the Fugitive Calendar. Such transfer shall be made even in those instances where other defendants in the case are not fugitive and the case is proceeding as to them, provided that where the judge determines that the presence of the fugitive defendant in such multiple defendant case is required for the trial of the non-fugitive defendants, and an order is entered to that effect, the fugitive defendant shall remain on the calendar of the judge.

(2) *Procedures for Removing Cases from the Fugitive Calendar.* Where a defendant on the Fugitive Calendar is arrested or appears and the judge to whom the case was assigned is still sitting and hearing criminal cases, the clerk shall promptly transfer the defendant from the Fugitive Calendar to the calendar of that judge. If the judge is either no longer sitting or is no longer receiving assignment of criminal cases, the following procedures shall be followed:

(A) Where the defendant is to be brought before a judge immediately following arrest or appearance, the United States Attorney shall have the defendant brought before the emergency judge who shall order the clerk to notify the Executive Committee of the need to have the defendant reassigned from the Fugitive Calendar.

(B) On being informed of the arrest or appearance of the defendant either as provided in (2)(A) or through other notification, the clerk shall promptly notify the Executive Committee of the need for an order directing the reassignment of the defendant.

(3) *Deferred Prosecution and the Fugitive Calendar.* Whenever subsequent to the filing of an indictment or information the judge approves a deferred prosecution for one or more of the defendants in the case and the case is not to be dismissed until the completion of the period covered by the deferred prosecution, the judge shall transfer the case to the Executive Committee for reassignment to the Fugitive Calendar. Following successful completion of the conditions of deferred prosecution or where the United States Attorney indicates that the conditions have not

been met and prosecution should be continued, the judge from whose calendar the case was reassigned shall notify the clerk of the need for an order of the Executive Committee reassigning the case from the Fugitive Calendar to the calendar of that judge.

(4) *Calendar Call of the Fugitive Calendar.* The Executive Committee may assign one or more judges for the purpose of making a periodic call of the cases on the Fugitive Calendar. The judge or judges assigned shall from time to time consult with the United States Attorney and the Attorney General to ascertain whether dismissals of particular criminal actions shall be deemed advisable.

(c) Reassignments and Assignments of Cases to the Chief Judge and Senior Judges. From time to time the Executive Committee may assign cases to the chief judge or to any senior judge. Such assignment may be performed in any of the following ways:

(1) The Executive Committee may direct the clerk to assign cases to the chief judge or to a senior judge in the same manner as cases are assigned to a regular active judge but limit the number of categories so assigned.

(2) The Executive Committee may direct the clerk to include the name of the chief judge or a senior judge in the assignment process of one or more assignment categories. In any order directing the assignment of new filings to the chief judge or a senior judge, the Executive Committee shall fix the frequency with which the name of the chief judge or senior judge shall appear in the process for the assignment category specified. The order shall also direct the clerk to assign cases in the assignment categories specified whenever that judge's name appears.

(3) The Executive Committee may, with the consent of the judge to whom such case or cases is assigned, direct that one or more cases be reassigned to the chief judge or to any senior judge.

(4) Where a case is reassigned from a senior judge pursuant to 28 USC § 294(b), the case shall be reassigned by lot to a regular active district judge.

(d) Reassignment by Agreement. Where two or more judges agree that the reassignment of one or more cases to one of them will enable the case or cases to be more efficiently administered and will serve to save judicial time, the cases involved may be transferred to the Executive Committee with a request for such reassignment. The request shall indicate briefly the reasons for such reassignment and specify whether or not the judge receiving the case is to return any case or cases to the Committee for reassignment to the transferring judge. If the Committee finds that the reassignment will enable a more efficient administration of the cases, it may then order the reassignment.

(e) Coordinated Pretrials in Complex Cases not Involving Multi–District Litigation. The Executive Committee may determine that it would be in the best interests of efficient judicial administration to hold a coordinated pretrial proceeding in a group of cases which either (1) are not related within the meaning of LR40.4(a) or (2) are related within the meaning of LR40.4(a) but reassignment is not appropriate under LR40.4(b). Where such a determination is made, the Committee will designate a judge to hold such a proceeding. The cases shall remain on the calendars of the judges to whom they were assigned at the start of the coordinated proceeding and only matters specified in the order of coordination shall be brought before the designated judge. All judges affected by such a coordinated pretrial proceeding shall be notified by the clerk.

(f) Recusals. (Amended July 7, 2000,)

(1) *General Procedures.* Except as otherwise provided in this section, whenever a case is transferred to the Executive Committee for reassignment following a recusal, the Committee shall direct the clerk to reassign the case by lot to a judge other than the judge who entered the recusal. A judge receiving a case on reassignment following a recusal shall promptly determine whether or not to enter a recusal. Where a recusal is entered, the judge shall promptly transfer the case back to the Committee which shall thereupon direct the clerk to reassign the case by lot to a judge other than those previously entering recusals. Where a recusal is not entered, the judge may transfer to the Committee for reassignment to the judge entering the initial recusal a case requiring a like amount of judicial effort for disposition. The Committee will reassign that case subject to verification that it will require like judicial effort.

(2) *Recusals With Equalization.* Where the reason for the recusal is included in one of the categories specified in this subsection, the judge entering the recusal may request that in lieu of receiving a like case from the receiving judge, the recusal be made part of the calendar equalization set out in IOP11(b). The categories of recusals for which this procedure may be used are as follows:

(A) cases in which a recusal is entered because a relative of the judge works for a law firm, or the U.S. Attorney's Office, which represents or is one of the parties to the case; and

(B) cases in which one of the parties is or was represented by a law firm with which the judge was associated within the previous five years.

(C) cases in which the judge determines that a recusal is required because one of the parties was previously represented by the judge.

(g) Calendar of Short Civil Trials. The calendar of short civil trials is a program intended to provide a list of cases that are ready for trial and where the trial is expected to take no more than five days. Cases on the list can be handled by visiting judges or by judges of the Court who as a result of unanticipated settlements find that they have available time to try a case.

(1) The following definitions shall apply to section (g):

(A) Judge: Any district judge of this Court on whose calendar there are civil cases pending.

(B) Listing Form: A form approved by the Executive Committee to be used by the assigned judge to effect the addition or removal of a case to or from the short civil trial calendar.

(C) Ready for Trial: A short civil trial case is ready for trial if (i) the final pretrial order has been entered and (ii) there are no unresolved pending motions other than motions *in limine* reserved for ruling at trial.

(D) Requesting Judge: A judge who requests a case from the short civil trial calendar or to whom such a case has been transferred but not reassigned.

(E) Short Civil Trial Case: A short civil trial case is a civil case that is ready for trial and it is estimated by the assigned judge at the time of entering the pretrial order that the trial will last no more than five days, including jury selection.

(F) Short Civil Trial Calendar: All cases in which a listing form has been received by the clerk that are still pending and available for reassignment to a requesting judge.

(G) Short Civil Trial Calendar Judge: The chief judge, or a judge designated by the chief judge, will be the short civil trial calendar judge. The short civil trial calendar judge will be responsible for coordinating the trial of cases on the short civil trial calendar.

(2) Any judge may place a short civil trial case on the short civil trial calendar by sending a completed listing form to the clerk. In order to assist the court in determining whether or not placing a case on the short civil trial calendar might be inappropriate, counsel will include in the final pretrial order form information concerning the anticipated circumstances of the trial that might impact scheduling.

(3) On receiving the listing form, the clerk shall forthwith docket the form and notify counsel and parties of the docketing in the manner provided by Fed.R.Civ.P. 77(d) for notice of orders or judgments. The clerk will include with the notice a reminder to parties of their right to consent to a reassignment of the case to the designated magistrate judge pursuant to 28 U.S.C. § 636(c) and LR73.1(b).

(4) Any judge, including any senior district judge or visiting judge designated to hold court in this District,

who is available to try a short civil case may request such a trial from the short civil trial calendar judge. The short civil trial calendar judge will forward the earliest filed case on the short civil trial calendar that fits the available trial time of the requesting judge. Any case so selected will be transferred to the requesting judge for pretrial review. Such transfer will serve as authority for the requesting judge to act in the case as if the case had been reassigned, although the case will remain on the docket of the assigned judge. The case will be reassigned to the requesting judge for all purposes if it is settled by that judge, or if that judge starts a trial in the case.

(5) If the requesting judge determines that a transferred case is not ready for trial, that judge will so inform the short civil trial calendar judge. The short civil trial calendar judge will so notify the assigned judge and may thereupon remove the case from the short civil trial calendar.

(6) Nothing in this rule shall preclude the assigned judge from settling or trying a case the judge has listed on the short civil trial calendar. If the assigned judge is able to resolve the case, the judge will forward a completed listing form to the clerk. The clerk will notify the short civil trial calendar judge that the case is to be removed from the short civil trial calendar.

(7) Motions brought in cases listed on the short civil trial calendar prior to its transfer to a requesting judge shall be heard by the assigned judge. Motions brought after the transfer but before the reassignment of the case to the requesting judge will be brought before the requesting judge. The requesting judge may thereupon send the motions to the assigned judge.

(8) When a case is disposed of following a trial conducted by a requesting judge who routinely participates in the assignment of civil cases filed in the Eastern Division, then that judge shall receive equalization in the form of one skip in the assignment deck of the same category as that of the case closed.

(h) Transfer of Motions by Agreement. A judge may with the agreement of the receiving judge transfer one or more pending motions to be ruled upon by the receiving judge without transferring the case. The transferring judge shall notify the Executive Committee of any transfer made under this rule. Such notice will be on a form approved by the Committee.

Notice of any transfer under this rule shall be sent to the parties. The notice shall indicate the name of the receiving judge. Any motion challenging the transfer on grounds other than the recusal of the receiving judge will not be entertained. Any such motion shall be filed with the receiving judge. Any motion for rehearing of a ruling by the receiving judge shall be presented to the receiving judge.

(i) Reassignments of Criminal Cases with Multiple Defendants. Except as provided by the Executive Committee's order reassigning a criminal case with multiple defendants, the reassignment order shall include all defendants.

(j) Other Reassignments and Transfers. If a case is reassigned from a judge who is temporarily not receiving cases pursuant to an order of the Executive Committee, the judge to whom the, case is reassigned shall receive equalization in the form of one skip in the assignment deck of the category in which the case was initially assigned. If a case is transferred to the Executive Committee for any reason not otherwise provided for in the local rules or the internal operating procedures and the Committee agrees that the case should be reassigned, it shall cause the case to be reassigned by lot. If the name of the transferring judge is drawn, another drawing shall be made. The judge who receives the case may transfer to the Committee a case or cases requiring a like amount of judicial effort to dispose of it or them, with the recommendation that it or they be reassigned to the calendar of the transferring judge.

(j) Order of Reassignment. Where one or more cases are to be reassigned pursuant to LR40.4, LR40.5, or sections (a), (b), (c), (d), (f), or (i) of this IOP, the assigned judge shall complete the appropriate reassignment transfer form. If the assigned judge is no longer sitting, the clerk shall complete the form. The transfer form will be given to the clerk who shall promptly transmit it to the chief judge. The chief judge may on receipt of the form enter an order on behalf of the Executive Committee directing that the case or cases be reassigned or may ask the full Committee to review the requested reassignment at the next meeting. A case will be deemed reassigned following the docketing of the order of the Executive Committee directing its reassignment.

[Amended effective March 3, 2011; February 27, 2014; May 22, 2014; December 23, 2014.]

IOP 14. MAGISTRATE JUDGES: REFERRALS & RECUSALS

A judge may refer a civil case to the designated magistrate judge pursuant to LR72.1 and LCrR50.3(d). In such instances, the judge shall specify any issue being referred to the magistrate judge.

[Amended effective May 31, 2011.]

IOP 15. BANKRUPTCY MATTERS

(a) Referral to Bankruptcy Judges. Pursuant to 28 U.S.C. § 157(a), any and all cases under Title 11 U.S.C. and any and all proceedings arising under Title 11 U.S.C. or arising in or related to any case under Title 11 U.S.C. are referred to the bankruptcy judges of this District.

(b) Assignment by Lot. Except as provided by sections C, D, E and F of this rule, each of the following shall be assigned by lot to a district judge:

(1) any motion (including a recommendation by a bankruptcy judge) for the withdrawal of the reference of a bankruptcy ("B") case or proceeding pursuant to 28 U.S.C. § 157(d);

(2) any motion (including a recommendation by a bankruptcy judge) for the withdrawal of the reference of an adversary ("A") proceeding pursuant to 28 U.S.C. § 157(d);

(3) any report and recommendation of a bankruptcy judge in a non-core proceeding filed pursuant to 28 U.S.C. § 157(c)(1); and

Where assigned by lot, petitions for withdrawal of reference, appeals, motions for leave to appeal, and applications for writs shall be assigned using the Civil II assignment category and reports and recommendations using the Civil III assignment category.

(c) Direct Assignment in Bankruptcy ("B") Cases. If in a bankruptcy ("B") case or set of related bankruptcy ("B") cases a report and recommendation referred to in (b)(3) is filed pursuant to the prior direction of a district judge, the report shall be assigned directly to the calendar of that judge.

If in a contested matter within a bankruptcy ("B") case a motion for withdrawal of reference, or a report and recommendation, or an appeal, or a motion for leave to file an interlocutory appeal, or an application for a writ referred to in (b)(1) or (b)(2), respectively, is filed and a motion, report, appeal, motion for leave to file an interlocutory appeal, or application for a writ referred to in (b)(1) or (b)(2), was previously filed in the same contested matter and assigned by lot to a district judge, then the subsequent motion, report, appeal, motion for leave to file an interlocutory appeal, or application for a writ shall be assigned directly to the calendar of that judge.

(d) Direct Assignment in Adversary ("A") Proceeding. If in an adversary ("A") proceeding a motion for withdrawal of reference, or a report and recommendation, or an appeal or a motion for leave to file an interlocutory appeal, or application for a writ referred to in (b)(1) or (b)(2), respectively, is filed and a motion, report, appeal, motion for leave to file an interlocutory appeal, or application for a writ referred to in (b)(1) or (b)(2) was previously filed in the same adversary ("A") proceeding and assigned by lot to a district judge, then the subsequent motion, report, appeal or motion for leave to file an interlocutory appeal, or application for a writ to be assigned shall be assigned directly to the calendar of that judge.

(e) Direct Assignment Following Remand. If in any bankruptcy ("B") case or in any adversary ("A") proceeding a district judge enters an order, opinion, or memorandum remanding a matter before that judge to the bankruptcy court for further proceedings, then any subsequent motion, report, motion for leave to file an interlocutory appeal, or application for a writ with respect to the matter remanded shall be assigned directly to the calendar of that judge.

(f) Relatedness. Where matters in the underlying bankruptcy case, or adversary proceedings associated with the underlying proceedings, or non-core proceedings associated with the underlying proceedings are pending on the calendars of two or more district judges, motions for relatedness may be filed to have the matters assigned to the calendar of one judge. The standards and procedures established by LR40.4 shall apply to such motions. For the purpose of determining the judge before whom such motion for relatedness should be filed, the term "lowest-numbered pending case" as used in LR40.4 shall refer to the petition initiating the bankruptcy case, the adversary proceeding, or the non-core proceeding with the earliest date and time of the filing with the bankruptcy clerk. The motion for relatedness shall include a listing of the dates and times of filing of each of the matters which movant is asking to be found related. Where a case is reassigned as related, it shall be treated on the same manner as a reassignment for relatedness pursuant to LR40.4 for the purposes of the equalization provisions of IOP11(b).

(g) Designation Sheet. The person filing the petition for withdrawal of reference, report and recommendation, appeal, motion for leave to appeal, or application for a writ shall complete the designation sheet required by LR3.1 and shall include on the sheet a list of any associated bankruptcy cases, adversary proceedings, non-core proceedings, appeals or motions for leave to appeal, or application for a writ from such proceedings previously assigned to one or more district judges.

IOP 16. INITIAL CALENDAR FOR NEW DISTRICT JUDGE

(a) Applicability of Procedures. These procedures expand upon the provisions of LR40.1(g). They apply only to the formation of the initial calendar of a new judge designated to sit in the Eastern Division. They are intended to assure that the initial calendar is a reasonable cross-section of the calendars of all of the judges in the Division. The exception to this goal is that no criminal cases shall be reassigned as part of the initial calendar. Instead, an additional number of civil cases equivalent to the number of criminal cases that would have been assigned shall be reassigned as part of the initial calendar.

(b) Number of Participating Judges. In general each regular active judge on full assignment participates in the reassignment of cases to form an initial calendar for any newly appointed judge to the extent of one share. The chief judge and each participating senior judge participate to the extent of one share weighted by the proportion of new civil filings that judge currently receives.

The chief judge routinely participates both in the reassignment of cases to form new calendars and in receiving cases reassigned when the calendar of another judge is eliminated or reduced. Usually, senior judges participate in the reassignment of cases to form new calendars only if (1) they are currently receiving a share of new filings and (2) they agree to receive reassignments in those instances where the calendar of another judge is eliminated or reduced. The Executive Committee will determine the participation of senior judges who are not currently receiving a share of new filings. For the purposes of these procedures, a senior judge is considered to be currently participating in the assignment of new cases unless there has been an order entered directing that the judge receive no new cases until further order of court.

The total of the number of participating judges receiving a full share of new civil cases plus the total of the weighted shares of those participating judges receiving less than a full share of new civil cases shall constitute the total participating judge equivalencies.

(c) Number of Pending Cases. The target value for the total number of cases to be reassigned to form the new calendar is the adjusted number of pending cases divided by the total participating judge equivalencies. The Executive Committee initiates the process by selecting the date on which the count of cases will be based.

For the process of creating an initial calendar, the adjusted number of pending cases on calendars of regular active judges will be the total number of civil and criminal cases reported as pending on the calendars of the participating judges on the date selected by the Executive Committee including any pending petitions for leave to proceed in forma pauperis, but net of any higher-numbered related cases or cases assigned to a multidistrict litigation ("MDL") docket. Pending cases filed by persons in custody that are directly assigned pursuant to LR40.3(b) are to be treated as a related set. The adjusted number of pending cases for the chief judge and participating senior judges will be determined in the same manner as regular active judges but may be weighted to reflect lower participation in the assignment of new cases. The Integrated Case Management System ("ICMS") will serve as the source for information on the pending cases.

The clerk will instruct the courtroom deputies assigned to the participating judge to submit a list of related cases shortly before the reassignment process is started. Failure to identify a case as a higher-numbered related case results in its remaining on the list used to select primary and secondary lists. Where

it is subsequently discovered that a case on the primary or secondary list was a higher-numbered related case, it is removed from the list. The related set is not reassigned in such circumstances. If the case appeared on the primary list, the appropriate substitution from the secondary list is made.

Cases pending before the chief judge and any of the senior judges participating are weighted on the basis of whether or not such judge retained his or her calendar on changing judicial status, *i.e.*, on becoming chief judge or taking senior status, and the extent of such judge's current participation in the assignment of new cases. The weighting is fixed as follows:

(1) each case is given a weight of 1.0, *i.e.*, counted in full, under the following conditions:

(A) civil cases where the judge disposed of a substantial proportion of his or her civil calendar on changing judicial status; and

(B) criminal cases where the judge disposed of a substantial proportion of his or her criminal calendar on changing judicial status and the judge is currently receiving new criminal cases, or where the judge retained his or her pending criminal cases on changing judicial status but the judge is not currently receiving new criminal cases.

(2) each case is given a weight equivalent to the current rate at which the judge participates in the assignment of new cases under the following conditions:

(A) civil cases where the judge retained his or her calendar and the judge is currently receiving new civil cases; and

(B) criminal cases where the judge retained his or her calendar of pending criminal cases on changing judicial status and the judge is receiving new criminal cases.

The adjusted total number of cases pending before the participating regular active judges on full assignment and the weighted total of the number of cases pending before the chief judge and senior judges is the final adjusted grand total. The adjusted total number of judges participating in the process is the sum of the number of participating regular active judges on full assignment, plus the number of new judges for whom initial calendars are to be formed, plus a weighted total for the chief judge and participating senior judges, where the weight applied to each is that at which they are currently participating in the assignment of new civil cases. The target calendar size is derived by dividing the adjusted grand total of cases pending by the adjusted total number of judges participating.

(d) Number of Cases to be Reassigned From Each Judge. The number of cases to be reassigned from each judge is calculated by dividing the target calendar by the sum of the number of participating regular active judges on full assignment plus the assignment equivalencies for the chief judge and participating judges. The result is rounded to the nearest integer.

(e) Primary & Secondary Lists.

(1) A calendar list is prepared for each participating judge. The list contains the case numbers and short title of all of the civil cases other than MDL cases pending on that judge's calendar. Higher-numbered related cases are included on the list, but only for the purpose of identifying any cases associated with the lower-numbered lead case. Each related set is counted as one case for the purpose of the selection process.

(2) The case numbers are sorted so that they are listed in case number order with the oldest case, *i.e.*, earliest case number, first.

(3) Cases that have previously been reassigned two or more times for any reason other than recusal, and cases that are motions to reduce sentence filed pursuant to 28 U.S.C. § 2255 are included on the list in the position determined by their age and in the count of cases. However, such cases are flagged so that the computer can identify them as cases not to be reassigned.

(4) The total, T, of the cases on the calendar list net of higher-numbered related cases is calculated.

(5) An interval number, I, is computed by dividing T by the number of cases to be reassigned from the calendar ("R"). As T/R will rarely result in an integer and the interval must be an integer, only the integer portion of T/R is taken.

(6) A primary start number, S1, is randomly selected from the set of numbers 1, 2, 3, . . . ,(I-2), (I-1),I. The random number generator used to select S1 is such that each number in the set has an equal chance of being selected.

(7) The primary lists consists of the S1th case, the (S1 + I)th case, the (S1 + 2I)th case, the (S1 + 3I)th case, . . . , and the [S1 + (R–1)I]th case, provided that if a flagged case is selected, e.g., one that was previously reassigned two or more times to form an initial calendar, the next lower-numbered case is then substituted. The computer keeps track of the cases so selected and flags them as they are selected.

(8) A secondary start number, S2, is selected in the same manner as the primary start number, except that it must be a number other than the primary start number.

(9) The secondary list is selected in a manner similar to that used to select the primary list.

(10) If as part of the process of forming either the primary or the secondary list the case selected is a flagged case, e.g., a case previously reassigned two or more times as part of the formation of an initial calendar, the next lower-numbered unflagged case is

selected. Should there be no lower-numbered unflagged case, the next higher-numbered unflagged case is selected.

(f) Review of Primary & Secondary Lists. The primary and secondary lists are sent to each of the participating judges. The cases on the primary list are those cases to be reassigned to form the initial calendar of the new judge. However, a case may be withheld from the primary list under certain circumstances. Where a case is to be withheld, the case on the secondary list with the case number closest to that of the case to be withheld will be substituted. As the reasons for withholding apply to cases on both lists, both should be reviewed by the judge.

Cases may be withheld from reassignment only if they meet one or more of the following conditions:

(1) the case is closed and the J.S. 6 statistical closing form has been received by the central Clerk's Office;

(2) the case has been reassigned to the calendar of another judge;

(3) the trial has started or has been completed;

(4) the case was remanded with instructions for action by the judge on whose calendar the case is pending at the time of the reassignment to form a new calendar;

(5) the case is found not to meet the criteria for inclusion in the pool of cases used to prepare the primary and secondary lists (e.g., the case is part of an MDL, the proceeding is not statistically reportable as a civil case).

In instances where a case is to be reassigned to a magistrate judge on consent of the parties, the case will be withheld from reassignment to the initial calendar only where the case has been transferred to the Executive Committee by the district judge from whose calendar the case is to be reassigned before the entry of the general order of reassignment.

In addition, where the new judge is coming from private practice or a position with an organization or agency that might have filed cases in this Court, a search will be made of ICMS records to identify all cases that the law firm, organization, or agency has pending before the Court. These cases are flagged and are skipped during the process of selecting cases for the primary and secondary lists in the same manner as higher-numbered related cases.

(g) Review of Substitutions. Whenever a case from the secondary list is to be substituted for a case on the primary list because the latter is to be withheld, the judge will indicate the reason the case is to be withheld. The Executive Committee shall decide whether or not a case is to be withheld in instances where it is unclear whether the reason given for withholding the case satisfies one or more of the conditions included in sections (e) and (f).

(h) Closed Cases. Where a case selected for reassignment is closed before it is reassigned to the initial calendar, the case with the closest case number on the secondary list is substituted for the closed case. Closings taking place after the date the cases have actually been reassigned are credited to the calendar of the new judge regardless of which judge closed the case and no substitutions are to be made for the case.

For the purposes of this section a case is considered closed when a J.S. 6 statistical reporting form indicating that the date of closing was prior to the date the new judge took office is received by the central Clerk's Office within a week of the date of closing.

(i) Recusals by New Judge. Recusals in cases assigned to a judge as part of an initial calendar will be reassigned to the calendar of the judge from which it was reassigned. That judge may transfer to the Executive Committee for reassignment to the recusing judge a case requiring a like amount of judicial effort for disposition.

[Amended effective May 22, 2014.]

Committee Comment

In a large multi-judge trial court that uses the random assignment process, the formation of the initial calendar of a new judge is a vital part of that process. Over the years the Court has adopted procedures that have steadily increased the randomness of the process. IOP16 and the *Comment* are based on these procedures. Because of the complexity of IOP16, the *Comment* is long. It has been broken into sections, each designated to correspond to the section of IOP16 being discussed.

(a) Applicability of Procedures. IOP16 is intended to provide a new judge with a calendar that is an average of that pending before the other judges. It applies only to the Eastern Division because currently there is only one regular active judge assigned to the Western Division.

Under these procedures cases are reassigned from the calendars of the sitting judges to form the initial calendar of the new judge. The process is timed so that the new calendar is ready when the newly appointed district judge enters on duty. Pursuant to LR40.1(b) "[t]he assignment of cases to calendars and judges and the preparation of calendars and supplements thereto shall be done solely under the direction of the Executive Committee by the clerk or a deputy clerk who is designated by the clerk as an assignment clerk." It is the usual practice for the Executive Committee to enter one order setting the process in motion and a second, following the selection, that specifies the cases to be reassigned to form the initial calendar.

Any set of procedures used to create a new calendar by reassigning cases from existing calendars has to provide for (1) the total number of cases to be reassigned, (2) the number of cases to be reassigned from each of the participating calendars, (3) the method of choice, (4) criteria for exempting cases falling within specified statuses prior to the actual reassignment, and (5) provisions for handling the need to make adjustments following the actual reassignment.

Practical considerations call for the elimination of cases falling within certain statuses. For example, it makes little sense to reassign a case that has been tried or a criminal case in which a guilty plea has been entered. The procedures provide for withholding cases in a limited number of such statuses.

(b) Number of Participating Judges. For the purposes of these procedures, a judge who is not receiving cases due to the periodic calendar adjustment program (*See* IOP18) is treated as a regular active judge on full assignment. Similarly, a senior judge may participate in new civil assignments to the extent of a three-quarter share which is received through the judge getting a full share during nine months of the year and no new cases for the remaining three months of the year. This judge would be considered currently on assignment for the purpose of participating in the reassignment to form a new calendar even if not actually receiving cases at the time, provided that the order taking the judge's name off the wheel indicated that it was for a set period and the name would be returned at the end of that period.

The following is an example of calculating the number of participating judge equivalents. 20 active judges participate in the process. Of these 17 are regular active judges on full assignment, one is a senior judge receiving a full share of civil cases, one is the chief judge receiving a one-half share of new civil cases, and one is a senior judge, also receiving a one-half share of new civil filings. The 17 regular active judges on full assignment and the senior judge receiving a full share of new civil cases each count as 1 participating judge equivalent. The chief judge and the senior judge receiving a one-half share of new civil filings each count as $\frac{1}{2}$ of a participating judge equivalent. The 20 judges thus total 19 participating judge equivalencies, *i.e.*, $17 + 1 + \frac{1}{2} + \frac{1}{2}$.

(c) Number of Pending Cases. In order to arrive at an average calendar size, some adjustments need to be made to the total number of cases pending. The most obvious adjustment involves related cases. A condition for reassigning cases as related required by LR40.4(b) is that "the handling of both cases by the same judge is likely to result in a substantial saving of judicial time and effort." Accordingly, the Court has determined that each set of related cases should be treated as one case for the purpose of forming an initial calendar. In order that a related set have the same chance of reassignment as any other case, only the lowest-numbered case in the set is included in the totals and in the list from which cases are picked. If the lowest-numbered case in the set is selected, all of the cases in the set are reassigned.

It is not unusual to discover that two or more of the cases in a related set were inadvertently included in the calendar list without the higher-numbered cases being flagged. This makes the likelihood that a related set will be selected greater than if the lowest-numbered case in the set is the only one listed. Where this has occurred and it is discovered that the higher-numbered case was selected for a primary or secondary list, the related set is not reassigned. A substitute is selected in a manner similar to that used where a case that is selected is closed before the reassignment.

Where two or more cases filed by a person in custody are pending on a judge's calendar and one or more of them was directly assigned to a judge's calendar pursuant to LR40.3(b), the cases are treated as a related set.

Under the standards governing case statistics approved by the Judicial Conference of the United States a petition for leave to proceed *in forma pauperis* is not counted as a case. Such a petition is counted as a case for the purposes of selecting an initial calendar.

Cases on MDL dockets are not included in the formation of an initial calendar because the handling of such a docket involves a degree of choice on the part of the judge. Traditionally, the regular docket reports circulated among the judges have separated MDL dockets from other civil cases.

The weight accorded the pending cases of the chief or a senior judge is adjusted based on both the level of that judge's participation in new case assignments and the action that judge took with respect to his or her pending calendar at the time that judge became the chief or a senior judge. It is common practice for judges to reduce the size of their pending calendar on becoming chief judge or taking senior status by an amount equal to the rate at which they will participate in new assignments. For example, the chief judge generally receive a one-half share of new civil cases. It is common practice for a judge who becomes the chief judge to reduce his or her pending calendar by one-half on assuming the office of chief judge.

Experience has shown that over time the number of cases processed by a judge correlates more strongly with the number of cases assigned to than the number pending before that judge. Accordingly, an adjustment is made to the calendars of the chief and participating senior judges that weighs each of their pending caseloads based on their current participation in the assignment process.

For example, assume that initial calendars are to be created for two new judges from cases pending on the calendars of 17 regular active judges on full assignment in the Eastern Division, the chief judge, and two senior judges. Assume that the chief judge disposed of part of his calendar on becoming chief judge and receives a one-half share of civil case assignments and no criminal case assignments, that senior judge A retained her calendar on taking senior status and receives a full share of new civil case assignments and no criminal case assignments, and that senior judge B disposed of part of his calendar on taking senior status and receives a one-half share of civil case assignments and no criminal case assignments. If the adjusted total number of civil and criminal cases pending before seventeen regular active judges on full assignment at the end the month selected were 5,974, and 451 of these were higher-numbered related cases, the preliminary adjusted grand total would be 5,974 less 451 or 5,523. Assume that the chief judge has a pending civil calendar of 150 cases of which 10 were higher-numbered related cases, and that senior judges A and B have pending civil calendars of 250 and 130 cases of which 19 and 10, respectively, were, higher-numbered related cases. The preliminary grand total would be adjusted by adding 140, i.e, 150 less 10, to take the chief judge's participation into account plus 351, i.e., 380 less 29, for senior judges A and B, resulting in a final grand total of 6,014, i.e., 5,523 plus 491. The adjusted number of participating judges is 21, i.e., 17 for the regular active judges on full assignment, plus ½ each for the chief judge and senior judge B, plus 1 for senior judge A, plus 2 for the new judges. The target calendar would be 6,014 divided by 21, or 286.38.

(d) Number of Cases to be Reassigned from Each Judge. In the example given above, the target calendar was 286.38 and the adjusted number of participating judges was 21. Of these two represented the new judge. Therefore, there were 19 judge equivalencies from whose calendars cases were to be reassigned. participating judge equivalencies other than the two new judges. 15 cases would be reassigned from the calendar of each judge on full assignment (286.93 divided by 19 equals 15.10. 15.10 rounded to the nearest integer is 15.) 7 cases would be reassigned from the calendar of the chief judge and a further 7 from the calendar of senior judge B as each receives a one-half share of new civil assignments. The total number of cases to be reassigned would be 284, i.e., 15 for each of the 17 regular active judges on full assignment, 7 for the chief judge, 15 for senior judge A, and 7 for senior judge B.

(e) Primary & Secondary Lists. Two sets of cases are selected from the each judge's list of pending cases. The first set forms the primary lists and the second the secondary list. The selection process is a form of stratified random selection process that selects the cases randomly but evenly spaced. In this way the initial calendar has a mix of cases by age that is the average for the Court. (The case number, the variable used to arrange the cases on the calendar list, is an accurate indicator of case age.)

The primary list is the list of cases intended to go to the new calendar. Experience has shown that there are always a small number of cases that for a variety of reasons—all specified in these procedures—should not be reassigned as part of an initial calendar. Accordingly, a secondary list is prepared using the same procedures as used to create the primary list. If a case on the primary list cannot be reassigned, then the case on the secondary list with the closest case number is substituted. (For purposes of these procedures the string of case numbers is assumed to be continuous so that the number following the last one assigned in year x is the first case number in year $(x+1)$. This is rarely of importance where a new case is involved, the most likely situation as the process results in many relatively new cases being selected for reassignment. Where the "closest case number" involves an old case, however, the single number sequence approach provides a fair and uniform manner for determining which of two old cases should be substituted.)

Subsection (e)(3) mentions two categories of cases which are included on the list and counted, but are not to be reassigned. These are motions to reduce sentence filed pursuant to 28 U.S.C. § 2255 and cases that have previously been reassigned two or more times to form an initial calendar. § 2255 motions are given a civil case number but are part of an underlying criminal proceeding. As the motions are assigned to the sentencing judge, reassignment is inappropriate.

The restriction of the number of times a case can be reassigned to form an initial calendar is a compromise between the goal of providing the new judge with a calendar which is an accurately reflection of an average calendar and the need to keep disruptive reassignments to a minimum. Experience showed that without such a limit a large proportion of the oldest cases being reassigned had been reassigned more than three times to make up an individual calendar system. The Court agreed to limit the number of such reassignments to two per case.

Subsections (e)(5) and (e)(6) establish the mechanism used to select cases. First an interval number, I, is selected. If the case count of a judge's calendar list is 293 and the judge is reassigning 15 cases, then I will be 19. A start number, S, is randomly selected from the numbers 1,2,3,...,17,18,19. Assume that 11 was selected as S. Then the 11th and every

19th case thereafter will be picked form the calendar list. The last case will be the 277th.

Because the interval number will rarely be an integer, there is a residual block of cases that has no chance of being selected. In the example given above, the 286th through the 293rd cases on the list have no chance of being selected. By definition this block of cases that have no chance of being selected must contain fewer than R cases. Furthermore, because of the way in which the selection process operates, the cases in this block are always the most recently filed cases on the calendar list.

(f) Review of Primary & Secondary Lists. The criteria for cases that may be withheld from reassignment are quite specific. The conditions specified for each category must exist. Potentially meeting the conditions is not sufficient. For example, the parties may indicate to the judge that the case will settle shortly. However, it can be withheld as closed only when there is a closing order and a J.S. 6 has been filed in the central Clerk's Office.

The reassignment of cases filed by the law firm or organization with which the new judge was recently associated would result in subsequent reassignments when the new judge entered recusals. For this reason they are, to the extent possible, identified and flagged as not to be reassigned.

(g) Review of Substitutions. The procedure makes explicit that the Executive Committee has reviewing authority over any substitutions proposed by a judge.

(h) Closed Cases. The process of creating calendars takes time. As a result, it is not unusual for some of the cases selected for reassignment to be closed by the judge from whom they are to be reassigned prior to the time of the reassignment. In such instances the case from the secondary list with the closest case number will be substituted for the closed case. As with subsection (f)(1), for a case to be considered closed under this section, the J.S. 6 statistical reporting form must have been received by the central Clerk's Office prior to the date of the reassignment or the date on which the new judge takes office, whichever is later.

(i) Recusals by New Judge. Where the new judge enters a recusal in a case reassigned to form that judge's initial calendar, it is reassigned to the judge from whose calendar it came. This minimizes the disruption to parties. The judge receiving the case is authorized to send to the Executive Committee for reassignment to the new judge a case requiring similar judicial effort.

IOP 17. INITIAL CALENDAR FOR NEW MAGISTRATE JUDGE

(a) General; Applicability of IOP16. An initial calendar shall be prepared under the direction of the Executive Committee for any newly-appointed magistrate judge. The calendar shall consist of referrals in civil cases made pursuant to LR72.1 and IOP14 and civil cases reassigned on consent pursuant to LR73.1. No referrals in criminal cases or criminal cases assigned to a magistrate judge shall be included in an initial calendar.

Except as provided in section (b), the provisions of IOP16 shall be followed in preparing the initial calen-

dar for a magistrate judge. Referrals and cases reassigned on consent shall be treated as two separate categories and separate target numbers and primary and secondary lists shall be prepared for each category. For the purpose of preparing the initial calendar for a magistrate judge, references to a regular active judge in IOP16 shall be taken to mean sitting magistrate judge. Referrals in criminal cases shall be included in the count of cases used to determine the target value for the number of civil referrals to be reassigned to form the initial calendar. Similarly, criminal cases assigned to magistrate judges will be included in the count used to determine the target value for the number of consent cases to be reassigned to form the initial calendar.

(b) Equalization and Initial Calendar Formation. The Executive Committee may use the formation of an initial calendar to equalize disparities in the calendars of magistrate judges. In the order directing the formation of an initial calendar for a magistrate judge the Executive Committee may direct that any of the following methods of determining the extent to which sitting magistrate judges may participate in the reassignment be used in lieu of the equal share participation rate established by IOP16:

(1) the participation may be limited to the magistrate judges most in need of equalization; or

(2) the participation may be based on the proportions of pending referrals or reassignments on consent rather than equal shares; or

(3) the participation may be based on the proportion of referrals or reassignments on consent received over a specified time period rather than pending numbers; or

(4) the participation may be based on such other method as the Executive Committee directs in order to achieve equalization of calendars among the magistrate judges.

Regardless of the method used, the referrals and cases to be reassigned will be selected from the calendars of the participating magistrate judges by lot in accordance with the procedures set out in IOP16.

Committee Comment

IOP17 applies only to the formation of the initial calendar of a magistrate judge assigned to the Eastern Division. Currently there is only one full-time magistrate judge assigned to the Western Division, so any new magistrate judge would simply replace a sitting judge and take over the latter's calendar. Section (a) of IOP17 provides that the procedures of IOP16 are, to the extent applicable, to be used in forming the initial calendar of a magistrate judge in the Eastern Division.

The calendar of a magistrate judge differs from that of a district judge in an important way. The calendar of a magistrate judge includes both referrals and cases reassigned on consent. The jurisdictional status of the latter is like that of the cases on the calendars of the district judges. The referrals, however, are simultaneously on the calendars of both a district and a magistrate judge. Accordingly, for the purpose of forming an initial calendar for a magistrate judge, the Court requires that referrals and reassignments on consent be kept separate. The initial calendar for the new magistrate judge will, therefore, involve two reassignment processes: one to select the referrals and the other to select the cases reassigned on consent.

There is another area in which the assignment of cases and referral of matters to magistrate judges differs from the assignment of new cases to regular active district judges. The system of assigning cases to district judges is designed to assure that each regular active judge receives the same number of new cases over time as each of the other regular active judges. Each magistrate judge in the Eastern Division is designated an equal number of times. However, a designation is a potential referral or reassignment on consent, not an actual referral or reassignment. Whether or not a case is referred is a result of many factors, case complexity and the calendar management style of the referring district judge, being just two of the more obvious. As a result, there often arises a significant variance among the magistrate judges in the numbers of referrals they receive. As civil consent cases frequently arise out of referrals, a similar variance occurs in the reassignment of cases on consent.

The formation of an initial calendar for a newly appointed magistrate judge provides and opportunity for the Court to address any calendar imbalances that have arisen among the magistrate judges because of variances in referral and reassignment rates. The default method of preparing an initial calendar is to use the procedures of IOP16, *i.e.*, the same system as that used to create the initial calendar of a new district judge. Under that system each magistrate judge would participate equally in the formation of the initial calendar. However, section (b) provides that the Executive Committee may depart from the equal participation approach of IOP16 and use the process of forming the initial calendar to equalize existing calendars. This may be done in one of four ways: (i) the participation may be limited to the magistrate judges most in need of equalization; or (ii) the participation may be based on the proportions of pending referrals or reassignments on consent rather than equal shares; or (iii) the participation may be based on the proportion of referrals or reassignments on consent received over a specified time period rather than pending numbers. The fourth alternative is simply a catch-all: "or by such other method as the Executive Committee directs in order to achieve equalization of calendars among the magistrate judges."

IOP 18. PERIODIC CALENDAR ADJUSTMENT PROGRAM (DISTRICT JUDGES)

(a) Participation. In order to participate in the program, a judge of the District must meet the following criteria:

(1) The judge is a regular active judge.

(2) The official duty station of the judge is Chicago.

(3) The judge entered on duty a minimum of 60 months preceding the months during which the judge is to be removed from the assignment process as part of the program.

(4) Where 2 or more judges are eligible to be removed from the assignment process under these procedures, they may agree to exchange scheduled adjustment periods for which they have been scheduled provided each of the judges is eligible to serve in the exchanged period.

(b) Order of Judges Within a Cycle. Each year the Executive Committee will enter an order directing the clerk to remove judges from the assignment process for periods of 3 months. Each such order will establish a cycle of four periods. The order of participation in each cycle will be based on the following criteria:

(1) Judges who have not previously participated in the calendar adjustment program shall be scheduled for the first period after they have met the eligibility criteria established in section (a) above.

(2) If two or more judges who have not previously participated are eligible for the same period, the order of their participation shall be based on seniority.

(3) The order of judges' names for any remaining periods in a cycle will be based on the length of time since their last participation in the calendar adjustment program; *i.e.*, the judge with the longest such interval will be assigned to the first available period.

(c) Sequence of Name Confidential. In order to permit the judges to plan to take best advantage of the opportunities offered by the program, a tentative list for 3 years will be issued to each judge at the time a copy of the order implementing the current periods is adopted. However, because knowledge that a judge may be removed from the assignment process might be used to permit judge shopping, the sequence should not be publicized.

(d) Exchanges of Periods. If 2 or more judges tentatively scheduled for the next year agree to change periods with other eligible judges as provided by subsection (a)(4), those involved should notify the chief judge so that the Executive Committee order can incorporate the agreement.

(e) Emergency Judge Schedule. Where a judge's emergency judge period would fall in a period during which the judge is scheduled to be removed from the assignment process under these procedures, the emergency judge assignment will be delayed to the next emergency judge period that falls outside of the non-assignment period.

[Amended July 7, 2000.]

Committee Comment

The essence of the periodic calendar readjustment program is that a judge is taken off the assignment wheel for a period of three months after having an aggregate of at least four years on the assignment wheel. The program is designed to give each judge a three month period approximately every four years where the judge can schedule matters without the pressure of monitoring new cases and the work associated with new cases such as petitions for preliminary injunctions.

The program only applies to the Eastern Division. In general, it has the effect of having one fewer judge on assignment at any point in time. Given that there are 21 judgeships authorized for that Division plus the active senior judges, the share of new cases of one judge divided among the remaining judges results in several additional cases per month for each of the others. The judges have agreed that the scheduling convenience permitted by the program outweighs the small increase in new assignments each receives when not off the wheel.

The program was initially adopted at the judges' meeting of 13 April 1989. It was subsequently amended at the judge's meetings of 17 April 1995 and June 29, 2000.

IOP 19. PERIODIC CALENDAR ADJUSTMENT PROGRAM (MAGISTRATE JUDGES)

(a) Introduction. The periodic calendar adjustment program for magistrate judges provides for a magistrate judge not to receive new referrals in civil or criminal cases, new civil cases reassigned on consent of the parties, or new criminal misdemeanor cases for a period of three months after five years of service.

(b) Participation. In order to participate in the program, a magistrate judge of the District must meet the following criteria:

(1) The magistrate judge is a full-time magistrate judge.

(2) The official duty station of the magistrate judge is Chicago.

(3) The magistrate judge has not previously participated in the program and entered on duty sixty months preceding the months during which the magistrate judge is to be removed from the assignment process as part of the program.

(4) The magistrate judge has previously participated in the program and an aggregate of fifty-one months (forty-eight months plus the three months of the previous adjustment period) has elapsed from the date the magistrate judge was last eligible to participate in the program.

(5) Where two or more magistrate judges are eligible to be removed from the assignment process under these procedures, the magistrate judge who has previously been removed the fewest times under this program will be scheduled first. Where two or more magistrate judges are eligible to be removed from the assignment process under these procedures and each was previously removed the same number of times, the most senior magistrate judge will be scheduled first.

(6) Where two or more magistrate judges are eligible to be removed from the assignment process under

these procedures, they may agree to exchange scheduled adjustment periods for which they have been scheduled in accordance with (5) above provided each of the magistrate judges is eligible to serve in the exchanged period.

(7) A magistrate judge may request to be removed from the assignment process during a period later than that for which the magistrate judge would be scheduled under these procedures provided that no magistrate judge is eligible for that later period.

(c) Order of Magistrate Judges Within Cycle. From time to time, the Executive Committee will enter an order directing the clerk to remove magistrate judges from the assignment process for periods of three months. The first magistrate judge to be removed shall be the most senior magistrate judge who meets the criteria set out in (b) above. The second magistrate judge to be removed shall be the next most senior magistrate judge meeting the criteria, etc.

(d) Sequence of Magistrate Judge Name Confidential. In order to permit the magistrate judges to plan to take best advantage of the opportunities offered by the program, a tentative list for three years will be issued to each magistrate judge at the time a copy of the order implementing the current periods is adopted. However, because knowledge that a magistrate judge may be removed from the assignment process might be used to permit magistrate judge shopping, the sequence should not be publicized.

(e) Order of Executive Committee. The Executive Committee will enter an order annually covering the next four periods. If two or more magistrate judges tentatively scheduled for the next year agree to change periods with other eligible magistrate judges as provided by (b)(6) above, those involved should notify the Chief Judge so that the order can incorporate the agreement.

(f) Conflicts Between Sabbatical and Magistrate Judge Assignment Cycles. A magistrate judge shall not serve as emergency magistrate judge, duty magistrate judge or federal enclave magistrate judge during a period when he or she is participating in the calendar adjustment program.

(g) Referrals and Reassignments on Consent Where the Designated Magistrate Judge is on Sabbatical. Except as provided for in section (h) below, during periods when a magistrate judge is participating in the calendar adjustment program, referrals and reassignments in cases where the magistrate judge has been designated pursuant to LR72.1 shall be randomly referred or reassigned to another magistrate judge.

The magistrate judge who receives a referral or case as provided for by this section shall become the designated magistrate judge in that case.

(h) Subsequent Referrals and Reassignments on Consent in Cases with Pending Referrals. Where a referral is pending in a case before a designated magistrate judge and either the case is to be reassigned on consent or a subsequent referral is to be made in that case during the period when the magistrate judge is participating in the calendar adjustment program, the reassignment or referral shall be made to that magistrate judge. Similarly, where a referral is pending before a designated magistrate judge in one or more cases in a related set of cases and a referral is to be made in another case that is part of the related set during the period when the magistrate judge is participating in the calendar adjustment program, the referral shall be made to that magistrate judge.

(i) Continuation of Designation at Filing. A magistrate judge who is participating in the periodic calendar adjustment program shall not be removed from the designation cycle provided for by LR72.1.

IOP 20. CONSENTS TO PROCEED BEFORE A MAGISTRATE JUDGE

(a) Notice Of Availability. Whenever a civil action is filed in this District, the clerk shall advise the person filing the complaint of the availability of a magistrate judge to exercise jurisdiction by informing the person that the magistrate judge consent form may be obtained on the Court's website. The plaintiff's counsel is responsible for advising the defendant or defendants of the availability of a magistrate judge to exercise jurisdiction.

(b) Notice to Newly Joined Party. Whenever a party is added to a case the district judge or magistrate judge to whom the case is assigned will direct the clerk to inform the additional party of the availability of a magistrate judge to exercise jurisdiction. If the additional party does not consent to proceed before a magistrate judge, the magistrate judge will transfer the case to the calendar of the district judge to whom the case was previously assigned.

(c) Joint Statements of Consent. Parties shall consent to proceed before a magistrate judge by filing a joint statement of consent. The joint statement shall be a form approved by the Executive Committee. Unless the form is completed in open court before the district or magistrate judge, the form shall be filed electronically. The joint statement shall be filed only after all parties have signed it.

[NOTE: Amended by General Order of May 26, 2006.]

IOP 21 TO IOP 24. [RESERVED.]

IOP 25. EMERGENCY DISTRICT JUDGE

(a) Designation of the Emergency Judge. At all times there shall be at least one judge of the Court assigned to act as emergency judge and perform the duties specified in LR77.2. The emergency judge shall be a regular active judge of the Court other than the chief judge or a judge whose duty station is outside the Eastern Division, provided that the chief judge may designate a senior judge to serve as emergency judge if such senior judge consents. No judge shall serve as emergency judge within the six months immediately after taking the oath of office. The chief judge may also serve as emergency judge.

There shall be two cycles for designating emergency judges: one for service during the summer sessions and the other for the balance of the year. Judges shall serve as emergency judge in order of seniority. No judge shall serve a second monthly term until all eligible judges have served a monthly term, nor shall any judge serve a second two week term until all eligible judges have served a two week term. The clerk shall maintain a record of the emergency judge periods served by each judge.

(b) Terms of Service. The term of service of an emergency judge shall start at 12:01 A.M. on Monday and end at midnight on the Sunday immediately preceding the Monday starting the next term of service. The length of service shall be as follows:

(1) during the summer sessions, *i.e.*, the fourteen week period beginning the first Monday in June, the term shall be two weeks; and

(2) during the balance of the year, the term shall be for one month starting with the first Monday of each month, provided that if the first Monday in September falls in the summer session, the September terms of service shall start with the second Monday in September.

(c) Preliminary Assignment Schedules. By 1 April of each year the clerk shall prepare and circulate among the judges preliminary schedules of emergency judges: one for the summer sessions of that year and one covering the service periods from the end of those summer sessions to the start of the next summer sessions. In preparing a preliminary schedule the clerk shall list for the first service period the most senior of the eligible judges who have not yet served in the current service cycle, for the next service period, the next most senior judge, etc. The clerk shall, where appropriate, modify this initial listing, to take into account the following:

(1) *New Judge Exception:* The clerk shall schedule any newly appointed judge who has never served as an emergency judge for the first service period starting not less than 6 months after that judge takes the oath of office. Where there are two or more such judges, the clerk shall schedule them in order of seniority. For the purpose of the records of service in emergency judge cycles kept by the clerk, each judge will be required to serve for a period in the emergen-

cy judge cycle in effect at the time the judge took the oath of office.

(2) *Recent Service Exception:* Even though the judge is otherwise eligible, the clerk shall not include a judge in the preliminary schedule who served as emergency judge in the previous period for which the lists are being prepared, *i.e.,* served as emergency judge in the last summer sessions where a schedule for the summer sessions is being prepared, or served as an emergency judge in the last regular set of service periods where a schedule for those periods is being prepared. The clerk shall re-schedule any judge covered by this exception to the first service in the preliminary lists for the next year.

(3) *IOP18(e) Exception:* If the service period for which a judge is initially scheduled falls within the period during which pursuant to IOP18 the judge is not receiving new assignments, the clerk shall list the judge in the first service period that starts after the IOP18 period ends.

Within 14 days of the date on which the preliminary lists were circulated, any judges agreeing to switch with all or part of a service period for which the judges were scheduled shall so inform the clerk. The clerk shall modify the preliminary schedules accordingly. Within 21 days of the date on which the preliminary lists were circulated, the clerk will prepare and forward to the chief judge a draft of a general order setting out the modified preliminary schedule for emergency judges for the next summer sessions and for the next period between the end of that summer sessions and the start of the next summer sessions.

(d) Formal Schedule Not Published. The order signed by the chief judge constitutes the formal schedule of emergency judge assignments for the period covered by the order. To minimize the potential for judge shopping, the formal schedule is not made public. At the beginning of each week the name of the emergency judge is made available for that week.

(e) Adjustments to Schedule. Should two or more judges agree to change all or part of their service periods after the order fixing the schedule has been entered, they must notify both the chief judge and the clerk. Where the change involves more than a few days, an amended order will be entered incorporating the change.

(f) Absence of Emergency Judge. In the event that the emergency judge will be out of town or otherwise unavailable, the emergency judge will arrange for another judge to act as emergency judge. Where such an arrangement is made, the emergency judge will promptly inform the chief judge and the clerk of the substitution. The chief judge may make such substitution if for any reason it has not been made and the scheduled emergency judge is unavailable.

Where the designated emergency judge is unable to serve as emergency judge due to illness and an order is entered removing the judge from the assignment system due to the same illness, for the purpose of subsequent designations as emergency judge, the designated judge will be considered to have served as emergency judge during the designated period regardless of the amount of time, if any, the judge actually served. The judge or judges assuming the judge's duties will not normally receive any additional credit for the service unless one judge served for the entire period and the chief judge instructs the clerk to credit both the originally designated judge and the serving judge with the period.

IOP 26. EMERGENCY MAGISTRATE JUDGE

(a) Designation Of The Emergency Magistrate Judge. At all times there shall be at least one magistrate judge of the Court assigned to act as emergency magistrate judge and perform the duties specified in LR77.2. Only a magistrate judge whose duty station is in the Eastern Division shall be assigned the duties of emergency magistrate judge. No magistrate judge shall serve as emergency magistrate judge within the six months immediately after taking the oath of office.

(b) Terms of Service. The term of service of an emergency magistrate judge shall be two weeks. It shall start at 12:01 A.M. on Monday and end at midnight on the Sunday immediately preceding the Monday starting the next term of service.

(c) Preliminary Assignment Schedules. The presiding magistrate judge in consultation with the other magistrate judges whose duty stations are in the Eastern Division shall be responsible for preparing a preliminary schedule of the assignments of emergency magistrate judge and federal enclave magistrate judge. These shall be prepared semi-annually in the form of an order to be signed by the chief judge on behalf of the Executive Committee. A copy of the schedule covering the period from the first Monday in July through the Sunday before the first Monday in January shall be delivered to the clerk by 1 May. A copy of the schedule covering the period from the first Monday in January through the Sunday before the first Monday in July shall be delivered to the clerk by 1 November. The clerk will place the preliminary schedule on the agenda of the next meeting of the Executive Committee scheduled after receipt of the preliminary schedules.

(d) Formal Schedule Not Published. With the approval of the Executive Committee the chief judge shall sign an order establishing assignment of emergency and federal enclave magistrate judges. The order signed by the chief judge constitutes the formal schedule of emergency and federal enclave magistrate judge assignments for the period covered by the order. To minimize the potential for judge shopping, the formal schedule is not made public. At the beginning of each week the name of the emergency magistrate judge is made available for that week.

(e) Adjustments to Schedule. Should two or more magistrate judges agree to change all or part of their service periods after the order fixing the schedule has been entered, they must notify the chief judge, the presiding magistrate judge, and the clerk. Where the change involves more than a few days, an amended order will be entered incorporating the change.

(f) Absence of Emergency Magistrate Judge. In the event that the emergency magistrate judge will be out of town or otherwise unavailable, the emergency magistrate judge will arrange for another magistrate judge to act as emergency magistrate judge. Where such an arrangement is made, the emergency magistrate judge will promptly inform the chief judge, the presiding magistrate judge, and the clerk of the substitution. The presiding magistrate judge with the approval of the chief judge may make such substitution if for any reason it has not been made and the scheduled emergency judge is unavailable.

IOP 27. ABSENCE OF ASSIGNED JUDGE

Any judge who plans to be absent from court on a regular business day, during the regular sessions of the Court, should arrange for a judge other than the emergency judge to hear non-emergency matters arising from cases on the judge's calendar. Where such arrangements are made, the judge should instruct the minute clerk to inform the Law Bulletin, so that the designation can be published in that periodical. A copy of the notice for the Law Bulletin should be given to the clerk so that inquiries directed to the clerk's office can be answered. The minute clerk should also post a notice on the door to the courtroom indicating the name of the judge who will hear non-emergency matters and the room number of that judge's courtroom.

IOP 28 TO IOP 29. [RESERVED.]

IOP 30. RESTRICTED DOCUMENTS

(a) Separate Filing Area for Restricted Documents. The clerk shall maintain restricted documents, sealed documents, and documents awaiting expunction as defined by LR26.2(a) separately from the files of documents to which access has not been restricted. Any area used to store documents to which access has been restricted shall be secure from entry by any persons other than the clerk or those designated in writing by the clerk as authorized to have access.

The clerk shall designate in writing deputies authorized to accept restricted documents either from chambers or for filing pursuant to protective orders.

Materials accepted for filing as restricted shall be maintained in a secure area until collected by one of the designated deputies. Where the materials so accepted are being filed pursuant to a protective order, the deputy accepting them will stamp the cover of the document with a FILED stamp indicating the date of filing.

(b) Handling Sealed Documents. Where a document ordered to be sealed, it is to be delivered for filing pursuant to LR5.9 with the seal on the enclosure intact. If the document is sent from chambers or returned from an appellate court with the seal broken, one of the deputies authorized to handle restricted materials pursuant to section (a) will forthwith deliver the document to the courtroom deputy assigned to the judicial officer to whose calendar the proceedings in which the sealed document was filed is assigned. If that judicial officer is no longer sitting, the deputy will forthwith deliver the document to the courtroom deputy assigned to the emergency judge. The courtroom deputy will promptly bring the document to the attention of the judge. The judicial officer will either order that the document be re-sealed, or order that it continue to be handled as a restricted document, but not as a sealed document, or enter such other order as required to indicate the status of the document. Where the document is to be re-sealed, the judicial officer or courtroom deputy will re-seal the document and transmit it to the appropriate deputy in the clerk's office.

Where under the terms of a protective order a party is permitted to inspect a sealed document and that party appears in the clerk's office and requests the document, one of the deputies authorized to handle restricted materials pursuant to section (a) will obtain the document and provide an area where the person may inspect the document other than in the public area of the clerk's office. The deputy will complete a form showing the date, description of the document, the name of the person requesting access to the document, a statement indicating that the deputy has checked the protective order and it does indeed authorize the person to inspect the document, and a statement that the deputy requested of and was shown identification by the person requesting access to the document. Any person wishing to break the seal and inspect the document must sign the form completed by the deputy to indicate that they are authorized to inspect the document and have broken the seal. After the person has completed the inspection, the deputy will follow the procedures set out in the previous paragraph for handling the re-sealing of the document.

Where a restricted document concerning a defendant is submitted electronically by the Pretrial Services Office, the electronic document will be destroyed by the Clerk of Court upon the disposition of the defendant.

(c) Grand Jury Records; Disposition. The clerk shall maintain documents arising out of or connected with grand jury proceedings separately from other restricted documents. The clerk shall designate in writing deputies authorized to accept grand jury documents for filing and authorized access to the area in which the documents are stored.

Such documents shall be maintained for not less than ten years following the date of filing or entry if not related to a specific grand jury proceeding. Documents in proceedings assigned a grand jury number shall be maintained for at least ten years following the commencement of the proceeding as indicated by the GJ number.

From time to time the clerk may petition the chief judge for leave to destroy documents arising out of or connected with grand jury proceedings. The petition shall contain a list of the GJ numbers for documents arising out of specific proceedings and a reasonable description of any documents other than those arising out of specific proceedings for which permission to destroy is sought. The clerk shall provide the United States attorney with a copy of the petition. If the United States attorney wishes to defer the destruction of some or all of the documents referred to in the petition, a written response to the petition setting forth the reasons for the requested deferral must be filed with the chief judge within 14 days of the date the copy of the clerk's petition was transmitted to the United States attorney. The chief judge may grant the petition for destruction, or direct that consideration of the destruction of some or all of the items specified in the petition be deferred for an additional year at the end of which the clerk may again petition for authority to destroy the documents.

The petition for leave to destroy the documents, the response of the United States attorney, and any order of the chief judge dealing with the petition and response are, except as otherwise ordered, restricted documents.

(d) Sanctions. Employees of the court are expressly forbidden to perform any of the following acts:

(1) entering an area designated for the storage of restricted documents without the appropriate written authorization required by sections (a) or (c);

(2) assisting any person who is not authorized access pursuant to sections (a) or (c) to an area designated for the storage of restricted documents to gain or to attempt to gain access to such an area;

(3) accepting for filing any restricted document when not specifically authorized to do so pursuant to section (a);

(4) permitting any person who is not specifically authorized to have access to a restricted document to examine such a document, or to provide such a person with a copy of such a document; and

(5) leaving a restricted document unattended in an area other than one specified by this procedure such that persons not authorized access to the document could readily gain access to it.

Employees of the court who knowingly perform any of these acts shall be subject to disciplinary action, including dismissal. Persons who are not employees of the court who seek to coerce or induce any employee of the Court to perform any of these acts shall be punished by contempt of court.

[Amended effective June 4, 2009; July 6, 2011.]

IOP 31. REGISTRY ACCOUNT

Fed.R.Civ.P. 67 requires the clerk to maintain an interest bearing registry account. The conditions and terms of the agreement between the clerk and the bank maintaining the registry account shall be approved by and be subject to the supervision of the Executive Committee. The relationship of the Court to these funds is custodial in nature, and the United States acts as a trustee for the rightful owners of such funds. The clerk, as the custodial agent for the United States, has no obligation to preserve and keep safe such funds for the depositor and the Court.

Any claimant entitled to any such money may, upon petition to the Court and upon notice to the United States attorney and full proof of the right thereto, obtain an order directing payment to him pursuant to 28 U.S.C. § 2042.

Payment of a registry fee is due and payable on funds held in the Courts' registry and invested in interest-bearing accounts. The fee is equal to the amount prescribed by the Judicial Conference based on the income earned on the invested funds throughout the life of the investments.

IOP 32. DISTRICT COURT FUND

The clerk shall be the trustee of the District Court Fund. Monies deposited in the Fund shall be used only for the benefit of the bench and bar in the administration of justice. All withdrawals from the fund shall require the approval of the chief judge or a judge designated by the chief judge.

APPENDICES

APPENDIX A. STANDING PRETRIAL PROCEDURE ORDER AND FORMS

STANDING ORDER ESTABLISHING PRETRIAL PROCEDURE

(Adopted Pursuant to General Order of 26 June 1985; Amended Pursuant to General Orders of 27 November 1991 and 9 March 1995)

1. Introduction. This pretrial procedure is intended to secure a just, speedy, and inexpensive determination of the issues. If the type of procedure described below does not appear calculated to achieve these ends in this case, counsel should seek an immediate conference with the judge and opposing counsel so that alternative possibilities may be discussed. Failure of either party to comply with the substance or the spirit of this *Standing Order* may result in dismissal of the action, default or other sanctions appropriate under Fed. R. Civ. P. 16 or 37, 28 U.S.C. § 1927 or any other applicable provisions.

Parties should also be aware that there may be variances in the forms and procedures used by each of the judges in implementing these procedures. Accordingly, parties should contact the minute clerk for the assigned judge for a copy of any standing order of that judge modifying these procedures.

2. Scheduling Conference. Within 60 days after the appearance of a defendant and within 90 days after the complaint has been served on a defendant in each civil case (other than categories of cases excepted by local General Rule 5.00), the court will usually set a scheduling conference (ordinarily in the form of a status hearing) as required by Fed.R.Civ.P. 16. At the conference, counsel should be *fully prepared* and have authority to discuss any questions regarding the case, including questions raised by the pleadings, jurisdiction, venue, pending motions, motions contemplated to be filed, the contemplated joinder of additional parties, the probable length of time needed for discovery and the possibility of settlement of the case. Counsel will have the opportunity to discuss any problems confronting them, including the need for time in which to prepare for trial.

3. Procedures for Complex or Protracted Discovery. If at any time during the scheduling conference or later status, hearings it appears that complex or protracted discovery will be sought, the court may

(a) determine that the *Manual on Complex Litigation 2d* be used as a guide for procedures to be followed in the case, or

(b) determine that discovery should proceed by phases, or

(c) require that the parties develop a joint written discovery plan under Fed. R.Civ.P. 26(f).

If the court elects to proceed with phased discovery, the first phase will address information necessary to evaluate the case, lay the foundation for a motion to dismiss or transfer, and explore settlement. At the end of the first phase, the court may require the parties to develop a joint written discovery plan under Fed.R.Civ.P. 26 (f) and this *Standing Order*. If the court requires parties to develop a discovery plan, such plan shall be as specific as possible concerning dates, time, and places discovery will be sought and as to the names of persons whose depositions will be taken. It shall also specify the parties' proposed discovery closing date. Once approved by the court, the plan may be amended only for good cause. Where the parties are unable to agree on a joint discovery plan, each shall submit a plan to the court. After reviewing the separate plans, the court may take such action as it deems appropriate to develop the plan. Where appropriate, the court may also set deadlines for filing and a time framework for the disposition of motions.

4. Discovery Closing Date. In cases subject to this *Standing Order,* the court will, at an appropriate point, set a discovery closing date. Except to the extent specified by the court on motion of either party, discovery must be *completed* before the discovery closing date. Discovery requested before the discovery closing date, but not scheduled for completion before the discovery closing date, does not comply with this order.

5. Settlement. Counsel and the parties are directed to undertake a good faith effort to settle that includes a thorough exploration of the prospects of settlement before undertaking the extensive labor of preparing the Order provided for in the next paragraph. The court may require that representatives of the parties with authority to bind them in settlement discussions be present or available by telephone during any settlement conference.

If the parties wish the court to participate in a settlement conference, counsel should ask the court or the minute clerk to schedule such conference. In a case where the trial will be conducted without a jury, particularly as the case nears the date set for trial, the preferred method of having the court preside over settlement talks is for the assigned judge to arrange for another judge to preside or to refer the task to a magistrate judge. If the case has not been settled and is placed on the court's trial calendar, settlement possibilities should continue to be explored throughout the period before trial. If the case is settled, counsel shall notify the minute clerk promptly and notice up the case for final order.

6. Final Pretrial Order. The court will schedule dates for submission of a proposed final pretrial order (Order) and final pretrial conference (Conference) in accordance with Fed.R.Civ.P. 16. In the period between notice and the date for submission of the pretrial order:

(a) Counsel for all parties are directed to meet in order to (1) reach agreement on any possible stipulations narrowing the issues of law and fact, (2) deal with non-stipulated issues in the manner stated in this paragraph and (3) exchange copies of documents that will be offered in evidence at the trial. The court may direct that counsel meet in person (face-to-face). It shall be the duty of counsel for plaintiff to initiate that meeting and the duty of other counsel to respond to plaintiff's counsel and to offer their full cooperation and assistance to fulfill both the substance and spirit of this standing order. If, after reasonable effort, any party cannot obtain the cooperation of other counsel, it shall be his or her duty to advise the court of this fact by appropriate means.

(b) Counsel's meeting shall be held sufficiently in advance of the date of the scheduled Conference with the court so that counsel for each party can furnish all other counsel with a statement (Statement) of the issues the party will offer evidence to support. The Statement will (1) eliminate any issues that appear in the pleadings about which there is no controversy, and (2) include all issues of law as well as ultimate issues of fact from the standpoint of each party.

(c) It is the obligation of counsel for plaintiff to prepare from the Statement a draft Order for submission to opposing counsel. Included in plaintiff's obligation for preparation of the Order is submission of it to opposing counsel in ample time for revision and timely filing. Full cooperation and assistance of all other counsel are required for proper preparation of the Order to fulfill both the substance and spirit of this Standing Order. All counsel will jointly submit the original and one copy of the final draft of the Order to the judge's chambers (or in open court, if so directed) on the date fixed for submission.

(d) All instructions and footnotes contained within the Final Pretrial Order form promulgated with this *Standing Order* must be followed. They will be binding on the parties at trial in the same manner as though repeated in the Order. If any counsel believes that any of the instructions and/or footnotes allow for any part of the Order to be deferred until after the Order itself is filed, that counsel shall file a motion seeking leave of court for such deferral.

(e) Any pending motions requiring determination in advance of trial (including, without limitation, motions *in limine,* disputes over specific jury instructions or the admissibility of any evidence at trial upon which the parties desire to present authorities and argument to the court) shall be specifically called to the court's attention not later than the date of submission of the Order.

(f) Counsel must consider the following matters during their conference:

(1) Jurisdiction (if any question exists in this respect, it must be identified in the Order);

(2) Propriety of parties; correctness of identity of legal entities; necessity for appointment of guardian, administrator, executor or other fiduciary, and validity of appointment if already made; correctness of designation of party as partnership, corporation or individual d/b/a trade name; and

(3) Questions of misjoinder or nonjoinder of parties.

7. **Final Pretrial Conference.** At the Conference each party shall be represented by the attorneys who will try the case (unless before the conference the court grants permission for other counsel to attend in their place). All attending attorneys will familiarize themselves with the pretrial rules and will come to the Conference with full authority to accomplish the purposes of F.R.Civ.P. 16 (including simplifying the issues, expediting the trial and saving expense to litigants). Counsel shall be prepared to discuss settlement possibilities at the Conference without the necessity of obtaining confirmatory authorization from their clients. If a party represented by counsel desires to be present at the Conference, that party's counsel must notify the adverse parties at least one week in advance of the conference. If a party is not going to be present at the Conference, that party's counsel shall use their best efforts to provide that the client can be contacted if necessary. Where counsel represents a governmental body, the court may for good cause shown authorize that counsel to attend the Conference even if unable to enter into settlement without consultation with counsel s client.

8. **Extensions of Time for Final Pretrial Order or Conference.** It is essential that parties adhere to the scheduled dates for the Order and Conference, for the Conference date governs the case's priority for trial. Because of the scarcity of Conference dates, courtesy to counsel in other cases also mandates no late changes in scheduling. Accordingly, *no* extensions of the Order and Conference dates will be granted without good cause, and no request for extension should be made less than 14 days before the scheduled Conference.

9. **Action Following Final Pretrial Conference.** At the conclusion of the Conference the court will enter an appropriate order reflecting the action taken, and the case will be added to the civil trial calendar. Although no further pretrial conference will ordinarily be held thereafter, a final conference may be requested by any of the parties or ordered by the court prior to trial. Any case ready for trial will be subject to trial as specified by the court.

10. **Documents Promulgated with the *Standing Order*.** Appended to this *Standing Order* are the following:

(a) a form of final pretrial order;

(b) a form for use as Schedule (c), the schedule of exhibits for the final pretrial order;

(c) a form of pretrial memorandum to be attached to the completed final pretrial order in personal injury cases;

(d) a form of pretrial memorandum to be attached to the completed final pretrial order in employment discrimination cases; and

(e) guidelines for preparing proposed findings of fact and conclusions of law.

Each of the forms is annotated to indicate the manner in which it is to be completed.

[Effective January 1, 2002.]

FORM LR 16.1.1.   FINAL PRETRIAL ORDER FORM
IN THE UNITED STATES DISTRICT COURT
FOR THE NORTHERN DISTRICT OF ILLINOIS
[*indicate Eastern or Western*] DIVISION

Plaintiff,[1]	)	
	)	
	)	
v.	)	Civil Action No.
	)	
	)	
Defendant.	)	Judge [*Insert name of*
	)	assigned judge*]*

FINAL PRETRIAL ORDER

This matter having come before the court at a pretrial conference held pursuant to Fed. R. Civ. P. ("Rule") 16, and [*insert name, address and telephone number*] having appeared as counsel for plaintiff(s) and [*insert name, address and telephone number*] having appeared as counsel for defendant(s), the following actions were taken:

(1) This is an action for [*insert nature of action, e.g., breach of contract, personal injury*] and the jurisdiction of the court is invoked under [*insert citation of statute on which jurisdiction based*].   Jurisdiction is (not) disputed.[2]

(2) The following stipulations and statements were submitted and are attached to and made a part of this Order:[3]

(a) a comprehensive stipulation or statement of all uncontested facts, which will become a part of the evidentiary record in the case (and which, in jury trials, may be read to the jury by the court or any party);[4]

(b) for jury trials a short agreed description of the case to be read to prospective jurors.

(c) except for rebuttal exhibits, schedules in the form set out in the attached Schedule (c) of—

(1) all exhibits (all exhibits shall be marked for identification before trial), including documents, summaries, charts and other items expected to be offered in evidence and

(2) any demonstrative evidence and experiments to be offered during trial;[5]

(d) a list or lists of names and addresses of the potential witnesses to be called by each party, with a statement of any objections to calling, or to the qualifications of, any witness identified on the list;[6]

(e) stipulations or statements setting forth the qualifications of each F.R. Evid. 702 witness in such form that the statement can be read to the jury at the time the F.R. Evid. 702 witness takes the stand;[7]

(f) a list of all depositions, and designated page and line numbers, to be read into evidence and statements of any objections thereto;[8]

(g) an itemized statement of damages;

(h)* for a jury trial, each party shall provide the following:

(i) trial briefs except as otherwise ordered by the court;[9]

(ii) one set of marked proposed jury instructions, verdict forms and special interrogatories, if any;[10] and

(iii) a list of the questions the party requests the court to ask prospective jurors in accordance with Fed.R.Civ.P. 47(a);

(i) a statement that each party has completed discovery, including the depositions of F.R. Evid. 702 witnesses (unless the court has previously ordered otherwise). Absent good cause shown, no further discovery shall be permitted;[11] and

(j) subject to full compliance with all the procedural requirements of Rule 37(a)(1), a brief summary of intended motions in limine. Any briefs in support of and responses to such motions shall be filed as directed by the Court.

(2.1) The following *optional* stipulations and statements were submitted and are attached to and made a part of this Order:

(k)* an agreed statement or statements by each party of the contested issues of fact and law and a statement or statements of contested issues of fact or law not agreed to;

(*l*)* waivers of any claims or defenses that have been abandoned by any party;

(m)* for a non-jury trial, each party shall provide proposed *Findings of Fact and Conclusions of Law* in duplicate (see guidelines available from the court's minute clerk or secretary);[12]

(3) Trial of this case is expected to take [*insert the number of days trial expected to take*] days. It will be listed on the trial calendar, to be tried when reached.

(4) [*Indicate the type of trial by placing an X in the appropriate box*]

    Jury ☐   Non-jury ☐

(5) The parties recommend that [*indicate the number of jurors recommended*][13] jurors be selected at the commencement of the trial.

(6) The parties [*insert "agree" or "do not agree" as appropriate*] that the issues of liability and damages [*insert "should" or "should not" as appropriate*] be bifurcated for trial. On motion of any party or on motion of the court, bifurcation may be ordered in either a jury or a non-jury trial.

(7) [*Pursuant to 28 U.S.C. § 636(c), parties may consent to the reassignment of this case to a magistrate judge who may conduct any or all proceedings in a jury or nonjury civil matter and order the entry of judgment in the case. Indicate below if the parties consent to such a reassignment.*]

    ☐ The parties consent to this case being reassigned to a magistrate judge for trial.

(8) This Order will control the course of the trial and may not be amended except by consent of the parties and the court, or by order of the court to prevent manifest injustice.

(9) Possibility of settlement of this case was considered by the parties.

_____

United States District Judge[14]

Date: _____

[Attorneys are to sign the form before presenting it to the court.]

_____   _____

Attorney for Plaintiff   Attorney for Defendant

Schedule (c)

Exhibits[15]

1. The following exhibits were offered by plaintiff, received in evidence and marked as indicated:

[*State identification number and brief description of each exhibit.*]

2. The following exhibits were offered by plaintiff and marked for identification. Defendant(s) objected to their receipt in evidence on the grounds stated:[16]

[*State identification number and brief description of each exhibit. Also state briefly the ground of objection, such as competency, relevancy or materiality, and the provision of Fed.R.Evid. relied upon. Also state briefly plaintiff's response to the objection, with appropriate reference to Fed.R.Evid.*]

3. The following exhibits were offered by defendant, received in evidence and marked as indicated:

[*State identification number and brief description of each exhibit.*]

4. The following exhibits were offered by defendant and marked for identification. Plaintiff objected to their receipt in evidence on the grounds stated:[17]

[*State identification number and brief description of each exhibit. Also state briefly the ground of objection, such as competency, relevancy or materiality, and the provision of Fed.R.Evid. relied upon. Also state briefly defendant's response to the objection, with appropriate reference to Fed.R.Evid.*]

5. Non-objected-to exhibits are received in evidence by operation of this Order. However, in jury trials, exhibits that have not been explicitly referred to in testimony or otherwise published to the jury prior to the close of all evidence or in argument are not in evidence.

[1] Singular forms are used throughout this document. Plural forms should be used as appropriate. Where a third-party defendant is joined pursuant to Rule 14(a), the Order may be suitably modified. In such cases, the caption and the statement of parties and counsel shall be modified to reflect the joiner.

[2] In diversity cases or other cases requiring a jurisdictional amount in controversy, the Order shall contain either a stipulation that the required jurisdictional amount is involved or a brief written statement citing evidence supporting the claim that such sum could reasonably be awarded.

[3] The asterisked (*) options shall not be required unless the court explicitly orders inclusion of one or more of them. On motion of any party or on the court's own motion, any other requirement of the Order may be waived.

[4] Counsel for plaintiff has the responsibility to prepare the initial draft of a proposed stipulation dealing with allegations in the complaint. Counsel for any counter-, cross- or third-party complainant has the same responsibility to prepare a stipulation dealing with allegations in that party's complaints. If the admissibility of any uncontested fact is challenged, the party objecting and the grounds for objection must be stated.

[5] Items not listed will not be admitted unless good cause is shown. Cumulative documents, particularly x-rays and photos, shall be omitted. Duplicate exhibits shall not be scheduled by different parties, but may be offered as joint exhibits. All parties shall stipulate to the authenticity of exhibits whenever possible, and this Order shall identify any exhibits whose authenticity has not been stipulated to and specific reasons for the party's failure so to stipulate. As the attached Schedule (c) form indicates, non-objected-to exhibits which have been explicitly referred to in testimony or stipulation or published to the jury are received in evidence by operation of this Order, without any need for further foundation testimony. Copies of exhibits shall be made available to opposing counsel and a bench book of exhibits shall be prepared and delivered to the court at the start of the trial unless excused by the court. If the trial is a jury trial and counsel desires to display exhibits to the members of the jury, sufficient copies of such exhibits must be made available so as to provide each juror with a copy, or alternatively, enlarged photographic copies or projected copies should be used.

[6] Each party shall indicate which witnesses *will* be called in the absence of reasonable notice to opposing counsel to the contrary, and which *may* be called as a possibility only. Any witness not listed will be precluded from testifying absent good cause shown, except that each party

reserves the right to call such rebuttal witnesses (who are not presently identifiable) as may be necessary, without prior notice to the opposing party.

[7] Only one F.R. Evid. 702 witness on each subject for each party will be permitted to testify absent good cause shown. If more than one F.R. Evid. 702 witness is listed, the subject matter of each expert's testimony shall be specified.

[8] If any party objects to the admissibility of any portion, both the name of the party objecting and the grounds shall be stated. Additionally, the parties shall be prepared to present to the court, at such time as directed to do so, a copy of all relevant portions of the deposition transcript to assist the court in ruling *in limine* on the objection. All irrelevant and redundant material including all colloquy between counsel shall be eliminated when the deposition is read at trial. If a video deposition is proposed to be used, opposing counsel must be so advised sufficiently before trial to permit any objections to be made and ruled on by the court, to allow objectionable material to be edited out of the film before trial.

[9] (*Note: The use of the asterisk (*) is explained in Footnote 3.*) No party's trial brief shall exceed 15 pages without prior approval of the court. Trial briefs are intended to provide full and complete disclosure of the parties' respective theories of the case. Accordingly, each trial brief shall include statements of—

(a) the nature of the case,

(b) the contested facts the party expects the evidence will establish,

(c) the party's theory of liability or defense based on those facts and the uncontested facts,

(d) the party's theory of damages or other relief in the event liability is established, and

(e) the party's theory of any anticipated motion for directed verdict.

The brief shall also include citations of authorities in support of each theory stated in the brief. Any theory of liability or defense that is not expressed in a party's trial brief will be deemed waived.

[10] *Agreed* instructions shall be presented by the parties whenever possible. Whether agreed or unagreed, each marked copy of an instruction shall indicate the proponent and supporting authority and shall be numbered. All objections to tendered instructions shall be in writing and include citations of authorities. Failure to object may constitute a waiver of any objection.

In diversity and other cases where Illinois law provides the rules of decision, use of Illinois Pattern Instructions ("IPI") as to all issues of substantive law is required. As to all other issues, and as to all issues of substantive law where Illinois law does not control, the following pattern jury instructions shall be used in the order listed, e.g., an instruction from (b) shall be used only if no such instruction exists in (a):

(a) the Seventh Circuit pattern jury instructions; or,

(b) any pattern jury instructions published by a federal court. (Care should be taken to make certain substantive instructions on federal questions conform to Seventh Circuit case law.)

At the time of trial, an unmarked original set of instructions and any special interrogatories (on 8½″ × 11″ sheets) shall be submitted to the court; to be sent to the jury room after being read to the jury. Supplemental requests for instructions during the course of the trial or at the conclusion of the evidence will be granted solely as to those matters that cannot be reasonably anticipated at the time of presentation of the initial set of instructions.

[11] If this is a case in which (contrary to the normal requirements) discovery has not been completed, this Order shall state what discovery remains to be completed by each party.

[12] These shall be separately stated in separately numbered paragraphs. Findings of Fact should contain a detailed listing of the relevant material facts the party intends to prove. They should not be in formal language, but should be in simple narrative form. Conclusions of Law should contain concise statements of the meaning or intent of the legal theories set forth by counsel.

[13] Rule 48 specifies that a civil jury shall consist of not fewer than six nor more than twelve jurors.

[14] Where the case has been reassigned on consent of parties to a magistrate judge for all purposes, the magistrate judge will, of course, sign the final pretrial order.

[15] As in the Final Pretrial Order form, references to "plaintiff" and "defendant" are intended to cover those instances where there are more than one of either.

[16] Copies of objected-to exhibits should be delivered to the court with this Order, to permit rulings *in limine* where possible.

[17] *See* footnote 17. [**Publisher's Note:** So in original. Probably should be "16".]

[Effective September 1, 1999. Amended effective July 1, 2008.]

Committee Comment

The amendment to the Final Pretrial Order Form will improve efficiency in litigation.

FORM LR 16.1.2. FORM OF PRETRIAL MEMORANDUM FOR USE IN PERSONAL INJURY CASES

IN THE UNITED STATES DISTRICT COURT
FOR THE NORTHERN DISTRICT OF ILLINOIS
———————— DIVISION

```
                    )
                    )
                    )
        v.          ) Civil Action No.
                    )
                    ) Judge [Insert name of assigned judge]
                    )
                    ) Plaintiff requests $____
                    ) Defendant offers $____
                    )
```

PRETRIAL MEMORANDUM

Plaintiff's Name: ——————
Age: ——————
Occupation: ——————
Marital status: ——————

Attorney for plaintiff [indicate name and phone number of trial attorney]:

————————————————————————
————————————————————————
————————————————————————

Attorney for defendant [indicate name and phone number of trial attorney]:

————————————————————————
————————————————————————
————————————————————————

Summary of injuries [note especially any permanent pathology]:

————————————————————————
————————————————————————
————————————————————————

Date, hour, and place of occurrence:

————————————————————————

Attending physicians:

————————————————————————

Hospitals:

————————————————————————

Place of employment:

————————————————————————
————————————————————————

Part A. Compensatory Damages [Parts A & B are to be completed by plaintiff's counsel.]
    1. Liquidated Damages:

    (a) Medical fees $_____

    (b) Hospital bills $_____

    (c) Loss of income $_____

    (d) Miscellaneous expenses $_____

        TOTAL $_____

2. What is the total amount of compensatory damages claimed
in this action? $_____

Part B. Punitive Damages

    a. Does the plaintiff claim punitive damages?

        Yes ☐   No ☐   If yes, how much? $_____

Brief Statement of Circumstances of Occurrence:

Plaintiff's view:

_____

_____

_____

_____

Defendant's view:

_____

_____

_____

_____

*[At the direction of the court the parties are to attach to this
memorandum any medical reports or other materials
useful for discussion at the pretrial conference.]*

[Effective September 1, 1999.]

FORM LR 16.1.3   FORM OF PRETRIAL MEMORANDUM FOR USE IN EMPLOYMENT DISCRIMINATION CASES

IN THE UNITED STATES DISTRICT COURT
FOR THE NORTHERN DISTRICT OF ILLINOIS
———— DIVISION

	)	Civil Action No.
	)	
v.	)	Judge [*Insert name of assigned judge*]
	)	
	)	

PRETRIAL MEMORANDUM

Attorney for plaintiff [*Indicate name and phone number of trial attorney*]:

_____

_____

Plaintiff's brief summary of claim and statement of employment action:

_____

_____

_____

Attorney for defendant [*Indicate name and phone number of trial attorney*]:

_____

_____

Defendant's brief summary of defenses and statement of employment action:

_____

_____

_____

[*Plaintiff's counsel will complete Part A, Plaintiff's Summary of Damages, and defendant's counsel will complete Part B, Defendant's Summary of Damages, Assuming Liability. As indicated in the title to Part B, defendant's counsel must complete the section using the assumption of liability, even though defendant disputes liability.*]

Part A. Plaintiff's Summary of Damages

1. Lost Wages and Benefits: [*For each year for which damages are claimed, indicate (A) the total wages and benefits that would have been earned working for defendant but for the discrimination, (B) the total wages, benefits, and other income earned in substitute employment that plaintiff was able to obtain, (C) additional wages and benefits defendant maintains plaintiff could have earned, and (D) the difference between (A) and the total of (B) + (C)*].

Year[1]	A Amounts Lost Due to Discrimination	B Amounts Earned in Substitute Employment	C Additional Amounts Could Have Earned	D Difference (A-(B + C))
19___	_____	_____	_____	_____
19___	_____	_____	_____	_____
		Total Lost Wages & Benefits:		$_____

2. (a) Attorneys Fees (to date): $_____

(b) Costs (to date): $ _____

3. Do you claim:
  (a) Pain, suffering, emotional injury, etc.?
    Yes ☐   No ☐   If yes, how much? $ _____
  (b) Punitive or liquidated (double) damages?
    Yes ☐   No ☐   If yes, how much? $ _____
  (c) Pre-judgment interest?[2]
    Yes ☐   No ☐   If yes, how much? $ _____

4. Do you claim any other kinds of damage?
    Yes ☐   No ☐   If yes, what kind and how
    much? _____ $ _____

5. Total Amount Claimed: $ _____

Part B. Defendant's Summary of Damages, Assuming Liability [*This portion is to be completed in good faith even though defendant disputes liability.*]

1. [*For each year for which damages are claimed, indicate (A) the total wages and benefits that would have been earned working for defendant but for the discrimination, (B) the total wages, benefits, and other income earned in substitute employment that plaintiff was able to obtain, (C) additional wages and benefits defendant maintains plaintiff could have earned, (D) other amounts received, such as disability or pension payments, and (E) the difference between (A) and the total of (B) + (C) + (D).*]

	A Amounts Lost Due to	B Amounts Earned in Substitute	C Additional Amounts Could Have	D Other Amounts	E Difference
Year[3]	Discrimination	Employment	Earned	Received	(A-(B+C+D))
19__	_____	_____	_____	_____	_____
19__	_____	_____	_____	_____	_____

Total Lost Wages & Benefits: $ _____

2. Does the defendant dispute the amount claimed for attorney's fees and costs?
    Yes ☐   No ☐   If yes, explain, giving estimated amount due:
_____
_____ $ _____

3. Does the defendant dispute the amount claimed for pain, suffering, emotional injury, etc.?
    Yes ☐   No ☐   If yes, explain, giving estimated amount due:
_____
_____ $ _____

4. Does the defendant dispute the claim for pre-judgment interest?
    Yes ☐   No ☐   If yes, explain, giving estimated amount due:
_____
_____ $ _____

5. Does the defendant dispute the claim for punitive damages?
    Yes ☐   No ☐   If yes, explain, giving estimated amount due:
_____
_____ $ _____

6. Does the defendant dispute any other claims for damages made by the plaintiff?
    Yes ☐   No ☐   If yes, explain, giving estimated amount due:
_____ $ _____
_____ $ _____

7. Total amount owed, assuming liability: $ _____
_____ $ _____
_____

---

[1] Only two years are shown. Use the appropriate number of years in completing the form.

[2] The inclusion of both liquidated damages and pre-judgment interest in this form is not intended to suggest that both are or are not recoverable.

3 Only two years are shown. Use the appropriate number of years in completing the form.

[Effective September 1, 1999.]

FORM LR 26.2.   MODEL CONFIDENTIALITY ORDER

UNITED STATES DISTRICT COURT
NORTHERN DISTRICT OF ILLINOIS

	)	
	)	
Plaintiff	)	
	)	
v.	)	Civil No.
	)	District Judge
	)	Magistrate Judge
	)	
Defendant	)	

[Agreed][1] Confidentiality Order

[if by agreement] The parties to this Agreed Confidentiality Order have agreed to the terms of this Order; accordingly, it is ORDERED:

[if not fully agreed] A party to this action has moved that the Court enter a confidentiality order. The Court has determined that the terms set forth herein are appropriate to protect the respective interests of the parties, the public, and the Court. Accordingly, it is ORDERED:

1. **Scope.** All materials produced or adduced in the course of discovery, including initial disclosures, responses to discovery requests, deposition testimony and exhibits, and information derived directly therefrom (hereinafter collectively "documents"), shall be subject to this Order concerning Confidential Information as defined below. This Order is subject to the Local Rules of this District and the Federal Rules of Civil Procedure on matters of procedure and calculation of time periods.

2. **Confidential Information.** As used in this Order, "Confidential Information" means information designated as "CONFIDENTIAL—SUBJECT TO PROTECTIVE ORDER" by the producing party that falls within one or more of the following categories: (a) information prohibited from disclosure by statute; (b) information that reveals trade secrets; (c) research, technical, commercial or financial information that the party has maintained as confidential; (d) medical information concerning any individual; (e) personal identity information; (f) income tax returns (including attached schedules and forms), W–2 forms and 1099 forms; or (g) personnel or employment records of a person who is not a party to the case[2] Information or documents that are available to the public may not be designated as Confidential Information.

3. **Designation.**

(a) A party may designate a document as Confidential Information for protection under this Order by placing or affixing the words "CONFIDENTIAL—SUBJECT TO PROTECTIVE ORDER" on the document and on all copies in a manner that will not interfere with the legibility of the document. As used in this Order, "copies" includes electronic images, duplicates, extracts, summaries or descriptions that contain the Confidential Information. The marking "CONFIDENTIAL—SUBJECT TO PROTECTIVE ORDER" shall be applied prior to or at the time of the documents are produced or disclosed. Applying the marking "CONFIDENTIAL—SUBJECT TO PROTECTIVE ORDER" to a document does not mean that the document has any status or protection by statute or otherwise except to the extent and for the purposes of this Order. Any copies that are made of any documents marked "CONFIDENTIAL—SUBJECT TO PROTECTIVE ORDER" shall also be so marked, except that indices, electronic databases or lists of documents that do not contain substantial portions or images

365

of the text of marked documents and do not otherwise disclose the substance of the Confidential Information are not required to be marked.

(b) The designation of a document as Confidential Information is a certification by an attorney or a party appearing pro se that the document contains Confidential Information as defined in this order.[3]

4. Depositions.[4]

Alternative A. Deposition testimony is protected by this Order only if designated as "CONFIDENTIAL—SUBJECT TO PROTECTIVE ORDER" on the record at the time the testimony is taken. Such designation shall be specific as to the portions that contain Confidential Information. Deposition testimony so designated shall be treated as Confidential Information protected by this Order until fourteen days after delivery of the transcript by the court reporter to any party or the witness. Within fourteen days after delivery of the transcript, a designating party may serve a Notice of Designation to all parties of record identifying the specific portions of the transcript that are designated Confidential Information, and thereafter those portions identified in the Notice of Designation shall be protected under the terms of this Order. The failure to serve a timely Notice of Designation waives any designation of deposition testimony as Confidential Information that was made on the record of the deposition, unless otherwise ordered by the Court.

Alternative B. Unless all parties agree on the record at the time the deposition testimony is taken, all deposition testimony taken in this case shall be treated as Confidential Information until the expiration of the following: No later than the fourteenth day after the transcript is delivered to any party or the witness, and in no event later than 60 days after the testimony was given, Within this time period, a party may serve a Notice of Designation to all parties of record as to specific portions of the testimony that are designated Confidential Information, and thereafter only those portions identified in the Notice of Designation shall be protected by the terms of this Order. The failure to serve a timely Notice of Designation shall waive any designation of testimony taken in that deposition as Confidential Information, unless otherwise ordered by the Court.

5. Protection of Confidential Material.

(a) General Protections. Confidential Information shall not be used or disclosed by the parties, counsel for the parties or any other persons identified in subparagraph (b) for any purpose whatsoever other than in this litigation, including any appeal thereof. **[INCLUDE IN PUTATIVE CLASS ACTION CASE:** In a putative class action, Confidential Information may be disclosed only to the named plaintiff(s) and not to any other member of the putative class unless and until a class including the putative member has been certified.]

(b) Limited Third–Party Disclosures. The parties and counsel for the parties shall not disclose or permit the disclosure of any Confidential Information to any third person or entity except as set forth in subparagraphs (1)–(9). Subject to these requirements, the following categories of persons may be allowed to review Confidential Information:

    (1) **Counsel.** Counsel for the parties and employees of counsel who have responsibility for the action;

    (2) **Parties.** Individual parties and employees of a party but only to the extent counsel determines in good faith that the employee's assistance is reasonably necessary to the conduct of the litigation in which the information is disclosed;

    (3) **The Court and its personnel;**

    (4) **Court Reporters and Recorders.** Court reporters and recorders engaged for depositions;

(5) **Contractors.** Those persons specifically engaged for the limited purpose of making copies of documents or organizing or processing documents, including outside vendors hired to process electronically stored documents;

(6) **Consultants and Experts.** Consultants, investigators, or experts employed by the parties or counsel for the parties to assist in the preparation and trial of this action but only after such persons have completed the certification contained in Attachment A, Acknowledgment of Understanding and Agreement to Be Bound;

(7) **Witnesses at Depositions.** During their depositions, witnesses in this action to whom disclosure is reasonably necessary. Witnesses shall not retain a copy of documents containing Confidential Information, except witnesses may receive a copy of all exhibits marked at their depositions in connection with review of the transcripts. Pages of transcribed deposition testimony or exhibits to depositions that are designated as Confidential Information pursuant to the process set out in this Order must be separately bound by the court reporter and may not be disclosed to anyone except as permitted under this Order.

(8) **Author or Recipient.** The author or recipient of the document (not including a person who received the document in the course of litigation); and

(9) **Others by Consent.** Other persons only by written consent of the producing party or upon order of the Court and on such conditions as may be agreed or ordered.

(c) **Control of Documents.** Counsel for the parties shall make reasonable efforts to prevent unauthorized or inadvertent disclosure of Confidential Information. Counsel shall maintain the originals of the forms signed by persons acknowledging their obligations under this Order for a period of three years after the termination of the case.

6. **Inadvertent Failure to Designate.** An inadvertent failure to designate a document as Confidential Information does not, standing alone, waive the right to so designate the document; provided, however, that a failure to serve a timely Notice of Designation of deposition testimony as required by this Order, even if inadvertent, waives any protection for deposition testimony. If a party designates a document as Confidential Information after it was initially produced, the receiving party, on notification of the designation, must make a reasonable effort to assure that the document is treated in accordance with the provisions of this Order. No party shall be found to have violated this Order for failing to maintain the confidentiality of material during a time when that material has not been designated Confidential Information, even where the failure to so designate was inadvertent and where the material is subsequently designated Confidential Information.

7. **Filing of Confidential Information.** This Order does not, by itself, authorize the filing of any document under seal. Any party wishing to file a document designated as Confidential Information in connection with a motion, brief or other submission to the Court must comply with LR26.2.

8. **No Greater Protection of Specific Documents.** Except on privilege grounds not addressed by this Order, no party may withhold information from discovery on the ground that it requires protection greater than that afforded by this Order unless the party moves for an order providing such special protection.

9. **Challenges by a Party to Designation as Confidential Information.** The designation of any material or document as Confidential Information is subject to challenge by any party. The following procedure shall apply to any such challenge.

(a) **Meet and Confer.** A party challenging the designation of Confidential Information must do so in good faith and must begin the process by conferring directly with counsel for the designating party. In conferring, the challenging party must explain the basis for its belief that the confidentiality designation was not proper and must give the designating party an opportunity to review the designated material, to reconsider the designation, and, if no change in designation is offered, to explain the basis for the designation. The designating party must respond to the challenge within five (5) business days.

(b) Judicial Intervention. A party that elects to challenge a confidentiality designation may file and serve a motion that identifies the challenged material and sets forth in detail the basis for the challenge. Each such motion must be accompanied by a competent declaration that affirms that the movant has complied with the meet and confer requirements of this procedure. The burden of persuasion in any such challenge proceeding shall be on the designating party. Until the Court rules on the challenge, all parties shall continue to treat the materials as Confidential Information under the terms of this Order.

10. Action by the Court. Applications to the Court for an order relating to materials or documents designated Confidential Information shall be by motion. Nothing in this Order or any action or agreement of a party under this Order limits the Court's power to make orders concerning the disclosure of documents produced in discovery or at trial.

11. Use of Confidential Documents or Information at Trial. Nothing in this Order shall be construed to affect the use of any document, material, or information at any trial or hearing. A party that intends to present or that anticipates that another party may present Confidential information at a hearing or trial shall bring that issue to the Court's and parties' attention by motion or in a pretrial memorandum without disclosing the Confidential Information. The Court may thereafter make such orders as are necessary to govern the use of such documents or information at trial.

12. Confidential Information Subpoenaed or Ordered Produced in Other Litigation.

(a) If a receiving party is served with a subpoena or an order issued in other litigation that would compel disclosure of any material or document designated in this action as Confidential Information, the receiving party must so notify the designating party, in writing, immediately and in no event more than three court days after receiving the subpoena or order. Such notification must include a copy of the subpoena or court order.

(b) The receiving party also must immediately inform in writing the party who caused the subpoena or order to issue in the other litigation that some or all of the material covered by the subpoena or order is the subject of this Order. In addition, the receiving party must deliver a copy of this Order promptly to the party in the other action that caused the subpoena to issue.

(c) The purpose of imposing these duties is to alert the interested persons to the existence of this Order and to afford the designating party in this case an opportunity to try to protect its Confidential Information in the court from which the subpoena or order issued. The designating party shall bear the burden and the expense of seeking protection in that court of its Confidential Information, and nothing in these provisions should be construed as authorizing or encouraging a receiving party in this action to disobey a lawful directive from another court. The obligations set forth in this paragraph remain in effect while the party has in its possession, custody or control Confidential Information by the other party to this case.

13. Challenges by Members of the Public to Sealing Orders. A party or interested member of the public has a right to challenge the sealing of particular documents that have been filed under seal, and the party asserting confidentiality will have the burden of demonstrating the propriety of filing under seal.

14. Obligations on Conclusion of Litigation.

(a) **Order Continues in Force.** Unless otherwise agreed or ordered, this Order shall remain in force after dismissal or entry of final judgment not subject to further appeal.

(b) **Obligations at Conclusion of Litigation.** Within sixty-three days after dismissal or entry of final judgment not subject to further appeal, all Confidential Information and documents marked "CONFIDENTIAL—SUBJECT TO PROTECTIVE ORDER" under this Order, including copies as defined in ¶ 3(a), shall be returned to the producing party unless: (1) the document has been offered into evidence or filed without restriction as to disclosure; (2) the parties agree to destruction to the extent practicable in lieu of return;[5] or (3) as to documents bearing the notations, summations, or other mental impressions of the receiving party, that party elects to destroy the documents and certifies to the producing party that it has done so.

(c) **Retention of Work Product and one set of Filed Documents.** Notwithstanding the above requirements to return or destroy documents, counsel may retain (1) attorney work product, including an index that refers or relates to designated Confidential Information so long as that work product does not duplicate verbatim substantial portions of Confidential Information, and (2) one complete set of all documents filed with the Court including those filed under seal. Any retained Confidential Information shall continue to be protected under this Order. An attorney may use his or her work product in subsequent litigation, provided that its use does not disclose or use Confidential Information.

(d) **Deletion of Documents Filed Under Seal from Electronic Case Filing (ECF) System.** Filings under seal shall be deleted from the ECF system only upon order of the Court.

15. **Order Subject to Modification.** This Order shall be subject to modification by the Court on its own initiative or on motion of a party or any other person with standing concerning the subject matter.

16. **No Prior Judicial Determination.** This Order is entered based on the representations and agreements of the parties and for the purpose of facilitating discovery. Nothing herein shall be construed or presented as a judicial determination that any document or material designated Confidential Information by counsel or the parties is entitled to protection under Rule 26(c) of the Federal Rules of Civil Procedure or otherwise until such time as the Court may rule on a specific document or issue.

17. **Persons Bound.** This Order shall take effect when entered and shall be binding upon all counsel of record and their law firms, the parties, and persons made subject to this Order by its terms.

So Ordered.

Dated: _____   _____
                                  U.S. District Judge
                                  U.S. Magistrate Judge

[Delete signature blocks if not wholly by agreement]
WE SO MOVE   **WE SO MOVE**
and agree to abide by the   **and agree to abide by the**
terms of this Order   **terms of this Order**

_____   _____
Signature   Signature

_____   _____
Printed Name   Printed Name

Counsel for: _____   Counsel for: _____

Dated: Dated:

_____   _____

ATTACHMENT A

UNITED STATES DISTRICT COURT
NORTHERN DISTRICT OF ILLINOIS

	)	
	)	Civil No.
Plaintiff	)	
	)	
	)	
	)	
Defendant	)	

ACKNOWLEDGMENT
AND
AGREEMENT TO BE BOUND

The undersigned hereby acknowledges that he/she has read the Confidentiality Order dated _____ in the above-captioned action and attached hereto, understands the terms thereof, and agrees to be bound by its terms. The undersigned submits to the jurisdiction of the United States District Court for the Northern District of Illinois in matters relating to the Confidentiality Order and understands that the terms of the Confidentiality Order obligate him/her to use materials designated as Confidential Information in accordance with the Order solely for the purposes of the above-captioned action, and not to disclose any such Confidential Information to any other person, firm or concern.

The undersigned acknowledges that violation of the Confidentiality Order may result in penalties for contempt of court.

Name: _____

Job Title: _____

Employer: _____

Business Address: _____

_____

_____

Date: _____ _____
                 Signature

ENTER:

FOR THE COURT

_____

Chief Judge

Dated at Chicago, Illinois this <u>18th</u> day of October, 2012

[Revised: October 18, 2012.]

1Counsel should include or delete language in brackets as necessary to the specific case. **Any other changes to this model order must be shown by redlining that indicates both deletions and additions to the model text.** Counsel may also modify this model order as appropriate for the circumstances of the case. This model order is for the convenience of the parties and the court and not intended to create a presumption in favor of the provisions in this model order and against alternative language proposed by the parties. The court will make the final decision on the terms of any order notwithstanding the agreement of the parties.

2If protection is sought for any other category of information, the additional category shall be described in paragraph 2 with the additional language redlined to show the change in the proposed Order.

3An attorney who reviews the documents and designates them as CONFIDENTIAL—SUBJECT TO PROTECTIVE ORDER must be admitted to the Bar of at least one state but need not be admitted to practice in the Northern District of Illinois unless the lawyer is appearing generally in the case on behalf of a party. By designating documents confidential pursuant to this Order, counsel submits to the jurisdiction and sanctions of this Court on the subject matter of the designation.

4The parties or movant seeking the order shall select one alternative for handling deposition testimony and delete by redlining the alternative provision that is not chosen.

5The parties may choose to agree that the receiving party shall destroy documents containing Confidential Information and certify the fact of destruction, and that the receiving party shall not be required to locate, isolate and return e-mails (including attachments to e-mails) that may include Confidential Information, or Confidential Information contained in deposition transcripts or drafts or final expert reports.

GUIDELINES FOR PROPOSED FINDINGS OF FACT AND CONCLUSIONS OF LAW

(a) Plaintiff shall first provide the court with proposed findings and conclusions, which shall have been served on each defendant. Each defendant shall then provide the court with answering proposals, which shall have been served on each plaintiff.

(b) Plaintiff's proposals shall include (a) a narrative statement of *all facts* proposed to be proved and (b) a concise statement of plaintiff's legal contentions and the authorities supporting them:

(1) Plaintiff's narrative statement of facts shall set forth in simple declarative sentences all the facts relied upon in support of plaintiff's claim for relief. It shall be complete in itself and shall contain no recitation of any witness' testimony or what any defendant stated or admitted in these or other proceedings, and no references to the pleadings or other documents or schedules as such. It may contain references in parentheses to the names of witnesses, depositions, pleadings, exhibits or other documents, but no party shall be required to admit or deny the accuracy of such references. It shall, so far as possible, contain no pejoratives, labels or legal conclusions. It shall be so constructed, in consecutively numbered paragraphs (though where appropriate a paragraph may contain more than one sentence), that each of the opposing parties will be able to admit or deny each separate sentence of the statement.

(2) Plaintiff's statement of legal contentions shall set forth all such plaintiff's contentions necessary to demonstrate the liability of each defendant to such plaintiff. Such contentions shall be separately, clearly and concisely stated in separately numbered paragraphs. Each paragraph shall be followed by citations of authorities in support thereof.

(c) Each defendant's answering proposals shall correspond to plaintiff's proposals:

(1) Each defendant's factual statement shall admit or deny each separate sentence contained in the narrative statement of fact of each plaintiff, except in instances where a portion of a sentence can be admitted and a portion denied. In those instances, each defendant shall state clearly the portion admitted and the portion denied. Each separate sentence of each defendant's response shall bear the same number as the corresponding sentence in the plaintiff's narrative statement of fact. In a separate portion of each defendant's narrative statement of facts, such defendant shall set forth all affirmative matter of a factual nature relied upon by such defendant, constructed in the same manner as the plaintiff's narrative statement of facts.

(2) Each defendant's separate statement of proposed conclusions of law shall respond directly to plaintiff's separate legal contentions and shall contain such additional contentions of the defendant as may be necessary to demonstrate the non-liability or limited liability of the defendant. Each defendant's statement of legal contentions shall be constructed in the same manner as is provided for the similar statement of each plaintiff.

[NOTE: This Guideline was amended by General Order of May 4, 2004]

[Effective January 1, 2002; Amended effective May 4, 2004.]

APPENDIX TO LOCAL RULE 54.3.   SAMPLE JOINT STATEMENT

Pursuant to section (e) of LR54.3, the parties submit the following Joint Statement with respect to the motion for fees and expenses filed by [*name of movant*]:

1. [*name of movant*] claims attorney's fees of $102,425 and related nontaxable expenses of $12,578.40. [*name of movant*] calculates this claim as follows:

Lawyer	Hours	Rate	Totals
Smith	300	$245	73,500
Jones	175	$110	19,250
Johnson	65	$ 95	6,175
Wilson (paralegal)	70	$ 50	3,500
Total			$ 102,425

2. The position of [*name of respondent*] is that fees should be awarded on the following basis:

Lawyer	Hours	Rate	Totals
Smith	200	$200	40,000
Jones	175	$110	19,250
Johnson	40	$ 95	3,800
Wilson	70	$ 50	3,500
Total			$ 66,550

Respondent's position is that related nontaxable expenses of $11,380.00 should be awarded.

3. The specific disputes remaining between the parties are the following:

(a) The appropriate hourly rate for Smith;

(b) Whether 100 hours spent by Smith and 25 hours spent by Johnson on the state claim should be compensated;

(c) Whether $1,198.40 spent on deposition transcripts of four specific witnesses (Banks, Davis, George, and Penny) should be compensable.

4. The underlying judgment in the case will not be appealed and the only remaining dispute in the litigation is the appropriate fee award.

FORM LR 65.1.   IRREVOCABLE STANDBY LETTER OF CREDIT

IN THE UNITED STATES DISTRICT COURT
FOR THE NORTHERN DISTRICT OF ILLINOIS
[*circle Eastern or Western*] DIVISION

Plaintiff,   )
)
) Civil Action No.
v   ) Judge [*Insert name of assigned judge*]
)
Defendant.   )
)

LETTER OF CREDIT NO: _____

DATE _____

BENEFICIARY: APPLICANT:

_____   _____

_____   _____

_____   _____

_____   _____

AMOUNT: _____

EXPIRATION DATE: _____

PURPOSE: _____

_____

_____

_____

_____

We, [FINANCIAL INSTITUTION], hereby establish our Irrevocable Standby Letter of Credit No: _____ for the account of _____ for an amount or amounts not to exceed in the aggregate U.S. $ _____ available by your drafts at sight and accompanied by a proper court order.

This letter of credit is unconditional and irrevocable.

[Adopted July 1, 2008.]

FORM LR 83.28. DECLARATION OF ADMISSIONS
TO PRACTICE REQUIRED BY LR 83.28(D)

DECLARATION OF ADMISSIONS TO PRACTICE

In Re _____

Disciplinary No. _____

    I, _____, am the attorney who has been served with an order to show cause why disciplinary action should not be taken in the above captioned matter.

    I am a member of the bar of this Court.

    I have been admitted to practice before the following state and federal courts, in the years, and under the license record numbers shown below:

    I declare under penalty of perjury that the foregoing is true and correct.

Executed on _____
                  (Date)

_____
                  (Signature)

_____
            (Full name—typed or printed)

_____

_____
            (Address of Record)

    This declaration must be signed, and delivered to the court with the attorney's answer to the order to show cause or any waiver of an answer. Failure to return this declaration may subject an attorney to further disciplinary action. Under 28 U.S.C. § 1746, this declaration under perjury has the same force and effect as a sworn declaration made under oath.

[Effective September 1, 1999.]

FORM LCrR 46.1. FORM TO BE COMPLETED BY THE PERSON DEPOSITING CASH TO SECURE A BOND

United States District Court
Northern District of Illinois
_____ Division

FORM TO BE COMPLETED BY THE PERSON DEPOSITING CASH
TO SECURE A BOND

Defendant's Name:_____

Case No:_____

I, *(Name of person depositing cash)* state that I am the person making the cash deposit of *(Amount of cash)* to secure the bond of defendant *(Name of the defendant whose bond is secured by this deposit)*.

I directed the Clerk of the Court to refund this cash deposit as follows *(Initial one or both and indicate the amount(s) to be refunded)*:

$*(Amount)* to me   *(Initials)*
$*(Amount)* to   *(Name of person to receive refund)* *(Initials)* of
                 (Street address)
                 (City, State and ZIP code)
                              (Signature of depositor)
Date: _____   *(Street address of depositor)*
Receipt No. ____   *(City, State and ZIP code of depositor)*

INSTRUCTIONS

1. *The person depositing cash with the clerk to secure the release of a defendant in a criminal case shall complete the form on the reverse. (The cashier will provide the receipt number.)*

2. *Refunds of cash deposits are governed by LCrR46.1(c).*

3. *The clerk will refund monies deposited without additional order of court only to the person or persons indicated on the reverse of this document.*

4. *In order to make the payment without specific order of court the clerk requires that this document, the original receipt, and the assignment, if any, be surrendered to the cashier at the time the request for refund was made.*

[Effective September 1, 1999.]

FORM LCrR 46.5(b)(2)   NON-DISCLOSURE AGREEMENT
FOR RESEARCH GROUPS
NON-DISCLOSURE AGREEMENT
FOR RESEARCH GROUPS

Whereas *(Name of person or organization)* has been granted access to records, reports and files of the Pretrial Services Agency *(Agency)* of the United States District Court for the *(name of district)* (District Court) hereby acknowledges and agrees that any information, including records, reports, files, or oral communications, it receives from the Agency with respect to criminal defendants is strictly confidential as provided by LCrR46.5, a copy of which is attached and is not to be disclosed to any parties, other than the Agency and Federal District Court, except in the matter of a research analysis and paper which shall not identify, directly or indirectly, the identities of any of the Agency subjects.

Upon a breach of this non-disclosure agreement, the Agency may withdraw access to its files and records by *(Name of person or organization)*, or take such lesser steps as are commensurate with the breach of confidentiality.

[Effective September 1, 1999.]

FORM LCrR 46.5(b)(3)   NON-DISCLOSURE AGREEMENT FOR ORGANIZATIONS PROVIDING CONTRACT SERVICES
TO BE ADDED AS COVENANT TO
CONTRACT NON–DISCLOSURE
AGREEMENT FOR CONTRACT SERVICES

(Name of person or organization) hereby acknowledges and agrees that any information, including records, reports, files, or oral communications, it receives from the Pretrial Services Agency (Agency) of the United States District Court for the *(Name of district)* (District Court) with respect to criminal defendants is strictly confidential as provided by LCrR46.5, a copy of which is attached, and is not to be disclosed, except as provided by that rule, to any parties, individuals or organizations, other than the Agency and District Court. *(Name of person or organization)* further agrees that it will not identify, directly or indirectly any individual Agency subject in any report of research, evaluation, periodic audits or studies, or in any articles for publication of any kind, or in any verbal disclosures, except in reports required by or to the referring Agency or the District Court.

It is understood and agreed that the Agency will be notified promptly by *(Name of person or organization)* of any subpoena or other request for information that pertains to Agency information.

Upon a breach of this non-disclosure agreement, the Agency is entitled to terminate the contract relationship with *(Name of person or organization)* or to take whatever lesser steps are necessary to prevent further breaches of this agreement.

[Effective September 1, 1999.]

APPENDIX B.   PROCEDURES FOR VOLUNTARY MEDIATION PROGRAM FOR LANHAM ACT CASES

UNITED STATES DISTRICT COURT
NORTHERN DISTRICT OF ILLINOIS
PROCEDURES FOR VOLUNTARY MEDIATION
PROGRAM
FOR LANHAM ACT CASES

Adopted Pursuant to Local Rule 16.3(b)

I.   SCREENING AND ASSIGNMENT OF CASES.

A.   Pursuant to Local Rule 16.3, cases that are filed under the Federal Trademark Act of 1946, 15 U.S.C. §§ 1051–1127 (the "Lanham Act"), shall be assigned to the program of court-annexed mediation (Program). Cases that are filed under seal pursuant to local General Rule 10L and cases that are under seal pursuant to court order shall not be assigned to the Program during the time they remain under seal. Any time periods specified in these procedures shall be adjusted to exclude periods when cases are under seal.

B.   Cases shall be assigned to the Program on the basis of information recorded in the Integrated Case Management System (ICMS). The information used for this purpose will be the nature of suit and cause of action recorded for each civil case. A computer program will be run on a weekly basis to identify all civil cases filed during the previous week where the cause of action entered in ICMS is a Lanham Act citation or the nature of suit code entered in ICMS is 840 (i.e., the nature of suit code for trademark cases).

C.   A member of the staff of the Clerk of Court will check the complaint for each case identified by the weekly computer program to verify that the complaint indicates that the case has been filed pursuant to the Lanham Act.

II.   NOTICE OF ASSIGNMENT

A.   For a case assigned to the Program, the Clerk shall provide notice of the assignment to the attorney who filed the action. If the case was commenced by a party filing pro se, the notice will be provided to the party. The notice will include a description of the Program. Along with the notice the Clerk will send a List of Lanham Act Organizations and Neutrals.

B.   The Clerk will notify the judge that the case has been assigned to the Program.

C.   Upon receiving the notice and accompanying material from the Clerk, each attorney notified as provided for in section II.A above must promptly provide a copy of the notice and accompanying descriptive material to that attorney's client and to the attorney for each defendant, if known, or to each defendant, if the attorney is not known. Defense attorneys must promptly provide copies of the material they receive to each party they represent.

III.   LIST OF LANHAM ACT ORGANIZATIONS AND NEUTRALS

A.   **Maintenance by the Clerk of a List of Lanham Act Organizations and Neutrals.** The Clerk of the Court shall maintain and make available to the public a List of Lanham Act Organizations and Neutrals consisting of the name, address, and telephone numbers of each organization and person who has filed with the clerk the certificate specified by section C of this rule, and whose name has not been withdrawn or removed pursuant to section E of this rule. The clerk shall further maintain and make available to the public a file containing the certificates filed by those persons whose names are included on the list of mediators. Inclusion on the list does not constitute certification by the Court of the qualifications of the organization or neutral.

B.   **Minimum Criteria.** No organization or person may file a certificate pursuant to paragraph C below or be included in the List of Lanham Act Organizations and Neutrals unless such person or organization meets the following minimum criteria:

(1) *For Organizations:*

a.   A minimum of three years involvement with alternative dispute resolution in providing, sponsoring or training neutrals; and

b.   Affiliation with two or more individuals who meet the minimum criteria set forth below.

(2) *For Individuals:*

a.   Five years or more experience in the practice of Lanham Act law; or

b.   Three years or more experience as a neutral (not necessarily in Lanham Act law).

C.   **Certificates.** An organization may be included in the List of Lanham Act Organizations and Neutrals by filing with the Clerk of this Court a certificate containing the following information:

(1) *For Organizations:*

a.   Name, address, and nature and duration of involvement in alternative dispute procedures and activities;

b.   procedures and programs for training individuals in techniques of mediation and arbitration;

c.   experience in training such individuals in connection with disputes under the Lanham Act;

d. experience in providing neutrals to mediate or arbitrate disputes under the Lanham Act;

e. names and addresses of individuals the organization represents are qualified by experience or training, or both, to mediate or arbitrate disputes under the Lanham Act, together with copies of their curricula vitae; and

f. representative cases (including citations to published decisions) in which the organization has participated, including the names and addresses of counsel and parties (unless such information is deemed confidential).

(2) *For Individuals:*

a. Name, address, and academic and legal education credentials;

b. years in the practice of Lanham Act law, including trademark and unfair competition law and false advertising law;

c. experience in mediating or arbitrating disputes under the Lanham Act, other intellectual property law disputes, or general commercial disputes;

d. a summary of Law School or C.L.E. courses in Lanham Act subject matter taken or taught, including seminars or meetings of the American Bar Association, ALI–ABA, American Intellectual Property Law Association, International (formerly The United States) Trademark Association, Practicing Law Institute, Chicago Bar Association, or other groups or organizations;

e. membership and committee activity in professional organizations dealing with intellectual property law, including the Lanham Act;

f. publications on Lanham Act or other intellectual property law subject matter;

g. Any other experience, including litigation experience, he or she believes relevant to serving as a neutral;

h. representative cases (including citations to published decisions) in which the individual has participated as a mediator or arbitrator, including the names and addresses of counsel and parties (unless such information is deemed confidential); and

i. a copy of his or her curriculum vitae.

D. Amendment and Updating. Any organization and individual who files a certificate with the Clerk shall promptly file amendments to the certificates, whenever necessary or appropriate, to disclose any substantial change in the information provided in the certificate. In addition, each such organization or individual shall file a complete, updated certificate at no more than five year intervals.

E. Withdrawal and Removal from the List of Lanham Act Organizations and Neutrals. Any or-

ganization or neutral may voluntarily withdraw from the List of Lanham Act organizations and neutrals at any time by providing written notification to the clerk of the Court, who shall thereupon remove the name of the organization or neutral from said List and remove that organization or neutral's certificate from the file of such certificates. If an organization or neutral fails to update his, her or its certificate pursuant to section D of this rule, or for good cause as certified to the clerk by the Chief Judge, the clerk shall remove the name of that organization or neutral from said List and remove that organization or neutral's certificate from the file of certificates.

IV. ATTORNEY CERTIFICATION

As soon as practicable but in no event later than 21 days after receiving the notice provided pursuant to section II.A, each attorney for a party shall file with the Clerk a certificate stating that the attorney has mailed or otherwise provided a copy of the notice and all information about the program to each party that the attorney represents in the action, or to the guardian or representative of each party.

V. NOTICE OF PARTICIPATION OR NON–PARTICIPATION

A. Nothing in these Procedures shall be construed to affect the time within which a party is to answer or otherwise plead to a complaint. If a pleading in lieu of answer, or a motion for a temporary restraining order or a preliminary injunction is filed before the notice of participation or non-participation required by subsection B of this section has been filed, the court may fix a new time by which the parties must file the joint notice, or may find that the case is not appropriate for the program and excuse the parties from filing the joint notice, or may enter such other order as may be appropriate. Such action by the court shall be in writing, or on the record.

The parties in cases assigned to the Program are not required to participate in the Program but are strongly encouraged to do so. At the earliest of the first scheduling conference, or 90 days from filing of the complaint, the parties in cases assigned to the Program will file a jointly written notice indicating one of the following:

(1) that they wish to participate in the Program;

(2) that they do not wish to participate in the Program; or

(3) that they are already participating in some other mediation program.

B. If the notice indicates that the parties do not wish to participate in the Program, a brief statement of the reason or reasons must be included in the notice. Such a statement shall not disclose the position of any individual party concerning participation in the

Program. If the notice indicates that the parties are participating in some other mediation program, the notice must provide a brief description of the nature of the program.

C. The judge to whom a case eligible for the Program is assigned may impose sanctions for failure to notify clients pursuant to paragraph II.C. and/or failure to file the notice pursuant to paragraphs V.A and B.

VI. MEDIATION PROCEDURE

A. Mediation is a flexible, nonbinding and confidential dispute resolution process in which an impartial and qualified neutral facilitates negotiations among the parties in an attempt to help them reach settlement.

B. The mediation process does not contemplate testimony by witnesses. The neutral does not review or rule upon questions of fact or law, or render any final decision in the case, but may provide an opinion on questions of fact or law, or on the merits of the case if the case if requested or if desirable.

C. The parties shall select a neutral and obtain the consent of the neutral to act as mediator not more than 14 days after the filing of the joint notice of participation. The parties may request an extension of time for good cause shown. The parties may agree to select a neutral from the List of Lanham Act Organizations and Neutrals provided with the notice of assignment. In the event the parties wish to participate in the Program, but cannot agree on a panel neutral, the parties may contact any organization or individual identified in the List, which or who will assist in selecting a neutral for them.

D. The neutral shall disqualify himself or herself in any case in which the circumstances listed in 28 U.S.C. § 455 exist, and would apply if the neutral were a judge.

E. The neutral shall select a time and a place for the mediation conference, and any adjourned mediation session, that is reasonably convenient for the parties, and shall give them at least 14 days written notice of the initial conference. Except as ordered by the court for good cause shown, the date of the first mediation conference shall be not later than 45 days after the filing of the joint notice of participation and the date of the last conference shall be not more than 30 days following the first conference. If the parties settle the case prior to the mediation conference, they shall promptly advise the neutral and the judge assigned to the case that a settlement has been reached.

F. The neutral may require the parties to submit memoranda, on a confidential basis and not served on the other parties, addressing the strengths and weaknesses in that party's case and the terms that party proposes for settlement.

G. The following individuals shall attend the mediation conference unless excused by the mediator:

(1) each party who is a natural person;

(2) for each party that is not a natural person, either

(a) a representative who is not the party's attorney of record and who has full authority to negotiate and settle the dispute on behalf of that party, or

(b) if the party is an entity that requires settlement approval by a committee, board or legislative body, a representative who has authority to recommend a settlement to the committee, board or legislative body;

(3) the attorney who has primary responsibility for each party's case; and

(4) any other entity determined by the mediator to be necessary for a full resolution of the dispute referred to mediation.

H. Except where a party has been excused as provided for by section VI.H. above, failure of an attorney or a party to attend the mediation conference as required shall be reported to the assigned judge and may result in the imposition of sanctions as the judge may find appropriate.

VII. REPORTING ON THE PROGRAM

A. Within 14 days following the conclusion of the mediation session, the neutral shall file a concise report with the court disclosing only whether required parties were present and the disposition of the case, including:

(1) the case settled;

(2) the parties agreed to adjourn for further mediation; or

(3) the neutral determined that the negotiations are at an impasse.

B. All written and oral communications made in connection with the mediation conference, including any statement made by any party, attorney or other participant, shall, in all respects, be privileged and not reported, recorded, placed in evidence, made known to the trial court or jury, or construed for any purpose as an admission. No party shall be bound by anything done or said at the conference unless a settlement is reached, in which event the agreement upon a settlement shall be reduced to writing and shall be binding upon all parties to that agreement. In addition, the parties are free to enter confidentiality agreements covering all information disclosed in memoranda and during the mediation session.

VIII. COSTS

A. Absent agreement to the contrary, the parties shall share equally all costs incurred as a result of the mediation, including the costs of the neutral's services, except that each party shall be responsible for its own attorneys' fees.

B. Neutrals shall be reimbursed for the expenses and compensated by the hourly rate disclosed by them during the selection process, or as agreed in writing in advance between the neutral and the parties.

C. Except as provided in section VIII.B., a neutral shall not charge or accept anything of value from any source whatsoever for or relating to his or her duties as a neutral.

[Effective September 1, 1999.]

APPENDIX C.   REGULATIONS PERTAINING TO TRIAL BAR ADMISSION*

(The following regulations were promulgated by the District Admissions Committee as interpretive and procedural guides to the admission rules. The District Admissions Committee was disbanded by the abrogation of General Rules 3.20, 3.21, 3.22 and 3.23 effective December 19, 1997. However, the following regulations remain in effect.)

D.A.C.REG.1. PARTICIPATION UNITS (LOCAL RULE 83.11)

Promulgated by the District Admissions Committee as an interpretive guide to definitions of "participations" and qualifying trial "days" as set forth in LR 83.11.

A. "Participation" and "Participates" Defined. The terms "participation" or "participates" as used in LR83.11, defining a participation unit, refer to an active and open involvement in the presentation of a case as contrasted with passive observation or rendition of services solely to another attorney who was actively involved. A minimum criterion for the requisite level of involvement contemplated by the rule for participation credit shall be that the applicant be present at the testimonial proceeding and prepared for and/or conducted the examination or cross examination of at least two (2) witnesses in the qualifying trial.

B. "One Day" Defined. The term "one day" as used in LR83.11, defining a qualifying trial refers to not less than three (3) hours of actual appearance time in open court during which testimony is taken and/or exhibits are offered. Notwithstanding the foregoing:

(1) In the event interruptions or recesses in a trial prevent attainment of the aforesaid 3–hour minimum in a single 24–hour day, it is permissible to aggregate appearance time in the same trial so as to achieve a total of three (3) hours, provided that such added appearance time is of the character referred to in the preceding paragraph B.

(2) In no event shall more than one (1) day of qualifying trial credit be claimed for any 24–hour day nor shall any appearance time in excess of three (3) hours be carried over to a subsequent day.

(3) A trial which is completed in less than three (3) hours shall be deemed to entail "one day" of credit if it is in all other respects a testimonial proceeding

under LR83.11 and if the applicant gave an opening statement and/or closing argument in the trial.

D.A.C.REG.2. OBSERVATION UNITS (LOCAL RULE 83.11)

Promulgated by the District Admissions Committee as an interpretive guide to observation units as set forth in LR83.11.

A. Basic Requirements for Receiving Credit for an Observation Unit. An applicant will be entitled to receive credit for an observation unit pursuant to LR83.11 if, in conjunction with a trial involving testimonial proceedings in a state or federal court within the scope of LR83.11 of the Local Rules of this Court and which constitutes as qualifying trial within the scope of LR83.11 of the Local Rules of this Court, he or she, at the time of the submission of the application:

(1) was supervised in the observation of the trial by counsel for one of the parties;

(2) became familiar with the factual and legal issues;

(3) attended a substantial amount of the court sessions during trial;

(4) observed any opening and closing arguments;

(5) observed a substantial portion of the direct testimony and cross examination presented by all parties;

(6) consulted with the supervising attorney from time to time; and

(7) is a member in good standing of the bar of this court.

B. Requirements for Supervising Attorney. The supervising attorney shall be required to complete an observation affidavit on behalf of the applicant attesting to the fulfillment of the above requirements and specifying certain other information regarding the trial which was the basis for the supervision. The supervising attorney must, at the time of the supervision, have been either admitted as a member of the trial bar of the Court or, should the supervision have taken place prior to such admission of the supervising attorney, give evidence of the equivalent of four (4) participation units achieved by affiant prior to the supervision activity.

C. "Substantial" Defined. The term "substantial," as used in paragraph A(3) and A(5) of this Regulation, is defined as at least fifty (50) percent of the court sessions and fifty (50) percent of the direct testimony and cross examination except that, if the trial lasted less than three (3) days, the term "substantial" shall be defined as having attended all court sessions and having observed all of the testimony presented.

D. Supervising Attorneys: No Remuneration, Limit on Numbers Supervised. There shall be no remuneration for supervising applicants for observation units, and the ratio of applicants to supervising attorneys shall not exceed three (3) to one (1), unless a greater ratio has been approved in advance by the District Admissions Committee.

D.A.C.REG.3.   SIMULATION UNITS (LOCAL RULE 83.11)

Promulgated by the District Admissions Committee as an interpretive guide to simulation units as set forth in LR83.11.

A. Trial Advocacy Programs & Simulation Units: General. A trial advocacy program will qualify a participant for simulation credit pursuant to LR83.11 if the focus of the program is experiential in accordance with paragraphs B and C below, with any lecture being incidental thereto and, in any event, comprising less than 25% of the program hours.

B. Standards for Trial Advocacy Programs. In general, to qualify the applicant for simulation unit credit, the trial advocacy program should, with respect to each unit of credit:

(1) provide the following hours of classroom or courtroom instruction:

(a) 24 hours in the case of a continuing education program for practicing lawyers; or

(b) 40 hours in the case of a law school program for second or third year law students.

(2) provide each participant the opportunity to do opening statements, closing arguments, direct and cross examination, and introduction of exhibits.

(3) provide each participant the opportunity to conduct one mock trial with a maximum of two participants on each side in which each participant examines at least one witness and gives an opening or closing argument.

(4) provide a ratio of participants to full-time or part-time instructors of not more than ten to one (10:1).

C. Approval of Simulation Unit in Certain Instances Where Trial Advocacy Program Does Not Meet the Standards. If a trial advocacy program does not meet the standards set forth in paragraph B above, an applicant, nonetheless, may be entitled to a simulation unit if it is demonstrated to the satisfaction of the District Admissions Committee, or a subcommittee thereof, that the program fulfills the objectives of providing the applicant with substantial hands-on experience in the phases of a trial set forth in paragraph B(2) above under competent supervision. In particular, the Committee, or a subcommittee thereof, shall consider the relationship between the hours of instruction and the participant/faculty ratio, the number of student presentations, the experience of the instructors, the syllabus for the program, and the quality of the instructional materials.

[Effective September 1, 1999.]

APPENDIX D.   PLAN FOR THE ADMINISTRATION OF THE DISTRICT COURT FUND*

*The Plan was initially adopted by the Court on Wednesday, 16 March 1983. It was subsequently amended on Thursday, 20 June 1985 and on January 12, 2001. A technical amendment was added on April 16, 2004.

PLAN FOR THE ADMINISTRATION OF THE DISTRICT COURT FUND

A. Creation of the Fund; Purpose of Plan. A District Court Fund was created by the General Rules of this court promulgated on April 13, 1965. Rule 6 A (iii) of those rules required newly admitted attorneys to pay to the Clerk a fee in addition to that established by the Judicial Conference of the United States pursuant to 28 U.S.C. § 1914. On July 12, 1982 new practice rules were promulgated including General

Rule 3.02. General Rule 3.02 replaced the earlier General Rule 6 A (iii) and required in addition to the fee for new attorneys, a fee for attorneys admitted to the trial bar of the court, the receipts from both fees to be deposited in the District Court Fund. This plan is adopted to provide procedures for the administration of funds deposited in the District Court Fund.

B. Advisory Committee. There shall be an advisory committee to advise the court on matters of policy relating to the administration of the fund. The committee shall consist of three judicial officers of the district, the Clerk of the court, and three attorneys. The judicial officers, one of whom shall serve as chairperson, shall be designated by the chief judge and shall include the district judge designated as liaison judge to the William J. Campbell Library. The three attorneys shall be designated by the chairpersons of the District Admissions and the District Performance Assistance Committees.

C. Custodian of the Fund. Pursuant to Internal Operating Procedure 32 the clerk of the court is the custodian of the District Court Fund. In the event of the death, retirement, or resignation of the clerk, the chief deputy clerk, or such other person as the chief judge designates, shall become the custodian until such time as the next clerk assumes office.

D. Duties and Responsibilities of the Custodian. The responsibilities of the custodian are as follows:

(1) to receive, safeguard, deposit, disburse, and account for all funds in accordance with the law, this plan, and the policies established by the court;

(2) to establish an accounting system for the fund;

(3) to insure that financial statements and operating reports are prepared in a timely fashion and to sign such statements and reports, thereby certifying that they accurately present the financial condition of the fund;

(4) to sign checks drawn on the fund, which checks shall be countersigned by the chief judge or a judge designated by him/her;

(5) to invest funds in accordance with the provisions of this plan; and

(6) to perform such other functions as may be required by the court.

E. Responsibilities upon Appointment of a Successor Custodian. When a successor custodian is appointed, the outgoing custodian should prepare and sign the following statements in conjunction with an exit audit or inspection conducted by an auditor or disinterested inspector designated by the chief judge:

(1) a statement of assets and liabilities;

(2) a statement of operations or of receipts and disbursements since the end of the period covered by the last statement of operations and net worth; and

(3) a statement of the balance in any fund accounts as of the date of transfer to the successor custodian.

The successor custodian will execute a receipt for all funds after being satisfied as to the accuracy of the statements and records provided by the outgoing custodian. Acceptance may be conditioned upon an audit and verification where circumstances warrant.

F. Audits and Inspections. The District Court Fund is subject to audit by the appropriate staff of the Administrative Office of the United States Courts or their contracted auditors. The chief judge may appoint an auditor or disinterested inspector (who may be a government employee) to conduct such audits as the court determines to be necessary. The written results of such audit or inspection will be provided to members of the advisory committee, each district judge, and, upon request, any member of the bar of the court.

In the event that the court orders a dissolution of the fund, a terminal audit or inspection will be performed and a written accounting rendered to the court.

G. Protection of the Fund's Assets. Except as otherwise provided in this plan, all receipts will be deposited in banks or savings institutions where accounts are insured by F.D.I.C. or F.S.L.I.C. Where practical and feasible the custodian shall place any substantial sums into interest bearing accounts, government securities, or a money market fund invested in government obligations. Such investment shall be at the direction of the advisory committee. Efforts should be made to maximize the return on investments consistent with the requirements of convenience and safety.

Funds held by the custodian must be segregated from all other monies in the custody of the clerk of the court, including other non-appropriated funds, if any.

H. Limitations on Use of Funds. Monies deposited in the fund must not be used to pay for materials or supplies available from statutory appropriations. Under no circumstances are such monies to be used to supplement the salary of any court officer or employee.

I. Uses of the Funds. In general the monies deposited in the fund are to be used for the benefit of the bench and bar in the administration of justice. Monies deposited in the fund may be used to pay for any of the following:

(1) the expenses related to attorney admission proceedings including expenses of the District Admissions Committee and expenses incurred in admissions ceremonies;

(2) the expenses of the District Performance Assistance Committee;

(3) the expenses related to attorney disciplinary proceedings, including the expenses of investigating counsel, and travel and witness fees in disciplinary proceedings;

(4) the cost of periodicals and publications purchased for the William J. Campbell library if appropriated funds are not available;

(5) the cost of anatomical charts and stands for courtroom use;

(6) the expenses associated with computerization of the library catalogue if appropriated funds are not available;

(7) the expenses associated with creating lawyer lounge facilities;

(8) the expenses of the plan's Advisory Committee;

(9) the expenses incurred by the custodian in performing his/her duties under the plan including the expense of a surety bond covering monies in the fund;

(10) the fees for services rendered by outside auditors or inspectors in auditing or inspecting the records of the fund;

(11) pursuant to the provisions of section J of this plan, the out-of-pocket expenses of attorneys appointed to represent indigent parties in civil proceedings in this court; and

(12) such other expenses as may from time to time be authorized by the full court or the Advisory Committee for the use and benefit of the bench and bar in the administration of justice.

J. Out-of-Pocket Expenses in Pro Bono Cases. In a civil case where an attorney is appointed to represent an indigent party, reasonable out-of-pocket expenses not otherwise recoverable may be paid for out of the fund, in accordance with regulations adopted by the full court or the Advisory Committee. Application to incur the expense or for reimbursement shall be on a form approved by the Executive Committee and available from the clerk.

Limits on the amounts to be reimbursed from the fund under this section for classes of expenses may be established in regulations adopted by the full court or the Advisory Committee. Except as provided in such regulations, no counsel appointed under LR83.36 of this court shall be reimbursed more than $3,000.00 for expenses incurred on behalf of any single party he or she was appointed to represent and no more than $7,000.00 shall be reimbursed for expenses incurred on behalf of multiple parties represented by appointed counsel in the same case. Only the expenses incurred by court appointed counsel on behalf of specific individuals are covered by this section.

K. Dissolution of the Fund. Should the court decide to dissolve the fund, the custodian will liquidate all outstanding obligations prior to the dissolution, including making provisions for the payment of any fees and expenses resulting from the required terminal audit or inspection. The court will direct the disposition of the assets of the fund in ways which fulfill the purpose of the fund.

[Adopted effective March 16, 1983. Amended June 20, 1985; January 12, 2001; April 16, 2004.]

APPENDIX E. THE DISTRICT COURT FUND REGULATIONS GOVERNING THE PREPAYMENT AND REIMBURSEMENT OF EXPENSES IN PRO BONO CASES*

* These Regulations were initially promulgated by the Court pursuant to the general order of June 27, 1985. They were amended by the general orders of November 1, 1990, April 1, 1991, and February 28, 2011. The Advisory Group added policies used in interpreting the Regulations. The policies were initially adopted on May 7, 1986 and amended in September 1992 and January 12, 2001. A copy of the policies is appended to the Regulations.

NOTE

Only counsel appointed by the court pursuant to Local Rule 83.36 are eligible to petition the court for the prepayment or reimbursement of expenses incurred in the preparation and presentation of the proceeding, subject to the restrictions of these regulations.

D.C.F. REG.1. ELIGIBILITY FOR PREPAYMENT OR REIMBURSEMENT OF EXPENSES

When a trial bar attorney has been appointed, pursuant to LR83.36, to represent an indigent party in a civil proceeding before this Court, that attorney shall be allowed to petition the Court for the prepayment or reimbursement of expenses incurred in the preparation and presentation of the proceeding, subject to the restrictions of these regulations.

D.C.F. REG.2. LIMITATIONS ON ELIGIBILITY

A. Not Applicable if C.J.A. Funds are Available. In any proceeding where expenses are covered by the Criminal Justice Act (Title 18 U.S.C. § 3006A), they shall be paid from such funds in accordance with C.J.A. guidelines and not from the District Court Fund.

B. Limit on Total Expenses Covered by Fund. The judge to whom the case is assigned is authorized to approve prepayments or reimbursements totaling $1,000.00. If the total of the prepayments or reimbursement requested and those already allowed exceed $1,000.00 the judge shall forward the request to the chief judge together with a recommendation. In no event will more than $3,000.00 in such expenses be paid for a party in any proceeding. Where two or more parties in the same proceeding are represented by counsel appointed pursuant to Local Rule 83.36, the limits established by this section shall apply to the costs incurred on behalf of each party, provided that in no proceeding shall the total amount paid from the Fund exceed $7,000.00, regardless of the number of parties so represented.

C. Limited to Civil Actions Before the District Court. Only those expenses associated with the preparation of a civil action in the U.S. District Court for the Northern District of Illinois shall be approved for reimbursement. No costs associated with the preparation or presentation of an appeal to the U.S. Court of Appeals or the U.S. Supreme Court shall be reimbursed from the District Court Fund unless otherwise approved by the Advisory Committee for the Administration of the District Court Fund and the Chief Judge of the U.S. District Court upon prior application by the appointed attorney.

D. Overhead Costs, Costs of Computer Assisted Legal Research, and Costs of Printing Briefs Not Covered. General office expenses, including personnel costs, rent, telephone services, secretarial help, office photocopying equipment, and any general expense that would normally be reflected in the fee charged to a client are not reimbursable from the District Court Fund. Any costs incurred in conducting computer assisted legal research is not reimbursable from the Fund. The expense of printing briefs, regardless of the printing method utilized, is not reimbursable.

E. Not Available to Pay Costs Awarded Against Party. Under no circumstances shall any payments be authorized from the Fund to pay for costs or fees taxed as part of a judgment obtained by an adverse party against a party for whom counsel was appointed pursuant to the rules of this Court.

F. Reimbursement and Prepayment Where Party Prevails. Except as provided by this section, no reimbursement shall be authorized from the Fund in those instances where the party for whom counsel was appointed prevails or accepts a settlement and the amount awarded to or accepted by the party exceeds $2,500.00. Where the amount awarded to or accepted by the party is more than $2,500.00 and no provision is made to cover the expenses incurred by court-appointed counsel that would otherwise be covered by these regulations, prepayments and reimbursements may be authorized within the limits of these regulations, but the total amount to be paid from the Fund shall be the amount authorized by these regulations less fifty cents for each dollar received by the party in excess of $2,500.00.

G. Prepayments in Excess of the Allowable Limits. In any instance where amounts have been prepaid from the Fund and the party for whom counsel was appointed prevails or accepts a settlement and the amount awarded or accepted exceeds $2,500.00, the Clerk will notify court-appointed counsel that the prepaid amounts are to be repaid to the District Court Fund. The Clerk will send a copy of the notice to the assigned judge. On receipt of such notice counsel will promptly remit the amount in excess of the limit.

D.C.F. REG.3. PROCEDURES FOR OBTAINING PREPAYMENTS OR REIMBURSEMENTS

A. Request for Authority to Incur Expense. For those expenses where authority to incur is required prior to incurring them, the request for authority to incur the expense shall be made by motion filed with the judge to whom the case is assigned. The motion shall set forth briefly the reason for the request and the estimated amount of the expense.

B. Request for Prepayment or Reimbursement of Expenses. Any request for the prepayment or reimbursement of expenses shall be on the voucher form approved by the Executive Committee and available on request from the clerk. The request shall be accompanied by sufficient documentation to permit the court to determine that the request is appropriate and reasonable and, where the request is for reimbursement, that the amounts have actually been paid out. The request shall be filed with the clerk's office. Requests may be made at any time during the pendency of the proceedings and up to thirty days following the entry of judgment in the proceedings. The assigned judge may, for good cause shown, extend the time for filing a request.

C. Requests for Reimbursement by Attorney No Longer Representing Party. Where an attorney appointed under this Court's pro bono rules is permitted to withdraw from representing the party in a proceeding and the attorney has incurred expenses which may be reimbursable under these regulations, he or she shall file a request for reimbursement within ninety days of the date of the entry of the order allowing the withdrawal. Except for good cause shown, the court will not allow reimbursement of expenses where the request was filed more than ninety days after the entry of the order of withdrawal.

D. Request May be Made Ex Parte. Any request made under sections A, B, or C of this regulation may be made ex parte.

E. Action by Assigned Judge and/or Chief Judge. The assigned judge or the chief judge may refuse to permit prepayment or disallow reimbursement of any expense based upon the absence of documentation that such expense is appropriate or reasonable or, where reimbursement is requested, was actually incurred.

F. Processing by Clerk. On receipt of the voucher form indicating amounts approved for prepayment or reimbursement, the clerk shall check to determine whether or not any payments had previously been made out of the Fund to cover expenses in the same proceeding. If no such payments had been made, the clerk shall promptly issue the required check or checks in the amount indicated on the voucher form or the limit set by these regulations, whichever is lower.

Where payments had previously been made from the Fund for expenses in the proceedings, the clerk will check to see if the amounts authorized by the current voucher together with amounts previously paid would require additional approval by the chief judge because the total exceeds the limits set by these regulations for amounts approvable by the assigned judge. Where such approval is required, the clerk shall promptly transmit the voucher to the chief judge. On receipt of the voucher from the chief judge, the clerk shall promptly issue the required check or checks in the amount indicated on the voucher form or limit set by these regulations, whichever is lower. If the chief judge disallowed any or all of the amounts requested, the clerk shall promptly transmit to the submitting attorney a copy of the voucher showing the action of the chief judge.

G. Amounts Paid From Fund To Be Reimbursed From Any Fee Award. Where a fee award is made by a judge to an appointed attorney, the attorney awarded fees shall upon receipt of the monies awarded promptly repay the Fund any amounts paid to him or her under these regulations.

[Amended effective February 28, 2011.]

D.C.F. REG. 4. EXPENSES AND COSTS COVERED BY REGULATIONS

A. C.J.A. Limits to Apply in Absence of Specific Limits. Except as specified by these regulations, the amounts and types of expenses covered by these regulations shall be governed by the guidelines for administering the Criminal Justice Act (18 U.S.C. § 3006A) (See also *Guide to Judiciary Policies and Procedures*, Volume VII, Section A, Chapters 2 and 3).

B. Deposition and Transcript Costs. The costs of transcripts or depositions shall not exceed the regular copy rate as established by the Judicial Conference of the United States and in effect at the time any transcript or deposition was filed unless some other rate was previously provided for by order of court. Except as otherwise ordered by the court, only the cost of the original of any transcript or deposition together with the cost of one copy each where needed by counsel and, for depositions, the copy provided to the court pursuant to Rule 54.1 of the Local Rules of this Court, shall be allowed.

C. Travel Expenses. Travel by privately owned automobile may be claimed at the rate currently prescribed for federal judiciary employees who use a private automobile for conduct of official business, plus parking fees, tolls, and similar expenses. Transportation other than by privately owned automobile may be claimed on an actual expense basis. Per diem in lieu of subsistence is not allowable; only actual expenses may be reimbursed. Actual expenses reason-

ably incurred shall be guided by the prevailing limitations placed upon travel and subsistence expenses of federal judiciary employees in accordance with existing government travel regulations.

D. Service of Papers; Witness Fees. Those fees for service of papers and the appearances of witnesses that are not otherwise avoided, waived or recoverable may be reimbursed from the District Court Fund.

E. Interpreter Services. Costs of interpreter services not otherwise avoided, waived, or recoverable may be reimbursed from the District Court Fund.

F. Costs of Photocopies, Photographs, Telephone Toll Calls, Telegrams. Except as provided by section D of Regulation 2, actual, out-of-pocket expenses incurred for items such as photocopying services, photographs, telephone toll calls, and telegrams necessary for the preparation of a case may be prepaid or reimbursed from the District Court Fund.

G. Other Expenses. Expenses other than those described in sections B through F of this regulation may be approved by the judge to whom the case is assigned. No single expense under this section exceeding $100 shall be reimbursed unless approval was obtained from the judge prior to the expenditure. When requesting reimbursement for any expenses under this section, a detailed description of the expenses should be attached to the petition for reimbursement filed with the judge.

POLICIES ADOPTED BY THE ADVISORY COMMITTEE REGARDING THE REGULATIONS

1) PAYMENT OF EXPENSES UNDER THE PROVISIONS OF SECTION I(12) OF THE PLAN FOR THE ADMINISTRATION OF THE DISTRICT COURT FUND

Monies deposited in the District Court Fund which are to be distributed under the provisions of section I(12) of the *Plan for the Administration of the District Court Fund* may be used to pay expenses incurred in relation to functions:

(a) where the nature of the function is primarily related to the operation of the United States District Court for the Northern District of Illinois, and

(b) where participation in the function is not restricted to members or employees of the United States District Court for the Northern District of Illinois, and/or persons receiving reimbursement of travel expenses from the United States Courts.

2) AUTHORITY OF CUSTODIAN TO MAKE DISBURSEMENTS UNDER THE PROVISIONS OF SECTION I(12) OF THE PLAN FOR THE ADMINISTRATION OF THE DISTRICT COURT FUND

The custodian of the fund shall be authorized to make disbursements up to, but not more than $200.00 per event for expenses for the use and benefit of the bench and bar in the administration of justice, notwithstanding the restrictions of section I, paragraph 12 of the *Plan for the Administration of the District Court Fund.* Such disbursements shall be subject to later review and approval by the full court or the District Court Fund Advisory Committee.

PLAN FOR RANDOM SELECTION OF JURORS

(As Revised September 2013)

1. **Purpose.** Pursuant to the Jury Selection and Service Act of 1968 (28 USC § 1861 *et seq.*), this Court adopts this Plan for the Random Selection and Service of Jurors in the United States District for the Northern District of Illinois (Plan). It is the purpose of the Jury Plan to implement the policies declared in the Jury Act, that all litigants in federal courts entitled to trial by jury shall have the right to grand and petit juries selected at random from a fair cross section of the community in the district or division wherein the court convenes, that all citizens shall have the opportunity to be considered for service on grand and petit juries in the district courts of the United States, and that all citizens shall have an obligation to serve as jurors when summoned for that purpose.

It is further the purpose of the Jury Plan to implement the prohibition against discrimination contained in 28 USC § 1862, which provides that no citizen shall be excluded from service as a grand or petit juror in the district courts of the United States on account of race, color, religion, sex, national origin, or economic status.

It is a violation of federal law, 28 USC § 1875, for an employer to discharge, threaten to discharge, intimidate or coerce any permanent employee by reason of such employee's jury service or the attendance or scheduled attendance in connection with such service in this court.

2. **Definitions.**

(a) For the purposes of this Plan, "Clerk" shall mean the Clerk of Court, any authorized deputy clerk, and any other person authorized by the Court to assist the Clerk in the performance of functions under this Plan.

(b) "Jury Administrator" shall mean the Jury Administrator for the Northern District of Illinois or his or her designees.

(c) In the Eastern Division of this District, "political subdivision" refers to the City of Chicago, the remainder of Cook County, the City of Aurora, the balance of Kane County, the balance of DuPage County, and the counties of Grundy, Kendall, Lake, La Salle, and Will. In the Western Division, "political subdivision" refers to the City of Rockford, the remainder of Winnebago County, and the counties of Boone, Carroll, De Kalb, Jo Daviess, Lee, McHenry, Ogle, Stephenson, and Whiteside.

3. **Application and Management.** Pursuant to 28 U.S.C. § 1869(e), separate master jury wheels are established for each Division of the Northern District of Illinois, as follows:

Eastern Division: the counties of Cook, Du Page, Will, Lake, Grundy, Kane, Kendall, and La Salle.

Western Division: the counties of McHenry, Boone, Winnebago, De Kalb, Ogle, Lee, Stephenson, Jo Daviess, Whiteside, and Carroll.

The provisions of the Jury Plan apply with equal force and effect to both Divisions of this District.

4. **Management and Supervision of Jury Selection Process.** The Clerk of Court, under the direction of the Chief Judge or his or her designee, is responsible for managing the jury selection process. The Jury Administrator is authorized to assist the Clerk in the management of the jury selection process.

5. **Random Selection from Lists of Registered Voters and Others.**

(a) The Court finds that a combination of official voter registration lists for the counties and cities in this district submitted annually to the Office of Voters Registration Illinois State Board of Elections for the State of Illinois in accordance with Illinois Laws and lists of persons licensed by the Illinois Secretary of State to drive motor vehicles and persons to whom the Illinois Secretary of State has issued a personal identification card, represents a fair cross section of the community in this District. The lists of registered voters in the District's political subdivisions are maintained as identified in Section 2(c) above.

(b) In order to implement the Court's policy, the names of persons to be considered for service as grand or petit jurors in each Division shall be selected at random from the lists of registered voters residing in that Division and persons licensed by the Illinois Secretary of State to drive motor vehicles and persons to whom the Illinois Secretary of State has issued a personal identification card.

6. Selecting Prospective Jurors for the Master Jury Wheel.

(a) The Court finds that electronic data processing methods can be effectively used for selecting names from the lists compiled pursuant to Section 5(a) above. Therefore, a properly programmed electronic data processing system may be used to select names from such lists for the master jury wheel, provided that each county or political subdivision is proportionately represented in the master wheel. The selection process may be carried out using either of the methods described in this section.

(b) The selection of names for the master jury wheel may be accomplished by a purely randomized process through a properly programmed electronic data processing system. The random selection of names from the source lists by Court staff or any outside contractor must ensure that each county is substantially proportionally represented in the master wheel in accordance with 28 USC § 1863(b)(3). The selection of names from the source lists must also ensure that the mathematical odds of any single name being picked are substantially equal.

(c) The selection of names for the master jury wheel may be carried out using a process based on a quotient and a randomly selected starting number as described below.

i. Determining a Quotient. After ascertaining the total number of registered voters for all counties within the Division, that total number is divided by the number of names needed for the jury wheel. The result, the ratio of selected to unselected names, is referred to as the quotient. For example, if it determined 5,000 names will be needed in the Western division master jury wheel to meet the Court's need for jurors over a two-year period, and if there are 100,000 names on all the lists for the Division as compiled pursuant to Section 5(a) above, the quotient would be 20 (100,000 total names divided by 5,000 names) and every 20th name should be placed in the Division's master jury wheel.

ii Determining a Starting Number. After determining the quotient, the clerk shall establish a starting number, which will identify the first name to be selected from the list compiled pursuant to Section 5(a) above. The randomly drawn starting number will be a number between one and the quotient. Pursuant to 28 U.S.C. § 1864(a) and guidelines established by the Judicial Conference of the United States Courts, the random selection of the starting number shall be made in public. As an example of how the quotient and starting number are used, if we assume the quotient to be 20 and the starting number is 8, the first name chosen from each county will be the 8th name on the list, the second name would be the 28th, the third name the 48th, and so on, until the end of the list is reached.

(d) The number of names initially added to the Master Jury Wheel shall be at least 50,000 names for the Eastern Division and 4,000 names for the Western Division. The Clerk shall refill the Master Jury Wheel every two years and within 120 days of receipt of the data from the State of Illinois in conformance with this Plan or at more frequent intervals as deemed necessary by the Clerk under the supervision of the Chief Judge. The Chief Judge, or his or her designee, may order that additional names be placed in the Master Jury Wheel at other times, as needed.

7. Drawing Names from the Master Jury Wheel and Completion of Juror Qualification Forms.

(a) *Juror Qualification Questionnaire.* Based on the Court's anticipated need for jurors, the Clerk shall prepare and mail a juror qualification questionnaire form to every person whose name is drawn from the master jury wheel, where the available address information indicates that the person resides within the District. Public notice of the mailing of qualification questionnaires shall be provided by the posting of information concerning the mailing on the Court's website. The mailing shall instruct the addressee to complete and return the form, duly signed and sworn, by mail to the Clerk within ten days in accordance with 28 U.S.C. § 1864(a).

(b) *Supplemental Draw for Undeliverable and Non–Responding Juror Qualification Forms.* For all qualification forms returned to the Court as "undeliverable" or those to which no response has been received (after the Clerk has sent a follow-up questionnaire to the person who has not responded), the Clerk shall issue the same number of new juror qualification forms to be mailed to addresses within the same zip code area to which the undeliverable or non-responding juror qualification forms had been sent. If qualification forms from the supplemental draw are returned undeliverable, no additional qualification forms will be issued. If no names from that zip code are available, no additional qualification form will be mailed. The Clerk shall draw these names for additional juror qualification forms from the Master Jury Wheel.

8. Qualifications, Exemptions, and Excuses from Jury Service.

(a) *Qualifications.* Under the supervision of the Chief Judge, the Clerk shall determine, solely on the basis of information provided on the juror qualification form and other competent evidence, whether a person is qualified for jury service, unqualified or exempt from service, or to be excused from jury service. The determination shall be noted on the juror qualification form or on supporting documentation, and recorded in automated records of the master jury wheel. The method used for this determination may be either mechanical or manual. Pursuant to 28 U.S.C. § 1865(b), any person shall be deemed qualified for jury service unless he or she:

(1) is not a citizen of the United States;

(2) is under eighteen years of age;

(3) has resided within this District for a period of less than one year;

(4) is unable to read, write, and understand the English language with a degree of proficiency sufficient to fill out satisfactorily the juror qualification form;

(5) is unable to speak the English language;

(6) is unable, by reason of mental or physical infirmity, to render satisfactory jury service; or

(7) is facing a pending charge for the commission of, or has been convicted in a state or federal court of, a crime punishable by imprisonment for more than one year, and his or her civil rights have been lost and have not been restored.

(b) *Exemptions.* The following persons are exempt from jury service pursuant to 28 U.S.C. § 1863(b)(6):

(1) members in active service in the armed forces of the United States;

(2) members of the fire or police departments of any state, district, territory, possession or subdivision thereof; and

(3) public officers in the executive, legislative, or judicial branches of the government of the United States, or any state, district, territory, or possession or subdivision thereof, who are actively engaged in the performance of official duties. Public officer shall mean a person who is either elected to public office or who is directly appointed by the person elected to public office.

(c) *Excuses.* Upon individual request, the Clerk shall excuse the following persons from jury service:

(1) any person over the age of seventy years;

(2) any person who has served as a juror in this court within the previous two years; or

(3) volunteer safety personnel who serve without compensation as firefighters or members of a rescue squad or ambulance crew for a public agency in accordance with 28 U.S.C. § 1863(b)(5)(B). Public agency shall mean the United States, the State of Illinois, or any unit of local government.

Under the supervision of the Chief Judge, the Clerk, upon individual request showing undue hardship or extreme inconvenience, may excuse any person from jury service for the period that such extreme hardship or inconvenience exists. Because such circumstances are often temporary in nature, decisions concerning requests to be excused will normally not be made until such time as a prospective juror is summoned for service. "Undue hardship or extreme inconvenience" shall mean the illness of the juror or a member of the juror's household; the active care and custody of a child under twelve years of age; the active full-time care of an aged or infirm person; business or recreational travel plans established before the receipt of the summons for jury service; or any other factor which the Clerk determines to be an undue hardship or to create an extreme inconvenience to the juror. Whenever possible, arrangements will be made with any juror who is excused from serving on a particular date for his or her service to be deferred to a specific future date.

9. Qualified Jury Wheel. The results of the screening of the juror qualification forms shall be recorded for the master jury wheels of each Division. Those persons not disqualified, barred, or excused pursuant to this Plan will be deemed qualified. The qualified juror wheel of each Division shall consist of the names of all qualified prospective jurors.

10. Miscellaneous.

(a) No person shall make public or disclose to any person, unless so ordered by a judge of this Court, the names drawn from the Qualified Jury Wheel to serve in this Court until the first day of the jurors' term of service. Any judge of this Court may order that the names of jurors involved in a trial presided over by that judge remain confidential if the interests of justice so require, to the extent allowed by law.

(b) The contents of records and documents used in connection with the jury selection process, including the juror qualification questionnaires, shall not be disclosed except as provided in 28 USC § 1867(f) and this Plan. Parties requesting access to these records shall petition the Court in writing setting forth the reasons for requesting access.

(c) The names of any jurors drawn from the Qualified Jury Wheel and selected to sit on a grand jury shall be kept confidential and not made public or disclosed to any person, except as otherwise authorized by an order issued by the Chief Judge.

(d) From time to time the Court may direct the Clerk to draw from the Qualified Jury Wheel for a Division such number of persons as may be required for grand and petit jury arrays or Special Panel arrays as provided for by LR 47.1(b). A "Special Panel" shall mean a list of prospective petit jurors drawn separately from the regular terms of jurors, which will be utilized for one or more specific trials upon order of a trial judge and the Chief Judge. If any special panel of jurors is not used for the trial for which the special panel was established, the jurors may be used for trials taking place during the regular term of service, or for another special panel. In such circumstances, the members of the special panel array may become a part of the regular array until that array is terminated.

(e) All records and documents compiled and used in the jury selection process shall be maintained and filed by the clerk, using intervals of time commencing with the proceedings to fill the master wheels and ending when all persons selected to serve before the wheels were emptied have completed their service. Said records shall be preserved for four years as required by 28 USC § 1868 and shall then be destroyed unless otherwise ordered by the Court.

(f) Where the Judicial Conference of the United States, the Administrative Office of the United States Courts, or the Federal Judicial Center approve experimental programs affecting the administrative aspects of jury service, the Executive Committee may determine that the Court shall participate in such programs. Where such participation requires a temporary suspension of one or more provisions of this Plan, the Executive Committee may direct that such provisions be suspended for the duration of the Court's participation in the experimental program. Any provisions temporarily suspended pursuant to this Section shall be reinstated upon the conclusion of the experimental program or upon a finding by the Executive Committee that the Court's participation in such experimental program shall end, whichever is sooner.

EFFECTIVE DATE This plan for jury selection shall be placed in operation after approval by the reviewing panel as provided in 28 USC § 1863 as amended by the Jury Selection and Service Act of 1968. Jury service under this plan shall be required upon special order of the Court at such time as processing of the juror qualification questionnaires has been completed.

This plan shall remain in force and effect until approval of one or more modifications of this plan by said reviewing panel. Modifications of this plan may be initiated by the Court and submitted to the reviewing panel for approval; and this plan shall be modified as and when directed by said reviewing panel.

Approved by the Full Court on September 20, 2013

Approved by the Judicial Council of the Seventh Circuit on October 23, 2013

[Adopted December 21, 2006. Revised effective March 19, 2007, as approved by the Judicial Council of the Seventh Circuit. Revised effective August 22, 2012, as approved by the Judicial Council of the Seventh Circuit. Revised effective October 23, 2013, as approved by the Judicial Council of the Seventh Circuit.]

GENERAL ORDERS AND NOTICES
THE JUDICIAL CONFERENCE POLICY REGARDING
THE AVAILABILITY OF TRANSCRIPTS OF
COURT PROCEEDINGS

The Judicial Conference implemented a policy regarding the availability of transcripts of court proceedings in September of 2007. This policy is limited to the redaction of specific personal identifiers from transcripts that are available for remote online viewing. Personal identifiers as outlined in FRCP 5.2 and FRCrP 49.1 include 1) individuals' social security numbers, 2) names of minor children, 3) financial account numbers, 4) dates of birth and 5) in criminal cases, the home address of an individual, a party or nonparty making the filing. Please review the rule for a complete listing and exceptions.

Availability. The court reporter or transcriber will e-file a copy of any transcript not later than three (3) business days after delivery to the requesting party. The transcript will be available at the Clerk's Office for electronic viewing only, for a period of 90 days after it is filed with the Clerk. The transcript will display a header "AVAILABLE AT THE PUBLIC TERMINAL FOR VIEWING ONLY."

After the 90-day period has ended, if no redactions are made, the original e-filed transcript will be available for viewing and copying in the Clerk's Office and for downloading from the court's CM/ECF system through the judiciary's PACER system.

Parties in the case who order the original transcript within the 90-day restriction period will be granted remote access to view the transcript as soon as it is filed.

Obtaining transcripts. During the 90-day period, a copy of the transcript may be purchased from the court reporter or transcriber at the rate established by the Judicial Conference [see Maximum Transcript Fees on our website]. An attorney who purchases the transcript from the court reporter or transcriber will have remote electronic access to the transcript through the court's CM/ECF system.

Redaction guidelines

Transcript Redaction Request. If a redaction is requested, counsel **must** e-file a Transcript Redaction Request within **twenty–one (21) calendar days** of the filing of the transcript. The Request must identify the personal data identifiers to be redacted by page/line number and description, for example Page 14, Line 21, SSN ending in 5111. NOTE: The request must not list the full personal identifier, e.g., the complete social security number.

The filing party must provide the court reporter or transcriber with a copy of the Transcript Redaction Request.

Efilers, make sure to use the correct event.

Request for additional redactions. If redaction of information other than personal identifiers is sought, the party must e-file a separate Motion to Redact Transcript with the Court. **Make sure you link the motion to the applicable transcript.**

The court reporter or transcriber must, within thirty-one (31) calendar days of the delivery of the transcript to the Clerk of Court, or longer if the court so orders, perform any requested redaction and file a redacted version of the transcript with the Clerk of Court.

Any party needing a copy of the unredacted transcript to review for redaction purposes may purchase a copy from the court reporter or transcriber or view the document at the Clerk's Office public terminal.

Remote Public Access to Transcripts. If a redacted transcript is filed with the Court, that redacted transcript will be remotely electronically available through PACER after 90 calendar days from the date of filing of the original transcript. If a redacted transcript is filed, the Clerk's Office will never make the original transcript publicly available. If the original transcript is filed without redaction, that original transcript will be remotely electronically available through PACER after 90 calendar days and may be copied at the Clerk's Office.

CJA Panel Attorneys. An attorney who is serving as "standby" counsel appointed to assist a pro se defendant in his or her defense in a criminal case must review the same portions of the transcript as if the pro se defendant were his or her client. If the transcript relates to a panel attorney representation pursuant to the Criminal Justice Act (CJA), including serving as standby counsel, the attorney conducting the review is entitled to compensation under the CJA for functions reasonably performed to fulfill the redaction obligation and for reimbursement for related reasonable expenses.

PACER fees. PACER fees will be applied both during and after the 90–day restriction period. Charges will not be capped at 30 pages ($2.40) as they are for other court documents, but will rather accrue for the entire transcript. The user will incur PACER charges for each time the transcript is accessed even though he/she may have purchased it from the court reporter or transcriber and obtained remote access through CM/ECF. There is no "free look" for transcripts.

Note: This policy applies to transcripts of events taking place in the court's courtrooms, not depositions taken outside of court or proceedings of state courts or other jurisdictions.

Attorneys are entirely responsible for identifying information to be redacted and notifying court reporters and transcribers. If there is no action by attorneys, no redaction will occur.

Transcript Costs. Pursuant to Local Rule 54.1(b), the Clerk of the Court is to publish the court reporter attendance fee that may be awarded in addition to the per page limit. Unless another rate was previously provided by order of the Court, the court reporter attendance fee shall not exceed $110 for one half day (4 hours or less), and $220 for a full day attendance fee.

Frequently Asked Questions. Click here to view a listing of frequently asked questions regarding the Judicial Conference policy on the availability of transcripts of Court proceedings on our web site www.ilnd.uscourts.gov.

Transcripts

Frequently Asked Questions

I purchased the original transcript and another party ordered a redacted transcript, will I automatically be given access to remotely view the redacted transcript?

Yes, the party in the case whom purchased the original transcript will automatically be granted access to remotely view the redacted transcript.

I purchased the redacted transcript, will I automatically be given access to remotely view the original transcript?

No. Your access will be limited to the redacted transcript.

Will the original transcript and the redacted transcript be available for remote viewing after the 90 day deadline has passed?

No. The original transcript will remain limited for remote viewing for parties in the case whom ordered the transcript. The redacted version of the transcript will be available for remote viewing to members of the public after the restriction period.

I'm an appellate attorney on a case, will I be given access to view transcripts?

Yes. After purchasing the transcript, you will be given access to remotely view the transcript. You will not be added to the individual case.

The media ordered the original transcript, will they be granted remote access to view the transcript?

No. At the end of the restriction period the public will be provided with remote electronic access to the transcript. If the transcript is redacted, only remote access to the redacted transcript will be given.

I filed my Notice of Intent to Request Redaction after the five (5) business day due date. Can I still file my Redacted Transcript Request?

Yes, the Redacted Transcript Request must be e-filed within twenty one (21) calendar days of the filing of the transcript.

[Amended effective May 30, 2013.]

LONG TRIAL EQUALIZATION PROCEDURES*

A. Definitions. The following definitions apply to these procedures:

(1) *Clerk.* The term *Clerk* shall mean the Clerk of the Court or a deputy or deputies expressly designated by the Clerk to perform the duties required of the Clerk by these procedures.

(2) *Criminal Proceeding.* The term *criminal proceeding* includes all activity in a criminal case from filing through termination. For the purposes of these procedures, once a criminal proceeding has been terminated, any subsequent proceeding initiated by a reopening will be treated as a separate proceeding.

(3) *Equalization Credit.* The term *equalization credit* shall mean a single skip in the process of assigning criminal cases for each equalization period. An equalization period consists of a minimum of two trial days with a combined total of at least nine trial hours in excess of the number of trial days and hours required for a qualifying trial.

(4) *Filing.* The term *filing* includes the initial filing at the time of the return of the indictment and any reopening subsequent to a termination.

(5) *Pending Case.* The term *pending case* includes any criminal case not terminated as defined in (7) below.

(6) *Qualifying Trial.* The term *qualifying trial* includes any trial or group of trials arising in a criminal proceeding held before the same judicial officer, with or without a jury, where the total number of trial days is at least fifteen and the total number of trial hours is at least 67.5.

(7) *Termination.* The term *termination* refers either to the statistical closing of a proceeding against a defendant in a manner specified by *Guide to Judiciary Policies and Procedures,* Volume XI, Chapter IV, Part IV, or to the transfer of a defendant to the Fugitive Calendar of the Executive Committee pursuant to local General Rule 2.30b. A criminal proceeding shall be considered terminated when all defendants are either terminated or transferred to the Fugitive Calendar.

(8) *Trial.* For the purposes of these procedures the terms *trial, trial day,* and *trial hour* shall be used in accordance with the definitions provided for completing the monthly JS–10 reports. (See *Guide to Judiciary Policies and Procedures,* Volume XI, Chapter VI.)

B. Equalization Procedures. Whenever the total number of trial days and trial hours in a criminal proceeding are sufficient to establish a qualifying trial, the minute clerk assigned to the judge before whom the qualifying trial has taken place shall notify the Clerk in writing. The minute clerk will also notify the Clerk in writing each time an equalization credit has been earned by the judge. The Clerk will prepare a form for use by the minute clerks in making such notification. Except in unusual situations, the Clerk is to be notified not later than the end of the business day following the day on which the qualifying trial is established or the equalization credit is earned.

The Clerk shall verify the data on the form submitted for mathematical accuracy and, to the extent that the times had previously been reported on a JS–10 report, for consistency with earlier reported amounts. Any discrepancies will be brought to the attention of the minute clerk.

Once the data has been verified and an equalization credit is to be given, the Clerk shall so indicate on the face of the form and transmit the form to the assignment clerk. The assignment clerk shall time stamp the form when it is received at the assignment desk. The form, once verified by the Clerk and time-stamped by the assignment clerk shall serve as authority to the assignment clerk to skip the next assignment card bearing the name of the judge receiving equalization credit, regardless of category.

Where there is more than one equalization credit form for the same judge, the assignment clerk shall arrange them in order so that the one bearing the earliest time-stamp is first and the one bearing the most recent time-stamp is last.

Whenever an indictment is to be assigned to a judge by lot in accordance with the Rules of this Court, the assignment clerk shall first check to see if there are any equalization credit forms on file with the assignment clerk. If there are none, the assignment shall proceed in accordance with the Rules. If there are forms, the assignment shall proceed in accordance with the Rules except that should a card be turned bearing the name of a judge to whom equalization credit is due, that card shall be skipped and the assignment clerk will pull another assignment card.

The assignment clerk will annotate any assignment card skipped under these procedures by writing on each card "Long Trial Equalization: [case number of case in which credit earned]." The assignment clerk will annotate each equalization credit form which resulted in an assignment card being skipped to indicate the date of the skipping and the assignment deck in which the card was skipped.

C. Effective Date of Application of Procedures. These procedures shall become effective with the entry of this order. They shall apply to all pending cases in which equalization credit has been earned.

[Dated: December 26, 1990.]

* [**Publisher's Note**: Title editorially supplied.]

ASSIGNMENT OF STUDENT LOAN AND OVERPAYMENT CASES*

By direction of the full Court met in Executive Session on Wednesday, 27 November 1991,

IT IS HEREBY ORDERED That the General Order entered on 23 February 1979 regarding the filing and assignment of civil complaints dealing with the alleged failure to repay student loans which were guaranteed by the Veterans' Administration and the Department of Health, Education and Welfare be, and it is hereby vacated.

IT IS FURTHER ORDERED That the Executive Committee Order entered on 22 October 1981 regarding the filing and assignment of civil complaints on behalf of the Veterans' Administration alleging a failure to repay an educational overpayment by a veteran be, and it is hereby vacated.

IT IS FURTHER ORDERED That

(a) Pursuant to 28 U.S.C. § 3008 the Court assigns its duties in proceedings under Chapter 176 of Title 28 of the United States Code [Federal Debt Collection Procedures Act of 1990 (Title XXXVI of Public Law 101–647, codified in 28 U.S.C. §§ 3001, et seq.)] to the United States magistrate judges of this Court.

(b) When a civil complaint is filed on behalf of the Veterans' Administration or the Department of Education alleging a failure to repay a student loan or failure to repay an educational overpayment, the person filing the complaint shall indicate its nature to the assignment clerk.

(c) The assignment clerk shall assign such complaints generally to the United States magistrate judges who shall supervise the pretrial of the case, forward a final pretrial order to such district judge as shall be assigned by lot at the close of discovery, and hear all supplemental post-judgment proceedings in cases not assigned to a district judge.

(d) Matters requiring the action of a judicial officer in such cases as are assigned generally shall be brought before the duty magistrate judge. The duty magistrate judge may take such action as is appropriate and consistent with (c) above, provided that where an answer or motion in lieu of answer is filed, or where hearings are required on post-judgment supplementary proceedings, the duty magistrate judge may direct the clerk to assign the case by lot to a magistrate judge in accordance with the Rules of this Court.

[Dated: November 27, 1991.]

* [**Publisher's Note**: Title editorially supplied.]

NOTICE REGARDING ACCESS TO ELECTRONIC CRIMINAL CASE FILES

Please be informed that documents filed in criminal cases in this court are now available to the public electronically.

You shall not include sensitive information in any document filed with the court. Any personal information not otherwise protected will be made available over the Internet via WebPACER. The following personal data identifiers **must** be partially redacted from the document whether it is filed traditionally or electronically: Social

Security numbers to the last four digits; financial account numbers to the last four digits; names of minor children to the initials; dates of birth to the year; and home addresses to the city and state.

In compliance with the E–Government Act of 2002, a party wishing to file a document containing the personal data identifiers specified above may file an unredacted document under seal. This document shall be retained by the court as part of the record. The court may, however, also require the party to file a redacted copy for the public file.

Because filings will be remotely, electronically available and may contain information implicating not only privacy but also personal security concerns, exercise caution when filing a document that contains any of the information listed below and consider accompanying any such filing with a motion to seal. Until the court has ruled on any motion to seal, no document that is the subject of a motion to seal, nor the motion itself or any response thereto, will be available electronically or in paper form.

- any personal identifying number, such as driver's license number;
- medical records, treatment and diagnosis;
- employment history;
- individual financial information;
- proprietary or trade secret information;
- information regarding an individual's cooperation with the government;
- information regarding the victim of any criminal activity;
- national security information; and
- sensitive security information as described in 49 U.S.C. § 114(s).

Counsel is strongly urged to share this notice with all clients so that an informed decision about the inclusion of certain materials may be made. If a redacted document is filed, it is the sole responsibility of counsel and the parties to be sure that all documents and pleadings comply with the rules of this court requiring redaction of personal data identifiers. **The clerk will not review filings for redaction.**

GENERAL ORDER 2011–22. [CAMERAS PILOT PROJECT]*

It appearing that the full Court met in executive session on Thursday, June 30, 2011 has elected to participate in the Cameras in the Courtroom Pilot Project authorized by the Judicial Conference of the United States Courts in September of 2010; therefore

IT IS HEREBY ORDERED That proceedings being recorded as part of the above-referenced pilot project are exempted from the provisions of Local Rule 83.1(c). Such recordings must be made subject to guidelines for the pilot program approved by the Judicial Conference.

[Dated: July 6, 2011.]

* [**Publisher's Note:** Title editorially supplied.]

12–0003. [GENERAL ORDER ON TRANSCRIPT COPY RATES]*

IT APPEARING That the Judicial Conference of the United States Courts has approved the transcript and transcript copy rates listed below; and

IT FURTHER APPEARING That the full Court met in executive session on January 25, 2012, and approved these rates; therefore

IT IS HEREBY ORDERED, pursuant to Title 28, U.S.C. § 753, the following transcript rates per page are prescribed by the Court and are effective for all transcripts requested on or after January 27, 2012.

	Original	Copy to Each Party	Additional Copy to Same Party
Ordinary Transcript (30 Day)	$3.65	$.90	$.60
Fourteen Day Transcript	$4.25	$.90	$.60
Expedited Transcript (7 Day)	$4.85	$.90	$.60
Daily Transcript	$6.05	$1.20	$.90
Hourly Transcript	$7.25	$1.20	$.90
Realtime Transcript	One feed; $3.05 per page; two-to-four feeds, are 2.10 per page; five or more feeds, $1.50 per page		

[Dated: January 26, 2012.]

* [**Publisher's Note:** Title editorially supplied.]

GENERAL ORDER 14–0024.   GENERAL ORDER ON ELECTRONIC CASE FILING

Meeting in executive session on November 16, 2004, the Court approved the following procedures for Electronic Case Filing (ECF). Revisions to these procedures were approved by the Court on May 19, 2005, May 21, 2006, October 25, 2007, April 30, 2009, July 6, 2011, March 20, 2014, and October 16, 2014.

I. Preamble

(A) **Whereas:**

(1) this court implemented the Case Management/Electronic Case Filing System in 2005;

(2) Federal Rules of Civil Procedure Rules 5, 77, and 79, and Federal Rules of Criminal Procedure Rules 49 and 55, now permit the creation, retention, and storage of court records and service of notice and court orders by electronic means; and

(3) This court has provided for the creation, retention, and storage of court records and service of notice and court orders by electronic means;

(B) The Court hereby enters this general order which may be referred to as the "General Order on Electronic Case Filing."

(C) This General Order shall be available through the Court Web Site. Any additional procedures established by the Clerk of the Court pursuant to this General Order are also available through the Court Web Site.

II. Definitions

(A) "Electronic Case Filing System" or "ECF" is the court's electronic system for receiving, recording, docketing, filing, and retrieving pleadings and other court documents in electronic form and for generating, recording, retrieving, and transmitting court orders and notices in electronic form.

(B) "E–Filer" is a person registered to use ECF in the Northern District of Illinois and who has been issued a login and password.

(C) "Notice of Electronic Filing" is the notice generated by ECF upon the completion of an electronic filing.

(D) "Court Web Site" is the official Internet web site of the United States District Court for the Northern District of Illinois, the present address of which is http://www.ilnd.uscourts.gov.

(E) A document is in "Compatible Format" if it is in Portable Document Format ("PDF") created by Adobe Acrobat or another similar and compatible program, or in such other format as the Clerk of the Court may designate and post on the Court Web Site.

(F) "Paper," when used in this General Order to describe forms, documents, etc., means a tangible, hard copy version in contrast to electronic versions.

III. Scope of Electronic Filing

(A) (1) All civil, criminal, and admiralty cases are assigned to ECF except those categories of cases specifically excepted below.

(2) The following categories of cases do not qualify to be assigned to ECF:

  (a) petty offenses;

  (b) grand jury matters;

  (c) sealed cases, until a point in the proceedings when the case is unsealed; and

  (d) any other specific case where the court expressly orders that it not be assigned to ECF, until a point in the proceedings that the court may order otherwise.

(B) (1) Except as expressly provided and in exceptional circumstances preventing an E–Filer from filing electronically, all petitions, motions, memoranda of law, or other pleadings and documents required to be filed with the court after September 30, 2005 in connection with a case assigned to ECF shall be electronically filed.

(2) The following categories of documents are not to be filed electronically:

  (a) charging documents in a criminal case, including superceding indictments, superceding informations, and superceding complaints;

  (b) warrants for arrest and summons in criminal cases;

  (c) all documents that require the signature of a criminal defendant;

  (d) sealed complaints;

  (e) bonds;

  (f) letters of request;

  (g) other designated documents in accordance with procedures established by the Clerk of the Court; and

  (h) documents that the court expressly orders or permits to be filed in paper form.

(3) Subject to restrictions on access approved by the Executive Committee, the following categories of documents shall be filed electronically:

  (a) administrative records;

  (b) state court records in a habeas corpus case;

  (c) restricted, sealed, or in camera documents;

  (d) ex parte motions;

  (e) pretrial services reports and presentence reports;

  (f) applications pursuant to Mutual Legal Assistance Treaties (MLATs).

(4) As to those documents listed in § III(B)(2) and any other documents filed in paper form, the Clerk of the Court may establish procedures for creating and storing electronic versions of such documents. Those procedures (a) may contain provisions for creating redacted versions of documents and (b) shall not provide for the maintenance of electronic versions of in camera documents unless the Clerk of the Court specifically determines that the then-current version of ECF contains adequate protections for securing and restricting access to such documents.

(C) Prior to filing an emergency motion or matter, as defined in Local Rule 77.2, an E–Filer shall contact the judge's courtroom deputy or chambers by telephone or in person. Chambers information, including standing orders, is posted on the Court Website.

(D) The Clerk of Court is hereby granted the authority to authorize refunds upon written request by a party who has inadvertently made erroneous or duplicate payments on line. All approved refunds shall be processed through the electronic credit card system. In the event that a particular attorney or law firm continues to make repeated mistakes when submitting fees and requesting refunds, the Clerk of Court may request that the Court issue an order to show cause why further requests for refunds should be considered. If a credit card transaction is invalid for any reason or if the credit card processing function in CM/ECF is experiencing problems, payment must be made within two business days. Summons will not be issued until the fee is paid by credit card, check, cash, or money order. If the case is an emergency filing, the filer must bring the paper document.

IV. Eligibility, Registration, and Passwords

(A) (1) Attorneys admitted to the bar of this court, including those admitted pro hac vice, and attorneys representing the United States in the attorney's official capacity, may register as E–Filers.

(2) Registration shall be in accordance with procedures established by the Clerk of the Court and shall require that the applicant provide his or her name, address, telephone number, Internet e-mail address, and a declaration that the applicant is admitted to the bar of this court or admitted pro hac vice. Registration also requires that the applicant have or obtain an account on the Public Access to Court Electronic Records ("PACER") system.

(B) (1) A party to a pending civil action who is not represented by an attorney and who is not under filing restrictions imposed by the Executive Committee of this Court, may register as an E–Filer solely for purposes of the case.

(2) Registration shall be in accordance with procedures established by the Clerk of the Court and shall require that the applicant identify the action as well as the name, address, telephone number, and Internet e-mail address of the applicant. Registration also requires that the applicant have or obtain an account on the Public Access to Court Electronic Records ("PACER") system.

(3) Parties who are in custody are not permitted to register as E–Filers. If, during the course of the action, a party who is registered as an E–Filer is placed in custody, the E–Filer shall promptly advise the Clerk of the Court to terminate the E–Filer's registration as an E–Filer.

(4) If, during the course of the action, the party retains an attorney who appears on the party's behalf, the attorney must advise the Clerk of the Court to terminate the party's registration as an E–Filer upon the attorney's appearance.

(C) Registration as an E–Filer constitutes consent to electronic service of all documents as provided in this General Order and in accordance with the Federal Rules of Civil Procedure and Federal Rules of Criminal Procedure. The Clerk of the Court shall use an electronic and/or paper registration form that contains an express consent to service by electronic means in accordance with Fed. R. Civ. P. 5(b)(2)(D) and Fed. R. Crim. P. 49(b).

(D) The Clerk of the Court may establish registration procedures that require an E–Filer applicant to complete on-line and/or in-person ECF training prior to being provided full access as an E–Filer.

(E) Once registration and/or training is completed in accordance with procedures established by the Clerk of the Court, the Clerk of the Court shall provide the E–Filer with notification of the E–Filer's login and password.

(F) E–Filers agree to protect the security of their passwords.

(1) An E–Filer shall immediately notify the Clerk of the Court if he or she learns that the E–Filer's password has been compromised.

(2) Use of the login and password is limited to the E–Filer and agents specifically authorized by the E–Filer. The E–Filer shall be responsible for all applicable charges associated with use of the E–Filer's password, and any documents filed by use of the password shall be deemed authorized and signed by the E–Filer.

(3) If the Clerk of the Court believes that an E–Filer's password has been compromised, the Clerk of the Court shall notify the E–Filer. In such instances, the Clerk of the Court may make necessary corrections to ECF and shall issue a new password to the E–Filer.

(4) E–Filers may be subject to sanctions for failure to comply with the provisions of this General Order or any ECF procedures established by the Clerk of the Court.

(G) It is the responsibility of the E–Filer to maintain adequate facilities and equipment to participate in ECF, including maintaining a current and active e-mail address. The E–Filer shall promptly provide written notification to the Clerk of the Court and opposing litigants in pending cases of any changes in the E–Filer's e-mail address. An E–Filer who lacks the necessary facilities, equipment, or active e-mail address, other than for a temporary period of limited duration, shall promptly seek withdrawal from ECF.

(H) An E–Filer may, for cause, be terminated from using ECF. The Clerk of the Court shall establish rules and procedures for such termination, which shall provide for review by petition to the Executive Committee of the court or a designated district judge or magistrate judge.

(I) (1) An E–Filer who is transferred to inactive status in accordance with LR 83.18 or suspended or disbarred pursuant to the court's disciplinary procedures, LR 83.25–.31, shall have his or her registration as an E–Filer automatically terminated.

(2) Following reinstatement under LR 83.18 or LR 83.30, a previously registered E–Filer must request reinstatement of his or her registration as an E–Filer. Such request must include then-current information as to the E–Filer's name, address, telephone number, and Internet e-mail address and any other information that may be required under procedures established by the Clerk of the Court.

V. Consequences of Electronic Filing

(A) Electronic transmission of a document to ECF consistent with these rules, together with the transmission of a Notice of Electronic Filing from the court, constitutes filing of the document for all purposes of the Federal Rules of Civil Procedure, the Federal Rules of Criminal Procedure, and the local rules of this court, and constitutes entry of the document on the docket kept by the Clerk of the Court under Fed. R. Civ. P. 58 and 79 and Fed. R. Crim. P. 49 and 55.

(B) When a document has been filed electronically or created by the court electronically, the official record is the electronic recording of the document as stored by the court.

(C) Where the Clerk determines that a legible scanned image cannot be produced of a document filed in paper form, the paper document shall be maintained as the official record of the court except as provided for in sections V(D) and V(E) below.

(D) Where a document filed in paper form is suitable for scanning, but one or more exhibits attached to the document cannot be readily scanned due to the quality of text or images included in the exhibit, the clerk may scan the document as provided for in section (B)(1) above and retain the exhibit in paper form.

(E) The filing party is bound by the document as filed. The Clerk of Court may, where necessary and appropriate, modify the docket to comply with quality control standards.

(F) Except in the case of documents first filed in paper form and subsequently submitted electronically under § III(B)(4), a document filed electronically is deemed filed at the date and time stated on the Notice of Electronic Filing from the court.

(G) Filing a document electronically does not alter the filing deadline for that document. Filing must be completed before midnight Central Time in the Northern District of Illinois in order to be considered timely filed that day. To the extent local rule or an order of the court requires filing with the court or service on an opposing party by a specific time of day, the document must be filed or served by that time of day to be timely and a courtesy copy submitted to the court within one business day.

VI. Entry of Court Orders

(A) (1) All orders, decrees, judgments, and proceedings of the court will be filed in accordance with this General Order which will constitute entry on the docket kept by the Clerk of the Court under Fed. R. Civ. P. 58 and 79 and Fed. R. Crim. P. 49 and 55. All signed orders will be filed electronically by the court or court personnel. Any order filed electronically by the court or court personnel without the original signature of a judge (or, where applicable, the Clerk of the Court) has the same force and effect as if the judge or Clerk of the Court had affixed the judge's or Clerk of the Court's signature to a paper copy of the order and it had been entered on the docket in the manner otherwise provided.

(2) The Clerk of the Court may establish additional procedures for filing, creating, and storing electronic versions of orders, decrees, and judgments.

(B) An E–Filer submitting a document electronically that requires a judge's signature must promptly deliver the document in such form as the judge requires.

VII. Documents, Attachments, and Exhibits

(A) E–Filers must file all documents in electronic form, except where this General Order or the court permits otherwise. All electronic documents must be submitted in Compatible Format. Each document filed electronically must be titled using one of the categories contained in ECF.

(B) Each exhibit or attachment must be filed as a separate document within the same entry.

(C) Individual documents filed electronically must not exceed 20 megabytes in size. Any document that exceeds the 20 megabyte limit must be broken into multiple PDF files. The 20 megabyte limitation applies to each individual component of the filing. For example, if a motion is filed with three related exhibits as attachments in one entry, each of the four files may be up to 20 megabytes in size. There is no limit to the aggregate total for multiple attachments within one filing.

(D) E–Filers may be excused from filing a particular component electronically under certain limited circumstances, such as when the component cannot be reduced to an electronic format. Such component shall not be filed electronically, but instead shall be filed with the Clerk of the Court and served upon the parties in accordance with the applicable Federal Rules of Civil Procedure or Federal Rules of Criminal Procedure and the local rules for filing and service of paper documents. E–Filers filing a paper component shall file electronically a Notice of Paper Filing setting forth the reason(s) why the component cannot be filed electronically.

(E) An E–Filer, unless otherwise instructed by the court, may submit as exhibits or attachments only those excerpts of the referenced documents that are directly germane to the matter under consideration by the court. Excerpted material must be clearly and prominently identified as such. E–Filers who file excerpts of documents as exhibits or attachments under this rule do so without prejudice to their right to timely file additional excerpts or the complete document. Responding parties may timely file additional excerpts or the complete document that they believe are directly germane.

(F) (1) Nothing in section VII of this General Order shall override the local rules regarding page limitations on specific types of documents. The pages of electronic documents should substantially comply with the page limitations contained in LR 5.2. Absent leave of court, the page limitations set forth in LR 7.1 apply to briefs filed in electronic form.

(2) Nothing in section VII of this General Order shall prevent the court from ordering that other rules will apply in a particular case.

VIII. Retention Requirements for Documents With Signatures of Persons Other Than E–Filers

(A) Documents that are electronically filed and require original signatures other than that of the E–Filer, *e.g*, affidavits, declarations, must be maintained in paper form by the E–Filer until 4 years after all time periods for appeals expire.

(B) On request of the court, the E–Filer must provide original documents for review.

IX. Signatures of E–Filers

(A) The user login and password required to transmit documents to ECF serve as the E–Filer's signature on all electronic documents filed with the court. They also serve as a signature for purposes of Fed. R. Civ. P. 11, the Federal Rules of Civil Procedure, the Federal Rules of Criminal Procedure, the local rules of this court, and any other purpose for which a signature is required in connection with proceedings before the court. Each document filed electronically must, if possible, indicate that it has been electronically filed. Electronically filed documents must include a signature block and must set forth the name, address, telephone number and the attorney's bar registration number, if applicable. In addition, the name of the E–Filer under whose login and password the document is submitted must be preceded by an "/s/" and typed in the space where the signature would otherwise appear.

(B) No E–Filer or other person may knowingly permit or cause to permit an E–Filer's password to be used by anyone other than an authorized agent of the E–Filer. Electronic filing may be delegated to an authorized agent, who may use the login and password to transmit a filing. However, use of the login and password to transmit the filing constitutes a signature by the E–Filer, even when the E–Filer does not perform the physical act of filing.

(C) In cases assigned to ECF, documents requiring signatures of more than one party must be electronically filed either by: (1) transmitting a scanned document containing all necessary signatures; (2) representing the consent of the other parties on the document; (3) identifying on the document the parties whose signatures are required and by the submission of a notice of endorsement by the other parties no later than three court days after filing; or (4) in any other manner approved by the court.

X. Service of Documents by Electronic Means

(A) All E–Filers shall maintain a current and active e-mail address to receive Notices of Electronic Filing through ECF.

(B) When a pleading or other document is filed electronically in a case assigned to ECF, ECF will automatically generate a Notice of Electronic Filing, which will automatically be transmitted by e-mail to all E–Filers in the case.

(C) Except where sealed documents are filed electronically, subject to the provisions of Fed. R. Civ. P. 5(b)(3), the Notice of Electronic Filing constitutes service under Fed. R. Civ. P. 5(b)(2)(D) and Fed. R. Crim. P. 49(b) as to all E–Filers in a case assigned to ECF.

(D) Parties to a case assigned to ECF, who are not E–Filers or represented by an E–Filer and who have not otherwise consented to service by electronic means under Fed. R. Civ. P. 5(b)(2)(D), are entitled to receive a paper copy of any electronically filed document. Service of such paper copy must be made in accordance with the Federal Rules of Civil Procedure, the Federal Rules of Criminal Procedure, and the local rules of this court.

(E) Where service is made as to any party who is not an E–Filer or is represented by an E–Filer, a certificate or affidavit of service must be included with all documents filed electronically. Such certificate or affidavit shall comply with LR 5.5 Such certificate or affidavit is not required as to any party who is an E–filer or is represented by an E–filer.

XI. Notice of Court Orders and Judgments

(A) Immediately upon the entry of an order or judgment in a case assigned to ECF, the Clerk of the Court will transmit to E–Filers in the case, in electronic form, a Notice of Electronic Filing. Electronic transmission of the Notice of Electronic Filing constitutes the notice required by Fed. R. Civ. P. 77(d) and Fed. R. Crim. P. 49(c). The Clerk of the Court must give notice in paper form to a person who is not an E–Filer or represented by an E–Filer in accordance with the Federal Rules of Civil Procedure, Federal Rules of Criminal Procedure, and the local rules of this court.

XII. Technical Failures

(A) An E–Filer whose filing is made untimely as a result of a technical failure may seek appropriate relief from the court.

(B) Any difficulty connecting to ECF and any other technical failure experienced should be immediately reported to the ECF Help Desk. The Court Web Site shall provide information as to how to contact the ECF Help Desk.

(C) Any court record, lost or destroyed, whether electronically filed or in paper format, will be restored pursuant to 28 U.S.C. § 1735 and § 1734.

XIII. Public Access

(A) Anyone desiring to view documents and court records maintained on ECF from a location other than the office of the Clerk of the Court, must have an account on the Public Access to Court Electronic Records ("PACER") system. Information about PACER, including applicable fees and how to register for it, may be found on the Court Web Site.

(B) The public will have electronic access to ECF at the offices of the Clerk of the Court for viewing during regular business hours. The offices of the Clerk of the

Court are located at 219 South Dearborn Street, Chicago, IL 60604 and 327 S. Church Street, Rockford, IL 61101.

(C) Paper copies and certified copies of the electronically maintained documents on ECF may be purchased at the offices of the Clerk of the Court. The fees for copying and certifying will be in accordance with 28 U.S.C. § 1930.

[Dated: October 16, 2014.]

INDEX TO UNITED STATES DISTRICT COURT
FOR THE NORTHERN DISTRICT OF ILLINOIS

Local Rules are cited as "LR___"
Criminal Rules are cited as "LCrR___"
Admiralty Rules are cited as "LRSup___"

ACTIONS AND PROCEEDINGS

ADMIRALTY

ALIENS

ALTERNATIVE DISPUTE RESOLUTION

APPEAL AND REVIEW

APPEARANCES

APPOINTMENTS

ARBITRATION AND AWARD

ARRAIGNMENT

ASSIGNMENT OF CASES

ATTACHMENT

ATTORNEY FEES

UNITED STATES BANKRUPTCY COURT FOR THE NORTHERN DISTRICT OF ILLINOIS

Including Amendments Received Through
April 1, 2015

RULE 1000–1. DEFINITIONS

(1) "Administrative Procedures" shall mean the Administrative Procedures for the Case Management/Electronic Case Filing System, adopted by the court on February 17, 2004, as amended;

(2) the "Bankruptcy Code" shall mean Title 11 of the United States Code, as amended;

(3) "Bankruptcy Court" shall mean the bankruptcy judges of the United States District Court for the Northern District of Illinois;

(4) "clerk" shall include the clerk of the court, any deputy clerk, and any member of a judge's staff who has taken the oath of office to perform the duties of a deputy clerk;

(5) "clerk of the court" shall mean the clerk of the court duly appointed by the Bankruptcy Court;

(6) "CM/ECF" shall mean the Case Management/Electronic Case Filing System;

(7) "courtroom deputy" shall mean the deputy clerk assigned to perform courtroom duties for a particular judge;

(8) the "date of presentment" shall refer to the day on which the motion is to be presented in open court according to the notice required by Rule 9013–1;

(9) "District Court" shall mean the United States District Court for the Northern District of Illinois;

(10) "District Court Local Rules" shall mean the Civil Rules promulgated by the District Court;

(11) "Executive Committee" shall mean the Executive Committee of the District Court;

(12) "judge" or "court" shall mean the judge assigned to a case or an adversary proceeding or any other judge sitting in that judge's stead;

(13) "motion" shall include all requests for relief by motion or application, other than applications to waive the filing fee or pay the filing fee in installments.

(14) "Rules" shall mean these Local Bankruptcy Rules and any amendments or additions thereto;

(15) "Rule ___" shall mean a rule within these Rules and any amendments and additions thereto;

(16) "trustee" shall mean the person appointed or elected to serve as case trustee under the Bankruptcy Code, but not the debtor in possession in a case under Chapter 11.

[Adopted effective December 1, 2008. Amended effective October 27, 2011; January 1, 2012.]

RULE 1000–2. SCOPE OF RULES

A. Scope of Rules. These Rules are promulgated by the District Court and the Bankruptcy Court pursuant to Fed. R. Civ. P. 83 and Fed. R. Bankr. P. 9029. They may be cited as "Local Bankruptcy Rules" and will govern procedure in the Bankruptcy Court, and in the District Court in all bankruptcy cases and proceedings as defined in 28 U.S.C. § 157, to the extent that they are not inconsistent with applicable law, the Federal Rules of Bankruptcy Procedure, or the Official Bankruptcy Forms. These Rules will be construed to secure the expeditious and economical administration of every case within the district under the Bankruptcy Code and the just, speedy, and inexpensive determination of every proceeding therein.

B. Previous Bankruptcy Rules Rescinded. All local bankruptcy rules adopted by the District Court and the Bankruptcy Court prior to the adoption of these Rules are rescinded.

C. Application of District Court Local Rules. The District Court Local Rules will apply to the Bankruptcy Court and bankruptcy cases only when the District Court Local Rules or these Rules so specify, or when applied by any judge to proceedings before that judge in situations not covered.

D. Additional Procedural Orders.

(1) In addition to these Rules, procedures in the Bankruptcy Court may also be governed by

(a) General Orders, issued by the court, applicable in all cases, and

(b) Standing Orders, issued by an individual judge, applicable in cases pending before that judge.

(2) The chief judge may issue, on behalf of the court, Administrative Orders governing matters such as hours of operation, court holidays, and case assignments.

(3) Administrative Procedures have been adopted by the court pursuant to Fed. R. Bankr. P. 5005 and Rule 5005–1(A).

[Adopted effective December 1, 2008.]

RULE 1006–1. PAYMENT OF FILING FEE IN INSTALLMENTS

A. Required Payments. If a debtor applies to pay the filing fee in installments pursuant to Fed. R. Bankr. P. 1006, the clerk may enter on behalf of the judge to whom the case is assigned the appropriate order, which will require four equal payments due 30, 60, 90, and 120 days after the petition is filed.

B. Notice to Creditors. If a debtor applies to pay the filing fee in installments, the clerk will not send notice of the commencement of the case or meeting of creditors to any party in interest until the order described in section A has been entered or the judge to whom the case is assigned has entered an order allowing the filing fee to be paid in installments.

[Adopted effective December 1, 2008.]

RULE 1006–2. PAYMENT OF FEES FOR ELECTRONIC FILINGS

Subject to Rule 1006–1, any document filed electronically must be accompanied by the appropriate fee.

[Adopted effective December 1, 2008.]

RULE 1006–3. PAYMENT OF FEES BY DEBTORS AND OTHER NON–REGISTRANTS

Subject to Rule 1006–1, any document filed on paper must be accompanied by the appropriate fee in the form of cash, cashier's check, certified check, or money order. The clerk may not accept personal, non-certified checks or credit cards from pro se parties or other non-registrants.

[Adopted effective December 1, 2008.]

RULE 1007–1. COMPUTER READABLE LISTS OF CREDITORS

In all voluntary cases filed under the Bankruptcy Code filed by parties other than pro se debtors, the petition for relief shall be accompanied by a list, in a computer readable format designed and published from time to time by the clerk, of the names and complete addresses, including zip codes, of the following:

(1) the debtor;

(2) the attorney of record;

(3) all secured and unsecured creditors; and

(4) all other parties in interest entitled to notice in the case.

Upon motion for cause shown, the court may excuse compliance with this Rule.

[Adopted effective December 1, 2008.]

RULE 1007–2. CLAIMS REGISTERS

A. Clerk to Supervise. The clerk will supervise preparation and maintenance of claims registers in all cases.

B. Claims Agent. On motion of the debtor or trustee, the court may authorize retention of a claims agent under 28 U.S.C. § 156(c) to prepare and maintain the claims register. In all cases with more than 500 creditors, the debtor must file a motion to employ a notice or claims agent approved by the clerk to perform this function. The claims register prepared and maintained by a claims agent retained under this Rule will be the official claims register of the court.

[Adopted effective December 1, 2008. Amended effective October 27, 2011; January 1, 2012.]

RULE 1009–1. NOTICE OF AMENDMENTS TO VOLUNTARY PETITIONS, LISTS OR SCHEDULES; NOTICE TO CREDITORS

The debtor must serve amendments to voluntary petitions, lists, or schedules under Fed. R. Bankr. P. 1009(a) on all creditors, the trustee, and in chapter 11 cases, on the United States Trustee and any official committee of unsecured creditors, and must file proof of such service with the clerk. In addition, if, after filing the petition, the debtor files the creditor list or adds any creditors to the schedules, the debtor must serve each such creditor, by first-class or certified mail, with a copy of the original notice of the meeting of creditors, and must file proof of such service with the clerk.

[Adopted effective December 1, 2008.]

RULE 1014–1. TRANSFERS

A. Time of Transfer. When an order is entered directing the clerk to transfer a matter to another district, the clerk shall delay the transfer of the case for fourteen days following the date that the order of transfer is docketed, except when the court directs that the case be transferred forthwith. In effecting the transfer, the clerk shall transmit a certified copy of the docket and order of transfer and the original of all other documents. The clerk shall note on the docket the date of the transfer.

B. Completion of Transfer. The filing of a motion under Fed. R. Bankr. P. 9023 with respect to an order of transfer referred to in section A of this Rule shall not serve to stop the transfer of the case. However, on motion, the court may direct the clerk not to complete the transfer process until a date certain or further order of court.

[Adopted effective December 1, 2008.]

RULE 1015–1. RELATED CASES

A. Relatedness Defined. Two or more cases are related if one of the following conditions is met:

(1) the debtors are husband and wife;

(2) the debtor was a debtor in a previous case under Chapter 11 of the Bankruptcy Code; or

(3) the cases involve persons or entities that are affiliates as defined in § 101(2) of the Bankruptcy Code.

B. Assignment of Related Case by Clerk at Filing. If two or more cases to be filed in this district at the same time are related, the attorney filing the cases must file a Certification of Relatedness in substantially the form posted on the court's website. If a case to be filed in this district is related to a case previously filed in this district, the attorney filing the case must file a Certification of Relatedness in substantially the form posted on the court's website. If the Certification of Relatedness shows that the cases are related, the clerk must directly assign the related cases to the same judge.

C. Transfer to Chief Judge for Reassignment as Related. A motion by a party in interest to transfer a case on the grounds of relatedness must be brought before the judge assigned to the higher-numbered case. If the cases are related, the judge must transfer the case to the chief judge for reassignment to the judge assigned the lower-numbered case. The judge assigned the higher-numbered related case may also transfer the case sua sponte to the chief judge for reassignment.

D. Effect of Filing County of Reassignments for Relatedness. No reassignment shall be made on the basis of section A(2) of this Rule if the case is pending in a county other than Cook County.

[Adopted effective December 1, 2008. Amended effective October 27, 2011; January 1, 2012.]

RULE 1017–1. CONVERSION FROM CHAPTER 13 TO CHAPTER 7

All notices of conversion of chapter 13 cases to chapter 7 cases, pursuant to § 1307(a) of the Bankruptcy Code and Fed. R. Bankr. P. 1017(f)(3), must be filed with the clerk's office, accompanied by: (1) proof of service on the designated chapter 13 standing trustee and the United States Trustee, and (2) any required fee.

[Adopted effective December 1, 2008.]

RULE 1017–2. MOTIONS OF PARTIES TO DISMISS CHAPTER 7 CASES

A. Procedure Generally. Any trustee or party in interest may move to dismiss a chapter 7 case by filing with the clerk each of the following:

(1) a completed request for notice of hearing on the form approved by the court and supplied by the clerk;

(2) a notice of motion with a certificate indicating service of the motion on the debtor, the United States Trustee, and any party on the notice list under Fed. R. Bankr. P. 2002(m); and

(3) the motion to dismiss.

B. Date of Presentment of Motion to Dismiss. The date of presentment of the motion to dismiss must be no less than 28 nor more than 35 days from the date the documents referred to in section A of this Rule are filed with the clerk. The date and time of presentment must be set for a date and time that the assigned judge normally hears new motions in chapter 7 cases.

C. Notice of Motion to Dismiss to be Sent by Clerk. Upon receipt of the documents referred to in section A of this Rule, the clerk will cause notice to be sent pursuant to Fed. R. Bankr. P. 2002(a)(4).

[Adopted effective December 1, 2008.]

RULE 1017–3. EFFECT OF DISMISSAL OF BANKRUPTCY CASE ON PENDING ADVERSARIES

Whenever a case under the Bankruptcy Code is dismissed, any adversary proceeding arising under, arising in, or related to the case then pending will be dismissed without prejudice unless otherwise ordered by the court either in the dismissal order or by separate order. Cases that have been removed to bankruptcy court shall be remanded to the courts from which they were removed.

[Adopted effective December 1, 2008.]

RULE 1019–1. CONVERSION BY ONE DEBTOR UNDER A JOINT PETITION

When only one of two joint debtors in a joint petition files a notice of intent or motion to convert, upon payment of any required additional filing fees, the clerk shall divide the case into two separate cases and assign a case number to the new case. The debtor seeking to convert his or her case shall give notice to the other debtor, as well as to all other parties entitled to notice under the Bankruptcy Code and Bankruptcy Rules, and shall be responsible for the payment of all required fees. Each debtor shall file within 14 days of division of the case all necessary

amendments to the schedules and statement of financial affairs.

[Adopted effective December 1, 2008. Amended effective October 27, 2011; January 1, 2012.]

RULE 1072–1. PLACES OF HOLDING COURT

Motions for cases assigned to the Geneva, Joliet, Waukegan, and Wheaton calendars shall be heard in those locations on the days on which court is held there. Emergency motions shall be noticed if possible for the days on which court is held in those locations, but if an emergency arises that must be heard on a day when court is not in session in the relevant location, the motion may be heard by the judge assigned to the case. Nothing in this rule shall prevent a judge from transferring a case or proceeding to Chicago or Rockford for hearing or trial.

[Adopted effective December 1, 2008.]

RULE 1073–1. ASSIGNMENT OF CASES

Except as provided in Rules 1073–4 and 1015–1, the clerk shall assign cases by lot to calendars of judges, both upon initial filing and upon reassignment, through use of any means approved by the court.

[Adopted effective December 1, 2008.]

RULE 1073–2. IMPOSITION OF SANCTIONS RELATING TO INTERFERENCE WITH THE ASSIGNMENT SYSTEM

A. Application of Sanctions to Employees of the Clerk's Office.

(1) No clerk or other employee of the clerk's office shall:

(a) reveal to any person the sequence of judges' names within the assignment system;

(b) reveal to any person the sequence of names of chapter 7 trustees designated by the United States Trustee; or

(c) number or assign any case or matter except as provided by these Rules.

(2) Any employee violating this provision shall be discharged from service. Any violation of this provision may also constitute contempt of court.

B. Application of Sanctions to Persons other than Employees.

(1) No person shall directly or indirectly cause or attempt to cause any clerk or other employee of the clerk's office:

(a) to reveal to any person the sequence of judges' names within the assignment system,

(b) to reveal to any person the sequence of names of Chapter 7 trustees designated by the United States Trustee, or

(c) to number or assign any case or matter, otherwise than as provided by these Rules.

(2) Any person who violates this provision may be charged with contempt of court.

[Adopted effective December 1, 2008.]

RULE 1073–3. REASSIGNMENT

A. Reassignment Generally. No case shall be transferred for reassignment from the calendar of a judge to the calendar of any other judge except as provided by these Rules or by other applicable law. Nothing in this Rule shall prohibit a judge from transferring a specific matter for hearing and determination by another judge in the interest of judicial efficiency and economy, or when exigency requires.

B. Reassignments by the Chief Judge. The chief judge may reassign cases or proceedings from and to any judge, and may decline to reassign related cases or proceedings under Rule 1015–1, in order to adjust case loads or otherwise to promote efficient judicial administration.

C. Limited Reassignments for Purposes of Coordinated Proceedings in Complex Cases. Two or more judges may determine that it would be efficient to hold coordinated proceedings in a group of matters that are not related within the meaning of Rule 1015–1. Where such a determination is made, those judges will designate one or more of themselves to conduct the proceedings. The matters shall remain on the calendars of the judges to whom they were assigned.

[Adopted effective December 1, 2008.]

RULE 1073–4. ASSIGNMENT OF JUDGE IN CHAPTER 9 CASES

Upon the filing of any case under chapter 9 of the Bankruptcy Code, the clerk will not assign such case to the calendar of any judge but will immediately inform the chief judge of such filing. The chief judge will then request that the chief judge of the Court of Appeals for the Seventh Circuit designate a bankruptcy judge to conduct the case.

[Adopted effective December 1, 2008.]

RULE 2002–1. RETURN OF MAILED NOTICES

Envelopes containing notices generated and mailed by the Bankruptcy Noticing Center will bear the return address of debtor's counsel or the debtor if pro se.

[Adopted effective December 1, 2008. Amended effective January 1, 2012.]

RULE 2015–1. DEFERRAL OF FILING FEES DUE FROM TRUSTEE

In an adversary proceeding, if the case trustee certifies to the clerk that the estate lacks the funds necessary to pay a filing fee, the clerk shall defer the filing fee without court order and enter the deferral on the docket. If the estate later receives funds sufficient to pay the deferred fees, the trustee shall then pay the fee.

[Adopted effective December 1, 2008.]

RULE 2016–1. DISCLOSURE OF AGREEMENTS BETWEEN DEBTORS AND THEIR ATTORNEYS

Every agreement between a debtor and an attorney for the debtor that pertains, directly or indirectly, to the compensation paid or given, or to be paid or given, to or for the benefit of the attorney must be in the form of a written document signed by the debtor and the attorney. Agreements subject to this rule include, but are not limited to, the Court–Approved Retention Agreement, other fee or expense agreements, wage assignments, and security agreements of all kinds. Each such agreement must be attached to the statement that must be filed under Fed. R. Bankr. P. 2016(b) in all bankruptcy cases. Any agreement entered into after the filing of the statement under Rule 2016(b) must be filed as a supplement to that statement within 14 days of the date the agreement is entered into.

[Effective October 27, 2011. Amended effective January 1, 2012.]

RULE 2070–1. SURETIES ON BONDS

A. Security For Bonds. Except as otherwise provided by law, every court-ordered bond or similar undertaking must be secured by:

(1) the deposit of cash or obligations of the United States in the amount of the bond;

(2) the undertaking or guaranty of a corporate surety holding a certificate of authority from the Secretary of the Treasury; or

(3) the undertaking or guaranty of two individual residents of the Northern District of Illinois.

B. Affidavit of Justification. A person executing a bond as a surety pursuant to section A(3) of this Rule must attach an affidavit of justification, giving the person's full name, occupation, residence, and business addresses and showing that the person owns real or personal property in this district which, after excluding property exempt from execution and deducting the person's debts, liabilities, and other obligations (including those which may arise by virtue of the person's suretyship on other bonds or undertakings), is properly valued at no less than twice the amount of the bond.

C. Restriction on Sureties. No member of the bar and no officer or employee of this court may act as surety in any action or proceedings in this court.

[Adopted effective December 1, 2008.]

RULE 2070–2. SUPERSEDEAS BOND

A. Judgment for a Sum Certain. Where judgment is for a sum of money only, a supersedeas bond shall be in the amount of the judgment plus one year's interest at the rate provided in 28 U.S.C. § 1961, plus $500 to cover costs. The bond amount fixed hereunder is without prejudice to any party's right to seek timely judicial determination of a higher or lower amount.

B. Condition of Bond; Satisfaction. The bond shall be conditioned for the satisfaction of the judgment in full, together with costs, interest, and damages for delay, if for any reason the appeal is dismissed or if the judgment is affirmed, and to satisfy in full such modification of the judgment and such costs, interest, and damages as the appellate court may adjudge and award.

[Adopted effective December 1, 2008.]

RULE 2090–1. APPEARANCE OF ATTORNEYS

A. Admission to District Court Required. Except as provided in Rules 2090–2 and 2090–3, an attorney appearing before this court must be admitted to practice before the District Court.

B. Circumstances Under Which Trial Bar Membership Required.

(1) If witnesses will testify at a proceeding, an attorney who is to participate as lead counsel or alone must be a member of the trial bar of the District Court if:

(a) the proceeding is an adversary proceeding governed by Fed. R. Bankr. P. 7001 *et seq.*, or

(b) the court on its own motion or on motion of a party in interest orders that a member of the trial bar shall participate.

(2) Where trial bar membership is required by this Rule, an attorney who is a member of the general bar, but not a member of the trial bar, may appear during testimonial proceedings only if accompanied and supervised by a member of the trial bar.

(3) On motion for cause shown, the court may excuse the trial bar requirement in particular cases, proceedings, or matters.

C. Exemption for Certain Officers Appearing in Their Official Capacity. The following officers appearing in their official capacity shall be entitled to appear in all matters before the court without admission to the trial bar of the District Court: the Attorney General of the United States, the United States Attorney for the Northern District of Illinois, the attorney general or other highest legal officer of any state, and the state's attorney of any county in the State of Illinois. This exception to membership in the trial bar shall apply to the persons who hold the above-described offices during their terms of office, not to their assistants.

[Adopted effective December 1, 2008.]

RULE 2090–2. REPRESENTATION BY SUPERVISED SENIOR LAW STUDENTS

A student in a law school who has been certified by the Director of the Administrative Office of the Illinois Courts to render services in accordance with Illinois Supreme Court Rule 711 may perform such services in this court under like conditions and under the supervision of a member of the trial bar of the District Court. In addition to the agencies specified in paragraph (b) of Illinois Supreme Court Rule 711, the law school student may render such services with the United States Attorney for this District, or the United States Trustee, or the legal staff of any agency of the United States government.

[Adopted effective December 1, 2008.]

RULE 2090–3. APPEARANCE BY ATTORNEYS NOT MEMBERS OF THE BAR OF THE DISTRICT COURT (PRO HAC VICE)

An attorney who is not a member of the bar of the District Court but who is a member in good standing of the bar of the highest court of any state or of any United States District Court may appear before this court after:

(1) completing the form application for leave to appear pro hac vice as prescribed by the District Court,

(2) paying the required fee to the clerk of the District Court, and

(3) filing the application and receipt for payment with the clerk of this court.

No order of court is required.

[Adopted effective December 1, 2008.]

RULE 2090–5. APPEARANCES

A. Individual Appearances; Appearances by Firms Prohibited.

(1) Filing a document electronically constitutes entering an appearance for the party on whose behalf the document is filed, and no further notice of appearance under Fed. R. Bankr. P. 9010(b) is required.

(2) Any other appearance must be filed by the attorney appearing using forms prescribed by the District Court.

(3) Only individual attorneys may file appearances. Appearances by firms are not allowed.

B. Appearance of Attorney for Debtor; Adversary Proceedings. Counsel who represents the debtor upon the filing of a petition in bankruptcy is deemed to appear as attorney of record on behalf of the debtor for all purposes in the bankruptcy case, including any contested matter and any audit, but is not deemed to appear in any adversary proceeding filed against the debtor.

C. Appearance by United States Attorney or United States Trustee. No appearance form need be filed by the United States Attorney or the United States Trustee or any of their assistants when appearing in the performance of their duties.

D. Appearance of Attorney for Other Parties. Once an attorney has appeared in a contested matter or an adversary proceeding, that attorney is the attorney of record for the party represented for all purposes incident to the matter or proceeding, unless a court orders otherwise.

[Adopted effective December 1, 2008. Amended effective October 27, 2011; January 1, 2012.]

RULE 2091–1. WITHDRAWAL, ADDITION, AND SUBSTITUTION OF COUNSEL

A. General Rule. An attorney of record may not withdraw, nor may other attorneys appear on behalf of the same party or as a substitute for the attorney of record, without first obtaining leave of court by motion, except that substitutions or additions may be made without motion where both counsel are of the same firm. Where the appearance indicates that pursuant to these Rules a member of the trial bar is acting as a supervisor or is accompanying a member of the bar, the member of the trial bar included in the appearance may not withdraw, nor may another member be added or substituted, without first obtaining leave of court. Any motion to withdraw must be served on the client as well as all parties of record.

B. Failure to Pay. In a case under Chapter 7 of the Bankruptcy Code, including a case converted from Chapter 13, where (1) the debtor's attorney has agreed to represent the debtor conditioned on the debtor entering into an agreement after the filing of the case to pay the attorney for services rendered after the filing of the case, and (2) the debtor refuses to enter into such an agreement, the court may allow the attorney to withdraw from representation of the debtor on motion of the attorney.

[Adopted effective December 1, 2008. Amended effective October 27, 2011; January 1, 2012.]

RULE 3007–1. OBJECTIONS TO CLAIMS

Subject to Fed. R. Bankr. P. 3007, objections to claims must be noticed for hearing as an original motion in accordance with Rule 9013–3 and must identify the claimant and claim number.

[Adopted effective December 1, 2008.]

RULE 3011–1. MOTIONS FOR PAYMENT OF UNCLAIMED FUNDS

All motions for payment of unclaimed funds under 28 U.S.C. § 2072 shall be filed before the chief judge or such other judge as the chief judge shall designate. All such motions shall be made in accordance with procedures established by the court and available to the public in the clerk's office and on the court's web site.

[Adopted effective December 1, 2008.]

RULE 3015–1. MODEL PLAN IN CHAPTER 13 CASES

In all cases filed under Chapter 13 of the Bankruptcy Code, the debtor's plan shall conform to the Model Plan adopted by the judges of this court, in effect on the date the case is filed. The Model Plan shall be available in the clerk's office and on the court's web site. The court may modify the Model Plan from time to time by duly adopted General Order, making the revised plan available in the clerk's office and on the court's web site no less than 30 days before its effective date.

[Adopted effective December 1, 2008.]

RULE 3016–1. DISCLOSURE STATEMENTS IN CHAPTER 11 CASES

Unless the court orders otherwise, the following requirements will apply to all disclosure statements or amended disclosure statements:

(1) Each disclosure statement must include the following:

(a) An introductory narrative summarizing the nature of the plan and including a clear description of the exact proposed treatment of each class showing total dollar amounts and timing of payments to be made under the plan, and all sources and amounts of funding thereof. The narrative should plainly identify all classes, the composition of each class (as to number and type of creditors), the amount of claims (specifying any that are known to be disputed and how they will be treated under the plan), and the amount (dollar and/or percentages) to go to each class. The distinction between pre- and post-petition creditors must be clear.

(b) A summary exhibit setting forth a liquidation analysis as if assets of the debtor were liquidated under chapter 7.

(2) Except where a liquidating plan is proposed, each disclosure statement must also include the following:

(a) A projected cash flow and budget showing all anticipated income and expenses including plan payments, spread over the life of the plan or three fiscal years, whichever is shorter;

(b) A narrative summarizing the scheduled assets and liabilities as of the date of filing in bankruptcy, reciting the financial history during the chapter 11 (including a summary of the financial reports filed), describing the mechanics of handling initial and subsequent disbursements under the plan, and identifying persons responsible for disbursements; and

(c) Consolidated annual financial statements (or copies of such statements for the years in question) covering at least one fiscal year prior to bankruptcy filing and each fiscal year of the debtor-in-possession period.

[Adopted effective December 1, 2008.]

RULE 3018–1. COUNTING CONFIRMATION BALLOTS IN CHAPTER 11 CASES

Unless the court orders otherwise, the following shall apply in all cases pending under chapter 11 of the Bankruptcy Code:

(1) Ballots accepting or rejecting a plan are to be filed with the clerk.

(2) Prior to the confirmation hearing, counsel for each plan proponent shall tally all ballots filed with the clerk and prepare a report of balloting which at a minimum shall include:

(a) a description of each class and whether or not it is impaired (for example, "Class I, unsecured creditors, impaired");

(b) for each impaired class, the number of ballots received, the number of ballots voting to accept and their aggregate dollar amount, and the number of ballots voting to reject and their aggregate dollar amount;

(c) a concluding paragraph indicating whether the plan has received sufficient acceptance to be confirmed;

(d) a completed ballot report form substantially similar to the one posted on the court's web site;

(e) appended to the completed ballot report form, copies of all ballots not counted for any reason and a statement as to why the same were not counted; and

(f) certification that all ballots were counted for the classes for which those ballots were filed except for ballots appended to the report.

(3) Counsel for each plan proponent shall:

(a) file the report of balloting on that plan with the clerk;

(b) serve notice of such filing together with a copy of the report on the United States Trustee, all parties on the service list, and all parties who have filed objections to confirmation.

(4) The notice and copy of the report shall be filed and served at least 3 days prior to the confirmation hearing. Proof of such service and a copy of the notice and report shall be filed with the clerk prior to the confirmation hearing.

[Adopted effective December 1, 2008. Amended effective October 27, 2011; January 1, 2012.]

RULE 3022–1. NOTICE TO CLOSE CASE OR ENTER FINAL DECREE IN CHAPTER 11 CASES

Unless the court orders otherwise, debtors or other parties in interest moving after chapter 11 plan confirmation either to close the case or enter a final decree shall (1) give notice of such motion to the United States Trustee, any chapter 11 trustee, and all creditors, and (2) state within the notice or motion the actual status of payments due to each class under the confirmed plan.

[Adopted effective December 1, 2008.]

RULE 4001–1. MOTIONS TO MODIFY STAY

A. Required Statement. All motions seeking relief from the automatic stay pursuant to § 362 of the Bankruptcy Code, must be accompanied by a completed copy of the Required Statement form available on the Court's web site (www.ilnb.uscourts.gov). Motions filed without the Required Statement may be stricken or denied without notice.

B. Date of Request. The date of the "request" for relief from the automatic stay referred to in § 362(e) of the Bankruptcy Code is deemed to be the date of presentment of the motion, provided that the movant has complied with applicable notice requirements.

[Adopted effective December 1, 2008.]

RULE 4001–2. CASH COLLATERAL AND FINANCING ORDERS

A. Motions.

(1) Except as provided in these Rules, all cash collateral and financing requests under §§ 363 and 364 of the Bankruptcy Code must be heard by motion filed pursuant to Fed. R. Bankr. P. 2002, 4001 and 9014 ("Financing Motions").

(2) *Provisions to be Highlighted.* All Financing Motions must (a) recite whether the proposed form of order or underlying cash collateral stipulation or loan agreement contains any provision of the type indicated below, (b) identify the location of any such provision in the proposed form of order, cash collateral stipulation or loan agreement, and (c) state the justification for the inclusion of such provision:

(a) Provisions that grant cross-collateralization protection (other than replacement liens or other adequate protection) to the pre-petition secured creditors (i.e., clauses that secure pre-petition debt by post-petition assets in which the secured creditor would not otherwise have a security interest by virtue of its pre-petition security agreement or applicable law).

(b) Provisions or findings of fact that bind the estate or all parties in interest with respect to the validity, perfection or amount of the secured creditor's pre-petition lien or debt or the waiver of claims against the secured creditor without first giving parties in interest at least 75 days from the entry of the order and the creditors' committee, if formed, at least 60 days from the date of its formation to investigate such matters.

(c) Provisions that seek to waive any rights the estate may have under § 506(c) of the Bankruptcy Code.

(d) Provisions that immediately grant to the pre-petition secured creditor liens on the debtor's claims and causes of action arising under §§ 544, 545, 547, 548, and 549 of the Bankruptcy Code.

(e) Provisions that deem pre-petition secured debt to be post-petition debt or that use post-petition loans from a pre-petition secured creditor to pay part or all of that secured creditor's pre-petition debt, other than as provided in § 552(b) of the Bankruptcy Code.

(f) Provisions that provide treatment for the professionals retained by a committee appointed by the United States Trustee different from that provided for the professionals retained by the debtor with respect to a professional fee carve-out, and provi-

sions that limit the committee counsel's use of the carve-out.

(g) Provisions that prime any secured lien, without the consent of that lienor.

(h) A declaration that the order does not impose lender liability on any secured creditor.

(i) Provisions that grant the lender expedited relief from the automatic stay in § 362 of the Bankruptcy Code, or relief from the automatic stay without further order of court.

(j) In jointly administered cases, provisions for joint and several liability on loans.

(3) All Financing Motions must also provide a summary of all provisions that must be highlighted under section (A)(2) of this Rule and a summary of the essential terms of the proposed use of cash collateral or financing, including the maximum borrowing available on a final basis, the interim borrowing limit, borrowing conditions, interest rate, maturity, events of default, use of funds limitations, and protections afforded under §§ 363 and 364 of the Bankruptcy Code.

(4) All Financing Motions must also provide a budget covering the time period in which the order will remain in effect. The budget must state in as much detail as is reasonably practical the amount of projected receipts and disbursements during the period covered by the budget.

(5) The court may deem unenforceable any provision not highlighted as required under section (A)(2) of this Rule.

B. Interim Orders.
In the absence of extraordinary circumstances, the court shall not approve interim financing orders that include any of the provisions previously identified in section (A)(2)(a) through (A)(2)(j) of this Rule.

C. Final Orders.
A final order shall be entered only after notice and a hearing pursuant to Fed. R. Bankr. P. 4001. If formation of a creditors' committee is anticipated, no final hearing shall be held until at least 7 days following the organizational meeting of the creditors' committee contemplated by § 1102 of the Bankruptcy Code unless the court orders otherwise.

[Adopted effective December 1, 2008. Amended effective October 27, 2011; January 1, 2012.]

RULE 4003–1. OBJECTIONS TO DEBTOR'S EXEMPTIONS

Subject to Fed. R. Bankr. P. 4003, objections to exemptions claimed by a debtor must be noticed for hearing as an original motion in accordance with Rule 9013–3.

[Adopted effective December 1, 2008.]

RULE 5005–1. METHOD OF FILING

A. Administrative Procedures. The court may adopt Administrative Procedures to permit filing, signing, service and verification of documents by electronic means in conformity therewith.

B. Electronic Case Filing. Pursuant to Fed. R. Bankr. P. 5005(a)(2), all documents must be filed in accordance with the Administrative Procedures.

C. Divisions of the District. The caption of each document must identify the division of the court to which the case is assigned.

D. Paper Documents. If paper documents are permitted or required by the Administrative Procedures, they must be filed at the office of the clerk in Chicago, Illinois, for Eastern Division cases, and the office of the clerk in Rockford, Illinois, for Western Division cases.

[Adopted effective December 1, 2008.]

Committee Note

Administrative Procedures were first adopted pursuant to this authorization on February 17, 2004.

The Northern District of Illinois has two divisions: the Eastern Division, headquartered in Chicago, and the Western Division, headquartered in Rockford. The Judicial Council determines the counties that fall within the Eastern and Western Divisions. At the time of adoption of this Rule, the counties were divided as follows:

Eastern Division: Cook, DuPage, Grundy, Kane, Kendall, Lake, LaSalle, and Will.

Western Division: Boone, Carroll, DeKalb, Jo Daviess, Lee, McHenry, Ogle, Stephenson, Whiteside, and Winnebago.

All Western Division cases are heard in Rockford. All Eastern Division chapter 11 cases and all Cook County cases are heard in Chicago. All DuPage County chapter 7 and chapter 13 cases are heard in Wheaton. All Kane County chapter 7 and chapter 13 cases are heard in Geneva. All Lake County chapter 7 and chapter 13 cases are heard in Waukegan. All chapter 7 and chapter 13 cases from Grundy, Kendall, LaSalle, and Will Counties are heard in Joliet.

RULE 5005–3. FORMAT OF DOCUMENTS FILED

A. Numbering Paragraphs in Pleadings. Allegations in any pleading must be made in numbered paragraphs, each of which must be limited, as far as practicable, to a statement of a single set of circumstances. Responses to pleadings must be made in numbered paragraphs, first setting forth the complete content of the paragraph to which the response is directed, and then setting forth the response.

B. Responses to Motions. A response to a motion must not be in the form of an answer to a complaint but must state in narrative form any reasons, legal or factual, why the motion should be denied, unless the judge orders otherwise.

C. Requirements.

(1) Each document filed on paper must be flat and unfolded on opaque, unglazed, white paper approximately 8½ × 11 inches in size. It must be plainly written, or typed, or printed, or prepared by means of a duplicating process, without erasures or interlineations which materially deface it, and must be secured by staples or other devices piercing the paper on the top at the left corner of the document. Paper clips or other clips not piercing the paper are not acceptable.

(2) Where the document is typed, line spacing must be at least 2 lines.

(3) Where the document is typed or printed:

(a) the size of the type in the document must be no smaller than 12 points, and

(b) the margins, left-hand, right-hand, top, and bottom, must each be no smaller than 1 inch.

(4) The first page of each document must bear the caption, descriptive title, and number of the action or proceeding in which it is filed, the case caption and chapter of the related bankruptcy case, the name of the judge to whom the case is assigned, and the next date and time, if any, that the matter is set.

(5) The final page of each document must contain the name, address, and telephone number of the attorney in active charge of the case as well as that of the attorney signing the pleading, or the address and telephone number of the individual party filing pro se.

(6) Copies of exhibits appended to documents filed must be legible.

(7) Each page of a document must be consecutively numbered.

(8) Each document filed electronically must be formatted similarly to documents filed on paper.

(9) Signatures on documents must comply with the Administrative Procedures (II–C).

(10) The caption of every document filed in cases heard in Joliet, DuPage County, Kane County, or Lake County must list the location where the case is heard (either Joliet, DuPage County, Kane County, or Lake County) in parentheses immediately below the name of the assigned judge.

D. Fifteen Page Limit. No motion, response to a motion, brief, or memorandum in excess of fifteen pages may be filed without prior approval of the court.

E. Documents Not Complying with Rule. If a document is filed in violation of this Rule, the court may order the filing of an amended document complying with this Rule. A judge may direct the filing of any communication to the court deemed appropriate for filing.

F. Proof of Service. All documents filed with the clerk must be accompanied by a proof of service consistent with Rules 7005–1 and 9013–1.

[Adopted effective December 1, 2008. Amended effective October 27, 2011; January 1, 2012.]

RULE 5005–4. RESTRICTED DOCUMENTS

A. Definitions. For the purpose of this Rule:

(1) "Restricted Document" means a document to which access has been restricted either by a court order or by law.

(2) "Redacted Document" means an altered form of a Restricted Document that may appear in the public record because portions of it have been deleted or obliterated.

(3) "Sealed Document" means a Restricted Document that the court has directed be maintained within a sealed enclosure such that access to the document requires breaking the seal of the enclosure.

(4) "Restricting Order" means any order restricting access to a document submitted to or filed with the clerk.

B. General Rule of Access. All documents filed with the clerk, both electronically and on paper, are accessible to the public unless covered by a Restricting Order.

C. Methods of Restriction.

(1) The court may order that a document not be filed but instead be submitted to the clerk as a Sealed Document.

(2) The court may order that a document be filed as a Redacted Document. When ordering that a Redacted Document be filed, the court may order that an unredacted version of the document be submitted to the clerk as a Sealed Document.

D. Filing and Submitting Restricted Documents.

(1) No attorney or party may file or submit a Restricted Document without prior order of the court specifying the particular document or portion of a document that may be filed as restricted.

(2) The final paragraph of any Restricting Order must contain (a) the identity of the persons entitled to access to the documents without further order of the court and (b) instructions for the disposition of the Restricted Documents following the conclusion of the case, consistent with section G of this Rule.

(3) A copy of the Restricting Order must be attached to a Sealed Document submitted to the clerk and to a Redacted Document filed with the clerk.

(4) The attorney or party submitting a Sealed Document to the clerk must present it in a sealed enclo-sure that conspicuously states on the face of the enclosure the attorney's or party's name and address, including the email address if the attorney is a registrant under CM/ECF, the caption of the case, and the title of the document.

E. Docket Entries. On written motion and for good cause, the court may order that the docket entry for a Restricted Document show only that the document was filed without any notation indicating its nature. Absent such an order a Restricted Document must be docketed in the same manner as any other document, except the entry will indicate that access to the document is restricted.

F. Inspection of Sealed Documents. The clerk must maintain a record, in a manner provided by internal operating procedures, of persons permitted access to Sealed Documents. Such procedures may require anyone seeking access to show identification and to sign a statement to the effect that they have been authorized to examine the Sealed Document. The clerk shall also keep a log of all such inspections.

G. Disposition of Sealed Documents. When a case is closed in which a Restricting Order has been entered, the clerk must maintain any Sealed Documents for a period of 63 days following the final disposition of the case including appeals. Except where the court, at the request of a party or on its own motion, orders otherwise, at the end of the 63–day period the clerk shall return any Sealed Documents to the submitting attorney or party. If reasonable attempts by the clerk to return the Sealed Documents are not successful, the clerk may destroy them.

[Adopted effective December 1, 2008.]

RULE 5070–1. CALENDARS

A. General. Bankruptcy cases, ancillary matters, and adversary proceedings assigned to a judge shall constitute the calendar of that judge.

B. Calendar of a Judge Who Dies, Resigns, or Retires. The calendar of a judge who dies, resigns, or retires shall be reassigned by the clerk as soon as possible under direction of the chief judge, either pro rata by lot among the remaining judges, or as necessary to promote efficient judicial administration.

C. Calendar for a Newly–Appointed Judge. A calendar shall be prepared for a newly-appointed judge to which cases shall be transferred by the clerk under direction of the chief judge in such number as the chief judge may determine, either by lot from the calendar of other judges, or by transfer in whole or part of the calendar of a judge who has died, retired, or resigned. If transfer is by lot from the calendar of other sitting judges, no case or proceeding shall be transferred if it is certified by a judge to be one on which that judge has engaged in such a level of judicial work that reassignment would adversely affect the efficient disposition of the matter.

[Adopted effective December 1, 2008.]

RULE 5070–2. PUBLICATION OF DAILY CALL

The omission of a matter from any published call in the *Chicago Daily Law Bulletin*, on the court's website, or otherwise shall not excuse counsel or parties pro se from attendance before the court on the date for which the matter is set.

[Adopted effective December 1, 2008.]

RULE 5073–1. USE OF PHOTOGRAPHIC, RADIO, AUDIO, AND TELEVISION EQUIPMENT IN THE COURT ENVIRONS

The taking of photographs, radio and television broadcasting, or taping in the court environs during the progress of or in connection with judicial proceedings before a bankruptcy judge, whether or not court is actually in session, is prohibited.

[Adopted effective December 1, 2008.]

RULE 5082–1. APPLICATIONS FOR COMPENSATION AND REIMBURSEMENT FOR PROFESSIONAL SERVICES IN CASES UNDER CHAPTERS 7, 9, 11 AND 12

A. Applications. Any application for interim or final compensation for services performed and reimbursement of expenses incurred by a professional person employed in a case filed under Chapter 7, 9, 11 or 12 of the Bankruptcy Code must begin with a completed and signed cover sheet in a form approved by the court and published by the clerk. The application must also include both a narrative summary and a detailed statement of the applicant's services for which compensation is sought.

B. Narrative Summary.

(1) The narrative summary must set forth the following for the period covered by the application:

(a) a summary list of all principal activities of the applicant, giving the total compensation requested in connection with each such activity;

(b) a separate description of each of the applicant's principal activities, including details as to individual tasks performed within such activity, and a description sufficient to demonstrate to the court that each task and activity is compensable in the amount sought;

(c) a statement of all time and total compensation sought in the application for preparation of the current or any prior application by that applicant for compensation;

(d) the name and position (partner, associate, paralegal, etc.) of each person who performed work on each task and activity, the approximate hours worked, and the total compensation sought for each person's work on each such separate task and activity;

(e) the hourly rate for each professional and paraprofessional for whom compensation is requested, with the total number of hours expended by each person and the total compensation sought for each;

(f) a statement of the compensation previously sought and allowed;

(g) the total amount of expenses for which reimbursement is sought, supported by a statement of those expenses, including any additional charges added to the actual cost to the applicant.

(2) The narrative summary must conclude with a statement as to whether the requested fees and expenses are sought to be merely allowed or both allowed and paid. If the latter, the narrative summary must state the source of the proposed payment.

C. Detailed Statement of Services. The applicant's detailed time records may constitute the detailed statement required by Fed. R. Bankr. P. 2016(a). Such statement must be divided by task and activity to match those set forth in the narrative description. Each time entry must state:

(1) the date the work was performed,

(2) the name of the person performing the work,

(3) a brief statement of the nature of the work,

(4) the time expended on the work in increments of tenth of an hour, and

(5) the fee charged for the work described in the entry.

D. Privileged Information and Work Product. If compliance with this Rule requires disclosure of privileged information or work product, the applicant may file a motion pursuant to Rule 5005–4, Restricted Documents.

E. Failure to Comply. Failure to comply with any part of this Rule may result in reduction of fees and expenses allowed. If a revised application is made necessary because of any failure to comply with provisions of this Rule, compensation may be denied or reduced for preparation of the revision. The court may also excuse or modify any of the requirements of this Rule.

[Adopted effective December 1, 2008. Amended effective October 27, 2011; January 1, 2012.]

RULE 5082–2. APPLICATIONS FOR COMPENSATION AND REIMBURSEMENT FOR PROFESSIONAL SERVICES IN CASES UNDER CHAPTER 13

A. Definitions. For the purpose of this Rule:

(1) "Court–Approved Retention Agreement" means Local Bankruptcy Form 23c.

(2) "Form Itemization" means Local Bankruptcy Forms 21 and 22.

(3) "Form Fee Application" means Local Bankruptcy Form 23.

(4) "Form Fee Order" means Local Bankruptcy Form 23a or 23b.

(5) "Flat Fee" means a fee not supported by an itemization of time and services.

(6) "Creditors Meeting Notice" means the Official Notice of Chapter 13 Bankruptcy Case, Meeting of Creditors, and Deadlines. (Official Form B9I.)

(7) "Original Confirmation Date" means the date of the confirmation hearing specified in the Creditors Meeting Notice.

B. Requirements.

(1) All requests for awards of compensation to debtor's counsel in chapter 13 cases must be made using the Form Fee Application, which must be accompanied by a completed Form Fee Order specifying the amounts requested.

(2) All requests for awards of compensation to debtor's counsel must include a certification that the disclosures required by Rule 2016–1 have been made.

(3) Applications for original fees must be noticed for hearing on the Original Confirmation Date at the time for confirmation hearing.

C. Flat Fees.

(1) If debtor's counsel and the debtor have entered into the Court–Approved Retention Agreement, counsel may apply for a Flat Fee not to exceed the amount authorized by the applicable General Order. If the Court–Approved Retention Agreement has been modified in any way, a Flat Fee will not be awarded.

(2) If debtor's counsel and the debtor have not entered into the Court–Approved Retention Agreement, the Form Fee Application must be accompanied by a completed Form Itemization.

(3) The Flat Fee will not be awarded if, in addition to the Court–Approved Retention Agreement, the debtor and an attorney for the debtor have entered into any other agreement in connection with the representation of the debtor in preparation for, during, or involving a Chapter 13 case, and the agreement provides for the attorney to receive

(a) any kind of compensation, reimbursement, or other payment, or

(b) any form of, or security for, compensation, reimbursement, or other payment

that varies from the Court–Approved Retention Agreement.

D. Notice.

(1) All fee applications must be filed with the clerk, served on the debtor, the trustee, and all creditors, and noticed for hearing as an original motion. However, a fee application need not be served on all creditors if

(a) the Creditor Meeting Notice is attached to the application, has been served on all creditors, and discloses the amount of original compensation sought; and

(b) the hearing on compensation is noticed for the Original Confirmation Date.

(2) Rule 9013–1(E)(2), which governs the dates for the presentment of motions, does not apply to requests under this Rule.

E. Compensation Following Dismissal.

(1) When a chapter 13 case is dismissed, the court will retain jurisdiction to hear requests from debtor's counsel as follows:

(a) In cases heard in Chicago and Rockford, jurisdiction will be retained for 30 days following the date of dismissal.

(b) In cases not heard in Chicago or Rockford, jurisdiction will be retained for 45 days following the date of dismissal.

(2) Notice of a request for compensation under this subsection E must be given in accordance with subsection D.

[Adopted effective December 1, 2008. Amended effective October 27, 2011; January 1, 2012.]

RULE 5096–1. EMERGENCY MATTERS; EMERGENCY JUDGE

A. Definitions. For the purpose of these Rules:

(1) "Emergency judge" means the judge assigned to perform the duties of emergency judge specified by any local rule or procedure adopted by the court.

(2) "Emergency motion" means a motion that arises from an occurrence that could not reasonably have been foreseen and requires immediate action to avoid serious and irreparable harm.

B. Duties of Emergency Judge. The emergency judge is responsible for hearing all emergency matters that arise outside of the regular business hours of the court. During regular business hours of the court, the emergency judge will hear emergency matters arising out of the cases assigned to the calendar of another judge when that judge is not sitting. The emergency judge will not hear emergency matters arising during regular business hours of the court when the assigned judge is sitting, except by agreement of the emergency judge at the request of the assigned judge.

C. Unavailability of the Emergency Judge. If the assigned judge and the emergency judge are unavailable, the person seeking to present an emergency motion must follow the procedure in the Administrative Procedures.

[Adopted effective December 1, 2008. Amended effective October 27, 2011; January 1, 2012.]

RULE 7005–1. PROOF OF SERVICE OF PAPERS

Unless another method is expressly required by these Rules or by applicable law, an attorney may prove service of papers by certificate, and other persons may prove service of papers by affidavit or by other proof satisfactory to the court.

[Adopted effective December 1, 2008.]

RULE 7016–1. CASE MANAGEMENT AND SCHEDULING CONFERENCES IN CHAPTER 11 CASES

The court on its own motion or on the motion of a party in interest may conduct case management and scheduling conferences at such times during a case as will further the expeditious and economical resolution of the case. At the conclusion of each such conference, the court shall enter case management or scheduling orders as may be required. Such orders may establish notice requirements, set dates on which motions and proceedings will be heard (omnibus hearing dates), establish procedures regarding payment and allowance of interim compensation under 11 U.S.C. § 331, set dates for filing the disclosure statement and plan, and address such other matters as may be appropriate.

[Adopted effective December 1, 2008.]

RULE 7020–1. MULTI–DEFENDANT AVOIDANCE ACTIONS

Claims under 11 U.S.C. §§ 547, 548, or 550 against multiple defendants may not be asserted in a single adversary proceeding, and a separate adversary proceeding asserting such claims must be commenced for each defendant, unless all of the claims in the adversary proceeding arise out of a transaction involving all of the defendants.

[Adopted effective December 1, 2008.]

RULE 7026–1. DISCOVERY MATERIALS

A. Definition. For the purposes of this Rule, the term "discovery materials" shall include all materials related to discovery under Fed. R. Civ. P. 26 through Fed. R. Civ. P. 36, made applicable to bankruptcy proceedings by Fed. R. Bankr. P. 7026 through Fed. R. Bankr. P. 7036 and Fed. R. Bankr. P. 9014, and to discovery taken under Fed. R. Bankr. P. 2004.

B. Discovery Materials Not to Be Filed Except By Order.

(1) Except as provided by this Rule or order of court, discovery materials shall not be filed with the clerk. The party serving discovery materials shall retain the original and be custodian of it. An original deposition shall be retained by the party who ordered it. The court, on its own motion, on motion of any party, or on motion by a non-party, may require the filing of any discovery materials or may make provision for a person to obtain a copy of discovery materials at the person's own expense.

(2) If discovery materials are received into evidence as exhibits, the attorney producing them will retain them unless the court orders them deposited with the clerk. When the court orders them deposited, they will be treated as exhibits subject to the provisions of Rule 9070–1.

[Adopted effective December 1, 2008.]

RULE 7033–1. INTERROGATORIES— FORMAT OF ANSWERS

A party responding to interrogatories shall set forth immediately preceding each answer or objection a full statement of the interrogatory to which the party is responding.

[Adopted effective December 1, 2008.]

RULE 7037–1. DISCOVERY MOTIONS

All motions under Rules 26 through 37 of the Federal Rules of Civil Procedure (made applicable by Fed. R. Bankr. P. 7026 through 7037) relating to a discovery dispute, including any motion under Fed. R. Bankr. P. 37(a) to compel discovery, must include a statement that:

(1) after consultation in person or by telephone, and after good faith attempts to resolve differences, the parties are unable to reach an accord; or

(2) counsel's attempts to engage in such a consultation were unsuccessful due to no fault of counsel.

Where consultation has occurred, the statement in the motion must recite the date, time, and place of the consultation, and the names of all persons participating. Where counsel was unsuccessful in engaging in the consultation, the statement in the motion must recite in detail the efforts counsel made to engage in the consultation.

[Adopted effective December 1, 2008.]

RULE 7041–1. NOTICE REQUIREMENTS FOR DISMISSAL OF PROCEEDINGS TO DENY OR REVOKE DISCHARGES

A. Requirements for Motion to Dismiss Adversary Proceeding to Deny or Revoke Discharge. No adversary proceeding objecting to or seeking to revoke a debtor's discharge under Sections 727, 1141, 1228, or 1328 of the Bankruptcy Code shall be dismissed except on motion and hearing after 21 days notice to the debtor, the United States Trustee, the trustee, if any, and all creditors and other parties of record. The motion shall either (1) state that no entity has promised, has given, or has received directly or indirectly any consideration to obtain or allow such dismissal or (2) specifically describe any such consideration promised, given, or received.

B. Additional Notice Requirements. The notice required under part A of this Rule must include a statement that the trustee or any creditors who wish to adopt and prosecute the adversary proceeding in question shall seek leave to do so at or before the hearing on the motion to dismiss.

C. Court's Discretion to Limit Notice. Nothing contained herein is intended to restrict the discretion of the court to limit notice to the debtor, the United States Trustee, the case trustee, if any, and such creditors or other parties as the judge may designate, or, for cause shown, to shorten the notice period.

[Adopted effective December 1, 2008. Amended effective October 27, 2011; January 1, 2012.]

RULE 7054–1. TAXATION OF COSTS

A. Time for Filing Bill of Costs. Within thirty days of the entry of a judgment allowing costs, the prevailing party shall file a bill of costs with the clerk and serve a copy of the bill on each adverse party. If the bill of costs is not filed within the thirty days, costs under 28 U.S.C. § 1920(1), other than those of the clerk, shall be deemed waived. The court may, on motion filed within the time provided for the filing of the bill of costs, extend the time for filing the bill.

B. Costs of Stenographic Transcripts. Subject to the provisions of Fed. R. Bankr. P. 7054, the necessary expenses of any prevailing party in obtaining all or any part of a transcript for use in a case, for purposes of a new trial, for amended findings, or for appeal shall be taxable as costs against the adverse party. The costs of the transcript or deposition shall not exceed the regular copy rate as established by the Judicial Conference of the United States in effect at the time the transcript or deposition was filed, unless some other rate was previously provided for by order of court. Except as otherwise ordered by the court, only the cost of the original and one copy of such transcript or deposition, and for depositions, the cost of the copy provided to the court, shall be allowed.

[Adopted effective December 1, 2008. Amended effective October 27, 2011; January 1, 2012.]

RULE 7054–2. SECURITY FOR COSTS

Upon good cause shown, the court may order the filing of a bond as security for costs. Except as ordered by the court, the bond will be secured in compliance with Rule 2070–1. The bond shall be conditioned to secure the payment of all fees which the party filing it must pay by law to the clerk, marshal, or other officer of the court and all costs of the action that the party filing it may be directed to pay to any other party.

[Adopted effective December 1, 2008.]

RULE 7055–2. CLERK NOT TO ENTER DEFAULT JUDGMENTS

Unless otherwise directed by a judge, the clerk shall not prepare or sign default judgments in any adversary proceeding or contested matter under Fed. R. Bankr. P. 9021 or Fed. R. Bankr. P. 7055. Such judgments shall be presented to the court for entry. Notwithstanding Fed. R. Bankr. P. 7055, a party seeking entry of judgment by default shall present a motion to the judge, rather than the clerk.

[Adopted effective December 1, 2008.]

RULE 7056–1. MOTIONS FOR SUMMARY JUDGMENT; MOVING PARTY

A. Supporting Documents Required. With each motion for summary judgment filed under Fed. R. Bankr. P. 7056, the moving party must serve and file a supporting memorandum of law and a statement of material facts as to which the moving party contends there is no genuine issue and that entitles the moving party to judgment as a matter of law, and that also includes:

(1) a description of the parties;

(2) all facts supporting venue and jurisdiction in this court; and

(3) any affidavits and other materials referred to in Fed. R. Civ. P. 56(e).

B. Form—Statement of Facts. The statement of facts must consist of short numbered paragraphs, including within each paragraph specific references to the affidavits, parts of the record, and other supporting materials relied upon to support the facts set forth in that paragraph. Failure to submit such a statement constitutes grounds for denial of the motion.

C. Subsequent Filings by Moving Party. If additional material facts are submitted by the opposing party pursuant to Rule 7056–2, the moving party may submit a concise reply in the form prescribed in Rule 7056–2 for response. All additional material facts set forth in the opposing party's statement filed under section A(2)(b) of Rule 7056–2 will be deemed admitted unless controverted by a statement of the moving party filed in reply.

[Adopted effective December 1, 2008. Amended effective October 27, 2011; January 1, 2012.]

RULE 7056–2. MOTIONS FOR SUMMARY JUDGMENT; OPPOSING PARTY

A. Supporting Documents Required. Each party opposing a motion for summary judgment under Fed. R. Bankr. P. 7056 shall serve and file the following:

(1) a supporting memorandum of law;

(2) a concise response to the movant's statement of facts that shall contain:

(a) a response to each numbered paragraph in the moving party's statement, including, in the case of any disagreement, specific references to the affidavits, parts of the record, and other supporting materials relied upon; and

(b) a statement, consisting of short numbered paragraphs, of any additional facts that require the denial of summary judgment, including references to the affidavits, parts of the record, and other supporting materials relied upon; and

(3) any opposing affidavits and other materials referred to in Fed. R. Civ. P. 56(e).

B. Effect. All material facts set forth in the statement required of the moving party will be deemed to be admitted unless controverted by the statement of the opposing party.

[Adopted effective December 1, 2008.]

RULE 9013–1. MOTIONS

A. General Requirements. Except as otherwise provided in these Rules or as ordered by the court:

(1) Every motion must be in the format required by section B of this Rule.

(2) Every motion must be filed with each of the items specified in section C of this Rule and must be filed no later than the date on which the motion is served. The date and time of filing a motion filed electronically are those shown on the Notice of Electronic Filing issued by the court's CM/ECF system. The date of filing a paper motion is the date on which the clerk receives the motion.

(3) Every motion must be served on parties in interest as required by section D of this Rule.

(4) Every motion must be presented by the movant as required by section E of this Rule.

B. Title and Format of Motions. Every motion must be titled as one of the events contained in the court's CM/ECF system, unless no event accurately describes the subject of the motion. Every motion must conform to the requirements of Rule 5005–3.

C. Items Required to be Filed with Motions. Every motion must be filed with the clerk of court, and the filing must include each of the items specified below.

(1) *Notice of Motion.* For all motions, a notice of motion, signed by the moving party or counsel for the moving party, and stating the date, time, and location of the motion's presentment to the court. The location must include the room number and full street address.

(2) *Exhibits.* If a motion refers to exhibits, legible copies of the exhibits must be attached to the motion, unless the court orders otherwise.

(3) *Certificate of Service.* Except for motions filed ex parte, a certificate of service stating the date on which the motion and each item filed with the motion were served. The certificate must also state:

(a) for each recipient who is a registrant with the court's CM/ECF system, the date of the filing and the name of the recipient, and

(b) for each recipient who is not a registrant with the court's CM/ECF system, the date, manner of service, and name and address of the recipient.

(4) *Ex Parte Affidavit.* For all motions filed ex parte, an affidavit showing cause for the filing of the motion ex parte.

(5) *Proposed Order.* For all motions, a proposed order in the form required by the Administrative Procedures, with a title specifying the relief granted in the order (e.g., "Order Granting Motion to Modify Stay" or "Order Extending the Time to Object to Discharge").

D. Service of Motions.

(1) *Service by Mail.* Where service of the notice of motion is by mail, the notice of motion must be mailed at least 7 days before the date of presentment.

(2) *Personal Service.* A notice of motion served personally must be served no later than 4:00 p.m. on the third day before the date of presentment. Personal service includes actual delivery and delivery by facsimile transmission ("fax").

(3) *Fax Service.* Where service is by fax, the certificate of service must be accompanied by an automatically generated statement confirming transmission. The statement must contain the date and time

of transmission, the telephone number to which the motion was transmitted, and an acknowledgment from the receiving fax machine that the transmission was received.

(4) *Service by the CM/ECF System.* In accordance with the Administrative Procedures for the Case Management/Electronic Case Filing System, electronic filing of a document constitutes service on any person who is a Registrant entitled to file documents using the Case Management/Electronic Case Filing System and who has filed a document in the case in electronic format via the System.

(5) *E-mail Service.* Except for service by the CM/ECF System as provided in this rule, service by electronic mail is prohibited.

E. Presentment of Motions.

(1) Except for emergency motions, and unless otherwise ordered by the court, every motion must be presented in court on a date and time when the judge assigned to the case regularly hears motions.

(2) The presentment of a motion must be no more than 30 days after the motion is filed, unless applicable statutes or rules require a longer notice period, in which case the date of presentment must be within 7 days after the expiration of the notice period.

F. Oral Argument. Oral argument on motions may be allowed in the court's discretion.

G. Failure to Comply. If a motion fails to comply with the provisions of this Rule in any respect, the court may, in its discretion, deny the motion.

H. Failure to Prosecute. If a movant fails to present the motion at the time set for presentment, the court may, in its discretion, deny the motion.

I. Request for Ruling. Any party may file a motion calling to the court's attention a matter that is fully briefed and ready for decision and requesting a status hearing.

[Adopted effective December 1, 2008. Amended effective October 27, 2011; January 1, 2012.]

RULE 9013–2 THROUGH 8. [RESERVED]

RULE 9013–9. ROUTINE AND UNCONTESTED MOTIONS

A. Routine Motion or Application Defined. A party presenting any of the following, upon required notice, may designate it as a "routine motion" or "routine application", as the case may be:

(1) request for payment of administrative expenses other than fees and reimbursement of expenses pursuant to section 330 or 331 of the Bankruptcy Code;

(2) motion to be added to the notice list under Rule 2002–2;

(3) motion to pay bond premium;

(4) motion to destroy books and records of a debtor;

(5) motion to extend time for filing complaints to determine dischargeability and objections to discharge;

(6) motion to extend by no more than 28 days the unexpired time to file an appearance, pleading, or response to a discovery request, provided that the motion states the next set court date and states that no court date will be affected by the extension;

(7) motion for leave to appear as an attorney or an additional attorney, or to substitute one attorney for another with the written consent of the client, except as to attorneys for a debtor in possession, trustee, or an official committee;

(8) motion to dismiss or withdraw all or any part of an adversary proceeding by agreement, which motion shall set forth any consideration promised or received for the dismissal or withdrawal and shall specify whether the dismissal or withdrawal is with or without prejudice, provided, however, that this subsection shall not apply to adversary proceedings under 11 U.S.C. § 727 (see Rule 7041–1) nor to any motion by a trustee that, if granted, would effectively abandon a cause of action;

(9) motion to avoid a lien pursuant to § 522(f) of the Bankruptcy Code;

(10) motion for leave to conduct examinations pursuant to Fed. R. Bankr. P. 2004, subject to Rule 7026–1;

(11) in cases under chapter 13 of the Bankruptcy Code, on notice to the standing trustee and all creditors:

(a) motion to increase the payments by the debtor into the plan; and

(b) motion to extend the duration of the plan, without reduction of periodic payments, where the proposed extension does not result in a duration of the plan beyond 60 months after the date of confirmation of the plan;

(12) motion by the trustee or debtor in possession, with notice to all creditors, to abandon property of the estate pursuant to § 554 of the Bankruptcy Code and Fed. R. Bankr. P. 6007(a); and

(13) motions by the debtor to dismiss under §§ 1208(b) or 1307(b) of the Bankruptcy Code.

B. Identifying Routine Motions or Applications; Proposed Order; Ruling Without Hearing. Each copy of a routine motion or routine application shall be designated as such in the heading below the caption and shall have appended to it a proposed order. The notice of a routine motion or routine application shall state in bold face type or capital letters that the appended proposed order may be entered by the judge without presentment in open court unless a party in interest notifies the judge of an objection thereto pursuant to section C of this Rule.

C. Order of Calling Routine Motions or Applications; Request for Hearing. Routine motions may be called by the courtroom deputy at the beginning of the motion call. If no party in interest requests a hearing, the court may enter an order granting relief in a form substantially similar to the proposed order without presentation of the motion or application in open court and without a hearing. If a hearing is requested, the motion or application shall not be granted routinely, but shall be heard in open court at the date and time noticed.

D. Uncontested Motion Defined. An "uncontested motion" is a motion properly noticed as to which all parties in interest entitled to notice have no objection to the relief sought by the movant, and the movant wishes the motion to be considered pursuant to this Rule.

E. Identifying Uncontested Motions; Proposed Order. An "uncontested motion" shall be designated as such in the heading below the caption and shall have appended to it either a proposed order signed by each party in interest entitled to notice of the motion or a certification of movant's counsel that each such party has no objection to entry of the proposed order.

F. Court May Rule on Uncontested Motion Without Hearing. The court may enter an order granting relief upon an uncontested motion in a form substantially similar to the movant's proposed order without presentation of the motion and without a hearing.

G. Procedure Where Court Declines to Grant Routine Motion or Application or Uncontested Motion. Before the commencement of the motion call, the court may post a list outside the courtroom of routine motions or applications and uncontested motions upon which ruling may be entered without hearing, if a hearing is not requested. Should the court decline to grant a routine motion or application or an uncontested motion without presentation in open court or a hearing, the movant or applicant shall present the same at the date and time noticed. If the movant or applicant fails to do so, the motion or application may be stricken or decided pursuant to Rule 9013–5.

H. Requirements of Notice Not Affected. Nothing in this Rule excuses the notice requirements for motions.

I. Individual Judge May Adopt Other Practices. Nothing in this Rule requires any judge to follow the procedures set forth herein.

[Adopted effective December 1, 2008. Amended effective October 27, 2011; January 1, 2012.]

RULE 9015–1. JURY TRIALS BEFORE BANKRUPTCY JUDGES

A. Designation of Bankruptcy Judges to Conduct Jury Trials. Each bankruptcy judge appointed or designated to hold court in this district is specially designated to conduct jury trials pursuant to 28 U.S.C. § 157(e). The District Court may for good cause withdraw the designation of any bankruptcy judge. Such withdrawal shall be in the form of a general order.

B. Consent. Any bankruptcy judge designated to conduct a jury trial may conduct such a trial in any case, proceeding, or matter that may be heard under 28 U.S.C. § 157, within which the right to a jury trial exists, only upon the consent of all parties. Whenever a party is added, the consent of each party must be of record, either in writing or recorded in open court. The filing of a consent does not preclude a party from challenging whether the demand was timely filed or whether the right to a jury trial exists.

C. Applicability of District Court Procedures. Jury trials shall be conducted in accordance with the procedures applicable to jury trials in the District Court.

[Adopted effective December 1, 2008.]

RULE 9016–1. ATTACHING A NOTE TO THE SUBPOENA IS PERMITTED

The validity of a subpoena shall not be affected by the attaching or delivering of a note or other memorandum containing instructions to a witness regarding the exact date, time, and place the witness is required to appear.

[Adopted effective December 1, 2008.]

RULE 9019–1. MOTIONS TO COMPROMISE OR SETTLE ADVERSARY PROCEEDINGS

A motion under Fed. R. Bankr. P. 9019 seeking approval of a compromise or settlement of an adversary proceeding must be filed in the bankruptcy case and not in the adversary proceeding.

[Effective October 27, 2011. Amended effective January 1, 2012.]

RULE 9020–1. CIVIL CONTEMPT OF COURT

A. Commencing Proceedings.

(1) A proceeding to adjudicate a person in civil contempt of court for conduct outside the presence of the court shall be commenced under Fed. R. Bankr. P. 9020 either on the court's own motion by order to show cause, or motion by a party in interest.

(2) A contempt motion shall be accompanied by an affidavit describing the alleged misconduct on which it is based, stating the total of any monetary claim occasioned thereby, and listing each special item of damage sought to be recovered. A reasonable counsel fee, necessitated by the contempt proceeding, may be included as an item of damage.

(3) If an order to show cause is entered, such order shall describe the misconduct on which it is based. It may also, upon necessity shown therein, direct the United States Marshal to arrest the alleged contemnor, and in that case shall fix the amount of bail and require that any bond signed by the alleged contemnor include as a condition of release that the alleged contemnor will comply with any order of the court directing the person to surrender.

(4) If the court initiates a contempt proceeding, the court may appoint an attorney to prosecute the contempt. If an attorney files a motion for contempt, that attorney is authorized to prosecute the contempt unless the court orders otherwise.

B. Order Where Found in Contempt.

(1) Should the alleged contemnor be found in civil contempt of court, an order will be entered:

(a) Reciting findings of fact upon which the adjudication is based or referring to findings recited orally from the bench;

(b) Setting forth the damages, if any, sustained by any injured party;

(c) Fixing any civil contempt award imposed by the court, which award shall include the damages found, and naming each person to whom such award is payable;

(d) Stating any acts that will purge or partially purge the contempt;

(e) Directing arrest of the contemnor by the United States Marshal and the confinement of the contemnor, should that be found appropriate, until the performance of some act fixed in the order and the payment of the award, or until the contemnor be otherwise discharged pursuant to law.

(2) Unless the order for contempt otherwise specifies, should confinement be ordered the place of confinement shall be either the Chicago Metropolitan Correctional Center in Chicago, Illinois, or the Winnebago County Jail in Rockford, Illinois. No party shall be required to pay or to advance to the Marshal any expenses for the upkeep of the prisoner. Upon such an order, the person shall not be detained in prison for a period exceeding 180 days. A certified copy of the order committing the contemnor shall be sufficient warrant to the Marshal for the arrest and confinement.

(3) Should a civil contempt award be entered, a party to whom it is payable will have the same remedies against property of the contemnor as if the award were a final judgment, and a formal final dollar judgment may also be separately entered. Should the United States Trustee initiate the proceeding by motion, or should the court initiate the proceeding by order to show cause, any contempt award ordered will be in favor of the United States of America unless otherwise ordered.

C. Discharge Where No Contempt. Where a finding of no contempt is entered, the alleged contemnor will be discharged from the proceeding.

[Adopted effective December 1, 2008.]

RULE 9021–1. SATISFACTION OF JUDGMENT AND DECREES

The clerk shall enter a satisfaction of judgment in any of the following circumstances:

(1) upon the filing of a statement of satisfaction of the judgment executed and acknowledged by (a) the judgment creditor, (b) the creditor's legal representative or assignee, with evidence of its authority; or (c) if the filing is within two years of the entry of the judgment, the creditor's attorney; or

(2) upon payment to the court of the amount of the judgment plus interest and costs, if the judgment is for money only; or

(3) if the judgment creditor is the United States, upon the filing of a statement of satisfaction executed by the United States Attorney; or

(4) upon receipt of a certified copy of a statement of satisfaction entered in another district.

[Adopted effective December 1, 2008.]

RULE 9027–1. REMAND

A. Time for Mailing of Order. When an order is entered directing that a matter be remanded to a state court, the clerk shall delay mailing the certified copy of the remand order for fourteen days following the date of docketing of the order of remand, provided that, where the court directs that the copy be mailed forthwith, no such delay shall occur.

B. Completion of Remand. The filing of a motion under Fed. R. Bankr. P. 9023 affecting an order of remand referred to in section A of this Rule shall not stop the remand of the case. However, on motion, the court may direct the clerk not to complete the remand process until a date certain or further order of court.

[Adopted effective December 1, 2008.]

RULE 9027–2. REMOVAL OF CASES FROM STATE COURT

A. Notice of Removal to Be Filed With Clerk of This Court. A party desiring to remove to this court, pursuant to 28 U.S.C. § 1452 and Fed. R. Bankr. P. 9027, a civil action or proceeding from a state court in this district shall file all required papers with the clerk.

B. Copy of Record to Be Filed With Clerk Within 21 Days. Within 21 days after filing the notice of removal, the petitioner shall file with the clerk a copy of all records and proceedings had in the state court.

[Adopted effective December 1, 2008. Amended effective October 27, 2011; January 1, 2012.]

RULE 9029–2. PROCEDURE FOR PROPOSING AMENDMENTS TO RULES

Amendments to these Rules may be proposed to the District Court by majority vote of all the judges.

[Adopted effective December 1, 2008.]

RULE 9029–3. INTERNAL OPERATING PROCEDURES

The judges may by majority vote adopt general orders of the court with respect to internal court and clerical administrative matters ("Internal Operating Procedures"), provided that no such general order of the court may conflict with applicable law, the Fed. R. Bankr. P., these Rules, or applicable local rules of the District Court. All such general orders and Internal Operating Procedures must be assigned numbers and be made public by the clerk.

[Adopted effective December 1, 2008.]

RULE 9029–4A. RULES OF PROFESSIONAL CONDUCT

The *Rules of Professional Conduct for the Northern District of Illinois*, as amended from time to time, shall apply in all proceedings and matters before this court.

[Former Rule 9029–4 adopted effective December 1, 2008. Redesignated as Rule 9029–4A effective November 22, 2011.]

RULE 9029–4B. ATTORNEY DISCIPLINARY PROCEEDINGS

A. Disciplinary Proceedings Generally.

(1) *Definitions.* The following definitions apply to the disciplinary Rules:

(a) "Misconduct" means any act or omission by an attorney that violates the disciplinary rules of the district court. Such an act or omission constitutes misconduct regardless of

(1) whether the attorney performed the act or omission individually or in concert with any other person or persons, or

(2) whether the act or omission occurred in the course of an attorney-client relationship.

(b) "Discipline" includes, but is not limited to, temporary or permanent suspension from practice before the bankruptcy court, reprimand, censure, or such other disciplinary action as the circumstances may warrant, including but not limited to restitution of funds, satisfactory completion of educational programs, compliance with treatment programs, and community service.

(2) *Jurisdiction.* Nothing in these Rules restricts the power of any judge over proceedings before that judge.

(3) *Attorneys Subject to Discipline.* By appearing in the bankruptcy court, an attorney, whether or not a member of the bar of the district court, submits to the disciplinary jurisdiction of the bankruptcy court for any alleged misconduct that the attorney commits.

(4) *Confidentiality.*

(a) Before a disciplinary proceeding is assigned to a judge pursuant to these Rules, the proceeding is confidential, except that the bankruptcy court may, on such terms as it deems appropriate, authorize the clerk of the court to disclose any information about the proceeding.

(b) After a disciplinary proceeding is assigned to a judge pursuant to these Rules, the record and hearings in the proceeding are public, and all materials submitted to the chief judge before the disciplinary proceeding was assigned must be filed with the clerk of the court, unless for good cause the judge to whom the disciplinary proceeding is assigned orders otherwise.

(c) A final order in a disciplinary proceeding is a public record.

B. Discipline of Attorneys for Misconduct.

(1) *Complaint of Misconduct.* A disciplinary proceeding is commenced by submitting a complaint of misconduct to the chief judge of the bankruptcy court. The complaint may be in the form of a letter. The complaint must state with particularity the nature of the alleged misconduct and must identify the Local Rule of the district court that has been violated. The chief judge must refer the complaint of misconduct to the bankruptcy court for consideration and appropriate action.

(2) *Request for a Response to a Complaint of Misconduct.* On receipt of a complaint of misconduct, the

435

bankruptcy court may forward a copy to the attorney and ask for a response within a set time. Any response must be submitted to the chief judge.

(3) *Action by the Bankruptcy Court on a Complaint of Misconduct.* On the basis of the complaint of misconduct and any response submitted, the bankruptcy court may, by a majority vote—

(a) determine that the complaint merits no further action and provide notice of this determination to the complainant and the attorney;

(b) direct that formal disciplinary proceedings be commenced; or

(c) take other appropriate action.

(4) *Statement of Charges.* If the bankruptcy court determines, based on allegations in the complaint of misconduct, and any response, that formal, disciplinary proceedings should be initiated, the bankruptcy court must issue a statement of charges against the attorney. The statement of charges must set forth the alleged misconduct and must require the attorney to show cause, within 28 days after service, why the attorney should not be disciplined.

(5) *Method of Service.* The clerk of the court must mail two copies of the statement of charges to the last known address of the attorney. One copy must be mailed by certified mail restricted to addressee only, return receipt requested. The other copy must be mailed by first class mail. If the statement of charges is returned as undeliverable, the clerk of the court must notify the chief judge. The bankruptcy court may direct that further, alternative attempts at service be made.

(6) *Date of Service.* For purposes of this rule, the date of service is

(a) the date of mailing, if service is by mail, or

(b) the date of delivery, if service is personal.

(7) *Answer to Statement of Charges.* Within 28 days after the date of service, the attorney who is the subject of the statement of charges must submit to the chief judge an answer to the statement of charges showing cause why the attorney should not be disciplined.

(8) *Appointment of the United States Trustee.* The bankruptcy court may appoint the United States Trustee for this region to investigate a complaint of misconduct and prosecute a statement of charges. The United States Trustee may decline the appointment and must notify the chief judge of that decision within 30 days. The bankruptcy court may then elect either to dismiss the proceeding or request that a member of the bar investigate the complaint of misconduct and prosecute the statement of charges.

(9) *Assignment to Judge for Hearing.* If, after the attorney has answered the statement of charges, the bankruptcy court determines by a majority vote that an evidentiary hearing is warranted, the chief judge will assign the disciplinary proceeding to a judge for hearing.

(10) *Subpoenas.* The United States Trustee or any other investigating or prosecuting attorney may cause subpoenas to be issued.

(11) *Hearing.* The Federal Rules of Evidence will apply in any hearing on a statement of charges. The burden is on the party prosecuting the complaint to demonstrate by a preponderance of the evidence that the attorney charged has committed misconduct.

(12) *Decision.* Upon completion of the hearing, the assigned judge must issue a written decision making findings of fact and conclusions of law, determining whether the attorney charged has committed misconduct, and if so, imposing appropriate discipline. A separate order imposing discipline must be entered in accordance with the written decision.

(13) *Appeal.* Entry of an order imposing the discipline is a final order, appealable as of right to the Executive Committee of the district court. Part VIII of the Federal Rules of Bankruptcy Procedure governs all appeals from disciplinary orders of the bankruptcy court, except that Rule 8001(f) of the Federal Rules of Bankruptcy Procedure does not apply.

C. Indefinite Suspension on Consent.

(1) *Declaration of Consent.* Any attorney who is the subject of a complaint of misconduct or a statement of charges may consent to indefinite suspension from practice before the bankruptcy court, but only by delivering to the chief judge a declaration stating that the attorney consents to indefinite suspension.

(2) *Order on Consent.* Upon receipt of the required declaration, the chief judge must enter an order indefinitely suspending the attorney. The order indefinitely suspending the attorney on consent is a matter of public record.

D. Reinstatement.

(1) *Reinstatement when Suspension is 90 Days or Fewer.* An attorney suspended for 90 days or fewer is automatically reinstated at the end of the period of suspension.

(2) *Reinstatement, when Suspension is more than 90 Days.* An attorney suspended for more than 90 days may not resume practice in the bankruptcy court until reinstated by order of the bankruptcy court in response to a petition for reinstatement. The attorney may petition for reinstatement at any time following the period of suspension.

(3) *Reinstatement when Suspension is for an Indefinite Period.* An attorney who is indefinitely suspended may not resume practice in the bankruptcy court until reinstatement by order of the bankruptcy court in response to a petition for reinstatement. The

attorney may petition for reinstatement any time after five years from the effective date of the suspension.

(4) *Presentation of Petition for Reinstatement.* A petition for reinstatement must be filed with the clerk of the court. The clerk must present the petition to the bankruptcy court which, by a majority vote, must either grant or deny the petition without an evidentiary hearing, or else determine the matter requires an evidentiary hearing before a judge of the bankruptcy court assigned by the chief judge.

(5) *Appointment of the United States Trustee.* Following the filing of a petition for reinstatement, the bankruptcy court may appoint the United States Trustee for this region to investigate the petition and support or oppose reinstatement. The United States Trustee may decline the appointment and must notify the chief judge of that decision within 30 days. The bankruptcy court may then request that a member of the bar investigate the petition and oppose or support reinstatement.

(6) *Hearing.* The Federal Rules of Evidence will apply in any hearing on a petition for reinstatement. The burden is on the petitioner to demonstrate by clear and convincing evidence that the petitioner has the requisite character and fitness to practice law before the bankruptcy court and that the petitioner's resumption of practice before the bankruptcy court will not be detrimental to the administration of justice.

(7) *Decision by Assigned Judge.* Upon completion of the hearing, the assigned judge must issue a written decision making findings of fact and conclusions of law and determining whether the petitioner should be reinstated. A separate order must be entered.

(8) *Conditions of Reinstatement.* If the petitioner fails to demonstrate fitness to resume the practice of law before the bankruptcy court, the petition for reinstatement must be denied. If the petitioner is found fit to resume practice before the bankruptcy court, the petitioner must be reinstated, but reinstatement may be subject to conditions, including but not limited to partial or complete restitution to parties harmed by the conduct that led to the suspension.

(9) *Appeal.* Entry of an order granting or denying a petition for reinstatement is a final order appealable as of right to the Executive Committee of the district court. Part VIII of the Federal Rules of Bankruptcy Procedure governs all appeals from disciplinary orders of the bankruptcy court, except that Rule 8001(f) of the Federal Rules of Bankruptcy Procedure does not apply.

(10) *Limitation on Successive Petitions for Reinstatement.* Following the denial of a petition for reinstatement, the petitioner may not file another petition for reinstatement until at least one year from the date of the order denying reinstatement.

E. Notice to Executive Committee and ARDC.

Following

(a) the entry of a final order imposing discipline or a final order granting or denying a petition for reinstatement, and

(b) the exhaustion of all appellate rights in connection with such an order, the clerk of the court must transmit a copy of the order to the Executive Committee of the District Court and to the Illinois Attorney Registration and Disciplinary Commission.

[Adopted effective November 22, 2011.]

RULE 9029–5. STANDING ORDERS OF INDIVIDUAL JUDGES

Nothing in these Rules shall limit the authority of each judge to issue standing orders generally applicable to administration or adjudication of cases and matters assigned to that judge without approval of the Bankruptcy Court or District Court, to the extent the standing orders are not in conflict with applicable law, the Fed. R. Bankr. P., these Rules, the Internal Operating Procedures, or local rules of the District Court. Each judge shall furnish copies of all standing orders to the clerk who will make them public.

[Adopted effective December 1, 2008.]

RULE 9029–6. ACTING CHIEF JUDGE

If the chief judge is absent from the District or is unable to perform his or her duties, such duties shall be performed by the judge in active service, present in the Eastern Division of the District and able and qualified to act, who is next in line of seniority based on the date of his or her first appointment. Such judge is designated as the acting chief judge on such occasions.

[Adopted effective December 1, 2008.]

RULE 9033–1. NON–CORE PROCEEDINGS—TRANSMITTAL TO THE DISTRICT COURT OF PROPOSED FINDINGS OF FACT AND CONCLUSIONS OF LAW

A. Time of Transmittal. The clerk shall transmit to the District Court the proposed findings of fact and conclusions of law filed pursuant to Fed. R. Bankr. P. 9033 upon the expiration of time for filing objections and any response thereto.

B. Procedures Following Transmittal. After transmission of proposed findings and conclusions to the District Court, no filings, except motions pursuant to Fed. R. Bankr. P. 9033(c), may be made in the Bankruptcy Court with respect to the non-core proceeding until after a dispositive ruling by the District Court. When findings of fact and conclusions of law are filed that do not completely resolve the non-core proceeding, the Bankruptcy Court retains jurisdiction over the remaining issues and parties.

[Adopted effective December 1, 2008.]

RULE 9037–1. MOTION TO REDACT PERSONAL INFORMATION

A motion to redact personal information prohibited under Fed. R. Bankr. P. 9037(a) should be filed without a notice of motion and without serving other parties. The motion must be accompanied by a redacted version of the filed document and a proposed order requiring the clerk to substitute the redacted document for the unredacted document. The judge should rule on the motion as soon as possible without holding a hearing unless there appears to be a reason to deny the motion, in which case the judge should set the matter for hearing with the movant as soon as possible.

[Effective October 27, 2011.]

RULE 9060–1. REFERRAL TO MEDIATION

(a) A party to any dispute pending before the court may, at any time, request entry of an order referring the dispute to mediation under these Rules by presenting to the court a motion for mediation, in the form appended to and made a part of this Rule. Each such motion shall be accompanied by a mediation agreement signed by the parties.

(b) The motion shall state whether the parties have agreed on a mediator. If the parties have not agreed on a mediator, the motion may name any mediator from the list maintained by the clerk pursuant to Rule 9060–5 whom a party wishes to exclude from service. Upon presentation of the motion for mediation, the court may enter an order referring the dispute to mediation under these Rules.

(c) These provisions do not apply when a sitting bankruptcy judge agrees to mediate a case assigned to another sitting bankruptcy judge, or when the parties use other types of alternate dispute resolution.

[Adopted effective December 1, 2008.]

Rule 9060–1 (Form): ADR Motion

[Case/Adversary Caption]

MOTION FOR MEDIATION

The undersigned party or Parties ("Parties") hereby request that this court enter an order referring the following dispute to mediation pursuant to the Local Bankruptcy Rules:

(brief description of the nature and status of the dispute)

1. Have the necessary Parties agreed upon mediation of this dispute? Yes/No

2. If the Parties have agreed upon a mediator, state the name, address and phone number of the mediator agreed upon:

_____

_____

_____

3. If the Parties do not notify the clerk that they have agreed upon a mediator, the Parties understand and agree that, then within seven (7) days of the entry of an order of reference to mediation, the clerk will randomly assign a mediator from the list of mediators maintained by the clerk pursuant to Local Bankruptcy Rule 9060–5A.

4. By agreeing to enter into mediation with the intention of reaching a consensual settlement of their dispute, the Parties and their counsel agree to be bound by the Local Bankruptcy Rules governing mediation and to proceed in a good faith effort to resolve this dispute.

Wherefore, the undersigned Parties and their counsel request that the court enter an order referring this dispute to mediation and granting such other relief as is just and proper.

Signed: _____   Print name: _____

_____   _____

Date:

Rule 9060–1 (Form): Bankruptcy Mediation Agreement

[Case/Adversary Caption]

BANKRUPTCY MEDIATION AGREEMENT

This is an agreement by and between _____ and _____ (hereinafter referred to as "the Parties") and their representatives. The Parties have agreed to enter into mediation with the intention of reaching a consensual settlement of their dispute.

1. The Parties agree to make complete and accurate disclosure of all information necessary for an understanding of each party's factual and legal position.

2. The Parties, together with their representatives and those in privity with them, agree to comply with the provisions of the local Bankruptcy Rules governing confidentiality and discovery of mediation proceedings, and further agree that disclosure by a party of privileged information to the mediator does not waive or otherwise adversely affect the privileged nature of

the information. However, nothing in this agreement shall be construed to prevent or excuse the Parties or those in privity with them from reporting matters such as crimes, imminent threats of bodily injury, or such other matters as to which the law imposes a duty to report.

3. The Parties and their representatives understand that the Mediator will not be offering legal advice to any party. Nor will the mediator be rendering any opinion or decision in connection with the mediation. The Mediator's role is to aid the parties in seeking a fair agreement in accordance with their respective interests. The Parties understand that they have a right to be represented by legal counsel in the mediation proceedings, and that such representation is recommended by the court. None of the Parties or those in privity with them will be permitted to employ the Mediator nor any attorney of his or her firm in any legal proceeding or other matter relating to the subject of the mediation, nor for any matter while the mediation is pending.

4. Any Party may withdraw this dispute from mediation at any time pursuant to Local Bankruptcy Rule 9060–3F.

5. The Parties agree to share the fees and expenses of the Mediator as follows: _____

_____.

However, any party who fails to comply with the Local Bankruptcy Rules governing mediation or the terms of this agreement without good cause will be responsible for any expenses of the other parties arising out of the failure to comply as determined by the court on notice with an opportunity for a hearing.

6. The Parties hereby release, indemnify and hold harmless the Mediator from any liability arising in connection with the performance of his or her duties as Mediator in accordance with this Agreement and the Local Bankruptcy Rules. However, nothing in this Agreement shall release the Mediator for liability arising from the willful derogation of his or her duties as mediator.

7. The Local Bankruptcy Rules governing mediation are expressly made a part of this agreement and are incorporated by reference herein. The Parties agree to be bound by these Rules.

8. The Parties agree that any dispute arising out of this mediation shall be heard and resolved by the bankruptcy judge, and the Parties expressly waive any requirement of the Federal Rules of Bankruptcy Procedure that relief pursuant to or arising out of this mediation be sought in the form of a complaint, and hereby consent to the application of Fed. R. Bankr. P. 9014 to any request for relief relating to this agreement. Furthermore, to the extent that any such request for relief is not a core proceeding under 28 U.S.C. § 157(b), the Parties hereby agree that a bankruptcy court may nevertheless enter appropriate orders and judgments with respect to the request for relief.

I have read, understand and agree to each of the provisions of this agreement.

SIGNED: _____ DATE: _____

SIGNED: _____ DATE: _____

[Adopted effective December 1, 2008.]

RULE 9060–2. SELECTION OF A MEDIATOR

A. Selection or Exclusion by the Parties. The parties to a dispute submitted to mediation under these Rules may select a person to serve as mediator, either by identifying that person in their motion for mediation, or by filing a designation of an agreed mediator with the clerk, within seven (7) days after entry of the order of reference to mediation. If the parties do not select a mediator, any party may file with the clerk, within six (6) days of the entry of the order of reference to mediation, a designation of any mediator from the list maintained by the clerk pursuant to Rule 9060–5(A) whom that party wishes to exclude from service as mediator.

B. Selection by the Clerk. If the parties do not select a mediator, the clerk shall randomly assign a mediator from the list maintained by the clerk pursuant to Rule 9060–5(A), other than a mediator whom a party has excluded in a motion for mediation or a designation filed under section A of this Rule.

C. Acceptance or Declination by the Mediator. The clerk shall promptly notify the person selected as mediator of the selection, including with the notification a copy of any motion for mediation and of the order referring the dispute to mediation. Within seven (7) days of the notification, the mediator selected (1) shall discuss with the parties his or her availability to serve and, if available, the terms of compensation under which he or she would be willing to serve; and (2) shall file with the clerk and serve on the parties to the dispute either (a) a statement of acceptance together with an affidavit of disinterestedness, or (b) a statement declining to serve as mediator.

D. Selection of an Alternative Mediator. Upon receipt of a statement of declination by the selected mediator, or upon the passage of seven (7) days from the notice of the selection without a response from the selected mediator, the clerk shall notify the parties that the selected mediator will not serve. Within seven (7) days of such a notice, the parties may select an alternative mediator or specify mediators for exclusion, pursuant to section A of this Rule. If the parties fail to make the selection within seven (7) days from the notice, the clerk shall make the selection of an alternate mediator pursuant to section B of this Rule. The alternate mediator shall be notified and shall respond as provided in section C of this Rule.

[Adopted effective December 1, 2008.]

RULE 9060–3. MEDIATION PROCEDURE

A. Effect of Mediation on Other Pending Matters. The referral of a dispute to mediation does not relieve the parties from complying with any other court orders or applicable law and rules. Referral to mediation does not stay or delay discovery, pre-trial hearing dates, or trial schedules unless otherwise provided by court order.

B. Scheduling of a Mediation Conference; Submission of Materials. After consulting with all counsel and any pro se parties, the mediator shall promptly schedule, at the earliest practicable date, a convenient time and place for an initial mediation conference, and shall give at least seven (7) days notice to all parties of the date, time and place of the initial mediation conference. The mediator may include in the notice of the initial mediation conference a direction to the parties to submit statements of their positions, copies of relevant documents, evidentiary exhibits, or other materials that the mediator believes will be helpful in the mediation process. The parties shall submit to the mediator all materials specified by the mediator and shall serve copies on all other parties, unless otherwise directed by the mediator, at least three days prior to the initial mediation conference.

C. Attendance at the Initial Mediation Conference. The following individuals shall attend the initial mediation conference unless excused by the mediator:

(1) each party who is a natural person;

(2) for each party that is not a natural person, either

(a) a representative, not the party's attorney of record, who has full authority to negotiate and settle the dispute on behalf of that party, or

(b) if the party is an entity that requires settlement approval by a committee, board or legislative body, a representative who has authority to recommend a settlement to the committee, board or legislative body;

(3) the attorney who has primary responsibility for each party's case; and

(4) any other entity determined by the mediator to be necessary for a full resolution of the dispute referred to mediation.

D. Conduct of the Initial Mediation Conference.

(1) The mediator shall preside over the initial mediation conference with full authority to determine the nature and order of presentations and the time, place, and structure of any proceedings. The mediator may direct that additional parties attend or that additional materials be submitted at any continuance of the mediation conference.

(2) Except as the mediator may direct, or as the mediation agreement provides, rules of evidence and procedure shall not apply to the mediation process.

(3) Except as specified in these Rules, no material submitted to the mediator or prepared in connection with any mediation conference shall be filed with the court as part of the mediation process.

E. Resignation of Mediator. The mediator may resign from the mediation at any time during the mediation process, by filing a notice of resignation with the clerk, with service on all parties, stating the reason for the resignation. A mediator who resigns shall forfeit his right to receive fees, unless the court determines that the resignation was proper and without any fault of the mediator. A new mediator will thereupon be selected in conformity with the provisions of Rule 9060–2D. The new mediator shall be served with a copy of the notice of resignation in addition to the other materials specified by Rule 9060–2C. The clerk shall attach a copy of the notice of resignation to the mediator's certificate maintained pursuant to Rule 9060–5A.

F. Withdrawal of a Dispute from Mediation. Any party may withdraw a dispute from mediation at any time upon the filing of a statement of withdrawal with the clerk. The clerk shall promptly notify the judge assigned to the case of the withdrawal.

[Adopted effective December 1, 2008.]

RULE 9060–4. POST MEDIATION PROCEDURES

A. Preparation of Documents Required to Implement Settlement. If the dispute referred to mediation is resolved, the parties, with the assistance of the mediator, shall determine who will prepare any document (e.g., agreements, stipulations, motions, or agreed orders) required to implement the resolution reached.

B. Report by the Mediator. Within seven (7) days after the mediator determines that the mediation is concluded, either by resolution or by withdrawal, the mediator shall file with the clerk and serve on the parties a report stating whether the dispute was resolved, and if so, who will prepare the documents required to implement the settlement.

[Adopted effective December 1, 2008.]

RULE 9060–5. LIST OF MEDIATORS

A. Maintenance by the Clerk of a List of Mediators and a File of Mediators' Certificates. The clerk shall maintain and make available to the public a list of mediators, consisting of the name, address, and telephone number of each person who has filed with the clerk the certificate specified by section B of this Rule, and whose name has not been withdrawn or removed pursuant to section D of this Rule. The clerk shall further maintain and make available to the public a file containing the certificates filed by those persons whose names are included on the list of mediators. Inclusion on the list does not constitute certification by the court of the qualifications of the mediator.

B. Filing and Form of Mediator's Certificate. Any adult may be included in the list of mediators maintained by the clerk pursuant to this Rule. To be included, such a person shall file with the clerk a completed mediator's certificate in the form appended to and made a part of this Rule. Each mediator included on the list shall promptly file amendments to the certificate, whenever necessary, to disclose any substantial change in the information provided in the certificate. In addition, each mediator included in the list shall file a complete, updated certificate at no more than three-year intervals.

C. Pro Bono Mediators. A person filing a completed mediator's certificate thereby agrees to accept at least one pro bono mediation per year pursuant to Rule 9060–7.

D. Withdrawal and Removal from the List of Mediators. Any mediator may voluntarily withdraw from the list of mediators at any time by providing written notification to the clerk, who shall remove the name of the mediator from the list of mediators and remove that mediator's certificate from the file of mediators' certificates. If a mediator fails to update his or her certificate pursuant to section B of this Rule, or if the chief judge notifies the clerk that a mediator has failed to accept at least one pro bono matter per year assigned to the mediator pursuant to Rule 9060–7, the clerk shall remove the name of the mediator from the list of mediators and remove the mediator's certificate from the file of mediator certificates.

Rule 9060–5 (Form): Mediator's Certificate

UNITED STATES BANKRUPTCY COURT NORTHERN DISTRICT OF ILLINOIS

MEDIATOR'S CERTIFICATE

I, the undersigned, hereby apply for designation on the List of Mediators in the United States Bankruptcy Court for the Northern District of Illinois. In making this application, I certify under penalty or perjury that all of the following information is true and correct.

A. Nature and level of training and experience in ADR and training programs you have completed: (include names, locations, dates, and CLE credit hours, where applicable, for any Alternative Dispute Resolution ("ADR").

_____

_____

_____

Nature and length of experience in bankruptcy (describe your experience as attorney, trustee, accountant, liquidator, reorganization specialist, assignee or in any other bankruptcy-related field in which you have special expertise):

_____

_____

_____

B. Professional licenses (identify any professional license that you hold relevant to your service as mediator or neutral, including the issuing body and the date first issued):

_____

_____

_____

C. Membership in professional organizations (identify any professional memberships relevant to your service as mediator or neutral to which you currently belong or have belonged in the past and state the time periods during which you were a member):

_____

_____

_____

D. (a) Have you ever been the subject of a finding of misconduct in a disciplinary proceeding that resulted in the suspension or revocation of your professional license or a public censure? _____

(b) Have you ever resigned from a professional organization while an investigation was pending into allegations of misconduct which would warrant discipline, suspension, disbarment or professional license revocation? _____

(c) Have you ever been removed for cause as a neutral? _____

(d) Have you ever been convicted of a felony? __

E.   If the answer to any part of question 5 is "Yes," set forth the circumstances surrounding the action in question, including the relevant dates and circumstances:

_____

_____

_____

_____

F.   Other relevant experience, skills, honors, publications, or other information:

_____

_____

_____

_____

G.   Counties in which you are available to conduct mediation conferences:

_____

_____

H.   General Affirmations:

(a) I have read the Local Bankruptcy Rules of the Bankruptcy Court for the Northern District of Illinois governing mediation.

(b) I agree to comply fully with the relevant provisions of the Local Bankruptcy Rules, as well as this court's General Orders and any modifications thereto, governing mediation.

(c) I will not accept appointment as a mediator in any proceeding or matter unless at the time of accepting the appointment:

(1) I qualify as a "Disinterested Person" as defined by 11 U.S.C. § 101, I am free of financial or other interests pursuant to 28 U.S.C. § 455 which would disqualify me if I were a judge, and I am unaware of any other reasons that would disqualify me as a mediator; or

(2) I have fully disclosed any potentially disqualifying circumstances and they have been waived by all parties.

(d) Upon learning that I am no longer qualified to serve as a mediator pursuant to Rule 9060–5D, I will immediately contact the clerk and any parties for whom I have accepted appointment as mediator.

(e) I consent to public disclosure of the information contained in this Application.

Date: _____ Signature: _____
                       Name: _____
                           (Print or Type)
                       Address: _____
                       Telephone: _____

[Adopted effective December 1, 2008.]

RULE 9060–6.   COMPENSATION

Before the commencement of the mediation conference, the mediator and the parties to the mediation shall enter into a written agreement setting forth the fees and expenses to be paid to the mediator by each party. A copy of the agreement shall be filed with the court. Nothing in these Rules relieves a mediator or any party to a mediation from complying with applicable sections of the Bankruptcy Code, the Federal Rules of Bankruptcy Procedure, and these Rules governing the retention and payment of professional persons.

[Adopted effective December 1, 2008.]

RULE 9060–7.   PRO BONO MEDIATION

If one or more of the parties to a dispute cannot afford to pay the fees of a mediator, but all parties have agreed to submit the matter to mediation, any party may present a motion to the chief judge, on notice to the other parties, to have the dispute designated for pro bono mediation. If the motion is granted, the chief judge shall appoint a mediator from the list maintained by the clerk and notify the mediator of the appointment. The appointed mediator shall respond in the manner specified by Rule 9060–2C, except that the mediator shall neither discuss nor receive compensation or reimbursement of expenses from any of the parties. If the mediator declines the appointment, the clerk shall so notify the chief judge, who shall appoint an alternate mediator.

[Adopted effective December 1, 2008.]

RULE 9060–8.   CONFIDENTIALITY

A. Confidentiality of Mediation Proceedings. The mediator, all parties, those in privity with them, and all non-party participants shall not divulge, outside of the mediation process, any oral or written information disclosed in the course of the mediation process, including but not limited to the following:

(1) views expressed or suggestions made by a party, the mediator, or a nonparty participant with respect to a possible resolution of the dispute;

(2) whether another participant indicated a willingness to accept a proposal or suggestion for resolution of the dispute;

(3) any statements, recommendations, or views of the mediator;

(4) any statements or admissions made in the course of the mediation;

(5) any documents prepared in connection with the mediation.

B. Admissibility. The matters described in Section A of this Rule are inadmissible in evidence in any proceeding before the court. Evidence or information otherwise admissible or discoverable does not become inadmissible or undiscoverable solely by reason of its disclosure or use in a mediation proceeding.

C. Prohibition Against Discovery. Subject to the second sentence in Section B of this Rule, no one may seek to discover from the mediator, a party, those in privity with them, or a non-party participant, except as otherwise provided in these Rules, any of the matters described in Section A of this Rule.

D. Waiver.

(1) The rule of confidentiality in Section A of this Rule may one be waived orally before a court reporter or in writing, if it is expressly waived by all parties to the mediation, and

(a) if it relates to actions or statements by the mediator, it is expressly waived by the mediator, or

(b) if it relates to actions or statements by a non-party participant, it is expressly waived by the non-party participant.

(2) A person who violates the rule of confidentiality in Section A of this Rule to the prejudice of another is precluded from asserting the rule to the extent necessary for the other to respond.

(3) A person who intentionally uses a mediation to plan, attempt to commit, or commit a crime may not assert the rule of confidentiality in Section A of this Rule.

[Adopted effective December 1, 2008.]

RULE 9060–9. MEDIATOR'S LIABILITY

The parties shall include in the mediation agreement a provision releasing, indemnifying and holding harmless the mediator from any liability arising in connection with the performance of his or her duties as mediator in accordance with these Rules, except liability for intentional violations of these Rules.

[Adopted effective December 1, 2008.]

RULE 9060–10. TERMINATION OF MEDIATION

Upon the filing of a mediator's report pursuant to Rule 9060–4B or the filing of a notice withdrawing a matter from mediation pursuant to Rule 9060–3F, the mediation will be terminated and the mediator relieved from further responsibilities in the mediation, without further court order.

[Adopted effective December 1, 2008.]

RULE 9060–11. OTHER DISPUTE RESOLUTION PROCEDURES

Nothing contained in these Rules is intended to prevent or discourage the parties or the court from employing any other method of dispute resolution.

[Adopted effective December 1, 2008.]

RULE 9060–12. EXTENSION OR REDUCTION OF DEADLINES

For cause, on motion, any party or mediator may request the court to extend or reduce any time limit provided for by these Rules for action to be taken in connection with the mediation process.

[Adopted effective December 1, 2008.]

RULE 9065–1. CHAPTER 13—COPIES OF ORDERS

In a chapter 13 case, if a copy of a proposed order submitted to the court for entry has not been served on the standing chapter 13 trustee, a copy must be supplied to the chapter 13 trustee in open court. When a draft order is to be submitted after a hearing, a copy shall be served on the chapter 13 trustee when the order is submitted to the court.

[Adopted effective December 1, 2008.]

RULE 9065–2. SERVICE OF COPIES OF PROOFS OF CLAIM IN CHAPTER 13 CASES

In all chapter 13 cases, if a claimant files a proof of claim alleging a security interest in any property of the debtor, the claimant shall serve a copy of the proof of claim on the debtor's attorney, or on the debtor, if pro se. Service shall be at the same time that the proof of claim is filed with the clerk.

[Adopted effective December 1, 2008.]

RULE 9070–1. CUSTODY OF EXHIBITS

A. Retention of Exhibits. Original exhibits shall be retained by the attorney or pro se party producing them unless the court orders them deposited with the clerk.

B. Exhibits Subject to Orders of Court. Original exhibits retained under section A of this Rule and original transcripts ordered by any party but not filed are subject to orders of the court. Upon request, parties shall make the exhibits and transcripts or copies thereof available to any other party to copy at its expense.

C. Removal of Exhibits. Exhibits that have been deposited with the clerk shall be removed by the party responsible for them (1) within ninety days after a final decision is rendered if no appeal is taken or (2) within thirty days after the mandate of the reviewing court is filed. Parties failing to comply with this Rule shall be notified by the clerk to remove their exhibits. Thirty days after such notice, the material shall be sold by the United States marshal or the clerk at public or private sale, or otherwise disposed of as the court directs. The net proceeds of any such sale shall be paid to the Treasurer of the United States.

D. Withdrawal of Exhibits; Receipt for Withdrawal. Exhibits deposited with the clerk shall not be withdrawn from the custody of the court except as provided by these Rules or upon order of court.

Parties withdrawing their exhibits from the court's custody shall give the clerk a signed receipt identifying the material taken, and the receipt shall be filed and docketed.

[Adopted effective December 1, 2008. Amended effective January 1, 2012.]

INTERNAL OPERATING PROCEDURES

IOP 1. SEAL OF THE COURT

The seal of this Court shall be circular, shall be two inches in diameter, and shall include the words "United States Bankruptcy Court for the Northern District of Illinois" in a circle surrounding a replica of the face or eagle side of the Great Seal of the United States.
[Effective June 1, 2003.]

Committee Note:

This IOP was formerly Local Bankruptcy Rule 200.

IOP 2. ACTING CHIEF JUDGE

If the chief judge is absent from the District or is unable to perform his or her duties, such duties shall be performed by the judge in active service, present in the Eastern Division of the District and able and qualified to act, who is next line of seniority based on the date of his or her first appointment. Such judge is designated as the acting chief judge on such occasions.
[Effective June 1, 2003.]

Committee Note:

This IOP was formerly Local Bankruptcy Rule 201.

IOP 3. RULE AMENDMENTS AND GENERAL ORDERS

A. Procedure For Proposing Amendments to Local Bankruptcy Rules. Amendments to the Local Bankruptcy Rules may be proposed to the District Court by majority vote of all the judges.

B. General Orders. Pursuant to 28 U.S.C. § 154(a) the judges shall by majority vote adopt general orders of the Court to determine the division of work among the judges. The judges may also by majority vote adopt general orders of the Court with respect to internal Court and clerical administrative matters, provided that no such general order of the Court shall conflict with applicable law, the Federal Rules of Bankruptcy Procedure, the Local Bankruptcy Rules, or the District Court Local Rules. All such general orders shall be assigned numbers and be made public by the clerk.

C. Standing Orders of Individual Judges. Nothing herein contained shall limit the authority of each judge to issue standing orders generally applicable to

the administration or adjudication of cases and matters assigned to that judge without approval of the Court or the District Court, to the extent the same are not in conflict with applicable law, the Federal Rules of Bankruptcy Procedure, the Local Bankruptcy Rules, or the District Court Local Rules. Copies of all standing orders will be supplied at the time of issuance to the clerk, who will make them public.

[Effective June 1, 2003.]

Committee Note:

This substance of this IOP was formerly contained in Local Bankruptcy Rule 203.

IOP 4. RECORDS OF THE COURT

A. Place of Keeping Records. The records and files of the Court shall be kept at Chicago and Rockford, Illinois and maintained by the clerk. From time to time the clerk shall, pursuant to an order of the chief judge, transfer records in closed cases to the Federal Records Center. In the Western Division, the judge senior in length of service among the bankruptcy judges permanently assigned to that Division may issue such order in the absence of an order of the chief judge.

B. Copies of Records. The clerk or any person or entity designated by order of court, on request and upon prepayment of costs, shall make copies of any document in the clerk's custody unless prohibited by law, court order, or a Local Bankruptcy Rule.

[Effective June 1, 2003.]

Committee Note:

This IOP was formerly Local Bankruptcy Rule 205. The Committee recommends that this IOP be deleted as unnecessary.

IOP 5. PROTECTION OF COMPUTERS

A. Use of Licensed Software. Only software properly licensed to the Court may be installed on any computer owned or rented by the Court. Such software may be installed on personal computers, and/or network computing systems owned and/or used by the Court, only by duly authorized members of the Court's Systems Department, except for such software that any judge wishes to use within the chambers of that judge and on laptops.

B. Scanning for Computer Viruses. Any diskettes introduced into any Court-owned or operated computers or into network computing systems must first be scanned for computer "viruses" by the Systems Department, unless the computer or system has been loaded with an automatic virus scanning software.

[Effective June 1, 2003.]

Committee Note:

This IOP was formerly Local Bankruptcy Rule 212. The Committee recommends that the IOP be deleted, as the subject matter is covered by the Computer User's Handbook.

IOP 6.   EMERGENCY JUDGE

A. Duties of Emergency Judge. The emergency judge will be responsible for hearing all emergency matters not previously assigned to a judge, and all emergency matters that arise at a time that the judge to whom the matter is assigned is absent. The emergency judge shall also act on matters in the absence of the assigned judge, unless the assigned judge has made arrangements to have matters in his or her cases heard by another judge, in which case that judge will hear the matters.

B. Designation of Emergency Judge. At all times there shall be at least one judge assigned to act as emergency judge. The judges shall serve as emergency judge for terms specified in paragraph C in order of seniority, unless they exchange or otherwise rearrange their duty periods by agreement. No judge shall serve as emergency judge within the ninety days immediately following taking the oath of office. The chief judge and any recall judge shall not be required to serve as emergency judge.

C. Terms of Service of Emergency Judge. The term of service of an emergency judge shall start at 12:01 A.M. on Monday and end at midnight on the Sunday immediately preceding the Monday starting the next term of emergency judge. The length of each term shall be set by general order of this Court.

D. Absence or Unavailability of Emergency Judge. Should any emergency judge be absent or unavailable during his or her term as emergency judge, that judge shall arrange with another judge to exercise the duties as emergency judge. The chief judge and the clerk shall be informed of the substitution.

E. Posting Notice Identifying Emergency Judge. A notice identifying the emergency judge shall be posted by the clerk. Committee Note: The substance of this IOP was formerly contained in Local Bankruptcy Rules 304 and 305. It is subject to the flexible approach of Local Bankruptcy Rule 1073–3

and IOP 7, which permit individual judges to exchange or otherwise rearrange their matters and duties to accommodate personal needs and exigencies.

[Effective June 1, 2003.]

IOP 7.   TEMPORARY ABSENCE OR UNAVAILABILITY OF THE ASSIGNED JUDGE

Any judge who plans to be absent from the Court should arrange for another judge to hear his or her matters and proceedings. Any judge whose workload makes it difficult to hear a particular matter in a case may arrange for another judge to sit in the place of the unavailable judge in that matter. A notice shall be posted indicating the name of the judge who will hear matters and the room number of that judge's courtroom. Copies of that notice will be supplied to the clerk of the Court and chief judge.

[Effective June 1, 2003.]

Committee Note:

The substance of this IOP was formerly contained in Local Bankruptcy Rule 307.

IOP 8.   CLASSES OF MATTERS

All cases and proceedings filed in this Court shall be assigned to one of the following two classes:

(1) Adversary Proceedings. (A), which includes all adversary proceedings and Security Investor Protection Act proceedings; and

(2) Bankruptcy. (B), which includes all bankruptcy cases or ancillary proceedings other than Security Investor Protection Act proceedings.

[Effective June 1, 2003.]

Committee Note:

This IOP was formerly Local Bankruptcy Rule 308.

IOP 9.   NUMBERING CASES AND PROCEEDINGS

Upon the filing of the initial paper in each case or proceeding, the clerk shall assign a permanent designation which shall indicate the year in which it was filed, the class to which it belongs, and the case or proceeding number, as follows:

(1) The year of filing will be indicated by the use of the last two digits of the calendar year in which the initial paper is filed.

(2) The class to which the matter belongs will be indicated by the use of the letter A for adversary or B for bankruptcy to indicate respectively the classes of proceedings or cases.

(3) The case number will be the next number in the appropriate class. There shall be a separate number series for each class. Each series in the Eastern Division will start each year with the number 1 and each used in the Western Division with the number 70001.

[Effective June 1, 2003.]

Committee Note:

The IOP is based on District Court IOP 10 (formerly local General Rule 2.12), and was formerly Local Bankruptcy Rule 309. The number in the last sentence of the IOP has been changed from 50001 to 70001. The IOP provides for a separate set of start numbers to distinguish Eastern Division cases from Western Division cases. For many years the start number for the Western Division has been 50001. The number is increased to 70001 as filings in the Eastern Division approach 50,000.

This IOP was submitted to the District Court. It is presently designated IOP2.

IOP 10. REASSIGNMENTS/RECUSALS AND TEMPORARY INCAPACITY OF A JUDGE

A. Recusals. Whenever a matter is transferred to the chief judge for reassignment following a recusal, the chief judge shall direct the clerk to reassign the matter by lot to a judge other than the judge who entered the recusal or a prior recusal in the matter.

B. Temporary Incapacity of a Judge. The chief judge may reassign a matter from any judge who, due to temporary incapacity, is unable to administer a full calendar. Such transfers may be made only after consultation with the affected judge unless circumstances make such consultation impractical. After the return of that judge, the chief judge may transfer all or some of the reassigned matters back to the original judge, after consultation with both judges involved and determination whether such transfer would adversely affect judicial economy.

[Effective June 1, 2003.]

Committee Note:

The substance of this IOP was formerly contained in sections C and D of Local Bankruptcy Rule 311.

IOP 11. REASSIGNMENT OF CHAPTER 13 CASES

Other than related cases, a chapter 13 case shall be reassigned to a judge who has the same standing trustee as the judge to whom the case was originally assigned.

[Effective June 1, 2003.]

Committee Note:

Standing trustees are assigned at the commencement of a case. If a judge recuses herself or himself or the case is otherwise to be reassigned, it should go back on the wheel as an original case with the proviso that it be reassigned by lot solely to judges who have the same standing trustee.

This IOP was submitted to the District Court. It is presently designated IOP3.

IOP 12. CLAIMS AND CLAIMS REGISTERS FOR CASES FILED BEFORE JANUARY 1, 2000

The duties placed on the chapter 13 standing trustees by this Internal Operating Procedure apply only to cases filed before January 1, 2000.

A. Proofs of Claim to be Filed with Clerk. Proofs of claims in cases under chapter 13 of the Bankruptcy Code shall be filed with the clerk. Such claims will be date and time stamped by the clerk as received, and made available by the clerk either on site or by delivery to the case standing trustee for copying. If delivered, the standing trustee shall promptly return the original claim to the clerk.

B. Standing Trustee to Maintain Claims Register. Standing trustees in all chapter 13 cases shall maintain a claims register of all claims filed in each case and may do so electronically. Each claim register shall include the name and address of each creditor; the amount claimed; whether the claim is secured or unsecured; whether the claim is administrative; and the sequence of payments provided under the debtor's plan or pursuant to any order of court.

C. Transfer of Claims: Recording, Notice of. The standing trustee shall record each transfer of a creditor's claims on the claims register, send notice of such transfer pursuant to Fed. R. Bankr. P. 3001(e)(2)(3) and (4), and promptly deliver all original filings with respect to such transfer to the clerk.

D. Trustee to Answer Inquiries re Claims Register. The standing trustees will promptly answer requests for information regarding claims registers, and will supply copies of such claim registers upon payment of any charges for actual costs of copying that are approved by the United States trustee.

E. Clerk to Establish Procedures; Report Deficiencies to Chief Judge. The clerk shall establish procedures and practices to inspect and verify the implementation of this Internal Operating Procedure, and shall promptly report any deficiencies in the compliance to the chief judge with copies to the United States trustee and to the standing trustee(s) affected. If the deficiencies affect the standing trustee in the Western Division, copies of the report shall be given promptly to the judge senior in length of service permanently assigned to that Division.

F. Standing Trustee and Employees Not Employees of Court. Nothing in this Internal Operating Procedure or the Local Bankruptcy Rules is intended to indicate that the standing trustees or persons employed by them are employees of the clerk or the United States of America, or that they have any right to compensation or benefits by reason of this rule.

[Effective June 1, 2003.]

Committee Note:

This IOP was formerly Local Bankruptcy Rule 1302. It was submitted to the District Court and it is presently designated IOP1.

The Clerk's Office maintains claims registers in cases filed on or after January 1, 2000. Very little activity is expected in cases filed before January 1, 2000, but this IOP should remain until such time as there are no remaining cases subject to the IOP. The Committee recommends that paragraph F become a Local Bankruptcy Rule.

IOP 13. CHAPTER 13—NOTICES SENT BY CHAPTER 13 TRUSTEES

A. Standing Trustee to File Certificate of Service With Clerk. When the chapter 13 standing trustee provides notice not otherwise provided directly by the clerk, the standing trustee shall file with the clerk within two business days of mailing each notice a certificate of service to which is appended a copy of the applicable notice and a list of the names and addresses of parties on whom it was served.

[Effective June 1, 2003.]

Committee Note:

This substance of this IOP was formerly contained in Local Bankruptcy Rule 1303.

IOP 14. FILING OF MOTIONS FOR WITHDRAWAL OF REFERENCE

If a motion for withdrawal of reference is filed pursuant to 28 U.S.C. § 157(d) and Fed. R. Bankr. P. 5011, the clerk will transmit that motion to the clerk of the District Court for assignment to a judge of that court pursuant to its rules.

[Effective June 1, 2003.]

Committee Note:

This IOP was formerly Local Bankruptcy Rule 1400.

Former Committee Note: This new rule specifies a procedure for the clerk to follow, a procedure not otherwise provided for by law or rule.

IOP 15. RESTRICTED DOCUMENTS

A. Separate Filing Area for Restricted Documents. The clerk shall maintain restricted documents, sealed documents, and documents awaiting expunction as defined by Rule 5005–4(a) separately from the files of documents to which access has not been restricted. Any area used to store documents to which access has been restricted shall be secure from entry by any persons other than the clerk or those designated in writing by the clerk as authorized to have access.

The clerk shall designate in writing deputies authorized to accept restricted documents either from chambers or for filing pursuant to protective orders.

Materials accepted for filing as restricted shall be maintained in a secure area until collected by one of the designated deputies. Where the materials so accepted are being filed pursuant to a protective order, the deputy accepting them will stamp the cover of the document with a FILED stamp indicating the date of filing.

B. Handling Sealed Documents. Where a document is ordered to be sealed, it is to be delivered for filing pursuant to Rule 5005–4 with the seal on the enclosure intact. If the document is sent from chambers or returned from another court with the seal broken, one of the deputies authorized to handle restricted materials pursuant to section (a) will forthwith deliver the document to the courtroom deputy assigned to the judge to whose calendar the proceedings in which the sealed document was filed is assigned. If that judge is no longer sitting, the deputy will forthwith deliver the document to the courtroom deputy assigned to the emergency judge. The courtroom deputy will promptly bring the document to the attention of the judge. The judge will either order that the document be re-sealed, or order that it continue to be handled as a restricted document, but not as a sealed document, or enter such other order as required to indicate the status of the document. Where the document is to be re-sealed, the judge or courtroom deputy will re-seal the document and transmit it to the appropriate deputy in the clerk's office.

Where under the terms of a protective order a party is permitted to inspect a sealed document and that party appears in the clerk's office and requests the document, one of the deputies authorized to handle restricted materials pursuant to section (a) will obtain the document and provide an area where the person may inspect the document other than in the public area of the clerk's office. The deputy will complete a form showing the date, description of the document, the name of the person requesting access to the document, a statement indicating the deputy has checked the protective order and it does indeed authorize the person to inspect the document, and a statement that the deputy requested of and was shown identification by the person requesting access to the document. Any person wishing to break the seal and inspect the document must sign the form completed by the deputy to indicate that they are authorized to inspect the document and have broken the seal. After the person has completed the inspection, the deputy will follow the procedures set out in the previous paragraph for handling the re-sealing of the document.

C. Sanctions. Employees of the court are expressly forbidden to perform any of the following acts:

(1) entering an area designated for the storage of restricted documents without the appropriate written authorization required by sections (a) or (c);

(2) Assisting any person who is not authorized access pursuant to section (a) to an area designated for the storage of restricted documents to gain or to attempt to gain access to such an area;

(3) Accepting for filing any restricted document when not specifically authorized to do so pursuant to section (a);

(4) permitting any person who is not specifically authorized to have access to a restricted document to examine such a document, or to provide such a person with a copy of such a document; and

(5) leaving a restricted document unattended in an area other than one specified by this procedure such that persons not authorized access to the document could readily gain access to it.

Employees of the court who knowingly perform any of these acts shall be subject to disciplinary action, including dismissal. Persons who are not employees of the court who seek to coerce or induce any employee of the Court to perform any of these acts shall be punished by contempt of court.

[Effective June 1, 2003.]

Committee Note:

This IOP is based on District Court IOP30, modified and adapted to bankruptcy procedures.

IOP 16. CLERK—DELEGATED FUNCTIONS OF

The clerk of the court and such deputies as the clerk may designate are authorized to sign and enter without further direction the following orders and notices, which are deemed to be of a ministerial nature:

(1) Orders and notices that establish meeting and hearing dates required or requested by a party in interest under the Code, including orders which fix the last dates for the filing of pleadings by parties in interest as to various matters, including objections to discharge, disclosure statements, and confirmations of plans, complaints to determine dischargeability of debts, and proofs of claim;

(2) Final decrees closing cases and discharging the trustees in all cases for which the trustee has reported that there is no estate to administer or for which an order has been entered by the court approving the final report and account of the trustee;

(3) Form notices concerning: the entry of an order for relief, the dismissal of a case, the revocation of the

discharge of a debtor, the filing of amended schedules, conversion of the case, asset determination and need to file proofs of claim, and form notice on the filing of the Trustee's Final Report, hearing on applications for fees, and the abandonment of property by the trustee;

(4) Orders permitting the payment of filing fees in installments and fixing the number, amount, and date of payment of each installment;

(5) Discharge orders and notices in Chapter 7 and Chapter 13 cases.

[Effective June 1, 2003.]

Committee Note:

This IOP formalizes present procedure used by the Bankruptcy Court, usually to enter large volumes of routine orders. This IOP does not preclude a judge from delegating the entry of orders to chambers staff by Standing Order.

IOP 17. UNCLAIMED FUNDS

A. Procedural Requirements for Payment of Funds.

(1) An application for payment of unclaimed funds must be in the form of a Motion to Withdraw Moneys under 28 U.S.C. Section 2042.

(2) The motion must be filed either by an individual, acting pro se, or by a licensed attorney-at-law, acting on behalf of an individual or corporation. Motions may not be filed by nonattorney locators on behalf of their clients, even if the clients provide a power of attorney to the locator.

(3) The motion must be submitted to the Chief Judge or such other Judge as the Chief Judge shall designate. The name of the Judge to whom the motion for payment is to be submitted shall be appropriately posted by the Clerk. The Procedural Requirements distributed will be modified to show the name of the Judge hearing motions respecting withdrawal of unclaimed funds.

(4) The motion must be submitted in accordance with the motion practice adopted by the Court and these procedural requirements. The hearing on the motion shall be at least 10 business days from the date of mailing of the notice, motion and proposed order to the parties identified in Step 5.

(5) Service of the notice of hearing and motion must be made to the Chief, Civil Division, U.S. Attorney's Office, 219 South Dearborn Street, Chicago, Illinois 60604, to Mr. Kenneth S. Gardner, Clerk of the U.S. Bankruptcy Court, Attention Fiscal Administrator, 219 South Dearborn Street, Chicago, Illinois 60604, to the trustee assigned to the case at issue, and to the United States Trustee, 227 West Monroe Street, Chicago, Illinois 60606.

(6) The movant or counsel for the movant is to appear on the date the motion is to be heard to see

whether funds are available and if any objections to the requests for withdrawal or hearing are presented. If the funds are available and if movant or counsel for the movant does not appear and no objections or requests for hearing are made, the Court may waive the movant's appearance and enter the appropriate order. If the fiscal officer reports that there are no funds available the motion will be denied. If an objection or request for hearing is made, the movant will be advised who made the objection or requested the hearing and the next Court date and time.

B. Forms. Suggested forms of notice, motion and order as well as the above procedures are available on the court's web site and in the clerk's office. Committee Note: In 1988 the court adopted by General Order procedures for the payment of previously unclaimed funds. These funds were deposited with the court on the closing of a case when claimants' checks were returned to the case trustee as undeliverable. These procedures were in response to numerous requests from "funds locator" firms. Several firms had requested and received permission from the Clerk to review the ledgers of the Court. Subsequent to these ledger reviews, the "locator" firms submitted requests for payment of previously unclaimed funds. As these requests took many forms, and as the law required a Court order for withdrawal of such funds, the matter was presented to the Bankruptcy Judges for adoption of a uniform procedure disposing of these requests. The Court has designated the Chief Judge to hear these motions or such Judge as the Chief Judge shall designate.

[Effective June 1, 2003.]

APPENDIX A.　SECTION 1126 BALLOT FORM

IN THE UNITED STATES BANKRUPTCY COURT FOR THE NORTHERN
DISTRICT OF ILLINOIS

CASE NAME _____ CASE NUMBER _____ CONFIRMATION
HEARING DATE _____

SECTION 1126 BALLOT REPORT FORM

	# BALLOTS CAST	# ACCEPTING	# REJECTING	$ ACCEPTING	$ REJECTING	CLASS ACCEPTING	CLASS REJECTING
CLASS I							
CLASS II							
CLASS III							
CLASS IV							

	YES	NO
PLAN ACCEPTED		

Please note the following provisions of Title 11.　Section 1126 of the United States Code

(c) A class of claims has accepted a plan if such plan has been accepted by creditors, other than any entity designated under subsection (e) of this section, that hold at least two-thirds in amount and more than one-half in number of the allowed claims of such class held by creditors, other than any entity designated under subsection (e) of this section, that have accepted or rejected such plan.

(d) A class of interests has accepted a plan if such plan has been accepted by holders of such interests, other than any entity designated under subsection (e) of this section, that hold at least two-thirds in amount of the allowed interests of such class held by holders of such interests, other than any entity designated under subsection (e) of this section, that have accepted or rejected such plan.

(e) On request of a party in interest, and after notice and a hearing, the court may designate any entity whose acceptance or rejection of such plan was not in good faith, or was not solicited or procured in good faith or in accordance with the provisions of this title.

_____
NAME OF PLAN PROPONENT

[Adopted effective December 1, 2008.]

GENERAL ORDERS

GENERAL ORDER NO. 05–05.
APPLICATION FOR PERMISSION TO
PAY FILING FEE IN INSTALLMENTS

IT IS HEREBY ORDERED, effective December 1, 2005:

A.　A voluntary petition by an individual shall be accepted for filing if accompanied by the debtor's signed application stating that the debtor is unable to pay the filing fee except in installments. The application shall state the proposed terms of the installments and that until the filing fee is paid in full, the debtor will not make any additional payment or transfer any additional property to an attorney or any other person for services in connection with the case.

B.   The clerk shall enter, on behalf of the judge to whom the case is assigned, an order granting leave to pay the filing fees providing the following terms of the agreement have been met:

1. the full filing fee shall be paid in four equal installment payments;

2. the first installment payment is to be paid within 30 days, and at least half of the filing fee must be paid within 60 days of the filing of the petition;

3. the final installment payment should be payable not later than 120 days after filing the petition.

[Dated: November 22, 2005.]

GENERAL ORDER NO. 07–02.   CHAPTER 13 ATTORNEY FEES*

The Bankruptcy Court for the Northern District of Illinois, having revised, as of May 1, 2007, both the model "Rights and Responsibilities Agreement Between Chapter 13 Debtors and Their Attorneys" (the "Model Retention Agreement"), and the form application for compensation of Chapter 13 professionals, required to be used pursuant to Local Bankruptcy Rule 5082-2 (Local Form No. 23, the "form application"), copies of which documents are available in the office of the Clerk of the Court, and which are published on the Court's website—www.ilnb.uscourts.gov,

IT IS HEREBY ORDERED THAT, as to cases filed on or after May 1, 2007, requests for awards of compensation to debtors' attorneys in Chapter 13 cases, pursuant to 11 U.S.C. 330(a)(4)(B), will be allowed without submission of an itemization of services rendered, provided that:

1. The completed form application reflects that the current (May 1, 2007) Model Retention Agreement has been entered into, and

2. The compensation sought does not exceed $3500 for all services required under the Model Retention Agreement through the completion of the case.

IT IS FURTHER ORDERED THAT in connection with such applications, if the debtor or the debtor's spouse was a debtor in a Chapter 13 case dismissed within one year of the current filing, the court may exercise its discretion to award a fee of less than $3500.

IT IS FURTHER ORDERED THAT if the form application fails to reflect that the current Model Retention Agreement has been entered into (requiring provision of services through completion of the case), or the compensation sought exceeds $3500, an itemization of all services provided by debtors' attorneys must be submitted with the application.

[Dated: April 26, 2007.]

* Suggested title added by publisher.

GENERAL ORDER NO. 08–01.   REGARDING PAY ADVICES*

Effective June 23, 2008

Filing of Payment Advices Pursuant to 11 U.S.C. § 521(a)(1)(B)(iv)

IT IS HEREBY ORDERED, effective as to cases filed on or after June 23, 2008, that copies of all payment advices or other evidence of payment received within 60 days before the date of the filing of the petition by the debtor from any employer of the debtor (1) shall not be filed with the court unless otherwise ordered, and (2) shall be provided to the trustee, to any creditor who timely requests copies of the payment advices or other evidence of payment, and, in Chapter 7 cases only, to the United States Trustee, at least seven days prior to the first date set for the meeting of creditors conducted pursuant to 11 U.S.C. § 341.   To be considered timely, a creditor's request must be received at least 15 days before the first date set for the meeting of creditors.

[Dated: February 27, 2008.]

* [**Publisher's Note:** *See also* General Order 10-01, *post.*]

GENERAL ORDER NO. 08–02. REGARDING ELECTRONIC FILING OF DOCUMENTS

IT IS HEREBY ORDERED that all attorneys must comply with the Administrative Procedures for the Case Management/Electronic Case Filing System, approved February 17, 2004 and amended from time to time, that require attorneys to file all documents in electronic format.

IT IS FURTHER ORDERED that failure to comply with the Administrative Procedures will result in the issuance of a notice of hearing of rule to show cause before the Chief Judge to the attorney responsible for filing documents in paper form. Failure to appear at the rule to show cause hearing may result in counsel being held in contempt of court and the imposition of other sanctions.

IT IS FURTHER ORDERED that, in accordance with the Administrative Procedures, individuals without legal representation may file documents in paper form.

[Dated: August 26, 2008.]

GENERAL ORDER NO. 10–01. FILING OF PAYMENT ADVICES PURSUANT TO 11 U.S.C. § 521(a)(1)(B)(iv)

IT IS HEREBY ORDERED that General Order No. 08–01, dated February 27, 2008, is amended as follows: Effective as to cases filed on or after June 23, 2008, copies of all payment advices or other evidence of payment received within 60 days before the date of the filing of the petition by the debtor from any employer of the debtor (1) shall not be filed with the court unless otherwise ordered, and (2) shall be provided to the trustee and to any creditor who timely requests copies of the payment advices or other evidence of payment, at least seven days prior to the first date set for the meeting of creditors conducted pursuant to 11 U.S.C. § 341. To be considered timely, a creditor's request must be received at least 15 days before the first date set for the meeting of creditors.

[Dated: April 21, 2010.]

GENERAL ORDER NO. 10–012. ADOPTION OF AMENDED INTERIM BANKRUPTCY RULE 1007–I*

IT APPEARING THAT the full Court met in executive session on Thursday, January 22, 2009 and adopted Interim Bankruptcy Rule 1007–I, Lists, Schedules, Statements, and Other Documents; Time Limits; Expiration of Temporary Means Testing Exclusion; and

IT FURTHER APPEARING THAT Interim Rule 1007–I included a time deadline, also contained in Bankruptcy Rule 1007, that has since been amended, effective December 1, 2010; and

IT FURTHER APPEARING THAT the Advisory Committee on Bankruptcy Rules and the Committee on Rules of Practice and Procedures together recommend that district courts revise Interim Rule 1007–I's deadline for filing the statement of completion effective December 1, 2010, consistent with the change to the time in Rule 1007; therefore

IT IS HEREBY ORDERED THAT the attached amended Interim Rule 1007–I ** is adopted by the Executive Committee of the United States District Court for the Northern District of Illinois in its entirety without change, effective December 1, 2010. General Order 09–001, adopting Interim Rule 1007–I and amended Form 22A,*** remains in effect in all other regards.

[Effective December 1, 2010.]

    * [**Publisher's Note:** Title editorially supplied.]

    ** [**Publisher's Note:** For the version of Interim Rule 1007-I in current effect before the Court, *see* General Order 12-0031, *post*.]

    *** [**Publisher's Note:** For Official Form 22A, please consult *West's Bankruptcy Code, Rules and Forms*.]

SECOND AMENDED GENERAL ORDER NO. 11–2. REGARDING DISCLOSURE OF AGREEMENTS BETWEEN DEBTORS AND THEIR ATTORNEYS IN CASES UNDER ALL CHAPTERS AND REGARDING COMPENSATION OF DEBTOR'S COUNSEL IN CHAPTER 13 CASES

The following requirements are imposed pending approval of Local Bankruptcy Rules by the District Court.

1. IT IS ORDERED that every agreement between a debtor and an attorney for the debtor in a case under ANY CHAPTER of the Bankruptcy Code that pertains, directly or indirectly, to the compensation paid or given, or to be paid or given, to or for the benefit of the attorney must be in the form of a written document signed by the debtor and the attorney. Agreements subject to this rule include, but are not limited to, the Court–Approved Retention Agreement as posted on the court's website, other fee or expense agreements, wage assignments, and security agreements of all kinds. Each such agreement must be attached to the statement that must be filed under Fed. R. Bankr. P. 2016(b) in all bankruptcy cases. Any agreement entered into after the filing of the statement under Rule 2016(b) must be filed as a supplement to that statement within 14 days of the date the agreement is entered into.

2. IT IS ORDERED that in Chapter 13 cases all requests for awards of compensation to debtor's counsel cases must include a certification that the disclosures required by paragraph 1 of this order have been made.

3. IT IS ORDERED that Flat Fees, as defined in Rule 5082–2, in Chapter 13 cases will not be awarded if, in addition to the Court–Approved Retention Agreement, the debtor and an attorney for the debtor have entered into any other agreement in connection with the representation of the debtor in preparation for, during, or involving a Chapter 13 case, and the agreement provides for the attorney to receive (a) any kind of compensation, reimbursement, or other payment, or (b) any form of, or security for, compensation, reimbursement, or other payment that varies from the Court–Approved Retention Agreement.

These requirements are effective for all cases filed after September 21, 2011.

[Effective April 15, 2011. Amended effective April 22, 2011; September 21, 2011.]

AMENDED GENERAL ORDER NO. 12–01. REGARDING PROCEDURES FOR EMERGENCY MOTIONS

IT IS HEREBY ORDERED, pending approval of a proposed Local Bankruptcy Rule regarding emergency motions, the following procedures are to be followed for setting a hearing on an emergency motion:

A. A motion may be treated as an emergency only if it arises from an occurrence that could not reasonably have been foreseen and requires immediate action to avoid serious and irreparable harm.

B.   A party seeking to present an emergency motion:

1.   must file an Application to Set Hearing on Emergency Motion that states the reasons that the motion should be heard on an emergency basis and the proposed time frame for presentment of the emergency motion;

2.   must attach the proposed emergency motion to the Application; and

3.   must not notice the Application for hearing and need not serve the Application.

C.   No response to the Application may be filed.

D.   After filing the Application and attached proposed motion specified in paragraph A, the movant must telephone the chambers of the judge assigned to the case of the filing of the Application. If the assigned judge is available to rule on the Application, the judge must promptly determine whether to grant the Application. If the judge assigned to the case is not available to rule on the Application, the movant should telephone the chambers of the emergency judge of the filing of the Application. If the emergency judge is available, the emergency judge must determine whether to grant the Application. If the emergency judge is not available, the movant may contact the clerk, using the emergency telephone numbers available on the court's web site if necessary, and the clerk must attempt to contact another judge to rule on the Application.

E.   If the Application to Set Hearing on Emergency Motion is granted, the movant must

1.   immediately notify all parties entitled to notice by phone, fax, or personal service of the date, time, and place of the hearing on the emergency motion; and

2.   file the emergency motion with:

(a) a notice of motion specifying the date, time, and place of the emergency hearing and a statement that the motion may be opposed on the basis that emergency treatment is not appropriate; and

(b) a certificate of service reflecting the date, time, and method of service of the notice of motion and the motion.

F.   If the Application to Set Hearing on Emergency Motion is denied, the movant must notice the motion in accordance with Rule 9013–1.

Dated: May 31, 2013

[Dated: September 18, 2012; effective October 1, 2012; June 1, 2013.]

GENERAL ORDER 12–0031. ADOPTION OF AMENDED INTERIM BANKRUPTCY RULE 1007–I.*

IT APPEARING THAT the full Court met in executive session on Thursday, November 29, 2012 and adopted Interim Bankruptcy Rule 1007–I, Lists, Schedules, Statements, and Other Documents; Time Limits; Expiration of Temporary Means Testing Exclusion; and

IT FURTHER APPEARING THAT Interim Rule 1007–I was amended on December 1, 2010; and

IT FURTHER APPEARING THAT the Advisory Committee on Bankruptcy Rules and the Committee on Rules of Practice and Procedures together recommend that district courts amend Interim Rule 1007–1 to provide a temporary exclusion from the bankruptcy means test for certain reservists and members of the National Guard; therefore

IT IS HEREBY ORDERED THAT the full Court, which met in Executive Session on November 29, 2012, approved the amendment to Interim Rule 1007–1, and

IT IS FURTHER ORDERED THAT all other provisions of General Order 09–001 as amended by General Order 10–012 remain in effect.

[Dated: December 5, 2012.]

* [**Publisher's Note:** Title editorially supplied.]

Interim Rule 1007–I.[1] Lists, Schedules, Statements, and Other Documents; Time Limits; Expiration of Temporary Means Testing Exclusion[2]

* * * * *

(b) Schedules, Statements, and Other Documents Required.

* * * * *

(4) *Unless either*: (A) § 707(b)(2)(D)(1) applies, or (B) § 707(b)(2)(D)(ii) applies and the exclusion from means testing granted therein extends beyond the period specified by Rule 1017(e), an individual debtor in a chapter 7 case shall file a statement of current monthly income prepared as prescribed by the appropriate Official Form, and, if the current monthly income exceeds the median family income for the applicable state and household size, the information, including calculations, required by § 707(b), prepared as prescribed by the appropriate Official Form.

* * * * *

(c) Time Limits. In a voluntary case, the schedules, statements, and other documents required by subdivision (b)(1), (4), (5), and (6) shall be filed with the petition or within 14 days thereafter, except as otherwise provided in subdivisions (d), (e), (f), (h), and (n) of this rule. In an involuntary case, the ~~list in subdivision (a)(2), and~~ the schedules, statements, and other documents required by subdivision (b)(1) shall be filed by the debtor within 14 days of the entry of the order for relief. In a voluntary case, the documents required by paragraphs (A), (C), and (D) of subdivision (b)(3) shall be filed with the petition. Unless the court orders otherwise, a debtor who has filed a statement under subdivision (b)(3)(B), shall file the documents required by subdivision (b)(3)(A) within 14 days of the order for relief. In a chapter 7 case, the debtor shall file the statement required by subdivision (b)(7) within 60 days after the first date set for the meeting of creditors under § 341 of the Code, and in a chapter 11 or 13 case no later than the date when the last payment was made by the debtor as required by the plan or the filing of a motion for a discharge under § 1141(d)(5)(B) or § 1328(b) of the Code. The court may, at any time and in its discretion, enlarge the time to file the statement required by subdivision (b)(7). The debtor shall file the statement required by subdivision (b)(8) no earlier than the date of the last payment made under the plan or the date of the filing of a motion for a discharge under §§ 1141(d)(5)(B), 1228(b), or 1328(b) of the Code. Lists, schedules, statements, and other documents filed prior to the conversion of a case to another chapter shall be deemed filed in the converted case unless the court directs otherwise. Except as provided in § 1116(3), any extension of time to file schedules, statements, and other documents required under this rule may be granted only on motion for cause shown and on notice to the United States trustee, any committee elected under § 705 or appointed under § 1102 of the Code, trustee, examiner, or other party as the court may direct. Notice of an extension shall be given to the United States trustee and to any committee, trustee, or other party as the court may direct.

* * * * *

(n) Time Limits for, and Notice to. Debtors Temporarily Excluded from Means Testing.

(1) An individual debtor who is temporarily excluded from means testing pursuant to § 707(b)(2)(D)(ii) of the Code shall file any statement and calculations required by subdivision (b)(4) no later than 14 days after the expiration of the temporary exclusion if the expiration occurs within the time specified by Rule 1017(e) for filing a motion pursuant to § 707(b)(2).

(2) If the temporary exclusion from means testing under § 707(b)(2)(D)(ii) terminates due to the circumstances specified in subdivision (n)(1), and if the debtor has not previously filed a statement and calculations required by subdivision (b)(4), the clerk shall promptly notify the debtor that the required statement and calculations must be filed within the time specified in subdivision (n)(1).

[1]Interim Rule 1007–I has been adopted by the bankruptcy courts to implement the National Guard and Reservists Debt Relief Act of 2008, Public Law No: 110–438, as amended by Public Law No. 112–64. The amended Act, which provides a temporary exclusion from the application of the means test for certain members of the National Guard and reserve components of the Armed Forces, applies to bankruptcy cases commenced in the seven-year period beginning December 19, 2008.

[2]Incorporates (1) time amendments to Rule 1007 which took effect on December 1, 2009, ~~and~~ (2) an amendment, effective December 1, 2010, which extended the time to file the statement of completion of a course in personal financial management in a chapter 7 case filed by an individual debtor, and (3) a conforming amendment, effective December 1, 2012, which removed an inconsistency created by the 2010 amendment.

GENERAL ORDER NO. 13–1. REGARDING FLAT FEES FOR DEBTOR'S COUNSEL IN CHAPTER 13 CASES

Pursuant to unanimous agreement by the judges of this court on July 9, 2013, IT IS HEREBY ORDERED that the maximum amount of the Flat Fee authorized for Chapter 13 debtor's counsel by Local Bankruptcy Rule 5082–2 is hereby increased to $4,000. This increase may be used in cases in which the Court Approved Retention Agreement is entered into on or after today's date.

[Dated: July 10, 2013.]

STANDING ORDERS

STANDING ORDER RE CHAPTER 13 PRE–CONFIRMATION ADEQUATE PROTECTION PAYMENTS

IT IS HEREBY ORDERED, effective as to all Chapter 13 cases filed on or after October 17, 2005, as follows:

(1) Payments of personal property leases governed by 11 U.S.C. § 1326(a)(1)(B) only shall be made directly by the debtor to the lessor if the debtor's plan so provides or if no plan provision addresses payment of the debtor's lease obligation. If the plan provides for payment of the lease obligation by the trustee, the debtor shall make the payment as part of the total payment to the trustee, and the trustee shall pay the lessor, both before and after confirmation.

(2) Pre-confirmation adequate protection payments governed by 11 U.S.C § 1326(a)(1)(C) shall only be made directly by the debtor to the secured creditor if the debtor's plan so provides or if no plan provision addresses payment of the secured claim. If the plan provides for payment of the secured claim by the trustee, the debtor shall make the payment as part of the total payment to the trustee, and the trustee shall pay the secured creditor, both before and after confirmation.

[Dated: August 15, 2005.]

STANDING ORDER. CHAPTER 13 FEE APPLICATIONS NOTICE AND HEARING REQUIRED

IT IS HEREBY ORDERED, effective December 1, 2004, as follows:

(1) All applications for original compensation must be noticed for hearing on the date of the confirmation hearing specified in the Notice of Meeting of Creditors (the "original confirmation date"). Failure to do so may result in reduced fees or no fees being awarded.

(2) All applications for compensation, whether original or supplemental, must be noticed for hearing as any original motion must be, unless the following paragraph authorizes limited service of the notice.

(3) If the Notice of Meeting of Creditors discloses the amount of original compensation requested and has been served on all parties in interest, and if the hearing on compensation is noticed for the original confirmation date, then the debtor's attorney need only serve the notice of the hearing on the debtor and the standing trustee, with a copy of the Notice of Meeting of Creditors attached.

[Dated: October 21, 2004.]

ECF PROCEDURES
ADMINISTRATIVE PROCEDURES FOR THE CASE MANAGEMENT/ELECTRONIC CASE FILING SYSTEM

As amended, Effective March 17, 2015

These Administrative Procedures are authorized by Federal Rules of Bankruptcy Procedure (Fed. R. Bankr. P.) 5005, 7005, 9029, and 9036, and Local Bankruptcy Rule 5005–1.

I. DESIGNATION OF CASES, PASSWORDS, REGISTRATION, AND APPEARANCE OF ATTORNEYS

I.A. Designation of Cases. All cases under title 11 of the United States Code, all adversary proceedings, and all ancillary matters filed or pending in the Northern District of Illinois ("Bankruptcy Cases") are assigned to the Case Management/Electronic Case Filing System ("System"). All documents in Bankruptcy Cases are maintained in electronic format. Except as provided otherwise herein, all petitions and other documents must be filed in electronic format via the System.

I.B. Passwords Required. To file documents in Bankruptcy Cases, an attorney or non-attorney bankruptcy trustee must obtain a login and password (collectively "Password") for electronic filing and viewing of documents in the System. Limited registrants, defined in paragraph I.C.7, must also obtain a Password.

I.C. Registration.

I.C.1. [reserved]

I.C.2. *Application Required.* To obtain a Password, an attorney, a non-attorney trustee, or a person seeking to be a Limited Registrant must fill out an on-line registration form and enroll in an appropriate training class offered by the clerk. The form is on the court's website: www.ilnb.uscourts.gov.

I.C.3. *Training.* The training class consists of a training session and a certification assignment. Upon completion of the training session, each applicant will receive a restricted password which will allow the trainee to complete the certification assignment. Within two weeks of completion of the training session, the applicant must complete the certification assignment and request activation of an unrestricted Password. Individuals with unrestricted Passwords are Registrants.

I.C.4. *Authorized Use of Passwords.* A Password may only be used by the Registrant to whom it is issued and by individuals authorized by the Registrant. A Registrant is responsible for all applicable charges associated with use of the Registrant's Password. Any documents filed using the Password will be deemed authorized and signed by the Registrant.

I.C.5. *Unauthorized Use of Passwords.* If a Registrant believes that the Registrant's Password has been or may be used by an unauthorized person, the Registrant must immediately notify the ECF Help Desk in the clerk's office—telephone (312) 408–7765. If the clerk believes that a Registrant's Password has been used improperly, the clerk will notify the Registrant. In all such instances, the clerk will make appropriate corrections to the System and issue a new Password to the Registrant.

I.C.6. *Withdrawal From Use of the System.* A Registrant may withdraw from use of the System, for cause, on order of the court. Any motion to withdraw from use of the System by a Registrant must be presented to the Chief Judge. If the motion is granted, the clerk will immediately cancel the Registrant's Password and delete the Registrant from all applicable electronic notice lists.

I.C.7. *Limited Registrants.* A Limited Registrant is a person who is authorized by the clerk to file electronically only proofs of claim, transfers of claim, withdrawals of claim, requests for service of notice, reaffirmation agreements, withdrawals of documents, change of address, Rule 3002.1 notices, personal financial management certificates, and ballots. These documents constitute the Limited Filing Documents. The court or clerk may authorize Limited Registrants for additional purposes.

If a Limited Registrant ceases to be an employee or agent of an entity on whose behalf documents are being electronically filed, or for any other reason ceases to be authorized to file electronically on behalf of that entity, the Limited Registrant must promptly contact the court and request the termination of filing privileges.

I.C.8. *Revocation of Password.* The clerk may invalidate the Password of an attorney who is disbarred or suspended.

The clerk must invalidate the Password of a Limited Registrant if it comes to the clerk's attention that the Limited Registrant is no longer an employee or agent of an entity authorized to file documents electronically.

I.D. Appearance of Attorneys.

I.D.1. *Local Bankruptcy Rules Not Altered.* These Administrative Procedures do not alter: (a) the requirement of Local Bankruptcy Rule 2090–1 that an attorney appearing before this court be admitted to practice before the District Court or (b) the procedure under Local Bankruptcy Rule 2090–3 for admission *pro hac vice.*

I.D.2. *Emergency Paper Filings Before Compliance.* In an emergency, an attorney not admitted to practice before the District Court and not having an office in this district may file documents in Bankruptcy Cases in paper form if it is impracticable to become a Registrant or engage local counsel prior to filing the documents. However, the paper filing must be followed by a motion seeking leave to file in paper form and showing cause for not becoming a Registrant and for not engaging local counsel in time to file the documents electronically. The motion seeking leave to file in paper must be presented to the Chief Judge. If the motion for leave is not granted within 14 days of the paper filing, the documents may be stricken by the court without prior notice. (See also paragraph II.A.4 regarding Emergency Matters.)

II. FILING AND SERVICE OF DOCUMENTS

II.A. Electronic Filing.

II.A.1. *Requirements.*

II.A.1.a. Electronic Filing Mandatory. Except as expressly provided in paragraph III, and except for circumstances that temporarily prevent a Registrant from filing electronically, all petitions, motions, applications, notices, pleadings, memoranda of law, and other documents filed with the court in connection with a Bankruptcy Case must be filed electronically. Individuals without legal representation may file documents in paper form with the clerk's office where the documents will be scanned into the System.

II.A.1.b. Time for Filing Motions. A motion must be filed no later than the date on which the motion is served.

II.A.1.c. Format All electronic documents must be submitted in Portable Document Format (.pdf).

II.A.1.d. Size Limit. Documents created electronically must not exceed the size specified and published on the Court's Internet website. A document which exceeds these limits must be broken into multiple .pdf files and filed as a document and attachments. A judge may order that other rules will apply in a particular case.

459

II.A.1.e. Title. Each document filed electronically must be titled as one of the events contained in the System, unless no event accurately describes the subject of the document.

II.A.1.f. Bookmarks. All initial bankruptcy petitions and supporting documents filed at the same time must be tagged with bookmarks, clearly labeled, generated by .pdf software to permit navigation to the following locations by clicking on the bookmarks:

(a) Summary of Schedules

(b) Schedule A Real Property

(c) Schedule B Personal Property

(d) Schedule C Exemptions

(e) Schedule D Secured Claims

(f) Schedule E Priority Claims

(g) Schedule F Unsecured Claims

(h) Schedule G Executory Contracts

(i) Schedule H Co-debtor

(j) Schedule I Income

(k) Schedule J Expenses

(*l*) Statement of Financial Affairs

(m) Statement of Intention

(n) Exhibit A (Business Declaration)

(*o*) Debtor Attorney Compensation

(p) Non-attorney Petition Preparer Certification

(q) List of Twenty Largest Creditors (chapter 11 cases).

II.A.2. *Date and Time of Filing.* The Notice of Electronic Filing issued by the System shows the date and time of filing. Documents filed electronically outside of normal business hours are deemed filed on the date and at the time the System files them. Documents filed before midnight on the date that is a deadline are considered timely, unless the judge, these Administrative Procedures, or Local Bankruptcy Rule specifically requires an earlier time.

II.A.3. *Creditor Lists.* Creditor lists must be submitted in electronic format as required by Local Bankruptcy Rule 1007–1.

II.A.4. *Emergency Matters.*

II.A.4.a. General Rule. Presentation of emergency motions is governed by Amended General Order 12–1, effective June 1, 2013.

II.A.4.b. Motions to Redact Personal Information. A motion to redact personal information prohibited under Fed. R. Bankr. P. 9037(A) should be filed without a notice of motion and without serving other parties. The motion must be accompanied by a redacted version of the filed document and a proposed order requiring the clerk to substitute the redacted document for the unredacted document. The judge should rule on the motion as soon as possible without holding a hearing unless there appears to be a reason to deny the motion, in which case the judge should set the matter for a hearing with the movant as soon as possible. Any registrant or limited registrant may file a motion to redact.

II.B. Notice and Service.

II.B.1. *E-mail Addresses.* All Registrants must maintain an active e-mail address to receive electronic notice and service from the System.

II.B.2. *Consent to Electronic Notice and Service.* Pursuant to Fed. R. Bankr. P. 7005 and 9036, registration as a Registrant constitutes waiver of the right to receive notice of hearings and service of documents by personal service or first class mail and further constitutes consent to receive notice and service electronically in those cases in which the Registrant has previously filed a document, except that electronic service is not sufficient service of (1) a complaint and summons in an adversary proceeding under Fed. R. Bankr. P. 7004 or (2) a subpoena under Fed. R. Bankr. P. 9016. Waiver of service and notice by first class mail applies to notice of the entry of an order or judgment under Fed. R. Bankr. P. 9022.

II.B.3. *Means and Effect of Electronic Service and Notice.*

II.B.3.a. General Rule. Whenever a document is filed, the System automatically sends notice of the filing via e-mail to the United States Trustee, the case trustee, and to all Registrants who have previously filed a document in the case (the "Electronic Notice"). The Electronic Notice allows the recipient to view the filed document once without charge. Unless otherwise provided herein, the Electronic Notice constitutes notice to and service on the Registrants to whom it is sent for those clients for which the Registrant has previously filed a document in the case.

II.B.3.b. Non–Registrants. Participants in the case who are not Registrants, or who are Registrants who have filed only Limited Filing Documents in the case, must be provided notice and service of any document filed electronically in accordance with the Federal Rules of Bankruptcy Procedure and the Local Bankruptcy Rules.

II.B.3.c. Special Rule–Local Presentment Rule. Nothing in these Administrative Procedures changes the requirement under Local Bankruptcy Rule 9013–1(D) that notice of intent to present a motion must be personally served at or before 4:00 p.m. of the third day preceding the date of presentment.

II.B.3.d. Special Rule–Emergency Motions. The Electronic Notice is not sufficient notice of an emergency motion which is being presented without complying with Local Rule 9013–1(D). See also II.A.4, above, and proposed Local Rule 9013–2.

II.B.4. *Certificate of Service.* Each motion must be accompanied by a certificate of service that complies with Local Bankruptcy Rule 9013–1(C).

II.B.5. *Limited Registrants and Limited Filing Documents.* The provisions of this paragraph, II.B, do not apply to Limited Registrants or to Registrants who have only filed Limited Filing Documents in the case who may not be served or given notice electronically. Limited Registrants must maintain accurate contact information including email address, mailing address, and telephone number.

II.B.6. *Withdrawal of Registrant from a Particular Case.* A Registrant who has filed documents in a particular case may be excused from the requirements of this paragraph, II.B, for that particular case by order, for cause, including that the Registrant is no longer involved in the matter. A Registrant seeking such relief must do so by motion and submit a proposed order entitled "Withdrawal of Registration from a Particular Case." If the Registrant later files another document in the case (other than a Limited Filing Document) the requirements of this paragraph, II.B, shall again apply to the Registrant in the case.

II.C. Signatures.

II.C.1. *Original Non–Attorney Signatures.* When an individual other than a Registrant is required to sign a document that is filed electronically, the Registrant shall include in a single filing with the document a scanned or otherwise electronically replicated copy of the document's signature page bearing the individual's original signature. By filing the document and signature page, the Registrant declares under penalty of perjury that the scanned signature was part of the original document. Once a document has been properly filed under this subsection, the original document bearing the individual's original signature need not be retained. The scanned signature may then be used with the same force and effect as the original signature under these rules and for any other purpose for which a signature is required in proceedings before the court.

II.C.2. *Original Attorney Signatures.* By using the Password to make an electronic filing, a Registrant is deemed to affix the Registrant's signature to the document for all purposes, including Fed. R. Bankr. P. 9011. Each filing must indicate a signature by the designation /s/, followed by the typed name of the Registrant. The typed name must be the name of the Registrant filing the document. Registrants who are attorneys must also include their complete mailing address, telephone number, and the name of the party the attorney represents. If the identifying information appearing in a document filed via the Internet is inconsistent with the identifying information supporting the Password with which the document was filed, the identifying information in the document will be disregarded, and the Registrant is responsible for the document for purposes of Fed. R. Bankr. P. 9011 and all other purposes.

II.C.3. *Paper Filings.* When documents listed above in paragraph II.C.1 are presented in paper form for scanning by the clerk, as permitted under paragraph II.A.1, the paper documents must contain original signatures, in a form that can be accurately scanned. The clerk will scan the paper documents into the System; the scanned image shall be the clerk's permanent record; and the paper documents may be discarded.

II.D. Fees Payable to the Clerk of the Court. All fees associated with electronic filings are payable at the time of filing. The System includes a procedure for automated payments to the United States Treasury. Details of the procedure are available on the court's website and from the clerk's office.

II.E. Orders.

II.E.1. *Proposed Orders Required.* Motions, applications, objections to claims, and other requests for relief that are filed electronically must include a proposed order as an electronic attachment.

II.E.2. *Format.* Proposed orders must be filed in the format required by the court, as published on the court's website.

II.E.3. *Minute Orders Prohibited.* Minute order forms must not be filed with any motion, application, objection to claim, or any other request for relief.

II.F. Correcting Docket Entries. After a document has been submitted and become part of the case record, the docket may only be corrected by the clerk. Corrections will be made by adding the correct docket entry with the appropriate document(s) referencing the incorrect docket entry.

II.G. Technical Failures. A Registrant whose filing is untimely because of a technical failure of the System may seek appropriate relief from the judge, or if no case is pending, from the Chief Judge. Relief will only be granted for cause. Any difficulty connecting to the System and any other technical failure experienced should be reported immediately to the ECF Help Desk. (Relief will not be given because of technical failures in the Registrant's office or equipment.)

III. EXCEPTIONS TO ELECTRONIC FILING– FILINGS USING PAPER DOCUMENTS

III.A. Restricted Documents. A motion to restrict access to documents pursuant to Local Bankruptcy Rule 5005–4 must be filed electronically, but the proposed Restricted Documents must not be filed with the clerk via the Internet. The proposed Restricted Documents should be submitted to the clerk on paper or on a disc, CD–rom, DVD, or other similar electronic medium.

III.B. Attorneys Without Financial Ability to File Electronically and Individuals Without Legal Representation.

III.B.1. *Financial Hardship–Attorneys.* An attorney may file an Application for Waiver of Electronic Filing Requirements seeking an exemption from electronic filing requirements. The application must be presented to the Chief Judge and must allege financial inability to access the equipment necessary to comply with paragraph II.A.1 above. The application will only be granted for cause.

III.B.2. *Procedure.* A waiver from electronic filing does not waive compliance with Local Bankruptcy Rules.

III.B.3. [reserved].

III.B.4. *Individuals Without Legal Representation.* An individual not represented by an attorney may file paper documents.

IV. PUBLIC ACCESS TO THE SYSTEM

IV.A. Internet Access. A Password provides Internet access to view only those documents included in the System maintained by the Bankruptcy Court for the Northern District of Illinois.

IV.B. Public Access at the Court. The public will be provided electronic access to view documents in the System without charge at each division of the clerk's office, during regular business hours, Monday through Friday.

IV.C. Paper Copies and Certified Copies. Paper copies and certified copies of electronically maintained documents may be purchased at the division offices of the clerk, 219 South Dearborn St., Chicago, IL 60604 and 327 S. Church St., Rockford, IL 61101. Fees for copying and certifying documents are charged pursuant to 28 U.S.C.§ 1930(b).

[Effective February 14, 2004. Amended effective January 18, 2005; August 2, 2005; March 20, 2007; December 16, 2008; May 14, 2010; March 15, 2011; January 1, 2012; November 1, 2012; November 1, 2014; March 17, 2015.]

FORMS

APPEARANCE

UNITED STATES BANKRUPTCY COURT
FOR THE NORTHERN DISTRICT OF ILLINOIS

In re Debtor(s)   )

)   Case No.

)

)

I, THE UNDERSIGNED, HEREBY FILE MY APPEARANCE AS ATTORNEY
FOR

_____

_____

_____

_____

Print Name on this Line	Firm Name
	FIRM ID NUMBER: _____
Signature	
ATTORNEY ID NUMBER _____	Street Address
	City State Zip
	Telephone _____

Trial Attorneys*

_____

                            Print Name

* Request is made for trial attorney to avoid possible conflicts in scheduling.

     DATED: _____

TYPE OF DEFENSE COUNSEL:

     CJA __, RETAINED __, SELF __, NONE OTHER __, PUB DEF __

FOR OFFICE USE ONLY:

     Party Code: P _____ D _____ TP _____

REQUEST FOR HEARING ON DISMISSAL

UNITED STATES BANKRUPTCY COURT
NORTHERN DISTRICT OF ILLINOIS

In re: Case No:
      Debtor   Chapter:

REQUEST FOR HEARING ON DISMISSAL

Please send notice (Complete remainder of form)

   Please Send Notice of Hearing on Dismissal under Rule 2002(a)(4) to the debtor(s), trustee, and all creditors in the following case:

Hearing Date: _____

Hearing Time: _____

Courtroom: _____

Judge: _____

Pursuant to Local Bankruptcy Rule 1017–2, a motion to dismiss shall be noticed no less than 28 calendar days from the date the motion is filed.

Date: Prepared by: _____
                                Movant's Attorney's Name: _____
                                Address:_____
                                _____
                                Telephone No. _____
                                Representing: _____

MOTION TO WITHDRAW MONEY UNDER 28 U.S.C. § 2042
UNITED STATES BANKRUPTCY COURT
NORTHERN DISTRICT OF ILLINOIS
EASTERN DIVISION

In Re:)
)
)   Bankruptcy Case No.
)
Debtor(s)   )

MOTION TO WITHDRAW MONEY
UNDER 28 U.S.C. § 2042

_____, claimant, moves this Court to order the withdrawal of moneys on deposit for this estate in the name of _____ and the payment of these moneys to claimant and in support of this motion states:

1. On _____, the trustee of this estate deposited the sum of $_____ belonging to the creditor with the Clerk of Court.

2. *(Please cross out the subparagraph that does not apply)* certify that the

    A. The claimant is the creditor in whose behalf these moneys were deposited and is entitled to the money deposited.

    B. The claimant is not the creditor but is entitled to payment of these moneys because *(please state the basis for your claim to the moneys)*

_____

_____

(Please attach a copy of any supporting document).

    C. Claimant is Debtor and is entitled to this money.

_____
Signature of Claimant or Attorney

_____
Printed Name

_____

_____
Mailing Address

Certification

I, _____, claimant, certify that the statements in the foregoing motion are true and correct.

_____

_____
Signature of Claimant and Last Four Digits of Claimant's Social Security Number or EIN

466

(i) If claimant is heir of decreased creditor, attach copies of death certificate and heirship order of court.

(ii) If claimant is assignee of creditor, attach copy of assignment.

(iii) If claimant is corporate successor of creditor, attach copies of all documents demonstrating such status.

(iv) If claimant is an agent of creditor for purposes of filing this application, attach a copy of the agency agreement.

(v) Attach other documents showing entitlement should none of the foregoing apply.

[Rev. 10/2011]

NOTICE OF MOTION

UNITED STATES BANKRUPTCY COURT
NORTHERN DISTRICT OF ILLINOIS
EASTERN DIVISION

In Re:)
)
)
)   Bankruptcy Case No.
)
)
Debtor(s)   )

NOTICE OF MOTION

To: Chief Civil Division   Mr. Jeffrey P. Allsteadt, Clerk
    U.S. Attorney's Office   Attention: Financial Administrator
    219 S. Dearborn Street   219 S. Dearborn Street
    Chicago, Illinois 60604   Chicago, Illinois 60604

    Trustee: _____   United States Trustee
    _____   227 W. Monroe, Suite 3350
    _____*   Chicago, Illinois 60604

Please take notice that on _____ at 10:00 A.M. (Please select a date at least ten (10) business days from the date of mailing this notice) I shall bring the above motion on for hearing before Judge Bruce W. Black, Courtroom 719, United States Courthouse, 219 South Dearborn Street, Chicago, Illinois 60604.

I certify that the motion and notice of motion were served on the person to whom notice is given by depositing copies in envelopes addressed to them with proper postage in the United States mail on _____.

                                          _____
                                          Signature of Claimant/Attorney/Movant *Insert name and address of case Trustee.*

[Rev. 10/2011]

467

UNITED STATES BANKRUPTCY COURT
NORTHERN DISTRICT OF ILLINOIS
EASTERN DIVISION

In Re:)

)

)

)   Bankruptcy Case No.

)

)

)

)

Debtor   )

ORDER GRANTING MOTION TO WITHDRAW UNCLAIMED FUNDS

IT IS HEREBY ORDERED that the Clerk of the United States Bankruptcy Court is directed to pay $_____ to _____ claimant in the above captioned case.

Last Four Digits of Claimant's Social Security Number or EIN _____.

_____

Bruce W. Black

United States Bankruptcy Judge

Dated:

Payment to be mailed to:

[Revised September 13, 2012.]

  * Insert name and address of case Trustee.

STATEMENT OF SOCIAL SECURITY OR EMPLOYEE
IDENTIFICATION NUMBER

UNITED STATES BANKRUPTCY COURT
NORTHERN DISTRICT OF ILLINOIS
EASTERN DIVISION

In Re:)
)
)   Bankruptcy Case No.
)
)
Debtor   )

STATEMENT OF SOCIAL SECURITY
EMPLOYEE IDENTIFICATION NUMBER

Name of claimant: _____
Claimant's Social Security or EI Number: _____
  I declare under penalty of perjury that the foregoing is true and correct.

                                    _____
                                    Signature of Claimant   Date

_____

Penalty for making a false statement: Fine of up to $250,000 or up to 5 years imprisonment or both. 18 U.S.C. §§ 152 and 3571.

[Dated: November 19, 2003.]

DECLARATION REGARDING ELECTRONIC FILING
PETITION AND ACCOMPANYING DOCUMENTS

01/2012   UNITED STATES BANKRUPTCY COURT
               NORTHERN DISTRICT OF ILLINOIS

IN RE:)   Chapter
)   Bankruptcy Case No.
)
)
          Debtor(s)   )

DECLARATION REGARDING ELECTRONIC FILING
PETITION AND ACCOMPANYING DOCUMENTS

DECLARATION OF PETITIONER(S)

A.   [To be completed in all cases]

    I (We), _____ and _____ the undersigned debtor(s), corporate officer, partner, or member hereby declare under penalty of perjury that (1) the information I(we) have given my (our) attorney is true and correct; (2) I(we) have reviewed the petition, statements, schedules, and other documents being filed with the petition; and (3) the documents are true and correct.

B.   [To be checked and applicable only if the petition is for a corporation or other limited liability entity.]

     ☐   I, _____, the undersigned, further declare under penalty of perjury that I have been authorized to file this petition on behalf of the debtor.

_____   _____
Printed or Typed Name of Debtor or   Printed or Typed Name of Joint Debtor
Representative

_____   _____
Signature of Debtor or Representative   Signature of Joint Debtor

_____   _____
Date   Date

[Revised on or about January 12, 2010; January 2012.]

REQUIRED STATEMENT TO ACCOMPANY ALL
MOTIONS FOR RELIEF FROM STAY

All Cases: Debtor(s) _____   Case No. _____   Chapter _____

All Cases: Moving Creditor _____   Date Case Filed _____

Nature of Relief Sought: ☐ Lift Stay   ☐ Annul Stay   ☐ Other (describe) _____

Chapter 13:   Date of Confirmation Hearing _____   or Date Plan Confirmed _____

Chapter 7:   ☐ No–Asset Report Filed on _____
             ☐ No–Asset Report not Filed, Date of Creditors Meeting _____

1. Collateral
    a.   ☐ Home
    b.   ☐ Car Year, Make, and Model _____
    c.   ☐ Other (describe) _____

2. Balance Owed as of Petition Date $ _____
    Total of all other Liens against Collateral $ _____

3. In chapter 13 cases, if a post-petition default is asserted in the motion, attach a payment
    history listing the amounts and dates of all payments received from the debtor(s) post-
    petition.

4. Estimated Value of Collateral (must be supplied in *all* cases) $ _____

5. Default
    a.   ☐ Pre–Petition Default
         Number of months _____   Amount $ _____

    b.   ☐ Post–Petition Default
         i.   ☐ On direct payments to the moving creditor
              Number of months _____   Amount $ _____

         ii. ☐ On payments to the Standing Chapter 13 Trustee
              Number of months _____   Amount $ _____

6. Other Allegations
    a.   ☐ Lack of Adequate Protection § 362(d)(1)
         i.   ☐ No insurance
         ii.   ☐ Taxes unpaid   Amount $ _____
         iii. ☐ Rapidly depreciating asset
         iv.   ☐ Other (describe) _____

    b.   ☐ No Equity and not Necessary for an Effective Reorganization § 362(d)(2)

    c.   ☐ Other "Cause" § 362(d)(1)
         i.   ☐ Bad Faith (describe) _____
         ii.   ☐ Multiple Filings
         iii. ☐ Other (describe) _____

    d.   Debtor's Statement of Intention regarding the Collateral

         i. ☐ Reaffirm   ii. ☐ Redeem   iii. ☐ Surrender   iv. ☐ No Statement of Intention Filed

Date: _____   _____
                                                Counsel for Movant

(Rev. 12/21/09)

[Revised on or about January 12, 2010.]

UNITED STATES DISTRICT COURT FOR THE CENTRAL DISTRICT OF ILLINOIS

Including Amendments Received Through
April 1, 2015

GENERAL AND CIVIL RULES

RULE 1.1. SCOPE OF THE RULES

(A) These Rules are known as the Local Rules of United States District Court for the Central District of Illinois. They may be cited as "CDIL–LR ____."

(B) These Rules became effective on January 20, 2010.

(C) These Rules apply in all proceedings in all of the courts in this district.

(D) These Rules supersede all previous Rules and orders promulgated by this court or any judge of this court, and will apply to all cases pending at the time these Rules become effective regardless of when the case was filed.

[Effective January 20, 2010.]

RULE 4.1. WAIVER OF SERVICE

When the Plaintiff elects to notify defendant(s) of the commencement of an action and requests that the defendant(s) waive service of a summons, proof of the written notice of lawsuit and request for waiver of service of summons, directed to the defendant(s), must be filed with the Clerk of this Court within 7 days of the mailing of the notice.

[Effective January 20, 2010.]

RULE 5.1. FORMAT OF FILINGS

The Court may strike any paper which does not conform to the following format:

In all cases except prisoner and other pro se cases and social security appeals,

(A) All documents filed with the Court must be double-spaced and must be formatted to standard 8½ by 11 inches in size.

(B) All documents must have one inch margins on all sides and each page must be numbered.

(C) Either a proportionally spaced or a monospaced typeface may be used. A proportionally spaced face must be 12–point or larger, in both body text and footnotes. A monospaced face may not contain more than 10½ characters per inch. All documents must be formatted in a plain, roman style. Italics may be used for emphasis.

(D) No pleading, motion, or other document may be transmitted to the court or the office of the clerk of the court by means of electronic facsimile.

[Adopted effective June 1, 1997. Amended October, 1998; January 1, 2002; January 20, 2010.]

RULE 5.2. ELECTRONIC FILING AUTHORIZED

Pursuant to Fed. R. Civ. P. 5(e), the court will accept for filing documents submitted, signed or verified by electronic means that comply with these Local Rules.

[Effective January 20, 2010.]

RULE 5.3. SERVICE BY ELECTRONIC MEANS AUTHORIZED

(A) Consent. Registration in the Court's Electronic Case Filing System constitutes a consent to electronic service and notice of all filed documents pursuant to Fed. R. Civ. P. 5(b)(2)(E). When a pleading or other paper is filed electronically, the "Notice of Electronic Filing" generated by the Court's Electronic Case Filing System constitutes service of that document on any person who is a registered participant in that System. The consent to electronic service applies only to service required under Fed. R. Civ. P. 5; it does not apply to service required under Fed. R. Civ. P. 4.

(B) Non–Registered Parties. A party who is not a registered participant of the System is entitled to a paper copy of any electronically filed pleading, document, or order. The filing party must therefore provide the non-registered party with the pleading, document, or order according to the Federal Rules of Civil Procedure. When mailing paper copies of documents that have been electronically filed, the filing party may include the "Notice of Electronic Filing" to provide the recipient with proof of the filing.

(C) Certificate of Service. A certificate of service on all parties entitled to service or notice is required, even when a party files a document electronically. The certificate must state the manner in which service or notice was accomplished on each party entitled to service or notice.

(D) Service by Mail. The three-day rule of Federal Rule of Civil Procedure 6(d) for service by mail also applies to service by electronic means.

[Effective January 20, 2010.]

RULE 5.4. DEFINITIONS FOR ELECTRONIC FILING

(A) "Case Management/Electronic Case Filing System," also referred to as "the System" or "CM/ECF," means the Internet-based system for filing documents and maintaining court files in the District Court for the Central District of Illinois.

(B) "Conventional filing" means submitting a document or pleading to the Court in paper or other non-electronic, tangible format. Documents submitted conventionally will be scanned, uploaded, filed and maintained in CM/ECF unless these Rules provide otherwise.

(C) "Electronic filing" means uploading a pleading or document directly from the registered user's computer in Adobe PDF format, using CM/ECF, to file that pleading or document in the Court's case file. Sending a document or pleading to the Court via e-mail does not constitute "electronic filing."

(D) "Notice of Electronic Filing" (or NEF) refers to the notice that is generated automatically by the CM/ECF System at the time a document is filed with the System, setting forth the time of filing, the name of the party and attorney filing the document, the type of document, the text of the docket entry, and an electronic link (hyperlink) to the filed document, which allows recipients to retrieve the document automatically.

(E) "PACER" (Public Access to Court Electronic Records) is the automated system that allows an individual to view, print, and download court docket information via the Internet.

(F) "PDF" refers to a document that exists in Portable Document Format. A document file created with a word processor, or a paper document that has been scanned, must be converted to portable document format before it can be electronically filed. Converted files contain the extension ".pdf".

[Effective January 20, 2010.]

RULE 5.5. SCOPE OF ELECTRONIC FILING

(A) Requirements. Unless otherwise provided by the court, all documents submitted for filing in civil cases in this district, no matter when a case was filed originally, must be filed electronically using CM/ECF.

(B) Exceptions.

(1) Unless the court, in its discretion, grants leave to a pro se filer to file electronically, pro se filers must file paper originals of all complaints, pleadings, motions, affidavits, briefs, and other documents. The Clerk's Office will scan these original documents into an electronic file in the System. The official court record will be the electronic file.

(2) The Clerk's Office will accept case initiating documents (i.e., complaints with civil cover sheets and summons, and notices of removal) delivered in person, sent by e-mail to the appropriate address listed in Local Rule 5.7(B), sent by United States mail or filed directly through CM/ECF.

(3) An attorney may apply to the assigned judge for permission to file documents conventionally. Even if the assigned judge initially grants an attorney permission to file documents conventionally, however, the assigned judge may withdraw that permission at any time during the pendency of a case and require the attorney to file documents electronically using the System.

(4) Any judge of this Court may deviate from the electronic filing procedures in specific cases, if deemed appropriate in the exercise of discretion, considering the need for the just, speedy, and inexpensive determination of matters pending before the Court.

[Effective January 20, 2010.]

RULE 5.6. ELIGIBILITY, REGISTRATION, AND PASSWORDS

Each attorney admitted to practice in the Central District of Illinois and pro se party given leave of court to proceed electronically must register for electronic filing and obtain a password. If a user comes to believe that the security of an existing password has been compromised and that a threat to the System exists, the user must change his or her password immediately. Additionally, if an attorney's or pro se party's e-mail address, mailing address, telephone number, or fax number changes after he or she registers for electronic filing, he or she must file notice of this change within 14 days and serve a copy of the notice on all other parties.

[Effective January 20, 2010.]

RULE 5.7. ELECTRONIC FILING PROCEDURES

(A) Pleadings and Documents Other Than Case Initiating Documents. All motions, pleadings, applications, briefs, memoranda of law, exhibits, or other documents in a civil case (except for complaints) must be electronically filed on the System except as otherwise provided by these Rules.

(1) A document submitted electronically will not be considered filed for purposes of the Federal Rules of Civil Procedure until the System-generated Notice of Electronic Filing has been sent electronically to the filing party.

(2) E–mailing a document to the Clerk's Office or to the assigned judge does not constitute "filing" of the document.

(3) A document filed electronically by 11:59 p.m. central standard time will be deemed filed on that date.

(B) Case Initiating Documents.

(1) The Clerk's Office will accept case initiating documents (i.e. complaints with civil cover sheets and summons, and notices of removal) sent by e-mail or directly into the CM/ECF system.

(a) A party submitting a case initiating document by e-mail for electronic filing must submit those documents in .pdf format to the proper divisional mailbox, as follows:

newcases.peoria@ilcd.uscourts.gov

newcases.urbana@ilcd.uscourts.gov

newcases.springfield@ilcd.uscourts.gov

newcases.rockisland@ilcd.uscourts.gov

(b) Payment of the filing fee must be made by cash, check, money order or credit card. Credit card payments may be made using pay.gov or by giving a credit card number, by phone, to the appropriate clerk's office.

(c) Case initiating documents submitted by e-mail will be deemed filed on the date that the complaint is received by e-mail or the date that the filing fee is paid, whichever is later.

(d) Case initiating documents filed by pro se plaintiffs will be deemed filed on the date received by the Clerk's Office. Legal issues regarding filing date or receipt of fees will be resolved by the Court.

(2) The Clerk's Office also will accept for filing case initiating documents sent by United States mail or delivered in person to the Clerk's Office when accompanied by the filing fee or a Petition to Proceed in forma pauperis. A case initiating document received in paper form will be scanned and uploaded by the Clerk's Office. Unless otherwise provided in these procedures, the paper documents will then be discarded.

(3) Only case initiating documents may be sent to the e-mail addresses listed above. If any other documents are sent to those e-mail addresses, the Clerk's Office will reply to the e-mail, notifying the party that the pleading has not been filed.

(4) A party may not electronically serve a case initiating document, but instead must effect service according to Fed. R. Civ. P. 4. Electronic service of a Notice of Filing does not constitute service of process where service of process is required by Fed. R. Civ. P. 4.

(C) Titling Docket Entries. The party electronically filing a pleading or other document is responsible for designating a docket entry title for the document by using one of the docket event categories prescribed by the court.

(D) Filing Problems.

(1) *Corrections.* Once a document is submitted and becomes part of the case docket, corrections to the docket are made only by the Clerk's Office. The System will not permit the filing party to make changes to the document or docket entry filed in error once the transaction has been accepted. <u>The filing party should not attempt to refile a document.</u> As soon as possible after an error is discovered, the filing party should contact the Clerk's Office with the case number and document number for which the correction is being requested. If appropriate, the Court will make an entry indicating that the document was filed in error. The filing party will be advised *if* the document needs to be refiled.

(2) *Technical Problems.*

(a) Technical Failures. The Clerk's Office will deem the Central District of Illinois CM/ECF site to be subject to a technical failure on a given day if the site is unable to accept filings continuously or intermittently over the course of any period of time greater than one hour after 10:00 a.m. that day. In the event a technical failure occurs, and despite the best efforts of the filing party a document cannot be filed electronically, the party should print (if possible) a copy of the error message received. As soon as possible, the party should file this message with a Declaration That Party Was Unable to File in a Timely Manner Due to Technical Difficulties.

(b) Filer's Problems. Problems on the filer's end, such as phone line problems, problems with the filer's Internet Service Provider (ISP) or hardware or software problems will neither constitute a technical failure nor excuse an untimely filing. If a party misses a filing deadline due to such problems, the document may be conventionally submitted, accompanied by a Declaration stating the reason for missing the deadline and a motion for leave to file instanter. The motion, document and declaration must be filed no later than 12:00 noon of the first day on which the Court is open for business following the original filing deadline. The Court will consider the matters stated in the declaration and order appropriate relief.

[Effective January 20, 2010.]

RULE 5.8. ATTACHMENTS AND EXHIBITS

(A) Size Limitations. Attachments and exhibits filed electronically must conform to the size limitations set forth on the Central District of Illinois CM/ECF login page. If a document with attachments and exhibits is longer than 30 pages, a courtesy paper copy must be provided to the presiding judge's chambers.

(B) Non–Trial Exhibits. A party may conventionally file exhibits which are not readily available in electronic form (e.g., blueprints, large maps). If possible, however, a filing party should scan a paper exhibit and file it electronically, in accordance with the size and scanning limitations set forth in these Rules. A party electronically submitting evidentiary materials must attach an index listing each item of evidence then being filed and identifying the motion or pleading to which it relates.

(C) Trial Exhibits. Trial exhibits will not be scanned into the electronic record unless specifically ordered by the Judge presiding over the matter.

[Effective January 20, 2010.]

RULE 5.9. COURT RECORD AND ORDERS

(A) Official Court Record. The Clerk's Office will not maintain a paper court file except as otherwise provided in these Rules. The official court record is the electronic file maintained by the court, supplemented with any documents or exhibits conventionally filed in accordance with these Rules.

(B) Orders.

(1) *Judges' Signatures.* The assigned judge or the Clerk's Office will electronically file all signed orders. Any order signed electronically has the same force and effect as if the judge had affixed the judge's signature to a paper copy of the order and it had been entered on the docket conventionally.

(2) *Proposed Orders.* Proposed orders must be submitted as attachments to motions. The presiding judge may request a copy of the proposed order be sent in Word or Word Perfect format (i.e., not .pdf) to the chambers e-mail address.

(3) *Text–Only Orders.* The assigned judge may grant routine orders by a text-only entry upon the docket. When text-only entries are made, no separate .pdf document will issue; the text-only entry will constitute the Court's only order on the matter. The System will generate a "Notice of Electronic Filing."

[Effective January 20, 2010.]

RULE 5.10. SEALED CASES, DOCUMENTS FOR IN CAMERA REVIEW, AND EX PARTE DOCUMENTS

(A) Filing Under Seal.

(1) *Sealed Cases.* All documents in sealed cases must be submitted conventionally to the Clerk's Office for filing.

(2) *Sealed Documents.* The Court does not approve of the filing of documents under seal as a general matter. A party who has a legal basis for filing a document under seal without prior court order must electronically file a motion for leave to file under seal. The motion must include an explanation of how the document meets the legal standards for filing sealed documents. The document in question may not be attached to the motion as an attachment but rather must be electronically filed contemporaneously using the separate docket event "Sealed Document." In the rare event that the motion itself must be filed under seal, the motion must be electronically filed using the docket event "Sealed Motion."

(3) *Service.* Parties must not use the Court's electronic notice facilities to serve documents in sealed cases or individually sealed documents. A publicly viewable Notice of Electronic Filing will be generated for a sealed document, but the document itself will not be viewable electronically. Service must be made in accordance with the Federal Rules of Civil Procedure and the Local Rules of this Court. A certificate of service must be attached to the filed document.

(4) *Denial of Requests to Seal.* In the event that a motion for leave to file under seal is denied, the document tendered will remain under seal, and it will not be considered by the presiding judge for any purpose. If the filer wishes to have the document considered by the Court, it must be re-filed in the normal fashion as an unsealed document. The Court may, in its discretion, order a sealed document to be made public if (1) the document is filed in disregard of legal standards, or (2) if the document is so intricately connected with a pending matter that the interests of justice are best served by doing so.

(B) Documents Submitted for In Camera Review. The Rules applicable to Sealed Documents also apply to documents submitted for in camera review.

(C) Ex Parte Submissions. A party who has a legal basis to file a submission without giving notice to other parties should file the submission electronically as either an "Ex Parte Document" or an "Ex Parte Motion."

[Effective January 20, 2010.]

RULE 5.11. PRIVACY

(A) **Redactions.** To address the privacy concerns created by Internet access to court documents, litigants must modify or partially redact certain personal data identifiers appearing in case initiating documents, pleadings, affidavits, or other papers. In addition to those set out in Fed. R. Civ. P. 5.2, these identifiers and the suggested modifications are as follows:

(1) *Addresses*: Use only City and State;

(2) *Signatures*: Use s/name; and

(3) *Driver's License numbers*: Use only last four numbers.

Litigants also should consider redacting or filing a motion to file under seal any document that contains information that might bring harm to anyone or should not be made public for law enforcement or security reasons.

(B) **Unredacted Documents and Reference Lists.** When redactions result in a documents' intent being unclear or if ordered by the Court, the filing party must file under seal an unredacted document or a reference list. A reference list must contain the complete personal data identifier(s) and the redacted identifier(s) to be used in its(their) place in the filing. If an unredacted version is not filed, the unredacted version of the document or the reference list must be retained by the filing party for one year after completion of the case, including all appeals. Upon a showing that the redacted information is both relevant and legitimately needed, the Court may, in its discretion, order the information disclosed to counsel for all parties.

(C) **Transcript Redactions.** Parties and attorneys may order transcripts. A court reporter then will file the transcripts electronically in CM/ECF. The transcript will be available for viewing at the Clerk's Office public terminal, but may not be copied nor reproduced by the Clerk's Office for a period of 90 days. A Notice of Filing of Official Transcript will be served on all parties. If any material should be redacted from a transcript, a party must file a Notice of Intent to Request Redaction within 7 days of the filing of the transcript. The responsibility for identifying material that should be redacted, in a transcript, lies solely with counsel and the parties. Within 21 days from the filing of the transcript, the parties must file under seal a Motion of Requested Redactions indicating where the material to be redacted is located, by page and line. If a party fails to follow the procedures for requesting redaction, the official tran-

scripts will be made available electronically to the public 90 days after the transcript was initially filed with the Clerk.

(D) **Pro Se Parties.** Documents filed in civil cases brought by pro se prisoners need not be redacted unless so ordered by the presiding Judge. Nonprisoner pro se parties must comply with the redaction Rules.

(E) **Social Security Cases.** Documents filed in social security cases need not be redacted unless so ordered by the presiding Judge.

[Effective January 20, 2010. Amended effective March 15, 2010.]

RULE 6.1. EXTENSIONS OF TIME

Any party seeking an extension of time for any reason must file a motion for such extension before the original deadline. Motions filed out of time will be denied, unless the presiding judge determines that such denial would create a substantial injustice. All such motions must state the amount of additional time requested, and must state whether opposing counsel has objection to the motion.

[Effective January 20, 2010.]

RULE 7.1. MOTIONS

(A) **Disposition of Motions: Oral Argument: Extension of Time.**

(1) Any motion (other than summary judgment motions, which are governed by subparagraph (D) of this Rule) may, in the court's discretion, be:

(a) scheduled for oral argument, either at a specified time or on a Motion Day as suggested in Fed. R. Civ. P. 78;

(b) scheduled for determination by telephone conference call;

(c) referred to a United States magistrate judge for determination or recommendation; or

(d) determined upon the pleadings and the motion papers without benefit of oral argument.

(2) A party desiring oral argument on a motion filed under subparagraph (B) of this Rule must so specify in the motion or opposition thereto and must state the reason why oral argument is desired.

(3) Motions for extensions of time must be filed within the original time allowed.

(B) **Memorandum of Law: Response; Reply; Length**

(1) Every motion raising a question of law (except summary judgment motions, which are governed by Subparagraph (D) of this Rule) must include a memorandum of law including a brief statement of the specific points or propositions of law and supporting

authorities upon which the moving party relies, and identifying the Rule under which the motion is filed.

(2) Any party opposing a motion filed pursuant to (B)(1) must file a response to the motion, including a brief statement of the specific points or propositions of law and supporting authorities upon which the responding party relies. The response must be filed within 14 days after service of the motion and memorandum. If no response is timely filed, the presiding judge will presume there is no opposition to the motion and may rule without further notice to the parties.

(3) No reply to the response is permitted.

(4)(a) A memorandum in support of and in response to a motion must be double-spaced and must not exceed 15 pages in length, unless it complies with the following type volume limitation.

(b) A memorandum that exceeds 15 pages in length will comply with the type volume limitation if

(1) it does not contain more than 7000 words or 45,000 characters, or

(2) it uses monospaced type and does not contain more than 650 lines of text.

(c) A memorandum submitted under the type volume limitation must include a certificate by counsel, or by an unrepresented party, that the memorandum complies with the type volume limitation. The certificate of compliance must state the number of words, characters or lines of type in the memorandum. The person who prepares the certificate of compliance may rely on the word or character count of the word processing system used to prepare the document.

(d) All headings, footnotes, and quotations count toward the page, word, character, and line limitations.

(C) **Supporting Documents.** If documentary evidence is to be offered in support of or in opposition to a motion, and if that evidence is conveniently susceptible of copying, copies thereof will be served and filed by the moving party with the motion and by the opposing party with the response thereto. If the evidence is not susceptible of convenient copying, the offering party instead will furnish to the court and to the adverse party, a concise summary of the contents and will immediately make the original available to the adverse party for examination.

(D) **Summary Judgment.** All motions for summary judgment and responses and replies thereto must comply with the requirements of this rule. Any filings not in compliance may be stricken by the court. The consequences for failing to comply are discussed thoroughly in *Waldridge v. American Hoechst Corp.*, 24 F.3d 918 (7th Cir. 1994). Motions for extension of time to file a motion for summary judgment or a response to a reply thereto will not be looked upon with favor; such motions may be summarily denied unless they are filed within the original time as allowed by this rule or by the scheduling order.

(1) *Motion for Summary Judgment.* Any party filing a motion for summary judgment pursuant to Fed. R. Civ. P. 56 and the scheduling order entered in the case, must include in that motion the following sections with appropriate headings:

(a) Introduction: Without citations, briefly summarize the legal and factual basis for the motion and the exact relief sought.

(b) Undisputed Material Facts: List and number each undisputed material fact which is the basis for the motion for summary judgment. Include as exhibits to the motion all relevant documentary evidence. For each fact asserted, provide citations to the documentary evidence that supports it, appropriately referencing the exhibit and page.

A WORD OF CAUTION: Material facts are only those facts which bear directly on the legal issue raised by the motion.

(c) Argument: Under an appropriate subheading for each separate point of law, explain the legal point, with citations to authorities, and why or how the application of that point to the undisputed material facts entitles movant to the relief sought.

(2) *Response to Motion for Summary Judgment*: Within 21 days after service of a motion for summary judgment, any party opposing the motion must file a response. A failure to respond will be deemed an admission of the motion. The response must include the following sections with appropriate headings:

(a) Introduction: Without citations, briefly summarize the legal and factual basis for opposition to the motion and the exact relief sought.

(b) Response to Undisputed Material Facts: In separate subsections state the following:

(1) Undisputed material facts: List by number each fact from Section B of the motion for summary judgment which is conceded to be undisputed and material.

(2) Disputed Material Facts: List by number each fact from Section B of the motion for summary judgment which is conceded to be material but is claimed to be disputed. Each claim of disputed fact must be supported by evidentiary documentation referenced by specific page. Include as exhibits all cited documentary evidence not already submitted by the movant.

(3) Disputed Immaterial Facts: List by number each fact from Section B of the motion for summary judgment which is claimed to be both immaterial and disputed. State the reason the fact is immaterial. Support the claim that the

fact is disputed with evidentiary documentation referenced by specific page. Include as exhibits all cited documentary evidence not already submitted by the movant.

(4) Undisputed Immaterial Facts: List by number each fact from Section B of the motion for summary judgment which is undisputed but is claimed to be immaterial. State the reason the fact is immaterial.

(5) Additional Material Facts: List and number each additional material fact raised in opposition to the motion for summary judgment. Each additional fact must be supported by evidentiary documentation referenced by specific page. Include as exhibits all relevant documentary evidence not already submitted by the movant.

(6) A failure to respond to any numbered fact will be deemed an admission of the fact.

(c) Argument: With or without additional citations to authorities, respond directly to the argument in the motion for summary judgment, for example, by explaining any disagreement with the movant's explanation of each point of law, why a point of law does not apply to the undisputed material facts, why its application does not entitle movant to relief or why, for other reasons, summary judgment should not be granted.

(3) *Movant's Reply*: Within 14 days after service of response, the movant may file a reply. The reply must include the following subsections, appropriately titled:

(a) Reply to Additional Material Facts. List by number the additional facts asserted in Section (b)(5) of the response. For each fact, state succinctly whether:

(1) it is conceded to be material and undisputed,

(2) it is conceded to be material but is disputed, in which case provide support the claim that the fact is disputed by providing citations to specific pages of evidentiary documentation. Include as exhibits all cited documentary evidence not already submitted,

(3) it is immaterial but disputed, in which case state the reason the the fact is immaterial and support the claim that the fact is disputed by providing citations to evidentiary documentation, attached as exhibits and referenced by specific page,

(4) it is immaterial and undisputed, in which case explain the reason it is immaterial,

(5) A failure to respond to any numbered fact will be deemed an admission of that fact.

(b) Argument. Succinctly and directly address any matters raised in the response with which the movant disagrees. THE REPLY WILL BE LIMITED TO NEW MATTERS RAISED IN THE RESPONSE AND MUST NOT RESTATE ARGUMENTS ALREADY RAISED IN THE MOTION.

(4) *Oral Arguments*. The Court may take the motion for summary judgment under advisement without oral argument or may schedule argument with appropriate notice to the parties. A party may file a request for oral argument and hearing at the time of filing either a motion or response pursuant to this Rule.

(5) *Page and Type Limitations*. Page and type volume limitations, as set forth in Rule 7.1(B)(4), apply to Section (1)(c) of the motion for summary judgment and to Section (2)(c) of the response to the motion. The argument section of a reply must not exceed five double-spaced pages in length.

(6) *Exceptions*. Local Rule 7.1(D) does not apply to pro se litigants, social security appeals, or any other case upon the showing of good cause.

(E) Amended Pleadings. Whenever an amended pleading is filed, any motion attacking the original pleading will be deemed moot unless specifically revived by the moving party within 14 days after the amended pleading is served.

[Effective January 20, 2010. Amended effective March 15, 2010.]

RULE 8.1. SOCIAL SECURITY CASES: REVIEW UNDER 42 U.S.C. § 405(g)

(A) Complaints: Contents. Any person seeking judicial review of a decision of the Commissioner of Social Security under Section 205(g) of the Social Security Act (42 U.S.C. § 405(g)) must provide, on a separate paper attached to the complaint served on the Commissioner of Social Security, the social security number of the worker on whose wage record the application for benefits was filed. The person must also state, in the complaint, that the social security number has been attached to the copy of the complaint served on the Commissioner of Social Security. Failure to provide a social security number to the Commissioner of Social Security will not be grounds for dismissal of the complaint.

(B) Complaints: Form of Allegation. In keeping with Fed. R. Civ. P. 84 and the Appendix of Forms to the Federal Rules of Civil Procedure, the following form of allegations in a complaint is considered sufficient for § 405(g) review cases in this court:

(1) The plaintiff is a resident of _____
                                     (City and State)

(2) The plaintiff complains of a decision which adversely affects (him) (her). The decision has become the final

decision of the Commissioner for purposes of judicial review and bears the following caption:

In the case of   Claim for

_____   _____

Claimant

_____

Wage Earner

(3) The plaintiff has exhausted administrative remedies in this matter and this court has jurisdiction for judicial review pursuant to 42 U.S.C. § 405(g).

WHEREFORE, plaintiff seeks judicial review by this court and the entry of judgment for such relief as may be proper, including costs.

(C) Responsive Pleading, Transcript of Proceedings. The respondent has 120 days from the date of service of summons within which to file a responsive pleading and transcript of administrative proceedings.

(D) Motions: Hearing. Within 30 days after the filing of the responsive pleading and transcript, the plaintiff must file a Motion for Summary Judgment and a Memorandum of Law which must state with particularity which findings of the Commissioner are contrary to law. The plaintiff must identify the statute, regulation or case law under which the Commissioner allegedly erred. The plaintiff must cite to the record by page number the factual evidence which supports the plaintiff's position. Arguing generally, "the decision of the Commissioner is not supported by substantial evidence" is not sufficient to meet this rule. Within 45 days thereafter, the defendant must file a Cross–Motion and Memorandum of Law which must specifically respond to the plaintiff's assertions and arguments. The defendant must cite to the record by page number the factual evidence which supports the decision of the Commissioner. The case may be set for hearing at the discretion of the presiding judge.

[Effective January 20, 2010.]

RULE 8.2. RULE ON POST–CONVICTION PROCEEDINGS IN CAPITAL PUNISHMENT CASES PURSUANT TO 28 U.S.C. SECTIONS 2254 AND 2255

(A) Operation, Scope, and Priority.

(1) This rule applies to post-conviction proceedings in all cases involving persons under sentence of capital punishment.

(2) The judge to whom a case is assigned will handle all matters pertaining to the case, including certificates of appealability, stays of execution, consideration of the merits, second or successive petitions when authorized by the court of appeals under 28 U.S.C. §§ 2244(b)(3), 2255(h), remands from the court of appeals or Supreme Court of the United States, and associated procedural matters. This rule does not limit a district judge's discretion to designate a magistrate judge, under 28 U.S.C. § 636, to perform appropriate tasks. An emergency judge may act when the designated district judge is unavailable.

(3) The judge must give priority to cases within the scope of this rule, using the time limitations in 28 U.S.C. § 2266(b) as guidelines when the section is not directly applicable.

(4) The judge may make changes in the procedures established by this rule when justice so requires.

(B) Notices and Required Documents.

(1) A petition or motion within the scope of this rule must:

    (a) Include all possible grounds for relief;

    (b) Inform the court of the execution date, if one has been set; and

    (c) In an action under 28 U.S.C. § 2254, inform the court how each issue raised was presented to the state tribunal and, if it was not presented, why the contention nonetheless should be treated as (i) exhausted, and (ii) not forfeited.

(2) As soon as a case is assigned to a judge, the district clerk must notify by telephone the judge, counsel for the parties, and the representatives designated under the next subsection. The district clerk also must inform counsel of the appropriate procedures and telephone numbers for emergency after-hours motions.

(3) The Attorneys General of states with persons under sentence of death, and the United States Attorneys of districts with persons under sentence of death, must designate representatives to receive notices in capital cases in addition to, or in lieu of, the government's assigned counsel, and must keep the court informed about the office and home telephone numbers of the designated representatives.

(4) The district clerk must notify the circuit clerk of the filing of a case within the scope of this rule, of any substantial development in the case, and of the filing of a notice of appeal. In all cases within the scope of this rule, the district court clerk must immediately transmit the record to the court of appeals following the filing of a notice of appeal. A supplemental record may be sent later if items are not currently available.

(5) Promptly after the filing of a case within the scope of this rule, the district clerk must furnish to petitioner or movant a copy of this rule, together with copies of Federal Rule of Appellate Procedure 22, and Seventh Circuit Rules 22 and 22.2.

(6) In all cases within the scope of this rule, the petitioner or movant must file, within 14 days after

filing the petition or motion, legible copies of the documents listed below. If a required document is not filed, the petitioner or movant must explain the omission.

(a) Copies of all state or federal court opinions, memorandum decisions, orders, transcripts of oral statements of reasons, and judgments involving any issue presented by the petition or motion, whether these decisions or opinions were rendered by trial or appellate courts, on direct or collateral review. If a decision or opinion has been published, a citation may be supplied in lieu of a copy.

(b) Copies of prior petitions or motions filed in state or federal court challenging the same conviction or sentence.

(c) If a prior petition has been filed in federal court, either (i) a copy of the court of appeals' order under 28 U.S.C. § 2244(b)(3) or § 2255(h) permitting a second or successive collateral attack, or (ii) an explanation of why prior approval of the court of appeals is not required.

(d) Any other documents that the judge requests.

(C) Preliminary Consideration.

(1) The district judge will promptly examine a petition or motion within the scope of this rule and, if appropriate, order the respondent to file an answer or other pleading or take such other action as the judge deems appropriate.

(2) If the judge determines that the petition or motion is a second or successive collateral attack for which prior approval of the court of appeals was required but not obtained, the judge will immediately dismiss the case for want of jurisdiction.

(3) If the court of appeals granted leave to file a second or successive collateral attack, the district judge must promptly determine in writing whether the criteria of 28 U.S.C. § 2244(b)(4) have been satisfied.

(D) Appointment of Counsel. Pursuant to 28 U.S.C. § 2255(g), counsel will be appointed for any person under a sentence of death who is financially unable to obtain representation, requests that counsel be appointed, and does not already have counsel appointed by a state under 28 U.S.C. § 2261.

(E) Stay of Execution.

(1) A stay of execution is granted automatically in some cases, and forbidden in others, by 28 U.S.C. § 2262. All requests with respect to stays of execution over which the court possesses discretion, or in which any party contends that § 2262 has not been followed, must be made by motion under this rule.

(2) Parties must endeavor to file motions with the court in writing and during normal business hours. Parties having emergency motions during nonbusiness hours must proceed as instructed under part (b)(2).

(3) A motion must be accompanied by legible copies of the documents required by part (b)(6), unless these documents have already been filed with the court or the movant supplies a reason for their omission. If the reason is lack of time to obtain or file the documents, then the movant must furnish them as soon as possible thereafter.

(4) If the attorney for the government has no objection to the motion for stay, the court must enter an order staying the execution.

(5) If the district judge concludes that an initial petition or motion is not frivolous, a stay of execution must be granted.

(6) An order granting or denying a stay of execution must be accompanied by a statement of the reasons for the decision.

(7) If the district court denies relief on the merits and an appeal is taken, then:

(a) if the judge denies a certificate of appealability, any previously issued stay must be vacated, and no new stay of execution may be entered; but

(b) if the judge issues a certificate of appealability, a stay of execution pending appeal must be granted.

(F) Clerk's List of Cases. The Clerk will maintain a list of cases within the scope of this rule.

[Effective January 20, 2010.]

RULE 11.1. TELEPHONE NUMBER ON PLEADINGS

In addition to the signature and address of the signing attorney or unrepresented party as required by Fed. R. Civ. P. 11, every pleading must show a telephone number where such attorney or party may be reached by telephone. For every pleading that is not electronically filed, the name of the filing party or attorney must be typed below the signature line.

[Effective January 20, 2010.]

RULE 11.2. DESIGNATION OF LEAD COUNSEL ON INITIAL PLEADING

When a party's initial pleading is filed, counsel must designate as lead counsel the attorney who will be responsible for receipt of telephone conference calls. Only one may be designated.

[Effective January 20, 2010.]

RULE 11.3. CERTIFICATE OF INTEREST

To enable the presiding judge to determine whether recusal is necessary or appropriate, an attorney for a non-governmental party or an amicus curiae must file a Certificate of Interest stating the following information:

(1) The full name of every party or amicus the attorney represents in the case;

(2) If such party or amicus is a corporation:

(a) its parent corporation, if any; and

(b) a list of corporate stockholders which are publicly held companies owning 10 percent or more of the stock of the party or amicus if it is a publicly held company.

(3) The name of all law firms whose partners or associates appear for a party or are expected to appear for the party in the case.

The certificate must be filed with the complaint or upon the first appearance of counsel in the case. The certificate must be in the following form:

[CAPTION]

The undersigned, counsel of record for [JOHN DOE, PLAINTIFF] furnishes the following in compliance with Rule 11.3 of this court.

[LISTED BY NUMBER CATEGORY]

DATE   ATTORNEY SIGNATURE

This rule does not apply to pro se litigants.

[Effective January 20, 2010.]

RULE 11.4.   ELECTRONIC SIGNATURES

(A) Signatures by Electronic Filers.

(1) Use of a log-in and password for electronic filing constitutes and has the same force and effect as the filer's signature for purposes of Fed. R. Civ. P. 11, the Local Rules of this Court, and any other purpose for which a signature may be required in connection with proceedings in this Court.

(2) Electronic filers should sign in the following manner: "s/ Jane Doe." Documents signed by an attorney must be filed using that attorney's log-in and password; they may not be filed using a log-in and password belonging to another attorney.

(3) Where multiple attorney signatures are required, such as on a joint motion or a stipulation, the filing attorney may enter the "s/" of the other attorneys to reflect their agreement with the contents of the documents.

(B) Signatures by Non–Electronic Filers.

(1) If an original document requires the signature[s] of one or more persons not registered for electronic filing (e.g., settlement agreement with a pro se party, or a witness' affidavit), the filing party or its attorney must initially confirm that the content of the document is acceptable to all persons required to sign the documents. Original signatures of all non-elec-

tronic filers must be obtained before the document is filed.

(2) The filing party must either redact the original signature[s] and efile the redacted version of the document, or provide the redacted version to the Clerk's Office for scanning and electronic filing. The filed document must indicate the identity of each non-registered signatory in the form "s/Jane Doe". A certificate of Service upon all parties and/or counsel of record must be filed with the document.

(3) The filing party must retain the original document until one year after the date that the judgment has become final by the conclusion of direct review or the expiration of the time for seeking such review has passed.

(4) The electronically filed document as it is maintained on the court's servers constitutes the official version of that record. The court will not maintain a paper copy of the original document except as otherwise provided in these Rules.

(C) Disputes Over Authenticity. Any party or non-filing signatory who disputes the authenticity of an electronically filed document or the signatures on that document must file an objection to the document within 14 days of receiving the notice that the document has been filed.

[Effective January 20, 2010. Amended effective March 15, 2010.]

RULE 12.1.   STATE OF ILLINOIS— TIME TO ANSWER

In all civil actions in which a claim is asserted against an official, employee, or agency of the State of Illinois, the defendant must file an answer or otherwise plead within 60 days after service of process in which the claim is asserted.

In prisoner civil rights cases where the plaintiff appears pro se, the answer and subsequent pleadings must be to the issues stated in the Case Management Order accompanying the process and complaint. A defendant need not parse the complaint and respond to it. The responsive pleading must be only to the issues stated in the court's Case Management Order issued after merit review of the complaint.

[Effective January 20, 2010.]

RULE 16.1.   PRETRIAL PROCEDURES

(A) Special Pretrial Conference. A special pretrial conference may be held at any time by the presiding judge on notice issued to the parties whenever it appears that such may aid in disposition or preparation for trial. The special pretrial conference will be by telephone conference unless otherwise directed by the presiding judge.

(B) Settlement Conference. The presiding judge may order the parties to submit to settlement conferences at any time if it appears that a case may be resolved by settlement. The settlement conference will be by personal appearance unless otherwise directed by the presiding judge. In addition to the attorney responsible for the actual trial of the case, someone with final settlement authority must attend the settlement conference, either in person or by telephone. The settlement conference in a matter to be tried to the court must be conducted by a judge who will not preside at the trial of the case.

(C) Cases Reported Settled. Whenever a party reports to the court that a civil action is settled, the presiding judge will enter an order dismissing the case without prejudice as settled, with leave to reopen within 35 days if the settlement is not finalized. The time to reopen may be extended by order of the presiding judge upon a showing of good cause.

(D) Cases With Intervening Bankruptcy.

(1) Whenever the presiding judge is advised that a bankruptcy under U.S.C. Title 11, or any other similar court-ordered reorganization of liquidation which stays ongoing debt collection proceedings, affects any party to any case filed in the district court of this district, the presiding judge will enter an order directing the parties to file within the clerk of this court a copy of the stay order. Until such order is filed, the presiding judge will keep the case on its active docket.

(2) After the stay order is filed, the presiding judge will enter an order directing the parties to show cause why the district court case should not be dismissed because of the pending bankruptcy, reorganization, or liquidation proceeding. The order to show cause will be returnable to a district judge at a date certain no less than 180 days from the date the stay order was filed with the clerk of this court. The time may be extended for good cause shown.

(3) It is the responsibility of the parties to the district court case to take whatever action is necessary to protect their interests in the bankruptcy, reorganization or liquidation proceedings. It is the further responsibility of the parties to lift the stay order or otherwise obtain relief from the bankruptcy, reorganization or liquidation proceeding and file with the district court a copy of the order allowing the district court case to proceed in order to prosecute the district court case. If such action is not taken the district court case will be dismissed.

(E) Final Pretrial Conference.

(1) A final pretrial conference will be scheduled by the presiding judge as soon as feasible after the date set for completion of discovery. Uncompleted discovery will not delay the final pretrial conference.

(2) Counsel for the parties or the parties, if not represented by counsel, must confer prior to the date set for final pretrial conference. They will explore the prospects of settlement and be prepared to report to the presiding judge at the final pretrial conference whether settlement is possible.

(3) The final pretrial conference will be by personal appearance unless otherwise directed by the presiding judge. Counsel who will actually try the case or parties not represented by counsel must appear at the final pretrial conference. Counsel and the parties must be authorized and prepared to enter such stipulations and agreements as may be appropriate.

(4) Prior to the date set for final pretrial conference, the parties must confer and prepare a proposed final pretrial order for presentation to the court at the conference unless otherwise ordered by the court. The form and content of the order are prescribed below and in Appendix 1.

(5) At the final pretrial conference, the presiding judge and counsel will consider the following:

(a) Simplification of the issues for trial;

(b) Any problems of evidence;

(c) Possible limitations of the number of expert witnesses;

(d) The desirability and timing of trial briefs;

(e) The prospects of settlement;

(f) Such other matters that may aid in the fair and expeditious trial and disposition of the action; and

(g) The possibility of trying the case on short notice. If the parties agree, the case will be put on a short notice calendar and may be called for trial on less than one-week notice.

(6) In cases to be tried to a jury, the parties must submit an agreed set of jury instructions. Instructions upon which the parties are unable to agree must be submitted separately by the parties, unless excused by the presiding judge. Each instruction must be appropriately numbered and on a separate sheet of 8½ by 11 size paper; must cover no more than one subject; must identify the source and authority upon which it is based; and must have the name of the party who submitted it noted at the bottom of the page.

(7) In bench trials, the parties must submit an agreed set of findings of fact and conclusions of law. Findings and conclusions upon which the parties are unable to agree must be submitted separately by the parties, unless excused by the presiding judge.

(8) Unless otherwise directed by the presiding judge, the parties must submit any trial briefs and motions in limine on or before 14 days prior to the scheduled start of trial. Untimely motions will not be considered unless good cause for delay can be shown to exist.

(F) Final Pretrial Order. Counsel for the plaintiff must prepare the order unless otherwise ordered by the presiding judge, and must submit it to opposing counsel at least 7 days prior to the date set for final pretrial conference. The pretrial order must contain the following:

(1) A brief statement of the nature of the case including the facts showing the basis for jurisdiction even if jurisdiction is not contested;

(2) A signed stipulation of uncontested material facts;

(3) A joint statement of uncontested issues of law;

(4) A joint statement of all contested material facts and issues of law;

(5) Stipulations regarding the use of depositions and the presentation of expert testimony;

(6) A list of all witnesses each party intends to call at trial. Failure to include a witness in the list may result in the witness being barred from offering testimony at trial;

(7) A list of exhibits each party intends to offer or use at trial. The court will assume that authentication proof for any listed exhibit is waived unless a specific objection to lack of authenticity is raised in the pretrial order. All other objections to exhibits must be specifically noted. Exhibits must be identified by number only and conform to the listing contained in the pretrial order;

(8) A list of all demonstrative aids intended for use in the trial. All foundation questions concerning those aids will be considered waived by the court unless specific objection is stated in the pretrial order.

(9) At the close of the pretrial conference, the parties and the presiding judge will sign the pretrial order. If changes or amendments to the order are required, the parties will complete the changes before they leave the courthouse, or the conference may be recessed to be continued in person within 14 days. The signed pretrial order takes the place of all prior pleadings. Any issue not contained in the final pretrial order will not be tried.

(10) A sample form of pretrial order is contained in Local Rules Appendix 1. The parties are admonished to conform their pretrial order to the sample format.

(G) Sanctions. Failure of counsel or parties, if not represented by counsel, to appear at any scheduled pretrial conference, including telephone conferences, or otherwise to comply with the provisions of this rule, may result in dismissal, default, awarding of attorney's fees and costs, and such other sanctions as may be appropriate.

[Effective January 20, 2010.]

RULE 16.2. SCHEDULING CONFERENCE AND ORDER

(A) Cases Covered. Within 90 days after the appearance of a defendant, all civil cases must have a conference pursuant to Federal Rule of Civil Procedure 16 to establish a scheduling order to govern case management except:

(1) Claims for relief within the admiralty and maritime jurisdiction as set forth in Fed. R. Civ. P. 9(h) and the Supplemental Rules for Certain Admiralty and Maritime Claims;

(2) Social Security cases filed under 42 U.S.C. § 405(g);

(3) Applications for writ of habeas corpus under 28 U.S.C. § 2254;

(4) Applications for review of sentence under 28 U.S.C. § 2255;

(5) Petitions brought by the United States to enforce a summons of the Internal Revenue Service;

(6) Appeals from rulings of a bankruptcy judge;

(7) Appeals from judgments of a United States magistrate judge;

(8) Naturalization proceedings filed as civil cases or proceedings to cancel or revoke citizenship;

(9) Requests for temporary retraining orders;

(10) Proceedings in bankruptcy;

(11) Proceedings to compel the giving of testimony or production of documents under a subpoena or summons issued by an officer; agency, or instrumentality of the United States not authorized to compel compliance;

(12) Proceedings to compel the giving of testimony or production of documents in this district in connection with discovery, or for perpetuation of testimony, for use in a matter pending or contemplated in a district court of another district;

(13) Proceedings for the temporary enforcement of orders of the National Labor Relations Board;

(14) Actions to enforce out-of-state judgments;

(15) Cases in which no service upon defendant(s) has been effected within 120 days of filing of the complaint;

(16) Other cases in which the court's review of the file indicates that the burden of a scheduling conference would exceed the administrative efficiency to be gained.

(17) The presiding judge may order a scheduling conference in any case.

(B) Order. At the conclusion of the scheduling conference, the presiding judge will enter an order setting forth the time limits as established at the conference. A copy of the order will be provided by the clerk of this court to each of the parties or their counsel.

(C) Scheduling by Telephone Conference. The scheduling conference may be held by a telephone conference call or the court may require personal appearance. Lead counsel must participate in the scheduling conference or inform the clerk of this court of substitute counsel before the time set for the conference. Whoever participates on behalf of a party is expected to be prepared to address the matters contemplated by the scheduling order and have full authority to bind the party as to such matters.

(D) Dates. The parties and their counsel are bound by the dates specified in the scheduling order absent a finding of due diligence and good cause for changing said dates.

(E) Scheduling Order. The scheduling order will contain certain deadlines for the following:

(1) Amendment of pleadings;

(2) Joinder of additional parties;

(3) Disclosure of expert witnesses;

(4) Completion of discovery;

(5) Filing of dispositive motions.

[Effective January 20, 2010.]

RULE 16.3. PRETRIAL PROCEDURES IN PRISONER AND DETAINEE CASES

The following procedures apply to civil cases filed by prisoners and civil detainees proceeding pro se. For purposes of this section, a "prisoner" is a person defined in 28 U.S.C. § 1915(h). A "civil detainee" is a person held in detention or committed to civil law, including but not limited to persons detained or civilly committed pursuant to the Illinois Sexually Violent Persons Commitment Act, 725 ILCS 207/1 et seq., or the Illinois Sexually Dangerous Persons Act, 725 ILCS 205/0.01 et seq.

(A) Complaint.

(1) Upon written request, the clerk of this court will provide each pro se plaintiff with a complaint form, a petition to proceed in forma pauperis and an instruction sheet. The plaintiff is not required to use the court's complaint form. No complaint will be rejected for filing because of improper form or because of failure to comply with Local Rules. However, failure to comply with Local Rules may result in dismissal of the plaintiff's case by the Court.

(2) The plaintiff's complaint may be handwritten or typed. However, the original complaint, as well as all pleadings, must be legible and signed by the plaintiff. If there is more than one plaintiff, each must sign the complaint. A complaint need not be notarized. How-ever, if the complaint contains false statements of material fact, the plaintiff may be subject to dismissal of the case or other sanctions.

(3) All copies of the original complaint provided by the plaintiff must be carbon copies or photocopies. No other copies, such as handwritten copies, will be accepted.

(4) The complaint should set forth a short and plain statement of the plaintiff's claim(s) showing that the plaintiff is entitled to relief. A short statement of names, dates and facts about what each defendant did will usually be enough. Legal argument and case citations are not necessary. If the Court requires additional information about a claim, the plaintiff will be ordered to provide a more complete statement. The complaint should also state what relief the plaintiff seeks, and if known, the grounds for the court's jurisdiction.

(5) The complaint should include the full first and last name of each defendant to be served and a full address where that defendant may be served, usually a work address. Failure of the plaintiff, without good cause, to timely and adequately identify a defendant for service will result in dismissal of that defendant from the case.

(6) The plaintiff should mail the complaint, along with the filing fee or the petition to proceed in forma pauperis, together in one package to: CLERK, U.S. DISTRICT COURT in the division in which the claim arose.

(7) The clerk will file the complaint upon receipt, regardless of the form of the complaint and regardless of whether the complaint is accompanied by payment of the filing fee or a petition to proceed in forma pauperis.

(B) Payment of Fees and Other Costs.

(1) If the plaintiff files a complaint without the filing fee or a petition to proceed in forma pauperis, a deficiency order will enter directing the plaintiff to either pay the filing fee or file a petition to proceed in forma pauperis. Failure to comply will result in dismissal of the case.

(2) If the plaintiff is a prisoner under 28 U.S.C. § 1915(h) and files a petition to proceed in forma pauperis which demonstrates inability to pay the filing fee, the petition will be granted and an initial partial filing fee will be assessed in accordance with 28 U.S.C. § 1915(b). The agency having custody of the plaintiff will be directed to pay the initial partial filing fee from the plaintiff's prison account and to forward monthly payments from that account in accordance with 28 U.S.C. § 1915(b). If the plaintiff is not a prisoner under 28 U.S.C. § 1915(h), this provision does not apply.

(3) All requests for file-stamped copies of documents must be accompanied by a stamped, self-addressed envelope and an extra copy to be file-stamped and returned.

(4) *Security for Costs.*

(a) In any case removed to this court under the provisions of 28 U.S.C. §§ 1441 or 1443 in which the plaintiff is a pro se prisoner who has been barred from proceeding in forma pauperis under the provisions of 28 U.S.C. § 1915(g), and who does not meet the exception of that section, the court may require security from the plaintiff for payment of costs.

(b) The court may require security for payment of costs from any plaintiff, regardless of whether that plaintiff is barred from proceeding in forma pauperis under 28 U.S.C. § 1915(g), where the court determines that such plaintiff: 1) has filed three or more prior actions in federal court that were dismissed as frivolous, malicious, or for failure to state a federal claim for relief; or, 2) has unpaid costs or sanctions assessed in a prior federal case. This section does not limit the court's power to require security in other appropriate cases.

(c) The security may be in the form of cash or a surety bond with corporate or justified sureties acceptable to the court. Failure by the plaintiff to provide the required security may result in the dismissal of the action.

(C) Case Management Order. If practicable, the Court will conduct a review of the complaint before service is ordered, and enter a Case Management Order delineating the viable claims stated, if any. At any time a Case Management Order is issued by the court defining the remaining claims in the case, the case will proceed solely on those claims identified in the Case Management Order. Any claims not defined in the Case Management Order will not be included in the case, except in the Court's discretion on motion by a party for good cause shown, or pursuant to Federal Rule of Civil Procedure 15.

(D) Service of Process. In cases proceeding in forma pauperis, after the complaint is filed and a Case Management Order enters, if any, a Scheduling Order will enter directing service of the complaint. Generally, waivers of service will be sought from the defendants in lieu of personal service. If a defendant fails to return a signed waiver of service, personal service will be attempted on that defendant, with the costs of personal service assessed against that defendant to the extent allowed under the Federal Rules of Civil Procedure.

If the full statutory filing fee is paid, the plaintiff is responsible for arranging for service.

(E) Answer.

(1) When the State of Illinois, any of its officers, agents, departments or employees is a defendant, a responsive pleading must be filed within 60 days of service or within 60 days of the date the waiver of service was sent, as the case may be. All other defendants, including officers and employees of counties and municipalities, must answer or otherwise plead within 21 days of personal service, or within 60 days after a waiver of service is sent, as the case may be. A motion to dismiss is not an answer. The answer must be considered a responsive pleading under Federal Rule of Civil Procedure 15(a) and should include all defenses appropriate under the Federal Rules. It is the responsibility of the individual named as a defendant to arrange for representation within that time limit. The Court will not extend the time for answer unless exceptional circumstances are shown. Default may be entered against defendants who do not answer within the time limits.

(2) In civil rights cases where the pro se plaintiff is a prisoner or civil detainee, the answer and subsequent pleadings will be to the issues stated in the Case Management Order accompanying the process and complaint, if such an order is entered. A defendant need not parse the complaint and respond to it. If no Case Management Order has entered, the responsive pleading will be to the complaint.

(F) Scheduling Conference. A scheduling order directing service of the complaint will also set the case for a scheduling conference. At the scheduling conference, the parties will be prepared to argue all pending motions; determine whether all parties have been correctly designated and properly served; discuss the course and progress of discovery and resolve any disputes; determine whether a jury demand has been timely filed; set firm dates for the completion of discovery and the filing of case-dispositive motions. At the conclusion of the scheduling conference, the court will set the matter for further status conference or will set scheduling deadlines. Scheduling conferences will be held by telephone or video unless otherwise ordered by the court.

(G) Status Conference. A status conference may be set at any time by the court. At a status conference the parties will be prepared to argue all pending motions; discuss the progress of discovery and resolve any disputes; review dates for the completion of discovery and the filing of case-dispositive motions. Status conferences will be held by telephone or video unless otherwise ordered by the court.

(H) Motions. The parties are responsible for filing motions within the deadlines set by the Court. Responses to motions must be filed within 14 days, or a party must file a timely motion for extension of time to respond, that is within the time set for response. Motions to file "instanter" are not viewed favorably by the Court and will not be allowed routinely. Motions will not be specially set or noticed for hearing. The court may rule on any motion after the time for response has passed, whether a response is on file or not. At his or her discretion, the presiding judge may set any motion for hearing.

(I) Final Pretrial Conference.

(1) As soon as practicable after the close of discovery and the resolution of dispositive motions, the presiding judge will set the case for final pretrial conference. All discovery MUST BE COMPLETED before the conference is held. Appropriate sanctions will be imposed upon any party failing to complete discovery as ordered. No case-dispositive motions will be accepted after the cut-off date for the filing of such motions, except by leave of court and a showing of extraordinary circumstances, e.g., a recently decided relevant court opinion or newly discovered evidence that with due diligence could not have been found during the time allotted for discovery. The conference must be by personal appearance, by telephone, or by video as directed by the Court, with the plaintiff, if not represented, and with the attorneys who will try the case.

(2) The following documents are to be prepared and exchanged between the litigants, BUT NOT FILED WITH THE COURT, at least 30 days before the date set for the final pretrial conference.

(a) A statement of uncontested facts.

(b) A statement of contested issues of fact and law.

(c) An itemized statement of damages (plaintiff only).

(d) A list of names and addresses of witnesses that each party intends to call to testify at trial, including the names of expert witnesses.

(e) A list of names and addresses of witnesses for whom subpoenas are requested, and a brief summary of the expected testimony of each such witness.

(f) A list of names, registration numbers (if applicable), and addresses of prisoner or detainee witnesses from whom writs of habeas corpus ad testificandum are requested, and a brief summary of the facts to which each such witness will testify.

(g) A list of exhibits, sequentially numbered, which each party intends to offer into evidence.

(h) A list of all demonstrative aids to be used at the trial.

(3) An attorney for the defendants must prepare a proposed final pretrial order based on the documents described above and must file the proposed final pretrial order at least 14 days before the final pretrial conference. A suggested form of the order is included as Appendix 2 to these Rules. As far as is practicable, the litigants are encouraged to resolve any disputes concerning the order prior to the conference.

When the plaintiff is represented by counsel, a final, agreed-to order will be presented at the conference.

(4) At the final pretrial conference, the presiding judge and the litigants will consider the following:

(a) The prospects of settlement. Plaintiff will make a definite demand for settlement and defendants will have authority to make a definite offer of settlement.

(b) Simplification of the issues for trial;

(c) The final witness lists, including the issuance of subpoenas and writs for witnesses;

(d) Any problems of evidence;

(e) Limitation on the number of expert witnesses;

(f) The desirability and timing of trial briefs;

(g) Such other matters that may aid in the fair and expeditious trial and disposition of the action;

(h) The estimated length of trial.

(5) In cases to be tried to a jury, the parties will submit an agreed set of jury instructions, unless otherwise directed by the court. Instructions upon which the parties are unable to agree will be submitted separately by each party, unless excused by the presiding judge. Each instruction will be appropriately numbered and on a separate sheet of 8½″ by 11″ (letter size) paper; will cover no more than one subject; will identify the source and authority upon which it is based; and will have the name of the party submitting it noted at the bottom of the page.

(6) Changes or amendments to the proposed final pretrial order will be made at the final pretrial conference. At the close of the pretrial conference, the parties and the presiding judge will sign the pretrial order. The court may direct that the parties' signatures be electronically affixed to the final pretrial order if the parties have not appeared in person for the final pretrial conference. The signed pretrial order takes the place of all prior pleadings. Any issue not contained in the final pretrial order WILL NOT BE TRIED. The parties are cautioned to consider the contents of the order very carefully, especially as to jury demand, types of damages sought, claims and defenses.

(7) A sample form of pretrial order is contained in Local Rules Appendix 2. The parties are cautioned to conform their pretrial order to the sample format.

(J) Sanctions. Failure of counsel or parties, if not represented by counsel, to appear at any scheduled pretrial conference, including telephone conferences, or otherwise to comply with the provisions of this Rule, may result in dismissal, default, awarding of attorney's fees and costs and such other sanctions as may be appropriate.

(K) Change of Address. Every pro se plaintiff must notify the clerk of this court in writing of any change of address during the entire pendency of his case. Failure to notify the clerk of a change of address will result in the dismissal of the case.

(L) **Waiver.** A plaintiff may request a waiver of any of the provisions of this rule by filing a motion with the clerk of this court stating in brief what requirements the plaintiff wants waived and why. The Court will consider each motion individually; however, motions to waive these requirements will not be routinely allowed.

[Effective January 20, 2010. Amended effective June 2, 2010.]

RULE 16.4. ALTERNATIVE DISPUTE RESOLUTION

(A) **General.** The court adopts these Rules pursuant to the Alternative Dispute Resolution Act of 1998 to make available to litigants a program of court-annexed dispute resolution processes designed to provide quick, inexpensive and satisfying alternatives to engaging in continuing litigation.

The court establishes mediation, summary jury trials and summary bench trials as the forms of alternative dispute resolution ("ADR") available to the litigants in this court. These are available in all civil actions, including adversary proceedings and contested matters in Bankruptcy being heard by the District Court, except those cases listed in CDIL–LR 16.2(A).

(B) **Definitions.** "Assigned judge" is the judge to whom the case is assigned for trial. The assigned judge will not preside over any form of ADR.

"Mediation" is a non-binding settlement process involving a neutral mediator who assists the parties to overcome obstacles to effective negotiation. In cases assigned to a district judge, the neutral mediator will normally be the magistrate judge to whom the case is referred.

"Summary jury trial" is a non-binding pretrial procedure in which the parties try their cases by narration to a jury with a judge presiding. The verdict or verdicts will serve as an aid in the settlement process.

"Summary bench trial" is a non-binding pretrial procedure consisting of a summarized presentation of a case to a judge whose decision and analysis will serve as an aid to the settlement process.

(C) **The ADR Administrator.** The "ADR Administrator" is a person appointed by the court with full authority and responsibility to direct the program created by these Rules. The ADR Administrator will:

(1) Oversee the operation of the ADR program in this court;

(2) Assign cases to various judges throughout the district for ADR processes;

(3) Prepare application for funding of the ADR program and administer any funds assigned; and

(4) Prepare such reports as may be required by the court or the Administrative Office of the U.S. courts concerning the operation of the program or the use of any funds allocated.

(D) **Referral to ADR.** Parties are encouraged to use the ADR process created by these Rules. At the initial Rule 16 conference, the presiding judge will inform the parties of the availability of ADR processes and will encourage the parties to participate in ADR at an appropriate time. All litigants in civil cases, except those in cases listed in CDIL–LR 16.2(A), are to consider the use of alternative dispute resolution processes at an appropriate stage of the litigation.

(E) **Mediation.**

(1) *Eligible Cases.* Any civil case, including adversary proceedings in bankruptcy, may be referred to mediation.

(2) *Reference to Mediation.* A case may be referred to mediation at any time but only on agreement of the parties.

(3) *Private Mediation.* Nothing in these Rules will prevent the parties from agreeing or contracting to utilize private mediation. The parties will notify the ADR Administrator upon initiating private mediation and within14 days after conclusion of private mediation.

(4) *Neutrality of Mediator.* If at any time the court-assigned mediator becomes aware of or a party raises an issue with respect to the mediator's neutrality, the mediator will either recuse himself or ask the ADR Administrator to determine the validity of the objection. In the event of recusal or well-founded objection, the ADR Administrator will designate another judge to act as mediator.

(5) *Written submissions to the mediator.* Within 7 days prior to the first mediation meeting, parties must submit to the mediator a memorandum setting forth their respective legal and factual positions. Such memoranda will be confidential and will not be disclosed to anyone.

(6) *Attendance.* The attorney who is primarily responsible for each party's case must personally attend all mediation conferences and must be prepared and authorized to discuss all relevant issues, including settlement. The parties must be present unless excused by the mediator. When a party's interest is represented by an insurance company, an authorized representative of the insurance company with full settlement authority must attend. Willful failure of a party to attend the mediation conference will be reported by the mediator to the ADR Administrator for transmittal to the assigned judge, who may impose appropriate sanctions.

(7) *Confidentiality.* The entire mediation process is confidential. Neither the parties nor the mediator may disclose information regarding the process, including terms of settlement, to the court or to third persons unless all parties otherwise agree. Parties, counsel and mediators may, however, respond to confidential inquiries or surveys by persons authorized by the court to evaluate the mediation program. Information provided in such inquiries will remain confidential and will not be identified with particular cases.

The mediation process will be treated as a compromise negotiation for purposes of the Federal Rules of Evidence and corresponding state Rules of evidence. The mediator is disqualified as a witness, consultant, attorney, or expert in any pending or future action relating to the dispute, including action between persons not parties to the mediation process.

(F) **Summary Jury Trial.** Any civil case triable by jury may be assigned for summary jury trial when all parties consent to such a proceeding. Such a proceeding will be conducted by a judge other than the assigned judge.

Summary jury trial is a flexible ADR process. The procedures to be followed should be set in advance by the judge who is to preside in light of the circumstances in the case.

[Effective January 20, 2010.]

RULE 26.2. IMPLEMENTATION OF FED. R. CIV. P. 26

(1) Fed. R. Civ. P. 26 controls the initial stages of discovery/disclosure in this court in all cases filed on or after January 1, 1994 with the exception of the categories of proceedings specified in Fed. R. Civ. P. 26(a)(1)(B). These categories are construed to include the following:

(a) Naturalization proceedings filed as civil cases or proceedings to cancel or revoke citizenship;

(b) Proceedings in bankruptcy;

(c) Proceedings to compel the giving of testimony or production of documents in this district in connection with discovery, or for perpetuation of testimony, for use in a matter pending or contemplated in a district court of another district;

(d) Actions to enforce out-of-state judgments;

(e) Cases exempted by the presiding judge on a case by case basis.

(2) The parties may not agree to opt out of the provisions of Fed. R. Civ. P. 26.

(3) Attorneys in all cases not exempt from Fed. R Civ. P. 26 will comply with Fed. R. Civ. P. 26(f) before the date set by the court for the initial scheduling conference. The parties must produce and file a proposed discovery plan which meets the requirements of Fed. R. Civ. P. 26(f). The attorney for the plaintiff is responsible for arranging the meeting and filing the proposed discovery plan.

[Effective January 20, 2010.]

RULE 26.3. FILING OF DISCOVERY OR DISCLOSURE MATERIALS

(A) Interrogatories under Fed. R. Civ. P. 33 and 26(b)(4), and the answers or objections thereto, requests for production or inspection under Fed. R. Civ. P. 34, and responses or objections thereto, requests for admission under Fed. R. Civ. P. 36, and responses and objections thereto, and depositions under Fed. R. Civ. P. 30 and 31 and disclosures under Rule 26, must not be filed with the clerk of this court except as hereinafter provided.

(B) The party responsible for the service of discovery materials must retain the originals as custodian.

(C) Any motion filed under Fed. R. Civ. P. 26(c) or 37 must be accompanied by the relevant portions of discovery material relied upon or in dispute.

(D) That portion of discovery material necessary to the consideration of a pretrial motion or for a final order on any issue must be filed contemporaneously with the motion or response to the motion and attached to the pleading as an exhibit thereto.

[Effective January 20, 2010.]

RULE 30.1. SCHEDULING OF DEPOSITIONS

In scheduling any deposition, counsel must make a good faith effort to coordinate with all opposing counsel the scheduling of a time that is mutually convenient to all opposing counsel and the parties. The signing and serving of a Notice of Deposition constitutes a certification by the attorney signing and serving the Notice of Deposition that the attorney has complied with this rule.

[Effective January 20, 2010.]

RULE 33.1. INTERROGATORIES

Answers or objections to interrogatories under Fed. R. Civ. P. 33 and 26(b)(4) must set forth in full the interrogatory being answered or objected to immediately preceding the answer or objection. Objections to interrogatories must not be filed with the clerk of this court except as exhibits to motions for protective order or motions to compel pursuant to Fed. R. Civ. P. 26(c) and 37.

[Effective January 20, 2010.]

RULE 37.3. DISCOVERY

(A) The requirement of Rule 37(a)(1) that the parties confer and attempt to resolve discovery disputes and so certify as part of any motion to compel do not apply to cases in which the plaintiff is incarcerated.

(B) The Court will entertain emergency oral motions involving discovery, at the discretion of the presiding judge. These motions will be heard by telephone conference.

[Effective January 20, 2010.]

RULE 38.1. EQUITABLE RELIEF OR JURY DEMAND

The plaintiff, in every civil action in which the complaint prays for any equitable relief, must mark upon the face of the complaint: "Equitable relief is sought;" and if a demand for jury trial under Fed. R. Civ. P. 38 is endorsed upon a pleading, the title of the pleading must include the words "and demand for jury trial."

[Effective January 20, 2010.]

RULE 40.1. ASSIGNMENT OF CASES AND PLACE OF FILING

(A) **Peoria.** All complaints and subsequent filings in cases which arise from the following counties: Bureau, Fulton, Hancock, Knox, Livingston, Marshall, McDonough, McLean, Peoria, Putnam, Stark, Tazewell, and Woodford will be filed at PEORIA, ILLINOIS, and heard by the judges of this court regularly sitting in PEORIA, ILLINOIS.

(B) **Springfield.** All complaints and subsequent filings in cases which arise from the following counties: Adams, Brown, Cass, Christian, DeWitt, Greene, Logan, Macoupin, Mason, Menard, Montgomery, Morgan, Pike, Sangamon, Schuyler, Scott, and Shelby, will be filed at SPRINGFIELD, ILLINOIS, and heard by judges of this court regularly sitting at SPRINGFIELD, ILLINOIS.

(C) **Rock Island.** All complaints and subsequent filings in cases which arise from the following counties: Henderson, Henry, Mercer, Rock Island, and Warren will be filed at ROCK ISLAND, ILLINOIS, and heard by the judges of this court regularly sitting at ROCK ISLAND, ILLINOIS.

(D) **Urbana.** All complaints and subsequent filings in cases which arise from the following counties: Champaign, Coles, Douglas, Edgar, Ford, Iroquois, Kankakee, Macon, Moultrie, Piatt, and Vermillion will be filed at URBANA, ILLINOIS, and heard by the judges of this court regularly sitting at URBANA, ILLINOIS.

(E) All complaints and subsequent filings in cases filed in the Central District of Illinois must identify in the caption of such pleading or document, the division in which the case is pending.

(F) As part of the statement of jurisdiction, the initial pleadings in each case must state the basis for filing in the division selected.

[Effective January 20, 2010.]

RULE 42.1. CONSOLIDATION AND TRANSFER OF RELATED CASES

When a party or counsel for a party knows that a newly filed case is related to another case already pending in the district, the parties are responsible for bringing the matter to the court's attention at the first opportunity but not later than the Rule 16 discovery conference or the first motion hearing, whichever occurs earliest. Consolidation of the cases will be considered at that time.

Later-filed cases may be transferred to the judge assigned to the first-filed suit, regardless of whether the cases are consolidated.

[Effective January 20, 2010.]

RULE 45.1. ISSUANCE OF BLANK SUBPOENAS

In a Civil Case, the Clerk must not issue blank subpoenas to a pro se party except upon order of the judge to whom the case is assigned.

Note on Use

Under Rule 45.2 ILCD, a pro se litigant may move the court, either orally or in writing, to issue a subpoena for specific witnesses or documents. The pro se litigant must present the court orally or in writing with a statement of what relevant information the documents contain or the person to be subpoenaed possesses.

[Effective January 20, 2010.]

RULE 47.2. COMMUNICATIONS WITH JURORS

(1) Before and during trial, no attorney, party or representative of either, may contact, converse or otherwise communicate with a juror or potential juror on any subject, whether pertaining to the case or not.

(2) No attorney, party, or representative of either may interrogate a juror after the verdict has been returned without prior approval of the presiding judge. Approval of the presiding judge may be sought only by application made by counsel orally in open court or upon written motion which states the grounds and the purpose of the interrogation. If a post-verdict interrogation of one or more of the members of the jury should be approved, the scope of the interrogation and other appropriate limitations upon

the interrogation will be determined by the presiding judge prior to the interrogation.

[Effective January 20, 2010.]

RULE 47.3. CONDUCT BEFORE THE JURY

All attempts to curry favor with jurors by fawning, flattery, or pretending solicitude for their personal comfort are unprofessional. Suggestions of counsel regarding the comfort or convenience of jurors and propositions to dispense with argument or peremptory challenges must be made to the presiding judge out of the jury's hearing.

[Effective January 20, 2010.]

RULE 48.1. NUMBER OF JURORS

In all jury cases, except as may be otherwise required by law or controlling Rule, the jury will consist of no less than six members.

[Effective January 20, 2010.]

RULE 51.1. PROPOSED INSTRUCTIONS TO JURY

(1) All requests for jury instructions not previously tendered must be submitted to the presiding judge at the conclusion of all the evidence with copies submitted to all parties.

(2) The instructions read to the jury by the presiding judge will accompany the jury to the jury room when the jury retires for deliberation unless otherwise determined by the presiding judge.

[Effective January 20, 2010.]

RULE 54.1. REQUESTS FOR ATTORNEYS FEES AND BILLS OF COSTS

(A) **Time for Requests.** In all civil cases, requests for attorneys fees must be filed no later than 14 days after entry of judgment. Bills of Costs must be filed within 30 days after entry of judgment.

(B) **Form.** Bills of costs and supporting documentation may be filed in any format, but must include Form AO–133 as a summary.

[Effective January 20, 2010.]

RULE 67.2. ORDERS DIRECTING INVESTMENT OF FUNDS BY THE CLERK

(A) Any order obtained by a party that directs the clerk of this court to invest in an interest-bearing account or instrument, funds deposited with the Reg-

istry Account of the court pursuant to 28 U.S.C. § 2041 will include the following:

(1) the amount to be invested;

(2) the name of the bank or financial institution where the funds are to be invested;

(3) the type of account or instrument in which the funds are to be invested; and

(4) the terms of the investment.

(B) Before an order is entered directing the Clerk of Court to invest Registry Funds in an interest-bearing account, counsel must file a copy of such proposed order with the Financial Deputy or Financial Administrator in the division where the action is pending. Failure of the party to serve a copy of the order to invest funds at interest will absolve the clerk and his or her deputies from any civil liability for the loss of any interest which might have been earned on the funds resulting from a late deposit due to failure to serve a copy of the order as required above.

(C) The clerk will invest the funds within 7 working days of the filing of the order. The 7–day limit may be extended by order of the court should the funds to be invested surpass the $100,000 FDIC insurance level.

(D) Before an order is entered directing the Clerk to release funds deposited in the Registry Funds of the court or in an interest-bearing account, the party must file a copy of such proposed order with the Financial Deputy or Financial Administrator in the division where the action is pending. The order must specify the amount to be paid, the name of the person or persons to whom payment is to be made, and the name and address of the person or persons to whom the check is to be delivered.

(E) The Clerk of Court will deduct from income earned on registry funds invested in interest-bearing accounts or instruments, a fee not exceeding that authorized by the Judicial Conference of the United States and set by the Director of the Administrative Office in accordance with the schedule which will be published periodically by the Director in the Federal Register. The fee will be withdrawn whenever income earned becomes available for deduction and will be deposited in the United States Treasury, without further order of the court. This assessment applies to all registry fund investments.

[Effective January 20, 2010.]

RULE 72.1. UNITED STATES MAGISTRATE JUDGES

(A) **Duties.** A magistrate judge in this district is authorized to perform all the duties in 28 U.S.C. § 636 and is designated to:

(1) upon the consent of the defendant, try either jury or non-jury cases of persons accused of misdemeanors and infractions committed within this district in accordance with 18 U.S.C. § 3401, and conduct all post-trial proceedings therein as may be warranted;

(2) conduct proceedings for commitment to another district and issue Commitments to Another District in accordance with Fed. R. Crim. P. 40;

(3) conduct extradition proceedings in accordance with 18 U.S.C. § 3184;

(4) order competency examinations of defendants pursuant to 18 U.S.C. § 4244;

(5) supervise proceedings conducted pursuant to letters of request, in accordance with 28 U.S.C. § 1782;

(6) hear and determine any non-dispositive pretrial motion pursuant to 28 U.S.C. § 636(b)(1)(A);

(7) conduct hearings, including such evidentiary hearings as are necessary or appropriate, and submit to a district judge proposed findings of fact and recommendations for the disposition of dispositive motions that are excepted in 28 U.S.C. § 636(b)(1)(A) in accordance with 28 U.S.C. § 636(b)(1)(B) and (C);

(8) exercise the powers enumerated in Rules 5, 8, 9 and 10 of the Rules Governing Section 2254 and Section 2255 Proceedings;

(9) upon the consent of the parties pursuant to 28 U.S.C. § 636(c), conduct any or all proceedings in a jury or non-jury civil matter and order the entry of judgment in the case;

(10) exercise general supervision of the civil and criminal calendars of the court, conduct calendar and status calls, and determine motions to expedite or postpone the trial of cases for the district judges;

(11) conduct pretrial conferences, settlement conferences, summary jury trials, omnibus hearings, and related pretrial proceedings;

(12) conduct arraignments in cases not triable by the magistrate judge to the extent of taking a not guilty plea or noting a defendant's intention to plead guilty or nolo contendere and ordering a presentence report in appropriate cases;

(13) receive grand jury returns in accordance with Fed. R. Crim. P. 6(f);

(14) upon the consent of the parties conduct voir dire and select petit juries for the court;

(15) accept petit jury verdicts in civil cases in the absence of a district judge;

(16) issue subpoenas, writs of habeas corpus ad testificandum or habeas corpus ad prosequendum, or other orders necessary to obtain the presence of parties or witnesses or evidence needed for court proceedings;

(17) order the exoneration or forfeiture of bonds;

(18) conduct proceedings for the collection of civil penalties of not more than $200 assessed under the Federal Boat Safety Act of 1971, in accordance with 46 U.S.C. § 1484(d);

(19) conduct examinations of judgment debtors, in accordance with Fed. R. Civ. P. 69;

(20) impose sanctions under Fed. R. Civ. P. 11, 16, and 37, except for dismissal or contempt;

(21) authorize the withdrawal of funds from the Court's Registry;

(22) perform any additional duty that is not inconsistent with the Constitution and laws of the United States;

(23) conduct scheduling conferences pursuant to Rule 16 and enter, vacate or modify scheduling orders;

(24) accept guilty pleas in felony cases with the consent of the defendant and the United States Attorney, order a presentence investigation report, and file a report and recommendation with the District Court.

[Effective January 20, 2010.]

RULE 72.2. REVIEW AND APPEAL FROM MAGISTRATE JUDGES

(A) Appeal of Non–Dispositive Matters. Any party may appeal from any order of a magistrate judge within 14 days after service of the order appealed from. Such an appeal must specifically designate the order appealed from and the basis for any objection. The appeal must be accompanied by a memorandum of law in support. Any party opposing the appeal must, within 14 days after service of the appeal, file a memorandum of law in opposition.

(B) Review of Dispositive Motions. Any party may object to a magistrate judge's report and recommendation by filing an objection in accordance with Fed. R. Civ. P. 72(b) within 14 days after service thereof. Such objection must specifically identify the portions of the report and recommendation to which objection is made and the basis for the objection and must be accompanied by a memorandum of law in support of the objection. Any party who opposes the objection must file a memorandum of law in opposition within 14 days after service of the objection. Failure to file an objection to a report and recommendation constitutes waiver of further review of the issue.

[Effective January 20, 2010.]

RULE 79.1. CUSTODY AND DISPOSITION OF MODELS AND EXHIBITS

(A) Custody. After being received into evidence, or offered and refused admission, all models, diagrams, exhibits and material forming part of the evidence in any cause pending or tried in this court, will be placed in the custody of the clerk of this court, unless otherwise ordered by the presiding judge.

(B) Removal. All models, diagrams, exhibits or material placed in the custody of the clerk of this court must be taken away by the attorney or party if not represented by an attorney, who offered them within 60 days after the case is decided unless an appeal is taken. In all cases in which an appeal is taken, they must be taken away within 30 days after the filing of the mandate of the reviewing court which disposes of the case. At the time of removal, a detailed receipt must be given to the clerk of this court and filed in the cause. If bulky exhibits are included in the evidence received or offered, the presiding judge may order that a photograph be taken of the bulky exhibit and the photograph be placed in the record in place of the bulky item.

(C) Neglect to Remove. If an attorney or a party, if not represented by an attorney, neglects to remove any models, diagrams, exhibits or materials within 30 days after notice from the clerk of this court, they may be sold by the clerk of this court at public or private sale or otherwise disposed of as the presiding judge may direct. If they are sold, the proceeds, less the expense of the sale, will be paid into the Registry of the Court pending further order of the presiding judge.

[Effective January 20, 2010.]

RULE 79.2. ACCESS TO RECORDS AND PAPERS

(A) Withdrawal of Original Documents. No person, other than an employee of this court in the exercise of official duty, will withdraw any original pleading, paper, record, model or exhibit from the custody of the clerk of this court or other employee of this court having custody thereof, except upon written order of a judge of this court, and upon leaving a proper receipt with the clerk of this court or employee.

(B) Public Access. Electronic access to the electronic docket and to documents filed in the System is available to the public at no charge at the Clerk's Office during regular business hours. A copy fee for an electronic reproduction is required in accordance with 28 U.S.C. § 1930. Public remote electronic access to the System for viewing purposes is limited to subscribers to the Public Access to Court Electronic Records ("PACER") system, which charges a user fee for remotely accessing certain detailed case information. Conventional copies and certified copies of electronically filed documents may be purchased by the public at the Clerk's Office. The fee for copying and certifying will be in accordance with 28 U.S.C. § 1914.

[Effective January 20, 2010.]

RULE 83.1. RULE MAKING

This court will from time to time adopt Local Rules of practice. When new Rules or amendments are proposed by the court, they will be offered for comment to the Local Rules Committee of the court. Local Rules will be adopted only after giving appropriate public notice and opportunity for comment. If emergency Rules are promulgated, they will be immediately sent to the Rules Committee for comment.

[Effective January 20, 2010.]

RULE 83.3. COURTROOM DECORUM

(1) During court proceedings, all attorneys may stand when speaking, unless otherwise directed by the presiding judge. All objections and comments thereon will be addressed to the presiding judge. There will be no oral confrontation between opposing counsel.

(2) During court proceedings, neither counsel nor parties may leave the courtroom without prior approval of the presiding judge.

[Effective January 20, 2010.]

RULE 83.5. ADMISSION TO PRACTICE

(A) Qualifications for Admission to Practice. Any attorney licensed to practice law in any state or in the District of Columbia must be admitted to practice generally in this court on written motion of a member in good standing of the bar of this court, or upon the attorney's own motion accompanied by certification of good standing from the state in which the attorney is licensed, and upon payment of the fees required by law and by Local Rule 83.5(E). On motion made at the time of the written motion for admission to practice, the presiding judge may waive the admission fees for any attorney employed full time by the United States, any state, or county.

Students of accredited law schools or law school graduates awaiting bar results may, upon written motion of a member in good standing of the bar of this court, be provisionally admitted to practice and may appear in this court under the supervision and direction of the sponsoring attorney. There will be no fee for provisional admission.

(B) Oath. All attorneys must, at the time of their admission to practice before this court, take an oath or affirmation to support the Constitution of the United States, faithfully to discharge their duties as attorneys and counselors, and to demean themselves uprightly and according to law and the recognized standards of ethics of the profession, and they must, under the direction of the clerk of this court, sign the oath of attorneys and pay the fees required by law and by Local Rule 83.5(E).

(C) Admission to Practice in All Divisions. Admission to practice generally in this court includes all divisions.

(D) Reciprocal Admission. Any attorney admitted to practice in District Courts of the Northern or Southern Districts of Illinois must be admitted to practice generally in this court upon the attorney's own motion accompanied by a copy of his/her admission certificate from the district in which the attorney is admitted, the attorney's certification that he/she is in good standing generally and upon payment of the fees required by law and Local Rule 83.5(E). Upon motion for reciprocal admission being allowed by the Court, movant will be summarily admitted to the CDIL bar.

(E) Fees Assessed Upon Admission. Each petitioner shall pay an admission fee upon the filing of the motion for admission, provided that in the event the petitioner is not admitted, the petitioner may request that the fee be refunded. The amount of the fee shall be established by the court, in conjunction with the fee prescribed by the Judicial Conference of the United States pursuant to 28 U.S.C. § 1914.

(F) Admission Pro Hac Vice. The court does not permit pro hac vice admissions generally. At the discretion of the presiding judge, an attorney who is duly licensed to practice in any state or the District of Columbia may file a motion seeking leave to participate in a case while his or her application for admission to practice in the Central District of Illinois is pending. The application for admission must be submitted contemporaneously with the motion for leave.

(G) Unauthorized Practice. All attorneys who appear in person or by filing pleadings in this court must be admitted to practice in this court in accordance with this Rule. Only attorneys so admitted may practice or file pleadings in this court. Except as provided in Local Rule 83.5(F), upon entry of appearance as an attorney of record, the entry of appearance must include a certification that the attorney is a member in good standing of the bar of this court.

Any person who, before his or her admission to the bar of this court, or during his or her suspension or disbarment, exercises in this district any of the privileges of a member of the bar in any action or proceedings pending in this court, or who pretends to be entitled to do so, may be adjudged guilty of contempt of court and appropriately sanctioned.

(H) Changes Reported to the Clerk of This Court. If at any time after admission any relevant circumstances change for an attorney (e.g., name, address, phone number, e-mail address, disciplinary status), he or she must notify the clerk of this court in writing of such change within 14 days.

(I) Admission. Admission may be in person, by mail, or electronically. Procedures for admission will be prescribed by the clerk of this court. Admission is deemed to be as of the date the oath card is received by the clerk.

(J) Pro Bono Panel. The Pro Bono Panel of this court consists of all attorneys admitted to practice in this court whose place of business is in the Central District of Illinois. Attorneys employed full time by the United States, the State of Illinois or a county are exempt from service on the panel. Attorneys appointed pro bono to represent litigants may not enter into any contingent fee arrangement with their clients concerning the subject case. Statutory fees and expenses may be awarded to a pro bono attorney as provided by law.

Any attorney appointed to represent an indigent party in a civil proceeding before this Court may petition the Court for reimbursement of expenses incurred in preparation and presentation of the proceeding, subject to the procedures and regulations contained in the plan of this Court adopted June 1, 2000, governing reimbursement of expenses from the District Court Fund.

[Effective January 20, 2010. Amended effective April 19, 2013.]

RULE 83.6. ATTORNEY DISCIPLINE

This court, in furtherance of its inherent power and responsibility to supervise the conduct of attorneys who are admitted to practice before it, promulgates the following Rule superseding all of its other Rules pertaining to disciplinary enforcement heretofore promulgated.

(A) Discipline. When it is shown to a judge of this court that any member of the bar of this court has been suspended or disbarred from practice in any other court of record, or has been guilty of conduct unbecoming a member of the bar of this court, the member will be subject to suspension, disbarment, or other appropriate disciplinary action by the court. The member will be afforded an opportunity to show good cause, within such time as the court will prescribe, why the member should not be suspended, disbarred, or otherwise disciplined. Upon the member's response to the Rule to show cause, and after hearing, if requested, or upon expiration of the time prescribed for a response if no response is made, the court will enter an appropriate order.

(B) Appointment of Counsel. The court will appoint an attorney from its pro bono panel to prosecute its interests under this Rule.

(C) Other Sanctions. Notwithstanding this Rule, but in supplement to it, the judges of this court may impose sanctions against a member of the bar of this court pursuant to Fed. R. Civ. P. 37 and 16 and initiate civil or criminal contempt proceedings when appropriate.

(D) Rules of Professional Conduct. The Rules of Professional Conduct adopted by this court are the Rules of Professional Conduct adopted by the Supreme Court of Illinois, as amended from time to time by that court, except as otherwise provided by specific Rule of this court after consideration of comments by representatives of bar associations within the state.

[Effective January 20, 2010.]

RULE 83.7. POSSESSION AND/OR USE OF ELECTRONIC DEVICES WITHIN THE COURTHOUSE

Definition. "Electronic Devices," as used within this Rule, includes cameras, video recorders, audio recorders, cellular or digital phones, palm pilots and PDAs, computers, and all similar electronic, cable, digital, computerized or other forms and methods of recording, transmitting, or communicating.

(A) Prohibitions. No electronic devices will be permitted into the courthouse subject to the exceptions below. To avert delays in security screening in the lobby, those entering the courthouse are strongly urged to heed this prohibition, because such devices will not be held within the courthouse.

News media representatives wishing to conduct interviews in relation to a court case may contact the presiding judge to seek permission to bring electronic equipment into the building for that purpose. If permission is granted, the judge will designate a specific area of the courthouse where such electronic equipment may be stored and used. After the interviews are completed the equipment must be immediately removed from the courthouse.

(B) Exceptions.

(1) This Rule may be suspended for naturalization or other ceremonial proceedings or otherwise as ordered by the presiding judge.

(2) Attorneys are allowed to possess and carry electronic devices within the courthouse (upon showing proper identification to court security personnel at the front desk) and in the courtrooms. However, such equipment will not be used in a courtroom without the permission of the presiding judge, and such equipment may not in any event be used to record or transmit court proceedings by audio, visual, or other means. Also, an attorney may not allow any other person (e.g., a client, whether in custody or not) to use the attorney's cell phone or other electronic device in the courthouse.

(3) This Rule does not apply to official court reporters in the performance of their official duties. Any use of recording or transcription services or equipment other than by the official court reporters must be approved by the presiding judge.

(4) This Rule does not apply to the United States Marshal, Deputy U.S. Marshals, Court Security Officers, law enforcement personnel known to Court Security Officers upon production of proper identification, and employees of the Illinois Department of Corrections who have transported state prisoners to court.

Note: This Rule does apply to prospective jurors.

[Effective January 20, 2010.]

RULE 83.8. PROHIBITION OF FIREARMS IN COURTROOMS

(A) No one, except a Deputy United States Marshal acting in the scope of employment, will possess any firearm or other weapon in any courtroom of this court.

(B) Deputy United States Marshals are directed to take and secure any firearm or other weapon from anyone, including law enforcement officers, before admittance to any courtroom.

(C) Law enforcement officers, other than employees of the United States Marshal Service, may possess firearms or other weapons in a courtroom in this district only with the express authorization of the United States Marshal or his or her designee.

[Effective January 20, 2010.]

RULE 83.9. COURT REPORTING FEES

A current schedule of transcript fees, as established by the Judicial Conference of the United States, is posted in each office of the clerk of this court and is available from the official court reporters.

[Effective January 20, 2010.]

RULE 83.10. STANDING COMMITTEES

(A) Committee on Local Rules. The court will appoint a committee from the bar of the district to review and give comment on Local Rules. The committee will meet at least once a year to review the existing Rules, propose any changes, and to give comment on changes proposed by the court.

(B) Advisory Committee Under the Civil Justice Reform Act. The court will appoint a committee from the district to carry out the duties required by the Civil Justice Reform Act of 1990, 28 U.S.C. § 471 et seq. The United States Attorney, or his or her designee, will be a permanent member; other members will serve not more than four years. Members will be representative geographically and of major litigation groups within the district. At least one member will be a non-attorney.

[Effective January 20, 2010.]

RULE 83.11. TRANSMISSION OF PLEADINGS BY FACSIMILE NOT ALLOWED

No pleading, motion, or other document shall be transmitted to the court or the office of the clerk of the court by means of electronic facsimile.

[Effective June 2, 2010.]

RULE 83.12. ADVANCE PAYMENT OF FEES

Except as may now or hereafter be required or permitted by law, by direction of the Judicial Conference of the United States, or by special order of the court in exceptional circumstances, the fees required by Section 1914 of Title 28 of the United States Code will be paid to the clerk of this court in advance of filing the document or documents involved.

[Effective January 20, 2010.]

RULE 83.13. PAYMENT OF COSTS IN ACTIONS BY POOR PERSONS

At the time application is made under 28 U.S.C. § 1915 for leave to commence any civil action without being required to prepay fees and costs or give security for the same, the applicant and his or her attorney must enter into an agreement to be filed with the court that any recovery secured in the action will be paid into the hands of the clerk of this court, who will pay therefrom all unpaid costs taxed against the plaintiff and remit the balance to the attorney of record for the plaintiff, or to the plaintiff if unrepresented. If the attorney has filed notice with the clerk that a contingent fee contract has been entered into by the plaintiff, the balance will be paid to the plaintiff and the attorney in accordance with the order of the presiding judge.

[Effective January 20, 2010.]

RULE 83.14. ASSESSMENT OF JURY COSTS

If for any reason attributable to counsel or parties, including settlement, the court is unable to commence a jury trial as scheduled where a panel of prospective jurors has reported for the voir dire, or a selected jury reports to try the case, all or part of the costs of the panel, including, but not limited to, mileage, attendance fees, and per diem for each juror reporting for service, may be assessed against the parties and attorneys responsible for the court's inability to proceed. Any monies collected as a result of assessment will be paid to the clerk of this court for transmittal to the Treasury of the United States.

[Effective January 20, 2010.]

RULE 83.15. DISTRICT COURT FUND

The District Court assesses attorneys a special fee determined by the Court at the time of admission to practice in this Court. This fee is established in Local Rule 83.5(E) and deposited in the District Court Fund. The Fund is administered in accordance with the Plan for the Establishment and Administration of the District Court Fund and Regulations Governing Reimbursement from the District Court Fund. The Clerk of this Court is the custodian of the District Court Fund.

[Effective January 20, 2010. Amended effective April 19, 2013.]

RULE 83.16. PRODUCTION AND DISCLOSURE OF DOCUMENTS AND TESTIMONY OF JUDICIAL PERSONNEL IN LEGAL PROCEEDINGS

(A) The purpose of the Rule is to implement the policy of the Judicial Conference of the United States with regard

(1) to the production or disclosure of official information or records by the federal judiciary, and

(2) the testimony of present or former judiciary personnel relating to any official information acquired by any such individual as part of the individual's performance of official duties, or by virtue of that individual's official status, in federal, state, or other legal proceedings.

Implementation of this Rule is subject to the regulations established by the Judicial Conference of the United States which are incorporated herein (a copy of such regulations can be obtained from the Clerk of the Court).

(B) Requests covered by this Rule include an order, subpoena, or other demand of a court or administrative or other authority, or competent jurisdiction, under color of law, or any other request by whatever method, for the production, disclosure, or release of information or records by the federal judiciary, or for the appearance and testimony of federal judicial personnel as witnesses as to matters arising out of the performance of their official duties, in legal proceedings. This includes requests for voluntary production or testimony in the absence of any legal process.

(C) This Rule does not apply to requests by members of the public, when properly made through the procedures established by the court for records or documents, such as court files or dockets, routinely made available to members of the public for inspection or copying.

(D) Any request for testimony or production of records must set forth a written statement by the party seeking the testimony of production of records containing an explanation of the nature of the testimony or records sought, the relevance of the testimony or records sought to the legal proceedings, and the reasons why the testimony or records sought, or the information contained therein, are not readily available from other sources or by other means. This explanation must contain sufficient information for the determining officer to decide whether or not federal judicial personnel should be allowed to testify or the records should be produced. Where the request does not contain an explanation sufficient for this purpose, the determining officer may deny the request or may ask the requester to provide additional information.

The request for testimony or production of records must be provided to the federal judicial personnel from whom testimony or production of records is sought at least 14 days in advance of the time by which the testimony or production of records is to be required. Failure to meet this requirement will provide a sufficient basis for denial of the request.

(E) In the case of a request directed to a district judge, or magistrate judge, or directed to a current or former member of such a judge's personal staff, the determining officer will be the district judge or magistrate judge.

(F) In the case of a request directed to an employee or former employee of a court office, such as the office of the clerk or the probation office, the determining officer will be the unit executive of the particular office. The unit executive consults with the chief judge of the district court for determination of all proper response to a request.

(G) In the case of presentence reports:

(1) In all criminal cases in which sentence is imposed, the presentence report will be made a part of the official court record. The original report, including the recommendation to the court and statement of reasons, will be placed under seal in the record. In the event of an appeal, the report, the recommendation, and the statement of reasons will be sent to the reviewing court under separate seal.

(2) A copy of the presentence report will be made available to appellate counsel on request, under the same terms and conditions as apply to use of the report by counsel in the trial court.

[Effective January 20, 2010.]

CRIMINAL RULES

RULE 12.1. PLEADINGS AND MOTIONS

(A) In the event a defendant desires to file any pretrial motion, the motion supported by a brief must be filed within 21 days of arraignment, or such later time as may be set by the presiding judge.

(B) All written pleadings, motions, and other papers in a criminal case filed in this district must be signed by the attorney of record, in the attorney's individual name, whose address, telephone number, and typed name will also be stated. A defendant who is not represented by counsel must sign pleadings in the same manner.

(C) The signature of an attorney or party constitutes a certificate by the signer that the signer has read the pleading, motion, or other paper; that, to the best of the signer's knowledge, information, and belief formed after reasonable inquiry, it is well-grounded in fact and is warranted by existing law or a good faith argument for the extension, modification, or reversal of existing law, and that it is not interposed for any improper purpose, such as to harass or to cause unnecessary delay or needless increase in the cost of litigation. If a pleading, motion, or other paper is not signed, it will be stricken unless it is signed promptly after the omission is called to the attention of the pleader or movant.

[Effective January 20, 2010.]

RULE 16.1. RULE FOR PRETRIAL DISCOVERY AND INSPECTION

(A) Within 7 days after the arraignment in any criminal case, the United States Attorney and the attorney(s) for the defendant(s) will confer, and, will comply with Federal Rule of Criminal Procedure 16.

(B) If, in the judgment of the United States Attorney, it would not be in the interests of justice to make any one or more disclosures as set forth in Section (A) as requested by counsel for the defendant(s), disclosure may be declined. A declination of any requested disclosure must be in writing directed to counsel for defendant(s), and signed by the Assistant United States Attorney in charge of the prosecution, and must specify the disclosure that is declined. A defendant seeking to challenge the declination will proceed pursuant to Section (D) below.

(C) If additional discovery or inspection is sought, attorney(s) for the defendant(s) will confer with the appropriate Assistant United States Attorney within 14 days of the arraignment (or such later time as may be set by the presiding judge for the filing of pretrial motions) with a view to satisfying those requests in a cooperative atmosphere without recourse to the court.

The request must be in writing, and the United States Attorney will respond in a like manner.

(D) In the event a defendant thereafter moves for additional discovery or inspection, a motion to compel discovery supported by a brief must be filed within 14 days of the arraignment (or such later time as may be set by the presiding judge for the filing of pretrial motions). It must contain:

(1) the statement that the prescribed conference was held;

(2) the date of the conference;

(3) the name of the Assistant United States Attorney with whom the conference was held; and

(4) the statement that agreement could not be reached concerning the discovery or inspection sought.

[Effective January 20, 2010.]

RULE 16.2. RULE FOR USE OF PRETRIAL DISCOVERY MATERIALS IN CRIMINAL CASES

(A) This Rule shall apply only to pretrial discovery materials (hereinafter, "materials") provided to the defendant:

(1) prior to a request by the defendant to the United States Attorney's Office for discovery pursuant to Rule 16 of the Federal Rules of Criminal Procedure or earlier than required by any other rule, statute, or the Constitution of the United States; or

(2) which the government is not obligated to provide to the defendant by rule, statute, or the Constitution of the United States.

(B) Any pretrial discovery materials provided to the defendant pursuant to this Rule:

(1) shall not be disseminated to any person or used for any purpose other than in direct relationship to the criminal case to which the discovery pertains;

(2) shall not be photocopied, recorded, imaged, or otherwise copied, except a single copy for use by defense counsel and a single copy for use by each of its agents;

(3) shall not be given to, or left in the possession of, the defendant, except to the extent that the defendant may review the discovery in the presence of defense counsel or its agents;

(4) shall be kept in the possession and control of defense counsel or its agents at all times;

(5) shall be returned to the United States Attorney's Office, including all copies, within ten days of the completion of the case before the Court or, if an appeal is taken, within ten days of the completion of the case in the United States Court of Appeals for the

Seventh Circuit or Supreme Court of the United States.

(C) This Rule applies to all materials in "hard copy" and on electronic media, as well as any "hard copies" created by defense counsel from electronic media.

(D) The requirements of this Rule may be modified in a particular case for good cause shown upon written agreement by the parties or by order of the Court.

(E) Violation of this Rule may result in contempt proceedings before the presiding judge.

[Effective June 10, 2013.]

COMMENTS

Section (A) limits the application of this Rule to discovery provided outside the requirements of Federal Rule of Criminal Procedure 16, applicable statutes, or the Constitution of the United States. It is the general practice of the United States Attorney in this District to provide discovery to defense counsel without a formal request or motion pursuant to Rule 16 and beyond what the government is required to disclose by that Rule, statute, or the Constitution. The administration of justice is served by this early and full disclosure. The purpose of this Rule is to encourage early and complete disclosure of material to defendants. A defendant may, however, avoid operation of this Rule by making a formal discovery request as provided for in Rule 16.

The Rule is designed to address concerns similar to those addressed by Illinois Supreme Court Rule 415(c). That rule, entitled "Custody of Materials," provides:

Any materials furnished to an attorney pursuant to these rules shall remain in his exclusive custody and be used only for the purposes of conducting his side of the case, and shall be subject to such other terms and conditions as the court may provide.

134 Ill.2d R. 415(c).

The committee comments for Rule 415(c) reflect the same concerns which this Court seeks to address by the Rule:

If the materials to be provided were to become, in effect, matters of public availability once they had been turned over to counsel for the limited purposes which pretrial disclosures are designed to serve, the administration of criminal justice would likely be prejudiced. Accordingly, this paragraph establishes a mandatory requirement in every case that the material which an attorney receives shall remain in his exclusive custody. While he will undoubtedly have to show it to, or at least discuss it with, others, he is not permitted to furnish them with copies or let them take it from his office.

134 Ill.2d R. 415(c), Committee Comments at 357.

Subsection (B)(1) prohibits dissemination or use of discovery unless it is in direct relationship to the case in which the materials are provided. Note that disclosure is not prohibited; only physical dissemination is prohibited. A defendant is free to discuss or disclose the contents of discovery with anyone, but may not physically distribute the discovery.

Subsection (B)(2) addresses copying materials. This subsection allows defense counsel to make a copy of the materials for himself and a copy for use by each of his agents.

Subsection (B)(3) prohibits materials from being left in the possession of a defendant but does not limit a defendant's right to review discovery in the presence of counsel. This limitation is consistent with the limitation set forth in Illinois Supreme Court Rule 415(c).

Subsection (B)(4), (B)(5), and Section (C) are self-explanatory.

Section (D) allows the Court or the parties by agreement to avoid operation of the Rule should there be a need in a particular case.

Section (E) is the penalty provision of the Rule.

RULE 32.1. IMPLEMENTATION OF SENTENCING GUIDELINES

The following procedures are established to govern sentencing proceedings under the Sentencing Reform Act of 1984, 18 U.S.C. § 3551, et seq.

(A) The sentencing hearing in each criminal case will be scheduled by the presiding judge no earlier than 70 days following the entry of a guilty plea or a verdict of guilty.

(B) It is the obligation of a complaining party to seek resolution of disputed factors or facts through opposing counsel and the assigned probation officer prior to the sentencing hearing.

(C) The presentence investigation report, the statement of reasons in the judgment of conviction, and the probation officer's sentencing recommendation will be sealed unless otherwise directed by the presiding judge.

(D) Unless otherwise ordered by the presiding judge, the probation officer's recommendation on the sentence will not be disclosed.

(E) The presiding judge may seal any other document related to sentencing, or a party may move to seal any such document in accordance with Local Rule 49.9(A).

[Effective January 20, 2010. Amended effective April 19, 2013.]

RULE 49.1. ELECTRONIC FILING AUTHORIZED

Pursuant to Fed. R. Crim. P. 49(b), the court will accept for filing documents submitted, signed or verified by electronic means that comply with the procedures established by this court.

[Effective January 20, 2010.]

RULE 49.2. DEFINITIONS FOR ELECTRONIC FILING

(A) "Case Management/Electronic Case Filing System," also referred to as "the System" or "CM/ECF," means the Internet-based system for filing documents

and maintaining court files in the District Court for the Central District of Illinois.

(B) "Conventional filing" means submitting a document or pleading to the Court or a party in paper or other non-electronic, tangible format. Documents submitted conventionally will be scanned, uploaded, filed and maintained in CM/ECF unless these Rules provide otherwise.

(C) "Electronic filing" means uploading a pleading or document directly from the registered user's computer in Adobe PDF format, using CM/ECF, to file that pleading or document in the Court's case file. Sending a document or pleading to the Court via e-mail does not constitute "electronic filing."

(D) "Notice of Electronic Filing" refers to the notice that is generated automatically by the CM/ECF System at the time a document is filed with the System, setting forth the time of filing, the name of the party and attorney filing the document, the type of document, the text of the docket entry, and an electronic link (hyperlink) to the filed document, which allows recipients to retrieve the document automatically.

(E) "PACER" (Public Access to Court Electronic Records) is the automated system that allows an individual to view, print, and download court docket information via the Internet.

(F) "PDF" refers to a document that exists in Portable Document Format. A document file created with a word processor, or a paper document that has been scanned, first must be converted to portable document format before it can be electronically filed. Converted files contain the extension ".pdf".

[Effective January 20, 2010.]

RULE 49.3. SERVICE BY ELECTRONIC MEANS AUTHORIZED

(A) **Consent.** Registration in the Court's Electronic Case Filing System constitutes a consent to electronic service and notice of all filed documents pursuant to Fed. R. Crim. P. 49(b). When a pleading or other paper is filed electronically, the "Notice of Electronic Filing" generated by the Court's Electronic Case Filing System constitutes service of that document on any person who is a registered participant in that System.

(B) **Non–Registered Parties.** A party who is not a registered participant of the System is entitled to a paper copy of any electronically filed pleading, document, or order. The filing party must therefore provide the non-registered party with the pleading, document, or order according to the Federal Rules of Criminal Procedure. When mailing paper copies of documents that have been electronically filed, the filing party may include the "Notice of Electronic Filing" to provide the recipient with proof of the filing.

(C) Certificate of Service. A certificate of service on all parties entitled to service or notice is required, even when a party files a document electronically. The certificate must state the manner in which service or notice was accomplished on each party entitled to service or notice.

(D) Service by Mail. The three-day Rule of Federal Rule of Criminal Procedure 45(c) for service by mail will also apply to service by electronic means.

[Effective January 20, 2010.]

RULE 49.4. SCOPE OF ELECTRONIC FILING

(A) Requirements. Unless otherwise provided by the court, all documents submitted for filing in criminal cases in this district, no matter when a case was filed originally, must be filed electronically using CM/ECF.

(B) Exceptions.

(1) All charging documents (including the complaint, information, indictment, and superseding indictment) must be filed conventionally and then uploaded by the Clerk.

(2) Unless the court, in its discretion, grants leave to a pro se filer to file electronically, pro se filers must file paper originals of all documents. The Clerk's Office will scan these original documents into an electronic file in the System. The official court record will be the electronic file.

(3) Juvenile criminal matters must be filed conventionally and under seal unless, after hearing, the Court Rules that the juvenile will be tried as an adult.

(4) An attorney may apply to the assigned judge for permission to file documents conventionally. Even if the assigned judge initially grants an attorney permission to file documents conventionally, however, the assigned judge may withdraw that permission at any time during the pendency of a case and require the attorney to file documents electronically using the System.

(5) Any judge of this Court may deviate from the electronic filing procedures in specific cases, if deemed appropriate in the exercise of discretion, considering the need for the just, speedy, and inexpensive determination of matters pending before the Court.

[Effective January 20, 2010.]

RULE 49.5. ELIGIBILITY, REGISTRATION, AND PASSWORDS

Each attorney admitted to practice in the Central District of Illinois and pro se party given leave of court to proceed electronically must register for electronic filing and obtain a password. If a user comes to believe that the security of an existing password has been compromised and that a threat to the System exists, the user must change his or her password immediately. Additionally, if an attorney's or pro se party's e-mail address, mailing address, telephone number, or fax number changes after he or she registers for electronic filing, he or she must file notice of this change within 14 days and serve a copy of the notice on all other parties.

[Effective January 20, 2010.]

RULE 49.6. ELECTRONIC FILING PROCEDURES

(A) Charging Documents. All charging documents (including the complaint, information, indictment, and superseding indictment) must be filed conventionally and then uploaded by the Clerk. All such documents must comply with the privacy policy set forth by these Rules.

(B) Pleadings and Documents Other Than Charging Documents.

(1) All subsequent pleadings, including motions, applications, briefs, memoranda of law, exhibits, or other documents in a criminal case must be electronically filed on the System except as otherwise provided by these Rules.

(2) A document submitted electronically will not be considered filed for purposes of the Federal Rules of Criminal Procedure until the System-generated Notice of Electronic Filing has been sent electronically to the filing party.

(3) E-mailing a document to the Clerk's Office or to the assigned judge will not constitute "filing" of the document.

(4) A document filed electronically by 11:59 p.m. central standard time will be deemed filed on that date.

(5) If filing a document requires leave of the court, such as filing a reply brief, the filing party must attach the proposed document as an exhibit to a motion to file. If the court then grants the motion to file, the Clerk will file the attached document electronically; the filing party should not do so.

(C) Titling Docket Entries. The party electronically filing a pleading or other document will be responsible for designating a docket entry title for the document by using one of the docket event categories prescribed by the court.

(D) Filing Problems.

(1) *Corrections.* Once a document is submitted and becomes part of the case docket, corrections to the docket are made only by the Clerk's Office. The

System will not permit the filing party to make changes to the document or docket entry filed in error once the transaction has been accepted. The filing party should not attempt to refile a document. As soon as possible after an error is discovered, the filing party should contact the Clerk's Office with the case number and document number for which the correction is being requested. If appropriate, the Court will make an entry indicating that the document was filed in error. The filing party will be advised *if* the document needs to be refiled.

(2) *Technical Problems.*

(a) Technical Failures. The Clerk's Office will deem the Central District of Illinois CM/ECF site to be subject to a technical failure on a given day if the site is unable to accept filings continuously or intermittently over the course of any period of time greater than one hour after 10:00 a.m. that day. In the event a technical failure occurs, and despite the best efforts of the filing party a document cannot be filed electronically, the party should print (if possible) a copy of the error message received. As soon as possible, the party should file this message with a Declaration That Party Was Unable to File in a Timely Manner Due to Technical Difficulties.

(b) Filer's Problems. Problems on the filer's end, such as phone line problems, problems with the filer's Internet Service Provider (ISP) or hardware or software problems, will neither constitute a technical failure nor excuse an untimely filing. If a party misses a filing deadline due to such problems, the document may be conventionally submitted, accompanied by a Declaration stating the reason for missing the deadline and a motion for leave to file instanter. The motion, document and declaration must be filed no later than 12:00 noon of the first day on which the Court is open for business following the original filing deadline. The Court will consider the matters stated in the declaration and order appropriate relief.

[Effective January 20, 2010.]

RULE 49.7. ATTACHMENTS AND EXHIBITS

(A) Size Limitations. Attachments and exhibits filed electronically must conform to the size limitations set forth on the Central District of Illinois CM/ECF login page. If attachments or exhibits are longer than 30 pages, a courtesy paper copy will be provided to the presiding judge's chambers.

(B) Non–Trial Exhibits. A party may conventionally file exhibits that are not readily available in electronic form (e.g., blueprints, large maps). If possible, however, a filing party should scan a paper exhibit and file it electronically, in accordance with the size and scanning limitations set forth in these Rules.

A party electronically submitting evidentiary materials to the Clerk's Office must attach an index listing each item of evidence then being filed and identifying the motion or pleading to which it relates.

(C) Trial Exhibits. Trial exhibits will not be scanned into the electronic record unless specifically ordered by the judge presiding over the matter.

[Effective January 20, 2010. Amended effective March 15, 2010.]

RULE 49.8. COURT RECORD AND ORDERS

(A) Official Court Record. The Clerk's Office will not maintain a paper court file except as otherwise provided in these Rules. The official court record is the electronic file maintained by the court, supplemented with any documents or exhibits conventionally filed in accordance with these Rules.

(1) The Clerk's Office will retain all original indictments, petitions to enter plea of guilty, plea agreements, and those documents requiring the signatures of non-attorneys (such as grand jury foreperson, defendants, third-party custodians, United States Marshals, officers from Probation, and other federal officers and agents). When these documents are filed conventionally, the Clerk's Office will scan them, upload them to the System, and retain the original documents in conventional format or sealed electronic format. Signatures of judiciary and justice department officials will be redacted by the filing party and replaced with "s/ name." Signatures of jurors on verdict forms and of the foreperson on indictments will be redacted by the Clerk before scanning and uploading. The electronic document as it is maintained on the Court's servers constitutes the official version of that record.

(2) Any party filing any original document conventionally (other than those listed above) must accompany such filing with a self-addressed, postage-paid envelope. The Clerk's Office will scan and upload the document filed into the System and then return the conventional document to the filing party in the self-addressed envelope. If a party fails to submit a self-addressed, postage-paid envelope with the conventionally filed document, the Clerk's Office will discard the documents after they are scanned and uploaded to the System. The electronic document as it is maintained on the Court's servers constitutes the official version of the document.

(B) Orders.

(1) *Judges' Signatures.* The assigned judge or the Clerk's Office must electronically file all signed orders. Any order signed electronically has the same force and effect as if the judge had affixed the judge's signature to a paper copy of the order and it had been entered on the docket conventionally.

(2) *Proposed Orders.* Proposed orders must be filed as attachments to motions. A filing party moving for issuance of a writ, warrant, or summons should advise the judge that a prompt ruling is required and submit the writ, warrant, or summons in .pdf form with the proposed order. The presiding judge may request a copy of the proposed order be sent in Word or Word Perfect format (i.e., not .pdf) to the chambers e-mail address.

(3) *Text–Only Orders.* The assigned judge may grant routine orders by a text-only entry upon the docket. When text-only entries are made, no separate .pdf document will issue; the text-only entry constitutes the Court's only order on the matter. The System will generate a "Notice of Electronic Filing."

[Effective January 20, 2010.]

RULE 49.9. SEALED CASES, DOCUMENTS FOR IN CAMERA REVIEW, AND EX PARTE DOCUMENTS

(A) Filing Under Seal.

(1) *Sealed Cases.* All documents in sealed cases must be submitted conventionally to the Clerk's Office for filing.

(2) *Sealed Documents.* The Court does not approve of filing of documents under seal as a general matter. A party who has a legal basis for filing a document under seal without prior court order must electronically file a motion for leave to file under seal. The motion must include an explanation of how the document meets the legal standards for filing sealed documents. The document in question may not be attached to the motion as an attachment but rather must be electronically filed contemporaneously using the separate docket event "Sealed Document." In the rare event that the motion itself must be filed under seal, the motion must be electronically filed using the docket event "Sealed Motion."

(3) *Service.* Parties must not use the Court's electronic notice facilities to serve documents in sealed cases or individually sealed documents. A publicly viewable Notice of Electronic Filing will be generated for a sealed document, but the document itself will not be viewable electronically. Service must be made in accordance with the Federal Rules of Criminal Procedure and the Local Rules of this Court. A certificate of service must be attached to the filed document.

(4) *Denial of Requests to Seal.* In the event that a motion for leave to file under seal is denied, the document tendered will remain under seal, and it will not be considered by the presiding judge for any purpose. If the filer wishes to have the document considered by the Court, it must be re-filed in the normal fashion as an unsealed document. The Court may, in its discretion, order a sealed document to be made public if (1) the document is filed in disregard of legal standards, or (2) the document is so intricately connected with a pending matter that the interests of justice are best served by doing so.

(B) Documents Submitted for In Camera Review. The Rules applicable to Sealed Documents also apply to documents submitted for in camera review.

(C) Ex Parte Submissions. A party who has a legal basis to file a submission without giving notice to other parties should file the submission electronically as either an "Ex Parte Document" or an "Ex Parte Motion."

[Effective January 20, 2010.]

RULE 49.10. ELECTRONIC SIGNATURES

(A) Signatures by Electronic Filers.

(1) Use of a log-in and password for electronic filing constitutes and has the same force and effect as the filer's signature for purposes of Fed. R. Civ. P. 11, the Local Rules of this Court, and any other purpose for which a signature may be required in connection with proceedings in this Court.

(2) Electronic filers should sign in the following manner: "s/Jane Doe." Documents signed by an attorney must be filed using that attorney's log-in and password; they may not be filed using a log-in and password belonging to another attorney.

(3) Where multiple attorney signatures are required, such as on a joint motion or a stipulation, the filing attorney may enter the "s/" of the other attorneys to reflect their agreement with the contents of the documents.

(B) Signatures by Non–Electronic Filers.

(1) If an original document requires the signature[s] of one or more persons not registered for electronic filing (e.g., settlement agreement with a pro se party, or a witness' affidavit), the filing party or its attorney must initially confirm that the content of the document is acceptable to all persons required to sign the documents. Original signatures of all non-electronic filers must be obtained before the document is filed.

(2) The filing party must either redact the original signature[s] and efile the redacted version of the document, or provide the redacted version to the Clerk's Office for scanning and electronic filing. The filed document must indicate the identity of each non-registered signatory in the form "s/Jane Doe". A certificate of Service upon all parties and/or counsel of record must be filed with the document.

(3) The filing party must retain the original document until one year after the date that the judgment has become final by the conclusion of direct review or

the expiration of the time for seeking such review has passed.

(4) The electronically filed document as it is maintained on the court's servers constitutes the official version of that record. The court will not maintain a paper copy of the original document except as otherwise provided in these Rules.

(C) Disputes Over Authenticity. Any party or non-filing signatory who disputes the authenticity of an electronically filed document or the signatures on that document must file an objection to the document within 14 days of receiving the notice that the document has been filed.

[Effective January 20, 2010. Amended effective March 15, 2010.]

RULE 49.11. ACCESS TO RECORDS AND PAPERS

(A) Withdrawal. No person, other than an employee of this court in the exercise of official duty, may withdraw any original pleading, paper, record, model or exhibit from the custody of the clerk of this court or other employee of this court having custody thereof, except upon written order of a judge of this court, and upon leaving a proper receipt with the clerk of this court or employee.

(B) Public Access.

(1) Electronic access to the electronic docket and to documents filed in the System is available for viewing to the public at no charge at the Clerk's Office during regular business hours. A copy fee for an electronic reproduction is required in accordance with 28 U.S.C. § 1930. Public remote electronic access to the System for viewing purposes is limited to subscribers to the Public Access to Court Electronic Records ("PACER") system, which charges a user fee for remotely accessing certain detailed case information. Conventional copies and certified copies of electronically filed documents may be purchased by the public at the Clerk's Office. The fee for copying and certifying will be in accordance with 28 U.S.C. § 1914.

(2) An exception to the prohibition on general public remote access is possible in a high-profile criminal case where the demand for documents may impose extraordinary demands on the Court's resources. The Court is authorized to provide Internet access to documents filed in such a case if all parties thereto consent and the trial judge finds that such access is warranted.

(C) Conventional Copies. Conventional copies and certified copies of electronically filed documents may be purchased by the public at the Clerk's Office.

The fee for copying and certifying will be in accordance with 28 U.S.C. § 1914.

[Effective January 20, 2010. Amended effective March 15, 2010.]

RULE 49.12 PRIVACY

(A) Redactions. To address the privacy concerns created by Internet access to court documents, litigants must modify or partially redact certain personal data identifiers appearing in case initiating documents, pleadings, affidavits, or other papers. In addition to those set out in Fed. R. Crim. P. 49.1, these identifiers and the suggested modifications are as follows:

(1) *Addresses*: Use only City and State;

(2) *Signatures*: Use s/name; and

(3) *Driver's License numbers*: Use only last four numbers.

Litigants also should consider redacting or filing a motion to file under seal any document that contains information that might bring harm to anyone or should not be made public for law enforcement or security reasons.

(B) Unredacted Documents and Reference Lists. When redactions result in a documents' intent being unclear or if ordered by the Court, the filing party must file under seal an unredacted document or a reference list. A reference list must contain the complete personal identifier(s) and the redacted identifiers(s) to be used in its(their) place in the filing. If an unredacted version is not filed, the unredacted version of the document or the reference list must be retained by the filing party for one year after completion of the case, including all appeals. Upon a showing that the redacted information is both relevant and legitimately needed, the Court may, in its discretion, order the information disclosed to counsel for all parties.

(C) Transcript Redactions. Parties and attorneys may order transcripts. A court reporter then will file the transcripts electronically in CM/ECF. The transcript will be available for viewing at the Clerk's Office public terminal, but may not be copied nor reproduced by the Clerk's Office for a period of 90 days. A Notice of Filing of Official Transcript will be served on all parties. If any material should be redacted from a transcript, a party must file a Notice of Intent to Request Redaction within 7 days of the filing of the transcript. The responsibility for identifying material that should be redacted, in a transcript, lies solely with counsel and the parties. Within 21 days from the filing of the transcript, the parties must file under seal a Motion of Requested Redactions indicating where the material to be redacted is located, by page and line. If a party fails to follow the procedures for requesting redaction, the official transcripts will be made available electronically to the public 90 days after the transcript was initially filed with the Clerk.

[Effective January 20, 2010. Amended effective March 15, 2010.]

RULE 57.2. CONFIDENTIAL PROBATION RECORDS

(A) Any person seeking release of any confidential records maintained by the U.S. Probation Office, including presentence and supervision records, must file a written request with the court for such records, which establishes with particularity the need for specific information in the records.

(B) Whenever a probation officer is subpoenaed to provide confidential information, he or she will apply to the presiding judge in writing for authority to release such information or provide testimony with regard to any confidential information. No disclosure will be made except upon an order issued by the presiding judge.

(1) In all criminal cases in which sentence is not imposed under the Sentencing Reform Act of 1984, 18 U.S.C. § 3551, et seq., when the presentence report has been requested by a reviewing court in connection with the appeal of a criminal conviction or sentence, the report must be sent to the reviewing court by the United States Probation Office by registered mail. The presentence report must be accompanied by a written request that the report be returned to the submitting office when it has served the court's purpose; that it be opened and examined in camera only, and that it not be made a part of the public record.

(2) In all criminal cases in which sentence is imposed under the provisions of the Sentencing Reform Act of 1984, 18 U.S.C. § 3551, et seq., the presentence report must be made a part of the official court record. The original report, including the recommendation to the court, must be placed under seal in the record. In the event of an appeal, the report and recommendation must be sent to the reviewing court under separate seal.

(3) A copy of the presentence report must be made available to appellate counsel on request, under the same terms and conditions as apply to use of the report by counsel in the trial court.

[Effective January 20, 2010.]

RULE 57.3. APPEARANCES IN CRIMINAL CASES

No attorney may appear on behalf of a criminal defendant unless the attorney is admitted to practice in this court and has filed a written entry of appearance in the case.

[Effective January 20, 2010.]

RULE 58.2. FORFEITURE OF COLLATERAL IN LIEU OF APPEARANCE

Except as hereinafter provided, a person who is charged with an infraction as defined in 18 U.S.C. § 19, and which is specifically listed in a schedule published by order of this court pursuant to this Rule, may, in lieu of appearance, post collateral in the amount specified in such schedule for the offense, waive appearance before a United States magistrate judge, and consent to forfeiture of the collateral as the fixed sum payment referred to in Rule 58(d) of the Federal Rules of Criminal Procedure.

If in the discretion of the law enforcement officer the offense is of an aggravated nature, the law enforcement officer, notwithstanding any other provision of this Rule, may, in the violation notice, require appearance, and any punishment established by law, including fine, imprisonment or probation, may be imposed upon conviction. Nothing contained in this Rule will prohibit a law enforcement officer from arresting a person for the commission of any offense, including those for which collateral may be posted and forfeited, and taking that person immediately before a United States magistrate judge or requiring the person charged to appear before a United States magistrate judge, as provided in the Federal Rules of Criminal Procedure.

[Effective January 20, 2010.]

BANKRUPTCY RULES

RULE 4.1. REFERENCE IN TITLE 11 CASES

All cases under Title 11, United States Code, and any or all proceedings arising under Title 11 or arising in or related to a case under Title 11 are referred to by* the bankruptcy judges for the district.

[Effective January 20, 2010.]

* So in original. Probably should read "are referred to the bankruptcy judges for the district".

RULE 4.2. JURY TRIAL PROCEDURES IN BANKRUPTCY COURT

The following procedures may apply to jury trials conducted by the bankruptcy court in this district.

(A) Designation of Bankruptcy Judges to Conduct Jury Trials. In bankruptcy cases filed on or after October 22, 1994, if the right to a jury trial applies in a proceeding that may be heard by a bankruptcy judge, the bankruptcy judges of this district are specially designated to exercise such jurisdiction, upon the express consent of all the parties, and upon compliance with all of the terms and conditions set forth in this Rule.

(B) Trial by Jury. Issues triable of right by jury will, if timely demanded, be by jury, unless the parties or their attorneys of record, by written stipulation filed with the court or by an oral stipulation made in open court and entered in the record, consent to trial by the court sitting without a jury.

(C) Demand.

(1) *Time; Forum.* Any party may demand a trial by jury of any issue triable by a jury by serving on the other parties a demand therefor in writing not later than 14 days after service of the last pleading directed to such issue. The demand may be endorsed on a pleading of the party. When a jury trial is demanded, it must be designated by the clerk in the docket as a jury matter.

(2) *Specification of Issues.* In the demand, a party may specify the issues to be so tried; otherwise, the demand will be deemed a demand for trial by jury of all the issues so triable. If the demand for trial by jury is directed to some of the issues, any other party, within 14 days after the service of the demand, or such lesser time as the court may order, may serve a demand for trial by jury of other or all of the issues.

(3) *Determination by Court.* On motion, or on its own initiative, the presiding judge may determine whether there is a right to trial by jury of the issues for which a jury trial is demanded or whether a demand for trial by jury will be granted.

(D) Waiver and Withdrawal. The failure of a party to serve a demand as required by this Rule and to file it as required by Federal Rule of Bankruptcy Procedure 5005, constitutes a waiver of trial by jury. A demand for trial by jury made as herein provided may not be withdrawn without the consent of all parties and the approval of the court.

(E) Trial by the Court. Issues not demanded for trial by jury will be tried by the court.

(F) Applicability of Certain of the Federal Rules of Civil Procedure. Federal Rules of Civil Procedure 47 through 51 will apply when a jury trial is conducted pursuant to this Rule.

[Effective January 20, 2010.]

APPENDIX TO RULES
APPENDIX 1.   PRE–TRIAL ORDER—CIVIL
FORM OF PRE–TRIAL ORDER: CIVIL

NOTE TO LITIGANTS: DO NOT FILL IN BLANKS ON THESE SHEETS. USE AS A GUIDE IN DRAFTING, AS YOU WOULD A FORM BOOK.

UNITED STATES DISTRICT COURT
CENTRAL DISTRICT OF ILLINOIS

Plaintiff	)	
	)	
	)	
vs.	)	CASE NO.
	)	
Defendant	)	

PRE–TRIAL ORDER

This matter having come before the Court at a pre-trial conference held pursuant to Rule 16 of the Federal Rules of Civil Procedure and Local Rule 16.1; and _____ having appeared as counsel for the plaintiff(s), or

the plaintiff having appeared pro se, and

_____ having appeared as counsel for the defendant(s),

(The listing of parties must be complete and appearances must show the individuals who were actually present.)

the following action was taken:

I. NATURE OF ACTION AND JURISDICTION

This is an action for _____ and the jurisdiction of the Court is invoked under _____. The jurisdiction of the Court is not disputed.

II. JOINT STATEMENT

A. JURISDICTION
B. UNCONTESTED ISSUES OF FACT
C. CONTESTED ISSUES OF FACT
D. CONTESTED ISSUES OF LAW
E. JURY DEMAND

III. PLAINTIFF'S STATEMENT

A. ITEMIZED STATEMENT OF DAMAGES

IV. WAIVER OF CLAIMS OR DEFENSES

(OR JURY DEMAND)

507

(If nothing is waived, leave this section out.)

V.   EXHIBITS ATTACHED

The following are attached as exhibits to this order and are made a part hereof:

A.   Stipulation of Uncontested facts and issues of law (signed by all parties).

B.   Plaintiff's Witness List (for each plaintiff).

C.   Defendant's Witness List (for each defendant).

D.   Plaintiff's Exhibit List (for each plaintiff).

E.   Defendant's Exhibit List (for each defendant).

F.   Joint Exhibit List.

G.   Proposed Jury Instructions (Joint) (or Findings and Conclusions).

H.   Plaintiff's Proposed Instructions (only if objections by defendant).

I.   Defendant's Proposed Instructions (only if objections by plaintiff).

VI.   GENERAL ADDITIONAL

The following additional action was taken:

[Recite amendments to pleadings, additional agreements of the parties on the qualifications of expert witnesses or any other subject, disposition of motions at the conference, etc., if necessary. If no such action was taken, leave this paragraph out of the Order.]

IT IS UNDERSTOOD BY THE PARTIES THAT:

The plaintiff(s) is (are) limited to ___ expert witnesses whose names and qualifications have been disclosed to the defendant(s). The defendant(s) is (are) limited to ___ expert witnesses whose names and qualifications have been disclosed to the plaintiff(s).

[This paragraph does not refer to treating or examining physicians or other highly trained witnesses who have actual knowledge of the case. It should be left out if no expert witnesses have been listed.]

Any Trial Briefs or Motions in limine must be filed as directed by the Court but in no event less than 14 days prior to trial. [Leave out if no trial briefs will be used.]

A party may supplement a list of witnesses or exhibits only upon good cause shown in a motion filed and served upon the other parties prior to trial; except that, upon the development of testimony fairly shown to be unexpected, any party may, with leave of court, call such contrary witnesses or use such exhibits as may be necessary to counter the unexpected evidence, although not previously listed, and without prior notice of any other party.

It is mutually estimated that the length of trial will not exceed ___ full days. The case will be listed on the trial calendar to be tried when reached.

Once a final version of this order has been approved by the Court, it may be modified at the trial of the action, or prior thereto, only to prevent manifest injustice. Such modification may be made either on motion of counsel for any party or on the Court's own motion.

[The foregoing three paragraphs must be contained in every order.]

Any additional proposed jury instructions shall be submitted to the Court within five days before the commencement of the trial, but there is reserved to counsel for the respective parties the right to submit supplemental proposals for instructions during the course of the trial or at the conclusion of the evidence on matters that could not reasonably have been anticipated.

[This paragraph should be left out in a non-jury case.]

IT IS SO ORDERED.

_____
JUDGE

ENTERED: _____

APPROVED AS TO FORM AND SUBSTANCE:

_____

Attorney for the Plaintiff(s)

_____

Attorney for the Defendant(s)

EXHIBIT LIST FOR PLAINTIFF/DEFENDANT/JOINT

(One for Each)

Counsel reminded to review Local Rule 5.11 regarding redactions.

Case Name:		Case No:	Page ___ of ___

No:	Description	Admit Without Objection	Authentication Waived	Objection

WITNESS LIST FOR PLAINTIFF/DEFENDANT

(One for Each)

Counsel reminded to review Local Rule 5.11 regarding redactions.

Case Name:	Case No:	Page ___ of ___

Witness Name	Address (City and State Only)	Expert	Adverse

[Effective January 20, 2010.]

APPENDIX 2. PRE–TRIAL ORDER—PRISONER
FORM OF PRE–TRIAL ORDER: PRISONER

NOTE TO LITIGANTS: DO NOT FILL IN BLANKS ON THESE SHEETS. USE THIS DOCUMENT AS A GUIDE IN DRAFTING YOUR PRETRIAL ORDER. IF THE PLAINTIFF IS PROCEEDING PRO SE, THE DEFENDANTS ARE REMINDED THEY BEAR THE RESPONSIBILITY FOR PREPARING THE JOINT PRETRIAL ORDER PURSUANT TO LOCAL RULE 16.3(I)(3).

UNITED STATES DISTRICT COURT
CENTRAL DISTRICT OF ILLINOIS

Plaintiff   )

)

        vs.   )   CASE NO.

)

Defendant   )

PRE–TRIAL ORDER

This matter having come before the Court at a pre-trial conference held pursuant to Rule 16 of the Federal Rules of Civil Procedure and Local Rule 16.3; and

_____ having appeared as counsel for the plaintiff(s), or

the plaintiff having appeared pro se, and

_____ having appeared as counsel for the defendant(s),

(The listing of parties must be complete).

the following action was taken:

I. NATURE OF ACTION

This is an action brought pursuant to 42 U.S.C. § 1983 for violations of the (i.e. list specific constitutional amendments) and violations of (if any other claims). The jurisdiction of the Court is invoked under Section 28 U.S.C. § 1331 and 28 U.S.C. § 1343. The jurisdiction of the Court is not disputed.

The plaintiff alleges (brief statement of case).

II. JOINT STATEMENT

A. JURISDICTION

B. UNCONTESTED ISSUES OF FACT

C. CONTESTED ISSUES OF FACT

D. CONTESTED ISSUES OF LAW

E. JURY DEMAND

III. PLAINTIFF'S STATEMENT

A. ITEMIZED STATEMENT OF DAMAGES

IV. WAIVER OF CLAIMS OR DEFENSES

(OR JURY DEMAND)

(If nothing is waived, leave this section out.)

V. EXHIBITS ATTACHED

The following are attached as exhibits to this order and are made a part hereof:

A. Stipulation of Uncontested facts and issues of law (signed by all parties).

B. Plaintiff's Witness List (for each plaintiff).

C. Defendant's Witness List (for each defendant).

D. Plaintiff's Exhibit List (for each plaintiff).

E. Defendant's Exhibit List (for each defendant).

F. Joint Exhibit List.

*G. Proposed Jury Instructions (Joint) (or Findings and Conclusions).

*H. Plaintiff's Proposed Instructions (only if objections by defendant).

*I. Defendant's Proposed Instructions (only if objections by plaintiff).

VI. GENERAL ADDITIONAL

The following additional action was taken:

1. The testimony of the following inmate witnesses is necessary for trial. The Clerk is directed to issue a Video Writ for the following inmate witnesses to appear by video conferencing:

    Inmate Name   Inmate No.   Current Correctional Center

2. The testimony of the following IDOC employees is necessary for trial. The defendants are ordered to produce these witnesses for trial.

    a) The following IDOC employees will appear by video conferencing. The Clerk is to directed to issue a Video Writ for their appearance during the trial:

        Name   Title   Current Correctional Center

    b) The defendants will produce the following IDOC employees to testify in person at trial:

        Name   Title   Current Correctional Center

3. The testimony of the following witnesses who are neither inmates nor employees is necessary for trial. The Clerk is directed to issue trial subpoenas for the following. The plaintiff must provide the witness fee and mileage fee to the witness.

[Recite amendments to pleadings, additional agreements of the parties on the qualifications of expert witnesses or any other subject, disposition of motions at the conference, etc., if necessary. If no such action was taken, leave this paragraph out of the Order.]

IT IS UNDERSTOOD BY THE PARTIES THAT:

The plaintiff(s) is (are) limited to ___ expert witnesses whose names and qualifications have been disclosed to the defendant(s). The defendant(s) is (are) limited to

___ expert witnesses whose names and qualifications have been disclosed to the plaintiff(s).

[This paragraph does not refer to treating or examining physicians or other highly trained witnesses who have <u>actual knowledge</u> of the case. It should be left out if no expert witnesses have been listed.]

Any Trial Briefs or Motions in limine shall be submitted no later than fourteen (14) days prior to the commencement of the trial. [Leave out if no trial briefs will be used.]

A party may supplement a list of witnesses or exhibits only upon good cause shown in a motion filed and served upon the other parties prior to trial; except that, upon the development of testimony fairly shown to be unexpected, any party may, with leave of court, call such contrary witnesses or use such exhibits as may be necessary to counter the unexpected evidence, although not previously listed, and without prior notice of any other party.

It is mutually estimated that the length of trial will not exceed ___ full days. The case will be listed on the trial calendar to be tried when reached.

This pre-trial order may be modified at the trial of the action, or prior thereto, to prevent manifest injustice. [Such modification may be made either on motion of counsel for any party or on the Court's own motion.]

[The foregoing three paragraphs must be contained in every order.]

Any additional proposed jury instructions shall be submitted to the Court within five days before the commencement of the trial, but there is reserved to the respective parties the right to submit supplemental proposals for instructions during the course of the trial or at the conclusion of the evidence on matters that could not reasonably have been anticipated.

[This paragraph should be left out in a non-jury case.]

IT IS SO ORDERED.

_____
JUDGE

ENTERED: _____

APPROVED AS TO FORM AND SUBSTANCE:

_____

Attorney for the Plaintiff(s)

_____

Attorney for the Defendant(s)

EXHIBIT LIST FOR PLAINTIFF/DEFENDANT/JOINT

(One for Each)

Parties reminded to review Local Rule 5.11 regarding redactions.

Case Name:		Case No:	Page ___ of ___

No:	Description	Admit Without Objection	Authentication Waived	Objection

WITNESS LIST FOR PLAINTIFF/DEFENDANT

(One for Each)

Parties reminded to review Local Rule 5.11 regarding redactions.

Case Name:		Case No:	Page ___ of ___

Witness Name	Address (City and State Only)	Expert	Adverse

Witness Name	Address (City and State Only)	Expert	Adverse

* Unless otherwise ordered by the Presiding Judge.

[Effective January 20, 2010.]

SELECTED ORDERS

STANDING ORDER CDIL–2. MANAGEMENT PLAN FOR COURT REPORTING SERVICES FOR THE CENTRAL DISTRICT OF ILLINOIS

The Official Court Reporter Plan dated December 21, 1987 is vacated, and the following plan is substituted as the Plan for the Central District of Illinois.

MANAGEMENT PLAN FOR COURT REPORTING SERVICES IN THE UNITED STATES DISTRICT COURT FOR THE CENTRAL DISTRICT OF ILLINOIS

A. Introduction. The Court desires through this Plan to achieve effective control and management of the official court reporters (court reporters). Recognizing the geography of this district and the fact that reporters are assigned to Judges in Peoria, Urbana, and Springfield, the reporters are to be supervised on a day to day basis by the Judge to whom he or she is assigned. Otherwise, the Clerk of Court (Clerk) is authorized administratively by the Court to supervise the combined court reporting operations of the Court.

The Plan is designed to:

1. obtain effective management of the court reporters by proper supervision and control;

2. make clear that court reporters though assigned to a particular judge, serve the court en banc and may be assigned when needed throughout the District for any active judge, senior judge, visiting district judge, or magistrate judge;

3. obtain the most effective utilization of the services of court reporters by equitable distribution of the workload at the same site;

4. avoid backlogs of transcript and assure prompt delivery of transcripts;

5. assure appointment and retention of fully-qualified court reporters and dismissal of court reporters who are no longer performing in a satisfactory manner;

6. minimize the use of contract reporters;

7. promote competency, loyalty, and dignity among the court reporters;

8. enhance the efficient operation of the court and further its mission.

B. Appointment and Dismissal of Court Reporters. The Court is presently authorized 5 official court reporters stationed in Peoria, Urbana, and Springfield.

The Clerk of Court has been designated by the Court to appoint court reporters with the approval of the Court. Court reporters shall be appointed in accordance with the provisions of the Court Reporter Act, 28 U.S.C. Section 753, and the policies and procedures of the Administrative Office of the United States Courts and the Judicial Conference of the United States. Only fully-qualified reporters shall be appointed as court reporters of this court. Newly appointed court reporters shall be subject to a probationary period of six months. Court reporters who do not perform in a competent and satisfactory manner shall be subject to dismissal by the Clerk.

In accordance with Judicial Conference guidelines, it is the policy of this Court that the Court en banc hires reporters to serve at the pleasure of the Court, regardless of the death, resignation, or retirement of an individual Judge. In the period between the occurrence of a judicial vacancy and appointment of a new Judge, reporters shall continue to serve other active judges, senior judges, and magistrate judges.

C. Duties of the Clerk.

1. The duties and responsibilities of the Clerk shall include, but shall not be limited to:

a. assignment and reassignment of official court reporters for the purpose of distributing fairly and equitably the workload of all reporters at the same site and assuring the best utilization of all reporters involved in the perfection of the record, subject to the provisions of paragraph D;

b. periodically reviewing transcripts to assure full compliance with format requirements of the Administrative Office of the United States Courts and the Judicial Conference of the United States;

c. periodically reviewing transcript billing to assure that authorized transcript rates are charged and that billing is in proper form, including the requirement of certification that the fee charged and the page format conforms to the requirements of the Judicial Conference of the United States;

d. determining compliance by all court reporters and recorders with the rules and regulations concerning the recording and filing of arraignments, pleas, and sentencings;

e. periodically reviewing the time records of the court reporters to assure proper maintenance and accuracy;

f. reviewing the records of the court reporters to assure the timely filing of all reports required by the Administrative Office of the United States Courts and the Judicial Conference of the United States;

g. requiring the court reporters to submit those reports mandated by the Judicial Conference to the Clerk for review and signature on a timely basis;

h. at least annually, filing with the Court a report concerning the work of the court reporters;

i. performing such other duties relating to court reporting services as shall be directed by the Court.

D. Assignment of Court Reporters.

1. Court reporters serve the Court en banc; therefore, it is within the discretion of the Clerk to assign and reassign court reporters to active judges, senior judges, visiting district judges, and magistrate judges, in a manner designed to equally distribute the total court reporting workload efficiently and cost effectively. When necessary and depending upon availability, a court reporter may be reassigned by the Clerk to another Judge of the Court, to a senior judge, or other judicial official. When necessary and in accordance with the policies of the Administrative Office of the United States Courts and the Judicial Conference of the United States, contract reporters will be utilized to meet the needs of the Court.

2. The use of contract reporters and per diem reporters shall be kept to an absolute minimum. Judicial Officers will minimize the travel of court reporters by utilizing official reporters stationed in other division, if available, when conducting proceedings in those division.

3. As employees of the Clerk's staff, each court reporter is assigned a regular tour of duty consisting of forty hours per week as specified by the Judge to whom he or she is assigned. An answering machine or voice mail shall be operational during any absence from their office. Court reporters shall be assigned in a manner which best meet the actual court reporting needs of the Court, regardless of whether the services are for active judges, senior judges, or other judicial officials.

4. Out-of-district travel of court reporters shall be kept to a minimum. Judicial Officers will utilize official reporters stationed in other districts, if available, when conducting proceedings in those districts.

5. Reporter services for senior and magistrate judges shall be provided through a combination of official reporters and contract court reporters.

E. Transcripts.

1.   Reporters shall require that all transcript orders be made in writing.   All transcript orders e-filed with the Court will immediately send a Notice of Electronic Filing (NEF) to the official court reporters.   The reporters may require a deposit, not to exceed the estimated costs of the transcript, before beginning work on the transcript.   Upon completion of the transcript and receipt of full payment, the court reporter shall deliver the transcript to the ordering party or parties in electronic or paper form.   The court reporter shall deliver on disk or e-mail the transcript to the Clerk of Court for e-filing within three days after delivery to the party or parties. Reporters shall make their records of transcript orders available to the Clerk upon request to insure that transcripts are being delivered promptly.

2.   Reporters shall not agree to "expedite" any transcript which will delay the preparation of transcripts necessary for appeal.   Unless otherwise directed by the clerk, transcripts in civil cases generally should be prepared in the order in which requests are received.   Preparation of criminal transcripts generally shall take precedence over preparation of civil transcripts.

3.   Production of daily and hourly transcripts shall not be subsidized by the Court.   If extra reporters are required to produce expedited transcripts, their fees shall be paid out of the earnings derived from those higher transcript rates established by the Judicial Conference of the United States.   Other court reporters may, however, assist with the production of daily and hourly transcripts when there are no other judicial proceedings to record, including those of magistrate judges, and where no transcript backlog will result.

4.   The rates charged for transcripts produced by court reporters must conform to the current fee schedule (Appendix A).

5.   Apportionment of accelerated transcript costs among parties in criminal cases is prohibited.

6.   Transcripts not delivered within the specified time periods prescribed by the Court are subject to a fee discount provision as follows:

a.   Transcripts ordered for District Court purposes shall be delivered within thirty (30) days.   Reporters who do not deliver transcript within thirty (30) days may charge only 90% of the prescribed fee unless an extension of time for the delivery of transcript has been granted by the Clerk of the District Court.   The extension of time, if granted, will not exceed fifteen (15) days, unless extraordinary circumstances exist as determined by the Clerk.

b.   Transcripts ordered for appeal purposes shall be delivered within thirty (30) days unless an extension of time for delivery of the transcript has been granted by the Clerk of the Court of Appeals.   Reporters who do not deliver transcripts within thirty (30) days may charge only 90% of the prescribed fee; reporters who do not deliver transcript within sixty (60) days may charge only 80% of the prescribed fee, unless a waiver of the sanction provision has been granted by the Clerk of the Court of Appeals.

7.   The original transcript must be submitted to the Clerk in .pdf format to be electronically filed in accordance with the E–Government Act of 2002 within three working days of delivery to the ordering party.   Access to the e-filed transcript shall be limited to the ordering party or view only in the Clerk's office for 90 days in accordance with Judicial Conference of the United States policies.   Due to privacy issues voir dire transcripts shall remain sealed through PACER, but may be viewed at the public terminal in the Clerk's Offices.

8.   Reporters are required to assure full compliance with format requirements of the Administrative Office of the United States Courts and the Judicial Conference of the United States.

F.   Magistrate Judges.   Proceedings before the U.S. Magistrate Judges may be recorded by electronic sound recording or by a court reporter.   The Magistrate Judge shall determine which technique is to be used in each case or hearing, taking into account the provisions of 28 U.S.C. 753(b) and 636 (c)(7).   Court reporters shall be used to record misdemeanor trials and related hearing before a U.S. Magistrate Judge if a timely demand for services of a court reporter is made.

G. Miscellaneous.

1. Court reporters shall not perform any private (freelance) work.

2. The work of the court reporters shall be "note-readable" so that the stenographic notes of a court reporter can be read by another reporter in the event of an emergency.

3. A copy of the court reporter's dictionary shall be filed in the court reporter note storage area on the file server and updated every six months.

4. A copy of the computerized steno notes and/or corresponding logs shall be kept in a location accessible by the clerk's staff in case of the unavailability of the court reporter for emergency production of transcript. The computerized steno notes and logs are to be filed with the Clerk of Court upon termination of employment. Transcripts will be produced by the Clerk's Office only in the event of unavailability or unwillingness of the court reporter to produce transcripts.

5. The marking, filing and storing of reporters' notes, compact disks, and recorded tapes shall be in accordance with the note storage procedures approved by this Court and outlined in this Plan (Appendix B).

6. Court reporters are encouraged to provide realtime translation upon request of parties, but must comply with the Realtime Reporting Standards promulgated by the Judicial Conference of the United States (Appendix C).

7. Court reporters shall earn annual leave in accordance with the provisions of the Leave Act, 5 U.S.C. Section 6301, et seq. Guidelines for the administration of leave are addressed in Chapter 3, of the Personnel Manual for the Central District of Illinois.

H. Authority of Clerk. The Clerk shall administer this Plan on behalf of the Court, and the Clerk is fully authorized and empowered to implement and carry out the terms of this Plan. The Clerk shall be responsible for the supervision of the work of the court reporters, and for compliance with all requirements of the Judicial Conference of the United States and of the Administrative Office of the United States Courts. This plan shall take effect upon approval of the Seventh Circuit Judicial Council and the Administrative Office of United States Courts.

[Dated: May 27, 2008.]

APPENDIX A

Transcript Fees

	Original	Copy to Each Party	Each Add'l Copy to the Same Party
Ordinary Transcript A transcript to be delivered within thirty (30) calendar days after receipt of an order	$3.65	$ .90	$ .60
14 Day Transcript A transcript to be delivered within fourteen (14) calendar days after receipt of an order	4.25	.90	.60

Expedited Transcript

	Original	Copy to Each Party	Each Add'l Copy to the Same Party
A transcript to be delivered within seven (7) calendar days after receipt of an order	4.85	.90	.60

Daily Transcript

A transcript to be delivered following adjournment and prior to the normal opening hour of the court on the following morning whether or not it actually is a court day.   6.05   1.20   .90

Hourly Transcript

A transcript of proceedings ordered under unusual circumstances to be delivered within two (2) hours.   7.25   1.20   .90

Realtime Transcript

A draft unedited transcript produced by a certified realtime reporter as a byproduct of realtime to be delivered electronically during proceedings or immediately following adjournment.   3.05   2.10 (Two to four feeds)
                                                       1.50 (Five or more feeds)

(Only Certified Realtime Reporters may charge for realtime services)

Transcript in CJA Cases

The multi-defendant cases involving CJA defendants, no more than one transcript should be purchased from the court reporter on behalf of CJA defendants. One of the appointed counsel or the Clerk of Court should arrange for the duplication, at commercially competitive rates, of enough copies of the transcript for each of the CJA defendants for whom a transcript has been approved. The cost of such duplication will be charged to the CJA appropriation. This policy would not preclude the furnishing of duplication services by the court reporter at the commercially competitive rate.

APPENDIX B

PROCEDURES FOR STORAGE OF COURT REPORTERS' PAPER NOTES, COMPACT DISKS, AND TAPES

All original notes and tapes are to be relegated to the Clerk of Court within 90 days after the conclusion of the proceeding. If a transcript is ordered in a case where the notes have been submitted to the Clerk, the court reporter shall retrieve the notes from storage and shall refile the notes when the transcript is filed.

Storage of Original Notes.

1. All notes are to be chronologically filed and placed in FRC boxes which can be obtained from the Clerk's Office.

2. The outside of the box should be marked with a label indicating the court reporter's name and calendar year, month and dates contained within.

3. If the notes for a particular month are too voluminous to be stored in one box, use as many boxes as necessary and identify them in sequence. Conversely, if the

notes for a particular month do not fill one box, several months' notes may be stored in the box as long as it is identified.

4. Each packet of notes is to be certified and should include the case number, case caption, presiding judge, date of proceeding and court reporter's name.

5. Each box of notes must contain a <u>Filing Certification Form for Original Notes</u> (Attachment 1). In order to maintain the security of original notes, it is recommended that each reporter place his/her notes in packets and secure them at the end of the day.

Storage of Original Tape Recordings.

The following procedure is to be followed if .wav files are not produced. In accordance with 28 U.S.C. § 753(b), court reporters are required to file with the Clerk of Court <u>either</u> a transcript <u>or</u> an electronic sound recording of all arraignments, pleas, and sentencings. Accordingly, all tape recordings of these proceedings are to be delivered to the Clerk of Court or Clerk's office staff within 90 days after the conclusion of a proceeding.

PROCEDURES FOR STORAGE OF COURT REPORTERS' PAPERLESS NOTES

With the use of new paperless stenograph machines, the court reporter must now provide the court with computer files of the steno notes rather than paper steno notes. To ensure that the notes are accessible to the court, standards relative to the file format, file name, file organization and media are included in the following general procedures for the handling of paperless steno notes.

Overview

1. Copying directly from the notes files created by the steno machine, the steno notes will be stored on one of the District network servers, ensuring that there is an off-site copy of the notes available, while also providing data redundancy.

2. The steno notes files will also be copied to the court reporter's personal computer to a folder named with the current month and year. Using the paperless steno machine's accompanying software, the court reporter will print the steno notes to an Adobe Acrobat PDF file, a recognized and accepted industry standard for document images, named with the date or date range of the proceedings.

3. At the end of each month, the court reporter will copy that month's PDF files and raw steno notes to a compact disk (CD). The CD will be clearly labeled as to its contents. The CD will be stored in the District-owned CD cabinet.

Standards

1. *Stored Notes on a Network Server.* The paperless stenograph machines write the notes to an electronic storage device. At least weekly, the court reporter will copy the files from the electronic storage to the designated district network folder. Under a shared network folder, each court reporter will have a folder named with the court reporter's name. In the court reporter's folder, the court reporter will create a sub-folder named with the date range of the notes it will contain. The naming convention of "ddmmyy-ddmmyy" will be used for the folder names. The court reporter will then copy the notes files from the electronic storage device to that folder. The next set of notes from the next storage device will be copied to a new folder named with that storage device date range.

2. *File Format for the Printed Image.* The court reporter will print each set of notes to Adobe PDF file. The notes print to the PDF file in three columns set at 8½ × 11 inches, and each column of notes is identical in appearance of notes on regular steno paper.

3. *Folder Names for Steno Notes and PDF Files on the Court Reporter's PC.* The raw notes files and the PDF files will be stored in a folder on the court reporter's computer, with a sub-folder created for each month and year. For

example, if the main steno note folder is C:StenoNotes, then the folders for the first three months of 2003 would be named c:stenonotesjan2003, c:stenonotes eb2003, and c:stenonotesmar2003. The court reporter will print the steno notes to PDF and save the PDF files, along with the raw steno notes files, in the appropriate month/year folder.

4. *Steno Notes and PDF File Names.* Adobe PDF files created from steno notes shall be named with the date or date range of the proceedings plus a dash character "-" plus the court reporter's initials (first-middle-last), in the format: ddmmyy-*fml*.pdf or ddmmyy-ddmmyy-*fml*.pdf. Steno notes files should follow this date-name convention, with the exception of the fact that the file extension will be the extension employed for steno notes created by the court reporter's particular CAT software.

5. *Creating Archive CD/DVDs.* All steno notes files plus all text, .WAV files for each month for each court reporter will be written to compact disk (CD/DVD). The court reporter will create CD/DVD labels to adhere to the month's CD/DVD. The CD/DVD labels will contain the court reporter's certification language as well as lines on which to provide the dates of the notes and the court reporter's signature.

6. **CD/DVD Storage.** Within thirty days following the close of a month, the court reporter will file that month's CD/DVD in a common CD/DVD storage cabinet designated by the court reporter supervisor.

(Attachment 1)

UNITED STATES DISTRICT COURT
CENTRAL DISTRICT OF ILLINOIS

FILING CERTIFICATION FORM FOR ORIGINAL NOTES

In accordance with 28 U.S.C. § 753, I hereby certify that the original notes tendered herein for filing with the Clerk of Court are the full, true and correct notes taken during oral proceedings in the United States District Court for the Central District of Illinois and includes District Court, Magistrate Court, and other official hearings held in said district.

_____   _____

(Date)   (Signature of Court Reporter)

APPENDIX C

Realtime Reporting Standards

1. **General Policy.** As adopted in March 1996, it is the policy of the Judicial Conference that effective June 1, 1996, a new category of "realtime unedited transcript" has been established. Realtime unedited transcript is defined as "a draft transcript produced by a Certified Realtime Reporter (CRR) as a byproduct of realtime to be delivered electronically during the proceedings or immediately following adjournment". Realtime includes the following services:

- The instantaneous translation of the proceedings on a computer monitor;

- The opportunity to scroll forward and backward, search the record for key words or phrases and mark portions of the text using viewer/annotation software; and

- The realtime unedited transcript on diskette delivered during the proceedings or at the end of the day.

When realtime services are requested by a party to the case, a CRR may charge and collect for realtime unedited transcript. CRRs should not sell realtime unedited transcript to anyone who is not a party to the case without prior approval of the presiding judge.

As adopted in March 1999, it is the policy of the Judicial Conference that a litigant who orders realtime services will be required to purchase an original certified transcript of the same pages of realtime unedited transcript at the regular rates (ordinary, expedited, daily, or hourly). Likewise, a litigant who orders a copy of a realtime unedited transcript will be required to purchase a certified copy of the same pages of realtime unedited copies at the regular copy rates (ordinary, expedited, daily, or hourly.) Judicial Conference policy on payments for transcripts ordered pursuant to the Criminal Justice Act (CJA) remains in effect.

2. **Qualifications of Reporters Who May Charge for Realtime Unedited Transcript.**

   a. *Judicial Conference Policy.* Official court reporters who have successfully completed the certified Realtime Reporter examination offered by the National Court Reporters Association (NCRA), or who have passed an equivalent qualifying examination, are recognized as Certified Realtime Reporters. CRRs are permitted, but not required, to sell realtime unedited uncertified transcript on diskette.

   b. *Equivalent Qualifying Examinations.* The CRR examination consists of five minutes of professionally audio-recorded dictation (straight matter) at variable speeds ranging from 180–200 words per minute. At a 96% accuracy rate, reporters must produce a simultaneous translation and display of live proceedings utilizing computer-aided translation within 5 seconds of stenotype input. Without editing, the reporter must produce an ASCII (computer language) text file on diskette. Reporters are required to provide all necessary personal equipment and software (computer, and display, write, cable, and realtime software). Any other qualifying examination must be equivalent to the NCRA examination.

3. **Production.** The transcript formal guidelines prescribed be the Judicial Conference apply to realtime unedited transcript with the following exceptions:

   a. Realtime unedited transcript must be clearly marked as such with a header or footer which appears at the top or bottom of each page of the transcript, or a computer-generated watermark on each page stating, "Realtime Unedited Transcript Only".

   b. The realtime unedited transcript should not include an appearance page, an index, or a certification.

   c. The diskette label may be of a different color than that used on diskettes containing the text of certified transcript and hand stamped with the words, "Realtime Unedited Transcript Only".

Realtime unedited transcript sold on computer diskette may be in ASCII format, or any other format requested by the ordering party and agreed to by the court reporter. It should include any notations made to the electronic file by the ordering party during the proceedings. Diskettes may not contain any protection or programming codes that would prevent copying or transferring the data.

All parties requesting realtime services shall be responsible for providing their own personal computers, viewer/annotation software, and monitors. Upon the request of the parties, reporters may make equipment and software available at no additional charge. The CRR shall provide wiring and data communications connections needed to provide realtime services to these persons. Parties should coordinate and pre-test their equipment with the CRR before official proceedings begin.

4. Distribution. A CRR providing realtime unedited transcript should offer comparable services to all parties to the proceeding. The primary purpose of realtime unedited transcript is to provide access to a draft transcript of the proceedings on diskette at the end of each day. It is not intended to be used in subsequent proceedings for impeachment or for any other purpose, including further distribution.

It should be noted that when realtime unedited transcript is provided, there may be two versions of the transcript for one proceeding—unofficial and official. The realtime unedited transcript may contain errors, some of which could change the accuracy or meaning of the testimony. A realtime unedited transcript will not satisfy the requirement for the reporter to provide or file a certified transcript with the district court clerk or as the record on appeal.

Realtime unedited transcript may only be distributed to ordering parties to the case. It should not be made available to the public, including news organizations or other non-participants. It is recommended that each CRR request that parties acknowledge receipt of a realtime unedited transcript by signing a disclaimer which explicitly states that the ordering party is aware that the realtime unedited transcript is not an official record of the court proceedings. A sample Realtime Unedited Transcript Disclaimer is attached (Attachment 2).

(Attachment 2)

SAMPLE

REALTIME UNEDITED TRANSCRIPT DISCLAIMER IN THE MATTER OF

_____

v.

_____

The following transcript(s) of proceedings, or any portion thereof, in the above-entitled matter, taken on any date, is being delivered UNEDITED and UNCERTI-FIED by the official court reporter at the request of _____.

The purchaser agrees not to disclose this realtime unedited transcript in any form (written or electronic) to anyone who has no connection to this case. This is an unofficial transcript which should NOT be relied upon for purposes of verbatim citation of testimony.

This transcript has not been checked, proofread or corrected. It is a draft transcript, NOT a certified transcript. As such, it may contain computer-generated mistranslations of stenotype code or electronic transmission errors, resulting in inaccurate or nonsensical word combinations, or untranslated stenotype symbols which cannot be deciphered by non-stenotypists. Corrections will be made in the preparation of the certified transcript, resulting in differences in content, page and line numbers, punctuation, and formatting.

This realtime unedited transcript contains no appearance page, certificate page, index, or certification.

_____   _____
Signature of Purchaser   Date

_____   _____
Signature of Official Reporter   Date

STANDING ORDER CDIL–3. PLAN FOR PROMPT DISPOSITION OF CRIMINAL CASES

Plan for prompt disposition of criminal cases

Final plan pursuant to Speedy Trial Act of 1974—18 U.S.C. § 3165(e)(3)

Section I. Introductory Material

DISTRICT COURT PLAN
FOR ACHIEVING PROMPT
DISPOSITION OF CRIMINAL CASES
(Effective July 1, 1980)

I. INTRODUCTORY MATERIAL

A. Adoption of Plan and Rules by the Court. Pursuant to the requirements of the Speedy Trial Act of 1974 (18 U.S.C. § 3165(e) as amended) the judges of the United States District Court for the Central District of Illinois have adopted the following District Plan for the Disposition of Criminal Cases. Section II of this Plan also adopts certain time limits, procedures, and rules for the disposition of the criminal cases and juvenile proceedings pursuant to Rule 50(b) of the Federal Rules of Criminal Procedure, the Speedy Trial Act of 1974 (18 U.S.C. Chapter 208) and the Federal Juvenile Delinquency Act (18 U.S.C. §§ 5036, 5037).

B. The Planning Group. This Plan has been adopted after consultation with the Speedy Trial Act Planning Group for the Central District of Illinois pursuant to 18 U.S.C. §§ 3165–3169.

The Planning Group consists of:

The Honorable Robert D. Morgan, Chief Judge of the Central District of Illinois and Chairman of the Planning Group.

The Honorable Bernard J. Ghiglieri, Jr., U.S. Magistrate of the Central District of Illinois.

Gerald D. Fines, United States Attorney for the Central District of Illinois.

Robert J. Kauffman, Clerk of the United States District Court for the Central District of Illinois.

Harry Marshall, U.S. Marshal for the District.

Glen Errion, Chief Probation Officer for the District.

David E. Booth, Federal Public Defender for the Central and Southern Districts of Illinois.

R. Michael Henderson, private attorney with substantial experience in civil litigation appointed pursuant to 18 U.S.C. § 3168(a) (as amended).

Gary T. Rafool, a private attorney with substantial experience in the defense of criminal cases appointed pursuant to 18 U.S.C. § 3168(a) (as amended).

John E. Nowak, Professor, University of Illinois College of Law, appointed as Reporter for the group pursuant to 18 U.S.C. § 3168.

C. Availability of the Plan. Copies of this Plan will be made available for inspection and copying at each office of the Clerk of the United States District Court for this District. Copies of Part II of this Plan wherein the Court adopts certain procedures for the disposition of criminal cases shall be furnished to all interested persons by the Clerk of the Court.

Section II.   Statement of Time Limits Adopted by the Court and Procedures for Implementing Them

II.   STATEMENT OF TIME LIMITS TO TAKE EFFECT JULY 1, 1980, AND PROCEDURES FOR IMPLEMENTING THEM

TIME LIMITS AND PROCEDURES FOR ACHIEVING PROMPT DISPOSITION OF CRIMINAL CASES

Effective July 1, 1980, the following shall constitute the Plan for achieving the prompt disposition of criminal cases in the Central District of Illinois including certain rules of procedure and discovery.

Pursuant to the requirements of Rule 50(b) of the Federal Rules of Criminal Procedure, the Speedy Trial Act of 1974 (18 U.S.C. Chapter 208), the Speedy Trial Act Amendments Act of 1979 (Pub. L. No. 96–43, 93 Stat. 327), and the Federal Juvenile Delinquency Act (18 U.S.C. §§ 5036, 5037), the judges of the United States District Court for the Central District of Illinois have adopted the following time limits and procedures to minimize undue delay and to further the prompt disposition of criminal cases and certain juvenile proceedings:

1. Applicability.

(a) *Offenses.* The time limits set forth herein are applicable to all criminal offenses triable in this court, including cases triable by United States Magistrates, except for petty offenses as defined in 18 U.S.C. § 1(3). Except as specifically provided, they are not applicable to proceedings under the Federal Juvenile Delinquency Act.

(b) *Persons.* The time limits are applicable to persons accused who have not been indicted or informed against as well as those who have, and the word "defendant" includes such persons unless the context indicates otherwise.

2. Priorities in Scheduling Criminal Cases. Preference shall be given to criminal proceedings as far as practicable as required by Rule 50(a) of the Federal Rules of Criminal Procedure. The trial of defendants in custody solely because they are awaiting trial and of high-risk defendants as defined in Section 5 should be given preference over other criminal cases.

3. Time Within Which an Indictment or Information Must be Filed.

(a) *Time Limits.* If an individual is arrested or served with a summons and the complaint charges an offense to be prosecuted in this District, any indictment or information subsequently filed in connection with such charge shall be filed within 30 days of arrest or service.

(b) *Measurement of Time Periods.* If a person has not been arrested or served with a summons on a Federal charge, an arrest will be deemed to have been made at such time as the person (i) is held in custody solely for the purpose of responding to a Federal charge; (ii) is delivered to the custody of a Federal official in connection with a Federal charge; or (iii) appears before a judicial officer in connection with a Federal charge.

(c) *Related Procedures.*

(1) At the time of the earliest appearance before a judicial officer of a person who has been arrested for an offense not charged in an indictment or information, the judicial officer shall establish for the record the date on which the arrest took place.

(2) In the absence of a showing to the contrary, a summons shall be considered to have been served on the date of service shown on the return thereof.

4. Time Within Which Trial Must Commence.

(a) *Time Limits.* The trial of a defendant shall commence not later than 70 days after the last to occur of the following dates:

(1) The date on which an indictment or information is filed in this District;

(2) The date on which a sealed indictment or information is unsealed; or

(3) The date of the defendant's first appearance before a judicial officer of this District.

(b) *Retrial; Trial After Reinstatement of an Indictment or Information.* The retrial of a defendant shall commence within 70 days from the date the order occasioning the retrial becomes final, as shall the trial of a defendant upon an indictment or information dismissed by a trial court and reinstated following an appeal. If the retrial or trial follows an appeal or collateral attack, the court may extend the period if unavailability of witnesses or other factors resulting from passage of time make trial within 70 days impractical. The extended period shall not exceed 180 days.

(c) *Withdrawal of Plea.* If a defendant enters a plea of guilty or nolo contendere to any or all charges in an indictment or information and is subsequently permitted to withdraw it, the time limit shall be determined for all counts as if the indictment or information were filed on the day the order permitting withdrawal of the plea became final.

(d) *Superseding Charges.* If, after an indictment or information has been filed, a complaint, indictment, or information is filed which charges the defendant with the same offense or with an offense required to be joined with that offense, the time limit applicable to the subsequent charge will be determined as follows:

(1) If the original indictment or information was dismissed on motion of the defendant before the filing of the subsequent charge, the time limit shall be determined without regard to the existence of the original charge.

(2) If the original indictment or information is pending at the time the subsequent charge is filed, the trial shall commence within the time limit for commencement of trial on the original indictment or information.

(3) If the original indictment or information was dismissed on motion of the United States Attorney before the filing of the subsequent charge, the trial shall commence within the time limit for commence of trial on the original indictment or information, but the period during which the defendant was not under charges shall be excluded from the computations. Such period is the period between the dismissal of the original indictment or information and the date the time would have commenced to run on the subsequent charge had there been no previous charge.

If the subsequent charge is contained in a complaint, the formal time limit within which an indictment or information must be obtained on the charge shall be determined without regard to the existence of the original indictment or information, but earlier action may in fact be required if the time limit for commencement of trial is to be satisfied.

(e) *Measurement of Time Periods.* For the purposes of this Section:

(1) If a defendant signs a written consent to be tried before a magistrate and no indictment or information charging the offense has been filed, the time limit shall run from the date of such consent.

(2) In the event of a transfer to this District under Rule 20 of the Federal Rules of Criminal Procedure, the indictment or information shall be deemed filed in this District when the papers in the proceeding or certified copies thereof are received by the Clerk.

(3) A trial in a jury case shall be deemed to commence at the beginning of voir dire.

(4) A trial in a non-jury case shall be deemed to commence on the day the case is called, provided that some step in the trial procedure immediately follows.

(f) *Related Procedures.*

(1) At the time of the defendant's earliest appearance before a judicial officer of this District, the officer will take appropriate steps to assure that the defendant is represented by counsel and shall appoint counsel where appropriate under the Criminal Justice Act and Rule 44 of the Federal Rules of Criminal Procedure.

(2) The court shall have sole responsibility for setting cases for trial after consultation with counsel. At the time of arraignment or as soon thereafter as is practicable, each case will be set for trial on a day certain or listed for trial on a weekly or other short-term calendar.

(3) Individual calendars shall be managed so that it will be reasonably anticipated that every criminal case set for trial will be reached during the week of original setting. A conflict in schedules of Assistant United States Attorneys or defense counsel will be ground for a continuance or delayed setting only if approved by the court and called to the court's attention at the earliest practicable time.

(4) In the event that a complaint, indictment, or information is filed against a defendant charged in a pending indictment or information or in an indictment or information dismissed on motion of the United States Attorney, the trial on the new charge shall commence within the time limit for commencement of trial on the original indictment or information unless the court finds that the new charge is not for the same offense charged in the original indictment or information or an offense required to be joined therewith.

(5) At the time of the filing of a complaint, indictment, or information described in paragraph (4), the United States Attorney shall give written notice to the Court of that circumstance and of his position with respect to the computation of the time limits.

(6) All pretrial hearings shall be conducted as soon after the arraignment as possible, consistent with the priorities of other matters on the court's criminal docket.

(7) Motions, discovery, and inspection shall commence following arraignment in accordance with Section 12.

5. Defendants in Custody and High–Risk Defendants.

(a) *Time Limits.* Notwithstanding any longer time periods that may be permitted under Sections 3 and 4, the following time limits will also be applicable to defendants in custody and high-risk defendants as herein defined:

(1) The trial of a defendant held in custody solely for the purpose of trial on a Federal charge shall commence within 90 days following the beginning of continuous custody.

(2) The trial of a high-risk defendant shall commence within 90 days of the designation as high-risk.

(b) *Definition of "High–Risk Defendant."* A high-risk defendant is one reasonably designated by the United States Attorney as posing a danger to himself or any other person or to the community.

(c) *Measurement of Time Periods.* For the purposes of this Section:

(1) A defendant is deemed to be in detention awaiting trial when he is arrested on a Federal charge or otherwise held for the purpose of responding to a Federal charge. Detention is deemed to be solely because the defendant is awaiting trial unless the person exercising custodial authority has an independent basis (not including a detainer) for continuing to hold the defendant.

(2) If a case is transferred pursuant to Rule 20 of the Federal Rules of Criminal Procedure and the defendant subsequently rejects disposition under Rule 20 or the court declines to accept the plea, a new period of continuous detention awaiting trial will begin at that time.

(3) A trial shall be deemed to commence as provided in Sections 4(e)(3) and 4(e)(4).

(d) *Related Procedures.*

(1) If a defendant is being held in custody solely for the purpose of awaiting trial, the United States Attorney shall advise the court at the earliest practicable time of the date of the beginning of such custody.

(2) The United States Attorney shall advise the court at the earliest practicable time (usually at the hearing with respect to bail) if the defendant is considered by him to be high-risk.

(3) If the court finds that the filing of a "high-risk" designation as a public record may result in prejudice to the defendant, it may order the designation sealed for such period as is necessary to protect the defendant's right to a fair trial, but not beyond the time that the court's judgment in the case becomes final. During the time the designation is under seal, it shall be made known to the defendant and his counsel but shall not be made known to other persons without the permission of the court.

6. Exclusion of Time From Computations.

(a) *Applicability.* In computing any time limit under Section 3, 4, or 5, the periods of delay set forth in 18 U.S.C. § 3161(h) shall be excluded. Such periods of delay shall not be excluded in computing the minimum period for commencement of trial under Section 7.

(b) *Records of Excludable Time.* The Clerk of the court shall enter on the docket, in the form prescribed by the Administrative Office of the United States Courts, information with respect to the excludable periods of time for each criminal defendant. With respect to proceedings prior to the filing of an indictment or information, excludable time shall be reported to the Clerk by the United States Attorney.

(c) *Pre–Indictment Procedures.*

(1) In the event that the United States Attorney anticipates that an indictment or information will not be filed within the time limit set forth in Section 3, he may file a written motion with the court for a determination of excludable time. In the event that the United States Attorney seeks a continuance under 18 U.S.C. § 3161(h)(8), he shall file a written motion with the court requesting such a continuance.

(2) The motion of the United States Attorney shall state (i) the period of time proposed for exclusion, and (ii) the basis of the proposed exclusion. If the motion is for a continuance under 18 U.S.C. § 3161(h)(8), it shall also state whether or not the defendant is being held in custody on the basis of the complaint. In appropriate circumstances, the motion may include a request that some or all of the supporting material be considered ex parte and in camera.

(3) The court may grant a continuance under 18 U.S.C. § 3161(h)(8) for either a specific period of time or a period to be determined by reference to an event (such as recovery from illness) not within the control of the government. If the

continuance is to a date not certain, the court shall require one or both parties to inform the court promptly when and if the circumstances that justify the continuance no longer exist. In addition, the court shall require one or both parties to file periodic reports bearing on the continued existence of such circumstances. The court shall determine the frequency of such reports in the light of the facts of the particular case.

(d) *Post–Indictment Procedures.*

(1) At each appearance of counsel before the court, counsel shall examine the Clerk's records of excludable time for completeness and accuracy and shall bring to the court's immediate attention any claim that the Clerk's record is in any way incorrect.

(2) In the event that the court continues a trial beyond the time limit set forth in Section 4 or 5, the court shall determine whether the limit may be recomputed by excluding time pursuant to 18 U.S.C. § 3161(h).

(3) If it is determined that a continuance is justified, the court shall set forth its findings in the record, either orally or in writing. If the continuance is granted under 18 U.S.C. § 3161(h)(8), the court shall also set forth its reasons for finding that the ends of justice served by granting the continuance outweigh the best interests of the public and the defendant in a speedy trial. If the continuance is to a date not certain, the court shall require one or both parties to inform the court promptly when and if the circumstances that justify the continuance no longer exist. In addition, the court shall require one or both parties to file periodic reports bearing on the continued existence of such circumstances. The court shall determine the frequency of such reports in the light of the facts of the particular case.

7. Minimum Period for Defense Preparation. Unless the defendant consents in writing to the contrary, the trial shall not commence earlier than 30 days from the date on which the indictment, information, or complaint is filed or, if later, from the date on which counsel first enters an appearance or on which the defendant expressly waives counsel and elects to proceed pro se. In circumstances in which the 70–day time limit for commencing trial on a charge in an indictment or information is determined by reference to an earlier indictment or information pursuant to Section 4(d), the 30–day minimum period shall also be determined by reference to the earlier indictment or information. When prosecution is resumed on an original indictment or information following a mistrial, appeal, or withdrawal of a guilty plea, a new 30–day minimum period will not begin to run. The court will in all cases schedule trials so as to permit defense counsel adequate preparation time in the light of all the circumstances.

8. Time Within Which Defendant Should be Sentenced.

(a) *Time Limit.* A defendant shall ordinarily be sentenced within 45 days of the date of his conviction or plea of guilty or nolo contendere.

(b) *Related Procedures.* If the defendant and his counsel consent thereto, a presentence investigation may be commenced prior to a plea of guilty or nolo contendere or a conviction.

9. Juvenile Proceedings.

(a) *Time Within Which Trial Must Commence.* An alleged delinquent who is in detention pending trial shall be brought to trial within 30 days of the date on which such detention was begun, as provided in 18 U.S.C. § 5036.

(b) *Time of Dispositional Hearing.* If a juvenile is adjudicated delinquent, a separate dispositional hearing shall be held no Later than 20 court days after trial, unless the court has ordered further study of the juvenile in accordance with 18 U.S.C. § 5037(c).

10. Sanctions.

(a) *Dismissal or Release from Custody.* Failure to comply with the requirements of Title I of the Speedy Trial Act may entitle the defendant to dismissal of the charges against him or to release from pretrial custody. Nothing in this Plan shall be construed to require that a case be dismissed or a defendant released from custody in circumstances in which such action would not be required by 18 U.S.C. §§ 3162 and 3164.

(b) *High–Risk Defendants.* A high-risk defendant whose trial has not commenced within the time limit set forth in 18 U.S.C. § 3164(b) shall, if the failure to commence trial was through no fault of the attorney for the government, have his release conditions automatically reviewed. A high-risk defendant who is found by the court to have intentionally delayed the trial of his case shall be subject to an order of the court modifying his nonfinancial conditions of release under Chapter 207 of Title 18 U.S.C., to ensure that he shall appear at trial as required.

(c) *Discipline of Attorneys.* In a case in which counsel (1) knowingly allows the case to be set for trial without disclosing the fact that a necessary witness would be unavailable for trial, (2) files a motion solely for the purpose of delay which he knows is frivolous and without merit, (3) makes a statement for the purpose of obtaining a continuance which he knows to be false and which is material to the granting of the continuance, or (4) otherwise willfully fails to proceed to trial without justification consistent with 18 U.S.C. § 3161, the court may punish such counsel as provided in 18 U.S.C. §§ 3162(b) and (c).

(d) *Alleged Juvenile Delinquents.* An alleged delinquent in custody whose trial has not commenced within the time limit set forth in 18 U.S.C. § 5036 shall be entitled to dismissal of his case pursuant to that Section unless the Attorney General shows that the delay was consented to or caused by the juvenile or his counsel, or would be in the interest of justice in the particular case.

11. Persons Serving Terms of Imprisonment. If the United States Attorney knows that a person charged with an offense is serving a term of imprisonment in any penal institution, he shall promptly seek to obtain the presence of the prisoner for trial, or cause a detainer to be filed, in accordance with the provisions of 18 U.S.C. § 3161(j).

12. Pretrial Motions, Discovery, and Inspection.

(a) Subject to the following provisions of this Section any and all pretrial motions may be filed after entry of a plea but must be filed within 20 days thereafter unless good cause for delay is shown in the motion.

(b) Except for good cause shown, the court may not extend the time for motions under Federal Rule of Criminal Procedure 12(b)(3) beyond 20 days after plea. Such motions will be ruled on promptly, so that the trial need not be delayed.

(c) Within five (5) days after arraignment, the United States Attorney and the defendant's attorney shall confer and, upon request, discovery and inspection shall be made by both parties in accordance with Federal Rule of Criminal Procedure 16.

(d) If in the judgment of the United States Attorney it would not be in the interests of justice to make any one or more disclosures set forth in paragraph (c) and requested by defendant's counsel, disclosure may be declined. A declination of any requested disclosure shall be in writing, directed to defendant's counsel, and signed personally by the United States Attorney or the Assistant United States Attorney handling the case, and shall specify the types of disclosures that are declined. If the defendant seeks to challenge the declination, he shall proceed pursuant to Subsection (e), below.

(e) *Additional Discovery or Inspection.* If additional discovery or inspection is sought, a defendant's attorney shall confer with the appropriate Assistant United States Attorney within ten (10) days of the arraignment, with a view to satisfying these requests in a cooperative atmosphere without recourse to the court. The request may be oral or written and the United States Attorney shall respond in like manner.

(f) In the event defendant thereafter moves for additional discovery or inspection, his motion shall be filed within the time set by the court for the filing of pretrial motions. It shall contain:

(1) The statement that the conference prescribed in (e), above, was held;

(2) The date of said conference;

(3) The name of the Assistant United States Attorney with whom conference was held; and

(4) The statement that agreement could not be reached concerning the discovery or inspection that is the subject of defendant's motion.

(g) Any duty of disclosure and discovery set forth in this Plan is a continuing one and the United States Attorney shall produce any additional information gained by the government.

(h) Any disclosure granted by the government pursuant to this Plan of material within the purview of Rule 16, Federal Rules of Criminal Procedure, shall be considered as relief sought by the defendant and granted by the court.

13. Effective Dates.

(a) The amendments to the Speedy Trial Act made by Public Law 96–43 became effective August 2, 1979. To the extent that this revision of the District's Plan does more than merely reflect the amendments, the revised Plan shall take effect upon approval of the reviewing panel designated in accordance with 18 U.S.C. § 3165(c). However, the dismissal sanction and the sanctions against attorneys authorized by 18 U.S.C. § 3162 and reflected in Sections 10(a) and (c) of this Plan shall apply only to defendants whose cases are commenced by arrest or summons on or after July 1, 1980, and to indictments and informations filed on or after that date.

(b) If a defendant was arrested or served with a summons before July 1, 1979, the time within which an information or indictment must be filed shall be determined under the Plan that was in effect at the time of such arrest or service.

(c) If a defendant was arraigned before August 2, 1979, the time within which the trial must commence shall be determined under the Plan that was in effect at the time of such arraignment.

(d) If a defendant was in custody on August 2, 1979, solely because he was awaiting trial, the 90–day period under Section 5 shall be computed from that date.

Section III. Summary of Experience Under the Act Within the District

III. SUMMARY OF EXPERIENCE UNDER THE ACT WITHIN THE DISTRICT.

A. Progress Towards Meeting the Permanent Time Limits. It is very difficult to quantify the progress of this District toward meeting the permanent time limits set by the 1979 amendments to the Speedy Trial Act. The reason for this difficulty is the fact that the district courts of Illinois were reorganized effective March 31, 1979, by the Federal District Court Reorganization Act of 1978 (P.L. 95–408; October 2, 1978). In that reorganization this District, which had heretofore been titled the Southern District of Illinois, became the Central District of Illinois and a portion of the old Eastern District became the new Southern District of Illinois. The data for 1977 and 1978 were compiled and reported in terms of the old district boundaries and titles. Neither the Clerks of the District Courts nor the Administrative Office of the United States Courts has sufficient time or resources to resort the earlier data to reflect the experience of the individual courts in the new district. This fact is referred to in the Fifth Report on the Implementation of Title I of the Speedy Trial Act of 1974, published by the Administrative Office on February 29, 1980, (see the appendix, page A–1, of that publication). The statistics regarding the case processing experience of this District following April 1, 1979, include data from cases that were terminated in this District but which had been on the docket of the District Court in Danville, Illinois, since the time when it was in the old Eastern District. This has made the evaluation of data quite difficult, but the Clerk of the Central District, Robert J. Kauffman, has compiled information on delays in each of the courts now in our District so that the Planning Group could make an accurate assessment of our progress toward meeting the new permanent time limits.

During the last six months of 1979 this District achieved total compliance with the permanent 30 day limit on the time from the arrest of a defendant to the filing of an indictment or information. In the first half of 1979 there was a significant percentage (38%) of the cases in which indictments were not filed within the 30 day period. However, the Planning Group has found that the delays in the early 1979 indictments resulted in part from the clearing of a temporary backlog of cases and problems encountered with the redistricting of the Illinois districts. Prior to 1979, the United States Attorney for this District had achieved compliance with the applicable time limit for indictments in approximately 90% of the cases. We expect no further problems with the United States Attorney being able to bring indictments within 30 "net" (nonexcludable) days from the arrest or service of summons upon a defendant.

The District had achieved almost perfect compliance with the previous 10 day time to arraignment limitation set by the Speedy Trial Act. However, that time period limitation has now been eliminated by the 1979 amendments to the Act.

As amended, the Speedy Trial Act requires the commencement of trial, or other disposition of a case, within a period of 30 to 70 days from indictment or, if later, the defendant's first appearance before a judicial officer in the District. Because the Act previously set a 10 day limit for arraignment and a 60 day limitation from arraignment to trial, the data kept by the Clerk and reported by the Administrative Office prior to 1979 does not reflect precisely the District's compliance with the new 30–70 day limitation. While it has been difficult to evaluate this data, the Planning Group has determined that the Central District of Illinois, as it is now constituted, has made excellent progress towards meeting this "time to trial" standard. We are hopeful that the District will have total compliance with the Act following July 1, 1980 (the new effective date for the new time limit sanctions). In the three years prior to June 30, 1979, this District had achieved compliance with the interim and transitional limits on the time from arraignment to trial in 90% of its cases. During the first six months of 1979, however, 22% of the terminated cases were not brought to trial within 70 net days from indictment or first appearance. This reported delay in case processing was in part attributable to difficulties in administering the redistricting and cases that were transferred in connection with the redistricting. In the last six months of 1979 all terminated cases complied with the 30–70 time to trial limitation.

B. Problems Encountered. Following the redistricting referred to in Part A of this Section, this District had to integrate a new district court into its administrative structure and process a number of cases which had originated in the old Eastern District of Illinois. The Planning Group has found that the most serious problems caused by the redistricting have now been dealt with and the criminal docket seems to be progressing in a highly efficient manner.

C. Incidence of and Reasons for, Requests or Allowances of Extension of Time Beyond District Standards. It is difficult to assess accurately the data on this subject for this District because of the redistricting and data evaluation problems referred to in Part A of this Section. In examining the reported incidence of delay we find that there has been very little exclusion of time in this District. This fact is referred to in the two versions of "Table 2" which are appended to this Plan. During the last six months of 1979 only one quarter of the defendants whose cases were terminated in this District had any reportable excludable time. In the previous twelve months only 36.9% of the defendants had excludable time reported in connection with their prosecutions. The Planning Group finds that there has been

534

no unnecessary exclusion of time in this District; most of the exclusions related to time when motions were heard or under consideration.

In one sense the low incidence of excludable time is laudable because it indicates that there has been little delay in the processing of cases in this District. However, this low incidence of excludable time may indicate that counsel for defendants, and the United States Attorneys office, have not fully reported to our Clerk all facts that might justify the notation of excludable time. A failure to report excludable time accurately to the Clerk may cause problems in the future (see Section D, below).

D. Cases Not in Compliance with the Limits—Reasons Why Exclusions Were Inadequate to Accommodate Periods of Delay. As reported in the previous parts of this Section of our Plan, this District has achieved total compliance with the time limitation for the bringing of indictments or informations. In the last six months of 1979 the District also achieved total compliance with the 70 day limitation on the time for commencing trial (or otherwise disposing of a case) following a defendant's indictment or first appearance.

During the first six months of 1979 approximately 20% of the terminated cases took longer than 70 net days from indictment or first appearance to trial or another disposition of a case. In examining the data for the cases which exceeded the 70 day "time to trial" limitation during the first half of 1979 it appears that a high percentage of the cases (7 of 13) originated in the Danville court; the initiation of those prosecutions predated the inclusion of that court in this district. Yet, it is difficult to determine the extent to which those cases are reflected in the data for the first six months of 1979 experience of this District. Most of the cases which took more than 70 days from indictment to trial involved multiple defendant litigation; several of the cases involved long periods of discovery and preparation in connection with charges of tax evasion or misappropriation of bank funds. The Planning Group believes that these "complex" cases may have involved more excludable time than was reported and that there may have been a failure on the part of counsel for the government and defendants to bring to the attention of the Clerk all facts that might have resulted in the notation of excludable time.

In the future it will be necessary for the office of the United States Attorney to work as closely as possible with the Clerk of the District Court to insure that all excludable time is reported and to bring to the attention of the court any need for a ruling on the existence of excludable time in a given case. Yet while we note this possible reporting problem, the Planning Group observes that any such problem appears to have been cured; the United States Attorney was in perfect compliance with the 30 day indictment-information time limit and that the court was able to process all defendants within 70 days (from indictment or first appearance) during the last six months of 1979.

E. The Effect on Criminal Justice Administration of the Prevailing Time Limits. As reported in our 1978 Plan, there has been no demonstrable effect of the Speedy Trial Act on the administration of criminal justice in this District. The Act has made the processing of cases somewhat more prompt than in previous years, but it has also made the scheduling of court time more difficult. There is no data to demonstrate that the system of criminal justice or any defendants have been helped or hurt by the existence of the Act and its time limits.

F. Effect of Compliance With the Time Limits on the Civil Calendar. In two of the three district court locations in this District the Speedy Trial Act has had little effect on the processing of the civil calendar. The ratio of criminal to civil cases at our District Courts in Danville and Peoria is such that there is sufficient time to hear civil cases promptly while leaving time open for the processing of the criminal docket at those courts in compliance with the terms of the Speedy Trial Act. However, the District's highest number of civil cases are filed at our district court in Springfield and the Speedy Trial Act has impaired the ability of the District to process those cases. The reason for this is a simple one: civil cases are set for trial at a time sufficient to allow for complete preparation by all parties and the appearance of all witnesses whereas criminal cases may be filed at a later time and require more immediate attention because they must be processed within the time limits set by the Speedy Trial Act. The requirements of the Act have resulted in our District Court in Springfield having to delay the previously arranged hearing of civil cases fairly frequently in order to hear criminal case motions or trials. The Planning Group notes, however, that the judges of this District have adjusted their calendars so that the overall processing of the civil docket has been efficient. But it is only the added effort of the judges which has mitigated the damage done to the efficient scheduling of civil cases by the Speedy Trial Act.

G. Frequency of Use of Sanctions Under 18 U.S.C. § 3164 (Release From Custody or Modification of Release Conditions). It has not been necessary in this District to invoke the sanctions under the time limits of the Speedy Trial Act to date.

Section IV. Changes in Practices and Procedures that Have Been or Will Be Adopted by the District Court to Expedite the Disposition of Criminal Cases in Accordance With 18 U.S.C. § 3167(b)

IV. STATEMENT OF PROCEDURES AND INNOVATIONS THAT HAVE BEEN OR WILL BE ADOPTED BY THE DISTRICT COURT TO EXPEDITE THE DISPOSITION OF CRIMINAL CASES IN ACCORDANCE WITH THE SPEEDY TRIAL ACT.

A. Court Rules. No changes in court rules have been adopted due to the Speedy Trial Act. However, it should be noted that the District has adopted open pretrial discovery and inspection rules which are designed to facilitate the processing of criminal cases; those rules are adopted in Section 11 of Part II of this Plan pursuant to Federal Rules of Criminal Procedure 16 and 50(b).

B. Case Reporting Systems–Office of the Clerk. As noted in our 1976 and 1978 District Plans, the Clerk of the District Court has developed a case tracking and reporting system which has greatly facilitated the processing of cases. The Clerk's office has created a listing of criminal cases which has a single line for each case that shows the relevant dates and occurrences that establish the time limits for each phase of that case under the Speedy Trial Act. A separate list of cases is kept for each judge and place of court within the District; copies of the list are sent to each judge every few weeks. It has been over four years since the Clerk began this tracking system and every criminal case in the District pending in the District now appears on these report sheets. This tracking of criminal cases has significantly increased the work of the Clerk and his assistants, but it has proved to be a most efficient method for assuring that cases are brought to trial within the applicable time limits.

Section V. Additional Resources Needed, if any, to Achieve Compliance with the Act by July 1, 1979 (18 U.S.C. § 3166(d))

V. STATEMENT OF ADDITIONAL RESOURCES NEEDED TO ACHIEVE COMPLIANCE WITH THE ACT.

A. Judgeships. In our 1978–79 Plan we reported on legislation then pending in Congress concerning the authorization of an additional judgeship for the then Eastern and Southern Districts of Illinois. Since that time the Districts for the United States District Courts for Illinois have been redrawn so that this District, the Central District of Illinois, is now a three judge District. While the presence of a third judge in the District has promoted the efficient case processing, the redistricting brought a significant increase in civil and criminal dockets for this District. Because the redistricting went into effect only one year ago it is too soon to determine whether the Central District will need an additional judgeship to keep pace with its caseload.

B. Magistrates. For slightly over two years our District has had a single full-time Magistrate, Charles H. Evans, whose work has proved invaluable in processing cases as well as trying cases within his jurisdiction. The District also has the services of four part-time magistrates. Authorization for, and appointment of an additional full-time magistrate probably would facilitate the processing of cases in this District. However, the Planning Group believes that the District needs more experience with the processing of cases following the recent expansion of magistrate jurisdiction in order to accurately assess whether an additional full-time magistrate is needed in this District.

C. Office of the Clerk of the District Court. In our 1978 Plan we reported that the Clerk would require an additional deputy clerk and increased stenographic assistance to assure compliance with the Speedy Trial Act. We renew that request. The intervening two years have demonstrated that the Act has put a severe strain on the Office of the Clerk. As reported in Part IV of this Plan, the Clerk of this District has created a case tracking and listing system which has greatly facilitated the processing of cases in compliance with the terms of the Speedy Trial Act. While the Clerk's office has been granted additional resources based on a case filing formula, the District still requires separate assistance for the Clerk to monitor and report the progress of cases in order to insure compliance with the permanent standards of the Speedy Trial Act.

D. "Supporting" Personnel. The Planning Group does not have any specific recommendations concerning the needs of those agencies whose functioning is necessary to the processing of cases in the District even though they are not formally a part of the Court administrative structure. However, it must be noted that, with increased size of this District, the workload of the offices of the United States Attorney, the Federal Public Defender (who serves both the Central and Southern Districts of Illinois), the Chief Probation Officer, and the United States Marshal has increased beyond that reflected merely by the number of cases now on the docket of this District. The Planning Group recommends that consideration be given to the awarding increased personnel to these agencies even though we have no specific recommendations on this subject at this time.

Section VI. Recommendations for Changes in Statutes, Rules, or Administrative Procedures (18 U.S.C. §§ 3166(b)(7), (d)(e))

VI. RECOMMENDATIONS FOR CHANGES IN STATUTES, RULES, OR ADMINISTRATIVE PROCEDURES.

In the District Plan submitted to the Reviewing Panel and Administrative Office in 1978 the Planning Group of this District (then titled the Southern District of Illinois) made a number of recommendations for changes to the Speedy Trial Act. Since that time the Act has been amended and it now expressly deals with some of the concerns expressed by the Planning Group in 1978. Accordingly, the Planning Group, at this time, does not have any recommendations for changes to the Speedy Trial Act, other federal statutes, any of the Federal Rules, or reporting requirements, procedures and forms.

Section VII. Incidence and Length of, Reasons for, and Remedies for Detention Prior to Trial (18 U.S.C. § 3166(b)(6))

VII. INCIDENCE AND LENGTH OF, REASONS FOR, AND REMEDIES FOR DETENTION PRIOR TO TRIAL.

It is unusual for a defendant to remain in Federal custody solely for the purpose of appearing at trial in this District. In the last six months of 1979 less than half of the defendants in this District spent any time in Federal custody prior to trial. Only 14 defendants spent more than 30 days in such custody and none was in custody more than 90 "net" days prior to trial (see Table 3 appended to this Plan). The reason for such detention has been that these defendants were unable to post bail in the amount set to fairly insure their appearance at trial.

Section VIII. Adoption; Effective Date

VIII. ADOPTION; EFFECTIVE DATE.

Pursuant to Rule 50(b) of the Federal Rules of Criminal Procedure, the Speedy Trial Act of 1974 (18 U.S.C. Chapter 208, as amended) and the Federal Juvenile Delinquency Act (18 U.S.C. §§ 5036, 5037) the foregoing is adopted as the District Court Plan for the disposition of criminal cases in the Central District of Illinois. This includes the adoption of certain rules and procedures for criminal cases contained in Part II of this Plan.

Upon approval of the reviewing panel designated in accordance with 18 U.S.C. § 3165(c) and Rule 50(b) of the Federal Rules of Criminal Procedure this Plan, and the time limits and procedures set forth herein, shall become effective on July 1, 1980, and shall supersede those previously in effect.

Section IX. Statistical Tables

[**Publisher's Note:** The Content in Section IX—Statistical Tables is omitted from this publication.]

[Dated May 1, 1980, approved by the Judicial Council of the Seventh Circuit June 13, 1980, and made effective July 1, 1980. Amended effective June 13, 1985; July 15, 1988; redesignated CDIL–3 on February 28, 1992.]

STANDING ORDER CDIL–7. ORDER ON DISPOSITION OF HABEAS CORPUS PETITIONS IN CAPITAL CASES

It is ordered by the Judges of this District that the District Court Rules for the Disposition of Petitions for Habeas Corpus pursuant to 28 U.S.C. § 2254 and § 2255 in Cases Involving Capital Punishment, as promulgated and amended by the Judicial Council of the Seventh Circuit Court of Appeals, and as set forth below, are hereby adopted by this District Court.

A. Operation and Scope.

1. These rules shall apply to habeas corpus petitions filed in United States District Courts within the Seventh Circuit brought pursuant to 28 U.S.C. § 2254 and § 2255 by petitioners under a sentence of capital punishment.

2. To the extent that these rules are inconsistent with the local rules of any of the United States District Courts within the Seventh Circuit, these rules shall apply.

3. The district judge to whom a case is assigned shall handle all matters pertaining to the case, including application for certificate of probable cause, motion for stay of execution, consideration of the merits, second or successive petitions, remands from the Supreme Court of the United States or the United States Court of Appeals, and all incidental or collateral matters. This rule does not limit a district judge's discretion to designate a magistrate judge, pursuant to 28 U.S.C. § 636, to perform such duties as the district judge deems appropriate or for an emergency judge to act in the absence of the assigned district judge.

4. If a second or successive petition is filed in another district court within the circuit, the judge to whom the second or successive petition is assigned ("second judge") shall communicate with the judge to whom earlier petitions were assigned ("first judge") and with the chief judge of the circuit. The chief judge shall, unless there is good reason not to do so, temporarily assign the first judge to serve as a

district judge in the other district for the assignment of the second or successive petitions.

5. Pursuant to the Criminal Justice Act, 18 U.S.C. § 3006A and 21 U.S.C. § 848(a), counsel shall be appointed for all prisoners in cases within the scope of these rules if the prisoner is not already represented by counsel, is financially unable to obtain representation, and requests that counsel be appointed.

6. If the district court grants or denies a stay of execution, it shall set forth the reasons for the decision.

7. The district judge to whom a case is assigned under these rules may make changes in procedures in any case when justice so requires.

B. Filing of a Petition.

8. Upon the filing of a petition within the scope of these rules, it shall be immediately assigned to a district judge under the usual practices of the court. The clerk shall immediately notify the judge of his or her assignment and shall thereafter promptly notify, by telephone, the designated representatives of the Attorney General of the state in which the petition is filed. The Attorneys General of Illinois and Indiana have the obligation to keep the court informed as to the office and home telephone numbers of their designated representatives.

9. In all petitions within the scope of this rule, the petitioner or movant shall file, within 10 days of the day of filing of the petition or motion, a legible copy of the documents listed below. If a required document is not filed, the petitioner or movant shall state the reason for the omission. The required documents are:

　　a. Prior petitions, with docket numbers, filed by petitioner in federal district court challenging the conviction and sentence challenged in the current petition;

　　b. a copy of, or a citation to, each state or federal court opinion, memorandum decision, order, transcript of oral statement of reasons, or judgment involving an issue presented in the petition; and

　　c. such other documents as the district court may request.

10. A petitioner shall include in his or her petition all possible grounds for relief and the scheduled execution date. If an issue is raised in a second or successive petition that was not raised in a prior petition, the petitioner shall state the reasons why the issue was not raised and why relief should nonetheless be granted.

11. If an issue is raised that has not been exhausted in state court, was never raised in state court or was not raised on direct appeal in state court, the petitioner shall state the reasons why the issue was not raised and why relief should nonetheless be granted.

12. Upon the filing of a petition within the scope of these rules, the district court clerk shall immediately provide the petitioner with a copy of these rules and a copy of Circuit Rule 22 adopted by the United States Court of Appeals for the Seventh Circuit.

13. The district court clerk shall notify the clerk of the Court of Appeals of the filing of a petition within the scope of these rules, of significant events and the progress of the case, and of any subsequent appeal of such case. The district court clerk shall send a copy of the final decision and any notice of appeal to the clerk of the state supreme court.

C. Preliminary Consideration by Judge.

14. The district judge shall promptly examine a petition within the scope of these rules and, if appropriate, order the respondent to file an answer or other pleading or take such other action as the judge deems appropriate.

15. If the district judge determines, after examination of the petition, that the petition is a second or successive petition raising issues previously decided by a federal court, the district judge shall enter an appropriate order with a written finding so stating.

D. Priority.

16. The district judge shall give priority on his or her calendar to scheduling and deciding cases within the scope of these rules.

E. Motions for Immediate Stay of Execution.

17. No motion for a stay of execution shall be filed unless accompanied by a petition for relief under 28 U.S.C. § 2254 or § 2255 which comports with these rules. The movant shall immediately notify opposing counsel by telephone of the filing.

18. The movant shall attach to the motion for stay a legible copy of the documents listed in Rule 9, unless the documents have already been filed with the court. If the movant asserts that time does not permit the filing of a written motion, he or she shall deliver to the clerk a legible copy of the listed documents as soon as possible. If a required document is not filed, the movant shall state the reason for the omission.

19. If the state has no objection to the motion for stay, the district court shall enter an order staying the execution.

20. If the district court determines that the petition or motion is not frivolous and a stay is requested, it shall enter an order staying the execution.

21. Following a decision on the merits, if the district court issues a certificate of probable cause, it shall enter an order staying the execution pending appeal. If the district court denies a certificate of probable cause, it shall not enter an order staying the execution pending appeal and it shall dissolve any stay of execution previously granted to petitioner by the district court.

22. Parties shall file motions with the district court clerk during the normal business hours of the clerk's office. The motion shall contain a brief account of the prior actions of any court or judge to which the motion or a substantially similar or related petition for relief has been submitted.

23. The district court shall adopt local rules setting forth the procedures for filing of emergency motions or applications when the district court clerk's office is closed.

F. Clerk's List of Cases.

24. The district court clerk shall maintain a separate list of all cases within the scope of these rules.

In accordance with Paragraph 23 above, the Judges of this District order that emergency motions or applications may be received by any District Judge of this District during times when the Clerk's Office is closed.

[Filed: March 2, 1992.]

ELECTRONIC CASE FILING

ELECTRONIC AVAILABILITY OF TRANSCRIPTS OF PROCEEDINGS BEFORE U.S. DISTRICT AND MAGISTRATE JUDGES

Transcripts of proceedings before the U.S. District Judges and Magistrate Judges in the Central District of Illinois taken by Official Court Reporters and Contract Reporters are now being filed with the court in electronic format. Electronic transcripts, once ordered by a party or attorney and produced by the Court Reporter, will be e-filed and available for viewing at the Clerk's Office public terminal, but may NOT be copied nor reproduced by the Clerk's Office for a period of 90 days. If no Notice of Intent to Request Redactions or Motion of Requested Redactions is filed, the restrictions will be removed after the 90 day period. The transcript will then be available remotely to view, download or print a copy from PACER at $.08 cents per page or from the Clerk's Office at a rate of $.10 per page.

During the initial 90 days after the transcript is e-filed, individuals wishing to purchase a copy of a transcript—in either paper or electronic form—must do so through the Court Reporter. Once an attorney on the case has purchased a transcript, the Court Reporter will notify the Clerk's office so the attorney will be given access to the transcript through the court's CM/ECF system.

This will apply to all transcripts of proceedings or parts of proceedings ordered on or after this date, regardless of when the proceeding took place. Please read this policy carefully. This policy establishes a procedure for counsel to request the redaction from the transcript of specific personal data identifiers before the transcript is made electronically available to the general public.

Whenever an official transcript of a proceeding has been filed by the Official Court Reporter or Contract Reporter, a Notice of Filing of Official Transcript will be served on all parties in the case. If necessary, a party must file a Notice of Intent to Request Redaction (sample attached) within seven (7) business days of the filing of the official transcript by the Court Reporter. If a party fails to request redaction within this time frame, the transcript will be made electronically available without redaction, 90 days after the transcript was initially filed with the Clerk. The e-filed transcript will be available for reviewing at the Clerk's Office public terminal or for purchase from the Court Reporter during this seven-day period in paper form or electronic form.

Counsel are strongly urged to share this notice with all clients so that an informed decision about the inclusion of certain materials may be made. **The responsibility for redacting personal identifiers rests solely with counsel and the parties. The Clerk and Court Reporter will not review each transcript for compliance with this rule.**

If a party files a Notice of Intent to Request Redaction, the transcript will not be made remotely electronically available to the general public until the redactions have been made. The e-filed transcript will be available for reviewing at the Clerk's Office public terminal or purchased from the Court Reporter during this time. Within 21 calendar days from the filing of the transcript with the Clerk, or longer if ordered by the Court, the parties must e-file with the Court a Motion of Requested Redactions indicating where the personal identifiers appear in the transcript by page and line and how they are to be redacted. Requests for Redactions other than personal identifiers will need to be ruled on by the Court. Access to this motion will be restricted to the Court and the attorneys of record in the case. For example, if a party wanted to redact the Social Security number 123–45–6789 appearing on page 12, line 9 of the transcript, the Statement of Requested Redactions would read: "Redact the Social Security number on page 12, line 9 to read xxx–xx–6789." A party is only responsible for reviewing and indicating the redactions in the testimony of the witnesses it called and its own statements (e.g. opening statements and closing arguments).

Only the following personal identifiers listed by the Judicial Conference in its policy on the Electronic Availability of Transcripts, may be redacted using a Statement of Requested Redactions submitted to the Court Reporter: All other requests for redaction shall be in a motion.

    1. Minors' names: use the minors' initials;

    2. Financial account numbers: use only the last four numbers of the account number;

    3. Social Security numbers: use only the last four numbers;

    4. Dates of birth: use only the year;

    5. Home addresses to the city and state.

If a party wants to redact other information, that party must move the Court for further redaction by separate motion served on all parties and the Court Reporter within the 21–day period. Counsel appointed pursuant to the Criminal Justice Act may claim compensation, at the applicable rate, for the time spent reviewing the transcript and preparing the Motion of Requested Redactions as well as for costs associated with obtaining a copy of the transcript.

IN THE UNITED STATES DISTRICT COURT FOR
THE CENTRAL DISTRICT OF ILLINOIS

	)	
	)	
Plaintiff(s)	)	
	)	
	)	
vs.	)	
	)	Case No.
	)	
	)	
Defendant(s)	)	
	)	

NOTICE OF INTENT TO REQUEST REDACTION

Notice is hereby given that a Motion of Requested Redactions shall be e-filed with the Court within 21 days from the filing of the transcript with the Clerk of Court. Access to the Motion of Requested Redactions will be restricted to the Court and attorneys of record in the case.

Date: _____

s/ _____

Address: _____

_____

_____

Telephone: _____

Fax: _____

Email: _____

CERTIFICATE OF SERVICE

I hereby certify that on ___Date___ , I electronically filed the foregoing with the Clerk of the Court using the CM/ECF system which will send notification of such filing to the following: _____, and I hereby certify that I have mailed by United States Postal Service the document to the following non CM/ECF participants: _____.

s/ _____

NOTE: To electronically file this document, you will find the event in our Case Management (CM/ECF) system, under Civil Events/Other Documents/Notice of Intent to Request Redaction and under Criminal Events/Notices/Notice of Intent to Request Redaction.

_____

**IN THE UNITED STATES DISTRICT COURT FOR
THE CENTRAL DISTRICT OF ILLINOIS**

Plaintiff(s)	))))
vs.	)) Case No.))
Defendant(s)	)))

REDACTION REQUEST—TRANSCRIPT

Pursuant to Judicial Conference policy, <u>(Plaintiff/Defendant Name)</u> requests redaction of transcript(s) on file in this case:

(Please list the document, page, and line number and a redacted identifier for each redaction necessary; *e.g.*, Doc. No. 15, Page 12, Line 9, Social Security No. to read xxx–xx–6130.)

Document No. of Transcript	Page No.	Line No(s).	Redacted Identifier

The undersigned understands that redaction of information other than personal identifiers listed below requires an order of the court.

Minors' names: use the minors' initials;

Financial account numbers: use only the last four numbers of the account number;

Social Security numbers: use only the last four numbers;

Dates of birth: use only the year;

Home addresses to the city and state.

Date: s/ _____

                               Address: _____

                                     _____

                                     Telephone: _____

                                     Fax: _____

                                     Email: _____

CERTIFICATE OF SERVICE

I hereby certify that on ___Date__, I electronically filed the foregoing with the Clerk of the Court using the CM/ECF system which will send notification of such filing to the following: _____, and I hereby certify that I have mailed by United States Postal Service the document to the following non CM/ECF participants: _____.

s/ _____

[Effective January 1, 2008. Revised May 6, 2008; August 14, 2008.]

Note

To electronically file this document, you will find the event in our Case Management (CM/ECF) system, under Civil or Criminal Events/Other Documents/Redaction Request— Transcript.

PLAN FOR THE RANDOM SELECTION OF JURORS
(Standing Order CDIL–4)

JURY SELECTION PLAN
OF THE UNITED STATES DISTRICT COURT
FOR THE CENTRAL DISTRICT OF ILLINOIS
FOR THE RANDOM SELECTION OF GRAND AND PETIT JURORS

(Amended January 20, 2009)

Pursuant to the Jury Selection and Service Act of 1968, as amended, 28 U.S.C. § 1861 et seq., "the Act," this Jury Selection Plan is hereby adopted by this court, subject to approval by the reviewing panel for the Seventh Circuit and to such rules and regulations as may be adopted from time to time by the Judicial Conference of the United States.

APPLICABILITY OF THE PLAN, 28 U.S.C. §§ 1861, 1863

This Plan applies to each of the divisions of this district as now established by law unless specifically indicated otherwise. The Central District of Illinois is hereby divided, for jury selection purposes, pursuant to Section 1869 of the Act, as follows:

The Peoria Division, consisting of the counties of: Bureau, Fulton, Hancock, Knox, Livingston, Marshall, McDonough, McLean, Peoria, Putnam, Stark, Tazewell and Woodford.

The Urbana Division, consisting of the counties of: Champaign, Coles, Douglas, Edgar, Ford, Iroquois, Kankakee, Macon, Moultrie, Piatt, and Vermilion.

The Springfield Division, consisting of the counties of: Adams, Brown, Cass, Christian, DeWitt, Greene, Logan, Macoupin, Mason, Menard, Montgomery, Morgan, Pike, Sangamon, Schuyler, Scott and Shelby.

The Rock Island Division, consisting of the counties of: Henderson, Henry, Mercer, Rock Island and Warren.

DECLARATION OF POLICY, 28 U.S.C. § 1861

It is the policy of the court that all litigants in this court entitled to trial by jury shall have the right to grand and petit juries selected at random from a fair cross-section of the community in each division where the court convenes, and that all citizens who reside within the district shall have the opportunity to be considered for service on grand and petit juries and they shall have an obligation to serve as jurors when summoned for that purpose.

DISCRIMINATION PROHIBITED, 28 U.S.C. § 1862

No citizen shall be excluded from service as a grand or petit juror in this court on account of race, color, religion, sex, national origin, or economic status.

MANAGEMENT AND SUPERVISION OF THE JURY SELECTION PROCESS, 28 U.S.C. § 1863(b)(1)

The clerk of the court shall manage the jury selection process under the supervision and control of the chief judge and each of the other judges presiding over the respective divisions of the court. In managing and supervising the jury selection process, the clerk is authorized to delegate duties as may be necessary in the jury selection process to deputy clerks.

METHOD AND MANNER OF RANDOM SELECTION, 28 U.S.C. § 1863(b)

The selection of names for the master jury wheel shall be accomplished by a purely randomized process through a properly programmed electronic data processing system. A properly programmed electronic data processing system for pure randomized selection shall also be used to select names from the master jury wheel for the purpose of determining qualification for jury service, and from the qualified wheel for summoning persons to serve as grand or petit jurors. In each instance, the randomized process ensures that the mathematical odds of any single name being picked are substantially equal.

Pursuant to 28 U.S.C. § 1861, all litigants "have the right to grand and petit jurors selected at random from a fair cross section of the community." The court uses a two-step process to select jurors. First, a master jury wheel is created by selecting names at random from the registered voter lists in each gubernatorial general election. Then names are randomly drawn periodically from the master jury wheel to receive juror qualification questionnaires. Individuals' answers to these questionnaires determine whether they are legally qualified to serve. If so, the names of those persons are put in a second wheel, a qualified jury wheel. As prospective jurors are needed for a specific trial or grand jury, juror summonses are sent to persons randomly selected from the qualified wheel. All of these selections are carried out through a properly programmed electronic data processing system for pure randomized selection. The pure randomized process ensures that the mathematical odds of any single name being picked are substantially equal.

MAINTAINING THE MASTER JURY WHEEL, 28 U.S.C. § 1863(b)(3) & (4)

The clerk shall maintain a master jury wheel for the district, with juror names from each of the four divisions of the wheel. The initial selection of names to fill the master jury wheel shall be of a sufficient number as may be deemed needed for a four-year period. The minimum number of names to be placed in the master jury wheel shall be at least one-half of 1% of the total number of names on the voter registration lists. The minimum number of names to be placed in the master jury wheel for each division will be as follows:

Peoria Division	30,000
Urbana Division	30,000
Springfield Division	30,000
Rock Island Division	6,000

The presiding judge in each division may order additional names to be placed in the master jury wheel for said division from time to time as necessary.

The number of names drawn from each county shall be substantially in the same proportion to the total number drawn from all counties within the division as the number of names on the county's voter registration list bears to the total number of names on the voter registration lists for each county within the division. For example, if there are 240,000 names on the voter registration list of all counties within the division, and there are 48,000 names on county "A's" list (twenty percent of the total), then the number of county "A's" names initially selected should be substantially twenty percent of the total number selected from all counties within the division.

After first determining the total number of names needed for the master jury wheel, and the proportionate share of names to be drawn from each particular county, the clerk shall proceed to make the initial selection of names.

The master jury wheel shall be refilled every four years using the names and addresses of all persons randomly selected from the lists of voters at the last gubernatorial general election. No later than June 1, the clerk shall begin selecting names for filling the qualified jury wheels from the newly filled master jury wheel and will cease selecting names from the prior master jury wheel.

JURY SELECTION SOURCES, 28 U.S.C. § 1863(b)(2) & (3)

The judges of the court find that the source from which the names of grand and petit jurors shall be selected at random shall be from the registered voter lists in each gubernatorial general election as maintained in the books or lists of (1) the office of the County Clerk in each county, (2) the office of the City Clerk in those cities which have separate registration lists or (3) the office of the State Board of Elections of the State of Illinois within the Central District of Illinois. The judges do further find that such lists represent a fair cross section of the communities in the district.

The clerk shall issue written instructions directing the Election Commission to provide a list of all registered voters in the district in electronic format ("voter data files"). The clerk shall also require the Election Commission to provide an affidavit stating that the voter data files contain a list of all registered voters in the district.

SELECTING THE NAMES BY AUTOMATED METHODS

The judges of this court find that electronic data processing methods can be advantageously used for selecting and copying names from the voters lists furnished by counties or the State Board of Elections which are submitted in machine readable forms such as magnetic tapes or magnetic discs. Therefore, a properly programmed electronic data processing system shall be used to select master wheel names from voter lists of any or all counties in the district, provided that the required proportions of names for each county are maintained as above described and the purely randomized selection process is followed.

Similarly, the judges of the court find that the Jury Management System (JMS) shall be used to select names from the master wheel of persons to be mailed qualification questionnaires, from the qualified wheel of persons to be summoned to serve as grand or petit jurors, and for the recording of names of prospective jurors and records needed by the court to administer the selection and payment of jurors.

DRAWING OF NAMES FROM THE MASTER JURY WHEEL; COMPLETION OF JUROR QUALIFICATION FORMS, 28 U.S.C. §§ 1863(b)(7), 1864(a), 1868 and 1869(k)

The clerk shall, either all at one time or at periodic intervals, utilize JMS to randomly draw a sufficient number of names from the master jury wheel to maintain an adequate number of names in the qualified jury wheel to meet the needs of the court. The clerk shall post a general notice for public review in the clerk's office and on the court's website explaining the process by which names are periodically and randomly drawn.

The number of names to be drawn from the master jury wheel shall be determined by the clerk based upon anticipated juror demands of the court, plus a margin of extra names sufficient to compensate for those individuals who will be ineligible or unavailable.

The lists of the names drawn shall not be exhibited to any person except as provided in the Act or this Plan. Lists of names so drawn are generated by JMS and are maintained in the clerk's office.

The clerk shall prepare, by means of JMS, and mail to every person whose name is so drawn, a juror qualification questionnaire form, accompanied by instructions to execute and return the questionnaire, duly signed and sworn to, by mail within ten days. At the option of the clerk, questionnaires may be mailed by the clerk's office or by a commercial mailing service. When the court implements the newest component to the JMS system, the on-line eJuror system, prospective jurors will have the option of completing their juror questionnaire on-line via the court's internet website. If any person fails to return a completed juror qualification form as instructed, the clerk may thereupon pursue the matter in accordance with 28 U.S.C. § 1864(a).

QUALIFICATIONS FOR JURY SERVICE, 28 U.S.C. § 1865(b)

Any person shall be deemed qualified to serve on grand and petit juries unless the person:

a. is not a citizen of the United States,[1] is not eighteen years old, or has not resided for a period of one year within the judicial district;

b. is unable to read, write, and understand the English language with a degree of proficiency sufficient to satisfactorily complete the juror qualification form;

c. is unable to speak the English language;

d. is incapable by reason of mental or physical infirmity of rendering satisfactory jury service; or

e. has a charge pending against him or her, or has been convicted in a state or federal court of record, for the commission of a crime punishable by imprisonment for more than one year and his or her civil rights have not been restored by pardon or amnesty.

EXEMPTIONS FROM JURY SERVICE, 28 U.S.C. §§ 1863(b)(6); 1869(i)

The judges of the court find members in active service in the armed forces of the United States, members of fire or police departments, and public officers in the executive, legislative, or judicial branches of the United States, or the State of Illinois, who are actively engaged in the performance of official duties shall be exempt from jury service under this Plan.

EXCUSE FROM JURY SERVICE UPON INDIVIDUAL REQUEST, 28 U.S.C. §§ 1863(b)(5)(A) & (B); 1866(e); 1869(j) and District Court Clerk's Manual Chapter 23

The judges of the court find that jury service by members of the following occupational classes or group of persons would entail undue hardship or extreme inconvenience to the members thereof, and the excuse of such members will not be inconsistent with the Act, as amended, and shall be granted upon individual request:

1. Persons over 70 years of age.

2. Persons who have, within the past two years, served on a federal grand or petit jury.

3. Persons having active care and custody of a child or children under 10 years of age whose health and/or safety would be jeopardized by their absence for jury service; or a person who is essential to the care of aged or infirm persons.

4. Any person whose services are so essential to the operation of a business, commercial, or agricultural enterprise that said enterprise must close if such person were required to perform jury duty.

5. Persons actively practicing or engaged full-time in one of the following: attorney or physician.

6. Volunteer safety personnel. Such personnel are defined as those who serve without compensation as firefighters or members of a rescue squad or ambulance crew for a public agency, meaning the United States, any state or territory of the United States or any unit of local government, department, or instrumentality of any of the foregoing.

DETERMINATION OF QUALIFICATIONS, EXEMPTIONS AND EXCUSES, 28 U.S.C. §§ 1865(a) & (b); 1866(c)

The presiding district judge or judges in each division, on their own initiative or upon recommendation of the clerk, shall determine solely on the basis of the information provided on the juror qualification questionnaire and other competent evidence whether a person is qualified, exempt, or to be excused from jury service. Such determination shall be entered in the space provided on the juror qualification questionnaire or shall appear on the appropriate database listing.

The clerk of court under the supervision of the court may determine whether persons are qualified, exempt or excused from jury service, with the exceptions of: (1) determining whether a person will be excused because his or her services are essential to the operation of a business, commercial or agricultural enterprise; (2) determining whether a person is disqualified because he or she is incapable by reason of mental or physical infirmity of rendering satisfactory jury service; and (3) any other determinations requiring the exercise of discretion. All matters of discretion are reserved for determination by the presiding judge unless the presiding judge specifically authorizes the clerk to make such determinations.

QUALIFIED JURY WHEELS AND SUMMONS FOR JURY SERVICE, 28 U.S.C. §§ 1863(b)(8); 1866; 1868

Separate qualified jury wheels shall be maintained in JMS for each division and the names of all persons drawn from the master jury wheel and not disqualified, exempt, or excused pursuant to this plan shall be placed in the qualified wheel. The clerk shall ensure that at all times an adequate number of names is contained in each such qualified jury wheel to meet the needs of the court.

From time to time as directed by the court, the clerk shall cause to be drawn at random, by means of JMS, from the qualified jury wheel of each division such number of names of persons as may be required for assignments to grand and petit jury panels. The clerk may prepare, by means of JMS, and mail to every person whose name is so drawn, a summons for jury service. At the option of the clerk, summonses may be mailed by the clerk's office or by a commercial mailing service.

As grand juries are required, the clerk shall order the drawing from the appropriate divisions' qualified wheels, a pro rata share of the total number of grand jurors needed to be summoned. Prospective grand jurors summoned to the Peoria division shall be drawn from the Peoria and Rock Island qualified wheels. Prospective grand jurors summoned to the Springfield division shall be drawn from the Springfield and Urbana qualified wheels.

For those who have been summoned for jury service, the clerk, in consultation with the presiding judge, is authorized to grant temporary excuses from jury service to jurors whose service on a particular day or days would create undue hardship or extreme inconvenience. The clerk is authorized to reinsert the names of those individuals temporarily excused back in the qualified wheel. Examples of undue hardship and extreme inconvenience are scheduled medical appointments, vacation plans, and business travel.

Names of persons summoned and appearing for service may be inserted in a panel assignment wheel, from which separate trial panels will be selected by lot. The clerk shall prepare for the use of the Court and counsel a separate list of names of persons assigned to each petit jury panel.

PENALTY FOR FAILURE TO APPEAR FOR JURY SUMMONS 28 U.S.C. § 1866(g)

The court finds any person summoned for jury service who fails to appear as directed may be ordered by the district court to appear and show cause for failure to comply with the summons. Any person who fails to show good cause for noncompliance with a summons may be fined not more than $1,000, imprisoned not more than three days, ordered to perform community service, or any combination thereof.

SUPPLEMENTAL ATTENDANCE FEE FOR PETIT JURORS SERVING ON LENGTHY TRIALS 28 U.S.C. § 1871(b)(2)

The court finds a petit juror required to attend more than thirty (30) days in hearing one case shall be paid an additional attendance fee of $10, for each day in excess of thirty days on which the juror is required to hear such case.

Effective October 1, 2009, the court finds a petit juror required to attend more than ten (10) days in hearing one case shall be paid an additional attendance fee of $ 10, for each day in excess of ten days on which the juror is required to hear such case.

FREQUENCY OF SERVICE, 28 U.S.C. § 1866(e)

In any two-year period, no person shall be required to (1) serve or attend court for prospective service as a petit juror for a total of more than thirty days, except when necessary to complete service in a particular case, or (2) to serve on more than one grand jury, or (3) to serve as both a grand and petit juror.

PENALTY FOR EMPLOYEES WHO RETALIATE AGAINST EMPLOYEES SERVING ON JURY DUTY 28 U.S.C. §§ 1875(b)(3)

No employer shall discharge, threaten to discharge, intimidate, or coerce any permanent employee by reason of such employee's jury service, or the attendance or scheduled attendance in connection with such service. Any employer who violates the provisions of this section shall be subject to a civil penalty of not more than $5,000 for each violation as to each employee, and may be ordered to perform community service.

RECORDS TO BE MAINTAINED BY THE CLERK AND MADE PUBLIC UPON REQUEST, 28 U.S.C. §§ 1863(a); 1867(f); 1868

The clerk shall retain the following documents:

- Jury Selection Plan
- Orders regarding refilling of the master jury wheel, petit juries, and grand juries
- Written instructions to State Election Commission to provide list of registered voters
- Affidavit from State Election Commission that instructions to provide list of registered voters were followed
- Voter data files
- Qualification questionnaires
- Individual petit jury and grand jury panel information

These records shall not be disclosed, except (1) pursuant to this Plan, or (2) pursuant to an order of the court finding disclosure is necessary in preparation of a motion challenging the selection of a jury, until the master jury wheel has been refilled and all persons selected as jurors from the prior master jury wheel have completed service. Parties who have obtained an order of disclosure shall be allowed to inspect, reproduce, and copy such records at reasonable times during the pendency of the motion challenging the selection of a jury.

Upon written order of the court, except when the court orders a longer retention period, these records can be disposed of four years after the master jury wheel has been refilled and all persons selected have completed jury service in accordance with 28 U.S.C. § 1868.

PUBLIC RELEASE OF JUROR INFORMATION, 28 U.S.C. § 1863(b)(7)

Information on jurors drawn from the qualified jury wheel and impaneled for criminal and civil trials shall be made public only upon approval of the presiding judge and only upon formal request. The presiding judge may keep juror information confidential in any case where the interests of justice so require. In cases in which the court has authorized the release of juror information only the names will be released without further identifying information.

[1] Notice of persons who identify themselves as non-citizens through the juror qualification process will be provided to appropriate election officials for verifying voter registration eligibility.

ORDER

In accordance with Title 28 U.S.C. Sections § 1861, et. seq., the United States District Court for the Central District of Illinois hereby adopts the revised Jury Selection Plan for the random selection of jurors. This plan becomes effective immediately.

IN THE UNITED STATES DISTRICT COURT
FOR THE CENTRAL DISTRICT OF ILLINOIS

IN RE: NOTICE REGARDING THE RANDOM SELECTION
OF GRAND AND PETIT JURORS

General Order: 09–1

Pursuant to 28 U.S.C. 1861, all litigants "have the right to grand and petit juries selected at random from a fair cross section of the community." The court uses a two-step process to select jurors. First, a master jury wheel is created by selecting names at random from the registered voter lists in each gubernatorial general election as maintained in the books or lists of (1) the office of the County Clerk in each county, (2) the office of the City Clerk in those cities which have separate registration lists or (3) the office of the State Board of Elections of the State of Illinois. Then names are randomly drawn periodically from the master jury wheel to receive juror qualification questionnaires. Individuals' answers to these questionnaires determine whether they are legally qualified to serve. If so, the names of those persons are put on a second wheel, a qualified jury wheel. As prospective jurors are needed for a specific trial or grand jury, juror summonses are sent to persons randomly selected from the qualified wheel. All of these selections are carried out through a properly programmed electronic data processing system for pure randomized selection. The pure randomized process ensures that the mathematical odds of any single name being picked are substantially equal.

[Entered: January 20, 2009.]

AMENDED CJA PLAN OF THE CENTRAL DISTRICT OF ILLINOIS PURSUANT TO THE CRIMINAL JUSTICE ACT OF 1964

Pursuant to the Criminal Justice Act of 1964 as amended, (CJA), (18 U.S.C. § 3006A) and the Guidelines for the Administration of the Criminal Justice Act, Volume VII, Guide to Judicial Policies and Procedures (CJA Guidelines), the Judges of the United States District Court for the Central District of Illinois adopt this Plan for furnishing representation in this court for any person financially unable to obtain adequate representation in accordance with the CJA.

I. STATEMENT OF POLICY

A. Objectives.

1. The objective of this Plan is to attain the ideal of equality before the law for all persons. Therefore, this Plan shall be administered so that those accused of crime, or otherwise eligible for services pursuant to the CJA, will not be deprived, because they are financially unable to pay for adequate representation, of any element of representation necessary to an adequate defense.

2. The further objective of this Plan is to particularize the requirements of the CJA and the CJA Guidelines and statutory requirements regarding representation in capital cases in a way that meets the needs of this District.

B. Compliance.

1. The Court, its Clerk, the Federal Public Defender Organization, and private attorneys appointed under the CJA shall comply with the CJA Guidelines approved by the Judicial Conference of the United States and/or its Committee on Defender Services and with this Plan.

2. Each private attorney shall be provided by the Clerk of the Court with a then current copy of this Plan upon the attorney's first appointment under the CJA or designation as a member of the Panel of private attorneys under the CJA (CJA Panel). The Clerk shall maintain a current copy of the CJA Guidelines for the use of members of the CJA Panel and shall make known to such attorneys its availability.

II. DEFINITIONS

A. "Representation" includes counsel, investigative, expert, and other services necessary to an adequate defense.

B. "Appointed attorney" includes private attorneys, the Federal Public Defender and staff attorneys of the Federal Public Defender Organization, and private attorneys who are members of the CJA panel.

III. PROVISION OF REPRESENTATION

A. Mandatory. Representation **shall** be provided for any financially eligible person who:

1. is charged with a felony or Class A misdemeanor;

2. is a juvenile alleged to have committed an act of juvenile delinquency which, if committed by an adult, would be a felony or Class A misdemeanor;

3. is charged with a violation of probation or faces modification, reduction, or enlargement of a condition or extension or revocation of a term of probation;

552

4. is under arrest, when such representation is required by law;

5. is subject to revocation of parole or is otherwise entitled to appointment of counsel in parole proceedings;

6. is charged with a violation of supervised release or faces modification, reduction, or enlargement of a condition or extension or revocation of a term of supervised release;

7. is subject to a mental condition hearing under chapter 313 of Title 18 of the United States Code;

8. is seeking to set aside or vacate a death sentence under sections 2254 or 2255 of Title 28 of the United States Code; or

9. is in custody as a material witness;

10. is entitled to appointment of counsel in verification of consent proceedings pursuant to a transfer of an offender to or from the United States for the execution of a penal sentence under section 4109 of Title 18 of the United States Code; or

11. is entitled to appointment of counsel under the Sixth Amendment to the Constitution, or faces loss of liberty in a case, and federal law requires the appointment of counsel.

B. Discretionary. Whenever a judge or magistrate judge determines that the interests of justice so require, representation **may** be provided for any financially eligible person who:

1. is charged with a petty offense (Class B or C misdemeanor, or an infraction) for which a sentence to confinement is authorized;

2. is charged with civil or criminal contempt who faces loss of liberty;

3. has been or will be called as a witness before a grand jury, a court, the Congress, or a federal agency or commission which has the power to compel testimony, where there is reason to believe, either prior to or during testimony, that the witness could be subject to criminal prosecution, a civil or criminal contempt proceeding, or faces loss of liberty;

4. is proposed by the United States Attorney for processing under a pretrial diversion program;

5. is seeking relief, other than to set aside or vacate a death sentence, under sections 2241, 2254, or 2255 of Title 28 of the United States Code;

6. is held for international extradition under chapter 209 of Title 18 of the United States Code; or

7. is in need of counsel in ancillary matters appropriate to the proceedings pursuant to 18 U.S.C. § 3006A(c).

C. When Counsel Shall Be Provided. Counsel shall be provided to eligible persons as soon as feasible, after they are taken into custody, when they appear before a judge or magistrate judge, when they are formally charged or notified of charges if formal charges are sealed, upon the filing of a motion or petition under sections 2241, 2254, or 2255 of Title 28 of the United States Code, or when a judge or magistrate judge otherwise considers appointment of counsel appropriate under the CJA, whichever occurs earliest.

D. Number of Counsel. More than one attorney may be appointed in any case determined by the Court to be extremely difficult. In a capital case, at least two attorneys shall be appointed.

E. Qualifications. Except as provided by Section 848(q)(7) of Title 21, United States Code at least one attorney appointed in a capital case shall meet the qualification requirements set forth in Sections 848(q)(5) and (6) of Title 21, United States Code. Pursuant to Section 848(q)(7), the presiding judicial officer, for good cause, may appoint an attorney who may not qualify under Section 848(q)(5) and (6), but who has the background, knowledge, and experience necessary to represent the defendant properly in a capital case, giving due consideration to the seriousness of the possible penalty and to the unique and complex nature of the litigation.

F. Eligibility for Representation.

1. The determination of eligibility for representation under the CJA is a judicial function to be performed by a federal judge after making appropriate inquiries concerning the person's financial condition.

2. The federal judge shall, in selecting and appointing counsel, either designate the Federal Public Defender, CJA Panel attorney, or, in death penalty habeas corpus cases, persons whose names are submitted by the Federal Public Defender.

3. If, at any time after appointment, counsel obtains information that a client is financially able to make payment, in whole or in part, for legal or other services in connection with his or her representation, and the source of the attorney's information is not protected as a privileged communication, counsel shall advise the Court.

IV. FEDERAL PUBLIC DEFENDER ORGANIZATION

A. Establishment.

1. The Federal Public Defender Organization for the Central District of Illinois, previously established in the district pursuant to the provisions of the CJA, is hereby recognized as the Federal Public Defender Organization for this district. The organization initially established offices in Peoria, and Springfield, Illinois. An office in Urbana is required and its establishment will be a priority of the FPD. An office will be established in Rock Island when expedient. Upon organization of the federal public defender's office, the federal public defender shall notify this court that he or she is available to accept appointments for representation.

2. The FPD shall be capable of providing legal services throughout the Central District and shall maintain its principal office in Peoria, Illinois.

B. Supervision of Defender Organization. The FPD shall be responsible for the supervision and management of the FPD office, and accordingly the FPD shall be appointed in all cases assigned to that organization for subsequent assignment to staff attorneys at the discretion of the FPD.

V. PRIVATE PANEL ATTORNEYS

This Plan also provides for the appointment and compensation of private counsel who are members of the CJA Panel, established by the Court as provided in § VIII A.

VI. APPOINTMENT OF COUNSEL AND CASE MANAGEMENT IN CAPITAL CASES

A. Applicability and Purpose. The provisions set forth in this section shall govern in all capital cases. For the purposes of this section, "capital cases," or "cases involving the death penalty," are those criminal cases in which the death penalty may be or is being sought by the prosecution, as well as proceedings under 28 U.S.C. § 2254 and 2255 seeking to vacate or set aside a death sentence, motions for a new trial, direct appeal, application for a writ of certiorari to the Supreme Court of the United States, all post-conviction proceedings, applications for stays of execution, competency proceedings, proceedings for executive or other clemency, and other appropriate motions and proceedings.

The provisions of this section shall be implemented by the presiding judge at the earliest opportunity in any potential capital case.

B. Trial Counsel.

1. *General Requirements.* Due to the complex, demanding, and protracted nature of death penalty proceedings, a defendant who is or has become financially unable to obtain capital representation and who applies for appointment of counsel at government expense shall be entitled, as required by 18 U.S.C. § 3005, to the assignment of at least two attorneys who meet the qualifications set forth in this section. At least one of the attorneys appointed to represent the defendant shall be learned in the law applicable to capital cases and, when applicable, qualified as pursuant to 21 U.S.C. § 848(q)(5) or 848(q)(6).

In cases where two or more defendants are to be tried jointly, the presiding judge shall appoint separate teams of counsel for each defendant. One member of the team shall be designated counsel and the other member(s) shall be identified as assistant counsel.

2. *Qualifications of Lead Counsel.* To be eligible for appointment as lead counsel in a capital case, an attorney must:

a.   be a member of the bar of this court, or must be admitted to practice pro hac vice based on his or her qualifications;

b.   have at least ten years experience in the field of federal criminal practice;

c.   have prior experience as sole or lead counsel in the trial of no fewer than three serious and complex felony cases that were tried to completion in federal court;

d.   have exemplary prior experience as counsel in a state or federal capital case;

e.   have demonstrated the necessary proficiency and commitment which exemplify the quality of representation appropriate to capital cases.

3. *Qualifications of Assistant Counsel.* To be eligible for appointment as assistant counsel in a capital case, an attorney must:

a.   be a member of the bar of this court, or be admitted to practice pro hac vice on the basis of his or her qualifications;

b.   have at least five years experience in the field of federal criminal practice;

c.   have prior experience as defense or prosecution counsel, demonstrating adequate proficiency in connection with serious and complex felony cases;

d.   have demonstrated the necessary proficiency and commitment which exemplify the quality of representation appropriate to the defense of capital cases.

4. *Special Appointments: Discretionary, Additional Counsel.* The presiding judge may, for good cause, appoint attorneys who do not meet this section's requirements, but whose background, knowledge, or experience would otherwise enable them to effectively represent a defendant in a capital case, provided that lead counsel for each defendant shall have distinguished prior experience as counsel in a capital case, as required by Subsection VI(B)(2) of this section.

Pursuant to 21 U.S.C. § 848(q)(4), if necessary for adequate representation, more than two attorneys may be appointed to represent a defendant in a capital case.

Where the defendant has counsel, the presiding judge may appoint additional counsel in order to ensure the adequate representation of the defendant. Appointment of additional counsel may take place during any stage in the proceedings.

C. Appointment Procedures.

1. *Appointment of Capital Trial Counsel.* Appointment of trial counsel shall occur no later than when a defendant appears in court and is charged with a federal criminal offense where the penalty of death is possible.

Before the appointment of counsel is made in a capital case, the judge presiding over the initial proceedings shall inform the Federal Public Defender for the Central District of Illinois that a capital case is pending and that counsel is needed. The Federal Public Defender shall provide the judge with the names of at least four attorneys who meet the guidelines for counsel in capital cases, as set forth in Section VI(B)(2).

The presiding judge shall either accept or reject the submitted names, and shall notify the Federal Public Defender of the decision. In the event that a recommendation is not accepted, the presiding judge shall consult with the Federal Public Defender to identify other qualified counsel acceptable to the Court.

The court may appoint counsel in advance of formal charges or habeas corpus petition being filed if it learns of a potential capital case prior to charges or habeas petition being filed or arrests being made. In order to protect the rights of an individual who is the subject of an investigation in a capital case, the presiding judge may assign interim counsel at his or her own initiative, or upon the request of any interested party.

2. *Appointment of Additional or Substitute Counsel.* In cases where counsel has been retained or appointed before the government filed notice of its intent to seek the death penalty, the appointment of additional or substitute counsel is permitted once the government files notice of intent to seek the death penalty. Appointment of additional or substitute counsel shall be made sufficiently in advance of trial to permit newly-appointed counsel an adequate opportunity to prepare.

3. *Termination of Appointment.* If, following the appointment of counsel in a capital case, it is determined that the death penalty will not be sought, the court may consider the question of the number of counsel and the rate of compensation needed for the duration of the proceeding. After considering whether the number of counsel initially appointed is necessary to ensure effective representation or to avoid disruption of the proceeding, the court may continue the appointments or reduce the number of appointed counsel.

After considering the need to fairly compensate appointed counsel, taking into account the commitment of time and resources appointed counsel has made and will continue to make, the court may continue to pay the previously approved rate, or prospectively reduce the rate.

D. Initial Status Conference and Case Management Schedule.

1. In all identified capital cases, the presiding judge shall promptly conduct an initial status conference to ensure the effective management of the case, including the appointment of counsel pursuant to this section.

2. Upon the return or unsealing of an indictment in a capital case, the court shall schedule a status conference to discuss issues and concerns related to the death penalty authorization process conducted by the Department of Justice. Among other matters, the conference should address the scheduling of the defendant's submissions to the United States Attorney, the meeting between the defense and the United States Attorney, and discovery that may be necessary before the defense can make any submission to the court or to the Department of Justice.

3. If the Attorney General's authorization decision delays the deadlines set in the court's schedule, the court may find that the Attorney General's death penalty notice issue did not provide the defense with a reasonable time to prepare for trial, as required by 18 U.S.C. § 3593(a).

4. In order to expedite compliance with this section, counsel shall become familiar with the United States Department of Justice protocol, practices, and procedures in capital cases.

E. Assessment of Costs and Fees.

1. *Counsel.* Counsel appointed pursuant to this section shall be compensated at a rate determined by the presiding judge to be reasonably necessary for qualified counsel to provide adequate representation in a capital case. At the time counsel are appointed, the court shall set an hourly rate of compensation pursuant to 21 U.S.C. § 848(q)(10)(A).

2. *Investigative, Mitigation, Expert, and Other Services.* Upon finding that investigative, mitigation, expert, or other services are necessary for the adequate representation of a defendant in a capital case, the presiding judge shall authorize counsel to obtain such services on behalf of the defendant and shall set the rate of compensation in consideration of the statutory limits.

Pursuant to the provisions of this section and the Criminal Justice Act, an interpreter shall be appointed to assist counsel if counsel is not fluent in the capital defendant's native language.

The presiding judge may authorize investigative, mitigation, expert, or other services, even if the services have already been obtained.

3. *Confidentiality.* Petitions for the payment of costs and fees, including the time and expense records of counsel, shall be heard ex parte and in camera. The petitions shall be placed under seal and shall be inaccessible to the prosecution and the public, absent court order or written waiver by the defendant, until disposition of the petition.

F. Procedures for Compensation.

1. *Compensation for Investigative, Mitigation, Expert, and Other Services.* Pursuant to 21 U.S.C. § 848(q)(10)(B), fees and expenses for investigative, expert, and other services in excess of the amount provided by statute must be certified by the presiding judge in order to provide fair compensation for services of an unusual character or duration. The amount of any excess payment must be approved by the Chief Judge of the Seventh Circuit Court of Appeals or his designee. The maximum statutory amount threshold applies to the total payments for investigative, expert, and other services in a case, not to each service individually.

2. *Forms.* Claims for compensation and reimbursement of expenses for services in death penalty proceedings should be submitted on CJA Form 30, "Death Penalty Proceedings: Appointment and Authority to Pay Court Appointed Counsel," and CJA Form 31, "Death Penalty Proceedings: Ex Parte Request for Authorization and Voucher for Expert and Other Services."

3. *Review of Vouchers.* Absent extraordinary circumstances, judges should act upon panel attorney and other compensation claims within thirty (30) days of submission.

4. *Interim Billing and Payment.* In the interest of justice and judicial economy, interim billing and payment shall be allowed in the court's discretion and encouraged for counsel, experts, and other services.

5. *Case Budgeting.* The presiding judge is encouraged to follow the budgeting procedure outlined in Section 6.02(F) of the *Guide to Judiciary Policies and Procedures: Appointment of Counsel in Criminal Cases.*

G. Other Considerations.

1. *Emergency Court Contacts.* In all capital cases where the death penalty has been authorized, the Clerk of the Court shall devise and implement a system for contacting the presiding judge, counsel for the parties, the United States Marshal for the Central District of Illinois or his representative, and the warden of the penal institution where the defendant is awaiting execution.

2. *Stays.* Upon the filing of a notice of appeal, motion for reconsideration, habeas corpus petition, or other such action which has the practical effect of challenging a sentence of death, the presiding judge shall issue a stay of execution pending final disposition of the matter, accompanied by any necessary findings. The Clerk shall immediately notify all parties, and the state or federal authorities responsible for implementing the defendant's sentence of death, of the stay. If notification is oral, it shall be followed by written notice. Unless vacated or modified, the stay will continue in effect until the expiration of all proceedings available to and elected by the defendant, including review by United States Supreme Court, unless otherwise ordered by the Court. The District Court shall

grant a prompt hearing as required by 28 U.S.C. § 2254 and 2255 and, as required by 18 U.S.C. § 3595(a) and 21 U.S.C. § 848(q)(1), the review in capital cases shall have priority over all other cases. The Clerk shall send notice to the parties and the state or federal authorities responsible for implementing the defendant's sentence of death when the stay imposed by this provision is no longer in effect.

3. *Pre–Bail Interviews.* CJA Counsel, or interim counsel appointed pursuant to this section, shall be present at each pre-bail interview with the defendant, and any other interview conducted by the United States Probation Office or any other office.

4. *Access to Defendant.* In light of the heightened necessity for attorney-client consultation in a capital case, the United States Marshals Service shall cooperate in providing counsel adequate access to the defendant.

VII. DUTIES OF LAW ENFORCEMENT AND RELATED AGENCIES

A. Presentation of Accused for Appointment of Counsel. Federal probation officers in this district, and those acting on their behalf, shall promptly ask any person who is in custody, or who otherwise may be entitled to counsel under the CJA, whether he or she is financially able to secure representation, and shall, in such cases in which the person indicates that he or she is not able, arrange to have the person promptly presented before a judge or magistrate judge of this Court for determination of financial eligibility and appointment of counsel.

B. Pretrial Interview. Recognizing the continuing excellent relationship between appointed counsel and the U.S. Probation Office in this District, this Plan encourages defense counsel and the Probation Office to continue to work together to accommodate the defendant's interest in speaking with an attorney at the earliest opportunity and the probation officer's interest in having sufficient time to obtain information relevant to the defendant's release status. To further this goal, the probation officer shall not discuss with the defendant any of the facts and circumstances of the defendant's arrest or the charges against the defendant.

C. Notice of Indictment or Criminal Information. Upon the return or unsealing of an indictment, the filing of a criminal information, or the filing of a petition to modify or revoke probation, the Clerk of the Court immediately shall mail or otherwise deliver a copy of the document to appointed counsel, or to the defendant if he or she is without counsel, at the address shown on defendant's bond papers or to the jail in which the defendant is incarcerated.

VIII. PLAN FOR THE COMPOSITION, ADMINISTRATION, AND MANAGEMENT OF THE PANEL OF PRIVATE ATTORNEYS UNDER THE CRIMINAL JUSTICE ACT

A. Composition of Panel of Private Attorneys.

1. *CJA Panel.*

a. Approval. The Court shall establish a panel of private attorneys (hereinafter referred to as the "CJA Panel") who are eligible and willing to be appointed to provide representation under the Criminal Justice Act. The Court shall approve attorneys for membership on the panel after receiving recommendations from the "Panel Selection Committee" and its sub-panels in each division established pursuant to Section VIII A 2(a) of this plan. Members of the CJA Panel shall serve at the pleasure of the Court.

b. Size. The Court shall fix, periodically, the size of the CJA panel. The panel shall be large enough to provide a sufficient number of experienced attorneys to handle the CJA caseload, yet small enough so that panel members will receive an adequate number of appointments to maintain their proficiency in federal criminal defense work, and thereby provide a high quality of representation.

c. Eligibility. Attorneys who serve on the CJA Panel must be members in good standing of the federal bar of this district and have demonstrated experience in, and knowledge of, the Federal Rules of Criminal Procedure, the Federal Rules of Evidence, and the Sentencing Guidelines.

d. Application. Application forms for membership on the CJA Panel shall be made available upon request by the Clerk of the Court. Completed applications shall be submitted to the Clerk of the Court who will transmit the applications to the chairperson and members of the Panel Selection Committee.

e. Equal Opportunity. All qualified attorneys shall be encouraged to participate in the furnishing of representation in CJA cases, without regard to race, color, religion, sex, age, national origin, or disabling condition.

2. *Panel Selection Committee.*

a. Membership. A Panel Selection Committee shall be established by the Court. The Committee shall consist of the chief district judge, one magistrate judge, the federal public defender, and one attorney who is willing to serve on the CJA Panel. The chief district judge shall be the chairperson. There shall be a sub-panel in each division appointed by the chief district judge consisting of the presiding district judge, one magistrate judge, the assigned federal defender for the division, and one attorney who is willing to serve on the CJA panel. The presiding district judge shall be the chairperson.

b. Duties.

(1) The Panel Selection Committee shall review applications for membership on the CJA Panel recommended by each sub-panel and shall make a recommendation to the Court regarding the applicant's worthiness for service on the panel. The Panel Selection Committee and sub-panels shall be permitted to gather information from any source for purposes of making a worthiness determination.

(2) The Panel Selection Committee and each sub-panel shall meet at least once a year to review the performance of each member of the CJA Panel and shall provide the Court with a list of attorneys recommended for retention on the CJA Panel.

(3) At its annual meeting, the Committee shall also review the operation and administration of the panel and sub-panels over the preceding year, and recommend to the Court any changes deemed necessary or appropriate by the Committee regarding the appointment process and panel management.

3. *CJA Training Panel.* The Panel Selection Committee may establish a "CJA Training Panel" consisting of attorneys who do not have the experience required for membership on the CJA Panel. Training Panel members may be assigned, by the Court, to assist members of the CJA Panel in a "second chair" capacity. Training Panel members are not eligible to receive appointments independently, and shall not be eligible to receive compensation for their services in assisting CJA Panel members without the approval of the presiding district judge. Prior service on the CJA Training Panel is not a requirement for membership on the CJA Panel, nor will service on the Training Panel guarantee admission of an attorney to the CJA Panel.

B. Selection for Appointment.

1. *Maintenance of List and Distribution of Appointments.* The Clerk of the Court shall maintain a current list of attorneys included on the CJA Panel, with current office addresses and telephone numbers, as well as a statement of qualifications and experience. The clerk shall furnish a copy of this list to each district judge, magistrate judge, and federal public defender.

2. *Method of Selection.* Appointments from the list of private attorneys should be made on a rotational basis, subject to the Court's discretion to make exceptions

due to the nature and complexity of the case, an attorney's experience, and geographical considerations. This procedure should result in a balanced distribution of appointments and compensation among the members of the CJA Panel, and quality representation for each CJA defendant.

C. Compensation—Filing of Vouchers.

1. Claims for compensation of private attorneys providing representation under the CJA shall be submitted on the appropriate CJA form, to the office of the Clerk of the Court. That office shall review the claim form for mathematical and technical accuracy and for conformity with the CJA Guidelines, and, if correct, shall forward the claim form to the appropriate district judge or magistrate judge. The court will exert its best effort to avoid delays in reviewing payment vouchers and in submitting them for further processing.

2. The maximum compensation with or without prior approval shall not exceed the maximum amount allowed under the CJA unless payment in excess of that amount is certified by the district judge or magistrate judge as "necessary to provide fair compensation for services of an unusual character or duration, and the amount of the excess payment is approved by the chief judge of the circuit."

3. Ex parte applications for services other than counsel made under this section shall be heard in camera and shall not be revealed without the consent of the person represented. The application shall be placed under seal until the final disposition of the case in the trial court, subject to further order of the court.

D. Appointment of Attorneys Not on the Panel. Subsection (B) of the CJA provides, in part, that counsel appointed pursuant to a local CJA plan must be:

selected from a panel of attorneys designated or approved by the court, or from a bar association, legal aid agency, or defender organization furnishing representation pursuant to the plan.

However, when the district judge presiding over the case, or the chief judge if a district judge has not yet been assigned to the case, or a magistrate judge determines that the appointment of an attorney, who is not a member of the CJA panel, is in the interest of justice, judicial economy, or continuity of representation, or there is some other compelling circumstance warranting his or her appointment, the attorney may be appointed to represent the defendant.

Consideration for preserving the integrity of the panel selection process suggests that such appointments should be made only in exceptional circumstances. Further, the attorney who may or may not maintain an office in this district, should possess such qualities as would qualify him or her for admission to this district's panel in the ordinary course of panel selection. Any suggestion not made through the FPD's ordinary course of assignments that a specific lawyer be appointed, shall come only from the defendant or the defendant's current attorney. The suggestion shall not be made by the U.S. Attorney's Office or by another law enforcement office or agency.

IX. DETERMINATION OF NEED FOR COUNSEL

A. Determination in Court. Upon the appearance of a person before a district judge or magistrate judge, or at any proceeding in which a person who is entitled to representation under the Plan appears without counsel, the judge or magistrate judge shall advise the person of the right to be represented by counsel throughout the case and that counsel will be appointed if the person is financially unable to afford adequate representation. If the person states that he or she wishes to be represented by appointed counsel, the judge or magistrate judge shall recess the proceedings and appoint the FPD or a CJA panel attorney forthwith. If the need for the assistance of counsel is immediate and apparent, counsel may be appointed and the financial inquiry may follow the appointment of counsel as soon thereafter as is practical. A defendant shall not have the right to select appointed counsel from the FPD staff or CJA panel.

B. Fact Finding. Unless it will result in undue delay, fact finding concerning the person's eligibility for appointment of counsel should be completed prior to the person's first appearance in court. Relevant information bearing on the person's financial eligibility should be reflected on a financial eligibility affidavit (CJA Form 23). Employees of law enforcement agencies or United States Attorney's offices should not participate in the completion of the CJA Form 23 or seek to obtain information from a person requesting the appointment of counsel concerning his or her eligibility.

All statements made by a person in requesting counsel or during the inquiry into eligibility shall be either (a) by affidavit sworn to before the court, a court clerk or deputy, or a notary public; or (b) under oath in open court.

C. Standards for Eligibility. In addition to the income and assets of a person seeking the appointment of counsel, the judge or magistrate judge shall also consider the cost of providing the person and the person's dependents with the necessities of life, and the cost of bail bond if financial conditions are imposed, or the amount of the cash the person is required to make to secure his or her release on bond.

D. Retroactivity of Appointment. Appointment of counsel may be made retroactive to include representation furnished pursuant to this Plan prior to appointment if the district judge or magistrate judge finds a person has been and is then financially unable to obtain an adequate defense, and that such earlier representation was authorized under the Plan. Compensation will be made retroactive to cover out-of-court time expended by the attorney during the prior period, and in addition cover compensation for services rendered from the time of initial presentation before a court. If the person represented is unavailable at the time counsel applies to the court for approval of retroactive appointment, the attorney may nevertheless submit his or her claim to the court for approval based on the person's financial condition at the time.

E. Multiple Representation. The district judge or magistrate judge shall appoint separate counsel for defendants having interests that cannot properly be represented by the same counsel, or when other good cause is shown. Ordinarily, unless good cause is shown or in the absence of a waiver on the record by the defendants, in a criminal prosecution involving more than one defendant or where separate charges arising out of the same or similar transactions are concurrently pending against two or more defendants, separate counsel should be appointed for each defendant.

F. Discretionary Appointments. Any financially eligible person for whom representation may be provided under this Plan may apply to the court or magistrate judge to be furnished representation based on a showing (1) that the interests of justice so require and (2) that such person is financially unable to obtain adequate representation. Such application shall be made on a CJA Form 23 unless another form is prescribed by the Judicial Conference of the United States or by Local Rule. If the party is not before the Court, the district judge or magistrate judge may, without requiring the personal appearance of the party for such purpose, act on the basis of the form alone, or the form as supplemented by such information as may be made available by an officer or custodian or other responsible officer, provided that such information is also made available to the party.

G. Waiver of Right to Counsel. All waivers of the right to counsel before a judge or magistrate judge shall be in writing on a form approved by the Chief Judge and shall be filed among the papers in the case. If a person knowingly waives the right to counsel, but refuses to sign the waiver form, the district judge or magistrate judge shall certify such fact to the Clerk of the Court for inclusion in the file.

A district judge or magistrate judge shall explain to a person waiving the right to counsel that such waiver will not prevent a request for the appointment of counsel at a later time or before the same or another judicial officer.

X. APPOINTMENT OF COUNSEL

A. Whenever it shall appear to the presiding district judge or magistrate judge at the time of arraignment or at any other time, that a party entitled to counsel is not represented by counsel and has not voluntarily waived the assistance of counsel, the district judge or magistrate judge shall determine whether such defendant is financially able to obtain counsel and, if not, whether the party wishes the judge to appoint counsel for the party. The judge may also make a discretionary appointment as provided in Section IX.F. of this Plan. If in either situation the judge concludes that counsel should be appointed, either the FPD will be designated or such appointment will be made from the CJA panel; provided, however, that in extraordinary situations, in the interest of justice, the judge may appoint any member of the bar of this court who would otherwise qualify to become a member of the Panel to represent such a party.

After conviction, if a defendant desires to waive his or her right of appeal, appointed counsel shall insure that such waiver is made intelligently and voluntarily, and shall obtain the signature of the defendant on a written waiver form to be approved by the chief judge, and shall cause the executed form to be filed with the other papers in the case.

B. Redetermination of Need. If at any stage of the proceeding prior to imposition of sentence, a district judge or magistrate judge shall find that a party for whom counsel has not previously been appointed under this Plan but who has retained private counsel, is financially unable to provide for continued representation, the judge or magistrate judge may appoint counsel for such party. The court will ordinarily not appoint the same attorney.

If at any time after appointment, counsel has reason to believe that a party is financially able to obtain counsel or to make partial payment for counsel, and the source of counsel's information is not protected as a privileged communication, counsel shall advise the Court. The Court will then take appropriate action, which may include permitting assigned counsel to continue to represent the party with part or all of the cost of representation defrayed by such defendant.

In such event, the amount so paid or payable by the party shall be considered by the court in determining the total compensation to be allowed to such attorney.

XI. INVESTIGATIVE, EXPERT, AND OTHER SERVICES

A. In Non–Capital Cases.

1. *With Prior Approval.* Counsel (whether or not appointed under the Criminal Justice Act) for a party who is financially unable to obtain investigative, expert, or other services necessary for an adequate defense, may request such services in an ex parte application submitted to the district judge before whom the case is pending, or before a magistrate judge who has jurisdiction (or if the judge otherwise refers such application to a magistrate judge for findings and report). Upon finding in an ex parte proceeding that the services are necessary, and that the person is financially unable to obtain them, the district judge or magistrate judge shall authorize counsel to obtain the services.

2. *Without Prior Approval.* Counsel appointed under the Criminal Justice Act may obtain, subject to later review, investigative, expert, or other services without prior authorization, if necessary for an adequate defense. The total cost of services obtained without prior authorization may not exceed the maximum amount then-allowed under the CJA Guidelines unless the presiding district judge or magistrate judge, in the interest of justice, finds in an *ex parte* proceeding that timely procurement of necessary services could not await prior authorization. The presiding judicial officer may then authorize such services *nunc pro tunc*.

3. *Maximum Compensation.* The maximum compensation with or without prior approval shall not exceed the maximum amount allowed under the CJA unless payment in excess of that amount is certified by the court or magistrate judge as "necessary to provide fair compensation for services of an unusual character or duration, and the amount of the excess payment is approved by the chief judge of the circuit."

B. In Capital Cases. The maximum compensation paid for investigative, expert, and other services in capital cases shall not exceed the statutory limitation on fees and expenses for these services, unless the payment in excess of that amount is certified as necessary by the presiding judicial officer.

C. Ex Parte Applications. Ex parte applications for services other than counsel made under this Section shall be heard in camera and shall not be revealed without the consent of the person represented. The application shall be placed under seal until the final disposition of the case in the trial court, subject to further order of the court.

XII. MISCELLANEOUS

A. Forms. Standard forms pertaining to the CJA and approved by the Judicial Conference of the United States or its Committee on Defender Services and prescribed and distributed by the Director of the Administrative Office of the United States Courts, shall be used, where applicable, in all proceedings under this Plan.

B. Compensation.

1. *Federal Public Defender Organization.* The Federal Public Defender shall receive such compensation as is fixed by the Court of Appeals at a rate not to exceed that of the U.S. Attorney for the district. The Federal Public Defender shall set the compensation for attorneys and other personnel of the Organization.

2. *Private CJA Attorneys.* Claims for compensation of private attorneys providing representation under the CJA shall be submitted on the appropriate CJA form to the Office of the Clerk. That Office shall review the claim form for mathematical and technical accuracy and for conformity with the CJA Guidelines, and, if correct, shall forward the claim form for the consideration of the appropriate judge or magistrate judge. The Court will exert its best effort to avoid delays in reviewing payment of vouchers and in submitting them for further processing.

3. *Supersession.* This Plan supersedes all prior Criminal Justice Act Plans of this Court.

[Filed March 9, 2004.]

UNITED STATES BANKRUPTCY COURT FOR THE CENTRAL DISTRICT OF ILLINOIS

Including Amendments Received Through
April 1, 2015

Publisher's Note

The United States Bankruptcy Court for the Central District of Illinois has no separate local rules. See Bankruptcy Rules 4.1 to 4.3 of the Local Rules of the United States District Court for the Central District of Illinois, ante.

Manual for Practitioners.

ELECTRONIC CASE FILING

General Orders Affecting Electronic Case Filing in the Central District of Illinois.

Privacy Protection Policy.

Director's Interim Guidance Regarding Tax Information Under 11 U.S.C. § 521.

Important Privacy Act Information.

ORDERS

In re Filing of Payment Advices Pursuant to 11 U.S.C. § 521(a)(1)(B)(iv).

In re Standing Order Regarding Credit Counseling.

Standing Order Regarding Attorney Fees for Debtors' Counsel in Chapter 13 and Chapter 7 Cases (Danville Division).

Standing Order Regarding Attorney Fees for Debtors' Counsel in Chapter 13 Cases (Peoria and Urbana Divisions).

Standing Order Regarding Attorney Fees for Debtor's Counsel in Chapter 7 and 13 Cases (Springfield Division).

Order In re Adoption of Revised Interim Bankruptcy Rule 1007–I.

Standing Order on Pretrial Conferences in Adversary Proceedings Presided Over by Judge William V. Altenberger.

Chief Judge Mary P. Gorman's Procedures for Cases Filed in the Springfield Division.

Order Pre–Trial Conference Rule.

Order Assignment of Cases.

In re Chapter 13 Pre–Confirmation Adequate Protection Payments.

General Order Re: Closure of Bankruptcy Court Operations in Danville, Illinois and Transfer of Bankruptcy Court Operations to Urbana, Illinois.

MANUAL FOR PRACTITIONERS

ADRIENNE D. ATKINS, CLERK

Revised March 23, 2015

This Manual was prepared by
the deputy clerks of the U.S. Bankruptcy Court
for the Central District of Illinois
to assist those who practice here.

OFFICE OPERATIONS

	URBANA COURT	PEORIA COURT
Judge:	Mary P. Gorman, Chief Judge (Ch.7s & 11s) Thomas L. Perkins (Ch. 12 & 13s)	Thomas L. Perkins William V. Altenberger
Address:	203 United States Courthouse 201 South Vine Street, Urbana, IL 61801	216 Federal Building 100 N.E. Monroe Street Peoria, IL 61602
Phone:	217/974–7330	309/671–7035

Office Hours:	Monday through Friday 8:00 a.m.—5:00 p.m.	Monday through Friday 8:00 a.m.—5:00 p.m.
Operations Manager:	Linda Blough	Michelle Heitzman

	SPRINGFIELD COURT	**CLERK OF THE COURT**
Judge:	Mary P. Gorman, Chief Judge	Adrienne D. Atkins
Address:	226 U.S. Courthouse 600 E. Monroe Street Springfield, IL 62701	226 U.S. Courthouse 600 E. Monroe Street Springfield, IL 62701
Phone:	217/492–4551	Phone: 217/492–4551
Office Hours:	Monday through Friday 8:00 a.m.—5:00 p.m.	
Operations Manager:	Gerald Miller	Chief Deputy Clerk: Jeff Gustafson
McVCIS	Phone: 866–222–8029	

SPECIAL NOTICES AND ALERTS

* Notice of an emergency or weather related closing of the Clerk's Office, including the cancellation or delay of court proceedings will appear at the court's website: www.ilcb.uscourts.gov

* A recorded voice message re: closing or delays will also be available by calling the main office phone numbers: Urbana 217–974–7330, Peoria 309–671–7035, Springfield 217–492–4551

* A broadcast email to all registered CM/ECF users will go out upon any emergency or weather related closing of the Clerk's Office.

* It is incumbent upon attorneys to check these sources and notify their clients accordingly.

* You should contact the Office of the US Trustee at 309–671–7854 regarding emergency or weather related cancellations of Meetings of Creditors.

BANKRUPTCY FEE SCHEDULE

The most current Bankruptcy Fee Schedule is located at www.ilcb.uscourts.gov under the Court Info tab.

LOCATIONS OF SECTION 341 MEETINGS

The County in which the petitioning debtor resides determines the location of the Section 341 Meeting.

URBANA DIVISION

Case numbers ___ –9 _____

County	Location of § 341 Meeting
Champaign	Urbana
Coles	Paris–Ch 7, Urbana—Ch. 13
Douglas	Paris–Ch 7, Urbana—Ch. 13
Edgar	Paris–Ch 7, Urbana–Ch. 13
Ford	Urbana
Iroquois	Kankakee

Kankakee	Kankakee
Livingston	Kankakee
Moultrie	Paris–Ch. 7, Urbana–Ch. 13
Piatt	Urbana
Vermilion	Urbana

Cases from the above counties are to be filed in Urbana, Illinois

Addresses of § 341 Meeting Locations:

Urbana

Urbana City Building
City Council Chambers
400 S. Vine Street
Urbana, IL 61801

Paris

Edgar County Courthouse
115 W. Court
Paris, IL 61944

Kankakee

Kankakee County Health Department
(Administrative/Environmental Entrance)
Conference Room
2390 W. Station Street
Kankakee, IL 60901

PEORIA DIVISION

Case numbers ___ –8 ____

County	Location of § 341 Meeting
Bureau	Peoria
Fulton	Peoria
Hancock	Galesburg
Henry	Rock Island
Knox	Galesburg
Marshall	Peoria
Peoria	Peoria
McDonough	Galesburg
Putnam	Peoria
Stark	Peoria
Tazewell	Peoria
Woodford	Peoria

Cases from the above counties are to be filed in Peoria, Illinois

County	Location of § 341 Meeting
Henderson	Galesburg
Mercer	Rock Island
Rock Island	Rock Island
Warren	Galesburg

Cases from the above counties may be filed in Peoria or Rock Island, Illinois

Addresses of § 341 Meeting Locations:

Peoria   Monmouth—Chapter 13 only

1105 Becker Building
401 Main Street
Peoria, IL 61602

100 W. Broadway
Warren County Courthouse
3rd Floor, #A
Monmouth, IL 61462

Rock Island
U.S. Post Office and Courthouse Building
211—19th Street
Courtroom 226
Rock Island, IL 61201

Galesburg—Chapter 7 only
Knox County Courthouse
200 S. Cherry Street
3rd Floor
Galesburg, IL 61401

SPRINGFIELD DIVISION

County	Location of § 341 Mtg.	County	Location of § 341 Mtg.	County	Location Of § 341 Mtg.
Adams	Quincy	DeWitt:			
Brown	Quincy	Clinton	Decatur	Macon	Decatur
Cass	Springfield	DeWitt	Decatur	Macoupin	Springfield
Christian:		Farmer City	Bloomington	Mason	Springfield
Assumption	Decatur	Kenney	Decatur	McLean	Bloomington
Bulpitt	Springfield	Lane	Decatur	Menard	Springfield
Clarksdale	Springfield	Wapella	Bloomington	Montgomery	Springfield
Dunkel	Decatur	Waynesville	Bloomington	Morgan	Springfield
Edinburg	Springfield	Weldon	Decatur	Pike	Quincy
Hewittsville	Springfield	Greene	Springfield	Sangamon	Springfield
Jeiseyville	Springfield	Logan:		Schuyler	Quincy
Kincaid	Springfield	Atlanta	Bloomington	Scott	Quincy
Langleyville	Springfield	Beason	Decatur	Shelby	Decatur
Millersville	Springfield	Broadwell	Springfield		
Morrisonville	Springfield	Chestnut	Decatur		
Mt. Auburn	Decatur	Cornland	Springfield		
Owaneco	Springfield	Elkhart	Springfield		
Palmer	Springfield	Emden	Springfield		
Pana	Springfield	Hartsburg	Bloomington		
Rosamond	Springfield	Lake Fork	Decatur		
Sharpsburg	Springfield	Latham	Decatur		
Stonington	Springfield	Lawndale	Bloomington		
Taylorville	Springfield	Lincoln	Springfield		
Tovey	Springfield	Middletown	Springfield		
Willeys	Springfield	Mt. Pulaski	Decatur		
		New Holland	Springfield		
		San Jose	Bloomington		

Cases from the above counties are to be filed in Springfield, Illinois

Addresses of § 341 meeting Locations:

Bloomington
Chapter 7, 12:   Law and Justice Center
                         Courtroom 3E
                         104 W. Front
                         Bloomington, IL 61701

Chapter 13:   Law and Justice Center
                         Courtroom 5B, 5th Floor
                         104 W. Front
                         Bloomington, IL 61701

Chapter 11:   Law and Justice Center
                         Operations Room
                         104 W. Front

Quincy
Chapter 7, 11, 12:   Courtroom 2D
                         Adams County Courthouse
                         521 Vermont
                         Quincy, IL 62301

Chapter 13:   Adams County Courthouse
                         2nd Floor, Small Jury Room
                         521 Vermont
                         Quincy, IL 62301

Springfield
Chapter 7, 11, 12, 13:   Illinois Building
                         607 E. Adams Street
                         1st Floor

568

Bloomington, IL 61701   Springfield, IL 62701

Decatur
Chapter 7, 11, 12, 13:   Macon County Courthouse
                          Courtroom 5C
                          253 E. Wood St.
                          Decatur, IL 62523

CENTRAL DISTRICT OF ILLINOIS TRUSTEES

CHAPTER 7   Glen R. Barmann, 200 E. Court Street, Kankakee, IL 60901
                 (815) 939–1133

                 Charles Covey, 700 Commerce Bank Building, Peoria, IL 61602
                 (309) 673–3807

                 A. Clay Cox, P.O. Box 3067, Bloomington, IL 61702–3067
                 (309) 828–7331

                 James R. Inghram, Bank of America Bldg., 529 Hampshire Street, Suite 409, Quincy, IL 62301
                 (217) 222–7420

                 Mariann Pogge, 3300 Hedley Road, Springfield, IL 62711
                 (217) 793–7412

                 Roger L. Prillaman, 220 West Main Street, Urbana, IL 61801
                 (217) 384–1300

                 Gary Rafool, 411 Hamilton Boulevard #1600, Peoria, IL 61602
                 (309) 673–5535

                 Jeana K. Reinbold, P.O. Box 7315, Springfield, IL 62791
                 (217) 801–4090

                 Jeffrey D. Richardson, 132 S. Water St., Suite 444, Decatur, IL 62523
                 (217) 425–1515

                 John L. Swartz, 1 W. Old State Capitol Plz, #600, P.O. Box 2117, Springfield, IL 62705
                 (217) 525–1571

                 Kristin L. Wilson, 600 Jackson Avenue, Charleston, IL 61020
                 (217) 345–3929

                 Pamela S. Wilcox, P.O. Box 1806, Galesburg, IL 61402
                 (309) 341–6036

CHAPTER 12   Michael Clark, 401 Main Street, Ste. 1130, Peoria, IL 61602–1241
                 (309) 674–6137

CHAPTER 13   Marsha L. Combs–Skinner, 108 S. Broadway, Newman, IL 61942
                 (217) 837–9730

                 Michael Clark, 401 Main Street, Ste. 1130, Peoria, IL 61602–1241
                 (309) 674–6137

                 John H. Germeraad, P.O. Box 257, Petersburg, IL 62675
                 (217) 632–4346

UNITED STATES TRUSTEE

Nancy J. Gargula
United States Trustee
Becker Building, Room 1100
401 Main
Peoria, IL 61602
(309) 671–7854

COMMONLY USED FEDERAL AND STATE AGENCY ADDRESSES

For all Chapters	**Internal Revenue Service** P.O. Box 7346 Philadelphia, PA 19101–7346
When scheduling Veterans Administration as a creditor, if no other address available use	**Veterans Administration** Regional Office POB 8136 536 S. Clark Chicago, IL 60680
When scheduling Farmers Home Administration, Dept. of Agriculture, ASCS—Farmers Home Administration, use as an additional address	**Farmers Home Administration** U.S. Dept. of Agriculture Illini Plaza, Suite 103 1817 S. Neil St. Champaign IL 61820
When scheduling Dept. of Agriculture, ASCS—Farmers Home Administration, ASCS, Commodity Credit Corp., use as an additional address	**USDA—IL State ASCS Office** 2305 W. Monroe St., #1 POB 19273 Springfield, IL 62794
When scheduling Federal Crop Insurance Corp., use as an additional address	**USDA—IL State ASCS Office** 2305 W. Monroe St., #2 Springfield, IL 62794
When scheduling Federal Housing Administration, use as an additional address	**Federal Housing Administration** Dept. of Housing & Urban Development Washington, D.C. 20411
When scheduling State of IL for taxes (R.O.T., Sales tax, Withholding tax, Income Tax, or if tax not designated)	**IL Dept. of Revenue** Bankruptcy Section P.O. Box 64338 Chicago, IL 60664–0338
When scheduling State of IL for unemployment taxes, payroll	**IL Dept. of Employment Security** Insolvency/Bkcy Subunit Field Audit Section 33 S. State St. Chicago, IL 60603 also add: **Attorney General** 33 S. State St. Room 992 Chicago, IL 60603
When scheduling State of IL for franchise tax	**State of IL** Corporation Dept. Franchise Tax Div. Springfield, IL 62706
When scheduling Dept. of Public Aid	**IL Dept. of Public Aid** Bureau of Collections Jesse B. Harris Bldg. 100 S. Grand Ave. East Springfield, IL 62762
When scheduling State of IL student loan	**IL State Scholarship Commission** 1755 Lake Cook Rd. Deerfield, IL 60015
When scheduling real estate and personal property taxes	**County Collector** ———————— County ————————, IL (zip code)
When debtor <u>engaged in business</u> of transporting persons or property, use as an additional address	**Chief Counsel** Transportation Audits GSA—General Law Division Room 4124 Washington, D.C. 20405
When debtor is a land developer, use as	**Dept. of Housing & Urban Development**

an additional address

Office of Interstate Land Sales Registration
Washington, D.C. 20410

When scheduling a component of U.S. Army,
use as an additional address

Commander
U.S. Army Finance & Acctg Center
Attn: FINCL
Indianapolis, IN 46249

When scheduling a component of U.S. Navy,
use as an additional address

Department of Navy
Navy Finance Center
Federal Bldg.
Cleveland, OH 44199

When scheduling Economic Development
Administration (Economic Development
Administration, U.S. Dept. of Commerce,
EDA), use as an additional address

**Ass't Chief Counsel for Litigation
 and Liquidation**
Economic Development Administration
Room 7106
U.S. Dept. of Commerce
Washington, D.C. 20230

When scheduling U.S. Postal Service, use
as an additional address

Postmaster General
U.S. Postal Service
475 L'Enfant Plaza
Washington, D.C. 20260

When scheduling a debt to the United States
other than for taxes BR 2002(j)

Name of Agency
c/o U.S. Attorney
318 South Sixth Street
Springfield, IL 62701–1626

SEARCH FEE GUIDELINES

You are encouraged to call the free computer line (VCIS), use PACER, or obtain free information in person with the use of Computer Terminals in each staffed office.

ALL REQUESTS MUST BE IN WRITING or IN PERSON
NO INFORMATION WILL BE GIVEN BY PHONE

SEARCH FEE OF $30.00 (paid in advance)

Any request requiring a physical search of court records in computer or in the case file by Deputy Clerk is considered a Search of Record and requires a $30.00 fee plus $ .50 per page of copywork paid in advance for:

All written requests; (See exceptions under "No Search Fee")

Information whether an entity is listed as a creditor;

Copies of petition, schedules, and other documents;

All in-person requests if Deputy Clerk must search the file for information. *No search fee if deputy retrieves file for person to view or if documents to be copied have been marked with paper clips by requesting party.*

NO SEARCH FEE TO OBTAIN:

Case Number when exact name of debtor is provided;

Date bankruptcy filed when exact name of debtor is provided;

Name of debtor when case number is provided;

Social Security number of debtor;

Whether case was filed as a voluntary case or an involuntary case;

Chapter Number of originally filed case;

Name of Debtor's Attorney;

Name of Trustee;

Whether the case is an Asset Case or a No Asset Case;

Date No Asset Report filed;

Date Final Report filed;

Date Discharge issued;

Date, Time and Place of Sec. 341 Meeting;

General Status of Case—Pending or Closed;

Date Notice of Appeal filed, if applicable.

COPYWORK POLICY

There are several ways to obtain copies of documents:

Print Electronic Records from your Personal Computer using PACER

You may print copies of documents, download documents to your own computer or search information in your case. The PACER system is available days, nights and weekends.

You must register to become a user at the PACER website (http://www.pacer.gov). There is a fee for copies of $.10 per page. A user is not billed until charges of $15 in a quarter have accrued. Most one-time users would not accrue enough charges to be billed for copies. You will find a full explanation of charges on the PACER website as well as directions for registration

Print Electronic Records at the Clerk's Office from Public Computer Terminals

You can print electronic records form the PACER (Public Access to Court Electronic Records) computer terminals located in each of our three offices. You will be charged $.10 cents per page. Please note, the Clerk's Office can only accept EXACT CHANGE and cannot make or give change.

Submit a Written Request by Email or Mail

You may send a written request for copies by email or mail to the office where your case was filed:

Copywork_Urb@ilcb.uscourts.gov

Copywork_Peo@ilcb.uscourts.gov

Copywork_Spr@ilcb.uscourts.gov

Your request must include:

Your name

The case number or name of debtor(s)

A description of the copies requested or document numbers

Once we receive your request, we will send you a statement of charges for the copywork. You will be charged $.50 per page for copies. If your request requires a search of the records, a $30.00 search fee is required.

After you receive the statement of charges, mail payment to the Clerk's Office via money order, cashier check, or company/firm check made payable to: Clerk, U.S. Bankruptcy Court. The Clerk's Office does not accept personal checks or cash through the mail.

After we receive payment, copies will be made and sent to you via email or first class mail. Please specify how you would like copies returned to you and provide the necessary information to do so. Please note: If you choose to have copies returned to you by email, your receipt will be sent by email as well.

ARCHIVED CASES

Cases closed prior to 2004 are stored in the Federal Records Center (FRC) in Chicago and copies may be obtained directly from the FRC. Contact the Clerk's Office to obtain location information.

PAYMENT BY CHECK OR CASH

Submit Money Order, Certified Check, Bank Cashier Check, or Business Check ONLY.

CHECKS:

Make payable to: Clerk, U.S. Bankruptcy Court

or

                         U.S. Bankruptcy Court

NOT ACCEPTED:

Personal Check

Third Party Check

Blank Check

Unsigned Check

Incorrect Amount—amount must be **EXACT**

Numerical Figure and Written Amount do not agree

Postdated Check

Check made payable to an unacceptable party—*See above*

NOTE—*There is a $53.00 service charge on all returned checks.*

CASH:

No Foreign Money accepted.

Must be **EXACT AMOUNT** only. We do not make change.

Cash payments accepted only in person at the counter.

Cash received in mail will be promptly returned.

INFORMATION ON ORDERING A TRANSCRIPT

Springfield Office

Requests for transcripts of proceedings held after 2/2007 must be submitted on the Transcript Order Form at http://www.uscourts.gov/uscourts/FormsAndFees/Forms/AO435.pdf. Please complete items 1–19 and return the form to the Bankruptcy Clerk's Office. Upon receipt of the completed form, you will be notified of the cost for the transcript. PREPAYMENT IS REQUIRED BEFORE ANY ORDER WILL BE PROCESSED.

Requests for transcripts of proceedings held between 11/2000 and 2/2007 must be sent directly to:

Carla Boehl
17804 Edwards Rd
Virden, IL 62690
217–965–3006

Please contact the Bankruptcy Clerk's Office at 217–492–4551 if you have questions regarding the procedures for ordering a transcript.

Peoria Office

Requests for transcripts must be submitted on the Transcript Order Form at http://www.uscourts.gov/uscourts/FormsAndFees/Forms/AO435.pdf. Please complete items 1–19 and return the form to the Bankruptcy Clerk's Office. Upon receipt of the completed form, you will be notified of the cost for the transcript. PREPAYMENT IS REQUIRED BEFORE ANY ORDER WILL BE PROCESSED.

Tape recordings of certain judicial hearings may be ordered by submitting your request in writing to the Bankruptcy Clerk's Office. You will then be notified of the total cost ($30.00 per tape). The Bankruptcy Clerk's Office does not transcribe tapes.

Please contact the Bankruptcy Clerk's Office at 309–671–7035 if you have questions regarding the procedures for ordering a transcript.

Urbana Office

Requests for transcripts of proceedings held after 4/18/95 must be submitted on the Transcript Order Form at http://www.uscourts.gov/uscourts/FormsAndFees/Forms/AO435.pdf. Please complete items 1–19 and return the form to the Bankruptcy Clerk's Office. Upon receipt of the completed form, you will be notified of the cost for the transcript. PREPAYMENT IS REQUIRED BEFORE ANY ORDER WILL BE PROCESSED.

Tape recordings of certain judicial hearings may be ordered by submitting your request in writing to the Bankruptcy Clerk's Office. You will then be notified of the total cost ($30.00 per tape). The Bankruptcy Clerk's Office does not transcribe tapes.

Requests for transcripts of proceedings held prior to 4/18/95 must sent directly to the Court Reporter as indicated below:

For proceedings held in Urbana or Paris	For proceedings held in Kankakee
Maninfior Court Reporting	Contact the Clerk's Office in
PO Box 1036	Urbana
Mattoon, IL 61938	
217–235–1127	

Please contact the Bankruptcy Clerk's Office, 217–974–7330, if you have questions regarding the procedures for ordering transcripts or tapes.

PACER

(Public Access to Court Electronic Records)

Web Version

Introduction

PACER is available on the Internet in a web-based format.

Note: Each court controls its own computer system and case information database; therefore, there will be some variations among jurisdictions as to the information offered.

Persons interested in utilizing this service must first register with the PACER Service Center at 800 676–6856. The website for the PACER Service Center is: http://pacer.uscourts.gov/

There is a charge of $.10/page for information retrieved from this site. A user is not billed until charges of $15 in a quarterly billing cycle have accrued. **Most one–time users would not accrue enough charges to be billed for copies.** You will find a full explanation of charges on the PACER website as well as directions for registration.

For more information: http://www.ilcb.uscourts.gov/obtaining-copies-documents-bankruptcy-case-file

REGISTRY OF MAILING ADDRESSES FOR STATE & GOVERNMENTAL UNITS

* Illinois Attorney General
33 S. State Street, Room 993
Chicago, IL 60603

* Illinois Attorney General
Revenue Litigation 500 S.
Second Street Springfield,
IL 62701

* U.S. Attorney General
U. S. Department of Justice 950
Pennsylvania Avenue, NW
Washington, DC 20530–0001

* U.S. Attorney
318 South Sixth Street
Springfield, IL 62701

*Illinois Capital Development Board
Chief Counsel
401 S. Spring St., 3rd Floor
Springfield, Illinois 62706

*Illinois Department of Human Services
General Counsel
100 W. Randolph, Suite 6–400
Chicago, Illinois 60601

*Illinois Department of Natural Resources
Chief Legal Counsel
1 Natural Resources Way
Springfield, Illinois 62703

*Illinois Department of Public Health
Division of Legal Services Attn:
Bankruptcy Notice 535 West
Jefferson, 5th Floor Springfield,
Illinois 62761

*Texas Workforce Commission
Bankruptcy Unit, Rm 556 101
E. 15th St.
Austin, TX 78778–0001

*Illinois Department of Employment Security
Insolvency/Bkcy Subunit Field
Audit Section
33 S. State St. 10th Floor
Chicago, IL 60603

*Treasurer of the State of Illinois
Office of the State Treasurer Legal
Department
James R. Thompson Center 100 W.
Randolph Street Suite 15–600
Chicago, Illinois 60601

* U.S. Securities and Exchange Commission
175 W. Jackson Blvd., Suite 900
Chicago, IL 60604

* Illinois Department of Revenue
Bankruptcy Section
P.O. Box 64338 Chicago, IL
60664–0338

* Internal Revenue Service
P.O. Box 7346 Philadelphia, PA
19101–7346

*Mississippi State Tax Commission
Bankruptcy Section
P.O. Box 22808 Jackson, MS
39225–2808

*U. S. Environmental Protection Agency
Richard L. Nagle
Bankruptcy Contact
US EPA Region 5 Mail Code: C–14J 77 W.
Jackson Blvd.
Chicago, IL 60604

*California Franchise Tax Board
Service of Adversary Proceedings: Chief
Counsel
Franchise Tax Board
c/o General Counsel Section
P.O. Box 1720, MS: A–260 Rancho Cordova,
CA 95741–1720

Bankruptcy Code § 505 Requests:
Franchise Tax Board
Bankruptcy Section, MS: A–340
PO Box 2952
Sacramento, CA 95812–2952

All Other Service and Notices:
Franchise Tax Board Bankruptcy
Section, MS: A–340 P.O. Box 2952
Sacramento, CA 95812–2952

11 U.S.C. § 505(b) Requests
Michigan Department of Treasury, Tax Policy Division ATTN:
Litigation Liaison
2nd Floor, Austin Building
430 West Allegan Street
Lansing, Michigan 48922

Oklahoma Tax Commission
Office of the General Counsel, Bankruptcy Section
120 N. Robinson, Ste. 2000W
Oklahoma City, OK 73102

McVCIS

(Multi–Court Voice Case Information System)

INTRODUCTION

McVCIS is a service provided by the federal bankruptcy courts which allows you to get information about any pending bankruptcy case filed in the Central District of Illinois by using a standard touch tone telephone. McVCIS, also allows you to search for case information in numerous other federal bankruptcy courts.

I. McVCIS

By dialing toll free 866–222–8029 from a touchtone phone, you may determine whether a party has filed for bankruptcy, and gain a considerable amount of case information. The service is available at all times. The information available includes debtor(s)' name(s), date of filing, chapter, attorney for the debtor, trustee (if any), date and time of the pending Sec. 341 Meeting, date of discharge, date of case closing, and general case status, such as "Awaiting 341 Meeting" or "Awaiting Discharge Order." Simply enter the debtor's name, last name first, using up to ten characters, and hit the # sign. Punctuation is irrelevant, and we recommend that you use all 10 characters allotted. If the debtor is a corporation, enter the first ten characters of the debtor's name and hit the # sign.

EQUIPMENT NEEDED

A touch-tone telephone

HOURS

The system is available 24 hours every day.

HOW TO USE McVCIS

To use McVCIS, simply follow these instructions:

1. For cases filed January 1, 2004 through current date—Dial 866–222–8029.

2. For most cases closed prior to January 1, 2004, contact the Clerk's Office for help.

3. When prompted to enter the state and division, say "Illinois Central"

4. Press 1 for instructions on how to use this system or say "help", press 2 to search by case number or say "case number", press 3 to search by participant's name or same "name", press 4 to search by participant's social security or say "social security number".

GENERAL INFORMATION

LOCAL RULES

There are no local rules in the Central District of Illinois Bankruptcy Court. The local rules of the U.S. District Court for the Central District of Illinois and the Federal Rules of Bankruptcy Procedure apply. The local District Court rules can be found at http://www.ilcd.uscourts.gov/. District Court's local rules may also be obtained in person at one of the District Clerk's Offices or by submitting a stamped, self addressed 9½″ × 12″ envelope with $4.95 postage prepaid to U.S. District Court, 151 U.S. Courthouse, 600 E. Monroe Street, Springfield, Illinois 62701.

INSTRUCTION PAMPHLETS AVAILABLE

There are pamphlets available in each of the divisional offices which briefly outline the basic information, filing requirements, and guidelines for preparing the creditor matrix for Chapter 7 and Chapter 13 bankruptcies.

EMERGENCY FILINGS

For emergency filings when the Clerk's Office is not open, contact the Clerk of Court, Adrienne D. Atkins at 217- 720–1881.

SETTING MATTERS FOR HEARING

The Clerk's Office will set matters for hearing on the first available court date. There is no need to formally request a hearing.

DISCHARGE ORDERS

Unless an objection has been filed, discharge orders will be mailed approximately eight weeks from the date the first meeting of creditors was originally set.

AMENDMENTS

When submitting amendments to the matrix, lists or schedules D, E, or F, please submit only the changes.

BANKRUPTCY NOTICING CENTERS AND UNDELIVERABLE MAIL

Many of our notices including 341 Notices and Discharges are now produced and mailed from the Bankruptcy Noticing Centers in Virginia and Utah. For this reason, the documents are being received several days later than the ones which are mailed locally. It is the responsibility of the Attorney for the Debtor to re-address and re-send undeliverable mail and then notify the Court as to any changes of address.

CM/ECF INFORMATION AND TIPS

Click the "ECF Helpdesk" tab from the court's website: http://www.ilcb.uscourts. gov

DEBTOR ELECTRONIC BANKRUPTCY NOTICING (DeBN)

Note: Only the court is authorized to send notices to the debtor through this DeBN program. All other parties, such as trustees and creditors, will continue to serve the debtor via U.S. mail or in person as required by court rules.

The U.S. Bankruptcy Court for the Central District of Illinois now offers debtors the opportunity to request receipt of court notices and orders via email, instead of U.S. mail, through a program called "Debtor Electronic Bankruptcy Noticing" or "DeBN."

DeBN provides the following advantages:

- **Faster**—You'll receive notices the same day they are filed by the court.
- **Convenient**—Access your notices any-where you have internet access.
- **No more lost paperwork**—Storing notices on your computer means never losing a paper copy.
- **Less paper clutter**—Helps the environment and reduces paper clutter in your home.
- **It is FREE!**

Pursuant to Federal Rule of Bankruptcy Procedure 9036, a party may make a written request for delivery of notices via email, instead of U.S. mail. Through the DeBN program, only notices and orders that have been filed by the court can be emailed to the debtor. Debtors requesting participation in the DeBN program must complete and file a Debtor's Electronic Noticing Request (DeBN) form with the court where their case is filed.

Go to www.ilcb.uscourts.gov/debn for more information and to download the request form.

[Effective March 13, 2012. Amended effective April 4, 2013; February 7, 2014; March 23, 2015.]

ELECTRONIC CASE FILING

GENERAL ORDERS AFFECTING ELECTRONIC CASE FILING IN THE CENTRAL DISTRICT OF ILLINOIS

IN THE UNITED STATES BANKRUPTCY COURT FOR THE CENTRAL DISTRICT OF ILLINOIS

Amended General Order Assigning All Cases to the Electronic Filing System Effective April 12, 2004

Pursuant to the court's Amended General Order Authorizing Electronic Case Filing entered January 7, 2004, all future, pending, and closed cases are hereby assigned to the Electronic Filing System effective April 12, 2004. The court will no longer accept paper documents for filing except from pro se debtors, certain creditor-claimants, and attorneys currently enrolled in a bankruptcy ECF training class in this district. Creditor-claimants such as credit card companies, financial institutions, and collection agencies who receive multiple bankruptcy notices annually are required to file electronically.

Attorneys who have attended an ECF training class shall have a 15 day grace period following the date of their class in which they may file paper documents.

[Dated: April 7, 2004. Amended January 10, 2007.]

Third Amended General Order Authorizing Electronic Case Filing

Federal Rules of Bankruptcy Procedure 5005(a)(2), 9011, 9029 and 9036 authorize this Court to establish practices and procedures for the filing, signing, maintaining, and verification of pleadings and papers, and sending of notices by electronic means.

NOW, THEREFORE IT IS ORDERED that:

1. Electronic Filing Authorized

The court will accept for filing documents submitted, signed or verified by electronic means that comply with procedures established by the court.

The court will designate which cases will be assigned to the "Electronic Filing System" (the court's system that receives documents filed in electronic form). Except as expressly provided and in exceptional circumstances preventing a "Filing User" (those who have a court-issued log-in and password to file documents electronically) from filing electronically, all petitions, motions, memoranda of law, or other pleadings and documents required to be filed with the court in connection with a case assigned to the Electronic Filing System must be electronically filed.

Notwithstanding the foregoing, pro se debtors, certain creditor-claimants, and attorneys currently enrolled in a bankruptcy electronic filing training class in this district are not required to electronically file pleadings and other papers in a case assigned to the System. Creditor-claimants such as credit card companies, financial institutions, and collection agencies who receive multiple bankruptcy notices annually are required to file electronically.

2. Eligibility, Registration, Passwords

Attorneys admitted to the bar of this court (including those admitted pro hac vice and attorneys authorized to represent the United States), United States trustees and their assistants, bankruptcy administrators and their assistants, private trustees, and others as the court deems appropriate, may register as Filing Users of the court's Electronic Filing System. Registration is in a form prescribed by the Clerk and requires the Filing User's name, address, telephone number, Internet e-mail address, and, in the case of an attorney, a declaration that the attorney is admitted to the bar of this court.

A party to a pending action who is not represented by an attorney may register as a Filing User in the Electronic Filing System solely for purpose of the action. Registration is in a form prescribed by the clerk and requires identification of the action as well as the name, address, telephone number and Internet e-mail address of the party. If, during the course of action, the party retains an attorney who appears on the party's behalf, the attorney must advise the clerk to terminate the party's registration as a Filing User upon the attorney's appearance.

Provided that a Filing User has an Internet e-mail address, registration as a Filing User constitutes: (1) waiver of the right to receive notice by first class mail and consent to electronic service, except with regard to the service of a summons and complaint under Fed.R.Bankr.P. 7004. Waiver of service and notice by first class mail applies to notice of the entry of an order or judgment under Fed.R.Bankr.P. 9022.

Once registration, which includes training provided by the court, is completed, the Filing User will receive notification of the user log-in and password. Filing Users agree to protect the security of their passwords and immediately notify the clerk if they learn that their password has been compromised. Users may be subject to sanctions for failure to comply with this provision.

3. Consequences of Electronic Filing

Electronic transmission of a document to the Electronic Filing System consistent with this Order, together with the transmission of a Notice of Electronic Filing from the court, constitutes filing of the document for all purposes of the Federal Rules of Bankruptcy Procedure and constitutes entry of the document on the docket kept by the clerk under Fed.R.Bankr.P. 5003.

Before filing a scanned document with the court, a Filing User must verify its legibility.

When a document has been filed electronically, the official record is the electronic recording of the document as stored by the court and the filing party is bound by the document as filed. A document filed electronically is deemed filed at the date and time stated on the Notice of Electronic Filing from the court.

Filing a document electronically does not alter the filing deadline for that document. Filing must be completed before midnight local time where the court is located in order to be considered timely filed that day.

4. Entry of Court Orders

All signed orders will be filed electronically by the court or by court personnel. Any order or other court-issued document filed electronically without the original signature of a judge has the same force and effect as if the judge had affixed the judge's signature to a paper copy of the order and it had been entered on the docket in a conventional manner.

Orders may also be issued as "text-only" entries on the docket, without an attached document. Such orders are official and binding.

The court may sign, seal and issue a summons electronically, although a summons may not be served electronically.

A Filing User submitting a document electronically that requires a judge's signature must promptly deliver the document in such form as the court requires.

5. Attachments and Exhibits

Filing users must submit in electronic form all documents referenced as exhibits or attachments. A Filing User must submit as exhibits or attachments only those excerpts of the referenced documents that are directly germane to the matter under consideration by the court. Excerpted material must be clearly and prominently identified as such. Filing Users who file excerpts of documents as exhibits or attachments do so without prejudice to their right to timely file additional excerpts or the complete document. Responding parties may timely file additional excerpts or the complete document that they believe are directly germane. The court may require parties to file additional excerpts or the complete document.

6. Transcripts

Transcripts shall be filed conventionally.

7. Sealed Documents

Documents ordered to be placed under seal must be filed conventionally, and not electronically, unless specifically authorized by the court. A motion to file documents under seal may be filed electronically unless prohibited by law. The order of the court authorizing the filing of documents under seal may be filed electronically unless prohibited by law. A paper copy of the order must be attached to the documents under seal and be delivered to the clerk.

8. Privacy Issues

In connection with the filing of any material in an action assigned to the Electronic Filing System, any person may apply by motion for an order limiting electronic access to or prohibiting the electronic filing of certain specifically-identified materials on the grounds that such material is subject to privacy interests and that electronic access or electronic filing in the action is likely to prejudice those privacy interests.

9. Retention Requirements

Documents that are electronically filed and require original signatures other than that of the Filing User must be maintained in paper form by the Filing User until all time periods for appeals expire. On request of the court, the Filing User must provide original documents for review.

10. Signatures

The user log-in and password required to submit documents to the Electronic Filing System serve as the Filing User's signature on all electronic documents filed with the court. They also serve as a signature for purposes of Federal Rules of Bankruptcy Procedure and any other purpose for which a signature is required in connection with proceedings before the court. Electronically filed documents must include a signature block and must set forth the name, address and telephone number. In addition, the name of the Filing User under whose log-in and password the document is submitted must be preceded by an "/s/" and typed in the space where the signature would otherwise appear, e.g. "/s/ Jane Doe", "/s/ John Doe".

No Filing User or other person may knowingly permit or cause to permit a Filing User's password to be used by anyone other than an authorized agent of the Filing User.

Documents containing the signature of non-Filing Users are to be filed electronically with the signature represented by a "s/" and the name typed in the space where a signature would otherwise appear, or as a scanned image.

Documents requiring signatures of more than one party must be electronically filed either by: (1) submitting a scanned document containing all necessary signatures; (2) representing the consent of the other parties on the document, provided the filing user retains the originally signed document; or (3) in any other manner approved by the court.

11. Service of Documents by Electronic Means

The "Notice of Electronic Filing" that is automatically generated by the court's Electronic Filing System constitutes service or notice of the filed document on Filing Users. Parties who are not Filing Users must be provided notice or service of any pleading or other document electronically filed in accordance with the Federal Rules of Bankruptcy Procedure and the local rules.

A certificate of service must be included with all documents filed electronically, indicating that service was accomplished through the Notice of Electronic Filing for parties and counsel who are Filing Users and indicating how service was accomplished on any party or counsel who is not a Filing User.

12. Notice of Court Orders and Judgments

Immediately upon the entry of an order or judgment in an action assigned to the Electronic Filing System, the clerk will transmit to Filing Users in the case, in electronic form, a Notice of Electronic Filing. Electronic transmission of the Notice of Electronic Filing constitutes the notice required by Fed.R.Bankr.P. 9022. The clerk must give notice to a person who has not consented to electronic service in paper form in accordance with the Federal Rules of Bankruptcy Procedure.

13. Technical Failures

A Filing User whose filing is made untimely as the result of a technical failure may seek appropriate relief from the court.

14. Public Access

Any person or organization, other than one registered as a Filing User, may access the Electronic Filing System at the court's Internet site (www.ilcb.uscourts. gov) by obtaining a PACER log-in and password. Those who have PACER access but who are not Filing Users may retrieve docket sheets and documents, but they may not file documents.

Information posted on the System must not be downloaded for uses inconsistent with the privacy concerns of any person.

[Dated: January 10, 2007.]

PRIVACY PROTECTION POLICY

Please adhere to this important Privacy Protection Policy

Federal Rule of Bankruptcy Procedure 9037 applies to all documents filed with the court. This policy requires parties in bankruptcy cases to modify or partially redact personal data identifiers contained in documents.

You **should not include sensitive information in any document filed with the court** unless such inclusion is required by the Federal Rules of Bankruptcy Procedure or Official Forms or the inclusion is otherwise necessary and relevant to the case. If sensitive information must be included, the following personal data identifiers **must be** partially redacted from the pleading:

- Social Security numbers
- Dates of birth
- Names of minor children
- Financial account numbers

In addition, exercise caution when filing documents that contain the following:

- Any personal identifying number, such as driver's license number:
- Medical records, treatment and diagnosis
- Proprietary or trade secret information

Official Form B–21 Statement of Social Security Number should not be included as part of the pdf you attach to the Voluntary Petition. Instead, the B–21 should be filed as a separate document using the event Bankruptcy>Miscellaneous>Statement of SSN. This event has a restricted access code associated with it and only court personnel may view the associated pdf.

Responsibility for redacting personal data identifiers from documents rests with the filers, not the court.

DIRECTOR'S INTERIM GUIDANCE REGARDING
TAX INFORMATION UNDER 11 U.S.C. § 521

Section 315(c) of the Bankruptcy Abuse Prevention and Consumer Protection Act of 2005 (the Act) mandates that the Director of the Administrative Office of the United States Courts establish procedures for safeguarding the confidentiality of tax information required to be provided under 11 U.S.C. § 521.[1] In accordance with the Act, the Director provides the following guidance on procedures to protect a debtor's tax information.[2]

I. No tax information filed with the bankruptcy court or otherwise provided by the debtor will be available to the public via the Internet, PACER, or CM/ECF.

In order for tax information to be electronically entered into a court's CM/ECF system, the "tax information" event must be selected from the CM/ECF event list. The "tax information" event limits access to the filed tax information to those users assigned "court" logins (i.e., judicial officers and court employees). All other users (including PACER users) will be limited to viewing a docket event on the docket report indicating that tax information has been filed. These other users will not be able to open and view the tax information.

II. Debtors providing tax information under 11 U.S.C. § 521 should redact personal information as set forth in the Judicial Conference's Policy on Privacy and Public Access to Electronic Case Files.

All tax information provided in accordance with section 521 of the Bankruptcy Code is subject to the Judicial Conference of the United States Policy on Privacy and Public Access to Electronic Case Files http://jnet.ao.dcn/it/ecf/privacy-policy.html ("JCUS policy") (JCUSSEP/OCT 01, pp. 49–50). In accordance with the JCUS policy, the debtor should take the following steps to redact personal identifiers in any tax information filed with the court or provided to the trustee or creditor(s), in either electronic or paper form:

-**Social Security numbers**. If an individual's social security number is included, only the last four digits of that number should appear;

-**Names of minor children**. If a minor child(ren) is/are identified by name, only the child(ren)'s initials should appear;

-**Dates of birth**. If an individual's date of birth is included, only the year should appear; and

-**Financial account numbers**. If financial account numbers are provided, only the last four digits of these numbers should appear.

Court employees are not responsible for redacting any of the personal identifying information. The responsibility for redacting personal identifiers rests solely with the debtor.

The court should make this Interim Guidance, implementing the JCUS policy, available to the public and members of the local bar.

III. Procedure for requesting and obtaining access to tax information filed with the bankruptcy court under 11 U.S.C. § 521(f).

To gain access to a debtor's tax information under 11 U.S.C. § 521(f), the United States trustee (or a bankruptcy administrator, if any), trustee, or party in interest, including a creditor, must follow the procedures set forth below.

A written request that a debtor file copies of tax returns with the court pursuant to

11 U.S.C. § 521(f) shall be filed with the court and served on the debtor and debtor's counsel, if any.

In order to obtain access to debtor's tax information that is filed with the bankruptcy court, the movant must file a motion with the court, which should include:

-a description of the movant's status in the case, to allow the court to ascertain whether the movant may properly be given access to the requested tax information;

-a description of the specific tax information sought;

-a statement indicating that the information cannot be obtained by the movant from any other sources; and

-a statement showing a demonstrated need for the tax information.

An order granting a motion for access to tax information should include language advising the movant that the tax information obtained is confidential and should condition dissemination of the tax information as appropriate under the circumstances of the particular case. At the discretion of the court, the order may state that sanctions may be imposed for improper use, disclosure, or dissemination of the tax information.

IV. Access to tax information when a motion for access has been granted

Local courts have authority to determine procedures, the details of which are within the discretion of the court, for transmitting the tax information to the movant when access has been granted.[3] Possible methods include mailing a hard copy, or developing procedures to view tax information at the clerk's office.

The transmission of the tax information to the movant, by whatever means the court deems appropriate, should be recorded as a docket event in CM/ECF so that the docket will reflect that the court has taken the action necessary to effect the provisions of its order granting access.

[Dated: September 20, 2005.]

[1] For purposes of the Director's Interim Guidance Regarding Tax Information Under 11 U.S.C. § 521 ("Interim Guidance"), the term "tax information" includes tax returns, transcripts of returns, amendments to returns and any other document containing tax information provided by the debtor under section 521 of title 11, United States Code.

[2] Interim Bankruptcy Rule 4002 (b)(5) provides that the debtor's obligation to provide tax information to the trustee or a copy of the information submitted to the trustee provided to a requesting creditor pursuant to 11 U.S.C. § 521(e)(2) is subject to the Interim Guidance. In addition, section 315(c)(1) of the Act authorizes the Director to promulgate guidance to protect the "confidentiality of any tax information required to be provided under this section," which encompasses information provided under section 521(e) and (f) of the Bankruptcy Code. Thus, except where expressly limited to tax information filed with the court, this Interim Guidance applies to any other document containing tax information required to be filed with the court or otherwise provided by the debtor under section 521 of the Bankruptcy Code.

[3] Administrative Office staff will explore the feasibility of including modifications in a future release of CM/ECF, which will provide access to a particular user that has been granted access to tax information by the court. Until such modifications can be incorporated into CM/ECF, local courts will need to determine how to provide access.

Important Privacy Act Information

The Judicial Conference of the United States adopted a policy in September 2001 regarding privacy and public access to electronic case files. This policy requires litigants in bankruptcy cases to modify or partially redact personal data identifiers contained in documents that will be made available electronically.

You **should not include sensitive information in any document filed with the court** unless such inclusion is required by the Federal Rules of Bankruptcy Procedure or Official Forms or the inclusion is otherwise necessary and relevant to the case. If sensitive information must be included, the following personal data identifiers **must be** partially redacted from the pleading:

* Social Security numbers
* Dates of birth

* Names of minor children

* Financial account numbers

In addition, exercise caution when filing documents that contain the following:

* Any personal identifying number, such as driver's license number:

* Medical records, treatment and diagnosis

* Proprietary or trade secret information

Official Form B-21 Statement of Social Security Number should not be included as part of the pdf you attach to the Voluntary Petition. Instead, the B-21 should be filed as a separate document using the event Bankruptcy>Miscellaneous>Statement of SSN. This event has a restricted access code associated with it and only court personnel may view the associated pdf.

Responsibility for redacting personal data identifiers from documents is with the filers and not the clerk's office.

[Dated: April 5, 2007.]

ORDERS

IN RE FILING OF PAYMENT ADVICES PURSUANT
TO 11 U.S.C. § 521(A)(1)(B)(IV)

IT IS HEREBY ORDERED, effective as to all cases filed on or after October 17, 2005, that copies of all payment advices or other evidence of payment received within 60 days before the date of the filing of the petition by the debtor from any employer of the debtor:

(1) shall not be filed with the Court unless otherwise ordered;

(2) shall be provided by the debtor to the trustee at least seven days before the first date set for the meeting of creditors conducted pursuant to 11 U.S.C. § 341; and

(3) shall be provided by the debtor promptly to any creditor who sends a written request to the debtor.

[Dated: October 5, 2005.]

IN RE STANDING ORDER REGARDING CREDIT COUNSELING

Pursuant to F.R.B.P. Interim Rule 1007(b)(3) and (c) and Section 521(b) of the Bankruptcy Code, an individual debtor is required to file with the petition in a voluntary case, Official Form 1. Exhibit D. *Individual Debtor's Statement of Compliance With Credit Counseling Agencies*, which must include one of the following:

(i) an attached certificate described in Section 521(b)(1) and the debt repayment plan, if any, described in Section 521(b)(2), or

(ii) an attached statement that the debtor has received the credit counseling briefing required by Section 109(h)(1), but does not have the certificate required by Section 521(b); or

(iii) an attached motion for determination by the court requesting a temporary waiver of the requirements of Section 109(h)(1) and an extension of time to comply; or

(iv) an attached motion for determination by the court to excuse the debtor entirely from the credit counseling requirements of Section 109(h)(1) because of incapacity, disability, or active military duty in a combat zone as defined by Section 109(h)(4).

584

For all individual and joint voluntary cases filed in the Central District of Illinois on the date of this Order and thereafter, **IT IS ORDERED** that the failure of any debtor to file one of the four filings specified above, **with the petition**, will result in automatic dismissal of the petition as to each such debtor without notice or hearing. In the event a case is so dismissed, it will not be treated as a filed case for purposes of Section 362(c)(3) or (4).

[Dated: October 4, 2006.]

STANDING ORDER REGARDING ATTORNEY FEES FOR DEBTORS' COUNSEL IN CHAPTER 13 AND CHAPTER 7 CASES (DANVILLE DIVISION)

The "no-look" fee in Chapter 13 cases is raised from $3,300 to $3,500. There will no longer be a set "no-look" fee for Chapter 7 cases.

This standing Order shall be applicable to cases filed on and after January 1, 2014.

DATED: January 14, 2014.

[Dated: December 15, 2009. Revised effective January 1, 2014.]

STANDING ORDER REGARDING ATTORNEY FEES FOR DEBTORS' COUNSEL IN CHAPTER 13 CASES (PEORIA AND URBANA DIVISIONS)

The Bankruptcy Court for the Central District of Illinois in the Peoria Division currently requires debtor's counsel to submit an itemized fee application in any Chapter 13 case where attorney fees sought exceed $3,300. Effective as of January 1, 2014, for Chapter 13 cases filed on and after that date, the review threshold will be increased by $200 and this Court will require an itemized fee application where the attorney fees sought exceed $3,500. Attorney fees in excess of $3,500 must be requested by application in accordance with Rule 2016 of the Federal Rules of Bankruptcy Procedure.

Allowed attorney fees shall be paid through the plan. However, the attorney may receive all or part of the allowed fees prior to the filing of the case, provided those fees are deducted from the total allowed fees to be paid through the confirmed plan. The allowed fees shall be paid by the Trustee ratably with other administrative expenses and priority claims.

This Court strongly disfavors plans that pay all or almost all of the distributions to the debtor's attorney. Attorneys are encouraged to charge a reduced fee to debtors who can afford only a minimal monthly payment. Where the full no-look fee of $3,500 is charged, the debtor's total plan payments should equal or exceed $5,400 (at least $150 per month for a 36–month plan), unless otherwise ordered by the Court.

The duties designated below are presumed to be included within the scope of services rendered by the attorney to the debtor. If an attorney fails to perform any required duty, the Court, upon notice and hearing, may order the attorney to disgorge all or any part of the fees received, as the Court, in its discretion, deems appropriate. Upon request or objection of an interested party, the Court will consider whether some or all of the debtor's attorney fees should be denied based on the circumstances of a particular case.

The debtor's attorney's duties in a Chapter 13 case include, but are not necessarily limited to, the following:

1. Consult with and advise the debtor about the differences and relative advantages and disadvantages of proceeding under Chapter 7 and Chapter 13.

2. Prepare and file the petition, statement of financial affairs, all schedules and Official Form 22C.

3. Prepare and file a Chapter 13 plan.

4. Upon information received from the debtor, take steps necessary to avoid the termination of, or to allow the reinstatement of, necessary utility services of the debtor by providing proof of filing of the petition to utility service creditors.

5. Take steps necessary to obtain the return of repossessed vehicles proposed to be retained by the debtor under the plan.

6. In the event of pending state or federal court litigation, notify creditor's attorneys, and appropriate court(s) in which the litigation is pending, that the bankruptcy case has been filed.

7. Send out an information letter to the debtor reminding the debtor to attend the 341 hearing, specifying the time and location of that hearing, and providing information advising the debtor as to the procedures of the 341 hearing.

8. Appear at the 341 meeting of creditors with the debtor and confer with the debtor to prepare him or her to appear at the 341 meeting.

9. Upon information received from the debtor, take steps necessary to terminate pending wage garnishments, including filing a Motion to Terminate Garnishment.

10. Attend all court hearings in the case, including the confirmation hearing.

11. Prepare all court mandated pre-trial statements, reports, briefs, etc.

12. Respond to objections to plan confirmation and, where necessary, prepare an amended plan.

13. Prepare, file, and serve necessary amended statements and schedules, in accordance with information submitted by the debtor, provided the debtor pays the Court's filing fee.

14. Prepare, file, and serve necessary motions to buy, sell, or refinance real property and vehicles, when appropriate.

15. Object to improper or invalid claims based upon documentation provided by the debtor.

16. File proofs of claims for creditors who fail to file claims, if it is in the debtor's best interest to file such a claim.

17. Advise and represent the debtor with respect to motions for relief from the automatic stay, for adequate protection, to terminate the co-debtor stay, and other contested matters.

18. Prepare, file, and serve motions to avoid liens on real or personal property.

19. Upon information received from the debtor, contact creditors who continue to communicate with the debtor after filing.

20. Pursuant to Section 1328(a), upon completion of plan payments, file a Certification of Payment of Domestic Support Obligation, if debtor(s) were required to pay a domestic support obligation during the pendency of the case.

21. Provide such other legal services as are necessary for the administration of the case before the Bankruptcy Court.

This Standing Order shall be applicable to cases filed on and after January 1, 2014.

DATED: December 3, 2013.

[Dated: December 3, 2009. Revised effective January 1, 2014.]

STANDING ORDER REGARDING ATTORNEY FEES FOR DEBTOR'S COUNSEL IN CHAPTER 7 AND 13 CASES (SPRINGFIELD DIVISION)

All attorneys representing individual debtors before this Court are reminded that they are "debt relief agencies" under the Code and, accordingly, must comply with the requirements for such agencies. *See* 11 U.S.C. § 101(12A); 11 U.S.C. § 528; *Milavitz, Gallop & Milavetz, P.A. v. U.S.*, 559 U.S. 229 (2010). Particular attention should be paid to the provisions of § 528 which require written fee contracts and full disclosure of all anticipated charges. *See* 11 U.S.C. § 528(a).

Since January 1, 2010, this Court's "no-look" flat fee for representation of a Chapter 13 debtor has been $3300. As of January 1, 2014, the "no-look" fee will become $3500 until further order of this Court. Attorneys may certainly charge less than the "no-look" flat fee. Further, attorneys are not required to represent Chapter 13 debtors for flat fees. However, attorneys who have not agreed with their debtor clients to accept fees at or below the "no-look" flat fee amount must request approval of their fees by itemized application. All fee applications must be made in accordance with Rule 2016 of the Federal Rules of Bankruptcy Procedure and the guidelines established by this Court. *See* Fed. R. Bankr. P. 2016(a); *In re Vancil Contracting, Inc.*, 2008 WL 207533 (Bankr. C.D. Ill. Jan. 25, 2008); *In re Minich*, 386 B.R. 723 (Bankr. C.D. Ill. 2008).

Attorneys are reminded of their duty to file complete and accurate disclosures of their fee agreements with their debtor clients. *See* Fed. R. Bankr. P. 2016(b); *In re Jackson*, 401 B.R. 333 (Bankr. N.D. Ill. 2009); *In re Kowalski*, 402 B.R. 843 (Bankr. N.D. Ill. 2009). This Court will not approve any award of fees, including the "no-look" flat fee amount, unless the attorney's own agreement with the debtor client provides for the payment of such fees.

Allowed attorney fees shall be paid through the plan. However, an attorney may receive all or part of the allowed fees prior to the filing of the case, provided those fees are deducted from the total allowed fees to be paid through the confirmed plan. The rate of payment of the fees through the plan shall not exceed the lesser of (1) 50% of the funds distributed by the trustee after payment of administrative expenses (including the trustee's fee), or (2) $350 per month, unless the Chapter 13 trustee recommends and the Court approves a larger monthly payment amount.

There may be instances where the allowed attorney fees in a case exceed 50% of the net funds to be distributed during the term of the plan and, therefore, at the rate of payment set forth above, the entire fee would not be paid in full during the term of the plan. In such event, and only in such event, the trustee may, without further order of the Court, increase the percentage at which allowed attorney fees are paid each month so that the fees are paid in full in approximately equal monthly installments during the term of the plan. Additionally, there may be instances where confirmed plans provide for precise amounts to be distributed monthly to priority or secured creditors, leaving insufficient funds available to distribute attorney fees at the rates stated above. In such cases, the attorney who filed the plan shall be deemed to have waived the right to the maximum monthly distribution allowable under this Order and the trustee may, without further order of the Court, distribute the attorneys fees in such cases in whatever periodic amounts he determines are appropriate, consistent with all other terms of both this Standing Order and the confirmed plan.

The duties designated below are presumed to be included within the scope of services rendered by the attorney to the debtor. If an attorney fails to perform any required duty, the Court, upon notice and hearing, may order the attorney to disgorge all or part of any fees received. Upon request of an interested party or sua sponte, the Court may consider whether an attorney's fees should be limited to an amount less than $3500 based on the circumstances of a particular case.

The debtor's attorney's duties in a Chapter 13 case include, but are not necessarily limited to, the following:

1. Consult with and advise the debtor about the differences and relative advantages and disadvantages of proceeding under Chapter 7 and Chapter 13.

2. Prepare and file the petition, statement of financial affairs, all schedules, and the creditor matrix.

3. Prepare and file a Chapter 13 plan.

4. Upon information received from the debtor, take all action necessary to avoid the termination of, or to require the reinstatement of, necessary utility services for the debtor.

5. File the necessary pleadings to obtain the return of repossessed vehicles proposed to be retained by the debtor under the plan.

6. In the event of pending state or federal court litigation, notify creditors' attorneys, and appropriate courts in which the litigation is pending, of the bankruptcy filing and the existence of the automatic stay.

7. Send out an information letter to the debtor reminding the debtor to attend the § 341 meeting, specifying the date, time, and location of the meeting, and providing information advising the debtor as to all necessary preparations for the § 341 meeting.

8. Collect from the debtor and deliver to the trustee all information required by statute to be provided prior to the § 341 meeting.

9. Appear at the § 341 meeting with the debtor.

10. Upon information received from the debtor, take steps necessary to terminate pending wage garnishments.

11. Attend all court hearings in the case.

12. Prepare all court mandated pre-trial statements, reports, briefs, etc.

13. Respond to objections to plan confirmation and, where necessary, prepare amended plans.

14. Prepare, file, and serve necessary amended statements and schedules, in accordance with information submitted by the debtor, provided the debtor pays any required filing fees.

15. Prepare, file, and serve necessary motions to buy, sell, or refinance real property and vehicles, when appropriate.

16. Review all claims promptly after the expiration of the claims bar date and file claims for creditors who failed to file claims, if it is in the debtor's best interest to do so.

17. Object to claims which should be disallowed in whole or in part.

18. Advise and represent the debtor with respect to motions for relief from the automatic stay, for adequate protection, to terminate the co-debtor stay, and other contested matters.

19. Prepare, file, and serve motions to avoid liens on real or personal property.

20. Upon information received from the debtor, contact creditors who continue to communicate with the debtor after filing.

21. Upon completion of plan payments, file a Certificate of Domestic Support Obligation if debtor was required to pay a domestic support obligation during the pendency of the case.

22. Provide such other legal services as are necessary for the administration of the case.

This Court will no longer set a "no-look" fee for Chapter 7 cases. However, this Court may, sua sponte, require an itemized fee application where the fees disclosed exceed the apparent value of the services rendered. Further, the panel trustees, the United States Trustee, and other parties in interest including the debtor, may request the filing of an itemized application or may file other pleadings as allowed by the Code and Rules challenging the reasonableness of any fee charged or expense incurred by a debtor's attorney. Debtors' attorneys are reminded of their obligation to fully disclose all fees paid by their clients and of their obligation to promptly supplement their disclosure if additional fees are paid which have not been previously disclosed. *See* Fed. R. Bankr. P. 2016(b). Debtors' attorneys are further reminded that the post-petition collection of attorney fees is prohibited inasmuch as pre-petition debts for legal fees are subject to discharge. *See In re Bethea*, 352 F.3d 1125, 1129 (7th Cir. 2003)

This Standing Order shall be applicable to cases filed on or after January 1, 2014.

DATED this 30th day of December, 2013.

[Dated: December 15, 2009; revised by order dated June 30, 2010. Revised effective January 1, 2012; by order dated December 15, 2011; January 1, 2014; by order dated December 30, 2013.]

GENERAL ORDER. IN RE ADOPTION OF REVISED INTERIM BANKRUPTCY RULE 1007–I

The Committee on Rules of Practice and Procedure and the Judicial Conference of the United States having approved Revised Interim Bankruptcy Rule 1007–I effective December I, 2010, **IT IS ORDERED** that Revised Interim Bankruptcy Rule 1007–I, is adopted by this Court, effective December 1, 2010.

Dated: November 15, 2010

Interim Rule 1007–I.[1] Lists, Schedules, Statements, and Other Documents; Time Limits; Expiration of Temporary Means Testing Exclusion[2]

* * * * *

(b) Schedules, Statements, and Other Documents Required.

* * * * *

(4) *Unless either*: (A) § 707(b)(2)(D)(i) applies, or (B) § 707(b)(2)(D)(ii) applies and the exclusion from means testing granted therein extends beyond the period specified by Rule 1017(e), an individual debtor in a chapter 7 case shall file a statement of current monthly income prepared as prescribed by the appropriate Official Form, and, if the current monthly income exceeds the median family income for the applicable state and household size, the information, including calculations, required by § 707(b), prepared as prescribed by the appropriate Official Form.

* * * * *

(c) Time Limits. In a voluntary case, the schedules, statements, and other documents required by subdivision (b)(1), (4), (5), and (6) shall be filed with the petition or within 14 days thereafter, except as otherwise provided in subdivisions (d), (e), (f), (h), and (n) of this rule. In an involuntary case, the list in subdivision (a)(2), and the schedules, statements, and other documents required by subdivision (b)(1) shall be filed by the debtor within 14 days of the entry of the order for relief. In a voluntary case, the documents required by paragraphs (A), (C), and (D) of subdivision (b)(3) shall be filed with the petition. Unless the court orders otherwise, a debtor who has filed a statement under subdivision (b)(3)(B), shall file the documents required by subdivision (b)(3)(A) within 14 days of the order for relief. In a chapter 7 case, the debtor shall file the statement required by subdivision (b)(7) within 60 days after the first date set for the meeting of creditors under § 341 of the Code, and in a chapter 11 or 13 case no later than the date when the last payment was made by the debtor as required by the plan or the filing of a motion for a discharge under § 1141(d)(5)(B) or § 1328(b) of the Code. The court may, at any time and in its discretion, enlarge the time to file the statement required by subdivision (b)(7). The debtor shall file the statement required by subdivision (b)(8) no earlier than the date of the last payment made under the plan or the date of the filing of a motion for a discharge under §§ 1141(d)(5)(B), 1228(b), or 1328(b) of the Code. Lists, schedules, statements, and other documents filed prior to the conversion of a case to another chapter shall be deemed filed in the converted case unless the court directs otherwise. Except as provided in § 1116(3), any extension of time to file schedules, statements, and other documents required under this rule may be granted only on motion for cause shown and on notice to the United States trustee, any committee elected under § 705 or appointed under § 1102 of the Code, trustee, examiner, or other party as the court may direct. Notice of an extension shall be given to the United States trustee and to any committee, trustee, or other party as the court may direct.

* * * * *

(n) Time Limits for, and Notice to, Debtors Temporarily Excluded From Means Testing.

(1) An individual debtor who is temporarily excluded from means testing pursuant to § 707(b)(2)(D)(ii) of the Code shall file any statement and calculations required by subdivision (b)(4) no later than 14 days after the expiration of the temporary exclusion if the expiration occurs within the time specified by Rule 1017(e) for filing a motion pursuant to § 707(b)(2).

(2) If the temporary exclusion from means testing under § 707(b)(2)(D)(ii) terminates due to the circumstances specified in subdivision (n)(1), and if the debtor has not previously filed a statement and calculations required by subdivision (b)(4), the clerk shall promptly notify the debtor that the required statement and calculations must be filed within the time specified in subdivision (n)(1).

[Dated: November 15, 2010.]

[1]Interim Rule 1007–I was adopted by the bankruptcy courts to implement the National Guard and Reservists Debt Relief Act of 2008, Public Law No: 110–438. The Act, which provides a temporary exclusion from the application of the means test for certain members of the National Guard and reserve components of the Armed Forces, applies to bankruptcy cases commenced in the three-year period beginning December 19, 2008.

[2]Incorporates (1) time amendments to Rule 1007 which took effect on December 1, 2009, and (2) an amendment, effective December 1, 2010, which extended the time to file the statement of completion of a course in personal financial management in a chapter 7 case filed by an individual debtor.

Committee Note

This rule is amended to take account of the enactment of the National Guard and Reservists Debt Relief Act of 2008, which amended § 707(b)(2)(D) of the Code to provide a temporary exclusion from the application of the means test for certain members of the National Guard and reserve components of the Armed Forces. This exclusion applies to qualifying debtors while they remain on active duty or are performing a homeland defense activity, and for a period of 540 days thereafter. For some debtors initially covered by the exclusion, the protection from means testing will expire while their chapter 7 cases are pending, and at a point when a timely motion to dismiss under § 707(b)(2) can still be filed. Under the amended rule, these debtors are required to file the statement and calculations required by subdivision (b)(4) no later than 14 days after the expiration of their exclusion.

Subdivisions (b)(4) and (c) are amended to relieve debtors qualifying for an exclusion under § 707(b)(2)(D)(ii) from the obligation to file a statement of current monthly income and required calculations within the time period specified in subdivision (c).

Subdivision (n)(1) is added to specify the time for filing of the information required by subdivision (b)(4) by a debtor who initially qualifies for the means test exclusion under § 707(b)(2)(D)(ii), but whose exclusion expires during the time that a motion to dismiss under § 707(b)(2) may still be made under Rule 1017(e). If, upon the expiration of the temporary exclusion, a debtor has not already filed the required statement and calculations, subdivision (n)(2) directs the clerk to provide prompt notice to the debtor of the time for filing as set forth in subdivision (n)(1).

STANDING ORDER ON PRETRIAL CONFERENCES IN ADVERSARY PROCEEDINGS PRESIDED OVER BY JUDGE WILLIAM V. ALTENBERGER

I.   A pretrial conference will be held on notice issued by the Court as soon as feasible after the return date of summons in each adversary proceeding.

A.   The pretrial conference shall be scheduled no less than 45 days from the date of the mailing of the notice. Counsel for all parties are directed to confer with all opposing counsel and together prepare in writing and file with the Court no less than five (5) working days prior to the pretrial conference a joint pretrial statement containing the following:

FOR PLAINTIFF

1.   A brief statement of the theory of each cause of action.

2.   A brief summary of plaintiff's contentions of facts in support of the cause(s) of action and the evidence to be relied upon to establish each of the facts contended.

FOR DEFENDANT

1.   A brief statement of the defense(s) including the theory of each defense.

2.   A brief summary of defendant's contentions of facts in support of the defense(s), and the evidence to be relied upon to establish each of the facts contended.

FOR ALL PARTIES

In addition, the joint document shall include or have attached to it the following:

1.   A statement of all admitted or uncontested facts.

2.   Each party's brief statement of contested facts.

3.   Each party's brief statement of contested legal issues.

4.   The affidavits or other documentary proof which each party submits in support of its contentions. All such affidavits or documents shall be exchanged by the parties at or before the time of filing of the PRETRIAL STATEMENT.

All of the above is to be incorporated in one document (with attachments) which is to be signed by all attorneys prior to the filing. It shall be the duty of counsel for plaintiff to initiate the conference and the duty of other counsel to respond to plaintiff's counsel and to offer their full cooperation and assistance.

B.   At such pretrial conference, which shall be attended by attorneys representing all parties who are authorized to enter into such agreements as may be appropriate, presumably the counsel who are to try the case, the Court and counsel will consider:

(1) Simplification of the issues;

(2) Any problems of evidence;

(3) Desirability of trial briefs;

(4) Prospects of settlement;

(5) Probable length of needed discovery;

(6) Such other matters as may aid in the fair and expeditious trial and disposition of the action; and

(7) The provisions of the pretrial order to be entered.

At the conclusion of the conference, the case will be set for trial, unless it appears to the Court that a further pretrial conference should be held. Ordinarily, the Court will enter a Pretrial Order reflecting the action taken and the agreements made at such conference, in the general form attached hereto. The Court may, however, direct counsel for plaintiff to prepare the Pretrial Order. In those instances, approval of such proposed order shall be obtained from counsel for all other parties by signature thereon, and such approved order will be entered by the Court upon submission.

II.   A pretrial conference will not be continued except for good cause shown in a written motion presented sufficiently in advance of the hearing for opposing counsel to be notified. Pretrials for Galesburg and Rock Island cases as well as Peoria cases involving an attorney from outside the tri-county area (Peoria–Tazewell–Woodford) will be scheduled for a telephonic conference call. Pretrials for all other cases will be held in Chambers and counsel must appear in person unless a request for conference call has been made and approved at least one week prior to the hearing date. Failure of counsel to appear or be available for any scheduled pretrial conference or otherwise to comply with the provisions of this order may result in dismissal or default as may be appropriate.

III.   This order is promulgated under Rule 16 of the Federal Rules of Civil Procedure, Rule 7016 of the Rules of Bankruptcy Procedure, Rule 10 of the published Rules of the District Court for the Central District of Illinois and Rule 2.04 of the Local Rules of Procedure of this Court.*

*[**Publisher's Note:** So in original. The U.S. Bankruptcy Court for the Central District of Illinois does not have local rules in current effect.]

[Dated: September 22, 1986.]

CHIEF JUDGE MARY P. GORMAN'S PROCEDURES FOR CASES FILED IN THE SPRINGFIELD DIVISION

Ex Parte Contacts Prohibited. Ex parte contacts are strictly prohibited. See Fed.R. Bankr. P. 9003(a). Any attempt by a party, an attorney, or their staff to contact the Court directly or through chambers staff to seek information about a pending case or advice about practicing before the Court is prohibited conduct. Neither Clerk's office staff nor chambers staff is authorized to grant oral requests for the continuance or rescheduling of a matter. Except in the case of an emergency, all requests for continuances or rescheduling must be made in writing and filed electronically.

Local Rules and Admission to Practice. The Local Rules for the United States District Court for the Central District of Illinois apply to proceedings before this Court and can be found online at www.ilcd.uscourts.gov. The United States Bankruptcy Court for the Central District of Illinois does not have separate local rules. Attorneys who intend to practice before this Court must be licensed to practice in the Central District of Illinois. For instructions on how to become admitted, see CDIL–LR 83.5. Pro Hac Vice admissions are governed by CDIL–LR 83.5(F).

Signature Requirement/Attorney Appearance. Every petition, pleading, written motion, and other paper except a list, schedule, or statement (and amendments thereto) must be signed by at least one attorney of record in the attorney's individual name. See Fed.R.Bankr.P. 9011. Petitions, lists, schedules, statements and all amendments thereto must be verified or contain an unsworn declaration by the debtor. See Fed.R.Bankr.P. 1008. Documents containing signatures may be filed as scanned images which show the actual signatures or may be filed with signatures represented by a "/s/" and the name typed in the space where a signature would otherwise appear as follows: /s/ First Name Last Name. Unsigned pleadings or pleadings where the above requirements are not strictly complied with are subject to being stricken without further notice.

Reference should also be made to paragraph 10 of the Third Amended General Order Authorizing Electronic Case Filing entered by the Bankruptcy Judges of the Central District of Illinois on January 10, 2007, for additional requirements regarding signatures and the retention of documents containing original signatures.

To be "of record" and authorized to sign pleadings, documents, or agreed orders on behalf of a party, every attorney, other than the attorney who filed the initial bankruptcy petition or the complaint in an adversary proceeding, must enter his or her appearance for the party. The Court will no longer process documents filed by attorneys who purport to represent a party but who have not formally appeared for that party. Further, every attorney who appears for a debtor must file a fee disclosure even if the attorney is not receiving or requesting additional fees. See 11 U.S.C. § 329(a); Fed. R. Bankr. P. 2016(b).

Service of Pleadings. Except as provided elsewhere in these Procedures, all pleadings should contain a certificate of service evidencing that the pleading has been served electronically, by mail, or by some other disclosed method on the parties and attorneys entitled to receive notice of the pleading. The fact that the Clerk of Court schedules and sends notice of all hearings and objection dates does not relieve the filer of a pleading of the obligation to serve the pleading as otherwise required.

For all contested matters as defined by Bankruptcy Rule 9014, the motion or request must be served in compliance with Bankruptcy Rule 7004. Corporations must be served as required under Rule 7004(b)(3) on an officer, managing or general agent, or on any agent authorized by appointment or by law to receive service of process. Insured depository institutions must be served as required under Rule 7004(h).

When service must be made on an agent authorized to accept service, service on an attorney for a creditor is sufficient only if the attorney is, in fact, the creditor's registered agent or, in the case of an insured depository institution, if the attorney has entered an appearance in the case. Fed. R. Bankr. P. 7004(h)(1). Service on an attorney who represented a creditor in a different case in a different court is not sufficient to comply with the Bankruptcy Rules.

A signed certificate of service should be filed with each pleading and should include the full name of each person served electronically and the full name and address of each person served by mail or otherwise. A certificate of service must state the precise manner of the service made on each party or entity. A certificate of service which states that service was made by one of several possible methods without specifying the actual method used is unacceptable and will be stricken. Any certificate of service which is docketed separately from the pleading served must also specifically identify the pleading served.

Failure to properly serve a pleading may result in the pleading being stricken without further notice.

The Clerk will no longer add new creditors, registered agents, or other persons or entities to the mailing matrix and will not change addresses or add alternate addresses to the mailing matrix based on certificates of service filed with motions or other documents. When a motion, notice, or other document must be served on a person or entity not previously included on the mailing matrix, the debtor may file an amended schedule and pay the requisite filing fee, if any, to update the mailing matrix. If the debtor does not update the mailing matrix, then the movant — whether the debtor or some other party in interest — must serve the motion, notice, or other documents directly and file a certificate of service evidencing compliance with the Bankruptcy Rules. Further, for many motions, service by the Clerk is not made on the entire mailing matrix but only upon the parties who appear to have an interest in the motion. Accordingly, registered agents, corporate officers and other similar persons added to the mailing matrix should be clearly identified as the agent of a particular creditor.

Applications to Employ Professionals. Applications to Employ Professional Persons are generally governed by Bankruptcy Rule 2014. Every Application should contain the information set forth in the Rule and every Application must be accompanied by the verified statement required by the Rule. Applications which are incomplete or not accompanied by the verified statement may be stricken without further notice.

Fee Applications. The Court strictly enforces the requirements set forth in the Bankruptcy Code and Rules regarding applications for an award of professional fees and expenses. See 11 U.S.C. § 330; Fed.R.Bankr.P. 2016; In re Vancil Contracting, Inc., 2008 WL 207533 (Bankr. C.D. Ill. Jan. 25, 2008); In re Minich, 386 B.R. 723 (Bankr. C.D. Ill. 2008).

Reference should also be made to this Court's Standing Order Re: Attorney Fees for Debtor's Counsel in Chapter 7 and Chapter 13 Cases—Springfield Division, for further guidance on when fee applications must be filed by debtors' attorneys in Chapter 7 and Chapter 13 cases.

Telephonic Hearings. The Court conducts a significant number of its non-evidentiary hearings via conference call. The Court considers conference call hearings to be of the same importance as hearings scheduled in court, and attorneys should prepare accordingly.

Chambers staff initiates all conference calls and attorneys are called at the contact phone number listed in the Court's ECF database. Attorneys may request to be called at a different phone number IF such information is provided to the Clerk's Office (217.492.4551) or chambers (217.492.4566) by 4:00 p.m. on the day before the call is scheduled to take place. Parties may also notify the Court that a substitute attorney will be appearing on a call by providing the name and phone number of the substituting attorney to the Clerk's Office or chambers by the deadline listed above. It is NOT acceptable to wait until the conference call is under way to provide an alternate phone number or the name and number of a substituting attorney. In emergency situations, alternate phone numbers and information regarding substituting attorneys may be provided to the Clerk's Office or chambers on the day of the hearing in advance of the call. However, no phone calls should be placed to chambers during the time that conference calls are scheduled. The Court's schedule is available elsewhere on this website.

The Court schedules a number of conference calls on each docket. Because of the large volume of calls, calls may not be made at the precise time shown on the hearing notice, in much the same way that in-court hearings do not always occur at the precise time they are set. As a general rule, attorneys should allow a 20–minute window before and after the scheduled time of the call in which to expect receipt of the call. Attorneys are strongly encouraged to make themselves available during that entire window, although no party will be defaulted if an attorney is not available before the scheduled time of the call. Parties MAY be defaulted if the attorney is unavailable at or after the time the call is scheduled, or if the attorney cannot be reached at the number provided (either via special instructions or on their ECF account). Exceptions to this procedure will not be made due to technical issues relating to a cell phone or cell phone service. It is the responsibility of an attorney appearing by cell phone to have a properly operating cell phone and to be at a location where cell phone service is available. All conference calls are recorded and attorneys must appear using telephonic equipment of sufficient quality that the Court's recording equipment is able to make a clear audio record of the call.

The Court rarely permits appearance by telephone by an attorney at an in-court hearing. Such requests must be made by motion and electronically filed at least 48 hours in advance of the hearing. The motion must state specific reasons why the attorney is unable to personally appear for the in-court hearing.

Hearings which involve a pro se party will rarely be held via conference call.

Motions for Summary Judgment. Strict compliance with CDIL–LR 7.1(D) is required. See In re Clayton, 369 B.R. 383 (Bankr. C.D. Ill. 2007).

Motions for Relief from Stay. Motions for Relief from Stay which seek relief with respect to property based on a perfected, secured interest in such property must have copies of all documents necessary to support movant's claim attached as exhibits. Copies of any documents which are required to be recorded in order to perfect a secured interest must include the recording information. Reference should be made to paragraph 5 of the Third Amended General Order Authorizing Electronic Case Filing signed by the Bankruptcy Judges of the Central District of Illinois on January 10, 2007, for further information about required attachments to motions. Motions for Relief from Stay filed without proper attachments may be stricken without further notice.

Motions Granted without Hearing in Chambers. Because the Clerk of Court sets all hearing and objection dates without attorneys being able to self-select available dates, the Court does consider motions for continuances, rescheduling, and extensions of time in chambers. The Court also considers some routine and uncontested matters in chambers.

Motions to continue specially set matters may also be considered in chambers. Motions to continue set matters must contain a specific reason for the request and state whether opposing counsel has been contacted regarding the request and consents to the request.

If the Court rules on a motion in chambers, a minute order or text order will be entered and attorneys will receive prompt electronic notification of the ruling. See Fed.R.Bankr.P. 9022(a). In the absence of an order from the Court, no party or attorney should assume that a matter has been or will be ruled on in chambers.

Chapter 13 Plans, Amended Plans, and Motions to Modify. All proposed Chapter 13 plans must be clearly labeled as Chapter 13 Plan or as First, Second, Third (and so forth) Amended Plan. Every proposed plan must be signed and dated. See Fed.R.Bankr.P. 3015(c), 9011. Plans and amended plans which do not meet these basic requirements may be stricken without further notice.

The Clerk of Court will send a copy of each plan or amended plan to all creditors and parties in interest with a notice scheduling an objection or hearing date. Accordingly, debtors do not need to include a certificate of service when filing a plan or amended plan.

Chapter 13 plans may contain provisions which resolve contested matters. If the creditor subject to such a plan provision is a corporation or insured depository institution, the plan and any notice setting an objection or hearing date regarding confirmation of the plan must be served in accordance with Bankruptcy Rule 7004. See Service of Pleadings above. Because the Clerk sends the plan and notices to creditors, debtors and their attorneys are responsible for including the proper addresses for such creditors on the mailing matrix. Alternatively, debtors and their attorneys may serve the plan and objection or hearing date notice on the creditor themselves and file a certificate of service evidencing compliance with Bankruptcy Rule 7004. The Clerk never sends notices by certified mail and, accordingly, to the extent service by that method is required, debtors and their attorneys will always be required to make that service themselves and file a certificate of service.

After a plan has been confirmed, it may be modified by motion. See 11 U.S.C. § 1329. Motions to Modify must also be signed and dated. See Fed.R.Bankr.P. 3015(c), 9011. Motions to Modify which do not meet these basic requirements may be stricken without further notice.

The Clerk of Court will send a copy of the Motion to Modify to all creditors and parties in interest with a notice scheduling an objection or hearing date. Accordingly, debtors do not need to include a certificate of service when filing a Motion to Modify. Again, the Clerk serves only the mailing matrix and, accordingly, to the extent a Motion to Modify seeks relief as to a corporation or insured depository institution, debtors and their attorneys are required to make sure that service of the Motion and notice of the objection or hearing date is properly effectuated and must file a certificate of service evidencing compliance with Bankruptcy Rule 7004.

Order Submission. At the conclusion of an in-court or telephonic hearing, if a proposed order granting the specific relief allowed has not previously been submitted, the Court generally will request that the prevailing party submit an order within a fixed period of time—usually 14 days. Likewise, when an objection date has been set on a motion or other pleading seeking relief and no objection has been timely filed, the Court will request an order be submitted within 14 days if one has not previously been submitted. The failure to submit an order within the time specified by the Court may result in the motion, request, application, objection, or other pleading being denied without further notice. Parties who are unable to submit an order within the set time frame should affirmatively request an extension of time to submit the required order.

Stricken Pleadings. Motions and other pleadings which are deficient in that they fail to meet the minimum requirements of the Bankruptcy Code and Rules or this Court's standing orders may be stricken. Likewise, as set forth herein, motions and other pleadings which are not properly served may be stricken. The striking of a pleading based on such defects is without prejudice to the refiling of a new motion or pleading seeking the same relief requested in the stricken pleading. The filing of a deficient pleading which is stricken, however, does not extend deadlines previously set by the Code, Rules, or court order. Filing fees paid for stricken pleadings are not refundable.

Sales by Debtors. Debtors (or debtors–in–possession) who want to sell property of the estate must file a detailed motion pursuant to § 363(b). If a sale is to be free and clear of liens, the motion must comply with the requirements of § 363(f). The specific liens subject to the motion and the basis for selling free and clear as to each particular lien, i.e. the applicable subsection of § 363(f), must be identified. A Notice of Intent to Sell must also be submitted which complies with the requirements of Bankruptcy Rule 2002(c)(1).

A sample Notice of Intent can be found in the Forms section of this website. Motions to Sell with the accompanying Notice of Intent must be filed not less than 30 days before an intended sale to ensure that sufficient notice can be provided to all parties in interest. Motions filed on weekends or late in the day will not be processed until the next business day, so movants should plan accordingly. Motions to shorten notice may be filed but generally are not favored.

Debtors must obtain authority to employ brokers or auctioneers before a sale can be authorized. No order authorizing a sale will be signed unless all professionals involved in the sale have been properly employed. After a sale, applications for compensation of the professionals involved should generally be filed. Applications for compensation must be served on the entire mailing matrix. As set forth below, under certain circumstances, the approval of professional compensation may be obtained through the filing of a Report of Sale without filing a separate application for compensation.

A Report of Sale per Bankruptcy Rule 6004(f)(1) must be filed for every sale. Service generally must be made only on the U.S. Trustee and case trustee. Orders generally are not required and will not be entered approving Reports of Sale. Because the Clerk traces for Reports of Sale to be filed, if a previously authorized sale does not close, a report of "no sale" should be filed.

When a professional such as a broker or auctioneer is to be compensated on a percentage basis as part of a sale, the compensation and itemized expenses of the professional may be specifically set forth in the Report of Sale and a separate application for compensation will not be required. In such case, the Report of Sale should also include a prayer for relief seeking approval of the compensation and expenses. When the Report of Sale is used in lieu of the application for compensation, service must be made on the entire mailing matrix. An order approving the Report of Sale and the specific compensation and expenses set forth therein should be submitted.

7 Day Orders. The practice in the Bankruptcy Court for the Central District of Illinois, Springfield Division, has been that when attorneys or parties failed to file pleadings or submit orders within the time by the Bankruptcy Code and Rules or by the Court, the Court routinely issued form orders granting an additional 7 days for compliance. The practice of the Court routinely issuing such 7 day extensions has been discontinued. Parties and their attorneys should comply with all statutory or court-ordered deadlines or affirmatively seek extensions of time to do so.

Mailing Matrix Required. Bankruptcy Rule 1007(a)(1) requires that a list containing the name and address of each entity included or to be included on Schedules D,E,F,G and H be filed with every voluntary petition. The list is commonly referred to as the mailing matrix. An extension of time to file the list may only be granted upon motion and for cause. See Fed. R. Bankr. P. 1007(a)(5). Any voluntary case filed without the required list or a motion seeking an extension of time for cause will be dismissed.

[Dated: March 1, 2009. Revised effective May 1, 2009; March 19, 2013; August 26, 2013; September 26, 2013.]

REVISED STANDING ORDER. PRE–TRIAL CONFERENCE RULE

In all cases filed and pending in the Danville Division of the United States Bankruptcy Court, counsel shall present to the Court, at least 2 days prior to pre-trial conference, a pre-trial memorandum containing the following information, to-wit:

(1) A statement of jurisdiction;

(2) An agreed statement of undisputed facts;

(3) An agreed statement of facts at issue;

(4) An agreed statement of issues of law to be resolved, and;

(5) A list of names and addresses of witnesses which each party intends to call to testify at trial, including the names of expert witnesses.

At the time of pre-trial conference, counsel shall assist the Court in forming a discovery calendar and scheduling the pending matter for trial. Failure to comply with the requirements of this standing order may result in the pre-trial conference allotment being vacated or appropriate sanctions being imposed against the unprepared party or both.

This revised order shall be effective upon filing in the Office of the U. S. Bankruptcy Court Clerk, Danville Division.

[Dated: January 4, 1989.]

GENERAL ORDER. ASSIGNMENT OF CASES

IT IS HEREBY ORDERED that all cases arising under Title 11, United States Code, and any or all proceedings arising under Title 11 or arising in or related to a case under Title 11, shall be assigned as follows:

(1) To the Bankruptcy Judge sitting in Danville, Illinois, all matters from the counties of: Champaign, Coles, Douglas, Edgar, Ford, Iroquois, Kankakee, Livingston, Moultrie, Piatt and Vermilion.

(2) To the Bankruptcy Judge sitting in Peoria, Illinois, all matters from the counties of: Bureau, Fulton, Hancock, Henderson, Henry, Knox, Marshall, Mercer, McDonough, Peoria, Putnam, Rock Island, Stark, Tazewell, Warren, and Woodford.

(3) To the Bankruptcy Judges sitting in Springfield, Illinois, all matters from the counties of: Adams, Brown, Cass, Christian, DeWitt, Greene, Logan, Macon, Macou-

pin, Mason, McLean, Menard, Montgomery, Morgan, Pike, Sangamon, Schuyler, Scott and Shelby.

[Dated: February 27, 1989.]

IN RE CHAPTER 13 PRE–CONFIRMATION ADEQUATE PROTECTION PAYMENTS

IT IS HEREBY ORDERED, effective as to all Chapter 13 cases filed on or after October 17, 2005, as follows:

(1) Pre-confirmation payments on leases of personal property governed by 11 U.S.C. § 1326(a)(1)(B) shall be made directly by the debtor to the lessor if the plan provides for the debtor to assume the lease. However, such payments shall not reduce the amount of the payments to be made to the trustee as proposed in the plan, since the plan must provide for all lease payments that come due postpetition to be paid direct by the debtor to the lessor, not through the trustee, and such payments should be shown as an expense on Schedule J. If the plan provides that the lease is to be rejected or does not provide any treatment of the lease, no payments shall be made to the lessor unless otherwise ordered by the Court.

(2) Pre-confirmation adequate protection payments governed by 11 U.S.C. § 1326(a)(1)(C) shall be made directly by the debtor to the secured creditor only if the plan provides for the debtor to retain the collateral and to pay the claim outside of the plan, not through the trustee, in which case the amount and due date of each adequate protection payment shall be as provided for in the contract between the parties. If the plan provides for payment of the secured claim by the trustee, the debtor shall pay the trustee the full payment required by the plan and the trustee shall make the monthly pre-confirmation payments to the secured creditor in the amount that the creditor would receive if the plan (or any amended plan) was confirmed as filed, to the extent of the available funds. All adequate protection payments shall be credited against the allowed secured claim. All such pre-confirmation adequate protection payments made by the trustee shall be subject to the trustee's percentage fee as set by the United States Trustee.

[Dated: August 2, 2006.]

GENERAL ORDER RE: CLOSURE OF BANKRUPTCY COURT OPERATIONS IN DANVILLE, ILLINOIS AND TRANSFER OF BANKRUPTCY COURT OPERATIONS TO URBANA, ILLINOIS

Effective June 1, 2014, the United States Bankruptcy Court for the Central District of Illinois shall move its operations from Danville, Illinois, to the United States Courthouse, 201 South Vine Street, Urbana, Illinois 61802. All cases then pending or thereafter filed where venue in the Central District of Illinois is based on a debtor's residence, place of business, or other connection to the Illinois counties of Champaign, Coles, Douglas, Edgar, Ford, Iroquois, Kankakee, Livingston, Moultrie, Piatt, or Vermilion shall be assigned to the new Urbana Division.

Effective June 1, 2014, all cases then pending in the Danville Division and all cases filed thereafter in the Urbana Division under Chapters 7 and 11 of Title 11 of the United States Code and all adversary proceedings related to Chapter 7 or Chapter 11 cases shall be assigned to Chief Judge Mary P. Gorman. Further, all cases then pending in the Danville Division and all cases filed thereafter in the Urbana Division under Chapters 12 and 13 of Title 11 of the United States Code and all adversary proceedings related to Chapter 12 or Chapter 13 cases, shall be assigned to Judge Thomas L. Perkins. Miscellaneous matters and other filings not specifically addressed above shall be assigned to Chief Judge Mary P. Gorman.

IT IS SO ORDERED.

[Dated: February 10, 2014.]

UNITED STATES DISTRICT COURT FOR THE SOUTHERN DISTRICT OF ILLINOIS

Including Amendments Received Through
April 1, 2015

Order

116. In re: Fee Payment Via Pay.Gov.
111. In re: Transcript Policy Amended November 2012.
107. In the Matter of: Redaction of Personal Data Identifiers From All Pleadings.
106. In re: New Transcript Policy.
96. In the Matter of Presentence Reports.
69. In re: Case Management/Electronic Case Filing.

Order

Notice Regarding Privacy and Public Access to Electronic Civil and Criminal Case Files and Requiring Compliance With Administrative Order #107.

PLAN FOR RANDOM SELECTION OF JURORS

CRIMINAL JUSTICE ACT PLAN

PLAN FOR PROMPT DISPOSITION OF CRIMINAL CASES (FINAL PLAN PURSUANT TO SPEEDY TRIAL PLAN ACT OF 1974 (18 U.S.C. § 3165(e)(3)))

TIMETABLE AND DEADLINES UNDER FEDERAL RULES AND CIVIL JUSTICE REFORM ACT

TIMETABLE AND DEADLINES UNDER FEDERAL RULES AND CIVIL JUSTICE REFORM ACT	
Service of Complaint	Within 120 days after complaint filed. [Fed. R. Civ. P. 4(m)]
Answer	Within 21 days after actual service of summons and complaint; OR Within 60 days if service has been waived (90 days if defendant was addressed outside any judicial district of the U.S.). [Fed. R. Civ. P. 12(a)(1)]
Initial Disclosures	At or within 14 days after the Rule 26(f) conference. [Fed. R. Civ. P. 26(a)(1)]
Report of the Parties to the Magistrate	Within 14 days after the parties' initial conference, and at least 7 days before the date of the scheduling and discovery conference. [Fed. R. Civ. P. 26(f); SDIL–LR 16.2(a)]
Discovery Cutoff	No later than 115 days before first day of presumptive trial month.
Dispositive Motion Deadline	No later than 100 days before first day of presumptive trial month.
Settlement Conference	The parties may request a settlement conference at any time. The court may set a settlement conference at its discretion at any time. Parties shall submit ex parte settlement statements to the Magistrate Judge 7 days before the settlement conference. [SDIL–LR 16.3(b)]
Final Pretrial Conference	No less than 7 days before presumptive trial date. Parties shall confer and jointly submit a signed proposed final pretrial order 3 days before the date of the final pretrial conference. [SDIL–LR 16.2(b)]

TIMETABLE AND DEADLINES UNDER FEDERAL RULES AND CIVIL JUSTICE REFORM ACT

Presumptive Trial Month	Track A: 8 to 10 months after first appearance of a defendant or default date. Track B: 11 to 14 months after first appearance of a defendant or default date. Track C: 15 to 18 months after first appearance of a defendant or default date. Track D: 19 to 24 months after first appearance of a defendant or default date. [SDIL–LR 16.1(a)]

[Effective March 1, 1999. Amended effective January 1, 2000; July 1, 2003; December 1, 2009.]

RULE 1.1. SCOPE OF RULES

(a) These rules shall be known as the Local Rules of the United States District Court for the Southern District of Illinois. Parties are encouraged to cite to these rules as "SDIL–LR."

(b) These rules became effective on December 1, 2009, and supersede all previous Local Rules. These rules shall apply in all civil and criminal proceedings in the Southern District of Illinois regardless of when the case was filed.

[Effective March 1, 1999. Amended effective January 1, 2000; July 1, 2003; December 1, 2009.]

RULE 3.1. PAYMENT OF FEES AND COSTS

(See 28 U.S.C. §§ 1911, 1915, 2254)

(a) **Advance Payment of Fees.** Except as may now or hereafter be required or permitted by law, by direction of the Judicial Conference of the United States, or by special Order of the Court in exceptional circumstances, all fees, including those fees required by 28 U.S.C. § 1914, shall be paid to the Clerk of Court in advance of filing the document or documents involved. On September 1, 2009, the Court implemented online fee payments via Pay.gov, and all fees shall be paid in accordance with the CM/ECF User's Manual in effect on the date of the filing. All electronic filers are required to use the Pay.gov Internet payment module in CM/ECF. Payments for filing fees, pro hac vice attorney admission fees, and notice of appeal fees must be paid by credit card over the Internet. Users will be automatically directed through the Pay.gov payment process. The Notice of Filing Fee Events List and the Notice of Refund Policy of Electronic Filing Fees is contained in the CM/ECF User's Manual or available online at www.

ilsd.uscourts.gov. All parties are strongly encouraged to read and have a working knowledge of the CM/ECF User's Manual and should stay current on all revisions to it.

(b) **In Forma Pauperis.** A petitioner or plaintiff who wishes to seek leave to file in forma pauperis under 28 U.S.C. § 1915 shall submit an affidavit which sets forth information to establish that he or she is unable to pay the fees and costs, shall sign and verify an oath or affirmation, and shall answer additional questions concerning his or her financial status as the Court may require. An example of an affidavit is contained in the Appendix of Forms to the Rules Governing Section 2254 cases in the United States District Courts titled "Model Form For Use in Applications for Habeas Corpus under 28 U.S.C. Section 2254." A blank copy of this affidavit as well as a form motion to proceed in forma pauperis may be obtained by sending a written request to the Clerk of Court at either the East St. Louis or Benton address listed in Local Rule 8.1(d).

A petitioner or plaintiff in custody must also submit a certified copy of his or her prison trust fund account statement for the six-month period preceding the filing of the complaint. All petitioners and plaintiffs are under a continuing obligation to keep the Clerk of Court and each opposing party informed of any change in his or her location. This shall be done in writing and not later than **7 days** after a transfer or other change in address occurs.

(c) **Payment of Costs and Court Order Waiving Costs.**

(1) At the time application is made under 28 U.S.C. § 1915 for leave to commence any civil action without being required to prepay fees and costs or give security for the same, the applicant and his or her attorney will be deemed to have entered into a stipulation that the recovery, if any, secured in the action shall be paid

to the Clerk of Court, who shall pay therefrom all unpaid costs taxed against plaintiff and remit the balance to plaintiff. If notice is filed with the Clerk of Court that an attorney's contingent fee contract has been entered into by plaintiff, the balance shall be paid to plaintiff and his or her attorney in accordance with an Order of the Court.

(2) Any person seeking leave to proceed in forma pauperis shall submit sufficient copies of the complaint to effect service upon all defendants. The original of the complaint shall be retained by the Clerk of Court. Upon good cause shown, this paragraph of the Local Rules may be waived by the Court at the time leave to proceed in forma pauperis is granted.

[Effective March 1, 1999. Amended effective January 1, 2000; July 1, 2003; December 1, 2009.]

RULE 5.1. SERVING AND FILING PLEADINGS AND OTHER PAPERS

(*See* **Fed. R. Civ. P. 5, 7.1, 11; Fed. R. Crim. P. 49**)

(a) Designation of Lead Counsel. When a party's initial pleading is filed, "Lead Counsel" shall be designated as the attorney for that party who will be responsible for receipt of service of every document required to be filed or served and for receipt of telephone conferences.

(b) General Format of Papers Presented for Filing. All pleadings, motions, documents, and other papers presented for filing shall be on 8½″ × 11″ white paper of good quality, flat and unfolded, and shall be plainly typewritten, printed, or prepared by a clearly legible duplication process and double-spaced, except for quoted material. Each page shall be numbered consecutively.

This rule does not apply to (a) exhibits submitted for filing and (b) documents filed in removed actions prior to removal from state court.

(c) Electronic Filing. All parties must file documents by electronic means that comply with procedures established by the Court unless specifically exempted for good cause shown. Filing a document electronically does not alter the filing deadline for that document. Filing must be completed before midnight (Central Time) to be considered timely filed that day, **unless a specific time is set by the Court.** Pursuant to Federal Rule of Civil Procedure 6(d) and Federal Rule of Criminal Procedure 45(c), whenever a document is served electronically, three days are added to the prescribed response time.

(d) Privacy Policy—*See Amended Administrative Order 107.* In order to promote electronic access to case files while also protecting personal privacy and other legitimate interests, parties shall refrain from including, or shall redact where inclusion is necessary, the following personal identifiers from all pleadings filed with the Clerk of Court, which includes exhibits attached thereto, unless otherwise ordered.

(1) *Social Security Numbers.* If an individual's social security number must be included, only the last four digits of that number should be used.

(2) *Names of Minor Children.* If the involvement of a minor child must be mentioned, only the initials of that child should be used.

(3) *Dates of Birth.* If an individual's date of birth must be included in a document, only the year should be used.

(4) *Drivers' License Numbers.* If a driver's license number must be included, only the last four digits should be used.

(5) *Financial Account Numbers.* If financial account numbers are relevant, only the last four digits should be used.

(6) *Home Addresses. In criminal cases only,* if home addresses must be used, only the city and state should be used. **[Limited to criminal cases only by interlineation on March 15, 2012—see Federal Rule of Civil Procedure 5.2, Federal Rule of Criminal Procedure 49.1, and Amended Administrative Order 107].**

The responsibility for redacting these personal identifiers rests solely with counsel and the parties. The Clerk of Court will not review each pleading for compliance with this rule. Counsel and the parties are cautioned that failure to redact these personal identifiers may subject them to discipline.

In compliance with the E–Government Act of 2002, a party wishing to file a document containing the personal data identifiers listed above **must file a redacted version in the public file** (file electronically for ECF cases or manually for non-ECF cases). In addition to the public filing, a party may file, but is not required to file, the personal data identifiers listed above by filing the information under seal in accordance with the directions below.

A party wishing to file the unredacted information may file either (a) a reference list under seal, or (b) an unredacted version of the document under seal. When a party finds it necessary to file the unredacted information under seal, the Court prefers a reference list to the filing of a complete document. The reference list shall contain the complete personal identifier(s) and the redacted identifier(s) used in its (their) place in the filing. All references in the case to the redacted identifiers included in the reference list will be construed to refer to the corresponding complete personal data identifier. The reference list must be filed under seal and may be amended as of right.

Parties are responsible for maintaining possession of original, unredacted documents and information redacted from publicly filed documents. Upon request, counsel may be required to furnish the unredacted information. (For further details, *See* Amended Administrative Order 107.)

[Effective March 1, 1999. Amended effective July 1, 2003; December 1, 2009.]

RULE 7.1. MOTION PRACTICE

(*See* Fed. R. Civ. P. 7, 56, 78; Fed. R. Crim. P. 12)

NOTE: The requirements for motions in class actions are located in SDIL–LR 23.1. To the extent anything in this Local Rule is in conflict with SDIL–LR 23.1, SDIL–LR 23.1 takes priority.

(a) A motion shall state its grounds with particularity and shall set forth the relief sought.

(b) Each motion shall include or have attached to it a certification that a copy has been properly served upon each party to the action as required by the Federal Rules of Civil Procedure and the Federal Rules of Criminal Procedure.

(c) Motions to remand, to dismiss, for judgment on the pleadings, for summary judgment, to suppress, and all post-trial motions shall be supported by a brief. The motion and brief may be combined into a single submission.

(1) An adverse party in a civil case shall have **30 days** after service of a motion listed above to file a response.

(2) An adverse party in a criminal case shall have **14 days** after service of a motion to suppress to file a response.

Failure to timely file a response to a motion may, in the Court's discretion, be considered an admission of the merits of the motion. Reply briefs, if any, shall be filed within **14 days** of the service of a response. **Reply briefs are not favored and should be filed only in exceptional circumstances.** The party filing the reply brief shall state the exceptional circumstances. Under no circumstances will sur-reply briefs be accepted. If a party believes it is necessary to supplement its brief with new authority due to a change in the law or facts that occurred after the filing of its brief, the party must seek leave of court to file a supplemental brief. The supplemental authority shall be filed in accordance with the supplemental authority provisions found in Federal Rule of Appellate Procedure 28(j).

(d) All briefs shall contain a short, concise statement of the party's position, together with citations to relevant legal authority and to the record. Allegations of fact not supported by citation may, in the Court's discretion, not be considered. No brief shall be submitted which is longer than 20 double-spaced typewritten pages in 12 point font. Reply briefs shall not exceed 5 pages. Requests for additional pages are not allowed.

(e) Any brief in support of or in opposition to a motion for summary judgment shall contain citation to relevant legal authority and to the record, together with any affidavits or documentary material designated pursuant to Federal Rule of Civil Procedure 56 supporting the party's position.

(f) All motions to dismiss, for judgment on the pleadings, and for summary judgment must be filed no later than **100 days** before the first day of the presumptive trial month.

(g) For all motions other than those listed in subsection (c) above, a supporting brief is not required. A party opposing a motion not listed in subsection (c) shall have **14 days** after service of the motion to file a written response. Failure to file a timely response to a motion may, in the Court's discretion, be considered an admission of the merits of the motion. A reply, if any, shall be filed within **7 days** of the service of the response. **Reply briefs are not favored and should be filed only in exceptional circumstances.** The party filing the reply brief shall state the exceptional circumstances. Under no circumstances will sur-reply briefs be accepted. If a party believes it is necessary to supplement its brief with new authority due to a change in the law or the facts that occurred after the filing of its brief, the party must seek leave of court to file a supplemental brief. The supplemental authority shall be filed in accordance with the supplemental authority provisions found in Federal Rule of Appellate Procedure 28(j).

(h) A party may not schedule or notice a hearing for oral argument on a pending motion. Any party desiring oral argument on a motion shall file a formal motion and state the reason why oral argument is requested. Any motion may be either:

(1) scheduled by the Court for oral argument at a specified time;

(2) scheduled for determination by telephone conference call;

(3) referred to a United States Magistrate Judge for determination or recommendation; or

(4) determined upon the pleadings and the motion papers without oral argument.

[Effective March 1, 1999. Amended effective July 1, 2003; December 1, 2009.]

RULE 8.1. PLEADINGS FILED BY PRISONERS

(*See* 42 U.S.C. § 1983; 28 U.S.C. §§ 1915, 2241, 2254, 2255; Fed. R. Civ. P. 1–15; Rules Governing Section 2254 Cases in the United States District Courts; Rules Governing Section 2255 Cases in the United States District Courts)

(a) Forms Available.

(1) *Civil Complaints and Habeas Corpus Pleadings.* Prisoners who wish to file a civil complaint under 42 U.S.C. § 1983, an application for writ of habeas corpus under 28 U.S.C. § 2241, a petition under 28 U.S.C. § 2254, or a motion under 28 U.S.C. § 2255 may obtain forms and instructions by sending a written request to the Clerk of Court at the East St. Louis address listed below. Prisoners who wish to file a civil complaint are referred to the Federal Rules of Civil Procedure generally, and in particular, Rules 1 through 15.

Prisoners who wish to file a petition under 28 U.S.C. § 2254 or a motion under 28 U.S.C. § 2255 are referred to the Rules Governing Section 2254 Cases in the United States District Courts and the Rules Governing Section 2255 Cases in the United States District Courts, respectively. The Court strongly urges plaintiffs to use the Court's complaint form.

(2) *In Forma Pauperis.* Prisoners who wish to proceed in forma pauperis—without prepayment of fees—may obtain forms and instructions by sending a written request to the Clerk of Court at the East St. Louis address listed below. (For further information regarding in forma pauperis status, see 28 U.S.C. § 1915 and Local Rule 3.1.)

(b) General Pleading Requirements. A complaint, petition, or motion filed by a prisoner shall be in writing, signed, and verified. The original pleading must be submitted with enough copies for each defendant or respondent as required by Federal Rule of Civil Procedure 4. All complaints, petitions, or motions, except motions under 28 U.S.C. § 2255, shall be filed with the Clerk of Court at the East St. Louis address.

Upon receipt of a complaint, petition, or motion, the Clerk of Court shall determine that the pleading has been properly completed and signed. The Clerk of Court will notify the designated District Judge of any pleading which fails to comply with any filing requirement of the Federal Rules of Civil Procedure. The Court, in its discretion, may strike and direct the return of any defective pleading.

(c) Court Addresses.

Clerk of Court
750 Missouri Avenue
P.O. Box 249
East St. Louis, Illinois 62202
(618) 482–9371

Clerk of Court
301 W. Main Street
Benton, IL 62812
(618) 439–7760

[Effective January 1, 2000. Amended effective July 1, 2003; December 1, 2009.]

RULE 9.1. PLEADINGS IN ACTIONS FOR REVIEW OF ADMINISTRATIVE DECISIONS

(*See* Fed. R. Civ. P. 8, 9, 84; 42 U.S.C. § 405)

(a) Any person seeking judicial review of a decision of the Commissioner of Social Security under Section 205(g) of the Social Security Act (42 U.S.C. § 405(g)) shall provide, on a separate paper attached to the complaint served on the Commissioner of Social Security, the last four digits of the social security number of the worker on whose wage record the application for benefits was filed. The person shall also state in the complaint that the complete social security number has been attached to the copy of the complaint served on the Commissioner of Social Security. Failure to provide a social security number to the Commissioner of Social Security will not be grounds for dismissal of the complaint.

(b) In keeping with Federal Rule of Civil Procedure 84 and the Appendix of Forms to the rules, the following form of allegations in the complaint is considered sufficient for § 405(g) review cases:

(1) Plaintiff is a resident of

City	State

(2) Plaintiff complains of a decision which adversely affects him/her. The decision has become the final decision of the Secretary for purposes of judicial review and bears the following caption:

In the Case of: Claim for:

Plaintiff	

Wage Earner	

(3) Plaintiff has exhausted administrative remedies in this matter, and this Court has jurisdiction for judicial review pursuant to 42 U.S.C. § 405(g).

(4) Defendant shall have **60 days** from the date of service of summons within which to file an answer and transcript of administrative proceedings.

(5) Within **30 days** after the filing of the answer and transcript, plaintiff shall file a brief which shall state with particularity which findings of the Commissioner are contrary to law. Within **30 days** thereafter, defendant shall file a brief which shall specifically respond to plaintiff's assertions and arguments. The case may be set for hearing at the Court's discretion.

[Effective March 1, 1999. Amended effective July 1, 2003; December 1, 2009.]

RULE 15.1. AMENDED PLEADINGS

(*See* Fed. R. Civ. P. 15)

A proposed amendment to a pleading or amended pleading itself must be submitted at the time the motion to amend is filed. Proposed pleadings must be submitted in accordance with the CM/ECF User's Manual Section 2.10 titled "Submitting a Proposed Document."

Section 2.10 provides that proposed orders, proposed amended complaints, proposed documents to be filed out of time, writs, post-judgment notices, and certain stipulations require court approval before actually being filed and given full effect. These documents must be attached to an e-mail sent to the presiding judge. The subject line of the e-mail must include the case number, the corresponding document number, and a brief description of the proposed document. Documents should be submitted in a format compatible with Microsoft Word [amended by interlineation to remove reference to WordPerfect and add Microsoft Word per Administrative Order No. 146] and served on all parties.

The e-mail addresses for submission of these documents are as follows:

Chief District Judge
   David R. Herndon   DRHpd@ilsd.uscourts.gov
District Judge J. Phil Gilbert   JPGpd@ilsd.uscourts.gov
District Judge G. Patrick Murphy   GPMpd@ilsd.uscourts.gov
District Judge Michael J. Reagan   MJRpd@ilsd.uscourts.gov
Senior District Judge
   William D. Stiehl   WDSpd@ilsd.uscourts.gov
Magistrate Judge Philip M. Frazier   PMFpd@ilsd.uscourts.gov
Magistrate Judge Clifford J. Proud   CJPpd@ilsd.uscourts.gov
Magistrate Judge
   Donald G. Wilkerson   DGWpd@ilsd.uscourts.gov

All new material in an amended pleading must be underlined. It is sufficient to simply underline the names of new parties the first place they appear in amended pleadings. Similarly, when new claims or defenses are raised by an amendment, it is sufficient that the number of the designated count or paragraph identifying the amendment be underlined.

[Effective March 1, 1999. Amended effective July 1, 2003; December 1, 2009.]

RULE 16.1. TRIAL DATES

(*See* 28 U.S.C. § 473 (a)(2)(B) and Appendix A, Fed. R. Crim. P. 50; 18 U.S.C. § 3161 et seq., 5036, 5037)

(a) Presumptive Trial Date. After the first appearance of a defendant or default date, whichever occurs first, the judicial officer to whom a case is assigned for trial will, in his or her discretion, assign a presumptive trial date to the case based on the following tracks of cases:

Track "A" The presumptive trial date will be set between 8–10 months after the first appearance of a defendant or default date, whichever occurs first. Track "A" shall include all cases exempt from the requirements of pretrial and settlement conferences by SDIL–LR 26.1. Prisoner habeas corpus petitions and any administrative review cases (i.e., social security) are not included in Track "A" assignments.

Track "B" The presumptive trial date will be set between 11–14 months after the first appearance of a defendant or default date, whichever occurs first. (Examples are simple tort and contract cases.)

Track "C" The presumptive trial date will be set between 15–18 months after the first appearance of a defendant or default date, whichever occurs first. (Examples are multi-party or complex issue cases including products liability, malpractice, antitrust, and patent cases.)

Track "D" The presumptive trial date will be set between 19–24 months after the first appearance of a defendant or default date, whichever occurs first. (Only proposed class actions will be assigned to Track "D.")

The presumptive trial date, which shall be for a specific month, will be communicated to the parties and, for cases assigned to Tracks "B," "C," and "D," shall be set forth in the notice to the parties of the date set for the initial pretrial and scheduling conference pursuant to Federal Rule of Civil Procedure 26(f) and also will be incorporated into the initial pretrial scheduling and discovery order.

(b) Firm Trial Date. On or before the presumptive trial date of a case assigned to Track "A," the judicial officer to whom the case is assigned shall set a firm trial date, and the parties shall be informed of this date. For cases in Tracks "B," "C," and "D," a firm trial date, which shall be for a specific week, shall be set at or before the final pretrial conference and incorporated into the final pretrial order (when required by the presiding judge).

(c) Continuances After Firm Trial Date Is Set. When the demands of the Speedy Trial Act, the unanticipated length of a civil trial, an emergency, or an unanticipated situation prevents the judicial officer to whom the case is assigned for trial from adhering to the firm trial date, the case will be given priority for trial during the next month or given an accelerated trial date.

(d) Parties Informed of Case Status. The Court will, from time to time, keep the attorneys/parties apprised of the trial date status of a case.

(e) Trial Dates in Criminal Cases. Trial dates in criminal cases are addressed in the District's "Plan for

Achieving Prompt Disposition of Criminal Cases."
(*See* Appendix A.)

[Effective March 1, 1999. Amended effective January 1,
2000; July 1, 2003; December 1, 2009.]

RULE 16.2. PRETRIAL CONFERENCES

(*See* Fed. R. Civ. P. 16, 26)

NOTE: The requirements for the scheduling and discovery report and pretrial conference in class actions are located in SDIL–LR 23.1. To the extent anything in this Local Rule is in conflict with SDIL–LR 23.1, SDIL–LR 23.1 takes priority.

(a) Initial Conference of the Parties; Submission of Report. At least **21 days** before any scheduling conference set by the Court, the attorneys (and any unrepresented parties) must confer in accordance with Federal Rule of Civil Procedure 26(f). Within **14 days** after conferring, and at least **7 days** before the date of the scheduling conference, a jointly prepared report must be submitted to the Magistrate Judge before whom the conference is set. (*See* Form: Joint Report of the Parties and Proposed Scheduling and Discovery Order.) The filing of motions will not eliminate the duty to comply with this rule.

(b) Final Pretrial Conference.

(1) Except in those cases listed in SDIL–LR 26.1(a), a final pretrial conference will be held before the judicial officer assigned to try the case not less than **7 days** prior to the presumptive trial date. The parties shall confer and jointly submit a signed proposed final pretrial order **3 days** before the date of the final pretrial conference unless otherwise directed by the presiding judge. The parties are encouraged to review the procedures for each judge as outlined on the Court's website.

(2) Lead trial counsel for each party with authority to bind the party shall be present at this conference.

(3) The following issues shall be discussed at the final pretrial conference and shall be included in the final pretrial order:

  (A) the firm trial date (*see* SDIL–LR 16.1(b));

  (B) stipulated and uncontroverted facts;

  (C) list of issues to be tried;

  (D) disclosure of all witnesses;

  (E) listing and exchange of copies of all exhibits;

  (F) pretrial rulings, where possible, on objections to evidence;

  (G) disposition of all outstanding motions;

  (H) elimination of unnecessary or redundant proof, including limitations on expert witnesses;

  (I) itemized statements of all damages by all parties;

  (J) bifurcation of the trial;

  (K) limits on the length of trial;

  (L) jury selection issues;

  (M) any issue which may facilitate and expedite the trial, for example, the feasibility of presenting testimony by a summary written statement; and

  (N) the date when proposed jury instructions shall be submitted to the Court and opposing counsel, which, unless otherwise ordered, shall be the first day of the trial.

(4) Trial briefs on any difficult, controverted factual or legal issue, including anticipated objections to evidence, shall be submitted to the Court at or before the final pretrial conference when possible.

[Effective March 1, 1999. Renumbered and amended effective January 1, 2000; July 1, 2003; December 1, 2009.]

RULE 16.3. SETTLEMENT CONFERENCES

(28 U.S.C. § 651, et seq.)

(a) Authorization of Alternative Methods of Dispute Resolution. To encourage and promote the use of alternative dispute resolution in this district, the parties shall use an early neutral evaluation in the form of a settlement conference in all civil cases except for the cases listed in SDIL–LR 26.1(a). The Court may, in its discretion, set any civil case for summary jury trial or other alternative method of dispute resolution which the Court may deem proper.

(b) Settlement Conference.

(1) The parties may request a settlement conference at any time. The Court may set a settlement conference at its discretion at any time during the course of the litigation.

(2) In addition to the lead counsel for each party, a representative of each party or the party's insurance company with authority to bind that party for settlement purposes shall be present in person.

(3) The notice of the settlement conference shall set forth the format of the conference, any requirement for information that must be submitted to the presiding judicial officer prior to the conference, and the types of documents or other information that must be brought to the conference.

(4) The statements or other communications made by any of the parties or their representatives in connection with the settlement conference shall remain confidential and shall not be admissible or used in any fashion in the trial of the case or any related case.

[Effective March 1, 1999. Renumbered and amended effective January 1, 2000; July 1, 2003; December 1, 2009.]

RULE 23.1. CLASS ACTIONS

(*See* Fed. R. Civ. P. 23)

(a) Scheduling and Discovery Conference. Proposed class actions pose complex scheduling and discovery issues which are not addressed by the standard "Joint Report of the Parties and Proposed Scheduling and Discovery Order." Accordingly, an initial scheduling and discovery conference with counsel for all parties may be set by the Court consistent with SDIL–LR 16.2.

The purpose of the scheduling and discovery conference is for the Magistrate Judge to identify the length and scope of discovery necessary for the fair and expeditious determination of whether the case can proceed as a class action. Discovery prior to class certification must be sufficient to permit the Court to determine whether the requirements of Federal Rule of Civil Procedure 23 are satisfied, including a preliminary inquiry into the merits of the case to ensure appropriate management of the case as a class action. In order to ensure that a class certification decision is issued as soon as practicable, however, priority shall be given to discovery on class certification issues.

After the scheduling conference, the Magistrate Judge shall enter the appropriate scheduling and discovery order in light of these concerns. Either party may move to have a second scheduling and discovery order entered after resolution of the motion for class certification.

(b) Joint Report. **Seven days** prior to any scheduling and discovery conference set by the Court, the parties shall submit a Joint Report of the Parties and Proposed Scheduling and Discovery Order (Class Action) consistent with the model found in the Forms section of these Local Rules. In the event the parties are unable to agree on a joint scheduling and discovery plan, the parties should each submit their Proposed Scheduling and Discovery Order and a memorandum in support of said order, addressing the issues in dispute **7 days** prior to the scheduling and discovery conference. The Magistrate Judge may adopt a Joint Report or issue a Scheduling and Discovery Order in lieu of proceeding with the scheduling and discovery conference.

(c) Motion Practice. The timetable for responding to a motion for class certification shall be established in the Joint Report or Scheduling and Discovery Order issued by the Court.

[Adopted effective July 1, 2003. Amended effective December 1, 2009.]

RULE 24.1. PROCEDURE FOR NOTIFICATION OF ANY CLAIM OF UNCONSTITUTIONALITY

(a) In any action, suit, or proceeding in which the United States or any agency, officer, or employee thereof is not a party and in which the constitutionality of an Act of Congress is drawn in question, or in any action, suit, or proceeding in which a state or any agency, officer, employee thereof is not a party and in which the constitutionality of any statute of that state is drawn in question, the party raising the constitutional issue shall notify the Court of the existence of the question either by checking the appropriate box on the Civil Cover Sheet or by stating on the pleading, immediately following the title of that pleading, "Claim of Unconstitutionality" or the equivalent.

(b) Failure to comply with this rule will not be grounds for waiving the constitutional issue or for waiving any other rights the party may have. Any notice provided under this rule, or lack of notice, will not serve as a substitute for, or as a waiver of, any pleading requirement set forth in the Federal Rules of Civil Procedure, the Federal Rules of Criminal Procedure, or any federal statute.

[Effective March 1, 1999. Amended effective July 1, 2003; December 1, 2009.]

RULE 26.1. INITIAL DISCLOSURE PRIOR TO DISCOVERY; FILING OF DISCLOSURE AND DISCOVERY; COOPERATIVE DISCOVERY

(*See* 28 U.S.C. § 473(a)(4)–(5); Fed. R. Civ. P. 26, 37; Fed. R. Crim. P. 12, 16)

(a) Implementation of Federal Rule of Civil Procedure 26. Federal Rule of Civil Procedure 26 shall control the initial stages of disclosure and discovery in all civil cases with the exception of the categories of proceedings specified in Federal Rule of Civil Procedure 26(a)(1)(B).

These categories are construed to include the following:

(1) prisoner habeas corpus petitions;

(2) prisoner civil rights cases;

(3) cases brought in which one of the parties appears pro se and is incarcerated;

(4) cases brought by the United States for collection on defaults of government loans and all mortgage foreclosure default loans;

(5) land condemnation cases;

(6) cases brought by the United States for condemnation or forfeiture against vehicles, airplanes, vessels, contaminated foods, drugs, cosmetics, and the like;

(7) cases brought to review the decision of administrative agencies (e.g., the Commissioner of Social Security);

(8) IRS enforcement actions;

(9) Freedom of Information Act cases;

(10) cases brought to collect civil penalties under the Federal Boat Safety Act of 1971;

(11) reviews of rulings of a Bankruptcy Judge or Magistrate Judge;

(12) suits to quash subpoenas; and

(13) proceedings filed as civil actions for admission to citizenship or to cancel or revoke citizenship.

The judicial officer to whom the case is assigned for trial may order an initial conference, a final pretrial conference, or a settlement conference in a case falling in one of the excluded categories if the judicial officer determines that the complexity of the case or some unusual factor warrants more extensive pretrial case management than is usually necessary for that type of case.

(b) Filing of Disclosure and Discovery.

(1) Interrogatories under Federal Rule of Civil Procedure 33 and the answers thereto, requests for production or inspection under Federal Rule of Civil Procedure 34, and depositions under Federal Rules of Civil Procedure 30 and 31 shall be served upon other counsel or parties but **shall not** be filed with the Clerk of Court. The party responsible for service of the discovery material shall retain the original and become the custodian thereof. Requests for admissions under Federal Rule of Civil Procedure 36 and responses thereto shall be served upon other counsel or parties and **shall** be filed with the Clerk of Court.

(2) Initial disclosures or discovery under Federal Rule of Civil Procedure 26(a) should be filed with the Clerk of Court upon Order of the Court or if a dispute arises over the disclosure or discovery.

(3) Any discovery motion filed pursuant to Federal Rules of Civil Procedure 26 through 37 shall have attached to it or the accompanying memorandum a copy of the actual discovery documents which are the subject of the motion or, in the alternative, set out in the memorandum a verbatim recitation of each interrogatory, request, answer, response, and/or objection which is the subject of the motion.

(4) If interrogatories, requests, answers, responses, or depositions are to be used at trial or are necessary to a pretrial motion which might result in a final order on any issue, the portions to be used shall be filed with the Clerk of Court at the outset of the trial or at the filing of the motion insofar as their use can be reasonably anticipated.

(5) When documentation of discovery not previously in the record is needed for appeal purposes, upon an application and order from the presiding judge or by stipulation of counsel, the necessary discovery papers shall be filed with the Clerk of Court.

(6) If a non-party requests to examine discovery materials and the presiding judge so orders, the parties will comply and make designated discovery material available for inspection.

(c) Duplicative Disclosure. At the time the duty to disclose arises, it may cover matters that have already been fully disclosed in the same civil action pursuant to an order, to a requirement of law, or otherwise. In that event, duplicative disclosure is not required and a statement that disclosure has already been made discharges the obligation imposed under this section.

(d) Cooperative Discovery Arrangements. Cooperative discovery arrangements in the interest of reducing delay and expense are mandated.

(e) Discovery in Criminal Cases. Parties in criminal cases shall comply with the Standard Order for Pretrial Discovery and Inspection.

[Effective March 1, 1999. Amended effective January 1, 2000; July 1, 2003; December 1, 2009.]

RULE 33.1. INTERROGATORIES

(*See* Fed. R. Civ. P. 33)

(a) Form. Under Federal Rule of Civil Procedure 33, answers or objections to interrogatories shall set forth in full the interrogatory being answered or objected to immediately preceding the answer or objection. Objections shall be served upon opposing counsel as a separate document entitled "Objections to Interrogatories," within the time provided by Federal Rule of Civil Procedure 33. Objections shall be accompanied by citation to legal authority. Objections shall not be filed with the Clerk of Court unless a motion to compel is submitted pursuant to Federal Rule of Civil Procedure 37.

(b) Copies Not Permitted. No photocopied or otherwise duplicated form containing interrogatories shall be served upon a party unless all interrogatories are consecutively numbered and applicable to the case in which the same are served. The intent and purpose of this rule is to prohibit the submission of photocopied or otherwise duplicated forms of "stock" interrogatories, except where the nature of the case or the number of the parties makes the use of such forms necessary and feasible.

(c) Sequential Numbering. All interrogatories served by a party, including supplemental interrogatories, shall be sequentially numbered. All subsequent sets of interrogatories shall be numbered commencing with the number immediately succeeding the one last used.

[Effective March 1, 1999. Amended effective July 1, 2003; December 1, 2009.]

RULE 40.1. CASE ASSIGNMENT AND TRIAL CALENDARS

(*See* Fed. R. Civ. P. 40, 79)

(a) Civil cases are randomly assigned to a District Judge pursuant to Administrative Order as from time to time amended by the Court. Any action taken to avoid the random assignment will subject that party and that party's attorney(s) to the full disciplinary power and sanctions of this Court.

(b) Criminal cases are randomly assigned to a District Judge by separate Benton and East St. Louis dockets.

[Effective March 1, 1999. Amended effective July 1, 2003; December 1, 2009.]

RULE 51.1. INSTRUCTIONS TO THE JURY

(*See* Fed. R. Civ. P. 49, 51; Fed. R. Crim. P. 30)

(a) In both civil and criminal cases, an electronic version of a party's proposed jury instructions should be submitted by e-mail to the presiding judicial officer. When required by the presiding judicial officer, an original and one copy of each proposed instruction also shall be submitted to the Court and duplicates shall be delivered to opposing counsel. The original of each instruction shall be on 8½″ × 11″ plain white paper without any designation or number. The copy shall be numbered and shall identify the authority supporting the instruction and which party tenders it. The parties are encouraged to review the procedures for each judge as outlined on the Court's website.

(b) In all cases, the Pattern Jury Instructions as approved by the Seventh Circuit Court of Appeals shall be used when available.

[Effective March 1, 1999. Amended effective July 1, 2003; December 1, 2009.]

RULE 53.1. COMMUNICATIONS WITH JURORS

Before and during trial, no attorney, party, or representative of either shall contact, converse, or otherwise communicate with a juror or potential juror on any subject, whether pertaining to the case or not.

No attorney, party, or representative of either may interrogate a juror after the verdict has been returned without prior approval of the presiding judge. Approval of the presiding judge shall be sought only by application made by counsel orally in open court or upon written motion which states the grounds and the purpose of the interrogation. If a post-verdict interrogation of one or more of the members of the jury is approved, the scope of the interrogation and other appropriate limitations upon the interrogation will be determined by the presiding judge prior to the interrogation.

[Effective July 1, 2003. Redesignated and amended, effective December 1, 2009.]

RULE 54.1. ASSESSMENT OF JURY COSTS

Whenever a civil case which has been set for jury trial is disposed of or settled by the parties, counsel shall immediately inform the chambers of the judge before whom the case is pending. When possible, notice of settlement shall be provided by no later than 3 p.m. on the last full court business day before the date the trial is scheduled. If for any reason attributable to counsel or the parties, including settlement or disposition of the matter, the Court is unable to commence a jury trial as scheduled, and a panel of prospective jurors has reported for service, or a selected jury has reported to hear the case, all costs incurred with respect to the jury, including per diem and mileage, may be assessed by the Court against all parties equally or against one or more of the parties, if it appears that the party was, or the parties were, responsible for the failure to notify the Court as required, or otherwise caused the Court's inability to proceed.

All money collected as a result of any assessment under this rule shall be paid to the Clerk of Court, who shall promptly remit said money to the Treasury of the United States of America.

[Effective March 1, 1999. Amended effective July 1, 2003; December 1, 2009.]

RULE 54.2. TAXATION OF COSTS

(*See* 28 U.S.C. §§ 1914, 1920, 1828; Fed. R. Civ. P. 54(d))

Not all trial expenses are taxable as costs. Only those items authorized by law may be taxed as costs. Costs shall be taxed in accordance with Federal Rule of Civil Procedure 54(d) and 28 U.S.C. § 1920.

Federal Rule of Civil Procedure 54(d)(1) provides that costs (other than attorneys' fees) should be allowed to the prevailing party, unless a federal statute, rule, or court order otherwise directs. Rule 54(d)(1) further provides that such costs may be taxed by the Clerk of Court "on 14 days' notice." Opposing counsel will be allowed **14 days** (from the date notice is given by the Clerk) in which to file any objections. If no objections are filed within the 14 day period, the Clerk of Court will tax the appropriate costs. If objections are timely filed, the matter will be reviewed and resolved by the presiding judge.

[Effective March 1, 1999. Amended effective January 1, 2000; July 1, 2003; December 1, 2009.]

RULE 54.3. CONTINUANCES

The Court may condition a continuance upon the payment of the expenses caused to the other parties and/or jury fees incurred by the Court.

[Effective March 1, 1999. Amended effective July 1, 2003; December 1, 2009.]

RULE 55.1. DEFAULT JUDGMENT

(*See* Fed. R. Civ. P. 55)

(a) Entry by Clerk. The Clerk of Court shall enter a default against any party who fails to respond to a complaint, crossclaim, or counterclaim within the time and in the manner provided by Federal Rule of Civil Procedure 12. The serving party shall give notice of the entry of default to the defaulting party by regular mail sent to the last known address of the defaulted party and shall certify to the Court that notice has been sent.

(b) Default Judgment. Any motion for default judgment pursuant to Federal Rule of Civil Procedure 55(b) shall contain a statement that a copy of the motion has been mailed to the last known address of the party from whom default judgment is sought. If the moving party knows, or reasonably should know, the identity of an attorney thought to represent the defaulted party, the motion shall also state that a copy has been mailed to that attorney.

[Effective December 1, 2009.]

RULE 72.1. ASSIGNMENT OF MATTERS TO MAGISTRATE JUDGES

(*See* 28 U.S.C. § 636, et seq.; Fed. R. Civ. P. 72, 73)

(a) Automatic References. The Clerk of Court shall refer the following matters to a Magistrate Judge upon filing:

(1) all pretrial motions for hearing and determination in accordance with the provisions of Federal Rule of Civil Procedure 72, with the exception of motions for injunctive relief, for judgment on the pleadings, for summary judgment, to dismiss, to remand, to permit maintenance of a class action, to dismiss for failure to state a claim upon which relief can be granted, to involuntarily dismiss an action, motions in limine regarding evidentiary matters, and for extensions of time with regard to matters pending before a District Judge. Upon entry of a pretrial order, all motions thereafter served shall be submitted to the assigned trial judge;

(2) all so-called "prisoner petitions" (e.g., petitions or complaints filed pursuant to 28 U.S.C. §§ 1331, 2241, and 2254 or 42 U.S.C. § 1983), which are filed by inmates during confinement;

(3) all requests for judicial review of a decision of the Commissioner of Social Security under Section 205(g) of the Social Security Act (42 U.S.C. § 405(g));

(4) all misdemeanor offenses occurring within the Southern District of Illinois which are prosecuted by criminal complaint;

(5) all petty offenses and all offenses involving Central Violations Bureau (CVB), which are offenses occurring on government property or reservations.

(6) all supplemental proceedings to discover assets and aid execution of judgments in civil cases pursuant to Federal Rule of Civil Procedure 69.

(b) Authorized References. With the consent of the parties, a Magistrate Judge is authorized to: (1) conduct voir dire and select petit juries for the District Court; (2) accept guilty pleas in felony cases, order presentence investigation reports, and file reports and recommendations with the District Court.

(c) Selected References. All other civil or criminal matters will be referred by a District Judge to a Magistrate Judge on a case-by-case basis.

[Effective March 1, 1999. Amended effective July 1, 2003; December 1, 2009.]

RULE 72.2. PROCEDURES BEFORE MAGISTRATE JUDGES

(*See* 28 U.S.C. § 636, et seq.; Fed. R. Civ. P. 72, 73)

(a) In General. In performing his or her duties, a Magistrate Judge shall conform to all applicable provisions of federal statutes and rules, to the general procedural rules of this Court, and to the requirements specified in any order of reference from a District Judge. All practice before a Magistrate Judge shall be in accordance with these Local Rules.

(b) Special Provisions for the Disposition of Civil Cases by a Magistrate Judge on Consent of the Parties—28 U.S.C. § 636(c).

(1) *Notice.* The Clerk of Court shall notify the parties in all civil cases that they may consent to have a Magistrate Judge conduct any or all proceedings in the case and order the entry of a final judgment. This notice shall be handed or mailed to plaintiff or his or her representative at the time an action is filed and to other parties as soon as practicable after service upon defendants. Additional notices may be furnished to the parties at later stages of the proceedings and may be included with pretrial notices and instructions.

(2) *Execution of Consent.* The Clerk of Court shall supply, with the notice, a consent form which may be used by the parties. An executed consent form shall be mailed to the Clerk of Court who will file the form

under seal. The executed consent form will be unsealed only if all parties consent to the reference to a Magistrate Judge. No Magistrate Judge, District Judge, or other court official may attempt to persuade or induce any party to consent to the reference of any matter to a Magistrate Judge. This rule shall not preclude a District Judge or Magistrate Judge from informing the parties that they have the option of consenting to a Magistrate Judge.

(3) *Reference.* If all parties file and execute consent forms agreeing to trial by a Magistrate Judge, the Clerk of Court shall transmit the forms to the District Judge to whom the case has been assigned for approval and referral of the case to a Magistrate Judge. Once the case has been assigned to a Magistrate Judge, the Magistrate Judge shall have the authority to conduct any and all proceedings to which the parties have consented and to direct the Clerk of Court to enter a final judgment in the same manner as if a District Judge had presided.

[Effective March 1, 1999. Amended effective July 1, 2003; December 1, 2009.]

RULE 73.1. REVIEW AND APPEAL OF MAGISTRATE JUDGES' ORDERS OR RECOMMENDATIONS

(*See* 28 U.S.C. § 636, et seq.; Fed. R. Civ. P. 72, 73)

(a) Appeal of Non–Dispositive Matters—28 U.S.C. § 636(b)(1)(A). Any party may appeal a Magistrate Judge's order determining a motion or matter within **14 days** after issuance of the Magistrate Judge's order, unless a different time is prescribed by the Magistrate Judge or a District Judge. The party shall file with the Clerk of Court and serve on all parties a written request for an appeal which shall specifically designate the order or part of the order that the parties wish the Court to reconsider. A District Judge shall reconsider the matter and shall set aside any portion of the Magistrate Judge's order found to be clearly erroneous or contrary to law. A District Judge may also reconsider sua sponte any matter determined by a Magistrate Judge under this rule.

(b) Review of Dispositive Motions and Prisoner Litigation—28 U.S.C. § 636(b)(1)(B). Any party may object to a Magistrate Judge's proposed dispositive findings, recommendations, or reports within **14 days** after being served with a copy. The objecting party shall file with the Clerk of Court and serve on all parties written objections which shall specifically identify the portions of the proposed findings, recommendations, or reports to which objection is made and the basis for the objections. Any party may respond to another party's objections within **14 days** after

being served with a copy. **Requests for extension of these deadlines are not favored.**

A District Judge shall make a de novo determination of those portions of the report or specified proposed findings or recommendations to which objection is made and may accept, reject, or modify, in whole or in part, the findings or recommendations made by the Magistrate Judge. The District Judge may conduct a new hearing, may consider the record developed before the Magistrate Judge, and may make a determination on the basis of that record. The District Judge may also receive further evidence, recall witnesses, or recommit the matter to the Magistrate Judge with instructions.

(c) Special Master Reports—28 U.S.C. § 636(b)(2). Any party may seek review of, or action on, a special master report filed by a Magistrate Judge in accordance with the provisions of Federal Rule of Civil Procedure 53(e).

(d) Appeal from Judgments in Misdemeanor Cases—18 U.S.C. § 3402; Fed. R. Crim. P. 58(g)(2)(B). A defendant may appeal a judgment of conviction by a Magistrate Judge in a misdemeanor case by filing a notice of appeal with the District Court within **14 days** after entry of the judgment, and by serving a copy of the notice upon the United States Attorney. The scope of the appeal shall be the same as on an appeal from a judgment of the District Court to the Court of Appeals.

(e) Appeal from Judgments in Civil Cases Disposed of on Consent of the Parties—28 U.S.C. § 636(c). Upon the entry of judgment in any civil case disposed of by a Magistrate Judge on consent of the parties under authority of 28 U.S.C. § 636(c), an aggrieved party may appeal directly to the United States Court of Appeals for the Seventh Circuit in the same manner as an appeal from any other judgment of this Court.

[Effective March 1, 1999. Amended effective July 1, 2003; December 1, 2009.]

RULE 79.1. CUSTODY AND DISPOSITION OF EXHIBITS

(a) During Trial. Unless the presiding judge orders otherwise, exhibits received into evidence at any trial or hearing shall be retained in the custody of the Clerk of Court for the duration of the proceeding.

(b) After Trial. Unless the presiding judge orders otherwise, exhibits shall not be retained by the Clerk of Court at the conclusion of the proceeding, but shall be retained in the custody of the respective attorneys who produced them in court. A detailed receipt shall be given to the Clerk of Court. Any exhibits not so removed may be destroyed or otherwise disposed of as the Clerk of Court may deem appropriate after **30 days** notice to counsel.

(c) Appeal. If an appeal is taken, parties shall make available all of the exhibits in their possession in order to prepare the record on appeal. The attorney who has custody of exhibits shall comply with Rule 10 of the Circuit Rules for the United States Court of Appeals for the Seventh Circuit and must ensure that exhibits to be included in the record which are not in the possession of the Clerk of Court in the district court are furnished to the Clerk of Court in the Seventh Circuit Court of Appeals as set forth in Rule 10.

[Effective March 1, 1999. Amended effective July 1, 2003; December 1, 2009.]

RULE 80.1. OFFICIAL TRANSCRIPTS

(*See* Fed. R. App. P. 10; 7th Cir. R. 10, 11)

Before producing an official transcript, a court reporter shall obtain a written request on a "Seventh Circuit Transcript Information Sheet" pursuant to Rule 10(b) of the Federal Rules of Appellate Procedure and Rule 10(c) of the Circuit Rules.

The written request shall contain the following pertinent data:

(a) a commitment of the party and his or her attorney to pay;

(b) the commitment of the party and his or her attorney that they will not directly or indirectly furnish the transcript or a copy of it to any other party or attorney in the action; and

(c) any other pertinent matter that is necessary for a clear understanding of the terms of the contract between the court reporter and the ordering party and his or her attorney.

[Effective March 1, 1999. Amended effective July 1, 2003; December 1, 2009.]

RULE 83.1. ADMISSION OF ATTORNEYS

(a) General Admission of Attorneys. Any attorney licensed to practice law in any state of the United States or the District of Columbia shall be admitted to practice generally in this Court upon payment of a $200.00 fee as required by law, and:

(1) a written motion of a member in good standing of the bar of this Court including the bar number of the member and all state bar numbers issued to the applicant; or

(2) the attorney's own motion accompanied by a Certificate of Good Standing from a state in which the attorney is licensed together with all state bar numbers issued to the applicant; or

(3) the attorney's own motion accompanied by a copy of the attorney's Certificate of Admission to Practice in the Northern or Central Districts of Illinois together with all state bar numbers issued to the applicant.

(b) Pro Hac Vice Admissions. Any attorney licensed to practice law in any state of the United States or the District of Columbia who does not wish to be admitted generally but wishes to be admitted for the purposes of a specific civil or criminal case only may, upon submission of a Motion to Appear *Pro Hac Vice* which contains a verified statement setting forth the state and federal bars of which the movant is a member in good standing, the bar number, if any, issued by each jurisdiction, and the required filing fee of $100.00 for *pro hac vice* motions, be permitted to appear of record and participate *pro hac vice*.

(c) Government Representation. Any attorney representing any governmental entity, whether federal, state, or municipal, may appear and participate in particular cases in his or her official capacity without the necessity of a motion for admission. The requirements of subparagraph (d) below, concerning nonresident counsel, shall apply.

(d) Non–Resident Counsel. It shall not be necessary for parties appearing by non-resident counsel to retain local counsel to represent them. At any time for good cause, upon the motion of any party, or upon its own motion, the Court may require that a non-resident attorney obtain local counsel to assist in the conduct of the case.

(e) Representation in Cases. In all cases filed in, removed to, or transferred to this Court, all parties, except governmental agencies or those appearing *pro se*, must be represented by a member of the bar of this Court. Service upon such attorney shall constitute service upon all other counsel appearing of record for the party.

Unless otherwise excepted by this rule, pleadings or other documents submitted by a party who is not represented by a member of the bar of this Court shall not be accepted by the Clerk of Court.

(f) Appearances. In all cases filed in, removed to, or transferred to this Court, all attorneys, including government attorneys, shall file a written entry of appearance before addressing the Court.

(g) Withdrawals. An attorney may not withdraw an entry of appearance for a party without leave of court and notice to all parties of record.

(1) *Notice to Court.* The motion for leave to withdraw shall be in writing and, unless another attorney is substituted, shall state the last known address of the party represented. The Court may deny the motion if granting it would delay the trial of the case or would otherwise be inequitable.

(2) *Notice to Parties.* Unless another attorney is substituted, a withdrawing attorney must give reasonable notice of the time and place of the presentation of

the motion for leave to withdraw to the party being represented at the party's last known business or residential address, by personal service or by certified mail. The notice shall advise the party being represented that he or she should retain other counsel and that within **21 days** of the entry of the order of withdrawal, the party or the new counsel shall file with the Clerk of Court a supplementary appearance that provides an address at which the party and/or the new counsel may receive service of documents related to the case.

If the motion for withdrawal is granted, the withdrawing attorney shall serve a copy of the order of withdrawal within **7 days** upon all counsel of record and upon unrepresented parties.

(h) Conduct. Conduct of attorneys admitted to practice in this Court is controlled by Local Rule 83.2.

(i) Duty of Attorneys to Accept Appointments. In testimonial proceedings arising out of matters pending before this Court, every member of the bar of this Court, as defined in subparagraph (a) of this rule, shall be available for appointment by the Court to represent or assist in the representation of those who cannot afford to hire an attorney. Appointments shall be made in such a manner that no member of the bar of this Court shall be required to accept more than one appointment during any twelve month period.

(j) Representation by Supervised Senior Law Students. A student in a law school who has been certified to render services pursuant to Illinois Supreme Court Rule 711 may, upon approval of the judge before whom the case is pending, perform such services in this Court as allowed by Rule 711 while under the supervision of an attorney authorized to practice in this Court. In addition to the agencies specified in paragraph (b) of Rule 711, the law school student may render services with the United States Attorney for this district, the legal staff of any agency of the United States government, or the Federal Public Defender for this district including any of its staff or panel attorneys.

(k) Registration Fee. When a fee is collected from an attorney for general admission to practice in this Court, the amount of $50.00 shall be retained by the Clerk of Court for use as set forth in this Court's *Plan for the Administration of the District Court Fund.* The balance of the fee collected from every general attorney admission shall be paid to the Treasury of the United States. The entire fee collected from a *pro hac vice* admission shall be retained by the Clerk of Court for use as set forth in this Court's *Plan for the Administration of the District Court Fund.*

[Effective March 1, 1999. Amended effective July 1, 2003; December 1, 2009.]

RULE 83.2.   CONDUCT OF ATTORNEYS

The Court, in furtherance of its inherent power and responsibility to supervise the conduct of attorneys admitted to practice before it, promulgates the following Rules of Disciplinary Enforcement superseding all of its other rules pertaining to disciplinary enforcement.

(a) For misconduct defined in these rules and for good cause shown, after notice and opportunity to be heard, any attorney admitted to practice before this Court may be disbarred, suspended from practice before this Court, reprimanded, or subjected to other disciplinary action as the circumstances may warrant.

(b) Acts or omissions by an attorney admitted to practice before this Court, individually or in concert with any other person or persons, which violate the Rules of Professional Conduct adopted by this Court shall constitute misconduct and shall be grounds for discipline, whether or not the act or omission occurred in the course of an attorney-client relationship. The Rules of Professional Conduct adopted by this Court are the Rules of Professional Conduct adopted by the Supreme Court of Illinois as amended from time to time, except as otherwise provided by specific rule of this Court.

(c) Whenever an attorney applies to be admitted or is admitted to this Court for purposes of a particular proceeding (pro hac vice), the attorney shall be deemed to have conferred disciplinary jurisdiction upon this Court for any alleged misconduct of that attorney arising in the course of, or in the preparation for, such proceeding.

[Effective December 1, 2009.]

RULE 83.3.   DISCIPLINARY ENFORCEMENT

(a) Disciplinary Proceedings.

(1) When misconduct or allegations of misconduct which, if substantiated, would warrant discipline on the part of an attorney admitted to practice before this Court shall come to the attention of a District Judge or Magistrate Judge, whether by complaint or otherwise, and the applicable procedure is not otherwise mandated by these rules, he or she shall refer the matter to counsel for investigation and the prosecution of a formal disciplinary proceeding or the formulation of such other recommendation as may be appropriate.

(2) Should counsel conclude after investigation and review that a formal disciplinary proceeding should not be initiated against the respondent-attorney because sufficient evidence is not present, or because there is pending another proceeding against the respondent-attorney, the disposition of which, in the judgment of the counsel, should be awaited before

further action by this Court is considered, or for any other valid reason, counsel shall file with the Court a recommendation for disposition of the matter, whether by dismissal, admonition, deferral, or otherwise, and set forth the reasons for his or her recommendation.

(3) To initiate formal disciplinary proceedings, counsel shall obtain an Order of this Court, upon a showing of probable cause, requiring the respondent-attorney to show cause within **30 days** after service of that order upon that attorney, personally or by mail, why the respondent-attorney should not be disciplined.

(4) Upon the respondent-attorney's answer to the order to show cause, if any issue of fact is raised or the respondent-attorney wishes to be heard in mitigation, this Court shall set the matter for prompt hearing before one or more judges of this Court, provided, however, that if the disciplinary proceeding is predicated upon the complaint of a judge of this Court, the hearing shall be conducted before one or more other judges of this Court appointed by the Chief Judge.

(5) *Criminal Contempt.* Notwithstanding any other provision of these rules, a District Judge may summarily punish a person who commits criminal contempt in its presence if he or she saw or heard the contemptuous conduct and so certifies; a Magistrate Judge may summarily punish a person as provided in 28 U.S.C. § 636(e). The contempt order must recite the facts, be signed by the Judge, and be filed with the Clerk of Court. (*See* Fed. R. Crim. P. 42(b); 28 U.S.C. § 1784.) If the misconduct has occurred outside the actual presence of the Court or where time is not of the essence, the provisions of Federal Rule of Criminal Procedure 42(a) may be applied.

(6) *Service of Paper and Other Notices.* Service of an order to show cause instituting a formal disciplinary proceeding shall be made by personal service or by registered or certified mail addressed to the respondent-attorney at the address shown in the most recent registration on file. Service of any other papers or notices required by these rules shall be deemed to have been made if such paper or notice is addressed to the respondent-attorney at the address shown on the most recent registration on file or to the respondent's attorney at the address indicated in the most recent pleading or other document filed in the course of any proceeding.

(7) *Appointment of Counsel.* Whenever counsel is to be appointed pursuant to these rules to investigate allegations of misconduct or prosecute disciplinary proceedings or in conjunction with a reinstatement petition filed by a disciplined attorney, this Court shall appoint as counsel one or more members of the bar of this Court to investigate allegations of misconduct or to prosecute disciplinary proceedings under these rules, provided, however, that the respondent-attorney may move to disqualify an attorney so appointed who

is or has been engaged as an adversary of the respondent-attorney in any matter. Counsel, once appointed, may not resign unless permission to do so is given by this Court.

(8) *Payment of Fees and Costs.* At the conclusion of any disciplinary investigation and prosecution, if any, under these rules, counsel may make application to this Court for an order awarding reasonable fees and reimbursing costs expended in the course of such disciplinary action or prosecution. Any such order shall be submitted to the Chief Judge, who may order payment of such amounts from the funds collected pursuant to Rule 83.1(k), as he or she may deem reasonable and just under the circumstances of each case.

(b) Attorneys Convicted of Crimes.

(1) Upon the filing with the Court of a certified copy of a judgment of conviction demonstrating that any attorney admitted to practice before the Court has been convicted of a serious crime, as hereinafter defined, in any court of the United States, the District of Columbia, or any state, territory, commonwealth, or possession of the United States, the Court shall immediately enter an order suspending that attorney, whether the conviction resulted from a plea of guilty or nolo contendere, from a verdict after trial or otherwise, regardless of the pendency of any appeal. A copy of such order shall immediately be served upon the attorney. Upon good cause shown, the Court may set aside such order when it appears to be in the interest of justice to do so.

(2) The term "serious crime" shall include any felony and any lesser crime, a necessary element of which, as determined by the statutory or common law definition of the crime in the jurisdiction where the judgment was entered, involves false swearing, misrepresentation, fraud, willful failure to file income tax returns, deceit, bribery, extortion, misappropriation, theft, or an attempt or a conspiracy or solicitation of another to commit a "serious crime."

(3) A certified copy of a judgment of conviction of an attorney for any crime shall be conclusive evidence of the commission of that crime in any disciplinary proceeding instituted against that attorney based upon the conviction.

(4) Upon the filing of a certified copy of a judgment of conviction of an attorney for a serious crime, the Court shall, in addition to suspending that attorney in accordance with the provisions of this rule, also refer the matter to counsel for the institution of a disciplinary proceeding in which the sole issue to be determined shall be the extent of the final discipline to be imposed as a result of the conduct resulting in the conviction, provided that a disciplinary proceeding so instituted will not be brought to final hearing until all appeals from the conviction are concluded.

(5) Upon the filing of a certified copy of a judgment of conviction of an attorney for a serious crime, the Court shall, in addition to suspending that attorney in accordance with the provisions of this rule, also refer the matter to counsel for the institution of a disciplinary proceeding before the Court in which the sole issue to be determined shall be the extent of the final discipline to be imposed as a result of the conduct resulting in the conviction, provided that a disciplinary proceeding so instituted will not be brought to final hearing until all appeals from the conviction are concluded.

Upon the filing of a certified copy of a judgment of conviction of an attorney for a crime not constituting a "serious crime," the Court may refer the matter to counsel for whatever action counsel may deem warranted, including the institution of a disciplinary proceeding in accordance with Rule 83.3(a), provided, however, that the Court may in its discretion make no reference with respect to convictions for minor offenses.

(6) An attorney suspended under the provisions of this rule will be reinstated immediately upon the filing of proof demonstrating that the underlying conviction of a serious crime has been reversed, but the reinstatement will not terminate any disciplinary proceeding brought in accordance with Rule 83.3(a) then pending against the attorney, the disposition of which shall be determined by the Court on the basis of all available evidence pertaining to both guilt and the extent of discipline to be imposed.

(c) Discipline Imposed by Other Court.

(1) Any attorney admitted to practice before this Court shall, upon being subjected to public discipline by any other court of the United States or the District of Columbia, or by a court of any state, territory, commonwealth, or possession of the United States, promptly inform the Clerk of Court.

(2) Upon the filing of a certified copy of a judgment or order demonstrating that an attorney admitted to practice before this Court has been disciplined by another court, this Court shall forthwith issue a notice directed to the attorney containing:

(i) a copy of the judgment or order from the other court; and

(ii) an order to show cause directing that the attorney inform this Court within **30 days** after service of that order upon the attorney, personally or by mail, of any claim by the attorney predicated upon the grounds set forth in (4) below that the imposition of the identical discipline by the Court would be unwarranted and the reasons why.

(3) In the event the discipline imposed in the other jurisdiction has been stayed there, any reciprocal discipline imposed by this Court shall be deferred until the stay expires.

(4) Upon the expiration of **30 days** from service of the notice issued pursuant to the provisions of (2) above, this Court shall impose the identical discipline unless the respondent-attorney demonstrates, or this Court finds, that upon the face of the record upon which the discipline in another jurisdiction is predicated, it clearly appears:

(A) that the procedure was so lacking in notice or opportunity to be heard as to constitute a deprivation of due process; or

(B) that there was such an infirmity of proof establishing the misconduct as to give rise to the clear conviction that this Court could not, consistent with its duty, accept as final the conclusion on that subject; or

(C) that the imposition of the same discipline by this Court would result in grave injustice; or

(D) that the misconduct established is deemed by this Court to warrant substantially different discipline. Where this Court determines that any of said elements exist, it shall enter such other order as it deems appropriate.

(5) In all other respects, a final adjudication in another court that an attorney has been guilty of misconduct shall establish conclusively the misconduct for purposes of a disciplinary proceeding in this Court.

(6) The Court may at any stage appoint counsel to prosecute the disciplinary proceedings.

(d) Disbarment on Consent or Resignation in Other Court.

(1) Any attorney admitted to practice before this Court who shall be disciplined on consent or resign from the bar of any other court of the United States or the District of Columbia, or from the bar of any state, territory, commonwealth, or possession of the United States while an investigation into allegations of misconduct is pending, shall, upon the filing with this Court of a certified copy of the judgment or order accepting such discipline on consent or resignation, be subject to the same action by this Court.

(2) Any attorney admitted to practice before this Court shall, upon being disciplined on consent or resigning from the bar of any other court of the United States or the District of Columbia, or from the bar of any state, territory, commonwealth, or possession of the United States while an investigation into allegations of misconduct is pending, promptly inform the Clerk of Court of such discipline on consent or resignation.

(e) Disbarment on Consent While Under Disciplinary Investigation or Prosecution.

(1) Any attorney admitted to practice before this Court who is the subject of an investigation into, or a pending proceeding involving, allegations of misconduct, may consent to discipline, but only by delivering

to this Court an affidavit stating that the attorney desires to consent to such discipline and that:

(A) the attorney's consent is freely and voluntarily rendered, the attorney is not being subjected to coercion or duress, and the attorney is fully aware of the implications of consenting;

(B) the attorney is aware that there is a pending investigation or proceeding involving allegations that there exist grounds for the attorney's discipline, the nature of which the attorney shall specifically set forth;

(C) the attorney acknowledges that the material facts so alleged are true; and

(D) the attorney so consents because the attorney knows that if the charges were predicated upon the matters under investigation, or if the proceedings were prosecuted, the attorney could not successfully defend himself.

(2) Upon receipt of the required affidavit, this Court shall enter an order of such discipline.

(3) The order disciplining the attorney on consent shall be a matter of public record. However, the affidavit required under the provisions of this rule shall not be publicly disclosed or made available for use in any other proceeding except upon Order of this Court.

(f) Duties of the Clerk of Court.

(1) Upon being informed that an attorney admitted to practice in this Court has been convicted of any crime, the Clerk of Court shall determine whether the court in which such conviction occurred has forwarded a certificate of the conviction. If a certificate has not been so forwarded, the Clerk of Court shall promptly obtain the certificate.

(2) Upon being informed that an attorney admitted to practice in this Court has been subjected to discipline by another court, the Clerk of Court shall determine whether a certified copy of the judgment or order has been filed with this Court, and, if not, the Clerk of Court shall promptly obtain the judgment or order.

(3) Whenever it appears that any person convicted of a crime or disbarred, suspended, censured, or disciplined on consent by this Court is admitted to practice law in any other jurisdiction or before any other court, the Clerk of Court shall, within **14 days** of that conviction, disbarment, suspension, censure, or discipline on consent, transmit to the disciplinary authority in such other jurisdiction or court, a certificate of the conviction or a certified copy of the judgment or order of disbarment, suspension, censure, or discipline on consent, as well as the last known office and residence addresses of the defendant or respondent.

(4) The Clerk of Court shall likewise promptly notify the National Discipline Data Bank operated by the American Bar Association of any order imposing public discipline upon any attorney to practice before this Court.

(g) Jurisdiction. Nothing contained in these rules shall be construed to deny to this Court such powers as are necessary for the Court to maintain control over proceedings conducted before it, such as proceedings for contempt under Title 18 of the United States Code or under Rule 42 of the Federal Rules of Criminal Procedure.

[Effective December 1, 2009.]

RULE 83.4. REINSTATEMENT OF ATTORNEYS

(a) After Disbarment or Suspension. An attorney suspended for three months or less shall be automatically reinstated at the end of the period of suspension upon filing with the Clerk of Court an affidavit of compliance with the provisions of the order suspending him or her. An attorney suspended for more than three months or disbarred may not resume practice until reinstated by Order of this Court.

(b) Time of Application Following Disbarment. A person who has been disbarred after hearing or by consent may not apply for reinstatement until the expiration of at least five years from the effective date of the disbarment.

(c) Hearing on Application. Petitions for reinstatement by a disbarred or suspended attorney under this rule shall be filed with the Chief Judge. Upon receipt of the petition, the Chief Judge shall promptly refer the petition to counsel and shall assign the matter for prompt hearing before one or more judges of this Court, provided, however, that if the disciplinary proceeding was predicated upon the complaint of a judge of this Court, the hearing shall be conducted before a panel of the remaining judges of this Court appointed by the Chief Judge. The judge or judges assigned to the matter shall, within **30 days** after referral, schedule a hearing at which the petitioner shall have the burden of demonstrating by clear and convincing evidence that he or she has the moral qualifications, competency, and learning in the law required for admission to practice law before this Court and that his or her resumption of the practice of law will not be detrimental to the integrity and standing of the bar or to the administration of justice or subversive of the public interest.

(d) Duty of Counsel. In all proceedings upon a petition for reinstatement, cross-examination of the witnesses of the respondent-attorney and the submission of evidence, if any, in opposition to the petition shall be conducted by counsel.

(e) Deposit for Costs of Proceeding. Petitions for reinstatement under this rule shall be accompanied by an advance cost deposit in an amount to be set by the

Court to cover anticipated costs of the reinstatement proceeding.

(f) Conditions of Reinstatement. If the petitioner is found unfit to resume the practice of law, the petition shall be dismissed. If the petitioner is found fit to resume the practice of law, the judgment shall reinstate him or her, provided that the judgment may make reinstatement conditional upon the payment of all or part of the costs of the proceedings and upon the making of partial or complete restitution to parties harmed by the petitioner whose conduct led to the suspension or disbarment. If the petitioner has been suspended or disbarred for five years or more, reinstatement may be conditioned, in the discretion of the judge or judges before whom the matter is heard, upon the furnishing of proof of competency and learning in the law, which proof may include certification by the bar examiners of a state or other jurisdiction of the attorney's successful completion of an examination for admission to practice subsequent to the date of suspension or disbarment.

(g) Successive Petitions. No petition for reinstatement under this rule shall be filed within one year following an adverse judgment upon a petition for reinstatement filed by or on behalf of the same person.

[Effective March 1, 1999. Amended effective July 1, 2003; December 1, 2009.]

RULE 83.5. AUDIO–VISUAL REPRODUCTIONS OF JUDICIAL PROCEEDINGS PROHIBITED

(See Fed. R. Crim. P. 53; 18 U.S.C. § 1508; 7th Cir. R. 55)

Unless otherwise authorized by Order of this Court, the taking of photographs, sound recordings (except by the official court reporters in the performance of their duties), and broadcasting by radio, television, or other means, in connection with any judicial proceeding on or from the same floor on which a courtroom is located is prohibited.

[Effective March 1, 1999. Amended effective July 1, 2003. Renumbered and amended effective December 1, 2009.]

RULE 83.6. FAIR TRIAL, FREE PRESS

(See Fed. R. Crim. P. 6, 12.1, 16, 32, 53; 18 U.S.C. § 3322; 28 U.S.C. §§ 566, 751, 753, 755, 956)

(a) Duties of Lawyers. It is the duty of the lawyer not to release or authorize the release of information or opinion for dissemination by any means of public communication, in connection with pending or imminent criminal litigation with which he or she is associated, if there is a reasonable likelihood that such dissemination will interfere with a fair trial or otherwise prejudice the due administration of justice. With respect to a grand jury or other pending investigation of any criminal matter, a lawyer participating in the investigation shall refrain from making any extrajudicial statement for dissemination by any means of public communication that goes beyond the public record or that is not necessary to inform the public that the investigation is underway, to describe the general scope of the investigation, to obtain assistance in the apprehension of a suspect, to warn the public of any dangers, or otherwise to aid in the investigation.

From the time of arrest, issuance of an arrest warrant, or the filing of a complaint, information, or indictment in any criminal matter until the commencement of trial or disposition without trial, a lawyer associated with the prosecution or defense shall not release or authorize the release of any extrajudicial statement for dissemination by any means of public communication relating to that matter and concerning:

(1) the prior criminal record (including arrests, indictments, or other charges of crime) or the character or reputation of the accused, except that the lawyer may make a factual statement of the accused's name, age, residence, occupation, and family status, and if the accused has not been apprehended, a lawyer associated with the prosecution may release any information necessary to aid in his or her apprehension or to warn the public of any dangers he or she may present;

(2) the existence or contents of any confession, admission, or statement given by the accused, or the refusal or failure of the accused to make any statement;

(3) the performance of any examinations or tests or the accused's refusal or failure to submit to an examination or test;

(4) the identity, testimony, or credibility of prospective witnesses, except that the lawyer may announce the identity of the victim if the announcement is not otherwise prohibited by law;

(5) the possibility of a plea of guilty or innocence or as to the merits of the case or the evidence in the case; or

(6) any opinion as to the accused's guilt or innocence or as to the merits of the case or the evidence in the case.

A lawyer may inform the public of developments in a case such as indictments and arrests, and communicate to the public the particulars of such matters. Additionally, a lawyer may inform the public that a hearing or trial has been scheduled and that his or her client pleads not guilty. During the trial of any criminal matter, including the period of selection of the jury, no lawyer associated with the prosecution or defense shall give or authorize any extrajudicial statement or interview relating to the trial or the parties or issues in the trial for dissemination by any means of public communication, except that the lawyer may quote from, or refer without comment to, public records in the case.

After the completion of a trial or disposition without trial of any criminal matter and prior to the imposition of sentence, a lawyer associated with the prosecution or defense shall refrain from making or authorizing any extrajudicial statement for dissemination by any means of public communication if there is a reasonable likelihood that such dissemination will affect the imposition of sentence.

Nothing in this rule is intended to preclude the formulation or application of more restrictive rules relating to the release of information about juvenile or other offenders, to preclude the holding of hearings or the lawful issuance of reports by legislative, administrative, or investigative bodies, or to preclude any lawyer from replying to charges of misconduct that are publicly made against him or her.

(b) Duties of Court Personnel. No personnel connected in any way with this Court or its operation, including, among others, marshals, deputy marshals, deputy clerks, bailiffs, secretaries, and court reporters, shall disclose to any person, without specific authorization by the presiding judge, any information relating to a pending criminal or civil case that is not a part of the public record. This prohibition applies specifically to the divulgence of information concerning arguments and hearings held in chambers or otherwise outside the presence of the public.

(c) Special Order in Certain Cases. In a widely publicized or sensational case, the Court, on motion of either party or on its own motion, may issue a special order governing such matters as extrajudicial statements by parties and witnesses which might interfere with the rights of the accused to a fair trial by an impartial jury, the seating and conduct in the courtroom of spectators and news media representatives, the management and sequestration of jurors and witnesses, and any other matters which the Court may deem appropriate for inclusion in such an order.

(d) Specific Directives or Orders of the Court May Include:

(1) directives regarding the clearing of entrances to and hallways in a courthouse and respecting the management of the jury and witnesses during the course of the trial to avoid their mingling with or being in the proximity of reporters, photographers, parties, lawyers, and others, both in entering and leaving the courtroom and courthouse, and during recesses in the trial;

(2) a specific directive that the jurors refrain from reading, listening to, or watching news reports concerning the case, and that they similarly refrain from discussing the case with anyone during the trial and

from communicating with others in any manner during their deliberations;

(3) sequestration of the jury on motion of any party or the Court, without disclosure of the identity of the movant;

(4) directive that the names and addresses of the jurors or prospective jurors not be publicly released, except as required by statute, and that no photographs be taken or sketch made of any juror within the environs of the Court;

(5) insulation of witnesses from news interviews during the trial period; and

(6) specific provisions regarding the seating of spectators and representatives of news media.

[Effective March 1, 1999. Amended effective July 1, 2003. Renumbered and amended effective December 1, 2009.]

RULE 83.7.   DEATH PENALTY CASES

(*See* 28 U.S.C. § 2261, et seq.)

(a) Operation, Scope, and Priority.

(1) This rule applies to post-conviction proceedings in all cases involving persons under sentence of capital punishment.

(2) The District Judge to whom a case is assigned will handle all matters pertaining to the case, including certificates of appealability, stays of execution, consideration of the merits, second or successive petitions when authorized by the Court of Appeals under 28 U.S.C. §§ 2244(b)(3), 2255 ¶8, remands from the Court of Appeals or Supreme Court of the United States, and associated procedural matters. This rule does not limit a District Judge's discretion to designate a Magistrate Judge, under 28 U.S.C. § 636, to perform appropriate tasks. An emergency judge may act when the designated District Judge is unavailable.

(3) The District Judge must give priority to cases within the scope of this rule, using the time limitations in 28 U.S.C. § 2266(b) as a guideline when that section is not directly applicable.

(4) The District Judge may make changes in the procedures established by this rule when justice so requires.

(b) Notices and Required Documents.

(1) A petition or motion within the scope of this rule must:

(A) include all possible grounds for relief;

(B) inform the Court of the execution date, if one has been set; and

(C) in an action under 28 U.S.C. § 2254, inform the Court how each issue raised was presented to the state tribunal and, if it was not presented, why the contention nonetheless should be treated as (i) exhausted, and (ii) not forfeited.

(2) As soon as a case is assigned to a District Judge, the Clerk of Court must notify by telephone the District Judge, counsel for the parties, and the representatives designated under the next subsection. The Clerk of Court also must inform counsel of the appropriate procedures and telephone numbers for emergency after-hours motions.

(3) The Attorney General of states with persons under sentence of death and the United States Attorneys of districts with persons under sentence of death must designate representatives to receive notices in capital cases in addition to, or in lieu of, the government's assigned counsel, and must keep the Court informed about the office and home telephone numbers of the designated representatives.

(4) The Clerk of Court in the district court must notify the Clerk of Court in the Seventh Circuit Court of Appeals of the filing of a case within the scope of this rule, of any substantial development in the case, and of the filing of a notice of appeal. In all cases within the scope of this rule, the Clerk of Court in the district court must immediately transmit the record to the Court of Appeals following the filing of a notice of appeal. A supplemental record may be sent later if items are not currently available.

(5) Promptly after the filing of a case within the scope of this rule, the Clerk of Court must furnish to petitioner or movant a copy of this rule, together with copies of Federal Rule of Appellate Procedure 22 and Seventh Circuit Rules 22 and 22.2.

(6) In all cases within the scope of this rule, the petitioner or movant must file, within **10 days** after filing the petition or motion, legible copies of the documents listed below:

(A) copies of all state or federal court opinions, memorandum decisions, orders (if a decision or opinion has been published, a citation may be supplied in lieu of a copy), transcripts of oral statements of reasons, and judgments involving any issue presented by the petition or motion, whether these decisions or opinions were rendered by trial or appellate courts, on direct or collateral review;

(B) copies of prior petitions or motions filed in state or federal court challenging the same conviction or sentence;

(C) if a prior petition has been filed in federal court, either (i) a copy of an Order issued by the Court of Appeals under 28 U.S.C. § 2244(b)(3) or § 2255 ¶8 permitting a second or successive collateral attack, or (ii) an explanation why prior approval of the Court of Appeals is not required; and

(D) any other documents that the presiding judge requests.

If a required document is not filed, the petitioner or movant must explain the omission to the Court.

(c) Preliminary Consideration.

(1) The District Judge will promptly examine a petition or motion within the scope of this rule and, if appropriate, order the respondent to file an answer or other pleading or take such other action as he or she deems appropriate.

(2) If the District Judge determines that the petition or motion is a second or successive collateral attack for which prior approval of the Court of Appeals was required but not obtained, he or she will immediately dismiss the case for want of jurisdiction.

(3) If the Court of Appeals granted leave to file a second or successive collateral attack, the District Judge must promptly determine in writing whether 28 U.S.C. § 2244(b)(4) has been satisfied.

(d) Appointment of Counsel. Pursuant to 18 U.S.C. § 3006A, 21 U.S.C. § 848(q), 28 U.S.C. § 2254(h), and 28 U.S.C. § 2255 ¶7, counsel will be appointed for any person under a sentence of death who is financially unable to obtain representation, requests that counsel be appointed, and does not already have counsel appointed by a state under 28 U.S.C. § 2261.

(e) Stay of Execution.

(1) A stay of execution is granted automatically in some cases and forbidden in others by 28 U.S.C. § 2262. All requests with respect to stays of execution over which the Court possesses discretion, or in which any party contends that § 2262 has not been followed, must be made by motion under this rule.

(2) Parties must endeavor to file motions with the Court in writing and during normal business hours. Parties having emergency motions during nonbusiness hours must proceed as instructed under part(b)(2).

(3) A motion must be accompanied by legible copies of the documents required by part (b)(6), unless these documents have already been filed with the Clerk of Court or the movant supplies a reason for their omission. If the reason is lack of time to obtain or file the documents, then the movant must furnish them as soon as possible.

(4) If the attorney for the government has no objection to the motion for stay, the Court must enter an order staying the execution.

(5) If the District Judge concludes that an initial petition or motion is not frivolous, a stay of execution must be granted.

(6) An order granting or denying a stay of execution must be accompanied by a statement of the reasons for the decision.

(7) If the District Court denies relief on the merits and an appeal is taken, then:

(A) if the Judge denies a certificate of appealability, any previously issued stay must be vacated, and no new stay of execution may be entered; but

(B) if the Judge issues a certificate of appealability, a stay of execution pending appeal must be granted.

(f) List of Cases. The Clerk of Court will maintain a list of cases within the scope of this rule.

[Effective March 1, 1999. Amended effective July 1, 2003. Renumbered and amended effective December 1, 2009.]

APPENDIX A.   CRIMINAL RULES

CR32.1.   CONFIDENTIAL PROBATION RECORDS

(*See* **Fed. R. Crim. P. 32; 18 U.S.C. § 3552**)

(a) Presentence Interview. The attorney for defendant will receive notice and a reasonable opportunity to attend any presentence investigation interview by the probation officer with defendant. Defense counsel has the burden of responding as promptly as possible to enable timely completion of the presentence report. If an undue delay is caused by defense counsel's unavailability, the probation officer will consult with the Court about proceeding with the interview without counsel.

(b) Presentence Report. The presentence report shall be mailed or otherwise provided to defendant's attorney and the attorney for the government at least **35 days** prior to the sentencing hearing in accordance with Federal Rule of Criminal Procedure 32. Defendant may waive the 35 day disclosure rule. The attorney for the government, attorney for defendant, and defendant shall acknowledge receipt of the presentence report on the Probation Form which is provided with the presentence report. The parties shall indicate whether the report is acceptable or that there are objections to the report. The Probation Form shall be filed with the Clerk of Court within **14 days** after receiving the presentence report. The Clerk of Court will provide a file-marked copy to the Probation Office.

Either party wishing to file objections to the presentence report must do so with the Clerk of Court within **14 days** after receiving the presentence report. The party filing objections must provide a copy to the Probation Office and opposing party. All responses to the objections must be served on the opposing party and the Probation Office within **7 days** of receipt of objections unless directed otherwise by the Court. The probation officer must submit the presentence report to the Court no later than **7 days** prior to disposition. The probation officer will also submit to the Court an addendum setting forth any unresolved objections and the officer's response to the objections. At the same time, the officer will furnish to defendant and counsel for both parties the revisions of the presentence report and the addendum. The probation officer's recommendation shall not be disclosed to either party and shall be sealed separate from the presentence report following disposition.

(c) Stipulation of Facts (Guilty Plea). Counsel for defendant and the attorney for the government may submit a written stipulation of facts pursuant to U.S.C.G. § 6B.1 that accompanies the plea agreement.

(d) Submission of Offense Conduct. The attorney for defendant and the attorney for the government may each file, with the Clerk of Court, a written version of the offense conduct not more than **14 days** after a guilty verdict. Each attorney shall provide a copy of his/her version to opposing counsel and to the Probation Office.

(e) Subpoena of Records and Testimony. When probation records, presentence reports, or testimony by a probation officer are requested by subpoena or other judicial process, the probation officer shall file a petition seeking instruction from the sentencing court for such disclosure. No disclosure will be authorized except upon an order issued by the sentencing court.

[Effective March 1, 1999. Amended effective July 1, 2003; December 1, 2009.]

CR50.1.   DISPOSITION OF CRIMINAL CASES; SPEEDY TRIAL

(*See* **Fed. R. Crim. P. 50; 18 U.S.C. § 3161, et seq.; 18 U.S.C. §§ 5036, 5037**)

The disposition of criminal cases shall be handled and disposed of in accordance with the District's *"Plan for Achieving Prompt Disposition of Criminal Cases."*

The *"Plan for Achieving Prompt Disposition of Criminal Cases,"* also called the Speedy Trial Plan, places special requirements on both the government and defendant regarding time which may be excluded from the time allowed by the Speedy Trial Plan, including an obligation for both parties to review the Clerk of Court's records of excusable time for completeness and accuracy.

The Clerk of Court shall enter judicial determinations of excusable time on the docket and in such other records as the Court may direct.

[Effective March 1, 1999. Amended effective July 1, 2003; December 1, 2009.]

APPENDIX B.   BANKRUPTCY CASES AND PROCEEDINGS

Historical and Statutory Notes

(See 28 U.S.C. § 157, 28 U.S.C. § 158, et seq.; 28 U.S.C. §§ 1334(c), 1452(b), 1412)

Br1001.1.   MATTERS DETERMINED BY THE BANKRUPTCY JUDGES

All cases under Title 11 of the United States Code, and any or all proceedings arising under Title 11 or arising in or related to a case under Title 11, are referred to the Bankruptcy Judge.

It is the intention of this Court that the Bankruptcy Judges be given the broadest possible authority to administer cases properly within their jurisdiction, and this rule shall be interpreted to achieve this end.

Motions for abstention, 28 U.S.C. § 1334(c); remand, 28 U.S.C. § 1452(b); transfer of venue, 28 U.S.C. § 157(b)(5); change of venue, 28 U.S.C. § 1412; withdrawal of reference, 28 U.S.C. § 157(d); and removal of cases under 28 U.S.C. § 1452(a) shall be filed with the Clerk of the Bankruptcy Court.

[Effective March 1, 1999. Amended effective January 1, 2000; July 1, 2003; December 1, 2009.]

Br9015.1.   JURY TRIAL

If the right to a jury trial applies in a proceeding that may be heard under Section 157 of Title 28, United States Code, by a Bankruptcy Judge, the Bankruptcy Judge for the Southern District of Illinois, as well as those Bankruptcy Judges sitting in this district by designation of the Circuit Council, are hereby specially designated to exercise such jurisdiction.

[Effective March 1, 1999. Amended effective July 1, 2003; December 1, 2009.]

Br9029.1.   ADOPTION OF LOCAL BANKRUPTCY RULES

The rules governing practice and procedure in all cases and proceedings within the District Court's bankruptcy jurisdiction shall be the Local Rules of the United States Bankruptcy Court for the Southern District of Illinois, adopted by Administrative Order in the District Court on February 1, 1989, in their present form or as amended or supplemented by the United States Bankruptcy Court in this District.

[Effective March 1, 1999. Amended effective July 1, 2003; December 1, 2009.]

ELECTRONIC FILING RULES

RULE 1.   SCOPE OF ELECTRONIC FILING

All cases, civil and criminal, are assigned to the Electronic Case Filing (ECF) system. Attorneys must utilize the ECF system, unless specifically exempted by the court for good cause shown. Pro se filers may, but do not have to, utilize the ECF system. Pro se filers who do not utilize the ECF system shall file all documents with the Clerk of Court by U.S. Mail or personal delivery to the Clerk's Office.

[Effective January 20, 2004.]

RULE 2.   ELIGIBILITY, REGISTRATION, PASSWORDS

Attorneys admitted to the bar of this court, including those admitted pro hac vice and attorneys authorized to represent the United States, must register as Filing Users of the court's ECF system or move for exemption. Registration is in a form prescribed by the clerk and requires the Filing User's name, address, telephone number, e-mail address, and a declaration that the attorney is admitted to the bar of this court. Registrants will be provided training. The ECF User's Manual is available at all times at www.ilsd.uscourts. gov.

No Filing User or other person may knowingly permit or cause to permit a Filing User's password to be used by anyone other than an authorized agent of the Filing User.

If the court permits, a party to a pending civil action who is not represented by an attorney may register as a Filing User in the ECF system solely for purposes of the action. Registration is in a form prescribed by the clerk and requires identification of the action as well as the name, address, telephone number, and e-mail address of the party. If, during the course of the action, the party retains an attorney who appears on the party's behalf, the attorney must advise the clerk to terminate the party's registration as a Filing User upon the attorney's appearance.

Provided that a Filing User has an internet e-mail address, registration as a Filing User constitutes consent to electronic service of all documents as provided in these rules in accordance with the Federal Rules of Civil Procedure and the Federal Rules of Criminal Procedure.

Once registration is completed, the Filing User will receive notification of the user log in and password. Filing Users agree to protect the security of their passwords and immediately notify the clerk if they learn that their password has been compromised. Users may be subject to sanctions for failure to comply with this provision.

[Effective January 20, 2004.]

RULE 3. CONSEQUENCES OF ELECTRONIC FILING

Electronic transmission of a document to the ECF system consistent with these rules, together with the transmission of a "Notice of Electronic Filing" from the court, constitutes filing of the document for all purposes of the Federal Rules of Civil Procedure, Federal Rules of Criminal Procedure, and the local rules of this court, and constitutes entry of the document on the docket kept by the clerk under Federal Rules of Civil Procedure 58 and 79 and Federal Rules of Criminal Procedure 49 and 55.

When a document has been filed electronically, the official record is the electronic recording of the document as stored by the court, and the filing party is bound by the document as filed. Except in the case of documents first filed in paper form and subsequently submitted electronically under Rule 1, a document filed electronically is deemed filed at the date and time stated on the "Notice of Electronic Filing" from the court.

Filing a document electronically does not alter the filing deadline for that document. Filing must be completed before midnight local time where the court is located in order to be considered timely filed that day, unless a specific time is set by the court. Pursuant to Federal Rule of Civil Procedure 6(e) and Federal Rule of Criminal Procedure 45(c), whenever something is served electronically, three days are added to the prescribed response period.

The filer is responsible for calculating the response time under the federal and/or local rules. The date generated by CM/ECF is a guideline only, and, if the Court has ordered the response to be filed on a date certain, the Court's order governs the response deadline.

[Effective January 20, 2004; revised effective September 9, 2010.]

RULE 4. ENTRY OF COURT ORDERS

All orders, judgments, minute entries, and notices filed in accordance with these rules will constitute entry on the docket kept by the clerk under Federal Rules of Civil Procedure 58 and 79 and Federal Rules of Criminal Procedure 49 and 55. Text-only entries on the docket, without an attached document, are official

and binding. Any order or other court-issued document filed electronically without the original signature of a judge or clerk has the same force and effect as if the judge or clerk had signed a paper copy of the document, and it had been entered on the docket in a conventional manner.

[Effective January 20, 2004.]

RULE 5. ATTACHMENTS, EXHIBITS, AND MAXIMUM SIZE OF FILINGS

All documents must be electronically filed. If the document exceeds 5.0 Mb (5120 Kb), then it must be divided into segments, with the first segment being the main document and all subsequent segments as attachments to the main document. Each segment should not exceed 5.0 Mb.

Service shall comport with Electronic Filing Rule 9.

[Effective January 20, 2004; Amended effective April 30, 2004; September 15, 2007.]

RULE 6. SEALED DOCUMENTS

When the court has ordered or otherwise allowed a document to be filed under seal, or when the law requires a document to be sealed (e.g., 18 U.S.C. § 3509(d); Fed. R. Crim. P. 6(e)), the document shall be electronically filed. The sealed PDF document must be attached to the event. Filing Users must bear ultimate responsibility for ensuring that information is properly redacted and/or sealed.

[Effective January 20, 2004; Amended effective April 30, 2004; April 30, 2006. Amended effective November 14, 2012.]

RULE 7. RETENTION REQUIREMENTS

Manually signed original documents scanned into the system by the attorney or party must be maintained by the filer for 5 years after final resolution of the action, including final disposition of all appeals. The original hard copy must be produced at any time when ordered by the court.

[Effective April 30, 2006. Amended effective September 2007; revised effective September 9, 2010.]

RULE 8. SIGNATURE

Upon registration, Filing Users automatically endorse their electronic signature for purposes of Federal Rule of Civil Procedure 11 specifically, the Federal Rules of Civil Procedure and the Federal Rules of Criminal Procedure generally, and the local rules. The Filing User's electronic signature also serves as a valid signature for purposes of unsworn declarations pursuant to 28 U.S.C. § 1746, service and filing pursuant to Federal Rule of Civil Procedure 5 and Federal

Rule of Criminal Procedure 49, and establishing perjury pursuant to 18 U.S.C. §§ 1621–1623. The "s/" name on the document and the filer's login ID must be the same or the document will be stricken.

[Effective January 20, 2004; redesignated effective April 30, 2006. Amended effective September 2007.]

RULE 9. SERVICE OF DOCUMENTS BY ELECTRONIC MEANS

All electronically filed documents, attachments, and exhibits should include a certificate of service in accordance with the Federal Rules of Civil Procedure, Federal Rules of Criminal Procedure, and local rules. Electronic service of the "Notice of Electronic Filing" constitutes service of the filed document and satisfies the certificate of service requirement, unless the filing party has actual knowledge of a technical failure resulting in non-receipt of a document.

A paper copy of any electronically filed document should be served upon attorneys who are exempted from utilizing the Electronic Case Filing system, as set out in Electronic Filing Rule 1, and pro se users not registered for electronic service. Service of any conventionally filed document must be made according to the Federal Rules of Civil Procedure, Federal Rules of Criminal Procedure, and local rules, and a certificate of service must be included on the document, indicating the manner in which each party was served.

[Effective January 20, 2004; Amended effective April 30, 2004; redesignated effective April 30, 2006; revised effective September 9, 2010.]

RULE 10. NOTICE OF COURT ORDERS AND JUDGMENTS

Immediately upon the entry of an order, judgment, minute entry, or notice in an action assigned to the ECF system, the clerk will transmit to Filing Users in the case, in electronic form, a "Notice of Electronic Filing." Electronic transmission of the "Notice of Electronic Filing" constitutes the notice required by Federal Rule of Civil Procedure 77(d) and Federal Rule of Criminal Procedure 49(c).

[Effective January 20, 2004; Amended effective April 30, 2004; redesignated effective April 30, 2006.]

RULE 11. TECHNICAL FAILURES

A Filing User whose filing is made untimely as the result of a technical failure may move for appropriate relief from the court. Technical failures cannot extend jurisdictional deadlines. Problems on the filer's end such as phone line problems, problems with the filer's Internet Service Provider (ISP), or hardware/software problems do not constitute a technical

failure or excuse an untimely filing. If a party misses a filing deadline because of such problems, a motion for leave to file *instanter*, accompanied by a signed Declaration stating the reason for missing the deadline, must be filed no later than 12:00 noon of the first day on which the Court is open for business following the original filing deadline. The Court will consider the matters stated in the declaration and order appropriate relief.

[Effective January 20, 2004; redesignated effective April 30, 2006; revised effective September 9, 2010.]

RULE 12. PUBLIC ACCESS AND FEES

A person may review at the Clerk's Office filings that have not been sealed by the court. A person may also access the ECF system at the court's Internet site https://www.ilsd.uscourts.gov/cmecf by obtaining a PACER log in and password. A person who has PACER access may retrieve docket sheets in civil and criminal cases and documents in all civil cases except social security cases and sealed cases. Only counsel of record may retrieve documents in social security cases and sealed cases.

Upon receipt of a "Notice of Electronic Filing," any Filing User will have one opportunity by way of a hyperlink to view and either print or download the document for free. Filing Users who already have electronically accessed a document once will be charged a per page fee from PACER.

[Effective January 20, 2004; redesignated and amended effective April 30, 2006. Amended effective September 2007.]

RULE 13. HYPERLINKS

Electronically filed documents may contain the following types of hyperlinks:

    1. Hyperlinks to other portions of the same document; and

    2. Hyperlinks to a location on the Internet that contains a source document for citation.

Hyperlinks to cited authority may not replace standard citation format. Complete citations must be included in the text of the filed document. Neither hyperlinks, nor any site to which it refers, shall be considered part of the record. Hyperlinks are simply convenient mechanics for accessing material cited in a filed document.

The court accepts no responsibility for, and does not endorse, any product, organization, or content at any hyperlinked site, or at any site to which that site may be linked. The court accepts no responsibility for the availability of any hyperlink.

[Effective April 30, 2006.]

FORMS

CERTIFICATE OF SERVICE

UNITED STATES DISTRICT COURT
SOUTHERN DISTRICT OF ILLINOIS

Plaintiff(s)

v.   Case Number:

Defendant(s)

CERTIFICATE OF SERVICE

     I hereby certify that on _____, I electronically filed _____ with the Clerk of Court using the CM/ECF system which will send notification of such filing(s) to the following:

and I hereby certify that on [date], I mailed by United States Postal Service, the document(s) to the following non-registered participants:

                                   Respectfully submitted,

                                   _____

                                   Name of Password Registrant

                                   _____

                                   Address

                                   _____

                                   City, State, Zip
                                   Phone: (__) _____
                                   Fax: (__) _____
                                   E-mail: _____@_____

                                   _____

                                   Attorney bar number (if applicable)

ENTRY OF APPEARANCE

Plaintiff(s)
      v.
Defendant(s)

)
)
) Case Number:
)
)
)

ENTRY OF APPEARANCE

To the Clerk of Court and all parties of record:

  I hereby enter my appearance as counsel for

DATED:

_____

Signature

_____

Name

_____

Address

_____

Phone Number

_____

Fax Number

_____

E–Mail Address

[Revised effective July, 2003; December 1, 2009; February 2011.]

625

UNIFORM TRIAL PRACTICE AND PROCEDURES
IN THE UNITED STATES DISTRICT COURT
FOR THE SOUTHERN DISTRICT OF ILLINOIS

	)	
	)	
Plaintiff(s),	)	
	)	
vs.	)	CIVIL NO.
	)	
	)	CJRA TRACK:
	)	PRESUMPTIVE TRIAL MONTH:
Defendant(s).	)	JUDGE:

UNIFORM TRIAL PRACTICE AND PROCEDURES

In conformity with the Civil Justice Reform Act of 1990 and in compliance with the Civil Justice Expenses and Delay Reduction Plan adopted by this Court, the following uniform procedures will apply to all civil cases filed in the Southern District of Illinois.

Scheduling Practice

Trial settings and other scheduling will vary depending on the track classification which was assigned to the case at the time of filing by the trial judge to whom the case is assigned. There are four tracks: "A," "B," "C," and "D." "A" cases are set for trial between 8–10 months after the date of first appearance of a defendant or the default date; "B" cases 11–14 months after the date of first appearance of a defendant or the default date; "C" cases 15–18 months after the date of first appearance of a defendant or the default date; and "D" cases 19–24 months after the date of first appearance of a defendant or the default date.

Except in cases exempted under SDIL–LR 26.1(a), the attorneys (and any unrepresented parties) must meet in accordance with SDIL–LR 16.2(a) at least **21 days** before any scheduling conference set by the Court to candidly discuss the issues in the case and potential discovery needs. Fed. R. Civ. P. 26(f). Within **14 days** after this meeting, and at least **7 days** before the date of the scheduling conference, the participants must submit a Joint Report of the Parties and Proposed Scheduling Order to the Magistrate Judge.

All track "B," "C," and "D" cases will be set for a scheduling and discovery conference before a Magistrate Judge within **40 days** after the track has been set by the District Judge. The scheduling conference may be canceled at the discretion of the Court following receipt of the Joint Report of the Parties regarding their initial meeting. The Magistrate Judge may approve the parties' Joint Report of Parties and Proposed Scheduling and Discovery Order, or enter a separate scheduling order, as circumstances require.

A final pretrial conference will be held by the trial judge at least **7 days** prior to the first day of the presumptive trial month. The parties shall confer and jointly submit a Final Pretrial Order **3 days** before the date of the final pretrial conference unless otherwise directed by the presiding judge.

Disclosures and Discovery Practice

Except in cases exempted under SDIL–LR 26.1, the parties shall comply with the initial disclosure requirements of Federal Rule of Civil Procedure 26(a). These disclosures must be supplemented by the parties, depending on the nature of the case and any limitations placed on discovery at the scheduling conference. The disclosures and supplementation are not to be filed with the Clerk of Court.

A party may not seek discovery from another source until: (a) the party seeking discovery has made its initial disclosures as required by Federal Rule of Civil Procedure 26(a), and, further, (b) the parties have met and conferred as required by SDIL–LR 16.2(a).

A party may not seek discovery from another party before such disclosures have been made by, or are due from, such other party. The cut-off date for all discovery, including experts and third parties, shall not be later than **115 days** prior to the first day of the month of the presumptive trial date. Disclosure of experts and discovery with reference to experts and other discovery dates will be set according to the Joint Report of the Parties following their initial meeting or at the scheduling and discovery conference before the Magistrate Judge.

Motion Practice

Motions to remand, to dismiss, for judgment on the pleadings, for summary judgment, and all post-trial motions shall be supported by a brief and filed with the Clerk of Court. Any adverse party shall have **30 days** after the service of the movant's brief in which to file and serve an answering brief.

Briefs shall be no longer than 20 double-spaced typewritten pages, 12 point font. Reply briefs, if any, shall be filed within **14 days** of the service of a response and shall be no longer than **5 pages**. Such briefs are not favored and should be filed only in exceptional circumstances. Under no circumstances will sur-reply briefs be accepted. If a party believes it is necessary to supplement its brief with new authority due to a change in the law or the facts that occurred after the filing of its brief, the party must seek leave of court to file a supplemental brief. The supplemental authority shall be filed in accordance with the supplemental authority provisions found in Federal Rule of Appellate Procedure 28(j).

For all motions other than those listed above, a supporting brief is not required. A party opposing such a motion shall have **14 days** after service to file a written response. Failure to file a timely response to a motion may, in the Court's discretion, be considered an admission of the merits of the motion. A reply, if any, shall be filed within **7 days** of the service of the response.

A party may not schedule or notice a hearing or oral argument on a pending motion. Any party desiring oral argument on a motion shall file a formal motion and state the reason why oral argument is requested. Any motion may be either (1) scheduled by the Court for oral argument at a specified time; (2) scheduled for determination by telephone conference call; (3) referred to a United States Magistrate Judge for determination or recommendation; or (4) determined upon the pleadings and the motions without benefit of oral argument.

FOR THE COURT:

NANCY J. ROSENSTENGEL,
CLERK OF COURT

[Revised effective July 1, 2003; December 1, 2009.]

NOTICE TO COUNSEL
IN THE UNITED STATES DISTRICT COURT
FOR THE SOUTHERN DISTRICT OF ILLINOIS

Plaintiff(s),)	
)	
vs.)	**CIVIL NO.**
)	
)	**CJRA TRACK:**
)	**PRESUMPTIVE TRIAL MONTH:**
Defendant(s).)	**JUDGE:**

NOTICE TO COUNSEL

Pursuant to SDIL–LR 16.1, the above-styled cause has been assigned as a "Track
_____" case. Therefore, you are hereby placed on notice that a presumptive
trial month has been set as indicated above. Pursuant to SDIL–LR 16.2(a) and
Federal Rule of Civil Procedure 26(f), an initial pretrial scheduling and discovery
conference is hereby set before:

Honorable _____,

Courtroom _____,

Date and Time _____.

The purposes of this conference are:

(1) To discuss the Joint Report of the Parties as to the proposed discovery plan;

(2) To discuss the possibility of settlement;

(3) To discuss the possibility of using a voluntary alternative dispute resolution
device (e.g., mediation, arbitration, summary jury trial, mini-trial) to resolve
the dispute;

(4) To discuss the complexity of the case and, if it is tried, the approximate
number of days necessary to complete the testimony;

(5) To confirm the presumptive date for the trial (see SDIL–LR 16.1(a));

(6) To set a cut-off date for completion of all discovery including experts'
discovery (or in the case of extraordinarily complex cases, the cut-off date for
completion of core discovery), which date shall be no later than **115 days**
before the first day of the month of the presumptive trial date;

(7) To establish a plan for the management of discovery in the case, including any
limitations on the use of the various discovery devices that may be agreed to
by the parties or ordered by the judicial officer presiding over the conference;

(8) To formulate, simplify, and narrow the issues;

(9) To discuss and set deadlines for amendments to the pleadings, including the
filing of third-party complaints, which deadline shall be no later than **90 days**
following this conference;

(10) To discuss the filing of potential motions and a schedule for their disposition,
including the cut-off date for filing dispositive motions;

(11) To set the approximate date of the settlement conference (see SDIL–LR
16.3(b));

(12) To set the approximate date of the final pretrial conference (see SDIL–LR
16.2(b));

(13) To consider the advisability of referring various matters to a Magistrate Judge or a Special Master;

(14) To discuss the advisability of one or more additional case management conferences prior to the final pretrial conference; and

(15) To cover any other procedural issues that the judicial officer hearing the case determines to be appropriate for the fair and efficient management of the litigation.

The Joint Report of Parties and Proposed Scheduling and Discovery Order, consented to and signed by each party or by an attorney of record, at the discretion of the assigned judicial officer, may be deemed to satisfy the requirements of SDIL–LR 16.2(a). All actions taken at the initial pretrial scheduling and discovery conference will be incorporated into a pretrial scheduling and discovery order, which shall be modified only by Order of Court.

The scheduling and discovery conference may, at the discretion of the Magistrate Judge, be canceled if the Magistrate Judge approves the parties' Joint Report of Parties and Proposed Scheduling and Discovery Order as submitted.

DATED:

NANCY J. ROSENSTENGEL,

CLERK

By: _____

Deputy Clerk

[Revised effective December 1, 2009.]

JOINT REPORT OF PARTIES AND PROPOSED
SCHEDULING AND DISCOVERY ORDER

IN THE UNITED STATES DISTRICT COURT
FOR THE SOUTHERN DISTRICT OF ILLINOIS

	)	
	)	
Plaintiff(s),	)	
	)	
vs.	)	**CIVIL NO.**
	)	
	)	**CJRA TRACK:**
	)	**PRESUMPTIVE TRIAL MONTH:**
Defendant(s).	)	**JUDGE:**

JOINT REPORT OF PARTIES AND PROPOSED
SCHEDULING AND DISCOVERY ORDER

Pursuant to Federal Rule of Civil Procedure 26(f) and SDIL–LR 16.2(a), an initial conference of the parties was held on _____ with attorneys and/or unrepresented parties _____ _____ participating.

SCHEDULING AND DISCOVERY PLANS WERE DISCUSSED AND AGREED TO AS FOLLOWS:

1. Initial interrogatories and requests to produce, pursuant to Federal Rules of Civil Procedure 33 and 34 shall be served on opposing parties by _____.

2. Plaintiff's deposition shall be taken by _____.

3. Defendant's deposition shall be taken by _____.

4. Motions to amend the pleadings, including the commencement of a third party action, shall be filed by _____ (which date shall be no later than **90 days** following the Scheduling and Discovery conference).

5. Expert witnesses shall be disclosed, along with a written report prepared and signed by the witness pursuant to Federal Rule of Civil Procedure 26(a)(2), as follows:
    Plaintiff's expert(s): _____.
    Defendant's expert(s): _____.
    Third Party expert(s): _____.

6. Depositions of expert witnesses must be taken by:
    Plaintiff's expert(s): _____.
    Defendant's expert(s): _____.
    Third Party expert(s): _____.

7. **Discovery** shall be completed by _____ (which date shall be no later than **115 days** before the first day of the month of the presumptive trial month). Any written interrogatories or request for production served after the date of the Scheduling and Discovery Order shall be served by a date that allows the served parties the full **30 days** as provided by the Federal Rules of Civil Procedure in which to answer or produce by the discovery cut-off date.

8. All **dispositive motions** shall be filed by _____ (which date shall be no later than **100 days** before the first day of the month of the presumptive trial month). Dispositive motions filed after this date will not be considered by the Court.

9. The Scheduling and Discovery Conference may, at the discretion of the Magistrate Judge, be canceled if the Magistrate Judge approves of the parties' proposed Scheduling and Discovery Order as submitted.

DATED:

_____
Attorney(s) for Plaintiff(s)

_____
Attorney(s) for Defendant(s)

———

IN THE UNITED STATES DISTRICT COURT
FOR THE SOUTHERN DISTRICT OF ILLINOIS

	)	
	)	
Plaintiff,	)	
	)	
vs.	)	**CIVIL NO.**
	)	
	)	**CJRA TRACK:**
	)	**PRESUMPTIVE TRIAL MONTH:**
Defendant.	)	**JUDGE:**

SCHEDULING AND DISCOVERY ORDER

Depositions upon oral examination, interrogatories, request for documents, and answers and responses thereto shall not be filed unless on Order of the Court. Disclosures or discovery under Rule 26(a) of the Federal Rules of Civil Procedure are to be filed with the Court only to the extent required by the final pretrial order, other order of the Court, or if a dispute arises over the disclosure or discovery.

Having reviewed the Report of the Parties and finding that the parties have complied with the requirements of Federal Rule of Civil Procedure 26(f) and SDIL–LR 16.2(a), the Court hereby approves and enters the Proposed Scheduling and Discovery Order as submitted by the parties/as modified at the Pretrial Scheduling and Discovery Conference.

A. A settlement conference is set before _____ in accordance with SDIL–LR 16.3(b) on _____ at _____ in _____.

B. A final pretrial conference is set for _____ at _____ before the trial judge in accordance with SDIL–LR16.2(b).

As initially set by the Court, the presumptive trial month is _____.

IT IS SO ORDERED.

DATED:

_____
United States Magistrate Judge

[Revised effective December 1, 2009.]

JOINT REPORT OF THE PARTIES AND PROPOSED SCHEDULING AND DISCOVERY ORDER
(CLASS ACTION)

**IN THE UNITED STATES DISTRICT COURT FOR
THE SOUTHERN DISTRICT OF ILLINOIS**

	)	
	)	
Plaintiff,	)	
	)	
vs.	)	CIVIL NO.
	)	
	)	CJRA TRACK:
	)	PRESUMPTIVE TRIAL MONTH:
Defendant.	)	JUDGE:

JOINT REPORT OF THE PARTIES AND PROPOSED SCHEDULING
AND DISCOVERY ORDER (CLASS ACTION)

Pursuant to Federal Rule of Civil Procedure 26(f), SDIL–LR 26.1, and SDIL–LR 23.1, an initial conference of the parties was held on _____ with attorneys _____ participating.

SCHEDULING AND DISCOVERY PLANS WERE DISCUSSED AND AGREED TO AS FOLLOWS:

1. Discovery prior to Class Certification must be sufficient to permit the Court to determine whether the requirements of Federal Rule of Civil Procedure 23 are satisfied, including a preliminary inquiry into the merits of the case to ensure appropriate management of the case as a Class Action. In order to ensure that a Class Certification decision be issued as soon as practicable, however, priority shall be given to discovery on class issues. Once Class Certification is decided, the Court may, upon motion of either party, enter a second scheduling and discovery order, if necessary.

2. Initial interrogatories and requests to produce, pursuant to Federal Rules of Civil Procedure 33 and 34 and SDIL–LR 33.1, shall be served on opposing parties by _____.
   Due to the nature of this case, the parties are exempted from compliance with Federal Rules of Civil Procedure 30(a)(2)(A) (10 deposition limit) and 33(a) (25 interrogatory limit).

3. Plaintiff(s)' depositions shall be taken by _____.

4. Defendant(s)' depositions shall be taken by _____.

5. Third Party actions must be commenced by _____.

6. Expert witnesses for Class Certification, if any, shall be disclosed, along with a written report prepared and signed by the witness pursuant to Federal Rule of Civil Procedure 26(a)(2), as follows:
   Plaintiff(s)' expert(s): _____.
   Defendant(s)' expert(s): _____.

7. Depositions of Class Certification expert witnesses must be taken by:
   Plaintiff(s)' expert(s): _____.
   Defendant(s)' expert(s): _____.

8. Plaintiff(s)' Motion for Class Certification and Memorandum in Support shall be filed by _____ and shall not exceed ___ pages.

9. Defendant(s)' Memorandum in Opposition to Class Certification shall be filed by _____ and shall not exceed ___ pages.

10. Plaintiff(s)' Reply Memorandum, if any, must be filed by _____ and shall not exceed ___ pages.

11. The Class Certification hearing will be set by separate notice.

12. Expert witnesses for trial, if any, shall be disclosed, along with a written report prepared and signed by the witness pursuant to Federal Rule of Civil Procedure 26(a)(2), as follows:
Plaintiff(s)' expert(s): _____.
Defendant(s)' expert(s): _____.
Plaintiff(s)' rebuttal expert(s): _____.

13. Depositions of trial expert witnesses must be taken by:
Plaintiff(s)' expert(s): _____.
Defendant(s)' expert(s): _____.
Plaintiff(s)' rebuttal expert(s): _____.

14. All discovery shall be completed by _____ (which date shall be no later than **115 days** before the first day of the presumptive trial month). Any written interrogatories or request for production served after the date set out in the Scheduling and Discovery Order shall be served by a date that allows the served parties the full 30 days as provided by the Federal Rules of Civil Procedure in which to answer or produce by the discovery cut-off date.

15. All dispositive motions shall be filed by _____ (which date shall be no later than **100 days** before the first day of the presumptive trial month). Dispositive motions filed after this date will not be considered by the Court.

DATED:

_____
Attorney(s) for Plaintiff(s)

_____
Attorney(s) for Defendant(s)

_____

IN THE UNITED STATES DISTRICT COURT
FOR THE SOUTHERN DISTRICT OF ILLINOIS

	)	
	)	
Plaintiff,	)	
	)	
vs.	)	**CIVIL NO.**
	)	
	)	**CJRA TRACK:**
	)	**PRESUMPTIVE TRIAL MONTH:**
Defendant.	)	**JUDGE:**

SCHEDULING AND DISCOVERY ORDER (CLASS ACTION)

Depositions upon oral examination, interrogatories, request for documents, and answers and responses thereto shall not be filed unless on order of the Court. Disclosures or discovery under Federal Rule Civil Procedure 26(a) and SDIL–LR 26.1 are to be filed with the Court only to the extent required by the final pretrial order, other order of the Court, or if a dispute arises over the disclosure or discovery. Having reviewed the Report of the Parties and finding that the parties have complied with the requirements of Federal Rule of Civil Procedure 26(f), SDIL–LR 26.1, and SDIL–LR 23.1, the Court hereby approves and enters the Proposed Scheduling and Discovery Order as submitted by the parties/as modified at the Pretrial Scheduling and Discovery Conference.

(　) A settlement conference is set before _____ in accordance with SDIL–LR 16.3(b) on _____ at _____ in _____.

(　) A Class Certification hearing is set for _____ at _____ before the trial judge.

(　) A final pretrial conference is set for _____ at _____ before the trial judge in accordance with SDIL–LR 16.2(b).

(　) As initially set by the Court, the presumptive trial month is _____.

DATED:

_____
United States Magistrate Judge

[Revised effective December 1, 2009.]

INSTRUCTIONS FOR PREPARING FINAL PRETRIAL ORDER

1. Although primary responsibility for the preparation of the Final Pretrial Order lies with plaintiff's attorney, full cooperation and assistance on the part of defendant's attorney is expected and required.

2. The parties are directed to stipulate to the authenticity of exhibits and shall indicate in the Final Pretrial Order those exhibits to which authenticity has not been stipulated and specific reasons why not.

3. The Final Pretrial Order should be submitted to the trial judge 3 days before the date of the Final Pretrial Conference or as otherwise directed by the Court. The parties are encouraged to review the procedures for each judge as outlined on the Court's website.

4. Failure to comply with the substance or intent of these instructions may result in appropriate sanctions pursuant to Federal Rules 16 or 37 and 28 U.S.C. § 1927, among others.

5. The Court greatly appreciates any and all efforts on the part of counsel to be brief and concise in preparing pretrial memoranda and findings of fact and conclusions of law.

[Revised effective December 1, 2009.]

FINAL PRETRIAL ORDER
IN THE UNITED STATES DISTRICT COURT
FOR THE SOUTHERN DISTRICT OF ILLINOIS

	)	
	)	
Plaintiff,	)	
	)	
vs.	)	**CIVIL NO.**
	)	
	)	
	)	**CJRA TRACK:**
	)	**PRESUMPTIVE TRIAL MONTH:**
Defendant.	)	**JUDGE:**

FINAL PRETRIAL ORDER

This matter is before the Court at a Final Pretrial Conference held pursuant to Rule 16 of the Federal Rules of Civil Procedure:

PLAINTIFF(S)' COUNSEL:
(Insert name, address, and telephone number)

DEFENDANT(S)' COUNSEL:
(Insert name, address, and telephone number)

I. NATURE OF THE CASE
The parties should prepare a brief statement of the nature of the case including the claims of the parties (personal injury, Federal Tort claim, breach of contract, etc.). The principal purpose of this statement is to assist the Court in explaining the case to prospective jurors.

II. JURISDICTION
   A.   This is an action for: (State the remedy sought, such as damages, injunctive, or declaratory relief.)

   B.   The jurisdiction of the Court is not disputed (or is disputed).

      1.   If not disputed, state the statutory, constitutional, or other basis of jurisdiction.

      2.   If disputed, the basis on which jurisdiction is contested.

III. UNCONTROVERTED FACTS
The following facts are not disputed or have been agreed to or stipulated to by the parties:

(This section should contain a comprehensive statement of facts which will become a part of the evidentiary record in the case and which, in jury trials, may be read to the jury.)

IV. AGREED TO ISSUES OF LAW
The parties agree that the following are the issues to be decided by the Court:

V. WITNESSES
   A.   List of witnesses plaintiff expects to call, including experts:

      1.   Expert witnesses.

      2.   Non-expert witnesses.

   B.   List of witnesses defendant expects to call, including experts:

      1.   Expert witnesses.

      2.   Non-expert witnesses.

If there are any third parties to the action, they should include an identical list of witnesses as that contained in parts A and B above.

    C.   *Rebuttal witnesses.* Each of the parties may call such rebuttal witnesses as may be necessary, without prior notice thereof to the other party.

VI. EXHIBITS

The parties shall prepare and append to the Final Pretrial Order a Pretrial Exhibit Stipulation, which shall be on a separate schedule. The Pretrial Exhibit Stipulation shall contain the style of the case, be entitled "Pretrial Exhibit Stipulation," shall contain each party's numbered list of trial exhibits, other than impeachment exhibits, with objections, if any, to each exhibit, including briefly the basis of the objection. All parties shall list their exhibits in numerical order. Where practicable, copies of all exhibits to which there is an objection will be submitted with the stipulation.

The burden for timely submission of a complete list is on plaintiff. Each party is to submit a pre-marked copy of each exhibit for the Court's use at trial. The list of exhibits shall be substantially in the following form:

PRETRIAL EXHIBIT STIPULATION

Plaintiff(s)' Exhibits

Number	Description	Objection	If objection, state grounds

Defendant(s)' Exhibits

Number	Description	Objection	If objection, state grounds

VII. DAMAGES

An itemized statement of all damages, including special damages.

VIII. BIFURCATED TRIAL

Indicate whether the parties desire a bifurcated trial and, if so, why.

IX. TRIAL BRIEFS

Trial briefs should be filed with the Court at the Final Pretrial Conference on any difficult factual or evidentiary issue and also set forth a party's theory of liability or defense.

X. LIMITATIONS, RESERVATIONS, AND OTHER MATTERS

    A. **Trial Date.** Trial of this cause is set for the week of _____.

    B. **Length of Trial.** The probable length of trial is ___ days. The case will be listed on the trial calendar to be tried when reached.

> **Mark Appropriate Box:**   JURY .... _____
>
> NON–JURY .... _____

    C. **Number of Jurors.** There shall be a minimum of six jurors.

    D. **Jury Voir Dire.** The Court will conduct voir dire. Limited participation by counsel may be permitted. If voir dire questions are to be tendered, they should be submitted with the Final Pretrial Order.

    E. **Jury Instructions.** All jury instructions shall be submitted as directed by the presiding judge and a copy delivered to opposing counsel.

IT IS ORDERED that the Final Pretrial Order may be modified at the trial of the action or before to prevent manifest injustice or for good cause shown. Such modification may be made either on application of counsel for the parties or on motion of the Court.

IT IS SO ORDERED.

DATED:

United States District Judge

[Revised effective December 1, 2009.]

INSTRUCTIONS FOR APPLYING FOR GENERAL ADMISSION TO THE UNITED STATES DISTRICT COURT FOR THE SOUTHERN DISTRICT OF ILLINOIS

READ THESE INSTRUCTIONS CAREFULLY

1. Pursuant to Local Rule 83.1(a), there are two ways an attorney may seek general admission to this district court. You may:

   - Ask a member in good standing of the bar of this court to file a motion on your behalf which includes the bar number of the member and all state bar numbers issued to you (*see* Local Rule 83.1(a)(1)); or

   - File your own motion accompanied by either (1) a Certificate of Good Standing from a state in which you are licensed together with all state bar numbers issued to you (*see* Local Rule 83.1(a)(2)); or (2) a copy of a Certificate of Admission to Practice in the Northern or Central District of Illinois (*see* Local Rule 83.1(a)(3)).

2. Once you decide whether another attorney will move for your admission or you will move on your own for reciprocal admission, complete the **appropriate motion** (attached), **Attorney Admission Questionnaire, AO153 Oath on Admission card** (*see* paragraph 3 below), **and Electronic Filing Registration Form.** Your admission packet, along with the $226.00 admission fee, should be mailed to the Clerk of Court at either courthouse address.

   Clerk of Court   **Clerk of Court**
   750 Missouri Avenue   **301 W. Main Street**
   P.O. Box 249   **Benton, IL 62812**
   East St. Louis, IL 62201

   Review the attached checklist to ensure you are submitting a complete admission packet. NOTE: If you have ever been admitted to practice pro hac vice on any case in this Court, the $126.00 pro hac vice fee is regarded as an installment which applies to your general admission fee. You will be required to pay the $100.00 balance for general admission.

3. You do not need to appear before a judge to be admitted, but if you would like to do so, bring the documents referenced above when you appear before the judge. If you do not appear before a judge, you will need to appear before a Notary Public to take the prescribed oath. **The Notary Public should sign and place the seal on the attached AO153 card.** If you choose to appear before a judge to take the oath, you should make an appointment by contacting one of the following Courtroom Deputy Clerks:

Courtroom Deputy	Phone Number	Judge	Courtroom Deputy	Phone Number	Judge
Benton	////////////////////	////////////////////////	**East St. Louis**	////////////////////	/////////////////////////////////
K. Jane Reynolds	(618) 439–7724	District Judge J. Phil Gilbert	Sara Jennings	(618) 482–9013	Chie f Judge David R. Herndon
Karen Metheney	(618) 439–7754	Magistrate Judge Philip M. Frazier	Linda McGovern	(618) 482–9309	District Judge G. Patrick Murphy
			Debbie DeRousse	(618) 482–9298	District Judge Michael J. Reagan
			Cheryl Ritter	(618) 482–9374	Senior District Judge William D. Stiehl
			Jackie Payton	(618) 482–9376	Magistrate Judge Donald G. Wilkerson
			Angie Vehlewald	(618) 482–9419	Magistrate Judge Stephen C. Williams

4. When admitted, you will receive a copy of the signed Order, a Certificate of Admission, and a receipt for your payment in the mail. The Clerk's Office will

prepare the order for the judge's signature; **it is not necessary for you to submit a proposed order.** You will receive an email with your CM/ECF login and password. Note that the Southern District of Illinois <u>does not</u> assign a separate federal bar number upon general admission.

5. If you need additional information or assistance regarding general admission procedures, please visit our website at www.ilsd.uscourts.gov and/or contact the clerk's office at (618) 482–9371 (East St. Louis) or (618) 439–7760 (Benton). The Local Rules are available on the website or may be purchased from the clerk's office for a fee.

UNITED STATES DISTRICT COURT
for the
Southern District of Illinois

In the Matter of the Admission   )
to Practice Generally of:)
)
)
_____)

MOTION FOR ADMISSION
TO PRACTICE GENERALLY

1. The undersigned attorney, a member in good standing, moves for the general admission of _____ to the United States District Court for the Southern District of Illinois.

2. The applicant for admission resides in _____ (city/state) and is licensed to practice law in the State(s) of _____. The state bar number(s) issued to applicant are: _____

3. Movant has known the applicant for ___ (years/months), and knows that s/he exhibits good moral character and general fitness to practice law. Movant recommends the applicant's admission to practice law in this district court.

Accordingly, movant asks that the court admit _____ to practice generally before this court pursuant to Southern District of Illinois Local Rule 83.1(a)(1).

Signed on: _____   _____
         Date   Signature of Movant

_____   _____
    Street Address   Printed Name

_____   _____
    City, State, Zip   Bar Number of Movant

UNITED STATES DISTRICT COURT
for the
Southern District of Illinois

In the Matter of the Admission)
to Practice Generally of:)
)
)
_____)

MOTION FOR RECIPROCAL ADMISSION TO PRACTICE GENERALLY

1. The undersigned attorney moves for general admission to the United States District Court for the Southern District of Illinois. In support of this motion, I have attached the following:

☐ Pursuant to Local Rule 83.1(a)(2), a Certificate of Good Standing from the State(s) of _____ where I am licensed to practice law; or

☐ Pursuant to Local Rule 83.1(a)(3), a copy of my Certificate of Admission in the Northern or Central District of Illinois.

2. The undersigned attorney resides in _____ (city/state) and is licensed to practice law in the State(s) of _____. The state bar number(s) issued to me are: _____.

Accordingly, I ask to be generally admitted to practice before this court.

Signed on: _____   _____
                          Date   Signature of Attorney

_____   _____
                   Street Address   Printed Name

_____
                   City, State, Zip

_____

UNITED STATES DISTRICT COURT
SOUTHERN DISTRICT OF ILLINOIS

ATTORNEY ADMISSION QUESTIONNAIRE

1. Full Name: _____
2. Affiliation/Firm Name: _____
3. Mailing Address: _____
4. Telephone Number: (__) __ Fax Number: (__) _____
5. Primary E-mail Address: _____
6. Secondary E-mail Address: _____
7. List all federal bar memberships, the date of admission, and your bar identification number, if any.

Jurisdiction   Date Admitted   Bar ID Number

_____

_____

_____

8. List all state bar memberships, the date of admission, and your bar identification number, if any.

    State   Date Admitted   Bar ID Number

_____

_____

_____

9. List the undergraduate schools you attended and the degrees you received, if any.

    Schools Attended   Degrees

_____

_____

_____

10. List the law school(s) you attended, the dates of attendance, and the degree you received, if any.

    Law Schools Attended   Degrees

_____

_____

_____

11. Have you read and become familiar with:

    a.   the law relating to jurisdiction and venue in a United States District Court?   ☐ Yes ☐ No

    b.   the Federal Rules of Civil Procedure?   ☐ Yes ☐ No

    c.   the Federal Rules of Criminal Procedure?   ☐ Yes ☐ No

    d.   the Federal Rules of Evidence?   ☐ Yes ☐ No

    e.   The Model Rules of Professional Responsibility of the American Bar Association or as adopted by the State of Illinois?   ☐ Yes ☐ No

    f.   The Standards of Professional Conduct within the Seventh Circuit?   ☐ Yes ☐ No

12. Have you assisted in the preparation of a civil or criminal case for trial?   ☐ Yes ☐ No

    If so, approximately how many times? _____

    Were any of the cases pending in federal court?   ☐ Yes ☐ No

13. Have you observed a complete hearing at which testimony was taken on the merits in a United States District Court?   ☐ Yes ☐ No

14. Would you be willing to join our pro bono panel of volunteers to represent indigent civil litigants on cases pending in the district?   ☐ Yes ☐ No

Applicant's Signature: _____ Date: _____

AO 153 (Rev. 6/96) Modified Southern District of Illinois (Rev. 3/ 2011)

NAME: (LAST, FIRST, MI)   SOCIAL SECURITY NO.

OATH ON ADMISSION

I, _____, DO SOLEMNLY SWEAR (OR AFFIRM) THAT AS AN ATTORNEY AND AS A COUNSELOR OF THIS COURT I WILL CONDUCT MYSELF UPRIGHTLY AND ACCORDING TO LAW, AND THAT I WILL SUPPORT THE CONSTITUTION OF THE UNITED STATES.

DATE: SIGNATURE: BAR I.D. NO.

COMPLETE REVERSE SIDE

AO 153 (Rev. 6/96) Modified Southern District of Illinois (Rev. 3/2011)

FIRM NAME   TEL. NO.

FIRM ADDRESS

CITY   STATE   ZIP CODE

SWORN AND SUBSCRIBED BEFORE ME,   DATE

ADMITTED ON MOTION OF: (Movant)

Checklist for Applying for General Admission to the United States District Court for the Southern District of Illinois

1. **MOTION FOR GENERAL ADMISSION**
   ☐ I have enclosed a completed Motion for Admission of Another to Practice Generally; or
   ☐ I have enclosed a Motion for Reciprocal Admission to Practice Generally and all necessary attachments.

2. **ATTORNEY ADMISSION QUESTIONNAIRE**
   ☐ I have enclosed a completed Attorney Admission Questionnaire.

3. **AO153 OATH ON ADMISSION CARD**
   ☐ I have appeared before a Notary Public and signed the AO153 Oath on Admission Card, and the notary has signed the card; or
   ☐ I have not attached a signed AO153 Oath on Admission Card, because I have contacted a courtroom deputy clerk to schedule a time to appear in person before a judge.

4. **ELECTRONIC FILING REGISTRATION**

☐ I have enclosed a completed Electronic Filing Registration Form;

☐ I have not submitted an Electronic Filing Registration Form because I already have a login/password in the Southern District of Illinois. My login is: _____.

5. FEE

☐ I have enclosed a check in the amount of $226.00 made payable to Clerk, U.S. District Court; or

☐ I have enclosed a check in the amount of $126.00 made payable to Clerk, U.S. District Court because I have already been admitted to practice pro hac vice in this Court, and the $100.00 pro hac vice fee was an installment to be applied to the general admission fee.

Once you have completed this checklist and the documents it references, mail it with your admission packet to either courthouse.

Clerk of Court   **Clerk of Court**
750 Missouri Avenue   **301 W. Main Street**
P.O. Box 249   **Benton, IL 62812**
East St. Louis, IL 62201

Upon admission, you will receive a copy of the signed Order, a Certificate of Admission, and a receipt for your payment in the mail. You will receive an email with your CM/ECF login and password.

[Revised effective February 2011.]

INSTRUCTIONS FOR APPLYING FOR PRO HAC VICE ADMISSION TO THE UNITED STATES DISTRICT COURT FOR THE SOUTHERN DISTRICT OF ILLINOIS

READ THESE INSTRUCTIONS CAREFULLY

1. Pursuant to Local Rule 83.1(b), an attorney licensed to practice law in any state of the United States or the District of Columbia who wishes to be admitted for the purpose of a specific civil or criminal case may file a motion for pro hac vice admission. The motion must contain a verified statement setting forth the state and federal bars of which the movant is a member in good standing, and the bar number, if any, issued by each jurisdiction. A sample motion is attached. You must also pay a filing fee of $100.00 per admission.

2. **If you do not already have a CM/ECF login and password issued by the Southern District of Illinois**, you first must complete an Electronic Filing Registration Form. This form can either be submitted online at the court's website, www.ilsd.uscourts.gov, or by mail to either courthouse.

> Clerk of Court
> 750 Missouri Avenue
> P.O. Box 249
> East St. Louis, IL 62201

> Clerk of Court
> 301 W. Main Street
> Benton, IL 62812

Please indicate on the form the case in which you plan to seek pro hac vice admission. You will receive an email with your CM/ECF login and password.

3. Once you have a CM/ECF login and password issued by the Southern District of Illinois, electronically file the motion in the case in which you seek pro hac vice admission. When filing the motion, you will be prompted to pay the $100.00 filing fee by credit card through the Pay.gov payment process.

4. Note that if more than one attorney seeks pro hac vice admission in the same case, each attorney must electronically file a motion to appear pro hac vice in the case and pay the $100.00 filing fee. Once an attorney has a CM/ECF login and password from the Southern District of Illinois, the attorney does not need to reapply for issuance of a login and password each time a motion for pro hac vice admission is electronically filed.

6.* If you need additional information or assistance regarding pro hac vice admission procedures, please visit our website at www.ilsd.uscourts. gov and/or contact the clerk's office at (618) 482–9371 (East St. Louis) or (618) 439–7760 (Benton). The Local Rules are available on the website or may be purchased from the clerk's office for a fee.

UNITED STATES DISTRICT COURT

for the

Southern District of Illinois

_____)	
Plaintiff(s))	
v.)	Case Number: _____
_____)	
Defendant(s))	

MOTION FOR PRO HAC VICE ADMISSION

Pursuant to Local Rule 83.1(b), the undersigned attorney moves for admission pro hac vice to the United States District Court for the Southern District of Illinois in order to appear as counsel of record in this case on behalf of _____.

In support of this motion, I state:

1. I am an attorney licensed to practice law and a member in good standing in the State(s) of _____. The state and federal bar numbers issued to me are: _____

2. I am familiar with the law, facts, and procedures relating to the subject matter of this litigation.

Accordingly, I ask to be admitted pro hac vice before this court.

Signed on: _____   _____
           Date   Signature of Movant

_____   _____
      Street Address   Printed Name

_____
      City, State, Zip

[Revised effective February 2011.]

    * So in original.

MOTION TO DEPOSIT MONEY WITH THE COURT
UNITED STATES DISTRICT COURT
for the
Southern District of Illinois

Plaintiff(s)	)	
v.	))	Case Number:
Defendant(s)	))	

MOTION TO DEPOSIT MONEY WITH THE COURT

Pursuant to Rule 67 of the Federal Rules of Civil Procedure, _____ moves the Court for an Order allowing the deposit of _____ with the Clerk of Court.

Dated:

_____

Signature

[Revised effective February 2011.]

NOTICE OF MANUAL FILING

UNITED STATES DISTRICT COURT
for the
Southern District of Illinois

Plaintiff(s)	)
v.	) Case Number:
Defendant(s)	)
	) Judge:

NOTICE OF MANUAL FILING

Please take notice that _____ has manually filed the following document or item: _____.

This document has not been filed electronically because:

☐ The document or item cannot be converted to an electronic format.

☐ _____ is excused from filing this document or item by court order.

☐ Other:

The document or item has been manually served on all parties.

_____
Name

_____
Firm

_____
Address

_____
City, State, Zip

_____
Phone

_____
E-mail

[Revised effective February 2011.]

ORDERS

ADMINISTRATIVE ORDER NO. 148. IN RE: PETITIONS FOR RETROACTIVE APPLICATION OF UNITED STATES SENTENCING GUIDELINES FOR CERTAIN CRACK COCAINE CONVICTIONS

HERNDON, CHIEF JUDGE:

This Order supersedes Administrative Order 137, which is hereby vacated.

As a result of the Fair Sentencing Act of 2010, this Court continues to receive motions asking it to examine, pursuant to 18 U.S.C. § 3582(c)(2), past sentences for the possibility of reductions. Often these requests include motions requesting that the Court appoint counsel to help the defendant navigate through the process.

The Seventh Circuit has now spoken to this issue and held in the case of *United States v. Foster*, ___ F.3d ___, 2013 WL 466201, *1 (7th Cir. (Ill.) Feb. 8, 2013), that a district court is not authorized by law to appoint counsel for a defendant in such an instance. As a consequence, of course, this Court will not appoint CJA Panel attorneys nor other outside attorneys to represent defendants in cases where the defendant is seeking a reduction in a sentence for conviction pursuant to 18 U.S.C. § 3582(c)(2). An exemption to this policy, of course, will be if an attorney volunteers to represent such a defendant pro bono.

However, as a service to the effected defendants, the Federal Public Defenders office is willing to enter its appearance on behalf of defendants who file such motions. The Clerk's office is directed to notify that office of any such filings. This appearance is voluntary on the part of that office initially but once the office appears the attorney client relationship naturally attaches. Should the public defenders office feel compelled to withdraw either because of a conflict or because it determines the petition is frivolous, the rule in *Foster* will effectively prevent the Court from appointing counsel for the defendant who has not convinced a lawyer to represent him pro bono.

With or without counsel, the Court, in consultation with the Probation office, will carefully review each motion to reduce sentence to determine if a reduction is in order under the law.

[Dated: February 13, 2013.]

ADMINISTRATIVE ORDER NO. 146. IN RE: DISTRICT COURT TRANSITION FROM WORDPERFECT TO WORD

ADMINISTRATIVE ORDER

On January 1, 2013, the United States District Court for the Southern District of Illinois will retire the word processing application WordPerfect and switch to Microsoft Word. Proposed documents will no longer be accepted in WordPerfect format and forms on the court's website will only be available in Word and Adobe formats. To the extent any local rule or user's manual requires a document to be submitted in WordPerfect format, that reference is amended by interlineation to require the use of Microsoft Word.

[Dated: November 19, 2012.]

ADMINISTRATIVE ORDER NO. 135. IN THE MATTER OF: AMENDING ADMINISTRATIVE ORDERS NO. 4 AND 134 CONCERNING THE DEPOSIT OF CERTAIN REGISTRY FUNDS DEPOSITED INTO INTEREST–BEARING ACCOUNTS

AMENDED ORDER REGARDING DEPOSIT AND INVESTMENT OF REGISTRY FUNDS

The Court, having determined that it is necessary to amend local procedures to reflect the transition of accountability and administration of the Court Registry Investment System ("CRIS") from the United States District Court for the Southern District of Texas to the Administrative Office of the United States Courts, as well as to ensure the continued uniformity in the deposit and investment of funds in the Court's Registry,

IT IS ORDERED that the following shall govern the receipt, deposit, and investment of registry funds:

I. Receipt of Funds

A. No money shall be sent to the Court or its officers for deposit in the Court's registry without a court order signed by the presiding judge in the case or proceeding.

B. Unless provided for elsewhere in this Order, all monies ordered to be paid to the Court or received by its officers in any case pending or adjudicated shall be deposited with the Treasurer of the United States in the name and to the credit of this Court pursuant to 28 U.S.C. § 2041 through depositories designated by the Treasury to accept such deposit on its behalf.

C. The party making the deposit or transferring funds to the Court's registry shall serve the order permitting the deposit or transfer on the Clerk of Court.

II. Investment of Registry Funds

A. Where, by order of the Court, funds on deposit with the Court are to be placed in some form of interest-bearing account, CRIS, administered by the Administrative Office of the United States Courts, shall be the only investment mechanism authorized.

B. Money from each case deposited in CRIS shall be "pooled" together with those on deposit with Treasury to the credit of other courts in CRIS and used to purchase Government Account Series securities through the Bureau of Public Debt, which will be held at Treasury, in an account in the name and to the credit of the Director of Administrative Office of the United States Courts, hereby designated as custodian for CRIS.

C. An account for each case will be established in CRIS titled in the name of the case giving rise to the investment in the fund. Income generated from fund investments will be distributed to each case based on the ratio each account's principal and earnings has to the aggregate principal and income total in the fund. Reports showing the interest earned and the principal amounts contributed in each case will be prepared and distributed to each court participating in CRIS and made available to litigants and/or their counsel.

III. Registry Investment Fee

A. The custodian is authorized and directed by this Order to deduct, for maintaining accounts in CRIS, the registry fee. The proper registry fee is to be determined on the basis of the rates published by the Director of the Administrative Office of United States Courts as approved by the Judicial Conference.

B. If registry fees were assessed against the case under the old 45–day requirement prior to deposit in CRIS, no additional registry fee will be assessed.

IV. Transition From Former Investment Procedure

This Order supercedes and abrogates all prior orders of this Court regarding the deposit and investment of registry funds.

[Dated: May 19, 2011.]

ADMINISTRATIVE ORDER NO. 116. IN RE: FEE PAYMENT VIA PAY.GOV

Effective September 1, 2009, the United States District Court for the Southern District of Illinois will implement fee payments via Pay.gov. All electronic case filers will be required to use the Pay.gov Internet payment module in CM/ECF. Payments for filing fees, pro hac vice attorney fees and notice of appeal fees must be paid by credit card over the Internet by ECF Users. Users will be automatically directed through the Pay.gov payment process. The Event List is attached as Exhibit A and Notice of Refund Policy is attached as Exhibit B. Further information regarding Pay.gov may be obtained on the Court's website at www.ilsd.uscourts. gov.

[Dated: August 18, 2009.]

EXHIBIT A

UNITED STATES DISTRICT COURT
FOR THE SOUTHERN DISTRICT OF ILLINOIS

PAY.GOV FILING FEE EVENTS

Civil
Notice of Appeal
Notice of Interlocutory Appeal
Notice of Cross Appeal
Complaint
Petition for Writ of Habeas Corpus
Notice of Removal
Motion to Appear PHV
Petition for Writ of Mandamus
Criminal
Notice of Appeal—Interlocutory
Notice of Appeal—Final Judgment
Notice of Appeal—Conditions of Release

EXHIBIT B

UNITED STATES DISTRICT COURT
SOUTHERN DISTRICT OF ILLINOIS

NOTICE OF REFUND POLICY OF ELECTRONIC FILING FEES

This Notice establishes procedures for the refunding of duplicate or erroneously paid filing fees which are generated during the electronic filing of documents. The Judicial Conference of the United States has generally prohibited the refunding of filing fees (JCUS_MAR 49). However, in March of 2005, the Judicial Conference of the United States issued guidance endorsing limited refund authority by the courts as a result of the increased likelihood of inadvertent, erroneous or duplicate payments made by parties using the Case Management/Electronic Case Files (CM/ECF) system. It further advised courts that determining appropriate policies and procedures for refunding erroneously applied filing fee payments be left to the sound discretion of each court.

The Clerk of the United States District Court for the Southern District of Illinois, or his designee, is authorized to refund all fees erroneously paid through the Pay.gov electronic filing fee tool in CM/ECF:

1. if discovered by the court or Clerk's office that a fee has been paid erroneously;

2. if an attorney files a motion for a refund and it can be determined by the Clerk or his designee that the fee has been erroneously paid.

Attorneys seeking a refund must electronically file a motion and supporting documentation must be attached, including a copy of the electronic payment receipt and the Notice(s) of Electronic Filing generated from the court's electronic case management system. The motion must include the name, address and telephone number of the party requesting the refund.

Upon order of the court, the Finance Department shall process the refund to the same credit card from which the erroneous payment was made and will forward notice of such to the Operations Department for recording to the docket. Refund checks will not be issued.

In the event that an attorney or law firm consistently errs when submitting fees and thereby repeatedly requests refunds, the court will consider remedial action and may issue an order to show cause as to why further requests for refunds should be considered.

[Dated: August 14 2009.]

ADMINISTRATIVE ORDER NO. 111. IN RE: TRANSCRIPT POLICY AMENDED NOVEMBER 2012

Effective today, the Court ADOPTS the attached Transcript Policy, as revised in November 2012, in compliance with the policy of the United States Judicial Conference.

[Dated: November 26, 2012.]

TRANSCRIPT POLICY

I. Introduction

The Judicial Conference of the United States has established a practice for redacting transcripts of court proceedings in compliance with the Federal Rules of Practice and Procedure. The policy set forth in this document reflects the local policy of the Southern District of Illinois and applies to all transcripts of proceedings filed in this Court on or after May 12, 2008, regardless of when the proceeding took place. To the extent this policy does not address or is inconsistent with the policy of the Judicial Conference, the policy of the Judicial Conference governs. The basic procedures, outlined in detail below, are as follows:

Note that special procedures, set forth in Section V below, apply to the voir dire examination portions of a transcript.

II. Notice to Attorneys and Parties to a Case

The best practice is to keep personal information out of the transcript. Counsel should take this into account when questioning witnesses or making statements in court. If information subject to this policy is mentioned in court, counsel may ask the judge to have it stricken from the record or partially redacted.

Anyone seeking a transcript of a court proceeding should contact the court reporter listed on the minutes of the proceeding (or the clerk's office if this information is needed). After receiving the proper forms and payment, the court reporter will prepare the transcript and deliver a copy to the requesting party in the format ordered. Within 3 days of delivery of the transcript to the requesting party, the court reporter will electronically file the transcript in the Case Management and Electronic Case Filing ("CM/ECF") system.

Once a prepared transcript is electronically filed in CM/ECF, attorneys in a case are (or, where there is a self-represented party, the party is) responsible for reviewing the transcript for the personal data identifiers required by the federal rules to be redacted and requesting redaction as set forth below. Within the first 90 days after a transcript is filed in CM/ECF (referred to herein as the "90–day restriction period"), a transcript may be reviewed for redaction purposes either by purchasing a copy from the court reporter or transcriber or by inspecting the transcript at either courthouse using the public terminal in the clerk's office. During this 90–day restriction period, both unredacted and redacted transcripts will be available at the public terminals in the clerk's office *for inspection only*. Employees of the clerk's office cannot make a copy of the transcript during the 90–day restriction period, and anyone requesting a copy of a transcript will be referred to the court reporter or transcriber who prepared it.

A party in the case who purchases the transcript during the 90–day restriction period will be given remote access to the transcript via CM/ECF and the Public Access to Court Electronic Records ("PACER") systems once satisfactory arrangements for payment have been made. Members of the public who purchase a transcript from the court reporter or transcriber will not be granted remote electronic access until after the 90–day restriction period ends.

At the end of the 90–day restriction period, the clerk's office will allow remote access to a redacted transcript, if the transcript was redacted during the 90–day restriction period, or to the unredacted transcript, if no redactions were requested.

PACER fees apply at all times when transcripts are accessed remotely. *Charges will accrue for the entire transcript.* Court reporters or transcribers may not charge an additional fee to redact a transcript.

III. Persons Responsible for Reviewing the Transcript

The following individuals are required to review the transcript for personal data that should be redacted:

- each party's attorney,
- "standby counsel" assisting a pro se defendant in a criminal case, and
- unrepresented parties.

Redaction responsibilities apply to attorneys even if the person requesting the transcript is a judge or a member of the media or public.

IV. Parts of the Transcript that Must be Reviewed

The parts of the transcript that must be reviewed include:

- opening and closing statements made on behalf of the represented party,
- any statements made by the party,
- the testimony of any witnesses called by the party,
- sentencing proceedings (both government and defense counsel), and
- any other portion of the transcript as ordered by the Court.

V. Voir Dire Examinations

This Court recognizes the need to protect jurors' privacy and restricts access to voir dire examinations. In the unusual case where an attorney elects to have voir dire transcribed, the court reporter or transcriber will file the voir dire portion of the transcript under seal as a separate document. The voir dire portion of the transcript will never be made available to the public remotely, even after the 90–day restriction period ends. For this reason, voir dire portions of a transcript are not subject to the redaction requirements set forth in this policy. The party requesting the voir dire transcript will have remote access to it only after purchasing a copy from the court reporter or transcriber. If the Court of Appeals orders the parties to provide the voir dire examination or orders a trial record containing voir dire information to be unsealed, the parties should immediately notify the judge who presided at the court proceeding.

VI. Personal Data to be Redacted

Personal data must be redacted as follows:

- **Social Security Numbers.** If an individual's social security number must be included in a document, only the last four digits of that number should be used.
- **Names of Minor Children.** If the involvement of a minor child must be mentioned, only the initials of that child should be used.
- **Dates of Birth**. If an individual's date of birth must be included in a document, only the year should be used.
- **Financial Account Numbers.** If financial account numbers are relevant, only the last four digits of these numbers should be used.
- **Home Addresses.** *In criminal cases only*, if home addresses must be used, use only the city and state.

Other personal information may be redacted only with leave of court. *See* Federal Rule of Civil Procedure 5.2 and Federal Rule of Criminal Procedure 49.1 and SDIL–LR 5.1.

VII. Notice of Intent to Request Redaction

Within *7 calendar days* after the court reporter or transcriber electronically files the official transcript, an attorney or unrepresented party must file a Notice of Intent to Request Redaction. If a Notice of Intent to Request Redaction is not filed during the 7 day period, the court will assume that redaction of personal data is not necessary, but the transcript will remain restricted until the 90–day restriction period ends.

VIII. Redaction Requests

If a Notice of Intent to Request Redaction is filed, an attorney or unrepresented party has *21 calendar days* from the filing of the official transcript to file a Redaction Request. The Redaction Request must list the places in the transcript (line and page number) where personal information to be redacted appears and should be worded in such a way that the personal information is not repeated (*i.e.*, "redact the Social Security number on page 12, line 9 to read xxx–xx–6789"). As set forth above, the transcript is available for inspection at the court's public terminal or for purchase from the court reporter or transcriber during this period, but it will not be available remotely to the public on PACER or for copying from the public terminals in the clerk's office until the 90–day restriction period has ended.

During the 21 day period, an attorney or unrepresented party may move for more time to request redactions and/or to redact information not set forth above. The transcript will not be available through PACER or for copying from the public terminals until the Court has ruled on any such motion. For good cause shown, the Court may extend the 21 day period.

If a Notice of Intent to Request Redaction was filed, but a Redaction Request is not received within 21 calendar days, the restrictions on remote access to the transcript will be lifted after the 90–day restriction period ends, and the transcript will be available remotely as if a Notice of Intent to Request Redaction had not been filed. *It is not the responsibility of the clerk's office to request or perform redactions. The responsibility rests on the attorneys to tell the court reporter where to redact and on the court reporter to perform requested redactions.*

IX. Redacted Transcript

The court reporter or transcriber must perform any requested redactions and electronically file a redacted version of the transcript no later than 31 calendar days after the filing of the transcript or 10 days after the Court rules on a motion addressing an issue related to redaction, whichever is longer. Remote electronic access to the redacted transcript will be available after the 90–day restriction period ends. The unredacted transcript will remain on the docket, but remote electronic access to it will be restricted to parties who purchased a copy of the transcript from the court reporter or transcriber.

X. Compensation of Criminal Justice Act Attorneys

Attorneys appointed under the Criminal Justice Act ("CJA") are eligible for compensation for reasonable time spent complying with this redaction policy and for reimbursement of related expenses. Examples of activities which could be covered include:

- the cost of obtaining the transcript,
- travel expenses to gain access to the transcript,
- time spent reviewing the transcript to determine the need for redaction,

- time spent and expenses incurred filing a notice of redaction,

- time spent on preparing and filing a Redaction Request, and

- time spent on motion practice relating to the transcript's redaction.

If a case involving a CJA representation has already been closed, and the original attorney (or standby counsel) is no longer available, a new attorney may be appointed under the CJA and compensated as outlined above. If the original appointed attorney is still available, but a final voucher for the underlying case has been filed, the attorney may file a supplemental voucher for compensation.

XI. Questions

Questions concerning this policy shall be directed to the clerk's office by calling 618/482–9371 (East St. Louis) or 618/439–7760 (Benton).

[Amended February 17, 2009; November 2012.]

AMENDED ADMINISTRATIVE ORDER NO. 107. IN THE MATTER OF: REDACTION OF PERSONAL DATA IDENTIFIERS FROM ALL PLEADINGS

In compliance with the policy of the Judicial Conference of the United States, the E–Government Act of 2002, Federal Rule of Civil Procedure 5.2, and Federal Rule of Criminal Procedure 49.1, and in order to promote electronic access to case files while also protecting personal privacy and other legitimate interests, a party or nonparty shall refrain from including, or shall partially redact where inclusion is necessary, the following personal data identifiers from all pleadings filed with the court, including exhibits, whether filed electronically or in paper form, unless otherwise ordered by the Court:

A. Social Security Numbers. If an individual's social security number must be included in a document, only the last four digits of that number should be used.

B. Names of Minor Children. If the involvement of a minor child must be mentioned, only the initials of that child should be used.

C. Dates of Birth. If an individual's date of birth must be included in a document, only the year should be used.

D. Financial Account Numbers. If financial account numbers are relevant, only the last four digits of these numbers should be used.

E. Home Addresses. In criminal cases only, if home addresses must be used, use only the city and state.

F. Driver's License Numbers. Use the last four numbers only.

A party or nonparty wishing to file a document containing the personal data identifiers listed above *must file a redacted version in the public file*. In addition to the public filing, a party or nonparty may, but is not required to file, the personal data identifiers listed above by filing (a) a reference list under seal, or (b) an unredacted version of the document under seal. A reference list shall contain the complete personal data identifier and the redacted identifier used in its place in the filing. All references in the case to the redacted identifiers included in the reference list will be construed to refer to the corresponding complete personal data identifier. The reference list must be filed under seal and may be amended as of right.

Filers are responsible for maintaining possession of original, unredacted documents and information redacted from publicly filed documents. Upon request, counsel may be required by the Court to furnish the unredacted information.

The responsibility for redacting these personal identifiers rests solely with counsel and the parties. The Clerk will not review each pleading for compliance with this rule.

[Dated: July 8, 2008. Amended effective March 15, 2012.]

ADMINISTRATIVE ORDER NO. 106. IN RE: NEW TRANSCRIPT POLICY

NEW TRANSCRIPT POLICY

Effective May 15, 2008

At its September 2007, as amended by the March 2008 session, the U.S. Judicial Conference approved a new policy regarding the availability of transcripts of court proceedings. A new release of CM/ECF, Version 3.2, includes software that facilitates the implementation of this policy.

I. Summary

The language from the Judicial Conference's September 2007 session states:

(1) A transcript provided to a court by a court reporter or transcriber will be available at the office of the clerk of court for inspection only, for a period of 90 days after it is delivered to the clerk.

(2) During the 90–day period, a copy of the transcript may be obtained from the court reporter or transcriber at the rate established by the Judicial Conference, the transcript will be available within the court for internal use, and an attorney who obtains the transcript from the court reporter or transcriber may obtain remote electronic access to the transcript through the court's CM/ECF system for purposes of creating hyperlinks to the transcript in court filings and for other purposes.

(3) After the 90–day period has ended, the filed transcript will be available for inspection and copying in the clerk's office and for download from the court's CM/ECF system through the judiciary's PACER system.

When the new transcript policy is implemented, transcripts must be compliant with the new Federal Privacy Rules, Civ. 5.2 and Crim. 49.1. The Judicial Conference approved procedures for applying redaction requirements to transcripts of court proceedings and the new CM/ECF Version 3.2 has been designed to include those procedures.

Under 28 U.S.C. § 753(b), the court reporter or transcriber must deliver promptly a certified copy of any transcript made to the clerk of court for the records of the court. The Notice of Electronic Filing (NEF) informs parties and attorneys of record of the 90–day restriction and how to obtain the transcript during the restriction period. The date when the transcript is submitted is the starting point for all deadlines related to the transcript.[1]

During the 90–day period (which may be extended by the court), access to the transcript in CM/ECF is restricted to four types of users:

- court staff;
- public terminal users;
- attorneys of record or parties who have purchased the transcript from the court reporter/transcriber; and
- other persons as directed by the court, e.g., appellate attorneys.

Except for public terminal viewers, persons authorized to view or download the transcript can also create hyperlinks to the transcripts.

II. Overview of the Process within CM/ECF

The Official Transcript which includes the Notice of Filing will be entered into CM/ECF. This notice included language that indicates that parties have 7 business days to file with the court a Notice of Intent to Request Redaction of this transcript. This notice is transmitted to the parties via the NEF. Redaction responsibilities apply to the attorneys even if the requestor of the transcript is a judge or a member of the public/media.

Any party needing to review the transcript for redaction purposes may purchase a copy from the court reporter/transcriber or view the transcript at the courthouse using the public terminal to CM/ECF. If a party purchases the transcript from the court reporter, and he or she is an attorney on the case, he or she will be given remote access to the transcript via CM/ECF and PACER. This access is provided via a utility program in CM/ECF. PACER fees apply at all times when accessing transcripts remotely. Access will be granted after payment is received by the court reporter. At which time the court reporter will also provide via email an electronic copy, a paper copy or both as designated by the requestor.

Within 7 business days of the filing in CM/ECF of the official transcript, each party wishing to redact a transcript must inform the court, by filing a Notice of Intent to Redact personal identifiers, as required by Fed.R.Crim.P.49.1 and Fed. R.Civ.P.5.2, from the electronic transcript of the court proceeding. If no such notice is filed within the allotted time, the court will assume redaction of personal identifiers from the transcript is not necessary.

Unless otherwise ordered by the court, the attorney must review the following portions of the transcript:

- opening and closing statements made on the party's behalf;
- statements of the party;
- the testimony of any witnesses called by the party
- sentencing proceedings (both government and defense counsel); and
- any other portion of the transcript as ordered by the court[2]

Only those identifiers listed in the rules can be redacted through this part of the process: Social Security numbers; financial account numbers; names of minor children; dates of birth; and home addresses of individuals.

If the transcript is related to a CJA representation, the attorney conducting the review is entitled to compensation under the CJA for functions reasonably performed to fulfill the redaction obligation and for reimbursement for related reasonable expenses.

If redaction is requested, a party is to submit a Redaction Request within 21 calendar days of the transcript's delivery to the clerk, or longer if a court so orders, a statement indicating where the personal identifiers to be redacted appear in the transcript. The court reporter or transcriber must redact the identifiers as directed by the party. These procedures are limited to redaction of the specific personal data identifiers listed in the rules. If an attorney wishes to redact additional information, he or she may make a motion to the court. The transcript will not be electronically available until the court has ruled on any such motions, even though the 90–day restriction period may have ended.

The court reporter or transcriber must, within 31 calendar days of the filing of the original transcript, or longer if the court so orders, perform the requested redactions, and file a redacted version of the transcript. The original unredacted electronic transcript will be retained as a restricted document. The court will monitor this deadline to ensure that the redacted transcript is available for parties and attorneys should there be an appeal.

III.   General Issues

A.   Purchase of the Transcript by the Public/Media. Members of the public, including the news media, who purchase a transcript from the court reporter within the 90–day restriction period, will not be granted remote electronic access during the restriction period. At the end of the restriction period, the public will be provided remote electronic access to the redacted transcript, or, if no redaction was done, to the transcript originally submitted, unless it was under seal.

B.   Miscellaneous Issues. If only part of the transcript is ordered, an attorney is not responsible for ordering and reviewing other parts of the proceedings.

Court reporters/transcribers are not responsible for identification of the need for or redaction of the transcripts. Redaction will be accomplished only with input from the attorneys who present the parties in the case. Attorneys are required to list the information to be redacted by page and line number.

The redaction-related documents (e.g., notice of intent to redact, etc.) should be in the court record to ensure that the changes to the transcript are documented and are available both to the court in which the transcript was created and the appellate court (for potential orders regarding any delay).

There is no obligation on the part of the clerk's office to perform any redaction. Instead, it rests on the attorneys to tell the court reporter where to redact, and on the court reporter to perform the redaction.

Standby counsel in pro-se cases are responsible to assist the pro-se litigant in complying with these rules.

The Court recognizes the need to protect jurors' privacy. As such, the voir dire will not be made part of the transcript filed with the Clerk's office absent a motion granted by the trial judge who will impose restrictions to insure juror privacy. In the event the Court of Appeals orders the parties to provide the voir dire, or orders a trial record containing the voir dire unsealed, the parties should immediately notify the trial judge who can then consider methods necessary to protect juror privacy.

C.   Compliance with Judicial Conference Policy. To the extent any of this rule does not address, or is or becomes inconsistent with Judicial Conference Policy, it is the Judicial Conference Policy that governs.

[Dated: May 9, 2008.]

1 Note: the special redaction procedures for transcripts and the 90–day restriction policy apply only to transcripts of federal courtroom proceedings.

2 Currently pending before the Judicial Conference is a recommendation to add a requirement that attorneys must specifically review "any transcript of a sentencing proceeding."

ADMINISTRATIVE ORDER NO. 96.   IN THE MATTER OF PRESENTENCE REPORTS

Federal Rule of Criminal Procedure 32 sets deadlines for the submission of Presentence Reports ("PSRs") and the filing of objections thereto. For instance, Rule 32(f)(1) provides that parties must object in writing within 14 days of receiving the PSR. Rule 32 does not specifically address when counsel must file a *response* to the objections to the PSR. Unless directed otherwise in a particular case, counsel are to file and serve responses to objections to the PSR within 7 calendar days of receiving the objections. Failure to timely file a response to objections may, in the Court's discretion, be considered an admission of the merits of the objection.

[Dated: January 18, 2007.]

ADMINISTRATIVE ORDER NO. 69. IN RE: CASE MANAGEMENT/ELECTRONIC CASE FILING

Mandatory Electronic Case Filing (ECF) began January 20, 2004. An aggressive and comprehensive notice campaign was initiated to educate counsel of the requirements of ECF. Compliance by counsel, as expected, has been excellent, but there are a few who are not yet registered as ECF users. Non-compliant counsel must register immediately. The Clerk of Court has been providing non-registered counsel with paper copies of orders. This is a time-consuming drain on the Clerk's limited resources. Accordingly, effective March 1, 2004, the Clerk's Office will no longer provide paper copies of orders to counsel except in special situations to be determined in the sound exercise of the Court and Clerk's discretion.

[Dated: February 23, 2004.]

NOTICE REGARDING PRIVACY AND PUBLIC ACCESS TO ELECTRONIC CIVIL AND CRIMINAL CASE FILES AND REQUIRING COMPLIANCE WITH ADMINISTRATIVE ORDER #107

The Office of the Clerk is now accepting electronically filed pleadings and making the content of these pleadings available on the court's Internet website via WebPACER. Any subscriber to WebPACER will be able to read, download, store and print the full content of electronically filed documents. The clerk's office will not make electronically available documents that have been sealed or otherwise restricted by court order.

You should not include sensitive information in any document filed with the Court unless such inclusion is necessary and relevant to the case. You must remember that any personal information not otherwise protected will be made available over the Internet via WebPACER. If sensitive information must be included, the following personal identifiers must be partially redacted from the document, whether it is filed traditionally or electronically:

1) Social Security Numbers. If an individual's social security number must be included in a document, only the last four digits of that number should be used.

2) Names of Minor Children. If the involvement of a minor child must be mentioned, only the initials of that child should be used.

3) Dates of Birth. If an individual's date of birth must be included in a document, only the year should be used.

4) Financial Account Numbers. If financial account numbers are relevant, only the last four digits of these numbers should be used.

5) Home Addresses. If home addresses must be used, use only the City and State (Criminal Cases Only).

6) Drivers License Numbers. Use the last four numbers only.

In compliance with the E–Government Act of 2002, a party wishing to file a document containing the personal data identifiers listed above must file a redacted version in the public file (file electronically for ECF cases or manually for non-ECF cases). **In addition to the public filing, a party may file, but is not required to file, the personal data identifiers listed above by filing the information under seal in accordance with the directions below.**

A party wishing to file the unredacted information with the court may file either **(a)** a reference list under seal, or **(b)** an unredacted version of the document under seal. **When a party finds it necessary to file the unredacted information under seal, the court prefers a reference list to the filing of a complete document.** The reference list shall contain the complete personal data identifier(s) and the redacted identifier(s) used in its (their) place in the filing. All references in the case to the redacted identifiers included in the reference list will be construed to refer to the corresponding complete personal data identifier. The reference list must be filed under seal and may be amended as of right. Parties are responsible for maintaining possession of original, unredacted documents, and information redacted from publicly filed documents. Upon request, counsel may be required by the Court to furnish the unredacted information.

In addition, exercise caution when filing documents that contain the following:

1) medical records, treatment and diagnosis

2) employment history

3) individual financial information

4) proprietary or trade secret information

5) information regarding an individual's cooperation with the government

6) information regarding the victim of any criminal activity

7) national security information

8) sensitive security information as described in 49 USC 114(s)

Counsel are strongly urged to share this notice with all clients so that an informed decision about the inclusion, redaction and/or exclusion of certain materials may be made. **It is the sole responsibility of counsel and the parties** to be sure that all documents comply with the rules of this Court requiring redaction of personal identifiers. **The Clerk will not review each document for compliance with this rule.**

PLAN FOR RANDOM SELECTION OF JURORS

Introduction

Pursuant to the Jury Selection and Service Act of 1968, 28 U.S.C. §§ 1861–1878, as amended, the following plan is adopted by this Court, subject to approval by the reviewing panel of the Judicial Council of the Seventh Circuit and to rules and regulations as may be adopted by the Judicial Conference of the United States.

All litigants entitled to a trial by jury shall have the right to petit and grand juries selected at random from a fair cross section of the community in the Southern District of Illinois where the Court convenes. All citizens residing within the Southern District of Illinois shall have the opportunity to be considered for service on petit and grand juries and shall have an obligation to serve as jurors when summoned. No citizen shall be excluded from service as a petit or grand juror based on race, color, religion, sex, national origin, or economic status.

Definitions

"Chief Judge" shall mean the Chief Judge of the United States District Court for the Southern District of Illinois or his/her designee.

"Clerk" and "Clerk of Court" shall mean the Clerk of the United States District Court for the Southern District of Illinois or any authorized deputy clerk who assists the Clerk in the performance of functions presented by the Jury Selection and Service Act or as set forth in this Plan.

"Master jury wheel" shall mean all names selected directly from official source lists in a manner described in this Plan.

"Qualified jury wheel" shall mean a group of jurors who, based solely on the information provided on the juror qualification questionnaire, have been deemed eligible for service.

"Petit jury" or "petit juror" shall mean a jury or juror summoned to serve at a civil or criminal trial.

"Grand jury" or "grand juror" shall mean a jury or juror summoned to serve at a grand jury proceeding.

Applicability of the Plan

For petit and grand jury selection purposes, the Southern District of Illinois is divided into the following divisions:

For the Court sitting at East St. Louis, jury selection will be from the counties of: Bond, Calhoun, Clinton, Fayette, Jersey, Madison, Marion, Monroe, Randolph, St. Clair, and Washington.

For the Court sitting at Benton, jury selection will be from the counties of: Alexander, Clark, Clay, Crawford, Cumberland, Edwards, Effingham, Franklin, Gallatin, Hamilton, Hardin, Jackson, Jasper, Jefferson, Johnson, Lawrence, Massac, Perry, Pope, Pulaski, Richland, Saline, Union, Wabash, Wayne, Williamson, and White.

Management and Supervision of the Jury Selection Process

The Clerk of Court shall manage the jury selection process under the supervision and control of the Chief Judge.

Jury Selection Sources

Juror names shall be selected from the general election voter registration lists and may be supplemented with lists of licensed drivers. These lists represent a fair cross section of the community in this District. Names of jurors shall be selected by randomized procedure from these lists within the counties comprising each jury division as set forth above. The registered voters list shall consist of those individuals who are of record as registered voters, as maintained by the County Clerk, City Clerk (if separate city lists exist), or the office of the State Board of Elections for the State of Illinois. The lists of licensed drivers will consist of licensed drivers eighteen years or older as recorded by the Illinois Secretary of State.

To the extent possible, elimination of duplicate names between the lists of registered voters and licensed drivers will be accomplished manually, through the use of a computer system, or through a combination of both.

Any reference to random selection in this Plan shall mean that all selections are part of a randomized procedure which ensures that:

- Names chosen will represent all segments of the source from which drawn.

- The mathematical odds of any single name being picked are substantially equalized.

- The possibility of human discretion or choice affecting the selection of any individual's name is eliminated.

The Master Jury Wheel—Method and Manner of Random Selection

At the option of the Clerk after consultation with the Chief Judge, the selection of names from complete source list databases in electronic media for the master jury wheel may be accomplished by a purely randomized process through a properly programmed electronic data processing system. Similarly, a properly programmed electronic data processing system for pure randomized selection may be used to select names from the master wheel for the purpose of summoning persons to serve as petit or grand jurors. The random selection of names from the source lists for inclusion in the master wheel by data computer personnel must ensure that each county within the jury division is substantially proportionally represented in the master jury wheel in accordance with 28 U.S.C. § 1863(b)(3). The selections of names from the source lists and the master wheel must also ensure that the mathematical odds of any single name being picked are substantially equal.

The Master Jury Wheel—Selection of Names by Electronic Method

The Court elects to use planned and programmed electronic methods in connection with the District's voter record source lists, licensed drivers source lists, master jury wheels, and qualified jury wheels. Names from all source lists will be randomly drawn by lot.

The Clerk will provide detailed instructions to local and state officials and to the vendor selected for electronic processing of the source lists into the master wheel. The Clerk will ensure that the instructions are specifically followed and that the vendor completes a Certificate of Compliance.

The Master Jury Wheel—Creation and Refilling

This Plan contemplates two master wheels. Jurors will be drawn from the wheel which contains names from each of the two jury divisions—East St. Louis and Benton. The names and addresses of all persons randomly selected from the source lists of voters at the last general election and licensed drivers shall be placed in each master jury wheel in electronic form as described above. Pursuant to 28 U.S.C. § 1863(b)(4), the minimum number of names to be placed in the master jury wheels shall be at least one-half of one percent (.5%) of the total number of names on all county source lists. Therefore, the minimum number of names in the East St. Louis jury division is 15,000, and the minimum number of names in the Benton jury division is 10,000.

The Chief Judge may order additional names to be placed in the master jury wheel for each place of Court, as necessary, and in accordance with the formula described above. The master and qualified jury wheels shall be emptied and refilled every two years, not later than June 1 of the year following a general election.

The Master Jury Wheel—Drawing Names

The Clerk shall draw at random from the master jury wheel the names of as many persons as may be required for jury service. The Clerk shall post a general notice for public review in the Clerk's Office and on the Court's website explaining the process by which names are periodically and randomly drawn.

If ordered by the Chief Judge, the Clerk may prepare an alphabetical list of the names drawn from the master jury wheel, but the list shall not be disclosed to any person except pursuant to this Plan, for use in challenging compliance with selection procedures pursuant to 28 U.S.C § 1867, or for maintenance and inspection of records pursuant to 28 U.S.C. § 1868.

Qualification and Summoning Procedure

Pursuant to 28 U.S.C § 1878, the Clerk shall use the optional one-step summoning and qualification procedure, in lieu of two separate procedures.

Completion of Juror Qualification Form

The Clerk shall utilize the juror qualification forms prescribed by the Administrative Office of the United States Courts and approved by the Judicial Conference of the United States. The Clerk shall mail to every person whose name is drawn from the master wheel a juror qualification form accompanied by instructions to fill out and return the form, duly signed and sworn, to the Clerk by mail or through the Court's internet website within ten days.

If the person is unable to fill out and return the form, another shall do it for him/her, indicate that s/he has done so, and explain why the summoned person is unable to complete the form. In any case in which it appears there is omission, ambiguity, or error, the Clerk shall return the form to the person with instructions to make corrections as necessary and return the form to the Clerk within ten days.

Any person who fails to return a completed juror qualification form as instructed will receive a reminder postcard to complete the juror qualification form. Any person who fails to return the juror qualification form within ten days after receiving the reminder postcard may be summoned by the Chief Judge to appear and complete the juror qualification form.

Qualifications for Jury Service

The Clerk, under supervision of the Chief Judge, shall determine on the basis of information provided on the juror qualification form and/or other competent evidence whether a person is unqualified for, exempt from, or otherwise should be excused from jury service. The Clerk shall enter the determination on the juror qualification form and in the juror's record in the Court's jury database, Jury Management System (JMS).

The Clerk shall deem any person qualified to serve on petit and grand juries unless s/he:

- Is not a citizen of the United States, is not at least eighteen years old, and has not resided in the Southern District of Illinois for the previous year;

- Is unable to read, write, and understand the English language with a degree of proficiency sufficient to fill out the juror qualification form;

- Is unable to speak the English language;

- Is incapable, by reason of mental or physical infirmity, to render satisfactory jury service; or

- Has a charge pending against him/her or has been convicted in a state or federal court of a crime punishable by imprisonment for more than one year and his/her civil rights have not been restored.

Exemption from Jury Service

Pursuant to 28 U.S.C § 1863(b)(6), the following groups are exempt and therefore barred from jury service:

- Members in active service in the Armed Forces of the United States, defined in 10 U.S.C. § 101(a)(4) as including the Army, Navy, Air Force, Marine Corps, Coast Guard, including full-time, active Armed Forces Reserves and National Guard;

- Members of the fire or police departments of any State, county, or city (not including volunteer, commercial departments, or correctional institutions);

- Public officers in the executive, legislative, or judicial branches of the Government of the United States, any State, county, or city, who are actively engaged in the performance of official duties.

Excuses Upon Individual Request

This Court finds that jury service by members of the following groups of persons, on individual request, would cause undue hardship or extreme inconvenience to the members of the groups, and excuse of these individuals is not inconsistent with 28 U.S.C. §§ 1861 and 1862:

- Persons over 70 years of age;
- Persons who have, within the previous two years, served on a federal petit or grand jury;
- Persons having active care and custody of a child or children under ten years of age whose health or safety would be jeopardized by their absence for jury service, and persons who are essential to the care of aged or infirm persons;
- Any person whose services are so essential to the operation of a business, commercial, or agricultural enterprise that the business must close or cease to function if the person were required to perform jury service;
- Persons serving as volunteer safety personnel, who serve without compensation for a public agency, such as volunteer police, firefighters, rescue squads, or ambulance crew.

In addition to the members of groups subject to excuse from jury service as provided above, any person summoned for jury service may be <u>temporarily</u> excused by the Clerk upon showing of undue hardship or extreme inconvenience. The names of those persons temporarily excused will be automatically re-summoned for the first petit jury panel scheduled to appear after termination of the period of temporary excuse.

The Qualified Jury Wheel

The Clerk shall place the names of those persons from the two master jury wheels who have not been disqualified, exempted, or excused pursuant to this Plan into qualified jury wheels to administer the selection and payment of jurors. The Clerk shall ensure that an adequate number of names shall be contained in each jury wheel. The number of names to be drawn shall be determined by the Clerk based upon anticipated juror demands by the Court, plus a number of additional names sufficient to compensate for the estimated number of juror qualification forms that will be undeliverable or not completed and returned.

The qualified wheels shall be maintained on the Court's jury database, JMS, which allows the Clerk to draw only a purely randomized number of jurors to be summoned, as directed by the Court. The Clerk shall post a public notice explaining the automated selection process.

Each grand jury panel will be selected by jury division and may sit in any place where the Court convenes. Grand juries will be selected yearly, or more often as required by the Court. The Clerk shall order the drawing of the total number of grand jurors needed to be summoned from either jury division's master wheel.

Selection of Petit and Grand Jurors

Petit jury panels drawn as provided in this Plan constitute a pool to be used by the Court in the jury division for which drawn and shall serve for one month or one trial. They shall then be excused from further service, unless otherwise ordered by the Court. Names of persons summoned and appearing for service will be selected by lot for each separate trial panel.

Grand jury panels drawn as provided in this Plan constitutes a pool to be used by the Court in the jury division for which drawn and shall serve for twelve consecutive months, unless otherwise extended by the Court.

Disclosure of Juror Names to Parties and the Public

On the first day of trial, the Clerk shall prepare for the use of the Court and counsel a separate list of names of persons drawn from the qualified jury wheel and assigned to each petit jury panel. The names of persons assigned to a petit jury panel or impaneled for a trial will not be disclosed except during voir dire examination, unless otherwise ordered by a Judge where the interests of justice so requires.

The Clerk shall prepare a separate list of names of persons assigned to each grand jury. After a grand jury has been obtained and sworn, the names and addresses of those on each grand jury should not be maintained in any public record or publicly disclosed except on order of the Chief Judge or the Judge at whose request the grand jury was ordered.

Frequency of Service

In any two year period, no person shall be required to:

- Serve or attend court for prospective service as a petit juror for a total of more than thirty days, except when necessary to complete service in a particular case; or
- Serve on more than one grand jury; or
- Serve as both a petit and grand juror.

Disclosure of Documents

The contents of records used by the Clerk in connection with the jury selection process during the life of the master wheel, including juror qualification questionnaires, shall not be disclosed or made available to the public or media, except to challenge compliance with selection procedures, pursuant to 28 U.S.C. § 1867(f).

After the master jury wheel is emptied and refilled, and after all persons selected to serve as jurors before the master wheel was emptied have completed their service, all records and papers compiled and maintained by the Clerk before the master wheel was emptied shall be preserved in the custody of the Clerk for four years or next cyclical audit, whichever is longer, and shall be available for public inspection for the purpose of determining the validity of the selection of any jury. Any documents related to the financial records of juror payments shall be disposed of six years and three months after the final juror payment transaction.

Juror Shortage

When there is an unanticipated shortage of available petit jurors drawn from the qualified jury wheel, the Chief Judge may order the United States Marshal to summon additional jurors from the lists of registered voters, actual voters, or licensed drivers, consistent with 28 U.S.C §§ 1861 and 1862.

Failure to Appear for Jury Service

Any person summoned for jury service who fails to appear as directed may be ordered to appear and show cause for failure to comply with the summons. Any person who fails to show good cause for noncompliance with a summons may be fined not more than $1,000, imprisoned not more than three days, ordered to perform community service, or any combination thereof.

[Dated: November 9, 2011.]

CRIMINAL JUSTICE ACT PLAN

I. Introduction

Pursuant to the Criminal Justice Act of 1964, as amended, 18 U.S.C. § 3006A (the "CJA"), and the "Guidelines for Administering the CJA and Related Statutes," contained in Chapter 7 of the *Guide to Judiciary Policy* (the "CJA Guidelines"), the United States District Court for the Southern District of Illinois adopts this Criminal Justice Act Plan (the "CJA Plan") to prescribe the procedures and requirements for furnishing representation in this Court to any person financially unable to obtain adequate representation in accordance with the CJA. This Plan supersedes all prior Criminal Justice Act Plans of this Court.

II. Objectives

The objective of this CJA Plan is to attain the ideal of equality before the law for all persons. It shall be administered so that those accused of a crime (or otherwise eligible for services pursuant to the CJA), will not be deprived of legal services because they are financially unable to pay for adequate representation or any element of representation necessary to an adequate defense. It is also the objective of this CJA Plan to particularize the requirements of the CJA, the USA Patriot Improvement and Reauthorization Act of 2005 (codified in part at 18 U.S.C. § 3599 — formerly the Anti–Drug Abuse Act of 1988), and the CJA Guidelines to meet the needs of this judicial district.

III. Definitions

"Appointed Attorney" includes private attorneys, the Federal Public Defender, and staff attorneys of the Federal Public Defender in this judicial district.

"Clerk" or **"Clerk of Court"** means the Clerk of the United States District Court for the Southern District of Illinois or her designee.

"Court" means the United States District Court for the Southern District of Illinois and includes any of the District Judges and Magistrate Judges assigned to this judicial district.

"Judicial Officer" includes a United States District Judge or a United States Magistrate Judge assigned to the Southern District of Illinois, a Judge designated to sit in the Southern District of Illinois, a Judge of the United States Court of Appeals for the Seventh Circuit, or a Justice of the United States Supreme Court.

"Representation" includes counsel and investigative, expert, and other services authorized by the CJA.

IV. Compliance

The Court, the Clerk of Court, the Federal Public Defender, and private attorneys appointed under the CJA shall comply with this CJA Plan and with the CJA Guidelines approved by the Judicial Conference of the United States and/or its Committee on Defender Services.

V. Provision of Representation

A. Timing. Counsel shall be provided to a financially eligible person as soon as feasible after the person is taken into custody, when the person first appears before a Judicial Officer, when the person is formally charged or notified of charges (if formal charges are sealed), or when a Judicial Officer otherwise considers appointment of counsel appropriate under the CJA, whichever occurs first.

B. Circumstances.

1. *Mandatory Representation.* Representation *shall* be provided for any financially eligible person who:

- is charged with a felony or a Class A misdemeanor;

- is a juvenile alleged to have committed an act of juvenile delinquency (as defined in 18 U.S.C. § 5031);

- is charged with a violation of probation or faces a change of a term or condition of probation (unless the modification sought is favorable to the probationer, and the government has not objected to the proposed change);

- is under arrest, when such representation is required by law;

- is charged with a violation of supervised release or faces modification, reduction, or enlargement of a condition, or extension or revocation of a term of supervised release (unless the change to the condition or term of supervised release is favorable to the offender, and the government has not objected to the proposed change);

- is subject to a mental condition hearing pursuant to 18 U.S.C. §§ 4241–4248;

- is in custody as a material witness;

- is entitled to appointment of counsel under the Sixth Amendment to the United States Constitution.

- faces loss of liberty in a case, and federal law requires the appointment of counsel;

- is entitled to appointment of counsel in a proceeding to transfer to or from a foreign country under 18 U.S.C. § 4109;

- is entitled to appointment of counsel in parole proceedings; or

- is seeking to set aside or vacate a death sentence under 28 U.S.C. §§ 2254 or 2255.

2. *Discretionary Representation.* Whenever a Judicial Officer determines that the interests of justice so require, representation may be provided for any financially eligible person who:

- is charged with a Class B or C misdemeanor, or an infraction for which a sentence to confinement is authorized;

- is seeking relief, other than to set aside or vacate a death sentence, under 28 U.S.C. §§ 2241, 2254, or 2255;

- is charged with civil or criminal contempt and faces loss of liberty;

- has been called as a witness before a grand jury, a court, the Congress, or a federal agency or commission which has the power to compel testimony, and there is reason to believe, either prior to or during testimony, that the witness could be subject to a criminal prosecution, a civil or criminal contempt proceeding, or face loss of liberty;

- is proposed by the United States Attorney for processing under a pretrial diversion program;

- is held for international extradition under 18 U.S.C. §§ 3181–3196.

3. *Ancillary Matters.* Representation may also be furnished for financially eligible persons in ancillary matters appropriate to the proceedings. *See Guide to Judiciary Policy, Volume 7, Chapter 2, § 210.20.30.*

C. Number of Counsel.

1. *Criminal Cases.* More than one attorney may be appointed in any case determined by the Court to be extremely difficult. In any case in which a defendant is charged with a crime which may be punishable by death, a defendant shall be entitled to at least two attorneys.

2. *Habeas Corpus Proceedings.* Pursuant to 18 U.S.C. § 3599(a)(2), a financially eligible person seeking to vacate or set aside a death sentence in proceedings under 28 U.S.C. §§ 2254 or 2255 is entitled to appointment of one or more qualified attorneys. Due to the complex, demanding, and protracted nature of death penalty proceedings, a Judicial Officer should consider appointing at least two attorneys.

D. Qualifications of Counsel. A Judicial Officer should ensure that all attorneys appointed in a federal death penalty case are well qualified, by virtue of their prior defense experience, training, and commitment, to serve as counsel in highly specialized and demanding litigation. Ordinarily, "learned" counsel, as that term is used in 18 U.S.C. § 3005, should have (1) distinguished prior experience in the trial, appeal, or post-conviction review of federal death penalty cases, or (2) distinguished prior experience in state death penalty trials, appeals, or post-conviction review that, in combination with co-counsel, will assure high-quality representation. When appointing counsel in federal capital prosecutions, the Court should consider the recommendation of the Federal Public Defender.

If an appointment is made in a death penalty case *before judgment*, at least one of the attorneys appointed must have been admitted to practice in this court for not less than five years and must have experience of at least three years in the actual trial of felony prosecutions. Pursuant to 18 U.S.C. § 3005, at least one of the attorneys appointed must be experienced in and knowledgeable about the defense of capital cases. If an appointment is made in a death penalty case *after judgment*, at least one of the attorneys appointed must have been admitted to practice in a federal court of appeals for not less than five years and must have experience of at least three years in handling federal appeals in felony cases. In appointing post-conviction counsel in a case where the defendant is sentenced to death, a Judicial Officer should consider the attorney's experience in federal post-conviction proceedings and capital post-conviction proceedings, as well as the general qualifications identified above.

If an attorney does not meet the qualifications set forth above, for good cause shown, the Court may appoint an attorney whose background, knowledge, or experience would otherwise enable him or her to properly represent the defendant, with due consideration to the seriousness of the possible penalty and to the unique and complex nature of the litigation.

E. Eligibility for Representation. The determination of eligibility for representation under the CJA is a judicial function to be performed by a Judicial Officer after making appropriate inquiries concerning the person's financial eligibility. If, at any time after appointment, counsel obtains information that a client is financially able to make payment, in whole or in part, for legal or other services in connection with his or her representation, and the source of the attorney's information is not protected as a privileged communication, counsel shall promptly advise the Court.

VI. Federal Public Defender Organization

The Federal Public Defender Organization for the Southern District of Illinois previously established in this district pursuant to the CJA, *see* 18 U.S.C. § 3006A(g)(2)(A), is recognized as the Federal Public Defender Organization for this district. The Federal Public Defender Organization shall maintain offices in East St. Louis and Benton, Illinois, and shall be capable of providing legal services throughout the Southern District of Illinois. The Federal Public Defender shall be responsible for the supervision and management of the Federal Public Defender Organization for this district, including the assignment of cases to staff attorneys at his discretion.

VII. Composition of Panel of Private Attorneys

A. Approval and Size. The Court has established a panel of private attorneys (hereinafter referred to as the "CJA Panel") who are eligible and willing to be appointed to provide representation under the CJA. Periodically, the Court shall fix the size of the CJA Panel. The CJA Panel shall be large enough to provide a sufficient number of experienced attorneys to handle the CJA caseload, yet small enough so that panel members will receive an adequate number of appointments to maintain their proficiency in federal criminal defense work and thereby provide a high quality of representation. The Federal Public Defender shall maintain a current list of attorneys included on the CJA Panel, with current office and email addresses and telephone numbers. The Federal Public Defender shall furnish a copy of this list to each District Judge and Magistrate Judge.

B. Qualifications. Attorneys who serve on a CJA Panel must be members in good standing of the bar of this court and have demonstrated experience in, and knowledge of, the Federal Rules of Criminal Procedure, the Federal Rules of Evidence, and the Sentencing Guidelines. Attorneys who serve on the CJA Panel will also be expected to have and maintain acceptable standards of competence, judgment, character, and demeanor to provide their clients with all the benefits of high quality legal counsel. All qualified attorneys shall furnish representation in CJA cases, without regard to race, color, religion, sex, age, national origin, sexual orientation, or disabling condition.

C. Application for Membership. Application forms for CJA Panel membership shall be made available upon request by the Federal Public Defender. Completed applications shall be submitted to the Federal Public Defender who will forward the applications to the Chairperson of the Panel Selection Committee.

D. Panel Selection Committee. A Panel Selection Committee shall be established by the Court. The Committee shall consist of one District Judge, one Magistrate Judge, one attorney who has served at least three years as a member of the CJA Panel, and the Federal Public Defender. The Committee shall select its own Chairperson. The Panel Selection Committee shall review applications for membership on the CJA Panel and shall make a recommendation to the Court regarding the applicant's worthiness for service on the CJA Panel. The Panel Selection Committee shall be permitted to gather information from any source for purposes of making a worthiness determination.

The Panel Selection Committee shall meet at least once a year to review the performance of each member of the CJA Panel and shall provide the Court with a list of attorneys recommended for retention on the CJA Panel. At its annual meeting, the Committee shall also review the operation and administration of the panel over the preceding year and recommend to the Court any changes deemed necessary or appropriate regarding the appointment process and panel management.

E. Appointments. When it is determined that there is a need for appointment of counsel, the District Judge or Magistrate Judge shall notify the Federal Public Defender of the need for counsel and the nature of the case. Appointments from the list of private panel attorneys should be made on a rotational basis, subject to the Court's discretion to make exceptions due to the nature and complexity of the case, an attorney's experience, and geographical considerations. This procedure should result in a balanced distribution of appointments and compensation among the members of the CJA Panel and quality representation for each defendant.

In the event of an emergency, i.e., weekends, holidays, or other non-working hours of the Federal Public Defender's office, a District Judge or Magistrate Judge may appoint any attorney from the current list. If a member of the CJA Panel is appointed out of sequence, the appointing District Judge or Magistrate Judge shall inform the Federal Public Defender of the attorney's name and date of appointment.

Where practical and cost effective, private attorneys from the CJA Panel will be appointed in a substantial proportion of the cases in which the accused is determined to be financially eligible for representation under the CJA. "Substantial" is defined as approximately 25% of the appointments under the CJA annually in the district.

The Federal Public Defender shall maintain a public record of assignments of private attorneys and, when appropriate, supporting statistical data.

VIII. Duties of Appointed Attorneys

Services rendered by an appointed attorney shall be commensurate with those rendered if counsel were privately employed by the person. Appointed attorneys shall conform to the highest standards of professional conduct, including but not limited to the provisions of the Rules of Professional Conduct adopted by the Supreme Court of the State of Illinois and other standards for professional conduct adopted by the Court.

Appointed attorneys may not require, request, or accept any payment or promise of payment or any other valuable consideration for representation under the appointment, unless such payment is approved by the Court.

Once counsel is appointed under the CJA, counsel shall continue the representation until: (1) the matter, including appeal and review by certiorari, is closed; (2) substitute counsel has filed a notice of appearance; (3) an order has been entered allowing or requiring the person represented to proceed pro se; or (4) the appointment is terminated by court order.

In cases involving a defendant charged with a crime punishable by death or post-conviction proceedings seeking to vacate or set aside a death sentence, unless replaced by similarly qualified counsel upon the attorney's own motion or upon motion of the defendant, each appointed attorney shall represent the defendant throughout every subsequent stage of available judicial proceedings, including pretrial proceedings, trial, sentencing, motions for new trial, appeals, applications for writ of certiorari to the Supreme Court of the United States, and all available post-conviction process, together with applications for stays of execution and other appropriate motions and procedures, and shall also represent the defendant in such competency proceedings and proceedings for executive or other clemency as may be available to the defendant.

IX. Duties of Law Enforcement and Related Agencies

Federal law enforcement and prosecutorial agencies, probation officers, and pretrial services officers in this district, and those acting on their behalf, shall promptly ask any person who is in custody or who otherwise may be entitled to counsel under the CJA, whether he or she is financially able to secure representation. If the person indicates that he or she is not able to secure representation, the agent or officer shall arrange to have the person promptly presented before a District Judge or a Magistrate Judge for determination of financial eligibility and appointment of counsel.

When practicable, unless the right to counsel is waived or the defendant otherwise consents to a pretrial interview without counsel, financially eligible defendants will be furnished an appointed attorney prior to being interviewed by a pretrial services officer. Appointed attorneys shall be accorded reasonable opportunity to confer with the accused before the pretrial services interview is conducted. The pretrial services officer will provide counsel notice and a reasonable opportunity to attend any interview of the defendant by the pretrial services officer prior to the initial pretrial release hearing or a detention hearing held under 18 U.S.C. § 3142(f).

X. Compensation

The CJA provides that the reviewing Judicial Officer shall fix the compensation and reimbursement to be paid to private counsel. Absent conflicts of interest, claims for compensation of private attorneys providing representation under the CJA shall be submitted to the office of the Federal Public Defender in a timely fashion. That office shall review the claim for mathematical and technical accuracy, for reasonableness, for recordation of statistical information, and for conformity with the CJA Guidelines. If correct, the Federal Public Defender shall forward the claim for consideration by the appropriate Judicial Officer. The Court will exert its best effort to avoid delays in reviewing payment vouchers.

In addition to reviewing the claim for mathematical and technical accuracy, the Federal Public Defender may recommend that the CJA Panel attorney submitting the claim supplement the voucher with a narrative statement regarding unusual services or other charges that require clarification before the Court reviews the claim. Whenever the claim for compensation exceeds the threshold amount of the district judge's authority (and must, therefore, be submitted to the Chief Judge of the Seventh Circuit for additional approval), the attorney shall provide a reasonably detailed statement as to why the representation was "extended or complex."

If a Judicial Officer determines that a claim for compensation should be reduced, appointed counsel should be provided (1) prior notice of the proposed reduction with a brief statement of the reason(s) for it, and (2) an opportunity to address the matter. Notice need not be given to appointed counsel when the reduction is based on mathematical or technical errors only.

XI. Miscellaneous

Each private attorney shall be provided a copy of this CJA Plan by the Federal Public Defender at the time the attorney is designated as a CJA Panel member. The Federal Public Defender also shall maintain a current copy of the CJA Guidelines for the use of members of the CJA Panel and shall make known to such attorneys its availability. The CJA Plan shall also be available for access by attorneys and the public on the Court's website, www. ilsd.uscourts.gov.

Standard forms pertaining to the CJA and approved by the Judicial Conference of the United States or its Committee on Defender Services and prescribed and distributed by the Director of the Administrative Office of the United States Courts shall be used, where applicable, in all proceedings under this Amended CJA Plan.

Nothing contained in this Plan or in the CJA Guidelines should be construed as requiring a hearing or as discouraging the Court from communicating informally with counsel about questions or concerns in person, telephonically, or electronically, as deemed appropriate or necessary.

This Plan, as amended this 2nd day of March, 2012, shall take effect when approved by the Judicial Council of the Seventh Circuit.

[Amended effective March 15, 2012.]

PLAN FOR PROMPT DISPOSITION OF CRIMINAL CASES (FINAL PLAN PURSUANT TO SPEEDY TRIAL PLAN ACT OF 1974 (18 U.S.C. § 3165(e)(3)))

I. INTRODUCTORY MATERIAL

A. Adoption of Plan and Rules by the Court. Pursuant to the requirements of the Speedy Trial Act of 1974 (18 U.S.C. § 3165(e) as amended) the judges of the United States District Court for the Southern District of Illinois have adopted the following District Plan for the Disposition of Criminal Cases. Section II of this plan also adopts certain time limits, procedures, and rules for the disposition of criminal cases and juvenile proceedings pursuant to Rule 50(b) of the Federal Rules of Criminal Procedure, the Speedy Trial Act of 1974 (18 U.S.C. Chapter 208) and the Federal Juvenile Delinquency Act (18 U.S.C. §§ 5036, 5037).

B. The Planning Group. This plan has been adopted after consultation with the Speedy Trial Act Planning Group for the Southern District of Illinois pursuant to 18 U.S.C. §§ 3165–3169.

The planning group consists of:

The Honorable J. Phil Gilbert, Chief Judge of the Southern District of Illinois

The Honorable Clifford J. Proud, United States Magistrate Judge

Michael Carr, Chief, Criminal Division, United States Attorney's Office
William Lucco, Esq.

Stuart J. O'Hare, Clerk, United States District Court

Paula G. Phillips, Esq.

Reneé E. Schooley, Assistant Federal Public Defender

Bruce Stewart, Esq.

Brian K. Trentman, Esq.

C. Availability of the Plan. Copies of this plan will be made available for inspection and copying at each office of the Clerk of the United States District Court for this district. Copies of Part II of this plan wherein the Court adopts certain procedures for the disposition of criminal cases shall be furnished to all interested persons by the Clerk of the Court.

Section II
Statement of Time Limits Adopted by the
Court and Procedures for Implementing
Them

II. STATEMENT OF TIME LIMITS TO TAKE EFFECT AND PROCEDURES FOR IMPLEMENTING THEM

Effective February 1, 1995, the following shall constitute the plan for achieving the prompt disposition of criminal cases in the Southern District of Illinois including certain rules of procedure and discovery.

Pursuant to the requirements of Rule 50(b) of the Federal Rules of Criminal Procedure, the Speedy Trial Act of 1974 (18 U.S.C. Chapter 208), the Speedy Trial Act Amendments Act of 1979 (Pub. L. No. 96–43, 93 Stat. 327), and the Federal Juvenile Delinquency Act (18 U.S.C. §§ 5036, 5037), the judges of the United States District Court for the Southern District of Illinois have adopted the following time limits and procedures to minimize undue delay and to further the prompt disposition of criminal cases and certain juvenile proceedings:

1. Applicability.

(a) *Offenses.* Pursuant to 18 U.S.C. §§ 3161 and 3172(2), the time limits set forth herein are applicable to all criminal offenses triable in this Court, including cases triable by United States Magistrates, except for Class B or C misdemeanors or infractions, as defined in 18 U.S.C. §§ 3559(a)(7), (8), and (9). Except as specifically provided, they are not applicable to proceedings under the Federal Juvenile Delinquency Act.

(b) *Persons.* The time limits are applicable to persons accused who have not been indicted or informed against as well as those who have, and the word defendant includes such persons unless the context indicates otherwise.

2. Priorities in Scheduling Criminal Cases. Preference shall be given to criminal proceedings as far as practicable as required by Rule 50(a) of the Federal

Rules of Criminal Procedure. The trial of defendants in custody solely because they are awaiting trial should be given preference over other criminal cases.

3. Time Within Which an Indictment or Information Must be Filed.

(a) *Time Limits.* If an individual is arrested or served with a summons and the complaint charges an offense to be prosecuted in this district, any indictment or information subsequently filed in connection with such charge shall be filed within 30 days of arrest or service.

(b) *Grand Jury Not in Session.* If the defendant is charged with a felony to be prosecuted in this district, and no grand jury in the district has been in session during the 30 day period prescribed in subsection (a), such period shall be extended an additional 30 days.

(c) *Measurement of Time Periods.* If a person has not been arrested or served with a summons on a Federal charge, an arrest will be deemed to have been made at such time as the person (i) is held in custody solely for the purpose of responding to a Federal charge; (ii) is delivered to the custody of a Federal official in connection with a Federal charge; or (iii) appears before a judicial officer in connection with a Federal charge

(d) *Related Procedures.*

(1) At the time of the earliest appearance before a judicial officer of a person who has been arrested for an offense not charged in an indictment or information, the judicial officer shall establish for the record the date on which the arrest took place.

(2) In the absence of a showing to the contrary, a summons shall be considered to have been served on the date of service shown on the return thereof.

4. Time Within Which Trial Must Commence.

(a) *Time limits.* The trial of a Defendant shall commence not later than 70 days after the last to occur of the following dates:

(1) The date on which an indictment or information is filed in this district,

(2) The date on which a sealed indictment or information is unsealed; or

(3) The date of the defendant's first appearance before a judicial officer of this district.

(b) *Retrial; Trial After Reinstatement of an Indictment or Information.* The retrial of a defendant shall commence within 70 days from the date the order occasioning the retrial becomes final, as shall the trial of a defendant upon an indictment or information dismissed by a trial court and reinstated following an appeal. If the retrial or trial follows an appeal or collateral attack, the Court may extend the period if unavailability of witnesses or other factors resulting from passage of time make trial within 70 days impractical. The extended period shall not exceed 180 days.

(c) *Withdrawal of Plea.* If a defendant enters a plea of guilty or nolo contenders to any or all charges in an indictment or information and is subsequently permitted to withdraw it, the time limit will be determined for all counts as if the indictment or information were filed on the day the order permitting withdrawal of the plea became final.

(d) *Superseding Charges.* If, after an indictment or information has been filed, a complaint, indictment, or information is filed which charges the defendant with the same offense or with an offense required to be joined with that offense, the time limit applicable to the subsequent charge will be determined as follows:

(1) If the original indictment or information was dismissed on motion of the defendant before the filing of the subsequent charge, the time limit shall be determined without regard to the existence of the original charge.

(2) If the original indictment or information is pending at the time the subsequent charge is filed, the trial shall commence within the time limit for commencement of trial on the original indictment or information.

(3) If the original indictment or information was dismissed on motion of the United States Attorney before the filing of the subsequent charge, the trial shall commence within the time limit for commencement of trial on the original indictment or information, but the period during which the defendant was not under charges shall be excluded from the computations. Such period is the period between the dismissal of the original indictment or information and the date the time would have commenced to run on the subsequent charge had there been no previous charge.

If the subsequent charge is contained in a complaint, the formal time limit within which an indictment or information must be obtained on the charge shall be determined without regard to the existence of the original indictment or information, but earlier action may in fact be required if the time limit for commencement of trial is to be satisfied.

(e) *Measurement of Time Periods for the Purposes of this Section.*

(1) If a defendant signs a written consent to be tried before a magistrate and no indictment or information charging the offense has been filed, the time limit shall run from the date of such consent.

(2) In the event of a transfer to this district under Rule 20 of the Federal Rules of Criminal Procedure, the indictment or information shall be deemed filed in this district when the papers in the proceeding or certified copies thereof are received by the Clerk.

(3) A trial in a jury case shall be deemed to commence at the beginning of voir dire.

(4) A trial in a non-jury case shall be deemed to commence on the day the case is called, provided that some step in the trial procedure immediately follows.

(f) *Related Procedures.*

(1) At the time of the defendant's earliest appearance before a judicial officer of this district, the officer will take appropriate steps to assure that the defendant is represented by counsel and shall appoint counsel where appropriate under the Criminal Justice Act and Rule 44 of the Federal Rules of Criminal Procedure.

(2) The Court shall have sole responsibility for setting cases for trial after consultation with counsel. At the time of arraignment or as soon thereafter as is practicable, each case will be set for trial on a day certain or listed for trial on a weekly or other short-term calendar.

(3) Individual calendars shall be managed so that it will be reasonably anticipated that every criminal case set for trial will be reached during the week of original setting. A conflict in schedules of Assistant United States Attorneys or defense counsel will be ground for a continuance or delayed setting only if approved by the Court and called to the Court's attention at the earliest practicable time.

(4) In the event that a complaint, indictment, or information is filed against a defendant charged in a pending indictment or information or in an indictment or information dismissed on motion of the United States Attorney, the trial on the new charge shall commence within the time limit for commencement of trial on the original indictment or information, unless the Court finds that the new charge is not for the same offense charged in the original indictment or information or an offense required to be joined therewith.

(5) At the time of the filing of a complaint, indictment, or information described in paragraph (4), the United States Attorney shall give written notice to the Court of that circumstance and of his position with respect to the computation of the time limits.

(6) All pretrial hearings shall be conducted as soon after the arraignment as possible, consistent with the priorities of other matters on the court's criminal docket.

(7) Motions, discovery, and inspection shall commence following arraignment in accordance with section 12.

5. Defendants in Custody.

(a) *Time Limits.* Notwithstanding any longer time periods that may be permitted under sections 3 and 4, the following time limit will also be applicable to defendants in custody:

The trial of a defendant held in custody solely for the purpose of trial on a Federal charge shall commence within 90 days following the beginning of continuous custody.

(b) *Measurement of Time Periods.* For the purposes of this section:

(1) A defendant is deemed to be in detention awaiting trial when he is arrested on a Federal charge or otherwise held for the purpose of responding to a Federal charge. Detention is deemed to be solely because the defendant is awaiting trial unless the person exercising custodial authority has an independent basis (not including a detainer) for continuing to hold the defendant.

(2) If a case is transferred pursuant to Rule 20 of the Federal Rules of Criminal Procedure and the defendant subsequently rejects disposition under Rule 20 or the Court declines to accept the plea, a new period of continuous detention awaiting trial will begin at that time.

(3) A trial shall be deemed to commence as provided in sections 4(e)(3) and 4(e)(4).

(c) *Related Procedure.* If a defendant is being held in custody solely for the purpose of awaiting trial, the United States Attorney shall advise the Court at the earliest practicable time of the date of the beginning of such custody.

6. Exclusion of Time from Computations.

(a) *Applicability.* In computing any time limit under sections 3, 4, or 5, the periods of delay set forth in 18 U.S.C. § 3161(h) shall be excluded. Such periods of delay shall not be excluded in computing the minimum period for commencement of trial under section 7.

(b) *Records of Excludable Time.* The Clerk of the Court shall enter on the docket, in the form prescribed by the Administrative Office of the United States Courts, information with respect to excludable periods of time for each criminal defendant. With respect to proceedings prior to the filing of an indictment or information, excludable time shall be reported to the Clerk by the United States Attorney.

(c) *Stipulations.*

(1) The attorney for the government and the attorney for the defendant may at any time enter into stipulations with respect to the accuracy of the docket entries recording excludable time.

(2) To the extent that the amount of time stipulated by the parties does not exceed the amount recorded on the docket for any excludable period of delay, the stipulation shall be conclusive as between the parties unless it has no basis in fact or law. It shall similarly be conclusive as to a codefendant for the limited purpose of determining, under 18 U.S.C. § 3161(h)(7), whether time has run against the defendant entering into the stipulation.

(3) To the extent that the amount of time stipulated exceeds the amount recorded on the docket, the stipulation shall have no effect unless approved by the Court.

(d) *Pre–Indictment Procedures.*

(1) In the event that the United States Attorney anticipates that an indictment or information will not be filed within the time limit set forth in section 3, he may file a written motion with the Court for a determination of excludable time. In the event that the United States Attorney seeks a continuance under 18 U.S.C. § 3161(h)(8), he shall file a written motion with the Court requesting such a continuance.

(2) The motion of the United States Attorney shall state (i) the period of time proposed for exclusion, and (ii) the basis of the proposed exclusion. If the motion is for a continuance under 18 U.S.C. § 3161(h)(8), it shall also state whether or not the defendant is being held in custody on the basis of the complaint. In appropriate circumstances, the motion may include a request that some or all of the supporting material be considered ex parte and in camera.

(3) The Court may grant a continuance under 18 U.S.C. § 3161(h)(8) for either a specific period of time or a period to be determined by reference to an event (such as recovery from illness) not within the control of the government. If the continuance is to a date not certain, the Court shall require one or both parties to inform the Court promptly when and if the circumstances that justify the continuance no longer exist. In addition, the Court shall require one or both parties to file periodic reports bearing on the continued existence of such circumstances. The Court shall determine the frequency of such reports in the light of the facts of the particular case.

(e) *Post–Indictment Procedures.*

(1) At each appearance of counsel before the court, counsel shall examine the Clerk's records of excludable time for completeness and accuracy and shall bring to the Court's immediate attention any claim that the Clerk's record is in any way incorrect.

(2) In the event that the Court continues a trial beyond the time limit set forth in sections 4 or 5, the Court shall determine whether the limit may be recomputed by excluding time pursuant to 18 U.S.C. § 3161(h).

(3) If it is determined that a continuance is justified, the Court shall set forth its findings in the record, either orally or in writing. If the continuance is granted under 18 U.S.C. § 3161(h)(8), the Court also set forth its reasons for finding that the ends of justice served by granting the continuance outweigh the best interests of the public and the defendant in a speedy trial. If the continuance is to a date not certain, the Court shall require one or both parties to inform the Court promptly when and if the circumstances that justify the continuance no longer exist. In addition, the Court shall require one or both parties to file periodic reports bearing on the continued existence of such circumstances. The Court shall determine the frequency of such reports in the light of the facts of the particular case.

(4) In an effort to ensure proper measurement of the 70 day time limit within which trial must commence, as set forth under section 4(a), the United States Attorney shall notify the Court in writing on the date, by his or her calculation, that there are 25 days remaining within which to commence trial.

7. Minimum Period for Defense Preparation. Unless the defendant consents in writing to the contrary, the trial shall not commerce earlier than 30 days from the date on which the indictment or information is filed or, if later, from the date on which counsel first enters an appearance or on which the defendant expressly waives counsel and elects to proceed pro se. In circumstances in which the 70 day time limit for commencing trial on a charge in an indictment or information is determined by reference to an earlier indictment or information pursuant to section 4(d), the 30 day minimum period will also be determined by reference to the earlier indictment or information. When prosecution is resumed on an original indictment or information following a mistrial, appeal, or withdrawal of a guilty plea, a new 30 day minimum period will not begin to run. The Court will in all cases schedule trials so as to permit defense counsel adequate preparation time in the light of all the circumstances.

8. Time Within Which Defendant Should Be Sentenced.

(a) *Time Limit.* A defendant shall ordinarily be sentenced within 90 days of the date of his conviction or plea of guilty or nolo contendere.

(b) *Related Procedures.* If the defendant and his counsel consent thereto, a presentence investigation may be commenced prior to a plea of guilty or nolo contendere or a conviction.

9. Juvenile Proceedings.

(a) *Time Within Which Trial Must Commence.* An alleged delinquent who is in detention pending trial shall be brought to trial within 30 days of the date on which such detention was begun, as provided in 18 U.S.C. § 5036.

(b) *Time of Dispositional Hearing.* If a juvenile is adjudicated delinquent, a separate dispositional hearing shall be held no later than 20 court days after trial unless the Court has ordered further study of the juvenile in accordance with 18 U.S.C. § 5037(c).

10. Sanctions.

(a) *Dismissal or Release from Custody.* Failure to comply with the requirements of Title I of the Speedy Trial Act may entitle the defendant to dismissal of the charges against him or to release from pretrial custody. Nothing in this plan shall be construed to require that a case be dismissed or a defendant released from custody in circumstances in which such action would not be required by 18 U.S.C. § 3162 and 3164.

(b) *High–Risk Defendants.* A high-risk defendant, as defined in 18 U.S.C. § 3164(a), whose trial has not commenced within the time limit set forth in 18 U.S.C. § 3164(b) shall, if the failure to commence trial was through no fault of the attorney for the government have his release conditions automatically reviewed. A high-risk defendant who is found by the Court to have intentionally delayed the trial of his case shall be subject to an order of the Court modifying his nonfinancial conditions of release under chapter 207 of Title 18, U.S.C. to ensure that he shall appear at trial as required.

(c) *Discipline of Attorneys.* In a case in which counsel (1) knowingly allows the case to be set for trial without disclosing the fact that a necessary witness would be unavailable for trial, (2) files a motion solely for the purpose of delay which he knows is frivolous and without merit, (3) makes a statement for the purpose of obtaining a continuance which he knows to be false and which is material to the granting of the continuance, or (4) otherwise willfully fails to proceed to trial without justification consistent with 18 U.S.C. § 3161, the Court may punish such counsel as provided in 18 U.S.C. §§ 3162(b) and (c).

(d) *Alleged Juvenile Delinquents.* An alleged delinquent in custody whose trial has not commenced within the time limit set forth in 18 U.S.C. § 5036 shall be entitled to dismissal of his case pursuant that section unless the Attorney General shows that the delay was consented to or caused by the juvenile or his counsel, or would be in the interest of justice in the particular case.

11. Persons Serving Terms of Imprisonment. If the United States Attorney knows that a person charged with an offense is serving a term of imprisonment in any penal institution, he shall promptly seek to obtain the presence of the prisoner for trial, or cause a detainer to be filed, in accordance with the provisions of 18 U.S.C. § 3161(j).

12. Pretrial Motions Discovery and Inspection.

(a) Subject to the following provisions of this section any and all pretrial motions may be filed after entry of a plea but must be filed within 10 days thereafter unless good cause for delay is shown in the motion.

(b) Except for good cause shown, the Court may not extend the time for motions under Federal Rule of Criminal Procedure 12(b)(3) beyond 10 days after plea. Such motions will be ruled on promptly, so that the trial need not be delayed.

(c) Within five (5) days after arraignment, the United States Attorney and the defendant's attorney shall confer and, upon request, discovery and inspection shall be made by both parties in accordance with Federal Rule of Criminal Procedure 16.

(d) If in the judgment of the United States Attorney it would not be in the interests of justice to make any one or more disclosures set forth in paragraph (c) and requested by defendant's counsel, disclosure may be declined. A declination of any requested disclosure shall be in writing, directed to defendant's counsel, and signed personally by the United States Attorney or the Assistant United States Attorney handling the case, and shall specify the types of disclosure that are declined. If the defendant seeks to challenge the declination, he shall proceed pursuant to subsection (e) below.

(e) If additional discovery or inspection is sought, defendant's attorney shall confer with the appropriate Assistant United States Attorney within ten (10) days of the arraignment, with a view to satisfying these requests in a cooperative atmosphere without recourse to the Court. The request may be oral or written and the United States Attorney shall respond in like manner.

(f) In the event defendant thereafter moves for additional discovery or inspection, his motion shall be filed within the time set by the Court for the filing, of pretrial motions. It shall contain:

(1) the statement that the conference prescribed in (e) above was held;

(2) the date of said conference;

(3) the name of the Assistant United States Attorney with whom conference was held; and

(4) the statement that agreement could not be reached concerning the discovery or inspection that is the subject of defendant's motion.

(g) Any duty of disclosure and discovery set forth in this plan is a continuing one and the United States Attorney shall produce any additional information gained by the government.

(h) Any disclosure granted by the government pursuant to this plan of material within the purview of Rule 16, Federal Rules of Criminal Procedure, shall be considered as relief sought by the defendant and granted by the Court.

Section III
Adoption and Effective Date

III. ADOPTION AND EFFECTIVE DATE

Pursuant to rule 50(b) of the Federal Rules of Criminal Procedure, the Speedy Trial Act of 1974 (18 U.S.C., chapter 208 as amended) and the Federal Juvenile Delinquency Act (18 U.S.C. §§ 5036, 5037) the foregoing is adopted as the District Court Plan for the Disposition of Criminal Cases in the Southern District of Illinois. This includes the adoption of certain rules and procedures for criminal cases contained in Part II of this plan.

Upon approval of the reviewing panel designated in accordance with 18 U.S.C. § 3165(c) and Rule 50(b) of the Federal Rules of Criminal Procedure this plan, and the time limits and procedures set forth herein, shall become effective on February 1, 1995 and shall supersede those previously in effect.

UNITED STATES BANKRUPTCY COURT FOR THE SOUTHERN DISTRICT OF ILLINOIS

Including Amendments Received
Through April 1, 2015

681

INTRODUCTION—SCOPE OF RULES

L.R. 1001. SCOPE OF RULES AND FORMS; SHORT TITLE

A. Title and Citation. These Rules are adopted pursuant to Rule 9029 of the Federal Rules of Bankruptcy Procedure to govern the local practice and procedures before the United States Bankruptcy Court for the Southern District of Illinois (the "Court"). These Rules shall be known as the "Local Rules of the Bankruptcy Court for the Southern District of Illinois" (the "Rules") and shall be cited as "S.D. Ill. LBR ___" herein. These Rules may be amended or supplemented from time to time by additional orders as the Court deems necessary. All references to provisions of the Bankruptcy Code are to Title 11 of the United States Code. All references to the District Court are to the United States District Court for the Southern District of Illinois.

B. Application. These Rules shall apply to all cases and proceedings in the United States Bankruptcy Court for the Southern District of Illinois except to the extent the Court determines application of the Rules would not be feasible or as otherwise more specifically provided herein. Failure to comply with these Rules may result in denial of the relief requested, dismissal, or other sanctions. To the extent that an order in a specific case conflicts with these Rules, the order in the case shall control.

C. Effective Date. These Rules become effective on June 1, 2012. The Rules governing chapter 13 plan contents shall be the rules in effect at the time the plan was originally filed. For previous versions of the rules, check the Court's website at www.ilsb. uscourts.gov or contact the Court.

D.   Relationship to Prior Rules/Orders; Actions Pending on Effective Date. These Rules supersede all previous rules and any conflicting Orders promulgated by this Court or any Judge of this Court. They shall govern all applicable proceedings brought in this Court after they take effect, and shall apply to all pending proceedings at the time they take effect, except to the extent that the Court determines that application thereof would not be feasible or would work injustice, in which event the former rules shall govern.

The General Orders, Standing Orders, and Administrative Orders listed in Appendix A of these Rules are repealed.

The superseding of any prior rule and repealing of any order shall not affect any act done pursuant to or obviate any act required thereby.

E.   Modification or Suspension of Rules. In specific cases or proceedings, the Court, upon its own motion or the motion of any party, may suspend or modify any of these Rules if the interests of justice so require.

F.   District Court Rules. Except as otherwise provided in these Rules, or as ordered by the Court in a particular case, the Local Rules of the United States District Court for the Southern District of Illinois are adopted and incorporated herein and shall apply to proceedings in the United States Bankruptcy Court for the Southern District of Illinois.

G.   Electronic Filing Rules and Chapter 13 Procedures Manual. The rules and procedures governing electronic filing are contained in a separate document entitled "Electronic Filing Rules." In addition, supplemental procedures, guidelines, and instructions applicable to chapter 13 cases are contained in a separate "Chapter 13 Procedures Manual." The Electronic Filing Rules and the Chapter 13 Procedures Manual are incorporated into and made a part of these Rules. Both will be maintained on the Court's website at www.ilsb.uscourts.gov. Reference in these Rules to any form, guideline or instruction in the Electronic Filing Rules or Chapter 13 Procedures Manual shall refer to the then-applicable form, guideline or instruction maintained by the Clerk of Court. All parties before the Court shall follow the procedures, guidelines and instructions set forth in the Electronic Filing Rules and Chapter 13 Procedures Manual and may be sanctioned for failing to do so.

H.   Conforming Changes. To the extent that the Federal Rules of Bankruptcy Procedure are revised from time to time, the Clerk of Court may revise these Rules to conform to such changes. The Clerk of Court will issue a public notice to advise of any such revision.

I. Nothing in these Rules precludes this Court from entering General Orders, Standing Orders, Administrative Orders or guidelines to supplement these Rules.

[Effective June 1, 2012.]

PART I.   COMMENCEMENT OF CASE; PROCEEDINGS RELATED TO PETITION AND ORDER FOR RELIEF

L.R. 1002–1.   NEW CASE FILING INFORMATION AND PDF DOCUMENTS

In any new case filed in this Court, if the information that is entered in the Court's electronic filing system is inconsistent with the attached PDF document(s), the information in the PDF document(s) will be considered the correct information and the PDF document(s) will control. The Clerk's office is authorized to correct the information in the electronic case file to match the information in the PDF document(s).

If notices or other documents are issued before the information in the electronic case file is corrected, and those notices or documents contain incorrect information, it is the responsibility of the person filing the case to notify creditors and parties in interest of this fact.

[Effective June 1, 2012.]

L.R. 1002–2.   MATRIX

A. The petitioner must file with the petition a mailing matrix of creditors listing the complete name, address, and zip code of each creditor. The matrix must be in a format prescribed in this Court's Style Guide for Electronic Case Filing, which can be found on the Court's website at www.ilsb.uscourts.gov. Attorneys who are registered CM/ECF participants are required to upload the creditor matrix in CM/ECF upon filing a petition for the commencement of a case. Pro se debtors must submit the matrix at the time of filing a petition for the commencement of a case, which shall be used for scanning the creditors into the computer.

B. When an attorney electronically files a petition as an emergency filing, the attorney must upload into CM/ECF the creditor information necessary to provide proper notice to all scheduled creditors. When a pro se debtor files a petition as an emergency filing, the debtor must submit the matrix at the time of filing, which shall be used for scanning the creditors into the computer.

C. The debtor shall also verify that the matrix includes all creditors listed on the schedules and submit, along with the petition, an appropriate verification similar to the one located on the Court's website at www.ilsb.uscourts.gov.

[Effective June 1, 2012.]

L.R. 1003. INVOLUNTARY PETITION

The burden to prosecute an involuntary petition rests with the petitioning creditors. Debtor shall file the schedules, statements and other documents required by Rule 1007 of the Federal Rules of Bankruptcy Procedure within 14 days of the entry of the order for relief. If debtor fails to do so, the petitioning creditors shall have 14 days thereafter to file the required schedules, statements and documents or a motion to appoint a responsible party to perform the duties of debtor. In the event the petitioning creditors fail to file either the required schedules and documents or a motion to appoint a responsible party, the Court may dismiss the involuntary petition for lack of prosecution.

[Effective June 1, 2012.]

L.R. 1006. FILING FEE

A. **Payment of Filing Fee in Installments.** Fifty percent of the filing fee shall be due at the time the petition is filed for debtors applying to pay the filing fee in installments.

B. **Waiver of Filing Fee.** The Court will post on the Court's website at www.ilsb.uscourts.gov the applicable poverty guidelines to be used in determining whether a debtor qualifies for a fee waiver pursuant to 28 U.S.C. § 1930(f). The order granting In Forma Pauperis status may be vacated if developments in the case demonstrate that waiver of the fee was unwarranted.

[Effective June 1, 2012.]

L.R. 1007–1. REQUIRED INFORMATION AND DOCUMENTATION FOR CASE TRUSTEES

A. **Information to be Served on Trustee.** For a list of the specific information and documents required by each Trustee, as well as whether the Trustee requires electronic or paper submission, consult the Court's website at www.ilsb.uscourts.gov.

B. **Other Documentation.** The debtor shall provide the documentation required by Rule 4002(b)(2) of the Federal Rules of Bankruptcy Procedure in the time and manner set forth by that Rule. If the debtor twice fails to provide the documentation in a timely

manner, the case will be dismissed without further hearing or notice, upon the filing of a motion to dismiss by the Trustee. The 10–day period set forth in Section 704(b)(1)(A) of the Bankruptcy Code shall be 10 days after the conclusion of the 341 meeting of creditors.

[Effective June 1, 2012.]

L.R. 1007–2. BANKRUPTCY CODE § 521(a)(1) FILING REQUIREMENTS

Effective as to cases filed on or after October 17, 2005, copies of all payment advices, or other evidence of payment, received by the debtor from any employer(s) of the debtor within 60 days prior to the date of the filing of the bankruptcy petition, (1) shall not be filed with the Court unless otherwise ordered; and (2) shall be provided to the Trustee, the United States Trustee if no Trustee has been appointed, and to any creditor who timely requests copies of payment advices, or other evidence of payment, at least 7 days before the first scheduled 341 meeting of creditors. To be considered timely, a creditor's request must be received at least 14 days before the first scheduled 341 meeting.

A. **Bankruptcy Code § 521(a)(1)(B)(iv).** The requirements of Section 521(a)(1)(B)(iv) of the Bankruptcy Code (that debtor provide copies of all payment advices or other evidence of payment received within 60 days before the date of the filing of the petition) is satisfied by providing to the Trustee (or the United States Trustee in a case where no Trustee has been appointed) at least 7 days before the first scheduled 341 meeting of creditors:

1. Payment advice(s) or other evidence of payment (which may be satisfied by providing less than "all payment advices or other evidence of payment received within 60 days before the date of the filing of the petition ..."—e.g. by providing a year-to-date statement that includes payments received within 60 days of the petition), or

2. A verified statement that the debtor did not receive payments to which Section 521(a)(1)(B)(iv) of the Bankruptcy Code applies.

3. Pay advices or other evidence of payment shall be arranged (1) separately for each debtor and (2) chronologically for each different employer.

4. Notwithstanding the foregoing, the Trustee may require that 6 months of pay advices or their evidence of payment (as defined in subsection 1 above) be provided to verify the current monthly income listed on Official Form B22A or B22C. Failure to provide this documentation shall not delay the commencement of the 341 meeting of creditors.

In no event shall the documents required by Section 521(a)(1)(B)(iv) of the Bankruptcy Code be provided later than 45 days after the date of the filing of the petition. If the 341 meeting is not set within 45 days of the filing of the petition, the 45–day deadline for providing payment advices to the Trustee (or the United States Trustee, if applicable) still applies. If the Trustee or the United States Trustee continues the 341 meeting to receive these documents, such continuance shall not be deemed a request or consent to extend the deadline of Section 521(i) of the Bankruptcy Code. Nothing in this Rule shall be construed as requiring the Trustee or the United States Trustee to continue the 341 meeting. Failure to provide the documents within the 45–day deadline shall be grounds for the Trustee or the United States Trustee (if applicable) to request dismissal. If the case is dismissed following such a request by the Trustee or the United States Trustee, and the debtor believes the case was dismissed in error, the debtor shall file any motion to reinstate the case within 14 days of the entry of the dismissal order. A case that has been dismissed for failure to file a required document or provide a required document to the Trustee or the United States Trustee will not be considered to be a case dismissed in error.

B. Bankruptcy Code § 521(a)(1)(B)(v). The requirement of Section 521(a)(1)(B)(v) of the Bankruptcy Code (statement of the amount of monthly net income, itemized to show how the amount is calculated) is satisfied by including such information in Schedule I.

C. Bankruptcy Code § 521(a)(1)(B)(vi). The requirement of Section 521(a)(1)(B)(vi) of the Bankruptcy Code (a statement disclosing any reasonably anticipated increase in income or expenditures over the next 12–month period following the date of the filing of the petition) is satisfied by including such information on the appropriate line item on Schedules I and J.

[Effective June 1, 2012.]

L.R. 1007–3. BANKRUPTCY CODE § 521 TAX RETURNS AND REQUESTS

Debtor shall provide the Trustee (or the United States Trustee if no Trustee has been appointed), no later than 7 days prior to the 341 meeting, a copy of the debtor's most recently filed federal and state tax returns, or a verified statement that such returns do not exist and the reason why the returns do not exist. The tax returns and/or verified statement shall not be filed with the Court. On request of a creditor under Section 521(e)(2)(A)(ii) of the Bankruptcy Code, the debtor shall provide copies of such tax returns to the creditor but shall not file the returns or an Exhibit Summary thereof with the Court. Failure to provide the Trustee (or the United States Trustee if applicable) with the required tax returns or a verified statement that such returns do not exist as set forth in this

Rule will result in the dismissal of the case without further notice, upon the filing of a motion to dismiss by the Trustee or the United States Trustee. Nothing in this Rule shall be construed as requiring the Trustee or the United States Trustee to continue the 341 meeting.

[Effective June 1, 2012.]

L.R. 1007–4. ADOPTION OF INTERIM RULE 1007–I OF THE FEDERAL RULES OF BANKRUPTCY PROCEDURE

Interim Rule 1007–I of the Federal Rules of Bankruptcy Procedure, along with all amendments thereto past and future, is adopted by this Court, effective December 19, 2008.

[Effective June 1, 2012.]

L.R. 1009. AMENDED SCHEDULES AND/OR MATRIX

A. Adding Creditors. If an amendment adds creditors, attorneys who are registered CM/ECF participants are required to upload creditor information for the additional creditors at the time of filing the amended document.

B. Content of Amended Schedules D, E, F or Matrix. Amended Schedules D, E, F and/or an amended matrix shall include only the names and addresses that have been newly added, or for which information has changed. Along with the amended schedule and/or matrix, the debtor shall file a signed declaration and/or verification (as applicable) for the amended schedule and/or matrix. If the debtor is deleting a creditor, the debtor must so state.

C. Service. The debtor shall serve the amended schedule and/or the amended matrix on the Trustee and on any entity affected thereby, in compliance with Rule 1009(a) of the Federal Rules of Bankruptcy Procedure. In addition, when the amendment adds creditors, the debtor shall also serve, on any newly added creditor, a copy of the last issued notice of commencement of case, and in any asset case, a proof of claim form and notice of the claims bar date. In chapter 13 cases, the debtor shall also serve a copy of the current chapter 13 plan on every newly added creditor included in the amended document. The debtor shall file a certificate of service listing the documents served. The debtor shall serve a copy of the amended schedules and/or matrix on any party requesting a copy of these documents.

D. Large Chapter 11 Cases. In any large chapter 11 case, or a chapter 7 case that has been converted from a chapter 11 case, in which the Court authorizes the debtor or a noticing agent to provide notice and maintain the creditor matrix, the following procedures shall apply to amended matrices:

1. When the matrix needs to be amended or corrected, the debtor shall file, in PDF format the amended or corrected matrix in the CM/ECF system. The debtor shall not upload this amended matrix into the CM/ECF system. The filed (not uploaded) amended matrix shall include all names and addresses comprising the most current list of the debtor's creditors.

2. To file the amended or corrected matrix, the debtor shall use the "Amended Creditor Matrix" event.

3. On conversion of a chapter 11 case or within 7 days of any request from the Court or any other party, the debtor shall file, in PDF format, and upload (as a text file) an amended matrix as set forth in these Rules.

[Effective June 1, 2012.]

L.R. 1015.   JOINT ADMINISTRATION AND AFFILIATED DEBTOR CASES

The debtor or a party in interest may request by motion that cases in this Court regarding a debtor and its affiliate(s) be jointly administered. A motion for joint administration shall be filed as early in the case as possible. Unnecessary delay may result in the Court's denial of the motion for joint administration. Such a motion shall be served on all creditors, the Trustee (if any), the Trustee's attorney, and any examiner in the case. The motion for joint administration shall be filed in the case requested to be designated as the lead case. Joint administration of a debtor and its affiliates, unless otherwise ordered by the Court, shall not be a substantive consolidation of the cases.

A. Designation of Lead Case. Unless otherwise stated in the order granting joint administration, when multiple affiliated cases are filed, the first case

filed (i.e., the case having the lowest case number) shall be designated as the lead case.

B. Docket. A single case docket and case file shall be maintained in the lead case after entry of the order for joint administration.

C. Style of Court Documents. Pleadings and other documents filed after entry of the order for joint administration shall be styled with the caption of the lead case, shall include the affiliated debtors from the jointly administered cases, and shall set forth the bankruptcy docket number of the lead case. Such documents shall be filed in the lead case only.

D. Claims. A separate claims register shall be maintained for each affiliated case. A proof of claim shall specifically state the name and case number of the debtor against which the claim is asserted. If claims are asserted against more than one of the affiliated debtors in a jointly administered case, a separate original proof of claim shall be filed in each case.

[Effective June 1, 2012.]

L.R. 1017.   MOTIONS TO REINSTATE FOLLOWING DISMISSAL ON TRUSTEE'S MOTION TO DISMISS FOR FAILURE TO MAKE PLAN PAYMENTS

The motion shall state the reason for failure to make payments and how debtor proposes to cure the arrearage. The motion shall also state whether the case was previously dismissed and reinstated and shall provide dates of any prior dismissals and orders of reinstatement. The debtor shall serve a copy of the motion on the Trustee, United States Trustee, and all parties in interest. No later than 7 days after the filing of the motion, the Trustee shall file a response to the motion, stating whether the Trustee consents or opposes reinstatement. Upon the filing of the Trustee's consent, the case may be reinstated without hearing.

[Effective June 1, 2012.]

PART II.   ADMINISTRATION AND NOTICE

L.R. 2002.   SERVICE/NOTICING

A. Noticing by Proponent. The proponent of the following matters will serve the notice required by Rule 2002 of the Federal Rules of Bankruptcy Procedure and shall forthwith file the notice with a certificate of service (the list is not intended to be all inclusive):

1. A proposed use, sale or lease of property of the estate other than in the ordinary course of business.

2. The time fixed to accept or reject a proposed modification of a chapter 12 or 13 plan.

3. A motion to allow temporary cessation/abatement of plan payments to the Trustee.

4. An application for compensation or reimbursement of expenses totaling in excess of $1,000.00.

5. A motion to compromise or settle a controversy, other than approval of an agreement pursuant to Rule 4001(d) of the Federal Rules of Bankruptcy Procedure.

6. A motion to retain a tax refund.

7. A motion for leave to modify/amend a mortgage.

8. A motion for abandonment.

9. A motion to redeem property.

10. A motion to avoid lien under Section 522(f) of the Bankruptcy Code.

B. Notices to the United States and its Agencies. Whenever these Rules or the Federal Rules of Bankruptcy Procedure require that notice be sent to the United States and/or its agencies, the notice shall be addressed in accordance with this Court's Electronic Filing Rules, which can be found on the Court's website at www.ilsb.uscourts.gov.

C. Mailing List. When the proponent is required to provide notice to all creditors, the proponent shall insure the current mailing matrix is used.

D. Certificate of Service. A certificate of service shall contain the full name and address of the persons/entities served by U.S. mail, or, if applicable, the certificate may state that "all creditors listed on the matrix have been served." A certificate of service shall contain the full name of the persons/entities served electronically as required by this Court's Electronic Filing Rules, which can be found on the Court's website at www.ilsb.uscourts.gov. The certificate of service shall be signed by the person completing service.

E. Notice of Preferred Addresses under Bankruptcy Code § 342(f) and National Creditor Registry Service. An entity and a notice provider may agree that when the notice provider is directed by the Court to give a notice to that entity, the notice provider shall give the notice to the entity in the manner agreed to and at the address or addresses the entity supplies to the notice provider. That address is conclusively presumed to be a proper address for the notice. The notice provider's failure to use the supplied address does not invalidate any notice that is otherwise effective under applicable law.

The filing of a notice of preferred address pursuant to Section 342(f) of the Bankruptcy Code by a creditor directly with the agency or agencies that provide noticing services for the Bankruptcy Court will constitute the filing of such a notice with the Court.

Registration with the National Creditor Registration Service must be accomplished through the agency that provides noticing services for the Bankruptcy Court. Forms and registration information are available at https://ncrs.uscourts.gov.

[Effective June 1, 2012.]

L.R. 2003. BANKRUPTCY CODE § 341 MEETINGS

A. Requests to Reschedule § 341 Meeting. All requests to continue or reschedule 341 meetings must first be directed to the United States Trustee in chapter 11 cases and to the assigned Trustee or interim Trustee, as appropriate, in chapter 7, 12 and 13 cases. Upon agreement between the proponent of the continuance and the appropriate Trustee, it is the responsibility of the proponent to immediately serve notice to all creditors and parties in interest, including the Court, of the new date, time and place of the rescheduled 341 meeting. The proponent shall file a certificate of service with the notice.

B. Requests to Reschedule § 341 Meetings within 7 Days of Meeting. Any request by the debtor to reschedule a 341 meeting within 7 days of the scheduled meeting will require either the debtor or his/her attorney to appear at the scheduled meeting to request that the meeting be rescheduled. If the appropriate Trustee consents to the rescheduling and announces at the regularly scheduled 341 meeting the new 341 meeting date, no further notice to the creditors and parties in interest is required, except that the appropriate Trustee shall advise the Court of the rescheduled hearing date, time and place by making a docket entry using the Court's CM/ECF system.

C. Continuance of the Bankruptcy Code § 341 Meeting Announced at Meeting. The Trustee or the United States Trustee may continue a 341 meeting from time to time by announcement at the regularly scheduled 341 meeting, with no further notice to the creditors and parties in interest being required, except that the appropriate Trustee shall advise the Court of the rescheduled hearing date, time and place by making a docket entry using the Court's CM/ECF system. The minimum amount of time for continuing a 341 meeting is 7 days.

D. Waiver of Attendance. A request by a debtor to be excused from attendance at the 341 meeting of creditors must be made in writing to the Office of the United States Trustee and copied to the case Trustee. The United States Trustee's acceptable grounds for waiver include: medical condition, imprisonment and military assignments that prevent attendance. Any application for waiver of attendance must include supporting documentation, e.g., doctor's letter, court order or military order. Waiver of personal appearance and permission to attend a 341 meeting by telephone must also be approved by the United States Trustee. To appear by telephone, the debtor must be sworn in and identified by a notary, court reporter or other person permitted by law to administer an oath.

E. Disputes. Prior to filing a motion seeking continuance of a 341 meeting or requesting that a joint debtor be excused from a 341 meeting, the movant shall seek such relief from the Trustee. The motion shall state relief from the Trustee has been denied. Failure to do so may result in the denial of the motion by the Court.

F. Failure to Attend the Bankruptcy Code § 341 Meeting. If the debtor in a voluntary case fails to attend the first scheduled 341 meeting without being excused, the Trustee shall list the date, time, and location for a continued 341 meeting by making a docket entry within the Court's CM/ECF system. The minimum amount of time for continuing a 341 meeting is 7 days. If the debtor fails to appear at the second 341 meeting without being excused, the Trustee may file a motion asking that the case be dismissed. The Court may consider the Trustee's motion without a hearing.

[Effective June 1, 2012.]

L.R. 2004. MOTIONS UNDER RULE 2004 OF THE FEDERAL RULES OF BANKRUPTCY PROCEDURE

A. Motion for Examination and/or Production. A motion under Rule 2004 of the Federal Rules of Bankruptcy Procedure may contain a request for an examination or for production of documents. In addition, in a motion for an examination, the moving party may request that the examinee be required to produce documents at the time and place of the examination or at such other time and place as set forth in the motion.

B. Conference Required. Prior to filing a motion for examination and/or for production of documents under Rule 2004 of the Federal Rules of Bankruptcy Procedure the moving party shall attempt to confer (in person or telephonically) with the proposed examinee or the examinee's counsel (if represented by counsel) to arrange for a mutually agreeable date, time, place and scope of an examination and/or production. If an agreement is reached, no motion shall be required.

C. Certification of Conference Required. All motions for examination and/or production under this Local Rule shall include a certification of the moving party that either (1) a conference was held as required and no agreement was reached, or (2) a conference was not held and an explanation as to why no conference was held.

D. Service and Notice Requirements. In addition to any other rules of service that generally apply, all motions for examination and/or production of documents shall be served upon the following parties, through their counsel, if represented: (1) the debtor; (2) the Trustee; (3) the United States Trustee; (4) all official committees; and (5) the proposed examinee and/or party producing documents. All such motions shall be accompanied by a notice of motion setting forth (1) an objection, response or answer deadline of 7 days from filing of the motion; and (2) the date, time and place of the hearing in the event an objection is filed.

[Effective June 1, 2012.]

L.R. 2015–1. DUTY OF CHAPTER 7 TRUSTEE UPON SALE OF PROPERTY

The Trustee shall file, within 14 days of the sale, a report of sale stating the property sold, to whom it was sold and the dollar amount for which the property was sold. An auctioneer's report may be substituted for the foregoing.

[Effective June 1, 2012.]

L.R. 2015–2. DUTY OF CHAPTER 7 TRUSTEE UPON DISMISSAL

In all dismissed cases, the Trustee shall file, within 14 days of the date of dismissal, a Report of Receipts and Disbursements, or, if applicable, a Report of No Receipts and Disbursements.

[Effective June 1, 2012.]

L.R. 2015–3. DUTY OF CHAPTER 7 TRUSTEE TO FILE INTERIM REPORTS

The chapter 7 Trustee shall file an Interim Report as frequently as required by the United States Trustee unless a Final Distribution has been filed and approved by the Court.

[Effective June 1, 2012.]

L.R. 2015–4. DUTY OF DEBTOR IN CHAPTER 11 CASE

A. Operating Reports. Chapter 11 debtors shall provide monthly operating reports to counsel for the Unsecured Creditors Committee and upon request, to any creditor.

B. Insurance Requirements—Debtor-in-Possession.

1. *General Requirements.* All debtors in a chapter 11 case in which no Trustee has been appointed shall:

    a. insure all estate assets against physical damage and loss with policy limits covering the asset values stated in the debtor's schedules;

    b. if applicable, maintain liability coverage for the debtor's operations and businesses;

    c. if applicable, and as appropriate or customary for the debtor's industry, maintain additional types of insurance (workers compensation, products liability, or professional liability); and

    d. require insurer(s) to notify the United States Trustee of any insurance claims or lapses of coverage.

2. *Proof of Insurance.* Upon request of any party, the Trustee, or the United States Trustee, the debtor shall provide proof of insurance, which shall include a certificate of insurance, binder, or other document(s) from the insurance carrier stating amounts, types and period of coverage, and notification of any secured party as loss payee. Failure to provide such proof shall give rise to a presumption that no insurance is in effect.

[Effective June 1, 2012.]

L.R. 2015–5. DUTY OF DEBTOR IN CHAPTER 12 CASE TO DISCLOSE DISPOSABLE INCOME

On the first anniversary of confirmation of a chapter 12 plan and not less frequently than annually thereafter, the debtor shall account to the Trustee for all disposable income as defined in Section 1225(b)(2) of the Bankruptcy Code. The debtor shall provide the Trustee with reasonable information, summaries, and documentation evidencing all receipts and disbursements of money and property over the prior year to enable the Trustee to determine whether the debtor has disposable income which should be applied to make plan payments under Section 1225(b)(1)(B) of the Bankruptcy Code. Failure to comply with this Rule shall be cause for dismissal or other appropriate action. Nothing in this Rule precludes the Trustee from obtaining an order of Court requiring disclosures more frequently than annually.

[Effective June 1, 2012.]

L.R. 2016–1. COMPENSATION OF PROFESSIONALS

A. Disclosure of Compensation and Pre–Petition Retainers. Pursuant to Section 329 of the Bankruptcy Code and Rule 2016(b) of the Federal Rules of Bankruptcy Procedure, an attorney representing a debtor in a case under any chapter shall file with the petition a statement disclosing compensation paid or agreed to be paid to such attorney for services in contemplation of or in connection with the case. Counsel shall serve the disclosure on the Trustee and United States Trustee. In chapter 13 cases, counsel shall serve only the Trustee. Until a case is closed, a supplemental fee disclosure statement shall be filed and served as required in this Rule either no later than 14 days after any payment not previously disclosed in a properly filed Disclosure of Compensation for Attorney for Debtor pursuant to Rule 2016(b) of the Federal Rules of Bankruptcy Procedure, or no later than 14 days after the agreement for such a payment. Monies received but not subsequently disclosed are subject to disgorgement.

B. Applications for Compensation. Except in flat fee chapter 13 cases as governed by the Chapter 13 Procedures Manual, all professionals employed under Sections 327 and 1103 of the Bankruptcy Code shall file an application for allowance of compensation following the guidelines in *In re Weidau's, Inc.,* 78 B.R. 904 (Bankr. S.D. Ill.1987). Applications for compensation may be denied if the professional seeking compensation has failed to obtain an order approving employment.

[Effective June 1, 2012.]

L.R. 2016–2. PAYMENT OF PROFESSIONAL FEES IN CHAPTER 11 CASES

A. General Requirements in Chapter 11 Cases. The requirements of Rule 2016–1 of these Rules apply in chapter 11 cases.

B. Monthly Bills (Fee Statements) in Chapter 11 Cases. If debtor's counsel desires to receive compensation on a monthly basis prior to allowance on an interim application, counsel shall file a motion to establish procedures for interim compensation and reimbursement of expenses of professionals. At the time the motion is filed, a separate notice shall be filed allowing 14 days from the date of filing to file objections. The motion and notice shall be served on all interested parties, including, but not limited to, the debtor; the United States Trustee; the Trustee (if any); the Trustee's attorney (if any); and counsel for the unsecured creditors committee or, if counsel has not been appointed, to the unsecured creditors committee. If no committee has been appointed, service shall also be made to the twenty largest unsecured creditors.

All monthly payments of fees and expenses are subject to approval, modifications or disgorgement on interim application, which may not be filed sooner than every 120 days and not less frequently than every 180 days. In any case that has been pending more than 180 days, no professional shall be permitted to receive payment on a monthly bill or fee statement unless such professional has filed one or more interim fee applications covering all services provided more than 180 days before the date of such monthly bill or fee statement. Counsel may file a motion to extend this period.

[Effective June 1, 2012.]

L.R. 2090. ATTORNEY ADMISSION

A. General Admission to Practice before the Bankruptcy Court. The bar of this Court shall consist of any attorney in good standing to practice before the United States District Court for the Southern District of Illinois. The requirements for attorney admission and standards concerning attorney discipline outlined in District Court's Local Rules 83.1

through 83.4 are adopted for this Court. Attorneys are required to read and remain familiar with:

1. These Local Rules, the Electronic Filing Rules, and the Chapter 13 Procedures Manual;

2. Local Rules of the United States District Court for the Southern District of Illinois, including the Rules of Disciplinary Enforcement, which can be found at www.ilsd.uscourts.gov;

3. Local Rules of Procedure for the Seventh Circuit Court of Appeals, which can be found at www.ca7.uscourts.gov;

4. Bankruptcy Code and Federal Rules of Bankruptcy Procedure;

5. Federal Rules of Civil Procedure;

6. Federal Rules of Evidence; and

7. Federal Rules of Appellate Procedure.

B. Admission Pro Hac Vice. Any attorney licensed to practice in any state of the United States or the District of Columbia who does not wish to be admitted generally, but wishes to be admitted for the purpose of a specific bankruptcy case or adversary proceeding only, must file a Motion to Appear Pro Hac Vice. The motion must contain a verified statement setting forth the state and federal bars of which the movant is a member in good standing and the bar number, if any, issued by each jurisdiction; and be accompanied by the filing fee for pro hac vice motions. Upon entry of the Court order granting the motion, the attorney will be permitted to appear of record and to participate pro hac vice.

C. Local Counsel. It shall not be necessary for parties appearing by non-resident counsel to retain local counsel to represent them. However, if local counsel is retained and appears in Court for non-resident counsel, then the Clerk of the Court shall enter the appearance of local counsel in the Court record. At each appearance, local counsel shall be fully apprised of, and conversant with, the facts and law concerning any case in which they appear. Local counsel shall also be required to have full authority to represent their clients as if they were non-resident counsel.

[Effective June 1, 2012.]

L.R. 2091. WITHDRAWAL AND SUBSTITUTION OF COUNSEL

A. Except as provided in subsection C of this Rule, an attorney of record may withdraw from a case, adversary proceeding, or contested matter only by way of a motion and order of the Court granting the attorney leave to withdraw. A motion to withdraw must be served upon (1) the attorney's client, (2) the Trustee, (3) the United States Trustee and (4) all

persons and entities having entered their appearances in the case, adversary proceeding or contested matter.

B. An order authorizing an attorney of record to withdraw may be granted without hearing if no objections to the motion to withdraw are filed within 7 days following the filing of the motion. If an objection to a motion to withdraw is filed, the Court will schedule a hearing to consider the motion and any objections thereto.

C. If new counsel is to be simultaneously substituted for a withdrawing attorney, then no motion to withdraw shall be necessary. Rather, a Notice for Substitution of Counsel shall be filed with the Court. Furthermore, the substituting counsel shall file a Form 2016(b) Disclosure of Compensation.

D. In a case under chapter 13, the Trustee shall cease payments to withdrawing counsel for the debtor upon entry of an order authorizing withdrawal or upon the filing of a Notice for Substitution of Counsel, as the case may be.

E. In a case under chapter 13, substitute counsel for the debtor shall be bound by withdrawing counsel's fee election unless the Court, on motion and for cause, orders otherwise. As such, absent a Court order to the contrary, and an amended plan if appropriate, the chapter 13 Trustee shall only disburse to substitute counsel those attorney's fees remaining unpaid, if any.

[Effective June 1, 2012.]

L.R. 2092. PROFESSIONAL CONDUCT AND OBLIGATIONS OF ATTORNEYS

A. Professional Conduct. The professional conduct of attorneys appearing before this Court shall be governed by the Rules of Professional Conduct adopted by the Supreme Court of Illinois, the Rules of Disciplinary Enforcement of the United States District Court for the Southern District of Illinois, and these Rules.

B. Duty to Confer. Every attorney appearing before this Court is required to attempt, in good faith, to communicate with opposing counsel in advance of appearing in any trial or hearing in a contested matter in an attempt to reach a settlement of the matter.

C. Obligations of Attorneys.

1. With respect to hearings, attorneys shall appear at all scheduled hearings, unless:

a. counsel advises the Court prior to the hearing that the matter has been resolved, and counsel has been excused;

b. at least one party appears and reports to the Court concerning resolution of the matter;

c. the Court has continued the matter; or

d. the Court has otherwise excused attendance.

2. Attorneys for debtors shall provide appropriate representation for the debtor at the 341 meeting. Failure of counsel to provide appropriate representation at any hearing or the 341 meeting is cause for the Court to reduce attorneys' fees or issue other sanctions. Counsel shall dress in courtroom attire when appearing at 341 meetings.

[Effective June 1, 2012.]

L.R. 2094. ATTORNEY DISCIPLINE

A. Disbarment or Suspension by another Court. Any attorney that has been admitted to practice in the United States District Court for the Southern District of Illinois that becomes disbarred or suspended from practicing law by any court shall automatically be disbarred or suspended in this Court for the same length of time as the attorney's disbarment or suspension in the original court. Any such attorney shall, immediately upon disbarment or suspension, notify the Clerk of Court of the disbarment or suspension in writing. Failure to do so shall subject the attorney to further sanctions by this Court.

B. Request for Reinstatement. Any attorney disbarred or suspended from practicing in this Court pursuant to subsection A of this Rule may file a motion with the Court requesting that the Court reinstate the attorney before the expiration of the disbarment or suspension in the original court. The Clerk of Court will then open a miscellaneous proceeding assigned to the Chief Judge of this Court. The Court will set a hearing at which the attorney will be required to show cause as to why the attorney should be reinstated in this Court.

C. Non-exclusivity. Nothing in this Rule shall preclude the Court from initiating its own attorney disciplinary proceedings regardless of whether an attorney has been disciplined by another court.

[Effective June 1, 2012.]

PART III–A. CLAIMS AND DISTRIBUTION TO CREDITORS

L.R. 3001. PROOF OF CLAIM— SUPPORTING INFORMATION

Rule 3001(c)(2)(C) of the Federal Rules of Bankruptcy Procedure also applies to non-residential mortgages.

[Effective June 1, 2012.]

L.R. 3002.1. NOTICE RELATING TO CLAIMS SECURED BY SECURITY INTEREST IN THE DEBTOR'S PRINCIPAL RESIDENCE

Rule 3002.1 of the Federal Rules of Bankruptcy Procedure also applies to non-residential mortgages.

[Effective June 1, 2012.]

L.R. 3003. FILING PROOF OF CLAIM OR EQUITY SECURITY INTEREST IN CHAPTER 11 CASES

Unless otherwise ordered, the claims bar date for any creditor or equity security holder whose claim or interest is not scheduled or is scheduled as disputed, contingent or unliquidated is 90 days following the first date set for the 341 meeting of creditors for nongovernmental units and 180 days after the date of the order for relief for governmental units.

[Effective June 1, 2012.]

L.R. 3004. FILING OF CLAIMS BY DEBTOR OR TRUSTEE

If the debtor or Trustee files a claim on behalf of a creditor pursuant to Rule 3004 of the Federal Rules of Bankruptcy Procedure, the debtor/Trustee shall serve the claim on the affected creditor and the creditor's attorney, if any. A certificate of service shall be filed with the claim. Any subsequent claim filed by the creditor supersedes the claim filed by the debtor/Trustee.

[Effective June 1, 2012.]

L.R. 3007. OBJECTIONS TO CLAIMS IN CHAPTER 13 CASES

In a chapter 13 case, a separate notice must be filed along with an objection to claim and must be served on all interested parties in accordance with the procedures set forth in the Chapter 13 Procedures Manual. The notice shall comply with the form found on the Court's website at www.ilsb.uscourts.gov.

[Effective June 1, 2012.]

PART III–B.   CHAPTER 11 AND 13 PLANS AND PROCEDURES FOR CONFIRMATION

L.R. 3015.   CHAPTER 13 PLANS AND PROCEDURES

The procedures, guidelines and instructions applicable to chapter 13 are contained in a separate "Chapter 13 Procedures Manual," which can be found on the Court's website at www.ilsb.uscourts.gov. The Manual is hereby incorporated into and made a part of these Rules.

[Effective June 1, 2012.]

L.R. 3016.   REQUIRED LANGUAGE IN CHAPTER 11 PLAN

Every chapter 11 plan shall contain a provision describing what property, if any, of the chapter 11 estate, which vests in the debtor upon confirmation, shall revest in the chapter 7 estate in the event that the chapter 11 case is converted to a chapter 7 case following confirmation, but before substantial consummation.

[Effective June 1, 2012.]

L.R. 3018.   ACCEPTANCE OR REJECTION OF CHAPTER 11 PLAN

A.   Form of Ballot. Unless a different ballot form has been approved by the Court, the plan proponent shall use the form available on the Court's website at www.ilsb.uscourts.gov. The ballot shall be distributed to creditors, shall include the address of the plan proponent or the party designated to receive ballots, and shall indicate that ballots should be received no later than the deadline established by the Court.

B.   Tabulation of Balloting; Report and Certification. The plan proponent shall tabulate the ballots and prepare a balloting report. The report shall list, for each class, the total number of claims voting, total dollar amount of claims accepting, and percentage of claims voting that accept the plan. The report shall also indicate, for each class, whether it is impaired or unimpaired and whether or not the requisite vote has been attained in each class. A sample "Ballot for Accepting or Rejecting Plan" and "Report of Balloting" can be found on the Court's website at www.ilsb. uscourts.gov. The Report of Balloting shall be certified by the plan proponent.

C.   Filing and Service. All ballots must be submitted to the attorney for the plan proponent at least 7 days before the confirmation hearing. The balloting report and certification shall be filed with the Court at least 3 days before the confirmation hearing. Copies of the report shall be served on the United States Trustee, the Service List, and parties filing objections to the plan.

D.   Rules for Tabulating Ballots. In tabulating the ballots, the following rules shall apply:

1.   Ballots that are not signed will not be counted either as an acceptance or rejection.

2.   Where the amount shown as owed on the ballot differs from the schedules, the amount shown on the schedules will be used, or if a proof of claim has been filed and allowed or deemed allowed, the amount shown on the proof of claim will be used for the purpose of determining the amount voting, unless the Court orders otherwise.

3.   Unless the Court orders otherwise, ballots that do not show a choice of either acceptance or rejection will not be counted either as an acceptance or rejection.

4.   Unless the Court orders otherwise, ballots that are received after the last date set for filing ballots will not be counted as either an acceptance or rejection.

[Effective June 1, 2012.]

L.R. 3022.   FINAL DECREE IN CHAPTER 11 CASES WHERE DEBTOR IS AN INDIVIDUAL (APPLICABLE TO CASES FILED ON OR AFTER OCTOBER 17, 2005)

A.   Application for Final Decree/Reports/Motion. If the debtor in a chapter 11 case is an individual and has completed all plan payments, then the debtor shall file the following documents:

1.   a report with the Court certifying that debtor has complied with the terms and conditions of the plan and that debtor is otherwise eligible for a discharge under Section 1141(d)(5) of the Bankruptcy Code;

2.   a motion for entry of discharge order; and

3.   an application for final decree pursuant to Rule 3022 of the Federal Rules of Bankruptcy Procedure.

In addition, debtor shall certify that all monthly operating reports have been filed. If the debtor is otherwise eligible, the Court shall issue a discharge as soon as practicable.

B.   Request for Discharge under Bankruptcy Code § 1141(d)(5)(B). If a discharge is sought under Section 1141(d)(5)(B) of the Bankruptcy Code, the debtor shall request entry of discharge by filing a motion for discharge, which shall be a contested matter governed by Rule 9014 of the Federal Rules of Bankruptcy Procedure. If the motion is granted, and if the debtor is otherwise eligible, the Clerk shall issue the discharge and the final decree closing the case.

C. Closing Case before Plan Payments Completed. If the debtor proposes to close the case before plan payments have been completed, and intends to reopen the case after plan completion to obtain a discharge, then the debtor shall file a motion to close the case and shall include in that motion a statement of the debtor's intent to reopen. The motion shall be accompanied by a notice giving all creditors 21 days from the date of filing within which to object to the motion. Upon the filing of a motion to reopen, the debtor shall be required to pay any fees due for reopening the case. After reopening, the debtor shall file the application for final decree and supporting documentation as required in subsection A of this Rule.

[Effective June 1, 2012.]

PART IV. THE DEBTOR: DUTIES AND BENEFITS

L.R. 4001–1. MOTIONS TO EXTEND OR IMPOSE THE STAY UNDER BANKRUPTCY CODE §§ 362(c)(3) OR (4)

Motions to extend or impose the automatic stay should be filed concurrently with the bankruptcy petition. A motion filed after the date of the filing of the petition may not receive a hearing date until after 30 days of the date of the filing of the petition.

The motion must include specific and sufficient facts to support the legal requirements for the motion as found in Sections 362(c)(3) or (4) of the Bankruptcy Code, as applicable.

[Effective June 1, 2012.]

L.R. 4001–2. MOTIONS FOR RELIEF FROM THE AUTOMATIC STAY

A motion for relief from stay must be filed as a separate pleading, except such motion may also include a request for abandonment or adequate protection, as well as a request for relief from the co-debtor stay.

A. Content of Motion for Relief from Stay. A motion for relief from stay shall:

1. name as respondents the debtor, the case Trustee (if one has been appointed) and, to the extent known to the moving party, any other entity that may have a legal or equitable interest in the property which is the subject of the motion;

2. state with particularity the grounds therefore and the relief sought;

3. state the value of the property, if known, and the amount of any known encumbrances thereon; and

4. if the motion is brought "for cause" rather than for "lack of equity," state the specific facts that constitute "cause."

B. Motion for Relief from the Automatic Stay to Foreclose on Collateral.

1. *General Provisions.* In a case filed under any chapter in which the movant is seeking to foreclose on collateral, the movant shall attach to the motion a separate statement that (1) lists any other entity/party that may have a legal or equitable interest in the property which is the subject of the motion; or (2) states that to the best of the movant's knowledge, information and belief, there are no such other entities/parties. Failure by the movant to include this statement shall result in the motion for relief from stay being stricken as deficient by the Court. In addition, the motion shall recite the specific statutory and factual basis on which relief is sought, including:

    a. the basis for the debt;

    b. the balance of the indebtedness on the petition date or otherwise;

    c. the date and manner of perfection, including book and page number, certificate of title, or UCC–1 recording. Documentation in support of a motion for relief shall be filed in accordance with this Court's Electronic Filing Rules, which can be found on the Court's website at www.ilsb.uscourts.gov; and

    d. if the motion is brought under Section 362(d)(2) of the Bankruptcy Code, the value of the collateral and the basis for the value.

2. *Chapter 13 Cases.*

    a. In a chapter 13 case in which the movant is seeking to foreclose on collateral, the motion shall also include:

        i. the balance due;

        ii. a breakdown of the amount due, including:

        (1) unpaid principal;

        (2) accrued interest from a specific date to a specific date;

        (3) late charges from a specific date to a specific date;

        (4) attorneys' fees;

        (5) advances for taxes, insurance and the like;

        (6) any other charges;

(7) specific months for which default is alleged; and

(8) evidence of perfection of the movant's lien or security interest.

b. Concurrent with the filing of the motion, the movant shall provide to the debtor, debtor's counsel, Trustee and the United States Trustee, a copy of the payment history for all post-petition payments to date. Failure to provide the payment history may result in the denial of the motion at the preliminary hearing.

C. Notice of Motion. A notice under this section must be filed as a separate document along with the motion and must be served on all respondents/interested parties. The notice shall comply with the form found on the Court's website at www.ilsb.uscourts.gov.

D. Incomplete Pleadings. Any motion for relief from stay not accompanied by the notice of motion and a certificate of service shall be stricken as deficient by the Court.

E. Opposition to Relief from Stay. Any pleading in opposition to the motion for relief from stay shall:

1. be filed and served on the movant, and on any entity or person known to have a legal or equitable interest in the property, not later than 14 days from the date of filing unless otherwise ordered;

2. identify the interest of the opposing party in the property;

3. state with particularity the grounds for the opposition; and

4. if filed by the debtor, state the value of the property specified in the motion and the amount of equity that would be realized by the debtor after deduction of all encumbrances.

F. Uncontested Motion. Unless an objection to a motion for relief from stay is timely filed, or unless the Court directs otherwise, an order granting the motion shall be entered without a hearing.

[Effective June 1, 2012.]

L.R. 4001-3. MOTIONS TO USE CASH COLLATERAL AND TO OBTAIN CREDIT

A. Provisions to be Disclosed. In addition to the provisions listed in Rules 4001(b)(1)(B) and (c)(1)(B) of the Federal Rules of Bankruptcy Procedure, any motion to use cash collateral or motion to obtain credit (collectively "Financing Motions") must also disclose the following:

1. *Cross–Collateralization of Pre–Petition Debt*: Provisions that grant cross-collateralization protection (other than replacement liens or other adequate pro-

tection) to the pre-petition secured creditor, i.e., clauses that secure pre-petition debt by post-petition assets in which the secured creditor does not assert a valid, perfected security interest by virtue of its pre-petition security agreement or applicable non-bankruptcy law, and provisions that deem pre-petition secured debt to be post-petition debt or that use post-petition loans from a pre-petition secured lender to pay all or part of that lender's pre-petition claim, other than as provided in Section 552(b) of the Bankruptcy Code;

2. *Professional Fee Provisions*: Provisions that grant a carve-out for professional fees, including the amount of the fee;

3. *Priming of Existing Liens*: Provisions that prime any secured lien;

4. *Loan Documentation Costs*: Provisions that call for the payment of fees or costs by the debtor other than reasonable attorney's fees for loan documentation;

5. *Plan Restrictions*: Provisions that limit, restrict, or otherwise affect the terms of a proposed plan of reorganization; and

6. *United States Trustee's Fees*: Payment of fees to the United States Trustee.

7. *Administrative Claims*: Existence of any administrative claim that is sought by the movant.

B. Summary of Essential Terms. All Financing Motions must also set forth, unless good cause is shown, the total dollar amount requested, the debtor's proposed budget for the use of the funds, an estimate of the value of the collateral which secures the creditor's asserted interest, the maximum borrowing available on an interim and final basis, the borrowing conditions, interest rate, fees, costs or other expenses to be borne by the debtor, maturity, limitations on the use of the funds, events of default and the protections afforded under Sections 363 and 364 of the Bankruptcy Code.

C. Interim Relief. The Court may grant relief on an interim and emergency basis to avoid immediate and irreparable harm to the estate pending a final hearing, provided that:

1. The party seeking interim and emergency relief files a motion which complies in all respects with this Rule and with Rule 9006–3 of these Rules, and which describes the reason(s) relief on an emergency basis is necessary and appropriate;

2. Counsel for the party seeking interim, emergency relief contacts the Judge's courtroom deputy to obtain a date and time for a hearing;

3. The motion and notice of hearing on the motion is served on all secured creditors, the United States Trustee, all parties who filed requests for notice, any examiner or Trustee appointed in the case, counsel for any official committee(s), and, if no committee of

unsecured creditors has been appointed, all creditors identified on the list of creditors filed pursuant to Rule 1007(d) of the Federal Rules of Bankruptcy Procedure;

4. The party seeking interim and emergency relief shall serve a copy of a proposed order granting the motion on all parties identified in the foregoing subsection.

5. Service of the motion and notice of hearing is made by one or more of the following means: (1) electronic mail, (2) facsimile transmission, or (3) overnight delivery;

6. The party seeking interim and emergency relief files a certificate of service which identifies the persons served with a copy of the motion and notice, and which, for each such person, specifies the method of service.

D. Proposed Order. A proposed order granting the motion must be submitted to the Court as a separate document in accordance with the Court's Electronic Filing Rules, which can be found on the Court's website at www.ilsb.uscourts.gov.

[Effective June 1, 2012.]

L.R. 4002. DEBTOR'S DUTIES: SCHEDULING PENDING LAWSUITS

The debtor shall include on Schedule F the name and address of any court (using the name and address of the applicable non-bankruptcy court) in which an action or post judgment proceeding is pending against the debtor at the time of the filing of debtor's bankruptcy petition. The debtor shall also include on Schedule F the names and addresses of the parties and counsel involved in that action or proceeding. These requirements are restricted to those actions which must be disclosed in response to questions 4(a) and 4(b) on the Statement of Financial Affairs. If an action against the debtor is commenced subsequent to the date of the order for relief, but prior to discharge, the debtor shall amend Schedule F, along with the matrix, as required above and shall provide notice to the parties identified above.

[Effective June 1, 2012.]

L.R. 4003. MOTION TO AVOID LIENS UNDER BANKRUPTCY CODE § 522(f)(1)

A. Requirements. Any debtor seeking to avoid a lien pursuant to Section 522 of the Bankruptcy Code shall file a separate written motion as to each alleged lien holder. The motion shall identify:

1. the lien to be avoided, its amount, and the date the debt that the lien secures was incurred;

2. the amount, listed separately, of all other liens on the property;

3. if applicable, the amount of the impaired exemption;

4. the statute allowing the exemption;

5. the value of the subject collateral; and

6. the specific statutory provision under which relief is sought.

Motions to avoid judicial liens shall also include the case number and the Court where the underlying judgment was entered, the date of the judgment, and shall list the common address of any real property affected by the lien.

B. Nonpossessory, Nonpurchase Money Security Interests in Household Goods. Motions to avoid a nonpossessory, nonpurchase money security interest in household goods under Section 522(f)(1)(B) of the Bankruptcy Code must, in addition to the requirements in subsection A of this Rule, specifically identify the household goods that are subject to the security interest sought to be avoided, referring to the definition of "household goods" provided in Section 522(f)(4) of the Bankruptcy Code.

C. Service and Notice. The debtor shall serve the motion and notice thereof on the lien holder, in accordance with Rule 9014(b) of the Federal Rules of Bankruptcy Procedure. The notice shall allow 21 days from the date of filing to file objections. The debtor shall file the notice and certificate of service with the Court.

[Effective June 1, 2012.]

L.R. 4004. OBTAINING DISCHARGE AFTER CASE CLOSED WITHOUT DISCHARGE FOR FAILURE TO FILE FINANCIAL MANAGEMENT CERTIFICATE

A debtor may file a motion to reopen a case in order to obtain a discharge where the discharge was not entered solely because the debtor failed to file an Official Form B23 pursuant to Rule 1007(b)(7) and (c) of the Federal Rules of Bankruptcy Procedure.

[Effective June 1, 2012.]

L.R. 4008. REAFFIRMATION HEARINGS

The discharge order will be entered by the Clerk no earlier than 14 days following the conclusion of the reaffirmation hearing.

[Effective June 1, 2012.]

PART V. COURT AND CLERK'S OFFICE OPERATIONS

L.R. 5001–1. COURT LOCATIONS, MAILING ADDRESSES AND HEARING LOCATIONS

There are two (2) court locations and Clerk's Offices in this District, with hearings being held at both locations. The mailing addresses and hearing locations are as follows:

U.S. Bankruptcy Court
Melvin Price Federal Courthouse
750 Missouri Avenue
East St. Louis, Illinois 62201
(618) 482–9400

U.S. Bankruptcy Court
Federal Courthouse
301 West Main Street
Benton, Illinois 62812
(618) 435–2200

[Effective June 1, 2012.]

L.R. 5001–2. COLLECTION OF FEES BY THE CLERK'S OFFICE

Except as otherwise provided by Rule 1006(b) and (c) of the Federal Rules of Bankruptcy Procedure and 28 U.S.C. § 1930(a)(6), all fees which the Clerk is required to collect are due and owing at the time of filing or in advance of performing any requested service.

The appropriate fee shall be in the form of credit card (only from attorneys or non-debtor parties), debit card, cash, or a cashier's check, money order or a check of the attorney for the debtor, made payable to "Clerk, U.S. Bankruptcy Court". Personal checks of the debtor will not be accepted by the Clerk's Office. Cash should not be sent through the mail. The Clerk is not responsible for the loss of cash allegedly mailed and not received in the Clerk's Office. Parties filing documents electronically which require a fee will submit the payment using an accepted credit/debit card via the internet as reflected in this Court's Electronic Filing Rules, which can be found on the Court's website at www.ilsb.uscourts.gov.

[Effective June 1, 2012.]

L.R. 5001–3. DISHONORED CHECKS

Upon a check or draft being returned by the depository upon which it is drawn for insufficient funds, the Clerk, without further order, may thereafter, for a period of 6 months, accept only cash, a cashier's check or money order from the person giving the dishonored check.

[Effective June 1, 2012.]

L.R. 5003. CASE INFORMATION

The Clerk's Office has installed a computerized Voice Case Information System (VCIS) which provides information on a case by dialing in from any touch-tone telephone. See the Court's website at www.ilsb.uscourts.gov for the telephone number and instructions on its use along with VCIS phone numbers for other Bankruptcy Courts.

Telephone inquiries to the regular business telephone line of the Clerk's Office requesting information that is readily available on VCIS will be directed to the VCIS telephone number.

[Effective June 1, 2012.]

L.R. 5005–1. FILING OF PAPERS: GENERAL REQUIREMENTS

A. Method of Filing. Effective September 3, 2002, the Court will no longer accept paper documents for filing, except from pro se filers. Any such pro se filer wishing to file a paper document may do so by bringing the document to the Clerk's Office in either East St. Louis or Benton during regular business hours. Assistance will be provided at those locations to aid such filers in scanning and entering such documents into the Court's electronic filing system.

B. Form. All petitions, pleadings and other papers offered for filing shall meet the following requirements:

1. *Legibility.* Papers shall be plainly and legibly typewritten, printed or reproduced on one side of the paper only.

2. *Caption: Official Forms.* The caption and form of all petitions, pleadings, schedules and other papers shall be in substantial compliance with the Federal Rules of Bankruptcy Procedure, Official Forms or Local Rules for the Southern District of Illinois. Each paper or set of papers filed shall bear the name of the debtor and chapter of the case. Each paper other than the petition shall also have the case number.

C. Signature. Every pleading and other paper shall be signed.

[Effective June 1, 2012.]

L.R. 5005–2. SIZE OF PAPERS

Papers submitted for filing shall be 8 ½″ by 11″ in size.

[Effective June 1, 2012.]

L.R. 5005–3. ELECTRONIC FILING POLICIES AND PROCEDURES

The Court has adopted Electronic Filing Rules to establish practices and procedures for filing, signing, maintaining and verification of pleadings and other documents by electronic means. The rules, as described in the Electronic Filing Rules, are incorporated into these Local Rules. The Electronic Filing Rules are available on the Court's website at www. ilsb.uscourts.gov. Amendments to the Electronic Filing Rules may be entered from time to time in keeping with the needs of the Court.

[Effective June 1, 2012.]

L.R. 5010. FEES FOR MOTIONS TO REOPEN

In any case in which a motion to reopen is filed, the filing fees prescribed by 28 U.S.C. § 1930(b) must be paid at the time the motion is filed, unless (1) the motion to reopen states that the purpose of reopening is to correct an administrative error or to file an action related to the debtor's discharge (such as a complaint to determine dischargeability or a motion for contempt for violation of the discharge injunction); or (2) a complaint to determine dischargeability and/or a motion for contempt for violation of the debtor's discharge injunction (which are considered actions related to the debtor's discharge) is filed simultaneously with the motion to reopen.

[Effective June 1, 2012.]

L.R. 5011. WITHDRAWAL OF REFERENCE

A. Time and Manner. A request to withdraw the reference of a case or proceeding, in whole or in part, other than a sua sponte request by the judge, shall be by motion. Absent leave of Court, a party filing a motion to withdraw the reference shall file the motion within 14 days of the filing of the first related pleading or response, or within 14 days of the pretrial order (if any), whichever is later, or shall be deemed to have waived such request.

B. Response. No later than 14 days after the filing of the motion to withdraw the reference, any other party may file and serve a response to such motion.

C. Place of Filing and Controlling Rules. A motion to withdraw the reference and all documents relating to the motion, including any responses thereto, shall be filed with the Bankruptcy Court (up until the time that the case is transferred) in the bankruptcy case or adversary proceeding in which reference is sought to be withdrawn using the caption of that bankruptcy case or adversary proceeding. The Clerk of Court will transmit the motion to withdraw the reference and all documents filed relating to the motion to the District Court. This Rule and the Local Rules of the United States District Court for the Southern District of Illinois regarding motion practice and bankruptcy court matters shall govern the motion to withdraw the reference and all proceedings related thereto.

[Effective June 1, 2012.]

PART VI. COLLECTION AND LIQUIDATION OF THE ESTATE

L.R. 6004–1. NOTICE OF PROPOSED SALE

In addition to the requirements of Rule 2002 of the Federal Rules of Bankruptcy Procedure, if the notice of a proposed sale is to a private party, the notice must also include a statement substantially as follows: "Any higher bids must be stated in writing and received by (proponent of motion) not later than (the same date as the last date to object to the proposed sale)."

[Effective June 1, 2012.]

L.R. 6004–2. LIQUIDATORS/AUCTIONEERS AND APPRAISERS

A. Bond Required. It is the responsibility of the Trustee to monitor the auctioneer or other liquidator and unless otherwise ordered by the Court, to assure that any auctioneer or other liquidator who will come into possession or control of any asset or proceeds of any asset of an estate, posts a bond with the United States Trustee on behalf of the United States of America, for the full value of the assets in the possession or control of the auctioneer or liquidator.

B. Report of Sale. The Trustee shall file a report of sale within 14 days of any sale. At the time of filing, the Trustee shall transmit a copy of the report of sale to the United States Trustee along with an itemized list of the property sold, the name of each purchaser, and the price received for each item or lot of inventory. The Trustee shall make available upon request said itemized list.

C. Application for Compensation. In the event the auctioneer or liquidator seeks compensation and costs of sale, an application for compensation containing a detailed itemization of requested compensation and actual expenses shall be filed with the Court.

D. Remittance of Gross Proceeds. Upon filing an application to employ an auctioneer or other liquidator and receiving Court approval, it is the responsibility of the Trustee to monitor the auctioneer or other liquidator, and to assure that, unless otherwise ordered by the Court, all gross sale proceeds are remitted to the Trustee within 14 days of the sale. Upon motion of any party in interest and for good cause shown, the Court may authorize the auctioneer or other liquidator to submit the net proceeds or to turn over to a secured creditor the net proceeds realized from the sale of that creditor's collateral.

E. Validity of Checks. The validity of any checks or bank drafts accepted by the auctioneer or other liquidator shall be the sole responsibility of the auctioneer or liquidator.

F. Separate Escrow Account. It is the responsibility of the Trustee to monitor the auctioneer or other liquidator, and to assure that, if the auctioneer or liquidator does not remit the entire sale proceeds to the Trustee within 14 days, and the proceeds of the property sold are $50,000.00 or more, the auctioneer or liquidator shall open a segregated escrow or trust account for deposit of the sale proceeds. This account shall be designated by the bankruptcy estate case name and shall require the co-signature of the Trustee for any withdrawals. If the proceeds of the sale are less than $50,000.00, the proceeds may be deposited in the auctioneer's or liquidator's trust or client fund account.

G. Appraiser Serving as Auctioneer or Liquidator. No appraiser, agent or employee of an appraiser who has been employed in a bankruptcy case may serve as the auctioneer or liquidator in that same case without the approval of the Court.

H. Auctioneer or Liquidator Purchasing at Sale. It is the responsibility of the Trustee to monitor and to assure that no auctioneer or other liquidator, or any agent, employee or family member of the auctioneer or liquidator employed in a case, purchase any asset from the estate.

[Effective June 1, 2012.]

L.R. 6007. ABANDONMENT OF PROPERTY

A motion for abandonment of property by a creditor will be granted without notice if the Trustee has filed a Report of No Distribution.

[Effective June 1, 2012.]

L.R. 6008. REDEMPTION OF PROPERTY

A. Filing and Certificate of Service. The debtor must file with the Court the motion for redemption, the notice, and a certificate of service.

B. Service and Notice. The debtor shall serve the motion and notice thereof on the lien holder and interested parties, in accordance with Rules 9014(b) and 7004 of the Federal Rules of Bankruptcy Procedure. The notice shall allow 21 days from the date of filing to file objections.

[Effective June 1, 2012.]

L.R. 6012. TRUSTEE PAYMENTS TO THE INTERNAL REVENUE SERVICE

Any duly appointed Trustee in a chapter 7 or chapter 13 bankruptcy case in this district who is remitting a nonelectronic payment to the United States Internal Revenue Service should direct the payment to the address found in the Internal Revenue Manual at Part 5, Chapter 9, Section 15.1, regardless of what address appears on the proof of claim.

[Effective June 1, 2012.]

PART VII. ADVERSARY PROCEEDINGS

L.R. 7004. SERVICE OF SUMMONS ON THE UNITED STATES AND ITS AGENCIES

Whenever service is required by the Federal Rules of Bankruptcy Procedure on the United States or its various agencies, the service shall be in accordance with this Court's Electronic Filing Rules, which can be found on the Court's website at www.ilsb.uscourts.gov.

[Effective June 1, 2012.]

L.R. 7016. PRE–TRIAL PROCEDURES

A. Duty to Exchange Witness and Exhibit Lists, and Exhibits. Parties to an adversary proceeding shall mark all exhibits prior to trial and shall prepare sufficient copies of the exhibits for all parties to refer to at trial, plus one copy each for the Judge, Law Clerk and Courtroom Deputy. The parties shall exchange all exhibits and supply paper copies to the Court at least 14 days prior to trial. Each party shall prepare and file at least 7 days prior to trial a written statement as to each exhibit indicating whether the party objects to the exhibit and, if so, the nature of the objection. Unless otherwise ordered, the parties shall exchange the names of all witnesses intended to be called at trial at least 7 days prior to trial.

B. Objections to Exhibits. Objections to the authenticity or genuineness of any document shall be made in writing no later than 72 hours prior to trial.

Failure to object to the authenticity or genuineness of a document does not waive any right to object on the basis of relevance at trial.

C. Briefs, Findings of Fact, Conclusions of Law. Unless a pre-trial order directs otherwise, the parties shall prepare and submit at least 14 days prior to trial proposed findings of fact, conclusions of law and briefs in support of their respective positions. The briefs shall contain a statement which outlines the burden of proof on each issue, who has the burden of proof, and why the burden of proof has or has not been sustained.

D. Failure to Comply. The Court may refuse consideration of or strike any pleading or other document, or take any other appropriate action, for failure to comply with the procedures set forth in subsections A, B or C of this Rule.

[Effective June 1, 2012.]

L.R. 7026–1. FILING AND SERVICE OF DISCOVERY MATERIALS

Because of the considerable cost to the parties of furnishing discovery materials, and the serious problems encountered with storage, the Court adopts the following procedure for filing of discovery materials with the Court:

A. If relief is sought under Rules 26(c) or 37 of the Federal Rules of Civil Procedure, concerning any disclosures, interrogatories, or requests for production or inspection, answers to interrogatories or responses to requests for production or inspection, copies of the portions of the disclosures, interrogatories, requests, answers or responses in dispute shall be filed with the Court contemporaneously with any motion filed under these Rules.

B. If disclosures, interrogatories, requests, answers, responses or depositions are to be used at trial or are necessary to a pre-trial motion which might result in a final order on any issue, the portions to be used shall be filed with the Court at the outset of the trial or at the filing of the motion insofar as their use can be reasonably anticipated.

[Effective June 1, 2012.]

L.R. 7026–2. MOTIONS TO COMPEL

Except as otherwise ordered, the Court will not entertain any motion under Rule 37 of the Federal Rules of Civil Procedure, unless, prior to the filing of the motion, counsel for the moving party has conferred or has made reasonable efforts to confer with opposing counsel concerning the matter in dispute. Counsel for the moving party shall file a statement establishing compliance with this Rule with any mo-

tion filed under Rule 37 of the Federal Rules of Civil Procedure.

[Effective June 1, 2012.]

L.R. 7041–1. DISMISSAL OF UNDER-LYING BANKRUPTCY CASE

Any pending adversary proceeding shall be dismissed 14 days following the date of dismissal of the underlying bankruptcy case, unless a party, within the same period, requests otherwise by written motion.

[Effective June 1, 2012.]

L.R. 7041–2. COMPLAINTS TO DENY OR REVOKE DISCHARGE: DISMISSAL OR SETTLEMENT

A. Contents and Service of Motion for, or Stipulation Regarding Voluntary Dismissal of Complaint to Deny or Revoke Discharge. Any dismissal, whether by motion or stipulation, of a complaint to deny or revoke the debtor's discharge pursuant to Section 727 of the Bankruptcy Code, shall be served on the United States Trustee, any case Trustee, counsel of record, and any party that has intervened in the adversary proceeding. The notice, motion or stipulation shall contain a recital concerning the consideration, if any, for the dismissal or the terms and conditions of any agreement concerning the dismissal. The moving party shall file, with the motion or stipulation, a separate notice giving all interested parties 21 days from the date of filing to object.

B. Objections to Dismissal. Unless the United States Trustee, the case Trustee, or another entity seeks to intervene or to be substituted for the plaintiff in the proceeding or objects to the dismissal within 21 days following the filing of the motion/stipulation, the Court may dismiss the complaint and/or close the adversary proceeding, upon such terms and conditions as it deems proper, without further notice or hearing.

[Effective June 1, 2012.]

L.R. 7055. DEFAULT JUDGMENT

A. Clerk's Entry of Default. A plaintiff seeking the Clerk of Court's entry of default shall follow the procedures set forth in Rule 7055 of the Federal Rules of Bankruptcy Procedure. To obtain the Clerk of Court's entry of default, the Court requires the filing of the following:

1. Request for Clerk of Court's entry of default; and

2. Verified Affidavit* supporting entitlement to entry of default.

*The affidavit shall contain:

a. The complete caption setting forth the name of the Court, the name of the parties, and bankruptcy and adversary case numbers;

b. Date of issuance of summons;

c. Statement of whether the Court fixed a deadline for filing an answer or motion, or whether the 30 or 35 day limit applies;

d. Date of service of the complaint;

e. Date of filing of affidavit or return of service;

f. Statement that no answer or motion has been received within the time limit fixed by the Court or by Rule 7012(a) of the Federal Rules of Bankruptcy Procedure;

g. Statement that the defendant is not in the military service (as required by the Soldier's & Sailor's Civil Relief Act, 50 U.S.C. App. § 521); and

h. Statement that the defendant is not a minor or an incompetent person as required by Rule 55(b)(1) of the Federal Rules of Civil Procedure.

If the plaintiff is entitled to entry of default, the Clerk's Office will complete the entry of default and serve a copy of the entry of default to the plaintiff.

B. Motion for Default Judgment. The movant shall file a separate motion for default judgment, and shall serve the motion on the party against whom the default judgment is requested by mail at the last known address.

C. Determining Amount of Judgment. If the claim to which no response was made is for a "sum certain," then the motion shall be accompanied by an affidavit showing the principal amount due and owing, not exceeding the amount sought in the claim, plus interest, if any, computed by the movant, with credit for all payments received to date clearly set forth, and costs, if any, pursuant to 28 U.S.C. § 1920. If the amount of the claim is not readily ascertainable or if the amount requested in the motion exceeds the amount stated in the claim, the Court may conduct a hearing on the motion for default judgment.

[Effective June 1, 2012.]

L.R. 7056. MOTIONS FOR SUMMARY JUDGMENT

A. Motion for Summary Judgment. A motion for summary judgment shall state with particularity, in separately numbered paragraphs, each material fact as to which the movant claims there is no genuine issue. Each such paragraph shall reference the pleading, discovery, affidavit or document that supports such fact. If the motion requires consideration of facts not appearing in the record, the party shall file all documentary evidence relied upon, including affidavits, as an attachment to the motion. The motion shall not refer to material facts not presented as evidence in support of the motion. The motion shall also state concisely the legal grounds on which relief should be granted.

B. Memorandum in Support. The moving party shall file with each motion for summary judgment a memorandum in support of the motion, including citations to any authorities upon which the party relies. Failure to file a memorandum in support of the motion may result in the entry of an order striking the motion.

C. Responses. Each party opposing a motion for summary judgment shall file a response specifically admitting or denying each of the movant's factual statements. The response shall include the reason for denial of any factual allegation and shall be supported by reference to the pleadings, discovery, affidavits or documents that support respondent's denial. The response shall further list in numbered paragraphs any additional facts that remain in dispute and those facts shall be supported by reference to the pleadings, discovery, affidavits or documents that support the respondent's allegations. If any response requires consideration of facts not appearing in the record, the party shall file with its response all documentary evidence relied upon, including affidavits, if applicable.

D. Memorandum in Support of Response. The respondent shall also file a memorandum in support of the response, including citations to authorities on which the respondent relies. Failure to file a memorandum in support of the response may result in the entry of an order striking the response.

E. Response Time. The response and memorandum in support of the response shall be filed within 21 days from the date the motion for summary judgment is filed.

F. Replies. The moving party may file a reply no later than 14 days after the response is filed. Additional replies may be filed by either party only with leave of Court. Any reply may address only matters raised in the response to which the reply relates.

G. Page Limits. Absent leave of Court, no pleading or memorandum regarding summary judgment shall exceed 20 numbered pages, exclusive of the signature page and attachments.

[Effective June 1, 2012.]

L.R. 7069. EXECUTION/ENFORCEMENT OF JUDGMENTS

A Trustee or debtor who seeks to enforce a judgment in an adversary proceeding or an order of turnover for the benefit of the bankruptcy estate may pursue collection in the Bankruptcy Court.

[Effective June 1, 2012.]

PART IX. GENERAL PROVISIONS AND MOTION PRACTICE

L.R. 9006–1. MOTIONS FOR RELIEF FROM STAY

Any objections to a motion for relief from stay shall be filed on or before 14 days from the date of filing unless otherwise ordered. This provision is to allow the Court time to meet the statutory hearing requirements of Section 362(e) of the Bankruptcy Code.

[Effective June 1, 2012.]

L.R. 9006–2. PROCEDURE FOR OBTAINING SHORTENED AND/OR LIMITED NOTICE

A. General Application. This provision shall govern the procedures to be followed for any matter as to which shortened notice or shortened notice and expedited hearing is requested pursuant to Rule 9006(c) of the Federal Rules of Bankruptcy Procedure (a "9006(c) Request"). The 9006(c) Request shall be considered by the Court without a hearing. If granted, the Court will issue an order shortening notice and/or setting an expedited hearing.

B. Filing Requirements. A 9006(c) Request shall be made by separate written motion, shall clearly refer to the matter to which it pertains (the "Underlying Motion"), shall specifically state the need for shortened notice or expedited treatment, shall state the time by which the notice is to be shortened or the expedited hearing is to be held, and shall briefly describe the relief requested in the Underlying Motion. The movant shall provide telephonic notice to the Clerk's Office of the filing of the 9006(c) Request and shall tender a proposed order.

C. Service and Distribution of 9006(c) Request, Underlying Motion and Order Shortening Notice and/or Setting Expedited Hearing. The movant shall serve, by fax, e-mail or hand delivery, the 9006(c) Request and the Underlying Motion, along with the Order Shortening Notice and/or Setting Expedited Hearing, on any party that has, or claims to have, an interest in the property to be affected by the relief requested in the Underlying Motion, parties required to receive notice under the applicable Federal Rule of Bankruptcy Procedure, and any other party as directed by the Court. If the matter is a contested matter within an adversary proceeding, service of the 9006(c) Request and the underlying Motion shall be made in the manner described above but only upon the parties to the adversary proceeding and any other party as directed by the Court.

[Effective June 1, 2012.]

L.R. 9006–3. EMERGENCY MOTIONS

Attorneys/participants seeking to schedule emergency motions or other expedited matters shall identify the same by using the word "emergency" in the title of the pleading; provide an explanation within the pleading as to the nature of the emergency; and use the word "emergency" in the docket text when electronically filing such pleading. Counsel shall immediately upon filing contact the Judge's courtroom deputy, who will advise chambers of the filing. Only upon being directed by the Court, counsel shall immediately issue and file a notice of the hearing with a certificate of service.

[Effective June 1, 2012.]

L.R. 9010. REPRESENTATION AND APPEARANCES

A. Appearances by Attorneys. The filing of any document (other than a proof of claim, a reaffirmation agreement, a request pursuant to Rule 2002(g) of the Federal Rules of Bankruptcy Procedure, or a creditor change of address) shall be deemed a general entry of appearance in that case by the attorney filing the document.

B. Appearance without Attorney—Corporation or Other Business Entities. A corporation, partnership, trust or other business entity, other than a sole proprietorship, may appear and act without counsel in a case or proceeding before this Court only for the purpose of attending the 341 meeting, filing a request for notice and service of documents, filing a change of address, filing a proof of claim, and submitting a ballot. For all other purposes, such entity shall appear and act only through an attorney.

[Effective June 1, 2012.]

L.R. 9011. SIGNING OF PAPERS

A. Signature Requirement and Attorney Information. If a party is represented by an attorney, every pleading filed and/or presented for filing shall be signed by the attorney of record in accordance with this Court's Electronic Filing Rules, which can be found on the Court's website at www.ilsb.uscourts.gov. Under the attorney's signature shall be typed the attorney's name, office address, e-mail address, telephone number, and state bar number.

B. Stipulations and Agreed Orders. Every stipulation and agreed order shall be signed by each interested party or their attorney of record.

[Effective June 1, 2012.]

L.R. 9013–1. FILING MOTIONS AND OBJECTIONS TO MOTIONS

A. Separate Motions and Objections. Every application, motion, or other request for an order from the Court, including motions initiating contested matters, shall be filed separately, except as provided in Rule 4001–2 of these Rules. Applications, motions and other requests shall state with particularity the order or relief sought, and shall contain a short and plain statement concerning the factual basis or grounds for the motion. Objections to separately filed motions must also be filed separately.

B. Stay Relief or Adequate Protection Motions. Motions seeking relief from the automatic stay or adequate protection may not be joined with any other objections or request for relief, except as provided in Rule 4001–2 of these Rules.

C. Content of Objections. Objections to any motion, application, or request shall contain a short, plain statement concerning the factual or legal basis for the objections. The failure to state a sufficient legal or factual basis for the objection may result in the objection being overruled without a hearing.

D. Duty to Confer. If a motion is contested, the movant shall confer with the respondent prior to the hearing to determine whether a consent order may be entered disposing of the motion, or in the alternative, to stipulate to as many facts and issues as possible.

[Effective June 1, 2012.]

L.R. 9013–2. CERTIFICATE OF SERVICE

A. Filing. All pleadings and papers filed in a bankruptcy case pursuant to Rules 9013 or 9014 of the Federal Rules of Bankruptcy Procedure shall comply with Rule 7005(d) of the Federal Rules of Bankruptcy Procedure.

B. Failure to Comply. The Court may refuse consideration of or strike any pleading or document for which a certificate of service has not been filed or which does not otherwise comply with subsection A above.

[Effective June 1, 2012.]

L.R. 9013–3. STIPULATIONS OR AGREEMENTS

In order to bring the matter before the Court, stipulations that are filed in a case must be accompanied by an appropriate motion to approve same. (This Rule does not apply if the stipulation is submitted pursuant to an order of the Court, and does not apply in adversary proceedings.) Stipulations that are filed without the appropriate motion will be processed as deficient by the Clerk's Office. If the stipulation is processed as deficient, it must be refiled when the motion to approve stipulation is filed.

[Effective June 1, 2012.]

L.R. 9013–4. PROPOSED ORDERS

With the exception of certain motions listed on the Court's website, all motions, applications, objections to claims in chapter 13 and chapter 11, and motions to approve stipulations or agreements must be accompanied by a proposed order. The order shall not be attached to the motion, application, etc., but shall be emailed to the Court in accordance with the Court's Electronic Filing Rules governing submission of proposed orders, which can be found on the Court's website at www.ilsb.uscourts.gov.

[Effective June 1, 2012.]

L.R. 9013–5. BRIEFS

A. Motions Requiring Briefs. Absent leave of Court, the following motions shall be supported by a brief: Motions to dismiss, motions to strike pleadings, motions for a more definite statement, and motions for judgment on the pleadings. (Briefs in support of motions for summary judgment are governed by Rule 7056 of these Rules.)

B. Motions that Do Not Require Briefs. The following motions do not require a brief: debtor's motion to voluntarily dismiss case; plaintiff's motion to voluntarily dismiss an adversary proceeding; motions to dismiss for failure to attend the 341 meeting of creditors; motions to dismiss for failure to comply with a Court order; motions to dismiss for failure to make chapter13 plan payments; and motions to avoid liens under Section 522(f) of the Bankruptcy Code.

C. Motions for Relief from Stay. At the preliminary hearing on a motion for relief from stay, the Court may order that briefs be filed prior to the trial date.

D. Time and Manner of Filing. Except as noted in subsection C of this Rule, briefs shall be filed at the time the corresponding motion is filed and shall be filed as a separate document. All briefs, including responsive briefs, shall contain a short, concise statement of the party's position and citations to any authorities upon which the party relies.

E. Responsive Briefs. Each party opposing the motion shall file a responsive brief within 14 days after the filing of the movant's brief. No brief beyond the responsive brief shall be filed except upon leave granted.

F. Page limits. Absent leave of Court, briefs shall not exceed 20 pages, exclusive of the signature page and attachments.

G. Failure to File Brief. If a party fails to file a brief in support of a motion as outlined above, the Court may enter an order striking or denying the motion. If an opposing party fails to file a responsive brief as outlined above, the Court may enter an order granting the relief sought in the motion.

[Effective June 1, 2012.]

L.R. 9014. APPLICABILITY OF BANKRUPTCY RULE 7016

Upon request, the Court may order that Rule 7016 of the Federal Rules of Bankruptcy Procedure shall apply in a contested matter.

[Effective June 1, 2012.]

L.R. 9015. JURY TRIALS

A. Authorization. Pursuant to District Court's Local Rule 9015.1, the District Court has authorized the Bankruptcy Judges of this District to conduct jury trials with the express consent of all parties.

B. Applicability of District Court Rules. Unless otherwise ordered by the Bankruptcy Court, the Local Rules of the United States District Court for the Southern District of Illinois governing jury trials shall apply.

C. Time for Consent. Unless, within 30 days after the demand for jury trial is filed, the other parties to the proceeding file a consent, the Bankruptcy Judge shall request that the District Court withdraw the reference of the matter. Even if all parties consent, the Bankruptcy Judge will determine whether the request for a jury trial is proper.

[Effective June 1, 2012.]

L.R. 9019. STIPULATIONS AND SETTLEMENTS

A. Notice to Court When Hearing is Set. When parties reach a settlement in a matter that has been set for hearing, the parties shall promptly notify the Court of the settlement and, within the time promised or as required by the Court, shall file the appropriate pleading and/or submit any proposed order concerning the settlement. The Court may extend the time for filing/submission upon request. Failure to file the settlement pleading or submit the proposed order may result in the Court taking such action as it deems appropriate, including granting or denying the requested relief.

B. Adversary Proceedings. When approval of a settlement or compromise is required by Rule 9019(a) or (b) of the Federal Rules of Bankruptcy Procedure, the movant shall file a motion to approve the settlement, along with the appropriate notice, in the adversary proceeding. In the event the settlement affects estate property, the movant shall also file a copy of the motion and notice in the bankruptcy case.

Settlements of complaints to deny or revoke discharge are governed by Rule 7041-2 of these Rules.

C. Matters Pending in Other Courts. Parties shall be required to file a motion/application to approve settlement of any civil action pending outside this Court.

[Effective June 1, 2012.]

L.R. 9027. REMOVAL

A. Removal when Bankruptcy Case Pending in this District. Removal of a matter pending in state court or in a district other than the Southern District of Illinois is accomplished by filing a notice of removal as an adversary proceeding in the bankruptcy case. If the matter is filed or pending before the District Court for this district, then a request to refer the matter to the Bankruptcy Court should be filed with the District Court.

B. Removal when Bankruptcy Case Pending in a Different District. A party seeking to remove a matter related to a bankruptcy case pending in another district should provide telephonic notice to the Bankruptcy Clerk of Court for the Southern District of Illinois prior to filing the removal.

[Effective June 1, 2012.]

L.R. 9034-1. TRANSMITTAL OF PLEADINGS, PAPERS, OBJECTIONS AND OTHER PAPERS TO THE UNITED STATES TRUSTEE

The mailing address and telephone number for the United States Trustee servicing the Southern District of Illinois can be found on the Court's website at www.ilsb.uscourts.gov.

[Effective June 1, 2012.]

L.R. 9034-2. MAILING ADDRESSES FOR UNITED STATES AND VARIOUS GOVERNMENT AGENCIES

Service to addresses for the United States and various government agencies shall be in accordance with this Court's Electronic Filing Rules, which can be found on the Court's website at www.ilsb.uscourts.gov.

[Effective June 1, 2012.]

L.R. 9037. PRIVACY PROTECTION FOR FILINGS MADE WITH THE COURT

The Court, on its own motion or on a motion for a protective order filed pursuant to Rule 9037(d) of the

Federal Rules of Bankruptcy Procedure, may rule on such motion without notice or hearing.

[Effective June 1, 2012.]

L.R. 9070. DISPOSITION OF EXHIBITS

The District Court's Local Rule 79.1 shall not apply. Exhibits admitted into evidence shall be held by the Court for a period of 14 days from the disposition of the matter. In the event an appeal is filed and the exhibits are not included in the designation of items on appeal, the exhibits shall be held by the Court until the disposition and expiration of the applicable appeal period.

[Effective June 1, 2012.]

APPENDICES

APPENDIX A

Repealed Orders:

General Order 11–5	Rule 3001(c)(2)(C) and Rule 3002.1 of the Federal Rules of Bankruptcy Procedure
General Order 11–4	Revised Uniform Chapter 13 Plan
General Order 11–3	Trustee Payments to the Internal Revenue Service
General Order 11–01	Attorney's Fees in Chapter 13 Proceedings
General Order 10–2	Amendment to General Order 08–7
General Order 09–4	Changes/Updates in Time Period Calculations in Local Rules and in Standing and General Orders
General Order 09–3	Chapter 13 Plans: Section 4(C) Governing Surrender of Property
General Order 09–2	Chapter 13 Confirmation Order: Change in Language
General Order 09–1	Amendment to General Order 08–4
General Order 08–7	Adoption of Interim Bankruptcy Rule 1007–I
General Order 08–5	Revised Uniform Chapter 13 Plan
General Order 08–4	Electronic Filing of Exhibits
General Order 08–3	Chapter 13/Changes in On–Going Mortgage Payments
General Order 08–2	Calculation of Trustee's Fee in Chapter 13 Cases
General Order 08–1	Chapter 13: Amended Plans, Amended Objections, Confirmation
General Order 07–8	Notice of Default in Chapter 13 Plan Payments
General Order 07–7	Notice of Default in Chapter 13 Plan Payments
General Order 07–6	Amended Plans in Chapter 13 Cases
Amended Standing Order 07–5	Chapter 13 Case Administration
General Order 07–04	Motion for Discharge in Chapter 13 Cases
General Order 07–03	Chapter 13/Distribution of Funds Upon Filing of Modified Plans After Confirmation
General Order 07–02	Chapter 13/Original Signatures
General Order 07–01	Chapter 13/Specified Monthly Payments
General Order 05–05	New Case Filing Information and PDF Documents
General Order 05–04	Attorney's Fees in Chapter 13 Proceedings
Administrative Order 05–03	Implementation of Notice of Preferred Addresses Under 11 U.S.C. § 342(f) and National Creditor Register Service
Amended General Order 05–02	Show Cause Procedure in Chapter 13 Cases
Standing Order 05–02	Filing of Payment Advices
Standing Order 05–01	Chapter 13 Case Administration
General Order 04–2	Dismissal and Reinstatement of Cases Upon Failure of Debtor(s) to Attend 341 Meetings of Creditors
General Order 04–1	Chapter 12 Filings
(No Number)	Amendment to Standing Order 1–94, entered 12/15/2003

[Effective June 1, 2012.]

ELECTRONIC FILING RULES

RULE 1. SCOPE OF ELECTRONIC FILING

All cases, bankruptcy and adversary, are assigned to the Electronic Case Filing (ECF) system. Attorneys must utilize the ECF system, unless specifically exempted by the Court for good cause shown. Pro se filers shall file all documents with the Clerk of Court by U.S. Mail or personal delivery to the Clerk's Office, or by using the Electronic Proof of Claims (ePOC) Program through the Court's website at www.ilsb.uscourts.gov.

[Amended effective March 4, 2013.]

RULE 2. ELIGIBILITY, REGISTRATION, AND PASSWORDS

ELIGIBILITY

Attorneys admitted to the bar of this Court, including those admitted pro hac vice and attorneys authorized to represent the United States, must register as ECF filers of the Court's ECF system or move for exemption. Each attorney admitted to practice in this Court shall be entitled to one system password to permit the attorney to participate in the electronic retrieval and filing of documents in accordance with the system. Any trustee who is also an attorney admitted to practice before this Court shall be entitled to one system password as an attorney and one system password as a trustee.

Limited filers (e.g. creditor, party in interest, transcriber, auditor, personal financial management course provider) may establish an account with the Court's

Case Management/Electronic Case Files (CM/ECF) system to electronically file documents in the Court's electronic files.

REGISTRATION

Each attorney/participant must complete the appropriate ECF registration form prescribed by the Clerk located on the Court's website. The forms may be duplicated for use.

All registration forms shall be returned to the Court by mail to United States Bankruptcy Court, Melvin Price United States Courthouse, 750 Missouri Avenue, East St Louis, IL 62201; Attn: CM/ECF Registration, or by fax to (618) 482–9417.

Registration as an ECF filer constitutes consent to electronic service of all electronically filed documents in accordance with the Federal Rules of Civil Procedure, Federal Rules of Bankruptcy Procedure, and the Local Rules of this Court.

PASSWORDS

Registrants will be provided training by the Court. Upon completion of the registration and training, the registrant will receive a password for the Court's Electronic Case Filing (ECF) system.

No ECF filer or other person may knowingly permit or cause to permit an ECF filer's password to be used by anyone other than an authorized agent of the ECF filer. If an employee of an ECF filer leaves their employment, the ECF filer must immediately notify the Court to activate a new password, remove the employee's e-mail address and add the e-mail address of the new employee, if applicable. ECF filers are also responsible for keeping their profile information current in the ECF system by notifying the Court of any modifications.

ECF filers agree to protect the security of their passwords and immediately notify the Clerk if they learn that their password has been compromised. Users may be subject to sanctions for failure to comply with this provision. To obtain a new password, contact the ECF Help Desk at (618) 482–9075.

[Amended effective June 1, 2012; December 1, 2013.]

RULE 3. TRAINING REQUIREMENTS

Each ECF filer must enroll in and complete a CM/ECF Filing User Training Program conducted by the Clerk. Selection and scheduling of applicants for CM/ECF training will be determined by the Clerk. The Clerk will use discretion in a fair and nondiscriminatory manner to ensure that all registrants are treated fairly.

The Court accepts training provided by another bankruptcy or district court and waives the classroom training requirement. ECF filers trained by other courts must indicate on the CM/ECF Registration Form the court in which they were trained.

Before registering to become an ECF user, review the CM/ECF Skills Checklist and Hardware/Software Requirements. Next download the ECF Registration Form and mail the form to the address listed on the form or fax it to (618) 482–9027. Once the form is received and reviewed, a Court representative will contact you with additional instructions.

Electronic Filers should also be familiar with the Court's Style Guide for Electronic Case Filing and the availability of answers to Frequently Asked Questions regarding Electronic Filing.

Individual requirements for obtaining an ID and password will be based on the following criteria:

1. You are registered as an ECF filer in another Court:

a. Complete and submit the ECF Registration Form, and

b. Complete required ECF Exercises.

2. You are not registered as an ECF filer in another Court:

a. Complete and submit the ECF Registration Form,

b. Complete ECF Training (classroom or Electronic Learning Modules), and

c. Complete required ECF Exercises.

RULE 4. PRIVACY ISSUES

In compliance with Federal Rules of Bankruptcy Procedure 9037, unless the Court orders otherwise, all filers must redact:

1. Social Security or taxpayer-identification numbers: Use last four digits only;

2. Dates of birth: Use year of birth only;

3. Names of minor children: Use the minor's initials;

4. Financial account numbers: Use last four digits only.

This requirement applies to all documents, including attachments. Failure to comply with this rule could result in the removal of electronic filing privileges. It is not the responsibility of the Clerk's Office to review documents filed with the Court for compliance with this rule.

RULE 5. SIGNATURES

This rule provides a means for the signature on pleadings and other documents through the mechanism of a password in compliance with S.D. Ill. LBR 9011. This rule also provides a means for the signature when filing a proof of claim or related document by electronic means directly with the Clerk using the Electronic Proof of Claims (ePOC) program through the Court's website at www.ilsb.uscourts.gov.

Signatures. Pursuant to Federal Rules of Civil Procedure 11, every pleading, motion, and other paper (except lists, schedules, statements or amendments thereto) shall be signed by at least one attorney of record or, if the party is not represented by an attorney, all papers shall be signed by the party.

The electronic filing of a pleading or other document by an attorney/participant who is registered in the Electronic Case Filing System, or by the attorney's or trustee's authorized filing agent, shall constitute the signature of that attorney/participant under Federal Rules of Bankruptcy Procedure 9011 and S.D. Ill. LBR 9011.

The filing of a proof of claim by electronic means directly with the Clerk using the Electronic Proof of Claims (ePOC) program shall constitute the filing claimant's approved signature by law, and the provisions of 18 U.S.C. § 152 shall apply to such filing. The filing of a claims related document by electronic means directly with the Clerk using ePOC shall constitute the filer's approved signature by law.

Electronically Filed Pleadings. Electronically filed pleadings requiring a signature shall either:

1. show an image of such signature as it appears on the original document, or

2. bear the name of the signatory preceded by an "/s/" or "s/" typed in the space where the signature would otherwise appear, as follows: "/s/ Jane Doe".

Registered Attorneys/Participants and Parties with Legal Representation. Petitions, schedules, statements, amendments, pleadings, affidavits, and other documents which must contain original signatures, or which require verification under Federal Rules of Bankruptcy Procedure 1008, or an unsworn declaration as provided in 28 U.S.C. § 1746, shall be filed electronically and in accordance with this Court's Electronic Filing Rules. The electronically filed document shall indicate a signature with the party's name typed in full, e.g., "/s/ Jane Doe".

In the case of a stipulation or other document to be signed by two or more persons, the following procedure shall be used:

The attorney/participant shall initially confirm that the content of the document is acceptable to all persons required to sign the document and shall obtain the actual signatures of all parties on the document.

The attorney/participant shall then file the document electronically, indicating the signatories, e.g. "/s/ Jane Doe", "/s/ John Doe", etc.

The attorney/participant who files the document shall retain the hard copy of the document containing the original signatures in accordance with Electronic Filing Rule 10.

Pro Se Debtors. Petitions, schedules, statements, amendments, pleadings, affidavits, and other documents which must contain original signatures, or which require verification under Federal Rules of Bankruptcy Procedure 1008, or an unsworn declaration as provided in 28 U.S.C. § 1746, must be submitted with full signature. These documents will be scanned by the Clerk's Office.

[Amended effective June 1, 2012; March 4, 2013.]

RULE 6. ATTACHMENTS, EXHIBITS, AND MAXIMUM SIZE OF FILINGS

Attachments. "Exhibits" as referenced below shall not be construed to include the following:

1. itemizations of fees and costs, and/or

2. affidavits.

The items listed above shall be filed with the relevant motion, application, or pleading as a single document, subject to the restrictions listed below under the Maximum Size of Filings section.

Exhibits. Exhibits (e.g., leases, promissory notes, mortgages, vehicle titles) may be filed electronically as a single document, subject to the restrictions listed below under the Maximum Size of Filings section.

A Summary of Exhibits may be filed electronically in lieu of filing the actual exhibits. The Summary of Exhibits shall enumerate and briefly describe each exhibit germane to the matter under consideration. The Summary of Exhibits shall conform with the Court's form Summary of Exhibits and shall be filed electronically as part of the document that references the exhibits (e.g., a proof of claim and a Summary of Exhibits shall be filed together electronically as a single document).

If a Summary of Exhibits is filed, the exhibits shall be served on interested parties and a certificate of service reflecting service of the exhibits shall appear on the Summary of Exhibits. Unless otherwise stated in the Pretrial Order or any other applicable Order issued by this Court, exhibits must be tendered to the Court at least fourteen days prior to the Court hearing to which they pertain.

Any Exhibit that is filed with the Court shall comply with the privacy protection requirements set forth in Federal Rules of Bankruptcy Procedure 9037.

Summary of Exhibits—Bankruptcy

Summary of Exhibits—Adversary

Maximum Size of Filings. If the document exceeds 5.0MB (5120KB), then it must be divided into segments, with the first segment being the main document and all subsequent segments as attachments to the main document. Each segment should not exceed 5.0MB.

[Effective October 12, 2011.]

RULE 7. ELECTRONIC FILING AND SERVICE OF DOCUMENTS, AND NOTICE TO THE UNITED STATES AND VARIOUS GOVERNMENT AGENCIES

Electronic Filing and Service of Documents. Electronically filed documents must conform to the preferred style practices for all users of the ECF system as prescribed in this Court's Style Guide for Electronic Case Filing.

Electronic transmission of a document to the ECF system consistent with these rules, along with the transmission of a Notice of Electronic Filing (NEF) from the Court, constitutes filing of the document for all purposes of the Federal Rules of Bankruptcy Procedure and the Local Rules of this Court, and constitutes entry of the document on the docket kept by the Clerk under Federal Rules of Bankruptcy Procedure 5003 and 9036. Likewise, the filing of a proof of claim or related document by electronic means directly with the Clerk using the Electronic Proof of Claims (ePOC) program through the Court's website at www.ilsb.uscourts.gov constitutes filing of the proof of claim or related document for all purposes of the Federal Rules of Bankruptcy Procedure and the Local Rules of this Court, and constitutes entry of the claim /document on the claims register/docket kept by the Clerk under Federal Rules of Bankruptcy Procedure 5003 and 9036.

When a document has been filed electronically, in accordance with the electronic filing procedures, the system will automatically generate a NEF at the time of docketing. The official record is the electronic recording of the document as stored by the Court, and the filing party is bound by the document as filed. A document filed electronically is deemed filed at the date and time stated on the NEF from the Court.

Filing a document electronically does not alter the filing deadline for that document. In accordance with Federal Rules of Bankruptcy Procedure 9006, filings must be completed before midnight local time where the Court is located in order to be considered timely filed that day, unless a specific time is set by the Court.

The filing party shall serve the document upon all persons entitled to notice or service in accordance with the applicable rules, or, if service by first class mail is permitted under the rules and the recipient of notice or service is a registered attorney/participant in the system, service of the NEF shall be the equivalent of service of the document by first class mail, postage prepaid.

Most sealed/restricted filings do not produce a Notice of Electronic Filing, and therefore, service by the filer of any such documents by an alternate method is required.

Nothing contained herein shall be construed to eliminate the necessity of service of the summons and complaint in accordance with the Federal Rules of Civil Procedure and the Federal Rules of Bankruptcy Procedure.

In chapter 7 cases, within seven (7) days after the filing of the bankruptcy petition, debtor (if proceeding pro se) or counsel for debtor shall serve a copy of the petition, schedules, statement of financial affairs, and statement of current monthly income and means test calculation on the chapter 7 trustee. See the Court's website at www.ilsb.uscourts.gov to determine if the Trustee requires electronic or paper submission.

Service Addresses. This Court maintains a list of creditor mailing addresses on its website for entities that have informed the Court of addresses where they wish to receive all bankruptcy correspondence. This list should be consulted prior to issuing service. These addresses should be substituted when service is required upon these entities. These addresses are subject to change should the party file a Notice of Preferred Address pursuant to 11 U.S.C. § 342(f) or § 342(e).

Notice to the United States and its Agencies. Whenever the Local Rules of Bankruptcy Procedure for the Southern District of Illinois or the Federal Rules of Bankruptcy Procedure require that notice be sent to the United States and/or its agencies, the notice shall be addressed to the United States Attorneys Office at the address as indicated in this Court's Creditor Mailing Addresses. In addition, a copy of the notice shall be sent directly to the Agency involved. If the Agency involved is the Internal Revenue Service, Small Business Administration, United States Department of Agriculture Rural Development, or United States Department of Agriculture Farm Services Agency (USDA–FSA), such notices shall be sent to the addresses in this Court's Creditor Mailing Addresses.

Service of Summons Upon the United States. Whenever service of summons is to be made upon the United States, a copy of the summons and complaint shall be sent by certified mail to both the United States Attorney General and the United States Attorneys Office, with a copy of the summons and complaint being mailed directly to the Agency involved. Such service shall be sent to the addresses in this Court's Creditor Mailing Addresses.

Service Upon State and Other Various Government Agencies. Whenever service is to be made upon the Illinois Department of Revenue or the Missouri Department of Revenue, such notice shall be sent to the address as indicated in this Court's Creditor Mailing Addresses.

[Amended effective June 1, 2012; March 4, 2013.]

RULE 8.   FEES PAYABLE TO THE CLERK

After successfully submitting a docket entry which requires a filing fee, the filer will be prompted to either pay the fee or continue filing. If the filer chooses to continue filing, the prompt will disappear, and they can continue using the electronic filing system. If the filer chooses to pay the filing fee, they will be prompted for their credit card information. After submitting their credit card information, the filing fee will be paid via the Internet directly to the U.S. Treasury, a transaction receipt will be displayed, and the receipt number will be docketed in the case immediately. All fees which the Clerk is required to collect are due and owing at the time of filing. Click here to view current filing fees.

If the filer fails to pay their outstanding fees after a 24–hour period, the filer will be "locked out". If this occurs, the only menu option available to the filer will be 'Internet Payments Due'. Once the fees are paid, the filer's account will be automatically unlocked. If you have questions about this process or experience problems paying your outstanding fees, please contact the Court at (618) 482–9075.

Electronically filed documents requiring a filing fee will be paid using an accepted credit/debit card via the Internet as part of the filing process. THE DEBTOR'S CARD MAY NOT BE USED TO MAKE THIS PAYMENT. Click here for more information on limitations and instructional videos.

RULE 9.   ORDERS

SUBMISSION OF ORDERS BY E–MAIL

When submitting a proposed order to the Court, attorneys/participants shall attach the proposed order to an e-mail message sent to one of the following addresses:

E-mail address for East St Louis: ESTLorders@ilsb.uscourts.gov
E-mail address for Benton: BENTONorders@ilsb.uscourts.gov

A PROPOSED ORDER MUST BE SUBMITTED AS AN ATTACHMENT TO AN E–MAIL MESSAGE. DO NOT FILE A MOTION/PLEADING THAT CONTAINS A PROPOSED ORDER WITHIN THE BODY OF THE MOTION/PLEADING OR AS AN ATTACHMENT TO A MOTION/PLEADING. DO NOT SUBMIT THE PROPOSED ORDER WITHIN THE BODY OF THE E–MAIL MESSAGE.

Only one proposed order may be submitted with each e-mail message (i.e., do not send an email message that has more than one proposed order attached to it).

The e-mail message to which the proposed order is attached must contain the following information in the "subject" line: (1) case name; (2) bankruptcy case number (include the adversary case number as well, if applicable); and (3) name of the order (the name of the order should describe the subject of the order, e.g., Order Granting Continuance, Order Granting Motion for Relief From Stay). If this is an agreed order or a proposed submitted from Court, this should be indicated in the subject line, as well.

The e-mail message to which the proposed order is attached must contain the following information in the body of the message: (1) the name of the attorney/participant submitting the proposed order; (2) the attorney/participant's telephone number; (3) the part(ies) he or she represents; and (4) the names of all parties and/or attorney/participants who have received a copy of the proposed order.

The proposed order must be in Word format and created (i.e., named or saved) using the following naming convention:

casenumber.doc

casenumber=the case number without hyphen

For example, 0255531.doc for a bankruptcy case, or 024993.doc for an adversary case.

AGREED ORDERS

An **agreed** order shall be submitted by e-mail and shall conform to the convention for stipulations as set forth in Electronic Fling Rule 5 under the Registered Attorneys/Participants and Parties with Legal Representation section.

SERVICE OF ORDERS

The following sentence must be included in <u>all</u> proposed orders (with the exception of final/appealable orders in adversary cases):

Counsel for the moving party shall serve a copy of this order by mail to all interested parties who were not served electronically.

NOTE: In adversary cases, the Clerk's office serves final/appealable orders.

[Amended effective June 1, 2012; November 14, 2012.]

RULE 10.   RETENTION REQUIREMENTS

Original executed petitions, schedules, statements of financial affairs, and stipulations or other documents signed by two or more persons must be retained by counsel until five (5) years after the closing of the case. Upon request of the Court, the attorney/participant must provide original documents for review.

Other documents should be retained until all matters relating thereto have been resolved or finalized.

The chapter 13 trustee is not required to maintain original signatures on pleadings, motions, orders, or other documents that are filed electronically.

RULE 11.   CONVENTIONAL FILING OF DOCUMENTS

Sealed Documents. Documents ordered to be placed under seal must be filed conventionally, and not electronically, unless specifically authorized by the Court. A motion to file documents under seal may be filed electronically unless prohibited by law.

Pro Se Debtors. A debtor without legal representation shall file petitions, schedules, motions, pleadings and any other documents conventionally in accordance with the Local Rules of the Bankruptcy Court for the Southern District of Illinois and other applicable filing rules.

RULE 12.   TECHNICAL FAILURE

In instances where a document must be filed immediately, but electronic filing cannot be accessed because of system failure within the attorney/participant's office or within the Court, the attorney/participant shall contact the appropriate office and speak with a deputy clerk to confirm that the system is not accessible, and state why an immediate filing is necessary.   The attorney/participant will make suitable arrangements for the filing to take place.

RULE 13.   PUBLIC ACCESS

The public may review at the Clerk's Office filings that have not been sealed or restricted by the Court.   Public terminals are available during regular business hours.

The public may also access the ECF system at the Court's Internet site https://ecf.ilsb.uscourts.gov by obtaining a PACER login and password.   A person who has PACER access may retrieve docket sheets and review documents filed in the system.

Registration for a PACER account may be made online at http://pacer.psc.uscourts.gov or by calling the PACER Service Center at (800) 676–6856.   Additional information about PACER is available on the Court's web site at http://www.ilsb.uscourts.gov/pacer.shtm.

Conventional and certified copies of electronically filed documents may be purchased at the Clerk's Office during regular business hours.   The fee for copying and certification will be in accordance with the provisions of 28 U.S.C. § 1930.

The Notice of Electronic Filing (NEF) contains a link to "one free look" of the filed documents.   It is recommended that the recipients of the NEF save the document for later viewing without incurring additional charges.   Please review the FAQ—Saving the 'One Free Look' document on the Court's web site.

RULE 14.   FILING OF FIRST DAY MOTIONS IN CHAPTER 11 CASES

First day Chapter 11 motions refer to a variety of pleadings filed with the initial case filing in order to keep the business functioning, to meet payroll, etc.   Motions filed in Chapter 11 cases within 48 hours of filing of the petition are considered first day motions.

To properly gather statistical information concerning Chapter 11 first day motions, first day motions shall be filed using designated Motion/Application events within the CM/ECF system.   In the instance of a motion being filed in which a descriptively titled event exists, the motion shall be filed using the applicable event. Examples: "Application to Employ" and "Motion to Use Cash Collateral".   Other first day motions shall be filed using the CM/ECF event under Motions/Applications of "Chapter 11 Continuation of Operations".   A description of the motion shall be typed into the available text box.

STYLE GUIDE FOR ELECTRONIC CASE FILING

December 2001

Revised 7/9/2012

Section-by-Section Comparison Chart

Change Code:
R = revised
D = deleted
A = addition

Type of Change	Date of Change	New or Revised Section(s)	Reason for Change
R	7/12/05	Introduction	Corrected two grammatical errors
R	7/12/05	Search Strategies	Clarified example of searching for debtors and corrected two grammatical errors
D	7/12/05	Adding Debtors	Removed redundant wording
D	7/12/05	Style Conventions for Addresses	Removed redundant wording and corrected grammatical error
R	7/12/05	Abbreviations—States and Territories	Corrected abbreviation for Marshall Islands, Micronesia, North Mariana Islands and Palau. Minnesota was missing
R	7/12/05	Street Designators	Added square and freeway. Reordered list to be alphabetical
R	3/10/08	Adding Debtors	Reworded sentence about names to make clearer
R	3/10/08	Adding Debtors	Modified SSN/TaxID prompts to match CM/ECF
A	3/10/08	Adding Plaintiffs and Defendants	Added sentence about alias(es)
A	3/10/08	Adding Creditors	Added sentence about alias(es)
A	3/10/08	Creditor/Party Filer Tips	Added sentence about party name(s) that contain an article
A	3/10/08	Street Designators	Added circle
R	7/09/12	Creditor matrix entries	Revised guidelines for adding creditors to matrix

United States Bankruptcy Court, Southern District of Illinois

This guide contains the preferred style practices for all users of the CM/ECF application in the Southern District of Illinois. The intention of the guide is to make everyone's task easier, whether they are entering data or querying the CM/ECF database. The application of a common set of styles when creating docket entries results in information being captured and displayed in more uniform and predictable ways, thus reducing confusion and errors. In addition, style consistency is the key to efficient searches in CM/ECF since successful queries require very exact matches on search data including punctuation and abbreviations.

The rule of thumb when using the CM/ECF application is to keep it simple. Using the least amount of punctuation and descriptive information as possible will further enhance uniformity.

Adding Parties

When adding new parties to the CM/ECF database, the names should conform with punctuation and spacing conventions adopted by the Southern District of Illinois Bankruptcy Court and listed in the **Style Conventions for Names** section of this guide.

Most of case opening in CM/ECF consists of adding the names of debtors, joint debtors, plaintiffs and defendants to cases. As cases progress, creditors and other parties are added. Access to this information is vital to the court, the bar, and the general public.

Searching for Parties

Make sure you do a thorough search of the CM/ECF database for a party before you add them to a case.

Before adding any party to a case, search for that party using appropriate "search clues". If the system finds the correct name, select it to help eliminate different versions of the same party name.

Even something as simple as "United States" can cause ambiguity if everyone is entering it differently. For instance, following this style guide can help avoid "United States" being in the database as "UNITED STATES", "U.S.", "US," "USA", "U.S.A.", or "U.S. of A."

Search Strategies

CM/ECF searches require exact text matches.

- When searching for debtors, the more search clues you provide, the more likely you are to find the exact person. For example, if you search for the last name of Grant, CM/ECF may return a list of a quite a few parties with that last name. However, if you search for the last name of Grant with a first name of Eugene, CM/ECF will return a single party.

- When searching for creditors, it may be necessary to conduct multiple searches. First, search for the creditor's entire name (e.g., "World Communications"). If that is not successful, you can search for part of the creditor's name (e.g., "World Comm" or just "World").

- When searching for a party, **DO NOT** use an asterisk in the search criteria as follows:

   Villa*

Using an asterisk will slow down the entire system.

- Finally, an unsuccessful search for A & A Metals might be successful if you search without special characters (e.g., A and A Metals).

Adding Debtors

Add debtors name(s) and address(es) using the Style Conventions for Names and Addresses found in this guide.

In most cases, you will NOT find debtors or joint debtors when you search the CM/ECF database. You will have to add them to the database and the case as a new party. One exception would be if the debtor and or joint debtor had previously filed a case.

If a debtor has a title, add the title in the "party text" box. Keep the following tips in mind when considering using a title.

Title Tips

1. The name of the debtor without the title will appear in docket text.

2. Titles will not appear on notices.

3. Titles will appear on the face of the docket report in upper and lower
case following the debtor name as shown below:

Jose Garza, Administrator of the Estate of Sylvia Garza

Alamo Limestone, a Texas Corporation

Catherine V. Ruiz, Official Administrator of Lottery Winnings

---

Make an entry in the SSN box or the Tax ID box even if the social security number
for an individual debtor or tax identification number for a business is unknown.
SSN/ITIN: 000–00–0000
TaxID/EIN: 00–0000000000

Adding Plaintiffs and Defendants

When you search for plaintiffs and defendants, you will probably find them in the
database.

If the complaint lists alias(es) for the plaintiff or defendant, add them separately
using the Alias(es) button and not as part of the name.

Adding Creditors

Add creditors to cases using names that are already in the CM/ECF database if at
all possible.

When you search for a creditor, you will probably find the party in the CM/ECF
database.

Creditors (such as Ford Motor Credit) are added to many different cases.
Ideally, there should be only one Ford Motor Credit party in the CM/ECF database.
This greatly simplifies searching when adding parties and querying cases.

For instance, it is better to add Ford Motor Credit to all cases even if that is not
the exact name used on a document being docketed. The idea is to avoid adding
name variations for a single creditor. For example:

- Ford Motor Credit
- Ford Motor Credit Company
- Ford Motor Credit Co.
- Ford Motor Credit Corporation
- Ford Motor Credit Company, Inc.
- Ford Motor Company
- Ford Motor Credit Corp.
- Ford Motors Credit Company
- Ford Motor Credit Company ("FMCC")

The proliferation of different names for the same creditor makes searching
frustrating and time consuming.

DO NOT add mailing addresses for creditors who have attorney representation.

DO NOT add titles for creditors.

DO NOT add alias(es) for creditors.

Make sure to select the creditor party role.

Style Conventions for Names

(These style conventions apply to all names entered in the CM/ECF application.)

Use upper and lower case for all names and capitalize the first letter in a proper noun.

Wallace D Smith

United Services Fidelity and Guaranty

Use single spacing between all names and/or initials. **The preferred method of entry is to omit the use of any punctuation.**

J J Jones

Smith Inc

C W Bradford Ltd

When typing names that have upper and lower case letters, **DO NOT** insert spaces.

Patricia DeLaGarza

Kathleen O'Brien (include apostrophe)

Patrick MacDougal

When typing hyphenated names, eliminate the hyphen and enter a space.

Mary Smith–Baker would be entered as Smith Baker in the last name field.

If an individual does NOT have a middle name, leave that field blank. **DO NOT** enter "NMI" (no middle initial).

If a party has multiple names such as Robert Kramer Johns Martin, add the extra names in the Middle Name box.

Last name:	Martin
Middle name:	Kramer Johns
First name:	Robert

DO NOT use the First or Middle name box when entering business names. Business names should be entered entirely in the Last Name box.

Spell out the word "and" when used in party names. **DO NOT** use the ampersand sign for "and".

B and D Company

Cameron and Associates

J and J Trucking

When entering a United States Government Agency, spell out United States.

United States Department of Agriculture

United States Attorney

United States Environmental Protection Agency

Creditor/Party Filer Tips

1. Make sure you search for existing creditors before adding new creditors/parties to the database.

2. **DO NOT** use <u>any</u> punctuation when specifying names.

   Example: *GMAC*

3. When a corporation has multiple locations, it is not necessary to include the name of the location in the party name.

Example: **Union Planters Bank**
US Bank

4. Try to make the name as short as possible. Shortening the name can prevent duplicates, prevent typograghical errors, and enhance uniformity.

Example: *American General Finance*
Norwest Financial

5. **DO NOT** include departments in the name.

6. All parties must be added individually.

7. If the business name begins with an article (A, An or The), enter the name without the article.

Example: The Franklin Mint Company as Franklin Mint Company The Chocolate Factory as Chocolate Factory

---

Style Conventions for Addresses

(These style conventions apply to all names entered in the CM/ECF application)

Abbreviate post office addresses without periods or a space between the P and O

PO Box 1359

PO Drawer 34321

Use integer numbers and not the spelling to designate numbered street names.

3224 E 26th St

425 6th St

1 Valley Plaza

If an address contains two directional words, abbreviate the first directional reference.

1093 N Belt West

Belleville, IL 62220

If the voluntary petition contains a mailing address for the *debtor* that differs from the street address, enter the mailing address listed on the voluntary petition, using the style guide specifications.

For example:

Street Address (DO NOT ENTER)	**Mailing Address (ENTER)**
John J Johnson	John J Johnson
4218 Elmwood Lane	PO Box 1477
Bentonville, AR 40453	Bentonville, AR 40453

It is preferred that you:
- *DO NOT include symbols such as c/o, &, %, #, etc.*
- *DO NOT include department numbers or descriptions (e.g. Certified Public Accountant, Examiner).*
- *Avoid the use of building names, suite numbers, floor numbers, firm names, and attention to information.*

When needed, use the second and/or third line of the address for building name, suite number, or floor.

Arthur Andersen and Associates
John Hancock Bldg Suite 2600
8723 Michigan Ave
Chicago, IL 60604

The city, state, and zip must be the only information on the last address line.

Use the full nine digit zip code if at all possible.

Foreign addresses must have the full name of the post office and country of destination printed in all capital letters.

The country name of APO destination must be the only information on the bottom line of the address.

Alfonso Diaz
Rio de Danubec y Rio Florido
CD JUAREZ, CHIHUAHUA
MEXICO 1050

Sgt John Smith
C Company 237 Armor
Unit 21103 Box 512
APO AE 09014

If the address contains an apartment number or suite number, *you simply type the number without the # symbol.*

Barbara Bixby
322 W Shady Ln Apt 334
Austin, TX 78701

The preferred format for telephone number is (210) 261–3851. Note the blank space between the area code and phone number.

Abbreviations

States & Territories

AL	Alabama		MT	Montana
AK	Alaska		NE	Nebraska
AZ	Arizona		NV	Nevada
AR	Arkansas		NH	New Hampshire
AS	American Samoa		NJ	New Jersey
CA	California		NM	New Mexico
CO	Colorado		NY	New York
CT	Connecticut		NC	North Carolina
DE	Delaware		ND	North Dakota
DC	District of Columbia		MP	N. Mariana Islands
FL	Florida		OH	Ohio
GA	Georgia		OK	Oklahoma
GU	Guam		OR	Oregon
HI	Hawaii		PW	Palau
ID	Idaho		PA	Pennsylvania
IL	Illinois		PR	Puerto Rico
IN	Indiana		RI	Rhode Island
IA	Iowa		SC	South Carolina
KS	Kansas		SD	South Dakota
KY	Kentucky		TN	Tennessee
LA	Louisiana		TX	Texas
ME	Maine		UT	Utah
MH	Marshall Islands		VT	Vermont
MD	Maryland		VA	Virginia
MA	Massachusetts		VI	Virgin Island
MX	Mexico		WA	Washington

MI	Michigan	WV	West Virginia
MN	Minnesota	WI	Wisconsin
FM	Federated States of Micronesia	WY	Wyoming
MS	Mississippi		
MO	Missouri		

Geographic Directions

North	= N	Northeast	= NE
South	= S	Southwest	= SW
East	= E	Southeast	= SE
West	= W	Northwest	= NW

Street Designators

Below is a list of the preferred street designators:

Use	Instead of
1st	First
2nd	Second
3rd	Third
Apt	Apartment
Ave	Avenue
Bldg	Building
Blvd	Boulevard
Center	Center
Circle	Circle
Ct	Court
Dr	Drive
Expwy	Expressway
Frwy	Freeway
Hwy	Highway
IH	Interstate Highway
Ln	Lane
Pkwy	Parkway
Place	Place
Road	Road
Route	Route
RR	Rural Route
Square	Square
St	Street
St	Saint

Creditor Matrix Specification

Matrix files must be in ASCII DOS text or text only files.

Margins (top, bottom, left, right) should be at least one (1) inch.

Each creditor must be separated by at least one blank line.

DO NOT include page numbers, headers, footers, etc.

All entries should conform to the style specifications in the Style Guide.

Each creditor name may contain no more than 50 characters including spaces. Each Address line maximum 5 lines may contain no more than 40 characters including spaces.

Names and addresses should be left justified (flush against the left margin, no leading blanks.)

Account numbers or "attention" lines should be placed on the second line of the name/address, *although the preferred method is that you omit account numbers and attention lines from the matrix.*

City, state and zip code must be on the last line.

There must be a comma placed immediately after the city name.

All states must be two-letter abbreviations.

Nine digit zip codes must be typed with a hyphen separating the two groups of digits.

[Revised July 9, 2012.]

ANNOUNCEMENT OF PROCEDURAL CHANGES—PRIVACY

Privacy amendments to the Federal Rules of Bankruptcy Procedure will take effect December 1, 2003. The amendments are designed to promote electronic access to case files while also protecting personal privacy. Below are some procedural changes that must be followed in order to comply with the privacy amendments.

A. Procedure for submission of debtor's Social Security number for petitions filed electronically in the Court's Case Management/Electronic Filing System (CM/ECF)

Note—this is a two part process:

1. Enter Social Security number into CM/ECF case opening screens. (CM/ECF Participants should submit the full Social Security number in the screens provided when inputting the case into CM/ECF or when using Case Upload.)

2. Submit the Statement of Social Security Number (Official Form 21). The statement of social security number **must** be submitted electronically as a separate, **private** document. To electronically submit Official Form 21, prepare the document as a PDF file. Select [Other] from the Bankruptcy Menu and then select the entry Statement of Social Security Number. (Attorneys will retain the signed paper copy of the Statement bearing debtor's original signature for a period of five years after the closing of the case. Upon request of the Court, the attorney must provide original documents for review.)

The docket report for a case will show that the "Statement of Social Security Number" was filed. However, the public will **not** be able to view the PDF document. In addition, there will be no "free look" through e-mail. If a user clicks on the document number link in the e-mail message, they will receive the error message: 'User access denied'.

B. Notice of meeting of creditors

CM/ECF version 2.3 will generate two versions of the 341 notice—one with the complete 9 digit SSN and a redacted version with only the last 4 digits. The version with the complete SSN will be sent to creditors, the trustee and US Trustee. The redacted version will be filed with the Court.

ORDERS

GENERAL ORDER 13–3. IN RE: AMENDED SCHEDULES

General Order 13–2 is hereby amended to change the effective date of the Order from December 15, 2013 to March 3, 2014. Accordingly, effective March 3, 2014, when an amended schedule or schedules are filed, all changes to the original schedule(s) shall be italicized or underlined (or lined through if deleting an item).

[Dated: December 30, 2013]

GENERAL ORDER 13–2. IN RE: AMENDED SCHEDULES

In addition to the requirements set forth in the Bankruptcy Code and Rules and in this Court's Local Rules, IT IS ORDERED as follows: When an amended schedule or schedules are filed, all changes to the original schedule(s) shall be italicized or underlined (or lined through if deleting an item). This Order shall become effective on December 15, 2013.

[Dated: December 5, 2013.]

GENERAL ORDER 13–1. IN RE: SUPPLEMENTAL SCHEDULES I AND J

Official Form B 6I (newly revised schedule I–Income) and Official Form B 6J (newly revised schedule J–Expenses) became effective on December 1, 2013. If, after the filing of the original schedules I and J, the debtor wishes to amend those schedules, the new forms require the debtor to indicate whether the schedule is (1) an *amended* filing, or (2) a *supplement* showing post-petition chapter 13 income or expenses.

IT IS ORDERED that use of the second option, *i.e.*, filing a *supplement* to schedule I or J, is not authorized in this Court. Instead, the Court's policy of requiring debtors to file an *amended* schedule I or J and to complete all sections of the amended schedule(s) shall remain in effect. All changes to the original schedules shall be italicized or underlined (or lined through if deleting an item). Schedules I and J that are filed as a supplement will be processed as deficient by the Clerk's Office.

[Dated: December 3, 2013.]

GENERAL ORDER 14–1. IN RE: CHAPTER 13 CASE TRUSTEE'S FEE

GENERAL ORDER FOR ADMINISTRATION OF CHAPTER 13 CASES

In light of a recent change in the United States Trustee Program's interpretation of 28 U.S.C. § 586(e)(2), the United States Bankruptcy Court for the Southern District of Illinois finds it necessary and beneficial to implement the following procedure for the administration of Chapter 13 cases.

IT IS HEREBY ORDERED that the Chapter 13 Trustees are authorized to begin collecting the statutory percentage fees upon receipt of plan payments in all Chapter 13 cases, regardless of when filed.

[Dated: October 1, 2014.]

GENERAL ORDER 14-2. IN RE: MOTIONS TO REDACT/MOTIONS TO RESTRICT ACCESS

The Judicial Conference has approved amendments to the Bankruptcy Court Miscellaneous Fee Schedule, Item 21. The amendments become effective on December 1, 2014. Pursuant to said amendments, a $25.00 filing fee will be charged for motions to redact or restrict access to personal identifying information protected by Bankruptcy Rule 9037. IT IS HEREBY ORDERED that the fee is waived if a debtor files the motion to redact or restrict access to protected information from records that were filed by a creditor in the case.

[Dated: October 28, 2014.]

CHAPTER 13 PROCEEDINGS—SELECTED FORMS
REVISED UNIFORM CHAPTER 13 PLAN

UNITED STATES BANKRUPTCY COURT
SOUTHERN DISTRICT OF ILLINOIS

In re:) Case No.
) ☐ Original Chapter 13 Plan
) ☐ Amended Plan Number _____
) (Changes must be underlined)
Debtor(s)) ☐ Limited Service Applicable

CHAPTER 13 PLAN AND NOTICE OF TIME TO OBJECT

CHAPTER 13 PROCEDURES MANUAL The provisions of the Court's Chapter 13 Procedures Manual are incorporated herein by reference and made part of this Plan. This manual is available at *www.ilsb.uscourts.gov.*

YOUR RIGHTS WILL BE AFFECTED You should read these papers carefully and discuss them with your attorney. Anyone opposing any provision of this Plan as set forth below must file a timely written objection. This Plan may be confirmed without further notice or hearing unless written objection is filed and served within 21 days after the conclusion of the 11 U.S.C. § 341(a) Meeting of Creditors. Objections to an amended Plan must be filed and served within 21 days after the date of filing of the amended Plan.

If you have a secured claim, this Plan may void or modify your lien if you do not object to the Plan.

THIS PLAN DOES NOT ALLOW CLAIMS A Creditor must file a timely Proof of Claim to receive distribution as set forth in this Plan. Even if the Plan provides for payment, no payment will be made unless a Proof of Claim is timely filed.

1. *PAYMENTS*

The Debtor submits to the Standing Chapter 13 Trustee all projected disposable income to be received within the applicable commitment period of the Plan. The payment schedule is as follows:

Start Month #	End Month #	Monthly Payment	Total

Total Months: _____   Grand Total Payments: _____

Wage Order Required: ☐ Yes ☐ No **The Debtor from whose check the payment is deducted:** _____
Employer's name, address, city, state, phone: _____
_____

☐ This Plan cures any previous arrearage in payments to the Chapter 13 Trustee under any prior Plan filed in this case.

IMPORTANT PAYMENT INFORMATION

NOTE: Plan payments to the Trustee must commence within 30 days of the filing of the petition. The Debtor must make direct payments to the Trustee by money order or cashier's check until the employer deduction begins. Include your name and case number on your money order or cashier's check. Contact the Trustee for the payment mailing address.

ORDER OF DISTRIBUTION

The following order of priority shall be utilized with respect to all payments received under the Plan terms:

1. Any unpaid portion of the filing fee;
2. Notice fees equal to $.50 per page of the Plan, multiplied by the number of creditors listed on the debtor's schedules;
3. The Trustee's fees for each disbursement, the percentage of which is fixed by the U.S. Trustee;
4. Ongoing mortgage payments on real estate;
5. Allowed administrative expenses;
6. Attorney's fees and other secured creditors as set forth in the Chapter 13 Procedures Manual;
7. Priority creditors as set forth in the Plan;
8. Any special class of unsecured creditors as set forth in the Plan; and
9. General unsecured creditors.

2. *ADMINISTRATIVE EXPENSES*

Administrative Creditor	Estimated Amount of Claim

ATTORNEY'S FEES

Attorney name: _____

☐ Flat fee through Plan $ ___ **OR**

☐ The Debtor's counsel elects to be paid on an hourly basis and will file a fee application(s) for approval of fees. No fees shall be disbursed until a fee application is approved by the Court. However, the Trustee shall reserve a total of $4,000.00 for payment toward such application, pursuant to the Order of Distribution and the Chapter 13 Procedures Manual.

3. *REAL ESTATE—CURING DEFAULTS AND MAINTAINING PAYMENTS*

Post-petition payments shall be made by the Trustee if (i) a pre-petition default exists; (ii) a post-petition, pre-confirmation default occurs; or (iii) a post-confirmation default arises that cannot be cured by the Debtor within six months. Otherwise, post-petition payments may be made directly by the Debtor to the creditor. Where the Trustee is disbursing the ongoing payments, the first mortgage payment to be disbursed will be that which becomes due in the second month after the month in which the petition is filed. In this situation, a mortgage holder should file a "pre-petition" claim that includes both the pre-petition arrearage and all post-petition contractual payments not disbursed by the Trustee as set forth above. Similarly, a Debtor must include the amount of any such payment(s) in the pre-petition arrearage calculation. (See the Chapter 13 Procedures Manual for examples and further instruction.)

For ongoing payments brought in due to a post-petition default, payments by the Trustee are to begin on the first due date after the month in which the amended or modified Plan is filed, or as otherwise ordered by the Court. All payments received from the Trustee must be credited by the creditor as the Plan directs. Pursuant to 11 U.S.C. § 524(i), ongoing post-petition mortgage payments tendered under the Plan by either the Trustee or the Debtor shall be credited by the holder and/or servicer of said claim only to such payments and may not be used for any other purpose without prior approval of the Court. Pursuant to 11 U.S.C. § 524(i), payments for pre-petition mortgage arrearages tendered under the Plan by the Trustee shall be credited by the holder and/or servicer of said claim only to such arrearages and may not be used for any other purpose without prior Court approval.

The Chapter 13 Procedures Manual sets forth the terms concerning notice of payment changes; notice of fees, expenses and charges; form and content of said notice; determination of fees, expenses or charges; notice of final cure payment; response to notice of final cure payment; determination of final cure and payment; and the consequences of the failure to notify. If a conflict arises between the terms set forth in the Chapter 13 Procedures Manual and any bankruptcy rule, the federal and local bankruptcy rule(s) shall supercede the Manual.

A) Payment of ongoing post-petition mortgage payments by the Debtor is as follows:

Creditor	Estimated Monthly Payment	Payment Start Date	Payment End Date

B) Payment of ongoing post-petition mortgage payments by the Trustee is as follows:

Creditor	Payment Address	Estimated Monthly Payment	Payment Start Date	Payment End Date

The estimated monthly payment amount referenced in Part 3A and 3B above may change based upon Proof(s) of Claim filed and/or subsequent Supplemental Proof(s) of Claim.

C) Payment of pre and/or post-petition arrearages, arising from a default in mortgage payments that were being made directly by the Debtor to the creditor, is as follows:

Creditor	Property Address	Lien No.	Estimated Amount of Claim

D) Payment of post-petition arrearages, arising from a default in Plan payments, is as follows:

Creditor	Total Amount of Post-petition Claim

Use of this section is more fully explained in the Chapter 13 Procedures Manual. In summary, this section should be used (i) when the ongoing mortgage payment is being disbursed by the Chapter 13 Trustee and (ii) the post-petition arrearage arises from a default by the Debtor in the Plan payments. Furthermore, the use of this section constitutes an affirmative representation by the filing party that the Debtor and creditor(s) have agreed to have this post-petition arrearage paid as a separate claim *unless the next box is checked.*

☐ By checking this box, the filing party represents that he or she has made reasonable and diligent efforts to secure an agreement with the creditor for the above-described treatment of this post-petition arrearage. Furthermore, upon request by any party in interest, the filing party shall provide a detailed, written explanation of the steps taken to attempt to secure an agreement with the creditor. Abuse of the letter and spirit of this provision may subject the filing party to any sanctions the Court deems appropriate.

If attorney's fees are to be sought in conjunction with this post- petition arrearage, a Proof of Claim for said fees must be filed with the Court and a separate agreed order submitted to the Court.

E) Real Estate Property Tax Claims shall be paid as follows: To the extent that taxes are due or will become due, they will be paid directly by the Debtor or pursuant to any applicable note and mortgage on the property.

F) Real Estate Secured Claims to which 11 U.S.C. § 506 Valuation is Applicable ("Cram Down Claims"):

Claims listed in this subsection are debts secured by real estate that is not the Debtor's primary residence. These claims will be paid either the value of the secured property as stated below or the secured amount of that claim as listed on the Proof of Claim, whichever is less, with interest as provided below. Any portion of a claim that exceeds the value of the secured property will be treated as an unsecured claim without the necessity of an objection.

Creditor Collateral	Value	Estimated Claim	Interest Rate	Estimated Monthly Payment

4. *SECURED CLAIMS AND VALUATION OF COLLATERAL UNDER 11 U.S.C. SECTION 506*

A) Secured Claims to which 11 U.S.C. § 506 Valuation is NOT Applicable ("910 Claims"):

Claims listed in this subsection are debts secured by a purchase-money security interest in a personal motor vehicle acquired for the personal use of the debtor, incurred within the 910 days preceding the date of the filing of the bankruptcy *or* debts secured by a purchase-money security interest in "any other thing of value" incurred within one year preceding the date of the filing of the bankruptcy. *These claims will be paid in full with interest as provided below.*

Creditor Collateral	Estimated Claim	Interest Rate	Estimated Monthly Payment

B) Secured Claims to which 11 U.S.C. § 506 Valuation is Applicable ("Cram Down Claims"):

Claims listed in this subsection are debts secured by personal property *not* described in the immediately preceding paragraph of this Plan. These claims will be paid either the value of the secured property as stated below or the secured amount of that claim as listed on the Proof of Claim, whichever is less, with interest as provided below. Any portion of a claim that exceeds the value of the secured property will be treated as an unsecured claim without the necessity of an objection.

Creditor Collateral	Value	Estimated Claim	Interest Rate	Estimated Monthly Payment

C) *Surrender of Property:*

This section allows for the surrender of collateral. The Debtor surrenders any and all right, title and interest in the following collateral. If the creditor believes that it may be entitled to a deficiency claim under applicable law, then the secured creditor must file its secured claim before the non-governmental claims bar date. Within 90 days following the claims bar date, the secured creditor shall file an amended Proof of Claim indicating the unsecured deficiency balance (if any), unless an extension is approved by the Court. Any objection to a timely filed deficiency claim shall be filed within 45 days of the date the deficiency claim was filed, or the same is deemed allowed. Absent leave of Court, deficiency claims filed outside of this 90–day period (or any extension granted by the Court) are deemed disallowed without action by any party. Upon entry of the Order lifting the automatic stay, the Debtor must reasonably cooperate with the creditor in either making the collateral available for pickup or in supplying information of the collateral's last known location.

Creditor	Collateral Surrendered	Estimated Monies Previously Paid by the Trustee

5. *SEPARATELY CLASSIFIED CLAIMS*

Creditor	Secured/ Unsecured	Estimated Claim	Interest Rate	Paid By

6. *EXECUTORY CONTRACTS AND UNEXPIRED LEASES*

All executory contracts and unexpired leases are ***rejected***, except the following which are assumed:

A) Payment of executory contracts and unexpired leases *directly* by the Debtor is as follows:

Creditor	Collateral	Monthly Payment	# of Payments Remaining

B) Payment of arrearages by the Trustee is as follows:

Creditor	Collateral	Address	Est. Claim	Int. Rate	Estimated Monthly Payment

Since the claims in Part 3F, 4A, 4B and 6B are based on the allowed claim amount, the estimated monthly payment in those sections is provided by the Debtor for reference only.

7. *PRIORITY CLAIMS*

A) Domestic Support Obligations:

The Debtor is required to pay all post-petition domestic support obligations directly to the holder of the claim and not through the Chapter 13 Plan.

1. Name of Debtor owing a domestic support obligation: _____

DSO Claimant Name	Address, City, State and ZIP	Estimated Arrearages	Current

B) Domestic Support Obligations Assigned to or Owed to a Governmental Unit Under 11 U.S.C. § 507(a)(1)(B):

Government Entity	Estimated Arrearages	Estimated Amount Paid	State Agency Case Number

C) Secured Income Tax Claims and Priority Claims Under 11 U.S.C. § 507:

All allowed secured tax obligations shall be paid in full by the Trustee as set forth herein. All allowed priority claims shall be paid in full by the Trustee as set forth herein, unless the creditor agrees otherwise:

Creditor	Priority/Secured	Estimated Claim Amount	Interest Rate (If Any)

8. *LONG–TERM DEBTS PAID DIRECTLY BY THE DEBTOR OR CO–DEBTOR TO THE CREDITOR*

Creditor	Basis for Treatment	Estimated Claim Amount	Monthly Payment	Number of Payments Remaining

9. *AVOIDANCE OF LIENS*

The Debtor will file a separate motion or adversary proceeding to avoid the following non-purchase money security interests, judicial liens, wholly unsecured mortgages or other liens that impair exemptions, and the Trustee shall make no distributions thereon.

Creditor	Collateral/Property	Amount of Lien to be Avoided

10. *UNSECURED CLAIMS*

The minimum amount the Debtor must pay to all classes of allowed non-priority unsecured claims is _____ or ☐ 100%.

11. *POST PETITION CLAIMS*

Post-petition claims shall not be paid by the Trustee unless the Debtor amends the Plan to specifically address such claims. Absent such an amendment, the Trustee shall not disburse any monies on said claims and these debts will not be discharged.

12. *LIEN RETENTION*

With respect to each allowed secured claim to be paid in full through the Plan, other than mortgage or long-term debts, the holder of such claim shall retain the lien securing its claim until the earlier of (i) the payment of the underlying debt determined under non-bankruptcy law; or (ii) entry of the discharge order under 11 U.S.C. § 1328.

13. *PROOF OF LIEN PERFECTION*

Any individual and/or entity filing a secured claim must provide the Chapter 13 Trustee, the Debtor, and Debtor's counsel with proof of lien perfection at the time its claim is filed and shall attach such documentation to its Proof of Claim pursuant to Bankruptcy Rule 3001.

14. *VESTING OF PROPERTY OF THE ESTATE*

Property of the estate shall revest in the Debtor upon confirmation of the Debtor's Plan, subject to the rights, if any, of the Trustee to assert a claim to additional property of the estate acquired by Debtor post-petition pursuant to 11 U.S.C. § 1306.

15. *PAYMENT NOTICES*

Creditors in Section 3 of this Plan (whose rights are not being modified) and in Section 6 of this Plan (Assumed Executory Contracts/Unexpired Leases) may continue to mail customary notices or coupons to the Debtor or Trustee notwithstanding the automatic stay.

16. *OBJECTIONS TO CLAIMS*

Absent leave of Court, any objection to a timely filed general unsecured claim shall be filed within 45 days following the expiration of the claims bar date for that claim. Objections to secured and/or amended claims shall be filed within 45 days from the applicable claims bar date or within forty-five 45 days from the date of filing of the claim, whichever is later.

17. *STAY RELIEF*

Notwithstanding any provision contained herein to the contrary, distribution to a secured creditor(s) who obtains relief from the automatic stay will terminate immediately upon entry of an Order lifting or terminating the stay, except to the extent that an unsecured deficiency claim is subsequently filed and allowed. Absent an Order of the Court, relief from the automatic stay shall also result in the Trustee ceasing distribution to all junior lien holders.

18. *DEBTOR REFUNDS*

Upon written request of the Debtor, the Trustee is authorized to refund to the Debtor, without Court approval, any *erroneous* overpayment of *regular* monthly payments received during the term of the Plan that have not been previously disbursed.

19. *PLAN NOT ALTERED FROM OFFICIAL FORM*

By filing this Plan, the Debtor and the Debtor's counsel represent that the Plan is the official form authorized by the Court. Changes, additions or deletions to this Plan are permitted *only* with Leave of Court.

20. *REASON(S) FOR AMENDMENT(S)*

Set forth a brief, concise statement of the reason(s) for the amendment(s). In addition, if there is a substantial change to the proposed Plan payments, or if the Trustee so requests, file an amended Schedule I & J.

_____

_____

_____

_____

Debtor's Declaration

I declare under penalty of perjury that the foregoing statements of value contained in this document are true and correct to the best of my knowledge and belief.

Dated: _____

Signature of the Debtor: _____

Signature of the Co-debtor: _____

Signature and Verification of Counsel for the Debtor

I have reviewed this plan and verify that it is proposed in good faith and, to the best of my knowledge and belief, does not include provisions or treatment that are forbidden by the Bankruptcy Code or Bankruptcy Rules.

Dated: _____

Signature of Counsel: _____

[Amended effective August 1, 2011.]

CHAPTER 13 PROCEDURES MANUAL

Accompanying the Uniform Chapter 13 Plan

This manual is divided into three parts. The first part governs general Chapter 13 practice within the Southern District of Illinois. The second part deals with the use and implementation of the new Uniform Chapter 13 Plan effective for all cases filed on or after August 1, 2011. The third part concerns new general requirements for Chapter 13 practice beginning with the implementation of the new Uniform Chapter 13 plan. All § references are to the Bankruptcy Code.

PART ONE—General Provisions Regarding Chapter 13 Practice

1) Conflict of Laws. If a conflict arises between the terms set forth in the Chapter 13 Procedures Manual and any bankruptcy rule, the national and local bankruptcy rule supersede the Chapter 13 Procedures Manual.

2) Uniform Chapter 13 Plans

A) *Mandatory Model Plan.* For all Chapter 13 cases filed in the Southern District of Illinois, the Court requires the use of the most current Uniform Chapter 13 Plan in use on the date of filing the original petition. Anyone filing an Amended Plan must always use the same version of the Uniform Chapter 13 Plan in use when the case was filed. Changes, additions, or deletions to the Plan, other than to add or delete creditor line boxes, are strictly prohibited without leave of Court. Uniform Plans, as well as their effective dates, can be found on the Court's website at *www. ilsb.uscourts.gov/forms.*

A prior version of the Uniform (standard) Chapter 13 Plan used in this District contains the following sentence in section 4(C): "Any claim by the creditors listed below will be deemed satisfied in full through surrender of the collateral." Said sentence is null and void and shall have no further force or effect in Chapter 13 cases pending in this Court.

B) *Designation on Chapter 13 Plans.* Each Amended Plan shall be titled "Amended Plan No. 1," "Amended Plan No. 2," etc., as is appropriate.

3) Signatures. Unless otherwise authorized by the Court, the Debtor and the Debtor's counsel are required to sign and date all Chapter 13 Plans prior to filing. Additionally, Debtor's counsel shall maintain the original documents containing the Debtor's "wet" signature in accordance with this Court's Electronic Filing Rules. Notwithstanding the foregoing, Debtor's counsel may request leave of Court, orally or in writing, to file an Amended Plan without obtaining the Debtor's wet signature if the amendment is being made solely to cure a typographical or technical error. **The plan must indicate, under the signature line(s), that leave of Court was so granted.** Failure to follow this procedure will result in the Clerk of Court processing the plan as deficient.

4) Minimum Monthly Chapter 13 Plan Payment. Unless otherwise ordered, the minimum monthly Chapter 13 Plan payment is $100.00.

5) Maximum Attorney's Fees for Cases Converted Pre–Confirmation. Notwithstanding counsel's fee selection (flat fee or fee application) for representation of the Debtor(s) in a Chapter 13 proceeding, absent leave of Court, counsel is prohibited from receiving more than $1,500.00 in attorney's fees for any case that converts, prior to confirmation, to a proceeding under Chapter 7. Unless otherwise ordered, upon entry of an Order of Conversion, the Chapter 13 Trustee shall use any remaining funds received pre-conversion to pay the balance of attorney's fees up to $1,500.00. The remaining monies on hand shall be refunded back to the Debtor.

If Debtor's counsel has previously been paid more than $1,500.00, upon the entry of an Order of Conversion, the Trustee shall file a Statement of Attorney's Fees Disbursed by the Chapter 13 Trustee.

6) Compliance With the Filing Requirement of 11 U.S.C. § 521(A)(1)

A) Copies of all payment advices, or other evidence of payment, received by the Debtor from any employer of the Debtor within 60 days prior to the date of the filing of the bankruptcy petition (i) shall not be filed with the Court unless otherwise ordered and (ii) shall be provided to the Trustee, the United States Trustee if no Trustee has been appointed, and to any creditor who timely requests copies of them, at least seven days before the § 341 meeting of creditors. To be considered timely, a creditor's request must be received at least 14 days before the first date set for the meeting of creditors.

B) The requirements of § 521(a)(1)(B)(iv) (copies of all payment advices or other evidence of payment received within 60 days before the date of the filing of the petition by the Debtor from any employer of the Debtor) are satisfied by providing to the Trustee, or the United States Trustee in a case where no Trustee has been appointed, at least seven days before the first date set for the § 341 meeting:

1) Payment advices or other evidence of payment. This requirement may be satisfied by providing less than "all payment advices or other evidence of payment received within 60 days before the date of the filing of the petition ..." by, for

example, providing a year-to-date statement that includes payments received within 60 days of the petition; or

2) A verified statement that the Debtor did not receive payments to which § 521(a)(1)(B)(iv) applies.

Pay advices or other evidence of payment shall be arranged (a) separately for each debtor and (b) chronologically for each different employer. Notwithstanding the foregoing, the Trustee may require that six months of pay advices or other evidence of payment as defined in subparagraph (1) above be provided to verify the current monthly income listed on Official Form B22A or B22C. Failure to provide this documentation shall not delay the commencement of the § 341 meeting of creditors.

In no event shall the documents required by § 521(a)(1)(B)(iv) be provided later than 45 days after the date of the filing of the petition. If the § 341 meeting is not set within 45 days of the filing of the petition, the 45-day deadline for providing payment advices to the Trustee (or the United States Trustee if applicable) still applies. If the Trustee or the United States Trustee continues the § 341 meeting to receive these documents, such continuance shall *not* be deemed a request or consent to extend the deadline of § 521(i). Nothing in this section is to be construed as requiring the Trustee or the United States Trustee to continue the § 341 meeting.

Failure to provide the documents within the 45-day deadline is grounds for the Trustee (or the United States Trustee if applicable) to request dismissal. If the case is dismissed following such a request by the Trustee or the United States Trustee, and the Debtor believes the case was dismissed in error, the Debtor shall file any motion to reinstate the case within 14 days of the entry of the dismissal order. A case that has been dismissed for failure to file a required document or provide a required document to the Trustee or the United States Trustee will not be considered to be a case dismissed in error.

C) *11 U.S.C. § 521(a)(1)(B)(v)*. The requirement of § 521(a)(1)(B)(v) (statement of the amount of monthly net income itemized to show how the amount is calculated) is satisfied by including such information on the Debtor's Schedule I.

D) *11 U.S.C. § 521(a)(1)(B)(vi)*. The requirement of § 521(a)(1)(B)(vi) (a statement disclosing any reasonably anticipated increase in income or expenditures over the 12-month period following the date of the filing of the petition) is satisfied by including such information on the appropriate line of Schedule J.

7) **Continuance of the § 341 Meeting Announced at the Meeting.** The Trustee or the United States Trustee may continue a § 341 meeting by announcement at the meeting. The Trustee or the United States Trustee shall list the continued date, time, and location for the continued meeting by making a docket entry using the Court's CM/ECF system. No further notice of the continued date is required. Unless otherwise agreed, the continued § 341 meeting will be set no earlier than 7 days after the prior § 341 meeting.

8) **Chapter 13 Plans: Confirmation Procedures**

A) *Deadline to File Objections to Confirmation of Plan and Original Confirmation Hearing.* Upon the timely filing of an objection to confirmation, whether by a creditor or the Chapter 13 Trustee, the Court will set a hearing date and provide notice thereof to all interested parties. An objection to the original Plan is considered timely if filed and served within 21 days after the date the § 341 meeting of creditors is concluded. Objections to Amended Plans filed prior to confirmation must be filed and served within 21 days after the date of filing the Amended Plan. Untimely objections may be summarily denied by the Court.

B) *Attendance at Confirmation Hearings.* The Debtor's attorney or the Debtor, if not represented by an attorney, and any party objecting to confirmation, shall attend the hearing set on such objections. The parties may contact the courtroom deputy in order to request an excused absence if an agreement has been reached prior to the hearing date, and if the Court is informed of this agreement by 3:30 p.m. the business day before the hearing. Absent such an excuse, failure to appear at the confirmation hearing may result in the overruling of the objection, or the denial of confirmation, and may subject counsel to further sanctions by the Court.

C) *Amended Plans Filed Prior to Confirmation in Response to Objections.* If the Debtor has no legal or factual basis to dispute the objection filed by the Trustee or a creditor, the Debtor shall file those documents necessary to cure the objection as soon as possible so as to expedite the confirmation process.

D) *Actions That Will Moot Pending Objections to Confirmation*

1) Amended Plans. The filing of an Amended Plan moots any pending objections to a previously filed Plan. If objections to a Plan are scheduled for hearing and an Amended Plan is filed, the hearing will be stricken from the docket upon either of the following: (1) entry of an Order mooting the objection, (2) counsel calling the Court and being excused from appearing. Nothing in this section is to be construed to prohibit an interested party from filing an objection to the Amended Plan.

2) Amended Objections to Plans. If a party files an amended objection to a Plan, any previous objections filed by that party are deemed moot. The Court will consider only those matters which have been raised in the amended objection.

3) Confirmation. If the Chapter 13 Trustee files a recommendation to confirm a Plan or orally recommends confirmation, that recommendation moots any objections previously filed by the Trustee.

E) *The Trustee's "Recommendation to Confirm" (East St. Louis) or "No Objection" (Benton) Filed Prior to Confirmation.* If the Trustee, after having reviewed the petition, schedules and Chapter 13 Plan, and after examining the Debtor at the § 341 meeting of creditors to ensure compliance with §§ 1322 and 1325, has no objection to a Plan prior to confirmation, whether an original or Amended Plan, he or she shall file a "Recommendation to Confirm" or "No Objection" to the relevant Plan. Such filing is to reference whether it is filed in response to an original Plan or an Amended Plan and, if an Amended Plan, the appropriate number listed on the Amended Plan. While it depends on the Trustee as to which named document is filed, this document shall be docketed as a Recommendation to Confirm. Such document shall be filed not later than 21 days after the conclusion of the § 341 meeting of creditors or, in the case of an Amended Plan filed prior to confirmation, within 21 days after the filing of the Amended Plan.

F) *Confirmation of Plan.* Upon the expiration of the time for objecting to a Plan and/or the resolution of all pending objections to a Plan, the Court will enter an order of confirmation, whether or not the Trustee's Recommendation to Confirm has been filed.

9) Amended Plans

A) *Generally.* Any amended or modified plan filed with the Court must be captioned as an "Amended Plan" and must indicate the "Amended Plan Number" (e.g., "Amended Plan No. 1"). The amended plan must contain all provisions of the plan. Motions seeking to amend only certain provisions of the plan will be summarily denied.

B) *Identification of Amendments.* Amendments to a Plan *must* be underlined if being added/modified or *lined through* if being deleted. Failure to identify any changes will result in the plan being noticed as deficient by the Clerk's office.

C) *Post–Confirmation Amended Plans Curing Delinquent Payments.* Any post-confirmation Amended Plans curing delinquent payments shall be filed in conformity with Sections 17(A) and 17(B) below governing Plan payment delinquency. Such plans shall include a "Total Paid In" (TPI) amount to be listed in the first tier of the funding provision by using the month number.

10) Service of Original and Amended Plans

A) *Original Plans*

1) Filed With the Petition. Notwithstanding any provision of the Local Rules, the Chapter 13 Trustee is responsible for serving a copy of the original Plan, as filed with the Clerk of the Court, on all creditors listed in the Debtor's schedules, provided that said Plan is filed contemporaneously with the petition.

2) Not Filed With the Petition. If the Plan is not filed with the petition, the Debtor shall serve a copy of the Plan on all parties listed on the Debtor's mailing matrix and file a certificate of service with the Court.

B) *Amended Plans Filed Prior to Confirmation*

1) If the claims bar date found in Bankruptcy Rule 3002(c) has not yet expired, the Debtor shall serve a copy of each Amended Plan on the Trustee, all creditors, and all parties listed on the Debtor's mailing matrix.

2) If the claims bar date found in Bankruptcy Rule 3002(c) has expired, the Debtor shall serve a copy of each Amended Plan on the Trustee, all parties who have filed a claim or a request for service, all secured creditors, or as otherwise required by this Manual.

C) *Post–Confirmation Modifications*

1) If the claims bar date found in Bankruptcy Rule 3002(c) has not yet expired, the Debtor shall serve a copy of each Amended Plan on the Trustee, all creditors, and all parties listed on the Debtor's mailing matrix.

2) If the claims bar date found in Bankruptcy Rule 3002(c) has expired, the Debtor shall serve a copy of each Amended Plan on the Trustee, all parties who have filed a claim or a request for service, all secured creditors, or as otherwise required by this Manual.

3) Debtor shall also file amended Schedules I and J to demonstrate that the Amended Plan is filed in good faith.

(D) *Limited Service of Certain Amended Plans.* Except as indicated in (iii) below, service of an Amended Plan may be limited to the Trustee if the proposed Amended Plan meets one of the following criteria:

1) The proposed Plan only changes the terms of the Plan by increasing the amount of the Plan payment or Plan duration; or,

2) The proposed Plan:

(i) Corrects errors in the funding paragraph; or

(ii) Changes the employer information;

(iii) Corrects collateral information due to typographical error (in this instance, the affected creditor must also be noticed);

(iv) Corrects any other scrivener's or mathematical errors that will not adversely and materially affect the timing, amount, and total payment on allowed claims; or

(v) Does not waive any missed plan payments.

If limited service is authorized, the front page of the Plan must so indicate by checking the box "Limited Service Applicable." If limited service is used and the box is not marked, the Clerk of Court will process the Plan as deficient.

11) Objections to Plans Amended After Confirmation

A) *Creditors.* Objections to Plans amended after confirmation shall be filed with the Court and served upon the Debtor, the Debtor's attorney (if any), and the Trustee no later than 21 days after the date the Amended Plan is filed.

B) *Chapter 13 Trustee.* The Trustee shall file, no later than 21 days after the date the Amended Plan is filed, a pleading either recommending approval of the Plan or objecting to it, referencing the specific modification number listed on the Plan.

C) *Moot Objections.* See Section 8(D).

D) *Attendance at Hearings on Objections to Plans Amended After Confirmation.* The Debtor's attorney or the Debtor, if not represented by an attorney, and any party objecting to the Amended Plan shall attend the hearing set on such objections. The parties may contact the courtroom deputy in order to request an excused absence if an agreement has been reached prior to the hearing date, and if the Court is informed of this agreement by 3:30 p.m. the business day before the hearing. Absent such an excuse, failure to appear at the hearing may result in the entry of an order overruling the objection or entry of an order denying approval of the Amended Plan, and may subject counsel to further sanctions by the Court.

12) How Chapter 13 Trustee Disbursements are Affected by the Timing of the Filing of an Amended Plan. If a modification of a Plan is received in the Trustee's office not later than three business days prior to the Trustee's next disbursement cycle, the Trustee is authorized, but not required, to distribute funds in accordance with the terms of the proposed modification commencing with that next disbursement, notwithstanding that an Order approving the modification has not yet been entered. Upon request of the Trustee, the Clerk of Court shall issue any wage deduction order consistent with such modification.

In the event that a Plan provision calls for the surrender of collateral on which the Trustee has been making payments, the Trustee shall reserve funds to that creditor until such time as the Order approving the modification is entered, at which time the reserve shall be released and funds distributed to other creditors pursuant to the modification of the Plan.

13) Distribution by the Chapter 13 Trustee in Circumstances of Insufficient Funds. In those circumstances where there are insufficient funds on hand to disburse the monthly payment amount, the Chapter 13 Trustee is authorized to disburse those funds pursuant to the Order of Distribution in the Uniform Plan in effect at that time.

14) Calculation of the Chapter 13 Trustee Fee. In calculating the amount of the Trustee's fee, the Debtor shall use the Chapter 13 Trustee's "effective percentage fee" in effect at the time the Plan is filed. It is the responsibility of counsel for the Debtor to monitor any changes in the fee and, if necessary, to amend the Plan to reflect any increase or decrease in the fee. The "effective percentage fee" is the fee based on the percentage allowed by the United States Trustee adjusted for certain factors (e.g. the Trustee's fee to pay the Trustee's fee). This information is available from each individual Trustee.

15) Chapter 13 Claim Objections. Absent leave of Court, any objection to a timely filed unsecured claim shall be filed within 45 days following the expiration of the claims bar date for that claim. Objections to secured and/or amended claims shall be filed within 45 days from the applicable claims bar date or within 45 days from the date of filing of the claim, whichever is later.

An objection to a proof of claim in a Chapter 13 case shall be served upon the claimant, any attorney who filed an entry of appearance for the claimant, the Trustee, the Debtor, and the Debtor's attorney (if any). Objections to claims in Chapter 13 cases will be heard only if a timely response in opposition is filed with the Court. The notice of objection shall state that any responsive pleading shall be filed with the Court, with a copy forwarded to all interested parties, no later than 30 days of the date of the notice, and that if no response is filed, the Court will enter an order sustaining the objection and disallowing or modifying the claim without further notice to any party.

16) Discharge in Chapter 13 Cases (Applicable only to cases filed on or after October 17, 2005)

A) *Trustee's Notice of Completion.* The Chapter 13 Trustee shall file a "Report of Plan Completion, Request for Termination of Wage Order and Notice Concerning Discharge" ("Trustee's Report/Notice") after all payments have been received.

B) *The Debtor's Required Pleadings.*   *Within 21 days of the filing of the Trustee's Report/Notice, eligible Debtors shall file a Motion and Notice to all creditors and parties in interest, pursuant to 11 U.S.C. § 1328 and Bankruptcy Rule 2002(f), setting forth their eligibility for discharge.   Failure to timely file said Motion and Notice will result in the Clerk of the Court closing this case without entry of an Order of Discharge.

*Prior to filing said Motion and Notice, the Debtor's counsel shall verify Debtor's eligibility to receive a discharge pursuant to 11 U.S.C. § 1328.

C) *Closing and Reopening.*   If the case is closed due to an eligible Debtor's failure to timely file the Motion and Notice as required by subparagraph B above, and the Motion and Notice are subsequently filed after the case has been closed, the Debtor must also simultaneously file a Motion to Reopen Case with the required filing fee.   The Motion to Reopen must set forth the reason(s) the case was closed without discharge.

(17) **Delinquent Plan Payments.** *Trustee's Notice of Default in Plan Payments and Options to Cure*

A) Upon a determination by the Chapter 13 Trustee that plan payments are delinquent, prior to the filing of a Motion to Dismiss for Failure to Make Plan Payments, the Trustee shall provide the Debtor and the Debtor's counsel (if any) with written notice of any default and options to cure.   Within 45 days thereafter, debtor(s) must exercise one of the following three options:

1) Make payment to the Trustee;

2) Enter into an Agreed Order, to be submitted to the Court, setting forth the manner in which the arrearages shall be cured and requiring future Plan payments to remain current for an agreed upon period of time; or

3) File an Amended Plan with the Court, curing the delinquency.   Note that, absent extraordinary circumstances, this option is not available if another Plan curing the delinquency has been filed within the past 12 months.

B) Failure by the Debtor to implement one of the foregoing options within 45 days will result in the Trustee filing a Motion to Dismiss with the Court.   Upon review of the Trustee's motion, the Court may dismiss the case without further notice or hearing.

18) **Motions to Reinstate Following Dismissal on the Trustee's Motion to Dismiss for Failure to Make Plan Payments.**   The motion shall state whether the case was previously dismissed and reinstated and shall provide dates of any prior dismissals and orders of reinstatement and the proposed manner in which the arrearage is to be cured.   The Debtor shall serve a copy of the motion on the Trustee, U.S. Trustee, and all parties in interest.

19) **Monthly Operating Reports in Chapter 13.**   Unless required by the Chapter 13 Trustee, § 1304(c) shall not apply.

20) **Obtaining Credit in Chapter 13 Cases**

A) *Dollar Limits.*   The Debtor may incur non-emergency, consumer debt up to $1,000.00 without written approval of the Trustee or Order of the Court.   Non-emergency, consumer debt exceeding $1,000.00 requires the approval of the Trustee or an Order of the Court, using the procedures set forth in subparagraphs (B) and (C) below.   Notwithstanding the foregoing, nothing shall prevent the Debtor from incurring reasonable and necessary medical expenses.

B) *Request Directed to Trustee.*   The Debtor shall first request approval to incur debt by written application to the Trustee.   Such request shall not be filed with the Court.   If approved by the Trustee, the Debtor may incur the debt in accordance with the terms and conditions approved by the Trustee.   If the Trustee has not directed use of a specific form, the application shall include the following information:

1) A statement of facts (or a proposed amended Schedule I and J) in support of the feasibility of the request;

2) A description of the item to be purchased or the collateral affected by the credit to be obtained;

3) The reasons why the Debtor has need for the credit; and

4) The terms of any financing involved, including the interest rate.

C) *Motion Directed to Court.* If the request is not approved by the Trustee, the Debtor may file a Motion to Incur Debt. The motion shall contain all of the information required to be included in the request by subparagraph (B) above and shall state that the Trustee has denied the request. The motion should be served on the Trustee.

21) Compliance with Requests for Information from the Chapter 13 Trustee. To assist the Trustee in determining compliance with the "best interest of creditors" test for confirmation of Chapter 13 Plans (*see 11 U.S.C. § 1325(a)(4)*), the Trustee may require that the Debtor submit a liquidation analysis, showing that the proposed distribution to unsecured creditors under the Plan is not less than the amount such creditors would receive in a Chapter 7 liquidation. Such information shall be provided to the Trustee within 10 days of his request. The failure to comply with the Trustee's request may be grounds for dismissal of the Debtor's case.

PART TWO—Specific Provisions of the Uniform Chapter 13 Plan for All Cases Filed On or After August 1, 2011

Claims Based Plan with Exceptions

Generally, this is a "claims based" Plan. As such, all allowed secured and priority claims will be paid the amount of their allowed secured/priority claim, except as provided in paragraph 4(B) of the Plan. The interest rate set forth in the Plan shall be binding on all parties upon confirmation/approval of the same Plan unless a timely written objection is filed.

1) Payments. This section establishes the payment schedule the Debtor will use to make his or her Plan payments. The first "Start Month #" will always be "1" and the "End Month #" will be the last month in which the Debtor will make that specific dollar amount of a monthly payment. The "Plan Payment Amount" is the monthly payment.

For example, if the Debtor proposes a 48–month plan, the "Start Month #" will be "1", the "End Month #" will be "48", and the total will be the Plan Payment Amount multiplied by 48. The additional lines will be utilized in circumstances where there is an unusual payment (e.g. lawsuit proceeds), the Plan Payment Amount changes due to a subsequent amendment, or in those certain circumstances where a step payment may be justified. An example is shown below:

Start Month #	End Month #	Monthly Payment	Total
1	33	200.00	6,600.00
34	60	300.00	8,100.00
Unknown lawsuit proceeds		Estimated	15,000.00
Total Months: 60		Grand Total Payments: 29,700.00	

The Debtor's employment information is self-explanatory. Absent leave of Court, entry of a wage withholding order is mandatory in all cases unless the Debtor's sole source of income is (i) Social Security benefits, (ii) retirement funds, (iii) unemployment benefits, (iv) self-employment, or (v) family assistance.

If the Debtor is amending the Plan to cure an arrearage in payments, the Debtor must so indicate in this section.

Order of Distribution

This sets forth the priority of payments to creditors. Unless the higher distribution level is an ongoing contractual monthly payment, all creditors must be paid in full in each category before disbursements will be made in a lower distribution level.

The first parties to be paid are the Court for any unpaid filing fees and the Chapter 13 Trustee's fees, including those for notice and mailing. Following the payment of these fees, ongoing monthly mortgage payments due after the Plan is filed will be paid. Treatment and payment of the monthly mortgage payments is set forth in greater detail below. Following mortgage payments, allowed administrative expenses will be paid. Following administrative expenses, attorney's fees and other secured creditors will be paid. The amount disbursed to each will be calculated as follows:

Based upon allowed secured claims, the attorney will receive ½ of the monies disbursed and the remaining ½ of the monies disbursed will be paid to allowed secured creditors on a pro rata basis. Pre-confirmation, the attorney shall not be entitled to receive more than $1,200.00 of their attorney's fees. Thereafter, commencing with the next regular disbursement and using the same disbursement calculation described above, the Trustee shall begin reserving the monies to be paid to the attorney until such time as the case has been confirmed. With the first regular disbursement after the case is confirmed, the Trustee shall release all funds on hold to the attorney and continue making monthly disbursements to the attorney until the remainder of the attorney's fees has been paid in full. Once the Debtor's attorney's fees have been paid in full, the secured creditors will begin to receive all the funds available, on a pro rata basis, until such time as each secured creditor's claim is paid in full. In those cases in which there are no secured creditors, the Debtor's attorney will be paid the entire amount of the monies to be disbursed each month until their fees are paid in full, subject to the pre-confirmation limit set forth above.

Following payment of attorney's fees and secured claims, the Trustee shall pay priority claims, followed by special classes of unsecured creditors as stated in the Plan and, finally, general unsecured creditors.

Interim Disbursements by the Chapter 13 Trustee as Adequate Protection Payments under 11 U.S.C. § 1326(a)(1)(C)

Commencing with the first regular disbursement after the conclusion of the Debtor's § 341 meeting of creditors, the Chapter 13 Trustee shall begin disbursement of the regular Plan payments received from, or on behalf of, the Debtor, to allowed claims pursuant to the Order of Distribution set forth in the Uniform Chapter 13 Plan.

2) Administrative Expenses

Administrative Creditor. For any allowed claim to be paid as an administrative expense, the Creditor's name and the estimated amount of the claim must be included in this section.

Attorney's Fees and Responsibilities. The Debtor shall indicate in this section whether the Debtor's attorney shall be paid a flat rate for representation during the entire case (with certain exceptions) or by filing a fee application. Once a Debtor elects either section, the Debtor is bound by the selection throughout the bankruptcy case, unless on motion, the Court orders otherwise.

A) *Flat Fees.* Effective for cases filed on or after January 19, 2011, if the Debtor elects to pay the attorney's fees on a flat fee schedule, then the maximum allowable flat fee for a non-business related bankruptcy is $4,000.00. The maximum flat fee for a business related bankruptcy is $4,500.00. A business bankruptcy is one in which the Debtor is engaged in business as defined by § 1304(a). Effective for cases filed October 17, 2005 through January 18, 2011, the maximum allowable flat fee is $3,500.00 for a non-business related bankruptcy and $4,000.00 for a business bankruptcy.

Upon notice, and if necessary, a hearing, the Court may award additional attorney's fees for the defense or prosecution of adversary proceedings by approving a fee application filed pursuant to the standards set forth by this Court in *In re Wiedau's, Inc.*, 78 B.R. 904 (Bankr.S.D.Ill.1987). Upon entry of such an award, the Plan shall be amended to pay such additional fees pursuant to the same terms set forth in the Order of Distribution.

B) *Hourly Fees.* Attorneys electing to be paid on an hourly basis must file a fee application for approval of fees. No fees shall be disbursed until a fee application is approved by the Court. However, the Trustee shall reserve a total of $4,000.00 for payment toward such application pursuant to the terms concerning payment of the attorney's fees as set forth in the Order of Distribution. The fee application must be made pursuant to the standards set forth by this Court in *In re Wiedau's, Inc.*, 78 B.R. 904 (Bankr.S.D.Ill.1987).

C) *The Debtor's and Attorney's Rights and Responsibilities.* Each Debtor and his or her counsel must execute a Rights and Responsibilities Form setting forth the minimum preparation and duties to be performed by the Debtor's counsel throughout the Chapter 13 bankruptcy. *See Appendix A.*

Failure to meet the requirements of the Rights and Responsibilities Form may result in any sanction the Court finds appropriate and reasonable under the circumstances including, but not limited to, disgorgement of fees and/or suspension of the attorney's right to practice before the Bankruptcy Court in this District.

Executed copies of this form shall be supplied upon request to the Court, the Chapter 13 Trustee, or the United States Trustee.

A Rule 2016(b) (Disclosure of Compensation of Attorney for Debtor) must be filed by every attorney entering an appearance on behalf of the Debtor. Care should be taken to ensure that the disclosures on this form are consistent with the attorney's fee amounts requested in the Chapter 13 Uniform Plan. This disclosure is a continuing obligation and must be updated during the pendency of the case to list any subsequent fees received by counsel directly from, or on behalf of, the Debtor, excluding those payments received from the Trustee pursuant to the terms of the Debtor's Plan.

3) Real Estate—Curing Defaults and Maintaining Payments

A) *Payment of Ongoing Mortgage Payments by the Trustee and Calculation of Pre-petition Mortgage Arrearage.* Post-petition payments shall be made by the Trustee if (i) a pre-petition default exists, (ii) a post-petition, pre-confirmation default occurs, or (iii) a post-confirmation default arises that cannot be cured by the Debtor within six months. Otherwise, post-petition payments may be made directly by the Debtor to the creditor. Where the Trustee is disbursing the ongoing payments, the first mortgage payment to be disbursed will be that which becomes due in the second month after the month in which the petition is filed. In this situation, a mortgage holder should file a "pre-petition" claim that includes both the pre-petition arrearage and all post-petition contractual payments not disbursed by the Trustee as set forth above. Similarly, the Debtor must include the amount of any such payment in the pre-petition arrearage calculation.

When the Trustee is to act as disbursing agent for the ongoing mortgage payments at the commencement of the case, the Debtor shall calculate any arrearage to include all post-petition payments that have become due from the date of filing up to and including the last day of the following month. For example, if a case is commenced on January 3rd (or any other month), the post-petition arrearage shall include all payments that come due from January 4th up to and including any payments that are to become due through the last day of February. Thus, assuming the Debtor's mortgage payment was due on the 10th of the month, the number of post-petition payments to be included in the arrearage would be two—the payment due on January 10th and the payment due on February 10th. Thereafter, the Trustee would start disbursing the ongoing mortgage payments commencing with the March 10th payment. *See Table Below.*

Filing Date	Mortgage Due Date	# Post–Petition Payments Included in Arrears Claim	# Mortgage Payments Disbursed by Trustee
3rd day of Month	1st day of Month	1	Proposed plan duration
3rd day of Month	10th day of Month	2	Proposed plan duration

As the Trustee disburses payment of ongoing mortgage payments with the prior month's disbursement (i.e., the April mortgage payment is paid with the March disbursement [further assuming funds are available, the § 341 meeting has been concluded, and the creditor has an allowed claim on file]), the number of ongoing mortgage payments to be disbursed by the Trustee would equal the proposed length of the Plan—i.e. for a 36 month Plan, the Trustee would disburse 36 ongoing mortgage payments.

If the Plan is subsequently amended to have the Trustee act as disbursing agent (i.e., the Debtor was initially making the payments directly), the payments by the Trustee are to begin on the first due date after the month in which the amended or modified Plan is filed or as otherwise ordered by the Court.

It shall be the duty of the Debtor(s) and his or her counsel to closely review each proof of claim filed by or on behalf of a mortgage company to ensure that said entity properly and correctly included any of the aforementioned payments in their arrearage claim.

No late charges, fees or other monetary amounts shall be assessed based on the timing of any payments made by the Trustee under the provisions of the Plan unless allowed by Order of the Court.

B) *The Amount of the Monthly Mortgage Payment.* If the Trustee is required to make current monthly payments, the Trustee is to pay the current monthly payment, as increased or decreased, as stated by the mortgage company in their original proof of claim and pursuant to any subsequent claim supplements. In the event the proof of claim does not set forth a current monthly payment amount, the Trustee shall pay the amount as set forth in the Debtor's plan.

C) *Monthly Mortgage Payment Change.* General Order 08–3 is repealed effective December 1, 2011.

D) *Payment of Pre–Petition Arrearages.* Absent an objection, the Trustee shall use the amount of the pre-petition arrearage listed in the mortgage holder's proof of claim.

E) *Payment of Post–Petition Arrearages.* The Debtor may propose an Amended Plan that seeks to pay, as a separate claim, any post-petition mortgage payments that have accrued after the date of the filing of the petition.

1) Subparagraph 3(C) of the Plan should be used for post-petition arrearages *only* when the Debtor seeks to include post-petition mortgage arrearages arising as a result of the Debtor's failure to timely pay such payments directly outside their Chapter 13 Plan.

2) Subparagraph 3(D) of the Plan should be used for post-petition mortgage arrears *only* (i) when the ongoing mortgage payments at issue were being disbursed by the Chapter 13 Trustee and (ii) the post-petition arrearage arises from a default by the Debtor in the Plan payments.

Unless otherwise indicated, the use of subparagraph 3(D) of the Plan constitutes an affirmative representation by the filing party that the Debtor and the affected creditor have agreed to have this post-petition arrearage paid as a separate claim. Prior to filing this Plan, the Debtor must use diligent efforts to attempt to contact the creditor to more accurately determine the arrearage, to avoid challenges to this treatment of post-petition mortgage arrearages and to make the process of approval of the Plan more efficient. At a minimum, the Debtor should attempt to contact the affected creditor and/or their counsel, if known, at least two times in writing and two times by phone using the best possible contact information before proceeding with the filing of an Amended Plan that proposes such treatment of their claim.

If, after making diligent efforts, the Debtor is unable to contact the creditor, the Debtor may represent that he or she has made reasonable and diligent efforts to secure an agreement with the creditor for the above-described treatment of this post-petition arrearage. This is done by checking the box in the plan. Further, upon request by any party in interest, the filing party shall provide a detailed written explanation of the steps taken to attempt to secure an agreement with the creditor. Abuse of the letter and spirit of this provision may subject the filing party to any sanctions the Court deems appropriate.

3) If attorney's fees are being sought in conjunction with this post-petition arrearage, a separate Agreed Order and supplemental proof of claim for the fees must be filed with the Court.

F) *Notice Relating to Claims Secured by a Security Interest in the Debtor's Principal Residence and Non-residential Mortgages*

1) In General. This section applies in a Chapter 13 case to claims that are (i) secured by a security interest in the Debtor's principal residence and (ii) provided for under § 1322(b)(5) in the Plan.

2) Notice of Payment Changes. **Rule 3002.1 of the Federal Rules of Bankruptcy Procedure also applies to nonresidential mortgages.**

The holder of the claim shall file and serve on the Debtor, the Debtor's counsel, and the Trustee a notice of any change in the payment amount, including any change that results from an interest rate or escrow account adjustment, no later than 21 days before a payment in the new amount is due.

(i) Upon filing of a Mortgagee's Notice, the Chapter 13 Trustee is authorized to commence disbursement of the payment amount set forth in the Mortgagee's Notice without the necessity of an Amended Plan having been filed, unless an objection to the Mortgagee's Notice is filed within twenty-one (21) days from the date the Mortgagee's Notice is filed. Should the Debtor(s) object to the Mortgagee's Notice, the Trustee shall reserve payment on the increased portion of the payment amount set forth in the Mortgagee's Notice until the objection is disposed of by the Court. This paragraph applies notwithstanding any Plan provision to the contrary, and regardless of the Plan version utilized by the Debtor(s).

(ii) If the Trustee subsequently determines any filed increase in the amount of the ongoing mortgage payment results in there being insufficient funding in the Plan to pay all classes of claims as required, the Trustee shall file a notice with the Court, or alternatively contact Debtor's counsel, alerting the parties of the failure of the Chapter 13 Plan to complete. If the Debtor fails to take any action with regard to the notice, the Trustee may seek dismissal of the case at the conclusion of the Plan term. Notwithstanding the foregoing, if any single payment change filed by the mortgage company results in an increase of the ongoing payment by more than $25.00 and no objection is filed by the Debtor within twenty-one (21) days from the date of the Mortgagee's Notice, a plan modification is required, whether filed by the Trustee or the Debtor. Said modification shall increase the Debtor's Plan payment and base amount accordingly. The Mortgage Payment Modification form can be obtained on the Court's website at www.ilsb.uscourts.gov.

3) Notice of Fees, Expenses and Charges. The holder of the claim shall file and serve on the Debtor, the Debtor's counsel, and the Trustee a notice itemizing all fees, expenses or charges (i) that were incurred in connection with the claim

after the bankruptcy case was filed and (ii) that the holder asserts are recoverable against the Debtor or against the Debtor's principal residence. The notice shall be served as soon as practical, and in no event, not later than the earlier of 180 days after the date on which the fees, expenses, or charges are incurred, or the date the case is closed.

4) Form and Content. A notice filed and served under subdivision (2) or (3) of this section shall be prepared as prescribed by the appropriate Official Form and filed as a supplement to the holder's proof of claim. The notice is not subject to Rule 3001(f).

5) Determination of Fees, Expenses or Charges. On motion of the Debtor or the Trustee filed within one year after service of a notice under subdivision (3) of this section, the Court shall, after notice and hearing, determine whether payment of any claimed fee, expense, or charge is required by the underlying agreement and applicable non-bankruptcy law to cure a default or maintain payments in accordance with § 1322(b)(5) of the Bankruptcy Code.

6) Notice of Final Cure Payment. Within 30 days after the Debtor completes all payments under the Plan, the Trustee shall file and serve on the holder of the claim, the Debtor, and the Debtor's counsel a notice stating that the Debtor has paid in full the amount required to cure any default on the claim. The notice shall also inform the holder of its obligation to file and serve a response under subdivision (7) of this section. If the Debtor contends that a final cure payment has been made and all Plan payments have been completed and the Trustee does not timely file and serve the notice required by this subdivision, the Debtor may file and serve the notice.

7) Response to Notice of Final Cure Payment. Within 21 days after service of the notice under subdivision (6) of this section, the holder shall file and serve on the Debtor, the Debtor's counsel, and the Trustee a statement indicating (i) whether it agrees that the Debtor has paid in full the amount required to cure the default on the claim and (ii) whether the Debtor is otherwise current on all payments consistent with § 1322(b)(5). The statement shall itemize the required cure or post-petition amounts, if any, that the holder contends remain unpaid as of the date of the statement. The statement shall be filed as a supplement to the holder's proof of claim and is not subject to Rule 3001(f).

8) Determination of Final Cure and Payment. On motion of the Debtor or Trustee, filed within 21 days after service of the statement under subdivision (7) above, the Court shall, after notice and hearing, determine whether the Debtor has cured the default and paid all required post-petition amounts.

9) Failure to Notify. If the holder of a claim fails to provide any information as required by subdivision (2), (3), or (7) of this rule, the Court may, after notice and hearing, take either or both of the following actions:

(i) Preclude the holder from presenting the omitted information, in any form, as evidence in any contested matter or adversary proceeding in the case, unless the Court determines that the failure was substantially justified or harmless; or

(ii) Award other appropriate relief including reasonable expenses and attorney's fees caused by the failure.

G) *Motions for Relief from the Automatic Stay of 11 U.S.C. §§ 362 and 1301 when Leases or Mortgages are Being Paid Directly by the Debtor.* If the Debtor is making direct, ongoing, post-petition payments to the lessor or mortgagee and the lessor or mortgagee subsequently seeks relief from the automatic stay based upon an alleged default in such direct payments by the Debtor, the parties shall comply with the following requirements:

1) The parties shall exchange any and all documentary evidence concerning the post-petition payment history of the Debtor at least 7 days prior to the preliminary hearing on the Motion for Relief; and

2) The parties shall have such evidence available at the preliminary hearing for presentation to the Court.

3) The failure to comply with the requirements of sub-paragraphs (1) and (2) may result in the Court taking such action as it deems appropriate, which may include the granting or denying of the relief sought in the Motion for Relief.

H) *Motions for Relief from the Automatic Stays of 11 U.S.C. §§ 362 and 1301 when Mortgages are Being Paid by the Trustee.* If the Debtor's Plan proposes that the Trustee act as disbursing agent for ongoing mortgage payments and the mortgagee subsequently seeks relief from the automatic stay based upon an alleged default in such payments, the mortgagee shall comply with the following requirements:

1) Prior to filing a Motion for Relief, the mortgagee or its agent shall review the Trustee's website to verify it has received all of the payments reflected therein; and

2) If, after review of the Trustee's website, the mortgagee determines there still exists a default in the ongoing mortgage payments, it may proceed with the filing of the Motion for Relief.

4) Secured Claims and Valuation of Collateral Under 11 U.S.C. § 506

A) *Secured Claims to which § 506 Valuation is NOT Applicable.* The amount listed in the "Claim Amount" is the amount proposed by the Debtor in the Plan. If the actual allowed claim is different from the amount specified and the Trustee determines that the Plan will still complete as proposed, the Trustee shall pay the actual amount of the allowed claim without the need for an Amended Plan.

B) *Secured Claims to which § 506 Valuation is Applicable.* The amount of a secured claim to be paid under this Plan is the lesser of the amount listed by the Debtor as the "Value" and the allowed secured portion of the holder's claim. If the Court orders a different amount than is shown, the Plan shall be deemed amended without the requirement of the filing of an Amended Plan unless the Trustee objects that the Plan will not complete as proposed. Any amended plan thereafter must use the amount ordered by the Court.

5) Separately Classified Claims.
This section deals primarily with the Co–Debtor's claims and is otherwise self explanatory.

6) Executory Contracts And Unexpired Leases.
This section is self explanatory.

7) Priority Claims.
Anytime a domestic support obligation (DSO) exists (even if the Debtor is current on payments) the DSO claimant must be listed in both the Plan and on Schedule E. The amount listed as the "Estimated Arrearage" is the arrearage amount proposed by the Debtor in the Plan. If the actual allowed claim is different from the estimated arrearage amount and the Trustee determines that the Plan will still complete as proposed, the Trustee shall pay the actual amount of the allowed claim without the need for an Amended Plan. If the Debtor is current on his or her DSO obligations then he should make an "X" under the word "Current. "

If the Plan addresses a DSO assigned or owed to a governmental unit under § 507(a)(1)(B), the Debtor should use section 7(B) of the Plan. If the Debtor proposes to treat this claim as a general unsecured creditor pursuant to § 1322(a)(4) then the Debtor should so indicate by inserting the word "NONE" under the language "Est. Amt. Paid." If so treated, the Debtor must also propose a Plan that satisfies the requirements of § 1322(a)(4).

Secured Income Tax Claims and 11 U.S.C. § 507 Priority Claims

This section is self-explanatory.

8) Long–Term Debts Paid Outside by the Debtor or Co–Debtor.
This section is self-explanatory.

9) Avoidance of Liens. This section is to identify creditors against whom the Debtor is proposing to either avoid or reduce their secured lien pursuant to law. This section does not constitute a judicial determination of whether these actions are allowed under the law.

10) Unsecured Claims. This section is designed to set forth the minimum amount the Debtor must pay to allowed general unsecured creditors pursuant to sections §§ 1325(a)(4) and 1325(b).

11–19) These sections are self-explanatory.

20) Reason(s) for Amendment(s). This section requires a brief, concise statement setting forth the reasons for any amendments of the Debtor's original Plan. The failure to complete this section on all Amended Plans will result in the Amended Plan being noticed as deficient by the Clerk's office. If there is a substantial change to the proposed Plan payments or upon the Trustee's request, the Debtor shall file an amended Schedule I and J.

PART THREE—*Additional General Requirements for All Cases Filed on or After August 1, 2011*

In addition to any duties imposed by law, rule or order, the Debtor must also perform the following duty concerning insurance on motor vehicles in Chapter 13 cases:

1) Insurance on Motor Vehicles in Chapter 13 Cases

A) *Required Coverage.* The Debtor in a Chapter 13 case shall maintain full-coverage insurance on any motor vehicle on which a lien exists to secure a debt, naming the lien holder as an additional loss-payee. The Debtor shall provide for a collision and comprehensive deductible of not more than $500.00. If the security agreement or other contract requires a deductible lower than $500.00, such contract will govern the amount of deductible the Debtor is required to maintain during the bankruptcy case.

B) *Proof of Insurance Coverage.* The Debtor in a Chapter 13 case shall provide the lien holder with proof of insurance providing full coverage, as listed in paragraph (A), from the date of the bankruptcy petition. If the insurance policy lapses during the pendency of the case, the Debtor shall be required to provide new proof of coverage which shall include proof of three months prepaid insurance. A copy of the policy or the policy declaration sheet and a copy of a receipt or similar payment statement from an insurance agent on company letterhead may be used as proof of coverage if the documents verify the terms of coverage and pre-payment of premiums.

APPENDIX A

Rights and Responsibilities of Chapter 13 Debtors and their Attorneys

It is important for those who file a bankruptcy under Chapter 13 to understand their responsibilities, as well as those of their attorney. As such, this document sets forth the services required to be performed by your attorney, as well as those responsibilities that are required and/or expected of you. In order to maintain a high standard of quality for the Debtors' counsel practicing in this district, the following requirements are mandatory for the Debtors' counsel in a Chapter 13 bankruptcy. These requirements are in addition to any others required by law, rule or order. Should a conflict arise between these rights and responsibilities and any law, rule or order, the law, rule or order shall supersede the conflict. Notwithstanding the foregoing, no provision, statement and/or clause contained herein shall be deemed as a limitation on the Debtors' counsel's responsibilities and/or obligations as set forth in the Bankruptcy Code.

Before the bankruptcy petition is filed, the attorney
will provide the following legal services:

1) The Debtor shall meet with an attorney for a reasonable period of time prior to the filing of the bankruptcy petition to review facts and to receive advice concerning the Debtor's bankruptcy and non-bankruptcy options and shall be present at the signing of the final documents.

2) Unless an emergency filing is necessitated by exigent circumstances, the Debtor's counsel must collect the following documents from the Debtor prior to filing, or document the inability to collect the same, subject to subparagraph (o) below:

a) Copies of all bank account statements (or similar documentation) from at least 60 days prior to the date of the filing of the bankruptcy petition (savings, checking, CDs, etc.).

b) Federal income tax returns, transcripts, or a completed affidavit declaring that the Debtor was not required to file tax returns for the tax year prior to the filing of the bankruptcy petition.

c) Federal income tax returns, transcripts, or a completed affidavit declaring that the Debtor was not required to file tax returns for the second through fourth years prior to the filing of the bankruptcy petition.

d) A copy of all payment advices or other evidence of payment the Debtor received within 60 days before the date of the filing of the petition from any employer of the Debtor, or an affidavit that no income was earned.

e) A copy of all payment advices or other evidence of payment the Debtor received within the six calendar months prior to filing the petition sufficient to calculate the Debtor's current monthly income pursuant to § 101(10A).

f) If the Debtor is self-employed, a profit and loss statement for the six months before the filing of the petition.

g) Copies of all billing statements for the Debtor's credit cards, medical bills, student loans, personal/payday loans, car loans, mortgages and other secured debts. Also, any utility bills on which the Debtor is *not* current. If the Debtor does not have a bill for a debt, the Debtor must provide a written statement of the (i) creditor's name, (ii) billing address, (iii) account number and (iv) amount owed.

h) A copy of any domestic support order that the Debtor has been ordered to pay.

i) Copies of final and signed divorce decrees and marital settlement agreements entered into in the two years prior to filing the bankruptcy petition.

j) Copies of any and all documentation concerning lawsuits or administrative proceedings the Debtor has been involved in within the last two years, regardless of the status or outcome of the suit.

k) If applicable, a statement from the county showing the current status of the Debtor's real estate/mobile home taxes. If the taxes have been purchased, the Debtor should provide a copy of the redemption certificate.

l) Copies of the most recent non-term life insurance statements in which the Debtor has an interest.

m) Copies of current statements regarding any non-retirement investments in which the Debtor has an interest.

n) Verification/information of the balance of any and all 401(k) loans.

o) If any of these documents are not available or present in the Debtor's counsel's file, then the Debtor and the Debtor's counsel should execute an affidavit stating that they both made reasonable efforts to obtain the documentation and were unable to comply. The affidavit must also list the documents not obtained.

3) The Debtor's counsel must complete an intake document which is reasonably detailed to ensure that the Debtor is asked the appropriate questions and given appropriate advice. There is no form intake document approved by the Court at present.

4) The Debtor's counsel must ensure that the Debtor has completed the required pre-petition credit counseling requirements or determine if the Debtor meets the standard for one of the exceptions to such requirements.

5) The Debtor's counsel must review the petition, schedules, supplemental local forms, Chapter 13 Plan and mailing matrix prior to the filing of said documents.

6) The Debtor's counsel must meet with the Debtor when they sign the final paperwork to be filed in their case.

7) The Debtor's counsel must review and sign all motions filed in the Debtor's case.

8) The Debtor's counsel shall timely provide the Debtor with a written executed contract that conforms to the requirements in the Bankruptcy Code and Rules.

After the bankruptcy petition is filed, the attorney will provide the following legal services:

1) Upon information received from the Debtor, take steps necessary to avoid the termination of, or to allow the reinstatement of, the Debtor's necessary utility services by providing faxed proof of filing of the petition to utility service creditors.

2) Take steps necessary to obtain the return of repossessed vehicles, which are necessary to the estate, including, but not limited to, the filing of Complaints to Compel Turnover.

3) In the event of pending state or federal court litigation, notify creditor's attorneys and the appropriate court in which the litigation is pending that the bankruptcy case has been filed.

4) Send out an information letter to the Debtor reminding the Debtor to attend the § 341 meeting, specifying the time and location of that meeting, and advising the Debtor as to the procedures of the § 341 meeting.

5) Appear at the § 341 meeting of creditors with the Debtor, confer with the Debtor to prepare him or her for the § 341 meeting, and advise the client to cure any arrears on Plan payments. Counsel will appear at all meetings dressed in professional attire.

6) Upon information received from the Debtor, take steps necessary to terminate pending wage garnishments, including filing a Motion to Terminate Garnishment.

7) Attend all court hearings relating to the Debtor's case, excluding adversary proceedings in which counsel is not retained.

8) Prepare and conduct all court mandated pre-trial conferences, reports, briefs, etc.

9) Address objections to Plan confirmation and, where necessary, prepare an Amended Plan.

10) Prepare, file, and serve necessary modifications to the Plan, which may include suspending, lowering, or increasing Plan payments.

11) Prepare, file, and serve necessary amended statements and schedules, in accordance with information submitted by the Debtor, provided the Debtor pays the Court's filing fee, unless the amendment or omission was due to the fault of Debtor's counsel.

12) Prepare, file, and serve necessary motions to buy, sell, or refinance real property when appropriate.

13) Review all proofs of claims filed and, if appropriate and in the Debtor's best interest, object to improper or invalid claims.

14) Timely file proofs of claims for creditors who fail to file claims if it is in the Debtor's best interest to file such a claim.

15) Represent the Debtor in motions for relief from stay and file an objection to such motions, if appropriate.

16) Where appropriate, prepare, file, and serve necessary motions to avoid liens on real or personal property.

17) Upon information received from the Debtor, contact creditors who continue to communicate with the Debtor after filing, by phone or in writing, and, if necessary and appropriate, file motions for sanctions, prepare testimony and exhibits, and appear for hearing.

18) If necessary, contact tax authorities or other third-parties to gather information necessary for the case. However, such contact shall not include the obtaining of the names, addresses, account numbers and other information necessary for the inclusion and filing of creditors on any schedule of the petition, as it is the duty of the Debtor to provide such information to counsel for the preparation of accurate bankruptcy schedules.

19) These rights and responsibilities do not include a requirement to represent the Debtor in an adversarial proceeding and the Debtor's attorney may require additional fees which must be approved by the Court.

20) Communicate with the Debtor—either by phone or by being available for office appointments—to discuss pending issues or matters in the present case.

21) Provide such other legal services as, in the attorney's sound judgment, are necessary for the prompt administration of the case before the Bankruptcy Court. Nothing contained herein shall be construed to bind the attorney to perform work that has no basis in law or fact or constitutes extraordinary proceedings within the context of a normal chapter 13 proceeding, such as adversary proceedings or other work that exceeds the scope of the attorney-client contract.

The requirements for payment of attorney's fees in Chapter 13 cases for the Southern District of Illinois provide for a flat-rate attorney fee of $4,000.00 for a non-business related Chapter 13 bankruptcy and $4,500.00 for a business bankruptcy as defined in § 1304, or for payment based on regular billing. Fees shall be paid through the Plan as provided for by the Confirmation Order. The attorney may receive part of the allowed fees prior to the filing of the case for the actual services performed prior to filing, provided said fees are deducted from the total allowed fees as paid through the confirmed Plan. The attorney may move to withdraw or the client may discharge the attorney at any time. The attorney agrees to perform substantially all duties designated above. If the attorney does not substantially perform all of the above duties inclusive, then, upon filing of a motion and after a hearing before the Court, the Court may order the attorney to disgorge all or any part of the fees received, as the Court, in its discretion, deems appropriate. If the case is not confirmed, then the attorney is allowed only those sums as set forth in the Chapter 13 Procedures Manual.

In addition to those duties and responsibilities set forth in 11 U.S.C. § 521, the Debtor(s) shall:

1) Keep their attorney informed of their current mailing address and contact information (including home, work and cell phone numbers). If the Debtor is proceeding pro se, the Debtor shall file a Notice of Change of Address with the Court.

2) Timely make all payments as called for by their Plan, whether through a wage deduction or directly, as set forth in the Plan.

3) Immediately notify their attorney of any wage garnishments or attachments of assets which occur or continue after the filing of the bankruptcy case.

4) Notify their attorney upon the loss of employment or other financial problems that may arise.

5) Notify their attorney if they are sued or contacted by a creditor (or a creditor's agent) after the bankruptcy case has been filed.

6) Contact their attorney before buying, refinancing or selling any real property or before entering into any long-term loan agreements to determine what steps must be taken to obtain the required approval for same.

7) Cooperate with their attorney in the preparation of all documents and attend all hearings, if required. This obligation includes timely responding to all letters and phone calls left by your attorney.

8) Comply with all other additional contractual obligations and terms with your attorney as specifically set forth in your attorney-client contract.

Dated: _____ _____
                                    Attorney for Debtor

Dated: _____ _____
                                    Debtor

[Effective August 1, 2011. Revised December 1, 2011.]

RULES OF PROCEDURE OF THE JUDICIAL PANEL ON MULTIDISTRICT LITIGATION

Renumbered and Amended Effective November 2, 1998

Including Amendments Effective
July 6, 2011

I. RULES FOR MULTIDISTRICT LITIGATION UNDER 28 U.S.C. § 1407

RULE 1.1 DEFINITIONS

(a) "Panel" means the members of the United States Judicial Panel on Multidistrict Litigation appointed by the Chief Justice of the United States pursuant to 28 U.S.C. § 1407.

(b) "Chair" means the Chair of the Panel appointed by the Chief Justice of the United States pursuant to Section 1407, or the member of the Panel properly designated to act as Chair.

(c) "Clerk of the Panel" means the official that the Panel appoints to that position. The Clerk of the Panel shall perform such duties that the Panel or the Panel Executive delegates.

(d) "Electronic Case Filing (ECF)" refers to the Panel's automated system that receives and stores documents filed in electronic form. All attorneys filing pleadings with the Panel must do so using ECF. All pro se individuals are non-ECF users, unless the Panel orders otherwise.

(e) "MDL" means a multidistrict litigation docket which the Panel is either considering or has created by transferring cases to a transferee district for coordinated or consolidated pretrial proceedings pursuant to Section 1407.

(f) "Panel Executive" means the official appointed to act as the Panel's Chief Executive and Legal Officer. The Panel Executive may appoint, with the

749

approval of the Panel, necessary deputies, clerical assistants and other employees to perform or assist in the performance of the duties of the Panel Executive. The Panel Executive, with the approval of the Panel, may make such delegations of authority as are necessary for the Panel's efficient operation.

(g) "Pleadings" means all papers, motions, responses, or replies of any kind filed with the Panel, including exhibits attached thereto, as well as all orders and notices that the Panel issues.

(h) "Tag-along action" refers to a civil action pending in a district court which involves common questions of fact with either (1) actions on a pending motion to transfer to create an MDL or (2) actions previously transferred to an existing MDL, and which the Panel would consider transferring under Section 1407.

(i) "Transferee district" is the federal district court to which the Panel transfers an action pursuant to Section 1407, for inclusion in an MDL.

(j) "Transferor district" is the federal district court where an action was pending prior to its transfer pursuant to Section 1407, for inclusion in an MDL, and where the Panel may remand that action at or before the conclusion of pretrial proceedings.

[Former Rule 1 adopted May 3, 1993, effective July 1, 1993. Renumbered Rule 1.1 September 1, 1998, effective November 2, 1998. Amended September 8, 2010, effective October 4, 2010.]

RULE 2.1   RULES AND PRACTICE

(a) Customary Practice. The Panel's customary practice shall govern, unless otherwise fixed by statute or these Rules.

(b) Failure to Comply With Rules. When a pleading does not comply with these Rules, the Clerk of the Panel may advise counsel of the deficiencies and set a date for full compliance. If counsel does not fully comply within the established time, the Clerk of the Panel shall file the non-complying pleading, but the Chair may thereafter order it stricken.

(c) Admission to Practice Before the Panel. Every member in good standing of the Bar of any district court of the United States is entitled to practice before the Panel, provided, however, that he or she has established and maintains a CM/ECF account with any United States federal court. Any attorney of record in any action transferred under Section 1407 may continue to represent his or her client in any district court of the United States to which such action is transferred. Parties are not required to obtain local counsel.

(d) Pendency of Motion or Conditional Order. The pendency of a motion, order to show cause, conditional transfer order or conditional remand order

before the Panel pursuant to 28 U.S.C. § 1407 does not affect or suspend orders and pretrial proceedings in any pending federal district court action and does not limit the pretrial jurisdiction of that court. An order to transfer or remand pursuant to 28 U.S.C. § 1407 shall be effective only upon its filing with the clerk of the transferee district court.

(e) Reassignment. If for any reason the transferee judge is unable to continue those responsibilities, the Panel shall make the reassignment of a new transferee judge.

[Former Rule 5 adopted May 3, 1993, effective July 1, 1993. Renumbered Rule 1.2 September 1, 1998, effective November 2, 1998. Former Rule 4 adopted May 3, 1993, effective July 1, 1993. Renumbered Rule 1.3 and amended September 1, 1998, effective November 2, 1998. Former Rule 6 adopted May 3, 1993, effective July 1, 1993. Renumbered Rule 1.4 September 1, 1998, effective November 2, 1998. Former Rule 18 adopted May 3, 1993, effective July 1, 1993. Renumbered Rule 1.5 September 1, 1998, effective November 2, 1998. Former Rules 1.2, 1.3, 1.4, and 1.5 redesignated and amended September 8, 2010, effective October 4, 2010.]

RULE 3.1   ELECTRONIC RECORDS AND FILES; COPY FEES

(a) Electronic Record. Effective October 4, 2010, the official Panel record shall be the electronic file maintained on the Panel's servers. This record includes, but is not limited to, Panel pleadings, documents filed in paper and then scanned and made part of the electronic record, and Panel orders and notices filed. The official record also includes any documents or exhibits that may be impractical to scan. These documents and exhibits shall be kept in the Panel offices.

(b) Maintaining Records. Records and files generated prior to October 4, 2010, may be (i) maintained at the Panel offices, (ii) temporarily or permanently removed to such places at such times as the Clerk of the Panel or the Chair shall direct, or (iii) transferred whenever appropriate to the Federal Records Center.

(c) Fees. The Clerk of the Panel may charge fees for duplicating records and files, as prescribed by the Judicial Conference of the United States.

[Former Rule 2 adopted May 3, 1993, effective July 1, 1993. Renumbered Rule 5.1 and amended September 1, 1998, effective November 2, 1998. Former Rule 5.1 redesignated and amended September 8, 2010, effective October 4, 2010.]

RULE 3.2   ECF USERS: FILING REQUIREMENTS

(a) Form of Pleadings. This Rule applies to pleadings that ECF users file with the Panel.

(i) Each pleading shall bear the heading "Before the United States Judicial Panel on Multidistrict Litigation," the identification "MDL No. ____" and the descriptive title designated by the Panel. If the Panel has not yet designated a title, counsel shall use an appropriate description.

(ii) The final page of each pleading shall contain the name, address, telephone number, fax number and email address of the attorney or party designated to receive service of pleadings in the case, and the name of each party represented.

(iii) Each brief submitted with a motion and any response to it shall not exceed 20 pages, exclusive of exhibits. Each reply shall not exceed 10 pages and shall address arguments raised in the response(s). Absent exceptional circumstances and those set forth in Rule 6.1(d), the Panel will not grant motions to exceed page limits.

(iv) Each pleading shall be typed in size 12 point font (for both text and footnotes), double spaced (text only), in a letter size document (8 ½ × 11 inch) with sequentially numbered pages.

(v) Each exhibit shall be separately numbered and clearly identified.

(vi) Proposed Panel orders shall not be submitted.

(b) Place of Filing. Counsel shall sign and verify all pleadings electronically in accordance with these Rules and the Panel's Administrative Policies and Procedures for Electronic Case Filing found at www. jpml.uscourts.gov. A pleading filed electronically constitutes a written document for the purpose of these Rules and the Federal Rules of Civil Procedure and is deemed the electronically signed original thereof. All pleadings, except by pro se litigants, shall conform with this Rule beginning on October 4, 2010.

(i)* Pleadings shall not be transmitted directly to any Panel member.

(c) Attorney Registration. Only attorneys identified, or to be identified, pursuant to Rule 4.1, shall file pleadings. Each of these attorneys must register as a Panel CM/ECF user through www.jpml.uscourts.gov. Registration/possession of a CM/ECF account with any United States federal court shall be deemed consent to receive electronic service of all Panel orders and notices as well as electronic service of pleadings from other parties before the Panel.

(d) Courtesy Copy of Specified Pleadings. Counsel shall serve the Clerk of the Panel, for delivery within 1 business day of filing, with a courtesy paper copy of any of the following pleadings: (i) a motion to transfer and its supporting brief; (ii) a response to a show cause order; (iii) a motion to vacate a conditional transfer order or a conditional remand order; (iv) any response, reply, supplemental information or interested party response related to the pleadings listed in (i), (ii) and (iii); and (v) a corporate disclosure statement. No courtesy copies of any other pleadings are required. Courtesy copies of pleadings totaling 10

pages or less (including any attachments) may be faxed to the Panel. The courtesy copy shall include all exhibits, shall be clearly marked "Courtesy Copy—Do Not File," shall contain the CM/ECF pleading number (if known), and shall be mailed or delivered to:

Clerk of the Panel
United States Judicial Panel on Multidistrict
 Litigation
Thurgood Marshall Federal Judiciary Building
One Columbus Circle, NE,
Room G–255, North Lobby
Washington, DC 20002–8041

(e) Privacy Protections. The privacy protections contained in Rule 5.2 of the Federal Rules of Civil Procedure shall apply to all Panel filings.

[Former Rule 3 adopted May 3, 1993, effective July 1, 1993. Renumbered Rule 5.11 and amended September 1, 1998, effective November 2, 1998; renumbered Rule 5.1.1 and amended March 25, 2010, effective April 1, 2010. Former Rule 7 adopted May 3, 1993, effective July 1, 1993. Renumbered Rule 5.12 and amended September 1, 1998, effective November 2, 1998. Amended April 2, 2001, effective April 2, 2001; paragraph (a) suspended in part by Order filed April 19, 2005; renumbered Rule 5.1.2 and amended March 25, 2010, effective April 1, 2010. Former Rule 9 adopted May 3, 1993, effective July 1, 1993. Renumbered Rule 7.1 and amended September 1, 1998, effective November 2, 1998. Amended April 2, 2001, effective April 2, 2001. Former Rules 5.1.1, 5.1.2, and 7.1 redesignated in part and amended September 8, 2010, effective October 4, 2010. Amended effective July 6, 2011.]

* So in original. No subdivision (ii) promulgated.

RULE 3.3 NON–ECF USERS: FILING REQUIREMENTS

(a) Definition of Non–ECF Users. Non–ECF users are all pro se individuals, unless the Panel orders otherwise. This Rule shall apply to all motions, responses and replies that non-ECF users file with the Panel.

(b) Form of Pleadings. Unless otherwise set forth in this Rule, the provisions of Rule 3.2 shall apply to non-ECF users.

(i) Each pleading shall be flat and unfolded; plainly written or typed in size 12 point font (for both text and footnotes), double spaced (text only), and printed single-sided on letter size (8 ½ × 11 inch) white paper with sequentially numbered pages; and fastened at the top-left corner without side binding or front or back covers.

(ii) Each exhibit shall be separately numbered and clearly identified. Any exhibits exceeding a cumulative total of 50 pages shall be bound separately.

(c) Place of Filing. File an original and one copy of all pleadings with the Clerk of the Panel by mailing or delivering to:

Clerk of the Panel

United States Judicial Panel on Multidistrict
  Litigation

Thurgood Marshall Federal Judiciary Building

One Columbus Circle, NE,

Room G–255, North Lobby

Washington, DC 20002–8041

(i) Pleadings not exceeding a total of 10 pages, including exhibits, may be faxed to the Panel office.

(ii) The Clerk of the Panel shall endorse the date for filing on all pleadings submitted for filing.

[Former Rule 3 adopted May 3, 1993, effective July 1, 1993. Renumbered Rule 5.11 and amended September 1, 1998, effective November 2, 1998; renumbered Rule 5.1.1 and amended March 25, 2010, effective April 1, 2010. Former Rule 7 adopted May 3, 1993, effective July 1, 1993. Renumbered Rule 5.12 and amended September 1, 1998, effective November 2, 1998. Amended April 2, 2001, effective April 2, 2001; paragraph (a) suspended in part by Order filed April 19, 2005; renumbered Rule 5.1.2 and amended March 25, 2010, effective April 1, 2010. Former Rule 9 adopted May 3, 1993, effective July 1, 1993. Renumbered Rule 7.1 and amended September 1, 1998, effective November 2, 1998. Amended April 2, 2001, effective April 2, 2001. Former Rules 5.1.1, 5.1.2, and 7.1 redesignated in part and amended September 8, 2010, effective October 4, 2010.]

RULE 4.1   SERVICE OF PLEADINGS

(a) Proof of Service. The Panel's notice of electronic filing shall constitute service of pleadings. Registration/possession by counsel of a CM/ECF account with any United States federal court shall be deemed consent to receive electronic service of all pleadings. All pleadings shall contain a proof of service on all other parties in all involved actions. The proof of service shall indicate the name and manner of service. If a party is not represented by counsel, the proof of service shall indicate the name of the party and the party's last known address. The proof of service shall indicate why any person named as a party in a constituent complaint was not served with the Section 1407 pleading.

(b) Service Upon Transferor Court. The proof of service pertaining to motions for a transfer or remand pursuant to 28 U.S.C. § 1407 shall certify that counsel has transmitted a copy of the motion for filing to the clerk of each district court where an affected action is pending.

(c) Notice of Appearance. Within 14 days after the issuance of a (i) notice of filing of a motion to initiate transfer under Rule 6.2, (ii) notice of filed opposition to a CTO under Rule 7.1, (iii) a show cause order under Rules* 8.1, (iv) notice of filed opposition to a CRO under Rule 10.2, or (v) notice of filing of a motion to remand under Rule 10.3, each party or designated attorney as required hereinafter shall file a Notice of Appearance notifying the Clerk of the Panel of the name, address and email address of the attor-

ney designated to file and receive service of all pleadings. Each party shall designate only one attorney. Any party not represented by counsel shall be served by mailing such pleadings to the party's last known address. Except in extraordinary circumstances, the Panel will not grant requests for an extension of time to file the Notice of Appearance.

(d) Liaison Counsel. If the transferee district court appoints liaison counsel, this Rule shall be satisfied by serving each party in each affected action and all liaison counsel. Liaison counsel shall receive copies of all Panel orders concerning their particular litigation and shall be responsible for distribution to the parties for whom he or she serves as liaison counsel.

[Former Rule 8 adopted May 3, 1993, effective July 1, 1993. Renumbered Rule 5.2 and amended September 1, 1998, effective November 2, 1998; March 26, 2009, effective December 1, 2009. Former Rule 5.2 redesignated and amended September 8, 2010, effective October 4, 2010. Technical revisions effective July 6, 2011.]

* So in original.

RULE 5.1   CORPORATE DISCLOSURE STATEMENT

(a) Requirements. A nongovernmental corporate party must file a disclosure statement that: (1) identifies any parent corporation and any publicly held corporation owning 10% or more of its stock; or (2) states that there is no such corporation.

(b) Deadline. A party shall file the corporate disclosure statement within 14 days after issuance of a notice of the filing of a motion to transfer or remand, an order to show cause, or a motion to vacate a conditional transfer order or a conditional remand order.

(c) Updating. Each party must update its corporate disclosure statement to reflect any change in the information therein (i) until the matter before the Panel is decided, and (ii) within 14 days after issuance of a notice of the filing of any subsequent motion to transfer or remand, order to show cause, or motion to vacate a conditional transfer order or a conditional remand order in that docket.

[Former Rule 2 adopted May 3, 1993, effective July 1, 1993. Renumbered Rule 5.1 and amended September 1, 1998, effective November 2, 1998. Former Rule 5.3 redesignated and amended September 8, 2010, effective October 4, 2010. Amended effective July 6, 2011.]

RULE 5.1.3   FILING OF PAPERS: COMPUTER GENERATED DISK REQUIRED [DELETED SEPT. 8, 2010, EFF. OCT. 4, 2010]

[Added May 22, 2000, effective June 1, 2000. And amended July 30, 2007, effective July 30, 2007; renumbered Rule 5.1.3 and amended March 25, 2010, effective April 1, 2010. Deleted September 8, 2010, effective October 4, 2010.]

RULE 6.1   MOTION PRACTICE

(a) Application. This Rule governs all motions requesting Panel action generally. More specific provisions may apply to motions to transfer (Rule 6.2), miscellaneous motions (Rule 6.3), conditional transfer orders (Rule 7.1), show cause orders (Rule 8.1), conditional remand orders (Rule 10.2) and motions to remand (Rule 10.3).

(b) Form of Motions. All motions shall briefly describe the action or relief sought and shall include:

(i) a brief which concisely states the background of the litigation and movant's factual and legal contentions;

(ii) a numbered schedule providing

(A) the complete name of each action involved, listing the full name of each party included as such on the district court's docket sheet, not shortened by the use of references such as "et al." or "etc.";

(B) the district court and division where each action is pending;

(C) the civil action number of each action; and

(D) the name of the judge assigned each action, if known;

(iii) a proof of service providing

(A) a service list listing the full name of each party included on the district court's docket sheet and the complaint, including opt-in plaintiffs not listed on the docket sheet; and

(B) in actions where there are 25 or more plaintiffs listed on the docket sheet, list the first named plaintiff with the reference "et al." if all the plaintiffs are represented by the same attorney(s);

(iv) a copy of all complaints and docket sheets for all actions listed on the Schedule; and

(v) exhibits, if any, identified by number or letter and a descriptive title.

(c) Responses and Joinders. Any other party may file a response within 21 days after filing of a motion. Failure to respond to a motion shall be treated as that party's acquiescence to it. A joinder in a motion shall not add any action to that motion.

(d) Replies. The movant may file a reply within 7 days after the lapse of the time period for filing a response. Where a movant is replying to more than one response in opposition, the movant may file a consolidated reply with a limit of 20 pages.

(e) Alteration of Time Periods. The Clerk of the Panel has the discretion to shorten or enlarge the time periods set forth in this Rule as necessary.

(f) Notification of Developments. Counsel shall promptly notify the Clerk of the Panel of any development that would partially or completely moot any Panel matter.

[Former Rule 10 adopted May 3, 1993, effective July 1, 1993. Renumbered Rule 7.2 and amended September 1, 1998, effective November 2, 1998. Amended April 2, 2001, effective April 2, 2001; March 26, 2009, December 1, 2009. Former Rule 7.2 redesignated in part and amended September 8, 2010, effective October 4, 2010.]

RULE 6.2   MOTIONS TO TRANSFER FOR COORDINATED OR CONSOLIDATED PRETRIAL PROCEEDINGS

(a) Initiation of Transfer. A party to an action may initiate proceedings to transfer under Section 1407 by filing a motion in accordance with these Rules. A copy of the motion shall be filed in each district court where the motion affects a pending action.

(b) Notice of Filing of Motion to Transfer. Upon receipt of a motion, the Clerk of the Panel shall issue a "Notice of Filing of Motion to Transfer" to the service list recipients. The Notice shall contain the following: the filing date of the motion, caption, MDL docket number, briefing schedule and pertinent Panel policies. After a motion is filed, the Clerk of the Panel shall consider any other pleading to be a response unless the pleading adds an action. The Clerk of the Panel may designate such a pleading as a motion, and distribute a briefing schedule applicable to all or some of the parties, as appropriate.

(c) Notice of Appearance. Within 14 days of issuance of a "Notice of the Filing of a Motion to Transfer," each party or designated attorney shall file a Notice of Appearance in accordance with Rule 4.1(c).

(d) Notice of Potential Tag-along Actions. Any party or counsel in a new group of actions under consideration for transfer under Section 1407 shall promptly notify the Clerk of the Panel of any potential tag-along actions in which that party is also named or in which that counsel appears.

(e) Interested Party Responses. Any party or counsel in one or more potential tag-along actions as well as amicus curiae may file a response to a pending motion to transfer. Such a pleading shall be deemed an Interested Party Response.

(f) Amendment to a Motion. Before amending a motion to transfer, a party shall first contact the Clerk of the Panel to ascertain whether such amendment is feasible and permissible considering the Panel's hearing schedule. Any such amendment shall be entitled "Amendment to Motion for Transfer," and shall clearly and specifically identify and describe the nature of the amendment.

(i) Where the amended motion includes new civil actions, the amending party shall file a "Schedule of Additional Actions" and a revised Proof of Service.

(ii) The Proof of Service shall state (A) that all new counsel have been served with a copy of the amendment and all previously-filed motion papers, and (B) that all counsel previously served with the original motion have been served with a copy of the amendment.

(iii) The Clerk of the Panel may designate the amendment with a different denomination (e.g., a notice of potential tag-along action(s)) and treatment.

(h) Oral Argument.* The Panel shall schedule oral arguments as needed and as set forth in Rule 11.1.

[Former Rule 10 adopted May 3, 1993, effective July 1, 1993. Renumbered Rule 7.2 and amended September 1, 1998, effective November 2, 1998. Amended April 2, 2001, effective April 2, 2001; March 26, 2009, December 1, 2009. Former Rule 15 adopted May 3, 1993, effective July 1, 1993. Renumbered Rule 6.2 and amended September 1, 1998, effective November 2, 1998. Former Rule 7.2 redesignated in part and amended September 8, 2010, effective October 4, 2010. Technical revisions effective July 6, 2011.]

* So in original.

RULE 6.3 MOTIONS FOR MISCELLANEOUS RELIEF

(a) Definition. Motions for miscellaneous relief include, but are not limited to, requests for extensions of time, exemption from ECF requirements, page limit extensions, or expedited consideration of any motion.

(b) Panel Action. The Panel, through the Clerk, may act upon any motion for miscellaneous relief, at any time, without waiting for a response. A motion for extension of time to file a pleading or perform an act under these Rules must state specifically the revised date sought and must be filed before the deadline for filing the pleading or performing the act. Any party aggrieved by the Clerk of the Panel's action may file objections for consideration. Absent exceptional circumstances, the Panel will not grant any extensions of time to file a notice of opposition to either a conditional transfer order or a conditional remand order.

[Former Rule 15 adopted May 3, 1993, effective July 1, 1993. Renumbered Rule 6.2 and amended September 1, 1998, effective November 2, 1998. Former Rule 6.2 redesignated and amended September 8, 2010, effective October 4, 2010.]

RULE 7.1 CONDITIONAL TRANSFER ORDERS (CTO) FOR TAG–ALONG ACTIONS

(a) Notice of Potential Tag-along Actions. Any party or counsel in actions previously transferred under Section 1407 shall promptly notify the Clerk of the Panel of any potential tag-along actions in which that party is also named or in which that counsel appears. The Panel has several options: (i) filing a CTO under Rule 7.1, (ii) filing a show cause order under Rule 8.1, or (iii) declining to act (Rule 7.1(b)(i)).

(b) Initiation of CTO. Upon learning of the pendency of a potential tag-along action, the Clerk of the Panel may enter a conditional order transferring that action to the previously designated transferee district court for the reasons expressed in the Panel's previous opinions and orders. The Clerk of the Panel shall serve this order on each party to the litigation but shall not send the order to the clerk of the transferee district court until 7 days after its entry.

(i)* If the Clerk of the Panel determines that a potential tag-along action is not appropriate for inclusion in an MDL proceeding and does not enter a CTO, an involved party may move for its transfer pursuant to Rule 6.1.

(c) Notice of Opposition to CTO. Any party opposing the transfer shall file a notice of opposition with the Clerk of the Panel within the 7–day period. In such event, the Clerk of the Panel shall not transmit the transfer order to the clerk of the transferee district court, but shall notify the parties of the briefing schedule.

(d) Failure to Respond. Failure to respond to a CTO shall be treated as that party's acquiescence to it.

(e) Notice of Appearance. Within 14 days after the issuance of a "Notice of Filed Opposition" to a CTO, each opposing party or designated attorney shall file a Notice of Appearance in accordance with Rule 4.1(c).

(f) Motion to Vacate CTO. Within 14 days of the filing of its notice of opposition, the party opposing transfer shall file a motion to vacate the CTO and brief in support thereof. The Clerk of the Panel shall set the motion for the next appropriate hearing session. Failure to file and serve a motion and brief shall be treated as withdrawal of the opposition and the Clerk of the Panel shall forthwith transmit the order to the clerk of the transferee district court.

(g) Notification of Developments. Parties to an action subject to a CTO shall notify the Clerk of the Panel if that action is no longer pending in its transferor district court.

(h) Effective Date of CTO. CTOs are effective when filed with the clerk of the transferee district court.

[Former Rule 12 adopted May 3, 1993, effective July 1, 1993. Renumbered Rule 7.4 and amended September 1, 1998, effective November 2, 1998. Amended April 2, 2001, effective April 2, 2001; March 26, 2009, December 1, 2009. Former Rule 7.4 redesignated and amended September 8, 2010, effective October 4, 2010. Technical revisions effective July 6, 2011.]

* So in original. No subdivision (ii) promulgated.

RULE 7.2 MISCELLANEOUS PROVISIONS CONCERNING TAG–ALONG ACTIONS

(a) Potential Tag-alongs in Transferee Court. Potential tag-along actions filed in the transferee district do not require Panel action. A party should request assignment of such actions to the Section 1407 transferee judge in accordance with applicable local rules.

(b) Failure to Serve. Failure to serve one or more of the defendants in a potential tag-along action with the complaint and summons as required by Rule 4 of the Federal Rules of Civil Procedure does not preclude transfer of such action under Section 1407. Such failure, however, may constitute grounds for denying the proposed transfer where prejudice can be shown. The failure of the Clerk of the Panel to serve a CTO on all plaintiffs or defendants or their counsel may constitute grounds for the Clerk to reinstate the CTO or for the aggrieved party to seek § 1407(c) remand.

[Former Rule 13 adopted May 3, 1993, effective July 1, 1993. Renumbered Rule 7.5 and amended September 1, 1998, effective November 2, 1998. Amended April 2, 2001, effective April 2, 2001. Former Rule 7.5 redesignated and amended September 8, 2010, effective October 4, 2010. Amended effective July 6, 2011.]

RULE 8.1 SHOW CAUSE ORDERS

(a) Entry of Show Cause Order. When transfer of multidistrict litigation is being considered on the initiative of the Panel pursuant to 28 U.S.C. § 1407(c)(i), the Clerk of the Panel may enter an order directing the parties to show cause why a certain civil action or actions should not be transferred for coordinated or consolidated pretrial proceedings. Any party shall also promptly notify the Clerk of the Panel whenever they learn of any other federal district court actions which are similar to those which the show cause order encompasses.

(b) Notice of Appearance. Within 14 days of the issuance of an order to show cause, each party or designated attorney shall file a Notice of Appearance in accordance with Rule 4.1(c).

(c) Responses. Unless otherwise provided by order, any party may file a response within 21 days of the filing of the show cause order. Failure to respond to a show cause order shall be treated as that party's acquiescence to the Panel action.

(d) Replies. Within 7 days after the lapse of the time period for filing a response, any party may file a reply.

(e) Notification of Developments. Counsel shall promptly notify the Clerk of the Panel of any develop-ment that would partially or completely moot any matter subject to a show cause order.

[Former Rule 7.3 adopted May 3, 1993, effective July 1, 1993. Renumbered Rule 7.3 and amended September 1, 1998, effective November 2, 1998; March 26, 2009, effective December 1, 2009. Former Rule 7.3 redesignated and amended September 8, 2010, effective October 4, 2010.]

RULE 9.1 TRANSFER OF FILES; NOTIFICATION REQUIREMENTS

(a) Notice to Transferee Court Clerk. The Clerk of the Panel, via a notice of electronic filing, will notify the clerk of the transferee district whenever a Panel transfer order should be filed in the transferee district court. Upon receipt of an electronically certified copy of a Panel transfer order from the clerk of the transferee district, the clerk of the transferor district shall transmit the record of each transferred action to the transferee district and then, unless Rule 9.1(b) applies, close the transferred action in the transferor district.

(b) Retention of Claims. If the transfer order provides for the separation and simultaneous remand of any claim, cross-claim, counterclaim, or third-party claim, the clerk of the transferor district shall retain jurisdiction over any such claim and shall not close the action.

(c) Notice to Clerk of Panel. The clerk of the transferee district shall promptly provide the Clerk of the Panel with the civil action numbers assigned to all transferred actions and the identity of liaison counsel, if or when designated. The clerk of the transferee district shall also promptly notify the Clerk of the Panel of any dispositive ruling that terminates a transferred action.

[Former Rule 19 adopted May 3, 1993, effective July 1, 1993. Renumbered Rule 1.6 and amended September 1, 1998, effective November 2, 1998. Former Rule 1.6 redesignated in part and amended September 8, 2010, effective October 4, 2010.]

RULE 10.1 TERMINATION AND REMAND

(a) Termination. Where the transferee district court terminates an action by valid order, including but not limited to summary judgment, judgment of dismissal and judgment upon stipulation, the transferee district court clerk shall transmit a copy of that order to the Clerk of the Panel. The terminated action shall not be remanded to the transferor court and the transferee court shall retain the original files and records unless the transferee judge or the Panel directs otherwise.

(b) Initiation of Remand. Typically, the transferee judge recommends remand of an action, or a part of it, to the transferor court at any time by filing a suggestion of remand with the Panel. However, the Panel may remand an action or any separable claim, cross-claim, counterclaim or third-party claim within it, upon

(i) the transferee court's suggestion of remand,

(ii) the Panel's own initiative by entry of an order to show cause, a conditional remand order or other appropriate order, or

(iii) motion of any party.

[Former Rule 14 adopted May 3, 1993, effective July 1, 1993. Renumbered Rule 7.6 and amended September 1, 1998, effective November 2, 1998. Amended April 2, 2001, effective April 2, 2001; March 26, 2009, effective December 1, 2009. Former Rule 7.6 redesignated in part and amended September 8, 2010, effective October 4, 2010.]

RULE 10.2   CONDITIONAL REMAND ORDERS (CRO)

(a) Entering a CRO. Upon the suggestion of the transferee judge or the Panel's own initiative, the Clerk of the Panel shall enter a conditional order remanding the action or actions to the transferor district court. The Clerk of the Panel shall serve this order on each party to the litigation but shall not send the order to the clerk of the transferee district court for 7 days from the entry thereof.

(i)* The Panel may, on its own initiative, also enter an order that the parties show cause why a matter should not be remanded. Rule 8.1 applies to responses and replies with respect to such a show cause order.

(b) Notice of Opposition. Any party opposing the CRO shall file a notice of opposition with the Clerk of the Panel within the 7–day period. In such event, the Clerk of the Panel shall not transmit the remand order to the clerk of the transferee district court and shall notify the parties of the briefing schedule.

(c) Failure to Respond. Failure to respond to a CRO shall be treated as that party's acquiescence to it.

(d) Notice of Appearance. Within 14 days after the issuance of a "Notice of Filed Opposition" to a CRO, each opposing party or designated attorney shall file a Notice of Appearance in accordance with Rule 4.1(c).

(e) Motion to Vacate CRO. Within 14 days of the filing of its notice of opposition, the party opposing remand shall file a motion to vacate the CRO and brief in support thereof. The Clerk of the Panel shall set the motion for the next appropriate Panel hearing session. Failure to file and serve a motion and brief shall be treated as a withdrawal of the opposition and the Clerk of the Panel shall forthwith transmit the order to the clerk of the transferee district court.

(f) Effective Date of CRO. CROs are not effective until filed with the clerk of the transferee district court.

[Former Rule 14 adopted May 3, 1993, effective July 1, 1993. Renumbered Rule 7.6 and amended September 1, 1998, effective November 2, 1998. Amended April 2, 2001, effective April 2, 2001; March 26, 2009, effective December 1, 2009. Former Rule 7.6 redesignated in part and amended September 8, 2010, effective October 4, 2010. Technical revisions effective July 6, 2011.]

* So in original. No subdivision (ii) promulgated.

RULE 10.3   MOTION TO REMAND

(a) Requirements of the Motion. If the Clerk of the Panel does not enter a CRO, a party may file a motion to remand to the transferor court pursuant to these Rules. Because the Panel is reluctant to order a remand absent the suggestion of the transferee judge, the motion must include:

(i) An affidavit reciting whether the movant has requested a suggestion of remand and the judge's response, whether the parties have completed common discovery and other pretrial proceedings, and whether the parties have complied with all transferee court orders.

(ii) A copy of the transferee district court's final pretrial order, if entered.

(b) Filing Copy of Motion. Counsel shall file a copy of the motion to remand in the affected transferee district court.

(c) Notice of Appearance. Within 14 days of the issuance of a "Notice of Filing" of a motion to remand, each party or designated attorney shall file a Notice of Appearance in accordance with Rule 4.1(c).

[Former Rule 14 adopted May 3, 1993, effective July 1, 1993. Renumbered Rule 7.6 and amended September 1, 1998, effective November 2, 1998. Amended April 2, 2001, effective April 2, 2001; March 26, 2009, effective December 1, 2009. Former Rule 7.6 redesignated in part and amended September 8, 2010, effective October 4, 2010. Technical revisions effective July 6, 2011.]

RULE 10.4   TRANSFER OF FILES ON REMAND

(a) Designating the Record. Upon receipt of an order to remand from the Clerk of the Panel, the parties shall furnish forthwith to the transferee district clerk a stipulation or designation of the contents of the record or part thereof to be remanded.

(b) Transfer of Files. Upon receipt of an order to remand from the Clerk of the Panel, the transferee district shall transmit to the clerk of the transferor district the following concerning each remanded action:

(i) a copy of the individual docket sheet for each action remanded;

(ii) a copy of the master docket sheet, if applicable;

(iii) the entire file for each action remanded, as originally received from the transferor district and augmented as set out in this Rule;

(iv) a copy of the final pretrial order, if applicable; and

(v) a "record on remand" as designated by the parties in accordance with 10.4(a).

[Former Rule 19 adopted May 3, 1993, effective July 1, 1993. Renumbered Rule 1.6 and amended September 1, 1998, effective November 2, 1998. Former Rule 1.6 redesignated in part and amended September 8, 2010, effective October 4, 2010.]

RULE 11.1 HEARING SESSIONS AND ORAL ARGUMENT

(a) Schedule. The Panel shall schedule sessions for oral argument and consideration of other matters as desirable or necessary. The Chair shall determine the time, place and agenda for each hearing session. The Clerk of the Panel shall give appropriate notice to counsel for all parties. The Panel may continue its consideration of any scheduled matters.

(b) Oral Argument Statement. Any party affected by a motion may file a separate statement setting forth reasons why oral argument should, or need not, be heard. Such statements shall be captioned "Reasons Why Oral Argument Should [Need Not] Be Heard" and shall be limited to 2 pages.

(i)* The parties affected by a motion to transfer may agree to waive oral argument. The Panel will take this into consideration in determining the need for oral argument.

(c) Hearing Session. The Panel shall not consider transfer or remand of any action pending in a federal district court when any party timely opposes such transfer or remand without first holding a hearing session for the presentation of oral argument. The Panel may dispense with oral argument if it determines that:

(i) the dispositive issue(s) have been authoritatively decided; or

(ii) the facts and legal arguments are adequately presented and oral argument would not significantly aid the decisional process.

Unless otherwise ordered, the Panel shall consider all other matters, such as a motion for reconsideration, upon the basis of the pleadings.

(d) Notification of Oral Argument. The Panel shall promptly notify counsel of those matters in which oral argument is scheduled, as well as those matters that the Panel will consider on the pleadings. The Clerk of the Panel shall require counsel to file and serve notice of their intent to either make or waive oral argument. Failure to do so shall be deemed a waiver of oral argument. If counsel does not attend oral argument, the matter shall not be rescheduled and that party's position shall be treated as submitted for decision on the basis of the pleadings filed.

(i) Absent Panel approval and for good cause shown, only those parties to actions who have filed a motion or written response to a motion or order shall be permitted to present oral argument.

(ii) The Panel will not receive oral testimony except upon notice, motion and an order expressly providing for it.

(e) Duty to Confer. Counsel in an action set for oral argument shall confer separately prior to that argument for the purpose of organizing their arguments and selecting representatives to present all views without duplication. Oral argument is a means for counsel to emphasize the key points of their arguments, and to update the Panel on any events since the conclusion of briefing.

(f) Time Limit for Oral Argument. Barring exceptional circumstances, the Panel shall allot a maximum of 20 minutes for oral argument in each matter. The time shall be divided among those with varying viewpoints. Counsel for the moving party or parties shall generally be heard first.

[Former Rule 16 adopted May 3, 1998, effective July 1, 1993. Renumbered Rule 16.1 and amended September 1, 1998, effective November 2, 1998. Amended April 2, 2001, effective April 2, 2001. Former Rule 16.1 redesignated and amended September 8, 2010, effective October 4, 2010.]

* So in original. No subdivision (ii) promulgated.

RULES 12 TO 15. [RESERVED]

II. RULES FOR MULTICIRCUIT PETITIONS FOR REVIEW UNDER 28 U.S.C. § 2112(a)(3)

RULE 25.1 DEFINITIONS

The Panel promulgates these Rules pursuant to its authority under 28 U.S.C. § 2112(a)(3) to provide a means for the random selection of one circuit court of appeals to hear consolidated petitions for review of agency decisions.

An "Agency" means an agency, board, commission or officer of the United States government, that has received two or more petitions for review in a circuit court of appeals to enjoin, set aside, suspend, modify or otherwise review or enforce an action.

[Former Rule 20 adopted May 3, 1993, effective July 1, 1993. Renumbered Rule 25.1 and amended September 1, 1998, effective November 2, 1998. Amended September 8, 2010, effective October 4, 2010.]

RULE 25.2 FILING OF NOTICES

(a) Submitting Notice. An affected agency shall submit a notice of multicircuit petitions for review pursuant to 28 U.S.C. § 2112(a)(3) to the Clerk of the Panel by electronic means in the manner these Rules require and in accordance with the Panel's Administrative Policies and Procedures for Electronic Case Filing, except that the portion of Rule 3.2(d) requiring a courtesy copy is suspended in its entirety.

(b) Accompaniments to Notices. All notices of multicircuit petitions for review shall include:

(i) a copy of each involved petition for review as the petition for review is defined in 28 U.S.C. § 2112(a)(2);

(ii) a schedule giving

(A) the date of the relevant agency order;

(B) the case name of each petition for review involved;

(C) the circuit court of appeals in which each petition for review is pending;

(D) the appellate docket number of each petition for review;

(E) the date of filing by the court of appeals of each petition for review; and

(F) the date of receipt by the agency of each petition for review; and

(iii) proof of service (*see* Rule 25.3).

(c) Scope of Notice. All notices of multicircuit petitions for review shall embrace exclusively petitions for review filed in the courts of appeals within 10 days after issuance of an agency order and received by the affected agency from the petitioners within that 10–day period.

(d) Filing at the Panel. The Clerk of the Panel shall file the notice of multicircuit petitions for review and endorse thereon the date of filing.

(e) Filing With Each Circuit Clerk. The affected agency shall file copies of notices of multicircuit petitions for review with the clerk of each circuit court of appeals in which a petition for review is pending.

[Former Rule 21 adopted May 3, 1993, effective July 1, 1993. Renumbered Rule 25.2 and amended September 1, 1998, effective November 2, 1998. Amended September 8, 2010, effective October 4, 2010. Technical revisions effective July 6, 2011.]

RULE 25.3 SERVICE OF NOTICES

(a) Proof of Service. Notices of multicircuit petitions for review shall include proof of service on all other parties in the petitions for review included in the notice. Rule 25 of the Federal Rules of Appellate Procedure governs service and proof of service. The proof of service shall state the name, address and email address of each person served and shall indicate the party represented by each and the manner in which service was accomplished on each party. If a party is not represented by counsel, the proof of service shall indicate the name of the party and his or her last known address. The affected party shall submit proof of service for filing with the Clerk of the Panel and shall send copies thereof to each person included within the proof of service.

(b) Service on Clerk of Circuit. The proof of service pertaining to notices of multicircuit petitions for review shall certify the affected party has mailed or delivered copies of the notices to the clerk of each circuit court of appeals in which a petition for review is pending that is included in the notice. The Clerk shall file the notice with the circuit court.

[Former Rule 22 adopted May 3, 1993, effective July 1, 1993. Renumbered Rule 25.3 September 1, 1998, effective November 2, 1998. Amended September 8, 2010, effective October 4, 2010.]

RULE 25.4 FORM OF NOTICES; PLACE OF FILING

(a) Unless otherwise provided here, Rule 3.2 governs the form of a notice of multicircuit petitions for review. Each notice shall bear the heading "Notice to the United States Judicial Panel on Multidistrict Litigation of Multicircuit Petitions for Review," followed by a brief caption identifying the involved agency, the relevant agency order, and the date of the order.

(b) Rule 3.2(b) and (c) govern the manner of filing a notice of multicircuit petitions for review.

[Former Rule 23 adopted May 3, 1993, effective July 1, 1993. Renumbered Rule 25.4 and amended September 1, 1998, effective November 2, 1998. Amended September 8, 2010, effective October 4, 2010.]

RULE 25.5 RANDOM SELECTION

(a) Selection Process. Upon filing a notice of multicircuit petitions for review, the Clerk of the Panel shall randomly select a circuit court of appeals from a drum containing an entry for each circuit wherein a constituent petition for review is pending. Multiple petitions for review pending in a single circuit shall be allotted only a single entry in the drum. A designated deputy other than the random selector shall witness the random selection. Thereafter, an order on behalf of the Panel shall be issued, signed by the random selector and the witness,

(i) consolidating the petitions for review in the court of appeals for the circuit that was randomly selected; and

(ii) designating that circuit as the one in which the record is to be filed pursuant to Rules 16 and 17 of the Federal Rules of Appellate Procedure.

(b) Effective Date. A consolidation of petitions for review shall be effective when the Clerk of the Panel enters the consolidation order.

[Former Rule 24 adopted May 3, 1993, effective July 1, 1993. Renumbered Rule 17.1 September 1, 1998, effective November 2, 1998. Former Rule 17.1 redesignated and amended September 8, 2010, effective October 4, 2010.]

RULE 25.6 SERVICE OF PANEL CONSOLIDATION ORDER

(a) The Clerk of the Panel shall serve the Panel's consolidation order on the affected agency through the individual or individuals, as identified in Rule 25.2(a), who submitted the notice of multicircuit petitions for review on behalf of the agency.

(b) That individual or individuals, or anyone else designated by the agency, shall promptly serve the Panel's consolidation order on all other parties in all petitions for review included in the Panel's consolidation order, and shall promptly submit a proof of that service to the Clerk of the Panel. Rule 25.3 governs service.

(c) The Clerk of the Panel shall serve the Panel's consolidation order on the clerks of all circuit courts of appeals that were among the candidates for the Panel's random selection.

[Former Rule 25 adopted May 3, 1993, effective July 1, 1993. Renumbered Rule 25.5 and amended September 1, 1998, effective November 2, 1998. Former Rule 25.5 redesignated and amended September 8, 2010, effective October 4, 2010.]

III. CONVERSION TABLE

New to Old:

New Rule / Previous Rule		New Rule / Previous Rule	
1.1	1.1	9.1	1.6
2.1	1.2, 1.3, 1.4, 1.5	10.1	7.6
3.1	5.1	10.2	7.6
3.2	5.1.1, 5.1.2, 7.1	10.3	7.6
3.3	5.1.1, 5.1.2, 7.1	10.4	1.6
4.1	5.2	11.1	16.1
5.1	5.3	25.1	25.1
6.1	7.2	25.2	25.1, 25.2
6.2	7.2	25.3	25.3
6.3	6.2	25.4	25.1, 25.4
7.1	7.4	25.5	17.1
7.2	7.5	25.6	25.5
8.1	7.3		

Old to New:

Previous Rule / New Rule		Previous Rule / New Rule	
1.1	1.1	7.1	3.2, 3.3
1.2	2.1	7.2	6.1
1.3	2.1	7.3	8.1
1.4	2.1	7.4	7.1
1.5	2.1	7.5	7.2
1.6	10.4	7.6	10.1
5.1	3.1	16.1	11.1
5.1.1	3.2, 3.3	17.1	25.5
5.1.2	3.2, 3.3	25.1	25.1, 25.2, 25.4
5.1.3	-	25.2	25.2
5.2	4.1	25.3	25.3
5.3	5.1	25.4	25.4
6.2	6.3	25.5	25.6

[October 2010.]

ELECTRONIC CASE FILING ADMINISTRATIVE POLICIES AND PROCEDURES

1. DEFINITIONS.

1.1 "ELECTRONIC FILING SYSTEM" (ECF) refers to the United States Judicial Panel on Multidistrict Litigation's (the Panel's) automated system that receives and stores documents filed in electronic form. The program is part of the CM/ECF (Case Management/Electronic Case Files) software which was developed for the Federal Judiciary by the Administrative Office of the United States Courts.

1.2 "CLERK OF THE PANEL" means the official appointed by the Panel to act as Clerk of the Panel and shall include those deputized by the Clerk of the Panel to perform or assist in the performance of the duties of the Clerk of the Panel.

1.3 "FILING USER" is an individual who has a Panel-issued login and password to file documents electronically. In accordance with Rule 1.4 of the Rules of Procedure of the United States Judicial Panel on Multidistrict Litigation (the Panel Rules), every member in good standing of the Bar of any district court of the United States is entitled to practice before the Judicial Panel on Multidistrict Litigation.

1.4 "NOTICE OF ELECTRONIC FILING" (NEF) is a notice automatically generated by the Electronic Filing System at the time a document is filed with the system, setting forth the time of filing, the date the document is entered on the docket, the name of the party and attorney filing the document, the type of document, the text of the docket entry, the name of the party and/or attorney receiving the notice, and an electronic link (hyperlink) to the filed document, which allows recipients to retrieve the document automatically. A document shall not be considered filed for the purposes of the Panel's Rules until the filing party receives a system generated Notice of Electronic Filing with a hyperlink to the electronically filed document.

1.5 "PACER" (Public Access to Court Electronic Records) is an automated system that allows an individual to view, print and download Panel docket information over the Internet.

1.6 "PDF" (Portable Document Format). A document file created with a word processor, or a paper document which has been scanned, must be converted to portable document format to be filed electronically with the Panel. Converted files contain the extension ".pdf".

1.7 "TECHNICAL FAILURE" is defined as a failure of Panel owned/leased hardware, software, and/or telecommunications facility which results in the inability of a Filing User to submit a filing electronically. Technical failure does not include malfunctioning of a Filing User's equipment.

2. SCOPE OF ELECTRONIC FILING.

(a) All multidistrict litigation matters (MDLs) brought before the Panel under 28 U.S.C. § 1407 shall be assigned to the Electronic Filing System. Effective October 1, 2010, all MDLs, proceedings, motions, memoranda of law and other pleadings or documents filed with the Panel in new and existing dockets must be filed using CM/ECF unless otherwise specified herein.

(b) The filing of all MDL papers shall be accomplished electronically under procedures outlined in the Panel's CM/ECF User Manual.

(c) A party proceeding pro se shall not file electronically, unless otherwise permitted by the Panel. Pro se filers shall file paper originals of all documents. The clerk's office will scan these original documents into the JPML's electronic system, unless otherwise sealed.

3. ELIGIBILITY, REGISTRATION, PASSWORDS.

(a) Any attorney admitted to the Bar of any United States district court is eligible to practice before the Panel. Unless otherwise exempt as set forth herein, to become a Filing User, an attorney must register as a Filing User by completing the prescribed registration form and submitting it to the Clerk of the Panel.

(b) Registration as a Filing User constitutes consent to electronic service of all documents filed with or issued by the Panel in accordance with the Panel Rules.

(c) By submitting the online registration form, the Filing Users certify that they have read and are familiar with the Panel Rules and these administrative policies and procedures governing electronic filing and the method of training in the System used prior to becoming a Filing User. Filing users must also have a PACER account. An individual may register more than one Internet email address. The clerk's office will email the login and password to the attorney.

(d) Once the registration is processed by the clerk, the Filing User shall protect the security of the User password and immediately notify the clerk if the Filing User learns that the password has been compromised. Filing Users may be subject to sanctions for failure to comply with this provision. After registering, attorneys may change their passwords. If an attorney comes to believe that the security of an existing password has been compromised and that a threat to the System exists, the attorney must change his or her password immediately.

(e) Exemptions from mandatory electronic filing may be granted upon submission of a written request to the clerk. The written request shall include a supporting affidavit showing a substantial undue hardship. Final authority to grant such request is vested in the Clerk of the Panel or his/her designee.

(f)(1) Each attorney is responsible for keeping his/her contact information up to date. If an attorney is leaving a law firm and is the attorney of record on an existing case and representation in the case will remain with the law firm, withdrawal and substitution of counsel must be made prior to the attorney's termination in the law firm, for the following reason:

The attorney leaving the firm has an email address with the law firm he or she is leaving on record with the Panel. This email address may be disabled by the law firm as soon as the attorney terminates his/her employment. The electronic notices in CM/ECF will continue to go to the terminated attorney's email address at the former firm. If the email address is disabled at the law firm, the attorney will not receive the electronic notice. If a withdrawal/substitution of counsel has not been filed prior to the attorney leaving the firm, the law firm should not disable the email account of the attorney leaving the firm until another attorney in the firm enters his/her appearance. The law firm should designate someone in the firm to check this email account for CM/ECF notices until substitution of counsel has been filed with the Panel.

(2) If the attorney leaving the firm is taking active cases from the firm, the attorney needs to change his/her email address as soon as possible, otherwise the attorney will not receive electronic notices from CM/ECF. The email will continue to be sent to the former law firm's email address still on record. Procedures for changing an email address may be found in the Panel's CM/ECF User Manual.

4. ELECTRONIC FILING AND SERVICE OF DOCUMENTS.

(a) Electronic transmission of a document to the Electronic Filing System in accordance with these procedures, together with the transmission of a (System) Notice of Electronic Filing from the Panel with a hyperlink to the electronically filed document, constitutes filing of the document for all purposes of the Panel Rules of Procedure.

(b) Emailing a document to the clerk's office does not constitute filing the document. A document shall not be considered filed until the System generates a Notice of Electronic Filing (NEF) with a hyperlink to the electronically filed document.

(c) Before filing a scanned document with the court, a Filing User must verify its legibility.

(d) When a document has been filed electronically, the official record of that document is the electronic recording as stored by the Panel and the filing party is bound by the document as filed. A document filed electronically is deemed filed on the date and time stated on the Notice of Electronic Filing (NEF) from the Panel.

(e) Filing a document electronically does not alter the filing deadline for that document. Filing must be completed before midnight, **EASTERN TIME**, in order to be considered timely filed that day. However, if time of day is of the essence, the Clerk of the Panel may order a document filed by a certain time.

(f) Upon the filing of a document, a docket entry will be created using the information provided by the Filing User. The clerk will, where necessary and appropriate, modify the docket entry description to comply with quality control standards. In the event a Filing User electronically files a document in the wrong MDL or associated civil action, or the incorrect PDF document is attached, the Clerk of the Panel, or his/her designee, shall be authorized to strike the document from the record. A notice of the action striking a document from the record shall be served on all parties in the case.

(g) By participating in the electronic filing process, the parties consent to the electronic service of all documents, and shall make available electronic mail addresses for service. Upon the filing of a document by a Filing User, a Notice of Electronic Filing (NEF), with a hyperlink to the electronic document and an email message will be automatically generated by the electronic filing system, and sent via electronic mail to the email addresses of all parties who have registered in the MDL. In addition to receiving email notifications of filing activity, the Filing User is strongly encouraged to sign on to the electronic filing system at regular intervals to check the docket in his/her MDL and/or civil action.

(h) If the filing of an electronically submitted document requires leave of the Panel, such as a request to file out-of-time, the attorney shall attach the proposed document as an attachment to the motion requesting leave to file. If the Clerk of the Panel grants the motion, the document will be electronically filed without further action by the Filing User.

(i) A certificate of service must be included with all documents filed electronically. Such certificate shall indicate that service was accomplished pursuant to the Panel's electronic filing procedures. Service by electronic mail shall constitute service pursuant to Panel Rule 5.2.

A party who is not a registered CM/ECF participant with any United States federal court is entitled to a paper copy of any electronically filed pleading, document, or order pursuant to Panel Rule 5.1.1.(b). The filing party must therefore provide the non-registered attorney or party, including a terminated party or attorney, if appropriate, with the pleading, document, or order pursuant to Panel Rule 5.2. Under the Rule, they can be served with a paper copy of the electronically filed document, or they can consent in writing to service by any other method, including other forms of electronic service such as fax or direct email.

The following is a suggested certificate of service for electronic filing:

CERTIFICATE OF SERVICE

On [Date], I electronically filed this document through the CM/ECF system, which will send a notice of electronic filing to: [Attorney Name (attach list if necessary)]; and I [mailed] [hand delivered] [faxed] this document and the notice of electronic filing to: [Attorney/Party Name], [Address], [Parties Represented], [Civil Action(s)] (attach list if necessary).

/s/ [typed name of attorney]

Attorney's name

Law Firm Name (if applicable)

Address

Phone Number

Fax Number

Attorney's Email address

Attorney for:

5. ENTRY OF PANEL DOCUMENTS.

(a) A document entered or issued by the Panel will be filed in accordance with these procedures and such filing shall constitute entry on the docket kept by the Clerk.

(b) All signed orders will be electronically filed or entered. An order containing the electronic signature of a Panel Judge or the Clerk of the Panel shall have the same force and effect as if the Panel Judge or Clerk of the Panel had affixed a signature to a paper copy of the order and the order had been entered on the docket in a conventional manner.

(c) Orders may also be issued as "text-only" entries on the docket, without an attached document. Such orders are official and binding.

6. NOTICE OF PANEL ORDERS AND NOTICES.

Immediately upon the entry of an order or notice by the Panel, the clerk will transmit to Filing Users in affected cases in the MDL, in electronic form, a Notice of Electronic Filing (NEF), with a hyperlink to the electronic document. Electronic transmission of the NEF, along with a hyperlink to the electronic document, constitutes the notice required by Panel Rule 5.2. The clerk must give notice in paper form to a pro se party or an attorney who is not a Filing User to the extent notice is required.

7. ATTACHMENTS AND EXHIBITS.

Documents referenced as exhibits or attachments shall be filed in accordance with these administrative policies and procedures and the Panel's CM/ECF User Manual, unless otherwise ordered by the Panel. A Filing User shall submit as exhibits or attachments only those excerpts of the referenced documents that are directly germane to the matter under consideration by the Panel. Excerpted material must be clearly and prominently identified as such. Filing Users who file excerpts of documents as exhibits or attachments under these procedures do so without prejudice to their right to file timely additional excerpts or the complete document. Responding parties may timely file additional excerpts or the complete document that they believe are directly germane. The Panel may require parties to file additional excerpts or the complete document.

8. SEALED DOCUMENTS.

To ensure proper storage of a document, a document subject to a sealing order must be filed with the Panel on paper in a sealed envelope marked "sealed", citing thereon the MDL docket number and title and the associated case caption and case number; or by attaching thereto a paper copy of the Panel's order sealing the document or a copy of the NEF citing the entry of the court's order sealing the document. The clerk may require the document to be accompanied by a disk or CD–ROM containing the document in .pdf format. Only a motion to file a document under seal may be filed electronically, unless prohibited by law. The order of the Panel authorizing the filing of documents under seal may be filed electronically, unless prohibited by law or otherwise directed by the Panel. If a document is filed under seal pursuant to the E–Government Act of 2002, the filing party is nevertheless required to file a redacted copy for the public record along with the unredacted sealed document.

9. SPECIAL FILING REQUIREMENTS AND EXCEPTIONS.

9.1   Special Filing Requirements

The documents listed below shall be presented for filing on paper. The clerk may require the document be accompanied by a disk or CD–ROM containing the document in .pdf format:

Sealed

MDL dockets involving Qui Tam Cases (under seal)

9.2 Exceptions

All documents shall be filed electronically unless otherwise ordered by the Panel or specifically exempt herein.

10. RETENTION REQUIREMENTS.

(a) A document that is electronically filed and requires an original signature other than that of the Filing User must be maintained in paper form by counsel and/or the firm representing the party on whose behalf the document was filed until one year after all periods for appeals expire. On request of the Panel, said counsel must provide the original document for review.

(b) The clerk's office may choose to discard certain documents brought to the clerk's office for filing in paper form after those documents are scanned and uploaded to the System (to include pro se filings). Therefore, counsel and pro se filers shall provide the Panel with a copy of the original documents with intrinsic value for scanning and maintain the original signature in accordance with 10(a).

11. SIGNATURES.

(a) The user login and password required to submit documents to the Electronic Filing System serve as the Filing User signature on all electronic documents filed with the court. They serve as a signature for purposes of the Panel Rules and any other purpose for which a signature is required in connection with proceedings before the Panel.

(b) Each document filed electronically must indicate in the caption that it has been electronically filed. An electronically filed document must include a signature block in compliance with Panel Rule 7.1(e), and must set forth the name, address, telephone number, fax number, and email address. In addition, the name of the Filing User under whose login and password the document is submitted must be preceded by an "/s/" and typed in the space where the signature would otherwise appear. No Filing User or other person may knowingly permit or cause to permit a Filing User password to be used by anyone other than an authorized agent of the Filing User.

(c) A document requiring signatures of more than one party must be filed either by:

(1) electronically filing a scanned document containing all necessary signatures; or

(2) representing the consent of the other parties on the document; or

(3) identifying on the document the party whose signature is required and by the submission of a notice of endorsement by the other parties no later than three (3) business days after filing; or

(4) any other manner approved by the Panel.

(d) A non-filing signatory or party who disputes the authenticity of an electronically filed document with a non-attorney signature, or the authenticity of the signature on that document; or the authenticity of an electronically filed document containing multiple signatures or the authenticity of the signature themselves, must file an objection to the document within fourteen (14) days of service of the document.

(e) Any party challenging the authenticity of an electronically filed document or the attorney's signature on that document must file an objection to the document within fourteen (14) days of service of the document.

(f) If a party wishes to challenge the authenticity of an electronically filed document or signature after the fourteen (14) day period, the party shall file a motion to seek a ruling from the Panel.

12. SERVICE OF DOCUMENTS BY ELECTRONIC MEANS.

12.1 Service

12.1.1 Filing User

Upon the electronic filing of a pleading or other document, the Panel's Electronic Case Filing System will automatically generate and send a Notice of Electronic Filing (NEF) to all Filing Users associated with that MDL and/or associated cases, along with a hyperlink to the electronic document. Transmission of the Notice of Electronic Filing with a hyperlink to the electronic document constitutes service of the filed document.

The NEF must include the time of filing, the date the document was entered on the docket, the name of the party and attorney filing the document, the type of document, the text of the docket entry, and an electronic link (hyperlink) to the filed document, allowing anyone receiving the notice by email to retrieve the document automatically. If the Filing User becomes aware that the NEF was not transmitted successfully to a party, or that the notice is deficient, *i.e.*, the electronic link to the document is defective, the filer shall serve the electronically filed document by email, hand, facsimile, or by first-class mail postage prepaid immediately upon notification of the NEF deficiency.

12.1.2 Individual who is not a Filing User

A non-registered participant is entitled to receive a paper copy of any electronically filed document from the party making such filing. Service of such paper copy must be made according to the Panel Rules.

13. TECHNICAL FAILURES.

(a) If the site is unable to accept filings continuously or intermittently for more than one (1) hour occurring after 12:00 noon Eastern Time that day, the Clerk of the Panel shall deem the Panel's Electronic Case Filing web site to be subject to a technical failure.

(b) If a Filing User experiences a technical failure as defined herein, the Filing User may submit the document to the Clerk of the Panel, provided that the document is accompanied by a certification, signed by the Filing User, that the Filing User has attempted to file the document electronically at least twice, with those unsuccessful attempts occurring at least one (1) hour apart after 12:00 noon Eastern Time that day. The Clerk may require the document to be accompanied by a disk or CD–ROM which contains the document in .pdf format.

(c) The initial point of contact for a Filing User experiencing technical difficulty filing a document electronically will be the Panel's CM/ECF Help Desk at the numbers listed on the Panel's web site and in the CM/ECF User Manual.

(d) A Filing User who suffers prejudice as a result of a technical failure as defined herein or a Filing User who cannot file a time-sensitive document electronically due to unforeseen technical difficulties, such as the malfunctioning of a Filing User's equipment, may seek relief from the Clerk of the Panel.

14. PUBLIC ACCESS.

14.1 (a) A person may receive information from the Electronic Filing System at the Panel's Internet site by obtaining a PACER login and password. A person who has PACER access may retrieve docket sheets and documents (unless otherwise sealed or restricted) in MDL dockets and associated civil cases. Any case or document under seal shall not be available electronically or through any other means.

(b) If a case or document has been restricted, a PACER user may retrieve the docket sheet over the Internet, but only a Filing User who is counsel of record may retrieve restricted documents electronically. However, a restricted case or document will be available for viewing by the public at the clerk's office.

(c) Electronic access to electronic docket sheets and all documents filed in the System, unless sealed, is available to the public for viewing at no charge during regular business hours at the clerk's office. A copy fee for an electronic reproduction is required in accordance with 28 U.S.C. § 1932.

(d) Conventional copies and certified copies of electronically filed documents may be purchased at the clerk's office. The fee for copying and certifying will be in accordance with 28 U.S.C. § 1932.

14.2 Sensitive Information

Since the public may access certain case information over the Internet through the Panel's Electronic Filing System, sensitive information should not be included in any document filed with the court unless such inclusion is necessary and relevant. In accordance with these Administrative Policies and Procedures, if sensitive information must be included, certain personal and identifying information such as Social Security numbers, financial account numbers, dates of birth and names of minor children shall be redacted from the pleading, whether it is filed electronically or on paper.

The Panel recognizes that parties may need to include in the record a document containing information such as driver's license number; medical records, treatment and diagnosis; employment history; individual financial information; and proprietary or trade secret information.

To avoid unnecessary disclosure of private, personal or financial information, a party may:

(a) **RESTRICTED MDL DOCKETS OR DOCUMENTS.**

File a "Motion to Seal" or "Motion to Seal Document". The motion must state the reason and show good cause for restricting remote access to the case. If the motion is granted, remote access to documents will be limited to Filing Users who are counsel of record. However, the MDL docket sheet and/or documents will be available for viewing by the public at the clerk's office.

(b) **EXHIBITS.**

File an exhibit containing private, personal or financial information as an attachment to a pleading entitled "Notice of Filing Restricted Exhibit". The notice and the attached exhibit shall be filed as a separate docket entry, rather than as an attachment to the pleading supported by the exhibit. Remote public access to the notice and exhibit will be limited to Filing Users who are counsel of record. The notice and exhibit will, however, be available for viewing by the public at the clerk's office.

(c) **DOCUMENTS UNDER SEAL.**

(1) File a redacted copy of a pleading or exhibit containing private, personal or financial infor-

mation, whether electronically or on paper, while concurrently filing an unredacted copy under seal. This document shall be retained by the Panel as part of the record.

OR

(2) File a reference list under seal. The reference list shall contain the complete personal data identifier(s) and the redacted identifier(s) used in its (their) place in the filing. All references in the case to the redacted identifier(s) included in the reference list will be construed to refer to the corresponding complete identifier. The reference list must be filed under seal, and may be amended as of right. It shall be retained by the Panel as part of the record.

(d) **MOTION TO SEAL.**

File a motion to seal the document or MDL associated case. The motion must state the reason and show good cause for sealing the document or MDL associated case. If the motion to seal is granted, the document or case under seal will not be available electronically or through any other means.

It is the sole responsibility of counsel and the parties to ensure that all documents filed with the Panel comply with these Administrative Policies and Procedures, regarding public access to electronic case files. The Clerk will not review any document for redaction.

Counsel are strongly urged to share this information with all clients so that an informed decision about the inclusion, redaction, and/or exclusion of certain materials may be made.

[Effective May 2010.]

FEDERAL COURTS MISCELLANEOUS FEE SCHEDULES

COURT OF APPEALS FEE SCHEDULE[1]

(Effective December 1, 2014)

The fees included in the Court of Appeals Miscellaneous Fee Schedule are to be charged for services provided by the courts of appeals.

- The United States should not be charged fees under this schedule, except as prescribed in Items 2, 4, and 5 when the information requested is available through remote electronic access.

- Federal agencies or programs that are funded from judiciary appropriations (agencies, organizations, and individuals providing services authorized by the Criminal Justice Act, 18 U.S.C. § 3006A, and bankruptcy administrators) should not be charged any fees under this schedule.

(1) For docketing a case on appeal or review, or docketing any other proceeding, $500.

- Each party filing a notice of appeal pays a separate fee to the district court, but parties filing a joint notice of appeal pay only one fee.

- There is no docketing fee for an application for an interlocutory appeal under 28 U.S.C. § 1292(b) or other petition for permission to appeal under Fed. R. App. P. 5, unless the appeal is allowed.

- There is no docketing fee for a direct bankruptcy appeal or a direct bankruptcy cross appeal, when the fee has been collected by the bankruptcy court in accordance with item 14 of the Bankruptcy Court Miscellaneous Fee Schedule.

- This fee is collected in addition to the statutory fee of $5 that is collected under 28 U.S.C. § 1917.

(2) For conducting a search of the court of appeals records, $30 per name or item searched. This fee applies to services rendered on behalf of the United States if the information requested is available through remote electronic access.

(3) For certification of any document, $11.

(4) For reproducing any document, $.50 per page. This fee applies to services rendered on behalf of the United States if the document requested is available through remote electronic access.

(5) For reproducing recordings of proceedings, regardless of the medium, $30, including the cost of materials. This fee applies to services rendered on behalf of the United States if the recording is available through remote electronic access.

(6) For reproducing the record in any appeal in which the court of appeals does not require an appendix pursuant to Fed. R. App. P. 30(f), $83.

(7) For retrieval of one box of records from a Federal Records Center, National Archives, or other storage location removed from the place of business of the court, $64. For retrievals involving multiple boxes, $39 for each additional box.

(8) For any payment returned or denied for insufficient funds, $53.

(9) For copies of opinions, a fee commensurate with the cost of printing, as fixed by each court.

(10) For copies of the local rules of court, a fee commensurate with the cost of distributing the copies. The court may also distribute copies of the local rules without charge.

(11) For filing:

- Any separate or joint notice of appeal or application for appeal from the Bankruptcy Appellate Panel, $5;

- A notice of the allowance of an appeal from the Bankruptcy Appellate Panel, $5.

(12) For counsel's requested use of the court's videoconferencing equipment in connection with each oral argument, the court may charge and collect a fee of $200 per remote location.

(13) For original admission of attorney to practice, including a certificate of admission, $176.

For a duplicate certificate of admission or certificate of good standing, $18.

1 Issued in accordance with 28 U.S.C. § 1913.

DISTRICT COURT FEE SCHEDULE[1]

(Effective December 1, 2014)

The fees included in the District Court Miscellaneous Fee Schedule are to be charged for services provided by the district courts.

- The United States should not be charged fees under this schedule, with the exception of those specifically prescribed in Items 2, 4 and 5, when the information requested is available through remote electronic access.

- Federal agencies or programs that are funded from judiciary appropriations (agencies, organizations, and individuals providing services authorized by the Criminal Justice Act, 18 U.S.C. § 3006 and bankruptcy administrators) should not be charged any fees under this schedule.

1. For filing any document that is not related to a pending case or proceeding, $46.

2. For conducting a search of the district court records, $30 per name or item searched. This fee applies to services rendered on behalf of the United States if the information requested is available through electronic access.

3. For certification of any document, $11. For exemplification of any document, $21.

4. For reproducing any record or paper, $.50 per page. This fee shall apply to paper copies made from either: (1) original documents; or (2) microfiche or microfilm reproductions of the original records. This fee shall apply to services rendered on behalf of the United States if the record or paper requested is available through electronic access.

5. For reproduction of an audio recording of a court proceeding, $30. This fee applies to services rendered on behalf of the United States, if the recording is available electronically.

6. For each microfiche sheet of film or microfilm jacket copy of any court record, where available, $6.

7. For retrieval of one box of records from a Federal Records Center, National Archives, or other storage location removed from the place of business of the court, $64. For retrievals involving multiple boxes, $39 for each additional box.

8. For any payment returned or denied for insufficient funds, $53.

9. For an appeal to a district judge from a judgment of conviction by a magistrate judge in a misdemeanor case, $37.

10. For original admission of attorneys to practice, $176 each, including a certificate of admission. For a duplicate certificate of admission or certificate of good standing, $18.

11. The court may charge and collect fees commensurate with the cost of providing copies of the local rules of court. The court may also distribute copies of the local rules without charge.

12. The clerk shall assess a charge for the handling of registry funds deposited with the court, to be assessed from interest earnings and in accordance with the detailed fee schedule issued by the Director of the Administrative Office of the United States Courts.

For management of registry funds invested through the Court Registry Investment System, a fee at a rate of 2.5 basis points shall be assessed from interest earnings.

13. For filing an action brought under Title III of the Cuban Liberty and Democratic Solidarity (LIBERTAD) Act of 1996, P.L. 104–114, 110 Stat. § 785

(1996), $6,355. (This fee is in addition to the filing fee prescribed in 28 U.S.C. § 1914(a) for instituting any civil action other than a writ of habeas corpus.)

14. Administrative fee for filing a civil action, suit, or proceeding in a district court, $50. This fee does not apply to applications for a writ of habeas corpus or to persons granted in forma pauperis status under 28 U.S.C. § 1915.

15. Processing fee for a petty offense charged on a federal violation notice, $25.

1 Issued in accordance with 28 U.S.C. § 1914.

BANKRUPTCY COURT MISCELLANEOUS FEE SCHEDULE[1]

(Effective December 1, 2014)

The fees included in the Bankruptcy Court Miscellaneous Fee Schedule are to be charged for services provided by the bankruptcy courts.

- The United States should not be charged fees under this schedule, with the exception of those specifically prescribed in Items 1, 3 and 5 when the information requested is available through remote electronic access.

- Federal agencies or programs that are funded from judiciary appropriations (agencies, organizations, and individuals providing services authorized by the Criminal Justice Act, 18 U.S.C. § 3006A, and bankruptcy administrators) should not be charged any fees under this schedule.

(1) For reproducing any document, $.50 per page. This fee applies to services rendered on behalf of the United States if the document requested is available through electronic access.

(2) For certification of any document, $11.
For exemplification of any document, $21.

(3) For reproduction of an audio recording of a court proceeding, $30. This fee applies to services rendered on behalf of the United States if the recording is available electronically.

(4) For filing an amendment to the debtor's schedules of creditors, lists of creditors, or mailing list, $30, except:

- The bankruptcy judge may, for good cause, waive the charge in any case.

- This fee must not be charged if—

  - the amendment is to change the address of a creditor or an attorney for a creditor listed on the schedules; or

  - the amendment is to add the name and address of an attorney for a creditor listed on the schedules.

(5) For conducting a search of the bankruptcy court records, $30 per name or item searched. This fee applies to services rendered on behalf of the United States if the information requested is available through electronic access.

(6) For filing a complaint, $350, except:

- If the trustee or debtor-in-possession files the complaint, the fee must be paid only by the estate, to the extent there is an estate.

- This fee must not be charged if—

  - the debtor is the plaintiff; or

  - a child support creditor or representative files the complaint and submits the form required by § 304(g) of the Bankruptcy Reform Act of 1994.

(7) For filing any document that is not related to a pending case or proceeding, $46.

(8) Administrative fee:

- For filing a petition under Chapter 7, 12, or 13, $75.

- For filing a petition under Chapter 9, 11, or 15, $550.

- When a motion to divide a joint case under Chapter 7, 12, or 13 is filed, $75.

- When a motion to divide a joint case under Chapter 11 is filed, $550.

(9) For payment to trustees pursuant to 11 U.S.C. § 330(b)(2), a $15 fee applies in the following circumstances:

- For filing a petition under Chapter 7.
- For filing a motion to reopen a Chapter 7 case.
- For filing a motion to divide a joint Chapter 7 case.
- For filing a motion to convert a case to a Chapter 7 case.
- For filing a notice of conversion to a Chapter 7 case.

(10) In addition to any fees imposed under Item 9, above, the following fees must be collected:

- For filing a motion to convert a Chapter 12 case to a Chapter 7 case or a notice of conversion pursuant to 11 U.S.C. § 1208(a), $45.
- For filing a motion to convert a Chapter 13 case to a Chapter 7 case or a notice of conversion pursuant to 11 U.S.C. § 1307(a), $10.

The fee amounts in this item are derived from the fees prescribed in 28 U.S.C. § 1930(a).

If the trustee files the motion to convert, the fee is payable only from the estate that exists prior to conversion.

If the filing fee for the chapter to which the case is requested to be converted is less than the fee paid at the commencement of the case, no refund may be provided.

(11) For filing a motion to reopen, the following fees apply:

- For filing a motion to reopen a Chapter 7 case, $245.
- For filing a motion to reopen a Chapter 9 case, $1167.
- For filing a motion to reopen a Chapter 11 case, $1167.
- For filing a motion to reopen a Chapter 12 case, $200.
- For filing a motion to reopen a Chapter 13 case, $235.
- For filing a motion to reopen a Chapter 15 case, $1167.

The fee amounts in this item are derived from the fees prescribed in 28 U.S.C. § 1930(a).

The reopening fee must be charged when a case has been closed without a discharge being entered.

The court may waive this fee under appropriate circumstances or may defer payment of the fee from trustees pending discovery of additional assets. If payment is deferred, the fee should be waived if no additional assets are discovered.

The reopening fee must not be charged in the following situations:

- to permit a party to file a complaint to obtain a determination under Rule 4007(b); or
- when a debtor files a motion to reopen a case based upon an alleged violation of the terms of the discharge under 11 U.S.C. § 524; or
- when the reopening is to correct an administrative error; or
- to redact a record already filed in a case, pursuant to Fed. R. Bankr. 9037, if redaction is the only reason for reopening.

(12) For retrieval of one box of records from a Federal Records Center, National Archives, or other storage location removed from the place of business of the court, $64. For retrievals involving multiple boxes, $39 for each additional box.

(13) For any payment returned or denied for insufficient funds, $53.

(14) For filing an appeal or cross appeal from a judgment, order, or decree, $293.

This fee is collected in addition to the statutory fee of $5 that is collected under 28 U.S.C. § 1930(c) when a notice of appeal is filed.

Parties filing a joint notice of appeal should pay only one fee.

If a trustee or debtor-in-possession is the appellant, the fee must be paid only by the estate, to the extent there is an estate.

Upon notice from the court of appeals that a direct appeal or direct cross-appeal has been authorized, an additional fee of $207 must be collected.

(15) For filing a case under Chapter 15 of the Bankruptcy Code, $1167.

This fee is derived from and equal to the fee prescribed in 28 U.S.C. § 1930(a)(3) for filing a case commenced under Chapter 11 of Title 11.

(16) The court may charge and collect fees commensurate with the cost of providing copies of the local rules of court. The court may also distribute copies of the local rules without charge.

(17) The clerk shall assess a charge for the handling of registry funds deposited with the court, to be assessed from interest earnings and in accordance with the detailed fee schedule issued by the Director of the Administrative Office of the United States Courts.

For management of registry funds invested through the Court Registry Investment System, a fee at a rate of 2.5 basis points shall be assessed from interest earnings.

(18) For a motion filed by the debtor to divide a joint case filed under 11 U.S.C. § 302, the following fees apply:

- For filing a motion to divide a joint Chapter 7 case, $245.
- For filing a motion to divide a joint Chapter 11 case, $1167.
- For filing a motion to divide a joint Chapter 12 case, $200.
- For filing a motion to divide a joint Chapter 13 case, $235.

These fees are derived from and equal to the filing fees prescribed in 28 U.S.C. § 1930(a).

(19) For filing the following motions, $176:

- To terminate, annul, modify or condition the automatic stay;
- To compel abandonment of property of the estate pursuant to Rule 6007(b) of the Federal Rules of Bankruptcy Procedure;
- To withdraw the reference of a case or proceeding under 28 U.S.C. § 157(d); or
- To sell property of the estate free and clear of liens under 11 U.S.C. § 363(f).

This fee must not be collected in the following situations:

- For a motion for relief from the co-debtor stay;
- For a stipulation for court approval of an agreement for relief from a stay; or
- For a motion filed by a child support creditor or its representative, if the form required by § 304(g) of the Bankruptcy Reform Act of 1994 is filed.

(20) For filing a transfer of claim, $25 per claim transferred.

(21) For filing a motion to redact a record, $25 per affected case. The court may waive this fee under appropriate circumstances.

1 Issued in accordance with 28 U.S.C. § 1930.

JUDICIAL PANEL ON MULTIDISTRICT LITIGATION FEE SCHEDULE[1]

(28 U.S.C. § 1932)

(Effective December 1, 2013)

Following are fees to be charged for services to be performed by the clerk of the Judicial Panel on Multidistrict Litigation. No fees are to be charged for services rendered on behalf of the United States, with the exception of those specifically prescribed in items 1 and 3. No fees under this schedule shall be charged to federal agencies or programs which are funded from judiciary appropriations, including, but not limited to, agencies, organizations, and individuals providing services authorized by the Criminal Justice Act, 18 U.S.C. § 3006A.

(1) For every search of the records of the court conducted by the clerk of the court or a deputy clerk, $30 per name or item searched. This fee shall apply to services rendered on behalf of the United States if the information requested is available through electronic access.

(2) For certification of any document or paper, whether the certification is made directly on the document or by separate instrument, $11.

(3) For reproducing any record or paper, $.50 per page. This fee shall apply to paper copies made from either: (1) original documents; or (2) microfiche or microfilm reproductions of the original records. This fee shall apply to services rendered on behalf of the United States if the record or paper requested is available through electronic access.

(4) For retrieval of one box of records from a Federal Records Center, National Archives, or other storage location removed from the place of business of the court, $64. For retrievals involving multiple boxes, $39 for each additional box.

(5) For any payment returned or denied for insufficient funds, $53.

[1] Issued in accordance with 28 U.S.C. § 1932.

ELECTRONIC PUBLIC ACCESS FEE SCHEDULE

(Issued in accordance with 28 U.S.C. §§ 1913, 1914, 1926, 1930, 1932)

(Effective December 1, 2013)

The fees included in the Electronic Public Access Fee Schedule are to be charged for providing electronic public access to court records.

Fees for Public Access to Court Electronic Records (PACER)

(1) Except as provided below, for electronic access to any case document, docket sheet, or case-specific report via PACER: $0.10 per page, not to exceed the fee for thirty pages.

(2) For electronic access to transcripts and non-case specific reports via PACER (such as reports obtained from the PACER Case Locator or docket activity reports): $0.10 per page.

(3) For electronic access to an audio file of a court hearing via PACER: $2.40 per audio file.

Fees for Courthouse Electronic Access

(4) For printing copies of any record or document accessed electronically at a public terminal in a courthouse: $0.10 per page.

PACER Service Center Fees

(5) For every search of court records conducted by the PACER Service Center, $30 per name or item searched.

(6) For the PACER Service Center to reproduce on paper any record pertaining to a PACER account, if this information is remotely available through electronic access: $0.50 per page.

(7) For any payment returned or denied for insufficient funds, $53.

Free Access and Exemptions

(8) **Automatic Fee Exemptions.**

- No fee is owed for electronic access to court data or audio files via PACER until an account holder accrues charges of more than $15.00 in a quarterly billing cycle.

- Parties in a case (including pro se litigants) and attorneys of record receive one free electronic copy, via the notice of electronic filing or notice of docket activity, of all documents filed electronically, if receipt is required by law or directed by the filer.

- No fee is charged for access to judicial opinions.

- No fee is charged for viewing case information or documents at courthouse public access terminals.

(9) **Discretionary Fee Exemptions.**

- Courts may exempt certain persons or classes of persons from payment of the user access fee. Examples of individuals and groups that a court may consider exempting include: indigents, bankruptcy case trustees, pro bono attorneys, pro bono alternative dispute resolution neutrals, Section 501(c)(3) not-for-profit organizations, and individual researchers associated with educational institutions. Courts should not, however, exempt individuals or groups that have the ability to pay the statutorily established access fee. Examples of individuals and groups that a court should not exempt include: local, state or federal government agencies, members of the media, privately paid attorneys or others who have the ability to pay the fee.

- In considering granting an exemption, courts must find:

- that those seeking an exemption have demonstrated that an exemption is necessary in order to avoid unreasonable burdens and to promote public access to information;

- that individual researchers requesting an exemption have shown that the defined research project is intended for scholarly research, that it is limited in scope, and that it is not intended for redistribution on the internet or for commercial purposes.

- If the court grants an exemption:

  - the user receiving the exemption must agree not to sell the data obtained as a result, and must not transfer any data obtained as the result of a fee exemption, unless expressly authorized by the court; and

  - the exemption should be granted for a definite period of time, should be limited in scope, and may be revoked at the discretion of the court granting the exemption.

- Courts may provide local court information at no cost (e.g., local rules, court forms, news items, court calendars, and other information) to benefit the public.

Applicability to the United States and State and Local Governments

(10) Unless otherwise authorized by the Judicial Conference, these fees must be charged to the United States, except to federal agencies or programs that are funded from judiciary appropriations (including, but not limited to, agencies, organizations, and individuals providing services authorized by the Criminal Justice Act [18 U.S.C. § 3006A], and bankruptcy administrators).

(11) The fee for printing copies of any record or document accessed electronically at a public terminal ($0.10 per page) described in (4) above does not apply to services rendered on behalf of the United States if the record requested is not remotely available through electronic access.

(12) The fee for local, state, and federal government entities, shall be $0.08 per page until April 1, 2015, after which time, the fee shall be $0.10 per page.

JUDICIAL CONFERENCE POLICY NOTES

The Electronic Public Access (EPA) fee and its exemptions are directly related to the requirement that the judiciary charge user-based fees for the development and maintenance of electronic public access services. The fee schedule provides examples of users that may not be able to afford reasonable user fees (such as indigents, bankruptcy case trustees, individual researchers associated with educational institutions, 501(c)(3) not-for-profit organizations, and court-appointed pro bono attorneys), but requires those seeking an exemption to demonstrate that an exemption is limited in scope and is necessary in order to avoid an unreasonable burden. In addition, the fee schedule includes examples of other entities that courts should not exempt from the fee (such as local, state or federal government agencies, members of the media, and attorneys). The goal is to provide courts with guidance in evaluating a requestor's ability to pay the fee.

Judicial Conference policy also limits exemptions in other ways. First, it requires exempted users to agree not to sell the data they receive through an exemption (unless expressly authorized by the court). This prohibition is not intended to bar a quote or reference to information received as a result of a fee exemption in a scholarly or other similar work. Second, it permits courts to grant exemptions for a definite period of time, to limit the scope of the exemptions, and to revoke exemptions. Third, it cautions that exemptions should be granted as the exception, not the rule, and prohibits courts from exempting all users from EPA fees.